SHAPING EU LAW THE BRITISH WAY:
UK ADVOCATES GENERAL AT THE
COURT OF JUSTICE OF THE EUROPEAN UNION

In this book, leading scholars of EU law, judges, and practitioners unpack the judicial reasoning offered by the UK Advocates General in over forty cases at the Court of Justice, which have influenced the shape of EU law. The authors place the Opinions in the wider context of the EU legal order, and mix praise with critique in order to determine the true contribution of the UK Advocates General, before hearing the concluding reflections by the UK Advocates General themselves.

The role of Advocates General at the Court of Justice of the European Union remains notoriously under-researched. With a few notable exceptions, not much ink has been spilled on analysing their contribution to the judicial discourse that emerges from the Court's *Palais* in Luxembourg. More generally, their impact on the shaping of EU law is only sporadically explored. This book fills the lacunae by offering an in-depth analysis of the way in which the UK Advocates General contributed to development of EU law during 47 years of the UK's membership of the EU.

During their terms of office, Advocates General Jean-Pierre Warner (1973–1981), Gordon Slynn (1981–1988), Francis Jacobs (1988–2006), and Eleanor Sharpston (2006–2020) delivered over 1400 Opinions. This staggering contribution of the four individuals and their cabinets of legal secretaries was supplemented by an Opinion of a then Judge of the Court of First Instance, David Edward, who was called to act as an Advocate General in two joined cases in what is now the General Court. With the last UK Advocate General departing from the Court of Justice in September 2020, an important era has ended. With this watershed moment, it is apt to take a look back and critically analyse the contribution to development of EU law made by the UK Advocates General, and to elucidate the lasting impact they have had on the nature of EU law.

REVIEWS

'For almost half a century British Advocates General brought rigour and creativity to the EU's highest court, while explaining its case law to a common law audience. This book analyses their contribution, and reminds us all of what we have lost.'

– David Anderson QC, Lord Anderson of Ipswich,
Brick Court Chambers and House of Lords.

'Advocates General are often the unsung heroes of EU law. They think hard and creatively. They write the first draft of the judgment which the courts can then work with – or against. The British Advocates General have contributed a lot to the development of EU law. This book shines an important light on the extraordinary influence.'

– Catherine Barnard,
Professor of European Union Law, University of Cambridge.

'The jury might still be out deliberating whether there is any distinctly British Way of exercising the role of Advocate General at the Court of Justice. What will nonetheless be obvious to any reader of this book is that selecting brilliant lawyers who did have the privilege of assisting the Court for extended periods of time born fruit, both in terms of enhancing the quality of judicial deliberations of the Court as well as in enabling a Member State to project own ideas, approaches, and legal culture onto the European level. This book is a fitting celebration of that achievement and of a group of remarkable jurists.'

– Michal Bobek,
Judge of the Supreme Administrative Court of the Czech Republic;
former Advocate General, Court of Justice of the European Union.

'The voice of the EU's apex court is a collective one and on occasion its reasoning suffers as a result. The Advocate General's voice is very much her or his own, and that single clear voice has often enhanced our understanding of the Court's judgments, or even convinced us that the Court has taken a false step. I have always thought that the British were amongst the leading exponents of the Advocate General's art. This book proves me right.'

– Derrick Wyatt QC,
formerly of Brick Court Chambers;
Emeritus Professor of Law, University of Oxford.

Shaping EU Law the British Way

UK Advocates General at the Court of Justice of the European Union

Edited by
Graham Butler
and
Adam Łazowski

·HART·

OXFORD · LONDON · NEW YORK · NEW DELHI · SYDNEY

HART PUBLISHING

Bloomsbury Publishing Plc

Kemp House, Chawley Park, Cumnor Hill, Oxford, OX2 9PH, UK

1385 Broadway, New York, NY 10018, USA

29 Earlsfort Terrace, Dublin 2, Ireland

HART PUBLISHING, the Hart/Stag logo, BLOOMSBURY and the Diana logo are
trademarks of Bloomsbury Publishing Plc

First published in Great Britain 2022

A catalogue record for this book is available from the British Library.

A catalogue record for this book is available from the Library of Congress.

Library of Congress Control Number: 2022943444

ISBN: HB: 978-1-50995-000-3
       ePDF: 978-1-50995-002-7
       ePub: 978-1-50995-001-0

Typeset by Compuscript Ltd, Shannon
Printed and bound in Great Britain by CPI Group (UK) Ltd, Croydon CR0 4YY

MIX
Paper from
responsible sources
FSC® C013604

To find out more about our authors and books visit www.hartpublishing.co.uk.
Here you will find extracts, author information, details of forthcoming events
and the option to sign up for our newsletters.

Shaping EU Law the British Way: UK Advocates General at the Court of Justice of the European Union

ABOUT

I N this book, leading scholars of EU law, judges, and practitioners unpack the judicial reasoning offered by the UK Advocates General in over 40 cases at the Court of Justice, which have influenced the shape of EU law. The authors place the Opinions in the wider context of the EU legal order, and mix praise with critique in order to determine the true contribution of the UK Advocates General, before hearing the concluding reflections by the UK Advocates General themselves.

The role of Advocates General at the Court of Justice of the European Union remains notoriously under-researched. With a few notable exceptions, not much ink has been spilled on analysing their contribution to the judicial discourse that emerges from the Court's *Palais* in Luxembourg. More generally, their impact on the shaping of EU law is only sporadically explored. This book fills the lacunae by offering an in-depth analysis of the way in which the UK Advocates General contributed to development of EU law during 47 years of UK's membership of the EU.

During their terms of office, Advocates General Jean-Pierre Warner (1973–1981), Gordon Slynn (1981–1988), Francis Jacobs (1988–2006), and Eleanor Sharpston (2006–2020) delivered over 1,400 Opinions. This staggering contribution of the four individuals and their cabinets of legal secretaries was supplemented by an Opinion of a then Judge of the Court of First Instance, David Edward, who was called to act as an Advocate General in two joined cases in what is now the General Court. With the last UK Advocate General departing from the Court of Justice in September 2020, an important era has ended. With this watershed moment, it is apt to take a look back and critically analyse the contribution to development of EU law made by the UK Advocates General, and to elucidate the lasting impact they have had on the nature of EU law.

EDITORS

Graham Butler, Associate Professor of Law, Aarhus University, Denmark.

Adam Łazowski, Professor of EU Law, University of Westminster, London, United Kingdom; Visiting Professor at College of Europe (Natolin, Poland) and Ivan Franko National University (Lviv, Ukraine).

Outline Table of Contents

PART III
GORDON SLYNN: EMBEDDING THE REVOLUTIONARY
DOCTRINES (1981–1988)

PART VI
ELEANOR SHARPSTON: THE LEGAL ORDER
PRE-AND POST-LISBON (2006–2020)

PART VII
AFTERWORDS

PART VIII
EU LAW WITHOUT UK ADVOCATES GENERAL

Detailed Table of Contents

PART III
GORDON SLYNN: EMBEDDING THE REVOLUTIONARY DOCTRINES (1981–1988)

PART IV
DAVID EDWARD: JUDGE ACTING AS ADVOCATE GENERAL
IN THE COURT OF FIRST INSTANCE (1992)

PART V
FRANCIS JACOBS: FROM EUROPEAN COMMUNITIES
TO EUROPEAN UNION (1988–2006)

PART VI
ELEANOR SHARPSTON: THE LEGAL ORDER
PRE-AND POST-LISBON (2006–2020)

PART VII
AFTERWORDS

PART VIII
EU LAW WITHOUT UK ADVOCATES GENERAL

List of Contributors

(Alphabetical by surname)

EDITORS

Graham Butler, Associate Professor of Law, Aarhus University, Denmark.

Adam Łazowski, Professor of EU Law, University of Westminster, London, United Kingdom; Visiting Professor at College of Europe (Natolin, Poland) and Ivan Franko National University (Lviv, Ukraine).

CONTRIBUTORS

Anthony Arnull, Barber Professor of Jurisprudence, University of Birmingham, United Kingdom; former Legal Secretary (*référendaire*) to Advocate General Jacobs, Court of Justice of the European Union, Luxembourg.

Carl Baudenbacher, Partner, Nobel Baudenbacher Law, Zurich/Brussels; Door Tenant Monckton Chambers, London, United Kingdom; Visiting Professor, London School of Economics, United Kingdom; President of the EFTA Court (2003–2017), Luxembourg; Full Professor Emeritus, University of St. Gallen, Switzerland.

Andrea Biondi, Professor of European Union Law and Director, Centre of European Law, King's College London, United Kingdom; Visiting Professor, Bocconi University, Milan, Italy; Visiting Professor, Luiss University, Rome, Italy; Academic Associate, 39 Essex Chambers, London, United Kingdom; Vice-Chair, Board of Appeal, European Union Agency for the Cooperation of Energy Regulators (ACER), Ljubljana, Slovenia.

Kieran Bradley, Judge, Administrative Tribunal of the Inter-American Development Bank, Washington, D.C., United States of America; former Judge, EU Civil Service Tribunal, Court of Justice of the European Union; former Special Adviser on Brexit, Court of Justice of the European Union, Luxembourg; Adjunct Professor, Trinity College Dublin, Ireland.

Graham Butler, Associate Professor of Law, Aarhus University, Denmark.

Tamara Ćapeta, Advocate General, Court of Justice of the European Union, Luxembourg; Professor of Law, University of Zagreb, Croatia.

Michael-James Clifton, Chef de Cabinet, Chambers of Judge Bernd Hammermann, EFTA Court, Luxembourg.

Anthony M Collins, Senior Counsel; Advocate General, Court of Justice of the European Union, Luxembourg; former Judge, General Court, Court of Justice of the European Union, Luxembourg.

John Cotter, Lecturer in Law, Keele University, United Kingdom.

Paul Craig, Professor Emeritus of English Law, St. John's College, University of Oxford, United Kingdom.

Adam Cygan, Professor of European Union Law, Leicester Law School, University Leicester, United Kingdom.

Sir Alan Dashwood, Queen's Counsel; Henderson Chambers, London, United Kingdom; former Legal Secretary (*référendaire*) to Advocate General Warner, Court of Justice of the European Union, Luxembourg; Emeritus Professor of European Law, University of Cambridge, United Kingdom.

Geert De Baere, Judge, General Court, Court of Justice of the European Union, Luxembourg; Associate Professor of Law, KU Leuven, Belgium.

Sir David Edward, Queen's Counsel; Former Judge, Court of Justice, Court of Justice of the European Union, and Court of First Instance, Luxembourg.

Piet Eeckhout, Professor of Law and Executive Dean, Faculty of Laws, University College London, United Kingdom; former Legal Secretary (*référendaire*) to Advocate General Jacobs, Court of Justice of the European Union, Luxembourg; Vice-Chair, Board of Appeal, European Union Agency for the Cooperation of Energy Regulators (ACER), Ljubljana, Slovenia.

Stefan Enchelmaier, Professor of European and Comparative Law, Lincoln College, University of Oxford, United Kingdom.

Elaine Fahey, Professor of Law and Jean Monnet Chair in Law and Transatlantic Relations, City Law School, City, University of London, United Kingdom.

Nial Fennelly, Senior Counsel; former Advocate General, Court of Justice of the European Union, Luxembourg; Former Justice, Supreme Court of Ireland, Dublin, Ireland.

James Flynn, Queen's Counsel; Brick Court Chambers, London, United Kingdom; former Legal Secretary (*référendaire*) to Advocate General Slynn, Court of Justice of the European Union, Luxembourg.

Eleni Frantziou, Associate Professor in Public Law and Human Rights, Durham Law School, Durham University, United Kingdom.

Vera Fritz, Marie Curie Fellow, University of Copenhagen, Denmark.

Laurence W Gormley, Professor, College of Europe, Bruges, Belgium; Professor Emeritus of European Law, University of Groningen, The Netherlands; Bencher of Middle Temple, London, United Kingdom.

Rosa Greaves, Professor Emeritus, University of Glasgow, United Kingdom.

Sir Francis G Jacobs, Queen's Counsel; former Advocate General, Court of Justice of the European Union, Luxembourg.

David T Keeling, Former Member of the Board of Appeal of the EU Intellectual Property Office (EUIPO), Alicante, Spain; former Member of the Board of Appeal of the European Patent Office (EPO), Munich, Germany; former Legal Secretary (*référendaire*) to Advocate General Jacobs, Court of Justice of the European Union, Luxembourg.

Jeff Kenner, Professor of Law and Chair of European Law, University of Nottingham, United Kingdom.

Dimitry Kochenov, Head, Rule of Law Working Group, CEU Democracy Institute, Budapest, Hungary; Professor of Legal Studies, CEU Department of Legal Studies, Vienna, Austria.

Theodore Konstadinides, Professor of Law, University of Essex, United Kingdom.

Panos Koutrakos, Professor of EU Law, City Law School, University of London, United Kingdom.

Mitchel de S-O-l'E Lasser, Jack G. Clarke Professor of Law, Cornell Law School, New York, United States of America.

Anna Łabędzka, Senior Lecturer in Law, Kingston University, London, United Kingdom.

Adam Łazowski, Professor of EU Law, University of Westminster, London, United Kingdom; Visiting Professor at College of Europe (Natolin, Poland) and Ivan Franko National University in Lviv (Ukraine).

Ronan McCrea, Professor of Constitutional and European Law, University College London, United Kingdom; former Legal Secretary (*référendaire*) to Advocate General Poiares Maduro, Court of Justice of the European Union, Luxembourg.

Valsamis Mitsilegas, Professor of European and Global Law, and Dean, School of Law and Social Justice, University of Liverpool, United Kingdom.

Niamh Nic Shuibhne, Professor of European Union Law, University of Edinburgh, United Kingdom.

Peter Oliver, Visiting Professor, Université Libre de Bruxelles, Belgium; former Legal Advisor, European Commission, Brussels, Belgium.

Aidan O'Neill, Advocate and Queen's Counsel; Scottish Bar (Ampersand Stable); Barrister and Queen's Counsel, Bar of England and Wales (Matrix Chambers); Barrister of Laws (Ireland).

Sébastien Platon, Professor of Public Law, University of Bordeaux, France.

Luca Rubini, Senior Research Fellow in International Law, School of Law, University of Turin, Italy; former Legal Secretary (*référendaire*) to Advocate General Jacobs, Court of Justice of the European Union, Luxembourg.

Daniel Sarmiento, Professor of European Union Law, Universidad Complutense of Madrid, Spain.

Eleanor Sharpston, Queen's Counsel; former Advocate General, Court of Justice of the European Union, Luxembourg.

Eleanor Spaventa, Professor of Law, Chair in EU Law, Director, Bocconi Lab in European Studies, School of Law, Bocconi University, Milan, Italy; Visiting Professor, College of Europe, Bruges, Belgium.

Steve Terrett, Director of Studies, British Law Centre, University of Warsaw, Poland.

Christa Tobler, Professor of European Law, Europa Institute, University of Basel, Switzerland; Europa Institute, Leiden University, The Netherlands.

Takis Tridimas, Professor of European Law, Director, Centre for European Law, King's College London, United Kingdom.

Alina Tryfonidou, Professor of European Law, Neapolis University Paphos, Cyprus; Visiting Professor of Law, University of Reading, United Kingdom.

Angela Ward, Legal Secretary (*Référendaire*), Court of Justice of the European Union, Luxembourg.

Stephen Weatherill, Emeritus Jacques Delors Professor of European Law, Somerville College, University of Oxford, United Kingdom.

Richard Whish, Emeritus Professor of Law, King's College London, United Kingdom.

Helen Xanthaki, Professor of Law, Dean of Postgraduate Laws Programmes, Faculty of Laws, University College London, United Kingdom; Senior Associate Research Fellow, Institute of Advanced Legal Studies, London, United Kingdom, President, International Association for Legislation.

Adrienne Yong, Senior Lecturer in Law, City, University of London, United Kingdom.

List of Abbreviations

AA	Association Agreement
ACCC	Aarhus Convention Compliance Committee
AAMS	Autonomous Administration of State Monopolies
ACER	European Union Agency for the Cooperation of Energy Regulators
AFSJ	Area of Freedom, Security, and Justice
AJCL	American Journal of Comparative Law
AG	Advocate General
AGs	Advocates General
AM&S	Australian Mining and Smelting
AUFF	Aarhus University Research Foundation
BIT	Bilateral Investment Treaty
CAP	Common Agricultural Policy
CCBE	Council of the Bars and Law Societies of Europe
CCP	Common Commercial Policy
CCT	Common Customs Tariff
CEE	Central and Eastern Europe
CETA	Comprehensive Economic and Trade Agreement between the EU and Canada
CFI	Court of First Instance
CFR	Charter of Fundamental Rights of the European Union
CFSP	Common Foreign and Security Policy
CILJ	Cornell International Law Journal
CJEL	Columbia Journal of European Law
CJEU	Court of Justice of the European Union
CLJ	Cambridge Law Journal
CLS	Critical legal studies
CMLRev	Common Market Law Review

CMO	Common Market Organisation
CoE	Council of Europe
COVID	Coronavirus Disease
CST	European Union Civil Service Tribunal
CUP	Cambridge University Press
CYELP	Croatian Yearbook of European Law and Policy
CYELS	Cambridge Yearbook of European Legal Studies
DG	Directorate-General
EA	Europe Agreement
EAEC	European Atomic Energy Community
EAGGF	European Agricultural Guidance and Guarantee Fund
EAT	Employment Appeal Tribunal
EAW	European Arrest Warrant
EBLR	European Business Law Review
ECB	European Central Bank
ECHR	European Convention of Human Rights and Fundamental Freedoms
ECSC	European Coal and Steel Community
ECtHR	European Court of Human Rights
EEA	European Economic Area
EC	European Community
ECB	European Central Bank
ECLR	European Competition Law Review
EEC	European Economic Community
EFARev	European Foreign Affairs Review
EFSA	European Food Safety Authority
EFTA	European Free Trade Association
EIPR	European Intellectual Property Review
EJIL	European Journal of International Law
ELJ	European Law Journal
ELRev	European Law Review
EPL	European Public Law
EPO	European Patent Office

ERPL	European Review of Public Law
ESA	EFTA Surveillance Authority
EStAL	European State Aid Law Quarterly
EU	European Union
EuConst	European Constitutional Law Review
EUI	European University Institute
EUIPO	European Union Intellectual Property Office
EUP	Edinburgh University Press
EUSFTA	Free Trade Agreement between the European Union and Singapore
FAO	Food and Agriculture Organization of the United Nations
FCO	Foreign and Commonwealth Office
FD	Framework Decision
FEBMA	Federation of European Bearing Manufacturers' Associations
FILJ	Fordham International Law Journal
FIT	Feed-in tariff
FMPA	EU-Swiss Agreement on the Free Movement of Persons
FYROM	Former Yugoslav Republic of Macedonia
GATT	General Agreement on Tariffs and Trade
GC	General Court
GLJ	German Law Journal
HAEU	Historical Archives of the European Union
HJRL	The Hague Journal on the Rule of Law
HUP	Harvard University Press
IBM	International Business Machines
ICJ	International Court of Justice
ICLQ	International and Comparative Law Quarterly
IGC	Inter-Governmental Conference
IJEL	Irish Journal of European Law
ILJ	Industrial Law Journal
IOLR	International Organisations Law Review
IPQ	Intellectual Property Quarterly
ISIA	Irish Studies in International Affairs

ISO	Import Standard Office
ISO	International Organization for Standardization
JAT	Yugoslav Airlines
JCMS	Journal of Common Market Studies
JR	Reporting Judge
JSPTL	Journal of the Society of Public Teachers of Law
KS	Norwegian Association of Local and Regional Authorities
LCD	Lord Chancellor's Department
LIEI	Legal Issues of Economic Integration
LO	Norwegian Federation of Trade Unions
LPICT	Law and Practice of International Courts and Tribunals
LPP	Legal professional privilege
LRB	London Review of Books
LQR	Law Quarterly Review
MEQR	Measures having equivalent effect of quantitative restrictions
MIBI	Motor Insurers' Bureau of Ireland
MJ	Maastricht Journal of European and Comparative Law
MLR	Modern Law Review
NATO	North Atlantic Treaty Organization
NJIL	Nordic Journal of International Law
NTF	Norwegian Transport Workers' Union
NTN	NTN Tokyo Bearing Company
NSK	Nippon Seiko KK
OFT	Office of Fair Trading
OHIM	Office for Harmonization in the Internal Market
OJ	Official Journal of the European Communities
OJ	Official Journal of the European Union
OJLS	Oxford Journal of Legal Studies
OUP	Oxford University Press
PCA	Partnership and Cooperation Agreement
PUP	Princeton University Press
QC	Queen's Counsel

QR	Quantitative restriction
REALaw	Review of European Administrative Law
RG	General assembly
RIA	Royal Irish Academy
SC	Senior Counsel
SCOTUS	Supreme Court of the United States of America
SEA	Single European Act
SSM	Single Supervisory Mechanism
TCA	Trade and Cooperation Agreement
TEU	Treaty on European Union
TFEU	Treaty on the Functioning of the European Union
TTIP	Transatlantic Trade and Investment Partnership
UK	United Kingdom
UKSC	Supreme Court of the United Kingdom
UN	United Nations
UNGA	United Nations General Assembly
UNSC	United Nations Security Council
UPC	Unified Patent Court
VCLT	Vienna Convention on the Law of Treaties
VJIL	Virginia Journal of International Law
WA	Withdrawal Agreement
WHO	World Health Organization
WTO	World Trade Organization
YPIL	Yearbook of Private International Law
YEL	Yearbook of European Law
YJIL	Yale Journal of International Law
YLJ	Yale Law Journal

Acknowledgements

WHAT may a Friday evening chat on a modern tool of communication lead to? Surely readers may come up with their own long lists of items. As the present volume demonstrates, such an innocent chat may result in a book. This venture started on one Friday in the early autumn of 2020. As things outside were getting darker by the hour, for real and figuratively, the editors were exchanging one idea after another. Fast forward, the concept of this book took shape and the proposal, with the list of authors, was ready in a matter of few weeks. The rest is history.

Whilst it is our names on the cover as curators and editors of this book, it is, firstly, the contributing authors that deserve our gratitude from the outset. We are very grateful to Francis Jacobs, David Edward, and Eleanor Sharpston who enriched the book with their afterwords, and to Anthony Collins for the foreword – Advocates General past and present. A big thank you also goes to other authors who enthusiastically accepted our invitations to take up Opinions that we suggested, or they preferred. In turn, they travelled back in time to analyse the Opinions of UK Advocates General and put them in a broader context, beyond the rulings of the Court that immediately followed. Among the authors, experiences and relationships to the cases and the Advocates General (AGs) varied widely. On the close side of things, some had worked at the Court in the early days, attended the oral hearings of the case in question, were involved with the cases on the side of an EU institution, assisted in writing the Opinion whilst working as a *référendaire* for the AG, and so forth. Others are even former or serving AGs. More distantly, some saw the value of AGs in other international systems or third countries, whilst others were not even born when the Opinions were delivered. In whatever relationship authors had to the Opinions they were analysing in this book however, each critiqued them for their merits (and imperfections), and put them into the broader perspective of EU law, legal reasoning, and adjudication in an environment such as that of the Court.

Many of the authors wrote their contributions during different periods of public health laws and guidelines given the ongoing COVID-19 pandemic that has obstructed many people's ordinary working and writing habits. In such times, support networks such as family, friends, and otherwise are appreciated even more. Yet despite the disruption that was caused, this book managed to come through unscathed, and we would extend our gratitude to everyone behind the scenes who managed to ensure this book came to fruition.

Several authors also helped us with suggestions for additional cases to include, and other authors acted as reviewers, in addition to us as editors, on offering substantive comments on the initial drafts of the chapters. In instances like these, authors went beyond the call of duty and for that we thank them very much indeed. Needless to say, all views expressed in each chapter are those of the author(s) of each chapter alone.

This book would not have been possible without our respective institutions – Aarhus University and the University of Westminster – indispensable havens of intellectual thought, freed from the otherwise busy world. Moreover, support from the Aarhus University Research Foundation (Aarhus Universitets Forskningsfond) (AUFF) is gratefully acknowledged as it provided a supporting basis for the publication of the book, which otherwise would not have been possible.

We also owe thanks to the team of superb archivists, in particular Valérie Mathevon, at the Historical Archives of the European Union (HAEU), located at the European University Institute (EUI) in Fiesole, near Florence, Italy. They were always on hand to provide us with the case files (minus, obviously, the deliberations of the Court) for some of the older cases. Files which were made available to us (and to the authors) provided some fascinating source material, including the original Opinions of the AGs that were initially typed up on a typewriter of some description. The case files held by the HAEU will be a treasure trove for future research in EU law that academia will begin to take seriously.

The editors are also very grateful to David Anderson, Catherine Barnard, Michal Bobek, and Derrick Wyatt for their endorsements.

This book would not be possible without Sinead Moloney and Sasha Jawed at Hart Publishing/Bloomsbury. From our initial dialogue about the book and its original approach, they understood its potential, and were swift with contracting it once we put all the pieces together. A word of thanks is also owed to the production manager, Tom Adams. They and the entire team at Hart make publishing with them a joy.

Last, but by no means least, our final and very special word of thanks goes to our own families, especially Katarina, Johan, and Ellen for Graham; and Anna for Adam. Adam is also very grateful to his parents who provided constant encouragement. Anyone leading a mission of scale knows the sacrifices that have to be made in preparing a book, and especially at the concluding phases of tying it all together; and the impact that this can have on immediate family as deadlines approach, and final twists have to be dealt with.

We hope this book will continue to see further research undertaken on the fascinating role of AGs within the Court, and the way in which they have shaped, and will continue to shape EU law.

Graham Butler and Adam Łazowski

Foreword

I N 1961, before the United Kingdom (UK) had done so, Ireland submitted its first application to join the six-nation European Economic Community (EEC).[1] Records disclose that Ireland's application received a cooler welcome than that of its larger, and then far more prosperous, neighbour. The veto in 1963 of Charles de Gaulle, President of France put an end to not-unfounded speculation that Ireland's application might be postponed, or even declined. Fifty years later, Ireland is a member of a 27-member European Union from which the UK has recently withdrawn. The numerous links that bind Ireland and the UK, amongst them a shared legal culture, notwithstanding the differences between their various legal systems, are perhaps sufficient to justify the editors' decision to bestow upon me the honour of penning this foreword.

At first blush, it appears incongruous to assess the contribution of Advocates General (AGs) to European Union law by reference to their Member States of origin. The number of AGs has always been well below that of the number of Member States. There is no equivalent direct legal link to that which exists between individual Member States and the nomination of judges of the Court. The Treaties emphasise the publically independent exercise of the functions of AGs. Moreover, 'the unbalanced system of rotation ordained by the larger Member States'[2] and the consequential time gap between the terms of office served by AGs nominated by smaller Member States, means that but a few Member States are in a position to nominate AGs for successive terms.

The regrettable withdrawal of the UK from the European Union provides a, hopefully singular, opportunity to assess what impact a series of AGs nominated by a single Member State may have on the development of EU law. For this timely and innovative initiative the editors deserve our congratulations. A particularly attractive aspect of the book is that one has the sense of embarking upon a quest, rather than confronting a thesis, leaving the reader to draw his or her own conclusions by reference to the excellent contributions contained within. It is in that spirit that I offer the following tentative reflections on the subject matter of this book.

An obvious starting point for an inquiry as to whether UK AGs shaped European Union law in a 'British way' is the dichotomy between the various civil law systems that apply on the European continent, and the common law that the British Empire propagated throughout the territories that were under its dominion at various times in the past. Whether that difference is a sufficient basis for an identifiably 'British' contribution to EU law is far from clear. Ireland and the UK acceded to Communities governed by a legal system that in the first 20 years of their existence had already established the foundations of a 'new legal order'.[3]

---

[1] Letter of Seán Lemass, Taoiseach (Prime Minister) to the President of the Council of the European Economic Community, 31 July 1961.

[2] See ch 3 below, by N Fennelly, 'Shaping EU Law: Ireland and the Common Law in Europe'.

[3] Case 26/62 NV *Algemene Transport- en Expeditie Onderneming van Gend & Loos v Netherlands Inland Revenue Administration* ECLI:EU:C:1963:1, p 12.

Upon their arrival in Luxembourg, the members of the Court nominated by the Irish and UK governments undertook to interpret and apply the law of the EEC, which consisted in elements adapted from various continental European legal systems. That included the interpretation and application of overarching principles derived from documents that enjoyed foundational legal status, an exercise with which UK lawyers would, at that time, have been unfamiliar. Like all of their colleagues at the Court, they thus were required to bend their minds to the exigencies of the Community legal order as it developed.

The contents of this book demonstrate that UK AGs met the challenge of interpreting and applying EU law with aplomb. Moreover, Irish and UK lawyers influenced the development of EU law in turn. The emphasis common law systems place on oral argument has become part of the fabric of EU law, much to its benefit. The development of a 'distinctive precedent-based methodology', as identified by Nial Fennelly, must have also been encouraged by the presence of practitioners of the common law doctrine of *stare decisis*. David T Keeling in this volume nevertheless identifies an important difference between the manner in which common law courts and the Court of Justice apply their respective methodologies. Whilst the former painstakingly examine precedents with a view to identifying contrasting strands in the case law, deciding upon which line to follow and, where it is not possible to distinguish precedent, overruling it, the latter at times appears to ignore judgments that it does not wish to follow in a given case. Opinions of UK AGs contain many fine examples of the first approach and none of the second.

Over three decades of professional involvement in EU law, almost half of it as a *référendaire* in the Court (1990–1999), a judge in the General Court (2013–2021), and now as Advocate General in the Court, I have observed that professional background, rather than nationality or legal system of origin, is often the strongest influence upon an individual's approach to the resolution and management of cases. On this approach, it may be more fruitful to examine whether the contributions of UK AGs display certain shared characteristics by reference to the training they have undergone, and the structure of the legal system in which they operated, prior to appointment.

Thus far, every one of the individuals nominated as members of the Court by the UK (and Ireland) share the experience of having practised as counsel at their respective Bars. As Vera Fritz's contribution makes clear, however, UK AGs were active contributors to European legal scholarship, a feature that distinguishes them from the majority of their fellow practitioners at the Bar.

Whilst the members of the Bars of Ireland and the constituent parts of the UK are justly renowned for their skill at oral advocacy, it is at times overlooked that a substantial part of a barrister's practice consists in the writing of legal opinions. Counsels' opinions are an essential element in the day-to-day operation of the legal system in Ireland and in the UK. There are many reasons why this is so. The accessibility of the Bar to the public, preserved through the operation of the 'cab-rank' rule, whereby counsel are under a professional obligation to take on cases sent to them. The readiness of state authorities in Ireland and in the UK to have recourse to, and to rely upon, the advice of independent legal practitioners in private practice. The relatively high cost of litigation, which pressurises parties into settling cases as early as possible. The recruitment of judges from the Bar and the daily interaction between Bar and Bench in open court, both of which facilitate members of the former predicting the approach that the latter might adopt. The preparation and submission of opinions fully engages the professional reputation of counsel. Qualities such as independent thought, clarity of analysis and stylistic precision are prized.

This does not change in the eventuality of appointment to judicial office, where judges are required to exercise independent judgement upon disputed issues of facts and law that arise before them, and to communicate that by way of the delivery in public of discursive judgments under their own name. One can readily appreciate the force of Alan Dashwood's observation in this volume that AG Warner considered that the role of AG was similar to that of a High Court judge, to seek out the legally correct answer in the case before him, and to explain clearly and succinctly how he arrived at it.

In contradistinction to many judges in national legal orders, AGs have invaluable human resources available to them in the form of the personnel of their cabinets. A sign of the importance of that engagement is that AGs Jacobs and Sharpston were *référendaires* to AGs General Warner and Slynn, respectively. Here again, an analogy may be drawn with the manner in which the Bar and, to a lesser extent, the Bench, rely upon the researches of counsel. As once observed by the late Donal Barrington, Ireland's first nominee to the Court of First Instance, a *référendaire* is akin to junior counsel, the judge being his/her leader. The analogy, like many of his musings, is sound, with the member of the Court having the added benefit that a *référendaire* is not normally required to allocate his/her time between the demands of a number of colleagues.

Years of practice in writing opinions and/or judgments, and applying the law to ascertained facts, is an ideal preparation for discharging the tasks of the post of AG. The application of that skill by expert practitioners of the art is perhaps the hallmark of the UK AGs and their identifiable contribution, as a group, to the development of EU law. It may be observed that those opinions of UK AGs that are considered to have broken new ground, or to have foreshadowed future trends in the law, more often than not sought to describe the law as it was at that time they were delivered. That the Court chose not to follow the point of view so expressed has no bearing upon its accuracy: as my colleague AG Ćapeta observes in her chapter:

> [w]ithin the limits allowed by the text, none of the multiple possible choices is 'right' or 'wrong'. ... The observer might find one of the interpretations more to his or her liking, but this does not make the other interpretation legally incorrect.[4]

Coherent expositions of what the law is, as distinct from hypothesising as to what it ought to be, are of themselves valuable contributions to ongoing debates on legal issues. The task of AGs is, above all, juridical.

Anthony M Collins
Advocate General
Court of Justice of the European Union, Luxembourg

---

[4] See ch 42 below, by T Ćapeta, 'The Notion of" Court or Tribunal of a Member State": Opinion of Advocate General Sharpston in Miles'.

Introduction

GRAHAM BUTLER AND ADAM ŁAZOWSKI

I. WHY UK ADVOCATES GENERAL?

ONE of the many consequences of Brexit is that the Court of Justice of the European Union lost the benefit of having at its disposal the UK judges and Advocates General.[1] On 31 January 2020, the term of UK judges at the Court of Justice[2] and the General Court came to an end.[3] This was followed by an abrupt and legally dubious early termination of the mandate of AG Sharpston on 10 September 2020. During their terms of office, AGs Jean-Pierre Warner (1973–81), Gordon Slynn (1981–88), Francis Jacobs (1988–2006), and Eleanor Sharpston (2006–2020) delivered over 1,400 Opinions. This contribution of the four individuals and their cabinets of legal secretaries (*référendaires*) was supplemented by an Opinion of a then Judge of the Court of First Instance, David Edward, who was called to act as an Advocate General during his brief judicial tenure at the Court of First Instance (before becoming a judge of the Court of Justice himself).

One of the critiques that we as editors heard whilst this book was being compiled was, 'well, what about the UK judges?' Indeed, few can doubt that the UK judges who served in the Court and General Court (formerly Court of First Instance) had also made a contribution. They too are part of the story of EU law, which should not be forgotten. That said, given the secrecy of the deliberations and the single judgment rule that has been in existence at the Court since its establishment, it is methodologically difficult, if not impossible, to measure the true influence and effect of individual judges at the Court. Thus, the story of the UK judges remains to be told elsewhere.

At first sight, as rightly pointed out by AG Collins in the Foreword to this book, it is perhaps a little strange that the contribution of certain members of the Court – AGs nominated by a specific Member State – is singled out. The reason is simple: Brexit. Termination of UK membership in the European Union was a watershed moment and it simply seemed apt to take a look back to show how UK Advocates General contributed to the shaping of EU law. Perhaps the urge came from the feeling shared by both editors, that despite all the legal turmoil that Brexit has created, the bad blood is only a one-sided picture of the UK's participation in the

---

[1] The UK's institutional involvement in the European Union ended on 31 January 2020.

[2] Five judges served at the Court from 1973–2020 (from EU accession to withdrawal): Alexander J Mackenzie Stuart (1973–88 (President, 1984–88)), Gordon Slynn (1988–92), David Edward (1992–2004), Konrad Schiemann (2004–12), and Christopher Vajda (2012–20).

[3] Four judges served from 1989–2020, from its creation to the UK's withdrawal from the EU: David Edward (1989–92), Christopher W Bellamy (1992–99), Nicholas Forwood (1999–2015), and Ian Stewart Forrester (2015–20). It is also worth mentioning that Paul Mahoney served as the first President (and Judge) of the EU Civil Service Tribunal (CST) (2005–11). The CST was dissolved in 2016.

integration through law endeavour. There is much more than meets the contemporary eye, and without a doubt, the UK, despite being a sometime troublemaker, also brought a lot of positive contributions to the development of the EU and its legal order. One way to demonstrate it is to give recognition to the enormous input of UK Advocates General. AG Collins has also reflected on the rather peculiar way of looking at EU law that the editors have selected as a frame for this book. As will be seen in later chapters throughout this volume, curiosity about the style of the book – which can humbly be claimed to be unique – is also felt by other authors. What is 'the British way', after all? As will be apparent to readers of the chapters of this book, the UK AGs did not really represent a 'British' view of EU law. Rather, in a much more anticipatory manner, they were just like any other EU lawyers at the Court, with their own skills, traditions, baggage of legal advocacy, and writing abilities. Their provenance shaped their work but, as readers will find out, all UK Advocates General, having reached their new habitat in Luxembourg, have greatly demonstrated their European credentials. Arguably, the notion of Britishness is mainly linked to the nationalities of UK Advocates General, although many of their contributions carry features known in common law. After all, Advocates General nominated by other Member States have too always brought their own flair to their judicial work at the Court. We come back to this point in the closing chapter of the book.

This volume therefore has many functions, but the overarching one is that it offers an in-depth analysis of the way in which the UK AGs contributed to the development of EU law during the 47 years of the UK's membership of the EU. Throughout this book, leading scholars of EU law, judges, and practitioners unpack the judicial reasoning offered by the UK Advocates General in almost 50 cases at the Court of Justice, which have influenced the shape of EU law. The authors place the Opinions in the wider context of the EU legal order, and mix praise with critique in order to determine the true contribution of the UK Advocates General, before hearing the concluding reflections by the UK Advocates General themselves towards the end of the book.

II. SELECTION OF OPINIONS

The fundamental challenge that the editors have faced from the beginning was where to start. How to select a solid sample from the over 1,400 Opinions of UK Advocates General? Such tasks are never easy and – surely – the results will not please everyone. The choice of Opinions commented on in the present volume was governed by the words of the great Spanish writer Miguel de Cervantes, who famously said that 'by a small sample we may judge of the whole piece'.[4] For the kite to fly, however, this small sample has to be representative. One of the difficulties was that the UK Advocates General served at different stages of European integration. For the duration of terms of AG Warner, AG Slynn, and a large part of the term of AG Jacobs, Opinions were compulsory. Consequently, many Opinions dealt with trivial and non-impactful cases. It was during the terms of AG Jacobs and AG Sharpston that EC law, later EU law, developed beyond recognition. This in turn brought a wider variety of cases to the Court, touching upon new areas of law. In turn, it allowed AG Jacobs and especially AG Sharpston to soar at altitudes not available to their predecessors, and to offer a very broad catalogue of Opinions.

---

[4] M de Cervantes, *Don Quixote de la Mancha (1605–1615)* Pt I, Book I, Ch 4.

The selection of Opinions attempts to find a balance between all these factors, and offers a rich selection of cases touching upon a wide variety of subject matters: Court procedures; enforcement of EU law at the national level; fundamental rights; free movement of goods; free movement of workers; Union citizenship; prohibition of discrimination; competition law; state aid law; EU criminal law; Common Commercial Policy; and, broadly, external relations of the European Union. By the same token, the editors aimed to find a good balance between Opinions where UK Advocates General were on the same page as the Court and Opinions where they were not. At the end of the day, it is not an objective selection, but a subjective one, based on the choices of the editors, taking into account the most gratefully received suggestions of authors.

III. WHAT TO EXPECT FROM THIS BOOK?

The opening part of this book sets the scene. To start with, the editors, and then Mitchel de S-O-l'E Lasser, put under the microscope the role of Advocates General. Former AG Fennelly takes readers on a historical journey to track milestones in the development of the common law and how it has reached the courtrooms in Luxembourg. In turn, Aidan O'Neill offers a sobering account of limits that the UK tradition of open justice has faced in the Court. One good example is the Opinion of AG Jacobs in *UPA*,[5] unsuccessfully pleading for the loosening up of the ridiculously strict *Plaumann* test,[6] which limits the *locus standi* under Article 263 TFEU to those highly skilled in legal acrobatics. The first part of the book ends with a chapter by Vera Fritz offering a detailed account of the professional careers of UK Advocates General.

Part II is dedicated to selected Opinions of AG Warner. Elaine Fahey, Stephen Weatherill, Graham Butler, Alan Dashwood, Christa Tobler, Rosa Greaves, Adam Cygan, Kieran Bradley, and James Flynn offer insights into Opinions touching upon different aspects of what was then EEC law.

Part III follows the footsteps of AG Slynn and his tenure, which the editors characterise as a period of embedding the revolutionary doctrines. Contributions of Daniel Sarmiento, Jeff Kenner, Graham Butler, Takis Tridimas, Eleanor Spaventa, John Cotter, Laurence W Gormley, and Steve Terrett introduce readers to Opinions of AG Slynn and their impact.

Part IV focuses on a rare bird, the Opinion of Judge Edward, who acted as AG in a case in the Court of First Instance. Analysis of this Opinion is offered by Richard Whish and, in the closing part of the book, also by Judge Edward himself.

Part V turns the attention to Opinions of AG Jacobs. A mere glance at the period in which he served at the bench, that is 1988–2006, makes one immediately realise what a journey it has been in all possible ways. This was the transition from the European Communities to the European Union, a period when both a deepening and widening of the European Union was in full swing. David T Keeling, Dimitry Kochenov, Adam Łazowski, Angela Ward and Graham Butler, Geert De Baere, Andrea Biondi, Piet Eeckhout, Carl Baudenbacher, Luca Rubini, Anthony Arnull, Peter Oliver, Stefan Enchelmaier, and Anna Łabędzka analyse Opinions delivered at different stages of this period of huge transitions.

---

[5] Opinion of AG Jacobs in Case C-50/00 P *Unión de Pequeños Agricultores v Council* ECLI:EU:C:2002:197. See ch 33.

[6] Case 25/62 *Plaumann* ECLI:EU:C:1963:17.

Part VI focuses on seminal Opinions of AG Sharpston. Helen Xanthaki and Adam Łazowski, Adrienne Yong, Paul Craig, Niamh Nic Shuibhne, Theodore Konstadinides, Tamara Ćapeta, Valsamis Mitsilegas, Ronan McCrea, Panos Koutrakos, Eleni Frantziou, Michael-James Clifton, Alina Tryfonidou, and Sébastien Platon take readers on a journey from status of non-published EU legislation through passenger rights, EU citizenship, environmental protection, non-admissible references for preliminary ruling, European Arrest Warrant, discrimination on grounds of religion or sexual orientation, asylum, competences to conclude trade agreements with third state, to the rule of law.

Part VII comprises respective afterwords by the former UK members of the Court of Justice (and Court of First Instance) who delivered Opinions: former Advocate General, Francis G Jacobs; former Judge, David Edward; and former Advocate General, Eleanor Sharpston.

In Part VIII, aptly titled 'EU Law Without UK Advocates General', the editors bring it all home, and once again return to the leitmotif of this book: shaping EU law the British way.

Part I

Setting the Scene

1

Let's Take the Canvass Out: Advocates General at the Court of Justice of the European Union

GRAHAM BUTLER AND ADAM ŁAZOWSKI

I have the honour of presenting an opinion on the first action to come before the Court of the first European Community, and I shall strive to carry out that task to the best of my ability, in the spirit in which it has been defined by the Statute of the Court.

Advocate General Maurice Lagrange

I. TWO FUNDAMENTAL QUESTIONS

THE endeavour of European Integration has come a long way since Maurice Lagrange delivered, in *France v High Authority*, the very first Opinion of an Advocate General (AG).[1] Shortly after that, the Court of Justice of the European Coal and Steel Community (ECSC) became one Court of Justice for the then three European Communities, later the European Union. Now two of the original European Communities belong to history books (the ECSC ceased to exist in 2002, and the Treaty of Lisbon incorporated the European Economic Community/the European Community into the European Union).[2] The legal landscape has changed beyond recognition, with EU law covering many areas which in the early days were either the domain of national law of Member States, or did not even exist at all.[3] Many actors, including the Court of Justice of the European Union (the Court, or CJEU), its judges, and Advocates General (AGs) have shaped this 'new legal order'.[4] For EU law

---

[1] Opinion of AG Lagrange in Case 1/54 *France v High Authority* ECLI:EU:C:1954:4. See further E Stein, 'The European Coal and Steel Community: The Beginning of Its Judicial Process' (1955) 55 *Columbia Law Review* 985. Interestingly, the author does not mention the Opinion of AG Lagrange at all. The Opinion is discussed, however, in N Burrows and R Greaves, *The Advocate General and EC Law* (Oxford, OUP, 2007) 61.

[2] On the evolution of the Court, see A Arnull, 'The Many Ages of the Court of Justice of the European Union' in C Kilpatrick and J Scott (eds), *New Legal Approaches to Studying the Court of Justice: Revisiting Law in Context* (Oxford, OUP, 2020); K Bradley, 'Judicial Reform and the European Court: Not a Numbers Game' in P Craig and G de Búrca (eds), *The Evolution of EU Law*, 3rd edn (Oxford, OUP, 2021).

[3] On the evolution of EU competences see, inter alia, M Claes and B de Witte, 'Competences: Codification and Contestation' in A Łazowski and S Blockmans (eds), *Research Handbook on EU Institutional Law* (Cheltenham, Edward Elgar, 2016).

[4] This notion was coined by the Court in the seminal Case 26/62 *Van Gend en Loos* ECLI:EU:C:1963:1.

novices, AGs are quite puzzling figures and, not surprisingly, two fundamental questions are often asked: who are AGs, and what is their role? A simple answer is, of course, that AGs are a part of the Court: they are members of the Court, just like the judges, and their function is to advise the Court on the cases at hand, to put the cases in the broader context of EU law, and to suggest solutions.[5] The reality, however, is far more nuanced, and deserves a more thorough analysis.

'So, you are a British Advocate General, aren't you? Jolly good, jolly good, and which regiment do you serve in?' was the exact question that AG Sharpston was asked by an English gentleman at a public function a few vintages ago.[6] By the appearance of things, she was not the first called on to respond to such a query. Something must have been in the air much earlier, as Jean-Pierre Warner, the first UK AG at the Court,[7] felt compelled to clarify that the AG 'is not an advocate any more than he is a General'.[8] Francis Jacobs, the longest serving UK AG, explained his role along the same lines.[9] For many, even inside the legal profession of any Member State, the concept of an AG may be puzzling or hard to comprehend. As noted in 2012 by Bobek, before he later became an AG himself some years thereafter:

> For most European lawyers educated outside of France, Belgium or the Netherlands, the idea of a fourth person in the court, permanently sitting, but being neither a judge nor a party, is somewhat odd.[10]

Despite the confusion that may arise, it is unquestionable that AGs are a well-established feature of the EU legal landscape. So, back to the two questions listed earlier, who are AGs, and what is their role?

II. APPOINTMENT OF ADVOCATES GENERAL

As a starting point, it is fitting to rehearse the rules governing the appointment of AGs. They are laid down in Article 253 TFEU. For a first-time reader, it quickly becomes apparent that they share many commonalities with the modus operandi applicable to the appointment of judges, which is regulated in the same provision.[11] The article sets out two different, alternative qualification grounds for potential appointees to be AG (or a judge). First, appointees may be persons 'who possess the qualifications required for appointment to the highest judicial offices

---

[5] The prototype of AGs was the *commissaire du gouvernement* in the French Council of State. The proposal came from the French government during the negotiations of the Treaty establishing the Coal and Steel Community, furthermore one of the two first AGs, AG Lagrange, had been prior *commissaire du gouvernement*. See A Dashwood, 'The Advocate General in the Court of Justice of the European Communities' (1982) 2 *Legal Studies* 202, 204–207.

[6] Eleanor Sharpston QC: First 100 Years Biography, available at www.youtube.com/watch?v=qGAIqnsiK7Q.

[7] The terms 'UK Advocates General' and 'British Advocates General' are used interchangeably. While, prima facie, it may not look as fully accurate, the fact of the matter is that the United Kingdom never appointed an AG from Northern Ireland. Hence, factually, accuracy is maintained. See ch 3.

[8] JP Warner, 'Some Aspects of the European Court of Justice' (1976) 14 *Journal of the Society of Public Teachers of Law* 14, 16.

[9] P Moser and K Sawyer, 'Introduction: Making Community Law. The Legacy of Advocate General Jacobs at the European Court of Justice' in P Moser and K Sawyer (eds), *Making Community Law: The Legacy of Advocate General Jacobs at the European Court of Justice* (Cheltenham, Edward Elgar, 2008) 1, 4.

[10] M Bobek, 'A Fourth in the Court: Why Are There Advocates General in the Court of Justice?' (2012) 14 *Cambridge Yearbook of European Legal Studies* 529, 530.

[11] Further on the appointment of judges and AGs (and, for comparison, judges of the European Court of Human Rights) see, inter alia, M Bobek (ed), *Selecting Europe's Judges: A Critical Review of the Appointment Procedures to the European Courts* (Oxford, OUP, 2015).

in their respective countries', or second, as clear from the use of *or*, in the alternative, appointees may be persons who 'are jurisconsults of recognised competence'.[12]

What a jurisconsult is must be given an autonomous definition as a matter of EU law, and is not subject to qualification by national law, or be in any way equated with qualification for national judicial office. The established practice of Member States nominating AGs means that candidates and appointed persons can be anyone who is familiar with the law, from legal academics, judges, civil servants, to even former politicians.[13] In other words, the threshold to be qualified to be a member of the Court, and thus an AG, is not terribly high.[14] Despite this, only persons who are sufficiently competent in EU law will pass the muster of the Article 255 TFEU panel, which determines the suitability of persons for membership of the Court.[15] About one in four candidates put forth for nomination by Member States do not get their stamp of approval of being sufficiently competent,[16] and thus, their nomination fails. Those who do receive approval are considered competent, and in turn, they are subject to a decision taken unanimously by the representatives of the governments of EU Member States.[17] It should be remembered that term of appointment for AGs, just like the judges at the Court, is six years. This term is renewable only in relation to the five AGs nominated by France, Germany, Italy, Spain, and Poland. The remaining six AGs positions[18] come from the other Member States, and are subject to an alphabetical rotation system,[19] which translates into a general non-renewability of their terms.[20]

---

[12] This was not the case for judges of the Court of Justice of ECSC. In fact, the first French judge was an economist, while the first Dutch judge was a trade union leader. See Warner (n 8) 17.

[13] A Arnull, *The European Union and Its Court of Justice*, 2nd edn (Oxford, OUP, 2006) 20. To prove this point, it is enough to make a quick *tour de table* of currently serving AGs. AG Szpunar, the first Advocate General has an academic background. Furthermore, prior to his appointment to the Court, he was a deputy minister of foreign affairs and agent of Poland before the Court. AG Kokott has primarily academic background; the same applies to AG Ćapeta. AG Campos Sánchez-Bordona, AG Richard de la Tour, AG Rantos, and AG Pikamäe have judicial backgrounds. AG Collins was a legal practitioner for most of his career prior to serving at the Court (though AG Collins was previously a judge in the General Court), while AG Medina, AG Pitruzzella, and AG Emiliou held various functions in the state administration (though AG Emiliou had started his career as an academic). Several AGs had worked earlier in their lives at the Court as *référendaires* to either judges or AGs, including Francis Jacobs and Eleanor Sharpston to AG Warner and AG and Judge Slynn respectively. Looking at the list of persons who have served as AGs previously, many were academics, including AG Van Gerven, AG Poiares Maduro, AG Trstenjak, AG Wahl, and AG Bobek.

[14] Rather bizarrely, and surely an error, to be a judge of the General Court, a person shall be someone 'who possess the ability required for appointment to high judicial office' (Art 254 TFEU, second para), but the 'jurisconsults of recognised competence' part that is applicable to the Court of Justice is omitted. Given that the Court of Justice is the appellant court of the General Court, it must be construed that 'jurisconsults of recognised competence' is enough for a person to be appointed to the General Court.

[15] See, inter alia, T Dumbrovský et al, 'Judicial Appointments: The Article 255 TFEU Advisory Panel and Selection Procedures in the Member States' (2014) 51 *CMLRev* 455.

[16] See Sixth activity report of the panel provided for by Art 255 TFEU, available at https://curia.europa.eu/jcms/upload/docs/application/pdf/2020-01/qcar19002enn_002_-_public.pdf.

[17] For the weaknesses in the design of Art 253 TFEU, see D Kochenov and G Butler, 'Independence of the Court of Justice of the European Union: Unchecked Member States power after the Sharpston Affair' (2021) *ELJ* 262.

[18] This number may be altered by the Council of the EU.

[19] The alphabetical rotation system follows the source languages of the Member States. Therefore, the alphabetical order is not necessarily the same as it would be in the English language. For example, Croatia is Hrvatska, Cyprus is Κύπρος, Austria is Österreich, and Finland is Suomi.

[20] The only person from the group of Member States that are subject to the rotation system has served twice as Advocate General was AG Mischo from Luxembourg (1986–1991 and 1997–2003). Bearing in mind that the EU now comprises 27 Member States, such an occurrence is quite unlikely in the future, though it should not be excluded, especially when younger AGs are appointed. For criticism of the general non-renewability of terms of the majority of AGs, see ch 50 by Jacobs in this volume.

Once appointed and sworn in, AGs are full members of the Court, with judges being judges, and AGs being AGs. As noted by Dashwood, historically 'the Advocates General took precedence after the Judges', this however was changed in 1974, when the ranks were equalised. Since then, precedence has been hinged upon time spent at the bench.[21] Initially, with only two AGs at the Court, there was no need to have a *primus inter pares*. This quite obviously changed when the number of AGs started to grow. Following the first enlargement of the European Communities, when the number of AGs was increased to four, the post of First AG was created. Until 2020, AGs used to rotate the position of First AG on an annual basis. To ensure more continuity, the renewable term of First AG has been increased to three years.[22] This function is currently held by AG Szpunar. The role of the First AG is not purely ceremonial. She/he is in charge of allocating cases among the team of AGs,[23] and has other important functions, such as the *le réexamen* procedure when specialised courts exist.[24]

III. THE ROLE OF ADVOCATES GENERAL: ASSIST BUT NOT SUBSTITUTE

No matter who holds the office of AG, the EU Treaties anticipate that it will be a 'person[] whose independence is beyond doubt'.[25] This is a pre-condition for successful performance of the role, which – as already alluded to – is to assist the Court. But what does that mean exactly?

The EU Treaties are rather vague as to the role of the AGs. They are 'to make, in open court, reasoned submissions on cases'.[26] What has been understood as 'reasoned submissions' has in turn become what are known as Opinions.[27] It might be thought that the assistance provided to judges would mean that they have a team of assistants or support staff to help them prepare a judgment for a case before them. But the EU Treaties provide that AGs are members of the Court, and must deliver their assistance publicly, which implies that they are not *fonctionnaires*. In fact, AG's cabinets are traditionally staffed with just as many *référendaires* as those of the judges. Today, both AGs and judges are housed in offices on the sixth and seventh floors of the Palais de Justice, and they attend the general meeting (*réunion générale*) of all members of the Court, where cases are discussed.[28]

In order to perform well, AGs need to be masters of both telescope and microscope.[29] Put differently, AGs have to be imaginative creatures. Their task is to equip the Court with solutions to the case at hand or – more broadly – to a pertinent legal issue. Often, this requires presentation of both the big picture and the small print. Venturing into unknown territories alongside familiar pastures is part of the job description. According to Weatherill, there are

---

[21] Dashwood (n 5) 203. See also Warner (n 8) 17.

[22] See Art 14 of the Rules of Procedure of the Court of Justice [2012] OJ L 265/1.

[23] Art 16 of the Rules of Procedure of the Court of Justice.

[24] See, inter alia, G Butler, 'An Interim Post-Mortem: Specialised Courts in the EU Judicial Architecture after the Civil Service Tribunal' (2020) 17 *International Organizations Law Review* 586.

[25] Art 19(2) TEU and Art 253 TFEU.

[26] Art 252 TFEU, second para. For interpretation by the Court itself see, inter alia, Order of the Court in Case C-17/98 *Emesa Sugar* ECLI:EU:C:2000:69.

[27] This rather unfortunate wording is a mistake in translation. According to Warner, the unofficial translation of the Treaties, which was used by the UK Foreign Office, employed the notion 'conclusions'. Alas, 'conclusions' became 'submissions' when the translation was finalised, and this mistranslation has never been corrected. See Warner (n 8) 16.

[28] Not to be confused with the deliberations in specific cases, which involve the sitting judges in a given case only.

[29] Paraphrased here are the words of the US Chief Justice Hughes, who described Justice Brandeis, also a member of the US Supreme Court, as a 'master of both microscope and telescope'. See RB Ginsburg, *My Own Words* (Simon & Schuster, 2016) 82.

five features of a good AG: clarity of expression; clarity of vision; contextual richness; leadership; and capacity to inspire.[30] It can be said that the role of the AG is to challenge the Court or, as put by Warner, referring to the speech of Donner (a former Dutch judge and President of the Court): 'the opinion of the Advocate-General [gives] the Judges something to "rub their minds against"'.[31] As experience proves, AGs may, in addition to the analysis of EU legislation, also reach to the national laws of Member States, the jurisprudence of the European Court of Human Rights, the EFTA Court,[32] or even go beyond European jurisdictions.[33]

But, most importantly, AGs in their Opinions include assessments of the previous jurisprudence of the Court. Being in full awareness of *jurisprudence constante*, a desideratum held dear by the judges, AGs may not only rehearse the existing jurisprudence but, in equal measure, praise or criticise it, and thus potentially ask the Court to overrule itself. As noted by Greaves, AGs are engaged in constant dialogue with the Court on matters of EU law.[34] AGs are also in constant dialogue with each other. This may happen, for instance, on a rare occasion when two Opinions are provided in a single case by the same AG,[35] or two different AGs,[36] which most interestingly may involve two AGs from the same Member State appointed in succession.[37] Another option is when similar cases are pending in parallel. An excellent example of this is the three Opinions of AGs on the compatibility of domestic rules on the use of goods with Article 34 TFEU, and the relevance of the *Keck* jurisprudence in this regard,[38] or Opinions in the first two headscarf cases.[39]

AGs have also a unique relationship with the world of academia. This is explored further at the end of this chapter, but for now it suffices to say that some AGs are EU legal scholars before and/or after joining the Court. Furthermore, many AGs regularly enrich their Opinions by citing academic articles and commentaries.[40] The judges in the Court, however, whilst

---

[30] S Weatherill, 'A Consumer's Appreciation of the Contribution of Advocate General Francis Jacobs to the Shaping of the EC's Legal Order' in P Moser and K Sawyer (eds), *Making Community Law: The Legacy of Advocate General Jacobs at the European Court of Justice* (Cheltenham, Edward Elgar, 2008) 28, 30–31.

[31] Warner (n 8) 19.

[32] See C Baudenbacher, 'The EFTA Court's Relationship with the Advocates General of the Court of Justice' in MT D'Alessio et al (eds), *De Rome à Lisbonne Les Juridictions de l'Union Européenne à La Croisée Des Chemins: Mélanges En l'honneur de Paolo Mengozzi* (Bruylant, 2013); C Baudenbacher, 'The EFTA Court, the ECJ, and the Latter's Advocates General – a Tale of Judicial Dialogue' in A Arnull et al (eds), *Continuity and Change in EU Law: Essays in Honour of Sir Francis Jacobs* (Oxford, OUP, 2008); P Mengozzi, 'The Advocates General and the EFTA Court' in EFTA Court (ed), *The EEA and the EFTA Court: Decentred Integration* (Oxford, Hart Publishing, 2014).

[33] See L Faircloth Peoples, 'The Influence of Foreign Law Cited in the Opinions of Advocates General on Community Law' (2009) 28 YEL 458.

[34] R Greaves, 'Reforming Some Aspects of the Role of Advocates General' in A Arnull et al (eds), *A Constitutional Order of States? Essays in EU Law in Honour of Alan Dashwood* (Oxford, Hart Publishing, 2011) 161, 169–70.

[35] See Opinion of AG Van Gerven in Joined Cases C-267/91 and C-268/91 *Keck* ECLI:EU:C:1992:448; Opinion of AG Van Gerven in Joined Cases C-267/91 and C-268/91 *Keck* ECLI:EU:C:1993:160.

[36] See Opinion of AG Léger in Case C-110/05 *Commission v Italy* ECLI:EU:C:2006:646; Opinion of AG Bot in Case C-110/05 *Commission v Italy* ECLI:EU:C:2006:646.

[37] See Opinion of AG Tizzano in Case C-170/04 *Rosengren* ECLI:EU:C:2006:213; Opinion of AG Mengozzi in Case C-170/04 *Rosengren* ECLI:EU:C:2006:213; Opinion of AG Warner in Case 155/79 *AM&S* ECLI:EU:C:1981:9; Opinion of AG Slynn in Case 155/79 *AM&S* ECLI:EU:C:1982:17. In relation to *AM&S* see ch 14.

[38] See Opinion of AG Léger in Case C-110/05 *Commission v Italy* ECLI:EU:C:2006:646; Opinion of AG Bot in Case C-110/05 *Commission v Italy* ECLI:EU:C:2006:646; and Opinion of AG Kokott in Case 142/05 *Mickelsson and Roos* ECLI:EU:C:2006:782.

[39] Opinion of AG Sharpston in Case C-188/15 *Bougnaoui* ECLI:EU:C:2016:2016:553; Opinion of AG Kokott in Case 157/15 *Achbita* ECLI:EU:C:2016:382. See ch 44.

[40] This, however, is not always the case. For instance, as noted by Mortelmans, AG Geelhoed – despite coming with years of academic experience under his belt – hardly ever referred to academic writing in his Opinions. See K Mortelmans, 'The Court under the Influence of its Advocates General: An Analysis of the Case Law on the Functioning of the Internal Market' (2005) 24 YEL 127, 137. That said, this is the exception, and the rule appears to be that most AGs do refer to academic works.

evidently making use of academic literature in the crafting of their judgments, do not openly cite such sources. The work of the AGs is thus more transparent and open.

Much can be said about the writing style of Opinions of the AGs, which frequently stands in stark contrast to the dry, often unreadable, style of the Court itself.[41] There are a number of reasons for the Court's difficult style of judgment writing. First, the judgments are products of collective work. With no dissenting opinions on the Court's menu, decisions of the Court are – in a way – negotiated within the assigned chamber handling the case. This is where the well-known rule of life: 'the more the merrier' is not fit for purpose. It is defeated by 'less is more'. Put in different terms, achieving consensus in the chamber of three or five judges may be tricky, but it becomes complicated when the Court sits as Grand Chamber or Full Court. The quality of the judgment may be the ultimate victim of the consensus, which may lead to pruning of the reasoning and some resort being had to creative ambiguity.[42] Since the deliberations of the judges are secret, very little is known about how consensus is reached in any given case. It is easy to imagine, though, that some cases will be relatively straightforward, whereas others may lead to a ding-dong between the judges. As Slynn euphemistically put it, 'this can be an absorbing and a highly creative experience'.[43]

In contrast, the Opinions of AGs are the result of their own work, and of course that of their *référendaires*. AGs may choose to write their Opinion in any official language of the EU,[44] while judges draft the master copy of the judgment and conduct their *délibéré* in French.[45] Thus, for ease of expression, AGs may (though they frequently do not) write in their mother tongue.

All of this, put together, shows that AGs have much more freedom to shape their Opinions to their liking. It, however, comes at the price of exposure. Whilst the judges adjudicate and deliver judgments as a collegiate body of judges, ranging from small three-judge chambers to the Full Court formation, with the public knowing only who the reporting judge (*juge rapporteur*) was, an AG has to deliver an Opinion in her/his own name. This means that the AGs – all 11 of them at the moment – are more likely to be known by name than many of their fellow members of the Court, ie, the judges. And, by this token, they are exposed to critique by the commentariat in particular professional and academic circles. It is fitting to note that the Opinions of AGs are made public, and in bygone era, were published jointly with judgments in the European Court Reports.[46]

It is essential to remember, however, that the Opinions of AGs are not binding on the Court. Furthermore, the Court – in express terms – does not regularly engage with the Opinions. At best, the Court contents itself with a mere cross reference to the Opinion of the AG, and this is a fairly recent occurrence. Still, Opinions of AGs are of highest relevance as they prepare

---

[41] See L Pierdominici, *The Mimetic Evolution of the Court of Justice of the EU: A Comparative Law Perspective* (London, Palgrave Macmillan, 2020) 317–50.

[42] On the role of Grand Chambers see M Bobek, 'What Are Grand Chambers for?' (2022) 23 *CYELS* 1.

[43] G Slynn, *Introducing a European Legal Order* (London, Stevens and Sons Ltd, 1992) 158.

[44] However, the established practice is that the Opinions of the AGs are typically drafted in one of the main languages of the EU: English, French, and German.

[45] See GF Mancini and DT Keeling, 'Language, Culture and Politics in the Life of the European Court of Justice' (1995) 1 *CJEL* 397, 397–98. For criticism of this outdated approach see A Arnull, 'The Working Language of the CJEU: Time for a Change?' (2018) 43 *ELRev* 904.

[46] As a matter of standard practice, Opinions are now published on the website of the Court on the date an Opinion is presented to the Court, and later in the Eur-Lex database.

the ground for the judgments and draw the attention of the judges to matters not yet explored or raised by the parties in written pleadings, or at oral hearings.[47] Opinions may also offer a combination of short- and long-term solutions that may be used by the Court in its future jurisprudence. In the words of Slynn, first an AG, and then a judge:

> As an advocate general, one always hoped that the function had some utility; as a judge I know it is very valuable in this kind of court to have a detailed first-round assessment on which the judges can work. The research, the analysis of fact and law, the direction indicated by the advocate general – even if not followed – are of considerable help.[48]

The audience of AGs is much broader, though. Their Opinions may be of good use also for lawyers, civil servants, and for the academic community. In extreme cases of poorly reasoned judgments of the Court, instead, the Opinions of the AGs have the potential to shed light on the reasons behind the final decision. As one of the present authors argued in an earlier contribution to the debate, in such cases the risk is that the fine line between advising and substituting the Court may be crossed.[49] This is not merely an abstract risk. It is typically said that the Opinions of the AGs are clearer, given the improved framing of the legal question before them, the broader context of the cases, and the novelty of the matters before them in the cases at hand.

It is no secret that the style of the Court's judgments often leaves much to be desired in terms of legal reasoning, with readers typically wanting more explanation of why the Court has reached a particular decision. It would be difficult to write judgments in a more technical and impersonal style than that adopted by the Court. One departing judge of the Court even noted that, 'our judgments … can hardly be said to be particularly reader-friendly. In fact, the operative part is not infrequently on the border of being incomprehensible'. He went on to note how the Court could begin to adapt the style of its judgments, bringing them closer to the Opinions of the AGs.[50]

In this sense, the AGs not only assist the Court, but also play a vital role by providing better jurisprudence, which lawyers working in the legal order can comprehend. One of the most well-known examples, where a very detailed AG Opinion was delivered, but the reasoning of the Court was appallingly thin, was *Ruiz Zambrano*.[51] There, AG Sharpston weighed up all the different approaches the Court could take on the question about the lack of a cross-border dimension in the case involving Union citizenship of Belgian national children in Belgium,[52] before offering her proposition on how the Court should rule the case. By contrast, there was no discussion whatsoever in the judgment of the Court. The reasoning was confined to just

---

[47] In extreme cases, the Opinions of AGs may end the proceedings at the Court. For instance the European Commission withdrew the case after the Opinion of the AG was delivered in Case C-13/07 *Commission v Council* ECLI:EU:C:2009:190 (*Accession of Vietnam to the WTO*), Opinion of AG Kokott. Furthermore, in November 2014, following an Opinion of AG Jääskinen, the UK government withdrew an action for annulment. The official line of the Whitehall was that the case would certainly be lost, and therefore there was no point in wasting any more taxpayers' money. See Opinion of AG Jääskinen in Case C-507/13 *UK v Parliament and Council* ECLI:EU:C:2014:2394.

[48] Slynn (n 43) 157.

[49] A Łazowski, 'Advocates General and Grand Chamber Cases: Assistance with the Touch of Substitution' (2012) 14 *CYELS* 635.

[50] CG Fernlund, 'Audience Solennelle de La Cour de Justice du 7 Octobre 2019 à l'occasion de La Cessation des Fonctions de M. Le Juge Rosas et M. Le Juge Fernlund et de l'entrée en Fonctions de MM. Niilo Jääskinen et Nils Wahl en Qualité de Juges à La Cour de Justice' (Luxembourg, 7 October 2019) 13.

[51] Case C-34/09 *Ruiz Zambrano* ECLI:EU:C:2011:124.

[52] Opinion of AG Sharpston in Case C-34/09 *Ruiz Zambrano* ECLI:EU:C:2010:560. For analysis see ch 40.

a few short paragraphs, and left more questions than answers. Yet *Ruiz Zambrano* has had a huge impact on the rights of Union citizens who find themselves with family members in precarious situations vis-à-vis the Member States.[53]

IV. SEVENTY YEARS OF ADVOCATES GENERAL: EVOLUTION THROUGH DECADES

The position of AGs has not remained static through the years. Whilst the expected function of the AG remains the same, the greater environs of the Court, and the way in which the AGs are organised, have undergone subtle changes over time.

As noted above, the first AGs were members of the Court of Justice of the ECSC. At these early stages of European integration, AGs as an institution lacked a legal anchor in the Treaty itself. Since the idea of adding AGs to the bench was a last-minute endeavour, their status was regulated only in the Statute of the Court. This, of course, changed soon after when the other two European Communities were created and by means of the Merger Treaty, one Court for all three organisations.[54] The 1970s saw some changes with regard to the number of AGs. Moreover, in 1974, the post of the First AG was established. The rule that the President of the Court would decide which AG was to be assigned a case was no longer fit for purpose,[55] and this role now belongs to the First AG.[56]

One of the most fundamental reforms affecting the role of AGs was introduced by the Treaty of Nice.[57] It was part and parcel of wider reform effort aimed at improving the functioning of the Court, including the then Court of First Instance.[58] The troubles at the Court caused by an increase in case numbers are well documented in the literature, and need no further rehearsing.[59] It is worth remembering, though, that from the early days of the European Communities, through to 2003, Opinions of AGs were required in almost all cases. While perfectly justified in the formational years of the European Communities, the system was not fit for purpose by the time the European Communities and the European Union entered into the new millennium. AGs became unnecessarily involved in trivial cases, including straightforward infractions brought by the European Commission for Member State failures to comply with directives, where the Member State would simply admit to the Court that it had not implemented them. Thus, giving the institution a choice to proceed with or without an Opinion was a very welcome change.

---

[53] See D Ferri and G Martinico, 'Revisiting the Ruiz Zambrano Doctrine and Exploring the Potential for Its Extensive Application' (2021) 27 *EPL* 685, and K Hyltén-Cavallius, 'Who Cares? Caregivers' Derived Residence Rights from Children in EU Free Movement Law' (2020) 57 *CMLRev* 399.

[54] Convention relative à certaines institutions communes aux Communautés Européennes, available at https://eur-lex.europa.eu/legal-content/FR/TXT/PDF/?uri=CELEX:11957K/TXT&from=EN.

[55] This is evident from the case files available from the Historical Archives of the European Union (HAEU) at the European University Institute (EUI) in Italy, which houses the archives of the Court.

[56] See Dashwood (n 5) 204.

[57] Treaty of Nice amending the Treaty on European Union, the Treaties establishing the European Communities and certain related acts, signed at Nice, 26 February 2001 [2001] C80/1. For an assessment see, inter alia, P Eeckhout, 'The European Courts after Nice' in M Andenas and J Usher (eds), *The Treaty of Nice and Beyond: Enlargement and Constitutional Reform* (Oxford, Hart Publishing, 2003).

[58] Support for such solution came from many participants in the debate. See, inter alia, W Van Gerven, 'The Role and Structure of the European Judiciary Now and in the Future' (1996) 21 *ELRev* 211, 222. However, for a recent opposite view advocating for the return of compulsory – or almost compulsory – Opinions of AGs, see Arnull (n 2) 44.

[59] See, for instance, P Craig, 'The Jurisdiction of the Community Courts Reconsidered' in G de Búrca and JHH Weiler (eds), *The European Court of Justice* (Oxford, OUP, 2001).

Today, AGs do not deliver Opinions in all cases, as previously required. Instead, whilst an AG is assigned to every case on the docket of the Court, once the case is allotted to an AG, it is up to each AG and their cabinet to suggest whether an Opinion is warranted. The decision on how to proceed is taken by the Court at the *réunion générale*. Rumour has it that sometimes this may lead to discussions between a *juge rapporteur* and an AG as to the right course of action. This innovation by the Treaty of Nice has meant that judicial resources have been freed up to ensure that only the more important cases, ones which raise new material questions of law, are pondered further. Today, the Statute of the Court provides that where the Court considers that a case 'raises no new point of law', the Court 'may decide, after hearing the [AG], that the case shall be determined without a submission from the [AG]'.[60] The result has been a drop-off in the number of Opinions, with Opinions now only delivered by AGs in a minority of cases. Put differently, Opinions are reserved for the flagship cases, which bring new elements to EU law.

All in all, however, the output of the 11 AGs remains impressive indeed. In 2017, the AGs delivered 323 Opinions. In 2018, they delivered 308 Opinions. The following year it was 311 Opinions, and in 2020, despite the COVID-19 pandemic, they delivered 239 Opinions. In 2021 they delivered 268 Opinions. With 11 AGs, the number of Opinions delivered has remained relatively steady. Just 10 years before, in 2008, there were 209 Opinions; in 2009 there were 206 Opinions; and in 2010, there were 211 Opinions.

Last but not least, it is worth noting a considerable change to proceedings under Article 218(11) TFEU, relating to the Opinion procedure in which the Court offers, at the request of a specified institution or Member State, *ex ante* judicial review of compatibility of international agreements with EU law.[61] Experience has proven that this is a powerful tool in the hands of the Court, and one which allows it to shape the wider contours of EU external action.[62] Traditionally, in such cases the Court renders an Opinion, as opposed to a typical judgment. Despite the name, the Opinion of the Court is binding. In the past, in the Opinion procedure cases, all AGs presented their views to the Court. They were not made available to the members of the public. In recent times, this practice has changed. Now the procedure follows the usual *modus operandi*. An AG is allocated to the case and presents a formal Opinion[63] or a View[64] before the Court completes the proceedings with its own Opinion of the Court. Given that the Opinion procedure is of seminal importance in the field of EU external relations law,[65] this is a welcome development.

V. THE POSSIBILITY FOR A JUDGE TO ACT AS AN ADVOCATE GENERAL IN THE GENERAL COURT

As is well known, there are no AGs at the General Court. Nor can AGs in the Court participate in proceedings at the General Court. The lack of AGs at the General Court has not, however,

---

[60] Art 20, fifth paragraph, Protocol (No 3) on the Statute of the Court of Justice of the European Union.

[61] See further G Butler, 'Pre-Ratification Judicial Review of International Agreements to be Concluded by the European Union' in M Derlén and J Lindholm (eds), *The Court of Justice of the European Union: Multidisciplinary Perspectives* (Oxford, Hart Publishing, 2018).

[62] In recent jurisprudence see, inter alia, *Opinion 2/15* ECLI:EU:C:2017:376. See ch 45.

[63] See for instance Opinion of AG Sharpston in *Opinion 2/15* ECLI:EU:C:2016:992.

[64] See for instance View of AG Jääskinen in *Opinion 1/13* ECLI:EU:C:2014:2292.

[65] See G Butler and RA Wessel (eds), *EU External Relations Law: The Cases in Context* (Oxford, Hart Publishing, 2022).

passed unnoticed. In fact, it was one of the items on the negotiating table when the Member States were shaping the future Court of First Instance (now the General Court). However, the view prevailed that, due to limited role of the court *in spe* and the fact that it would not have the role in developing EU law (despite the fact that it actually would), there was no need to have AGs on the bench of the Court of First Instance. Yet, should a need potentially arise, the option of asking one of the judges to act as an AG in individual cases was created.[66]

The basic framework is provided in Article 49, first paragraph of the Statute of the Court of Justice.[67] Further rules are elaborated in the Rules of Procedure of the General Court, which envisage that one of the judges may serve as an AG if the case is particularly difficult or factually complex.[68] It is notable that not all judges of the General Court may be called to serve as the AG. The exceptions include the President of the Court, as well as presidents of chambers who are barred from doing so. The right of initiative is vested in the hands of the chamber to which the case is allocated, which has to request approval from the General Court Plenum (all judges). Once the green light is given, an AG will be appointed from the pool of eligible judges by the President of the General Court.[69] As per Article 112 of the Rules of Procedure, Opinions are communicated to the parties, and once that happens, the oral part of the procedure comes to an end.

In reality, this option has been hardly ever utilised in the General Court. In fact, after experiments in the early 1990s, which resulted in a total of four Opinions – it has not been put in motion since.[70] Judge Edward remains the last person to have been a judge in the General Court (then Court of First Instance) in 1992 in delivering an Opinion when acting as an AG.[71] Given the reforms to the General Court in recent years, including, inter alia, an expansion of the General Court to now include two judges nominated by each Member State, there is no reason why, with such added resources and a potentially underworked judiciary, Opinions could not return to the General Court. AGs would not be appointed to the General Court, but judges, in specific cases, could be called upon to fulfil that function.

Why this procedure has only ever been utilised on four occasions remains a mystery. Support for the return of judges acting as AGs in specific cases in the General Court is thin on the ground,[72] despite the many arguments debating whether the novelty of such action would be a welcome return. Nonetheless, genuine consideration must be given to improving the quality of judgments from the General Court, as the types of cases it hears continue to be expanded. After all, today, the General Court is the administrative court of the Union, with a broad mandate. Contemporary cases raise more novel questions of EU law than were previously heard at the General Court, and go beyond its original remit of dealing with a limited array of direct actions.

---

[66] See, inter alia, LN Brown and T Kennedy, *Brown & Jacobs The Court of Justice of the European Communities*, 5th edn (Sweet & Maxwell, 2000) 82.

[67] Protocol No 3 on the Statute of the Court of Justice [2016] OJ C202/1.

[68] Art 30 of Rules of Procedure of the General Court [2015] OJ L105/1.

[69] Art 31 of Rules of Procedure of the General Court.

[70] Opinion of Mr Kirschner, Judge in the Court of First Instance, in Case T-51/89 *Tetra Pak* ECLI:EU:T:1990:15; Opinion of Judge Biancarelli of the Court of First Instance in Case T-120/89 *Stahlwerke Peine-Salzgitter* ECLI:EU:T:1991:6; Opinion of Mr Vesterdorf acting as Advocate General in Case T-1/89 *Rhône-Poulenc* ECLI:EU:T:1991:38; Opinion of Judge Edward acting as Advocate General in Case T-24/90 *Automec* and Case T-28/90 *Asia Motor France* ECLI:EU:T:1992:39.

[71] See R Greaves, 'Judge Edward Acting as Advocate General' in M Hoskins and W Robinson (eds), *A True European: Essays for Judge David Edward* (Oxford, Hart Publishing, 2003). See chs 23 and 51.

[72] Exceptionally, see P Nihoul, 'The General Court at a Crossroad' in F Amtenbrink et al (eds), *The Internal Market and the Future of European Integration: Essays in Honour of Laurence W Gormley* (Cambridge, CUP, 2018) 399, 403–404.

VI. ADVOCATES GENERAL AND ACADEMIA

There is no doubt that there is an unspoken of, but very real relationship between the AGs and the academic community. As already mentioned, some of the AGs come from the world of academia, or were a part of it at some point in their careers. But there is, of course, much more to it than that. Many scholars, including the editors of this book, follow developments at the Court on a daily basis and eagerly await – in equal measure – Opinions of AGs and judgments of the Court. At a basic level of research, Opinions provide anticipatory guidance to the forthcoming judgments on the docket of the Court, owing to the fact that they are published usually months before the Court delivers its judgments. For the Court, whilst there is obviously value in a given chamber having the Opinion of an AG to hand, it is somewhat difficult to conceal the reality: that the AGs are sometimes – and it is their job to be – a bit of nuisance for the judges, despite providing useful advice. As noted by Ritter, 'Advocates-General act to some extent as intermediaries between the Court and the academic world'.[73]

Whilst AGs are perhaps individually well known in EU legal circles, their actual role remains, as we argue, under-researched. Given that AGs have been part of the Court since its very inception in the 1950s, this is not easily excusable. With a few notable exceptions, not much ink has been spilled on analysing their contribution to the judicial discourse that emerges from the Palais de Justice on the Kirchberg Plateau in Luxembourg. An overview of the existing literature reveals a few strands.

First, there are a number of publications introducing, in a general fashion, the function of the AGs.[74] Not surprisingly, several contributions that fall into this category were prepared either by AGs themselves, or by their former *référendaires*, who – to paraphrase Oscar Wilde – could resist anything but temptation, in taking upon their shoulders the task of popularising the work of the AGs.[75] A second and less populated strand in the existing literature covers publications focusing on the impact of AGs on particular areas of EU law,[76] or the work of selected AGs.[77] The third strand is literature on the Court, where – for reasons which deserve

---

[73] C Ritter, 'A New Look at the Role and Impact of Advocates-General – Collectively and Individually' (2006) 12 *CJEL* 751, 759.

[74] See, inter alia, K Borgsmidt, 'The Advocate General at the European Court of Justice' (1988) 13 *ELRev* 106; A Albors-Llorens, 'Securing Trust in the Court of Justice of the EU: The Influence of the Advocates General' (2011–2012) 14 *CYELS* 509; L Clément-Wilz, 'The Advocate General: A Key Actor of the Court of Justice of the European Union' (2011–2012) 14 *CYELS* 587; A Hinarejos, 'Social Legitimacy and the Court of Justice of the EU: Some Reflections on the Role of the Advocate General' (2011–2012) 14 *CYELS* 615; S Turenne, 'Advocate Generals' Opinions or Separate Opinions? Judicial Engagement in the CJEU' (2011–2012) 14 *CYELS* 723; Greaves (n 34); Ritter (n 73); Bobek (n 10).

[75] See, inter alia, Warner (n 8); FG Jacobs, 'Advocates General and Judges in the European Court of Justice' in D O'Keeffe and A Bavasso (eds), *Judicial Review in European Union Law: Liber Amicorum in Honour of Lord Slynn of Hadley* (The Hague: Kluwer Law International, 2000); E Sharpston, 'The Changing Role of the Advocate General' in A Arnull et al (eds), *Continuity and Change in EU Law: Essays in Honour of Sir Francis Jacobs* (Oxford, OUP, 2008); N Fennelly, 'Reflections of an Irish Advocate General' (1996) 5 *Irish Journal of European Law* 5; P Léger, 'Law in the European Union: The Role of the Advocate General' (2004) 10 *The Journal of Legislative Studies* 1; M Damon, 'The Role of the Advocate General at the Court of Justice of the European Communities' in S Shetreet (ed), *The Role of Courts in Society* (Leiden, Martinus Nijhoff, 1988); M Szpunar, 'Zur Rolle des Generalanwalts im aktuellen System der EU-Gerichtsbarkeit' in B Łukańko and A Thiele (eds) *In Reformprozesse der Europäischen Gerichtsbarkeit: Herausforderungen aus deutscher und polnischer Sicht* (Tübingen, Mohr Siebeck, 2019); T Tridimas, 'The Role of the Advocate General in the Development of Community Law: Some Reflections' (1997) 34 *CMLRev* 1349; Dashwood (n 5).

[76] See, inter alia, T Ćapeta, 'The Advocate General: Bringing Clarity to CJEU Decisions? A Case-Study of Mangold and Kücükdeveci (2011–2012) 14 *CYELS* 563; HW Micklitz, *The Politics of Judicial Co-operation in the EU: Sunday Trading, Equal Treatment and Good Faith* (Cambridge, CUP, 2003) 108–121, 244–257; Mortelmans (n 40).

[77] See P Moser and K Sawyer (eds), *Making Community Law: The Legacy of Advocate General Jacobs at the European Court of Justice* (Cheltenham, Edward Elgar, 2008); R Greaves, 'Selected Opinions Delivered by Advocate Lagrange (2003–2004) 6 *Cambridge Yearbook of European Legal Studies* 83; V Korah, 'Advocate General Jacobs'

no further explanation – the role of AGs is discussed.[78] All three strands have happily met in the seminal work of Burrows and Greaves.[79]

Finally, there are two further strands: case notes and, more recently, contributions to the blogosphere, focusing on particular Opinions of AGs. As far as the case notes are concerned, Opinions of AGs are usually discussed alongside judgments, with the centre of gravity frequently often placed on the latter. Blogs and a wide variety of online publications give opportunities for immediate and rushed assessments. Sometimes it is hard to curb the urge to contribute to the debate. These two stands have one thing in common: academic commentary is published shortly after the Opinion is published, or at a slightly later stage when the judgment has also been delivered. Neither allows for an assessment of the impact of a new development for shaping of EU law in the middle or long term, though a bit of speculation in contemporary debate is always welcome. When the ink is not yet dry, it is difficult to assess whether certain Opinions of AGs (and perhaps also judgments) are period pieces, or whether they will contribute to future cases at the Court, perhaps even leading to changes in primary or secondary legislation.

The question that readers may be asking themselves now is, where does this book fit? To which strand does this book on UK AGs belong? In fact, it is a mix of all. This book offers a series of tailor-made chapters, focusing on selected Opinions of UK AGs, but written with the benefit of hindsight. Put differently, this book looks back and critically analyses the contribution to the development of EU law made by the UK AGs, and attempts to elucidate the lasting impact they have had on EU law.

Contribution to Competition Law' (2005) 29 *Fordham International Law Journal* 716; Burrows and Greaves (n 1) 59–166.

[78] See, inter alia, Brown and Kennedy (n 66) 64–74.

[79] Burrows and Greaves (n 1).

2

Framing Exercises: The Role of the Advocates General

MITCHEL DE S-O-L'E LASSER

I. INTRODUCTION

I T HAS LONG been common knowledge that the high courts of different jurisdictions deploy different modes of reasoning. Yet the received wisdom about common law/civil law difference, as elaborated in the classic comparative law literature, was, at best, highly misleading. That wisdom outlined a well-worn dichotomy. The common law was the domain of the judge, who ruled via case law established in transparently and pragmatically reasoned judgments. The civil law, by contrast, was the realm of positive law and academic scholarship, where legislative commands – properly rationalised and directed by academic doctrine – were mechanically applied by purportedly passive judges writing in highly formalistic syllogisms.

In efforts to demonstrate the misguided simplicity of this supposed dichotomy, little proved more useful than focusing on the roles played by two important, though largely ignored judicial players in the French high courts and at the Court: the Advocates General (or *Commissaire de gouvernement* [CdG][1]) and the Reporting Judge.[2] To examine their work was necessarily to challenge the traditional dichotomy between common law and civil law legality, bequeathed by the canonical works of the comparative law discipline: for here were French and EU judges working at the very centre of the decision-making process of their respective high courts, yet arguing explicitly in terms of precedent, policy, equity, pragmatic social needs, and so on. What a pleasure it is, therefore, to come back to these issues once again, albeit after more time than one would like to admit and under circumstances that are fundamentally disheartening: the nationalist British decision to excise itself from the rest of Europe.

This volume, which assesses the rich contributions made to EU law by the distinguished British AGs at the Court,[3] accordingly raises an intriguing theoretical puzzle: to what extent were these contributions distinctively British? In other words, did the British AGs add something to the development of EU law that went beyond fine lawyering, and if so, was this a

---

[1] In response to pressures from European Court of Human Rights (ECtHR), the French *Conseil d'Etat* renamed the CdG the 'rapporteur public'. See Décret n° 2009-14 du 7 janvier 2009 relatif au rapporteur public des juridictions administratives et au déroulement de l'audience devant ces juridictions.

[2] See M Lasser, *Judicial Deliberations: A Comparative Analysis of Judicial Transparency and Legitimacy* (Oxford, OUP, 2004) 168–74.

[3] Unfortunately, one might almost speak of gifts left behind.

function of their common law heritage? This chapter prepares the ground for how one might fruitfully address this question.

The last 20 years have generated a mature international literature on the role played by the AGs at the Court.[4] This volume adds a great deal to this literature by offering a series of richly detailed chapters that examine the Opinions of the British AGs in high-impact cases before the Court. But do these Opinions constitute a specifically British, common law contribution? In order to address this question, one might reasonably undertake to synthesise the empirical findings presented in this book's detailed studies. This chapter adopts a different approach. It takes a step back in order to address a preliminary question: how are we to understand the role of the AGs in the first place?

This chapter examines how the existing literature on the role of the AGs is fundamentally, if latently, framed by our traditional understandings of the common law/civil law dichotomy. It argues that this literature raises three distinct, though interrelated, framing issues, each of which highlights a major feature of common law/civil law difference as classically understood. The first is the difference between a legal system dominated by judges and one led by scholars. The second is the distinction between transparent and opaque judicial decision-writing. And the third is the division between legal systems in which judicial decisions establish case law, and those that do not.

The purpose of the ensuing exercise is not to argue in favour or against the understanding suggested by one or the other side of any of these three distinctions. It is instead to recognise that in each instance, there exists an analytic choice to be made about how one wishes to conceive of common law/civil law difference, and thus, a choice to be made concerning how one wishes to conceive of the role that the AGs may play, do play, and perhaps should play, in the decision-making process of the Court. By unearthing the presuppositions that the existing literature deploys regarding the common law/civil law dichotomy, one can better grasp how these assumptions frame the analysis of the role actually and/or potentially played by the AGs. Only once one has wrestled through these threshold issues can it be fruitfully addressed whether the Opinions of the British AGs constitute a specifically British, common law contribution to EU law in general, and to the Court in particular.

II. FRAME #1: A LEGAL SYSTEM OF JUDGES OR SCHOLARS

The first conceptual frame underlying the existing literature on the AGs is the difference between a legal system dominated by judges and one led by scholars. This judge/scholar division represents of course one of the classic comparative law prisms for describing the difference between common law and civil law legal systems. As Merryman wrote in the 'Scholars' chapter of his canonical *The Civil Law Tradition*:

> This is what we mean when we say that the legal scholar is the great man of the civil law. Legislators, executives, administrators, judges, and lawyers all come under his influence. He molds the civil law tradition and the formal materials of the law into a model of the legal system. He teaches this model to law students and writes about it in books and articles. Legislators and judges accept his idea of what law is, and, when they make or apply law, they use concepts he has developed. Thus although legal scholarship is not a formal source of law, the doctrine carries immense authority.

---

[4] A list of citations will not be provided here, as the references are made throughout this volume.

In the United States, where the legislature is also theoretically supreme, there is a well-known saying (originated by a judge) that the law is what the judges say it is. This is, properly understood, a realistic statement of fact .... In a similar sense it is reasonably accurate to say the law in a civil law jurisdiction is what the scholars say it is.[5]

According to this understanding, one of the defining differences between common law and civil law legal systems lies in which 'protagonist' exercises the primary leadership role: the common law judge and the civil law scholar.

For present purposes, the question is where this dichotomy leaves the analysis of the Court's AGs. Are they to be thought of as judges or scholars? This categorisation problem surfaces over and over again in the literature. In one of the earlier articles on the AGs, Dashwood wrestled with the issue with characteristic sensitivity. He began by pointing to the Treaty rules for AG appointments:

> The rules on the appointment of Advocates General are the same as for the Judges. They must be 'persons whose independence is beyond doubt and who possess the qualifications required for appointment to the highest judicial offices in their respective countries or who are jurisconsults of recognised competence'. The un-English word 'jurisconsults' opens up the un-English possibility of appointing Professors to the Court.[6]

This passage expertly conveys the professional and conceptual complexity in play. On the one hand, the AGs are judge-like: they are appointed in the same way as the sitting judges. On the other hand, they (and, for that matter, the judges) are potentially academics: they may be professors. And finally, this academic-judicial combination is prototypically 'un-English'. The judicial/academic distinction is thus explicitly mapped onto the common law/civil law divide.

But Dashwood is not done mining the intersection of these two intersecting veins (ie the judicial/academic and the common law/civil law). As a practical matter, the AGs have long informed the Court's judges in a manner highly reminiscent of Roman jurisconsults, especially given the inability of the judges 'to rely on the same standard of professional assistance from the Bar that is available to national courts'.[7] But the AGs have also functioned in some respects as judges of first instance. Thus, an Opinion of an AG 'constitutes a first, independent stage in the making of the decision'. Indeed, '[t]he intervention of the opinion between the hearing and the judgment means that, in effect, all cases are judicially considered twice over'.[8] The net result is that the AG functions as – but is not – a judge of first instance, which is most confusing to the forthright common lawyer: 'English counsel are most prone to think of the Advocate General as a first instance judge, and to be shocked when they find that he cannot be treated as one'.[9]

Bobek traces this in-between quality of the AG to the French CdG, who bridges the judicial and academic spheres:

> In an uncodified system of rules such as French administrative law, the CdGs had indeed functioned, for a considerable time, as a type of 'law professor': individuals in a privileged position, having strategic overview of the case law, systematically pushing for development of certain areas of law. From this point of view, it could be suggested that CdGs find themselves effectively standing in between the

---

[5] JH Merryman, *The Civil Law Tradition*, 2nd edn (California, Stanford University Press, 1985) 56, 60.
[6] A Dashwood, 'The Advocate General in the Court of Justice of the European Communities' (1982) 2 *Legal Studies* 202, 203 (footnote omitted).
[7] ibid, p 212.
[8] ibid, p 213.
[9] ibid.

judicial and the academic world. On this account, the former president of the '*Section du contentieux*' of the [Conseil d'Etat] provided at least one 'positive' definition: a CdG is the favourite (*bien-aimé*) of the public law academia who will have always the tendency to overestimate his role.[10]

Bobek preserves the liminal quality of the CdGs by referring to them neither as judges nor as scholars, but as 'fourths in the court' who, even if they perform the seemingly judicial function of being 'the first one who has a 'full go' at a case, developing legal arguments in detail, which will inevitably shape any later discussion' in a manner that recalls the role of the reporting judge in German or Central European jurisdictions,[11] nonetheless represent the 'natural ally' of legal academics: 'From the point of view of the academics, in contrast to the Court, the AGs quote us, talk to us in their Opinions. In a number of cases, past and present, AGs have even been one of us'.[12]

AG Sharpston does very much the same, referring to the AG's role as 'quasi-judicial':

> In a world in which not all cases are properly pleaded and judges do not have the leisure to trawl through the extensive academic literature in the hopes of finding something interesting and pertinent, the Advocate General continues to provide open, public reflection on the present state of the case law, the possible directions in which that case law might now go and reasoned suggestions as to why it would be better for the case law to move in one direction rather than another.[13]

To Sharpston and Bobek, the AGs personify the link between the judicial and the academic realms.

III. FRAME #2: TRANSPARENT VS. OPAQUE JUDICIAL DECISIONS

The second conceptual frame underlying the existing literature on the AGs is the difference between judicial systems that offer individual and transparently reasoned judgments, and those that generate collegial and opaque ones. This stylistic division represents, as does the judge/scholar distinction, one of the foundational comparative law prisms for describing the difference between common law and civil law legal systems.

The transparency/opacity distinction is, of course, never more relevant than in the analysis of French judicial decision-making. The disapproval by the Anglo-American jurist before the short, unsigned, single-sentence judicial syllogism of the French *Cour de cassation* has long defined the comparative law discipline in the English language. As Dawson wrote over 50 years ago:

> What is missing? An observer from an English-speaking country might be inclined to say some stress on the absence of dissenting or concurring opinion. The responsibility for personal, independent judgment that is cast on the doctrinal writer and is preserved in theory for lower courts is not carried through to public expression of deviant views by members of the courts themselves. This is true not only of the Court of Cassation but of the collegiate courts at subordinate levels.[14]

French judges do not properly explain their judgments, which leaves a gaping informational hole: 'Continuity with past decisions, trends for the future, and the decisive factors in each

---

[10] M Bobek, 'A Fourth in the Court: Why Are There Advocates General in the Court of Justice?' (2011–2012) 14 *CYELS* 529, 540.

[11] ibid, p 553.

[12] ibid, p 561. Indeed, Bobek may have been prophetic: he was appointed AG in 2015.

[13] See E Sharpston, 'The Changing Role of the Advocate General' in A Arnull et al (eds), *Continuity and Change in EU Law: Essays in Honour of Sir Francis Jacobs* (Oxford, OUP, 2008) 20, 33.

[14] J Dawson, *The Oracles of Law* (Michigan, University of Michigan Press, 1968) 406.

particular case are left to be deciphered by others – chiefly by the writers of analytic notes published in the law reports'.[15] Worse, the judicial refusal to explain interpretive judgments represents a failure to take responsibility for, and thus be constrained by, them:

> These constraints can become effective only if courts accept a responsibility to the legal system as a whole, to maintain its order and consistency while constantly engaged in new creation. So far as time and insight permit, we expect each individual court opinion to weave itself into the seamless web.[16]

The judicial transparency question, which thus represents a fundamental – and unabashedly value-laden – issue in the comparative literature, surfaces repeatedly in the debates over the Court's AGs. The underlying reason is simple: loosely modelled on the French *Conseil d'Etat*, the Court generates unsigned, collegial, and relatively opaque decisions that are vaguely reminiscent of their French antecedents. As Weiler forcefully argued:

> [A]s regards the style of judgments, I think the Court should abandon the cryptic, Cartesian style which still characterizes many of its decisions and move to the more discursive, analytic and conversational style associated more with the common law world – though practiced by others as well, notably the German Constitutional court.[17]

The Opinions of the AGs might help remedy this state of affairs.[18]

The analysis offered by Ćapeta does not offer much cause for optimism. Ćapeta contributes a delightful, if ruthless, critique of the explanatory role supposedly played by the AGs.[19] Working painstakingly through the Court's age discrimination jurisprudence, she demonstrates irrefutably (and somewhat wryly) that the Opinions of AGs do not in fact do anything to clarify the Court's reasoning in its decisions. Methodically analysing the interpretive confusion left by the courts' *Mangold* and later judgments, she bluntly concludes: 'The above discussion demonstrates that the Court's rulings [...] have not been not clarified through any AG Opinion to date'.[20]

Indeed, how could an Opinion of an AG in a given case clarify the Court's judgment? As Ćapeta explains: 'When AGs give their Opinion in a case, they cannot and do not take issue with the Court's arguments in that case, as their Opinion precedes the judgment'.[21] Written before the Court deliberates and renders judgment, an Opinion of an AG is perhaps best compared to 'any other academic article on the issue'.[22] And yet, it would be a mistake to treat the AG as an academic. Leaving aside the fact that the AGs are members of the Court appointed in exactly the same manner as their judicial colleagues, the AGs and the sitting judges of the Court also share the same institutional and professional space:

> Yet unlike academic commentators, AGs are present at the CJEU on a daily basis. Thus, even if they do not participate in the deliberations and, therefore, can only guess as to the judicial treatment of their arguments, they are still part of the same jurisprudential space as the judges: they all work in the same court.[23]

---

[15] ibid, p 410.

[16] ibid, p 414.

[17] JHH Weiler, 'Epilogue: The Judicial Après-Nice' in G de Búrca and JHH Weiler (eds), *The European Court of Justice* (Oxford, OUP, 2002) 215, 225 (citations omitted).

[18] Łazowski goes so far as to suggest that when the Court's judgments are particularly brief and uninformative, the Opinions of the AGs all but substitute for them. See A Łazowski, 'Advocates General and Grand Chamber Cases: Assistance with the Touch of Substitution' (2011–2012) 14 *CYELS* 635, 654.

[19] T Ćapeta, 'Advocate General: Bringing Clarity to CJEU Decisions: A Case-Study of Mangold and Kükükdeveci' (2011–2012) 14 *CYELS* 563. Amusingly, Ćapeta was recently appointed AG at the Court.

[20] ibid, p 582.

[21] ibid, p 585.

[22] ibid, p 586.

[23] ibid.

Though prized by academics, the published work of the AGs emerges from within the walls of the Court.

Turenne is not significantly more sanguine than Ćapeta about the Opinions of AGs doing much to improve the regrettable opacity of the Court's judgments. Arguing that the Court needs to deploy 'persuasive authority' if it is to enlist the support of the national courts in its endeavour to develop European constitutional law, she questions whether this can be accomplished 'within the current civil law based framework of a terse and single-voiced judgment from the Court'.[24] Unlike '[t]he Anglo-American judgment[, which] displays the process of elaboration of the solution, where the reader checks whether there was unanimity or a majority of judges behind the decision', '[m]ost continental systems have formally (as in the case of Hungary or Spain), or informally, developed various constraints on the formulation and publication of dissenting opinions'.[25] Saddled by this civilian tradition, the Court cannot hope to succeed in persuading national courts to adopt the Court's interpretive positions on such contested issues as fundamental rights:

> In this context, the Aristotelian syllogism traditionally used to justify the brevity of the French judicial discourse – the template for the Court's judicial style – is no longer pertinent. It seems inevitable, then, that the Court's lapidary reasoning be criticised, for failing to seek to persuade on complex and sensitive issues.[26]

Although the AGs could in theory make up for the Court's failure to provide sufficient information in its terse judgments, Turenne joins Ćapeta in bemoaning their failure to do so. As Ćapeta explains: 'The main reason for this, however, does not lie with the Advocates General, but rather in the non-responsiveness of the Court to their Opinions'.[27] The 'absence of any reaction from the Court to [the AGs'] efforts' thus dooms the Court to maintaining the judicial opacity that characterises the French civil law tradition from which it is derived; and this severely hampers the legitimacy of its judgments.[28]

In conclusion, these analyses offer a second conceptual dichotomy for grasping the theory and practice of the AGs role at the Court: the distinction between individual and transparently reasoned judgments on the one hand, and collegial and opaque ones on the other. And as these analyses explain quite forthrightly, this dichotomy flows directly from the distinction between common law and civil law jurisdictions.

IV. FRAME #3: JUDICIAL CASE LAW VS. JUDICIAL INTERPRETATIONS

The third and final frame that tends to structure the existing literature on the AGs has to do with the legal status to accord to the Court's decisions. Much of that literature hinges on whether or not the Court's decisions should be understood as creating binding case law. Needless to say, this conceptual and doctrinal division represents one of the foundational comparative law prisms for describing the difference between common law and civil law legal systems.

---

[24] S Turenne, 'Advocate Generals' Opinions or Separate Opinions: Judicial Engagement in the CJEU' (2011–2012) 14 *CYELS* 723, 726.
[25] ibid, p 736.
[26] ibid, p 731.
[27] Ćapeta (n 19) 785–86. See also Turenne (n 24) 727, 740.
[28] Ćapeta (n 19) 770, 774, 786.

No one contests that case law is one of the defining hallmarks of the common law tradition.[29] The issue is how to conceptualise judicial output in civilian jurisdictions. There are at least two approaches open to the comparatist. The first is to take civil law legal systems – including even the French, which plays the role of purist on this front – at their word: judicial decisions do not, and cannot, make law. As the French Civil Code states unequivocally: 'It is forbidden for judges to make pronouncements [to rule] by means of general and regulatory provisions on the cases submitted to them'.[30]

The second approach is to refuse to accept such normative statements at face value. By adopting a more materialist perspective, the comparatist can focus instead on the practical reality that judges develop, institute, apply and eventually modify judicial norms that effectively govern large swaths of the civilian legal universe. This second approach comes in several variants, ranging from ones that decry civilian judicial hypocrisy,[31] to others that arguably laud civilian clarity and efficiency.[32] And of course, the distinction between the two basic comparative approaches may not be as stark as one might at first suppose. After all, just because civilian judges may not make law as a matter of principle does not mean that their judgments may not wield a great deal of authority in practice. And just because they do so does not necessarily mean that civilian theory is either misguided or dishonest: the definitional and categorical distinctions may hold important symbolic and practical value.[33]

Why does this time-worn comparative law debate matter for the purposes of understanding the role played by the AGs at the Court? Because the literature assessing that role hinges on underlying conceptions of the Court's own function in the European legal/constitutional order. Take the following passage by Dashwood:

> Secondly, opinions of Advocates General stand as legal authorities in their own right. By the phrase 'legal authority' I mean an expression of view on a point of law, normally by the holder of a judicial office but possibly also by a learned author, which commands attention, quite apart from any intrinsic merit, simply because it was uttered by that person. Opinions of Advocates General are frequently cited by counsel and in the legal literature as authorities in this sense. Now, the Court of Justice has no doctrine of binding precedent as we do in England, although once a point has been settled by a line of decisions (Fr: *jurisprudence constante*) it is difficult to shift the Judges from it. Where all authority is persuasive, relative weight becomes crucial. Clearly, on an issue considered in both the judgment and the opinion the former will outweigh the latter, and if the answers that are given coincide, the opinion will disappear from view as an authority, although it may still serve the ancillary, clarificatory purpose that I have described. The opinion comes into its own where the judgment either differs from it on the point in question or fails to deal with the point altogether.[34]

This exceptionally sensitive passage takes the first approach. It takes civilians at their word: '[T]he Court of Justice has no doctrine of binding precedent as we do in England'. Having adopted this perspective, Dashwood can conceptualise the role of the AGs as both dialogical and diachronic: the AGs offer weighty contributions to ongoing debates over what the law might be.

---

[29] See ch 3.

[30] *Code Civil*, Art 5. Other foundational rules, such as those that forbid judges to interfere with the political branches and that deny the binding effect of judicial decisions on unrelated cases, flesh out the point. See *Code de l'organisation judiciaire* tit. II. an. 10, Aug. 16-24. 1790, Arts 10 and 13; Code civil Art 1355.

[31] See Dawson (n 14); Merryman (n 5).

[32] See M Wells, 'French and American Judicial Opinions' (1994) 19 *Yale Journal of International Law* 81.

[33] See Lasser (n 2) 168–74.

[34] Dashwood (n 6) 214.

This perspective is to be distinguished from the second approach, which is well illustrated in the following passage by Ćapeta:

> The starting proposition is that the legitimacy of CJEU decisions depends on the clarity of their reasoning. Although there may be other ways of legitimating court decisions, I argue that a politically non-accountable court such as the CJEU, whose rulings are nonetheless generally accepted to make law, can win public trust only if its decisions are properly reasoned. The only reason why the public would trust such a court is if it shows clearly that it has thought over its final decision, and explains why it decided to follow that specific path. Then, even if one does not agree with the decision, one will still see it as legitimate.[35]

As should be readily apparent, Ćapeta's working assumption about the law-making power of the Court transforms the expectations regarding the role to be played by the AG. If the Court is a law-making institution, and if its legitimacy hinges on the reasoning of its judgments, then the AG had better contribute significantly to the public explanation of the reasoning lying behind those judgments.

Finally, nothing stops the analysis from blending the two approaches, treating the Court's output as case law, even when respectfully recognising the Court's refusal to do so. Tridimas thus argues:

> Opinions bear an invisible influence on the case law, the evolution of which can best be understood as a collective effort, namely as resulting from the dialectical interplay between opinions and judgments. …

> One of the most important aspects of [the AG's] role is to consider, where necessary, issues of legal principle independently of the facts of the case [as well as] to take into account the wider implications of its ruling and its repercussions on the fabric of the law. Thus, the opinion is designed to contribute to more coherent and cogent case law. That function, it is submitted, is of particular importance given especially the tendency of the Court to deny the normative function of its judgments and may in itself justify the existence of the office of the advocate general.[36]

As all of these analyses demonstrate quite clearly, the role that the AG is expected to play is fundamentally shaped by the underlying understanding of the Court's own role and methods.

V. CONCLUSIONS

This chapter has shown that the debates over the proper role of the AGs are heavily informed by a series of interrelated presuppositions about judicial decision-making that are themselves intimately tied to traditional understandings of the common law/civil law divide. To question whether the contributions of the Court's British AGs were distinctively British is therefore necessarily to intervene in a discussion over the nature and methods of judicial decision-making in different jurisdictions.

The existing literature regarding the AGs demonstrates the ongoing pertinence of these mutually informing distinctions, however oversimplified they may be. In particular, this literature is dominated by three canonical dichotomies: the difference between a legal system dominated by judges and one led by scholars, the distinction between transparent and opaque

---

[35] Ćapeta (n 19) 564 (footnotes omitted).
[36] T Tridimas, 'The Role of the Advocate General in the Development of Community Law: Some Reflections' (1997) 34 *CMLRev* 1349, 1363–64.

judicial decision-writing, and the division between legal systems in which judicial decisions establish case law and those in which they do not.

In a hermeneutic field constructed in this manner, everything depends on one's working assumptions. If the Court is understood to play a leading (and arguably preeminent) role in the European constitutional arena via the elaboration of its binding case law, then demands will likely be felt to explain and justify these normative decisions in a sustained and public manner. And to the extent that the Court is not thought to engage sufficiently in such public debate on its own, it should not be surprising that the AGs would be understood as judicial and urged to partake actively in this endeavour.[37] If, on the other hand, the Court is understood to play a merely collaborative legal role, then the AGs can instead be conceived as but one set of influential voices among many who work together in the ongoing development of EU law.

The question, then, is how one *should* conceive of the Court and its AGs. My default methodological inclination – which is by no means orthodoxy within the theory and practice of the comparative law discipline – is to take seriously the conceptual, methodological, and professional definitions that are endemic within the legal system under consideration. To come to terms with a legal system involves trying to come to terms with such ideas and practices and to do so in the terms of that legal system. Only then can one hope to acquire sufficient insight to be in the position to translate them in a reasonably faithful and effective manner to outsiders. If, to pick the most straightforward example, the French have traditionally insisted that their judges did not and could not make law, it is probably malpractice for a US comparatist to apply mechanically the American realist aphorism that 'law is what the judge says it is' in order to insist that they do.[38] As a general matter, therefore, one should take conceptual, methodological, and professional definitions seriously.

For this reason, it is atypical for this author to argue that it might be wise *not* to get involved in such definitional debates when discussing the role of the Court's AGs. There exist, however, two good reasons for such avoidance in this instance. First, these definitional debates would likely offer little of substantive value. The reason is straightforward: there simply does not exist sufficiently widespread agreement within the EU legal order about the status of Opinions of the AGs – or, for that matter, of decisions of the Court – for one to be able to conclude that the AGs and their Opinions are fundamentally scholarly or judicial in nature, create or do not create law, and so on. As this chapter has shown, the literature is characteristically divided on such matters. In this regard, the EU legal space is actually rather different than the national ones, in which centuries of juristic debate have tended to yield rather settled (if perpetually evolving) conceptual, methodological, and professional fields.[39] It is therefore not only difficult, but also probably descriptively inaccurate, to conclude that the AGs are properly understood as 'really' academic or judicial in nature, or that the Court really does (or does not) make law, and so on. However one were to come out on such issues, one would likely be unfaithful to the fundamentally unsettled and contested nature of the European legal universe, in which so many legal cultures and traditions are constantly in play. There actually exists little in the way of general consensus on such matters; and there exists no fundamentally

---

[37] Bobek does a very good job of describing how the literature has a tendency to describe the AGs' role in such a manner as to remedy perceived shortcomings of the Court. See Bobek (n 10) 559.

[38] See Lasser (n 2) 175–79.

[39] Needless to say, these relatively settled national fields include their fair share of internal schisms; but even these ongoing arguments are characteristically patterned in their own right, even if the patterns do shift over time. For an analysis of such patterns of agreement and disagreement in the contemporary French and European context, see M Lasser, *Judicial Transformations: The Rights Revolution in the Courts of Europe* (Oxford, OUP, 2009).

authoritative set of legal materials on which to rely. To make confident descriptive statements probably accomplishes little more than to expose one's prior assumptions.

The second reason for avoiding such definitional debates when discussing the role of the Court's AGs is that those debates have proven to be fundamentally, if latently, framed by our traditional – and terribly oversimplified – understandings of the common law/civil law dichotomy. This chapter demonstrated how this dichotomy has established the guiding intellectual framework for making sense of the Court and its AGs, underlining three classic common law/civil law distinctions: judicial vs. academic leadership, transparent vs. opaque judicial decision-writing, and binding case law or not. There is, of course, a certain grain of truth in such simple distinctions. But to use them uncritically when trying to consider whether the Opinions of the British AGs constitute a specifically British, common law contribution to the development of EU law is to falsify the data and to predetermine one's conclusions.

Take the similarly clichéd distinction between deductive (civil law) and pragmatic (common law) judicial decision-making. To apply it mechanically when considering the contribution of the British AGs will likely lead to one of two similarly tautological conclusions. If one accepts the distinction at face value, then the deeply pragmatic Opinion of AG Warner in *Walrave and Koch*,[40] to pick an early example, or of AG Jacobs in *Schmidberger*,[41] to pick a later one, are *ipso facto* characteristically common law contributions to the development of EU law. But this would be silly: the Civilians AGs at the Court (or, for that matter, at the French *Cour de cassation*) offer no less pragmatic arguments.[42] Conversely, does the existence of such pragmatic and transparently argued civilian Opinions mean, then, that there has been no specifically British contribution? Absolutely not. It only means that if one were to locate a distinctively British contribution, the way to do so would probably not lie in mechanically reiterating the received wisdom regarding common law/civil law difference.

A final, melancholy thought. This is a book that recognises and celebrates the contributions made by the British AGs at the Court. One did not need to witness the recent shameful acts committed under the Stars and Stripes (never mind the Stars and Bars) at the US Capitol on 6 January 2021 to recognise the dangers lurking behind knee-jerk flag waving. In a similar vein: there is no pressing need to classify the contributions made by the British AGs as British, except to underline the British loss. They were important contributions made by thoughtful and committed jurists. They inured to the benefit of people in 28 different countries. How sad that they will now only benefit people in 27.

---

[40] Opinion of AG Warner in Case 36/74 *Walrave* ECLI:EU:C:1974:111. See ch 7.

[41] Opinion of AG Jacobs in Case C-112/00 *Schmidberger* ECLI:EU:C:2002:437. See ch 34.

[42] See, eg, Opinion of AG Van Gerven in Case C-70/88 *Parliament v Council* ECLI:EU:C:1991:270; Opinion of AG Poiares Maduro in Case C-438/05 *Viking* ECLI:EU:C:2007:292. For French examples, Lasser (n 2) 27–61, 166–202.

3

Shaping EU Law: Ireland and the Common Law in Europe

NIAL FENNELLY*

I. INTRODUCTION

THIS BOOK MARKS a historic and unprecedented event. The United Kingdom of Great Britain and Northern Ireland, following a vote of its people, has left the European Union, ending almost half a century of membership. Being of Irish nationality, the present writer is not one of the 'UK Advocates General' of the title. He had, however, the enormous privilege of serving as an Advocate General (AG), on terms of fruitful friendship and cooperation in company with one of the most distinguished holders of that office, AG Francis Jacobs. The invitation to contribute to this volume comes as a special honour.

The title, 'Shaping EU Law the *British* Way' (emphasis added) invites comment. No adjective exists to describe the condition of belonging to the UK. The word, British, does not serve, since it does not include the part of the United Kingdom called Northern Ireland. More pertinently, the distinctive legal heritage which might be loosely called British, and which was brought by the UK to the EEC from 1973, was that of the common law of England, which does not include Scotland, which has its own distinct legal heritage. Anomalies abound.

This work includes, very appropriately, a study of: 'Bringing the Common Law to Luxembourg …', given that Ireland shares this heritage of the common law, whose history will be recalled, before adverting to the European dimension.

II. IRELAND: THE FIRST ADVENTURE OF THE COMMON LAW; THE NORMANS TO ELIZABETH

Ireland has frequently been described as the site of the first adventure of the common law.[1] Scholars have traced the transplantation of the nascent common law of England to Irish soil

---

* The author wishes to thank Judge Kieran Bradley, Mr. Justice Gerard Hogan, and Advocate General Anthony Collins for their comments on drafts of this chapter.
[1] See WJ Johnston, 'The First Adventure of the Common Law' (1920) 36 *Law Quarterly Review* 9. Johnston had been a judge of the Irish County Court, part of the (then) United Kingdom. He later served as a judge successively of the High Court and Supreme Court of the Irish Free State and, finally, of Ireland. Judge Johnston appears to have coined the expression, used in his title. See J McEldowney and P O'Higgins (eds), *The Common Law Tradition: Essays in Irish Legal History* (Newbridge, Irish Academic Press, 1990) 20. See also the address of President Michael D Higgins to the delegates of the Law Commission, 5 July 2012.

variously to lost Royal Charters,[2] and even to the (probably apocryphal) Papal Bull *Laudabiliter* of 1155, whereby the only ever English Pope, Adrian IV (also known as Hadrian IV), purported to authorise King Henry II to invade Ireland (which Henry did in 1171). Sir Edward Coke quoted Matthew of Paris as having said, improbably one might think, that 'the just and honourable laws of England were joyfully received and obeyed by the Irish'.[3] Various Royal instruments typically proclaimed that 'the laws of England were by all freely received and confirmed'.[4]

In reality, the common law applied until the seventeenth century, only to the area under English rule surrounding Dublin, known as the Pale, and 'in the first instance, extended to Ireland solely for the benefit of the colonists'.[5] For the rest, even by 1556, the King's 'council had but a very irregular and tenuous jurisdiction over the areas outside the Pale ...'.[6] By 1578, however, 'the legal system had been extended ... to include a far greater territory under the common law'. The Irish 'adventure' was not, of course, viewed from the position of the supposed Irish beneficiaries of the common law entirely voluntary. The judiciary of the lordship of Ireland 'was a colonial judiciary', whose 'primary purpose was to serve the English colony and of English colonists in Ireland'.[7] However, it has also been suggested that the process of introducing the common law to Ireland acted reciprocally as 'a significant factor in the creation of the literature of the early common law',[8] even if the objective was to bring the people to 'the obedience of English and the English Empire'.[9]

For several hundred years, the common law coexisted with native Irish Brehon law.[10] In the Tudor and Stuart periods, English political power was consolidated over the entire of Ireland. Gaelic power ended with the 'Flight of the Earls', the last survivors of the Irish nobility, in 1607.

'It was the law', as Sir John Davies noted, 'that would make Ireland English'.[11] Davies, as law officer of the Crown 'played a major role in consolidating the Elizabethan conquest of the island'.[12] Thus, the common law of England was firmly embedded in Ireland from the commencement of the seventeenth century.

The common law had not yet travelled to the rest of the world. The pilgrim fathers had not yet sailed in the Mayflower to Massachusetts. More than a century was to elapse before Captain James Cook mapped what were to become New Zealand and Australia. The common law was not to reach the Indian sub-continent until the eighteenth century. Ultimately, what is now known as the common law came to prevail in the United States, Canada, Australia,

---

[2] P Brand, 'Ireland and the Literature of the Early Common law' (1981) 16 *Irish Jurist* 95. He refers to a lost charter of King John of 1210.

[3] Johnston (n 1) 9. See Coke upon Littleton, 19th edn, Vol I, 141 a and b.

[4] Brand (n 2) 99, citing references to a council held by King Henry II at Lismore (Waterford) in 1171. See generally the website of the Courts Service of Ireland.

[5] Johnston (n 1) 9.

[6] JG Crawford, *Anglicizing the Government of Ireland: The Irish Privy Council and the Expansion of Tudor Rule 1556–1578* (Newbridge, Irish Academic Press, 1995) 176.

[7] P Brand, 'The Birth and Early Development of a Colonial Judiciary in Ireland: The Judges of the Lordship of Ireland' in N Osborough (ed), *Explorations in Law and History* (Newbridge, Irish Academic Press, 1995).

[8] Brand, ibid, p 113.

[9] J Ohlmeyer, *Making Ireland English* (New Haven, Yale University Press, 2012) 212. The quotation is from the Calendar of State Papers relating to Ireland (14 vols, London, 1860–1911). Sir John Davies (1569–1626) served as Attorney General for Ireland from 1606 to 1619. See *Dictionary of Irish Biography* (Royal Irish Academy) vol 3, 70.

[10] N Osborough, 'Roman Law in Ireland' (1990–1992) 25–27 *Irish Jurist* 218.

[11] Quoted in Ohlmeyer (n 9) 212.

[12] N Osborough, *An Island's Law: A Bibliographical Guide to Ireland's Legal Past* (Dublin, Four Courts Press, 2013) 16.

New Zealand, partly in the Indian sub-continent and such other far-flung parts of the world as Singapore, Hong Kong, and several countries of the Caribbean.

III. THE COMMON LAW SETTLES IN IRELAND: ELIZABETH TO VICTORIA

Meantime, Ireland continued to practise the common law under English rule. This meant, in particular, that most appointments to the Irish bench were of Englishmen. Most strikingly, in a country which had, in great majority, retained the Catholic religion following the Reformation, no Catholics were, or could be, appointed to the Irish bench from the reign of Elizabeth I to Victoria, except for a short period during the reign of James II. Thus, it was possible for the Lord Chancellor of Ireland to declare about 1760 from the bench that 'the laws did not presume a Roman Catholic to exist in Ireland …'.[13] The Act of Union of 1800 abolished the Irish Parliament, and Ireland became part of the newly created United Kingdom of Great Britain and Ireland.[14]

Important change came following the grant in 1829 of Catholic Emancipation.[15] The first Catholic was appointed to the bench in 1837.[16] In the following 50 years, many more Catholics were appointed. There was no reason to differentiate between judges on grounds of religious faith: 'whether they were Roman Catholics or protestant those raised to the bench had passed through the same mill …'.[17] During the nineteenth century, Irish courts and judges became assimilated and a single system of common law had come to apply to the entire country.

Daniel O'Connell's great success as a lawyer, as well as a political leader, demonstrated the potentialities of the courts and the law.[18] The people came to recognise courts and systems of the common law. Progressively, the common law became the accepted, and indeed the only recognised system of law. A judge could seek guidance from 'our common law …'.[19] Chief Baron Palles, the greatest of the Irish Judges, who is reputed to have said repeatedly, echoing statements to similar effect attributed by Coke, many centuries earlier, to Matthew of Paris: 'We should be supremely grateful to those Normans, who introduced us to the common law'.[20]

IV. THE COMMON LAW IN INDEPENDENT IRELAND: 1922–1973

The nineteenth and the early twentieth century have been described as 'the great formative phase of the common law …'.[21] Irish courts continued to follow the principles of the common law and 'the Irish system of courts was, securely as it seemed, locked into the English judicial structure'. Most fundamentally decisions of the courts of the common law were binding on courts later deciding the same point arising on the same facts, the principle of *stare decisis*.

---

[13] F Erlington Ball, *The Judges in Ireland, 1221–1921. Vol II* (Dublin, The Round Hall Press, 1993) 152 (first published by John Murray (London, 1926)). The declaration is attributed to Lord Bowes, Lord Chancellor from 1757 to 1759.

[14] See R Keane 'The Role of the Law Lords in relation to Ireland' in L Blom-Cooper et al (eds), *The Judicial House of Lords 1876–2009* (Oxford, OUP, 2009).

[15] Roman Catholic Relief Act 1829.

[16] Michael O'Loghlen was appointed as Master of the Rolls.

[17] Ball (n 13) 283.

[18] See P Geoghegan, 'Daniel O'Connell and the Law' in FM Larkin and N Dawson (eds), *Lawyers, the Law and History* (Dublin, Four Courts Press, 2013).

[19] Lord O'Brien of Kilfenora, Lord Chief Justice, in *The Queen v Drury* [1894] 2 IR 489 at 496.

[20] Quoted, without citation, in VTH Delany, *Christopher Palles* (Dublin, Allen Figgis, 1960).

[21] R Keane, 'Judges as Lawmakers: The Irish Experience' (2004) 4 *Judicial Studies Institute Journal* 1.

They also generally followed decisions of the English courts. During this period, the ultimate appeal from the Irish courts was to the House of Lords sitting at Westminster.

This adherence to the common law did not end when Ireland, save for Northern Ireland, attained independence in 1922. The Irish Free State was established with effect from 6th December 1922. Ireland adopted a new Constitution in 1937. The Constitutions of 1922 and 1937 each provided that existing laws should continue to be 'of full force and effect' until repealed or amended, but subject to an important proviso that any such law should not be inconsistent with the Constitution itself. This provision acted (and acts) as a filter applied to all existing laws which applied to Ireland at the date of coming into effect of the Constitution. The courts ruled that 'that by virtue of Article 73 [of the 1922 Constitution] all such laws as were in force immediately before the 6th December 1922, continued and remained in force except so far as they were inconsistent with the Constitution …'.[22]

In January 1923, the Executive Council (Government of the Irish Free State) established a Committee to recommend the new courts structure. There was one moment of hesitation. The President wrote to that Committee describing the system of justice of the 'administration lately ended' in unflattering terms. Its 'nomenclature were only to be understood by the student of the history of Southern Britain. It had not struck root in this Nation'. The Committee was encouraged to 'constitute a system of judiciary and an administration of law and justice …. after a pattern of our designing'. In the event, that Committee tersely recommended the establishment of a judicial system which replicated the former one in almost every respect, down to the wearing of wigs and the form of address.[23]

The approach generally taken by the Irish courts after 1922 was typified by the statement of a judge, who had been a member of the Irish Free State Constitution Commission which had drafted the Constitution, to the effect that Article 73 had 'been intended to set up the new State with the least possible change in the previously existing law, and that Article 73 should be so construed as to effectuate this intention …'. The 'fullest possible effect should be given to Article 73, and … the previously existing laws should be regarded as still subsisting unless they are clearly inconsistent with the Constitution'.[24] In spite of the greatest political and constitutional change, 'it was intended that the existing body of law should be carried forward with as little dislocation as possible'.[25]

Generally, therefore, following the establishment of the Irish Free State in 1922, and the adoption of the present Constitution in 1937, the Irish courts followed and applied the decisions delivered prior to 1922 by Irish courts, but also, where applicable, by English courts. It was held in a number of cases that '[d]ecisions of the House of Lords upon law common to England and Ireland given before the coming into operation of the Constitution of 1922 are of binding force until effect has been altered by our Legislature'.[26]

Neither the Constitution of the Irish Free State nor that of Ireland of 1937 made any mention of the common law. It was left to be deduced, from case to case, and from the reference

---

[22] Per Lord Sankey in *Performing Rights Society Ltd v Bray UDC* [1928] IR 506.

[23] These external marks have now been abandoned. Their passing did not affect the continued adherence to the common law.

[24] *The State (Kennedy) v Little* [1931] IR 39. See also *Fogarty v O'Donoghue* [1926] IR 531; *The State (McCarthy) v Lennon* [1936] IR 485; *Exham v Beamish* [1939] IR 336; *Cork County Council and Burke v Commissioners of Public Works; Mayo-Perrott v Mayo-Perrott* [1958] IR 205.

[25] *Laurentiu v Minister for Justice* [1999] 4 IR 26 at 8, per Keane J.

[26] Per Murnaghan J in *Minister for Finance v O'Brien* [1949] IR 91 at 116. See also *Corry v National Union of Vintners, Grocers and Allied Trades Assistants* [1950] IR 315.

to 'laws in force' in each case that the framers intended that the system of the common law was to be maintained. Thus, it was not only that any existing legal provision, statutory or otherwise, was to continue in force. In essence, all existing legal arrangements were to continue. As it was expressed by Keane CJ, the Constitution 'provided for the retention of the common law in the Irish law, of which it had formed a central part since its first migration from its homeland in the twelfth century'.[27] It also followed, he added, that: 'No doubt it was envisaged that the Irish courts would continue to develop the common law, as they had done since independence, in the light of changing social conditions in Ireland and decisions in other common law jurisdictions'.[28]

To a very large extent, existing judicial conduct rules and practices, from before 1922, continued to be observed thereafter. 'It is no small tribute to the adaptability and acceptability of the common law', according to one writer, 'that no sharp break was made with the pre-existing system'.[29] Above all, the system retained the distinctive features of the common law, namely the binding effect of precedent, the rule of *stare decisis*. As was stated in one case, it 'is grounded on the [need for] certainty, stability and predictability of law ...'.[30] The Supreme Court, however, decided that, however, important and desirable these objectives were, they could not restrain a court of final appeal from declining to follow an earlier decision which it considered to have been clearly erroneous.[31] The Court, nonetheless, preserved the normal application of the principle of precedent and held that:

> a decision of the full Supreme Court ... given in a fully-argued case and on a consideration of all the relevant materials, should not normally be overruled merely because a later Court inclines to a different conclusion.[32]

The Irish courts have consistently acknowledged, expressly or implicitly the key essential characteristics of the common law, notably its capacity for organic development in response to changing social and economic conditions, such that 'novel judicial decisions are not uncommonly referred to as judge-made law'.[33] There are limits flowing from the underlying principle of *stare decisis*. AG Hogan, when a judge of the High Court, noted that 'incremental change and development are standard features of the common law method ...'.[34] Nonetheless, he continued, 'the courts are broadly speaking, confined to the general parameters of the law [in that case] of torts as they existed ...' at the date of the coming into effect of the Constitution.[35]

V. IRELAND AND UK JOIN THE EUROPEAN COMMUNITIES: 1973

The common law of Ireland from 1922 was, in its essence, the common law of England, and was the same system as continues to apply as far afield as New Zealand, Canada, Singapore, and Jamaica. In these and other countries of the common law, provisions of national constitutions

---

[27] Per Keane J in *Iarnród Eireann v Ireland* [1996] 3 IR 321 at 366–67.
[28] ibid.
[29] S Henchy, 'Precedent in the Irish Supreme Court' (1963) 25 *MLR* 544, 545. The author later became a judge of the High Court and the Supreme Court.
[30] Per Keane CJ in *O'Brien v Mirror Group Newspapers* [2001] IR 1.
[31] *Attorney General v Ryan's Car Hire Ltd.* [1965] IR 642.
[32] *Mogul of Ireland v Tipperary (NR) County Council* [1976] IR 260 at 272.
[33] Per Lardner J in *RT v VP (Orse) VT)* [1990] 1 IR 545 at 558.
[34] *Healy v Stepstone Mortgage Finance Ltd* [2014] IEHC 134.
[35] ibid.

often prevail over the common law, whose content is also subject to legislative change. These considerations do not alter the essence, which is that the system is that of the common law. This was the system which Ireland, in the company of the United Kingdom, brought to the European Communities in 1973. It is a habit of thought rather than a set of dogmas or rigid rules. It is pragmatic rather than dogmatic. As Wendell Holmes, put it, 'the life of the law has not been logic: it has been experience'.[36]

This then was the state of the common law in Ireland when, in company with the UK, it became a Member State on 1 January 1973. These were the first two Member States of the common law to join what was to become the EU. Now, after Brexit, Ireland is the sole carrier of the flag of the common law, with the partial exceptions of Malta and Cyprus.

Of course, while every Member State had the right to have a judge at the Court, a certain number of designated Member States have enjoyed the right to nominate an AG. From 1973 to 1981 AGs came only from the four largest Member States. Nominations by the remaining Members States have been subjected to a system of rotation since 1981. One important corollary of this was that an AG from a larger Member State could be reappointed at the end of their term. An AG from a smaller Member State could not serve beyond a single six-year term, thus limiting their capacity to develop knowledge and experience. In the result, there was no AG from Ireland until 1995, some 22 years after Ireland's accession, when the fortunate appointee was the present author,[37] then a Senior Counsel at the Irish Bar. Ireland was, of course, represented on the bench of the Court, initially, by a distinguished former Chief Justice, Cearbhall Ó Dálaigh,[38] and a number of distinguished successors.

VI. THE COMMON LAW IN THE EUROPEAN COMMUNITIES: FOLLOWING PRECEDENT

The UK and Ireland, as Member States of the common law were, of course, acceding to a Community comprising, up to then, six Member States, all of them from the civil law tradition. France is generally seen as the embodiment of that system of law. Denmark also acceded at the same time.

Much misunderstanding surrounds the word, 'jurisprudence', whether in English or French. Robespierre is said to have told the *Assemblée constituante* in 1790 that the word 'must be expurgated from the French language', and that it was 'nothing more than law-making'.[39] In English, the word means the study, science, or theory of law. This indeed corresponded with the old or historic meaning of the term, whereas a French dictionary of law renders it 'in a more modern and precise sense' as 'the solution suggested by a combination of sufficiently consistent decisions delivered by courts on a legal question'.[40] The classical French position, stated by Montesquieu, was that the judge was to act as 'la bouche de la loi'.[41] That view

---

[36] O Wendell Holmes JR, *The Common Law* (Cambridge, MA, Harvard University Press 2009).

[37] See, N Fennelly, 'Reflections of an Irish Advocate General' (1996) 5 *Irish Journal of European Law* 5.

[38] Judge Ó Dálaigh resigned to become President of Ireland in 1974. He was replaced by Judge Aindrias Ó Caoimh.

[39] Quoted and translated by Bradley in K Bradley, 'Vertical Precedent at the European Court of Justice: When Push Comes to Shove' in K Bradley et al (eds), *Of Courts and Constitutions: Liber Amicorum in Honour of Nial Fennelly* (Oxford, Hart Publishing, 2014).

[40] *Lexique de termes juridiques*, 6th edn (Paris, Dalloz, 1985), author's translation.

[41] T Tridimas, 'Precedent and the Court of Justice; A Jurisprudence of Doubt?' in J Dickson and P Eleftheriadis (eds), *Philosophical Foundations of European Union Law* (Oxford, OUP, 2012). At 308 Tridimas says: 'The expression comes from Montesquieu's seminal work De L'esprit des lois (1748) [which] stated that judges should be 'the mouth that pronounces the words of the law, inanimate beings who can moderate neither its force nor its rigour (see Montesquieu, *The Spirit of the Laws* Cambridge: Cambridge University Press, 1989, bk II, Ch 6, 156)'.

has been described as representing 'the other extreme', from the common law position.[42] The practice of the judgments of the Court is to translate the French term, *jurisprudence*, into the English 'case law', a result which glosses over centuries of conflict.

One would have thought that the language and reasoning of the modern Court was a world away from the France of the revolutionary period. Nonetheless, there survives an almost spiritual link with the philosophy of the French system. The Court, according to more than one writer, was modelled on the French *Conseil d'Etat* with the consequence that precedent played little role in its legal reasoning.[43] Tridimas states: 'The Court did not view reference to precedent as being part of its reasoning, in contrast to Advocates General who, from an early stage, saw analysis of previous case law as a core part of their function'.[44]

VII. ANALYSIS OF PRECEDENT AT THE EUROPEAN COURT: *VAN GEND EN LOOS*

It is outside the scope of this contribution and surpasses the ambition of the present writer to emulate the many impressive academic studies of the emergence of the practice of the following of precedent at the Court.[45] The author will, nonetheless, make some brief comments on *Van Gend en Loos*.[46] The author will also recall an Opinion he delivered as AG, in which he presumed, unsuccessfully as it happened, to advise the Court to depart from one of its own earlier decisions, a practice that AG Jacobs had once done quite successfully.[47] Finally, the author will comment on the ultimate practice of precedent at the Court, and as to whether it reflects the influence of the common law.

The Member States were generally believed to have bound themselves by classical international agreements, which were binding in international law but which had no implications for their domestic legal systems, or for individuals. The Court, however, in 1963, took a radical leap in the case of *Van Gend en Loos*, barely five years after the entry into force of the Treaty of Rome. It decided to rule that certain articles of the EEC Treaty 'produce direct effects and create individual rights which national courts must protect ...'.[48] This was the precedent without precedent. The Community thereby became a club consisting not only of its Member States, but also of their nationals.

Van Gend en Loos was a ground-breaking decision. It depended for its force and effect on the use of the unique and innovative mechanism of the reference for preliminary ruling under what is now Article 267 TFEU. Availing of that facility, individuals were enabled to invoke the principle that provisions of the EU Treaties were capable of having direct effect and of being relied upon by individuals in national law. It required very little reflection to conclude that such provisions must necessarily be accorded primacy over conflicting provisions of national law.

However, it was not without some hesitation that the decision became recognised as a precedent. In *Da Costa*,[49] the Court was asked effectively identical questions, also via Article 177 EEC (now Article 267 TFEU), concerning the interpretation of Article 12 EEC. AG Lagrange,

---

[42] Keane (n 21) 8.
[43] Tridimas (n 41) 307.
[44] Tridimas (n 41) 308.
[45] See ch 2.
[46] Case 26/62 *Van Gend en Loos* ECLI:EU:C:1963:1.
[47] See ch 24.
[48] At para 13 of judgment in *Van Gend en Loos*.
[49] Joined Cases 28, 29 and 30/62 *Da Costa* ECLI:EU:C:1963:6.

in his Opinion, abstained from recognising that *Van Gend en Loos* was binding as a precedent. His view was that:

> [T]he Court of Justice should ... remain free when giving its future judgments. However important the judgment which it is led to give on some point may be, whatever may be the abstract character which the interpretation of some provision of the Treaty may present – or appear to present – the golden rule of res judicata should be preserved: it is from the moral authority of its decisions, and not from the legal authority of res judicata, that a jurisdiction like ours should derive its force [...].[50]

The Court declined the invitation of the Commission to dismiss the reference for preliminary ruling in *Da Costa* on the ground that the questions referred had already been decided in in the judgment in *Van Gend en Loos*. The national court has, it ruled, the right to make a further reference, 'if it considers it desirable to refer questions of interpretation to the Court again'.[51] Thus, in a decision of some obscurity and, without according it the status of precedent, the Court, entrenched *Van Gend en Loos* in the legal and constitutional system of the Community.

AG Lagrange, in his Opinion in the next celebrated case of *Costa v Enel*,[52] cited the language of *Van Gend en Loos*. He reminded the Court that it had decided 'that Articles 12 and 31 of the EEC Treaty produce direct effects and create individual rights which national courts must protect, [and that] you yourselves have declared that they are, to use the hallowed expression, self-executing'. It surprises the common lawyer in this author that the AG, in effect, advised the Court, so very discreetly, by the use of the phrase, 'as the court has said', that the Court follow its reasoning in *Van Gend en Loos*, but without formally citing that case or even mentioning its name. Judge Andreas Donner, who had been President of the Court in 1963, writing extra-judicially, but more explicitly in 1968, described *Van Gend en Loos* as 'the fundamental precedent for the entire jurisprudence that followed'.[53]

The practice of citing earlier judgments was, without intending to be critical, haphazard and did not follow any explicit set of rules. One of the earliest examples of the practice was in 1979 in the *Simmenthal* judgment.[54] Thereafter, the Court more frequently cited earlier judgments, often briefly, in support of its current statement.

The Court had moved on, some 25 years later. Its *Opinion 1/91*[55] on the Agreement creating the European Economic Area (EEA), the Court suggested a more developed understanding of the practice of precedent, when it ruled:

> As the Court of Justice has consistently held, the Community treaties established a new legal order for the benefit of which the States have limited their sovereign rights, in ever wider fields, and the subjects of which comprise not only the Member States but also their nationals ... The essential characteristics of the Community legal order which has thus been established are in particular its primacy over the law of the Member States and the direct effect of a whole series of provisions which are applicable to their nationals and to the Member States themselves.[56]

The principle of primacy was, it seems, an inevitable corollary of direct effect established in *Van Gend en Loos*. Without it, the Treaties would, in the view of one writer, 'rapidly have

---

[50] Opinion of AG Lagrange in Joined Cases 28, 29 and 30/62 *Da Costa* ECLI:EU:C:1963:2, p 42.

[51] At p 38 of the judgment in *Da Costa*.

[52] Case 6/64 *Costa v ENEL* ECLI:EU:C:1964:66.

[53] AM Donner, *The Role of the Lawyer in the European Communities* (Edinburgh, Edinburgh University Press, 1968) 72, as quoted in W Phelan, *Great Judgments of the European Court of Justice: Rethinking the Landmark Decisions of the Foundational Period* (Cambridge, CUP, 2019) 37.

[54] Case 92/78 *Simmenthal v Commission* ECLI:EU:C:1979:53.

[55] *Opinion 1/91* ECLI:EU:C:1991:490.

[56] Para 21 of *Opinion 1/91*.

become a dead letter and in all probability the Community would have been dissolved long ago'.[57] This appears to echo the language of AG Lagrange in his Opinion in *Costa v Enel*.[58] Commenting on the possibility that a decision of the Italian Constitutional Court which would allow Italian laws to evade the jurisdiction of the Court by rendering inadmissible references for preliminary ruling from Italian courts, he expressed the view that there would be 'disastrous consequences' if that precedent were maintained and that it 'would risk ... the functioning of the system of institutions established by the Treaty and, as a consequence, the very future of the Common Market'.[59]

The decisive importance of *Van Gend en Loos* is not ignored by those hostile to the European Union, or indeed to the entire European project. The writer, Perry Anderson, in a series of articles in the London Review of Books in 2020 and 2021,[60] applies the word 'coup' to the decision in *Van Gend en Loos*. He explains that he meant 'an action taken suddenly by stealth, catching its victims unawares, and confronting them with a fait accompli that cannot be reversed'.[61] Use of this description for a decision duly taken in open court, following a full hearing of the parties, and the public delivery of the contrary Opinion of the AG, seems nothing less than a travesty.

Van Gend en Loos constituted then a giant step in the functioning of the European Community. It conferred on individuals the right to rely directly on provisions of the Treaties in their national courts. This created what has been called a 'Europe of judges'. It expanded the possibilities of the procedure of reference for preliminary with consequent enhancement of the power of the Court to extend individual rights.

VIII. AN UNPERSUASIVE OPINION: *MERCK V PRIMECROWN*

This was the context in which, this writer, entered the lists in 1996 in the joined cases of *Merck v Primecrown*,[62] unsuccessfully seeking to persuade the Court to depart from its existing case-law, which forbade the owners of patent rights from seeking to prevent parallel imports from other Member States in which they had placed their products on the market at a time when the products in question did not enjoy patent protection in that other Member State.

In this author's Opinion, it recalled that the courts of the then two common law jurisdictions of the Community, the United Kingdom and Ireland, followed the doctrine of precedent or *stare decisis*. While, at least in the case of Ireland, the following of precedent was the normal, indeed almost universal practice, the courts of final appeal could depart from their own previous judgments for compelling reasons, where there was compelling reason not to follow the earlier decision. It is not here relevant to explore the differences, real or merely perceived, between this approach and that expounded by AG Lagrange. It is more relevant to note the response of the Court, when it gave judgment after this author's Opinion.[63]

---

[57] DT Keeling, 'In Praise of Judicial Activism. But What Does it Mean? And Has the European Court of Justice Ever Practised It?' in *Scritti in onore di Giuseppe Federico Mancini*, vol II (Milan, Giuffrè Editore, 1998) 532.

[58] Opinion of AG Lagrange in Case 6/64 *Costa v ENEL* ECLI:EU:C:1964:51.

[59] At p 605 of the Opinion of AG Lagrange in *Costa v ENEL*.

[60] P Anderson, 'The European Coup' (2020) 42 *London Review of Books*; P Anderson, 'Ever Closer Union?' (2021) 43 *London Review of Books*; P Anderson, 'The Breakaway' (2021) 43 *London Review of Books*.

[61] ibid.

[62] Opinion of AG Fennelly in Joined Cases C-267/95 and C-268/95 *Merck* ECLI:EU:C:1996:228.

[63] Joined Cases C-267/95 and C-268/95 *Merck* ECLI:EU:C:1996:468.

The Court gave detailed and serious consideration to whether the arguments advanced by Merck were such as to 'call in question the reasoning on which the Court [had] based' what it described as the 'rule in Merck'.[64] It recalled its reasoning in the earlier case in some detail. It concluded that 'the arguments put forward' had not shown that the Court had been wrong in the earlier case 'in its assessment of the balance between the principle of free movement of goods in the Community and the principle of protection of patentees' rights'.[65]

It is not easy to reach a clear conclusion from reading the judgment in *Merck* as to whether there is a principle of precedent in Community law (now EU law). On the one hand, the Court refers at least twice to the 'rule in Merck', which seems to imply that the Court was referring to a *rule* of law, something more than a mere decision in an individual case. It also referred to earlier case-law which had been cited in its prior judgment. On the other hand, the Court conducted a detailed analysis of the reasoning in the earlier *Merck v Stephar*, suggesting that it was not in any sense treating it as having independent binding effect. The word 'precedent' does not occur in the judgment. A fair conclusion may be that the Court adhered fairly closely to the advice AG Lagrange had given in *Da Costa*: The Court is not bound to follow its earlier judgments. Normally, however, it will follow its earlier decisions, but is free to change when it is persuaded that it should.

IX. SETTLED CASE LAW AT THE COURT

The *Merck* litigation belongs to a quarter of a century ago, but it contains the two strands of evolving judicial thinking at the Court. Firstly, the Court emerged from the civil law tradition, which did not recognise the notion of precedent, at least when formulated as a doctrine. Secondly, nonetheless, the Court was led by its decisions in concrete cases to develop its own distinctive precedent-based methodology. When a corpus of case law was formulated in rulings on important subjects, it was necessarily driven to seek solutions to pending disputes by reference to its earlier judgments, which thereby became in effect recognised as having the status of precedent.

The Court came to use the formula, 'settled case law', or in French, '*jurisprudence constante*'. The expression had a subtly different meaning more redolent of French law. Tridimas reaches a striking conclusion:

> The picture that emerges is that of a judicial behaviour which is close in result, albeit not in methodology, to that of Anglo-Saxon supreme courts which adhere to the doctrine of stare decisis.[66]

While fully accepting the substance of this statement, the present author finds it difficult to resist a respectful comment on his use of the description, Anglo-Saxon, as a synonym for common law. Ireland is now the only common law Member State in the European Union, but it is not and never was Anglo-Saxon. More importantly, as this author understands history, the common law was a product not of the Anglo-Saxons, but of the Normans.

---

[64] Case 187/80 *Merck* ECLI:EU:C:1981:180.
[65] See paras 33–37 of the Judgment in Joined Cases C-267/95 and C-268/95 *Merck*.
[66] Tridimas (n 41) 308.

X. THE BRITISH HAVE GONE: LEFT ALL ALONE; THE PRECIOUS STONE

The departure from the European Union of the Member State which gave birth to the common law ranks unmistakably as a legal event of the first importance. An obvious and regrettable result is that the common law will be represented among the AGs only when the unbalanced system of rotation ordained by the larger Member States permits it. Ireland was allowed to nominate an Advocate General in 1995, after 22 years of membership and the again in 2018, after a lapse of a further 23 years. Thus it is that, during the term of the second Irish Advocate General, we may view the state of the common law in the European Union.

AG Hogan took office in 2018. He was a resolute proponent of the common law during his remarkable Irish judicial career. He wrote, for example, of:

> the common law's preference for incremental step-by-step change through case law, coupled with a distaste for reliance on overarching general principles which are not deeply rooted in the continuous, historical fabric of the case law ....[67]

More recently, he has expressed deep concern that legislative harmonising proposals at EU level could 'represent a major cultural shift in our entire private law' by requiring courts to give effect to broad general principles, rather than adhering to the historic and incremental habits of the common law.[68] He has speculated that the common law systems in Europe will be pulled apart in opposite directions, even that the common law is in danger of being swamped. He asks whether Ireland will, over time, cease to be a common law country in any true sense of the term. Perhaps, he suggests in a more light-hearted vein, Ireland could find itself in a position like the State of Louisiana, which is an island of civil law among forty-nine common law states in the United States. He might also have cited the case of the Province of Québec in Canada.

These concerns expressed so eloquently by one of our greatest and most profound legal thinkers deserve great respect. This author is however hopeful that the common law in Ireland will continue to survive and to serve its people. It is possible, in this author's belief, to be reassured by the very fact that each Member State will continue to establish and maintain its own courts, requiring it to apply its own laws. Ireland will, as a common law Member State, continue to apply the rules and follow the practices of the common law in its courts. In the article already cited, AG Hogan acknowledged that 'broadly speaking ... the last sixty years or so ... has not changed the fabric of the 28 legal systems: they remain recognizably either common law or civil law jurisdictions'.[69] The courts of the Member States continue to avail of the procedure of reference for preliminary ruling. Some two-thirds in number of the cases decided by the Court continue to be initiated through this route, which is deeply rooted in the legal systems of the Members States. EU law respects national procedural autonomy. It ought to be added that both Louisiana and Québec continue to practise civil law after more than 200 years, and that it took an invasion to remove the Brehon law in Ireland.

It must here be noted that Advocate General Hogan has vacated his office on returning to Ireland as a Judge on the Supreme Court of Ireland. His position as Advocate General has been assumed by Judge Anthony Collins from 5 October 2021 to the end of Advocate General Hogan's term on 8 October 2024.

---

[67] *Flynn v Breccia* [2017] IECA 74.
[68] G Hogan, 'Laws in Common' (2019) 24 *The Bar Review* 22.
[69] ibid, p 22.

While none of the above is to question the great and growing influence of EU law, one of the outstanding features of the European system is its steadfast defence of the principle of the rule of law. This author believes that Ireland will continue to follow the system of the common law brought to us by the Norman invaders some 800 years ago. Ireland continues to share the island of Ireland with Northern Ireland, a part of the United Kingdom, which proudly retains the common law. Perhaps Ireland is not, after all, left entirely alone. Ireland may, in the words of John of Gaunt be a 'precious stone set in a silver sea'.[70]

---

[70] John of Gaunt in Shakespeare's *Richard II*, Act II, Scene 1.

4

Culture Clash? The UK Tradition of Open Justice and the Court of Justice of the European Union

AIDAN O'NEILL

I. INTRODUCTION

THIS CHAPTER OFFERS a survey of the extent to which aspects – which are common in and to the courts in the four political territories (and separate legal jurisdictions of Northern Ireland, Scotland, England and Wales) which currently make up the United Kingdom – of legal practice associated with the principle of 'open justice', have (or have not) translated in and to the practice of the Court of Justice of the European Union (the Court). The practices considered are: the requirements of standing to bring a case to the courts; public access to formal pleadings and other papers before the court; the naming (or anonymising) of litigants before the court; and the importance afforded to oral hearings before the courts.

II. THE OPEN JUSTICE AND THE PRINCIPLE IN THE UK CONSTITUTION

In June 1693, the Scottish Parliament (at that point the legislature of, and representative body for, the independent Scottish nation) passed two statutes mandating that justice be done with 'open doors' both in civil cases[1] and in relation to criminal proceedings[2] in the higher courts in Scotland. Although these were statutes passed by the Scottish Parliament before the 1707 Parliamentary Union between Scotland and England, their provisions were referred to and relied upon by the Scottish Law Lord, Lord Shaw of Dunfermline, in *Scott v Scott*,[3] in which

---

[1] The Court of Session (Scotland) Act 1693 remains on the statute book and in force in Scotland. It specifies that in all time coming all proceedings before the Court of Session 'shall be considered reasoned advised and voted' on by the Court of Session judge with 'open doors' that is to say where parties, their lawyers and the public at large are allowed to be present, other than exceptional cases when the judges will be permitted to order the removal of all persons, other the parties and their lawyers, from the court and for the hearing to be held behind closed doors (or 'in camera').

[2] The Scottish Parliament's Act Anent Advising Criminal Processes with Open Doors of 12 June 1693 applied to criminal procedure before Scotland's High Court of Justiciary while providing that 'in the cases of rape, adultery and the like the said Commissioners [of Justiciary] may continue their former use and custom, by causing remove all persons, except parties and procurators, at the leading of the probation, as they shall see cause'.

[3] *Scott v Scott* [1913] AC 417.

the Appellate Committee of the House of Lords ruled that the courts of England and Wales had no general power to order, even in the interests of public decency and at the request of the parties,[4] that a matrimonial cause be heard in private before them.

Interestingly, in his judgment, Lord Shaw noted that the two Scottish statutes of 1693 were passed as part of Scotland's (Glorious) Revolutionary settlement 'to secure civil liberties *against judges* as well as against the Crown'. The fact that among the factors behind the overthrow of James II and VII from the thrones of England and of Scotland were concerns about the role played by judges under his regime is confirmed by, among other things, the terms of Article 9 of the English Bill of Rights 1688, which assert 'that the Freedom of Speech and Debates or Proceedings in Parliament ought not to be impeached or questioned *in any Court* or Place out of Parliament', and by the Scottish Claim of Right 1689 declaring 'that it is the right and privilege of the subjects to protest for remedy of law to the King and Parliament against sentences pronounced by the Lords of Session', a provision which subsequently formed the basis for the post-1707 House of Lords to exercise an appellate jurisdiction from decisions of the Court of Session.

The open justice principle is, then, seen as one means of ensuring that the judges themselves do not abuse their judicial power; for, as Jeremy Bentham put it, publicity 'keeps the judge himself, while trying, under trial',[5] a sentiment echoed by the now President of the UK Supreme Court, the Scottish judge Lord Reed who, again relying on the 1693 Scottish statutes, noted in *A v British Broadcasting Corporation*:

> Society depends on the courts to act as guardians of the rule of law. *Sed quis custodiet ipsos custodes?* Who is to guard the guardians? In a democracy, where the exercise of public authority depends on the consent of the people governed, the answer must lie in the openness of the courts to public scrutiny.[6]

Open justice has been said to have two key elements. The first is that in principle proceedings are to be heard, and evidence given in public. To enhance public interest and understanding of what is going on in court, this will generally mean public access to the documents spoken to by counsel or otherwise relied upon in court,[7] as well as information as to the identity (usually

---

[4] *cf R v Westminster City Council, ex p P* (1998) 31 HLR 154 per Sir Christopher Staughton at 163: 'when both sides agreed that information should be kept from the public, that was when the court had to be most vigilant ...'.

[5] See Jeremy Bentham, *Works*, vol 4 (1843) 316, quoted in *L v L – re ancillary financial relief and anonymity* [2015] EWHC 2621 (Fam), [2016] 1 WLR 1259 by Mostyn J at § 5. Similarly in *Lilly Icos Ltd v Pfizer Ltd (2)* [2002] 1 WLR 2253 the Court of Appeal set out (at para 25(i)) the general principle of open justice as follows: '25 i) The court should start from the principle that very good reasons are required for departing from the normal rule of publicity. That is the normal rule because, as Lord Diplock put it in *Home Office v Harman* [1983] AC 280 at 303C, citing both Jeremy Bentham and Lord Shaw of Dunfermline in *Scott v Scott* [1913] AC 417, "Publicity is the very soul of justice. It is the keenest spur to exertion, and the surest of all guards against improbity. It keeps the judge himself, while trying, under trial." The already very strong English jurisprudence to this effect has only been reinforced by the addition to it of this country's obligations under Arts 6 and 10 of the European Convention on Human Rights.' Interestingly in Case C-245/20 *X and Z v Autoriteit Persoonsgegevens* ECLI:EU:C:2021:822 while Advocate General Bobek opens his Opinion of 6 October 2021 with the same citation of Bentham, he chooses to *omit* the passage referring to publicity as necessary to keep the judge himself, while trying, under trial.

[6] *A v British Broadcasting Corpn* [2014] UKSC 25, [2015] AC 588, para 23.

[7] See *Dring v Cape Intermediate Holdings Ltd* [2019] UKSC 38 [2020] AC 629 confirming that in principle all courts and tribunals in the UK had an inherent jurisdiction to determine what the constitutional principle of open justice required in terms of access to documents or other information placed before that court or tribunal in question and that the default position – subject only to contrary statute or rules of court or countervailing public interest considerations – was that the public should be allowed access, not only to the parties written submissions and arguments, but also to the documents which had been placed before the court and referred to during the hearing.

the names) of the parties litigating.[8] The second element is that the judges have an obligation, once proceedings have ended, to announce their decisions to the public, and give an account – in the form of a published reasoned judgment – setting out just why they have reached the particular decision.[9] In this way, it is hoped the probity of the judges will be secured, the likelihood of witnesses telling the truth increased, and public understanding about (and therefore it is thought confidence in) the legal process enhanced. All this was expressed extrajudicially by the Associate Justice of the US Supreme Court, Louis Brandeis, who in 1913 observed that:

> Publicity is justly commended as a remedy for social and industrial diseases. Sunlight is said to be the best of disinfectants; electric light the most efficient policeman.[10]

This understanding of the open justice principle permeates the understanding of how justice requires to be done and to be seen to be done in the UK.[11] It affects among other things: the access to justice rules concerning when and by whom and for what purpose recourse might be had to the courts; the importance afforded by these courts to oral hearings; the unwillingness of the courts too readily to grant anonymity to litigants or parties before them; and the readiness of the courts to allow for dissenting judgments in multi-judge cases at all levels of the national judicial hierarchies within the (British) Union polity.

The approach taken by the courts in the UK on these matters differs, in significant respects, from the practices of and procedures before the Court. It may be that this difference in approach left it open for the Court and its case law to be misunderstood and misrepresented in the UK's legal, political, and journalistic circles as embodying an alien curial cultural tradition. This may ultimately have contributed to the apparent popular disaffection with the 'European Court' which marked the Brexit referendum campaign, and fuelled the political desire to escape its jurisdiction.

So – in a manner which perhaps runs wholly contrary to the overarching theme of this book – this chapter may be understood as outlining a failure or *lack* of influence of the UK's legal traditions on the workings, self-understanding, and self-presentation of the Court.

III. OPEN JUSTICE AND ACCESS TO JUSTICE THROUGH LEGAL STANDING

The courts in the UK have increasingly operated on the basis that the constitutional principle of open justice requires the dismantling of older rules which created barriers against access to

---

[8] See eg *Practice Guidance of the Court of Appeal of England and Wales re Anonymity in Asylum and Immigration Cases* [2022] 1 WLR 2103 at para 2: 'The starting point for the consideration of anonymity orders is open justice. This principle promotes the rule of law and public confidence in the legal system. Given the importance of open justice, appellants should generally expect to be named in proceedings in the Court of Appeal. Any departure from this principle will need to be justified.'

[9] *MH v Mental Health Tribunal* [2019] CSIH 14, 2019 SC 432, paras 18–20: 'Open justice has two key elements. The first is that proceedings are heard and determined in public. The second is that the public has access to judicial determinations, including any reasons for them and the identity of the parties'.

[10] L Brandeis, 'What Publicity Can Do' *Harper's Weekly* (New York, 20 December 1913) 10.

[11] See *BBC v Chair of the Scottish Child Abuse Inquiry* [2002] CSIH 5, 2022 SLT 385 at paras 44–45: 'The principle of open justice is a cornerstone of the legal system. Public scrutiny of courts and tribunals facilitates public confidence in the system and helps to ensure that they are carrying out their functions properly. It would require very special circumstances before a court or tribunal would be justified in prohibiting publication of the existence of a case pending before it. Sensitive and confidential material can legitimately be restricted, but very often it can be dealt with satisfactorily by anonymising the identity of the parties rather than concealing the subject matter of the dispute. Even then, Lord Rodger's answer to his own question "What's in a name ?" ("A lot !") should be borne firmly in mind: *Re Guardian News and Media* [2010] UKSC 1 [2010] 2 AC 697 at para 63.'

justice. Thus there are now very liberal rules on standing across the legal systems of the UK, at least in public law cases. In *Walton v Scottish Ministers*, in a case that concerned issues around compliance with EU law requirements for environmental impact assessments of planned major road trunk networks, Lord Reed observed:

> In many contexts it will be necessary for a person to demonstrate some particular interest in order to demonstrate that he is not a mere busybody. Not every member of the public can complain of every potential breach of duty by a public body. But there may also be cases in which *any individual, simply as a citizen, will have sufficient interest to bring a public authority's violation of the law to the attention of the court, without having to demonstrate any greater impact upon himself than upon other members of the public.* The rule of law would not be maintained if, because everyone was equally affected by an unlawful act, no-one was able to bring proceedings to challenge it.[12]

An example of an NGO being regarded as having sufficient interest effectively to be able to act as an enforcer of EU environmental law – even in the face of inaction from the Commission – is seen in *R (ClientEarth) v Secretary of State for the Environment, Food and Rural Affairs*[13] where, in the face of an admitted breach by the UK Government of EU law setting limits on permissible levels of nitrogen dioxide polluting emissions, the UK Supreme Court felt able to issue a mandatory order requiring the Secretary of State to prepare new air quality plans under Article 23(1) of Directive 2008/50/EC in accordance with a defined timetable set by the court, to end with delivery of the revised plans to the Commission not later than 31 December 2015, so as to ensure the effective remedy required by EU law.

A greater readiness on the part of the UK courts to give apparently general advisory opinions as part of the principle of open justice may also be seen in *Wightman v Secretary of State for Exiting the European Union*[14] in which the First Division of the Court of Session was faced with a question of EU law, namely whether or not Article 50 TEU allowed for the possibility of a Member State which had duly notified its intention to leave the EU, to withdraw that notification and so remain in the Union. The UK Government objected that this was a purely hypothetical and academic (and premature) question, since, it said, that even if it were possible for the Article 50 TEU notification to be revoked, the UK had no intention of so doing. The First Division rejected this claim, and held that it was a matter of considerable practical important for Parliament to know whether they could still, as a matter of EU law, stop the withdrawal of the UK from the EU in the event that Parliament considered the terms of any Withdrawal Agreement negotiated between the UK and the EU to be unacceptable. In reaching this view, the First Division made important observations on the principle of access to justice before the UK courts, with the Lord President (Carloway) noting:

> The courts exist as one of the three pillars of the state to provide rulings on what the law is and how it should be applied. That is their fundamental function. The principle of access to justice *dictates that, as a generality, anyone, who wishes to do so, can apply to the court to determine what the law is in a given situation.* The court must issue that determination publicly.[15]

Because the issue raised before was one of EU law on which there was significant dispute and no clear precedent, the First Division accordingly made a reference to the Court on this point of law. The UK Government again argued before the Court that the question referred by the

---

[12] *Walton v Scottish Ministers* [2012] UKSC 44, [2013] PTSR 51, para 94, emphasis added.
[13] *R (ClientEarth) v Secretary of State for the Environment, Food and Rural Affairs* [2015] UKSC 28, [2015] PTSR 909.
[14] *Wightman v Secretary of State for Exiting the European Union* [2018] CSIH 62, 2019 SC 111.
[15] ibid, para 21.

Scottish Court should simply not be answered. In *Wightman*,[16] the Court held that it was not for it to take a different view from the Inner House (which was satisfied that the question met an objective need for the purpose of settling a real dispute), and ruled that a Member State could unilaterally revoke its earlier notification of its intention to leave the EU for as long as a withdrawal agreement concluded between that State and the Union had not entered into force (or, if no such agreement had been concluded, for as long as the period laid down in Article 50(3) TEU of two years unless extended by agreement with the EU, had not expired).

The generous approach to the open justice principle seen in decision of the UK courts, has *not*, however, been matched in the case law of the Court as regards direct access to that court. Article 263 TFEU allows that a private party may have *locus standi* to bring such an annulment action in respect of an EU decision or regulation of direct and individual concern to him. Yet the possibility of strategic litigation proceeding by direct action brought by private parties before the Court is severely limited by the fact that the Court strictly and narrowly construes these standing requirements.[17] In *Inuit*,[18] a post-Lisbon judgment, the Grand Chamber of the Court confirmed that interest groups/NGOs have no standing to challenge the validity of general legislative measures adopted by the EU legislature. This decision also confirmed that while a direct action can be brought in the Court to review the lawfulness of a *failure to act* on the part of any EU institution or agency pursuant to Article 263 TFEU, and that direct actions can also be brought pursuant to Article 265 TFEU to challenge the legality of an EU measure, in both cases, the same restrictive standing provisions apply. And even if these strict rules on standing are met, the Court has held that there still remains a need to demonstrate an *interest* in having the contested act annulled. An interest in bringing proceedings and *locus standi* are distinct conditions for admissibility which must be satisfied by a natural or legal person *cumulatively* in order to be admissible to bring an action for annulment under the fourth paragraph of Article 263 TFEU.[19]

In *Stichting Natuur en Milieu*,[20] the Court held that Article 9(3) of the Aarhus Convention did not contain any unconditional and sufficiently precise obligation capable of directly regulating the legal position of individuals, and it was not therefore capable of being relied upon as the basis for an action for annulment.[21] In *Carvalho*,[22] (Sixth Chamber, 25 March 2021) the Court adjudicated in a small chamber of just three judges, without holding an oral hearing, and dispensing with any written Opinion from the Advocate General (AG), dismissed an attempt by a consortium of individual environmental activists to challenge the compatibility of the EU's legislative package regulating continued greenhouse gas emissions within

---

[16] Case C-621/18 *Wightman* ECLI:EU:C:2018:999.

[17] See Case C-50/00 P *Unión de Pequeños Agricultores* ECLI:EU:C:2002:462. See ch 33.

[18] Case C-583/11 P *Inuit Tapiriit Kanatami* ECLI:EU:C:2013:625.

[19] See, to that effect, judgments in Case C-132/12 P *Stichting Woonpunt* ECLI:EU:C:2014:100, paras 67–68, and in Case C-133/12 P *Stichting Woonlinie* ECLI:EU:C:2014:105, paras 54–55.

[20] Joined Cases C-404/12 P and C-405/12 P *Council and Commission v Stichting Natuur en Milieu* ECLI:EU:C: 2015:5. See A Thies, 'The Impact of Obligations under International Agreements on the (Judicial) Review of EU Measures: Stichting Natuur En Milieu and Pesticide Action Network Europe' in G Butler and RA Wessel (eds), *EU External Relations Law: The Cases in Context* (Oxford, Hart Publishing, 2022).

[21] Contrast with Case C-240/09 *Lesoochranárske zoskupenie VLK* ECLI:EU:C:2011:125 and Case C-243/15 *Lesoochranárske zoskupenie VLK* ECLI:EU:C:2016:838, in both of which the Grand Chamber of the Court effectively ruled that national environmental NGOs could effectively pray in aid Aarhus Convention principles on access to justice through the medium of EU law to require the disapplication of national rules of procedure which restricted their participation as parties before the national courts seeking to enforce EU environmental law against the Member States.

[22] Case C-565/19 P *Armando Carvalho* ECLI:EU:C:2021:252.

Member States with the EU international climate change obligations under the Kyoto Protocol Agreement and the Paris Agreement, on the grounds of lack of standing. The activists submitted that the right to bring an action before the Court must be given a teleological interpretation so that the law on climate change could be properly enforced. The Court however stated that:

> 69. According to settled case-law, the Courts of the European Union may not, without going beyond their jurisdiction, interpret the conditions under which an individual may institute proceedings against an act of the Union in a way which has the effect of setting aside those conditions, which are expressly laid down in the FEU Treaty, even in the light of the principle of effective judicial protection (see, to that effect, judgment of 1 April 2004, *Commission* v *Jégo-Quéré*, C-263/02 P, EU:C:2004:210, paragraph 36).

> 70. It follows that, even if the appellants are requesting that the judgment in resulting from the judgment of 15 July 1963, *Plaumann* v *Commission* (25/62, EU:C:1963:17 be adapted so as to enable the acts at issue to be contested in the present case, such an adaptation must be rejected inasmuch as it is contrary to the provisions laid down in the FEU Treaty regarding the admissibility of actions for annulment, such as that set out in the fourth paragraph of Article 263 TFEU ....

> 76. ... [T]he appellants cannot ask the Court of Justice to set aside such conditions, which are expressly laid down in the FEU Treaty, and, in particular, to adapt the criterion of individual concern as defined by the judgment in *Plaumann*, in order that they may have access to an effective remedy.

> 77. In that regard, it should be borne in mind ... that the protection conferred by Article 47 of the Charter does not require that an individual should have an unconditional entitlement to bring an action for annulment of such a legislative act of the Union directly before the Courts of the European Union (see, to that effect, judgment of 3 October 2013, *Inuit Tapiriit Kanatami and Others* v *Parliament and Council*, C-583/11 P, EU:C:2013:625, paragraph 105).

> 78. Although the conditions of admissibility laid down in the fourth paragraph of Article 263 TFEU must be interpreted in the light of the fundamental right to effective judicial protection, such an interpretation cannot have the effect of setting aside the conditions expressly laid down in that Treaty (see, to that effect, judgments of 25 July 2002, *Unión de Pequeños Agricultores* v *Council*, C-50/00 P, EU:C:2002:462, paragraph 44, and of 1 April 2004, *Commission* v *Jégo-Quéré*, C-263/02 P, EU:C:2004:210, paragraph 36).

Now, all this reasoning and reference to past case law may be thought to show a proper judicial deference to the provisions of the EU Treaties which limit the extent of the Court's jurisdiction. The problem, however, is that the Court has not consistently shown any such deference in other contexts – indeed, quite the contrary. In performing its task of 'interpretation' of the EU Treaties, the Court has, in a variety of contexts, effectively inserted new provisions into the Treaties.

The series of cases relating to the involvement of the Parliament in the EU legislative and judicial processes is a prime example. With no support in the original wording of the then EC Treaty (now TFEU), the Court has found: that the Parliament had a right to intervene in cases before the Court,[23] and that it had *locus standi* to raise actions for failure to act under Article 175 of the EC Treaty (now, as amended, Article 265 TFEU);[24] that the Court can review the legality of the activities of the Parliament under Article 173 of the EC Treaty (now, after similar *ex post facto* amendment, Article 263 TFEU),[25] and that the Parliament was competent to bring actions against other EU institutions under Article 173 of the EC Treaty (subsequently

---

[23] Case 139/79 *Maizena GmbH* ECLI:EU:C:1980:250.
[24] Case 13/83 *Parliament v Council* ECLI:EU:C:1985:220.
[25] Case 294/83 *Les Verts* ECLI:EU:C:1986:166. See also, Case 34/86 *Council v Parliament* ECLI:EU:C:1986:291.

after amendment Article 263 TFEU) in order to defend its own powers and privileges.[26] In effect, the Court has re-written the EU Treaties as regards the position of the Parliament. The Member States subsequently agreed to an amendment of the terms of Articles 173 and 175 of the then EC Treaty at the 1993 Inter-Governmental Conference (IGC) at Maastricht, to bring the wording of these Treaty provisions into line with the Court's case law.

Although it was the EU Treaties which originally gave rise to the EU legal order, the articles of these Treaties are themselves interpreted in the light of what is required of a specifically legal order. Thus, where the EU Treaties have appeared to the Court to contain contradictions or gaps, the Court, as creator and guardian of this new legal order, has felt justified in removing the contradictions and filling in the gaps, even if this results in ignoring or adding to the original wording. As the then AG Mancini stated in his Opinion in *Les Verts*:

> [T]he obligation to observe the law takes precedence over the strict terms of the written law. Whenever required in the interests of judicial protection, the Court is prepared to correct or complete rules which limit its powers in the name of the principle which defines its mission.[27]

In similar vein, Judge Koopmans of the Court, has observed:

> The obligation to follow the applicable texts seems less compelling to the Court when the simple fact of applying these texts would counteract the protection of a right considered as fundamental. In such a case, even a Treaty text cannot always form an obstacle to a judicial strategy aimed at upholding fundamental rights. To that degree, the value-oriented approach prevails.[28]

The Court is highly sensitive to political, economic, and academic reactions to its judgments, and it has a tendency to depart from previous decisions, or to halt or slow down the development of a line of case law, where these have not been well-received in the outside world.[29] This of course leaves the Court open to accusations of inconsistency when, after a period of judicial creativity and teleological reasoning, it subsequently relies on the *precise* wording of the languages,[30] either of the EU Treaties or of secondary EU legislation[31] and proclaims that the EU has the power attributed to it by its Treaty and no more. One noted example of this

---

[26] Case 70/88 *Parliament v Council* ECLI:EU:C:1991:373. See also, Case C-295/90 *Parliament v Council* ECLI:EU:C:1992:294.

[27] Opinion of AG Mancini in Case 294/83 *Les Verts* ECLI:EU:C:1985:483, at 1350.

[28] T Koopmans, 'The Theory of Interpretation and the Court of Justice' in D O'Keeffe and A Bavasso (eds), *Judicial Review in the European Union Law: Volume 1 of Liber Amicorum in Honour of Lord Slynn of Hadley* (The Hague, Kluwer Law International, 2000) 54.

[29] See eg the Court's change of position on the relationship between pre-Maastricht Arts 130s and 100a of the EC Treaty (now Art 192 TFEU and Art 114 TFEU respectively) as between Case C-300/89 *Commission v Council* ECLI:EU:C:1991:244, and Case C-155/91 *Commission v Council* ECLI:EU:C:1993:98. See also, the slowing down of the application of the principle of equal treatment to occupational pensions heralded in, Case 262/88 *Barber* ECLI:EU:C:1990:209, which is evident in the Court's judgment in Case C-152/91 *Neath* ECLI:EU:C:1993:949. Further examples of the Court's responsiveness to criticism are given in A Arnull, *The European Union and its Court of Justice*, 2nd edn (Oxford, OUP, 2006) 639–67.

[30] As the Court has also noted in Case C-263/08 *Djurgården-Lilla Värtans Miljöskyddsförening* ECLI:EU:C:2009:631, para 25: 'It is clear from settled case-law that the need for an application, and hence a uniform interpretation, of the provisions of Community law requires that, in cases of doubt, the text of a provision must not be considered in isolation in one of its versions, but, on the contrary, should be interpreted and applied in the light of the versions existing in the other official languages'.

[31] A certain 'textual scrupulousness' in relation to EU secondary legislation may also be seen in the unsuccessful attempts to apply the Equal Treatment Directive (76/207/EEC) to cases involving discrimination on grounds of sexual orientation in Case C-249/96 *Grant* ECLI:EU:C:1998:63, and in Case T-264/97 *D v Council* ECLI:EU:T:1999:13, and on appeal to the Court as Joined Cases C-122/99 P and C-125/99 P, *D and Sweden v Council* ECLI:EU:C:2001:304 (notwithstanding the earlier extension of the same legislation by the Court to pre-operative trans* individuals in Case C-13/94 *P v S and Cornwall County Council* ECLI:EU:C:1996:170.

is the Court's finding – after years of repeating that the substantive content of the European Convention on Human Rights (ECHR) could be regarded as forming part of the general principles of EU law – that, even following Member States amendment of the EU Treaties to provide in Article 6(2) TEU that 'the Union shall accede to the European Convention for the Protection of Human Rights and Fundamental Freedoms. Such accession shall not affect the Union's competences as defined in the Treaties'[32] – it was simply not competent for the EU itself to become a party to the ECHR (and thereby bring the Court itself directly under the jurisdictional oversight of the European Court of Human Rights (ECtHR)).[33]

Thus, individuals are faced then with a court which will, when it chooses, apply the black letter of the law, but in other cases, adopt an innovative approach to reach what it considers to be the proper result, regardless of the specific constraints or terms of the text. This variable approach by the Court has led to allegations that it is over-stepping its judicial role to further a political agenda of further integration, and limitation on the powers of individual Member States. Rasmussen, the noted veteran critic of the Court, observed:

> When judges recast the law in a radically innovative, ground-breaking and adventurous fashion, they do a lot more than create legal uncertainty and unpredictability. They divert from courts' purposes, their organization, their procedures, their institutional *raison d'être*, the judging personnel's education, their training and all other resources. This action is not only constitutionally illegitimate but squarely illegal because it violates the other fundamental constitutional separation-of-powers pact. This endowed certain functions of government on the judiciary while it vested law- and policy-making functions in other, typically elected and democratically responsible institutions.
>
> Courts' raison d'être is the best possible discharge of their duty to apply, in most cases, the legislator's laws to the facts of concrete cases and conflicts, hereby upholding the rule of law. Of course, while applying the law the courts interpret and fill gaps in it, utilizing their margins of discretion to best transform the legislator's legal messages to actual legal facts. To randomly rewrite or reconstruct the constitution and/or the entire legal system to make it consonant with the whims of judicial majorities is to substitute the rule of men to the rule of law.[34]

IV. OPEN JUSTICE AND PUBLIC ACCESS TO COURT DOCUMENTS

In an Order in *Tobacco Advertising I*,[35] the Court stated that the parties in action before the Court are, in principle, free to disclose their own written submissions (which would include any documents appended thereto). The Court observed:

> So far as infringement of the principle of confidentiality is concerned, there is no rule or provision under which parties to proceedings are authorised to or prevented from disclosing their own written submissions to third parties. Apart from exceptional cases where disclosure of a document might adversely affect the proper administration of justice, which is not the case here, the principle is that parties are free to disclose their own written submissions.[36]

---

[32] In *Opinion 2/94* ECLI:EU:C:1996:140, the Court stated that it was beyond the competence of the EU *in the absence of express Treaty provisions* to accede as a body to the ECHR.

[33] See *Opinion 2/13* ECLI:EU:C:2014:2454.

[34] H Rasmussen and L Nan Rasmussen, 'Comment on Katalin Kelemen – Activist EU Court "Feeds" on the Existing Ban on Dissenting Opinions: Lifting the Ban is Likely to Improve the Quality of EU Judgments' (2013) 14 *German Law Journal* 1373.

[35] Case C-376/98 *Germany v Parliament and Council* ECLI:EU:C:2000:181.

[36] ibid, para 10.

In his Opinion in *Sweden and API v Commission*, AG Maduro stated that the Court should take the opportunity of expressly departing from and overruling this Order on the basis that 'if the decision to release documents is left to the parties, they may be too cautious in releasing documents where they fear damage to their own interests and too ready to release documents that might cause harm to their adversaries'.[37] In its judgment however, the Grand Chamber of the Court did not expressly follow the approach of the AG Maduro, nor did it explicitly overrule the Order in the earlier *Tobacco Advertising I* case. Instead, it ruled that third parties had no right of access to pleadings submitted to the Court as a matter of EU law, and justified such non-disclosure on the grounds of the 'need to ensure that, throughout the court proceedings, the exchange of argument by the parties and the deliberations of the court in the case before it take place in an atmosphere of total serenity' to avoid 'exposing judicial activities to external pressure, albeit only in the perception of the public'.[38] By way of further justification, the Court noted that the terms of what is now Article 15(3) TFEU obliged the Court only to exercise its administrative tasks in accordance with the principle of transparency, and read from that by implication that it was therefore intended that it conduct its judicial tasks in accordance with the principle of opacity, otherwise 'the effectiveness of the [Treaty] exclusion of the Court of Justice from the institutions to which the principle of transparency applies … would be largely frustrated'.[39]

Trying to reconcile the Order in *Tobacco Advertising I* in 2000 with the observations of the Grand Chamber in its 2010 judgment, one could say that in the *Sweden* case, the Court simply established that third parties have no general right of access to the pleadings upon which the Court is proceeding in pending cases. Nor is the Court bound by the general principle of transparency. The Order of 2000 makes it plain, however, that it is open to a party to proceedings before the Court to makes its own pleadings public should it choose to do so. In its decision in *Sweden and API v Commission*, the Court seemed to set little store by the idea of compliance with the principle of transparency in decision making – at least in the context of proceedings before the Court – as being in itself of overriding public interest, and summarily dismissed 'mere claims' made by API to the effect that the public's right to be informed about important issues of EU law – such as those concerning competition, and about issues which are of great political interest raised by infringement proceedings against Member States – should 'prevail over the protection of the court proceedings'. Instead, in the Grand Chamber's view,

> it is only where the particular circumstances of the case substantiate a finding that the principle of transparency is especially pressing that that principle can constitute an overriding public interest capable of prevailing over the need for protection of the disputed documents and, accordingly, capable of justifying their disclosure.[40]

This judgment, stating that there is no public right of access to written pleadings before the Court is difficult to justify, particularly against the apparent lack of transparency in the Court's actual reasoning in so many cases, given the requirement for unanimous non-dissenting judgments which too often conceal more than they reveal in Delphic prose. The approach of the Court is particularly difficult to justify within the context of the United Kingdom where it has

---

[37] Opinion of AG Maduro in Joined Cases C-514/07 P, C-528/07 P, and C-532/07 P *Sweden and API v Commission* ECLI:EU:C:2009:592.

[38] Joined Cases C-514/07 P, C-528/07 P, and C-532/07 P *Sweden and API v Commission* ECLI:EU:C:2010:541, para 93.

[39] ibid, para 95.

[40] ibid, para 156.

been a constant theme of the courts that the right of open justice require that the public should be able to scrutinise both written and oral evidence, and argument, upon which a court of law has been invited to arrive at its decision.

The achievement of that purpose requires that a member of the public, who is an observer, should be afforded access to the same written submissions and witness statements, given to the judge and referred to in open court. What this means is that there is a strong presumption in favour of all court papers lodged with the court (including parties arguments and the court pleadings) to be released and made available to the public and to the press on request. Thus, in *GIO Personal Investment Services Ltd v Liverpool and London Steamship P&I Association Ltd*,[41] Potter LJ noted:

> If, as in the instant case, an opening speech is dispensed with in favour of a written opening (or a skeleton argument treated as such) which is not read out, or even summarised, in open court before the calling of the evidence, it seems to me impossible to avoid the conclusion that an important part of the judicial process, namely the instruction of the judge in the issues of the case, has in fact taken place in the privacy of his room and not in open court. In such a case, I have no doubt that, on application from a member of the press or public in the course of the trial, it is within the inherent jurisdiction of the court to require that there be made available to such applicant a copy of the written opening or skeleton argument submitted to the judge.[42]

Interestingly, in *R (Mohammed) v Secretary of State for Foreign & Commonwealth Affairs*,[43] the Court of Appeal once again referenced the idea of publicity and open justice being a necessary part of the checks on possible judicial abuse of power. Lord Judge CJ stated:

> 38. Justice must be done between the parties. The public must be able to enter any court to see that justice is being done in that court, by a tribunal conscientiously doing its best to do justice according to law. *For that reason, every judge sitting in judgment is on trial*. So it should be, and any exceptions to the principle must be closely limited. In reality very few citizens can scrutinise the judicial process: that scrutiny is performed by the media, whether newspapers or television, acting on behalf of the body of citizens. Without the commitment of an independent media the operation of the principle of open justice would be irremediably diminished.
>
> 39. There is however a distinct aspect of the principle which goes beyond proper scrutiny of the processes of the courts and the judiciary. The principle has a wider resonance, which reflects the distinctive contribution made by the open administration of justice to what President Roosevelt described in 1941 as the
>
> '... first freedom, freedom of speech and expression'.
>
> In litigation, particularly litigation between the executive and any of its manifestations and the citizen, the principle of open justice represents an element of democratic accountability, and the vigorous manifestation of the principle of freedom of expression. Ultimately it supports the rule of law itself. Where the court is satisfied that the executive has misconducted itself, or acted so as to facilitate misconduct by others, all these strands, democratic accountability, freedom of expression, and the rule of law are closely engaged.

---

[41] *GIO Personal Investment Services Ltd v Liverpool and London Steamship P&I Association Ltd* [1999] 1 WLR 984.

[42] At 996E–G. Similarly in *R v Howell* [2003] EWCA Crim 486, Judge LJ said, at para 197: 'Subject to questions arising in connection with written submissions on [public interest immunity] applications, or any other express justification for non-disclosure on the basis that the written submissions would not properly have been deployed in open court, we have concluded that the principle of open justice leads inexorably to the conclusion that written skeleton arguments, or those parts of the skeleton arguments adopted by counsel and treated by the court as forming part of his oral submissions, should be disclosed if and when a request to do so is received'.

[43] *R (Mohammed) v Secretary of State for Foreign & Commonwealth Affairs* [2010] EWCA Civ 158, [2011] QB 218.

There appears to be a profound philosophical divergence between the assumptions embodied in the judgment of the Court in *Sweden and API v Commission* in which the paramount need to preserve the 'serenity' of proceedings is seen as justification for shielding it from public gaze, and the starting point for the UK courts which is that judicial power requires to be held to public account, just as much as other forms of power in the state.

V. OPEN JUSTICE AND THE NAMING OF LITIGANTS

In re S, Lord Steyn observed:

> From a newspaper's point of view a report of a sensational trial without revealing the identity of the defendant would be a very much disembodied trial. If the newspapers choose not to contest such an injunction, they are less likely to give prominence to reports of the trial. Certainly, readers will be less interested and editors will act accordingly. *Informed debate about criminal justice will suffer.*[44] (emphasis added)

As seen, the UK courts emphasise the importance of the principle of open justice as the primary means of facilitating public confidence in the civil and criminal justice. It has been seen to be a necessary corollary of the open justice principle in the UK that the presumption should be that those who are parties to civil litigation or criminal trial should in principle be named, rather than anonymised by court order.[45] One rationale given for this is that the press require to name names in order to attract readers and hence promote continued scrutiny of the justice system.[46] Accordingly, as the Lord President (Carloway) noted in *Anwar v Secretary of State for Business, Energy and Industrial Strategy*:

> Unless the circumstances are life threatening or might result in the party being subjected to inhuman or degrading treatment, it is for the court to balance the competing rights of respect for privacy and open justice/transparency. The presumption is for open justice. It is not enough for anonymisation to be convenient or even desirable. It must be 'a matter of necessity in order to avoid the subordination of the ends of justice to the means'.[47]

The UK courts have also been clear that the possibility of some sectors of the press abusing their freedom to report court proceedings cannot, of itself, be a sufficient reason for curtailing that freedom for all members of the press. Instead, the possibility of abuse is therefore simply one factor to be taken into account when considering whether an anonymity order is a proportionate restriction on press freedom in any particular situation.[48]

Again, however, a startling contrast can be seen between the practice and presumptions of the UK courts in favour of naming names, and the practice and presumption of the Court of anonymising at least those cases that come before it by way of preliminary reference from Member State courts. It had long been the practice of the Court to replace the names of asylum seekers, children, and other individuals in sensitive litigation by initials of some description.

---

[44] *Re S* [2004] UKHL 47, [2005] 1 AC 593, at 608, para 34.

[45] See eg *Xanthopoulos v Rakshina* [2022] EWFC 30 per Mostyn J at para 128: 'The correct question is not: "Why is it in the public interest that the parties should be named?", but rather: "Why is it in the public interest that the parties should be anonymous?" If the correct question is asked then the burden of proof rightly falls on the party seeking to prevent names being published rather than on the party or journalist/blogger seeking to publish them.'

[46] *MH v Mental Health Tribunal* [2019] CSIH 14, 2019 SC 432, para 20.

[47] *Anwar v Secretary of State for Business, Energy and Industrial Strategy* [2019] CSIH 43, 2020 SC 95.

[48] *Re Guardian News and Media Ltd* [2010] UKSC 1, [2010] 2 AC 697, per Lord Rodger of Earlsferry, para 72.

Other cases were otherwise referred to by the name of parties involved. This was in line with the Article 95 of the Court's Rules of Procedure, which reads:

> 1. Where anonymity has been granted by the referring court or tribunal, the Court shall respect that anonymity in the proceedings pending before it.
>
> 2. At the request of the referring court or tribunal, at the duly reasoned request of a party to the main proceedings or of its own motion, the Court may also, if it considers it necessary, render anonymous one or more persons or entities concerned by the case.

In June 2018, the Court issued a press release announcing that with effect from 1 July 2018, the Court would in all requests for preliminary rulings replace, in all its public documents:

> the names of natural persons involved in the case by initials and would remove any additional element likely to permit identification of the persons concerned. This change would apply to all publications made as part of the handling of the case, from its lodging until its closure (notices to the Official Journal, Opinions, judgments …), and to the name of the case. The new practice would not apply to legal persons which could however expressly request anonymisation.

This change in the Court's practice did not involve, at the time, any amendment of its Rules of Procedure (which would have required the approval of the Council by virtue of Article 253 TFEU), and it is not clear whether or not there was any prior consultation with potentially interested parties, such as the other EU institutions (including the EU's Fundamental Rights Agency), the Member States, or the Council of the Bars and Law Societies of Europe (CCBE) as the professional body for the lawyers representing litigants before the court. In any event, the practice is now more formally set out in the Court's 2020 Practice Directions as follows:

> In order to ensure optimal protection of personal data, in particular in connection with material published by the Court concerning the cases that are brought before it, the Court as a general rule deals with preliminary ruling cases in anonymised form. This approach means in practice that, unless there are special circumstances, the Court will redact the names of individuals mentioned in the request for a preliminary ruling and, if necessary, other information that may enable them to be identified, if the referring court or tribunal did not do so before submitting its request. All interested persons referred to in Article 23 of the Statute are requested to respect, in their written observations or oral submissions, the anonymity thus conferred.[49]

In the Official Journal for 8 November 2019, the Court's Recommendations to National Courts and Tribunals in relation to their initiation of preliminary reference now provides that 'in order to ensure optimal protection of personal data' in the Court's case handling the referring court or tribunal 'is invited to anonymise the case by replacing, for example using initials or a combination of letters, the names of individuals referred to in the request and by redacting information that might enable them to be identified'.[50] Interestingly, this reference to the national courts being 'invited' replaces the previous 2018 recommendation's claim that it was 'necessary' to anonymise, presumably to blunt critics that the Court was purporting to impose its views and practice – at least when a case is before the Court – on the proper approach to anonymising cases on Member State courts, regardless of the general practice within the national jurisdictions.[51] But even this 'invitation' has the potential for the paradoxical result

---

[49] (2020) OJ L 42 I/4 (14 February 2020), para 7.

[50] (2019) OJ C 380/01 (8 November 2019), emphasis added.

[51] In Case C-245/20 *X and Z v Autoriteit Persoonsgegevens* ECLI:EU:C:2022:216, the Court ruled that the 'open justice' practice of the courts of the Netherlands (done with a view to assisting journalists in better reporting on court cases being heard before them) of allowing the press to access on the date of a court hearing certain procedural

of a case being named at the national level, anonymised on a reference to the Court, but then assuming its original name when the national court deals with the reference back from the Court. Such name switching looks, if anything, to be a recipe for confusion.

What does not seem to have been (sufficiently) taken into account by the Court in its insistence on having preliminary references case before it involving natural persons referred by random and intentionally misleading initials (to prevent jigsaw identification) and/or by keywords, means that, in one stroke, the jurisprudence of the Court is rendered more opaque, more difficult to research, almost impossible to remember. 'What is in a case-name?', it might be asked. 'A lot', is the answer, when it concerns a corpus of judge made law which has developed over time. The naming of cases is essential to ensuring the transparency of the Court's work which in many ways has resembled a common law court in its effective creation and constant re-development of legal doctrine in building upon its past case law.

No-one denies that there can be case in which these general transparency considerations may in specific circumstances give way to the needs to preserve the privacy of particular individual litigants. Somewhat shockingly, one of the cases in which the UK courts felt it necessary to conceal the identities of litigants was *R (Miller) v Secretary of State for Exiting the EU*,[52] the challenge to the attempt by the UK Government to trigger the process for the withdrawal of the United Kingdom from the EU without prior legislative authorisation from the UK Parliament. In the light of threats made against the individuals in whose names the challenge had originally been brought, the UK Supreme Court made an order forbidding the publication of the names or any other means of identifying those claims whose identities were not already public. They also permitted the still-named lead claimant, Gina Miller, to attend court accompanied by two personal bodyguards. But as Lord Reed noted in in *A v BBC Scotland*:

> [T]he court has to carry out a balancing exercise which will be fact specific. Central to the court's evaluation will be the purpose of the open justice principle, the potential value of the information in question in advancing that purpose and, conversely, any risk of harm which its disclosure may cause to the maintenance of an effective judicial process or to the legitimate interests of others.[53]

The problem with the Court's new practice and requirements on case anonymisation – at least from the perspective of UK lawyers – is that the Court seems simply to have ignored and failed to take into account the positive benefits associated with the naming of cases.[54] The impression given is that transparency and open justice are not values by which the Court sets great store, and that for lawyers trained in the UK, traditions of open justice are a source of some concern and discomfort.

VI. OPEN JUSTICE AND ORAL HEARINGS

In *R (Siddiqui) v Lord Chancellor*, Sir Timothy Lloyd observed that 'the oral hearing procedure lies at the heart of English civil procedure, much more so perhaps than in the case of some

---

documents in those cases scheduled before the court for that day (including court documents containing personal data such as the names and addresses and national identification number of individual litigants) was *not* (yet) unlawful as a matter of EU law.

[52] *R (Miller) v Secretary of State for Exiting the EU* [2017] UKSC 5, [2018] AC 61.

[53] *A v BBC Scotland* [2014] UKSC 25, 2014 SC (UKSC) 151, para 41.

[54] The protection of personal data in connection with publications relating to judicial proceedings before the Court of Justice, Note produced by the Court of Justice of the European Union, available June 2021.

continental jurisdictions'.[55] In *Sengupta v Holmes*, Laws LJ explained what, from a judicial perspective, were the primary benefits of oral hearings, in noting that:

> [O]ral argument is perhaps the most powerful force there is, in our legal process, to promote a change of mind by a judge. That judges in fact change their minds under the influence of oral argument is not an arcane feature of the system; it is at the centre of it. .... It is a commonplace for a hearing to start with a clear expression of view by the judge or judges, which may strongly favour one side; it would not cross the mind of counsel on the other side then to suggest that the judge should recuse himself; rather, he knows where he is, and the position he has to meet. He often meets it.[56]

In the same case of *Sengupta*, Keene LJ extolled the benefits of the court's hearing public oral argument, over it simply privately considering the papers and deciding a case on the basis of the pleadings and arguments presented to it solely in written form:

> [T]the benefit enjoyed by the court of listening to oral argument ... is a fundamental part of our system of justice and it is a process which as a matter of common experience can be markedly more effective than written argument. It will be evident from what has been said earlier in this judgment that, before hearing oral argument in this case, I had some considerable sympathy for the applicant's arguments. The process of oral debate has persuaded me that those arguments are unsound. I mention this simply as one example of the impact which oral submissions may have under our system on the decision-making process. Yet it is a feature absent from the process by which the decision by the single judge on the papers is arrived at.[57]

In *Wasif v Secretary of State for the Home*, Underhill LJ noted that the potential value of an oral renewal hearing did not lie only in the power of oral advocacy.[58] It is also provided an opportunity for the parties, under judicial questioning, to address the perceived weaknesses in the claim which may not always have been anticipated or addressed in the pleadings or written arguments. And in *R (Detention Action) v First-Tier Tribunal*, a case in which the Court of Appeal struck down the fast-track regime applying to asylum and immigration appeals in the First-Tier Tribunal and Upper Tribunal as being structurally unfair, Lord Dyson MR made the following more general remarks:

> [T]he rules must secure that the proceedings are handled quickly and efficiently, but in a way which ensures that justice is done in the particular proceedings and that the system is accessible and fair. Speed and efficiency do not trump justice and fairness. Justice and fairness are paramount.[59]

The drive towards open justice in the UK has meant that it is now standard practice for oral hearing (at least before the UK Supreme Court) to be streamed live online from the court's own website, with the footage being made available more generally to broadcasters. And video on demand recordings of oral hearings from 2017 at the UK Supreme Court are also available to view from its website. The 3-day hearing held before the full bench of eleven judges of the UK Supreme Court in *R (Miller) v Prime Minister/Cherry v Advocate General for Scotland*[60]

---

[55] *R (Siddiqui) v Lord Chancellor* [2019] EWCA Civ 1040, para 8.

[56] *Sengupta v Holmes* [2002] EWCA Civ 1104, para 38.

[57] ibid, para 47.

[58] *Wasif v Secretary of State for the Home Department* [2016] EWCA Civ 82, [2016] 1 WLR 2793, para 17(3).

[59] *R (Detention Action) v First-Tier Tribunal* [2015] EWCA Civ 840, [2015] 1 WLR 5341, para 22.

[60] *R (Miller) v Prime Minister/Cherry v Advocate General for Scotland* [2019] UKSC 41, [2020] AC 373. The UKSC judges were: Baroness Hale of Richmond PSC, Lord Reed DPSC, Lord Kerr of Tonaghmore, Lord Wilson, Lord Carnwath, Lord Hodge, Lady Black, Lord Lloyd-Jones, Lady Arden, Lord Kitchin, and Lord Sales JJSC.

attracted a large national and international audience who followed the proceedings (and the delivery of the judgment) both online, and on live television.[61]

At the Court, oral hearings may, but need not, be held. Article 76 of the Court's consolidated Rules of Procedure provides that parties have to submit 'reasoned requests for a hearing' which set out a real assessment of the benefits of having an oral hearing (indicating among other things the documentary elements or arguments which the requesting party considers it necessary to develop or challenge more fully at the hearing). If the court is of the view, after hearing from the Judge Rapporteur and the AG, that it has sufficient information from reading the written pleadings or observations lodged to allow it to give a ruling, then it may refuse the request, and dispense with a hearing. But the Court's 2020 Practice Directions also make it clear that that a hearing will be arranged by the Court, even on its own motion and without any reasoned request, whenever it considers that holding a hearing would be likely to contribute to a better understanding of the case and the issues raised by it.

Interestingly, the Court's Practice Directions do not suggest that an oral hearing may be arranged only when it might assist *the Court* better to understand the case. There appears instead to be an implicit acceptance of the role of oral hearings as public theatre, as a way in which the public at large may come better to understand a case and the issues raised by it. Certainly the oral hearing that was arranged before a Full Court of 25 judges[62] and one AG[63] in *Wightman* constituted a grand, constructive, and illuminating public event in which the questioning of the advocates for all parties from so many of the judges illustrated both the Court's profound engagement with the issues raised in that case, and the seriousness with which they regarded these question of both transnational constitutional law and politics.[64]

VII. CONCLUSION: PLATO V ARISTOTLE?

The differences outlined above between the UK courts' and the Court's respective understandings of their commonly accepted principle that 'justice should not only be done, but should manifestly and undoubtedly be seen to be done'[65] may reflect a basic difference in the dominant judicial philosophical approach which, for want of better terms, might be characterised

---

[61] In the interest of full disclosure, this author advised and acted for the applicants in *Cherry* and appeared as senior counsel and argued for them at all stages of the case before the Outer House of the Court of Session, the Inner House of the Court of Session and the UKSC.

[62] The judges of the Court were: President K Lenaerts; Vice-President R Silva de Lapuerta; Presidents of Chambers J-C Bonichot, A Arabadjiev, A Prechal, M Vilaras, E Regan, T von Danwitz, C Toader, F Biltgen, K Jürimäe, C Lycourgos, Judges A Rosas, E Juhàsz, M Ilesic, J Malenovsky, L Bay Larsen, M Safjan, D Svàlby, C G Fernlund, C Vajda, S Rodin, P G Xuereb, N Piçarra, L S Rossi.

[63] The AG was M Campos Sánchez-Bordona.

[64] In the interest of full disclosure, this author advised and acted for the applicants in *Wightman*, and appeared as senior counsel and argued for them at all stages of the case before the Outer House of the Court of Session, the Inner House of the Court of Session, and at the Court.

[65] *R v Sussex Justices, ex p McCarthy* [1924] 1 KB 256 at 259, quoted approvingly by AG Tanchev in his Opinion in Joined Cases C-585/18, C-624/18 and C-625/18 *AK* ECLI:EU:C:2019:551, concerning the independence and impartiality of the Disciplinary Chamber of the Polish Supreme Court at para 120: 'As I observed in my Opinions in Case C-619/18 *European Commission v Republic of Poland* and Case C-192/18 *European Commission v Republic of Poland* the independence and impartiality of a judge under Article 6(1) ECHR extends to an objective assessment of whether the tribunal itself offers sufficient guarantees to exclude any legitimate doubt in respect of its impartiality. Appearances are of a certain importance, so that "justice must not only be done, it must also be seen to be done"'.

as 'Aristotelian' versus 'Platonic'. In *Plato and Aristotle on Constitutionalism*, Polin identified the distinction thus:

> What are the significant differences in the political theory of Plato and Aristotle?
>
> First it seems Aristotle at all times advocated the supremacy of the rule of law, rather than rule by the judgment of a super-wise man he knew to be non-existent or by an elite group unrestrained by law.
>
> But Plato always tried so to hedge that his system would produce at least in hypothetical theory the rule of a savant or a council of elite elder statesmen or philosopher-rulers whose qualifications were supposedly wisdom and virtue and who would have the ultimate political power in the State. ... Such ruler or rules seemingly would be guided by, but not rigidly restrained by, positive law or custom.[66]

Using this terminology, the 'Platonic' approach to judging may (somewhat crudely be characterised or caricatured) as one in which the judges are understood as being a species of wise philosopher kings operating – beyond the contingent, the mundane and the purely political – in the realm of the ideal, of celestial perfection, where they can intuit the good, or the right or just result. Justice becomes, in a sense, oracular and the act of judging anonymous and impersonal. The one right (legal) answer is handed down from on high to be applied in the best way it can be to the specific facts in the messy real world of shadows and caves. In relation to the approach to the interpretation of legal texts, a tendency of the Platonic approach precisely because it is consequentialist – the achievement of the good end or the better realisation of the *telos* justifies the means – such that adherence to the strict letter of the rules become less important if this might lead to what the judges hearing the case consider to be an undesirable or unwanted result. The legal text is thus subordinated to the just result. Justice is done because the just/right end result is achieved.

The 'Aristotelian' approach to judging may be said, by contrast, to be one rooted in the earth and the messy particulars of real life and the individual case, and the clarities and obscurities of legal texts. It focuses on the particular rather than the universal. On this approach one begins and ends with the facts and the text. It is in following and respecting the form and structure of the legal text as laid down that justice is done and achieved. The Aristotelian approach assumes that every legal answer is provisional, and may require to be revisited and re-argued and that judges can and sometimes indeed must publicly dissent from what fellow judges deem to be the right answer.[67] It is an approach which values process – arguing the law

---

[66] R Polin, *Plato and Aristotle on Constitutionalism* (Abingdon, Routledge Revivals, 2020) 277–78.

[67] See eg *Liversidge v Anderson* [1942] AC 206 per Lord Atkin (dissenting) at 244: 'I view with apprehension the attitude of judges who on a mere question of construction when face to face with claims involving the liberty of the subject show themselves more executive minded than the executive. ... In this country, amid the clash of arms, the laws are not silent. They may be changed, but they speak the same language in war as in peace. It has always been one of the pillars of freedom, one of the principles of liberty for which on recent authority we are now fighting, that the judges are no respecters of persons and stand between the subject and any attempted encroachments on his liberty by the executive, alert to see that any coercive action is justified in law'. See to similar effect *R (Zadig) v Halliday* [1917] AC 260 per Lord Shaw of Dunfermline (dissenting) at 289: '[L]et the public end sanctify, as may be the case, this private wrong: the generality of a power to issue a regulation covers the case; it is *intra vires*. We shall have to consider in a little while how much on this principle of generality, – this principle that during the war the Government may do what it likes – how much is repealed. Let us pursue the inquiry as to how much the power embraces. Against regulations, in their generality, as thus construed, nothing can stand. No rights, be they as ancient as *Magna Carta*, no laws, be they as deep as the foundations of the Constitution: all are swept aside by the generality of the power vested in the Executive to issue 'regulations.' '*Silent enim, leges inter arma.*'

in court and clearly reasoning the law in judgment. It is predicated on judges *not* being all-seeing and all-wise.[68] The Aristotelian judge lets the rules guide one to the particular, whether initially desired or not; the problem being that the result may not be the most workable and indeed one which the judge would personally prefer not to reach. Yet a wholly 'black letter' approach may not be the best guard against legislative tyranny, and the 'austerity of tabulated legalism'[69] may lead to a result which give legal cover to injustice in the particular case, contrary to the protection of fundamental rights and constitutional values in accordance with the rule of law – leading to corrosive allegations of an unrepresentative and 'out of touch' judiciary.

It should always be borne in mind that this suggested distinction between the Platonists' result driven approach and the Aristotelians' rule structured approach is an attempt to capture an 'ideal type' or tendency and is not meant to constitute a complete characterisation or prediction as to how any individual UK judge will decide in any particular case as contrasted with the approach which the Court would take to the same facts and law. It is however intended to cut across the normal crude characterisation of judicial philosophies as either 'pro-European integration' as opposed to 'nationalist-sovereigntist' approach. Individual judges of whatever predisposition or pedigree or court can (at different times) be Platonists or Aristotelian, to a greater or lesser degree.

In its Order in *Emesa Sugar*, the Grand Chamber of the Court observed of the office of AG that it is their:

> duty is to make, in open court, acting with complete impartiality and independence, reasoned submissions on cases brought before the Court of Justice, in order to assist the Court in the performance of the task assigned to it, which is to ensure that in the interpretation and application of the Treaty, the law is observed.[70]

It may be that the role specifically of AGs in general (not just those hailing from, or trained in, any of the legal systems of the United Kingdom) may usefully be understood as one in which in their Opinions the 'Aristotelian assumptions' (which, on the account as outlined above, may be said to characterise much of the judicial practice and approach to open justice in the UK) are mediated and explained and set out before a judicial tribunal whose decision-making procedures are more to characterised by reference to a high Platonic vision, the better for justice to be done and to be seen to be done.

---

[68] Thomas Aquinas makes the following observations on the proper (Aristotelian) relationship between judges and legislators at IaIIae q 95,1 resp 2–3: 'As Aristotle says (in Rhetoric I, I. I 354a31), "it is better that all issues be regulated by law than to be left to the decision of judges". Three reasons may be given: first, because it is easier to find the few wise persons who suffice to frame rightful laws than the many to judge aright about every single case; secondly, because framing the law allows for a long time during which to ponder over what they should enforce, whereas judgments on particular facts are about cases which suddenly blow up. It is easier to see what is right by taking many cases into consideration than by relying on one solitary case; thirdly, because lawgivers judge on the general lie of the land and with an eye to the future, whereas judges have to decide on the cases before them, about which they can be affected by love or hate or some partiality, and this can impair their judgment .... [I]t is better, wherever possible, to draw up laws on matters to be judged and to leave as little as possible to individual discretion. As Aristotle also notes (in Rhetoric I, I. I354b13), some individual features, which cannot be covered by general laws have to be left to judges, such as questions of fact and the like'.

[69] In the words of Lord Wilberforce in *Minister of Home Affairs v Fisher* [1980] AC 319, at 328.

[70] Case C-17/98 *Emesa Sugar* ECLI:EU:C:2000:69, para 13.

5

The History and Biographies of the UK Advocates General

VERA FRITZ

I. INTRODUCTION

DURING THE FIRST decades of the European integration process, AG posts were reserved for the larger and the more influential Member States. When the six founding states established the European Coal and Steel Community (ECSC) in 1952, France and Germany received the privilege of selecting candidates for the two available AG posts.[1] France attributed the role to one of the drafters of the ECSC Treaty who had played a key part in the creation of the AG function at the Court during the negotiations, Maurice Lagrange, a member of the French Conseil d'Etat.[2] The other AG post, to be nominated by Germany, was given to Karl Roemer, a lawyer who had worked as a legal counsellor for the German Ministry of Foreign Affairs on the liberation of prisoners of war held in France.[3]

The third largest country, Italy, received the Presidency of the Court in compensation for not nominating an AG. However, ever since the implementation of this arrangement, the Italian government was under the impression that it was unfair, and requested the appointment of an AG to be nominated by them.[4] The six Member States found a temporary solution in 1958 by providing Italy with a second judge position at the Court. A decade and a half later, the accession of the UK to the European Communities represented an occasion to revise the distribution of AG posts. All four of the then largest member states, ie France, Germany, the UK, and Italy, were now allowed to nominate an AG. When Greece joined the European Communities in 1981, the Member States created a fifth AG post, which was rotated between the remaining Member States. Declaration No. 38 annexed to the Treaty of Lisbon opened

---

[1] This decision was the result an informal agreement between the Member States. According to Article 32 of the ECSC Treaty, the members of the Court were appointed by common accord of all six Member States, for a period of six years. It is noteworthy that Italy had also proposed a candidate for the AG posts to be filled in 1952, namely Riccardo Monaco, who would later become a judge at the Court. See, Archives nationales de Luxembourg, AE 11374, Note à Monsieur le Ministre des Affaires étrangères, 27 June 1952.

[2] A Boerger-De Smedt, 'La Cour de Justice dans les négociations du traité de Paris instituant la CECA' (2008) 14 *Journal of European Integration History* 7.

[3] For detailed biographies of both Maurice Lagrange and Karl Roemer, see V Fritz, *Juges et avocats généraux de la Cour de Justice de l'Union européenne. Une approche biographique de l'histoire d'une révolution juridique* (Frankfurt am Main, Vittorio Klostermann, 2018).

[4] National Archives of the Netherlands, 2.05.118, 20025, Memorandum van JURA aan M en T via DGES, 17 February 1958.

the door to the Court to ask for three more AGs and recorded the Member States' political agreement that, in that event, Poland would join the group of large Member States that always have the right to nominate a candidate to a vacant post. In 2013, following such a request from the Court, the Council duly agreed to increase the number of AGs from 8 to 11.[5] When the UK left the EU in January 2020, the AG post ordinarily occupied by a candidate nominated by the UK became a rotating one. Today, a total of five Member States have the understanding of being able to nominate a candidate to the 'permanent' AG posts: France, Germany, Italy, Poland, and Spain.

Compared to AGs from other Member States, the British AGs, especially the most recent two, served particularly long terms at the Court. In almost 50 years of membership, the UK only nominated four AGs: Jean-Pierre Warner (1973–1981), Gordon Slynn (1981–1988), who later also became an ECJ judge (1988–1992), Francis Geoffrey Jacobs (1988–2006) and Eleanor Sharpston (2006–2020). This chapter will outline the career paths of these four British AGs. Additionally, it will highlight Judge David Alexander Ogilvy Edward, who, as portrayed in Part IV of this book, acted as an AG in 1992, when he was a member of the Court of First Instance (CFI) (1989–1992).

II. THE CAREER PATHS OF THE UK AGS AT THE COURT

The first British AG at the Court, Jean-Pierre Warner (1924–2005), took his oath in Luxembourg on 9 January 1973, together with the first British judge and future president of the Court, Alexander J. Mackenzie Stuart.[6] Among his AG colleagues counted several other relative newcomers to the role: the AG Henri Mayras of France had been appointed less than one year earlier than Warner, and his Italian colleague, Alberto Trabucchi, previously a judge of the Court, became an AG on the same day that Warner arrived at the Court. One of the original AGs, Karl Roemer, was replaced shortly afterwards by Gerhard Reischl. Thus, a largely renewed group of AGs started out at the Court in 1973.[7]

A clear advantage for Warner in the carrying out of his new role was the fact that he already perfectly mastered French. Born in Kensington, London, to a British father and a French mother, he had moved to France as a young child, and had received a French education until the age of 14. In 1938, he had returned to England and attended Harrow school in London. He later went to Trinity College, Cambridge, to read history. During World War II, he was commissioned into the rifle brigade, and served in Lord Mountbatten's staff in the Far East. When he was demobilised in 1947, he returned to Trinity College to read law.[8]

Warner became a member of Lincoln's Inn, and was called to the Bar in 1950. He subsequently established a successful practice specialising in the fields of trust and fiscal law. In 1961, he became a junior counsel to the Registry of restrictive trading agreements. He appeared in this role in many cases in the Restrictive Practices Court, and acquired vast experience in competition law, which was going to be of great help at the Court. In 1964, he was recruited

---

[5] Council Decision 2013/336/EU of 25 June 2013 increasing the number of Advocates-General of the Court of Justice of the European Union [2013] OJ L179/92.

[6] Also joining the Court on that day were Max Sørensen and Cearbhall Ó Dálaigh, as judges, arising from the accession of Denmark and Ireland to the EU.

[7] Contrary to the judges, however, AGs do not work as a team. They handle their cases individually, with their law clerks.

[8] J Lever, 'Warner, Sir Jean-Pierre Frank Eugene (1925–2006)', *Oxford Dictionary of National Biography*; 'Sir Jean-Pierre Warner' *The Times* (23 February 2005).

as junior counsel to the Treasury, a position also known as the 'Treasury devil', in chancery matters. In 1972, shortly before he became an AG, he was appointed Queen's Counsel (QC).[9] Throughout these years of activity as a barrister and counsellor, he was also a non-executive director of the family firm of silk fabric manufacturers.[10] Unfortunately, not much is known about the recruitment process that led Warner to be selected as one of the two first British members of the Court; however, his appointment as Treasury devil was a clear indication that he had been earmarked as a candidate for the senior judiciary. His mandate was renewed in 1979, and he presented his Opinion in over 200 cases during the eight years that he spent at the Court. Moreover, he and Judge Mackenzie Stuart, as the first UK members of the Court, took very seriously the task of helping to educate present and future members of the legal professions of the country in their new role as subjects of the EU legal order. They fulfilled numerous invitations to speak to professional groups and to groups of academics and students, and hosted carefully planned visits to the Court by UK judges twice yearly.

Warner's successor, AG Sir Gordon Slynn (1930–2009), was also a specialist of competition law, although he had initially planned on being a teacher.[11] Born in the town of Runcorn (Cheshire), Slynn took a degree in English history and French at Goldsmiths College, University of London, and acquired his teaching qualifications. In 1951, he decided to change his career path, joined Gray's Inn, and took a law degree at Trinity College, Cambridge. Five years later, he was called to the Bar and developed a commercial practice. In 1967, he was appointed junior counsel to the Ministry of Labour. The following year, he became, as Warner, a Treasury devil, however, in common law. This role as leading counsel led him to act on several occasions as a defendant of the British government before the European Court of Human Rights (ECtHR). In 1974, Slynn took silk as a QC, and continued to work as a leading counsel to the Treasury. Two years later, he started a judicial career as a judge in the Queen's Bench division, and was knighted. In 1978, he progressed to the position of president of the Employment Appeal Tribunal, in which he remained until his appointment as an AG at the Court in 1981. Similarly to Jean-Pierre Warner, Sir Gordon Slynn was fluent in French already before he came to the Court.[12] He acted as an AG until 1988, presenting almost 300 Opinions. In turn, the British government then nominated him to be judge at the Court. He remained at the Court until 1992, taking on the role of reporting judge in over 60 cases.

The two subsequent AGs nominated by the UK were already trained in European law before their appointment as AGs. They also had a strong grasp of what their role consisted of, since both had worked as law clerks (*référendaires*) for the two previous British AGs. Francis Jacobs, born in 1939 in Cliftonville, Kent, started his career as a lecturer in jurisprudence at the University of Glasgow (1963–65) and a lecturer in law at the London School of Economics (1965–69).

Jacobs' first experience in international organisations occurred at the European Commission of Human Rights, at which he worked as an official in the Secretariat from 1969

---

[9] He would undoubtedly have taken Silk much earlier, had he not been serving as Treasury devil.

[10] J Lever, 'Warner, Sir Jean-Pierre Frank Eugene (1925–2006)', *Oxford Dictionary of National Biography*; 'Sir Jean-Pierre Warner' *The Times* (23 February 2005).

[11] For biographical information on Sir Gordon Slynn, see M Beloff, 'Slynn, Gordon, Baron Slynn of Hadley (1930–2009)', *Oxford Dictionary of National Biography*; L Blom-Cooper, 'Lord Slynn of Hadley, Liberal law lord, judge and advocate-general of the European Court of justice' *The Guardian* (London, 21 May 2009).

[12] His wife since 1962, Odile Marie Henriette Boutin, was French.

to 1972.[13] He then moved to Luxembourg to work as a law clerk for AG Warner. He returned to England in 1974 on appointment to the new Chair of European Law at the University of London, tenable at King's College. From 1981 to 1988 he was also Director of the Centre of European Law. Having been called to the Bar at the Middle Temple in 1964, he also practised as a barrister, and was appointed QC in 1984. Thus, Jacobs could count on a solid expertise in both European Human Rights and Community law when he became an AG. He also came to the Court with an important record of publications. In the mid-1970s, he had, among others, published a book and several articles on the preliminary ruling procedure,[14] as well as a book on the European Convention on Human Rights (ECHR), and another on European law and the individual.[15] His most commonly known publication from this period was, arguably, the monograph that he co-authored with Lionel Neville Brown, *The Court of Justice of the European Communities* (1977).[16] Jacobs was the AG nominated by the UK at the Court from 1988 to 2006, and presented close to 600 Opinions.

Eleanor Sharpston, the last British AG to serve at the Court, was born in 1955 in London. She was the first and only woman to be nominated to the Court by the UK. She moved to Brazil when she was a young child, and spent her adolescent years in Geneva and then Vienna, where her father worked for the United Nations Industrial Development Organization.[17] She read economics, languages, economics again, and law at King's College, Cambridge. After obtaining her degree, she taught and researched at Corpus Christi College, Oxford (1977–1980), and was called to the Bar by the Middle Temple in 1980. As her Inn's Sir Peter Bristow Scholar, she enjoyed the opportunity to work as a *Stagiaire* (trainee) with John Temple Lang in the European Commission's Legal Service and then in AG Slynn's chambers in Luxembourg. In an interview of 2015, she explained that quite early on she had had the ambition to specialise in European law, but that it had been difficult, as a woman, to get a tenancy in chambers in London with that specialty.[18] After the Bristow award, Sharpston moved to Brussels and after a short six-month stint in a local law firm became the junior member of Jeremy Lever QC's Brussels chamber. At a moment when her practice was in decline, she got advance notice from

[13] For biographical information on Sir Francis Jacobs, see 29(4) *Fordham International Law Journal*, which paid tribute to his attainments in the field of European law. See especially RJ Goebel, 'Dedication to Advocate General Francis Jacobs' (2006) 29 *Fordham International Law Journal* 589. See also JH Jackson, 'Introduction to Sir Francis G. Jacobs' Essay' (2008) 11 *Journal of International Economic Law* 3; P Moser and K Sawyer (eds), *Making Community Law: The Legacy of Advocate General Jacobs at the European Court of Justice* (Cheltenham, Edward Elgar, 2008); A Arnull et al (eds), *Continuity and Change in EU Law: Essays in Honour of Sir Francis Jacobs* (Oxford, OUP, 2008).

[14] FG Jacobs and A Durand, *References to the European Court: Practice and Procedure* (London, Butterworths, 1975); FG Jacobs, 'When to Refer to the European Court' (1974) 90 *LQR* 486; FG Jacobs 'Jurisdiction and Procedure in Preliminary Rulings' (1976) 1 *ELRev* 391; FG Jacobs 'Which Courts and Tribunals are Bound to Refer to the European Court?' (1977) 2 *ELRev* 119. For later publications on this same topic, see, inter alia, FG Jacobs, 'References to the Court of Justice: The Way Forward?' in N Colneric et al (eds), *Une communauté de droit: Festschrift für Gil Carlos Rodríguez Iglesias* (Berlin, BWV, 2003); FG Jacobs, 'Further Reform of the Preliminary Ruling Procedure: Towards a "green light" system?' in C Gaitanides et al (eds), *Europa und seine Verfassung: Festschrift für Manfred Zuleeg zum siebzigsten Geburtstag* (Baden-Baden, Nomos, 2005).

[15] FG Jacobs, *The European Convention on Human Rights* (Oxford, Clarendon 1975); FG Jacobs, *European Law and the Individual* (Amsterdam, North-Holland, 1976).

[16] L Neville Brown and FG Jacobs, *The Court of Justice of the European Communities* (London, Sweet & Maxwell, 1977).

[17] Eleanor Sharpston has explained her personal and professional trajectory in several interviews. See, among others, 'Interview with Eleanor Sharpston' (2012) 11 *Competition Law Insight* 3 (issue 9) and 5 (issue 10), as well as the interview conducted by Alison Maitland in 2015 in the framework of the history project The First Hundred Years, https://first100years.org.uk/eleanor-sharpston/. See also the interview by Professor Alan MacFarlane of 27 November 2015, www.youtube.com/watch?v=pnQKDRa0Ows.

[18] Interview with Eleanor Sharpston, conducted by Alison Maitland in 2015.

John Temple Lang about the opening of new law clerk positions at the Court. She drove on her motorbike from London to Luxembourg to see the AG Slynn in person, and asked him for the job.[19] The strategy paid off, and she worked in Slynn's team of *référendaires* for several years (1987–1990).

In 1990, Eleanor Sharpston eventually got a full tenancy at 4 Paper Buildings in London. Simultaneously, with her (re)launched EU practice at the London Bar, she was also the Director of European Legal Studies at University College London, where she lectured in EC and Comparative law (1990–1992). She continued her academic journey as a lecturer (1992–1998) and later affiliated lecturer (1998–2005) at the University of Cambridge, where she was also a senior research fellow at the Centre for European Legal Studies (1998–2005). From 1992 to 2010, she was also a Fellow of King's College, Cambridge. This academic activity led her to publishing several pieces on a variety of EU-related topics, among which the most substantial was a book on interim and substantive relief in claims under Community law.[20] Most of her fee-earning activity as a barrister was dedicated to EU law, appearing as counsel for the United Kingdom in numerous cases before the Court, but she also had a large pro bono practice in human rights cases. Eleanor Sharpston took silk as a QC in 1999, and became a bencher of Middle Temple in 2005.

As regards her appointment as an AG at the Court of Justice, Sharpston has declared that she became aware of a public advertisement in *The Times*, announcing that AG Jacobs was retiring, and that candidates could apply for the position. Having decided at the very last moment to put her hat into the ring, she resorted once again to her motorbike to hand-deliver the application herself. After an interview with members of the House of Lords, civil servants from the Foreign and Commonwealth Office (FCO), and the Lord Chancellor's Department (LCD), as well as a representative of civic society, she was chosen to become the UK's next AG and serve the remaining three and a half years of the mandate of AG Jacobs. Eleanor Sharpston was then later reappointed to a new full six-year mandate in 2009. She was not formally interviewed as that mandate drew to an end.[21] Despite political concerns expressed about her within the Whitehall machine on the grounds that she had, as a barrister, prosecuted the Metric Martyr Steve Thoburn in 2001/2002 (and was therefore, presumably, 'suspect' as being too pro-European), she was renominated in 2015. During the 14 and a half years that she was an AG, she presented over 350 Opinions.

Sharpston's work as an AG came to an end prematurely in the context of the UK's withdrawal from the European Union. Whilst Judge Vajda left the Court on 31 January 2020, the last day in which the UK was a Member State, the remaining 27 Member States moved to dismiss Sharpston in September 2020. Since the judges and AGs are officially appointed by common accord, and not by one particular Member State, the legality of this decision has been questioned.[22] While EU primary law creates a connection between the judges and the Member

---

[19] ibid.

[20] E Sharpston, *Interim and Substantive Relief in Claims under Community Law* (London, Butterworths, 1993).

[21] 'When we were coming up to the point of my renewal, I wondered what would happen. In fact, absolutely nothing happened in the sense that nobody even picked up the telephone and talked to me about it': 'Interview with Eleanor Sharpston' (2012); *Competition Law Insight*, n 17.

[22] See eg D Halberstam, 'Could there be a Rule of Law Problem at the EU Court of Justice?' (*Verfassungsblog*, 23 February 2020); D Kochenov and G Butler, 'Independence of the Court of Justice of the European Union: Unchecked Member States power after the Sharpston Affair' (2021) *ELJ* 262; S Bohnert, 'Predictable and Unsatisfying. The Sharpston Saga: the CJEU's Orders in Cases C-684/20 P and C-684/20 P' (*Verfassungsblog*, 20 June 2021).

States, by stating that the Court shall consist of one judge from each Member State,[23] it does not hold such a clause regarding AGs, whose job description is that they are there to 'assist' the Court.

While this challenging legal situation created by a Member State's withdrawal from the Union was unprecedented, AG Sharpston and Judge Vajda at the Court, and Judge Forrester at the General Court, were in fact, not the first to have their terms ended prematurely. When the Italian Alberto Trabucchi became an AG in 1973, he also had not completely finished his mandate as a judge.[24] Trabucchi himself had in 1962 replaced Judge Nicola Catalano, who had been asked to resign from the Court by the Italian government.[25] Previously, in 1958, when the First Merger Treaty (1957) had transformed the ECSC Court of Justice into the Court of Justice of the European Communities, the mandates of two judges, Massimo Pilotti, who was also the President of the Court, and Adrianus Van Kleffens, were terminated two months before their official end.[26] A third judge, Petrus Serrarens, an international trade unionist, was removed three years and two months before the end of his term, to make room for a second Italian judge.[27] He threatened to challenge his removal before the Court, but eventually did not do so. Eleanor Sharpston decided to bring proceedings,[28] arguing that her removal represented an interference with the autonomy and independence of the Court. However, her legal actions were dismissed by her former judge colleagues.[29]

A short overview of judge David Alexander Ogilvy Edward, who acted as an AG in two cases in 1992, is also necessary. Sir David Edward was born in 1934 in Perth, a small city in central Scotland.[30] After studying classics at the University of Oxford, and reading law at the University of Edinburgh, he was admitted to the Scottish Faculty of Advocates, the Scots Bar, in 1962. He worked on many cases together with the future judge of the Court, AJ ('Jack') Mackenzie Stuart, who worked at the Scots Bar as a QC when Edward was a junior advocate.[31] Edward became a QC himself in 1974. From 1967 to 1977, he was also Clerk, and then Treasurer of the Faculty of Advocates.

David Edward came in contact with European law for the first time as Clerk of Faculty when he became aware of the Commission proposal for a Directive on the provision of services by lawyers, which did not take account of the peculiarities of the British and Irish professions. He took over Mackenzie Stuart's role as member of the Consultative Committee (later Council) of Bars and Law Societies of the European Community (CCBE), and later becoming the leader

---

[23] Art 19(2) TEU.

[24] His term as a judge was ended on 12 December 1972.

[25] For a detailed account of this replacement, see Fritz (n 3) 113.

[26] Pilotti and Van Kleffens were appointed in December 1952, but their successors took up their office in October 1958.

[27] In 1952, the Member States had decided to limit the first mandates of some members of the Court to three years to avoid a complete renewal of the bench in 1958. Serrarens had been drawn by lot to count among those who were only appointed until 1955. His mandate was then renewed, which meant that he should legally stay at the Court until 1961. For a detailed account of these discussions, see Fritz (n 3) 102–109.

[28] Case T-180/20 *Sharpston* ECLI:EU:T:2020:473; Case T-184/20 *Sharpston* ECLI:EU:T:2020:474; Case T-550/20 *Sharpston* ECLI:EU:T:2020:475. On 6 August 2021 Sharpston issued a personal statement about the proceedings, which was taken up and analysed by Joshua Rozenberg ('A Lawyer Writes') 'EU court undermines its independence. British advocate general says Court of Justice acted politically in sacking her'.

[29] For the concluding dismissing Orders, see Case C-684/20 P *Sharpston* ECLI:EU:C:2021:486; and Case C-685/20 P *Sharpston* ECLI:EU:C:2021:485.

[30] For in-depth biographical information on judge Edward, see the Judge David Edward Oral History Website hosted by the Sturm College of Law (University of Denver), which proposes a large collection of personal documents, photographs, publications and speeches of judge Edward, as well as videos and transcripts of a series of interviews conducted in 2005 by Don C Smith. See www.law.du.edu/judge-david-edward-oral-history.

[31] Interview with David Edward by Professor Don C Smith, 2005, Part 2.

of the British delegation from 1978 to 1980, the President. For the CCBE, he prepared a study of the law professional confidentiality[32] and later appeared before the Court in the *AM&S* case,[33] in which CCBE had asked to intervene because it raised important questions regarding lawyer-client confidentiality. Edward later also appeared for the Commission and the United Kingdom at the same Court.[34] In 1981, he appeared in one of the EEC's biggest antitrust policy cases, launched by the European Commission against the Corporation International Business Machines (IBM) for abuse of dominant position.[35] The specialisation in EU competition law that he drew from these cases allowed him to build an academic career, alongside his career at the Bar. In 1985, he was appointed Salvesen Professor of European Institutions and Director of the Europa Institute at the University of Edinburgh School of Law. He remained in this position until 1989, when he became a judge at the newly created Court of First Instance.

Edward has described the process of his appointment to the CFI as relatively simple: he was asked whether he was interested in the position by the Lord Advocate, the equivalent to the Attorney General in Scotland. He later also received a letter from the foreign secretary Geoffrey Howe, asking whether he would accept appointment. When he confirmed his interest, he was formally nominated to the position.[36] He took his oath at the Court along with the 11 other first judges of the CFI on 25 September 1989. While AGs play a central role in the Court of Justice, they have no equivalents at the General Court (what was back then the Court of First Instance). If an independent opinion in a case is deemed necessary, one of the judges may be asked to take on the AG role ad hoc. David Edward, being a CFI judge, was designated to act as an AG in two cases, *Automec II* and *Asia Motor France*,[37] in which he delivered a single Opinion. So far, this was the last of four occasions on which an Opinion was delivered by a judge of the Court of First Instance/the General Court, acting as an AG. Three years after his first appointment as judge at the CFI, he was appointed a judge at the Court, having been invited to accept nomination by the then Lord Advocate (Lord Rodger of Earlsferry). He remained in this position until 2004.

III. THE BRITISH AG'S CONTRIBUTION TO EUROPEAN LEGAL SCHOLARSHIP

The AGs nominated by the UK to the Court have been active contributors to European legal scholarship. AG Warner was a General Rapporteur at the 1968 FIDE Congress in Copenhagen, and was a regular speaker at academic and professional conferences. Sir Gordon Slynn published several pieces on competition law,[38] as well as general reflections on the role and the functioning of the Court,[39] and the development of Community Law.[40] He also contributed to

---

[32] *The Professional Secret, Confidentiality and Legal Professional Privilege* (CCBE, 1993), described by AG Warner as 'a remarkable feat of comparative law'.

[33] Case 155/79 *AM&S* ECLI:EU:C:1982:157. See ch 14.

[34] Case 270/80 *Polydor* ECLI:EU:C:1982:43; Case C-12/86 *Demirel* ECLI:EU:C:1987:400.

[35] Case 60/81 *IBM* ECLI:EU:C:1981:264.

[36] Interview with David Edward (n 31).

[37] Case T-24/90 *Automec* ECLI:EU:T:1992:97; Case T-28/90 *Asia Motor France* ECLI:EU:T:1992:98. See chs 23 and 51.

[38] G Slynn, 'EEC Competition Law from the Perspective of the Court of Justice' in *Annual Proceedings of the Fordham Corporate Law Institute, Antitrust and trade policy in the US and the EC*, vol 1985, 1986; G Slynn et al, *Procedural Aspects of EC Competition Law* (Maastricht, European Institute of Public Administration, 1995).

[39] G Slynn, 'The Court of Justice of the European Communities' (1984) 33 *ICLQ* 409; G Slynn, 'What is a European Community Law Judge?' (1993) 52 *CLJ* 234.

[40] G Slynn, 'Aspects of the Law of the European Economic Community' (1985) 18 *Cornell International Law Journal* 1.

popularisation of EU law not only in the United Kingdom but also in many other countries. For instance, in 1991 Sir Gordon Slynn delivered the Hamlyn Lectures.[41] Furthermore, Lord Slynn supported the British Law Centre, a Warsaw based joint venture of the University of Cambridge and the University of Warsaw.[42] For 13 years he also served as the President of the Judicial Panel of Central and Eastern European Moot Court Competition, sharing his wisdom, knowledge, and sense of humour with hundreds of young lawyers.[43]

Sir Francis Jacobs had, as mentioned above, already published extensively on Community Law before he became an AG, and continued to give lectures and publish while he was working at the Court, as well as after he retired. Among the topics that he researched and reflected on the most count European human rights and the protection of individuals in European law as overarching issues.[44] However, he has also published on the role of the Court in general, including his personal experience and views from inside.[45] Among his most noted scholarly contributions counts the monograph which he published the year after his departure from the Court, *The Sovereignty of Law: The European Way*, based on his Hamlyn lectures.[46] In more recent years, Jacobs has continued to publish his views on the future of the Court and the EU.[47]

Judge David Edward, who acted once as AG in the CFI, has been an equally prolific author, and has published on a broad variety of topics, ranging from the legal profession within the Communities, to the impact of the Single Act on European institutions,[48] freedom of movement[49] and competition and environmental law,[50] to cite just a few.[51] Together with Robert

---

[41] See G Slynn, *Introducing a European Legal Order* (London, Sweet & Maxwell, 1992).

[42] See further on the history of the British Law Centre: www.britishlawcentre.co.uk/blc/. It is worth noting that many of its alumni in Poland, and other Central and Eastern European countries, are now practising lawyers. Two of them, Krystyna Kowalik-Bańczyk and Maciej Szpunar, are respectively a judge at the General Court and an AG at the Court of Justice. Michal Bobek was the AG at the Court of Justice in years 2015–2021.

[43] See further https://ceemc.co.uk/history/.

[44] See, inter alia, FG Jacobs, 'Between Luxembourg and Strasbourg: Dialogue between the European Court of Human Rights and the European Court of Justice' in A Epiney et al (eds), *Die Herausforderung von Grenzen: Festschrift für Roland Bieber* (Baden-Baden, Nomos, 2007); FG Jacobs, 'Human Rights in the European Union: The Role of the Court of Justice' (2001) 26 *ELRev* 331; FG Jacobs, 'Access to Justice as a Fundamental Right in European Law' in GC Rodriguez Iglesias et al (eds), *Mélanges en hommage à Fernand Schockweiler* (Baden-Baden, Nomos, 1999); FG Jacobs, 'The Protection of Human Rights in the Member States of the European Community: The Impact of the Case Law of the Court of Justice' in J O'Reilly (ed), *Human Rights and Constitutional Law: Essays in Honour of Brian Walsh* (Dublin, Round Hall, 1992); FG Jacobs, 'Citizenship of the European Union – A Legal Analysis' (2007) 13 *ELJ* 591; FG Jacobs, 'Access by Individuals to Judicial Review in EU Law' in H Koch et al (eds), *Europe: The New Legal Realism: Essays in Honour of Hjalte Rasmussen* (Copenhagen, Djøf, 2010).

[45] See, inter alia, FG Jacobs, 'Is the Court of Justice of the European Communities a Constitutional Court?' in D Curtin and D O'Keeffe (eds), *Constitutional Adjudication in European Community and National Law: Essays for the Hon. Mr. Justice T.F. O'Higgins* (London, Butterworths, 1992); FG Jacobs, 'A View from the Court' (2005) 16 *European Business Law Review* 467.

[46] FG Jacobs, *The Sovereignty of Law: The European Way* (Cambridge, CUP, 2007).

[47] FG Jacobs, 'The Court of Justice in the Twenty-first Century: Challenges Ahead for the Judicial System?' in A Rosas et al (eds), *The Court of Justice and the Construction of Europe* (The Hague, Asser Press/Springer, 2013); FG Jacobs, 'The Lisbon Treaty and the Court of Justice: The Judicial System of the European Union: Some Suggestions for the Future' in U Leanzo et al (eds), *Scritti in onore di Giuseppe Tesauro*, vol 2 (Editoriale scientifica, 2014).

[48] D Edward, 'The Impact of the Single Act on the Institutions' (1987) 24 *CMLRev* 19.

[49] D Edward, 'Freedom of Movement for the Regulated Professions' in R White et al (eds), *Current Issues in European and International Law: Essays in Memory of Frank Dowrick* (London, Sweet & Maxwell, 1990).

[50] D Edward, 'Perspectives on Competition Law. Problems and Solutions' (1999) 23 *Fordham International Law Journal* 274; D Edward, 'Constitutional Rules of Community Law in EEC Competition Cases' (1989) 13 *Fordham International Law Journal* 111; D Edward and W Robinson, 'The Court of Justice and Environmental Protection' in DS MacDougall et al (eds), *European Community Energy Law: Selected Topics* (The Hague, Kluwer Law International, 1994).

[51] A broad collection of Edward's publications can be found at the David Edward Oral History website: www.law.du.edu/judge-david-edward-oral-history/description-project.

Lane, he has also published a book on European Union Law, which has been reedited several times.[52]

Last but not least, Eleanor Sharpston has published, among others on European Union citizenship,[53] as well as on the areas freedom, security and justice.[54] Moreover, as some of her predecessors, she has offered her general views on the role of AGs and the Court.[55]

IV. LIFE AFTER THE COURT

All of the AGs nominated by the UK continued to be professionally active after they had left the Court. Jean-Pierre Warner was appointed a judge in the chancery division of the High Court of Justice in London (1981), and knighted. The following year, he also became a judge at the UK restrictive practices court. He retired from the High Court in 1994, and died in Chelsea, in 2005.

AG Slynn left the Court to become a Lord of Appeal in Ordinary – a Law Lord – and took the title Baron Slynn of Hadley.[56] In 2002, he retired from this function, but continued to work as an arbitrator, and an accredited mediator. Every year for two weeks, he was also a president of the Court of Appeal of the Solomon Islands. From 1999 to 2004, he presided the Slynn Foundation, a charity working all over Europe (today also the Arab world) to enhance the rule of law, which organised many workshops on EU law and practice, as well as human rights law. He passed away in Kensington, London, in 2009.

AG Jacobs was appointed to the Privy Council, and knighted shortly before he left the Court in 2006. Back in the UK, he resumed the position as Professor of Law at King's College London. He was also President of the European Law Institute, and the United Kingdom Association for European Law, as well as a Trustee at the British Institute of International and Comparative Law, and a Governor at the Institute of Human Rights.

Judge David Edward was appointed to the Privy Council, sat as an associate judge in the Inner House of the Court of Session, Scotland's court of appeal for civil, commercial, and administrative cases, and resumed academic life as Chairman of the Europa Institute at the University of Edinburgh. As former AG Jacobs, he has also been active in various other law associations and committees.

---

[52] Latest edition: D Edward and R Lane, *Edward and Lane on European Union Law* (Cheltenham, Edward Elgar, 2014).

[53] E Sharpston, 'Citizenship and Fundamental Rights: Pandora's Box or a Natural Step Towards Maturity' in P Cardonnel et al (eds), *Constitutionalising the EU Judicial System: Essays in Honour of Pernilla Lindh* (Oxford, Hart Publishing, 2012); E Sharpston, 'European Citizenship and Social Rights? The Views of the Advocates General and the Court' in C Calliess (ed), *Europäische Solidarität und nationale Identität: Überlegungen im Kontext der Krise im Euroraum* (Tübingen, Mohr Siebeck, 2013); D Sarmiento and E Sharpston, 'European Citizenship and its New Union: Time to Move on?' in D Kochenov (ed), *EU Citizenship and Federalism: The Role of Rights* (Cambridge, CUP, 2017).

[54] E Sharpston, 'The Future of the Area of Freedom, Security and Justice' in M Dougan and S Currie (eds), *50 Years of the European Treaties: Looking Back and Thinking Forward* (Oxford, Hart Publishing, 2009); E Sharpston, 'First Steps towards an EU Jurisprudence on the Area of Freedom, Security and Justice (AFSJ)' in J Iliopoulos-Strangas et al (eds), *Rules of Law, Freedom and Security in Europe* (Baden-Baden, Nomos, 2010).

[55] E Sharpston, 'The Changing Role of the Advocate General' in A Arnull et al (eds), *Continuity and Change in EU Law: Essays in Honour of Sir Francis Jacobs* (Oxford, OUP, 2008); E Sharpston and G De Baere, 'The Court of Justice as a Constitutional Adjudicator: A Constitutional order of States?' in A Arnull et al (eds), *A Constitutional Order of States? Essays in EU Law in Honour of Alan Dashwood* (Oxford, Hart Publishing, 2011); E Sharpston, 'Making the Court of Justice of the European Union More Productive' (2014) 21 *Maastricht Journal of European and Comparative Law* 763.

[56] For more detailed information on Slynn's activity as a law lord, see M Beloff, 'Slynn, Gordon, Baron Slynn of Hadley (1930–2009)', *Oxford Dictionary of National Biography*.

Alongside her role at the CJEU, AG Sharpston continued to be an educator, delivering guest lectures and conference keynote speeches around Europe. In the footsteps of Sir Gordon Slynn, AG Sharpston has served as the President of the Central and Eastern European Moot Court Competition since 2009. In 2020, Eleanor Sharpston also delivered the Hamlyn Lectures.[57] All these activities continued after the termination of her mandate at the Court. In March 2021 AG Sharpston has been appointed an adjunct professor at the Trinity College Dublin School of Law in Ireland. It is notable that before, during, and after her time at the Court, Eleanor Sharpston has always found time for her passions. She is a keen violinist and has a black belt in Karate.[58]

V. CONCLUSIONS

In almost 50 years of EEC/EU membership, the UK AGs have undoubtedly made a major contribution to the development of EU law, both inside and outside the Court. The task of the first AG nominated by the UK, Jean-Pierre Warner, was certainly not an easy one, since the function has no equivalent in the English legal system, and he had to quickly familiarise with an important bulk of EC law. AG Slynn was equally not a specialist of EC law when he came to the Court. Yet, as this book shows, he managed, as Warner, to provide authoritative Opinions on cases. AGs Jacobs and Sharpston have through their particularly long terms, 18 years for the former and fourteen for the latter, provided masterful conclusions on cases touching upon all EU law fields. AG Jacobs and AG Sharpston also count, as Judge David Edwards, among the most eminent British EU law scholars. AG Sharpston was the first and only woman to be appointed to the Court by the UK, and she was a particularly vocal member of the institution, always willing to explain her work at academic conferences, as well as to visitors, and the press. She was also the first and only member of the institution to take legal actions against the premature termination of her six-year mandate, sparking an intense and most certainly useful debate about the independence of the Court from the Member States.

---

[57] E Sharpston, *The Great Experiment: Constructing a European Union under the Rule of Law from a Group of Diverse Sovereign States* (Cambridge, CUP, forthcoming).

[58] During her studies she was a member of the Oxford University ladies' rowing team, which won the annual Cambridge v Oxford rowing competition on the River Thames in southwest London. This was duly recorded on the cover of *The Times* newspaper, which caused the future Advocate General a great deal of trouble (see interview Women in Law, First Hundred Years, www.youtube.com/watch?v=qGAIqnsiK7Q).

Part II

Jean-Pierre Warner: The Early Days of Community Law (1973–1981)

6

Accession to the Communities, and Compensation under the Common Agricultural Policy: Opinion of Advocate General Warner in Ireland v Council

ELAINE FAHEY*

I. INTRODUCTION

THE PROCEEDINGS IN *Ireland v Council*[1] concerned the Act on Conditions of Accession of Denmark, Ireland, and the United Kingdom to the European Communities,[2] and related to derogations provided therein regulating transitional systems of compensation. The derogations set up a transitional regime of diminishing compensatory amounts for certain agricultural products.[3] The applicant state, Ireland, in proceedings brought against the

---

* The author is grateful to Ivanka Karaivanova for research assistance.

[1] Case 151/73 *Ireland v Council* ECLI:EU:C:1974:23. For an overview see pp 287–288.

[2] Act on Conditions of Accession was a part of the Accession Treaty. See Treaty between the Kingdom of Belgium, the Federal Republic of Germany, the French Republic, the Italian Republic, the Grand Duchy of Luxembourg, the Kingdom of the Netherlands (Member States of the European Communities), the Kingdom of Denmark, Ireland, the Kingdom of Norway and the United Kingdom of Great Britain and Northern Ireland concerning the accession of the Kingdom of Denmark, Ireland, the Kingdom of Norway and the United Kingdom of Great Britain and Northern Ireland to the European Economic Community and to the European Atomic Energy Community [1972] OJ L73/5.

[3] The transitional regime was laid down in Art 65 of the Act. It read as follows:

'1. A compensatory amount shall be fixed for fruit and vegetables in respect of which:

(a) the new Member State concerned applied, during 1971, quantitative restrictions or measures having equivalent effect,

(b) a common basic price is fixed, and

(c) the producer price in that new Member State appreciably exceeds the basic price applicable in the Community as originally constituted during the period preceding the application of the Community system to the new Member States.

2. The producer price referred to in paragraph 1(c) shall be calculated by applying to the national data of the new Member State concerned the principles set out in Article 4(2) of Regulation No 159/66/EEC laying down additional provisions in respect of the common organisation of the market in fruit and vegetables.

3. The compensatory amount shall apply only during the period for which the basic price is in force.'

Council, sought an order declaring void Regulation 1365/73 of 21 May 1973 relating to the fixing of compensatory amounts for tomatoes.[4]

The production of tomatoes on a commercial scale in the Community was almost entirely, at the time, outside in the open in the south, in Southern France and Italy; wholly under glass in the north, in Ireland, the UK, the Netherlands, and Denmark; and partly in the outside in the open and partly under glass in northern France, Belgium, Luxembourg, and West Germany. It thus raised an interesting question about the normalisation of Community standards after the first enlargement in light of such considerable divergences.

The place of glass house tomatoes thus resulted in the case at hand in a notable Irish victory in the proceedings very shortly after entry to the Communities. It exposed tense engagement with a highly protected economy affected acutely by liberalisation of its markets, only to be protected by the Act on Conditions of Accession and the operation of a compensation system. It is one of the earliest Irish proceedings against a European Union (EU) institution. Subsequently, Ireland did not litigate much against the Council directly.[5] Instead, it has a wealth of litigation initiated against the Commission, of at least 200 cases at the time of writing and a lengthy history of intervening in support of UK-led or UK-related proceedings, although a fuller discussion is beyond the scope of the chapter.[6] With accession to the Communities, an extraordinary increase in agricultural incomes was predicted between 1970 and 1980 in Ireland.[7] The proceedings in *Ireland v Council* arguably demonstrate significant tensions at the entry point of Ireland to the common market and the liberalisation of agriculture and trade that was to follow, given the highly protected nature of the Irish economy at the time.

The proceedings in *Ireland v Council* also raised inter-institutional tension as to the accession process, and sought to bring clarity and legal certainty related to issues thought to have been agreed with states, but also the fairness of the process of accession. A compensatory amount was fixed regarding fruit and vegetables, where a basic price was set. It was anticipated that the lower agricultural prices existing in the UK, Ireland, and Denmark would necessitate difficult outcomes and systems as they transitioned into membership.[8] At the time of the first

---

[4] Regulation (EEC) No 1365/73 of the Council of 21 May 1973 supplementing, as regards cauliflowers and tomatoes, Regulation (EEC) No 228/73 laying down general rules for the system of compensatory amounts for fruit and vegetables [1973] OJ L137/1.

[5] A rare example was Case C-301/06 *Ireland v Parliament and Council* ECLI:EU:C:2009:68. See E Fahey, *Practice and Procedure in Preliminary References to Europe* (First Law, 2007); E Fahey, *EU Law in Ireland* (Dublin, Clarus Press, 2010).

[6] See, e.g., via a Curia search in June 2021, Case C-199/03 *Ireland v Commission* ECLI:EU:C:2005:548; Case C-339/00 *Ireland v Commission* ECLI:EU:C:2003:545; Case C-239/97 *Ireland v Commission* ECLI:EU:C:1998:213; Case C-238/96 *Ireland v Commission* ECLI:EU:C:1998:451; Joined Cases C-296/93 and C-307/93 *France and Ireland v Commission* ECLI:EU:C:1996:65; Case 239/86 *Ireland v Commission* ECLI:EU:C:1987:554; Case 242/86 *Ireland v Commission* ECLI:EU:C:1988:288; Case 337/85 *Ireland v Commission* ECLI:EU:C:1987:453; Case 325/85 *Ireland v Commission* ECLI:EU:C:1987:546, almost all of which related to clearance of accounts of European Agricultural Guidance and Guarantee Fund (EAGGF) or agriculture and fisheries more generally. See also the case law before the General Court particularly related to state aid: Joined Cases T-778/16 and T-892/16 *Ireland and Others v Commission* ECLI:EU:T:2020:338; Joined Cases T-778/16 and T-892/16 *Ireland and Others v Commission* ECLI:EU:T:2020:338; Joined Cases T-129/07 and T-130/07 *Ireland and Aughinish Alumina Ltd v Commission* ECLI:EU:T:2019:610; Joined Cases T-50/06, T-56/06, T-60/06, T-62/06 and T-69/06 *Ireland and Others v Commission* ECLI:EU:T:2007:383; Joined Cases T-50/06 RENV, T-56/06 RENV, T-60/06 RENV, T-62/06 RENV and T-69/06 RENV *Ireland and Others v Commission* ECLI:EU:T:2012:134; Joined Cases T-50/06 RENV II and T-69/06 RENV II *Ireland and Aughinish Alumina Ltd v Commission* ECLI:EU:T:2016:227. There are other proceedings brought by Ireland against the Commission but later discontinued by it: see eg Case T-56/05 *Ireland v Commission* ECLI:EU:T:2006:134.

[7] See generally J Lee, *Ireland 1912–1985: Politics and Society* (Cambridge, CUP, 1990) 463; P Drudy and D McAleese, *Ireland and the European Community* (Cambridge, CUP, 1984).

[8] G Olmi, 'Agriculture and Fisheries in the Treaty of Brussels of January 22, 1972' (1972) 9 CMLRev 293, 296.

application of Ireland to join the European Economic Community (EEC) in January 1963, the majority of actors in Ireland realised that it could not prosper in economic isolation. As regards agriculture, it was felt that Irish advantage in British markets, its long-standing closest market, was in decline, and that the Common Agricultural Policy (CAP) offered guaranteed high prices to farmers, an expanded consumer market and new trading opportunities for such agricultural products.[9] In a largely agricultural economy, the CAP was central to the benefits derived by Ireland entering the EEC, with 30 per cent of the workforce engaged in agriculture, and with Ireland exporting half of its agricultural production at the time.[10] The proceedings related to a more significant dispute as to the Act on Conditions of Accession and tomatoes, with respect to compensation than might be apparent from its status as a historical precedent or its reporting.

AG Warner was to make an extraordinary impact upon the role of the AGs.[11] These proceedings were at an early point in his career as AG, and are thus of much historical value as to the nature of developments taking place.[12] They are also of some interest given the applicant, a new Member State, was challenging the conditions for new entrants as applied in accession frameworks.[13]

II. BACKGROUND, CONTEXT, AND FACTS

Before accession, tomato growers in Ireland were protected by a prohibition imposed annually on the importation of tomatoes during a period when domestic supplies were sufficient to meet demand. During this period, no tomatoes could be imported into Ireland without a licence, resulting in extremely low levels of imports. Irish tomatoes growers were further protected by duties on imports of tomatoes. A basic amount fixed in Regulation of 1365/73 was less than these duties. These duties were reducible over the period after accession. Imports were deductible from the basic amounts in computing compensatory amounts. The result was to leave no compensatory amount payable on imports of tomatoes in to Ireland, at all, from other Member States.

In the proceedings, the Government of Ireland argued that the contested Regulation made no mention of the application of conversion factors set out in the Regulation 2515/69[14] before the ratification of the Accession Treaty (including one of its parts, that is the Act on Conditions of Accession). The use of conversion factors for fixing compensatory amounts to be applied in respect of fruit and vegetables was not contemplated by Ireland. Ireland challenged the process for the new Member States related to tomatoes grown under glass. All tomatoes in Ireland were grown under glass given the climate, and were thus significantly protected before entry into the common market by temporary measures prohibiting imports, or making the

---

[9] G Murphy, 'Government Interest Groups and the Irish Move to Europe 1957–1963' (1997) 8 *Irish Studies in International Affairs* 57.

[10] E Moxon Browne, 'Ireland in the EEC' (1975) 31(1) *The World Today* 424, 426.

[11] See A Dashwood, 'The Advocate General in the Court of Justice of the European Communities' (1982) 2 *Legal Studies* 202, citing an unpublished lecture of Warner 'The Role of the Advocate General at the European Court of Justice' which was delivered in Luxembourg on 19 November 1976.

[12] This chapter relies upon Historical Archives of the European Union (HAEU) at the European University Institute (EUI) on the case (682 pages of proceedings) as well as Lee (n 7) and also for background context J McMahon and M Cardwell (eds), *Research Handbook on EU Agricultural Law* (Cheltenham, Edward Elgar, 2015).

[13] *cf* Case C-273/04 *Poland v Council* ECLI:EU:C:2007:622.

[14] Regulation 604/71 of the Commission of 23 March 1971 fixing the list of representative producer markets for the products listed in Annex I to Regulation 159/66/EEC [1971] OJ L70/9.

latter subject to customs duty.[15] Ireland argued that if the conversion factor was legal, it was incorrectly applied in this instance. The Council, as the defendant of the legal act, argued that the content and scope of the principle referred to in the Act of Accession did not require interpretation by the Court.[16] Ireland produced forms from the Commission that had been drawn up to calculate basic prices for fruit and vegetables for the 1969–1971 period, *not* mentioning the distinction to be drawn between glasshouse and open field cultivation. The Council argued that the Commission, and not the Council, was the author of these forms, and argued that any distinction was not material or thought necessary to be elaborated.[17]

III. THE OPINION OF AG WARNER

AG Warner delivered his Opinion on 19 February 1974,[18] shortly before the Court would deliver its judgment on 21 March 1974. He stated in a careful and detailed Opinion, but with occasional bursts of frankness that 'oddly', the Regulation of greatest importance in the proceedings, was no longer in force, ie Regulation 159/66,[19] amended by Regulation 2515/69[20] on 9 December 1969.[21] He noted – perhaps of more historical interest – that there was no authentic English text of either of these regulations, and only unofficial translations.[22] He outlined nonetheless how the Regulation envisaged two stages of intervention in support of the market in tomatoes as to organisation of producers and intervention, when the Commission declared the market was in a state of crisis. In the Regulation, a basic price was formulated to serve as a starting point in the calculation of withdrawal prices, buying in prices, and reimbursements to Member States. However, in practice, the Council fixed prices for tomatoes only for the months of June to November in each year.

Ireland had complained that the relevant recitals of Regulation 1365/73 were 'cryptic', so as not to amount as to a proper statement of the Council's reasons for adopting the figures that it did. AG Warner expressed himself 'in sympathy' with this complaint, because he stated that one had to go to the Council's pleadings in order to ascertain the reasoning.[23] In fact, the adoption of the reasoning by the Council was to defeat the object of Articles 65 and 66 of the Act on Conditions of Accession in the view of Ireland was to temper the procedures in new Member States who, before accession, were protected by quantitative restrictions.

AG Warner preferred the submission of Ireland, that it could not be organised in interpreting Articles 65 and 66 of the Act on Conditions of Accession that the common basic prices were fixed for reference types.[24] Ireland had vigorously denied that the different method of production was an issue, pointing to the case of Belgium. AG Warner noted that contention of the Council seemed surprising, given the succulence of French or Italian tomatoes ripened

---

[15] Page 306 of the Opinion.
[16] Page 292 of the Judgment.
[17] Page 293 of the Judgment.
[18] Opinion of AG Warner in Case 151/73 *Ireland v Council* ECLI:EU:C:1974:14.
[19] Règlement n° 159/66/CEE du Conseil, du 25 octobre 1966, portant dispositions complémentaires pour l'organisation commune des marchés dans le secteur des fruits et legumes [1966] OJ 192/3286.
[20] Règlement (CEE) n° 2515/69 du Conseil, du 9 décembre 1969, modifiant le règlement n° 159/66/CEE portant dispositions complémentaires pour l'organisation commune des marchés dans le secteur des fruits et legumes [1969] OJ L318/10 (no official English text of the Regulation).
[21] Page 302.
[22] ibid.
[23] Page 306.
[24] Pages 309–10.

in the sun, in contrast to the 'dreariness of the almost plastic products of [the] Northern glasshouses'.[25] AG Warner initially considered that the Court had to resolve, as a preparatory matter, the issue of whether tomatoes grown under glass, and those grown outside in the open, were commercially different products.[26] However, at a later stage, as he openly admitted in the Opinion, he experienced a change of heart and therefore argued that:

> The relevant question is thus not whether tomatoes grown under glass and those grown in the open have different commercial characteristics in some general sense, but whether the Irish tomatoes for which producer prices are to be fixed under Article 65 [of Act on Conditions of Accession] have characteristics differing from those by which the reference types are defined.[27]

AG Warner accepted the submission of Ireland that it was wrong to apply the conversion factor to the Irish producer price for this amounted to fixing a producer price for non-existent product, namely open field tomatoes. If an adjustment was to be made, he held, it had to be made to the common basic price for tomatoes generally, so as to obtain a notional common basic price for glasshouse tomatoes, for which Irish producer price for the same tomatoes could be compared. AG Warner argued that Ireland's production of tomatoes and its export of them was 'infinitesimal' in relation to production in the Community as a whole, and any substantial increase in those exports would necessitate investment in new glasshouses and heating plants.[28] It is notable that neither side had asked the Court to exercise its jurisdiction under Article 174 EEC Treaty (now Article 264 TFEU) to state which of the effects of the regulation to be declared void.[29] Nonetheless, AG Warner concluded that it would be hardly possible to 'unscramble' the effects on Ireland's and Denmark's trade in tomatoes.[30] He advised the Court to declare Regulation 1365/73 void as it related to tomatoes, and to state that the effects of the Regulation would be considered definitive.

IV. ANALYSIS

The proceedings ultimately related to one of the few cases taken by Ireland against the EU institutions. Whatever doubts existed as to the impact of accession with respect to increased competition from imports, sovereignty and neutrality, it was abundantly clear that there were no reservations with respect to the huge gains expected to accrue to Irish agriculture from higher prices paid under the CAP. For this alone, the issue was worth litigating.

On one level, the Irish economy appeared that it would be badly affected by a decision to compensate only tomatoes grown outdoors. At the time, however, the brutal reality was that the number of tomatoes grown in Ireland was relatively low, amounting to nothing more than could be considered negligible. The dispute, with hindsight, was the revealing of a protected economy becoming exposed to significant new European agriculture rules, and the challenge of modelling compensation for those changes. The Opinion of AG Warner here was a modicum of clarity and certainty.[31] Within it were traces of evidence of AG Warner harbouring certain

---

[25] Page 308.
[26] ibid.
[27] ibid.
[28] Page 309.
[29] Page 309.
[30] Page 310.
[31] Pages 288–93 of the Judgment.

sympathy for new entrants to the Community, given that northern Europe enjoyed differing climates and agriculture fortunes compared to those of the original six Member States.

A. The Judgment

In the judgment of the Court, the Court declared Regulation 1365/73 to be void, to the extent that it provided for the application of a conversion factor to the producer price, which in consequence fixed the compensatory amount to be applied in Ireland to tomatoes for fresh delivery to the consumers. The Court found that the system of compensatory amounts laid down in Article 65 of the Act on Conditions of Accession was to facilitate the gradual adaptation of the new Member States to EEC rules, in particular the Common Agriculture Policy. The Court reiterated the protective function of the compensatory amounts, which were designed to supersede national measures for the protection of the market.[32] The Court stated that the compensatory amounts were to offer Irish tomato producers a measure of protection against imports of tomatoes from the Community as originally constituted.[33] It stated further that tomatoes grown outside in the open were, in a commercial sense, different produce from those grown under glass, and that the adoption of conversion factors affected the level of the relevant compensatory amount in a way which was unfavourable for the new Member States. The contested Regulation had not provided for a reference to the Act on Conditions of Accession for the application of conversion factors to the producer price in the new Member State. The Court held that the extension of principles in Article 4(2) of Regulation 159/66 would disregard the spirit and the letter of Article 64(2) of the Act on Conditions of Accession.[34]

B. Effect on Future Case Law

The case remains of interest, more for its timing and subject field and outcome, than the actual content of its judgment. Ultimately, the case provides evidence of benevolence to newcomers affected by the extreme variety of regulatory spaces covering agriculture in the then EEC. It is also an early example of significant inter-institutional tension as to the process of accession. As noted above, the proceedings demonstrated tensions at the entry point of Ireland to the common market and the liberalisation of agriculture and trade that was to follow, given the highly protected nature of the Irish economy.

However, the case also suggests a highly misleading stance as to Irish engagement with the EU institutions through EU law and litigation, which ultimately would not be carried out. The Opinion of the AG was of much significance for its insightful 'take' on the nature of the challenges posed for the new Member States. *Ireland v Council* was cited by the Commission during the proceedings in the later case of *Commission v UK (Potatoes)*.[35] That case related to litigation by the Commission against the UK with respect to similar agricultural law issues, namely sheepmeat and potatoes, arising from the Act on Conditions of Accession.[36]

---

[32] Para 13 of the Judgment.

[33] Para 14 of the Judgment.

[34] Para 17 of the Opinion.

[35] See Opinion of AG Mayras in Case 231/78 *Commission v UK* ECLI:EU:C:1979:101, p 1465.

[36] The actions of intervening parties are of much interest there in the Opinion of AG Mayras, who undertook an assessment of the alignment of interests of the Netherlands, UK, and France to warrant intervention: See p 1464 of the Opinion.

Other future related case law would deal with other similar complaints, yet considerably later on and without citation of the commented Opinion of AG Warner or judgment of the Court.[37] In the relative scheme of things, the Opinion of AG Warner was arguably not of much jurisprudential significance, but more of historical interest as to the dynamics of accession and the power dynamics taking effect in agriculture being rebalanced in the Court room. It also aligns well with understanding the nature of transitional arrangements designed to facilitate the entry of new Member States into the Common Agricultural Policy.

---

[37] See eg Case 6/78 *Union française de céréales v Hauptzollamt Hamburg-Jonas* ECLI:EU:C:1978:154; Opinion of AG Capotorti in Case 6/78 *Union française de céréales v Hauptzollamt Hamburg-Jonas* ECLI:EU:C:1978:138; Case 250/80 *Schumacher* ECLI:EU:C:1981:246; Opinion of AG Capotorti in Case 250/80 *Schumacher* ECLI:EU:C:1981:212; Joined Cases 71/84 and 72/84 *Surcouf* ECLI:EU:C:1985:363; Opinion of AG Lenz in Joined Cases 71/84 and 72/84 *Surcouf* ECLI:EU:C:1985:191.

7

Horizontal Application of EU Law, Non-discrimination on Grounds of Nationality, and EU Sports Law: Opinion of Advocate General Warner in Walrave and Koch

STEPHEN WEATHERILL

I. INTRODUCTION

AT ITS HEART, *Walrave and Koch* was a dispute about how, if at all, the rule of non-discrimination on grounds of nationality applied to the composition of representative sports teams.[1] The ruling exerted transformative significance in the development of two areas of (what we today call) EU law. First, *Walrave and Koch* was the first case in which the Court ruled that the Treaty provisions on the free movement of workers and services are capable of horizontal application in proceedings before national courts – that is, they bind private parties, not just public authorities. Second, it was the first case in which the Court was asked to apply EU law to the practices of a governing body in sport.

The case has stood the test of time. Even today, it is frequently cited by the Court itself. In the determination of how far EU law should be treated as directly applicable to private parties, the Court has over time moved in important respects beyond *Walrave and Koch*, as will be explained. Even so, the ruling in *Walrave and Koch* retains foundational importance. For example, in *AMS* and in *Egenberger*, important cases concerning the horizontal application of the Charter of Fundamental Rights decided by the Court in 2014 and 2018 respectively, both Advocates General were induced to reach back to 1974 to investigate the roots of EU law's engagement with private legal relations nurtured by *Walrave and Koch*.[2] So too, as will be explained, the treatment of sport has been adjusted since *Walrave and Koch*, but the ruling remains unavoidable in the Court's contemporary job of mediating the

---

[1] Case 36/74 *Walrave and Koch* ECLI:EU:C:1974:140; Opinion of AG Warner in Case 36/74 *Walrave and Koch* ECLI:EU:C:1974:111
[2] Opinion of AG Cruz Villalón in Case C-176/12 *Association de médiation sociale* ECLI:EU:C:2013:491; Opinion of AG Tanchev in Case C-414/16 *Egenberger* ECLI:EU:C:2017:851.

demands of the EU's internal market and sporting specificity recognised by Article 165 TFEU. Accordingly, the Court's 2019 ruling in *TopFit e.V. v Daniele Biffi* drew explicitly on *Walrave and Koch*.[3]

So *Walrave and Koch* endures, but on these points, it is important as the first word, not the last. The style of both the Opinion of AG Warner and the ruling of the Court is strikingly laconic to the modern eye, and some of the reasoning is unsatisfyingly thin. This chapter provides an opportunity to take a trip back to a time when much of what EU lawyers know today was as yet undiscovered.

II. BACKGROUND, CONTEXT, AND FACTS

Walrave and Koch was a dispute between two athletes and the governing body of their sport. The sport was paced cycling, involving a team of two persons, one providing the lead on a motorcycle to the second riding a bicycle. The provision of a slipstream by the pacer allows the cyclist to travel much faster than would be possible riding solo. The cyclist needs power and endurance, while the skill of the pacer lies in travelling fast enough, but not too fast.

The background is helpfully amplified by the Opinion of AG Warner. The Court is typically much less concerned to provide factual context in its ruling, although the treatment of the 'Facts' in the hard copy version of the European Court Reports is also illuminating,[4] and the case dossier held in the Historical Archives of the European Union (HAEU) at the European University Institute (EUI) provides 828 pages of (often turgid and occasionally quirky) material. Walrave and Koch were highly regarded Dutch pacers who had usually, for want of top level Dutch cyclists competing in the sport, teamed up with Belgian or German cyclists. The dispute arose as a result of a requirement, introduced with effect from 1973 by the governing body, the UCI, that the pacer in the world championships should hold the same nationality as the cyclist. In short, they were required to be a national team.

The UCI's new rule limited Walrave and Koch's commercial freedom, and reduced their earning power, and they complained that they were victims of nationality-based discrimination. It was perfectly obvious that the requirement discriminated on the basis of nationality. EU law prohibits any discrimination on the basis of nationality within the scope of application of the EU Treaties. That prohibition was at the time contained in Article 7 EEC (now Article 18 TFEU). The obligation to co-operate with a fellow national, and not to team up with a national of another state, injected a clear cross-border dimension to the matter, bringing free movement law into play, although it was not clear whether the pacers were workers, or providers of services. The referring court in Utrecht asked questions about both relevant Treaty provisions, Articles 48 and 59 EEC as they then were, today in amended form as Articles 45 and 56 TFEU.

The key legal questions to be addressed were whether the relevant Treaty provisions applied to the practices of private parties generally, and to those active in the field of sport in particular; and, if they did, whether the discrimination practised fell foul of the requirements of EU law. Esoteric though the particular sport undoubtedly was, the issue was potentially huge in its impact. If EU law did preclude such an arrangement, and instead required that governing bodies operating within the EU shall permit selection of representative teams only on the basis

---

[3] Case C-22/18 *TopFit* ECLI:EU:C:2019:497.
[4] [1974] ECR 1405, 1407–16.

of quality of performance and not nationality of the athlete, the very idea of international representative sports events would be called into question. Would EU law prohibit football's World Cup?

III. THE OPINION OF AG WARNER

The opening paragraph of AG Warner's short six-page Opinion immediately identified that although the detail of the dispute concerned paced cycling, the matter is 'of general importance in professional sport'.[5] He then proceeded to explain the nature of the sport, its regulatory structure, the economic impact of the rule change on participants in general, and on Walrave and Koch in particular. Weighing in at fewer than 3500 words, the Opinion is considerably shorter than this comment on it. This is a long-gone world in which opinions and judgments were kept brief. The Opinion is remarkably brisk, crisp, and self-confident. Less generously put, it is thin in its reasoning and inadequately sensitive to the intellectual challenges involved. It is a window on a distant past when understanding about the nature and effect of key provisions of substantive EU law was still in the process of formation.

Article 48 EEC (now Article 45 TFEU), he stated, has direct effect and binds not only public authorities, as decided a few months previously in *Commission v France*,[6] which he cites, but also private parties. This, he stated, was doubted by no one – and '[t]he reason why Article [45 TFEU] binds everyone is that its provisions are in general terms'. No further elaboration is offered – no case law or doctrine is cited!

AG Warner then turned to Article 59 EEC (now Article 56 TFEU) on services, which, he stated, had not been the subject of any previous ruling addressing its direct effect generally, or its application to private parties in particular. Here too, he declared he had 'no doubt' that Article 56 TFEU has direct effect, before turning to the matter of its application to private parties which, he reported, the UCI queried and the Commission opposed. But he considered that the general terms of Article 56 TFEU militated against any such restriction on its scope. He therefore concluded that Articles 45 and 56 TFEU should be interpreted in parallel, and that both apply to the practices of private parties.

He then quickly set aside the objection that the UCI's rules operate in countries which are not members of the EU. This was true, but this did not block the application of EU law on EU territory. On this point the Opinion is entirely convincing.

The AG then turned to the final point, which was whether an 'exception' – a word he uses without any explanation – should be made from the Treaty provisions forbidding nationality-based discrimination in the case of limiting national teams to nationals of the relevant state. His answer – yes. But why? He drew on a test governing the implication of terms into contracts which he explained was adopted 'in the laws of some of our countries', though it was, in truth, a tool of English common law. The test was to ask what reply would an 'officious bystander' have received, had he or she asked those signing the EU Treaties whether it precluded selection for national teams on the basis of nationality? That reply would, he thought, have been 'Of course not!'. This, for AG Warner, was a matter of 'common sense', the point 'so obvious it did not need to be stated'. He then left it to the referring national court to decide whether the pacer and the cyclist were truly a 'team', but assuming they were, his Opinion clearly carried

---

[5] Page 1422 of the Opinion.
[6] Case 167/73 *Commission v France* ECLI:EU:C:1974:35.

the message that Walrave and Koch's complaint must fail. The UCI could not be prevented from applying its nationality-based rule by resort to EU law.

IV. ANALYSIS

The most striking aspect of the Opinion is how quick AG Warner was to assume that the application of the Treaty provisions to private parties raised no issue of principle. This was new territory for the Court's case law, and it was highly significant in fixing the reach of EU law, but he treated it as if it was trivially straightforward.

It is correct that a textual reading of both Articles 48 and 59 EEC reveals no explicit limitation on the entities that are bound by the provisions. And the mood of the times was plainly favourable to treating key Treaty provisions as apt for application to private parties, as much as they were to public authorities. Sixteen months later in *Defrenne*, the Court decided that Article 119 EEC (today Article 157 TFEU), which provided that each Member State shall maintain the application of the principle that men and women shall receive equal pay for equal work, should be applied by national courts, not only to actions of public authorities, but also to agreements intended to regulate paid labour collectively and to contracts between individuals.[7] That readiness to look beyond an express textual connection to Member States, and only to Member States, was a much bigger and bolder step than that taken in *Walrave and Koch*, and seen in that light, the finding that what is now Articles 45 and 56 TFEU were capable of horizontal application was no surprise.

But AG Warner's analysis was nonetheless troublingly rudimentary. There were competing values in play, most of all the claim to autonomy upon which a private party would typically seek to rely in order to resist subjection to public regulation. Perhaps the importance of securing EU values of non-discrimination and free movement transcended such concerns, especially in the context of private bodies as powerful as an international sports federation. But, even allowing for the fact that this was very early in the development of the law, the Opinion of AG Warner was disappointingly bare of any appreciation that there were choices about priorities to be made. Nor did he mention the structural concern internal to EU law that subjecting the activities of private parties to the free movement provisions may cause friction with the application of the Treaty competition rules to the same practices.

As far as sport was concerned, the thin quality of the reasoning was also the most remarkable feature of the Opinion. The appeal to the expectations of those who negotiated the Treaty, and more broadly, to common sense, was based on a general intuition that the achievement of the objectives of the Treaty did not entail that international representative sport should be suppressed as unlawful discrimination. But the lack of any intellectually rigorous engagement with why this was so is troubling, and unhelpful to those looking for a principled basis upon which the law was to develop in future. In particular, the use of the word 'exception' by AG Warner seems misleading. What he appeared to intend, in his Opinion, was not an 'exception' to the application of EU law in the sense that matters such as public policy or public health provide exceptions to the basic rule of free movement in provisions such as (today) Articles 36, 45(3), 52(1) or 62 TFEU, but rather, and more broadly, either a reason for in some way placing the matter beyond the reach of the Treaties, or for treating it as falling

---

[7] Case 43/75 *Defrenne* ECLI:EU:C:1976:56.

within the scope of the Treaties, but not contrary to their demands. Whilst the matter was poorly articulated by AG Warner, it should, however, be appreciated that this was the first time that the intersection of sport and EU law had ever needed to be addressed at the Court, and more modern trends, according to which obstacles to trade are assessed with full awareness of the particular context in which they arise and operate, were many years away from being judicially developed.

The Court reached the same destination as AG Warner in *Walrave and Koch*, in the sense that the Court too found a way to ensure that EU law did not prohibit representative sport involving national teams. However, the ruling, which stretched over 36 paragraphs, was structured quite differently from the Opinion. In truth, the Court's ruling seemed to have only drawn very lightly on the advice supplied to it by its AG in the case at hand.

A. The Importance of Economic Activity

The Court preferred to begin by addressing whether the matter fell within the scope of the Treaties. Sport, at the time, was not even mentioned in the Treaties, and in fact, it would not be until 2009, when the amending Treaty of Lisbon entered into force, that it secured explicit recognition as a matter with which the EU engages.[8] The ruling in *Walrave and Koch* was therefore foundationally important in explaining how and why EU law affects sport, even in the absence of any explicit direction to that effect in the Treaties. At paragraph 4 of its judgment in *Walrave and Koch*, the Court declared that:

> Having regard to the objectives of the Community, the practice of sport is subject to Community law only in so far as it constitutes an economic activity within the meaning of Article 2 of the Treaty.

The Court's starting point was therefore whether the EU has competence to engage with sport. In the modern era, the Court would cite Article 5 TEU, the principle of conferral, which directs that the Union shall act only within the limits of the competences conferred upon it by the Member States in the Treaties to attain the objectives set out therein. It is its character as 'economic activity' which, in the approach taken by *Walrave and Koch*, took sport over that threshold, and subjected it to review against standards mandated by EU law, most of all, non-discrimination on grounds of nationality and free movement.

The Court's chosen phrase, that EU law applies 'only' in so far as sport constitutes an economic activity, was deceptive. Sport readily constitutes an economic activity, and plainly, it did in the particular circumstances of professional sport which generated the dispute. The question then was to determine which Treaty provisions would apply. Given the presence of gainful employment or remunerated service, it was either Article 48 EEC or Article 59 EEC which was at stake.[9] The Court stated that both gave effect to the general rule against discrimination based on nationality contained in Article 7 EEC.[10] So it did not matter exactly which Treaty provision applied, because work and services were subject to the identical rule forbidding nationality discrimination.[11]

---

[8] Now, Arts 6 and 165 TFEU.
[9] Para 5 of the Judgment.
[10] Paras 6, 16, 23–24, 32.
[11] ibid.

B. Application to Private Parties

The Court, in contrast to AG Warner, examined with some care the question whether the Treaty prohibitions extended to the practices of bodies which were not governed by public law. It found that they did. They applied not only to actions of public authorities, but also to 'rules of any other nature aimed at regulating in a collective manner gainful employment and the provision of services'.[12] The Court gave two reasons for this, neither of which had been broached by AG Warner. First, the fundamental objective of abolishing obstacles to free movement 'would be compromised if the abolition of barriers of national origin could be neutralised by obstacles resulting from the exercise of their legal autonomy by associations or organisations which do not come under public law'.[13] Second, the pattern of regulation of working conditions by public action and by private agreement showed variations between Member States. Therefore any limitation of the Treaty freedoms to the control of acts of a public nature alone would cause an inequality in application.[14]

The Court's approach, though reaching the same conclusion on the scope of application of the Treaty provisions on the free movement of workers and services, was fuller and more satisfying than AG Warner's thin claim that there was 'no doubt' about the Treaty provisions' aptitude for horizontal application. The Court also noted the 'general nature' of the terms of Article 59 EEC (now Article 56 TFEU), which did not address or limit the source of restrictions to be abolished,[15] which was a nod to the textual approach of AG Warner. Here, however, its main point was to insist on a parallel interpretation of Articles 48 and 59 EEC. The Court made clear that both implement the rule of non-discrimination on the basis of nationality, and both contain an unconditional prohibition which created individual rights which national courts must protect. This was still unsatisfying because it failed to engage with the competing value of private autonomy, and because it ignored possible friction with competition law. Yet the Court worked harder than AG Warner to explain just why it believed that the free movement rules were not limited to control of acts of public authorities.

The UCI's practices were therefore subject to review. The Court, like AG Warner, convincingly disposed of the argument that the UCI's activities were not confined to the territory of the EU by observing that in so far as they did take effect on the territory of the EU, they were required to comply with EU law.

C. The Specificity of Sport

This left only the question of whether there was anything special about discrimination arising in the composition of sports teams which might justify a modified application of EU law. The Court addressed this in a way that was quite different from AG Warner, though no less intellectually unsatisfying. Both Court and AG were however agreed that EU law did *not* forbid discrimination in the selection of a national team. The Court stated that the prohibition against nationality-based discrimination 'does not affect the composition of sport teams, in particular national teams, the formation of which is a question of purely sporting interest and

---

[12] Para 17.
[13] Para 18.
[14] Para 19.
[15] Para 20.

as such has nothing to do with economic activity'.[16] This thinly explained formula, devoid of any cited authority, did not seem to purport to be an exception to the normal application of the EU's rules, but rather, was a claim that the practices in question lay outside the bounds of the EU Treaties. The EU only had the competences conferred on it by its Treaties, so the Court's denial of an economic context aimed to locate the UCI's rules beyond the reach of EU law.

The Court was plainly anxious that it might be tearing a hole in the legal protection provided by EU law, and so it added that this restriction on the scope of the Treaty provisions in question must 'remain limited to its proper objective'.[17] And it reserved to the national court the question whether what was before it was truly a 'team' event eligible for approval in this way.[18] The narrower the concept of 'team', the less significant the curtailment in the application of the normal expectation of non-discrimination on grounds of nationality. But the Court had clearly found a way to ensure that football's World Cup was not incompatible with EU law, despite the fact that it was (and is) existentially based on a value – selection on the basis of nationality – which is in normal circumstances treated as incompatible with EU law.

The Court took a different route to the same destination as AG Warner: nationality discrimination in sport is a special case. But neither approach impresses. AG Warner's appeal to common sense and the intervention of the officious bystander deserves criticism for lacking intellectual rigour, but the Court's claim that the formation of teams is a question of purely sporting interest, and as such, has nothing to do with economic activity, was worse, because it was simply not true. Walrave and Koch had brought the case *precisely* because the UCI's rules damaged their economic opportunities! Only in subsequent case law, considered below, would a superior understanding emerge of just why EU law does not oppose national teams.

D. Effect on Future Case Law

Walrave and Koch has proved influential in the development of two distinct strands of case law, first, that dealing with the scope of the 'horizontal' application of Treaty provisions and, second, that concerning the review of sporting practices conducted under EU law. In neither instance has *Walrave and Koch* proved the last word. This is perfectly understandable given how little of what we grapple with today in these two areas had reached the surface of judicial decision-making or academic debate in 1974.

The logic of the Court's ruling, supported in a less fully articulated form by AG Warner, held that the relevant Treaty provisions achieve their maximum effect, and that they are not subverted by local variations in the scope of the public sector, by being treated as apt for direct application to actions of private parties aimed at regulating economic activity in a collective manner. This has proved long-lasting, and is today firmly entrenched in EU law. The Court has never deviated from its pioneering insistence in *Walrave and Koch* that the Treaty provisions on the free movement of persons and the free movement of services are capable of horizontal direct effect.[19] The case, and the reasoning contained in it, is frequently cited in support of this

---

[16] Para 8.
[17] Para 9.
[18] Para 10.
[19] See, S Enchelmaier, 'Horizontality: The Application of the Four Freedoms to Restrictions Imposed by Private Parties' in P Koutrakos and J Snell (eds), *Research Handbook on the Law of the EU's Internal Market* (Cheltenham, Edward Elgar, 2017).

proposition in relation not only to governing bodies in sport,[20] but also other private bodies which establish standards such as a trade union,[21] and an organisation regulating access to a profession.[22]

The Court, though not AG Warner, carefully focused on collective practices of private parties, and that has been the typical pattern of subsequent case law in which private parties have been treated as bound by free movement law.[23] On a couple of occasions, the Court has even suggested that a unilateral act by a private party is capable of falling within the scope of free movement law, at least where workers are concerned.[24] However, the case law remains too thin for that extension to be taken as clearly established.

The principal oddity in the case law on free movement is that the Court has consistently refused to treat the rules on the free movement of *goods* as capable of direct application to private parties.[25] The logic of *Walrave and Koch* – that the relevant Treaty provisions achieve their maximum effect and that they are not subverted by local variations in the scope of the public sector by treating them as apt for direct application to private parties – applies equally to cases involving restrictions on the free movement of goods as it does to those involving the free movement of natural and legal persons. Yet the Court has never been tempted to make that apparently logical extension. Moreover, it has never tried to explain why the Treaty freedoms should be divided in this way. Perhaps people are different.[26]

The inquiry in *Walrave and Koch* was confined to the particular matter of nationality-based discrimination as a potential violation of the Treaty freedoms. Free movement law would soon break the banks of that limited paradigm. The precise definition of a restriction to free movement remains a matter of intense debate, but there is no doubt today that across all the freedoms, it is broader in scope than a mere non-discrimination norm.[27] But in the identification of the entities which are subject to the obligations imposed by the Treaty freedoms on workers and services, *Walrave and Koch* remains an important touchstone. Its core is good law.

For the law of sport the ruling's legacy is more mixed. The Court's identification of sport as subject to EU law in so far as it constitutes an economic activity remains foundationally important. Moreover the conclusion in *Walrave and Koch* that nationality-based discrimination in international representative sport is not incompatible with EU law would also be reached today. But the reasoning employed would be different. AG Warner struggled to articulate a clear basis for his 'common sense' view, while the Court's claim that nationality-based rules are a matter of purely sporting interest which have nothing to do with economic activity is simply unsustainable. An athlete's profile is raised by playing international representative sport, all the more so in a successful team, and this has commercial consequences in markets for sponsorship and exploitation of image rights. Above all, as explained by AG Warner, Walrave and Koch themselves suffered financially by being restricted to pacing only Dutch cyclists in world

---

[20] Case C-415/93 *Bosman* ECLI:EU:C:1995:463; Joined Cases C-51/96 and C-191/97 *Deliège* ECLI:EU:C:2000:199; Case C-22/18 *TopFit* (n 3).

[21] Case C-438/05 *Viking* ECLI:EU:C:2007:772.

[22] Case C-309/99 *Wouters* ECLI:EU:C:2002:98.

[23] See case law cited in nn 19–21.

[24] Case C-281/98 *Angonese* ECLI:EU:C:2000:296; Case C-94/07 *Raccanelli* ECLI:EU:C:2008:425.

[25] eg, Case C-159/00 *Sapod Audic* ECLI:EU:C:2002:343; Case C-573/12 *Ålands Vindkraft* ECLI:EU:C:2014:2037.

[26] *cf* H Schepel, 'Constitutionalising the Market, Marketising the Constitution, and to Tell the Difference' (2012) 18 *ELJ* 177 (which begins with *Walrave and Koch*).

[27] See S Weatherill, *The Internal Market as a Legal Concept* (Oxford, OUP, 2017) ch 6.

championship events, which showed that the Court's depiction of selection rules as divorced from economic activity was false.

The Court repeated this unfortunate line of analysis 20 years later in the famous *Bosman* case, in which it refused to extend to *club* football any concession to apply eligibility rules founded on nationality. *Bosman* was a fuller and more detailed ruling than *Walrave and Koch*, but shared with it the flawed reasoning that the Treaty provisions concerning freedom of movement for persons 'do not prevent the adoption of rules or practices excluding foreign players from certain matches for reasons which are not of an economic nature, which relate to the particular nature and context of such matches and are thus of sporting interest only'.[28]

This formula is as unpersuasive as it was when introduced in *Walrave and Koch*. The reasons underpinning the adopted rules may not be 'of an economic nature', but such rules plainly exert economic effects. It is intellectually deceptive to describe them as 'of sporting interest only'. *Bosman* shares with *Walrave and Koch* a readiness to integrate the peculiar features of sport into the interpretation and application of EU law, but it also shares with it a poorly articulated basis for how and why this is so. Most of all, both rulings make the mistake of assuming there is a sharp division to be drawn between economic rules and sporting rules. In reality, few sporting rules are devoid of economic implications. It took until 2006 for the Court to shift its analytical focus to a case-by-case examination of the place of organisational rules in sport under EU law, and away from a preoccupation with the unhelpful notion of the 'purely sporting' rule.

This occurred in *Meca-Medina and Majcen v Commission*[29] which concerned anti-doping procedures. The Court held that a rule that is inherent and necessary in the organisation of sport survives condemnation pursuant to EU law – not because it exerts no economic effect (an anti-doping sanction clearly does!), but rather because EU law is interpreted in a manner which is respectful of the specific organisational demands of sport. This reflects Article 165 TFEU, introduced into the EU Treaties with effect from 2009, which asserts that sport has a 'specific nature'. This is how *Walrave and Koch* should have been handled. And it nearly was. The account of the proceedings recorded in the hard copy of the European Court Reports notes that 'such discrimination is inherent in the concept of a national team',[30] but this shining insight is then ignored. Had this interpretative approach been embraced by AG Warner and the Court, EU sports law would from its beginning have taken a more coherent developmental path towards its current model of 'conditional autonomy', according to which sport, when it comes into contact with EU internal market law, is allowed to pursue its own model of regulation on condition that a sufficiently compelling explanation is provided for the patterns chosen.[31]

---

[28] Case C-415/93 *Bosman*, para 127.
[29] Case C-519/04 P *Meca-Medina and Majcen v Commission* ECLI:EU:C:2006:492.
[30] [1974] ECR 1405, 1410.
[31] See S Weatherill, *Principles and Practice in EU Sports Law* (Oxford, OUP, 2017).

8

Reconciling the Special Provision on State Monopolies with the General Provisions on the Free Movement of Goods: Opinion of Advocate General Warner in Manghera

GRAHAM BUTLER

I. INTRODUCTION

THE FIRST FREEDOM contained in EU free movement law – goods – has given rise to some of the most seminal cases in EU law, featuring all of the UK Advocates General at the Court, as seen in many other chapters in this volume. Whilst Articles 28–30 TFEU cover customs union provisions concerning the free movement of goods, which in the mainstream literature are called fiscal measures; and Articles 34–36 TFEU ('the general provisions') cover quantitative respects on imports and exports, and measures having equivalent effect, which are called non-fiscal or regulatory measures; there is also the final provision concerning goods contained in Article 37 TFEU ('the special provision') concerning state monopolies of a commercial character (state monopolies). This special provision has long suffered from relative obscurity, and is indeed a curious creature.[1]

The general provisions concerning the free movement of goods (Articles 34–36 TFEU) can now be seen as largely settled case law, barring technical bits and pieces that remain to be resolved, especially as regards mutual recognition.[2] Whilst it always remains possible for changes in the case law, to put simply for now, when dealing with Article 34 TFEU concerning quantitative restrictions on *imports* and measures having equivalent effect, the Court reads Article 34 TFEU as being a *restrictions* test, with its famous (or infamous) exclusion of 'certain selling arrangements' doctrine from *Keck*[3] still in situ, as well as the Court's market access

---

[1] See G Butler, 'State Monopolies and the Free Movement of Goods in EU Law: Getting Beyond Obscure Clarity' (2021) 48 *LIEI* 285.

[2] See eg P Oliver, 'Mutual Recognition: Addressing Some Outstanding Conundrums' in A Albors-Llorens et al (eds), *Cassis de Dijon. 40 Years On* (Oxford, Hart Publishing, 2021).

[3] Joined Cases C-267/91 and C-268/91 *Keck* ECLI:EU:C:1993:905.

doctrine, as elaborated in *Commission v Italy (Trailers)*,[4] playing a crucial role in ensuring that Article 34 TFEU is given true effect in the Member States.

By contrast, in relation to the similar provision on quantitative restrictions on *exports* and measures having equivalent effect, the Court reads Article 35 TFEU as being merely a *discrimination* test, and not one concerning broader restrictions.[5] Article 36 TFEU acts as a potential basis for Member States to derogate, upon written (listed) grounds, from Articles 34–35 TFEU, subject to the general principles of EU law. The judgment of the Court in *Cassis de Dijon* created a further basis to derogate from Articles 34–35 TFEU through unwritten (unlisted) grounds, in what are called 'mandatory requirements', 'rules of reason', 'imperative requirements' or 'overriding reasons in the public interest'.

Where then, was there to be a place for Article 37 TFEU, the special provision concerning the free movement of goods and state monopolies, within the jurisprudence of the Court? How were national measures concerning state monopolies, for which there was no shortage of at the time of the Union's creation in the original six Member States, to be tested as regards their compatibility with the free movement provisions in what when then the EEC Treaty (now TFEU)? Were national measures to be scrutinised under the general provisions of Articles 34–36 TFEU, or under the special provision of Article 37 TFEU, or alternatively, both? Moreover, if national measures were to be only scrutinised under the special provision of Article 37 TFEU alone, was the test under Article 37 TFEU to be a mere *discrimination* test, in line with the *exports* provision of Article 35 TFEU, or what it to be a more comprehensive *restrictions* test, in line with the *imports* provision of Article 34 TFEU? The TFEU has never provided any answers to these questions. Thus, it has been up to the Court to adjudicate on such questions as matters came before it.

The earliest cases under Article 37 TFEU that were referred by national courts under the preliminary ruling procedure, regrettably, did not give many concrete answers to these questions, including in *Manghera*, the case at hand.[6] However, as will be demonstrated, the Opinion of AG Warner that he delivered in 1976 offered remarkable foresight for where, in fact, the case law has *de facto* ended up in the modern era.[7] Whilst there continues to be uncertainty about the relevance of Article 37 TFEU as concerning the free movement of goods for how national measures are to be tested against it, the Opinion of AG Warner offered an early insight into the problematic nature of Article 37 TFEU, and for why, the Court, whilst not taking up AG Warner's *obiter dictum* comments in *Manghera* at the time, has in fact come around to his way of thinking about the free movement of goods provisions collectively. The Court has now realised that Article 37 TFEU is unworkable, and thus, is currently declining to adjudicate on it.

II. BACKGROUND, CONTEXT, AND FACTS

At the time that *Manghera* was lodged at the Court, there were only a small number of cases in which the Court had adjudicated on the basis of Article 37 TFEU when dealing with state

---

[4] Case C-110/05 *Commission v Italy* ECLI:EU:C:2009:66 (*Trailers*).

[5] See Case C-205/07 *Gysbrechts* ECLI:EU:C:2008:730; Case C-15/15 *New Valmar* ECLI:EU:C:2016:464. See also M Szydło, 'Export Restrictions within the Structure of Free Movement of Goods: Reconsideration of an Old Paradigm' (2010) 47 *CMLRev* 753.

[6] Case 59/75 *Manghera* ECLI:EU:C:1976:14. Before *Manghera*, there was Case 13/70 *Cinzano* ECLI:EU:C:1970:110; Case 82/71 *SAIL* ECLI:EU:C:1972:20; Case 155/73 *Sacchi* ECLI:EU:C:1974:40.

[7] Opinion of AG Warner in Case 59/75 *Manghera* ECLI:EU:C:1976:1.

monopolies in the realm of goods. These were the *Cinzano*, *SAIL*, *Sacchi*, and others where Article 37 TFEU appeared in some way.[8] Therein stood many unanswered questions about the meaning and scope of this special provision that national courts would inevitably need answers to, for these initial cases saw the Court act minimally, in refusing to give expansive reasoning on the place of Article 37 TFEU within the free movement of goods provisions as a whole. As AG Warner himself noted in *Manghera*, the then Article 37 EEC (now Article 37 TFEU) had 'been the subject of controversy almost ever since the EEC Treaty was signed'.[9] What he meant by this is uncertain, but it is likely that the incongruent wording of the provision, as elaborated below, was a starting point.

The *Manghera* case was a request for a preliminary ruling under what was then Article 177 EEC (now Article 267 TFEU) that arrived at the Court from the Investigating Judge at the Tribunal of Como in Italy. At issue before the national court was, at the time, a state tobacco monopoly called the *Amministrazione autonoma dei monopoli di Stato* (Autonomous Administration of State Monopolies) (AAMS), which had existed before the creation of the then European Communities, and possessed exclusive rights to 'manufacture, prepare, import and sell' tobacco within the Member State. Given the powers of AAMS under the Italian law, it was extremely difficult for tobacco products from outside Italy to be lawfully imported, marketed, and subsequently sold in Italy, and thus, the national measures were a potential barrier to trade. Whilst there was doubt about the compatibility of AAMS's rights with EU law, therein lay opportunities for illicit conduct for private operators to try and circumvent the national measures.

Before the referring national court were individuals who had been accused by national authorities of smuggling cigarettes into Italy by; firstly, evading duties owed; but also secondly, and crucially, infringing upon the exclusive rights of the AAMS monopoly to import certain types of goods – tobacco products. Though unclear from public documents relating to the case such as the Opinion of AG Warner and the judgment of the Court, the smuggled cigarettes were, apparently manufactured in other EU Member States. However, the case file[10] has subsequently revealed that the confiscated goods at issue totalled 52,500 kilograms, and had numerous different states of origin, from both Member States and non-Member States (third countries) alike.[11]

As for the alleged smugglers that had been apprehended with the goods in question, the individuals were detained by Italian law enforcement authorities trying to import cigarettes into Italy, contrary to the law of that Member State. Some of the accused were born in Switzerland, though it is unclear from the case file as to the nationalities of all of them. Mr. Manghera himself was a Swiss national, and therefore, not a national of a Member State. However, the nationality of the accused was immaterial, as the case concerned goods and the special provision concerning the free movement of goods, and not the nationality of the accused.

---

[8] NB: Art 37 TFEU (then Art 37 EEC) appeared in a few older cases, but these cases were not 'Article 37 EEC' cases, per se. Two of such examples included Case 6/64 *Costa v ENEL* ECLI:EU:C:1964:66 and Case 20/64 *Albatros v Sopéco* ECLI:EU:C:1965:8. In the latter case the Court did not deal with Art 37 EEC, but yet its AG did. See Opinion of AG Gand in Case 20/64 *Albatros v Sopéco* ECLI:EU:C:1964:85.

[9] At p 106.

[10] Now open for public inspection at the archives of the Court kept at the Historical Archives of the European Union (HAEU) at the European University Institute (EUI) in Fiesole (outside Florence, Italy).

[11] Of these, the goods were categorised in the case file as follows: 17,500 kg Marlboro cigarettes (origin: USA), 14,000 kg Muratti cigarettes (origin: USA), 10,000 kg Peer cigarettes (origin: West Germany), 6,000 kg Gallant cigarettes (origin: USA), 3,000 kg Astor cigarettes (origin: West Germany), 1,000 kg H.B cigarettes (origin: West Germany), 0,500 kg Kent cigarettes (origin: United Kingdom (UK)), and 0,500 kg Parisiennes cigarettes (origin: France).

The referring court had sought guidance on firstly, the proper interpretation of Article 37(1) TFEU; and secondly, the effect of a Council Resolution that was adopted after the ending of the transition period that Article 37 TFEU had built into it. That resulted in four questions being put to the Court, to only which the Court sought it as necessary to answer question 1, 2, and 4. They were as follows:

> 1) Was the special provision of Article 37(1) [TFEU] to be interpreted as meaning that, with effect from the date when the transitional period expired, AAMS should have been reorganised in such a way as to eliminate even the possibility of any discrimination, with consequential extinction of the exclusives right for AAMS to import tobacco from other Member States?
>
> 2) Did the special provision of Article 37(1) [TFEU] have direct effect, so that an individual could invoke it before a national court?
>
> 4) Could a Council Resolution, published in the Official Journal (OJ), vary the effect of the special provision of Article 37(1) [TFEU]?

Thus, for the purposes of state monopolies, all that was being challenged in *Manghera* was the exclusive import rights of AAMS, and, furthermore, a clarification was being sought as to direct effect of Article 37 TFEU. However, as already mentioned, the key issue was the fundamental place of Article 37 TFEU within the overall set of Treaty provisions concerning the free movement of goods.

As it stood at the time of *Manghera*, the then Article 37(1) EEC (now Article 37(1) TFEU) read:

> Member States shall progressively adjust any State monopolies of a commercial character so as to ensure that when the transitional period has ended no discrimination regarding the conditions under which goods are procured and marketed exists between nationals of Member States.
>
> The provisions of this article shall apply to any body through which a Member State, in law or in fact, either directly or indirectly supervises, determines or appreciably influences imports or exports between Member States. These provisions shall likewise apply to monopolies delegated by the State to others.

This concerned adjustments that needed to be made by Member States to state monopolies. But therein lay an even more important issue concerning the test that was to be applied. On face value, and on a textual reading, Article 37 TFEU, as a whole, was unclear about what it actually demanded of the Member States when the broader scheme of Article 37 TFEU was examined. Whilst Article 37(1) TFEU spoke of *discrimination*, Article 37(2) TFEU, by contrast, spoke of *restrictions*.

At the time, Article 37(2) TFEU read:

> Member States shall refrain from introducing any new measure which is contrary to the principles laid down in paragraph 1 or which restricts the scope of the Articles dealing with the abolition of customs duties and quantitative restrictions between Member States.

Therefore, beyond the specific questions of the referring Court in *Manghera*, the Court was offered an opportunity to clarify how the special provision of Article 37 TFEU was to be interpreted, and more generally, how to reconcile its relationship with the general provisions of Articles 34–36 TFEU. Whilst, the Court rested on a discrimination reading, which, whilst ensuring that the exclusive right to import goods from other Member States had to be eliminated, it ultimately did not define the relationship of the special provision with the general provisions on movement of goods.

Remarkably, despite the incongruity of Article 37(1) TFEU and Article 37(2) TFEU, the wording of these two subsections remains the same in the post-Lisbon legal order, just as they have since their inclusion in the Treaty of Rome. It has never undergone any significant improvement in the lifecycle of amendments to EU primary law.[12]

III. THE OPINION OF AG WARNER

The Opinion of AG Warner in *Manghera* was noteworthy for his pondering beyond the strict confines of the case at hand. Furthermore, he looked at Article 37 TFEU through a broader lens, and highlighted the inherent difficulties that surround the provision in question. Yet first, he had to assist the Court in answering the questions submitted by the referring court. AG Warner began by stating his views on the answer to the second question, which – to his mind – did not present 'any difficulty'.[13] He argued:

> I have no doubt that Article 37(1) [TFEU] has had, since the end of the transitional period, direct effect in the original Member States. My reasons for holding this view are the same as those expressed by … [AG] Roemer in Case 82/71 the *SAIL* case … and by … [AG] Reischl in Case 45/75 *Rewe-Zentrale v Hauptzollamt Landau* (in which Your Lordships have not yet delivered Judgment).[14]

In finding that Article 37(1) TFEU enjoyed direct effect, he drew his conclusions from a prior assertion of the Court in *Costa v ENEL*,[15] which confirmed that Article 37(2) TFEU enjoyed direct effect. He then noted that '[i]t is indeed noteworthy that no-one who has submitted observations to the Court in this case has contended otherwise'.[16] For AG Warner the answer to the fourth question put by the referring court was 'even clearer'.[17] He argued that a Council Resolution of any description would always be considered as 'essentially[,] a political act', and thus, '[m]anifestly[,] a mere Resolution of the Council cannot alter the Treaty'.[18]

From there, the issue before for AG Warner and ultimately for the Court was the compatibility of AAMS's exclusive right of import with the overall presumption of the TFEU which was to secure the free movement of goods. The Italian government, intervening, argued that Article 37(1) TFEU meant a state monopoly only had to be 'adjusted', and not 'abolished', and consequently, pleaded that the Court rule that as a result of such an interpretation, AAMS's exclusive import right could be maintained.

AG Warner, however, set out the flaws of such an interpretation. For him, initially concurring with the Italian government, Article 37(1) TFEU did not require state monopolies themselves to be abolished. However, this time contrary to the views of the Italian government, he understood Article 37(1) TFEU as meaning that 'nor does it, in terms, require them to be preserved'.[19] For AG Warner, such adjustment entailed that it excluded 'any []discrimination regarding the conditions under which goods are procured and marketed', which meant for AAMS, it had to be 'adjusted[] out of existence by the end of the transitional period'.[20]

---

[12] The only time when the provision in question was substantively amended was by the Treaty of Amsterdam, with the old subparagraphs of the then Art 37(3) EC, Art 37(5) EC, and Art 37(6) EC, all of which related to transition periods of former times, being removed. Art 37(4) EC then became Art 37(3) EC. Briefly between two treaties, it became 'Art 31', but post-Lisbon, is 'Art 37' once again as Article 37 TFEU.

[13] At p 105.

[14] At p 106.

[15] Case 6/64 *Costa v ENEL* ECLI:EU:C:1964:66, p 597. A similar view was expressed in the Opinion of AG Lagrange in Case 6/64 *Costa v ENEL* ECLI:EU:C:1964:51, p 613.

[16] At p 105.

[17] At p 106.

[18] ibid.

[19] At p 107.

[20] ibid.

AG Warner essentially endorsed Article 37(1) TFEU as a mere discrimination test, rather than a broader restrictions one. For him:

> a [s]tate monopoly that involved no such discrimination at all (if ever there was one) required no 'adjustment' whatever. Thus, in every case the only relevant question can be whether the possession by a [s]tate monopoly of an exclusive right to import involves a discrimination as between nationals of Member States regarding the conditions under which goods are procured and marketed.[21]

From there, however, he went on to distinguish different types of state monopolies that may exist. Firstly, whilst an import monopoly cannot be compatible with Article 37(1) TFEU and thus it should be abolished. However, adjustments resulting in abolition would not be needed for other forms of state monopolies, such as a manufacturing monopoly, or retail monopoly, which could indeed be adjusted. On why he supported the view that *import* monopolies were incompatible, he relied on the pleas of the Commission:

> a [s]tate monopoly that retains an exclusive right to import is in practice in a position to discriminate against goods from other countries, not only in obvious ways, but also in day to day decisions about pricing, advertising, deliveries and so forth. Such discrimination is difficult to detect or prevent and the Commission's experience over many years of seeking to secure observance of the provisions of Article 37 [TFEU] has led it to the conclusion that this cannot satisfactorily be obtained short of the abolition of exclusive rights of importation.[22]

Therefore, for AG Warner, the immediate answers were clear: Article 37(1) TFEU required the elimination of exclusive import rights by a state monopoly (and thus, an import monopoly was incompatible with Article 37 TFEU, Article 37(1) TFEU had direct effect, and a Council Resolution could not materially alter the effect of Article 37(1) TFEU.

Then, however, came AG Warner's most important observation, which, with hindsight, demonstrated a remarkable view of how Article 37 TFEU was to be seen within the general scheme of the free movement of goods. Despite having just stated earlier in his Opinion that Article 37(1) TFEU was essentially a *discrimination* test only, and not a *restrictions* test, he nonetheless stated:

> It would, I think, be odd if, whilst Articles 34–36 [TFEU] precluded potential restrictions on trade between Member States, Article 37 [TFEU] did not.[23]

This was the real kicker of AG Warner, in taking his examination of the legal issues at stake beyond a mere discrimination analysis. Firstly, he moved the scope of Article 37 TFEU to potential hindrances; and secondly, he was inclined to imply that Article 37 TFEU was not merely concerned with discrimination alone, but rather, of being about restrictions, more broadly. For this assertion, he drew upon the observations of two former AGs. In *Albatros v Sopéco* in particular, AG Gand stated that:

> Either we [the Court] analyse the [state monopoly] system covered by Article 37 [TFEU] into its constituent parts and apply directly to each of the elements which comprise the monopoly the rules of the preceding Articles [Articles 34–36 TFEU] under the conditions determined by those Articles, …, or else we consider that Article 37 [TFEU] is only directly applicable to the case of monopolies and like organi[s]ations; which is not to say that the application of the rules contained in the preceding Articles [Articles 34–36 TFEU] is entirely excluded, but that these Articles are applicable through Article 37 [TFEU] in so far as the latter refers to them.[24]

---

[21] ibid.
[22] At pp 107–108.
[23] At p 108.
[24] Opinion of AG Gand in Case 20/64 *Albatros v Sopéco* ECLI:EU:C:1964:85, p 45.

AG Warner was convinced by such assertions by noting that AG Gand had 'showed how Article 37 [TFEU] completes the preceding Articles dealing with the elimination of quantitative restrictions on the movement of goods between Member States'.[25] AG Warner also restated the famous diktat of the Court in *Dassonville* – '[a]ll trading rules enacted by Member States which are capable of hindering, directly or indirectly, actually or potentially, intra-Community trade are to be considered as measures having an effect equivalent to quantitative restrictions'[26] – as potentially encompassing a broader restrictions test. In other words, taking an academic perspective, rather than one strictly confined to the case at hand, AG Warner theoretically saw the problematic essence of Article 37 TFEU, and thus, thought that national measures could be subjected to the general provisions of Articles 34–36 TFEU.

IV. ANALYSIS

On substance, the Opinion of AG Warner in *Manghera* was followed by the Court.[27] It ruled that exclusive import rights of state monopolies as regards trade in goods were incompatible with Article 37(1) TFEU, Article 37(1) TFEU had direct effect (in the same way it confirmed that Article 37(2) TFEU in *Costa v ENEL*), and that a Council Resolution cannot alter EU primary law. In other words, AG Warner was substantively followed in full, but the Court ignored his *obiter dictum*.

The judgment of the Court was not very surprising, even in hindsight. Indeed, as cases come and go on the docket of the Court, *Manghera* cannot really be seen as a difficult case, given it had straightforward facts, the Court adjudicated clearly for the time, and it provided a tangible judgment for the referring court to work with thereafter. The exclusive rights of import were clearly incompatible with Article 37 TFEU because having a manufacturing capacity, along with an exclusive import right, effectively sealed off any competition from goods that had their origin in other Member States altogether.

Although it will never be known for sure, there is a likelihood that in *Manghera*, the Italian court opted to send a reference for preliminary ruling to use the Court as a shield. Arguably, it did not want to rule by itself that the AAMS state monopoly, with exclusive import rights, was incompatible with the TFEU. This would have been a drastic step that could have put it at the collision course with various national entities. Be it as it may, at that stage of European integration, it did not take very much for national courts to find an uncertainty justifying referrals to the Court under Article 177 EEC (now Article 267 TFEU).

A. The Special Provision of Article 37 TFEU: A Discrimination Test, or a Restrictions Test?

The Court (echoing AG Warner) ruled that under Article 37(1) TFEU, Member States:

> must progressively adjust any [s]tate monopolies of a commercial character so as to ensure that when the transitional period has ended[,] no *discrimination* regarding the conditions under which goods are procured and marketed exists between the nationals of Member States.[28] (emphasis added)

---

[25] At p 108.
[26] Case 8/74 *Dassonville* ECLI:EU:C:1974:82, para 5.
[27] Case 59/75 *Manghera* ECLI:EU:C:1976:14.
[28] Para 4.

It further stated that, 'this provision [Article 37(1) TFEU] prescribes in mandatory terms that they must be adjusted in such a way as to ensure that when the transitional period has ended such *discrimination* shall cease to exist' (emphasis added).[29] However, from there, which up to that point had appeared to be the Court stating that Article 37(1) TFEU was to be a discrimination test, it then began to trip over itself. In the very next paragraphs, it stated:

> For the purposes of interpreting Article 37 [TFEU] as regards the nature and scope of the adjustment prescribed *it must be considered in its context in relation to* the other paragraphs of the same article and in *its place in the general scheme of the … Treaty*.[30] (emphasis added)

That is to say, for the Court, a broader restrictions test *could* be applied, by making an overall analysis of the free movement of goods provisions more generally, such as Articles 34–36 TFEU. The Court continued:

> This article [Article 37 TFEU] comes under the title on the free movement of goods and in particular under Chapter II on the abolition of quantitative restrictions between Member States …[31]

> Furthermore, Article 37(2) [TFEU] refers to the obligation on all Member States to refrain … from introducing any new measures likely to restrict the scope of the articles dealing with the *abolition of* customs duties and *quantitative restrictions between Member States…*[32] (emphasis added)

> It follows … that the obligation laid down in … [Article 37(1) TFEU] … aims at ensuring compliance with the fundamental rule of the free movement of goods throughout the common market, in particulary [sic] by the *abolition of quantitative restrictions and measures having equivalent effect in trade between Member States*.[33] (emphasis added)

Even though the Court stated that Article 37(4) TFEU provided for a discrimination test, it also clearly toyed, in paras 6–9 of the judgment, with a restrictions test. If, in the alternative, the Court had adjudicated in *Manghera* under Article 34 TFEU, then the Court would have had no choice but to apply a *restrictions* test. As a whole therefore, *Manghera* appeared uncertain as to which test was to apply – a discrimination test or a restrictions test. This was the Court, regrettably, providing profound uncertainty. Whilst AG Warner had said a discrimination test applied, he had thereafter expressed some dissatisfaction with such a narrow approach. The Court, by contrast, gave an indeterminate answer on the applicable test.

In *Rewe v Hauptzollamt Landau/Pfalz*, shortly thereafter, clarity came, at least as regards Article 37(1) TFEU. There, the Court stated that, it was 'not concerned exclusively with quantitative restrictions but prohibits any *discrimination*' (emphasis added).[34] The Court slightly wavered in *Hansen*, similar to how it did in *Manghera*, when it stated that Article 37 TFEU was 'intended to render the sales policy of a [s]tate monopoly subject to the requirements of the free movement of goods and of the equal opportunities which must be accorded to products imported from other Member States'.[35] However, ever since, it has remained steadfast when adjudicating on Article 37 TFEU – which it has not in some time – that is it merely a discrimination test that applies under the special provision, and not a restrictions test.

---

[29] Para 5.
[30] Para 6.
[31] Para 7.
[32] Para 8.
[33] Para 9.
[34] Case 45/75 *Rewe v Hauptzollamt Landau/Pfalz* ECLI:EU:C:1976:22, para 26.
[35] Case 91/78 *Hansen* ECLI:EU:C:1979:65, para 13.

B. The Special Provision of Article 37 TFEU and the General Provisions of Articles 34–36 TFEU

In *Manghera*, the Court adjudicated on the basis of the special provision of Article 37 TFEU, as the national court had asked; and not on the basis of the general provisions of Articles 34–36 TFEU. This was as AG Warner had proposed. However, AG Warner did hint at the end, in his *obiter dicta*, that Article 37 TFEU was not without issues, and should perhaps be viewed in a broader light of other provisions, for which he was eminently correct. In fact, over the time, the Court's jurisprudence on Article 37 TFEU wavered, and became inconsistent.

The case law can be broken up into three time periods. Firstly, the early case law up to 1979, when the Court examined all national measures relating to state monopolies under Article 37 TFEU, and did not engage in a separability exercise. *Manghera* was of this 'early era', when the Court did not subject national measures to the general provisions of Articles 34–36 TFEU. This early case law was neatly summarised in *Miritz*, where the Court stated that Article 37 TFEU was:

> not limited to imports or exports which are directly subject to the monopoly but covers *all measures* which are connected with its existence and affect trade between Member States in certain products, *whether or not subject to the monopoly*.[36] (emphasis added)

Thereafter, however, the Court had a change of heart, without directly acknowledging it was overturning itself.[37] Its judgment in *Cassis de Dijon* marked the second stage of Article 37 TFEU's life, which can be called the 'middle era'. Here, the Court overturned *Miritz* (and de facto *Manghera*) on the point of what provision of the free movement of goods that national measures are to be scrutinised under. The Court was now of the position that Article 37 TFEU was:

> irrelevant with regard to national provisions *which do not concern the exercise by a public monopoly of its specific function*, ... but apply in a general manner to the production and marketing of ... [goods].[38] (emphasis added)

This new approach of the middle era meant that the compatibility of national measures with the free movement of goods provisions were in turn to be examined cumulatively under Article 34 TFEU first, and Article 37 TFEU second, or vice versa. In other words, *Cassis de Dijon* created the idea that a separability test was to exist.[39] This new approach was quickly affirmed in *Peureux I*, where the Court stated, with more clarity, that Article 37 TFEU:

> concern[s] only activities intrinsically connected with the specific business of the [state] monopoly and ... irrelevant to national provisions which have no connexion with such specific business.[40]

From there however, the Court had again changed its case law, spurning both the early and middle era for what can now to called the 'modern era'. Instead, the Court now assesses all national measures related to state monopolies under the general provisions of

---

[36] Case 91/75 *Miritz* ECLI:EU:C:1976:23.

[37] By contrast, on the Court overturning itself in an honest and open fashion, see ch 24.

[38] Case 120/78 *Cassis de Dijon* ECLI:EU:C:1979:42, para 7.

[39] On the separability exercise, see Butler (n 1) 290–97.

[40] Case 86/78 *Peureux I* ECLI:EU:C:1979:64, para 35.

Articles 34–36 TFEU alone, with a deliberate position of not assessing any national measures under the special provision of Article 37 TFEU.

The first sign of this new approach was seen in *Rosengren*, where the Court considered the national measures on import restrictions for private use (different but similar in some way to *Manghera* on prohibition of imports in contravention of a state monopoly's exclusive rights). This time however, the Court stated that the national measures at issue:

> under which private individuals are prohibited from importing alcoholic beverages, must be assessed in the light of Article [34 TFEU] and not in the light of Article [37 TFEU].[41]

The Court's position of assessing the national measures under the general provisions on the free movement of goods in *Rosengren* was evident too when it came to potential justifications grounds for the Member State's national measures. It then stated that the prohibition of private imports was:

> in the light of the alleged objective, that is to say, limiting generally the consumption of alcohol in the interest of protecting the health and life of humans, that prohibition, because of the rather marginal nature of its effects in that regard, must be considered unsuitable for achievement of that objective.[42]

As such, no separability test to was to engaged with, all national measures were to be examined under the general provisions of Articles 34–36 TFEU. Moreover, no 'public interest aim' that the Court put forward in *Franzén* was invoked on the basis of Article 37 TFEU. Thus, *Rosengren* was a step away from the middle era case law. Two subsequent judgments in *ANETT* and *Visnapuu* cases confirmed the existence of the modern era.

In *ANETT*, the Court was asked to determine the applicability of the free movement of goods provisions with national measures that prohibited tobacco retailers from importing tobacco products from other Member States. Despite pleas that it was an Article 37 TFEU situation from the Spanish government (and, strangely adopting the same position, the Commission), the Court stated that the national measures:

> cannot be regarded as a rule relating to the existence or the operation of the monopoly. Accordingly, Article 37 TFEU is irrelevant for the purposes of determining whether such a prohibition is compatible with EU law, in particular with the provisions of the Treaty relating to free movement of goods.[43]

The 'irrelevant' terminology was quite strong language, seen as affirmation that the modern era had well and truly arrived. If there was any doubt, *Visnapuu* was the confirmation that the Court had shied from its use of the special provision of Article 37 TFEU altogether from the early and middle eras. At the end of its discussion of its case law concerning it, the Court merely stated that, '[t]he file before the Court does not contain enough information' for the Court to have given a ruling under Article 37 TFEU. Instead, the Court held:

> In the light of the foregoing, it is necessary to examine whether legislation of a Member State, such as that at issue in the main proceedings, … constitutes a measure having equivalent effect to a quantitative restriction on imports within the meaning of Article 34 TFEU.[44]

---

[41] Case C-170/04 *Rosengren* ECLI:EU:C:2007:313, para 27.
[42] Para 47 of the judgment in *Rosengren*.
[43] Case C-456/10 *ANETT* ECLI:EU:C:2012:241, para 30.
[44] Case C-198/14 *Visnapuu* ECLI:EU:C:2015:751, para 97.

In other words, the Court in *Visnapuu* provided an interpretation of Articles 34–36 TFEU only, and provided no interpretative guidance on Article 37 TFEU – the third such case in a row of doing so. The Court thus now goes out of its way to avoid adjudicating on the basis of Article 37 TFEU, and instead subjects national measures to the general provisions of Articles 34–36 TFEU only. This approach of the modern era, rejecting the use of Article 37 TFEU altogether, is a development that AG Warner would have approved of, given his Opinion in *Manghera*.

C. Article 37 TFEU and the Advocates General

Article 37 TFEU cases throughout the different eras have seen quite a number of instances where the AGs have delivered Opinions that offered alternative views to those of the cases at hand. It can even be said that this case law, on the finite details of EU free movement law, is where AGs have provide their most value. In addition to AG Warner's almost throw-away remarks concluding his Opinion in *Manghera*, two subsequent AGs have endorsed his approach, one explicitly, and another implicitly.

In *Commission v Italy (Manufactured Tobacco)*, AG Rozès explicitly stated:

> as elucidated by the exceptionally clear Opinion of Mr Advocate General Warner [in *Manghera*] – the unity of the concept of a measure having equivalent effect in Articles 37 [TFEU] and 34 [TFEU] appears, in my view, to be beyond doubt.[45]

As she otherwise put it:

> [t]he reference thus made by the Court to the concept of a measure having an effect equivalent to quantitative restrictions on imports raises the question as to whether or not that concept should be endowed with the same meaning in Article 37 [TFEU] as it has in Article 34 [TFEU]. In my opinion, the Court's case-law requires an affirmative reply to that question.[46]

AG Rozès, just like AG Warner, saw the potential contradiction between the special provision and the general provisions, and thus saw beyond a simple discrimination reading of Article 37 TFEU. In *Hanner*, the Opinion of AG Léger is also noteworthy in this regard. He stated that 'the Court has adopted that particular understanding of 'discrimination' in its case-law'[47] under Article 37 TFEU, and that, contrary to the Court, stated in *Hanner* that:

> [i]t follows that the concept of 'discrimination' in Article [37 TFEU] refers to *all obstacles to the free movement of goods*. Those obstacles may take a variety of forms, such as customs duties or charges having equivalent effect within the meaning of Article [30 TFEU], quantitative restrictions or measures having equivalent effect within the meaning of Article [34 TFEU] or discriminatory internal taxation within the meaning of Article [110 TFEU].[48]

For AG Léger implicitly, like AGs Warner and Rozès before him, Article 37 TFEU was to akin to a restrictions test, rather than a simple discrimination test. Collectively, these AGs, and AG Gand in *Albatros v Sopéco*, all came to the realisation, well before the Court did, that

---

[45] Opinion of AG Rozès in Case 78/82 *Commission v Italy* ECLI:EU:C:1983:109 (*Manufactured Tobacco*), pp 1975–76.
[46] Page 1975 of the Opinion of AG Rozès.
[47] Opinion of AG Léger in Case C-438/02 *Hanner* ECLI:EU:C:2004:317, para 64.
[48] Para 86 of the Opinion of AG Léger.

Article 37 TFEU was unworkable, long before the Court eventually came around to a related view in *Rosengren*, *ANETT*, and *Visnapuu*. Up until then, the Court was blind to the problems of Article 37 TFEU, or at least, not honest enough to admit so.

D. The State of State Monopolies of a Commercial Character in the Case Law

Manghera was not the first state monopolies case on the basis of Article 37 TFEU to have reached the Court, and nor was it the last.[49] State monopolies are anything but a memory in some Member States, as there are many state monopolies that continue to exist, rather bizarrely, given the EU is essentially an open market economy, and state monopolies are obstacles to inter-state trade.

What was particularly notable about the *obiter dicta* in the Opinion of AG Warner in *Manghera* was entirely correct, given that the Court has indirectly, but obscurely come around to his way of handling state monopolies as regards their (in)compatibility with the general regime of free movement within the internal market. It is submitted that the modern era of case law, and the result in *Rosengren*, *ANETT*, and *Visnapuu* is the best possible way of adjudicating on state monopolies whilst the provision is still in the EU Treaties. Indeed, the Court should continue to ignore Article 37 TFEU until such a time it is removed from the EU Treaties. Should national measures need to be checked against the free movement of goods provisions in the future, and there is every reason to believe national courts will still refer to questions about state monopolies, the Court should continue this trajectory of utilising the Articles 34–36 TFEU only.

Prior to this modern era, state monopolies of a commercial character provided some unfortunate case law. For example, in *Franzén*, the Court went out of its way to create derogation grounds *within* Article 37 TFEU for state monopolies that pursue a 'public interest aim',[50] which the Court has only half-heartedly endorsed in full in subsequent case law on select points of that judgment. *Franzén* was a poorly reasoned and highly political judgment of the Court, appearing to go to some lengths and out of its way to save a retail monopoly on alcoholic goods, known as *Systembolaget* in Sweden, for the then newly-acceded Member State in the 1990s.

There was absolutely no basis in the EU Treaties for the Court's reasoning in *Franzén*, and the Opinion of AG Elmer was wrongfully spurned by the Court.[51] AG Elmer had meticulously (and correctly) argued that the way in which *Systembolaget* was formed and operated was contrary to EU law under both the special provision of Article 37 TFEU, as well as the general provision of Article 34 TFEU, and could not be saved by Article 36 TFEU, given that more proportionate grounds (or measures less restrictive) of protecting health could be found.[52] In other words, the state monopoly should have been totally disbanded, and the retail market liberalised. If *Franzén* was to be re-tested, there can still be hope the Court would explicitly overturn *Franzén*, and thus force the Member State to bring *Systembolaget* to its logical end,

---

[49] See D Wyatt, 'New Light on Article 37 EEC' (1976) 1 *ELRev* 307.

[50] For criticism of the *Franzén* judgment, and why parts of it are no longer concerned to be good law, see Butler (n 1) 297–300.

[51] Opinion of AG Elmer in Case C-189/95 *Franzén* ECLI:EU:C:1997:101.

[52] For even more trenchant criticism of the *Franzén* judgment, see Opinion of AG Léger in Case C-438/02 *Hanner* ECLI:EU:C:2004:317, paras 40–81, who systematically picks apart the flawed judgment. See also, G Butler, *Alcoholic Goods and Sweden: The EU Law of Private Imports, Retail Sale, and State Monopolies* (Stockholm, SIEPS, 2022).

for its essence is not able to be saved by written justification grounds in Article 36 TFEU, or other unwritten grounds.

AG Warner's *obiter dictum* in *Manghera* has had some jurisprudential value, lasting well beyond his tenure at the Court. The case law of the modern era, having moved away from adjudicating on the basis of Article 37 TFEU altogether, is ultimately in line with the *obiter* comments of AG Warner. Historically, the Court struggled for consistency over time in its Article 37 TFEU adjudication, and this implies, if anything, that at some basic level, applying Article 37 TFEU is unworkable. At the earliest opportunity, it would be helpful for the Court to add to its modern era of case law in *Rosengren*, *ANETT*, and *Visnapuu*, and finally put Article 37 TFEU to rest.

9

Equivalence and Effectiveness in the Enforcement of EU Rights: Opinion of Advocate General Warner in Rewe

ALAN DASHWOOD

I. INTRODUCTION

JEAN-PIERRE WARNER (known to friends and colleagues as J-P) was AG at the Court from the accession of the United Kingdom to the then European Communities on 1 January 1973 until 1982, during what may be described as the Court's 'heroic age', when it was building its reputation as the final authority on questions of EU law, worthy of the respect of the grandest national tribunals. This author had the immense privilege of serving as J-P's Legal Secretary (*référendaire*) at the Court for some three years, from 1978 to 1980.[1]

The 1970s was the period in which the Court was working out, with intellectual courage and imagination, the implications for the establishment of the common market envisaged by the EEC Treaty of the great constitutional principles of direct effect and the primacy of Community law, which had first been enunciated in *Van Gen den Loos*[2] and *Costa v ENEL*.[3] Landmark cases, confirming the existence and clarifying the scope of the directly effective rights of free movement and equal treatment derived from the EEC Treaty, included *Reyners* (1974) on the right of establishment,[4] *van Binsbergen* (1974) on freedom to provide services,[5] *van Duyn* (1974) on the free movement of workers and the direct effect of directives,[6] *Defrenne* (1978) on equal pay for men and women,[7] and *Cassis de Dijon* (1979) on mutual recognition of marketing standards for goods.[8] However, as the old Latin tag has it, *ubi remedium, ibi ius*: having a remedy means having a right. The Court recognised that, in the absence of remedies prescribed by Community law, the effective enforcement of Community rights could only be ensured through the courts of the Member States. The Court's initial instinct appears to have

---

[1] See A Dashwood, 'The Advocate General in the Court of Justice of the European Communities' (1982) 2 *Legal Studies* 202.
[2] Case 26/62 *Van Gend en Loos* ECLI:EU:C:1963:1.
[3] Case 6/64 *Costa v ENEL* ECLI:EU:C:1964:66.
[4] Case 2/74 *Reyners* ECLI:EU:C:1974:68.
[5] Cae 33/74 *van Binsbergen* ECLI:EU:C:1974:131.
[6] Case 41/74 *van Duyn* ECLI:EU:C:1974:133.
[7] Case 149/77 *Defrenne* ECLI:EU:C:1978:130.
[8] Case 120/78 *Cassis de Dijon* ECLI:EU:C:1979:42.

been to leave it entirely for national courts to determine the appropriate remedy and apply the relevant procedural rules provided for under their domestic legal systems.[9] As the number of cases began to increase, however, the need was evidently perceived to develop a framework within which the national enforcement of Community rights would take place subject to certain requirements imposed by Community law. The ruling by the Court in *Rewe*, and in the parallel *Comet* case,[10] marked the beginning of this process.

II. BACKGROUND, CONTEXT, AND FACTS

AG Warner gave a single Opinion[11] relating to both *Rewe* and *Comet* since, as he explained, the two cases raised essentially the same question:

> where a Member State has, in breach of Community law, exacted from a trader a charge having equivalent effect to a customs duty, either on exports to or on imports from another Member State, may that State, in proceedings brought in its own courts by that trader for recovery of the amount unlawfully charged, plead a limitation period prescribed by its own national law?.

The referring court in the *Rewe* case was the German Federal Administrative Court. The main proceedings concerned a challenge against notices of assessment to a charge for phytosanitary inspection in 1968 in respect of apples imported into Germany from France, and a claim for the reimbursement of the charge which had been paid. Similar charges had been held in a previous case to be charges having an equivalent effect to customs duties on imports,[12] and the relevant German authority conceded that those in issue here were unlawful. However, AG Warner pointed out, that was not, as had been suggested in argument, by virtue of the relevant provision of the EEC Treaty, Article 13(2) EEC, which provided for the progressive abolition of such charges during the EEC's transitional period, and had only become directly effective after that period ended on 31 December 1969; the imposition of the charges had been rendered unlawful through the direct effect of a provision contained in one of the original structural measures of the common agricultural policy (CAP), on the common organisation of the market in fruit and vegetables,[13] which required their abolition as from 1 January 1967.

In resisting the claim, the German authorities relied on the limitation period for challenging administrative decisions of the kind in question, which was normally a month or, in certain circumstances, a year. The importer's legal challenge was mounted only in February 1973 which, the AG remarked, was 'well after the expiry of either limitation period'. He noted further that lower German courts had held the importer's claim to be out of time, rejecting the contrary argument that a right conferred by Community law could not be barred by any provision of national law. While agreeing with that ruling, the *Bundesverwaltungsgericht* felt bound under the third paragraph of Article 177 EEC (now Article 267 TFEU), as the court of final resort in the proceedings, to refer to the Court a question asking whether there would still be a right under Community law, arising from the infringement of the prohibition on charges having an effect equivalent to customs duties by

---

[9] See below the authorities discussed by AG Warner in the Opinion which is the subject of this study.
[10] Case 45/76 *Comet* ECLI:EU:C:1976:191.
[11] Opinion of AG Warner in Case 33/76 *Rewe* ECLI:EU:C:1976:167.
[12] Case 39/73 *Rewe-Zentralfinanz* ECLI:EU:C:1973:105.
[13] Art 13(1) of Council Regulation No 159/66/EEC (Règlement n° 159/66/CEE du Conseil, du 25 octobre 1966, portant dispositions complémentaires pour l'organisation commune des marchés dans le secteur des fruits et legumes [1966] OJ 192/3286).

an administrative body of a Member State, to the annulment of the administrative measure, and/or to reimbursement of the amount paid, even if under the rules of procedure of the national law the time-limit for contesting the validity of the measure was past. Two subsidiary questions were: whether that would be the case at least if the Court had already ruled that there had been an infringement of the prohibition; and whether, if a right to a refund existed, interest should be paid on the amount and, if so, from what date and at what rate.

In the parallel case, *Comet*, the offending charge was levied by a Dutch authority on exports of bulbs and corms of flowering plants to Germany, its purpose being to finance publicity for these products. Once again, it was common ground that the charge was unlawful, this time for the infringement of a prohibition, effective from 1 July 1968, which was contained in the original CAP structural measure on the market in live trees and other plants, bulbs, roots and the like, cut flowers and ornamental foliage.[14] Notices of assessment to the charge were issued in respect of exports effected between the Autumn of 1968 and the Spring of 1969; these were paid by the exporter, who only lodged an appeal against the assessments in 1975. The limitation period for such appeals being 30 days, the defendant authority pleaded before the competent administrative tribunal that the claim was time-barred. AG Warner noted that the tribunal had previously rejected the argument that a Community right could not be overridden by such a rule of national law, and was disposed to do the same again, had its attention not been drawn to the reference in *Rewe*. Accordingly, the Tribunal referred a question to the Court to similar effect as the main question of the *Bundesverwaltungsgericht*.

III. THE OPINION OF AG WARNER

AG Warner, J-P, was a devoted European. Like his colleague, Jack Mackenzie Stuart, the first UK judge on the Court, he had fought in World War II as a young soldier, and regarded the establishment of the European Communities as the antidote to the terrible history of European nationalism. A common lawyer through and through, he was meticulous in his analysis of case law and in teasing out the meaning of legislation, though sensitive to the need for an embryonic legal order to draw on a wider range of sources, notably Member States' legal experience. He did not have a grandiose view of his role, but saw it as rather similar to that of a High Court Judge, looking for the legally correct answer to the case before him, and explaining clearly and succinctly how he arrived at it. Those characteristics were to the fore in his Opinion in *Rewe* and *Comet*.

The analysis in the Opinion begins with a strong assertion of the principles of primacy and direct effect as they applied in *Rewe* and *Comet*:

> I do not doubt, My Lords, that provisions such as those of Article 13(1) of Regulation No 159/96 and Article 10(1) of Regulation No 234/68, which abolished or prohibited charges having an effect equivalent to customs duties from a certain date, invalidated national legislation purporting to impose such charges after that date. Nor do I doubt that such provisions had direct effect in the legal systems of the Member States in the sense of conferring on private persons rights that the national courts must uphold.[15]

---

[14] Art 10(1) of Council Regulation (EEC) No 234/68 (Regulation (EEC) No 234/68 of the Council of 27 February 1968 on the establishment of a common organisation of the market in live trees and other plants, bulbs, roots and the like, cut flowers and ornamental foliage [1968] OJ L55/1). As the Court of Justice pointed out, charges having equivalent effect to quantitative restrictions on exports between Member States had, in fact, been prohibited by Art 16 EEC from the end of the first stage of the transitional period, ie 1 January 1962: see judgment in *Comet*, para 5.

[15] At p 2002 of the Opinion.

The AG went on, however, to express the view that it was 'for the national law of each Member State to determine the nature and extent of the remedies available in the Courts of that State to give effect to those rights',[16] citing copious authorities for that proposition, going back to an ECSC case, *Humblet v Belgium* in 1960.[17] In that case, the Court held that whether an official of the ECSC was entitled to be awarded interest in respect of income tax exacted by the tax authorities of Belgium in breach of the ECSC's Protocol on Privileges and Immunities fell to be determined by Belgian legislation.[18] A similar position had been taken by the Court in cases concerning other aspects of the enforcement of Community rights conferred on individuals, namely: the choice of appropriate remedies;[19] the classification of claims for the purpose of determining which national court should have jurisdiction over them;[20] and the conditions governing State liability for damage caused to an individual by an infringement of Community law.[21] As already intimated, in these earlier cases the applicability of national remedies and procedural rules was affirmed by the Court without qualification and as a given, with little or no supporting argument.

Recourse to national rules and procedures, the AG reasoned, was a matter of common sense, where Community law confined itself to prohibiting an act on the part of Member States and to saying that private persons were entitled to rely on the prohibition in their national courts, without itself prescribing the procedures available to them for this purpose. The suggestion that this would be to allow national law to override Community law was wrong; it should be seen, rather, as 'a situation in which Community law and national law operate in combination, the latter taking over where the former leaves off, and working out its consequences'.[22]

Two other authorities cited by AG Warner were *Mutualities Chretiennes*, where a right to recover advances of benefits under a Regulation on social security was held to be subject to the different periods of limitation prescribed by the laws of different Member States,[23] and *Roquette*, where it was held that an entitlement to interest in respect of levies imposed under Community Regulations, to which a trader had been wrongly assessed, must be settled in accordance with national law.[24] By comparison, he suggested, *Rewe* and *Comet* might, in a way, be considered *a fortiori*, being concerned, not with levies imposed by Community law, but by national law.

The authority chiefly relied upon by the claimants was the famous *Rheinmuhlen* case,[25] in which AG Warner had himself been the AG.[26] The substantive issues in the case related to

---

[16] ibid.

[17] Case C-6/60-IMM *Humblet* ECLI:EU:C:1960:48.

[18] ibid, p 569.

[19] Case 28/67 *Firma Molkerei-Zentrale* ECLI:EU:C:1968:17, 154; Case 34/67 *Firma Gebrüder Lück* ECLI:EU:C:1968:24, 251; Case 120/73 *Lorenz* ECLI:EU:C:1973:152, para 9.

[20] Case 13/68 *Salgoil* ECLI:EU:C:1968:54, p 463.

[21] Case 60/75 *Russo* ECLI:EU:C:1976: 9, para 9.

[22] At p 2003 of the Opinion.

[23] Case 35/74 *Rzepa* ECLI:EU:C:1974:118, para 13.

[24] Case 26/74 *Roquette Frères* ECLI:EU:C:1976:69, para 12.

[25] Case 166/73 *Rheinmuhlen-Dusseldorf* ECLI:EU:C:1974:3. It was referred to the Court by the German Federal Finance Court (*Bundesfinanzhof*). There had been an earlier reference to the Court (Case 146/73 *Rheinmühlen-Düsseldorf* ECLI:EU:C:1974:12), by a lower German court, the Finanzgericht of Hesse, relating to a matter on which a decision by the latter had been overruled by the *Bundesfinanzhof*, whose decisions were binding on it. The claimants had appealed to the *Budesfunanzhof* against the referral decision by the lower court, leading to the reference in Case 166/73.

[26] He gave a single Opinion relating to both cases. See Opinion of AG Warner in Case 166/73 *Rheinmühlen-Düsseldorf* and Case 146/73 *Rheinmühlen-Düsseldorf* ECLI:EU:C:1973:162.

the conditions governing the entitlement of grain traders to export refunds under the then applicable CAP legislation. The Court was asked whether the second paragraph of Article 177 EEC gave a lower national court a completely unfettered right to address questions to the Court, or whether it left unaffected rules of domestic law to the contrary whereby a court was bound on points of law by the judgments of courts superior to it. The Court held that such a rule of domestic law could not of itself take away the power of referral provided for by Article 177 EEC. This did not prevent the decision to make a reference from being the subject of an appeal under the national system but, in the interests of clarity and legal certainty, the Court would continue to give full effect to such a decision until it was withdrawn.[27] The decision in *Rheinmuhlen* had shown, the claimants argued, that Community law was capable of overriding national procedural law.

AG Warner provided a detailed rebuttal to the claimants' argument. The national rule was overridden in *Rheinmuhlen* because it was incompatible with the express provision of Community procedural law contained in Article 177 EEC. For the claimants to get home with their argument, they would have had to establish a similar incompatibility: that Community law not only invalidated the levies to which they were assessed but itself conferred a right of action for restitution of those levies; and, moreover, one which could not be limited by any provision of national law. No such independent right of action was conferred on claimants by Community law. Nor, even if a right had been conferred, was there any Community procedural law applicable to its exercise, with which national procedural law could be incompatible. The logic of the claimants' position would mean that no limitation period could be applicable at all to their right of action, which would have been inconsistent with the common legal traditions of the Member States and with the approach of Community law itself, as exemplified in Article 173 EEC (now Article 263 TFEU).[28] The *reductio ad absurdum* of that position would be that an action brought by the claimants for restitution of the levies could not be dismissed by the national court on any procedural ground whatsoever, not even for want of prosecution.

The final authorities that AG Warner considered were two well-known decisions of national courts affirming the primacy and direct effect of Community law, the *Le Ski* and *Café Jacques Vabre* cases.[29] Far from aiding the claimants, he pointed out, the question at issue in *Rewe* and *Comet* was not ever broached in those cases; indeed, the national courts that decided them assumed relevant rules of national procedural law to be applicable. His discussion of the two cases ends with the statement:

> Of course, when I say that, in circumstances such as those of these cases, the remedies and procedures that must be invoked are those prescribed by national law, I do not mean that it is open to the legislature of a Member State specifically to deprive of their remedies under such law persons who have been the victims of a breach by that State of Community law.[30]

This was the only reference in the Opinion to the issue for which the ruling in *Rewe* and *Comet* was to become famous, namely the limitation placed by the Court on the procedural autonomy of Member States in the enforcement of rights derived from EU law.

---

[27] AG Warner had taken a different view from the Court in his Opinion. In the light of a full and careful analysis of the issue, he reached the firm conclusion that an order for reference should not be capable of being appealed to a higher national court.

[28] A reference to the limitation period of two months provided for by Art 263 TFEU, sixth paragraph.

[29] *Etat Belge* v SA *Fomagerie Franco-Suisse 'Le Ski'*, Cour de Cassation of Belgium (JT 1971, p 460); *Administration des Douanes* v *Societe 'Café Jacques Vabre'*, Cour de Cassation of France (D 1975 J 497).

[30] At p 2004.

In the result, AG Warner concluded that the Court should answer the main question – whether there was any provision of Community law preventing the respective national authorities in *Rewe* and *Comet* from relying on the fact that the time limits for challenging the decisions in issue had elapsed – in the negative. This meant that the third question, as to whether interest should be paid on the amounts wrongfully exacted, did not arise. As to the second question – the relevance of the fact that the Court had already ruled on the incompatibility with Community law of charges of the kind in question – he was very clear that the right of private persons to be reimbursed charges levied in breach of Community law could not depend on the existence or absence of a ruling by the Court concerning the charges in question. As he put it, '[a] ruling of this Court declares the law; it does not make it'.[31]

IV. ANALYSIS

A. The Principles of Equivalence and Effectiveness

The Court gave separate but substantially identical judgments in *Rewe* and *Comet*. Compared with the Court's more recent practice, both judgments were extremely brief. In the style of the time, no authorities were cited, the arguments of the parties were not examined, and there was no reference to the Opinion of AG Warner.

The Court only found it necessary to answer the main question regarding reliance on time limits to defeat claims based on Community law. In doing so, it grasped the opportunity to enlarge on the bare statements in its earlier case law that, in the absence of Community rules on the subject, the designation of the courts with jurisdiction to hear such claims, and the procedural rules governing remedies for pursuing them, were matters for the domestic legal system of each Member State. The role given to national courts in ensuring the legal protection of directly effective Community rights was said to be an application of 'the principle of cooperation laid down in Article 5 of the Treaty' (Article 5 EEC, corresponding to sincere cooperation under Article 4(3) TEU today).[32] The Court recalled that there were legislative means available, in the form of harmonisation measures adopted under then Articles 100–102 EEC,[33] or of supplementary powers created under then Article 235 EEC,[34] if differences between the relevant provisions of Member States' legal systems were likely to distort or harm the functioning of the common market. However, the chief significance of the rulings in *Rewe* and *Comet* lay in the identification of two essential requirements that national standards of judicial protection for Community rights must meet. The first requirement was that the conditions governing actions at law for the enforcement of Community rights 'cannot be less favourable than those relating to similar actions of a domestic nature';[35] this has come to be known as 'the principle of equivalence'. The second requirement was that such conditions must not make it 'impossible in practice to exercise the rights which the national courts are obliged to protect'.[36] In later case law, beginning with the judgment in *San Giorgio*, this requirement was significantly reinforced, as one that the applicable national remedies and procedural rules must not render

---

[31] At p 2005.
[32] Para 5 of Judgment in *Rewe*.
[33] The corresponding, though substantially amended, provisions are now Arts 114–118 TFEU.
[34] The corresponding provision, again substantially amended, is now Art 352 TFEU, known as the flexibility clause.
[35] Para 5 of Judgment in *Rewe*.
[36] ibid.

the exercise of EU rights 'virtually impossible *or excessively difficult*'.[37] It has come to be known as 'the principle of effectiveness'.[38]

The enunciation of the principles of equivalence and effectiveness in *Rewe* and *Comet* amounted to an assertion by the Court of the power to review national standards of protection for EU rights, although before the reinforcement of the effectiveness principle the criteria to be applied for this purpose were extremely narrow. The Court said that limitation periods would comply with the effectiveness principle, if reasonable, observing that the prescription of such time-limits for actions of a fiscal nature was 'an application of the fundamental principle of legal certainty protecting both the tax-payer and the administration concerned'.[39] It raised no objection to the application of the national limitation periods in question in the proceedings, though they were very short (respectively one month or 30 days). As noted below, the addition of the phrase 'or excessively difficult' to the effectiveness principle as it was originally formulated in *Rewe* and *Comet*, would greatly extend the scope of the Court's power of review.

It is not surprising that the Opinion of AG Warner contained no mention of the two principles, neither of which featured in any of the case law that he analysed for the Court. It was not his style to speculate as to how the law should develop in the future, but to help the Court find the right answer to the case before it. On the matter of equivalence, he doubtless assumed (and there was no reason to believe otherwise) that the limitation periods prescribed by the relevant German and Dutch legislation were being applied to the reimbursement of the charges levied in breach of Community law under the same conditions as they would be in the case of breaches of national fiscal legislation. More importantly, the almost throwaway remark that it was not, of course, open to a Member State's legislature 'specifically to deprive of their remedies under [national] law persons who have been the victims of a breach by that State of Community law', may have been the inspiration for the initial tentative formulation by the Court of the principle of effectiveness.

B. Effect on Future Case Law

There is now a very large body of case law on the employment of national remedies and procedural rules for the enforcement of rights derived from EU law. The bulk of these cases raise the issue whether, pursuant to the reinforced principle of effectiveness, there are grounds for disapplying, with respect to the EU rights being litigated, national procedural rules that exclude or limit the scope of the national remedies otherwise normally available. Such rules include: limitation periods, as in *Rewe* and *Comet*; restrictions on the retrospective effect of claims;[40] restrictions on the introduction of new pleas in legal proceedings;[41] unjust enrichment;[42] and

---

[37] Case 199/82 *San Giorgio* ECLI:EU:C:1983:318. The Court held that Community law did not prevent the application of a rule on 'unjust enrichment' disallowing recovery of an illegally levied charge which the trader concerned had passed on to customers. This was on condition that the means of proof prescribed by the national legal system must not make it virtually impossible or excessively difficult to secure repayment.

[38] The current formulation of the two principles can be found in, eg, Joined Cases C-397 and 410/98 *Metallgesellschaft Ltd and Hoechst* ECLI:EU:C:2001:134, para 86.

[39] Para 5 of *Rewe* Judgment.

[40] See, eg, Case C-338/91 *Steenhorst-Neerings* ECLI:EU:C:1993:857, concerning a restriction imposed by the Netherlands social security law on the payment of disability benefits to a period no earlier than a year prior to a given claim.

[41] See, eg, Case C-312/93 *Peterbroeck* ECLI:EU:C:1995:437, concerning a time limit for the lodging of new pleas.

[42] See, eg, Case 199/82 *San Giorgio* (n 37).

ceilings on the amount recoverable for certain claims, or the denial of the possibility of interest on sums awarded.[43] In another important line of cases, the Court has, in effect, supplemented the remedies available to the national courts: for example, by insisting that the national courts have power to grant interim relief, where needed to ensure the effectiveness of an eventual judgment on the existence of an EU right, even if this would not be available for the protection of national rights;[44] and, most radically, through the development of the doctrine of State liability in damages for losses caused to individuals by a Member State's infringement of its EU obligations.[45] *Rewe* and *Comet*, as the judgments in which the Court, following up the hint given by AG Warner, first spelled out that there may be limits to national procedural autonomy where EU rights are at stake, may justly be seen as the ancestors of that case law.

The Court may appear sometimes to have forgotten the lesson which can be drawn from *Rewe* and *Comet*, that caution must be exercised in interfering with the operation of procedural rules that often reflect basic constitutional choices by Member States or matters of legitimate public concern such as the proper use of financial resources. A notorious instance was the decision in *Emmott*,[46] where the Court ruled that, so long as a Member State had not properly transposed a directive into its national legal system, the national authorities would be prevented from invoking a limitation period prescribed by national law (even a reasonable one) in proceedings for the enforcement of rights conferred by the directive on an individual. This seemed to mean that claims based on directly effective rights under an EU directive could never be time-barred. *Emmott* was, however, soon distinguished in *Steenhorst-Neerings*,[47] regarding a restriction on a claim for arrears of disability benefits, which the Court judged acceptable, as promoting sound administration and helping to preserve the financial balance of the social security scheme; this in spite of the fact that the claim arose from a Member State's alleged failure properly to implement an EU directive. Subsequently, the Court has effectively disavowed the principle enunciated in *Emmott*, explaining its decision in the case by the fact that the national authorities defending the claim in question had discouraged the claimant from initiating proceedings, pending a possibly relevant ruling by the Court, which caused her to miss the deadline for seeking relief.[48] The resulting rule was the perfectly sensible one, that a time limit cannot be relied upon to defeat a claim based on an EU right, where conduct of the party invoking the time limit was responsible for its breach by the claimant.

On the whole, and certainly in the Court's more recent practice, decisions seeming to encroach on a Member State's procedural autonomy can usually be justified by the particular context in which the protection of an EU right calls for an appropriate national remedy.[49] The likelihood of such cases arising is greater than at the time of *Rewe* and *Comet*, since EU law has become so much more complex, in particular through its extension to the fields of equal treatment, and social and employment law. A telling example is *Magorrian*.[50] Relevant UK legislation had the effect of limiting, to two years prior to the date of application, the period of

---

[43] See, eg, Case C-271/91 *Marshall* ECLI:EU:C:1993:335, concerning the ceiling imposed by UK legislation on compensation, and the tribunal's inability to award interest, in a case of unlawful dismissal involving sex discrimination.

[44] Case C-213/89 *Factortame* ECLI:EU:C:1990:257.

[45] Joined Cases C-6 and C-9/90 *Francovich* ECLI:EU:C:1991:428; Joined Cases C-46/93 and C-48/93 *Brasserie du Pêcheur* ECLI:EU:C:1996:79.

[46] Case C-208/90 *Emmott* ECLI:EU:C:1991:333.

[47] Case C-338/91 *Steenhorst-Neerings* (n 40).

[48] See Case C-188/95 *Fantask* ECLI:EU:C:1997:580.

[49] See the discussion in A Dashwood et al, *Wyatt and Dashwood's EU Law*, 6th edn (Oxford, Hart Publishing, 2011) 299–302.

[50] Case C-246/96 *Magorrian and Cunningham* ECLI:EU:C:1997:605. See also Case C-78/98 *Preston* ECLI:EU:C:2000:247.

pensionable service in respect of which the claimants' right to membership of an occupational pension scheme, wrongly denied on discriminatory grounds, could be recognised retrospectively. The time limit meant that, unlike their male colleagues, the claimants' future pension entitlement would not reflect the total period of their actual service. It had to be disapplied, to ensure for the claimants the effectiveness of the EU right of equal access to their occupational pension scheme.[51]

While such cases were far outside the experience of J-P during his time as an AG, the example he set, of rigorous analysis of the case law and any relevant legislation, following the argument wherever it might lead to a legally compelling solution of the particular issues before the Court, remains as relevant as ever.

---

[51] The Court distinguished *Steenhorst-Neerings*, on the ground that the rule in question did not deprive the claimant of her right under EU law, namely the right to a disability benefit, but merely limited the period prior to the commencement of proceedings in respect of which arrears of benefits could be backdated: see Case C-246/96 *Magorrian*, para 43.

10

Previous Criminal Convictions and Public Policy Exceptions: Opinion of Advocate General Warner *in* Bouchereau

CHRISTA TOBLER

I. INTRODUCTION

T HE RIGHT TO free movement of persons and services is subject to three statutory
derogations: public policy, public security and public health.[1] At the time of the
Bouchereau case,[2] Articles 3(1) and (2) of Directive 64/221[3] provided:

Measures taken on grounds of public policy or of public security shall be based exclusively on the
personal conduct of the individual concerned. Previous criminal convictions shall not in themselves
constitute grounds for the taking of such measures.

Today, the first part of Article 27(2) of Directive 2004/38,[4] its successor, consists of practically the same text, though now also including a reference to the principle of proportionality.
Importantly, the provision continues with a part that was as yet missing in Directive 64/221,
namely:

The personal conduct of the individual concerned must represent a genuine, present and sufficiently
serious threat affecting one of the fundamental interests of society. Justifications that are isolated
from the particulars of the case or that rely on considerations of general prevention shall not be
accepted.

The first sentence of this addition stems from the *Bouchereau* judgment. In charge of writing
the Opinion on this case was AG Warner. At that time, there was no impediment to AGs

---

[1] Public policy and public security are also part of the much longer list of potential derogations under Art 36 TFEU;
see eg chs 17 and 22.

[2] Case 30/77 *Bouchereau* ECLI:EU:C:1977:172; Opinion of AG Warner in Case 30/77 *Bouchereau*
ECLI:EU:C:1977:141.

[3] Directive 64/221/EEC on the co-ordination of special measures concerning the movement and residence of foreign
nationals which are justified on grounds of public policy, public security and public health, OJ English Special Edition
Series I Chapter 1963–1964, p 117.

[4] Directive 2004/38/EC on the right of citizens of the Union and their family members to move and reside freely
within the territory of the Member States amending Regulation (EEC) No 1612/68 and repealing Directives 64/221/EEC,
68/360/EEC, 72/194/EEC, 73/148/EEC, 75/34/EEC, 75/35/EEC, 90/364/EEC, 90/365/EEC and 93/96/EEC [2004]
OJ L158/77.

delivering Opinions in cases from Member States which had nominated them to the Court. Like the *Bouchereau* case, AG Warner combined French and British elements: born to a French mother and an English father, he studied both in France and the UK. This international background will undoubtedly have helped him in his work at the Court.[5] Before comparing his opinion on *Bouchereau* to the Court's judgment, the facts and issues of the case will be summarised below.

II. BACKGROUND, CONTEXT, AND FACTS

In 1976, Mr Bouchereau, a French national employed in the UK, found himself in court on charge of unlawful possession of drugs. As this was not his first drug offence, the national court considered making a recommendation to the Home Secretary for his expulsion from the UK. Under UK law, such a recommendation was a necessary step towards expulsion. It was, however, not binding on the Home Secretary.

Faced with the threat of expulsion, Mr. Bouchereau claimed that Community law on the free movement for workers prevented such a recommendation from being made in his case. This led the national court – the first UK *criminal* court to do so[6] – to request a preliminary ruling from the Court on three questions, which can be summarised as follows: 1) is an action of a national court such as a recommendation for expulsion a 'measure' within the meaning of Article 3(1) of Directive 64/221? 2) what is the meaning of the expression 'not in themselves' in relation to previous criminal convictions in Article 3(2) of the Directive? and, 3) what is the meaning of 'public policy' in Article 48(3) of the EEC Treaty (now Article 45(3) TFEU)?

In this chapter, the first of these questions is not further discussed. Suffice it to note, AG Warner's statement that the recommendation in question had legal effects for the defendant,[7] and the Court's finding that any action that affects the rights of persons comes within the field of application of the rules on the free movement for workers.[8] The chapter thus focuses on the second and the third questions only.

III. THE OPINION OF AG WARNER

A. Relevance of Previous Criminal Convictions

With respect to the relevance of previous criminal convictions, the national court enquired specifically whether the words 'in themselves' in Article 3(2) of Directive 64/221 meant that previous criminal convictions were solely relevant in so far as they manifested a *present or future propensity* to act in a manner contrary to public policy or public security. Before the Court, this interpretation was favoured by Mr. Bouchereau and the Commission. Counsel for the prosecution argued that future tendencies of the person in question must remain irrelevant; instead, past personal conduct that resulted in a criminal conviction must form the basis for any subsequent decision to restrict the freedom of movement of the person concerned.

---

[5] See ch 5.

[6] The first reference for a preliminary ruling from the UK was Case 41/74 *van Duyn* ECLI:EU:C:1974:133.

[7] Page 2021 of the Opinion.

[8] Para 21 of the Judgment.

Similarly, the UK Government maintained that the nature and gravity of past conduct must be relevant.

AG Warner essentially agreed with this latter view: whilst a previous conviction cannot of its own form the basis for a decision to restrict free movement, past conduct can and must be taken into account. Even without any clear propensity, a previous act may have caused such deep public revulsion that public policy demands departure, 'just as a man may exclude from his house a guest, even a relative, who has behaved in an excessively offensive fashion'.[9] In terms of the general formula to be used, the AG argued in favour of the approach set out by the Court in *Rutili*: restrictive measures must be allowed where a person's 'presence or conduct constitutes a genuine and sufficiently serious threat to public policy'.[10] Considering that the last four words read oddly, the AG instead suggested 'a threat to the requirements of public policy' instead.

The Court did take up this last point, but used a different formula: the existence of a previous criminal conviction can only be taken into account in so far as the circumstances which gave rise to that conviction are evidence of personal conduct constituting a present threat to the requirements of public policy. The Court agreed that, although in general a finding that such a threat exists implies the existence in the individual concerned of a propensity to act in the same way in the future, it is possible that past conduct alone may constitute such a threat.[11]

With this definition, the Court departed from the *Rutili* formula, which had mentioned both conduct *and* presence. In fact, the wording of Article 3 of Directive 64/221 only mentioned conduct. Further, it is submitted that the Court's finding in *Bouchereau* implies that it rejected AG Warner's 'house guest' approach. Indeed, the focus in *Bouchereau* was not on past conduct alone, but rather on what such conduct meant in terms of a *present* threat. This was different from an approach where revulsion caused by a previous act sufficed to exclude a person. Accordingly, the Member States could not be compared to hosts who are free to decide whom they want to admit to, or ban from, their home. Rather, they have agreed on common rules which circumscribe their room for action. As a result, these common rules elevated workers exercising free movement above the station of guests. In his Opinion in the earlier *Bonsignore* case, AG Mayras spoke of a 'privileged class of aliens constituted by workers who are nationals of Common Market Countries'.[12]

From a modern EU perspective, nationals of other Member States who make use of the right to free movement are not 'guests', but rather, fellow Union citizens. According to the Court, this status calls for a particularly narrow interpretation of the derogations to free movement.[13] At the time of *Bonsignore*, and *Bouchereau*, Union citizenship did not yet exist. At the most, one could have spoken about 'market citizens', a term that tends to be criticised in modern academic writing. For example, it has been argued that the notion of a market citizen in the case law has led to a commodification of the individual, and that this case law has represented a turn away from the fundamental principles of dignity, the rule of law, and fundamental rights protection.[14] However, if seen in a historical context, and in contrast to the house guest approach, the concept at least has the advantage of seeing people as 'citizens'. Indeed, writing at the time of *Bouchereau*, others argued that the restrictions

---

[9] Page 2022.
[10] Page 2022.
[11] Paras 28 and 29 of the Judgment.
[12] Opinion of AG Mayras in Case 67/74 *Bonsignore* ECLI:EU:C:1975:22, p 316.
[13] Joined Cases C-482/01 and C-493/01 *Orfanopoulos* ECLI:EU:C:2004:262, para 65.
[14] D Kochenov, 'The Oxymoron of 'Market Citizenship' and the Future of the Union' in F Amtenbrink et al (eds), *The Internal Market and the Future of European Integration: Essays in Honour of Laurence W Gormley* (Cambridge, CUP, 2019). See also eg N Nic Shuibhne, 'The Resilience of EU Market Citizenship' (2010) 47 *CMLRev* 1597.

defined, by the Court, with respect to expulsion should be regarded as 'an opening of new horizons to Community nationals, as a source for wider rights for these citizens to move freely within the Community, as a promising step forward on the road of integration, in other words, as a new dimension to inter-human relationships'.[15] In this more positive sense, the limited concept of 'market citizens' is still relevant in the framework of what the EU's political institutions term the 'extended internal market',[16] as established notably through the European Economic Area (EEA) Agreement,[17] and the EU-Swiss market access agreements, among them the Agreement on the Free Movement of Persons (FMPA).[18] Here, too, people who make use of their free movement rights are more than house guests, who can be kept out at will.

B. The Meaning of 'Public Policy'

With respect to the concept of public policy under Article 48(3) of the EEC Treaty, the national court in *Bouchereau* asked about three possible understandings: must the term be understood '(a) as including reasons of state even where no breach of the public peace or order is threatened, or (b) in a narrower sense in which is incorporated the concept of some threatened breach of public peace, order or security, or (c) in some other wider sense'? Mr. Bouchereau and the Commission advocated a strict interpretation along the lines of version (b). Nobody argued that virtually every type of 'reason of state' could be relevant within the meaning of version (a), not even the UK Government, which favoured an interpretation along the lines of version (c).

AG Warner appeared to be puzzled by the language used by the national court. Noting that 'reasons of state' is not an expression that belongs to English legal terminology, he suspected that what the national court might have meant, in terms of English law, was close to 'justification on grounds of public interest wider than breaches of the peace and public order', as suggested by the UK Government.[19] As for Community law, the AG noted that whilst the term 'peace' appeared in the English language version of the *Bonsignore* judgment, this was a mistranslation of the authentic German text, which used a different term, namely 'öffentliche Ordnung', which corresponded to 'public order'.[20]

With respect to public policy, AG Warner emphasised the function of this concept as a ground for making an exception to the principle of non-discrimination under Community law. Apart from that, the concept had been deliberately left to be defined and developed by secondary law and case law. With respect to the latter, AG Warner referred to *Van Duyn*[21] and *Rutili*,[22] where the Court said that the Member States' discretion in determining the requirements of public policy in the light of their national needs is subject to control by the

---

[15] A Barav and S Thomson, 'Deportation of EEC Nationals from the United Kingdom in the Light of the Bouchereau Case' (1977) 4 *LIEI* 37, 37.

[16] See Council, 'Conclusions on a homogeneous extended single market and EU relations with Non-EU Western European countries' (2018), www.consilium.europa.eu/en/press/press-releases/2018/12/11/council-conclusions-on-a-homogeneous-extended-single-market-and-eu-relations-with-non-eu-western-european-countries/.

[17] European Economic Area Agreement [1994] OJ L1/3.

[18] Agreement of 21 June 1999 between the European Community and its Member States, of the one part, and the Swiss Confederation, of the other, on the free movement of persons [2002] OJ L114/6.

[19] Page 2023.

[20] Para 6 of the Judgment in *Bonsignore*.

[21] Case 41/74 *van Duyn* ECLI:EU:C:1974:133.

[22] Case 36/75 *Rutili* ECLI:EU:C:1975:137.

Community institutions. As for secondary law, the annex to Directive 64/221 at that time listed drug addiction as a disease that might threaten public policy or public security.[23] Noting that there was no evidence that Mr. Bouchereau was in fact a drug addict, AG Warner nevertheless went on to delve into the distinction under English law between drug addiction (considered an illness) and drug possession (a criminal offence with expulsion as a possible consequence), and compared this with other national legal orders. The AG also mentioned the fictional case of a person who is at once a scientologist (obviously a reference to the *van Duyn* case) and a drug addict: according to AG Warner, under the English law in force at the time, such a person could clearly be expelled on the ground of association with scientology, though not on the ground of drug addiction[24] (an assessment that was rejected in an annotation on *Bouchereau*).[25]

Finally, in terms of how the Court should answer the national court's question, AG Warner thought that perhaps it would be enough to state that 'public policy is not limited to the threatened breach of public peace, order or security', as had been suggested by the UK government. However, according to the AG, 'it might be more helpful if the Court were somewhat more specific and added that that concept is not to be interpreted as excluding, as a potential ground for limiting the rights conferred on a worker by that Article, the fact of his having been found repeatedly in unlawful possession of harmful drugs'.[26] Yet, the Court did not proceed in this manner, and it is submitted that this was quite logical. After all, for the issue of previous crimes there was (and is) a specific provision on the level of secondary law. As stated, the exception of public policy had been the subject of Directive 64/221, 'which is intended to delimit more precisely the scope of the exception'.[27]

The Court shared with AG Warner the common starting point of public policy being part of a derogation rule which, as such, must be interpreted strictly. Within the limits of Community law, the Member States enjoyed an area of discretion which allowed them to take into account differences in the circumstances in different Member States and between different time periods. Against this backdrop, the Court's definition of public policy was as follows:

> In so far as it may justify certain restrictions on the free movement of persons subject to Community law, recourse by a national authority to the concept of public policy presupposes, in any event, the existence, in addition to the perturbation to the social order which any infringement of the law involves, of a genuine and sufficiently serious threat affecting one of the fundamental interests of society.[28]

As noted at the time, the final part of this definition part arms migrants 'with considerable protection against arbitrary treatment. [...] while national communities are free to safeguard local values, it is only when the fundamental of these are put at risk that the public policy proviso may be invoked. Mr. Bouchereau, convicted of possessing small quantities of LSD and amphetamines, was eventually considered by the learned Magistrate, in the light of the judgment of the Court of Justice, as posing no such threat to the requirements of English public policy'.[29]

---

[23] Directive 2004/38 no longer contains such an annex; Art 29 instead refers to the World Health Organization.

[24] Page 2027 of the Opinion.

[25] D Wyatt, 'Case 30/77, Regina v. Pierre Bouchereau. Preliminary ruling of 27 October 1977 on request of the Marlborough Street Magistrates' Court, London. (1977) ECR 1999' (1978) 15 *CMLRev* 214, 226.

[26] At p 2028 of the Opinion.

[27] L Neville Brown, 'The Linguistic Regime of the European Communities: Some Problems of Law and Language Problems of Law and Language' (1981) 15 *Valparaiso University Law Review* 319, 328. In relation to *Bouchereau*, the article deals with the different language versions for the term 'measure' in Directive 64/221.

[28] Para 35.

[29] Wyatt (n 25) 225.

IV. ANALYSIS

A. A Genuine and Sufficiently Serious Threat Affecting One of the Fundamental Interests of Society

Following *Bouchereau*, the reference to 'a genuine and sufficiently serious threat affecting one of the fundamental interests of society' in the Court's definition of the concept of public policy became standard in the context of the free movement of persons and services. For example, the Court used it in the *Adoui* case,[30] where it also corrected *van Duyn*, stating that conduct may not be considered as being of a sufficiently serious nature to justify restrictions on the admission to, or residence within, the territory of a Member State of a national of another Member State in a case where the former Member State does not adopt, with respect to the same conduct on the part of its own nationals, repressive measures or other genuine and effective measures intended to combat such conduct. Accordingly, modern academic writing considers the Court's approach in *van Duyn* to have been incorrect.[31] Eventually, the reference to 'a genuine and sufficiently serious threat affecting one of the fundamental interests of society' was codified in Article 27(2) of Directive 2004/38.

Through the EEA and the EU-Swiss association regimes, the Court's definition also made its way into the extended internal market. For example, the EFTA Court (which is in charge of EEA cases that arise in Iceland, Liechtenstein, and Norway) quoted the *Bouchereau* definition in *Rainford-Towning*,[32] and *Wahl*.[33] In Switzerland, the Federal Tribunal regularly refers to the *Bouchereau* definition.[34]

B. Expulsion Based on Previous Criminal Convictions

Following *Bouchereau*, the Court revisited the issue of expulsion and criminal convictions on several occasions. Leading cases from the time before Directive 2004/38 were *Calfa* and *Orfanopoulos*,[35] both concerning drug addicts. In *Calfa*,[36] the Court accepted that a Member State may consider the use of drugs a danger for society such as to justify special measures against non-nationals who contravene its laws. However, expulsion as an automatic consequence of a criminal conviction, without any account being taken of the personal conduct of the offender or of the danger which that person represents for the requirements of public policy, was not acceptable. This was confirmed in *Orfanopoulos*, where the Court again emphasised the relevance of exclusively personal conduct, which must be examined on a case-by-case basis.

In the context of Directive 2004/38, elsewhere, the link of the issue with Article 28 on the protection against expulsion and with the procedural safeguards under Article 31 and others of the Directive has been pointed to.[37] The former required that a balance must be

---

[30] Joined Cases 115/81 and 116/81 *Adoui* ECLI:EU:C:1982:183, para 8.
[31] E Guild et al, *The EU Citizenship Directive*, 2nd edn (Oxford, OUP, 2019) 260.
[32] Case E-3/98 *Rainford-Towning*, EFTA Court, para 42.
[33] Case E-15/12 *Wahl*, EFTA Court, para 85.
[34] BGE 129 II 215 (cons. 7.3) is an early example.
[35] Guild et al (n 31) 263 ff.
[36] Case C-348/96 *Calfa* ECLI:EU:C:2004:262.
[37] N Nic Shuibhne, 'Exceptions to the Free Movement Rules' in C Barnard and S Peers (eds), *European Union Law*, 3rd edn (Oxford, OUP, 2020) 510, 536 ff.

struck between the threat to public policy and public security, and the fundamental rights of the individual concerned, as evidenced by case law such as *Tsakouridis*[38] concerning drug offences, and *PI*[39] involving sexual abuse of a family member. In *PI*, the Court made a link to Article 83(1) TFEU.

The modern standard of EU law on these matters, as set out in Directive 2004/38, has been incorporated into EEA law, with a limiting declaration regarding future EU case law on Union citizenship.[40] In its case law concerning expulsion, the EFTA Court follows the CJEU. The beginning of the operative part of the EFTA Court's judgment in *Norway v L*[41] provides an illustrative example:

> Permanent exclusion orders are, in principle, not contrary to EEA law, provided that they satisfy the conditions set out in Articles 27 and 28 of [Directive 2004/38] and may be lifted in accordance with Article 32 thereof. An expulsion measure must be based on an individual examination. As regards EEA nationals who have legally resided for a period of more than 10 years in the host State, expulsions may only be adopted, pursuant to Articles 27 and 28(3) of Directive 2004/38/EC, on imperative grounds of public security, in circumstances where the personal conduct of the individual concerned poses an exceptionally serious threat that an expulsion measure is necessary for the protection of one of the fundamental interests of society. This is provided that such protection cannot be attained by less strict means, having regard to the length of residence of the EEA national in the host State, and in particular to the serious negative consequences such a measure may have for an EEA national and his/her family members who have become genuinely integrated into the host State. Any subsequent exclusion decision must be limited to what is necessary to safeguard the fundamental interest that the expulsion intended to protect. The exclusion decision must adhere to the principle of proportionality.[42]

In contrast to the EEA Agreement, the EU-Swiss FMPA has not been updated in the light of Directive 2004/38.[43] A draft Institutional Agreement that would have introduced a framework for a dynamic updating system, among others, for the FMPA was shelved by the Swiss Government in May 2021.[44] Instead, the derogation provision of Article 5 in Annex I to the FMPA still refers to Directive 64/221.[45]

In its case law on criminal convictions and expulsion, the Federal Tribunal accepts the Court's stance on the need for a case-by-case assessment. However, beyond that, the Tribunal has taken the view that the different context of the FMPA, as compared to EU law, justifies a different interpretation. In other words, it applies what in EU law is known as the

---

[38] Case C-145/09 *Tsakouridis* ECLI:EU:C:2010:708.

[39] Case C-348/09 *PI* ECLI:EU:C:2012:300.

[40] Decision of the EEA Joint Committee No 158/2007 of 7 December 2007 amending Annex V (Free movement of workers) and Annex VIII (Right of establishment) to the EEA Agreement [2008] OJ L124/20. See K Fløistad, 'Article 28 Free Movement of Workers' in F Arnesen et al (eds), *Agreement on the European Economic Area: EEA Agreement. A Commentary* (Munich, CH Beck, 2018).

[41] Case E-2/20 *L*, EFTA Court, para 38.

[42] In contrast, in the context of return cases the EFTA Court takes a different approach in order to guarantee substantive homogeneity with EU law in terms of the rights of citizens; see eg C Tobler, 'Free Movement of Persons in the EU v. in the EEA: Of Effect-Related Homogeneity and a Reversed *Polydor* Principle' in N Cambien et al (eds), *European Citizenship under Stress: Social Justice, Brexit and Other Challenges* (Leiden, Brill Nijhoff, 2020).

[43] The EU-Swiss Agreement on Free Movement of Persons belongs to the category of static agreements, that is with no legal obligation to update in case of changes to EU law.

[44] See Federal Council, No signing of the Swiss-EU institutional agreement, media release 26 May 2021, www.admin.ch/gov/en/start/documentation/media-releases.msg-id-83705.html.

[45] M Oesch, *Switzerland and the European Union: General Framework, Bilateral Agreements, Autonomous Adaptation* (Baden-Baden, Nomos, 2018) 70.

Polydor approach.[46] More specifically, in Case BGE 145 IV 364, the Tribunal referred to the Court's statement in *Graf and Engel* according to which the concept of public order must be interpreted in the specific framework of the FMPA with its economic objective.[47] Noting that the Member States founded the EU to achieve an ever-closer union, the Tribunal stated that the Court's interpretation on expulsion in EU law is due to the integrative dynamic application, which intends the harmonisation and deepening of the Union. The Tribunal continued (BGE 145 IV 364, cons. 3.8 and 3.9; English translation by DeepL):

> According to the current legal situation, Switzerland does not have to take into account this nuance of this case law (teleological reduction of the normative content of Art. 5 para. 1 Annex I FMPA) for criminal law, as the interpretation under Union law is not to be automatically adopted [...]. Moreover, the criminal expulsion of criminals lacks significance under any title of the FMPA and the bilateral agreements. The criminal expulsion has neither an economic nor a migration law component.

This last sentence has been heavily criticised in Swiss academic writing.[48] Obviously, an expulsion has immediate consequences for the economic possibilities of workers who have exercised free movement. Most likely, the statement has to be seen against the backdrop of a Swiss constitutional initiative on the expulsion of non-nationals if they commit certain crimes. It is interesting to note that, in the debate on this initiative, the house guest approach was expressly used.[49] The initiative carried. In practice, the rules following from it are applied with a certain restraint, but tensions with the FMPA remain.[50]

C. Effect on Future Case Law

The *Bouchereau* case has undoubtedly shaped free movement law in the EU's extended internal market. How much did AG Warner contribute to this judgment? On a general level, it has been noted that AG Warner, the first AG trained in a common law jurisdiction, 'patiently anglicized some of the Court's procedures',[51] for example by asking questions on the submissions before the Court. He did so in the *Bouchereau* case, where – in the words of the judge *rapporteur* – he entered into a regular 'dialogue' with the representative of the UK.[52]

In terms of substance, the Court took up his suggestion regarding the language to be used in defining public policy, and it acknowledged that it is possible that past conduct alone may indicate a present threat. However, the Court did not follow the Opinion of AG Warner

---

[46] See eg, C Tobler, 'Context-related Interpretation of Association Agreements. The Polydor Principle in a Comparative Perspective: EEA Law, Ankara Association Law and Market Access Agreements between Switzerland and the EU' in D Thym and M Zoeteweij-Turhan (eds), *Rights of Third-Country Nationals under EU Association Agreements: Degrees of Free Movement and Citizenship* (Leiden, Brill Nijhoff, 2015).

[47] Case C-506/10 *Graf and Engel* ECLI:EU:C:2011:643, para 32.

[48] Bommer remarks somewhat sarcastically that in order to arrive at this view, one must very resolutely disregard the effect of a criminal expulsion for the person affected by it. See F Bommer, 'Die Rechtsprechung des Bundesgerichts zum materiellen Strafrecht im Jahr 2019' (2020) *Zeitschrift des Bernischen Juristenvereins* 499, 515. Critical also A Epiney, 'Strafrechtliche Landesverweisung und FZA', *Jusletter* 22 May 2019; S Progin-Theuerkauf, 'Expulsion pénale et ALCP' (2020) *Zeitschrift für schweizerisches Recht* 35.

[49] 'Those who become criminals and thus abuse our hospitality must leave', www.svp.ch/wp-content/uploads/200722-Positionspapier-Nichtumsetzung-Ausschaffungsinitiative-1.pdf.

[50] In addition to the authors mentioned in n 48, see eg S Gless et al, 'Ein fächerübergreifendes Prüfprogramm für die obligatorische Landesverweisung nach Art. 66a StGB' (2018) *forumpoenale* 97.

[51] N Burrows and R Greaves, *The Advocate General and EC Law* (Oxford, OUP, 2007) 166.

[52] CJEU, Dossier de la procédure original: affaire 30/77, p 30, European University Institute, *Historical Archive of the European Union 1977*.

on certain other points, among them, notably, the 'house guest' approach. This, the Court rejected, which is a subtle but important difference between the Opinion and the judgment. Finally, AG Warner struggled with differences in language and concepts. At the time, this was referred to as 'a perennial problem of language and translation'.[53] Indeed, in modern academic writing, this issue is still discussed. Thus, elsewhere, it has been written that:

> 'Public policy' is a very unsatisfactory translation of *ordre public, öffentliche Ordnung, openbare orde* and *ordine pubblico*, all of which have well-established and specific meanings in the national law of other member states which are neither rendered by 'public policy' nor necessarily equivalent to the meaning to be given to the term in Union law. In this context 'public order' would probably be better, except that it comes with its own baggage in English.[54]

---

[53] J Usher, 'How Fundamental is Public Policy?' (1977) 2 *ELRev* 449, 453.
[54] D Edward and R Lane, *Edward and Lane on European Union Law* (Cheltenham, Edward Elgar, 2013) 627 fn 674.

11

Rights of Undertakings in EU Antidumping Proceedings: Opinion of Advocate General Warner in Bearings I

ROSA GREAVES

I. INTRODUCTION

THE ADOPTION OF antidumping legislation by national governments goes back to 1904 when Article 19 of the Customs Law of Canada was enacted. Internationally, dumping and countervailing duties have been regulated since the adoption of Article VI of GATT which came into force in 1948. An agreement to implement Article VI was signed in 1968, which led to the adoption of the Antidumping Code. In essence, the GATT allows a contracting state to levy, on any dumped product, an antidumping duty not greater in amount than the margin of dumping in respect of such product. In its simplistic form, dumping in international trade arises where products are exported at a price below which they are sold in the country of production or manufacture.[1] This pricing discrimination in international trade is considered to be an unfair commercial practice.

The EU adopted its first antidumping measure in 1968, exercising its exclusive competence in matters of external commercial policy.[2] Regulation No 459/68 (the Antidumping Regulation) was adopted in conformity with the Antidumping Code, setting out the specific roles of the Council and Commission in implementing the EU's antidumping regime.[3] The Commission was granted investigative powers to determine whether specific products from non-EU states, third countries, were being sold in the EU at a price less than the comparable price in the exporting country of origin. An investigation normally began with a complaint from a European undertaking or organisation. Once the Commission established there has been dumping, which caused or is likely to cause material injury to an EU industry (a causal

---

[1] An undertaking is considered to be dumping a product if it exports the product at a price lower than the normal value of the product. The normal value is either the product's price as sold on the home market of the undertaking, or a price based on the cost of production and profit.

[2] Art 113 EEC Treaty, currently – after several revisions – Art 207 TFEU.

[3] Regulation (EEC) No 459/68 of the Council of 5 April 1968 on protection against dumping or the granting of bounties or subsidies by countries which are not members of the European Economic Community [1968] OJ L93/1. The current EU antidumping regime is governed by Council Regulation (EU) 2016/1036 of the European Parliament and of the Council of 8 June 2016 on protection against dumped products from countries not members of the European Union (codification) [2016] OJ L176/21.

link is necessary), then a definitive antidumping duty, usually in the form of an ad valorem duty, was applied to the imported product, as long as it was in the EU's interest to do so. This remains the case today. As an interim measure, provisional duties could be imposed which were not immediately collected, but the importers had to provide security to the amount specified.

In the Japanese *Bearings I* cases,[4] the Court was asked to consider, for the first time, the EU antidumping legislation. The parties sought, inter alia, declarations that Regulation 1778/77, which ended the antidumping investigation against the manufacturers and importers of ball bearings and tapered roller bearings from Japan, to be void, in whole, or in part.[5] The Court delivered separate judgments, but AG Warner delivered a single Opinion for all the five cases.[6]

The key issues addressed in the Opinion concerned: first, the standing of the parties to seek an annulment of a general applicable EU measure (ie a regulation) imposing an antidumping duty on specific products; secondly, the procedural safeguards for the parties concerned which were set out in paragraphs (2), (4) and 6 of Article 10 of the Antidumping Regulation; and, thirdly, the legality under the Antidumping Regulation of accepting from the parties an undertaking which puts an end to the dumping investigations but, at the same time, imposing a definitive duty though suspended.

Of all the three issues, the greatest impact of the Opinion of AG Warner was on the development of procedural safeguards. In *Bearings I*, it was established that the Commission had failed to notify the applicants of details which would have been relevant to their defence, including: the alleged dumping margins and their methods of calculation; the use of constructed values instead of domestic prices; the manner in which injury had been determined. As a result of judicial criticism strongly articulated by AG Warner, the existing Antidumping Regulation was amended to provide improved procedural rights for undertakings whose products were subject to antidumping investigations.[7]

II. BACKGROUND, CONTEXT, AND FACTS

From the late 1960s onwards, European manufacturers faced strong competition emerging from the Far East, where manufacturers, with modernised factories and cheaper labour, gained efficiencies that enabled them to offer highly competitively priced products to European importers. The European industries responded, often through their trade associations, by complaining of unfairness, alleging the imported products were being dumped, ie sold below their normal value, in order to penetrate the EU market, and to force the EU competitors to exit the market.

---

[4] Case 113/77 *NTN Toyo Bearing Co* ECLI:EU:C:1979:91; Case 118/77 *Import Standard Office (ISO)* ECLI:EU:C:1979:92; Case 119/77 *Nippon Seiko* ECLI:EU:C:1979:93; Case 120/77 *Koyo Seiko* ECLI:EU:C:1979:94; Case 121/77 *Nachi Fujikoshi Corpn* ECLI:EU:C:1979:95.

[5] Council Regulation (EEC) No 1778/77 of 26 July 1977 concerning the application of the anti-dumping duty on ball bearings and tapered roller bearings originating in Japan [1977] OJ L196/1.

[6] Opinion of AG Warner in Case 113/77 *NTN Toyo Bearing Company*, Case 118/77 *Import Standard Office (ISO)*, Case 119/77 *Nippon Seiko*, Case 120/77 *Koyo Seiko*, Case 121/77 *Nachi Fujikoshi Corpn* ECLI:EU:C:1979:39. For a case analysis, see A Dashwood, 'Case 113/77, *NTN Toyo Bearing Co. Ltd. and others v. Council* (1979) ECR 1185; Case 118/77, *Import Standard Office v. Council*' (1980) 17 CMLRev 119.

[7] Council Regulation (EEC) No 1681/79 of 1 August 1979 amending Regulation (EEC) No 459/68 on protection against dumping or the granting of bounties or subsidies by countries which are not members of the European Economic Community [1979] OJ L196/1.

At the time Japanese manufacturers were the major source of ball bearings and tapered roller bearings, with some 95 per cent of exports to the EU being produced by four major manufacturers: NTN Tokyo Bearing Company Ltd (NTN); Nippon Seiko KK (NSK); Koyo Seiko Company Ltd (Koyo); and Nachi Fujikoski Corporation (Nachi). There were also nine other smaller manufacturers, and, together, they were members of the Japan Bearing Industrial Association. In Europe, the manufacture of ball bearings took place mainly in France, Western Germany, and the United Kingdom, with some minor production in other Member States.[8] Although there were thousands of types and sizes of ball bearings and tapered roller bearings, they were all prescribed under agreed international standards, and therefore, interchangeable. The Japanese manufacturers concentrated their competition on those types of bearings which were in very high demand, and could be manufactured cheaply where long production runs were possible.

In 1976, the Federation of European Bearing Manufacturers' Associations (FEBMA) submitted a complaint to the European Commission alleging that dumping was taking place and causing injury. After consultation with the EU Member States, antidumping proceedings were opened, and an investigation was carried out resulting in a provisional antidumping duty of 20 per cent being imposed on all ball bearings and tapered roller bearings originating in Japan,[9] with the percentage fixed at 10 per cent for the products manufactured and exported by Nachi and Koyo. The Commission continued with further investigations, which included on the spot inspections of the European subsidiaries of the Japanese companies, and of the four major Japanese manufacturers offices in Japan. After further discussions between the Commission officials and the Japanese producers, the four major Japanese manufacturers agreed to give undertakings to the Commission that they would increase prices. A definitive measure, Council Regulation (EEC) No 1778/77, was then adopted applying antidumping duty on ball bearings and tapered roller bearings originating from Japan.[10] On the same date that this Regulation was adopted, the Commission accepted the undertakings given by the Japanese manufacturers. The undertakings were signed after the proposal had been sent to the Council, but before the Council had acted.

The Regulation imposed a definitive duty of 15 per cent (Article 1) but its application was suspended as long the price undertakings provided by the four major Japanese manufacturers were observed (Article 2). Furthermore, Article 3 authorised the collection of the amounts of provisional duty from the four major Japanese manufacturers to the extent that they did not exceed the 15 per cent duty imposed in Article 1. The actions for judicial review were brought before the Court of Justice by the four Japanese manufacturers and by a number of EU importers of these products to challenge the validity of Regulation 1778/77 in whole or in part. The applicants relied on the second paragraph of 173 EEC (now Article 263 TFEU) as to their standing to challenge the Council Regulation which was by its very nature classified as a general act. In *NTN Tokyo* Case the applicants sought only the annulment of Article 3 of Regulation 1778/77 arguing that the provision was not justified given undertakings had been given and accepted. Alternatively, they claimed that the dumping complaint had not been sufficiently established in law in accordance with the GATT Code and EU law.[11]

---

[8] Belgium, Denmark, Ireland, Luxembourg and the Netherlands. Italy had been given authorisation by the Commission to exclude imports of Japanese bearings that were in free circulation in other Member States.

[9] Commission Regulation (EEC) No 261/77 of 4 February 1977 imposing a provisional anti-dumping duty on ball bearings, tapered roller bearings and parts thereof originating in Japan [1977] OJ L34/60.

[10] See n 5.

[11] In Case 118/77 *ISO* sought a declaration that Regulation 1778/77 was void. In Case 119/77 *NSK* claimed nullity of Regulation 1778/77 and requested compensation. In Case 120/77 *Koyo Seiko* argued for a declaration that

III. THE OPINION OF AG WARNER

As already noted above, AG Warner delivered a single Opinion covering all the issues raised in the five cases. The analysis below will consider the Opinion of the AG in respect of the matters raised in the case of *NTN Tokyo* (Case 113/77), and on the critical views expressed by AG Warner on the lack of procedural safeguards in EU antidumping investigations.

The AG and the Court were broadly in agreement in respect of the admissibility of the actions,[12] and reached the same conclusions on substance, namely that both Article 3 and Regulation 1778/77 itself should be annulled. The Court concluded that Article 3 amounted to a 'collective decision relating to named addressees',[13] and that 'it is unlawful for one and the same anti-dumping investigation to be terminated on the one hand by the Commission's accepting an undertaking from the exporter or exporters to revise their prices at the same time as, on the other hand, by the imposition on the part of the Council, at the proposal of the Commission, of a definitive anti-dumping duty'.[14] The acceptance of undertakings terminated the proceedings according to Article 14 of the Antidumping Regulation. In the other four judgments, the Court decided in favour of the applicants, annulling Regulation 1778/77.[15]

However, as already indicated above, the most significant and influential aspect of the Opinion of AG Warner was the detailed and robust critique he provided of the manner in which the Commission undertook its antidumping investigation. He found the proceedings to have lacked transparency by failing to inform the appellants as to how the various prices had been computed, and thus preventing the appellants from being able to defend themselves. He considered such behaviour to be a breach of an essential procedural requirement as listed in what is now Article 263 TFEU.

IV. ANALYSIS

As in most cases, especially at the time,[16] the Court in the *Bearings I* judgments made no reference to the Opinion of the AG. Apart from the issue of admissibility, which was relevant to all five cases, the Court confined its *NTN Tokyo* judgment to the shortest possible route to a decision, namely giving the applicants what they had asked for, the annulment of Article 3. Thus in the *NTN Tokyo* the Court made no reference to the procedural irregularities pleaded by the appellants which were more pertinent to the legality of the Regulation itself. The Court focused on interpreting two articles in the Regulation (Articles 14(2) and Article 17), ruling it unlawful to terminate an antidumping investigation under one article and, at the same time, to impose a definitive antidumping duty under another article.[17]

Regulation 1778/77 was void. Finally, in Case 121/77 *NACHI* claimed that either Regulation 1778/77 or its Art 3 was void.

[12] They differed on the standing of the importer (Case 118/77, *ISO*). The Court did not follow the AG, and ruled that, in this particular case, *ISO* was not just an importer, but an exclusive one, so individually and directly concerned.

[13] Para 11. The AG considered the Regulation itself to be a hybrid measure. See section IV.A below.

[14] Para 17.

[15] In *NTN Tokyo*, the applicants sought the annulment only of Art 3 of the Regulation. The annulment of Regulation 1778/77 was sought in the other four *Bearings I* cases.

[16] For further analysis of the case law at that time, P Didier, 'EEC Anti-dumping Rules and Practices' (1980) 17 *CMLRev* 349; R Greaves, 'Judicial Review of Anti-Dumping Cases by European Court of Justice' (1985) 10 *ELRev* 135.

[17] Para 17 of the *NTN Tokyo* Judgment.

As for the Opinion of AG Warner, the most striking feature was his criticism of the Commission's exercise of its powers under Regulation 459/68. He concluded that the process lacked transparency, and failed to provide procedural safeguards to the undertakings involved in the investigation. It is not surprising that AG Warner expressed his views strongly on these matters, as AG Warner was a common law trained advocate from a legal system where procedural rights are fundamental to its legal system. He had already argued for rules of natural justice to be upheld by the Court in earlier cases where the Commission had carried out investigations of alleged breaches of the EU competition rules (now Articles 101 and 102 TFEU).[18] In many ways, investigations into alleged antidumping or anticompetitive practices are very similar.

The analysis provided below focuses first on the two issues which concerned the *NTN Tokyo* case: admissibility of the action (Section IV.A) and the lawfulness of the collection of the provisional duty after an acceptance of retrospective undertakings (Section IV.B). The subsequent sections thereafter focus on two failures identified and criticised by AG Warner. Section IV.C considers the lack of transparency of the antidumping investigation, whilst Section IV.D focuses on the rights to be heard and to be informed that should be embedded in antidumping investigations given the Commission's wide discretion. The Opinion of AG Warner is important for its criticism of the manner in which the Commission undertook dumping investigations. It is this forensic and detailed attack on the process that had material impact as to how the Commission discharged its role in future antidumping investigations. For example, the Antidumping Regulation was immediately amended to provide procedural safeguards along the lines proposed by the AG.[19]

A. Admissibility of the Action for Annulment

Antidumping duties are imposed by the Council after an investigation is carried out by the Commission to establish that dumping has taken place, and injury has been suffered by a European industry. The duties are imposed by regulation, a binding legislative act of general applicability, not addressed to individuals.

The question of admissibility of the action was robustly challenged by the Council. The Council requested the issue to be adjudicated separately from the substance, but was unsuccessful.[20] Detailed pleadings on admissibility were exchanged between the Council, the various applicants, and the intervener (FEBMA). The Council argued that antidumping measures are measures of commercial policy or international trade, and not subject to judicial review in the same manner as administrative acts. Thus, only privileged parties such as Member States or certain EU institutions have an automatic right to challenge their validity.

Nevertheless, under Article 173 EEC, natural or legal persons were able to challenge a regulation if they meet three conditions: show the act was really a decision; that it concerned

---

[18] In a number of Opinions delivered in earlier cases concerning the application of EU competition rules, AG Warner had already pressed for procedural safeguards for undertakings participating in a Commission investigation. In Case 17/74 *Transocean Marine Paint Association* ECLI:EU:C:106, AG Warner submitted that the *audi alteram partem* principle was at stake: 'the right to be heard forms part of those rights which "the law" referred to in Article [220] of the Treaty upholds, and of which, accordingly, it is the duty of this Court to ensure its observance' (at p 1089).

[19] See n 7.

[20] By Order of the President of the Court dated 12 April 1978, the preliminary objection made by the Council was joined to the main case.

them directly; and that it concerned them individually. Prior to the ruling in *NTN Tokyo*, there was uncertainty and controversy as to whether producers/manufacturers and importers could ever satisfy the conditions.

AG Warner reviewed prior relevant judgments of the Court, and approached the issue by categorising the applicants into three groups: the four major Japanese manufacturers; the subsidiaries and affiliates of these four Japanese manufacturers; and the independent importers. He examined the provisions of Regulation 1778/77 in detail, and concluded that the Japanese manufacturers and their subsidiaries and affiliates, who were named in the Regulation, were directly and individually concerned with the key provisions of this Regulation which 'has all the characteristics of a decision affecting particular persons on the basis of their own conduct'.[21] He considered this Regulation to be a hybrid instrument, but was careful to state that he did not consider every regulation imposing a definitive antidumping duty or providing for the collection of a provisional duty entitled the exporters concerned to have standing to challenge its validity. The Court followed the Opinion of AG Warner on this point, ruling that Article 3 constitutes a 'collective decision' in the context of the named addressees.[22] However, contrary to the AG's view, the Court ruled the action admissible also for ISO (the applicant in Case 118/77), who was an independent but exclusive importer. The Court reasoned that although the collection of provisional duties are of direct concern to all importers of the bearings, Article 3 had a special feature, namely that it did not concern all importers, but only those who had imported products manufactured by the named four Japanese undertakings in that article. Thus, the Court concluded all actions were admissible.

B. The Effect of an Acceptance of Undertakings Offered on the Closure of Antidumping Proceedings

As far as the applicants in *NTN Tokyo* were concerned, the legal consequence of the Commission having accepted the undertakings offered was the core argument of their application for annulment of Article 3 of the Regulation. Simply put, the argument was that the Council and the Commission could not lawfully accept undertakings concerning revised prices that were retrospective, and, at the same time, order the collection of the provisional duty. Furthermore, the regulation imposing the recovery, Regulation 1778/77, provided no reasoning as to why this had been done. The Opinion of AG Warner undertook a thorough analysis of the options available to the Commission to decide what to do with provisional duty when dumping and injury are established. He outlined three possible scenarios as to how the Commission might exercise its discretion in such a situation. He was indeed sympathetic to the difficulties facing the Council and the Commission in exercising their discretion, but he concluded the decision they took was arbitrary. He identified three main arguments submitted by the Council, but dismissed them all.

AG Warner's conclusions were followed by the Court, though via a more direct route. The Court focussed on the wording of Article 14(1) and (2)(a) of Council Regulation 459/68 (concerning the termination of proceedings) to mean that an undertaking by an exporter to revise prices, when accepted by Commission, terminated the proceedings. Thus, once the proceedings were terminated in accordance with Article 14(2)(a), the process ended. For the

[21] At pp 1245–46 of the Opinion.
[22] See n 13.

Court, neither the Council nor the Commission could resort to another provision of the Antidumping Regulation, namely Article 17, as authority to recover definitively amounts secured by way of provisional duty. The Court ruled that 'a combination of measures which are by their very nature contradictory would in fact be incompatible with the system laid down in the basic regulation'.[23]

C. Lack of Transparency in Dumping Investigations

AG Warner was very critical of the Commission's failure to disclose the methodology used for its price calculations and adjustments. He strongly condemned the lateness of the Commission to admit it had constructed the domestic prices. Such tardiness denied the Japanese exporters an opportunity during the investigation to make representations. Furthermore, by not revealing the relevant information until rejoinders were submitted in Cases 119/77 and 120/77, the Commission prevented these issues being properly discussed in the pleadings, and hindered the ability of the Court to reach conclusions on the issues.

In order to establish that there had been dumping, and to determine the dumping margin, the starting point was to calculate the domestic and the export price of the alleged dumped products as set out in Article 3 of the Antidumping Regulation. However, it became clear during the oral hearing and in the answers provided by the Commission to questions asked by the Court, that the Commission failed to disclose to the applicants the methods they used. This information was particularly important in this investigation, given the calculations were not straight forward for a number of reasons. First, the large number of different types of bearings which were sold in the EU (circa. 3,500) had to be reduced to a manageable number. The Commission decided to focus on the 16 representative types, which were selected by the complainants. Secondly, in order to determine the domestic and the export prices, the Commission decided to use weighted average prices since the investigation found considerable variations in price on individual transactions, even in respect of the same product from the same supplier. Furthermore, given the affiliation between the four major Japanese manufacturers and the importers, the export price had to be constructed as provided in the Antidumping Regulation.[24]

However, the Commission took the view that it had no obligation to disclose the calculations or anything to do with them, as for example, how they had used figures supplied by the manufacturers. The applicants struggled in not being able to question the Commission's findings during the investigation given the lack of information as to the method and figures used. For example, it was only during the proceedings before the Court, when submitting its rejoinder in one of the five cases,[25] that the Commission disclosed the percentage deductions it had made for costs from the resale of prices of each of the subsidiaries of the Japanese manufacturers. Similarly, only in the rejoinder, did the Commission state that after sending the proposal to the Council for the adoption of Regulation 1778/77, it had made further variations in the calculations without revealing what they were. Furthermore, the Commission updated domestic prices back to January 1977, and made further adjustments to the domestic price in May and June 1977, without informing the parties concerned. The above are only a few examples of the lack of transparency in antidumping investigations.

---

[23] Para 20 of the *NTN Tokyo* Judgment.
[24] Article 3(3).
[25] Case 119/77 NSK.

D. Procedural Safeguards: The Right to be Heard

It is evident that AG Warner was passionate about the right of parties under a Commission investigation to have procedural safeguards and, in particular, the right to be heard, and to know the evidence upon which the Commission will come to a decision. He considered the right to be heard to be a fundamental right based on the traditions of the EU Member States and, therefore, part of EU law. AG Warner stated:

> It is a fundamental principle of [EU] law that, before any individual measure or decision is taken, of such a nature as directly to affect the interests of a particular person, that person has a right to be heard by the responsible authority; and it is part and parcel of that principle that, in order to enable him effectively to exercise that right, the person concerned is entitled to be informed of the facts and considerations on the basis of which the authority is minded to act. That principle, which is enshrined in many a Judgment of this Court, and which applies regardless of whether there is a specific legislative text requiring its application, was re-asserted by the Court only yesterday in Case 85/76 *Hoffmann-La Roche& Co. AG v Commission*.[26]

He concluded that the Commission's duty in an antidumping investigation was to inform the parties 'as clearly and as fully as the circumstances permitted',[27] what was the case and evidence against them. His precise words demonstrate his frustration as to how the Commission handled the investigation. For him, it was conclusive proof of failure given that 'to this day, none of the Applicants (nor this Court) knows the actual margins of dumping the Commission, as a result of the investigations preceding the adoption of Regulation No 1778/77, found to have been practised by each of the Big Four nor whereabouts in the [EU] it found those margins to have been practised. Much less do any of those Applicants (or we) know how, precisely, those margins were calculated'.[28] Thus, the AG had no hesitation in concluding that an infringement of an essential procedural requirement within the meaning of what is now Article 263 TFEU had occurred, and therefore the Regulation itself should be declared void.

AG Warner was right in pressing for such a right in antidumping investigations where an administrative body (the Commission) acts as investigator, depositor of information, prosecutor, and judge. The EU's antidumping regime not only empowers the Commission to investigate and analyse complex economic situations, but also grants it a wide discretion to propose to the Council that a definitive duty be imposed on specific products from a named third country. Those undertakings, whose interests are directly affected, should have a right to access the evidence against them and to be heard.

E. Effect on Subsequent Antidumping Legislation and Case Law

The Opinion of AG Warner in *Bearings I* had an impact on the development of the EU's antidumping law both in terms of legislation and case law. Within three months, a Commission proposal for an amendment of the Antidumping Regulation was tabled, acknowledging that experience had shown that concepts contained in the Regulation needed clarification and drawing the attention of the Council specifically to the 'guidance given recently by the European

---

[26] At p 1261.
[27] At p 1265.
[28] At p 1265.

Court of Justice and in particular by the opinions expressed by the Advocate General'.[29] In August 1979, Regulation (EEC) No 1681/79 was adopted amending the Antidumping Regulation.[30] Article 3 and Article 4(1), (2) and (3) were replaced by new provisions. The new Article 3 clarified the meaning of the concepts of 'export rice' and 'normal value' of the product and set out detailed rules as to how these prices were to be established under a number of different scenarios. The new Article 4(1), (2) an (3) expanded the evidence needed to establish injury to a European industry. Thus, the Commission's discretion was reduced.

AG Warner was also highly critical of the lack of procedural safeguards to protect those being investigated. This was acknowledged by replacing Article 10(4) with a new text setting out, in detail, the various rights that complainants, importers, and exporters have to access information, and in accordance with a precise timetable to prevent delays in supply. As demonstrated above, there is clear evidence that AG Warner's criticisms led to greater disclosure of information and transparency, as well as recognition that the imposition of antidumping duties is the result of an administrative investigation, the results of which can have legal and detrimental effects on the undertakings concerned. This was an important concession for the EU to recognise that antidumping measures may have their legal basis in the EU's Common Commercial Policy (Article 207 TFEU), but its implementation remains an administrative procedure subject to the EU's legal order and all that such entails, namely, due process, procedural safeguards, and judicial review by the Court.

As far as the impact of the Opinion is concerned on subsequent case law, this is less clear. Less than 10 years later, in *Bearings II* cases,[31] the Court significantly retreated from reviewing the Commission's discretion in dumping investigations.[32] Nevertheless, until *Bearings II*, it is submitted the Court was generous in allowing producers, exporters and complainants to challenge regulations imposing antidumping duties. If the producers and exporters were expressly named in the regulation, then they clearly had automatic standing.[33] Producers and exporters were also granted standing when they could demonstrate they had been identified in the regulation or, they had participated in the Commission's investigation.[34]

However, the same generosity was not evident in respect of importers who are normally not identified in the regulation. In *Alusuisse Italia v Council and Commission*,[35] the Court denied standing to an importer, distinguishing the *Bearings I* case on the grounds the importer in *Alusuisse* was not an *exclusive* importer of the named producers who had been dumping products in the EU market. Yet as regards the complainant, as mentioned above, antidumping investigations start as a result of a complaint from an EU industry. Questions rightly arise about the extent that complainants have standing to challenge either a Commission refusal to

---

[29] Commission, 'Proposal for a Council Regulation (EEC) amending Regulation (EEC) No 459/68 on protection against dumping or the granting of bounties or subsidies by countries which are not members of the European Economic Community' COM (1979) 304 final.

[30] See n 7. For a discussion of the amendments see P De Smedt, 'The EEC Anti-dumping Policy: New Developments' (1980) 14 *The International Lawyer* 223.

[31] Appeals by the same Japanese undertakings as for *Bearings I*, but with different outcomes. The Court found in favour of the Council and the Commission on almost every procedural and substantial point raised by the Applicants. See eg Case 240/84 *NTN Toyo Bearing Co* ECLI:EU:C:1987:202.

[32] For a comprehensive review of the antidumping case law see JK Lockett, 'EEC Antidumping Law and Trade Policy after *Ballbearings II*: Discretionary Decisions Masquerading as Legal Process' (1987) 8 *Northwestern Journal of International Law and Business* 365.

[33] Case 236/81 *Celanese Chemical Co* ECLI:EU:C:1982:115.

[34] Joined Cases 239/82 and 275/82 *Allied Corpn* ECLI:EU:C:1984:68.

[35] Case 307/81 *Alusuisse Italia* ECLI:EU:C:1982:115.

investigate, or a Commission's finding at the end of an investigation. In *FEDIOL*,[36] the Court ruled that a complainant had a legitimate interest and had standing to seek judicial review of a Commission decision not to investigate the complaint. Finally, in *Timex*,[37] standing was allowed to a complainant, who was not named in the regulation, to challenge a regulation imposing an antidumping duty considered by the complainant to have been insufficient.

In conclusion, the main contribution of the Opinion of AG Warner in *Bearings I* to the development of EU antidumping law lies in the immediate amendment to the Antidumping Regulation which reduced the Commission's unfettered discretion, and strengthened the rights of undertakings in antidumping investigations.

---

[36] Case 191/82 *FEDIOL* ECLI:EU:C:1983:259.
[37] Case 264/82 *Timex* ECLI:EU:C:1985:119.

12

Free Movement of Goods and the Public Morality Exception: Opinion of Advocate General *Warner in* Henn and Darby

ADAM CYGAN

I. INTRODUCTION

THE EUROPEAN UNION comprises a customs union which covers all trade in goods, and which involves the prohibition between Member States of customs duties on imports and exports and of all charges having equivalent effect, as well as the adoption of a common customs tariff in their relations with third countries, with no derogations written into the text of the EU Treaties. In addition, quantitative restrictions on imports and exports between Member States, and all measures having equivalent effect, are also prohibited, but subject to the derogations within Article 36 TFEU[1] on grounds of public morality, public policy or public security; the protection of health and life of humans, animals or plants; the protection of national treasures possessing artistic, historic or archaeological value; or the protection of industrial and commercial property. In relation to the justification of public morality, which was at issue in the case of *Henn and Darby*,[2] the Court sought to maintain a balance between the protection of free movement rights and a recognition that moral sensitivities, protected through national laws, cannot be completely ignored.

The list of derogations in Article 36 TFEU, all of which relate to non-economic interests,[3] are interpreted narrowly by the Court. Moreover, any measure, including one for the protection of public morality, must also respect the principle of proportionality and the burden of proof in justifying the measures adopted under Article 36 TFEU lies with the Member State.[4] However, when a Member State provides convincing justifications, it is then for the Commission to show that the measures taken are not appropriate in that particular case.[5]

---

[1] The Court has also developed the *Cassis de Dijon* line of indistinctly applicable derogations, mandatory requirements, which are broader than those contained in Art 36 TFEU, eg protection of the environment and the consumer, etc.

[2] Case 34/79 *Henn and Darby* ECLI:EU:C:1979:295, p 3795; Opinion of AG Warner in Case 34/79 *Henn and Darby* ECLI:EU:C:1979:246.

[3] Case C-120/95 *Nicolas Decker* ECLI:EU:C:1998:167; Case 72/83 *Campus Oil* ECLI:EU:C:1984:256. On the application of the public policy derogation in *Campus Oil* see ch 17.

[4] Case 251/78 *Firma Denkavit* ECLI:EU:C:1979:252.

[5] Case C-55/99 *Commission v France* ECLI:EU:C:2000:693.

Even if a measure is justifiable under Article 36 TFEU, it must not, according to the second sentence of Article 36 TFEU, 'constitute a means of arbitrary discrimination or a disguised restriction on trade between Member States'. This second part of Article 36 TFEU was designed to avoid abuse on the part of Member States. As the Court stated in *Henn and Darby*, 'the function of the second sentence of Article [36 TFEU] is to prevent restrictions on trade based on the grounds mentioned in the first sentence from being diverted from their proper purpose and used in such a way as to create discrimination in respect of goods originating in other Member States or indirectly to protect certain national products',[6] i.e., to adopt what are essentially protectionist measures.

Member States may therefore decide to ban a product on grounds that it infringes standards of public morality. While it is up to each Member State to set the standards enabling goods to comply with national provisions concerning morality, discretion must be exercised in conformity with the obligations arising under EU law. For example, any prohibition on imports of products, the marketing of which is restricted but not prohibited, will be discriminatory and in breach of the free movement of goods provisions. Most of the cases, including *Henn and Darby*, involved facts where the Court admitted that the public morality justification concerns obscene or indecent articles, and where the Member State argued that there was no domestic market for the goods at all.[7] In other cases where the public morality justification has been invoked, other interlinked justifications were found, for example, a public interest justification in gambling cases,[8] or the protection of minors in the case of marking of videos and DVDs with an age restriction.[9] These cases confirm that the public morality exception is to be very narrowly construed.

II. BACKGROUND, CONTEXT, AND FACTS

Henn and Darby was the first preliminary reference made to the Court by the House of Lords.[10] It was also the first case in which the Court was called upon to consider the scope of the exception in Article 36 TFEU for prohibitions or restrictions on the free movement of goods between Member States which were to be justified on grounds of public morality. The facts of the case concerned the importation of pornographic material into the UK, which was on sale in other Member States, but for which there was no legal market in the UK. Henn and Darby imported a range of pornographic materials from the Netherlands, having originated in Denmark, Germany, and Sweden (the last of which was not an EU Member State at the time), and they were charged with fraudulently evading the prohibition on the importation of indecent or obscene articles, contrary to Section 42 Customs Consolidation Act 1876 and Section 304 Customs and Excise Act 1952. In particular, Section 42 of the 1876 prohibited the *importation* into the UK of 'indecent or obscene' articles, and provided that articles imported contrary to the prohibition shall be forfeited and may be destroyed or otherwise disposed of as the Commissioners of Customs may direct. Section 304 of the 1952 Act also made it a criminal offence for any person to be in any way 'knowingly concerned in the fraudulent evasion or attempted evasion of the prohibition on importation'.

---

[6] Page 3815 of the Judgment.

[7] See also, Case 121/85 *Conegate* ECLI:EU:C:1986:114. See ch 21.

[8] See further, Case C-275/92 *Schindler* ECLI:EU:C:1994:119; Case C-124/97 *Markku Juhani Läärä* ECLI:EU:C:1999:435; Case C-98/14 *Berlington Hungary Tanácsadó és Szolgáltató kft* ECLI:EU:C:2015:386.

[9] Case C-244/06 *Dynamic Medien Vertriebs GmbH* ECLI:EU:C:2008:85.

[10] *R v Henn and Darby* [1981] AC 850.

At the outset of the trial, an application was made to the trial judge by counsel acting for both defendants to quash the charges relating to the infringement of the 1876 Act. Relying on the direct effect of EU law, the defendants argued that following accession of the United Kingdom to the EU, by reason of Section 2(1) and Schedule I, part 1, paragraph 2 of the European Communities Act 1972, Article 34 TFEU invalidated Section 42 of the Customs Consolidation Act 1876, in so far as it related to goods coming from another EU Member State. But this application was rejected by the trial judge. The appellants thus pleaded 'Not Guilty' to the charge, and though the application was renewed at the end of the case for the prosecution, it was again rejected. Both appellants were convicted, and on 15 July 1977 they were sentenced, with Henn receiving a custodial term of 18 months imprisonment, and Darby was sentenced to two years imprisonment. They were further ordered to pay a financial penalty.

Both appellants appealed against their convictions. The appeals were heard by the Court of Appeal (Criminal Division) on 4 to 7 July 1978.[11] The Court of Appeal refused to refer any questions to the Court under the preliminary reference procedure under what is now Article 267 TFEU, and dismissed the appeals, and refused leave to appeal to the House of Lords. The Court of Appeal certified, in accordance with Section 33 of the Criminal Appeal Act 1968, that a point of law of general public importance was involved in the appeals, namely 'Whether s.42 of the Customs Consolidation Act 1876 is effective to prevent the importation of pornographic articles from Holland, notwithstanding Articles [34 and 36 TFEU]'.[12] In response to this point of law, the Court of Appeal answered that import restrictions which are *prima facie* in conflict with Article 34 TFEU may be imposed on articles of an indecent or obscene character on the grounds of public morality as determined by the Member State, under Article 36 TFEU. Moreover, Lord Widgery in the Court of Appeal held,[13] incorrectly in the view of the House of Lords and Court, that the reference in Article 34 TFEU to quantitative restrictions did not include a total prohibition on imports, and so, in his view, this provision of the EU Treaties was not relevant in this case.

On 9 November 1978, leave to appeal was granted to both appellants by an Appeal Committee of the House of Lords. On 29 January 1979, on the hearing of the appeals, the House determined that a question of interpretation of Article 36 TFEU *did* arise, and should be referred to the Court in accordance with what is now Article 267 TFEU. The House of Lords considered that the case raised questions of whether a total ban on imports may constitute a quantitative restriction within the meaning of Article 34 TFEU. Lord Diplock in particular highlighted that, under the *Dassonville*[14] formula, the free movement of goods had been, *prima facie*, impeded by the total ban. Secondly, the House of Lords asked if the answer to this question is in the affirmative, did the first sentence of Article 36 TFEU upon its true construction mean that a Member State may lawfully impose prohibitions on the importation of goods from another Member State which are of an indecent or obscene character as understood by the laws of that Member State. In total, the House of Lords referred seven questions the Court. On the reference, the Court held that, (1) the restriction was *prima facie* a restriction in conflict with Article 34 TFEU, but, (2) a Member State could nevertheless impose such restrictions under Article 36 TFEU on the grounds of public morality, as determined by the Member State in accordance with its own values and applying the approximate domestic law.

---

[11] *R v Henn and Darby* [1978] 1 WLR 1031.
[12] ibid, at 1033.
[13] ibid, at 1037.
[14] Case 8/74 *Dassonville* ECLI:EU:C:1974:82.

On receipt of the judgment of the Court by the House of Lords, their Lordships held that the jury had correctly found this pornographic material as falling within the prohibition of the 1876 Act, and that there had been no arbitrary discrimination or disguised restriction on trade within the second sentence of Article 36 TFEU.[15] The appeal was therefore dismissed, and the House of Lords upheld the convictions. Moreover, the trial jury had also found, in relation to other counts against the appellants, that the materials were of such a character as to fall under the prohibition contained within the Obscene Publications Acts of 1959 and 1964 which prevented the *publication* and *dissemination* of these types of materials in the UK, irrespective of their source.[16] On this application of the UK legislation and Article 36 TFEU, it followed that there had not been any arbitrary discrimination or disguised restriction of trade between Member States under Article 34 TFEU. Thus, while it was important to recognise that the 1876 and 1959 and 1964 Acts have somewhat different purposes, and could apply to different types of materials, it was relevant to note that many materials in this case fell within the ambit of all of these laws. Under this statutory regime, there was no lawful market in the UK for these types of materials, whether imported or domestically produced materials.

III. THE OPINION OF AG WARNER

Both the Opinion of AG Warner and the judgment of the Court were pragmatic responses to the application of the public morality exception to the free movement rules.[17] The recognition that this derogation raised sensitive questions of what constitutes 'public morality', and that its understanding may vary across the Member States, was implicit in the Opinion and the judgment.[18] That said, both the AG and the Court recognised that, when assessing whether a Member State has satisfied the public morality exception, this must be done within the framework of the EU free movement rules, and that the use of this justification should not be for the purposes of a disguised restriction of trade. Thus, the identification of a public morality justification must be a *genuine* one, which manifests itself through both policy and legal restrictions that operate in a non-discriminatory manner. However, the reasoning on how to arrive at this assessment of the national measures differed between that of the AG and the Court.

In his Opinion, AG Warner stated that Article 36 TFEU is to be interpreted strictly because 'it comes directly from the fundamental principle of free movement of goods within the EU'.[19] In assessing the compatibility of the UK legislation with Article 36 TFEU, the AG adopted what could be described as a 'reasonableness test', which required that national laws prohibit the same domestic articles, and that this prohibition must be reasonable. Non-discrimination was important, but the requirement that the restriction must also be reasonable meant that the restriction must be proportionate.[20] This requirement of proportionality, as explained by AG Warner, was very much along the lines of the subsequent

---

[15] *R v Henn and Darby* [1981] AC 850 at 904.

[16] The scope of these Acts is expansive, applying to anything to be viewed or read, including sound recordings, films, or other records of a picture or pictures. Moreover, the geographical scope of the Obscene Publications Acts is very broad, applying to any materials or articles distributed, sold, or otherwise 'published' within the borders of the UK.

[17] See further D Doukas, 'Morality, Free Movement and Judicial Restraint at the European Court of Justice' in P Koutrakos et al (eds), *Exceptions from EU Free Movement Law: Derogation, Justification and Proportionality* (Oxford, Hart Publishing, 2016).

[18] See G McFarlane, 'Indecency and Obscenity: The View from Europe' (1990) 140 *New Law Journal* 50.

[19] At p 3824.

[20] ibid, p 3795.

reasoning of AG Jacobs in *Leclerc*,[21] and should be the least restrictive measure by which the objective could be attained, and that there were no alternative means available to the UK. On the facts of the case, especially because of the complete legal prohibition on the import, manufacture, and sale of the goods in the UK, AG Warner concluded that the UK had satisfied this requirement of reasonableness through its total ban.

Though arriving at broadly the same conclusion as the AG, that the ban could be justified under Article 36 TFEU, the Court focused on the 'intent' of the UK legislation, rather than whether it was reasonable and proportionate. For the Court, the primary issue was whether the objective and purpose of the UK legislation was to protect public morality. The Court held that though UK customs laws were stricter than the domestic laws, which had prohibited the sale and distribution of pornographic material, the customs law could not be considered as a measure the purpose of which was to arbitrarily discriminate against goods from other states, or to protect a national product.[22] In the light of the development of the Court's case law, especially in relation to proportionality, non-discrimination, and market access,[23] the AG's approach would be viewed as the preferable interpretation. This was especially true, in this instance, because the legislation at issue, the Customs Consolidation Act, was enacted in 1876, and it is questionable whether it was really possible for the Court to determine the legislative intent of legislation that is comparatively old.

IV. ANALYSIS

The EU aims to preclude national measures if they discriminate against imported goods in a protectionist manner in order to overcome obstacles that divergences among national standards may otherwise present. Yet, even when goods lawfully enter or are manufactured in the EU's internal market, Member States may still impose, as a matter of exception to the general rule, diverging standards for moral reasons. To this extent, Member States enjoy a considerable margin of discretion when it comes to the moral demarcation of the internal market space of free movement, demonstrated by a 'hands off approach' of the Court in its case law that addresses the justification of *genuine* public morality exceptions.[24]

On the facts, the public morality exception had an explicit objective in *Henn and Darby*, and the Court held that 'in principle, it is for each Member State to determine in accordance with its own scale of values and judgment of its appropriate form, the requirements of public morality in its territory'.[25] Thus, a Member State must first establish the existence of a threat to public morality covered by the first sentence of Article 36 TFEU. Thereafter, it was necessary to demonstrate, in addition, that the national measures taken to protect public morality correspond with the demands of the second sentence of Article 36 TFEU, which included an assessment of the principles of proportionality.

---

[21] Opinion of AG Jacobs in Case C-412/93 *Leclerc-Siplec* ECLI:EU:C:1994:393, p 179. See ch 35.

[22] For an argument that the law in *Henn and Darby* did discriminate against the imported goods, see L Catchpole and A Barav, 'The Public Morality Exception and the Free Movement of Goods: Justification of a Dual Standard in National Legislation?' (1980) 1 *LIEI* 1.

[23] See eg Case 405/98 *Gourmet International* ECLI:EU:C:2001:135.

[24] Compare the reasoning in Case 121/85 *Conegate*, p 1007, with that in Case 34/79 *Henn and Darby*, p 3797.

[25] At p 3813 of the Judgment.

A. The Public Morality Exception and the Free Movement of Goods

The general structure of Article 36 TFEU offers a list of potential justifications, including that of public morality, but Article 36 TFEU also issues a stern warning that any justification will be scrutinised carefully to ensure that it is genuine. A justification on grounds of public morality allows the maintenance of barriers to inter-EU trade that are hostile to the free movement of goods, and in in common with other derogations such as those in Article 45(3) TFEU as regards the free movement of workers, to be interpreted narrowly. Furthermore, the Court was absolutely unwilling to extend the scope of available heads of justification in Article 36 TFEU beyond those specifically laid down.[26] On this point, the Court confirmed Lord Diplock's view, and rejected the interpretation of the Court of Appeal that Article 36 TFEU embraces only a partial, but not a total prohibition on imports.[27]

Thus, for a claim of public morality under Article 36 TFEU to be successful, the UK needed to demonstrate unequivocally that the pornography in question was not lawfully available within the UK, and that the UK actively prevented the availability of such materials. In the absence of effective internal controls of such obscene material in the UK, it would be readily apparent that the alleged claim of an impact on public morality would be no more than a restriction that protected domestic trade from competition.[28] Putting aside the variation in rules across the jurisdictions of the UK, the House of Lords, applying the reasoning of the Court, was satisfied that there was in existence a UK-wide internal ban on this type of pornographic material.[29] On this narrow and prescriptive application of the public morality derogation in Article 36 TFEU, the measures taken by the UK were justified and compatible with EU law, and so the convictions of both Henn and Darby stood.

B. Public Morality and the Test of 'Reasonableness'

Despite the different reasoning, the Opinion of AG Warner and the judgment of the Court both 'walked the tightrope' of balancing competing interests of national law and EU law, and recognised that questions of public morality were often rooted in domestic religious or historical traditions.[30] AG Warner pointed out that other derogations in Article 36 TFEU, namely the protection of indications of origin, of consumers generally, and of the health and life of humans, animals or plants, were matters which were capable of an objective assessment, in order to determine whether the Member States' action was justified. Moreover, these

---

[26] See Case 113/80 *Commission v Ireland* ECLI:EU:C:1981:139, p 1625 and Case 72/83 *Campus Oil*, p 2727.

[27] *R v Henn and Darby* [1981] AC 850 at 904–906.

[28] The Obscene Publications Acts did not extend to Scotland or to Northern Ireland. Although the laws regulating and restricting obscenity were not uniform throughout the United Kingdom, the Court held that these variations were irrelevant. The fundamental concepts that they embodied were still to be understood as being uniformly applied. See p 3813 of the Judgment.

[29] The Court indicated that notwithstanding national diversity, for these purposes a unitary view of the UK's system could be taken by looking at the overall scope. It would have been far more integrationist but challenging regional diversity if the it had insisted that the UK could impose restrictions no stricter than the most relaxed applied anywhere in the UK.

[30] See further F de Witte, 'Sex, Drugs & EU Law: The Recognition of Moral and Ethical Diversity in EU Law' (2013) 50 *CMLRev* 1545. De Witte states that the Court is sometimes called upon to rule on the interaction of EU law with 'national norms that express a certain moral, ethical or cultural value'. He further explains, such category of norms 'ascribe a normative quality to a particular type of life, and typically reflect a communal, political understanding of what is "good"'.

are also derogations for which, the AG considered, it was possible for the EU to prescribe a solution through the adoption of harmonising legislation that would be applicable uniformly in all Member States, and which would eliminate the need for Member States to resort to national prohibitions and restrictions permitted by Article 36 TFEU.[31]

By contrast, with respect to the public morality derogation, AG Warner recognised that a different approach was required. This was because, in his view, the concept of 'public morality' was not one that can be made the subject of objective assessment, or of an EU-wide definition.[32] Morality was to be understood, for him, as a matter of individual opinion, rather than of expert opinion. When deciding upon the right approach to the interpretation of the phrase 'justified on grounds of public morality', AG Warner looked for assistance from the European Convention on Human Rights (ECHR). By drawing upon the case law of the European Court of Human Rights (ECtHR), the AG formed part of a tradition within the Court, in which the Court's judgments were benchmarked against compatibility with the standard of protection of rights under the ECHR, a strategy which the Court had already used in order to promote legitimacy of its judgments.[33] AG Warner referred to paragraphs 48 and 49 of the judgment of the ECtHR in *Handyside*,[34] where the ECtHR considered the proper interpretation of Article 10 ECHR concerning freedom of expression. Specifically, the ECtHR considered the proper interpretation of the exception Article 10(2) ECHR which provided for 'such ... restrictions or penalties as are prescribed by law and are necessary in a democratic society ... for the protection of ... morals ...'.

In addressing the issue in *Henn and Darby* concerning the understanding of the concept of 'public morality', AG Warner quoted directly from *Handyside*. In doing so, the AG could be said to interpret the understanding of public morality in EU law through an interpretation which chimes with a principle of subsidiarity in the broader sense, namely, that questions of 'public morality' which reflected national values, and would be more appropriately decided at the national level, rather than EU level. He stated:

> In particular, it is not possible to find in the domestic law of the various Contracting States a uniform European conception of morals. The view taken by their respective laws of the requirements of morals varies from time to time and from place to place, especially in our era which is characterized by a rapid and far-reaching evolution of opinions on the subject. By reason of their direct and continuous contact with the vital forces of their countries, State authorities are in principle in a better position than the international judge to give an opinion on the exact content of these requirements as well as on the 'necessity' of a 'restriction' or 'penalty' intended to meet them. The Court notes at this juncture that ... the adjective 'necessary', within the meaning of Article 10 para. 2, is not synonymous with 'indispensable'....[35]

The reference to *Handyside* by AG Warner was important because it simultaneously provided latitude to recognise the definition of public morality in the UK, while still leaving room to manoeuvre in order to recognise the importance of free movement rights. The AG stated that Article 36 TFEU was to be interpreted strictly because it came directly from the fundamental principle of free movement of goods within the EU Treaties.[36] To this extent, his aim to define

---

[31] Page 3820 of the Opinion.
[32] ibid, p 3821.
[33] Case 11/70 *Internationale Handelsgesellschaft* ECLI:EU:C:1970:114.
[34] *Handyside v United Kingdom* (1979) 1 EHRR 737.
[35] At pp 3821–22.
[36] ibid, p 3823.

the outer limits of the public morality derogation was an exercise in balancing the competing interests of national rules and EU fundamental freedoms. The AG viewed the interpretation of Article 10 ECHR by the ECtHR as offering a solution in the case through the margin of discretion under Article 10 (2) ECHR for contracting states, but that also, this discretion was not without limits. As he put it:

> Consequently, Article 10 para. 2 leaves to the Contracting States a margin of appreciation .... Nevertheless, Article 10 para. 2 does not give the Contracting States an unlimited power of appreciation .... The domestic margin of appreciation ... goes hand in hand with a European supervision .... This means, amongst other things, that every ... 'restriction' or 'penalty' imposed in this sphere must be *proportionate* to the legitimate aim pursued.[37] (emphasis added)

The reliance on this part of the ECtHR's *Handyside* judgment was significant because, notwithstanding the recognition that Member States preserved a discretion to define their own policies, standards, and values with respect to public morality, the concept of public morality must, nevertheless, still have a clear boundary. Implicit in this was the need for proportionality of national measures and that alternative, less restrictive means, should be used if possible. As AG Warner noted, this limit to the margin of appreciation had already been recognised by the Court when it had applied the public policy derogation within Article 45 TFEU in judgments such as *van Duyn*[38] and *Bouchereau*.[39] In these judgments, the Court considered that the use of the public policy derogation by Member States in the free movement of persons case law should be benchmarked against the principle of proportionality, and that national measures should not go beyond what is necessary to achieve the objective sought by the Member State. In doing so, AG Warner explained that, in a case such as *Henn and Darby*, where the application of Article 36 TFEU was at issue, reasonableness and proportionality are 'the same concept' or that, at least, 'proportionality is an aspect of reasonableness'.[40]

Following on from this, though the AG accepted that the margin of appreciation for public morality has been cast wide, and arguably wider than the public policy derogation under Article 45 TFEU, there would still need to be a boundary. Accordingly, it would be for the Court to consider the point at which national rules may become a restriction on trade under Article 34 TFEU, and an assessment of the reasonableness and proportionality of those national rules would be required. On this analysis, the AG noted that in the case of a book that was prohibited by the Customs Consolidation Act, but legally sold in England, it would be difficult to conclude that the discrimination was justified under Article 36 TFEU.[41]

C. The Intention of National Legislation

In his analysis, AG Warner therefore offered a different solution to that adopted by the Court when seeking to reconcile these two competing interests of public morality and the fundamental right of free movement. The Court's reasoning adopted a test in which it considered the intention and purpose of the UK legislation and, in particular, whether the laws in question

---

[37] ibid, p 3824.
[38] Case 41/74 *van Duyn* ECLI:EU:C:1974:133.
[39] Case 30/77 *Bouchereau* ECLI:EU:C:1977:172. See ch 10.
[40] At p 3831.
[41] At p 3832.

have the 'purpose' of arbitrarily discriminating against the goods of other Member States.[42] In *Henn and Darby*, the primary argument of the UK government was that the prohibition on the importation of indecent or obscene publications in the Customs Consolidation Act 1876 ban was justified on grounds coming within the public morality exception in Article 36 TFEU. Thus, the Court had to determine what factors would enable it to determine that the ban was justified. Unlike the AG, who considered whether the ban on grounds of public morality was reasonable and proportionate, the Court focused on the *purpose* of the second sentence of Article 36 TFEU, which stated that restrictions under any of the derogations within Article 36 TFEU shall not 'constitute a means of arbitrary discrimination or a disguised restriction on trade between Member States'.[43]

It is clear from this that the overriding objective of the second sentence was (and is) to prevent Member States from adopting domestic laws which may constitute arbitrary discrimination, or are protectionist, whilst suggesting that the purpose of that legislation was to protect public morality. But in order for the Court to do this, it first had to arrive at a clear understanding of what the intention of the legislature was when it adopted the law. The Court, having weighed up the facts, came to the conclusion the UK Parliament had the primary purpose of protecting public morality when it legislated for the Customs Consolidation Act 1876. Moreover, the Court further stated that the fact that the 1876 Act, which restricted importation, was stricter than the domestic laws which concerned the sale and distribution of such goods did not, *per se*, suggest that the 1876 Act was deliberately designed to arbitrarily discriminate against goods from other states, or to protect a national product.[44] Thus, the implication from the Court was clear: in order to breach Article 36 TFEU, lawmakers must have actually intended to unfairly discriminate or to protect a national product through the domestic legislation.

While the Court's reasoning may be viewed as pragmatic, like the AG, the Court was also mindful of the cultural, political, and legal sensitivities of the case, and thus, the reasoning was not without some difficulty. For example, measuring the precise intention of a legislature is difficult, even in a state such as the UK where guidance for the drafting of parliamentary legislation emphasises the importance of expressing with clarity Parliament's intention,[45] and which is designed to keep judicial interpretation to a minimum.[46] Furthermore, though the Customs Consolidation Act 1876 clearly had the intention to prevent the importation of goods which violated public morality, the legislation was passed in 1876. On the question of whether Parliament's intention from 1876 was clearly ascertainable, in particular, on the question considered by the Court that this legislation was intended to discriminate against goods from other states, there must be some doubt.[47]

---

[42] Pages 3815–17.

[43] ibid, p 3815. For more on the relationship between the two sentences of Art 36 TFEU, see JHH Weiler, 'Europornography – First Reference of the House of Lords to the European Court of Justice' (1981) 44 *MLR* 91, 92.

[44] At p 3815.

[45] Office of the Parliamentary Counsel Drafting Guidance, June 2020, pp 1–3, available at https://assets. publishing.service.gov.uk/government/uploads/system/uploads/attachment_data/file/892409/OPC_drafting_guidance_June_2020-1.pdf.

[46] There is one exception to this arising from the judgment in *Pepper v Hart* [1993] AC 593, whereby, if primary legislation is ambiguous or obscure the courts may, in certain circumstances, take account of statements made in Parliament by ministers or other promoters of a Bill in construing the application of that legislation. However, such legislative construction was not an alternative, throughout UK membership of the EU, to a UK court seeking a preliminary reference under Art 267 TFEU by which a UK court would seek clarification on the interpretation and application of EU law in instances of ambiguity or uncertainty. Arguably this was the position of the House of Lords in *Henn and Darby* when it made the preliminary reference request.

[47] See further CG McClister, 'Prohibition of Obscene Imports in the United Kingdom – A Violation of Article 36 of the Treaty Establishing the European Community?' (1995) 13 *Penn State International Law Review* 329.

The Court's judgment thus concluded that a prohibition of certain imports was justified, so long as there was no intentional abuse of Article 36 TFEU, which it considered was the UK's position in *Henn and Darby*.[48] But this reasoning was only relevant in circumstances when a restriction only needs only be justified because there is discriminatory treatment between national and foreign goods. If, as on the facts of this case, the imported goods are also prohibited domestically, there could be no actual discrimination on the part of the Member State, because the imported products and domestic goods were regulated in an identical manner. However, looking at the intention of the legislation, as the Court did, when there is no lawful product in the goods, is problematic. If there were to be a lawful domestic trade in the goods there, this would have been arbitrary discrimination, regardless of what the legislature intended to achieve.

Perhaps what distinguishes the AG's reasoning from the Court's is that the AG was prepared to consider the purpose of the public morality exception in Article 36 TFEU. AG Warner expressly rejected the approach subsequently adopted by the Court to consider the intention of the legislation. He noted that:

> Although the expression 'a means of arbitrary discrimination' in the second sentence of Article 36 may seem at first sight to call for an enquiry into the intentions of those who enacted the measure under consideration .... I cannot believe that the authors of Article 36 meant its application to depend on the outcome of such an enquiry, which would manifestly be impracticable, and indeed unrealistic, in most cases.[49]

What is clear from this statement is that AG Warner focused on where the boundary of public morality lay, thereby taking a more 'universal' approach to this derogation and its future application. This would, in most instances, be in circumstances where the facts were less clear cut than in *Henn and Darby*, where there may exist different treatment of imported and domestic products, and the subject matter of such a dispute would not involve strong pornographic material, where a total prohibition on importation was not unreasonable. But it would not be unreasonable to assume that public opinion may also come to a conclusion that even if the UK's actions did breach Article 36 TFEU, and were overtly discriminatory, preventing the importation of such pornographic material was ultimately a good thing, and that such action would not be disproportionate.

The Court, perhaps mindful of this risk of 'moral outrage', and not wanting to get involved in a debate about what constitutes 'public morality' within the UK, or any other Member State for that matter, adopted a more 'one-dimensional' approach through its legislative intent reasoning than the reasonableness and proportionality tests in the Opinion of AG Warner. Had the Court followed the AG's reasoning, this would almost certainly have necessitated the Court making some value judgments about UK standards of public morality. Legislative intent provided the Court with a convenient strategy, through which it could sidestep such questions of reasonableness and the outer reaches of the public morality derogation, and instead focus on the narrower question of the purpose of the UK legislation which, on the facts, was unquestionably within the Article 36 TFEU derogation. The Court, however, recognised that questions of reasonableness of national measures were also important, and a derogation by a Member State on grounds of public morality could necessitate that, in the future, it would examine the scope and application of Article 36 TFEU derogations.[50] But implicit in the

---

[48] At p 3817.
[49] ibid, p 3827.
[50] ibid, p 3815.

Court's approach was that this was for another day, when the subject matter at issue before the Court would be less sensitive, and when a decision to deny a Member State the derogation may be less controversial.

D. Effect on Future Case Law

The concept of 'public morality', which both the AG and Court accepted, varied across the Member States, and left open the possibility that this Article 36 TFEU derogation could be used liberally by Member States. Several years after *Henn and Darby*, the application of the derogation arose again in *Conegate*, which concerned the import of life-size inflatable dolls from Germany. When the goods were seized, Conegate argued this was a violation of Article 34 TFEU, an argument which following *Henn and Darby*, could not be readily opposed. The UK, pursuing the precedent of *Henn and Darby*, argued that its action was justified on grounds of public morality.

On a preliminary reference, to the Court observed that a Member State was permitted by the EU Treaties to make its own assessment of what constitutes public morality in its own territory. But unlike in *Henn and Darby*, where there was no lawful market for the goods in question, in *Conegate*, the seized imported goods could be lawfully manufactured and marketed in the UK. Thus, the Court examined the UK's internal trade regulations, and to this extent, the judgment followed *Henn and Darby*. In the UK's different internal jurisdictions, the law relating to such goods was not uniform, and though there existed certain restrictions on the sale of such goods, for example, only through licensed shops to person over 18 years of age, and the goods could not be visible to the public, this did not constitute a prohibition on manufacture and marketing in the UK as understood in *Henn and Darby*. For this reason, the UK was unable to rely on the public morality derogation in Article 36 TFEU to prevent importation of the dolls.[51]

So, what is the difference between *Henn and Darby* and *Conegate*? The primary distinction arises from the test of reasonableness and proportionality that was fundamental to the Opinion of AG Warner, and lies in the element of discrimination against the imported goods. A conviction in *Conegate*, through the recognition that the outer limits of the public morality derogation were the same as in *Henn and Darby*, would undoubtedly have resulted in the application of harsher rules to an importer than to an exclusively domestic trader. The national measures were thus within the scope of Article 34 TFEU in *Conegate*. They were disproportionate and alternative less restrictive means were available, and indeed already used for the sale of such goods through licensed outlets to persons over the age of 18 only. The State though retaining the power to define morality, and select those elements which it deems necessary to protect remains, as AG Warner stated, within the ambit of Article 36 TFEU. Though different standards of morality do exist across the Member States, there must be equal treatment of all goods and any measures seeking to restrict imported goods must be proportionate.[52]

Public morality remains to this day a difficult concept for the Court, because the Court remains reluctant to engage in moral or ethical questions, and instead focuses its judgments on

---

[51] Conegate was awarded costs, but agreed not to pursue an action for damages to compensate it for the unlawful seizure of its goods. See ch 21.

[52] See further Doukas (n 17).

the more objective question of whether free movement rights have been infringed.[53] In doing so, the Court continues to adopt the reasoning of AG Warner and apply the reasonableness and proportionality principles to national measures, and whether alternative means exists to those measures employed by the state. This reasoning has been developed to apply beyond the narrow public morality Article 36 TFEU derogation at issue in *Henn and Darby*, and is clearly apparent in the line of the post-*Keck*[54] market access cases such as *Leclerc, Gourmet International, D'Agostini,*[55] *Commission v Italy (Trailers)*[56] and *Mickelson and Roos.*[57] In preventing discriminatory barriers to trade, the Court has found proportionality and alternative means very useful principles by which to strike down discriminatory measures which prevent or even hinder goods accessing a Member State.

Notwithstanding the broader judicial legacy of *Henn and Darby*, and in particular AG Warner's application of proportionality and alternative means principles to Article 36 TFEU, it will be the understanding of how to apply 'public morality' in EU law for which the case is arguably most significant. Despite the AG's application of proportionality, the Court continues to be more hesitant in applying this principle, presumably because by doing so, it would be reducing national laws relating to public morality to mere regulatory instruments, rather than acknowledging that they express what the Member State believes to be genuine matters of principle and of collective determination. The Court was perhaps mindful of the criticism it would face if a ban on pornography was based on whether such prohibition was an adequate means to achieve a certain goal, ie uphold public morality and general public 'goodness', instead of approaching the issue as a matter of principle. To avoid this, the Court proceeds by framing some issues as involving moral, ethical, or cultural choices, and then deferring to national authorities, as it did in *Henn and Darby*.

But what comes within the scope of public morality and therefore potentially subject to a 'hands-off' approach by the Court? *Henn and Darby* was factually clear-cut because it concerned the import of pornographic material which the Member State deems to be harmful to the public, and was ultimately why the Court reaches a different conclusion in *Conegate*. A decade after the public morality question arose in *Henn and Darby*, the Court addressed the question of public morality within the context of gambling, and in *Schindler* the Court stated that 'it is not possible to disregard the moral, religious or cultural aspects of lotteries, like other types of gambling, in all the Member States'.[58] In the light of this, the Court was of the view that national authorities ought to 'maintain a sufficient degree of latitude to determine what is required to protect the players and, more generally, in the light of the *specific social and cultural features of each Member State*, to maintain order in society, as regards the manner in which lotteries are operated, the size of the stakes, and the allocation of the profits they yield' (emphasis added).[59]

---

[53] See eg Case C-159/90 *The Society for the Protection of Unborn Children Ireland (SPUC) v Grogan* ECLI:EU:C:1991:378; Case 506/06 *Mayr* ECLI:EU:C:2008:119. In the latter case the Court confirmed that it would not decide questions of an ethical nature in very sensitive fields, which are determined by Member States 'multiple traditions and value systems, such as the definition of the human embryo'.

[54] Joined Cases C-267/91 and C-268/91 *Keck and Mithouard* ECLI:EU:C:1993:905.

[55] Case C-34/95 *De Agostini* ECLI:EU:C:1997:344.

[56] Case C-110/05 *Commission v Italy* ECLI:EU:C:2009:66 (*Trailers*).

[57] Case C-142/05 *Mickelsson and Roos* ECLI:EU:C:2009:336.

[58] Case C-275/92 *Schindler*, at paras 58–60.

[59] ibid, para 61.

Following this assessment, it was then a matter for national authorities to determine whether lottery operators should be limited or completely prohibited. As in *Henn and Darby*, the Court in *Schindler* deferred to national sensitivities, and to this date, maintains this 'subsidiarity' form of reasoning when it comes to the domestic regulation of gambling. In doing so, the Court has established a link between the nature of the issue before it, and the intensity of its review as it arguably did in its assessment of Article 36 TFEU in *Henn and Darby*.[60] This factual assessment/value judgment methodology allows the Court to distinguish the scope of application of the free movement rules from that of the national law. Where moral or cultural choices are involved, the Court steps back from the value judgments of Member States, provided that they are non-discriminatory and proportionate in their application, will be permitted to limit free movement rights.[61] AG Warner's legacy was therefore to ensure that when it comes to the Court considering national legislation, it does so in manner which recognises the need for a *genuine* public morality objective, and not one which may constitute a disguised restriction on trade.

---

[60] In Case C-244/06 *Dynamic Medien Vertriebs GmbH* concerning the protection of minors, the Court justified the margin of appreciation by reference to the diversity of conceptions of public morality across the EU. The Court stated that 'as that conception may vary from one Member State to another on the basis of, inter alia, moral or cultural views, Member States must be recognized as having a definite margin of discretion'. See Case C-244/06 *Dynamic Medien Vertriebs GmbH* ECLI:EU:C:2008:85.

[61] See further T Marzal, 'From Hercules to Pareto: of Bathos, Proportionality, and EU Law' (2017) 15 *International Journal of Constitutional Law* 621.

13

An Expedient of Proceedings: Opinion of Advocate General Warner in Foglia v Novello I

KIERAN BRADLEY

I. INTRODUCTION

ARTICLE 267 TFEU does not impose explicit restrictions on a national court's prerogative to refer a question of Union law to the Court of Justice for a preliminary ruling, beyond a prima facie assessment that 'a decision on the question is necessary for it to give judgment'. Prior to *Foglia I*, the Court had refused to provide preliminary rulings in only a handful of particularly egregious cases, where the questions referred were merely speculative or had no link with Union law.[1]

The reference in *Foglia I* appeared to raise two orders of problem. In the first place, the Court was in effect invited by a court of one Member State to rule on the compatibility with EEC law (now EU law) of the legislation of a different Member State. Second, the factual and procedural context in which the question arose had all the markings of an artifice, a legal construction which appears to have been dreamt up by the parties with the primary intention of producing a ruling that would suit both of them, one in the context of the instant dispute and one more generally.

II. BACKGROUND, CONTEXT, AND FACTS

The facts, as stated in the judgment[2] and Opinion,[3] arose in early 1979 when Mariella Novello ordered 'some cases of Italian liqueur wines' from Pasquale Foglia, a local wine merchant in Santa Vittoria d'Alba, Italy, for delivery to a party resident across the border in Menton, France. At the time, French law taxed imported liqueur wines (with a small number of exceptions which are not here relevant) at a much higher rate than indigenous wines with similar characteristics and alcohol content. For more than a decade, the Commission had been pursuing the French Republic, with a conspicuous lack of success, to induce it to equalise

---

[1] See Section IV.B below.
[2] Case 104/79 *Foglia* ECLI:EU:C:1980:73 (*Foglia I*).
[3] Opinion of AG Warner in Case 104/79 *Foglia I* ECLI:EU:C:1980:22. The facts are examined in more detail below in Section IV.F.

the tax treatment of national and imported liqueur wines. Infringement proceedings were first launched in 1975; the Commission informed the Court that it had notified the reasoned opinion to France in mid-August 1979, though the Court was not to rule on the action for several years to come.[4]

The contract between buyer and seller specified that Novello would not be liable for any charges imposed by the French authorities which were 'contrary to the free movement of goods or at all events not due'. A similar clause was included in the contract between Foglia and Danzas SpA for the transport of the wine to France. Danzas delivered the wine to Menton having paid the French consumption tax; Foglia nonetheless paid the transport carrier's bill in full, including the amount of the tax. He subsequently initiated proceedings against Novello when she refused to reimburse the amount paid in respect of the French tax.

Before the Pretore[5] di Bra, Foglia argued that Danzas should also be joined in the proceedings. The Pretore took the view that both the joinder and the principal question of Novello's liability depended on whether the consumption tax imposed by the French legislation was compatible with EEC law. Having concluded that there was evidence of 'serious discrimination' against Italian liqueur wines, the Pretore referred five questions to the Court, largely concerning the interpretation of different substantive Treaty provisions.

III. THE OPINION OF AG WARNER

After a brief explanation of the French legislation on taxing wine, AG Warner noted that, while they might hesitate to do so, national courts may be unable to avoid ruling on the compatibility with EEC law of the legislation of another Member State. What gave the AG pause in the present case was the fact that 'there was no dispute between the only parties to the [national] proceedings', as both Foglia and Novello contended that the French legislation violated EEC law: Novello because of her financial interest in escaping liability for payment of the tax, and Foglia because he wished to be able to sell Italian liqueur wines in France more competitively.[6]

Turning to Article 177 EEC (now Article 267 TFEU), the AG noted that the discretion of the national court to assess whether 'a decision on the question is necessary to enable it to give judgment' was conditional on a question of EEC law's having been raised in the first place; this provision did not 'confer on [national courts] an unlimited power to refer cases to this Court'. Where there is no dispute between the parties to civil proceedings, then there 'is not ... really a question at all'.[7] He was conscious of breaking new ground in inviting the Court to reject the questions referred for this reason, given that the assessment of the relevance of such questions was considered to be the exclusive province of the national court. While this was a 'salutary rule', he considered it not to be absolute; the Court had never admitted a question 'notwithstanding that the parties ... were *ad idem* as to the answer to it and they alone were interested in the answer to it'.[8]

---

[4] Case 196/85 *Commission v France* ECLI:EU:C:1987:182 (*Natural sweet wines and liqueur wines*); see Section IV.G below.

[5] For reasons which are not clear, the term '*Pretore*' in Italian was translated as 'Pretura' in the English-language court report; the more usual 'Pretore', which is used in the English version of Case 244/80 *Foglia II* ECLI:EU:C:1981:302, is preferred here. On this latter case, see ch 15.

[6] ibid, p 764.

[7] ibid, p 765.

[8] ibid, p 766.

In his view, such a reference 'would have no chance of being adequately argued in this Court', as the government would be absent from the proceedings in the national court, where the facts are found and the national legal context determined, and the proceedings would be conducted in a language other than that its advisers were accustomed to using. While the Court had admitted a number of questions referred to it in *ex parte* proceedings (all from Italian courts), AG Warner viewed that line of authority as not very satisfactory, even if he had himself followed it in a recent case as representing the law.[9] He took comfort in the fact that it was clear that in these cases there had been a 'genuine dispute' between the parties, and that none had raised the compatibility with EEC law of the legislation of Member State other than that of the referring court. Moreover, in two cases where there had arguably been no real dispute between the parties, the Court had declined to answer all the questions referred.[10]

In a brief judgment, the Court followed the AG's proposal to decline jurisdiction on the ground of the absence of a genuine dispute between the parties.

IV. ANALYSIS

A. Reactions to *Foglia I*

The judgment in *Foglia I*[11] unleashed a barrage of negative academic criticism which was exceedingly rare, if not unheard of, at the time; in many cases, the Opinion was also singled out for opprobrium. It has remained a punchbag amongst Court decisions ever since. For one contemporary commentator, the judgment represented a form of 'censorship' of preliminary ruling requests from national courts; if the message was not clear from the title, the terms 'censor' and 'censorship' appear a further four times in the body of the article.[12] The judgment was seen as posing 'a threat to the usefulness of Article 177 proceedings', while the Court's reasoning was considered 'unprecedented and unjustified'.[13] With a reserve which perhaps reflected his then status as a member of the Legal Service of the Commission, another commentator found it to be 'an enigmatic and troublesome ruling which could have more than disturbing consequences for the operation of the Community legal order'.[14] In a more neutral vein, a future Vice-President of the Court noted that the judgment was 'destined to stoke numerous polemics, and provoke the opposition of those who supported the entirely different approach the Court has followed heretofore'.[15]

---

[9] Opinion of AG Warner in Case 70/77 *Simmenthal* ECLI:EU:C:1978:33.

[10] ibid, pp 766–68.

[11] The present chapter examines the first *Foglia* judgment in its historical context; the wider implications of this litigation are discussed in ch 15.

[12] A Barav, 'Preliminary Censorship? The Judgment of the European Court in Foglia v Novello' (1980) 6 *ELRev* 443.

[13] C Gray, 'Advisory Opinions and the European Court of Justice' (1983) 8 *ELRev* 24, 30, and 39; the author's trenchant views might carry more weight were they not accompanied by an attempt to prove that the Court provides 'advisory' opinions on envisaged international agreements under what is now Art 218(11) TFEU, which is, of course, incorrect.

[14] G Bebr, 'The existence of a genuine dispute: an indispensable precondition for the jurisdiction of the Court under Article 177 EEC Treaty?' (1980) 17 *CMLRev* 525, 525–26.

[15] A Tizzano, 'Litiges fictifs et competence préjudicielle de la Cour de justice européenne' (1981) 85 *Revue générale de droit international public* 514. All citations from materials in French or Italian are free translations by the author.

Later commentary is similarly unkind to the decision, which has been described as 'an aberration in the history of a highly deferential and welcoming court'.[16] While not castigating them specifically, the two *Foglia* judgments were lumped together with other preliminary ruling requests the Court had ruled inadmissible, thereby 'sen[ding] a confusing signal to national courts at precisely the moment when the Community is expanding further, and when national courts are being encouraged to become "Community law courts"'.[17]

B. *Le Revirement* – What Just Happened?

The purportedly unprecedented character of the Court's stance was a source of surprise, not to say indignation, amongst the commentariat, and had clearly troubled AG Warner himself. He therefore sought, in the best common law tradition, carefully to 'distinguish' *Foglia I* from existing case law, concluding that the Court 'would [not] be departing from any previous decision'.[18] The judgment was nonetheless stigmatised as 'a drastic and significant departure from established principles governing the procedure for preliminary rulings [which] upsets the balance hitherto carefully preserved between the European Court and national courts and tribunals …'.[19] This author sought to parry the AG's thrust that the Court had never admitted a case where the parties were *ad idem* by noting that:

> [t]here is no case where the Court held that a question *might not* be referred to it when the parties to the main action were *ad idem* as to the answer and they alone were interested in it.[20]

Cumulatively the *Foglia* cases were seen as 'dramatic events which disturb the smooth operation of the preliminary ruling procedure'.[21] For other commentators, the Court had not followed 'its well-established case law', and had 'modified its categorical view' on its competence to review the questions referred and their relevance to the national litigation,[22] and the judgment, 'the first case in which the ECJ declined jurisdiction in an Article 177 reference – came as a shock'.[23]

For the keen Court-watcher, the precedential value of its judgments is something of a minefield: academic and judicial treatment of the subject 'reveals a remarkable degree of disagreement on virtually every aspect of the question'.[24] While the Treaty was silent on the matter, as the Court of a Community set up by six states from civil law traditions, and whose procedures were primarily[25] modelled on those of the French *Conseil d'État*, the expectation can only have been that it was not so bound. Nor is there any particular reason the judicial institution of

---

[16] T Tridimas, 'Knocking on Heaven's Door: fragmentation, efficiency and defiance in the preliminary reference procedure' (2003) 40 *CMLRev* 9, 22–23.

[17] C Barnard and E Sharpston, 'The Changing Face of Article 177 References' (1997) 34 *CMLRev* 1113, 1169.

[18] See n 3, p 769.

[19] Barav (n 12) 467.

[20] Barav (n 12) (emphasis in original); of course, by then there was one such case.

[21] A Barav, 'Imbroglio Préjudiciel, à propos des arrêts de la Cour de justice dans l'affaire Foglia c/ Novello' (1982) 18 *Revue trimestrielle de droit européen* 431.

[22] Bebr (n 14) 530.

[23] Barnard and Sharpston (n 17) 1121; *Foglia I* was not in fact the first such case, see below.

[24] ÁG Tóth, 'The Authority of Judgments of the European Court of Justice: Binding Force and Legal Effects' (1984) 4 *YEL* 1, 2.

[25] Though not exclusively so; see L Pierdominici, *The Mimetic Evolution of the Court of Justice of the EU* (London, Palgrave MacMillan, 2020) 56 and the references provided.

a relatively new and then rapidly developing legal order should have tied its own hands for the future in the name of some sort of putative infallibility, in the way the Appellate Committee of the House of Lords did for the century preceding its Practice Direction of 1966.[26] As early as *Da Costa*, the Court rejected the view, then propounded by the Commission, that an existing preliminary ruling on a particular point of law rendered nugatory (to be 'dismissed for lack of substance') a subsequent request for a ruling on the same matter; it held that Article 177 EEC 'always allows a national court, if it considers it desirable, to refer questions of interpretation to the Court again'.[27] Such a possibility would have little sense if the Court were unable, as a matter of law, to depart from its earlier ruling.

The evolution of both the relevant Treaty provisions and the Court's case law confirms the absence of any doctrine of binding precedent. Thus, the 'development of Union law' is one of the grounds on which the Court may decide to hear an appeal from a decision of the General Court in a case which had previously been considered by an independent board of appeal in one of the Union's agencies empowered to take legally-binding individual decisions.[28] Albeit rare, such reversals of previous case law (*'revirements'*) may be found scattered throughout the Court reports, whether the Court merely 'reconsider[ed] the interpretation' it had previously adopted of the relevant legal provisions,[29] or, more bluntly, admitted that its finding in the instant judgment is 'contrary to what ha[d] previously been decided'.[30]

The ruling in *Foglia I* was, in any case, not quite so unprecedented as some of the comments might lead one to believe. Some months before the facts in *Foglia*, the Court had refused to provide an interpretation of Article 237 EEC (now Article 49 TEU) in circumstances which are analogous in several relevant respects to those in the Italian case.[31] Two private parties had provided that the right of termination of their contract for services depended on a Court ruling on whether the accession of Spain and Portugal was 'practicable in law'. The Court held that its jurisdiction:

> cannot be altered ... by agreements between private persons tending to compel the courts of the Member States to request a preliminary ruling by depriving them of the independent exercise of the discretion which they are given by the second paragraph of Article 177.[32]

The Court had also previously ruled that it 'clearly' had no jurisdiction to provide the rulings requested on two occasions by the Acting Judge of the Tribunal d'Instance, Hayange, on the status of national judges, because the facts had revealed that the disputes at issue had no connection with the interpretation or validity of any provisions of EEC law.[33] In each case, the questions did raise matters of EEC law,[34] but in circumstances where it was obvious that the

---

[26] *Beamish v Beamish* (1859–1861) HLR 274 and *London Street Tramways v London County Council* [1898] AC 375; [1966] All ER 77.

[27] Joined Cases 28-30/62 *Da Costa* ECLI:EU:C:1963:6, p 38.

[28] Art 58a, 3rd para, Statute of the Court of Justice of the European Union [2016] OJ C202/210.

[29] Case C-10/89 *HAG* ECLI:EU:C:1990:358, reversing the judgment in Case 192/73 *Hag* ECLI:EU:C:1974:72. See ch 24.

[30] Joined Cases C-267/91 and C-268/91 *Keck* ECLI:EU:C:1993:905, para. 16; see also Case C-70/88 *Parliament v Council* ECLI:EU:C:1991:373, reversing Case 302/87 *Parliament v Council* ECLI:EU:C:1988:461.

[31] Case 93/78 *Mattheus* ECLI:EU:C:1978:206.

[32] Judgment in Case 93/78 *Mattheus*, para 5 (incorrectly numbered '6' in the English version of European Court Reports).

[33] Case 105/79 *Godard* ECLI:EU:C:1979:168; Case 68/80 *Sonacotra* ECLI:EU:C:1980:67.

[34] In recent times, the Court has interpreted on Art 50 TEU, which it considers to be the 'counterpart' of Art 49 TEU which was at issue in *Mattheus v Doego* (see Case C-621/18 *Wightman* ECLI:EU:C:2018:999) and has established a voluminous case law on the status of national judges under Union law (see eg Case C-791/19 *Commission v Poland* ECLI:EU:C:2021:596 (*Disciplinary regime for Judges*)).

answers were not 'necessary to enable [the national courts] to settle genuine disputes which are brought before them'.[35]

Contemporary commentators simply denied any parallels between these rulings and *Foglia I*.[36] While viewing *Foglia I* as being the first open manifestation of a reversal of case law on the requirements for a preliminary ruling request, Tizzano noted that the possibility of such a '*revirement*' had been on the cards for some time.[37] As we shall see, it was the facts of the case in *Foglia* which were 'unprecedented', and which justified the AG's proposal to decline jurisdiction.[38]

C. 'Increasing the Margin of Impunity for Member States'

The Opinion and the judgment also were criticised as undermining the possibility for private parties to rely on the preliminary ruling procedure indirectly to challenge national legislation by the interpretation of Community provisions, the 'vigilance of individuals' which had been trumpeted in *Van Gend en Loos*.[39] This restriction could 'increase the margin of impunity for Member States which had failed to comply with their Treaty obligations', and weaken the protection of individual rights.[40]

> Limiting the application of directly effective Community rules … to the courts of the defaulting Member State … would have deplorable consequences for an effective operation of the Community legal order in general and for its uniform efficacy in particular.[41]

This view seems rather overstated, and may reflect the 'shock' effect of the judgment in the academic world. In fact, the Court did not deal explicitly with this point. While noting that French legislation was being contested in an Italian court, the Court only did so incidentally in describing the procedural scenario while had led it to determine that this was an artificial 'expedient'. The relevant sentence of the judgment commences '[i]t thus appears that the parties …', and the remainder of the phrase does not bear the hallmarks of a judicial determination.[42] For his part, AG Warner explicitly acknowledged that the compatibility with EEC law of the legislation of one Member State could indeed be questioned in the courts of another Member State and the matter referred to the Court, but opined that this should not come about as the result of a misuse of the judicial process.[43]

D. 'Re-writing Article 177 EEC'

In the flurry of reactions, both at the time and subsequently, the harshest words were reserved for what was seen as the Court's purported willingness to review the relevance of the questions

---

[35] Judgment, para 11.
[36] Bebr (n 14) 525; Barav (n 12) 456.
[37] Tizzano (n 15) 514 and 520. See also De Wyatt, 'Following up Foglia: why the Court is right to stick to its guns' (1981) 6 *ELRev* 447.
[38] Section IV.E below.
[39] Case 26/62 *Van Gend en Loos* ECLI:EU:C:1963:1, p 13.
[40] Tizzano (n 15) 523, 521–24; Barav (n 12) 460–67.
[41] Bebr (n 14) 536–37.
[42] First sentence of para 11 of the Judgment. See also Case 244/80 *Foglia II*, paras 22–24.
[43] ibid, pp 766–67.

raised by the national court. Requiring the existence of a 'genuine dispute between the parties rather than ... the mere existence of a question of Community law ... is to allow the Court to censor the reasons for which the reference was made'.[44] The Court had taken account of certain elements of the national case-file in order to conclude that the litigation was fabricated: '[i]n a sense it went even further than merely reviewing the relevance of the questions raised. It reviewed the very nature of a dispute'.[45] This 'interference' by the Court would deprive the national court of an exclusive competence it heretofore enjoyed by virtue of Article 177 EEC not only to judge whether there is a 'question' of Community law, but to evaluate the possibly artificial character of the judicial procedure pending before it.[46]

The Court, however, based its ruling exclusively on the preliminary issue of whether the dispute which had given rise to the reference was genuine. Having determined it was not, the Court took no account of the content or relevance of the questions themselves, leaving intact the national courts' competence in this regard. If its reasoning is rather scant, it may be that the Court considered the matter to be manifest, and that a detailed examination of the nature of the dispute would have been unnecessary and even inappropriate, as liable to give the impression that the Court was reviewing the questions themselves. Under the standard test, 'questions relating to EU law enjoy a presumption of relevance' which may be overturned 'only where it is quite obvious' that the EU law question bears no relation to the facts of the case, or raises a hypothetical problem, or where the factual or legal background provided to the Court is insufficient.[47] In *Foglia II*, the Court explained that its earlier judgment did 'not in any way trespass on the prerogatives of the national court but makes it possible to prevent the application of the procedure ... for purposes other than those appropriate for it'.[48]

E. AG Warner's 'Harsh Appraisal' versus a *Cui Bono?* Analysis

For some, denying the existence of a real dispute was tantamount to holding that 'the Pretore was misguided in entertaining the claim [which] clearly exceeds the Court's jurisdiction under Article [177 EEC]', and portraying him in effect as a knave or a fool.[49] It has been suggested in this regard that '[i]t was Advocate General Warner's harsh appraisal of the referring court's questions that moved the Court into taking a strict approach on terms of jurisdiction' in the earlier case.[50] But was the appraisal of the artificial character of the dispute, which is the crux of the Court's ruling in *Foglia I*, really so harsh? And who was at the origin of the indemnification clause in the contracts for sale of the wine and its transportation to France?

To resolve this latter question, the principle of *cui bono?* may be of some assistance. While well known to readers of classical detective fiction, in the context of legal proceedings it has an even more venerable and relevant pedigree; no less a figure than Cicero attributed it to one Lucius Cassius Longinus Ravilla, a celebrated Roman judge of the latter part of the 2nd century BCE. Under this principle, to identify the perpetrator of an act, one should ascertain who stands to benefit, or benefit most, from the consequences of the act.

---

[44] Barav (n 12) 452.
[45] Bebr (n 14) 532.
[46] Tizzano (n 15) 525.
[47] See, eg, Case C-621/18 *Wightman* (n 34), para 27.
[48] Case 244/80 *Foglia II*, para 18.
[49] Barav (12) 457; Tizzano (n 15) 527, saw the judge as facing an uncomfortable choice of being seen as either '*un naïf ou ... un complice de la comédie mise en scène par les parties*'.
[50] See ch 15.

While the facts of *Foglia I* are usually presented rather summarily, the Court was at pains to underline that its decision was based on 'the circumstances of this case', which therefore merit closer examination.[51] At the time of the facts, Ms. Novello was just 20 years old; her order comprised no fewer than 108 bottles of liqueur wine[52] – enough to keep a small *débit de vins* stocked up in liqueur wine for weeks, if not months – and came to just under EUR 1000 in today's prices, with a similar sum due for the French tax. It is of course possible that Novello was just a well-heeled young citizen sending an exceptionally generous gift to a particularly thirsty compatriot, or perhaps she was about to embark on a career in the exportation of wine or in European Community law, and wished to gain some practical experience. Whatever Novello's personal circumstances, if Foglia did not actively persuade her to make such a substantial order, it must have seemed like a godsend for his campaign against the consumption tax.

Danzas had no obvious incentive to agree to such a clause in its contract with Foglia; this would in effect have obliged it either to accept liability for the French tax – which must have dwarfed its potential profit from the transaction – or to challenge the validity of the tax on behalf of the wine producers of Italy, an initiative of highly uncertain outcome. One possible explanation is that Danzas was confident that it would not in the end be required to bear the financial burden of the tax, which is in fact what transpired.

Whatever the motivation of Novello's exorbitant order and Danzas' heroic abnegation, the legal construct was designed to ensure that regardless of the ruling of the courts, Foglia would not be obliged to pay the reviled consumption tax, even though as a professional dealer in Italian wines with export ambitions, his long-term gain from the proceedings was potentially much greater than that of either of the other parties. In this light, his reimbursement to Danzas, which contradicted head-on the terms of the indemnification clause, served both to maintain good commercial relations with his transport company, and to provide him with an economic interest in proceeding against Novello. While his reimbursement to Danzas presupposed that the French tax was compatible with EEC law, Foglia had claimed to be 'neutral' before the Pretore, and strenuously urged its incompatibility before the Court.

Little wonder that Foglia's position aroused the suspicions of the Court; all the questions at the hearing were addressed to his counsel, though few answers were forthcoming. Tellingly, he was unable to explain why his client had paid Danzas the amount of the tax; he did not deny that the parties had already envisaged that the Pretore would refer a question to the Court at the time the sale was agreed, but did not confirm it either, hiding behind his apparently total ignorance of the relevant facts. He did, however, as much as admit that Foglia was at the origin of the indemnification clause: Foglia was 'a sufficiently educated person and well aware of the existence of the Common Market ... Foglia Wines is a large enough company to be aware of the problems' caused by differential taxes on wine in the various Member States.[53] While it was unnecessary for the Court, or AG Warner, to come to an explicit finding on the point, there were clear grounds for considering that Foglia or his counsel had drafted the indemnification clause, which featured in both contracts he concluded, and ostensibly put him in a 'heads I win, tails you lose' situation as regards the payment of the French tax. The Court was not prepared to accept this instance of 'cakeism' *avant la lettre*.

---

[51] *Dossier de procédure original: affaire* 104/79, CJUE-4065, Historical Archives of the European Union (HAEU) at the European University Institute (EUI). See also, T Pavone, *The Ghostwriters: Lawyers and the Politics Behind the Judicial Construction of Europe* (Cambridge: CUP, 2022) 168–70.

[52] While different figures for the size of the order were referred to, Foglia's counsel was quite specific in his written pleadings: 12 bottles each of Aleatico, Lacrima Cristi, Moscato Passito, and Malvasia, and 60 bottles of Marsala Superiore.

[53] Transcript of the hearing, CJUE-4065 n 51, 359–60.

F. In Praise of *Foglia*

In proposing that the Court not answer the questions referred by the Pretore di Bra, AG Warner sought to save national courts from instrumentalisation by the parties, and indirectly to save the Court from a similar fate at the hands of those courts, as in *Mattheus v Doego*. Like any court of last instance, the Court must 'remain the final arbiter of its own jurisdiction', and may raise the matter of its own motion if need be.[54] Under this view, references for preliminary rulings should be subject to procedural requirements for the same reasons as direct actions:

> (i) upholding the legitimate interests of public authorities whose acts are called into question; and
> (ii) safeguarding the integrity of the judicial proceedings involved.[55]

This approach is consistent with the Court's rules of procedure, though on its face the relevant rule goes to admissibility rather than jurisdiction;[56] formulating a provision to cover the particular circumstances of *Foglia I* would test even the Court.

There is much merit in the conclusion that 'the jurisdictional rules affirmed in *Foglia* are correct in principle and amount to a valuable long-stop against abuse of process in exceptional cases'.[57] More generally, the ruling serves to remind national courts that cooperation is a two-way process; the national court must 'have regard to the proper function of the Court of Justice in this field'.[58] Why should the Court alone be 'highly deferential and welcoming',[59] while national judges fail to exercise the minimum of discretion required to ensure they are not being set up?

That said, with the benefit of hindsight, *Foglia I* can be seen as being an outlier; it did not herald a major change in the operation of the preliminary ruling procedure, still less a form of 'censorship' of the content or relevance of the questions, or serve a docket control function.[60] Having made the point, the Court has subsequently proved fairly indulgent on the matter of the genuine character of national disputes, even where these might appear somewhat fishy; jurisdiction will only be refused where there is sufficient evidence that 'the proceedings are obviously artificial or collusive'.[61] Moreover, while it may have appeared 'singularly fragile' at the time, the preliminary ruling procedure has not merely survived *Foglia*, but thrived, to the extent that the volume of requests may soon test the limits of the Court's capacity properly to answer them.[62]

G. Postscript

The present author had the privilege of meeting AG Warner at a lunch organised by the Court for visiting students in 1978. The small talk threw up a query as to who was more important,

---

[54] Wyatt (n 37) 448.
[55] ibid.
[56] Art 94 of the Rules of Procedure of the Court of Justice [2020] OJ L 265/1.
[57] Wyatt (n 37) 449.
[58] Case 244/80 *Foglia II*, para 20.
[59] Tridimas (n 16).
[60] See P Craig, *UK, EU and Global Administrative Law: Foundations and Challenges* (Cambridge, CUP, 2015) 431.
[61] Opinion of AG Fennelly in Case C-97/98 *Jägerskiöld* ECLI:EU:C:1999:315, para 13. The Court agreed ECLI:EU:C:1999:515, para 25.
[62] Barav (n 12) 443. On the rise in the volume of references, see K Bradley, 'Judicial Reform and the European Court: Not a Numbers Game' in P Craig and G de Búrca (eds), *The Evolution of EU Law*, 3rd edn (Oxford, OUP, 2021) 156; C Donnelly and T de la Mare, 'Preliminary Rulings and EU Legal Integration: Evolution and Continuity' in Craig and de Búrca, ibid, p 228.

a judge or an Advocate General? Looking at the visitor over the top of his glasses, AG Warner replied: 'there are nine judges, but only four Advocates General. You can work it out'.

While the Court refused to rule on the compatibility with EEC law of the French tax in either *Foglia* case, it eventually did so in *Commission v France (Natural sweet wines and liqueur wines)* mentioned above. This resulted in a very rare defeat for the Commission on the merits in infringement proceedings, when the Court found that the contested French tax advantages pursued legitimate economic and social objectives, and that there was 'nothing in the evidence … to suggest the application of the scheme in fact gives preference to French wines'.[63]

---

[63] Case 196/85 *Commission v France* (n 4), para 10.

14

Legal Professional Privilege in EU Competition Law: Opinions of Advocates General Warner and Slynn in AM&S Europe

JAMES FLYNN

I. PERSONAL INTRODUCTION

THE INVITATION TO write about the Opinions in *AM&S Europe* was irresistible. I knew AG Warner, who received me courteously when I was the Middle Temple Bristow Scholar in 1980, I attended the first hearing in *AM&S* while in pupillage,[1] and later worked for three years for AG (and then Judge) Slynn (from whom I learned much about law and presentation). It is by definition unusual for two AGs to give opinions in the same case, so *AM&S* presents the opportunity to compare and contrast their styles. Issues of legal professional privilege (LPP) in competition proceedings have recurred often in my practice, most notably when I reprised the 'Edward' role of representing the Council of Bars and Law Societies of Europe (CCBE) in *Akzo Nobel*,[2] in which the Court (and before it, the Court of First Instance (CFI) as it then was) firmly declined the opportunity to revisit the AM&S approach to the LPP status of 'in-house' counsel. The topic has recently enjoyed a flare-up as a consequence of Brexit, but that is another story.[3]

II. BACKGROUND, CONTEXT, AND FACTS

The litigation arose from an inspection (colloquially, a dawn raid, though they almost never were) at AM&S's premises in the English port of Bristol. 'AM&S' stood, significantly, for 'Australian Mining and Smelting'. The inspection was carried out by the European Commission under the powers set out in the then applicable Regulation 17, Article 14 of which entitled it to examine and take copies of business records relating to the subject matter of the inspection.[4] Simplifying somewhat, AM&S withheld a number of identified documents on the basis that they contained or referred to legal advice. The Commission considered that only it (through its inspector) was competent to decide whether the relevant documents were protected. It issued a

---

[1] That hearing took place on Wednesday 19 November 1980. My diary records that I travelled from London by night ferry to Ostend and took a cabin.

[2] Case C-550/07 P *Akzo Nobel* ECLI:EU:C:2010:512.

[3] A readable survey of the issues is available at www.lawsociety.org.uk/en/topics/brexit/eu-lpp-after-brexit.

[4] EEC Council Regulation No 17: First Regulation implementing Articles 85 and 86 of the Treaty [1962] OJ L13/204.

decision ordering AM&S to produce them. AM&S brought proceedings before the Court for the annulment of that order. Interventions were permitted from France, the United Kingdom, and the CCBE. The CCBE was represented by David Edward QC, then its immediate past President, and the author in 1976 of the eponymous report on 'the Professional Secret'.[5]

The dispute as framed by the principal parties concerned the procedure to be followed when there was a claim that documents should not be relied on by the Commission because they contained confidential advice. They agreed in their pleadings that this was a narrow dispute. The Commission's position was that, by means of an answer to a question in the European Parliament given in 1978, it had set out its stall: there was no express legislative protection of legal confidence at Community level, but, wishing to be 'fair', the Commission would not 'use' as evidence of an infringement any document genuinely containing strictly legal advice, and if it came across such papers, would not copy them. However, it had the responsibility (which no-one else could discharge) of verifying for itself whether any document had that status. That entitled it, if it chose, to read the whole of the documents, not just selected parts proffered by the company under investigation. AM&S objected, in essence, that if the Commission's officials examined the documents, they would not be able to put their contents out of mind, and so it was imperative that the decision on the status of the documents be taken by someone neutral.

Although presenting the case on this narrow basis, the principal parties agreed that there was some protection for confidential legal advice in Community law, but essentially agreed to disagree about its scope. The intervening Member States argued respectively, but not in detail, that there was protection at Community level (per the United Kingdom), and that there was not (per the French government).

This was, if not the first, one of the principal missteps in the course of this curious case. The Court plainly found it unsatisfactory: it ordered the parties and intervening governments to come to the hearing prepared to address the question of 'the existence and scope of the principle of professional privilege in Community competition law', on which the CCBE was said to have given a full statement of its views in its intervention. AG Warner[6] approvingly quoted from the CCBE intervention the phrase that 'procedural questions do not arise *in vacuo*', and the deduction that it was therefore necessary to decide whether there was a Community principle protecting, *as of right*, disclosure of confidential advice, and the scope of any such principle before the question of the appropriate procedure could be answered. So a major issue, if not the main issue, of the case was argued orally, and not in writing.

Worse was to come. At the first hearing, the Commission stated that it was unable to address the question of principle, and left it to the wisdom of the Court. It stood by the answer it had given to the European Parliament, and would engage on the procedural issues.

III. THE OPINIONS OF AGS WARNER AND SLYNN

A. The Opinion of AG Warner

AG Warner began by rehearsing the law and the facts, and made reference to public statements by the Commission or its officials.[7] He called the Edward Report a remarkable work of

---

[5] David Edward went on to even greater distinction, as can be seen elsewhere in this volume.
[6] Opinion of AG Warner in Case 155/79 *AM&S Europe* ECLI:EU:C:1981:9, p 1630.
[7] ibid, pp 1620–21.

comparative law, but then, in a loftily back-handed way, said that it proceeded on a mistaken premise, namely that there was a fundamental distinction between the laws of the 'Original Six' and those of the states which joined the Community in the first accession. According to AG Warner, this failed to recognise substantial differences, on the one hand, between the laws of the Original Six, which the report brought out and, on the other, between the laws of Scotland and England, which it overlooked.[8]

Turning to the issue of principle, AG Warner began by stating some general considerations, before reviewing in some detail the law of England, and to a lesser extent of France and Belgium, which had received particular attention at the hearing, and for the rest, largely referred the Court to the Edward Report. His appreciation, in line with the Edward Report, which he endorsed to that extent, was that the differences between the national systems were not really differences of result, but of approach conditioned by different national traditions and ways of organising the legal profession. It was not necessary to find exactly the same approach in each Member State for there to be a Community principle.

AG Warner disagreed with AM&S and the CCBE that the protection of confidentiality in legal advice was a human right, notably as it was a right which could be limited or overridden by legislation, but he agreed that it could not be denied just because there was no express mention of such protection in Regulation 17.[9] Accordingly, he concluded that, as a matter of Community law, the Commission's powers under Regulation 17 had to be exercised subject to a right of the undertaking under investigation to claim[10] confidentiality in communications made for the purpose of seeking or giving legal advice.[11] Strikingly, in view of future developments, he was not specific about the concept of a 'lawyer' for these purposes, although his overall assessment was plainly made by reference to the recognised national professions such as that of 'avocat' or 'barrister'; but he regarded the differences between them at national level as not going to what he called the 'heart of the matter'.[12]

With that, he examined the questions of procedure. The Commission had stuck to its hard line: only it, through its inspector, could determine whether a given document was one that the Commission would disregard, and the Court's only opportunity to review the Commission's treatment of a confidential document would be at the time of an appeal against a final infringement decision. It sought to palliate the position by stressing that inspectors would be instructed to minimise their examination of documents (while reserving the possibility of reading the whole) and to put privileged contents out of mind. The Commission also indicated that it would consider legislative amendment, and take account of any remarks the Court might make.[13]

AG Warner was unimpressed. The Commission could not change (Council) Regulation 17, and it was not the Court's task to suggest improvements, but rather to declare the law as it stood. Someone other than the Commission had to rule in the event of disagreement. The Commission had misunderstood the fundamental nature of the protection: where it applied, it had to be complete, and was breached by any disclosure.[14] However, AG Warner was also

---

[8] ibid, p 1622.

[9] ibid, pp 1636–37.

[10] This recognises that the 'privilege' is that of the client, not the lawyer, and can be waived.

[11] Opinion of AG Warner in Case 155/79 *AM&S Europe* ECLI:EU:C:1981:9, p 1637.

[12] ibid, p 1633.

[13] ibid, p 1637.

[14] ibid, pp 1638–39. See also the clear statement in para 25 of the *Akzo Nobel* judgment: 'Any breach of legal professional privilege in the course of investigations does not take place when the Commission relies on a privileged document in a decision on the merits, but when such a document is seized by one of its officials.'

opposed to the ultimate solution put forward by AM&S, of referring the issue to an independent lawyer. There was no provision in the legislation for a neutral third party to bear such a decisive role, and the Court could not give its imprimatur to such improvisation.[15]

His answer to the conundrum was to have recourse to the national courts, who were required under Regulation 17 to give any necessary assistance to the Commission in its investigations and would be obliged to apply Community law, not national law, in doing so.[16] Perhaps with hindsight, this approach should be reconsidered on its merits, which would provide a readily available forum in all inspections (many 'dawn raids' open with the issue of a warrant by a national court), and is surely better than the 'quick look' theory still advanced by the Commission in *Akzo Nobel*, as if nothing had happened in 1982.

In keeping with the rather abstract basis on which the case had been presented, and implicitly assuming that continuing disputes about the documents could be referred to national courts, AG Warner recommended the Court to set aside the production order, and award costs to AM&S, the United Kingdom, and the CCBE.[17]

AG Warner delivered his Opinion on 20 January 1981. Since at that point the composition of the Court was not the same as when the case was submitted and the hearing took place, the Court quickly reopened the oral procedure to allow AG Warner to redeliver his Opinion on 28 January 1981. However, the Court plainly felt that the case was left in an unsatisfactory state. The allegedly privileged documents were not before the Court; it only had AM&S's description of them in a schedule sent to the Commission after the inspection. Only a week after AG Warner redelivered his Opinion, the Court issued an order[18] reopening the oral procedure (for the second time) for a further hearing, and requiring AM&S to send the documents to the Court in a sealed envelope. The order provided for the Court to draw up a report on the documents 'in a form which it considers appropriate so as not to prejudice its final decision', and specified that the parties would be heard on questions to be particularised before the hearing.

AM&S provided the documents in the famous sealed envelope, and the President directed that it should be opened in the presence of the Judge Rapporteur (Judge Bosco) and the AG (now Slynn), along with the Deputy Registrar. The report produced in accordance with the Court's order is an important document that should be more widely known, as it is difficult to make sense of the eventual ruling without it.[19] It noted that as well as the documents themselves, the applicant provided a short description (essentially the schedule that the Court had already seen). Certain of the documents were not provided to the Court at all, as the privilege claim had been withdrawn and they had already been handed over to the Commission; identified passages in some provided documents had also been disclosed to the Commission. The Court's report describes the remainder, document by document, in an abstract way (for example, in relation to the first document, stating that it was drawn up by a (named) solicitor in the UK, who was head of the legal department of a sister subsidiary of AM&S, and was a request for oral advice from two (named) barristers in private practice). It did not specify the matter on which advice was sought, or the tenor of any advice given, but noted that many of the documents referred to a transfer of shares in a non-group company established outside the

---

[15] ibid, pp 1639–40.

[16] ibid, pp 1640–41.

[17] ibid, p 1642. Those were the days.

[18] Set out in the European Court Reports at pp 1616–19: confusingly the Order appears after the Court's judgment (which it of course preceded) and just before the Opinion, which it post-dated.

[19] The report can be found in the Court's case file held in the Historical Archives of the EU, under the guardianship of the European University Institute. Regrettably, the transcript from the first hearing has for unstated reasons been kept confidential, but the transcript of the second hearing is there, and most amusing it is too.

Community to a group subsidiary established in the Community, and that the 'application of Community law to that transaction is occasionally envisaged in those documents.'[20]

That report was sent to all parties, and the case set down for hearing. The notice to the parties[21] is remarkable for the detailed issues that they were asked to address, based on the Court's categorisation of the various documents in the envelope. The parties were invited to state orally, at the hearing, their views on the 'legislation, academic opinion, and case-law in the various Member States' on the extent of protection, in public investigations made for the purpose of detecting offences of an economic nature, especially in the field of competition, to correspondence passing between various categories of lawyer and client. It was also noted that since the composition of the Court had changed since the first hearing, the parties were at liberty to 'put afresh' the factual and legal arguments they had advanced during the first hearing.

This was plainly an ambitious agenda. As noted below, the hearing proved somewhat indigestible, and indeed had its farcical elements, despite the heroic efforts of all involved.

B. The Opinion of AG Slynn

Picking up where AG Warner had left off, AG Slynn dived straight into a detailed description of the documents,[22] grouping them neatly into three categories, respectively (i) asking for, (ii) giving and (iii) summarising advice.[23]

AG Slynn then considered what questions needed to be addressed at the stage the proceedings had reached.[24] He noted the Commission's evolving stance: unable to take a position at the time of the first hearing, it had moved slightly by the time of the second hearing to acknowledge that there was a general principle of protection of confidence in communications relating to defence rights after a proceeding has begun. Undertakings could rely on the Commission's statement (in its answer to the Parliament) that it would not make use of such documents as evidence of an infringement, but it still insisted that only the inspector could decide whether a document had protected status. In stating the Commission's position, it is significant that AG Slynn expressly noted its acceptance that the term 'lawyer' embraced both a lawyer in private practice, and a salaried lawyer employed by a company who was subject to the same regime of professional ethics and discipline.[25]

Like AG Warner, AG Slynn considered that the narrow basis on which AM&S and the Commission had sought to litigate was unworkable, and preferred the view of the CCBE and the French government that there had first to be an answer to the question of principle: was there protection of legal confidence in the circumstances, and what was the scope of that protection. Only then could the question of appropriate procedure be addressed. For that reason, he disclaimed the temptation of relying on the Commission's concession that it would

---

[20] The full text of the Court's Order of 4 February 1981, to which the report was attached, is not available online. The curious reader therefore has to go to ECR, or the EUI Archive, to access the material. In the meantime, it is hoped this oversight on the Court's website could be rectified.

[21] See pp 1603–1604 of the case report, which is important as an insight into the thinking of the Court and perhaps principally its redoubtable Judge Rapporteur.

[22] Opinion of AG Slynn in Case 155/79 *AM&S* ECLI:EU:C:1982:17. See pp 1643–44 of the case report, which is vital for an understanding of the judgment, in the absence of the actual schedule or the Court's report on it.

[23] ibid, pp 1643–44.

[24] ibid, p 1645.

[25] ibid, pp 1645–48.

not 'use' documents numbered 1-10 on the list: it still had to be determined whether or not they were entitled to do so.[26]

As regards the question of principle, AG Slynn began with a detailed account of the correct method for discerning a general principle in Community law, essentially noting that the general principles were not limited to fundamental rights and could be deduced on a qualitative basis without requiring a similar outcome in a preponderance of Member States. He stated:

> It is, in my view, important not to fasten too closely on a detailed comparison of particular labels or rules. What matters is the overall picture.[27]

It was easy to state the divergences between national laws on the topic of protection of legal confidence, and hard to state the content of any particular national law. He noted the wide disparity of views at the hearing where, for example, the French government had argued that the Edward report was wrong on French law, but its agent had, according to AG Slynn, misunderstood the laws of the United Kingdom. Sir Gordon gave a high-level summary of the position in each Member State, based principally on the statement agreed between AM&S, the Commission, and the CCBE.[28] From that, AG Slynn drew the conclusion that, despite considerable variances, it was:

> plain that there exists in all the Member States a recognition that the public interest and the proper administration of justice demand as a general rule that a client should be able to speak freely, frankly and fully to his lawyer.[29]

He also noted the:

> advantages to a society which evolves complex law reaching into all the business affairs of persons, real or legal, that they should be able to know what they can do under the law, what is forbidden, where they must tread circumspectly, where they run risks.[30]

Protection of legal confidence should accordingly be declared a principle of EC law.

As regards the nature of the 'lawyer' in question, he again noted and endorsed the Commission's position that where an employed lawyer remains a member of the profession, and is subject to its discipline and ethics, he should be treated in the same way as a lawyer in private practice. He specified that protection depended on the lawyer acting as such (and not for example as company secretary). AG Slynn opined that confidentiality should extend to communications between lawyers qualified in different jurisdictions about the affairs of their mutual or respective clients; he plainly did not consider this statement to be limited to lawyers who were members of one of the Community professions.[31]

He then considered whether the general principle should yield in the context of competition investigations. Reviewing Member State laws on that topic, he concluded that the protection was mostly maintained in that context, and despite doubts in a few cases, nowhere was it definitively excluded. Neither the legislative history of Regulation 17 nor the notionally administrative (as opposed to judicial) nature of the Commission's investigations led to any different conclusion.[32]

---

[26] ibid, p 1647.
[27] ibid, p 1650.
[28] ibid, pp 1650–54.
[29] ibid, p 1654.
[30] ibid.
[31] ibid, p 1655.
[32] ibid, pp 1656–60.

Turning to the subsidiary procedural question, AG Slynn was adamant that the determination whether a document was privileged could not be left either to the investigated undertaking or to the inspector. The Commission's undertaking not to 'use' documents it had read would always leave doubt as to their impact on officials. The possibility of annulling the eventual infringement decision was unsatisfactory, not least on account of delay and cost.[33]

He did not reject out of hand AG Warner's proposal to have recourse to national courts, although he noted that in some systems such determinations fell to the *bâtonnier*, not courts. Overall, however, he thought the better solution was the one adopted in the case, of the Commission taking a procedural decision which could be appealed to the Court.[34]

AG Slynn therefore concluded that, except in so far as some of the documents went beyond merely noting advice, the contested production order had to be set aside, with costs awarded in the same way as suggested by AG Warner.

IV. ANALYSIS

Put shortly, in its famous judgment, the Court discerned from the laws of Member States (which it did not discuss individually) a general principle of protection of confidential exchanges for the purpose of securing legal advice, provided that (i) the exchanges pursued the client's right of defence and (ii) the advice came from an independent lawyer, namely a member of one of the professions listed in the Community legislation on legal services who was not bound to the client by a contract of employment.[35] Regulation 17 had to be read as subject to that principle. In the event of a dispute, a solution had to be found at Community level, as had been done in the case itself, and not through private arbitration or the national courts. As to the specific documents, the Court was untroubled by the fact that the exchanges substantially pre-dated the inspection and held that, where the advice came from an independent Community lawyer, the documents need not be produced. The decision was accordingly set aside in part, and each party was ordered to bear its own costs.

A. Substance

On the question of principle, the Judgment was narrower than anyone seems to have expected and, in this author's view, is parochial. On the question of procedure, experience suggests that the Warner solution has attractions over the current dispensation.

The Court's order itself is gnomic. It specified AM&S's production obligations[36] by reference to a schedule not reproduced in the report. Some assistance is obtainable from the Opinion of AG Slynn, but he did not tether his analysis to the numbered documents either. With the benefit of the Court's report and the schedule, it can be seen that AM&S was ordered to produce all the documents prepared by non-lawyers and, critically, also some documents whose 'use' the Commission (implicitly accepting that they should be within the scope of protection) had renounced.[37] The schedule shows that they extended beyond advice from

---

[33] ibid, pp 1661–63.
[34] ibid, p 1663.
[35] Case 155/79 *AM&S* ECLI:EU:C:1982:157, para 21.
[36] The case file shows that the Court returned all the documents to AM&S along with the judgment, pointing out in the covering letter that the order required some of them to be produced to the Commission.
[37] ie, documents 1–10.

'Community' lawyers to advice from both in-house and third country lawyers, indeed from third country in-house lawyers (Australian solicitors, *in casu*).[38]

It is clear that, for both AGs (as well as for the Commission at the time), those were irrelevant distinctions.[39] AG Slynn's caveat at the end of his Opinion concerned the extent to which the executive notes went beyond summarising legal advice.[40]

B. Style

A short word on style. The Warner Opinion, coming at the very end of his tenure, is urbane and conversational, a speech to be read to an audience of equals. It is charming that he says to the judges that they will be so familiar with Article 14 (notably from the *National Panasonic* case[41]) that he does not need to quote it. The Slynn Opinion, an early work, descends more into details and shows its workings, perhaps therefore more exhibiting the contribution of the *référendaires*. Nevertheless, the quotations given above are absolutely in his unforgettable voice.

C. Case Management

The Court's grip on the case was distinctly unorthodox. Its request for oral answers at the first hearing was a perfect recipe for confusion, compounded by the Commission's refusal to engage. The resulting obscurity clearly precipitated the call for the underlying documents, only a week after the redelivered Opinion of AG Warner. If AG Warner was blindsided, so it seems was AG Slynn, who would surely have said more on the status of the relevant 'lawyer' if he had appreciated that the Court's inclination was to legislate as it did. Nevertheless, the notice to the parties convening the second hearing clearly set out an analytical framework in which such issues could be raised and decided.

The Court refused to adjourn or allow written answers. As the transcript reveals, the resumed hearing opened with the nowadays unthinkable spectacle of junior counsel for AM&S[42] reading on to the record a lengthy statement agreed between AM&S, the Commission, and the CCBE, on the scope of various national laws on the protection of legal confidence. The hearing overran terribly, and resumed later in the week (with the hearing in *Nungesser* in between, and the Luxembourg autumn weather preventing the return of the UK Attorney General).[43] A spirited attempt by counsel for the French government to detail features of Member State law undermining any general principle at Community level faced testy, not to say rude, interventions from several judges, riled by perceived misrepresentation of their home rules. Despite its refusal to allow written submissions, which would surely have increased the serenity of the

---

[38] Specifically, documents 2, 3, and 10.

[39] This could be called a quintessentially English or common law approach. An interesting recent judgment reviews the authorities: *Tatneft v Bogolyubov* (Moulder J) [2020] EWHC 2437 (Comm).

[40] See his comment on document 13 on p 1661 of the case report.

[41] Case 136/79 *Panasonic* ECLI:EU:C:1980:169. As it happens, that was the first hearing of the Court this author attended, as a *stagiaire* in the Commission Legal Service under the wing of the great John Temple Lang.

[42] Now Lord Bellamy QC, later a judge of the Court of First Instance (succeeding Judge Edward), and thereafter, the first President of the United Kingdom's Competition Appeal Tribunal.

[43] Case 258/78 *Nungesser* ECLI:EU:C:1982:211.

proceedings, the Court accepted hand-ups, including a note from the Federal Cartel Office of Germany (*Bundeskartellamt*), in translation with manuscript emendations, and various judgments from the United States and Australia. As an object lesson in how not to handle a complex case, *AM&S* would take some bettering.

D. Legacy

Subsequent case law has filled in a few gaps, notably addressing the issues of internal notes and summaries of advice received.[44] However, the line in the sand drawn by the Court in *AM&S* as to the type of lawyer whose advice is covered by LPP has remained unchanged for nearly 40 years, despite pertinent developments in Union legislation on the nature of regulated legal practice in the services and establishment context.

The Court repulsed a determined effort to extend the scope of LPP to advice given by in-house lawyers in *Akzo Nobel*.

The Commission, despite its relatively liberal position on scope at the time of *AM&S*, retreated to a position of no advance on *AM&S*, and indeed suggested that if *AM&S* was to be reconsidered, it was relevant to note that there had been national developments in the other direction. The Commission has never been willing to grasp the nettle and press for improved standards of national ethical rules for lawyers, or to engage in bilateral negotiations with third countries on this issue,[45] and its treatment of advice from external counsel in private practice qualified in other jurisdictions is more the stuff of unspoken convention than rules.

The extension of the *AM&S* rule advocated in *Akzo Nobel* by the CCBE, namely that advice from a lawyer who was subject to the professional disciplinary regime of one of the professions recognised in the relevant EU legislation (as was the Dutch employed *advocaat* in *Akzo Nobel*) should be covered by LPP, was a modest re-focussing on the lawyer's status as a regulated EU legal professional, rather than his or her employment status.

The cause of widening the scope of the privilege, Monnet-style, by modest increments was not served by the plethora of interventions from other representative bodies, pressing for a wider recognition of the standards and ethics of in-house and third country counsel. The Court dug itself in, making statements about the degree of independence available even to regulated employed lawyers for which it had absolutely no evidence.

There seems to be no realistic likelihood of the Court changing the *AM&S* 'rule'. Both AG Warner and AG Slynn would plainly have found this regrettable.

---

[44] See Order in Case T-30/89 *Hilti* ECLI:EU:T:1990:27, which is essentially in line with the proposals of AG Slynn in relation to documents 11 onwards in *AM&S*.

[45] On this, see J Temple Lang, 'The AM&S Judgment' in M Hoskins and W Robinson (eds), *A True European: Essays for Judge David Edward* (Oxford, Hart Publishing, 2003). John Temple Lang had a long and distinguished career in the Commission, but his role as the Commission's agent in *AM&S* must have been thankless and frustrating, and in this chapter, one senses that in full.

Part III

Gordon Slynn: Embedding the Revolutionary Doctrines (1981–1988)

15

Artificial Arrangements and References for a Preliminary Ruling: Opinion of Advocate General Slynn in Foglia v Novello II

DANIEL SARMIENTO

I. INTRODUCTION

F OGLIA II WAS the second attempt of the District Court of Bra, Italy in trying to obtain a reply from the Court in a case which had the appearance of a fabrication.[1] The saga of *Foglia v Novello* in its first and second consecutive judgments, gave the Court an opportunity to insert some discipline into the procedure when parties and national judges seemed eager to obtain rulings from the Court, irrespective of the reality of the dispute in the main proceedings. In *Foglia II*, the Court set the tone and content of such case law, and this doctrine is in force still as of today, although very exceptionally applied in practice.

In *Foglia II*, AG Slynn happened not to be the same AG who gave an Opinion in *Foglia I*. Whilst AG Warner took a restrictive line in *Foglia I* that was followed by the Court in the first case,[2] and ensued in the Court's lack of jurisdiction, AG Slynn took a different view from his predecessor. He was not followed by the Court. Nevertheless, the force of AG Slynn's arguments have resonated within the walls of the *Palais du Kirchberg*, and, more than 40 years since its delivery, many of the Opinion's arguments are now part of the case-law, leaving the two *Foglia* judgments of the Court in a rather isolated corner, hardly applicable in reality. The Opinion of AG Slynn in *Foglia II* is a good example of how an AG's proposals may not be taken immediately into account, but they might be in a near or in a distant future, thus paving the way for future inroads in the case-law. The Opinion of AG Slynn here in *Foglia II* also demonstrates quite a different position to that of his predecessor, when compared to the Opinion of AG Warner in *Foglia I*.

II. BACKGROUND, CONTEXT, AND FACTS

The case in *Foglia* was based on the same facts that triggered the reference in *Foglia I*. Mr Foglia, an Italian wine merchant, received a purchase order from Ms Novello, for the

---

[1] Case 244/80 *Foglia II* ECLI:EU:C:1981:302.
[2] Case 104/79 *Foglia I* ECLI:EU:C:1980:73. See also Opinion of AG Warner in Case 104/79 *Foglia I* ECLI:EU:C:1980:22. See ch 13.

delivery of the goods to a third party in France. In the contract between Mr Foglia and Ms Novello, it was made clear that the purchaser would assume no charge whatsoever resulting from any levy of tax or custom duties deemed contrary to the EEC Treaty. A similar contractual clause was agreed between Mr Foglia and the company entrusted with the transport and delivery of the goods in France. When the transport company delivered the goods following payment of a French levy, the amount was not contested before the French authorities and it was passed on to Ms Novello, who refused payment. Mr Foglia brought Ms Novello to civil court, requesting payment, although the contractual clause made it clear that no illegal levy was to apply to the party.

At the time of the relevant facts, the French *Code Général des Impôts* provided for an additional levy to be applied to wines which did not come under the category of *'vins doux naturels'*, a levy that had been applicable mostly to Italian wines, thus producing a serious competitive disadvantage on Italian wines *vis-à-vis* French wines. This levy had been questioned by the Commission with little success, and France had managed to delay proceedings and any opposition to the levy. It was obvious that the infringement procedure in the hands of the Commission was not being used effectively, to the despair of Italian wine producers and exporters.

In *Foglia I*, the *Pretura di Bra* referred the case to the Court, pointing to the fact that in proceedings between private parties, it was essential to determine whether the French *Code Général des Impôts* was in conformity with the EEC Treaty (now TFEU). If not, Ms Novello would be under no obligation to face payment, nor would Mr Foglia, nor, for that matter, the transport and delivery company that delivered the goods in France. However, following AG Warner's advice, the Court decided that such a case bore no links with a genuine dispute deserving of the interpretation of EEC law (now EU law).

According to the Court, the case as presented in *Foglia I* had been fabricated through the introduction of a contractual clause by both parties, in proceedings over which they both agreed on the outcome. The transport and delivery company had not challenged the levies in France, as it could have well done. To make matters more convoluted, the Italian judge was asking about the compatibility with EEC law (now EU law) of a national provision of *another* Member State. As a result, the Court declined its own jurisdiction, and stated that:

> a situation in which the Court was obliged by the expedient of arrangements like those described above to give rulings would jeopardize the whole system of legal remedies available to private individuals to enable them to protect themselves against tax provisions which are contrary to the Treaty.[3]

The result in *Foglia I* was a declaration of no jurisdiction by the Court, thus leaving the matter settled, and creating a precedent on the limits of the preliminary reference procedure when parties have no genuine dispute to solve among them and there is evidence of a fabrication. This outcome surprised commentators, as portrayed in Bebr in 1981.[4] For the first time, the Court was showing its lack of willingness to engage with a national court, paving the way to a possibly more restrictive approach towards judicial dialogue through preliminary references.

The *Pretura di Bra* did not give up on Mr Foglia's claim, and referred yet a second request for a preliminary reference, this time showing the Court the implications of its ruling in *Foglia I*, and seeking advice on how to handle the consequences of the new and stricter approach towards judicial cooperation. In its order for reference, the District Court pointed out that

---

[3] ibid, para 11.

[4] G Bebr, 'The existence of a genuine dispute: an indispensable precondition for the jurisdiction of the Court under Art. 177 EEC Treaty?' (1980) 17 *CMLRev* 530. See also, G Bebr, 'The possible implications of Foglia v. Novello II' (1982) 19 *CMLRev* 421.

the ruling in *Foglia I* created a significant obstacle to the procedural rights of the parties, whose right to be granted a declaratory ruling was now frustrated by the Court's lack of appetite towards litigation in which parties had no real conflict between them. Consequently, the *Pretura di Bra* decided to refer the case to the Constitutional Court of Italy, so that the high constitutional jurisdiction had a say on the constitutionality of these procedural limitations.[5] Only as a matter of precaution did the *Pretura di Bra* decide to refer, once again, the matter to the Court, this time highlighting the implications that the strict approach of the Court would have for the parties in the main proceedings.

The *Pretura di Bra*'s questions in the reference for a preliminary ruling focused on three points: first, the scope of Article 177 EEC and the powers of the national court when the Court declined to rule on a case on grounds as the ones in *Foglia I*; second, whether national courts had the power under Community law to review national provisions of another Member State; and third, how to articulate the participation of that other Member State, particularly in the course of national proceedings.

III. THE OPINION OF AG SLYNN

The Opinion of AG Slynn in *Foglia II* was a balanced and pragmatic legal text that departed from his predecessor's strict approach towards national proceedings presumably fabricated by the parties.[6] While AG Warner openly dismissed the intentions of Mr Foglia and Ms Novello, and took a harsh approach towards arrangements in which parties do not dispute, but seek in common agreement a ruling of the Court, AG Slynn focused more closely on the role played by the referring court and the textual content of Article 177 EEC.

As a result, AG Slynn considered that the preliminary reference procedure did not confer on the Court a power to double-guess the parties' intentions. On the contrary, if the referring judge concluded that a decision was necessary to rule on the case, a matter of what was then Community law should be addressed, if subject to interpretation, to the Court. According to AG Slynn:

> the judge has concluded that a question of Community law has to be decided for him to give judgment on the claim, and on the cross claim for a declaration. In my opinion, against this background, he is [...] entitled to refer a question to the Court pursuant to Article 177. It does not seem to me that he is barred from doing so because of the absence of a contention in the case.[7]

The apparent contradiction between this statement, and the Court's ruling in *Foglia I* was, according to AG Slynn, justified on the grounds of the new documents and further explanations provided by the *Pretura di Bra* in *Foglia II*. This new round of information seemed sufficient for AG Slynn to provide to the Court with material to give a ruling on the substance. This feature also allowed the AG to address the second question for a preliminary reference in a very simple way: if the Court declined jurisdiction on the answer the questions referred by the national court, the latter is of course in a position to rule on the case. However, if a question of interpretation of Union law surfaces, the national court still has the power to make yet another question for a preliminary reference. Since the second round of questions in *Foglia II* provided enough information to override the Court's concerns in *Foglia I*, the AG astutely found a way

---

[5] Page 3051 of Judgment in Case 244/80 *Foglia II*.
[6] Opinion of AG Slynn in Case 244/80 *Foglia II* ECLI:EU:C:1981:175.
[7] Page 3072.

to respond to the second question for reference in a way that left the query unresolved but, at the same time, accepting the premise of the referring court.

On the second and third issues raised by the *Pretura di Bra*, concerning the intervention of the Member State whose legislation might come under question in the courts of another Member State, the AG solved the matter with characteristic grace and common sense. The right of Member States to intervene in proceedings under Article 177 EEC was to be considered a sufficient safeguard to ensure the rights of the Member State whose legislation was under review.[8] The fact that the main proceedings were *inter privatos* allowed the AG to dissipate concerns about this kind of indirect review of legislation of another Member State, with the argument that national courts in civil and commercial litigation are used to interpret law of another Member State. The ruling of the national court would not bind the Member State, but rather, only the parties to the case. And if the case was ever to reach the Court through the preliminary ruling procedure, the Member State's right to intervene would be guaranteed.[9]

Finally, AG Slynn took issue with the substance, in contrast with the Court and AG Warner's position in *Foglia I*, who ruled only on the jurisdictional point. The question as to France's additional levy imposed on a third category of wine liquors that, de facto, targeted Italian wines, had been the source of discontent throughout the proceedings, although left unaddressed until the Opinion of AG Slynn was published. Unsurprisingly, in the Opinion he came to the conclusion that the French scheme had sufficient elements to conclude that it could be in violation of Article 95 EEC (now Article 110 TFEU). Following settled case-law on the matter,[10] the French law was considered to be contrary to Union law, even if the classification of goods was made by reference to the objective characteristics of the products, 'provided that the domestic and imported products have similar characteristics and meet the same needs from the point of view of consumers, or provided that both are in competition, even partial, indirect or potential'.[11] In sum, AG Slynn agreed with Mr Foglia, Ms Novello, the delivery company, and the *Pretore di Bra*, in concluding that the French levies breached Union law, and should have never been paid.

IV. ANALYSIS

The Opinion of AG Slynn in case *Foglia II* was a worthy example of how the AG can keep his/her distance from the Court, and at the same time, play a constructive role for the future. Whilst his interpretation of EEC law in the case at hand was not followed, it paved the way to a much more flexible and understanding approach on the part of the Court in future cases in which apparent fabrications could be deduced. It could even be said that the Court's ruling in case *Foglia II* is nowadays an exception to a rule, with the rule being a flexible and pragmatic approach, as suggested by AG Slynn.

A. Artificial Arrangements and Article 267 TFEU

The case law on wholly artificial arrangements and preliminary reference procedures has remained mostly as an exceptional safeguard, with hardly any practical effect. This said, the

---

[8] Page 3073.
[9] Page 3074.
[10] Case 27/67 *Firma Fink-Frucht* ECLI:EU:C:1968:22; Case 168/78 *Commission v France* ECLI:EU:C:1980:51.
[11] Pages 3076-77.

case law features, rightly, in the literature on the preliminary reference procedure.[12] Cases *Foglia I* and *Foglia II* acted as a warning sign to imaginative parties and national jurisdictions hoping to make use of the Court's jurisdiction to solve legal queries, but not to solve genuine disputes. It could be argued that the two cases were precautionary signals, but not much more. The times at which the Court has rejected its own jurisdiction on these grounds have been exceptional, hardly a confirmation of what seemed back in 1981 as a more restrictive and rigorous oversight of national references.[13] The Opinion of AG Slynn was a powerful counterweight to this strict approach, but in such a way, through a subtle and elegant approach, has reinforced the position of the AG more generally, and, seen with the benefit of hindsight, weakened the force of the judgment of the Court in *Foglia II*.

The first aspect that should be highlighted from the Opinion of the AG Slynn was its radical departure from his predecessor's position in *Foglia I*. It was AG's Warner harsh appraisal of the referring court's questions that moved the Court into taking a strict approach in terms of jurisdiction. By contrast, and without ever mentioning the fact that he was departing from the position of his predecessor, AG Slynn subtly rejected such an approach, and opted for a more flexible and practical perspective. First, he considered that the second request for a preliminary reference provided the Court with sufficient information to give a ruling, as a means to override the fact that case *Foglia I* had ended in a declaration of no jurisdiction. Second, AG Slynn reversed the principle and considered whether the answer coming from the Court would be useful to the parties, and his conclusion was in the positive. In other words, instead of focusing on how much of an interest do the parties have and thus enter into the complex terrain of fact and party strategies, the AG Slynn focused only on the practical role that an answer would have for the referring court.

These two findings were important to understand later developments. The AG's flexibility in inviting the Court to look into the case for a second time was probably decisive in the fact that the reference was not rejected once again on a lack of jurisdiction. Instead, the Court decided to reply to the *Pretura di Bra* in detail, quite a departure from *Foglia I*, and the findings of the judgment provided four answers to the referring court. The Court could have simply stated in its conclusion that it lacked jurisdiction to answer the questions referred by the *Pretura di Bra*, but instead it decided to directly address the issues and reply in detail. The AG could have openly stated his disagreement with AG Warner and the judgment of the Court in *Foglia I*. Instead, his approach was to affirm that the new information provided allowed him to rule on the merits and to argue in support of the Court's jurisdiction. This non-combative approach towards precedent was an intelligent way to seduce the Court into changing or rebalancing its case-law. In case *Foglia II*, while the case-law was not amended, it was certainly rebalanced. As it will be pointed in section IV.D below, the approach finally taken by the judgment has turned the *Foglia v Novello* doctrine on wholly artificial arrangements into an exception in the case-law, rather than a general rule.

---

[12] See, *inter alia*, M Broberg and N Fenger, *Broberg and Fenger on Preliminary References to the European Court of Justice*, 3rd edn (Oxford, OUP, 2021) 186–93.

[13] After close inspection of the development of the case-law since the *Foglia* cases, this is the impression of N Wahl, L Prete, 'The Gatekeepers of Article 267 TFEU: on jurisdiction and admissibility of references for preliminary rulings' (2018) 55 *CMLRev* 511. At p 532 the authors argue: 'After those first cases, in fact, the principles remained on paper only. Indeed, the Court required the collusive or fictitious nature of the dispute to be manifest, something which is extremely difficult to ascertain.'

B. Review of the Law of Another Member State by National Courts

The other major point on which AG Slynn focused in his Opinion in case *Foglia II* was the review of legislation of a Member State in national proceedings in *another* Member State. This was a question that was addressed in case *Foglia I* by categorically discarding the power of national courts to undergo this kind of review. However, AG Slynn disagreed, and came to the conclusion that this was part of the normal course of events in European litigation. In fact, he considered that national courts were accustomed to interpret law from beyond the immediate jurisdiction, particularly in civil and commercial litigation, so nothing should stop them from undergoing a review of such rules if they happen to be in breach of EEC law (now EU law). In sum, the power to review of law of another Member State in breach of Union law should be in the toolkit of national court, in contrast with the Court's finding in case *Foglia I*, which immediately took stock with the fact that Danzas, the transport company in France, did not challenge payment of the French levy when it had the occasion.

In *Foglia II*, despite the AG Slynn's willingness to accept the principle, the Court departed from his position, and stated that it:

> must display special vigilance when, in the course of proceedings between individuals, a question is referred to it with a view to permitting the national court to decide whether the legislation of another Member State is in accordance with Community law.[14]

In other words, the Court accepted that in certain cases, it will be possible for a national court to undergo the review of the law of another Member State, but at the same time, it highlighted the 'special vigilance' that it will apply if the national court is ever to raise the matter to the Court.

On this point, a dialogue between the Court and the AG ensued. While the AG emphasised the fact that law from another jurisdiction is regularly interpreted by national courts in civil and commercial proceedings, the Court replied that that may be the case in litigation *inter privatos*, but it is certainly not the usual practice of administrative litigation in which the defendant party is a public authority. The same applied to the fact that in a preliminary reference, there would be a chance for the Member State to be heard in the proceedings, while that may not be the case in national court.

While the AG considered the procedural safeguards under Article 177 EEC to be sufficient, the Court was highly reluctant to suggest that that solution would be satisfactory for the Member State whose legislation was to come under review. But the interesting point was that, resulting from this tacit conversation between the Court and its AG, the outcome ended up being quite similar, although articulated on opposite terms. In other words, while the AG Slynn supported review of law of another Member State by national courts, the Court did not. But in the end, *Foglia II* ended up acting as a warning sign, because the Court's position was one of 'special vigilance' before these kinds of moves, not a prohibition falling upon national courts. In sum, while the AG Slynn advocated in support of this type of review, and the Court looked at it with reluctance and suspicion, the truth is that today, as a matter of principle, national courts are entitled to ask such questions, and if the Court is willing, it can reply to queries in which the indirect review of national legislation of another Member State is at stake.

---

[14] Para 30 of the Judgment in Case 244/80 *Foglia II*.

C. Ruling on the Substance

It was obvious that the Court's answer in case *Foglia I* was not satisfactory for the *Pretura di Bra*. AG Slynn was fully aware of this, though he did not voice it explicitly in his Opinion. The pragmatic approach taken in the procedural questions for reference is evidence of the AG Slynn's willingness to go into the substance of the case, which he did. He could have done it on a subsidiary basis, even if he agreed in the end with AG Warner (which he did not). In his Opinion in case *Foglia II*, AG Slynn not only explained, in detail, why the references needed to be replied on procedural grounds, but he also took a close look into the merits of the substantive issues and concluded that the *Pretura di Bra*'s suspicions (as well as Mr Foglia's and Ms Novello's) were correct.

The Opinion of AG Slynn in *Foglia II* explored the conformity of the French levy on liquor wine consumption, and he applied the conventional standards developed by the case-law to date at that time. As a result, AG Slynn proposed to the Court that it should review the French provisions by undertaking a substantive approach that looked at the direct or indirect effect of the measure, as well as the terms in which the goods were comparable in the market. This framework led AG Slynn to suggest that the French provisions were not in line with EEC law, thus confirming the underlying concern in Foglia and Novello's contractual arrangements.[15]

To go into the substance of the case seemed like an obvious choice once the AG admitted that the Court had jurisdiction to rule on the case. However, this approach also reinforced the arguments put forward by the AG to confirm the Court's jurisdiction. In the same way that AG Warner's strict approach led him not to deal with the substance (although he could have done so on subsidiary terms, in case he was not followed by the Court on the points of jurisdiction), AG Slynn's decision to tackle the substance reinforced considerably his willingness to hear the case, and invited the Court to give a ruling on the substance. In a certain way, the fact that Foglia and Novello were right, as a matter of law, in making contractual arrangement, could have diluted the concerns about the artificiality of the case. It was true that in the end the Court decided to remain attached to its first position and declined to rule on the case, but the degree of reasoning, the detail and the fact that it did not simply declare itself lacking jurisdiction, was probably the result of the Opinion of AG Slynn pointing in the exact opposite direction.

D. Effect on Future Case Law

The Opinion of AG Slynn is an excellent example of how an AG can subtly shape the direction of the Court's case law, even in areas in which the case-law seems to be settled. The case-law certainly seemed to be settled after case *Foglia I*, once AG Warner and the Court laconically refused to confirm jurisdiction. The terms in which the Court reasoned its second decision in the case, with a similar outcome as in case *Foglia I*, is a tribute to AG Slynn's persuasive Opinion. The Court could not simply repeat what it had argued in case *Foglia I*. After witnessing the frustration of the referring court, and with the Opinion of AG Slynn pursuing the opposite outcome and a convincing argument as to the substance, the Court had to give sound arguments to justify its decision. The fact that the judgment's conclusive answers to the *Pretura di Bra* do not simply highlight the Court's lack of jurisdiction, but on the contrary, it provided

---

[15] Pages 3076-77.

detailed answers to each of the individual questions referred on points of procedure, is proof of the impact of the Opinion in the Court's final decision.

But the Opinion has lived on, and has played an important role in conditioning the Court's temptation to develop the restrictive approach in the *Foglia v Novello* cases any further. Although the principles set in both judgments point towards a hard look of references in which suspicions of artificial arrangements might have been involved, the truth is that these precedents have hardly ever been applied again. The Court will highlight that it will take special precautions to avoid being instrumentalised, but in practice, the shadow of *Foglia v Novello* has not found any continuation. The doctrine stands as a shadow, whilst the real figure creating the luminic effect remains missing. There have been many occasions in which the Court could have taken a hard look, as it did in the two *Foglia v Novello* cases (cases *Chen*,[16] *Mangold*,[17] *Chain v Atlanco*,[18] to name but a few). The fact that the Court has kept far from any attempts at reviving and putting into action the *Foglia v Novello* test, demonstrates that the Opinion of AG Slynn was vindicated in the end. It could be said that, in practice and at the present time, the case-law on artificial arrangements is more clearly portrayed in the Opinion of the AG than in the judgment itself. Once again, only by looking into an Opinion can the case law of the Court be really understood.

---

[16] Case C-200/02 *Zhu and Chen* ECLI:EU:C:2004:639.
[17] Case C-144/04 *Mangold* ECLI:EU:C:2005:709.
[18] Case C-189/14 *Chain* ECLI:EU:C:2015:432.

16

The Intrinsic Value of Part-time Work in the Construction of the Internal Market: Opinion of Advocate General Slynn in Levin

JEFF KENNER

I. INTRODUCTION

Ms LEVIN WAS a British national who moved to the Netherlands with her South African husband in 1977. She had sufficient resources to live on without working but chose to work regularly as a chambermaid at hotels in Amsterdam. Despite this, Ms Levin was deemed not to be in employment and refused a residence permit. On 9 April 1979, Ms Levin applied to the Secretary of State for Justice for reconsideration of the decision. On that day, Ms Levin resumed work as a chambermaid working approximately 20 hours a week for a net income of 130 guilders per week.[1] In the absence of a reply, Ms Levin's application was rejected on the ground that such a limited amount of work for a small sum of money was insufficient for subsistence, because it was below the level of the minimum wage. Under Dutch law, Ms Levin was not a 'favoured EEC citizen' covered by the free movement provisions in the EEC Treaty (now TFEU). Ms Levin challenged the decision contending that she was pursuing an activity as an employed person and, moreover, it was irrelevant that her income was below the subsistence level, as she had other resources to support herself.

The *Raad van Staat*, the Judicial Division of the Council of State, referred three questions to the Court, neatly reformulated by AG Slynn in the Opinion issued on 20 January 1982.[2] The first question was whether a national of a Member State, who undertook work in another Member State but earned an income from that work below the minimum subsistence level in that state, fell within the scope of the provisions on freedom of movement for workers contained in Article 48 EEC (now Article 45 TFEU)? Secondly, would the answer to the first question be different if the individual had recourse to other resources that brought them to, or above, the minimum level of subsistence in that state or if they chose to live below that level? Thirdly, assuming that the first question was answered in the affirmative, can the right of the

---

[1] Equivalent to €53.50 in 2020. See 'Value of the Guilder versus the Euro', International Institute of Social History, https://iisg.amsterdam/en/research/projects/hpw/calculate.php. The facts are based on evidence provided by Ms Levin's counsel which was not challenged by the respondent.

[2] Opinion of AG Slynn in Case 53/81 *Levin* ECLI:EU:C:1982:10, p 1054.

worker to free movement be relied upon if her/his chief motive for residing in that state is for a purpose other than the pursuit of an activity or provision of services to a limited extent?

II. BACKGROUND AND CONTEXT

When *Levin* was lodged before the Court on 10 March 1981, the prevailing mood in the Community was intensely pessimistic. In a bleak report, the Economic and Social Committee noted rising unemployment, growing economic and social inequalities, a lack of solidarity between Member States, and institutional inertia to such an extent that 'the political will to attain the underlying objectives of the Community [was] lacking'.[3] In the early 1980s, before the Delors' Commission[4] and publication of the White Paper on 'Completing the Internal Market',[5] there appeared to be little prospect of fully realising the economic and social potential of unhindered free movement of persons in the Community. Whereas there had been optimism in the 1960s that the adoption of Regulation 1612/68 and related instruments[6] had reinvigorated the concept of free movement as 'a fundamental right of workers and their families',[7] and even established an 'incipient form of European citizenship',[8] by the dawn of the 1980s, the Community concept of the 'worker' and its limits had yet to be mapped out. The Commission's proposal to extend the personal scope of free movement by providing for a general right of residence for nationals of Member States in the territory of another Member State had stalled in the Council.[9] Debate about imbuing free movement with a right of European citizenship was mainly confined to articles in academic journals[10] and federalist motions of the European Parliament.[11]

However, *Levin* was about more than speeding up the construction of the single market or giving definition to a nascent European citizenship. In the 1970s, there had been rapid deindustrialisation, dislocation and change in the structure of the European labour market brought about by multiple factors including neo-liberal policies, the growth of further and higher education, and technological innovation. One of the consequences of what we now call globalisation was a shift from, on the one hand, the homogenous 'standard' employment relationship, where workers, typically male and unionised, worked full-time on a permanent

---

[3] 'Prospects for the 80s', Bull ESC 10/81, 5-12, 5. See J Kenner, *EU Employment Law* (Oxford, Hart Publishing, 2003) 71–73.

[4] J Delors, President of the Commission, 1985–1995.

[5] Commission, 'Completing the Internal Market. White Paper from the Commission to the European Council' COM (85) 310 final.

[6] Regulation (EEC) No 1612/68 of the Council of 15 October 1968 on freedom of movement for workers within the Community [1968] OJ L257/2; Council Directive 68/360/EEC of 15 October 1968 on the abolition of restrictions on movement and residence within the Community for workers of Member States and their families [1968] OJ L257/13; Council Directive 64/220/EEC of 25 February 1964 on the abolition of restrictions on movement and residence within the Community for nationals of Member States with regard to establishment and the provision of services [1964] OJ 56/845 (amended by Council Directive 73/148 [1973] OJ L172/14); Council Directive 64/221/EEC of 25 February 1964 on the co-ordination of special measures concerning the movement and residence of foreign nationals which are justified on grounds of public policy, public security or public health [1964] OJ 56/850.

[7] Regulation 1612/68, third recital of the preamble.

[8] L Sandri, 'Free Movement of Workers in the European Community', Bull EC 11/68, 5–9. Sandri was Commission Vice-President.

[9] Commission, 'Proposal for a Council Directive on a right of residence for nationals of Member States in the territory of another Member State' [1979] OJ C201/14.

[10] AC Evans, 'European Citizenship' (1982) 45 *MLR* 497.

[11] European Parliament, 'Draft Treaty establishing the European Union' [1984] OJ C77/33, 36.

basis for the same concern for their entire career with security, decent pay, and a pension, to, on the other hand, heterogeneous 'non-standard' employment, such as part-time, fixed term, and agency work, often with multiple employers and interspersed with periods of unemployment. Non-standard work was typically performed by women, young people, migrants, and other vulnerable workers.[12] It was often low paid, insecure, and, if there was a pension, it was meagre. The labour market was becoming more flexible,[13] creating diverse employment opportunities, but bifurcated between protected 'insiders' and precarious 'outsiders'.[14]

Fundamentally, *Levin* concerned the intrinsic value of part-time work and other forms of precarious employment. The decision to deny Ms Levin a work permit required AG Slynn and the Court to address the unfairness of excluding non-standard migrant workers and their family members from the European social model of access to free movement in order to seek employment with contingent labour rights. AG Slynn, appointed to the Court in 1981, was relatively new to his position when allocated *Levin*, but was vastly experienced in employment matters having served in the UK as junior counsel to the Ministry of Labour, a judge, and, from 1978 to 1981, President of the Employment Appeal Tribunal.[15] This grounding in employment law and understanding of the world of work served AG Slynn well in the formulation of the Opinion.

III. THE OPINION OF AG SLYNN

AG Slynn was admirably succinct in answering the first question on whether to include a person performing low paid part-time work within the meaning of 'workers' in Article 48 EEC. Two principles, established in *Hoekstra*,[16] applied to the construction of Article 48 EEC and subsidiary provisions on free movement for workers in the Community's implementing acts. First, the meaning of 'workers' was solely a matter of EC law, and second, 'unless there are compelling reasons to the contrary, a "worker" should be defined in such a way as to avoid as far as possible variations between Member States'.[17] Giving a Community scope to the term 'workers' in Article 48 EEC was therefore necessary to prevent a Member State from being able to 'eliminate at will' the protection afforded by the Community to the 'migrant worker'.[18]

Then, AG Slynn sought to put flesh on the bones of *Hoekstra*. AG Slynn emphasised that any derogations from the principle of free movement must be strictly construed and warned the Court to be slow to introduce any limits that would 'cut down the ordinary and natural meaning of the word "worker"'.[19] Referring to Article 3(3) of Directive 68/360 on the abolition

---

[12] Kenner (n 3) 300–301; U Mückenberger, 'Non-standard Forms of Work and the Role of Changes in Labour and Social Security Regulation' (1989) 17 *International Journal of the Sociology of Law* 381; G Bosch, 'Towards a New Standard Employment Relationship in Western Europe' (2004) 42 *British Journal of Industrial Relations* 618; E Ales et al (eds), *Core and Contingent Work in the European Union: A Comparative Analysis* (Oxford, Hart Publishing, 2017).

[13] J Kenner, 'New Frontiers in EU Labour Law: From Flexicurity to Flex-Security' in M Dougan and S Currie (eds), *50 Years of the European Treaties: Looking Forward and Thinking Back* (Oxford, Hart Publishing, 2009).

[14] I Florczak and M Otto, 'Precarious Work and Labour Regulation in the EU: Current Reality and Perspectives' in J Kenner et al (eds), *Precarious Work: The Challenge for Labour Law in Europe* (Cheltenham, Edward Elgar, 2019) 1–2.

[15] See ch 5.

[16] Case 75/63 *Hoekstra* ECLI:EU:C:1964:19, 184.

[17] Opinion of AG Slynn in Case 53/81 *Levin* ECLI:EU:C:1982:10, p 1058.

[18] ibid, p 1058, citing Case 75/63 *Hoekstra*, p 184.

[19] ibid, p 1059, citing Case 152/73 *Sotgiu* ECLI:EU:C:1974:13, para 4; Case 36/75 *Rutili* ECLI:EU:C:1975:137, paras 16, 27.

of restrictions on workers' free movement and residence, the AG observed that Member States were required to issue a residence permit and an entry document upon proof of employment. The Directive did not restrict 'the type of work, the number of hours or the wage'.[20] Moreover, under Article 2(2) of Directive 64/221 on limitations in Article 48(3) EEC on grounds of public policy, public security and public health, 'such grounds shall not be invoked to service economic ends'. Finally, the overarching Regulation 1612/68 'emphasises the right of *all* workers to pursue the activity of their choice'.[21] Having stressed the need for an inclusive approach to the 'worker' concept, AG Slynn issued the most powerful passage of the Opinion revealing an acute understanding of the realities of 'work':

> It seems to me to be too restrictive an interpretation to read "worker" as meaning only a full-time worker. I find it impossible to accept the argument that a part-time worker as such is not a worker within the meaning of Article 48. Such a result would in present circumstances exclude a very large, and probably increasing number of persons from the rights conferred by Article 48 and the Regulation and Directives to which reference has been made. The group includes not only women, the elderly and disabled who, for personal reasons might wish only to work part- time, but also women and men who would prefer to work full time but are obliged to accept part-time work. In the absence of clear words, excluding part-time workers from such rights, I do not believe that they were intended to be deprived of those rights.[22]

Moreover, by excluding part-time workers, a Member State could discriminate against nationals of other Member States and, if the definition of full-time work in that Member State was laid down in legislation, there could 'inevitably be substantial restrictions on the mobility of labour which the Treaty sets out to eradicate'.[23] The same logic meant that it was not 'possible' to read into Community legislation an alternative task for the Court to set a 'fixed minima' of hours worked or wages earned before a person was deemed a 'worker'.[24] AG Slynn rejected the suggestion that 'universal criteria' could be applied to 'divide the genuine part-time worker from the person who took a job for a few hours a week as a front in order to benefit from the rights conferred on workers'.[25] This passage was important when we compare the approach of the AG with that of the Court below. Avoiding such a distinction, the AG proffered a clear, inclusive answer to the first question:

> It seems to me that a person who is offered employment and who accepts it is a worker for the purpose of the legislation even though he earns less than the wage which is regarded as the minimum necessary in the State in question to enable the cost of subsistence to be met.[26]

AG Slynn dispatched the second question speedily, agreeing with the Commission's argument that the existence of private means to enable the person to bring their earnings up to the minimum subsistence level of the state was not a 'relevant factor' in construing Article 48 EEC.[27]

Turning to the third question on whether the worker must show that the work they undertake is their main purpose or dominant intention, AG Slynn gave a convoluted and somewhat meandering answer. Under Dutch law, as noted in the Court's report on the facts, the EEC citizen was required to have the 'subjective will' to pursue an occupation and, it was contended,

---

[20] ibid, p 1059.
[21] ibid, AG Slynn's emphasis.
[22] ibid.
[23] ibid, p 1060.
[24] ibid.
[25] ibid.
[26] ibid.
[27] ibid.

that this was absent because Ms Levin took up employment in order to enable her husband to have a right of residence.[28] The AG highlighted Article 48(3)(b), concerning the right to move freely 'for the purpose of' accepting employment, and Article 48(3)(c), the right to stay 'for the purpose of' employment, and similar language in implementing measures.[29] On this basis, 'the worker must show he wishes to enter and reside for the purpose of employment' and such a purpose must be 'genuine' and 'substantial'.[30] Taking up part-time work on pay less than the subsistence level can be genuine or substantial as it will increase the worker's standard of living and 'a hope of more hours and pay later may exist'.[31] For AG Slynn, such a 'worker' can be differentiated from a person whose real purpose is to study or retire and, therefore, may not be entering for the purposes of employment 'even if as a device he takes on a few hours' work each week or from time to time'.[32] AG Slynn opined that '[the] fewer hours worked, the more difficult it may be to establish that work is such a genuine and substantial purpose'.[33] Also, in the context of the limitations in Article 48(3) EEC, a 'low income' may be considered along with other factors such as a criminal record.[34]

At this point, AG Slynn provided more clarity by stating that 'although the purpose of working must be a genuine and substantial purpose, I do not think that it has to be shown to be the dominant or principal purpose'.[35] Indeed a person may wish to work in a Member State because of a family connection or the quality of the health or education system and having such reasons as the prime motivation 'does not prevent the purpose of work from being a genuine and substantial one'.[36] From this, it can be implied that it would be legitimate if Ms Levin's principal motive for working was to secure her husband's status as a lawful resident.

IV. ANALYSIS

AG Slynn offered lucid and persuasive advice to the Court on the first two questions. Establishing a broad, inclusive Community-wide interpretation of 'workers' validated part-time work as important for the individual in raising their standard of living and useful for the market integration process even if the worker earns less than the subsistence level in the host Member State. If followed by the Court, it prevented that state from imposing definitions of part-time or full-time work that may discriminate against nationals of other Member States. It recognised that part-time work and other forms of non-standard work may be a necessary choice or the only option for the most marginalised.

AG Slynn's answer to the third question was problematic, however, in requiring an examination of the person's motive for entering and staying in another Member State. It would impose a burden of proof on the person to show that the purpose of their work was 'genuine' and 'substantial'. Such ambiguous language might lead to arbitrary interpretations of a person's motives for working based on prejudice. Sufrin observes that 'such gradations of motive would

---

[28] Judgment in Case 53/81 *Levin* ECLI:EU:C:1982:105, pp 1037–38.
[29] Page 1060 of the Opinion. See Art 1 of Directive 64/221; first recital of the preamble to Regulation 1612/68; Art 2 of Directive 68/360.
[30] ibid.
[31] ibid, p 1061.
[32] ibid.
[33] ibid.
[34] ibid.
[35] ibid.
[36] ibid.

be unworkable' and 'unless motive was also relevant to full-time workers there would be discrimination between them and part-timers'.[37]

A. The Judgment

The Court restricted its consideration to the issue of free movement for workers in employment. It resisted the Commission's suggestion that it should take the opportunity to consider the position of nationals of another Member State who were unemployed but seeking work in the host Member State.[38]

When addressing the first question, the Court followed AG Slynn in applying the principle that it was necessary to give the terms 'worker' and 'activity as an employed person' a Community meaning to prevent free movement from being frustrated by making it subject to criteria, such as the level of minimum wage.[39] The Court emphasised the right of all workers to freely pursue their chosen activity and the unconditional nature of the right of residence drawing on the same legislative sources as the AG.[40] Giving 'full scope' to these terms conformed with the objectives of the Treaties of 'promoting throughout the Community a harmonious development of economic activities and a raising of the standard of living'.[41] Hence, the Court evinced the AG's reasoning on the intrinsic value of part-time work:

> Since part-time employment, although it may provide an income lower than what is considered to be the minimum level for subsistence, constitutes for a large number of persons an effective means of improving their living conditions, the effectiveness of Community law would be impaired and the achievement of the objectives of the Treaty would be jeopardised if the enjoyment of rights conferred by the principle of freedom of movement for workers were reserved solely to persons engaged in full-time employment and earning, as a result, a wage at least equivalent to the guaranteed minimum wage in the sector under consideration.[42]

Thus, a part-time worker was pursuing an 'activity as an employed person', even if the remuneration was below the minimum guaranteed level for that activity and, neatly addressing the second question, there was 'no distinction' between those who managed to subsist on their income from that activity and those who supplemented it with other income 'whether the latter is derived from property or from the employment of a member of their family who accompanies them'. This was an important elaboration which recognised that free movement would not be hindered if a third-country family member was the main earner in the worker's household and anticipated the subsequent legislative recognition of the right of a family member of an EU citizen to work in the host Member State and be treated equally with nationals of that state.[43]

---

[37] BE Sufrin, 'When is a Worker a Worker?' (1983) 46 *MLR* 495, 497.

[38] The Court, at p 1043 of the Judgment, notes the Commission's reference to an interpretative Council declaration, issued when adopting Regulation 1612/68 and Directive 68/360, allowing for a three-month period of work seeking. Later, in Case C-292/89 *Antonissen* ECLI:EU:C:1991:80, it was established that the worker category in Art 48 EEC (now Art 45 TFEU) was not exhaustive. It encompassed a period for work seekers to access the labour market.

[39] Paras 11–12 of the Judgment, applying *Hoekstra*.

[40] Opinion, p 1059.

[41] Para 15 of the Judgment, referring to Arts 2 and 3 EEC.

[42] ibid.

[43] Arts 23 and 24 of Directive 2004/38/EC of the European Parliament and of the Council of 29 April 2004 on the right of citizens of the Union and their family members to move and reside freely within the territory of the Member States amending Regulation (EEC) No 1612/68 and repealing Directives 64/221/EEC, 68/360/EEC, 72/194/EEC, 73/148/EEC, 75/34/EEC, 75/35/EEC, 90/364/EEC, 90/365/EEC and 93/96/EEC [2004] OJ L158/77.

At this point, the Court, unlike the AG, sought to distinguish between two types of activities based on whether the individuals in question are 'persons who pursue or are desirous of pursuing an *economic activity*'.[44] The rules that guarantee freedom of movement for workers 'cover only the pursuit of effective and genuine activities, to the exclusion of activities on such a small scale as to be regarded as purely marginal and ancillary'.[45] AG Slynn, by contrast, deployed the term 'genuine part-time worker' but rejected a 'fixed minima' or the use of 'universal criteria' to exclude marginal workers on a low income. The AG's approach would cover all those who were offered and accepted employment, even if the wage was below the subsistence level.[46] The Court's test is problematic because even a minimal amount of remunerated work can be economically important for an individual, which left the meaning of the term 'effective and genuine' uncertain.[47] The Court's test, equating 'effective and genuine' work with economic activity, has been criticised by O'Brien, not only because it has 'developed its own internal logic, becoming an accepted practice with fixed terms and concepts',[48] but also, it 'squeezes social concerns out of the definitional process and shuts out any positive equality duty'.[49] This critique is briefly examined in the next section.

Turning to the third question, on the relevance of the motive of the individual pursuing employment, the Court provided a more straightforward answer than AG Slynn. For the Court it was 'inherent' in the principle of free movement for workers that the freedom 'may be relied upon by persons who actually pursue or seriously wish to pursue activities as employed persons'.[50] Therefore, so long as the 'condition' of 'effective and genuine activity as an employed person' is satisfied, the motives of the worker in seeking employment in the host state 'are of no account and must not be taken into consideration'.[51] The Court's approach is preferable to AG Slynn's attempt to identify a 'genuine and substantial purpose' for employment,[52] although the term 'seriously wish to pursue' is not without its difficulties. For the Court, it is the economic activity that must be 'genuine' not its objective although either the AG's or the Court's test might lead to similar outcomes. Nevertheless, the Court's firm rejection of motive as a factor limits the scope for narrow moral judgments being applied by national courts.

B. Effect on Future Case Law

40 years on, *Levin* remains the starting point in cases concerning the scope of 'workers' in Article 45 TFEU. The Opinion of AG Slynn and the judgment of the Court interweave the economic dimension of free movement, based on remuneration for work as an economic activity, with its social purpose, contributing to improving the worker's standard of living and recognising the intrinsic value of part-time work for the migrant worker, even if low paid or supplemental to other income. Recognition of low paid work in *Levin* has been a catalyst for the inclusion of more precarious workers within the 'worker' construct.

---

[44] Para 17 of the Judgment. Emphasis added.
[45] ibid.
[46] Opinion, p 1060.
[47] Sufrin (n 37) 497.
[48] C O'Brien, 'Social Blind Spots and Monocular Policy Making: The ECJ's Migrant Worker Model' (2009) 46 *CMLRev* 1107, 1117.
[49] ibid, 1128.
[50] Para 21 of the Judgment.
[51] Para 22 of the Judgment.
[52] Opinion, pp 1080–81.

In *Kempf*,[53] the Netherlands refused a residence permit, this time to a German national giving approximately twelve piano lessons a week. Here, however, Mr Kempf did not have a supplemental income and was reliant on social security benefits, which, according to the Netherlands, meant that the work was not 'effective and genuine'. However, the Court found the case indistinguishable from *Levin* because the part-time work was regarded by the referring court not to be marginal and ancillary and, therefore, as Mr Kempf was a 'genuine' part-time worker it did not matter that the supplemental income was from public funds.[54]

While the 'effective and genuine' test may have been a reflex by the Court in response to concerns of some Member States about an influx of labour from Member States with less generous levels of social assistance,[55] the Court has not adopted a narrow economic approach based on a minimum number of hours worked.[56] For example, work for remuneration in kind, such as provision of food, accommodation and expenses, can be deemed 'economic activity',[57] establishing the principle that neither the *sui generis* nature of the employment relationship, nor the level of productivity, the origin of the funds, or the limited amount of remuneration 'can have any consequence in regard to whether or not the person is a worker'.[58] Thus, training is 'work' if the trainee is sufficiently familiar with their work to be 'effective',[59] and ten hours of work per week can be effective and genuine.[60] *Levin* has been reinforced in cases in which subjective factors such as the conduct of the worker have been declared not to be relevant to status.[61] This guidance is important as ultimately what is 'effective and genuine' is a matter to be decided by the national court.[62]

The case law discussed above demonstrates that the test is not about the amount of remuneration or hours worked, but rather, whether there is a 'genuine intention to work',[63] as opposed to some other intention such as study.[64] The consequences can be seen in *Bettray*, where the Court put an unnecessary gloss on the 'effective and genuine test' to exclude a worker on an ex-offender rehabilitation scheme from Article 45 TFEU on the basis that he was not in 'employment under normal conditions',[65] or using the term of AG Jacobs, not part of the 'normal labour market' because he was not in competition with other workers for employment.[66] AG Jacobs emphasised the unusual nature of the case, and distinguished it from a situation where a disabled worker 'cannot work under normal conditions', but is 'none the less engaged by way of employment in an effective and genuine activity'.[67] Nevertheless, as O'Brien observes, the 'disapprobation of "work" that exhibits a primarily social purpose is likely to impact adversely on disabled workers … who may themselves see work in terms of social interaction rather than material rewards'.[68] This ties with O'Brien's broader critique

---

[53] Case 139/85 *Kempf* ECLI:EU:C:1986:223.
[54] ibid, para 14.
[55] P Craig and G de Búrca, *EU Law: Text, Cases and Materials*, 7th edn (Oxford, OUP, 2020) 815.
[56] O'Brien (n 48) 1116.
[57] Case 196/87 *Steymann* ECLI:EU:C:1988:475, para 12.
[58] Case C-188/00 *Kurz* ECLI:EU:C:2002:694, para 32.
[59] *Kurz*, ibid; Case C-357/89 *Raulin* ECLI:EU:C:1992:87; Case C-3/90 *Bernini* ECLI:EU:C:1992:89.
[60] Case C-171/88 *Rinner-Kühn* ECLI:EU:C:1989:328.
[61] Case C-413/01 *Ninni-Orasche* ECLI:EU:C:2003:600.
[62] See Case C-276/07 *Delay* ECLI:EU:C: 2008:282.
[63] E Johnson and D O'Keeffe, 'From Discrimination to Obstacles to Free Movement: Recent Developments Concerning the Free Movement of Workers 1989–1994' (1994) 31 *CMLRev* 1313, 1318.
[64] Case C-94/07 *Raccanelli* ECLI:EU:C:2008:425.
[65] Case 344/87 *Bettray* ECLI:EU:C:1989:226, para 18. Distinguished in Case C-456/02 *Trojani* ECLI:EU:C:2004:488.
[66] Opinion of AG Jacobs in Case 344/87 *Bettray* ECLI:EU:C:1989:113 para 32.
[67] ibid, para 23.
[68] O'Brien (n 48) 1131.

that the Court's focus on 'economic activity' excludes social objectives outside its internal market frame of reference.[69]

Levin needs updating to reflect the development of Union citizenship, the widening of the social provisions in the TFEU, and the adoption of a positive disability duty based on a 'social model' which removes barriers to the labour market.[70] The 'normal labour market' test 'contradicts Community social objectives, such as the promotion of occupational mobility and social inclusion of carers'.[71] O'Brien[72] cites cases where an informal carer,[73] or person receiving a care allowance,[74] have been found not to be 'workers'. There is a danger that the Court will fall back on the argument that such free movers are now covered by their right of citizenship in Article 21 TFEU, which is more limited for those not included under the economic tests for Articles 45, 49 or 57 TFEU (see below). Consequently, '[e]quating care with economic inactivity risks in certain cases locking carers out of the jobs market'.[75] Moreover, as precarity rises with increasing use of zero hours contracts and the growth of the gig economy, workers from other Member States on low incomes and in insecure jobs are at heightened risk of exclusion from the EU's legal framework of equal treatment.[76]

Nevertheless, *Levin* provided a springboard for a broad, inclusive definition of 'worker' in cases where it is necessary to distinguish a 'worker' in an employment relationship under Article 45 TFEU from a person pursuing an activity as a self-employed person within the scope of the right of establishment, Article 49 TFEU, or a provider of services, Articles 56–57 TFEU. In *Lawrie-Blum*, the Court established an objective test whereby the essential feature of an employment relationship is that 'for a certain period of time a person performs services for and under the direction of another person in return for which he receives remuneration'.[77] Usefully, this wide test has been applied horizontally beyond the internal market to cover the term 'work' under the equal pay principle in Article 157 TFEU,[78] and when 'worker' is used in EU social policy legislation without reference to national definitions of 'worker' or 'employee',[79] it has been given an autonomous meaning specific to EU social law to prevent Member States from imposing a more restrictive interpretation. Unlike with Article 45 TFEU it is not necessary to refer to an 'economic activity'. Rather, the term 'worker' must be defined 'in accordance with objective criteria which distinguish the employment relationship by reference to the rights and duties of the persons concerned'.[80] Thus, a person classified as self-employed under national

---

[69] ibid, 1107.

[70] See UN, 'Convention on the Rights of Persons with Disabilities', UN General Assembly Resolution, A/RES/61/106, 13 Dec 2006, entered into force on 3 May 2008, www.un.org/disabilities/convention/conventionfull.shtml. It was incorporated into EU law under Council Decision 2010/48/EC of 26 November 2009 concerning the conclusion, by the European Community, of the United Nations Convention on the Rights of Persons with Disabilities [2010] OJ L23/35.

[71] O'Brien (n 48) 1107.

[72] ibid, 1118–19.

[73] Case C-77/95 *Züchner* ECLI:EU:C:1996:425.

[74] Joined Cases C-502/01 & C-31/02 *Gaumain-Cerri and Barth* ECLI:EU:C:2004:413.

[75] O'Brien (n 48) 1119.

[76] C O'Brien, 'Civis Capitalist Sum: Class as the New Guiding Principle of EU Free Movement Rights' (2016) 53 CMLRev 937.

[77] Case 66/85 *Lawrie-Blum* ECLI:EU:C:1986:284.

[78] Case C-256/01 *Allonby* ECLI:EU:C:2004:18.

[79] See Art 2(1) of Directive 2003/88/EC of the European Parliament and of the Council of 4 November 2003 concerning certain aspects of the organisation of working time [2003] OJ L299/9; Art 2 of Council Directive 92/85/EEC of 19 October 1992 on the introduction of measures to encourage improvements in the safety and health at work of pregnant workers and workers who have recently given birth or are breastfeeding (tenth individual Directive within the meaning of Article 16 (1) of Directive 89/391/EEC) [1992] OJ L348/1.

[80] Case C-147/17 *Sindicatul Familia Constanţa* ECLI:EU:C:2018:926, para 41.

law may be recognised as a 'worker' under EU law and protected by the applicable EU social legislation without the need to show 'economic activity' as a factor of market integration. The horizontal 'worker' test has been found to include workers as diverse as company directors,[81] musicians,[82] and foster parents.[83] This case law indicates that is not essential for there to be subordination in the employment relationship. The Court has preferred a broad meaning of 'worker' that includes all those who have an employment relationship in which they are not wholly autonomous.[84]

Finally, it is worth recalling the inertia in the Community in the early 1980s. The Commission had plans for a series of directives to provide for equal treatment of atypical workers, including between part-time and full-time workers carrying out comparable work with the same employer. AG Slynn's vision of the intrinsic value of part-time work in *Levin*, which was settled case law by the late 1980s, provided impetus for the Commission to move forward. By 1990, it had published its first legislative proposal on part-time work,[85] which was eventually to bear fruit in an adapted form in 1997 by means of a Directive implementing a Framework Agreement between the social partners.[86]

---

[81] Case C-232/09 *Danosa* ECLI:EU:C:2010:674.

[82] Case C-413/13 *FNV Kunsten Informatie en Media* ECLI:EU:C:2014:2411.

[83] Case C-147/17 *Sindicatul Familia Constanța* ECLI:EU:C:2018:926.

[84] J Kenner, 'Recent Court of Justice Judgments on Working Time' (2019) 20 *ERA Forum* 259, 262.

[85] Commission, 'Proposal for a Council Directive on certain employment relationships with regard to working conditions' (COM) 90 228 final.

[86] Council Directive 97/81/EC of 15 December 1997 concerning the Framework Agreement on part-time work concluded by UNICE, CEEP and the ETUC – Annex: Framework agreement on part-time work [1998] OJ L14/9.

17

Free Movement of Goods and the Public Security Exception: Opinion of Advocate General Slynn in Campus Oil

GRAHAM BUTLER

I. INTRODUCTION

ARTICLE 36 TFEU contains a number of listed grounds upon which Member States may attempt to rely upon, to justify national measures that derogate from giving effect to the free movement of goods. One of these listed grounds is public security, and is specifically contained in the respective internal market freedoms provisions in the EU Treaties. Prior to *Campus Oil*, the 'public security' term, at least in regards to the free movement of goods, had not been interpreted or applied by the Court. Thus, with AG Slynn assigned to the case, it afforded him the opportunity to give the first judicial pronouncement of the Court on how public security was to be understood in this regard to this foremost freedom.[1] Given this first mover advantage, AG Slynn had the opportunity to shape the interpretation of the concept within internal market law, beyond merely the case at hand, but more broadly on the notion of security and EU law.

The question in *Campus Oil* was, essentially, how far the public security (*sécurité publique*) exception extended for Member States to derogate from the premise of free movement. There were and are two opposing views. On the one end of the spectrum is the view that public security is a delicate matter for the nation state to protect and defend its interests. On the other end of that spectrum is a narrower structural view that sees any measure of a Member State, in the name of public security, as hampering the effectiveness of free movement. Where the case law on this matter comes down is ultimately a matter of several considerations, commencing in *Campus Oil* as regards trade in goods. The *Campus Oil* case is essentially known for how Member States may successfully invoke the public security exception, but simultaneously, how that its invocation must be sufficiently justified, in light of given circumstances.

II. BACKGROUND, CONTEXT, AND FACTS

During the 1970s, there were several oil shocks that resulted in extreme volatility in the price of petroleum. Not only did pricing fluctuate, but shortages were evident, which threatened

---

[1] Opinion of AG Slynn in Case 72/83 *Campus Oil* ECLI:EU:C:1984:154.

the normal functioning of societies around the world. The then EC Member States were not immune to such events, and famously, many had its residents queuing outside of petroleum stations to fill their motor vehicles arising from the shortages. In 1971, prior to the accession of the Ireland to the then European Communities, Irish law through the Fuels (Control of Supplies) Act 1971 (the 1971 Act) allowed for the national government to enact regulation and control of the supply and distribution of fuels and for the control, regulation, restriction or prohibition of the import or export of fuels.[2] However, this was only where 'common good necessitate the control by the Minister on behalf of the State of the supply and distribution of fuel'.[3] In other words, only exceptional situations could necessitate such action.

As a result of subsequent oil shocks, further measures were taken by the Member State on foot of the 1971 Act,[4] and it was thus alleged by the applicants that the Member State was acting in violation of then Article 30 EEC (now Article 34 TFEU) and Article 31 EEC (since repealed).[5] The nationals measures in question mandated that importers of oil had to purchase 35% of the good from a state-owned oil refinery within the Member State. The Member State in question had recently acquired the Whitegate Oil Refinery in County Cork on the south coast, the Member State's only oil refinery, from four major multinational oil companies. The Member State only acquired the oil refinery to prevent its closure by its prior owners, and had done so in consultation with the European Commission.

The national measures in place, in effect, meant that economic operators in the petroleum business, within the Member State, had to purchase a certain percentage of their goods from the state-owned oil refinery, with a fixed price set by that Member State, even if a more competitive price was available for that good – refined oil – in other Member States. The nub of the issue, from a free movement of goods perspective, therefore, was that the traders were being compelled into purchasing a good domestically, that they might otherwise purchase on the open market from other Member States.

Given that the national measures were clearly captured by Article 34 TFEU, though disputed, but it was uncertain where such a derogation could be justified, the referring national court under the Article 177 EEC (now Article 267 TFEU) preliminary reference procedure wanted to know whether it was permissible for the Member State to invoke the public security exception within Article 36 TFEU, to derogate from the free movement of goods and their import from other Member States under Article 34 TFEU. Whilst there would be unlisted grounds to derogate from Articles 34–35 TFEU, the grounds of mandatory requirements that were uncovered in *Cassis de Dijon*,[6] by contrast, *Campus Oil* offered AG Slynn and the Court the first real opportunity to give an understanding of what is meant by public security within the then Article 36 EEC (now Article 36 TFEU). However, the case did not just turn on public security alone, but also concerned the concept of a public policy exception, which was and is also listed in Article 36 TFEU.

---

[2] Fuels (Control of Supplies) Act, 1971. Number 3 of 1971. Amended by Fuels (Control of Supplies) Act, 1982. Number 18 of 1982.

[3] Art 2(1), Fuels (Control of Supplies) Act, 1971. Number 3 of 1971.

[4] Petroleum Oils (Control of Supply and Distribution) (Continuance) Order, 1982, Number 81 of 1982; Fuels (Control of Supplies) Order 1982. Number 280 of 1982; and, Petroleum Oils (Regulation or Control of Acquisition, Supply, Distribution or Marketing) Order, 1983. Number 1 of 183.

[5] Art 31 EEC was a transition period provision, and is no longer in the EU Treaties.

[6] Case 120/78 *Cassis de Dijon* ECLI:EU:C:1979:42.

III. THE OPINION OF AG SLYNN

By-and-large, the AG and Court were in agreement, though differing somewhat, as the analysis below elucidates. AG Slynn had no hesitation in finding that the national measure in question was a measure having equivalent effect of a quantitative restriction within the meaning of the then Article 30 EEC (now Article 34 TFEU).[7] The Member State had tried to convince the opposite. In essence, Ireland had argued that the goods in question – oil – was not *made* in the Member State, but rather, that it was only *refined*, and that consequently, there was no discrimination in place, given the source of the product was not a domestic good.

Unsurprisingly, AG Slynn did not accept this purely discriminatory reading of Article 34 TFEU, pointing to *Dassonville*,[8] in which he stated covered neither just discriminatory measures nor protectionist measures, but rather, the broader concept of hindering intra-Union trade.[9] Not only that he said, it was also discriminatory, given the compulsion to buy from a specific point in that Member State. From there however, he proceeded to permit the Member State to nonetheless derogate from Article 34 TFEU, using Article 36 TFEU and its public security exception, on the basis of the specific facts and circumstances before the Court. AG Slynn said such national measures were 'justified under Article 36 [TFEU] on the grounds of public security, and thereby not precluded by Article [34 TFEU], *if it is necessary, other than on economic grounds, to maintain essential services and supplies*' (emphasis added),[10] and that '[i]t will not be necessary for this purpose where the requisite oil supplies can be ensured by other means which are less restrictive of imports, such as the keeping of stocks'.[11]

IV. ANALYSIS

The proceedings before the national court in *Campus Oil* gave rise to considerable controversy. As a matter of national law in the Member State from which the preliminary reference originated, *Campus Oil* has legendary status. It is known for its role in the case law on interlocutory injunctions (interim measures),[12] but more importantly, the case is considered a landmark judgment of the Supreme Court of Ireland on how an order for a preliminary reference from a lower instance national court cannot be subject to an appeal.[13] It was alleged that the referring national court, the High Court of Ireland, with the judge in question, Murphy J, had made the reference for a preliminary ruling prematurely, on the basis that all facts underlying the dispute had not been affirmatively established.

In passing, AG Slynn noted that this was not the case, and notwithstanding the dispute in the referring court about the *full* extent of the facts, AG Slynn said '[i]n my view the learned

---

[7] ibid, p 2761.
[8] Case 8/74 *Dassonville* ECLI:EU:C:1974:82, para 5.
[9] ibid, p 2760.
[10] ibid, pp 2767–68.
[11] ibid.
[12] For just a selection of the commentary, see E Fahey, *Practice and Procedure in Preliminary References to Europe: 30 Years of Article 234 EC Case Law from the Irish Courts* (First Law, 2007) 98–104; BME McMahon and F Murphy, *European Community Law in Ireland* (London, Butterworths, 1989) 227–28; G Hogan et al, *Kelly: The Irish Constitution*, 5th edn (London, Bloomsbury Professional, 2018) 600, 670, 1112–23, 1138.
[13] For praise of this outcome (as opposed to the reasoning offered), see G Butler and J Cotter, 'Just Say No! Appeals Against Orders for a Preliminary Reference' (2020) 26 *EPL* 615, 622–26.

judge was entitled to refer the ... question in the way and at the stage he did'.[14] However, it is evident from comparing the Opinion of AG Slynn in *Campus Oil*, to that of the judgment of the Court, that AG Slynn was more willing to hold back on certain aspects of the case given the ongoing appeal at national level. By contrast, the Court was undeterred by this.[15]

Moreover, after AG Slynn had delivered his Opinion in *Campus Oil*, but prior to the Court rendering its judgment, the Commission had launched infringement proceedings before the Court against the Member State.[16] It can be construed that this action may have tried to indirectly assert pressure on the Court in reaching its judgment in *Campus Oil*.[17] However, the infringement was later discontinued, despite the fact that it would have been a lot more interesting, for the Court would have had to make a final determination itself in such a direct action, and not merely just ask the national court to apply the Court's interpretation of EU law in a preliminary reference case.

Nonetheless, the pure EU law aspects of the case are worthy of reflection. Section IV.A considers the use of the public security exception, whilst section IV.B contemplates the scope of the public policy exception, which is also a listed ground in Article 36 TFEU. Section IV.C critiques the economic aims non-exception for the free movement of goods, with section IV.D analysing the relevance of secondary law in the legal space at the time of *Campus Oil*. Section IV.E deliberates on the fact that the Court does not see any goods as being 'special', and conclusively, section IV.F reflects on the relevance of *Campus Oil* in the contemporary era, and demonstrates the continued relevance of the strict scrutiny approach of AG Slynn (and the Court) to public security exception in free movement law.

A. The Public Security Exception and the Free Movement of Goods

Campus Oil is most well-known for its contribution to understanding what is meant by a public security exception within the meaning of Article 36 TFEU, from the free movement of goods contained in Articles 34–35 TFEU.[18] The Opinion of AG Slynn in *Campus Oil* stated that a national measure that is taken on public security grounds, in itself, is not enough to

---

[14] ibid, p 2761.

[15] A point made in P Oliver, 'A Review of the Case Law of the Court of Justice on Articles 30 to 36 EEC in 1984' (1985) 22 *CMLRev* 301, 311.

[16] Case 126/84 *Commission v Ireland*, lodged at the Court in May 1984. This was between the delivered of the Opinion of AG Slynn on 10 April 1984, and the delivery of the judgment of the Court on 10 July 1984.

[17] However, it has otherwise been suggested there may have been practical difficulties on part of the Commission for not having lodged an infringement action sooner, prior to a dispute on the matter reaching the Court via the preliminary reference mechanism. K Mortelmans, 'Case 72/83, Campus Oil Limited and Others v. The Minister for Industry and Energy, and Others, Judgment of 10 July 1984, (1984) 3 C.M.L.R. 544.' (1984) 21 *CMLRev* 687, 711.

[18] Beyond the Opinion of AG Slynn in *Campus Oil*, the case has another interesting angle, for the purposes of this book, and EU law more generally. First, in the national proceedings before the High Court of Ireland, representing the applicants was John Cooke, who was later to be a judge of the Court of First Instance (later, the EU General Court). Representing the defendant, the state, was Nial Fennelly, who would later become AG Fennelly in 1995. Intervening in *Campus Oil*, as counsel for the UK, was a certain Francis Jacobs, who would later succeed AG Slynn in 1988, and become AG Jacobs. AG Fennelly and AG Jacobs served concurrently in the late 1990s. Mr Justice Fennelly later said that in *Campus Oil*, 'Mr Jacobs, as he then was, played no small part in persuading the Court to interpret the notion of "public security" in Article 36 [TFEU] ... as possibly encompassing the restrictions on trade adopted by the Irish government'. See N Fennelly, 'The Effect of European Community Law on Irish Law and the Irish Constitution' in A Arnull et al (eds), *Continuity and Change in EU Law: Essays in Honour of Sir Francis Jacobs* (Oxford, OUP, 2008) 454.

justify the measure in question. He later said that any derogation from the freedoms had to be properly justified, and specifically, and categorically of the view that '[n]o lesser test should be accepted'.[19]

Given the grounds offered by the Member State in trying to justify its measures, AG Slynn stated in *Campus Oil* that 'at the present day, the provision of adequate oil supplies has to be accepted as being crucial to the well-being of the State, for the maintenance of essential services and supplies. It is a fundamental and, by proper means, legitimate interest of the State to protect the supply of oil, which for some purposes has no substitute and for that reason may be different from other products which have been referred to'.[20] AG Slynn therefore concluded that a limited public security exception could exist, but with caution, through a proportionality assessment. In his own words:

> [s]uch legislation will be justified under Article 36 [TFEU] on the grounds of public security, and thereby not precluded by Article [34 TFEU], *if it is necessary, other than on economic grounds, to maintain essential services and supplies. It will not be necessary for this purpose where the requisite oil supplies can be ensured by other means which are less restrictive of imports, such as the keeping of stocks*'[21] (emphasis added)

Thus, AG Slynn's contextual approach favoured towards giving the benefit of the doubt to the Member State in invoking the public security exception, but was not all encompassing, and was not to be construed as an open-ended licence for the Member State to invoke the derogation, and that strict scrutiny had to apply to any invocation. It is fair to say that AG Slynn was more sceptical about the use of the public security exception than how the Court ultimately ruled. In contrast with the reasonably strict approach of AG Slynn, the approach of the Court in *Campus Oil* was much more widely encompassing, with it capturing more than public security within 'public security'. The Court said that '*[a]n interruption of supplies of petroleum products*, with the resultant dangers for the country's existence, *could therefore seriously affect the public security* that Article 36 [TFEU] allows States to protect' (emphasis added).[22] The Court furthermore stated 'in the light of the seriousness of the consequences that an interruption in supplies of petroleum products may have for a country's existence, the aim of ensuring a minimum supply of petroleum products *at all times*... and thus as capable of constituting an objective covered by the concept of public security' (emphasis added).[23] AG Slynn was narrower, and more correct. As put in subsequent analysis of *Campus Oil*, '[t]he Court seem[ed] to have elevated the public security heading to a level at which, once it has been made out that a measure can be justified under that heading, other effects of the measure can be ignored'.[24]

In *Campus Oil*, both AG Slynn and the Court found a legitimate aim, and the proportionality of that legitimate aim. The Court inserted some proportionality standards to be given to

---

[19] G Slynn, 'The Concept of the Free Movement of Goods and the Reservation for National Action under Art. 36 EEC Treaty' in J Schwarze (ed), *Discretionary Powers of the Member States in the Field of Economic Policies and their Limits under the EEC Treaty* (Baden-Baden, Nomos, 1988).

[20] Page 2763.

[21] Page 2768.

[22] Case 72/83 *Campus Oil* ECLI:EU:C:1984:256, para 34.

[23] Para 35.

[24] LW Gormley, *Prohibiting Restrictions on Trade within the European Economic Community: The Theory and Application of Articles 30–36 of the EEC Treaty* (Amsterdam, Elsevier Science, 1985) 136.

the national court,[25] following AG Slynn. Whilst the Court was happy to leave the proportionality assessment to the referring judge, AG Slynn was clear to put the Member State back in its box about the extent to which it had tried to construe public security. He stated that:

> [c]ontrary to what counsel for the Irish Government's submission appeared to be, justification is not established by the mere fact that the Government in its discretion decided to adopt these particular measures.[26]

Ever since *Campus Oil*, and following AG Slynn's narrative, it has been noted that in public security cases, the Court has been keen to give detailed criteria to national courts on how to engage in proportionality exercises in public security cases.[27]

Many years thereafter in *Campus Oil*, for example, in *Richardt*, the Court expanded the public security exception to cover the exports dimension of the free movement of goods in an Article 35 TFEU situation. Specifically, and expanding on *Campus Oil*, the Court said that 'it is necessary to state … that the concept of public security within the meaning of Article 36 [TFEU] … covers both a Member State's internal security and its external security'.[28] But yet the Court has also been keen to contain wider potential use of the public security exception across the freedoms. In *Sirdar*, it tried to summarise its prior jurisprudence on the matter. There, the Court felt compelled to state that the public security exception only applies in 'exceptional and clearly defined cases',[29] referring to all the public security exceptions, including that of goods, even though *Sirdar* was a case concerning equal treatment. The Court elaborated further in *Kreil*, saying that '[i]t is not possible to infer … there is inherent in the Treaty a general exception excluding from the scope of [Union] law all measures taken for reasons of public security'.[30] This concurs with AG Slynn in *Campus Oil* of the public security exception being drawn reasonably narrowly.

What is not talked about in either the Opinion of AG Slynn and nor the Court's judgment in *Campus Oil* is *when* a public security exception may be invoked by a Member State. In *Campus Oil*, excessive pre-emotive measures in the name of public security where taken, when in fact, it looked like an artificially protectionist economic measure to ensure a single oil refinery in the Member State would not operate at a loss. A correct construal of a public security exception, on consideration of when it can be invoked, is that excessive pre-emptive measures are to be prohibited, and only upon the production of compelling evidence of public security being imminently threatened can the exception be properly invoked. This could, and should have been addressed in *Campus Oil*.

B. The Public Policy Exception and the Free Movement of Goods

The aforementioned public security exception was only one of the two considered grounds in Article 36 TFEU that was considered as regards derogation grounds from the application of Article 34 TFEU. The public policy (*ordre public*) exception was also invoked by the Member State in question, as a fallback, should the public security exception have not been entertained by the Court.

---

[25] Para 51.

[26] Page 2764.

[27] See P Koutrakos, 'Public Security Exceptions and EU Free Movement Law' in P Koutrakos et al (eds), *Exceptions from EU Free Movement Law: Derogation, Justification and Proportionality* (Oxford, Hart Publishing, 2016).

[28] Case C-367/89 *Richardt* ECLI:EU:C:1991:376, para 22.

[29] Case C-273/97 *Sirdar* ECLI:EU:C:1999:523, para 16.

[30] Case C-285/98 *Kreil* ECLI:EU:C:2000:2, para 16.

AG Slynn was even more cautious on the use of public policy grounds in Article 36 TFEU to justify a derogation from Article 34 TFEU, much more so than he was on the public security exception. For AG Slynn, in his own words:

> [i]if less rigorous standards are adopted, it will be all too easy for 'public policy' ... to be used in such a way as to diminish the basic concept of a common market between Member States.[31]

In other words, public policy grounds should be subject to even stricter scrutiny than the public security exception. In stating so, he relied upon the judgment of Burrough J in the British courts in *Richardson v Mellish*, which stated that '[p]ublic policy is a very unruly horse, and when you get astride, you never know where it will carry you'.[32]

It is therefore surprising the position that AG Slynn ultimately took to the public policy exception, in saying that if the public security exception was not applicable in the case at hand, he would have been nonetheless satisfied to consider the case on the public policy exception ground.[33] Analysis of this assertion of AG Slynn has been, rightly, less than fully favourable. AG Slynn was consequently cautioning the Court of 'mounting the beast',[34] given the same considerations would equally apply to public security, but yet was nonetheless considering mounting it himself. Similarly, it has been said that an overall general ground of public policy would stand to be 'easily abused by Member States'.[35] It is thus a struggle to understand the logic of AG Slynn on this point. Thankfully, it was not considered further by the Court in *Campus Oil*, and paid due diligence to AG Slynn's own warning that he appeared not to pay attention to himself.[36]

Another reason why the Court did not want to touch the public policy exception, in respect of the free movement of goods, might have been because it previously blundered the public policy exception within the free movement of workers. A number of years beforehand in *Van Duyn*,[37] the Court gave extremely wide latitude to the Member State's understanding of the public policy exception there, before rolling back that extensive discretion to Member States in *Adoui*.[38] This toying with the public policy exception, which ultimately failed, was clearly in the background regarding the reasoning of AG Slynn and the Court in *Campus Oil*, demonstrating an unwilling to give such wide latitude as it did in *Van Duyn*, where it said that 'the concept of public policy may vary from one country to another and from one period to another, and it is therefore necessary in this matter to allow the ... [Member States] ... an area of discretion within the limits imposed by the Treaty'.[39] In the present era, the distinction to be drawn between public security and public policy has never been truly settled.[40]

C. Economic Aims Non-exception and the Free Movement of Goods

One reading of the *Campus Oil* judgment was that Member States could advance a derogation from Article 34 TFEU, with it being justified on economic aims when coupled with public

---

[31] Page 2767.
[32] *Richardson v Mellish* (1824) 2 Bing 229, Burrough J.
[33] Page 2764.
[34] S Weatherill and P Beaumont, *EC Law*, 3rd edn (London, Penguin, 1993) 399.
[35] McMahon and Murphy (n 12) 348.
[36] Para 33.
[37] Case 41/74 *Van Duyn* ECLI:EU:C:1974:133, paras 18–23.
[38] Joined Cases 115/81 and 116/81 *Adoui* ECLI:EU:C:1982:183, paras 5–9.
[39] Case 41/74 *Van Duyn*, para 18.
[40] D Edward and R Lane, *Edward and Lane on European Union Law* (Cheltenham, Edward Elgar, 2013) 464–65.

security concerns, notwithstanding that economic aims were not within the scope of Article 36 TFEU.[41] From the get-go, economic aims could not be stated as a ground for derogating from the free movement of goods, as affirmed in early case law such as *Commission v Italy (Pork)*. There, the Court said that Article 36 TFEU is 'directed to eventualities of a noneconomic kind which are not liable to prejudice the principles laid down by Articles [34–35 TFEU], as the last sentence of … [Article 36 TFEU] … confirms', and that 'it does not establish a generic protective'.[42]

Therefore, *Campus Oil* posed some difficult questions about the non-reliance of Member States on economic grounds to justify restrictions on the free movement of goods, when coupled with the permissible grounds listed in Article 36 TFEU, including public security. *Campus Oil*, in part, had to figure this relationship out. The applicants (and the Commission, intervening) were of the view that the national measure was merely an economic one, and could not rely upon Article 36 TFEU accordingly. They were furthermore of the view that even if the public policy or public security exceptions could potentially be relied upon, the Member State had not demonstrated any threat to public security to necessitate the national measure. It has even been claimed that the public security exception in *Campus Oil* was 'dreamed up'[43] when the case had to be defended before the Court, when in fact, the national measures were just a 'job security exception' at the oil refinery – an economic aim – which was not permitted.

Albeit there were hints that the national measures were not public security matters, but rather, economic justification grounds, both AG Slynn and the Court gave the Member State the benefit of the doubt, and adjudicated on the assumption that the public security exception grounds were genuine. The Court did not consider where the burden of proof lay, but AG Slynn was unequivocal in that it lay with the Member State.[44] He also said that Article 36 TFEU could not be invoked for purely economic ends, citing *Duphar*,[45] but both he and Court did not delve it this much further, and did not eliminate any further doubt that a purely economic aim of the Member State did not have a bearing on the case. Consequently, post-*Campus Oil*, it was not sufficiently clear that a purely economic aim could not be relied upon, even when a Member State was to also rely upon a list ground in Article 36 TFEU.

This conclusion in *Campus Oil* can be directly compared to the *Cullet* case, decided mere months after *Campus Oil*, where AG VerLoren van Themaat in *Cullet* said that 'it is quite impossible … to classify … [economic measures] … under any of the grounds set out in Article 36 [TFEU] …'.[46] He went on to note that, quite drastically, that if such grounds were 'accepted as justification, the existence of the four fundamental freedoms of the Treaty could no longer be relied upon'.[47] In *Campus Oil* therefore, the Court likely did not mean to imply that purely economic aims could be a factor in allowing a derogation from Article 34 TFEU. Neither, it is submitted, was that the intention of the curt analysis on this point in *Campus Oil* by AG Slynn, as is clear from his later extra-judicial writings.

---

[41] G de Búrca, 'The Principle of Proportionality and Its Application in EC Law' (1993) 13 *YEL* 105, 133.

[42] Case 7/61 *Commission v Italy* ECLI:EU:C:1961:31 (*Pork*). Moreover, see P Oliver, 'When, If Ever, Can Restrictions on Free Movement Be Justified on Economic Grounds?' (2016) 41 *ELRev* 147.

[43] LW Gormley, 'Comments on the Energy Sector' in J Stuyck and AJ Vossestein (eds), *State Entrepreneurship, National Monopolies and European Community Law* (Deventer, Kluwer Law and Taxation Publishers, 1993).

[44] This was consistent with the Court's judgment in Case 174/82 *Sandoz* ECLI:EU:C:1983:213, para 22.

[45] Case 238/82 *Duphar* ECLI:EU:C:1984:45.

[46] Opinion of AG VerLoren van Themaat in Case 231/83 *Cullet v Leclerc* ECLI:EU:C:1984:322, p 312.

[47] ibid.

Later, some years after *Campus Oil*, AG Slynn, soon to be Judge Slynn,[48] said that Article 36 TFEU 'is not meant as an easy escape route for a Member State which seeks to rely on one of the various factors which are there set out'.[49] This was despite AG Slynn agreeing that the Member State in *Campus Oil*, to which the Court agreed to allow the public security exception to be successfully invoked. Writing some years after that again, Judge Slynn singled out *Campus Oil* as a case that, notwithstanding the law, that there was, admittedly 'economic and political factors' that were at play.[50]

D. The Existence of Secondary Law

If the EU legislature has harmonised, usually partly, an area of policy, and thus becoming an area that is the subject of secondary law, it is no longer possible for Member States to fall back on the permissible derogations in that policy area that are contained within EU primary law. In the case at hand, the good in question was subject to secondary law, as regards supply of oil. Directive 72/425,[51] amending a prior directive,[52] in particular, demanded that Member States keep oil supplies to a level of approximately 90 days, either in each Member State itself, or through arrangement with another Member State.

Therefore, it is curious, with hindsight, that both AG Slynn and the Court were willing to pay less heed to this fact that primary law derogations – Article 36 TFEU in *Campus Oil* – could still be used to undermine a freedom where there was extensive secondary law. AG Slynn refused to accept that there was *sufficient* secondary law in play, and in turn, said that Article 36 TFEU could indeed be relied upon by the Member State. Specifically, he stated that the EU secondary law provided an extensive basis for ensuring oil supplies in the Union, but that nothing in those arrangements contributed 'to ensuring that oil shortages in the [Union] are dealt with on a [Union] basis'.[53]

In this vein, AG Slynn and the Court who followed the AG in *Campus Oil* can be criticised for not paying enough attention to EU secondary law that prevented the Member State from using the listed ground of public security in Article 36 TFEU. In light of *Campus Oil* therefore, it has specifically been said that it would be 'difficult to imagine that any directive (or any national measure, for that matter) could give an unconditional assurance that the interest in question would be protected in all circumstances: no such standards are possible in human affairs'.[54] More critically, if *Campus Oil* were to be followed more broadly on this point, then EU secondary law would not always eliminate the possibility for Member States to fall back on Article 36 TFEU, curtailing the true effects of harmonisation.

---

[48] AG Slynn was Advocate General at the Court from 26 February 1981 to 6 October 1988, and Judge from 7 October 1988 to 10 March 1992. See ch 5.

[49] Slynn (n 19) 21–22.

[50] G Slynn, *Introducing a European Legal Order* (London, Stevens and Sons, 1992) 52.

[51] Council Directive 72/425/EEC of 19 December 1972 amending the Council Directive of 20 December 1968 imposing an obligation on Member States of the EEC to maintain minimum stocks of crude oil and/or petroleum products [1972] OJ L291/154.

[52] Council Directive 68/414/EEC of 20 December 1968 imposing an obligation on Member States of the EEC to maintain minimum stocks of crude oil and/or petroleum products [1968] L308/14.

[53] Page 2765.

[54] J Currall, 'Some Aspects of the Relation between Articles 30–36 and Article 100 of the EEC Treaty, with a Closer Look at Optional Harmonisation' (1984) 4 *YEL* 169, 189.

E. The Non-existence of Special Goods

On whether oil is a special good, or to use the term in the plea of the Member State defending its measure, that oil is 'the lifeblood of the country', a number of grounds were advanced. It was argued that the Member State in question was a non-aligned neutral country, not a member of NATO, that the Member State was highly dependent on the good without any domestic production. Moreover, the Member State said that the national measures were only temporary until another arrangement was found. The United Kingdom intervened, in support of Ireland, said that whilst derogations from the free movement of goods should be construed narrowly, they cannot be so narrow as to render the actual effect of the derogation illusionary.

What the Court did say, of which AG Slynn did not, is that there cannot be such a thing as special goods. In particular, the Court said that notwithstanding the claim of the defendant Member State regarding the importance of petroleum products to the Member State, 'it is sufficient to note that the Treaty applies the principle of free movement to all goods',[55] and that '[g]oods cannot therefore be considered exempt from the application of that fundamental principle merely because they are of particular importance for the life or the economy of a Member State'.[56] Rather, all goods coming within Article 34 TFEU, and the use of the public security exception in Article 36 TFEU, would be highly circumstantial, which must be proportionate in light of objective considerations in order to be justified. Many years later, the essence of *Campus Oil* was confirmed in *PrussenElektra*, though there, AG Jacobs, the successor to AG Slynn, noted that petroleum products – oil – had a 'special economic role',[57] but is not the same as going a special *good*, it did not mean it demand any exceptional treatment.

F. Effect on Future Case Law

The determination on the public security exception within *Campus Oil*, as regards goods, would obviously be highly relevant across the other freedoms where the identical ground is put forth as a basis for justification. This was indeed recognised by AG Cosmas in *Albore*, a free movement of capital case, who said that 'the term 'public security' [was] used by the framers … to designate the same dimension of the public interest' across the freedoms.[58] However, with the potential breadth given to Member States in *Campus Oil*, and a Member State's success in relying upon it to justify a derogation from inter-state commerce, it was not long after *Campus Oil* before another Member State tried to invoke it. Accordingly, the judgment of the Court in *Campus Oil* was labelled as 'awkward',[59] and not easily applied to other cases involving the public security exception.

Around the same time as *Campus Oil* in another case, *Cullet*, another Member State attempted to use the public security exception as a basis for justifying minimum prices of petroleum in the name of avoid unrest amongst retailers of petroleum products, and arguing that the true market price of fuel would have endangered social order, triggering violence. Much like in *Campus Oil*, there were clearly protectionist economic considerations at play.

---

[55] Para 17.
[56] ibid.
[57] Case C-379/98 *PreussenElektra* ECLI:EU:C:2000:585, para 209.
[58] Opinion of AG Cosmas in Case C-423/98 *Albore* ECLI:EU:C:2000:158, para 47.
[59] Opinion of AG Tesauro in Case C-347/88 *Commission v Greece* ECLI:EU:C:1990:225, para 27.

In *Cullet* however, France was unsuccessful in invoking the public security exception, unlike Ireland in *Campus Oil*, who was successful.

AG VerLoren van Themaat in *Cullet* noted how the public security justification ground in Article 36 TFEU, affirmatively established and successfully invoked *Campus Oil*, should not necessarily be drawn too widely, and drew caution on the wider implications of *Campus Oil*, by noting that 'I think certain crucial differences of fact militate against applying that judgment [*Campus Oil*] by analogy in the present case [*Cullet*]'.[60] In *Cullet*, the Court took a different approach compared to *Campus Oil* also, and did not accept the Member State's justification. The Court stated that France 'ha[d] not shown that it would be unable, using the means at its disposal, to deal with the consequences which an amendment of the rules in question in accordance with the principles set out above would have upon public order and security'.[61]

Even outside the scope of the free movement of oil, but related to energy policy more generally, the issue of public security arose again in the *Electricity* cases.[62] There, AG Cosmas shared AG Slynn's view from *Campus Oil* that not too much breadth should be given to the public security exception.[63] The argument that *Campus Oil* should be understood as 'limited to the peculiar situation that prevails in the energy market in the [Union]',[64] is only half the truth however. Whilst it is a limited basis upon which the Member States can try to invoke, the *Campus Oil* nonetheless did prove that the public security exception is a ground that can be successfully invoked, and was not necessarily tied to energy, as *Richardt* later proved.[65]

In light of nearly 40 years since *Campus Oil* was delivered, it has been doubted whether the rationale of the justification ground accepted by the Court in *Campus Oil* would stand if *Campus Oil* were to be reheard today.[66] In *Greek Oil Supplies I*[67] and *Greek Oil Supplies II*,[68] though 10 years apart, the Court stood behind the assertion of oil supplies as coming within the scope of public security exception in Article 36 TFEU, as it initially established in *Campus Oil*. However, contrary to its judgment in *Campus Oil*, the proportionality assessment had clearly changed. The Court did not stand fully behind *Campus Oil* in *Greek Oil Supplies I*, and was willing to distinguish it. In *Greek Oil Supplies I*, the Court said, '[h]owever, it must be pointed out that Greece has not shown that if the [s]tate's rights with regard to the importation and marketing of petroleum products were not maintained in force, the public-sector refineries would be unable to dispose of their products on the market at competitive prices and thereby ensure their continued operation. Consequently, the argument relied upon in that regard by Greece must be dismissed'.[69]

---

[60] Opinion of AG VerLoren van Themaat in Case 231/83 *Cullet*, p 313.

[61] Para 33 of Judgment in Case 231/83 *Cullet*. According to Enchelmaier, the Court's judgment here was 'cryptic[]'. See S Enchelmaier, 'Article 36 TEU: General' in P Oliver (ed), *Oliver on Free Movement of Goods in the European Union*, 5th edn (Oxford, Hart Publishing, 2010) 252. It ought to be noted that the AG was also of the same view, but was keen to draw the distinction between *Campus Oil* and *Cullet*. See Opinion of AG VerLoren van Themaat in Case 231/83 *Cullet*, pp 313–14.

[62] Case C-157/94 *Commission v Netherlands* ECLI:EU:C:1997:499; Case C-158/94 *Commission v Italy* ECLI:EU:C:1997:500; Case C-159/94 *Commission v France* ECLI:EU:C:1997:501; Case C-160/94 *Commission v Spain* ECLI:EU:C:1997:502.

[63] Opinion of AG Cosmas in Case C-157/94 *Commission v Netherlands* ECLI:EU:C:1996:449, paras 81–82.

[64] Weatherill and Beaumont (n 34) 404.

[65] Case C-367/89 *Richardt* ECLI:EU:C:1991:376.

[66] P Oliver, 'Free Movement of Goods in the Labyrinth of Energy Policy and Capacity Mechanisms' in L Hancher et al (eds), *Capacity Mechanisms in the EU Energy Market: Law, Policy, and Economics* (Oxford, OUP, 2015) 211.

[67] Case C-347/88 *Commission v Greece* ECLI:EU:C:1990:470.

[68] Case C-398/98 *Commission v Greece* ECLI:EU:C:2001:565.

[69] Case C-347/88 *Commission v Greece* ECLI:EU:C:1990:470, para 49.

Thereafter in *Greek Oil Supplies II*,[70] the Court further demonstrated how hard it actually is to rely upon *Campus Oil*. That is to say, *Campus Oil* appears as a last resort for reliance on the public security exception, and not the first point in which Member States can rely upon as a line of defence. AG Ruiz-Jarabo Colomer was unequivocal. He stated that '[t]o my mind, the arguments which the ... [Member State] ... puts forward in the present proceedings in order to justify its legislation on grounds of national security lack the force of those put forward at the material time by the Irish Government [in *Campus Oil*] in order to justify national legislation which adversely affected imports of petroleum products into Ireland and which convinced the Court of Justice that one of the justifying grounds set out in Article 36 [TFEU] ... was present'.[71]

Thus, the Court has been turning slowly in the direction of AG Slynn over time, applying much more detailed scrutiny to the Member States, ensuring a public security exception is genuine, proportionate, and suitable; and not just a mask for economic aims. This demonstrates that the Opinion of AG Slynn in *Campus Oil* has mostly aged well, and has ensured that not too much room for manoeuvre is given to Member States for invoking the public security exception.

---

[70] Case C-398/98 *Commission v Greece* ECLI:EU:C:2001:565, paras 29–32.
[71] Opinion of AG Ruiz-Jarabo Colomer in Case C-398/98 *Commission v Greece* ECLI:EU:C:2001:96, para 48.

18

Ants Working Hard, and the Free Movement of Legal Services as Professional Activities: Opinion of Advocate General Slynn in Klopp

TAKIS TRIDIMAS

I. INTRODUCTION

*K*LOPP[1] IS A key case from the formative years of the right of establishment. The case delineated the scope of Article 52 EEC and venturing, if reticently, beyond discrimination on grounds of nationality, it brought home the impact of direct effect of what is now Article 49 TFEU. *Klopp* had an important signalling function. It granted EU primary law a strong constraining effect on state power to regulate professional activities, thereby relativising the importance of harmonisation directives. It also set in motion a line of authorities that expanded the reach of the right of establishment to indistinctly applicable measures, and infused liberal standards on professional regulation challenging established paths of dependency.

The Opinion of AG Slynn,[2] with which the judgment was fully aligned, has all the hallmarks of an Opinion delivered by a common lawyer at the relatively early years of the representation of the Anglo-Saxon tradition in the European bench. Concise but thorough, it is dispute-centred, rather than principle setting. Coming from an earlier era, there was little precedent to rely on, and there were no references to scholarly discourse. In terms of style, it tied in with his other Opinions, as demonstrated elsewhere in this book. AG Slynn was one of the few member of the Court to inter-change as both an AG and a judge.[3] He made a distinct contribution in, among others, the development of the free movement of persons,[4] and was instrumental in advancing the role of the oral hearing in proceedings at the Court. More broadly, he was an advocate of European law in the United Kingdom, and highly influential in promoting the role of the English Bar in Europe, bridging the common-civil law divide.

---

[1] Case 107/83 *Klopp* ECLI:EU:C:1984:270.
[2] Opinion of AG Slynn in Case 107/83 *Klopp* ECLI:EU:C:1984:174.
[3] See ch 5.
[4] AG Slynn delivered Opinions in, among others, the following cases: Case 197/86 *Brown* ECLI:EU:C:1987:375; Case 39/86 *Lair* ECLI:EU:C:1987:373; Case 24/86 *Blaizot* ECLI:EU:C:1987:372; Case 309/85 *Barra* ECLI:EU:C:1987:368; Case 293/85 *Commission v Belgium* ECLI:EU:C:1987:367; Case 139/85 *Kempf* ECLI:EU:C:1986:158; Case 293/83 *Gravier* ECLI:EU:C:1985:15; Joined Cases 35–36/82 *Morson and Jhanjan* ECLI:EU:C:1982:339; Case 53/81 *Levin* ECLI:EU:C:1982:10. For an assessment, see RCA White, 'Revisiting Free Movement of Workers' (2011) 33 *Fordham International Law Journal* 1564.

His Opinion in *Klopp* provided an important building block for *Vlassopoulou*[5] and *Gebbard*.[6] Neither of these cases could have been decided the same way, had Mr. Klopp failed in his claim. Thus, although the holding of the Court in *Klopp* does not represent the culmination of a line of case law, it was a *sine qua non* for its subsequent development and the modern understanding of the internal market. *Klopp* belongs to the category of cases where not only did the Court agree with the AG as to the outcome, but also the grounds of the judgment endorse fully the reasoning of the Opinion.

II. BACKGROUND, CONTEXT, AND FACTS

Mr Klopp was a German national who was a qualified lawyer both in Germany and France, and maintained an office in Düsseldorf. The Paris Bar refused him admission on the ground that, under its rules, *avocats* must have their chambers only in one place. The Court held that, even in the absence of any harmonisation directive, the right of establishment prevents the host state from denying to nationals of other Member States the right to exercise the legal profession solely on the ground that they maintain chambers simultaneously in another Member State.[7] *Klopp* came at a time when the European Economic Community emerged from *lourder*. Throughout the 1970s, the requirement of unanimity in Council voting, in combination with political disagreement or indifference, resulted in low legislative output. Stagnation rather than progress characterised the common market project. Whilst political action fell short of the commitments made in the Treaties, the judicial vision of Europe was guided by the peremptory language of the latter. Given that, traditionally, inter-state trade in goods was economically more important than trade in services, it is no surprise that the first battle ground was in the area of the former. *Dassonville*[8] had already unleashed the great potential of negative integration. It is not an accident that *Klopp* comes few months after the seminal *Cassis de Dijon*. As the underlying model of integration, based on market access and proportionality, began to morph in relation to goods, the tension between state power and market freedom expanded into other areas. It is in this context that the findings of the Opinion of AG Slynn and the judgment of the Court should be assessed.

III. THE OPINION OF AG SLYNN

In an earlier work, this author classified the functions of AGs as follows:

'(a) they assist the Court in the preparation of the case, e.g. by suggesting what is the appropriate formation to hear the case or whether any written questions should be put to the parties;
(b) they propose a solution;
(c) they provide legal grounds to justify that solution, in particular, by linking it to the sources of law, including case law, and placing it within the matrix of existing authority;
(d) they may opine on such points of law incidental to the case as they think fit and or make a critical assessment of the case law or comment on the development of the law more generally.'[9]

---

[5] Case C-340/89 *Vlassopoulou* ECLI:EU:C:1991:193.
[6] Case C-55/94 *Gebhard* ECLI:EU:C:1995:411.
[7] Para 22.
[8] Case 8/74 *Dassonville* ECLI:EU:C:1974:82.
[9] T Tridimas, 'The Influence of the Advocate General in the Development of Community Law: Some Reflections' (1997) 34 *CMLRev* 1349, 1358.

Whilst, in a specific case, the first type of contribution stated above may be difficult to discern for an observer outside the Court, the last three types can be determined on the basis of the court reports. The second and the third function are evident in the Opinion of AG Slynn in *Klopp*. The Opinion proved persuasive and was fully endorsed by the Court. The last function, which is not (and should not) be an attribute of all Opinions, is less present. This is partly the result of the specific case, which did not readily lend itself to wider pronouncements, and partly reflects the more general, dispute-specific, approach of AG Slynn. Be this as it may, his understanding of the right of establishment and, more broadly, economic integration was anything but narrow.

The Court made four findings in relation to all of which it followed the Opinion of the AG:

(a) it confirmed that Article 49 TFEU produces direct effect despite the absence of any harmonisation legislation;
(b) it held that freedom of establishment includes the right to maintain a professional basis in more than one Member States simultaneously;
(c) it suggested that the freedom goes beyond the principle of non-discrimination on grounds of nationality; and,
(d) it held that, in the interests of the administration of justice, the host state may impose restrictions on the way lawyers practice but such restrictions must be proportionate.

The interplay of the Opinion of AG Slynn and the judgment of the Court in relation to each of those findings merits attention.

A. Treaty Rights and Harmonisation Directives

The question posed in *Klopp* was whether, in the absence of any directive coordinating provisions governing access to and exercise of the legal profession, the single chambers rule of the Paris Bar was compatible with the right of establishment. The reference came from the *Cour de Cassation*, manifesting its openness towards EU law in contrast to the guarded approach of the *Conseil d'Etat*, which, for several years, kept its distance from the Court.

In answer to the question, the Court referred to the general programme for the abolition of restrictions on freedom of establishment adopted by the Council in 1961,[10] and pointed out that, although a directive had been adopted governing lawyers freedom to provide services,[11] no directive on freedom of establishment for lawyers has been adopted. However, following the Opinion of the AG, it reiterated *Reyners*.[12] Article 49 TFEU imposes an obligation to attain a precise result the fulfilment of which must be made easier by, but not dependent on, the implementation of a programme of progressive measures. Consequently, the fact that the Council had failed to issue a directive cannot serve to justify failure to meet the obligation.[13] As AG Slynn pointed out, the Court had already made it clear that Article 49 TFEU had direct effect and created a basic right not dependent on the issue of directives.

---

[10] Council, 'General Programme for the abolition of restrictions on freedom of establishment' [1962] OJ 36/7.
[11] Council Directive 77/249/EEC of 22 March 1977 to facilitate the effective exercise by lawyers of freedom to provide services [1977] OJ L 78/17.
[12] Case 2/74 *Reyners* ECLI:EU:C:1974:68.
[13] Para 10.

Although in *Reyners*, and *Van Binsbergen*,[14] the Court had already dissociated the direct effect of the right of establishment and the freedom to provide services from the adoption of harmonisation directives, *Klopp* went a step further. In *Reyners*, Belgian law squarely discriminated against a Dutch lawyer on grounds of nationality. The prohibition of such discrimination was the very minimum of the right of establishment and could not be said to be dependent on the adoption of harmonisation legislation. In *Klopp*, by contrast, Article 49 TFEU was invoked to set aside a provision of the host state which had nothing to do with nationality, but governed the way the profession was to be exercised in the national territory and which *prima facie* fall within the remit of that state's competence. It related more closely than the Belgian rule in *Reyners* to the exercise of, rather than access to, the profession. In that respect, *Klopp* extended the autonomous effect Article 49 TFEU increasing its independence from legislative action.

In *van Binsbergen*, Dutch law prohibited a lawyer based in Belgium from offering services in the Netherlands. Although the lawyer was a Dutch national, the law entailed discrimination on grounds of the place of residence nullifying the freedom to provide services. It interfered with a core aspect of that freedom which could not be said to be dependent on the adoption of harmonisation legislation. To some extent, *Klopp* had been foreshadowed by *van Binsbergen*, but its integrationist potential was greater given that it relates to the right of establishment rather that services. The closest precedent was *Thieffry*.[15] The Paris Bar had refused admission to a Belgian advocate, although his Belgian law diploma had been recognised by a French university as equivalent to the French law degree, and he had passed the French professional examinations for advocates. The Court held that the refusal to admit him was an unjustified restriction on the right of establishment. *Klopp* was essentially the first case under the right of establishment to concern requirements for the exercise of a professional activity other than professional qualifications.[16]

B. The Right to Secondary Establishment

The most impactful finding in *Klopp* is that freedom of establishment includes the right to maintain a professional basis in more than one Member State simultaneously. The reasoning of the AG Slynn was twofold. First, the right to secondary establishment was expressly stated in Article 52 EEC (now Article 49 TFEU) in relation to companies. This was a specific statement of a general principle applicable equally to the liberal professions. Secondly, if it were otherwise, it would mean that a person may only exercise the right of establishment in the host state at the expense of losing the right to carry out a professional activity at the home state. As AG Slynn put it, the intention of the Treaty was to allow multiple establishments, and it was 'quite impossible' to read it otherwise. As he put it:

> Article 52 [EEC, now 49 TFEU] gives a right of establishment in another Member State; it does not take away any right which may exist in the national's own Member State. Nor does it make renunciation of the latter the price of the former.[17]

---

[14] Case 33/74 *Van Binsbergen* ECLI:EU:C:1974:121.
[15] Case 71/76 *Thieffry* ECLI:EU:C:1977:55.
[16] See also LW Gormley, 'Freedom to Practise at the Bar in More than One Member State' (1984) 9 *ELRev* 439.
[17] See the Opinion in *Klopp* ECLI:EU:C:1984:174, at 2994.

C. The National Neutrality Characterisation of the Restriction

A distinct aspect of the case is that the rules of the Paris Bar were nationality neutral. They required that *avocats* must maintain only one office which must be within the territorial jurisdiction of the regional court where they were registered. The restriction thus applied without distinction between French nationals and those of other Member States. Nonetheless, both AG Slynn and the Court found the rules to infringe the right of establishment. This aspect of the case requires further analysis.

There were three possible types of discrimination involved.

First, difference in treatment on grounds of nationality. However, as stated, the rules applied without distinction and there was no direct discrimination.

Secondly, difference in treatment between lawyers maintaining more than one office within France and lawyers maintaining more than one office in France and in another Member State. This issue did not appear to occupy the Court. AG Slynn expressly excluded it from the scope of his inquiry, noting that the internal effect of the rules had nothing to do 'even obliquely' with their effect on inter-state situations.[18]

Thirdly, difference in treatment between outgoing and incoming lawyers. There was some uncertainty as to whether, even though the Paris Bar refused Mr. Klopp admission on the ground he had chambers in Germany, in practice it allowed its members to have a second set of chambers in other countries. The Court neutralised the issue by stating that it was for the national court to determine whether in reality the rules of the Paris Bar were discriminatory, and answered the question irrespective of whether they involved discrimination in this respect. AG Slynn referred to this type of differential treatment as part of his proportionality inquiry, and not as part of establishing whether a restriction existed.

The key point is that neither the AG nor the Court based their reasoning on the existence of any of the above types of differential treatment. They found the rules of the Paris Bar to be a restriction, despite their non-discriminatory character, thus taking the first step towards recognition that the right of establishment may extend beyond discrimination. This had already been recognised in relation to the free movement of goods,[19] but not openly in relation to Article 49 TFEU, although, to some extent, *Thieffry* and *van Binsbergen* had foreshadowed that Articles 49 and 56 TFEU are not tied to nationality discrimination. In *Thieffry*, the reason for rejecting admission to the Paris Bar was not the Belgian nationality of the applicant, but his lack of a French diploma. Also in *van Binsbergen*, the Court had accepted that the freedom to provide services could be invoked against the host state by one of its own nationals who had exercised free movement. Indeed, AG Slynn referred to *Thieffry* in support of the conclusion that Article 49 TFEU extended beyond discrimination on grounds of nationality.

Nonetheless, as it has been pointed out, *Klopp* did not establish unequivocally that, as a general rule, Article 49 TFEU covers non-discriminatory restrictions. The finding could be read more narrowly as referring only to non-discriminatory rules that prevent secondary establishment.[20] Indeed, both the AG and the Court took care to refer to the text of Article 49 TFEU. Such references, and some subsequent judgments,[21] support a narrow reading of their finding.

---

[18] Op cit at 2993.

[19] Case 120/78 *Cassis de Dijon* ECLI:EU:C:1979:42.

[20] See P Craig and G de Búrca, *EU law, Text, Cases and Materials*, 2nd edn (Oxford, OUP, 1998) 745.

[21] See Case C-145/99 *Commission v Italy* ECLI:EU:C:2002:142, discussed below, and Case 182/83 *Fearon* ECLI:EU:C:1984:335.

D. Exceptions in the Interests of the Administration of Justice

Building on *Thieffry* and *Van Binsbergen*, AG Slynn accepted that, in the interests of the due administration of justice and compliance with professional ethics, the host state may impose restrictions. Such restrictions however must be objectively justified. Foreshadowing convergence among the freedoms, the AG referred to *Van Binsbergen* stating that, even though the case was concerned with the provision of services, a similar rule must apply to freedom of establishment. There is a noticeable absence of reference to the derogation clause of Article 52 TFEU and an equally conspicuous, albeit silent, following of *Cassis de Dijon*. AG Slynn and the Court found that the French rules did not meet the requirement of proportionality. The AG made a much lengthier analysis of possible justifications, and engaged in detail with the arguments of the French government and the Paris Bar.

The single chambers rule was said to be justified on two grounds: the need to ensure that lawyers maintain sufficient contact with their clients and the courts, and the need to abide by rules of the professional conduct. The AG dismissed both on proportionality grounds. He pointed out that members of the Paris Bar could have secondary chambers in the area where they were registered within the bounds of the respective *tribunal de grande instance*. They could also appear to plead orally before courts in other parts of France. He accepted on the evidence that some members of the Paris Bar also belonged to another Bar in another Member State, and this was tolerated.

Modern methods of communication, as they existed at that time, rendered physical presence on a permanent basis less than necessary. The market could take care of failures. If a lawyer, having offices in two Member States, were to default on his obligations to the court or to his clients, 'he would not survive long'.[22] Similarly, the need to comply with rules of the Bar and possible conflicts arising from the application of conduct rules of two separate Bars could not justify a priori refusal of admission.

Although the Opinion of AG Slynn made reference to the less restrictive alternative principle, the proportionality analysis did not display the nuanced complexity that characterised subsequent case law. Still, *Klopp* represented the triumph of proportionality vis-à-vis a narrow nationality discrimination criterion as the defining model for distinguishing between acceptable and unacceptable obstacles to the right of establishment. The rule of the Paris Bar was a classic manifestation of professional protectionism, incompatible with the liberal outlook of the internal market. *Klopp* is also an outcome case. The AG and the Court did not simply provide guidelines to the referring court, but established that the French rule was incompatible with EU law.

E. Legacy

The Opinion of AG Slynn in *Klopp* contributed to laying down the principles which govern the compatibility of national professional rules with free movement, in particular, the interaction of the regulation of legal services with the right of establishment. Given that the judgment of the Court was fully in line with the Opinion of AG Slynn, the two have to be seen as a unit. *Klopp* is part of a generation of cases delivered in the formative years of the right of establishment and its value has to be seen in the cumulative effect of successive rulings. It provided the

---

[22] Op cit n 17, at 2996.

building blocks for *Vlassopoulou, Gebhard*, and even *Wouters*.[23] Following *Klopp*, two issues arose. The first pertained to the types of professional rules that come within the ambit of the ruling. The second pertained to the extent to which the legal profession could be considered distinct from other professional activities.

In relation to the first issue, it will be noted that the Court has been preoccupied mostly with two categories of restrictions: those pertaining to academic and professional qualifications, and those imposed in the interests of professional integrity. The first is subject to EU legislation,[24] but the underlying principles of mutual recognition was firmly established in *Vlassopoulou*. In the absence of EU rules harmonising the conditions of access to a profession, the host state is subject to positive obligations. It must take into consideration diplomas and other evidence of qualifications which the person concerned has acquired to exercise the same profession in another Member State and make a comparison between the specialised knowledge and abilities certified therefrom and the knowledge and qualifications required by the national rules. If that comparative examination results in the finding that the knowledge and qualifications acquired correspond to those required by the national provisions, the Member State must recognise that diploma as fulfilling the requirements laid down by its law. If, on the other hand, the comparison reveals only partial correspondence, the host state may require the persons concerned to show that they have acquired the knowledge and qualifications which are lacking. But even in this case, the national authorities must assess whether the knowledge acquired in the host Member State during a course of study or by way of practical experience is sufficient to make up for the knowledge which is lacking.[25] *Vlassopoulou* essentially provided an overarching positive duty of mutual recognition that operates by default and complements legislation, advancing the cooperative model of integration the key levers of which are found in primary law. It also opened the way for the liberal approach of 'gradual assimilation of knowledge' through the practice of law[26] provided by Directive 98/5.[27]

In relation to the second issue identified above, the question is this: would professional rules restricting access or the exercise of other professions be subject to the same constraints? *Klopp* had an important export value since it was itself the manifestation of a wider philosophy of the internal market gravitating towards the market access and proportionality requirements. The starting point in relation to all professions is the same. Although Member States are competent to regulate their exercise, their discretion is subject to the general disciplines of the internal market. All measures which prohibit, impede, or render less attractive the exercise of the freedoms of establishment are treated as restrictions and need to be justified.[28] Beyond that, the inquiry is fact specific.

In *Wouters*, the Court found Dutch rules prohibiting inter-disciplinary practices, ie lawyers and accountants practising together, compatible with EU law. It held that the lawyers' duty of professional secrecy conflicted with the duty of accountants to certify accounts and disclose their views on the reliability of financial statements. Thus, the need to guarantee the

---

[23] Case C-309/99 *Wouters* ECLI:EU:C:2002:98.

[24] See Directive 2005/36/EC of the European Parliament and of the Council of 7 September 2005 on the recognition of professional qualifications [2005] L255/22.

[25] Paras 17–21 of Judgment in *Vlassopoulou*.

[26] Case C-168/98 *Luxemburg v Parliament and Council* ECLI:EU:C:2000:598, para 43.

[27] Directive 98/5/EC to facilitate practice of the profession of lawyer on a permanent basis in a Member State other than that in which the qualification was obtained [1998] OJ L77/36.

[28] See eg Case C-442/02 *CaixaBank* ECLI:EU:C:2004:586, para 11; Case C-55/94 *Gebhard*, para 37; Case C-79/01 *Payroll* ECLI:EU:C:2002:592, para 26.

independence of lawyers made the Dutch rules a justifiable restriction on competition, and also on free movement. In some respects, the Court has recognised the distinctiveness of the legal profession. It has thus been held that the *Wouters* principle does not allow a Member State to prohibit the exercise of accounting activities in conjunction with the activities of an insurance broker, or an estate agent, or with any banking or financial services activity, since consideration of independence that apply to the legal profession did not arise.[29]

It is interesting that legal services have been the subject of a relatively high number of rulings.[30] *Klopp* challenged entrenched professional interests, and the basic principles of the case law continued to encounter opposition many years after the ruling. In *Commission v Italy*,[31] the Court held that Italy had breached its obligations under Articles 49 and 56 TFEU by requiring lawyers to reside in the judicial district where the Bar at which they were enrolled was attached, and by prohibiting lawyers established in other Member States from having in Italy the infrastructure needed to provide their services. In *Cipolla*, the Court held that the fixing by legislation of minimum lawyers fees, from which there can be no derogation, was a restriction on the freedom to provide services because it deprived lawyers established in other Member States of the possibility of charging lower fees, and also limited the choice of service recipients in Italy. It left it to the national court to determine whether, in light of the specific conditions of the local market, the restriction was justified in the interests of avoiding excessive competition among lawyers.[32]

Klopp laid the foundations for subsequent developments, but the evolution of the case law was not necessarily linear. Three years later, the *Biology Laboratories* case tempered the scope of *Klopp* by linking Article 49 TFEU to discrimination on grounds of nationality.[33] Belgian law provided that all the members and directors of private biology laboratories providing clinical services had to be individuals that were authorised as doctors or pharmacists. Otherwise, their services could not be reimbursed by social security schemes. In the Commission's view, this inhibited the right of establishment because it made it impossible for companies established in other Member States to set up secondary establishments in Belgium. The Court nonetheless found the Belgian law to be in conformity with Article 49 TFEU, relying on a criterion of discrimination. Belgian law applied without distinction on grounds of nationality since it did not prevent doctors or pharmacists who are nationals of other Member States from establishing themselves in Belgium and operating there a laboratory to carry out clinical analyses qualifying for reimbursement under the social security system. The judgment interpreted Article 49 TFEU as relying on a criterion of discrimination, rather than access to the market, with AG Lenz finding 'nothing' in *Klopp* to suggest that indistinctly applicable measures are covered by Article 49 TFEU.[34] It was not until *Gebhard* that the Court unequivocally established that national professional requirements, liable to hinder or make less attractive the exercise of fundamental freedoms guaranteed by the Treaty, are caught by the right of establishment and must fulfil certain conditions to survive scrutiny.[35]

---

[29] Case C-384/18 *Commission v Belgium* ECLI:EU:C:2020:124.

[30] See eg for a recent illustration, Case C-218/19 *Onofrei* ECLI:EU:C:2020:1034 and for earlier cases, see, among others, Case C-3/95 *Reisebüro Broede* ECLI:EU:C:1996:487; Case C-168/98 *Luxembourg v Parliament and Council*.

[31] Case C-145/99 *Commission v Italy* ECLI:EU:C:2002:142.

[32] Joined Cases C-94/04 and C-202/04 *Cipolla and Others* ECLI:EU:C:2006:758.

[33] Case 221/85 *Commission v Belgium* ECLI:EU:C:1987:81.

[34] Opinion of AG Lenz in Case 221/85 *Commission v Belgium* ECLI:EU:C:1986:456, p 731.

[35] As per para 37 the conditions are the following: they must be applied in a non-discriminatory manner; they must be justified by imperative requirements in the general interest; they must be suitable for securing the attainment of the objective which they pursue; and they must not go beyond what is necessary in order to attain it.

Although not one of the most often quoted judgments, *Klopp* has been referred to in a number of subsequent decisions of the Court. Such references appear to have been only to the judgment, and not to the Opinion of the AG since, as stated, the two overlap completely. It has been used as authority mostly in support of the principle that EU law permits a person to hold more than one place of professional establishment within the EU,[36] even 'without the need to apply a strict definition of permanence'.[37] It has also been cited, inter alia, in support of the principle, that although Member States are free to set the professional requisites for the exercise of the legal profession, their scope for manoeuvre is circumscribed by EU law,[38] and that the proper administration of justice may justify restrictions on the right of establishment and the freedom to provide services and the freedom of workers.[39]

F. Conclusion

The Opinion of AG Slynn in *Klopp* did not represent the culmination of a judicial trend, but rather an important building block in the gradual development of the right of establishment and its constraining effect on the regulation of professional activities by national law. Its influence lies in its cumulative effect, rather than as a single point of reference. *Gebhard* completed a journey that started in *Reyners*, but in which a significant stop was the Opinion of AG Slynn in *Klopp*. In Lord Neuberger's figurative distinction between common lawyers who work as ants vis-à-vis civil lawyers who work as spiders,[40] the Opinion of the AG in *Klopp* was the work of an ant. Exacting, methodical and convincing, it adds one stone into the integration edifice. It confirmed the need for judicial balancing, without presuppositions or general pronouncements as to the limits of state power.

---

[36] See eg Case C-171/02 *Commission v Portugal* ECLI:EU:C:2004:270, para 42; Opinion of AG Mazák in Case C-64/08 *Engelmann* ECLI:EU:C:2010:79, para 28; Opinion of AG Kokott in Case C-514/03 *Commission v Spain* ECLI:EU:C:2005:438, para 49.

[37] Opinion of AG Colomer in Case C-310/07 *Holmqvist* ECLI:EU:C:2008:314, para 33.

[38] Case C-202/84 op cit, n 32, at para 82 of the AG Opinion.

[39] See para 34 of the Judgment in *Onofrei*.

[40] See Lord Neuberger, 'Judges and Professors – Ships Passing through the Night?', speech delivered at the Max Planck Institute, Hamburg, 9 July 2012, www.judiciary.uk/wp-content/uploads/JCO/Documents/Speeches/mr-speech-hamburg-lecture-09072012.pdf.

19

Blurring the Boundaries of the Free Movement of Goods: Opinion of Advocate General Slynn in Cinéthèque

ELEANOR SPAVENTA

I. INTRODUCTION

Article 34 TFEU (Article 30 EEC, when this case was decided) prohibits quantitative restrictions on import (ie bans or quotas) and measures having equivalent effect on quantitative restrictions on imports. The latter concept was, and is, not defined in the EU Treaties, so that it fell upon the Court to determine which rules Article 34 TFEU caught. As it is all too well known, the Court did so in the *Dassonville* case, clarifying that all measures which directly or indirectly, actually or potentially, affect intra-Community trade are measures having equivalent effect for the purposes of Article 34 TFEU.[1] In the subsequent case of *Cassis de Dijon*, the Court further clarified the ambit of application of the Treaty free movement of goods provisions.[2]

First of all, it held that obstacles could arise simply because of the existence of different regulatory standards between Member States. If traders have to comply with 27 different set of rules the free flow of goods within the EU would be significantly affected. Secondly, the Court also acknowledged that, whereas normally, goods that had been lawfully produced and marketed in another Member State should be able to be sold in the importing Member State, in certain circumstances, this might not be so. In particular, where the rules of the importing Member State seek to protect a mandatory requirement of public interest, such as consumer protection or fiscal supervision, then that rule is compatible with the EU Treaties, provided that it is also necessary and proportionate to achieve the stated aim.

The *Dassonville* and *Cassis de Dijon* case law lies at the very foundation of the internal market: the free circulation of goods first, and services later, is guaranteed, not so much from imposing one single standard across the EU, but rather, by the mutual recognition of regulatory standards existing across the Member States. It is only in limited circumstances that the importing Member State can require that the imported product also complies with its own regulatory standard: as a result, free movement is greatly enhanced, and costs greatly reduced.[3]

---

[1] Case 8/74 *Dassonville* ECLI:EU:C:1974:82.

[2] Case 120/78 *Cassis de Dijon* ECLI:EU:C:1979:42.

[3] Commission, 'Communication from the Commission concerning the consequences of the judgment given by the Court of Justice on 20 February 1979 in Case 120/78 ("Cassis de Dijon")' [1980] OJ C256/2.

This very successful model, however, is of more difficult application when the rules imposed by the importing Member State do not regulate the product, *per se*, but rather, the way that products can be placed on the market (what will later become the dichotomy between product requirements and selling arrangements). The question in this respect, one that was raised implicitly in *Cinéthèque*, is whether compliance with any rule imposed by the importing Member State should be considered a potential obstacle to intra-Community trade, or rather, whether there are areas which, lacking discrimination, fall within the regulatory autonomy of the Member States.

Cinéthèque, a precursor to the 'Sunday Trading' cases, is important (if often overlooked) exactly for this reason: it signalled the first step towards a broad and indiscriminate interpretation of the notion of measure having equivalent effect to a restriction on imports. It is because of the interpretation given by the Court in *Cinéthèque* that traders were able to attack rules that merely regulated 'how and when' goods could be sold, with the consequent confusion about the boundaries of the free movement of goods provisions in the EU Treaties. It is because of the broad interpretation in *Cinéthèque* that national courts struggled to assess the proportionality of non-discriminatory rules that might have an effect on trade, but not specifically on intra-Community trade.[4]

The 'Sunday Trading' saga, as it became known, was resolved comparatively quickly – it took eight years and a handful of cases for the Court to backtrack in the *Keck* ruling. And yet, that period highlighted the tensions, still present, within the free movement provisions. As mentioned, the functioning of the internal market relies significantly, if not predominantly, on negative integration, ie on the principle whereby goods and services can move freely from one Member State to the other, rather than on positive integration, ie the imposition of one single rule for all of the Member States. Yet there is no doubting that negative integration serves not only the purpose of facilitating trade, but also that of maintaining a healthy regulatory diversity within the European Union. But inevitably, compliance with rules always entails costs, be those compliance costs, opportunity costs, legal costs, and so forth. The ongoing issue then is the extent to which additional costs associated with negative integration (and inherent in exporting to other markets) can be tolerated, or rather, are to be construed always as barriers which need justifying. As shall be seen below, these issues were already discussed to a certain extent by AG Slynn in his Opinion.[5] Had the Court followed his lead, it would have avoided finding itself in the blind alley of the 'Sunday Trading' cases, and perhaps, it would have also helped in shaping the interpretation of the free movement provisions along clearer lines.

II. BACKGROUND, CONTEXT, AND FACTS

Younger readers might struggle to relate to the facts in *Cinéthèque*: the rules at issue required a minimum time gap between the release of movies/films in cinemas, and the release of the same movie/film on videotapes, regardless of whether the copyright holder wanted to release the videotapes at an earlier stage. The rationale underpinning those rules, then commonplace across Member States, was the fear that videotapes, which opened up an entirely new market for 'private' enjoyment of movies/films, could threaten distribution of movies in cinemas, to the detriment not only of the film industry as a whole, but also of that particular form of

---

[4] See Opinion of AG Tesauro in Case C-292/92 *Hünermund* ECLI:EU:C:1993:863.
[5] Opinion of AG Slynn in Joined Cases 60 and 61/84 *Cinéthèque* ECLI:EU:C:1985:122.

cultural experience that arises from the collective enjoyment of artistic production. After all, why would viewers pay for expensive cinema tickets when they could just buy or hire a videotape? Of course, the context is now obsolete given the technological developments that allow for consumption of movies and programmes on demand; and yet, the legal issues raised by the *Cinéthèque* case are still actual: to what extent should the EU Treaties interfere with rules that regulate the market without imposing discrimination or a differential burden on intra-state trade? This question is constitutional in nature: the broader the interpretation of the free movement provisions, the more intense the scrutiny over national legislation with the consequent loss in national regulatory autonomy.

III. THE OPINION OF AG SLYNN

AG Slynn considered with care the main issue at hand, whether the measure should indeed be considered as a measure having equivalent effect to a quantitative restriction on imports. He clarified that only if that was the case, would it be necessary to proceed to the second step of analysis, which was that of justification. He started by stressing the fact that even though the rules at issue did not expressly ban either import or export of the video tapes, that did not exhaust the analysis of the effect of the measures. That was because since the delay meant that for the first 12 months from the release of the movie/film, there would be little point in import-ing the tapes, as those could neither be sold nor hired. He then proceeded to assess whether, even absent discrimination, such measures could fall within the scope of Article 34 TFEU.

In this respect, AG Slynn recalled the existing case law of the Court and divided rules falling within the scope of Article 34 TFEU in three categories: rules forbidding or restricting imports quantitatively;[6] discriminatory rules;[7] and rules which 'although not directed to importation as such but covering both national good and imports' require producers or distributors to take 'additional steps to those which he would normally and lawfully take in the marketing of his goods, which thereby render importation more difficult, so that imports may be restricted and national producers *be given protection in practice*' (emphasis added).[8] In that event, the meas-ure could still be justified pursuant to the mandatory requirements doctrine. AG Slynn then argued that, on the other hand, where there are no EU standards, where a 'national measure is not specifically directed at imports, does not discriminate against imports, does not make it any more difficult for an importer to sell his products that it is for a domestic producer, and gives no protection to domestic producers' then, *prima facie*, it would not fall within the scope of Article 34 TFEU, even if 'it does in fact lead to a *restriction or reduction of imports*' (emphasis added).[9] In AG Slynn's view, the effect of the measures at issue was exactly that of restricting/reducing imports without discrimination or protectionism, and therefore, the rules fell outside the scope of the EU Treaties altogether, and did not need to be justified.

In the alternative however, AG Slynn stated that if the measure had to be justified, it would be done on the basis of it being necessary for the maintenance of the movies/films industry and the supply of movies/films to the consumer. He then analysed whether the measures fell within the scope of the free movement of services, and found that since they were non-discriminatory,

---

[6] Eg Case 34/79 *Henn and Darby* ECLI:EU:C:1979:295. See ch 12.
[7] Eg Case 113/80 *Commission v Ireland* ECLI:EU:C:1981:139.
[8] Opinion of AG Slynn in *Cinéthèque*, p 2611.
[9] ibid.

they fell outside the services provisions.[10] If a different conclusion were to be reached, they would be equally justified in his view. Finally, in relation to the contention that the measures unduly restricted freedom of expression, as protected by Article 10 of the European Convention on Human Rights (ECHR), accepting that if the EU Treaties applied then justifications had to be construed in the light of the ECHR, he found that Article 10 ECHR had not been violated. This was at a time before the EU's Charter of Fundamental Rights came to be.

The Court did not follow AG Slynn's main finding, namely, that the rules fell altogether outside the scope of the EU Treaties. Rather, after having acknowledged that the rules applied without distinction, and their purpose was not to regulate trade patterns or to favour domestic production, the Court found that the mere difference in regulatory standards could give raise to barriers to intra-Community trade. Therefore, the Court said the national measure was compatible with the EU Treaties, only insofar as it was necessary and proportionate to the attainment of the pursued objective. Since that was the case, the rules were justified. The Court also dismissed the fundamental rights issue, pointing out that the rules (because justified) fell within the jurisdiction of the national legislator, so that the Court had no power to assess the compatibility of the rules with the ECHR.

IV. ANALYSIS

The *Cinéthèque* ruling signalled the first step towards a considerable expansion of the notion of a measure having equivalent effect, which would lead in the late 80s and early 90s to great confusion when traders sought to attack rules that merely regulated trade,[11] and national courts differed in their assessment of the proportionality of such rules.[12] The Opinion of AG Slynn is interesting in this respect, exactly because it was a precursor for the turn in the Court's interpretation in *Keck*.[13]

A. The Definition of a Measure Having Equivalent Effect: How Far Beyond Discrimination?

It has been remarked above that the definition of what constitutes a measure having equivalent effect fell squarely within the hermeneutic monopoly of the Court. Here, it is important to understand the twin operation of *Dassonville* and *Cassis de Dijon*: the definition in *Dassonville*, brought within the remit of the EU Treaties even measures that only indirectly and potentially affected intra-Community trade, a broad formula capable of encompassing a wide range of

---

[10] It was not until the ruling in Case C-76/90 *Säger* ECLI:EU:C:1991:331, that non-discriminatory rules were brought within the scope of the free movement of services provisions.

[11] Case C-145/88 *Torfaen* ECLI:EU:C:1989:593; Case C-312/89 *Union départementale des syndicats CGT de l'Aisne* ECLI:EU:C:1991:93; Case C-306/88 *Rochdale Borough Council* ECLI:EU:C:1992:510; C-169/91 *Council of the City of Stoke on Trent and Norwich City Council* ECLI:EU:C:1992:519.

[12] See A Arnull, 'What Shall We Do on Sunday?' (1991) 16 *ELRev* 112. The 'Sunday Trading' cases gave raise to a very lively academic debate; see eg LW Gormley, '"Actually or Potentially, Directly or Indirectly"? Obstacles to the Free Movement of Goods' (1989) 9 *YEL* 197; EL White, 'In Search of the Limits of Article 30 EEC Treaty' (1989) 26 *CMLRev* 235; K Mortelmans, 'Article 30 of the EEC Treaty and Legislation relating to Market Circumstances: Time to Consider a New Definition?' (1991) 28 *CMLRev* 115; D Chalmers, 'Free Movement of Goods within the European Community: An Unhealthy Addiction to Scotch Whisky?' (1993) 42 *ICLQ* 269; P Oliver, 'Some Further Reflections on the Scope of Articles 28–30 (ex 30–36) EC' (1999) 36 *CMLRev* 783; J Steiner, 'Drawing the Line: Uses and Abuses of Article 30 EEC' (1992) 29 *CMLRev* 749.

[13] Joined Cases C-267/91 and C-268/91 *Keck* ECLI:EU:C:1993:905.

rules. *Cassis de Dijon* clarified, however, that a violation of Article 34 TFEU would occur only to the extent to which the rule was not necessary to achieve a mandatory requirement of public interest in a proportionate way. More crucially, it also clarified that mere differences in regulatory standards might give rise to obstacles to intra-Community trade: the most persuasive interpretation of the reasons behind this choice was the theory of double regulatory burden.

If a product has already been regulated and was safe for consumers in the exporting Member State, then there must be a compelling public interest to require that it complies, additionally, with the rules of the importing Member State. The principle of mutual recognition of regulatory standards is then rooted in the concept of mutual trust: Member States must trust each other's regulatory policies and standards. In this respect, the notion of discrimination was neither particularly relevant nor helpful: what mattered was the additional burden on the importer that has already complied with one set of rules.[14] However, the equation double regulatory burden/different regulatory standard with obstacle to intra-Community trade only worked for certain rules and in particular, as clarified in *Keck*, in relation to those rules which are similar in nature to those already complied with in the home Member State. Yet, the *Dassonville/Cassis de Dijon* formula, also because of the factual circumstances underpinning those two cases, did not contain any such qualification.

The rules in *Cinéthèque* then could be interpreted either way, and, in this author's view, the strength of the Opinion of AG Slynn rested exactly in a more careful analysis of the need to establish at least some *specific* effect on *intra-Community* trade before a rule is deemed to be an obstacle. Here, in order to give a more precise indication of when a measure would have to be justified, the AG pointed out that a rule which neither discriminates in favour of nor protects domestic production, should not be considered to fall within the EU Treaties only because it leads to a restriction or reduction on imports. And, despite the fact that the Court decided not to follow the Opinion of AG Slynn, the latter had been influential in shaping the thinking of AGs in subsequent cases. In particular, in trying to exclude the applicability of Article 34 TFEU to the Sunday trading rules, AG Van Gerven argued that when a national rule only increased the difficulty in penetrating the market, then it should fall within the EU Treaties, only if 'it appears from the entire legal and economic context that the economic interweaving of national markets sought by the Treaty is thereby threatened. In such a case, the compartmentalisation of the market should be made sufficiently probable by a number of quantitative factors which show that the application of the rule makes it more difficult to penetrate the market, thereby rendering the market so inaccessible (expensive, unprofitable) that it must be feared that the majority of imported goods will disappear from the market'.[15] Arguably, AG Slynn's test was easier and clearer to apply, and his interpretation was prescient to the extent to which it stressed that a mere reduction or restriction on imports was not sufficient to trigger the EU Treaties.[16]

---

[14] See in particular, N Bernard, 'La libre circulation des marchandises, des personnes et des services dans le Traité CE sous l'angle de la compétence' (1998) 33 *Cahiers de droit europeen* 11; and N Barnard, *Multi Level Governance in the European Union* (Kluwer Law International, 2002) ch 2.

[15] Opinion of AG Van Gerven in Case C-145/88 *Torfaen Borough Council* ECLI:EU:C:1989:279,. In favour of straightforward application of *Dassonville*, see LW Gormley, 'Case 145/88, Torfaen Borough Council v. B&Q PLC (formerly B&Q Retail Ltd.), Preliminary reference under Art. 177 EEC by the Cwmbran Magistrates' Court on the interpretation of Arts. 30 & 36 EEC. Judgment of the Court of Justice of the European Communities of 23 November 1989' (1990) 27 *CMLRev* 141; LW Gormley, 'Recent Case Law on the Free Movement of Good: Some Hot Potatoes' (1990) 27 *CMLRev* 825.

[16] This same approach was then adopted by White (n 12). See Opinion of AG Tesauro in Case C-292/92 *Hünermund* ECLI:EU:C:1993:863.

As it is well known, in *Keck*, the Court finally accepted this approach, but also in order to ensure ease of applicability, worked around a system of presumptions, so that product requirements would always be caught by Article 34 TFEU, whereas selling arrangements rules that just regulate when and how a product can be sold, must be justified only if directly or indirectly discriminatory. In more recent times though, it has been clarified that the dichotomy of product requirements/certain selling arrangements does not exhaust the range of measures that might come to the attention of the Court. Thus, the Court further clarified that certain selling arrangements, and in particular, those regulating sales over the internet or banning advertisement, might have an effect on intra-Community trade relevant for the purposes of Article 34 TFEU, either because they affect market access or because they are inherently indirectly discriminatory;[17] that rules fixing prices at a certain level, including minimum or maximum, are measures having equivalent effect and must be justified;[18] and that measures which regulate when and how a product can be used might also fall within the scope of Article 34 TFEU if and when they affect market access.[19] Arguably, the rules in *Cinéthèque* would now fall within the latter category, and fall within the scope of Article 34 TFEU to the extent to which they affect market access.

B. Fundamental Rights and Justifications

The other issue, only touched upon in the Opinion of AG Slynn and the judgment of the Court in *Cinéthèque*, concerned the relationship between the EU Treaties, national rules, and fundamental rights as then protected by the general principles of EU law, and now by the Charter. The issue was and is one of primary importance: on the one hand, there was no mention of fundamental rights in the original EU Treaties. This was in line with the functional approach adopted in relation to European integration: fundamental rights were contained in a parallel Treaty which was never ratified.[20] On the other hand, given the law making and administrative powers vested in the then Community, coupled with the principles of direct effect and primacy, fundamental rights had to be recognised as general principles of Union law, to ensure that the

---

[17] Eg Case C-405/98 *Gourmet* ECLI:EU:C:2001:135; Case C-322/01 *Deutscher Apothekerverband* ECLI:EU:C:2003:664. See ch 35.

[18] Eg Case C-333/14 *Scotch Whisky Association* ECLI:EU:C:2015:845; Case C-148/15 *Deutsche Parkinson Vereinigung* ECLI:EU:C:2016:776.

[19] Case C-110/05 *Commission v Italy* ECLI:EU:C:2009:66 (*Trailers*); Case C-142/05 *Mickelsson and Roos* ECLI:EU:C:2009:336. See E Spaventa, 'Leaving Keck behind? The Free Movement of Goods after the Rulings in Commission v Italy and Mickelsson and Roos' (2009) 34 *ELRev* 914; P Wennerås and KB Moen, 'Selling Arrangements, Keeping Keck' (2010) 35 *ELRev* 387; S Enchelmaier, 'Moped Trailers, Mickelsson & Roos, Gysbrechts: the ECJ's Case Law on Goods Keeps on Moving' (2010) 29 *YEL* 190; P Oliver, 'Of Trailers and Jet Skis: Is the Case Law on Article 34 TFEU Hurtling in a New Direction?' (2010) 33 *Fordham International Law Journal* 1423; LW Gormley, 'Free Movement of Goods and Their Use: What Is the Use of It?' (2010) 33 *Fordham International Law Journal* 1589; T Horsley, 'Unearthing Buried Treasure: Art. 34 TFEU and the Exclusionary Rules' (2012) 37 *ELRev* 734; MS Jansson and H Kalimo, 'De Minimis Meets "Market Access": Transformations in the Substance – and the Syntax – of EU Free Movement Law?' (2014) 51 *CMLRev* 523; LW Gormley, 'Inconsistencies and Misconceptions in the Free Movement of Goods' (2015) 40 *ELRev* 925; R Schütze, 'Of Types and Tests: Towards a Unitary Doctrinal Framework for Article 34 TFEU?' (2016) 41 *ELRev* 826.

[20] Joint Declaration by the European Parliament, the Council and the Commission concerning the protection of fundamental rights and the European convention for the protection of human rights and fundamental freedoms [1977] OJ C103/1.

EU institutions were bound by a similar standard to that applicable in the domestic context by virtue of both domestic constitutions and ECHR.[21]

Whereas this development was fairly uncontested and endorsed by the political institutions in the 1977 declaration,[22] the Court went further. In *Rutili*,[23] the general principles of Community law as encapsulated in the ECHR, were mentioned in relation to national measures restricting the free movement of workers. In *Cinéthèque*, then, one of the issues raised by the claimant concerned whether the French rules also constituted a restriction on freedom of expression, as guaranteed by Article 10 ECHR. AG Slynn proceeded along the twin analysis as per above: if the measure did not fall within the scope of Article 34 TFEU, as he had argued, then the issue of compatibility with the general principles of Community law would not arise. A measure falling entirely within the scope of national law would be assessed only in relation to the domestic constitutional system. On the other hand, if the measure was found to be a measure having equivalent effect in need of justification, then the matter would be different: once a national measure has to be justified, either pursuant to derogations in the EU Treaties, or by the mandatory requirements doctrine, then it fell within the EU constitutional framework, and it had to be consistent with its constitutional values. This interpretation, rejected by the Court in *Cinéthèque*, but accepted in later case law, if consistent with its premises, is not so straightforward, since it signals a significant interference with national discretion in a field which is extremely culturally sensitive, that of the balancing between fundamental rights and other values.

Take, for instance, the judgment in *Familiapress*.[24] Here, Austrian rules prohibited offering consumes free gifts linked to the sale of goods or supply of services; an Austrian publication brought proceedings against a German magazine that was offering prizes for the correct completion of a crossword puzzle on the grounds that it breached the aforementioned law. The Court found that the application of the rule to German publications would entail the need to alter the content of the publication, and was therefore to be qualified as a product requirement, consequently falling automatically within the definition of a measure having equivalent effect. Turning to the justification of the measure, the Court accepted the Austrian Government and Commission's claim that it could be potentially justified by the need to ensure press diversity, as an expression of Article 10 ECHR. Crucially though, the Court also pointed out that in order to be justified, the measure also needed to comply with freedom of expression, also enshrined in Article 10 ECHR. It left it to the national court to then determine whether the balance between the two aspects inherent in Article 10 ECHR (press diversity and freedom of expression) had been correctly struck by the rules at issue. Whereas the same balancing act would arguably be necessary within the context of domestic constitutional law, *Familiapress* clarified that now such assessment becomes a matter of EU law. Furthermore, in *Schmidberger*, the Court found that even the exercise of a right protected by the national Constitution could be qualified as a measure having equivalent effect.[25] In that case, actions of demonstrators exercising their constitutionally protected freedom of expression were construed as a barrier to

---

[21] Case 29/69 *Stauder* ECLI:EU:C:1969:57; Case 11/70 *Internationale Handelsgesellschaft* ECLI:EU:C:1970:114; Case 4/73 *Nold* ECLI:EU:C:1974:51.

[22] Joint Declaration by the European Parliament, the Council and the Commission concerning the protection of fundamental rights and the European convention for the protection of human rights and fundamental freedoms [1977] OJ C103/1.

[23] Case 36/75 *Rutili* ECLI:EU:C:1975:137.

[24] Case C-368/95 *Familiapress* ECLI:EU:C:1997:325.

[25] Case C-112/00 *Schmidberget* ECLI:EU:C:2003:333. See ch 34.

the free movement of goods since such action prevented traffic on the Brenner motorway. This time, the exercise of domestic fundamental rights was cast directly against the free movement right, and, once again, the balancing act between competing interests was catapulted from the domestic to the European dimension.[26]

Furthermore, even when the EU fundamental right performs its traditional function, that of curtailing the discretion of the decision maker to protect the individual, matters might not be so straightforward. Thus, if the market freedoms are given a very broad interpretation, then the intrusion of EU fundamental rights in domestic systems also becomes more pervasive. Here, take for instance the case of *Carpenter*.[27] Mr Carpenter was married to a third country national who was facing a deportation order for having overstayed her entry permit. The situation had a very tenuous link to free movement. Mr Carpenter was a British national self-employed and resident in the UK; however, the Court found that since he provided services also for clients established in other Member States, there was a sufficient cross-border link for the matter to fall within the scope of the free movement of services. It further found that the 'separation of Mr and Mrs Carpenter would be detrimental to their family life and, therefore, to the conditions under which Mr Carpenter exercises a fundamental freedom',[28] so that the deportation of Mrs Carpenter could be construed as a barrier to intra-Community provision of services.

In assessing the justification for such a barrier, the need to control unlawful migration, the Court also examined the issue of fundamental rights and found that the deportation of Mrs Carpenter would be inconsistent with Article 8 ECHR. The *Carpenter* case is a good example of the wide-ranging effect of the broad interpretation of free movement provisions/applicability of fundamental rights might have on regulatory choices, also in spheres that are in theory a matter reserved to the national regulator.

Despite the protestations of the Member States, however, this approach has persisted, and indeed, it has been codified in Article 51 of the Charter which specifies that the latter applies also to Member States when they are implementing EU law. The Court has clarified that the notion of implementation also encompasses those instances in which the Member State is limiting a free movement right.[29]

C. Conclusions

The Opinion of AG Slynn in *Cinéthèque* is interesting for two reasons: first of all, it noted how a mere restriction on trade should not necessarily be interpreted as a barrier to the free movement of goods. As mentioned above, it would take eight years to the Court to realise its mistake and adopt this approach in the *Keck* ruling. Secondly, the AG found that fundamental rights should be applicable in assessing whether the rule is justified pursuant to the mandatory requirements doctrine or derogations in the EU Treaties. Here again, the Court did not follow the AG, and yet some 10 years later adopted the same approach, an approach which is still followed. It is then clear that the Opinion of AG Slynn anticipated fundamental developments in the case law on the free movement of goods.

---

[26] And this led to real problems, see Case C-438/05 *Viking* ECLI:EU:C:2007:772; Case C-341/05 *Laval* ECLI:EU:C:2007:809.

[27] Case C-60/00 *Carpenter* ECLI:EU:C:2002:434.

[28] ibid, para 39.

[29] For an outline of when the Charter applies to acts of the Member States, see Case C-206/13 *Siragusa* ECLI:EU:C:2014:126.

20

Formal-Style Reasoning and its Progeny: Opinion of Advocate General Slynn in Marshall I

JOHN COTTER

I. INTRODUCTION

MARSHALL I is a case that contains multitudes.[1] It is, on one plane, an episode in Helen Marshall's long campaign in English and European courts to secure protection for herself (and other women) against discriminatory retirement policies. On another level, *Marshall I* has been utilised to demonstrate the oft-superior protections provided to citizens by EU law when compared to national law.[2] However, those interested in the EU's 'constitutional' law may have different associations with the case. It was in *Marshall I*, on the invitation of AG Slynn, that the Court ruled that directives are incapable of enjoying horizontal direct effect. This development has been widely criticised.[3] It is also a judgment from which the Court has arguably been trying to recover ever since, even if it has shown no inclination to revisit it directly.[4]

This chapter commences by setting out the background, context, and the facts in *Marshall I*, before summarising the Opinion of AG Slynn. The Opinion on the discrimination aspect is then considered. Thereafter, the 'constitutional' dimension of the Opinion is analysed as it relates to the effect of directives. The argument is then advanced that the Opinion is a prime example of what the American legal realist Karl Llewellyn dubbed 'Formal-Style' judging, carrying with it the negative consequences that Llewellyn associated with that style. The chapter concludes with a brief account of the significance of the Opinion in subsequent cases.

---

[1] Case 152/84 *Marshall* ECLI:EU:C:1986:84; Opinion of AG Slynn in Case 152/84 *Marshall* ECLI:EU:C:1985:345.

[2] Indeed, the Court on social media used the case as an example of the institution's contribution in advancing equal treatment for women on International Women's Day in 2021: https://twitter.com/EUCourtPress/status/1368837608130904064.

[3] See, for instance, Opinion of AG van Gerven in Case C-271/91 *Marshall* ECLI:EU:C:1993:30; Opinion of AG Lenz in Case C-91/92 *Faccini Dori* ECLI:EU:C:1994:45; Case C-413/15 *Farrell* ECLI:EU:C:2017:492. For a selection of academic commentary see J Coppel, 'Rights, Duties and the End of Marshall' (1994) 57 *MLR* 859; T Tridimas, 'Horizontal Effect of Directives: A Missed Opportunity?' (1994) 19 *ELRev* 621; R Mastroianni, 'On the Distinction Between Vertical and Horizontal Direct Effects of Community Directives: What Role for the Principle of Equality?' (1999) 5 *EPL* 417. See generally, S Prechal, *Directives in EC Law* (Oxford, OUP, 2005). See also ch 46.

[4] Case C-91/92 *Faccini Dori* ECLI:EU:C:1994:292; Case C-201/02 *Wells* ECLI:EU:C:2004:12.

II. BACKGROUND, CONTEXT, AND FACTS

1975 saw two significant milestones in the progression of gender equality in British society: in February, Margaret Thatcher became the first female leader of the opposition, and in November, the Sex Discrimination Act 1975 (the 1975 Act), which prohibited forms of work-place discrimination between men and women, received royal assent. Though the 1975 Act was regarded as radical at the time,[5] only three months later in February 1976, the then EEC adopted Directive 76/207,[6] which – as subsequent events would demonstrate – offered superior protection to women against discrimination. Despite being obliged to implement the Equal Treatment Directive, the UK failed to do so, which led ultimately to some women in the UK suffering discrimination, and having to turn to the Court to vindicate their EU law rights.[7] Helen Marshall was one such woman.

Helen Marshall was employed by Southampton and South-West Hampshire Area Health Authority (Teaching) (the 'Authority') from June 1966, working as a senior dietitian from 1974, until her dismissal at age 62 in 1980.[8] Around 1975, the Authority adopted a written policy (which was an implied term of Ms Marshall's contract) that female employees would retire at the age at which social security pensions became payable, which pursuant to the Social Security Act 1975, was 65 for men, but 60 for women. After waiving this policy for two years in respect of Ms Marshall, the Authority dismissed Ms Marshall against her wishes on 31 March 1980, with the sole reason being the written policy. Ms Marshall commenced proceedings against the Authority (which the Court of Appeal later determined to be an 'emanation of the State') before the Industrial Tribunal, claiming that her dismissal constituted unlawful discrimination contrary to the 1975 Act and Directive 76/207. At the relevant time, the UK had not specifically implemented the Directive nor had it adopted measures pursuant to Article 5(2)(b) thereof to ensure that provisions in individual contracts of employment which were contrary to the principle of equal treatment could be declared null and void or be amended. Moreover, the 1975 Act did not afford as high a level of protection to a woman in Ms Marshall's predicament, since section 6(4) of the 1975 Act provided that the prohibition of discrimination against women in the context of employment did 'not apply to provision in relation to death or retirement'.

The Industrial Tribunal rejected Ms Marshall's claim based on the 1975 Act due to the exemption in section 6(4). However, the Tribunal upheld Ms Marshall's claim based on the violation of the equal treatment principle under the Directive. On appeal, the Employment Appeal Tribunal rejected both claims, ruling that the Directive could not be relied upon before a UK court or tribunal. Upon Ms Marshall's appeal to the Court of Appeal, two questions were referred to the Court: first, whether Ms Marshall's dismissal was an act of discrimination prohibited by the Equal Treatment Directive, and; second, if so, whether the Directive could be relied upon by Ms Marshall before a national court or tribunal, notwithstanding any inconsistency between the Directive and section 6(4). Before the Court, Ms Marshall and the Commission argued that both questions should be answered in the affirmative, whereas the Authority and the UK argued the opposite.

---

[5] See, for instance, this archived BBC piece on the 1975 Act from 29 December 1975: http://news.bbc.co.uk/onthisday/hi/dates/stories/december/29/newsid_2547000/2547249.stm.

[6] Council Directive 76/207/EEC of 9 February 1976 on the implementation of the principle of equal treatment for men and women as regards access to employment, vocational training and promotion, and working conditions [1976] OJ L39/40.

[7] Another such judgment of major EU legal significance was rendered in Case C-188/89 *Foster* ECLI:EU:C:1990:313.

[8] The facts of the case were set out at pp 725–27 of the Opinion.

III. THE OPINION OF AG SLYNN

Prior to addressing both questions, AG Slynn recalled previous judgments of the Court in which it had ruled that the elimination of discrimination based on sex formed 'part of the fundamental rights the observance of which the Court has a duty to ensure ...'.[9] Turning to the first question, AG Slynn first opined that the principle of equal treatment for men and women as regards 'working conditions' would apply to a provision in a person's contract requiring them to retire at a certain age.[10] Secondly, AG Slynn reasoned that a differential in terms of age of retirement for men and women would, on the face of it, constitute a breach of Article 5(1), ie a failure to guarantee the same conditions with discrimination on the grounds of sex.[11] Satisfied on the facts that Ms Marshall would not have been dismissed in the same circumstances had she been a man, AG Slynn concluded that there was a prima facie failure by her employer to comply with Article 5(1).[12]

The AG then considered two arguments raised by the Authority and the UK in favour of rebutting the prima facie finding of discrimination.[13] The first argument was that the dispute was one concerning social security, and that pursuant to Article 1(1) and (2), it was for the Council to adopt further provisions to deal with such matters. The only instrument that had been adopted at the relevant time was Directive 79/7,[14] which, under Article 7, expressly allowed Member States to exclude from its scope 'the determination of pensionable age ...'. AG Slynn, however, while acknowledging that the two were often factually linked, distinguished retirement age from pensionable age, concluding that the fixing of a retirement age was not the determination of pensionable age, and therefore not subject to exclusion from the scope of the principle of equal treatment for men and women.[15] The second argument was that the previous judgment in *Burton*[16] permitted discrimination between men and women as regards retirement age. Again, however, AG Slynn distinguished that case from the present one, reasoning that *Burton* concerned a social security context, and that a judicial finding that 'access at different ages to benefits in the context of social security is in certain circumstances not discrimination', did not mean that different retirement ages for men and women were not discriminatory.[17]

Moving to the second question, AG Slynn commenced his observations by noting that the 1975 Act was inconsistent with the Equal Treatment Directive.[18] AG Slynn then considered the extent of the national court's duty to construe national legislation harmoniously with the Directive. Applying the previous judgment on the duty of harmonious interpretation in *von Colson*,[19] AG Slynn concluded that the duty applied only to national legislation adopted to implement the Directive, and would not apply to legislation, like the 1975 Act, which predated the Directive.[20] Given that harmonious interpretation was impossible, AG Slynn then

---

[9] pp 727–28 of the Opinion.
[10] ibid, pp 728–29.
[11] ibid, p 729.
[12] ibid.
[13] ibid, pp 729–31.
[14] Council Directive 79/7/EEC of 19 December 1978 on the progressive implementation of the principle of equal treatment for men and women in matters of social security [1979] OJ L 6/24.
[15] At pp 729–30 of the Opinion.
[16] Case 19/81 *Burton* ECLI:EU:C:1982:58.
[17] At pp 730–31 of the Opinion.
[18] ibid, pp 731–32.
[19] Case 14/83 *Von Colson* ECLI:EU:C:1984:153.
[20] At pp 732–33 of the Opinion.

turned his attention to the question of whether the Equal Treatment Directive could enjoy direct effect. Applying the Court's longstanding test of sufficient precision and unconditionality, AG Slynn concluded that both criteria were met in respect of the Article 5(1) prohibition.[21]

Having determined that the relevant provision enjoyed direct effect, the AG addressed the matter as to whether a directive could be relied upon by an individual in a national court or tribunal against a non-state entity ('horizontal direct effect'). The AG effectively dismissed the generally framed paragraph 23 of the Court's judgment in *Becker*,[22] which appeared supportive of the idea of horizontal direct effect, to focus on the more specifically drafted paragraphs 24 and 25. Paragraph 24 of the *Becker* judgment contained a prohibition on Member States being allowed to plead their own failure to implement a directive against an individual to justify a failure to perform its obligations under that directive.[23] In paragraph 25 of *Becker*, the Court had ruled that a directive that enjoyed direct effect could 'be relied upon as against any national provision *or* in so far as the provisions define rights which individuals are able to assert against the State'. Based on these two paragraphs, AG Slynn concluded that a directive could only be relied upon by an individual before a national court in a situation like that in the case before him: where a Member State was relying on its own failure to implement a directive to deny an individual the rights they were entitled to under that directive. For AG Slynn, it was '[a]s against the State in default the litigant could assert those rights'.[24]

Arguing, therefore, that the possibility of horizontal direct effect of directives should be excluded, the AG sought to justify this view further. First, AG Slynn pointed to the fact that a directive is addressed to the Member States, and not to the individual, thereby placing obligations on the former only. To bolster this point, the AG referred to the fact that a directive does not have to be notified to individuals, and was published in the *Official Journal* 'by way of information' only.[25] Secondly, again drawing upon *Becker*, AG Slynn reiterated that an individual could only utilise a directive 'to enable rights to be claimed … against the State in default'.[26] Utilising the language of estoppel, a principle that the Court had turned to before,[27] the AG added that such rights could be asserted 'either as a sword or as a shield'.[28] Thirdly, AG Slynn asserted that to allow horizontal direct effect of directives would be to 'blur the distinction between regulations and directives' provided for in the EU Treaties.[29] Finally, the AG observed that it was not the role of the Court to declare national laws to be void; rather, the Court could declare national law to be incompatible with Community law when national courts were obliged not to apply conflicting national law. In this connection, AG Slynn added that where a Member State failed to comply, it was for the Commission to commence infringement proceedings.[30]

Having excluded the possibility of horizontal direct effect, it then became necessary for the AG to consider what constituted 'the state' in this context. This consideration was of direct relevance to Ms Marshall's case, since she had instituted proceedings against the Authority, rather than against the UK. Turning to this issue, AG Slynn opined that the term 'state' must be

---

[21] At p 733 of the Opinion.
[22] Case 8/81 *Becker* ECLI:EU:C:1982:7.
[23] The so-called 'estoppel theory', first identified in Case 148/78 *Ratti* ECLI:EU:C:1979:110. See Prechal (n 3) 220–26.
[24] At p 734 of the Opinion.
[25] ibid.
[26] ibid.
[27] The first example in the context of the direct effect of directives in case law being Case 148/77 *Ratti* (n 23).
[28] At p 734 of the Opinion.
[29] ibid.
[30] ibid, pp 734–35.

'taken broadly, as including all organs of the State'.[31] Moreover, he added that in employment matters, the term would, in the context of the Equal Treatment Directive, include 'all employees of such organs and not just the central civil service'.[32] AG Slynn continued by rejecting the argument that a distinction should be made between the state as an employer and the state acting in another capacity. The AG noted also that a state employer could not be regarded as being in an analogous position to a private employer, given that the state can legislate, whereas the latter could not.[33] As regards the Authority, AG Slynn noted that as a health authority it was a Crown body, and that Ms Marshall was regarded by the Employment Appeal Tribunal as having been in effect employed by the state.[34] The AG noted also that the Court of Appeal in its order for reference had described the Authority as 'an emanation of the State'.[35]

IV. ANALYSIS

The analysis of AG Slynn's Opinion that follows is divided in four and focusses primarily, though not exclusively, on the doctrinal legal reasoning utilised by the Advocate General to justify his conclusions. First, the Advocate General's views on the question of whether the Equal Treatment Directive prohibited retirement policies such as that at issue are examined. Secondly, AG Slynn's reasoning on the 'constitutional' question relating to the effect of directives is considered. Thereafter, the Opinion is analysed in terms of its judicial style, and the consequences flowing from that style. Finally, the Opinion's legacy in the Court's case law is examined.

A. The Substantive Dispute: Discriminatory Retirement Policies and the Equal Treatment Directive

Over 35 years later, AG Slynn's Opinion, which was effectively adopted by the Court, has a legacy that may be compartmentalised. The finding that a retirement policy such as that applied to Ms Marshall was discrimination has come to be regarded as a landmark in the Court's equal treatment and employment rights jurisprudence.[36] The effluxion of time, and the progress made in the intervening years, can lead however to hindsight bias or a sense that the outcome was inevitable. That would be wrong. It must be recalled that Ms Marshall had been unsuccessful, in whole or in part, before two domestic tribunals, and that there were questions of EU law of such an indeterminate nature that the Court of Appeal referred them to the Court. Moreover, one cannot ignore the fact that both Ms Marshall's employer and the UK advanced what at the very least were plausible legal arguments in favour of their preferred outcome.

AG Slynn's method of proffering his opinion as regards the first question will be one familiar to advocates: the AG engaged directly with the points that had been raised by the Authority and the UK to rebut a prima facie finding of unlawful discrimination, despatching them swiftly

---

[31] At p 735 of the Opinion.
[32] ibid.
[33] ibid.
[34] ibid.
[35] ibid, pp 735–36.
[36] Coppel (n 3); Tridimas (n 3); Mastroianni (n 3).

and clinically. The attempt to conflate retirement age and pensionable age, and so escape the prohibition of discrimination, was met by the AG not with reliance on legal authority, but on what might be termed an approach based on first principles: AG Slynn simply rejected the notion that there must be a legal link between retirement and pension ages merely because there exists frequently a factual link. AG Slynn dismissed the argument based on the Court's decision in *Burton* in a manner typical of the common law tradition: a simple distinguishing of both cases on their facts. The Court's ruling in *Burton* that access to social security at different ages would not, in certain circumstances, constitute discrimination did not mean that differing retirement ages would not be discriminatory.

The influence of the Opinion of AG Slynn on the Court's judgment is obvious, with the Court essentially mirroring in more concise form the reasoning of the Opinion, focusing on the fundamental importance of the principle of equality of treatment, before distinguishing retirement age and pensionable age to dismiss the application of Directive 79/7 and the *Burton* case.[37] Both AG Slynn and the Court made what might have been a legal question of some complexity in other hands look like light work.

B. The 'Constitutional' Context: Horizontal Direct Effect of Directives and State Authorities

If AG Slynn's Opinion as it related to the discrimination aspect of the case, and its effective adoption by the Court, have become part of the Court's outcome-legitimacy lore, the same is not quite true of the Opinion's 'constitutional' dimension. The AG's view that directives should not be afforded horizontal direct effect, a position that was also adopted by the Court, has attracted considerable criticism from other Advocates General (AGs) and many EU-law scholars since.[38] If one focuses on the minute details of AG Slynn's purely legal reasoning in *Marshall I*, there is much that is open to criticism. One problem that pervades AG Slynn's treatment of the second question is his selective and otherwise questionable use of previous judgments, specifically the *von Colson* and *Becker* rulings.

Famously in *von Colson*, the Court had ruled that 'in applying the national law and in particular the provisions of a national law specifically introduced in order to implement [a directive], national courts are required to interpret their national law in the light of the wording and the purpose of the directive in order to achieve the result referred to in the third paragraph of [Article 288 TFEU]'.[39] Despite that fact that the Court's exposition of this general rule had not limited the duty of harmonious interpretation to national measures adopted specifically to implement a directive, AG Slynn elected to sever that general rule from what he termed the 'operative part' of the judgment, in which the Court in the final sentence of its ruling had stated that it was for the national court to interpret and apply harmoniously the legislation adopted for the implementation of the Equal Treatment Directive.[40] On a purely literal reading of *von Colson*, this interpretation makes little sense. The Court had clearly established a binding general rule, which had in no way been limited to national law intended specifically to implement a directive, and the final sentence of the judgment was evidently a reference to the fact that the national rule at issue in *von Colson* was such a rule. In any event, AG Slynn's

---

[37] At pp 743–46 of the Opinion.
[38] Coppel (n 3); Tridimas (n 3); Mastroianni (n 3).
[39] Case 14/83 *von Colson*, para 26.
[40] ibid, para 28.

attempt to restrict what has come to be known as the doctrine of indirect effect was to be short-lived. In *Marleasing*,[41] the Court would rule that the harmonious interpretation duty applied to a national law, whether adopted before or after the directive at issue.[42]

AG Slynn's doctrinal justifications for excluding the possibility of horizontal direct effect of directives, which are built heavily on the *Becker* ruling, are also less than satisfactory. Once again, the AG engaged in an interpretation of a judgment that is difficult to reconcile with a literal reading of the ruling. In *Becker*, a case in which AG Slynn had also provided an Opinion, the Court confirmed that directives could enjoy vertical direct effect, and established the conditions required for provisions of a directive to be afforded such effect. Paragraph 25 of *Becker* became central to AG Slynn's reasoning in *Marshall I*, and is worth setting out in full:

> Thus, wherever the provisions of a directive appear, as far as their subject-matter is concerned, to be unconditional and sufficiently precise, those provisions may, in the absence of implementing measures adopted within the prescribed period, be relied upon as against any national provision which is incompatible with the directive *or* in so far as the provisions define rights which individuals are able to assert against the State. (emphasis added).

A literal reading of this paragraph suggests that an unimplemented directive could be relied upon before a national court in two circumstances: (1) as against any incompatible national provision; *or*, (2) as a source of rights to assert against the state. Paragraph 25 stated these possibilities as alternatives, and in no way limits the first alternative to utilisation of a directive against a state. While acknowledging this interpretation, AG Slynn swiftly limited the possibility of direct effect of directives as applying solely to situations where the defendant is the state. There is a lack of reasoning as to why the wording of paragraph 25, which is inconvenient for the AG's conclusion, can be dispensed with. Instead, the AG turned – quite legitimately – to rely indirectly on the wording of what is now Article 288 TFEU, and the fact that directives are addressed to Member States, rather than individuals. This raises the question as to why AG Slynn utilised *Becker* at all, since it appears, if anything, to contradict his general conclusion. Indeed, the Court in its judgment in *Marshall I*, chose wisely (if unsatisfactorily) to sidestep this problem by simply ignoring the phrasing of paragraph 25 of *Becker*, and pinning its reliance primarily on the provision from the EU Treaties.[43] The grammatical approach adopted by both the AG and the Court in its interpretation of the EU Treaties in this context is striking as being atypical of the Court's traditional approach. Indeed, the institutionally out-of-character nature of the Opinion of AG Slynn, when considered in the context of the Court's historical jurisprudence on direct effect, is underlined in his final comments on horizontal direct effect, in which he asserted, '[i]f the Member State is in default it is for the Commission to proceed under Article 169 [now Article 258 TFEU] of the Treaty'.[44] Such a sentiment bears little resemblance to the judicial- and citizen-empowering approach of the Court in cases such as *Van Gend en Loos*,[45] in which the Court had afforded to nationals of the Member States and national courts a key role, via the preliminary reference procedure, in the enforcement of EU law.[46]

AG Slynn's analysis of the issue of what constitutes the 'state', a matter that only became live due to the rejection of the possibility of horizontal direct effective of directives, is also

---

[41] Case C-106/89 *Marleasing* ECLI:EU:C:1990:395.

[42] In Joined Cases C-397/01 to C-403/01 *Pfeiffer and others* ECLI:EU:C:2004:584, the Court confirmed that the interpretative obligation applied to the entire national legal system.

[43] Paras 46–48 of the Judgment.

[44] At pp 734–35 of the Opinion.

[45] Case 26/62 *Van Gend en Loos* ECLI:EU:C:1963:1.

[46] See generally, JHH Weiler, 'The Transformation of Europe' (1991) 100 *YLJ* 2403.

open to some criticism. In a manner that would cause foreseeable issues regarding the uniform application of EU law, AG Slynn chose to provide very little guidance as to what would constitute the 'state' as a matter of EU law. Rather, the AG elected to remark that the concept of the state 'must be taken broadly, as including all organs of the State', a definitional economy that would come back to haunt the Court on more than one occasion.[47]

The Court in its judgment arrived at the same conclusion as AG Slynn on the question of horizontal direct effect, but in its customary manner, took a far less circuitous route to get there. Neglecting to comment upon the extent of the harmonious interpretation duty, the Court dismissed the possibility of horizontal direct effect of directives in three terse paragraphs.[48] Unlike AG Slynn, the Court chose to forego an analysis of previous cases (beyond simple citation) in doing so, focusing instead on the wording of what is now Article 288 TFEU, and the fact that Member States were the addressees of directives, thereby – as mentioned previously – sidestepping paragraph 25 of *Becker*. Similarly, the Court passed on the opportunity to elaborate upon the meaning of the concept of the state in this context, contenting itself merely to remark that the Court of Appeal in the order for reference had already concluded that the Authority was an emanation of the state.[49] Both the AG and the Court had left room for at least one sequel.

C. The Opinion of AG Slynn as Formal-Style Reasoning par Excellence

In retrospect, it may be said that the Opinion of AG Slynn, delivered on 18 September 1985, typified a mid-1980s minimalist *zeitgeist* at the Court, which appears at odds with the more expansive and consequences-focused jurisprudence of the Court in the 1960s and 1970s. February of the following year, the same month in which the judgment in *Marshall I* was handed down, saw the signing of the Single European Act, which heralded a new era of greater legislative effectiveness at European level, one in which the Court's prior expansive (or activist, depending on perspective) approach was perhaps no longer as justifiable. Academically, the Court was also coming under much more unflattering scrutiny, with Rasmussen's compelling criticism of the legitimacy of the Court's alleged activism, published in 1986, being a landmark moment.[50]

In an article published in October 1986, Judge Thijmen Koopmans, himself one of the seven judges in *Marshall I*, suggested that European lawyers, and by implication, the Court itself, ought to adopt what he described as a more minimalist conception of the lawyer's role.[51] Taking a cyclical view of legal development, Koopmans opined that European legal integration had moved from an approach dominated by institutionalism to one where instrumentalism achieved prominence.[52] Koopmans characterised institutionalism as a belief that EU institutions were 'the centrepiece of the European construction'[53] and argued this credo was evident in the Court's reasoning in 1960s cases like *Van Gend en Loos* and *Costa v ENEL*.[54] By way of

---

[47] Most famously in Case C-188/89 *Foster*, and Case C-413/15 *Farrell*.
[48] Paras 46–48 of the Judgment.
[49] ibid, para 50.
[50] H Rasmussen, *On Law and Policy in the European Court of Justice: A Comparative Study in Judicial Policymaking* (Leiden, Martinus Nijhoff, 1986).
[51] T Koopmans, 'The Role of Law in the Next State of European Integration' (1986) 35 *ICLQ* 925.
[52] ibid, pp 926–27.
[53] ibid, p 927.
[54] Case 6/64 *Costa v ENEL* ECLI:EU:C:1964:66.

contrast, instrumentalism was an approach 'where the law serves to promote the Community's ends', and was evident in 1970s judgments such as *Reyners*,[55] *Petroni*,[56] and *Cassis de Dijon*.[57] Evidently sceptical of instrumentalism and its claims that law could deliver social change, Koopmans argued that the instrumentalists' Panglossian outlook had given way to a less optimistic, more minimalist conception of the law's role. Rather than act as 'a high priest in a world of norms and principles', the lawyer should reduce their role to be 'more like a troubleshooter in the case of conflict'.[58] He suggested the minimalist approach may already have been taking shape at the Court.[59]

The Opinion of AG Slynn and the judgment in *Marshall I* appear to fit in with this minimalist conception of the Court's role. Scholars with an interest in American legal realism may also note the similarity of Koopmans' categorisations with Karl Llewellyn's 'Period Style'. In *The Common Law Tradition*, Llewellyn argued that one of two styles of judging, the 'Grand Style' and the 'Formal Style', each with their own differing conceptions of courts' role, tended to dominate American appellate decision-making in any one era.[60] The 'Grand Style', characterised by more open, purposive reasoning, had dominated in the formative era of America's legal order, and was, according to Llewellyn, re-emerging at the beginning of the 1960s.[61] This style was also distinguished by its wider conception of the judicial role and a focus on the wider prospective effects of judgments, thereby seeming to align with Koopmans' instrumentalism. By way of contrast, the 'Formal Style', typified by more literal, dogmatic reasoning, and associated with greater judicial conservativism – like Koopmans' minimalism – tended to dominate in times of doctrinal consolidation.[62]

While judgments of the Court have always tended to conform to the more superficial indicia of the 'Formal Style', such as outward use of the declaratory theory of the judicial function, judgments of the 1960s and 1970s in what might be described as 'constitutional' matters had demonstrated a clear consequentialist approach, which had openly sought optimal legal solutions for the uniformity and effectiveness of EU law. The Opinion of AG Slynn in *Marshall I*, however, especially as regards horizontal direct effect, lacks this instrumentalist approach almost entirely. Indeed, the Opinion may be characterised as 'Formal Style' judging *par excellence*, relying as it does on (often questionable) doctrinal distinctions and uncharacteristically literal interpretations of provisions of the EU Treaties, with relatively little focus on the consequences of the outcome for the future direction of the Court's jurisprudence or for the effectiveness of directives at national level. As the nomenclature of the judicial styles would suggest, Llewellyn had a clear preference for 'Grand-Style' judging, which he believed,

---

[55] Case 2/74 *Reyners* ECLI:EU:C:1974:68.
[56] Case 24/75 *Petroni* ECLI:EU:C:1975:129.
[57] Case 120/78 *Cassis de Dijon* ECLI:EU:C:1979:42.
[58] Koopmans (n 51) 930.
[59] ibid, p 931.
[60] KN Llewellyn, *The Common Law Tradition: Deciding Appeals* (London, Little Brown, 1960) 35–45.
[61] ibid, pp 41–45.
[62] ibid, pp 38–41. For an excellent and accessible account of Llewellyn's theories in *The Common Law Tradition* (including a rationalisation of the 'Period Style'), see W Twining, *Karl Llewellyn and the Realist Movement* (Cambridge, CUP 2012) 203–69. Twining noted that the 'Period Style' presented some diagnostic issues in the English context, since judges in England tend to use formalistic means, even when delivering ground-breaking judgments that might be characterised as 'Grand Style' in terms of consequence (pp 214–15). It is perhaps worth mentioning, at this juncture, that *Marshall I* is dominated by British actors: other than the Commission, no non-British actors intervened in the proceedings; the AG was British (English); and, the President of the Court, Mackenzie Stuart, was also British (though, it should be noted, from the Scottish legal tradition). The practice of AGs delivering Opinions in references originating from their own Member State appears to have been discontinued in the intervening years.

with its dual concern for legal doctrine and the purpose of the rules, created more prospective legal certainty.[63]

It may be argued that the minimalist or 'Formal Style' approach adopted by AG Slynn in *Marshall I*, in terms of its myopic focus on legal doctrine and lack of consideration – at least on the surface – of the forward-facing consequences, led ultimately to a series of subsequent cases in which the Court attempted to mitigate the effects of the problems the eventual ruling created. It could be argued that many of these problems might have been avoided had a more instrumentalist or 'Grand Style' approach been taken by AG Slynn and the Court. A brief account of the post-*Marshall I* case law is provided below.

D. Effect on Future Case Law

The judgment in *Marshall I*, which was favourable to Ms Marshall on all counts, was not the end of her struggle. The Court of Appeal would remit the case to the Industrial Tribunal to consider the question of compensation, which the Tribunal capped pursuant to section 65 of the 1975 Act. The controversy concerning the adequacy of the remedy would ultimately reach the House of Lords, which referred questions to the Court, one of which sought clarity on whether the compensation cap was compatible with Article 6 of the Equal Treatment Directive. The judgment of the Court of Justice in *Marshall II*, delivered in August 1993, over 13 years after the unlawful dismissal, would again favour Ms Marshall, and was another important landmark in the Court's jurisprudence on the effectiveness of EU law remedies.

The effect of the 'constitutional' dimension of the Opinion of AG Slynn in *Marshall I* on the subsequent case law of the Court is common knowledge (to EU lawyers at any rate), and it would be impossible to narrate the entire story here. This author has been known to tell students in lectures, having finished covering *Marshall I*, that if the Court had decided the horizontal direct effect point differently, most of the rest of the lecture and usually the next one too would be unnecessary. The Court in cases such as *Dori* and *Wells* has refused to revisit this aspect of *Marshall I*, despite the pleas of AGs. The failure to recognise the possibility of horizontal direct effect of directives would leave a judicial protection gap, however, which the Court would attempt to fill with increasingly complex solutions.[64]

The need, resulting from the exclusion of horizontal direct effect of directives, to determine what constitutes an 'emanation of the state' also led to something of a jurisprudential muddle. As mentioned previously, neither AG Slynn nor the Court provided much in the way of guidance on that point. The Court would be confronted again with this question shortly after in another British case, *Foster*. However, that judgment would contain a contradiction on its face as to whether the criteria identified by the Court were cumulative or alternative, a question which was resolved in favour of the latter interpretation in *Farrell* in 2017.

In summation, the legacy of the Opinion of AG Slynn in *Marshall I* was of a dual nature. On one hand, it is a milestone in the Court's record as an institution that has done much to

---

[63] Llewellyn (n 60) 37–38.

[64] Craig and de Búrca list six such doctrinal devices: a broad concept of the state; the expansion of the doctrine of indirect effect; the development of incidental horizontal effects (for instance, Case C-194/94 *CIA Security* ECLI:EU:C:1996:172); the utilisation of general principles of EU law, most famously (or infamously) in Case C-144/04 *Mangold* ECLI:EU:C:2005:709; the inception of horizontal direct effect of fundamental rights; and, the development of state liability in damages (Joined Cases C-6/90 and C-9/90 *Francovich* ECLI:EU:C:1991:428). See P Craig, G de Búrca, *EU Law: Text, Cases, and Materials (UK Version)*, 7th edn (Oxford, OUP, 2020) 248–67.

protect equal treatment and individual employment rights. On the other, however, the overly minimalistic or formalistic approach that was taken by AG Slynn on the question of horizontal direct effect, which appears not – at least on the face of the Opinion – to have considered the forward-facing consequences of that view, has left a legacy of unnecessary and convoluted case law in its wake.

21

Free Movement of Goods and Double Standards in Public Morality: Opinion of Advocate General Slynn in Conegate

LAURENCE W GORMLEY

I. INTRODUCTION

C ONEGATE IS OF legal interest principally because of double standards in public morality for imports; put more widely, this means that justifications for barriers to the free
movement of goods must operate on a level playing-field that does not treat imports
more harshly than domestic products. The case is also memorable, at least anecdotally, for an
observation by AG Slynn during the oral hearing, and the sequel to the judgment is a good
illustration of pragmatic policy in enforcement, with the Commission using its discretion
not to commence infringement proceedings, despite legally inadequate compliance with the
judgment.

II. BACKGROUND, CONTEXT, AND FACTS

Two consignments of goods described as 'window display models' arrived at Heathrow Airport
in London from Germany on 7 and 11 October 1982. On investigation at customs, the consignments were found to contain 48 'Love Love' dolls', 432 'Miss World Special' dolls, and 10
'Rubber Lady' dolls, as well as 12 'sexy vacuum flasks'.[1] The customs officer involved took the
view that these goods were indecent or obscene within the meaning of section 42 of the Customs
Consolidation Act 1876,[2] and thus liable to forfeiture under section 49 of the Customs and
Excise Management Act 1979.[3] Forfeiture was granted by the Uxbridge Magistrates Court – a
civil proceeding – and Conegate's appeal to the Crown Court at Southwark was unsuccessful.
The Crown Court found, first, that the articles were indeed indecent or obscene and, secondly,
rejected Conegate's argument that the objects could not be seized and forfeited because of the

---

[1] The latter are articles resembling normal vacuum flasks for drinks, but with an unusual content which pops up
on a spring when the flask is opened. The figures come from the case stated by the Crown Court at Southwark for the
High Court (see [1987] QB 254 at 256).

[2] 39 & 40 Vict 1876 c 36.

[3] 1979 c 2.

application of the European Communities Act 1972 and the EEC Treaty. This second point was the subject of appeal to the High Court, which referred four questions to the Court. Three of these were related directly to the free movement of goods,[4] the fourth concerned the interpretation of Article 234 EEC (now, after amendment, Article 351 TFEU).

After the written pleadings by Conegate, the UK, and the Commission, the hearing took place on 21 January 1986. Counsel for Conegate observed that his clients had been importing the type of merchandise involved for some time, without any problems, and the case was merely brought because of the seizure of this consignment. Counsel for the UK dryly observed that these items were new to him, whereupon AG Slynn said 'I suppose we'd better watch what we say'.[5] Discreet smiles in the courtroom, even from some of the normally more po-faced judges. At the end of the hearing, after a short adjournment, AG Slynn delivered his Opinion. This was even then unusual, and is nowadays no longer done. The answers to the questions posed were clear, and he had, of course, already drafted his Opinion: not for nothing did he enjoy the reputation of a *jurist de grande itesse vitesse*.[6]

III. THE OPINION OF AG SLYNN

The parties were *ad idem* that the exercise of the power of seizure was prima facie a quantitative restriction on imports within the meaning of Article 30 EEC (now Article 34 TFEU), so AG Slynn turned immediately to examine the alleged justification on the ground of public morality under the first sentence of Article 36 EEC (now Article 36 TFEU), even though the national court had referred to Article 36 EEC as interpreted by the Court in *Henn & Darby*.[7] Only if it could be justified would it be necessary to examine whether the prohibition was a means of arbitrary discrimination or a disguised restriction on trade between Member States, and thus caught by the second sentence of Article 36 EEC (now Article 36 TFEU). This might have been the case if, for example, the grounds of public morality or public policy were not the true reason for the adoption of the prohibition.

As EC law stood at the time of the case,[8] the learned AG noted that it was up to the Member States to decide what standards of public morality they wanted to uphold, even if this meant that one Member State's legislation was more restrictive than that of other Member States, as attitudes varied from place to place and from time to time. While AG Slynn felt that it was clear that restrictions or prohibitions on obscene and indecent publications, articles, or activities were capable of being justified on the grounds of public morality, he recalled that Article 36 EEC (now Article 36 TFEU) had always been strictly construed and applied, which meant that it was for the Member State relying on a prohibition to justify it. A Member State which set its own standards for public morality was thus obliged, in justifying a prohibition on

---

[4] Space limits militate against reproducing the three questions in full, but they are to be found in the Judgment (para 6) and at p 1009 of the Opinion of AG Slynn. See Case 121/85 *Conegate* ECLI:EU:C:1986:114; Opinion of AG Slynn in Case 121/85 *Conegate* ECLI:EU:C:1986:21.

[5] Personal recollection. The present author was the desk officer in DG III of the European Commission, dealing with *Conegate*.

[6] L Blom-Cooper, 'Lord Slynn of Hadley, Liberal law lord, judge and advocate-general of the European Court of Justice' *The Guardian* (London, 21 May 2009) www.theguardian.com/uk/2009/may/21/obituary-lord-slynn-hadley; RJ Goebel, 'Introduction: In Honor of Gordon Slynn, UK Law Lord and Judge of the EC Court of Justice' (2011) 33 *Fordham International Law Journal* 1335.

[7] Case 34/79 *Henn and Darby* ECLI:EU:C:1979:295.

[8] This has not changed since!

imports, to do so in the light of the circumstances prevailing, and against the standards which it adopted in its own territory in respect to its domestic production and distribution. AG Slynn clearly felt that a proportionality test was necessary.

The UK had submitted that, based on *Henn & Darby*,[9] it was allowed to adopt a unitary approach to Article 36 EEC, based on the strictest approach applied within that Member State, when, whatever the differences and possibilities for exemptions, there were laws which banned or restricted, on grounds of public reality, the domestic production and distribution of goods the importation of which it was also sought to prevent. *Henn & Darby* was concerned with films and magazines which involved scenes of child abuse and of intercourse between humans and animals, acts which in themselves constituted criminal conduct,[10] wholly independently of any finding that the articles concerned were indecent or obscene under customs legislation.

The articles in *Conegate*, however, were of a very different kind indeed. AG Slynn opined that a prohibition on imports could not be justified under Article 36 EEC on the grounds of public morality unless a broadly comparable standard were accepted. For AG Slynn, whether by statute or administrative act, for imports and domestic production; having one rule for imports and a different one for the sale of domestically manufactured goods, which between them exclude imports from other Member States was, he felt, insufficient to establish a justification over prohibition and imports within the meaning of Article 36 EEC.[11] To have a different approach as to public morality from that in respect of public policy would be quite wrong, as counsel for the United Kingdom accepted.

AG Slynn then turned to examine whether broadly comparable standards were adopted, pointedly observing that it would be inappropriate to look through the eyes of a mediaeval schoolmen or to demand that the same techniques or provisions be adopted in respect of domestic production as in respect of imports.[12] He felt that a ban on domestic production and sales would not have to be absolute to justify a prohibition on imports; limited exceptions might be acceptable – for example, the publication of obscene articles could be 'justified by the public good on the ground that it is in the interests of science, literature, art or learning, or of other objects of general concern'.[13] It was the substance of the standards which mattered.

The parties agreed that different legislation applied to different parts of the UK: in Northern Ireland, only the sending of obscene and indecent articles by post was prohibited; in the Isle of Man (part of the UK for these purposes), the sale, distribution, and exhibition for gain of obscene and indecent material was prohibited; in Scotland, there was disagreement as to the legal position.

However, in England and Wales (the largest part of the UK), the manufacture and sale of the *Conegate* articles was not prohibited by the Obscene Publications Act 1959, nor were the manufacture or possession of goods of this kind prohibited. There was no general prohibition

---

[9] ibid, at para 21 of that Judgment: 'Whatever may be the differences between the laws on this subject in force in the different constituent parts of the United Kingdom, and notwithstanding the fact that they contain certain exceptions of limited scope, these laws, taken as a whole, have as their purpose the prohibition, or at least, the restraining, of the manufacture and marketing of publications or articles of an indecent or obscene character.'

[10] See Opinion of AG Warner in Case 34/79 *Henn and Darby* ECLI:EU:C:1979:246, p 3819, para 5 (quotation from the Agreed Statement of Facts). See ch 12.

[11] AG Slynn noted that this approach followed that in Joined Cases 115 and 116/81 *Adoui* ECLI:EU:C:1982:183, para 8.

[12] See, as to equivalent, but not identical measures: in relation to health protection, Case 4/75 *Rewe Zentralfinanz* ECLI:EU:C:1975:98, para 8; in relation to public policy, concerning persons, Case 41/74 *Van Duyn* ECLI:EU:C:1974:133, paras 19–24.

[13] Obscene Publications Act 1959 (1959 c 66), s 4.

on their sale or distribution, accepting them to be obscene or indecent, although they could not be sent by post, nor, under the Indecent Displays (Control) Act 1981,[14] could they be displayed in a public place or so as to be visible in a public place. That latter Act was one of several steps taken by the Thatcher government in one of its periodic fits of moral outrage.

Another was the Local Government (Miscellaneous Provisions) Act 1982.[15] Section 2 of that act empowered local authorities to adopt the powers set out in Schedule 3 to that Act, which enabled the local authority to restrict the number of sex shops in its area by introducing licensing; the number could even be set at zero. Where the local authority had adopted Schedule 3, goods of the type involved could be sold in licenced sex shops subject to compliance with certain conditions, but in any event not to persons aged under 18, such goods could still be sold in unlicensed premises (it seemed to persons of any age), as long as the sale of those articles did not comprise to a significant degree the business of the premises. Where a local authority had not adopted schedule 3, the goods involved in *Conegate* could be sold from any premises, again, it seemed, to persons of any age. It appeared that the parties agreed that, even though no figures were available, a substantial percentage of, if not most, local authorities had not adopted these powers.

AG Slynn had little difficulty in concluding that while there was no doubt that the UK legislation against obscene and indecent material was indeed adopted in the interests of public morality and had become increasingly restrictive in recent years, as far as it related to the licensing of premises for the sale of articles such as those involved in *Conegate*; only in the Isle of Man and perhaps in Scotland was there a prohibition on sale comparable with the prohibition on imports contained in the customs legislation relied on by the Crown in this case.

It was plain, and the parties agreed on this point, that two different standards were applied: one standard for imports, and one for domestic production and sale. AG Slynn correctly gave short shrift to the argument that the type of articles concerned did not seem to be manufactured in the UK:[16] the manufacture of such goods was not prohibited, nor was there any evidence adduced that they were seized from points of retail sale, even if a power to do so existed. AG Slynn felt that it was not enough for the United Kingdom to argue that the import ban was justified because there was a general hostility to obscene and indecent articles, but there were no effective means of preventing their manufacture and sale from domestic outlets in the UK. In the greater part of the UK there was no legal bar on the manufacture and sale of domestic products comparable to that on imports.

The AG then discussed whether, had he concluded that the ban was justified on the grounds of public morality, the second sentence of Article 36 EEC would have defeated the justification. In *Henn & Darby*, the Court had stated that, in the light of the existing laws in relation to obscene publications:

> it is permissible to conclude, on a comprehensive view, that there is no lawful trade in the goods concerned in that case in the United Kingdom. A prohibition on imports which may in certain respects be more strict than some of the laws applied within the United Kingdom cannot therefore be regarded as amounting to a measure designed to give indirect protection to some national product or

---

[14] 1981 c 42. As to exceptions, see s 1(3)–(5).

[15] 1982 c 30.

[16] Conegate had indicated that it had looked at commencing production in the United Kingdom, but 'blow-up dolls' could not be produced economically to compete with those manufactured in the Far East. The articles concerned had been placed in free circulation in the Community in the then West Germany and imported from there into the United Kingdom.

aimed at creating arbitrary discrimination between goods of this type depending on whether they are produced within the national territory or another Member State.[17]

Thus, on a comprehensive view, because the legislation sought to prohibit or at least restrain the manufacture and marketing of publications and films of an obscene or indecent character, the Court had concluded, in *Henn & Darby*, that there was no lawful trade in such publications and films, even if there were limited exceptions and variations.

Returning to the circumstances in *Conegate*, AG Slynn found that the same might be true of Scotland and of the Isle of Man in respect of the articles concerned, but it could not, however, be said of Northern Ireland, and England and Wales. In relation to England and Wales, there was not so much a prohibition on sale as a partial restriction, and control of retail sales outlets had only been partly implemented. At least to an extent, it could be compared with restrictions on sales outlets for goods such as alcohol and tobacco. Even though the UK government clearly disapproved of the retail sale of the type of goods involved in *Conegate*, sale to anyone aged 18 or over was possible in licensed sex shops in areas where licensing applied, and in any other shops in those areas if the trade in such goods did not form part a significant part of the business of those shops, and generally at premises elsewhere, provided that there was no unlawful display of the articles involved. It was simply not possible to say that there was no lawful trade in such goods in the UK within the meaning of the judgment in *Henn & Darby*. For AG Slynn, the conclusion followed therefore that, although there was no intention in the customs legislation to discriminate against goods from other Member States in order to protect domestic production, there was arbitrary discrimination within the meaning of the second sentence of Article 36 EEC, which meant that the justification on grounds of public morality in the first sentence could not be relied upon.

AG Slynn went on to observe that this did not mean that the goods in *Conegate* could be sold freely in the UK. They were subject to the controls and limits which applied generally to the sale and distribution of other obscene or indecent obscene and indecent articles of a similar kind within the UK. Finally, he emphasised that his conclusion did not mean that Community law compelled the UK to admit these objects from other Member States indefinitely; it merely did so as long as there was no effective ban on the manufacture and sale of domestic products of the same kind.

The fourth question, about the effect of two international conventions,[18] did not detain him long. The parties did not deal with this in their oral submissions, and it seemed doubtful whether the conventions were relevant to the case: it was not concerned with publications which were the principal subject matter of the Geneva Convention, and the goods were not sent by post, so the Universal Postal Convention did not apply. Moreover, the Commission had observed that Germany had denounced the Geneva Convention before the relevant facts in this case, and the renewal of the Universal Postal Convention was concluded after the accession of the UK to the EEC, so Article 234 EEC (now Article 351 TFEU) was irrelevant. AG Slynn opined that the obligations under those two conventions could not in any event override the obligations of one Member State to another, whatever the effect of those conventions were in relation to third states. Moreover, he felt the question posed added nothing to that posed as the final question in *Henn & Darby*, and he proposed that it be answered in the same manner.

---

[17] Para 21 of the Judgment.

[18] The Geneva Convention for the Suppression of Traffic in Obscene Publications (Geneva, 12 September 1923, as amended, Lake Success, New York, 12 November 1947), https://treaties.un.org/doc/Treaties/1950/02/19500202%20 06-19%20AM/Ch_VIII_02p.pdf; the Universal Postal Convention (renewed at Lausanne, 5 July 1974, 1005 UNTS 53 (No 14723, https://treaties.un.org/doc/Publication/UNTS/Volume%201239/v1239.pdf).

IV. ANALYSIS

This Opinion treaded carefully, but still made mincemeat of the UK's arguments, demolishing them courteously but convincingly. The questions posed were rather cumbersomely phrased, but AG Slynn went straight to core point about the applicability of Article 36 EEC, examining first whether the public morality justification could be made out. This was sensible, as if it could not, there was no need to go further. The Opinion demonstrated a neat balancing act; AG Slynn examined each aspect clearly, but also dealt with the 'what if' scenario, looking to see whether the second sentence of Article 36 EEC would have operated to prevent the UK from relying on the public morality justification, had he found it to be prima facie made out.

AG Slynn's reasoning and conclusion on public morality were firmly framed in the context of the first sentence of Article 36 EEC. In modern case-law, the Court has started to speak in terms of consistency being required,[19] and it was this inconsistency that was fatal to the argument that the prohibition of imports was justified. The absurdities of the argument had already been well-exposed by AG Warner in *Henn & Darby*:

> Perhaps the most glaring disparity lies in the fact that, although an obscene book may be lawfully on sale in English bookshops, for instance because its publication is judged to be for the public good on the ground of its scientific value or literary merit, the identical book may not be imported into England.[20]

AG Warner also went on to:

> doubt if the application of [the proportionality] test would justify the prohibition of the importation into the United Kingdom of a book that was lawfully on sale in English bookshops. Clearly it would be unreasonable and disproportionate to forbid the importation of such a book just because of the risk that it might be displayed in an English street or put on sale in Scotland or the Isle of Man. Those very same risks flow from the publication of the book in England.[21]

The Court, however, turned a proverbial deaf ear.

In *Henn & Darby* the Court's conclusion that there was no lawful trade in indecent or obscene articles has been the subject of much criticism,[22] as was its observation that if a prohibition on importation were justifiable on grounds of public morality, and if it were imposed with that purpose, then the enforcement of it could not be affected by the second sentence of Article 36 EEC. The Court's approach in *Henn & Darby* emptied the second sentence of Article 36 EEC of all substance, and was out of step with the Court's own normal approach to that sentence.[23] Fortunately, that approach has not been followed by the Court since.

Even though the national court paid so much attention to it, *Henn & Darby* was of limited assistance, not least because the type of articles to which it related was so entirely different from those involved in *Conegate*. It is not surprising therefore that the AG looked at the EEC Treaty itself, rather than be dazzled by the poverty of legal reasoning in *Henn & Darby*. That

---

[19] eg in relation to services, Case C-500/06 *Corporación Dermoestética* ECLI:EU:C:2008:421, para 39; Case C-169/07 *Hartlauer* ECLI:EU:C:2009:141, para 55; Case C-169/08 *Presidente del Consiglio dei Ministri* ECLI:EU:C:2009:709, para 42; Case C-390/12 *Pfleger and Others* ECLI:EU:C:2014:281, para 54.

[20] Pages 3828–29 of the Opinion of AG Warner in Case 34/79 *Henn and Darby*. See ch 12.

[21] Page 3831 of the Opinion of AG Warner in Case 34/79 *Henn and Darby*.

[22] eg L Catchpole and A Barav, 'The Public Morality Exception and Free Movement of Goods: Justification of a Dual Standard in National Legislation?' (1980) 7 *LIEI* 1; LW Gormley, *Prohibiting Restrictions on Trade within the EEC* (Elsevier, 1985) 126–28.

[23] LW Gormley, 'The Answer, My Friend, Is Blowing in the Wind' (1986) 11 *ELRev* 443, 447.

'a general hostility to obscene and indecent articles' was not a legitimate argument when no concrete steps were taken to prevent or deter the manufacture or sale of the *Conegate* type of goods. This was later confirmed in a different context (hostility to live transport of veal calves) in *Compassion in World Farming*.[24]

A. The Judgment

In a relatively brief judgment, the Court dealt swiftly with the issues. It observed that the first question raised initially the general problem of whether a provision on the importation of certain goods could be justified on grounds of public morality where the legislation of the Member State concerned contained no prohibition on the manufacture or marketing of the same products within the national territory. Article 36 EEC clearly provided that the free movement of goods provisions of the treaty did not preclude import prohibitions on imports justified on grounds of public morality. The Court noted that it had already made clear in *Henn & Darby* that, in principle, it was for each Member State to determine the requirements of public morality in its territory in accordance with its own scale of values and in the form selected by it. Yet that was no *carte blanche*, and the Court observed that:

> the fact that goods cause offence cannot be regarded as sufficiently serious to justify restrictions on the free movement of goods where the Member State concerned does not adopt with respect to the same goods manufactured or marketed within its territory, penal measures or other serious and effective measures intended to prevent the distribution of such goods in its territory.[25]

It therefore followed that a Member State could not rely on grounds of public morality to prohibit the importation of goods from other Member States when its legislation contained no prohibition on the manufacture or marketing of the same goods on its territory.

Whether and to what extent the UK legislation contained such a prohibition, was naturally, a matter for the referring national court. Nevertheless, the Court observed that the question whether there was such a prohibition in a Member State comprised of different constituent parts, each of which had its own internal legislation, could only be resolved by taking all the relevant legislation into consideration. It was not necessary for this purpose that the manufacturing and marketing of the product whose importation had been prohibited should be prohibited in the territory of *all* the constituent parts, but it had at least to be possible to conclude from the applicable rules, taken as a whole, that their purpose was in substance to prohibit the manufacture and marketing of the products concerned.

In the case at hand, the Court noted that the High Court had carefully defined the substance of the national legislation, noting that the goods in question could be manufactured freely and marketed subject only to certain restrictions: an absolute prohibition on the transmission of such goods by post; a restriction on their public display, and, in certain areas of the UK (some parts of England and Wales), a system of licensing of premises for the sale of those goods to customers aged 18 and over. These restrictions, said the Court, could not be regarded as

---

[24] Case C-1/96 *Compassion in World Farming* ECLI:EU:C:1998:113, paras 67–68: 'In any event, a Member State cannot rely on the views or the behaviour of a section of national public opinion, as CIWF maintains, in order unilaterally to challenge a harmonising measure adopted by the Community institutions. Therefore, reliance on Article 36 for the protection of public order or public morality in circumstances such as those involved in the instant case is also ruled out.'

[25] Para 15 of the Judgment.

equivalent in substance to a prohibition on manufacture and marketing. The fact that no articles of the type to which the case related were manufactured in the UK did not exclude the possibility such articles being manufactured there; it did not lead to a different assessment of the situation. In these circumstances, the UK could not rely on the grounds of public morality in Article 36 EEC to prohibit the importation of this type of goods. That did not prevent the UK authorities from applying to those goods, once imported, the same restrictions on marketing which replied to similar products manufactured and marketed within the country. With that conclusion, the matter was disposed of, and it was unnecessary to answer the remaining questions on Articles 30-36 EEC.

On Article 234 EEC, the Court simply followed the Commission's view: agreements concluded before the entry into force of the EEC Treaty could not be relied upon in relations to justify restrictions on trade between Member States. As there were no rights of non-Member States, or questions about the observance of obligations under such agreements involved, the Court could formulate its conclusion briefly.[26]

B. Analysis of the Judgment

In contrast to the judgment in *Henn & Darby*, the Court's reasoning in *Conegate* was clearly based on the first sentence of Article 36 EEC (rather than on the second sentence); the public and morality justification simply had not been made out, given the difference in the domestic approach and the approach taken to imported goods. The already Court's key statement that:

> the fact that goods cause offence cannot be regarded as sufficiently serious to justify restrictions on free movement of goods where the legislation of the Member State concerned contains no prohibition on the manufacture or marketing of the same products within the national territory penal measures or other serious and effective measures intended to prevent the distribution of such goods in its territory,[27]

parallels the approach, in relation to public policy justifications in the free movement of persons, that the conduct of the person concerned must pose 'a genuine and sufficiently serious threat'.[28] In particular, it parallels *Adoui & Cornuaille*, in which the Court observed that:

> conduct may not be considered as being of a sufficiently serious nature to justify restrictions on the admission to or residence within the territory of a Member State of a national of another Member State in a case where the former Member State does not adopt, with respect to the same conduct on the part of its own nationals repressive measures or other genuine and effective measures intended to combat such conduct.[29]

This firmly brought the case law on public morality in line with that on public policy. The Court could perhaps have found that the provision as such were justifiable on the grounds of

---

[26] It did recall in full its ruling in Case 812/79 *Burgoa* ECLI:EU:C:1980:231, but did not mention *Henn and Darby*, or the points mentioned by AG Slynn. See P Koutrakos, 'International Agreements Concluded by Member States prior to their EU Accession: Burgoa' in G Butler and RA Wessel, *EU External Relations Law: The Cases in Context* (Oxford, Hart Publishing, 2022).

[27] Para 15 of the Judgment.

[28] See eg Case 36/75 *Rutili* ECLI:EU:C:1975:137, para 28; Case 30/77 *Bouchereau* ECLI:EU:C:1977:172, para 35, and Joined Cases 115 and 116/81 *Adoui*, para 8.

[29] Joined Cases 115 and 116/81 *Adoui*, para 8. See also, in relation to free movement of goods, Case 40/82 *Commission v UK*, para 38 (final sentence), 'The deduction must be made that the 1981 measures did not form part of a seriously considered health policy.'

public morality, but were unacceptable because the difference in treatment of domestic and imported goods was irrational, thus concluding that there was an arbitrary discrimination within the meaning of the second sentence of Article 36 EEC, but this was never really likely in view of the Opinion of AG Slynn. Whether the justification was as such made out was examined in relation to the first sentence of Article 36 EEC; the second sentence dealt with whether an ostensible justification was being misused. In common with the other first sentence justifications (and, indeed the case-law-based justifications) for barriers to free movement, public morality considerations were not a set of reserved powers; the choices made were subject to scrutiny for compliance with Community, now EU law, by the Court.

C. Subsequent Developments

As both the AG and the Court pointed out, it was open to the UK authorities to apply the same restrictions on marketing to the goods concerned in *Conegate* which were applied to similar products manufactured and marketed within its territory. When the case returned to the High Court, Kennedy J had little difficulty in concluding that the conviction had to be quashed, and the goods concerned had to be returned.[30]

As a result of the Court's judgment in *Conegate*, the UK issued instructions to customs officers not to seize goods of the type to which the judgment related. This was not good compliance with the judgment, as mere administrative instructions can be withdrawn at the whim of the administration, and offer no legal certainty at all.[31] The Commission could have required legislative action to be taken to correct the offending discrepancy, but there was a risk that the UK government might, if pressed, prohibit the manufacture and sale on its territory of the *Conegate* type of articles, rather than amend the customs legislation so as specifically to permit the importation of such articles. The feeling in Brussels was that the Commission had rather better things to do than push the UK into a corner on this matter (imagine certain sections of the press having a field day with headlines claiming, no matter how wrongly, 'European Commission says we've all got to have blow-up dolls!'). On the basis that there were no new complaints coming in about people being prevented from importing this type of article, the Internal Market Directorate General advised the Commission to simply close the file.[32] If there were complaints in the future, appropriate action could always be taken. The Commission was wise enough to agree to this proposal. This saga is a good example of the Commission exercising its discretion to decide whether it is opportune to bring infringement proceedings.

---

[30] *Conegate Ltd v Customs & Excise Commrs* [1987] QB 254, 272–74.
[31] See Case 167/73 *Commission v France* ECLI:EU:C:1974:35, paras 40–48.3.
[32] Personal knowledge (the present author proposed this step).

22

To Beer, Or Not to Beer? That is the Public Health Question: Opinion of Advocate General Slynn in Commission v Germany (Beer Purity)

STEVE TERRETT

I. INTRODUCTION

I N 1516, IN the Bavarian city of Ingolstadt, a Bavarian Duke, William IV, proclaimed the *Reinheitsgebot* (Beer Purity Law). This regulated beer production, by prohibiting the use of ingredients other than barley, hops, and water. Whether the *Reinheitsgebot* was, as a brochure from the Ingolstadt tourist information centre claims, 'the first food regulation of the modern era',[1] is less important than the fact that it ultimately resulted in the case analysed here. Ingolstadt is also famous as being the location of Mary Shelley's novel, *Frankenstein: The Modern Prometheus*. When it was published in 1818, many were horrified at the prospect of science gone-too-far and monstrous creations threatening human safety. Such fears also continued to exist many centuries later, albeit in relation to fluid abominations.

In 1982, the European Commission formally notified Germany[2] that its legislation, based on the *Reinheitsgebot*, contravened the free movement of goods, particularly Article 30 EC (now Article 34 TFEU). Regardless of their historical-cultural importance,[3] national laws restricting manufacturing methods and name-designations were measures equivalent to quantitative restrictions (MEQRs) requiring justification. Germany's defence of its beer purity laws echoed the fears of many who read Mary Shelly's novel. Beers from elsewhere, using ingredients and additives that were prohibited in Germany, were the liquid equivalent of Frankenstein's monster. Germany defended its national laws as necessary to protect public health and avoid consumer confusion, on the basis of what is now Article 36 TFEU.

---

[1] To avoid accusations of pro-European bias in this alco-historical introduction, it should be noted that the first beer (*kui*) was probably brewed in ancient China in around 7,000 BC, or perhaps as early as 10,000 BC in ancient Iran. The likelihood of Europeans having 'discovered' beer or beer regulations is perhaps as likely as Europeans having 'discovered' America.

[2] The Commission launched almost identical proceedings against Greece, whose legislation also prohibited imports of beer containing additives. However, the backstory of Greece's law is nowhere near as mystical as the Reinheitsgebot, which perhaps explains the comparative anonymity of Case 176/84 *Commission v Greece* ECLI:EU:C:1987:125.

[3] On the importance of beer to Germany's national and cultural identity, see N MacGregor, *Germany: Memories of a Nation* (London, Penguin, 2016) 174–76.

Beer Purity[4] was not the first case to deal with measures having equivalent effect to quantitative restrictions or to discuss consumer protection and public health justifications. Nonetheless, AG Slynn's pragmatic approach is an important contribution to the ongoing debate on how to strike an appropriate balance between two competing factors.[5] On the one hand, the Member States may have genuine concerns for food and product safety and should be entitled to enforce their own standards until EU legislation fully harmonises the relevant area. On the other hand, public health and consumer protection justifications may be abused by Member States to shield their national products from foreign competition or crystallise existing preferences to keep their consumers buying familiar domestic products instead of experimenting.

Food quality standards were one reason why the EU and the United States were unable to conclude the Transatlantic Trade and Investment Partnership (TTIP) after three years of negotiations.[6] Until the EU-UK Trade and Cooperation Agreement was concluded,[7] many feared that Brexit would result in UK stores being stocked with foods made according to lower standards. Ferocious debate continues, to this day, on whether non-animal milks (made from nuts, rice, oats, etc) should be forced to be sold as 'juice', rather than 'milk', or whether vegan sausages or burgers should instead be called 'vegetable tubes' or 'veggie-discs'. The *Beer Purity* case neither started nor ended such debate, but it played an important part in identifying the legitimate boundaries of national legislative autonomy over foodstuff regulation.

II. BACKGROUND, CONTEXT AND FACTS

The case occurred during a pivotal period of development in the Union's history. The adoption of EU harmonising measures under Article 100 EC (now Article 115 TFEU) required unanimous approval. Completion of the internal market seemed as elusive as the pot of gold at rainbow's end.[8] Attempts to adopt EU harmonising laws on beer and additives had already failed,[9] and the Commission was devoting more time to combatting market restrictions via infringement proceedings, rather than detailed legislative proposals. When proceedings were lodged in July 1984, an ad hoc Committee on Institutional Affairs to the European Council (the 'Dooge Committee') was already working on a report,[10] which led to a Commission White Paper describing a 'new approach' to market integration.[11] It fixed 1992 as the common market's completion date. When AG Slynn delivered his Opinion in September 1986, the Single

---

[4] Case 178/84 *Commission v Germany* ECLI:EU:C:1987:126 (*Beer Purity*).

[5] Opinion of AG Slynn in Case 178/84 *Commission v Germany* ECLI:EU:C:1986:324 (*Beer Purity*).

[6] TTIP negotiations commenced in July 2013 and ended in October 2016, before being halted by the US in 2018 and declared 'obsolete and no longer relevant' by the Commission in 2019.

[7] Trade and Cooperation Agreement Between the European Union and the European Atomic Energy Community, of the one part, and the United Kingdom of Great Britain and Northern Ireland, of the other part [2021] OJ L 149/10.

[8] For discussion of the procedural and substantive difficulties created by the original version of Art 100 TEC (now Art 115 TFEU) see P Craig and G de Búrca, *EU Law: Text, Cases and Materials*, 3rd edn (Oxford, OUP, 2003) 1171. Art 100 EEC Treaty stated: 'The Council shall, acting unanimously on a proposal from the Commission, issued directives for the approximation of such laws, regulations or administrative provisions of the Member States as directly affect the establishment of the common market.'

[9] See HL Clark, 'The Free Movement of Goods and Regulation for Public Health and Consumer Protection in the EEC: The West German Beer Purity Case' (1988) 28 *Virginia Journal of International Law* 753, 757.

[10] Report from the ad hoc Committee on Institutional Affairs (Brussels, 29–30 March 1985).

[11] Commission, 'Completing the Internal Market: White Paper from the Commission to the European Council' COM (1985) 310. On the 'new approach' see paras 61–79.

European Act (SEA) had already been ratified by all Member States except Ireland.[12] The SEA entered into force in July 1987, after the Court's judgment in March of that year.[13]

The Commission was determined not only to improve the EU's legislative capacity, but also to demonstrate the effectiveness of infringement proceedings. Challenging Germany's restrictions on beer imports provided an opportunity to show that completing the common market may require even the largest Member States to repeal centuries-old regulations which affect culturally significant products. In the few years preceding *Beer Purity*, the Court had ruled on infringement actions concerning restrictions on imports of curds,[14] vinegar,[15] and woodworking machines.[16] Earlier in 1987, it ruled on the legality of restricting imports of low-quality meat cuts,[17] allowing non-EU goods to be released onto the EU market in instalments after entering the EU on a single entry form,[18] and Italy's delay in implementing directives on cattle and swine inoculations.[19] Contemporary preliminary references from national courts had asked the Court to consider price-fixing of books,[20] butter-labelling laws[21] and the classification of scientific equipment within the common external tariff.[22] Each such issue was important, but none came remotely close to being a showcase statement of intent as challenging Germany's 400-year old beer purity laws, which had achieved notoriety in the international press as flagrant trade barriers.[23] AG Slynn was typically understated when describing the case as 'an important one'.[24]

The restrictions, ultimately deemed unlawful, were contained in two separate statutes. The first was the Beer Duty Act 1952, the contemporary embodiment of the *Reinheitsgebot*.[25] Article 9 stated that only barley malt, hops, yeast, and water may be used in beer production.[26] Whilst not specifically referring to additives, AG Slynn interpreted this *a contrario* as precluding their use. Article 9, read in conjunction with related secondary legislation,[27] prevented the use of rice, maize, or sorghum malts in beer. Article 9 did not apply to breweries producing beer purely for consumption on their own premises (*Hausbrauer*), and could be disapplied

---

[12] Ireland's ratification was delayed by a constitutional challenge initiated against its European Communities (Amendment) Act 1986, intended to implement the SEA 1986 into Irish law. For details, see para 8 of *Crotty v An Taoiseach* [1987] IESC 4, [1987] IR 713. For an academic appraisal see G Hogan, 'The Supreme Court and the Single European Act' (1987) 22 *Irish Jurist* 55; J Temple Lang, 'The Irish Court Case which delayed the Single European Act: Crotty v An Taoiseach and Others' (1987) 24 *CMLRev* 709.

[13] The SEA was signed in Luxembourg on 17 February 1986 and in The Hague on 28 February 1986, but only entered into force on 1 July 1987.

[14] Case 35/84 *Commission v Italy* ECLI:EU:C:1986:59.

[15] Case 281/83 *Commission v Italy* ECLI:EU:C:1985:407.

[16] Case 188/84 *Commission v France* ECLI:EU:C:1986:43.

[17] Case 124/85 *Commission v Greece* ECLI:EU:C:1986:490.

[18] Case 275/85 *Commission v Italy* ECLI:EU:C:1987:37.

[19] Case 364/85 *Commission v Italy* ECLI:EU:C:1987:51.

[20] Case 168/86 *Rousseau* ECLI:EU:C:1987:107.

[21] Case 98/86 *Mathot* ECLI:EU:C:1987:89.

[22] Case 13/84 *Control Data v Commission* ECLI:EU:C:1987:16.

[23] For further discussion, see Clark (n 9) 754.

[24] At p 1246 of the Opinion.

[25] The 1952 Act (*Biersteuergesetz*) was as amended by the *Zolländerungsgesetz* (Customs Law [Amendment] Act) on 12 September 1980.

[26] For top-fermented beer (*Einfach bier*), other malts and technically pure cane, beet or invert sugar, and glucose and colorants obtained from those sugars, could also be used. Moreover, secondary legislation (the *Zusatzstoff-Zulassungsverordnung* or Order Authorising the Use of Certain Additives) permitted saccharin to be used in *Einfach bier*. However, only 15% of beer sales in Germany concerned top-fermented beer. Far more common was bottom-fermentation beer, ie a light, lager-type beer.

[27] Art 17(4) of the *Durchführungsbestimmungen zum Biersteuergesetz* (Implementing Provisions to the Biersteuergesetz) of 14 March 1952, [1952] I Bgbl. 153, cited in the Judgment, para 5.

upon an application in individual cases regarding: (i) the manufacture of special beers; (ii) beer intended for export; and (iii) beer intended for scientific experiments.

Article 9 only applied, per se, to German beer, but Article 10 stated that only drinks complying with Article 9 could market themselves as beer (*bier*). This applied to both German and non-German beers. Contraventions of both Articles 9 and 10 were punishable by a fine. These two Articles, therefore, prevented any beer produced with rice, maize or additives from being sold in Germany as 'bier'.

The Foodstuffs Law 1974 contained further restrictions which complicated life for non-German beer producers. Article 11 prohibited the use of any additive in foodstuffs, unless the additive in question: (i) had received prior authorisation; and (ii) was completely eliminated from the foodstuff by the time of consumption or existed only as a technically unavoidable and technologically insignificant residue, negligible from the point of view of health, odour and taste. Article 12 permitted regulations to be adopted: (i) to authorise certain additives generally or for specific foodstuffs or uses; and (ii) to establish a maximum content or purity standard of particular additives. Such authorisations included *lex generalis* rules permitting certain additives in all foodstuffs and *lex specialis* regulations on particular foodstuffs such as wine, meat, fruit juice, and syrups. No equivalent existed for beer. Most significantly, Article 47 prohibited the importation of products containing non-authorised additives.

III. THE OPINION OF AG SLYNN

Unsurprisingly, both AG Slynn and the Court deemed both sets of restrictions to be unlawful measures having equivalent effect, thereby infringing Article 30 EEC. It was irrelevant that they applied to both domestic and imported beer, and that any trader could, regardless of nationality, produce beer which complied with German law and sell its product as 'bier'. They clearly made life more difficult for beers from other Member States which, apart from Greece, allowed beer to contain additives or to be made using rice or maize.[28]

The designation rules, effectively preventing non-German products from being sold as 'bier', were incapable of justification because consumers could be protected by less restrictive labelling rules. However, the public health defence was more debatable. In principle, until fully-harmonising EU law existed, Member States retained autonomy to regulate foodstuffs safety. They were entitled to be concerned about the types and amounts of additives consumed by their consumers. They were not precluded from restricting certain additives merely because they were permitted elsewhere. However, such restrictions must be a proportionate response to a genuine health risk, rather than arbitrary discrimination or disguised trade restrictions. Germany's desire to protect public health was legitimate in principle, but the absence of any realistic evidence of a public health risk, plus some confusing exceptions to the national restrictions, led AG Slynn and the Court to conclude that its blanket prohibitions were disproportionate. Just as theoretical arguments may convince a listener about the virtues of flying, only to lose credibility when applied to the concrete example of the Hindenburg zeppelin, Germany's theoretically legitimate justification for regulating foodstuffs went up in flames when applied to the concrete example of beer.

Aside from its importance to free movement of goods jurisprudence, the Opinion of AG Slynn also adopted a more liberal attitude than the hitherto case law on how strictly the

---

[28] Report for the Hearing in Case 178/84 *Commission v Germany* ECLI:EU:C:1986:34, p 1230.

Commission's reasoned opinion must be interpreted when identifying the national measures challenged in infringement proceedings. Although the Commission's reasoned opinion only explicitly mentioned the Beer Duty Act, AG Slynn argued, and the Court agreed, that the infringement proceedings also applied to the Foodstuffs Law.

IV. ANALYSIS

The analyses of AG Slynn and the Court follow the same pattern, which is also reflected in the sections below. Section 4.1 discusses the Commission's failure to explicitly mention the Foodstuffs Law in its reasoned opinion. Section 4.2 then analyses the categorisation of the German beer purity rules as unlawful measures having equivalent effect. Section 4.3 deals with the consumer protection justification. Section 4.4 discusses the public health justification. Section 4.5 offers some conclusions regarding the impact of the *Beer Purity* case on future case law.

A. Omitting the Foodstuffs Law from the Commission's Reasoned Opinion

Some confusion existed about precisely which national law(s) the Commission had challenged. During informal discussions, and until the Commission issued a formal notification and reasoned opinion, the only legislation discussed was the Beer Duty Act. However, when proceedings commenced, Germany argued that the unlawful restrictions arose from the Foodstuffs Law. Beer was subject to both the *lex specialis* production rules in the Beer Duty Act and the *lex generalis* rules of the Foodstuffs Law, so the restrictions were contained in '... separate but complementary pieces of legislation ...',[29] only one of which was mentioned in the reasoned opinion.

Germany's contention that the Commission was precluded from adding new grounds of challenge, or widening the scope of its reasoned opinion once proceedings commenced, was supported by authority.[30] If the Foodstuffs Law was the true source of the allegedly unlawful restrictions, surely the Commission's claim must fail for having omitted any reference to that statute? In *Commission v Italy (Wool)*,[31] the Court thought it would be unfair to adversely affect a Member State's rights of defence by allowing the Commission to expand its allegations beyond those in its reasoned opinion once proceedings had commenced. Accordingly, the Commission could either continue with the allegations in its reasoned opinion, or end the proceedings and commence new proceedings based on an expanded reasoned opinion.

AG Slynn preferred a more pragmatic approach. For him, the Commission's challenge should be viewed 'in substance if not in form', as if it were against both statutes. Although its letter of formal notice referred solely to the Beer Duty Act, it clearly sought to challenge the prohibition on importing and selling non-German beers containing additives. There was no doubt about the *substance* of the alleged infringement, so if those restrictions resulted from other statutes, they too were the intended object of the infringement action. From the

---

[29] Para 19 of the Judgment.
[30] See Case 232/78 *Commission v France* ECLI:EU:C:1979:215; Case 124/81 *Commission v UK* ECLI:EU:C:1983:30; Case 123/76 *Commission v Italy* ECLI:EU:C:1977:128. For discussion of the procedural limits applicable to reasoned opinions, see K Lenaerts et al, *EU Procedural Law* (Oxford, OUP, 2014) 186–91.
[31] Case 7/69 *Commission v Italy* ECLI:EU:C:1970:15, para 5.

outset, Germany sought to justify its prohibitions on the basis of public health risks caused by consuming additives. Whilst not explicitly mentioning the Foodstuffs Law, Germany's defence specifically covered issues dealt with in that statute. The Court concluded that Germany had 'understood and acknowledged that the subject matter of the proceedings also covered the absolute ban on the use of additives'.[32] As that ban was contained in the Foodstuffs Law, both parties had implicitly acknowledged that this statute was relevant, despite neither having referred to it, *expressis verbis*, until the proceedings commenced.

This was not a case where the Commission sought to expand the scope of the proceedings,[33] but conversely, where the Member State had. The Commission had 'picked up the [Foodstuffs Law] gauntlet thrown down in defence',[34] and both statutes had been debated at great length without objection from either side. The public health and consumer protection defences were 'hotly, and … voluminously contested'.[35] If the proceedings ignored the Foodstuffs Law, it would simply result in new proceedings being initiated against Germany, with identical issues to those lengthily discussed in these proceedings, at Germany's instigation.

AG Slynn's pragmatic approach reflected a practical sense of justice, derived perhaps from his experience of the common law's preference for practical solutions over grand, immutable theories. His concern that justice be efficient, whilst preserving the litigants' rights, was reminiscent of English law's approach to civil justice in general.[36] It is impossible to know whether the Court would anyway have adopted this less rigid view of the Commission's duty to provide reasons, but it agreed with AG's Slynn's matter-of-fact approach and confirmed that Germany had not been denied its right to a fair hearing.

B. Germany's Beer Purity Rules Constitute Unlawful Measures Having Equivalent Effect

It was unsurprising that the restrictions in both statutes were categorised as unlawful measures having equivalent effect. *Beer Purity* was decided 12 years after *Dassonville*,[37] in which the Court's expansive interpretation of (what is now) Article 34 TFEU extended to cover indistinctly applicable rules. This was 'a bold move'[38] at the time, 'devoid of any references to its previous jurisprudence',[39] but by 1986, it was standard orthodoxy. Germany's beer purity rules were clearly 'capable of hindering, directly or indirectly, actually or potentially, intra-[Union] trade …'.[40] Accordingly, it was perplexing that Germany originally argued that its restrictions fell outside the scope of the EU Treaties because they created a 'relative rather than an absolute ban', capable of being avoided by any trader complying with the purity rules, regardless of nationality. However, by the time proceedings commenced, Germany had conceded that both sets of restrictions were measures having equivalent effect and required justification.[41]

---

[32] Para 23 of the Judgment.

[33] See Case 51/83 *Commission v Italy* ECLI:EU:C:1984:261. The Court refused to allow the Commission to expand infringement proceedings, initiated against Italy for unlawfully restricting gelatine use in sweets, so as to challenge a similar restriction on meat products and ice-cream.

[34] At p 1247 of the Opinion.

[35] ibid.

[36] For example, the overriding objective of civil justice in the Civil Procedure Rules of England and Wales was (and is) inter alia, to enable a court to deal with cases expeditiously and fairly, to save expense, and to deal with cases proportionately.

[37] Case 8/74 *Dassonville* ECLI:EU:C:1974:82.

[38] Craig and de Búrca (n 8) 660.

[39] R Schütze, '"Re-Reading" Dassonville: Meaning and Understanding in the History of European Law' (2018) 24 *ELJ* 376, 397–407.

[40] Para 5 of *Dassonville* Judgment.

[41] Para 29 of the Judgment.

C. Rules on Designating Products as 'Beer'

Beer production, fine dining, and legal argumentation seem to share at least one common trait: sometimes, *less is more*. During the pre-litigation stage, Germany argued that its prohibition on using the designation 'bier' was justified on public health grounds. AG Slynn described it as 'plainly right' that Germany subsequently abandoned this argument. He dismissively referred to suggestions that unwashed rice or millet might cause illnesses. Such unsubstantiated allegations could not discharge Germany's burden of proof that this restriction was necessary.[42]

Instead, Germany relied on a consumer protection justification. Consumers in Germany would wrongly conclude that all products sold as 'bier' complied with the Reinheitsgebot's purity rules, even if they contained additives. This was reminiscent of Germany's unsuccessful argument in *Cassis de Dijon*,[43] and AG Slynn rightly rejected this re-hashing of the same argument, based on *Cassis* and other cases.[44] Germany was perhaps not exactly a recidivist, but it certainly 'had form' with such arguments, as criminal law barristers would say. Generic names like 'bier' could not be reserved solely for products complying with domestic standards, if the same generic name was used to describe similar products in other Member States. Compelling importers to think-up alternative names would be ridiculous. 'Fermented barley juice' would be unlikely to generate the same consumer pulling power as 'bier'. AG Slynn's description of beer as an 'aqueous extract of cereal grains with the addition of hops'[45] sounded just as unappealing as contemporary suggestions for renaming vegan foodstuffs.

Germany's argument that 'bier' was a generic term was rejected outright. AG Slynn noted that the Beer Duty Act referred to 'bier' for export, despite it being exempt from the purity restrictions. The Court added that the EU's Common Customs Tariff (CCT) uses 'bier' as a generic term denoting fermented beverage manufactured from malted barley, either alone or with added rice or maize. Both AG Slynn and the Court concluded that German consumers could be protected by adequate labelling, either on beer bottles and cans, or on beer taps where beer was poured directly into an empty glass, such as at a bar. Other German legislation required certain information to be displayed on casks or beer taps, so it was a 'complete exaggeration'[46] to deny its adequacy here.

The Court also cross-referenced its earlier case law on discriminatory taxation,[47] noting that rules such as Article 10 crystallised consumer habits and consolidated advantages held by domestic products, rather than encouraging consumer tastes to evolve. It suggested that, even if Germany replaced the prohibition with a labelling requirement, it must 'not entail negative assessments for beers not complying with the requirements of Article 9'.[48] This was eminently sensible. Imagine the impact of a label on German beer saying 'made in accordance with the Reinheitsgebot', and one on imported beers saying 'contains additives not permitted in German beers'. Perhaps the Court was pre-emptively dealing with a potential future case, to save everyone the time of recycling these arguments in future years.

---

[42] Case 227/82 *Van Bennekom* ECLI:EU:C:1983:354; Case 174/82 *Sandoz* ECLI:EU:C:1983:213, para 22.

[43] Case 120/78 *Cassis de Dijon* ECLI:EU:C:1979:42.

[44] Case 12/74 *Commission v Germany* ECLI:EU:C:1975:23; Case 193/80 *Commission v Italy* ECLI:EU:C:1981:298; Case 27/80 *Fietje* ECLI:EU:C:1980:293; Case 182/84 *Miro* ECLI:EU:C:1985:470.

[45] At p 1250 of the Opinion.

[46] At p 1252 of the Opinion.

[47] Case 170/78 *Commission v UK* ECLI:EU:C:1980:53. See also C Barnard, *The Substantive Law of the EU: The Four Freedoms*, 6th edn (Oxford, OUP, 2019) 61.

[48] Para 35 of the Judgment.

D. Prohibiting the Sale of Beer Containing Additives

AG Slynn acknowledged that Germany's concerns about food safety was, in principle, 'largely legitimate'.[49] Member States were entitled to be concerned about the excessive use of additives, their interaction with other additives, or with alcohol, and the cumulative effects of consuming additives in multiple products. They were entitled to take account of national dietary specificities, such as high beer consumption in Germany,[50] and, in principle, to decide what degree of protection was required until EU harmonising legislation existed. This much was acknowledged in previous cases. In *Sandoz*, the Netherlands were entitled to maintain rules requiring vitamin-enriched foodstuffs to receive authorisation prior to sale. In *Motte*,[51] similar rules were justified regarding food colourants. In *Muller*,[52] France was permitted to retain a system of administrative approvals for foodstuffs containing emulsifiers, stabilizers, thickeners and gelling agents.[53] However, Member States must always ensure that their trade restrictions comply with EU law. Such compliance depends upon three factors: (i) the absence of full harmonisation at an EU level; (ii) the existence of a genuine public health threat;[54] and (iii) the proportionality of the response.

Regarding the first factor, Germany's desire to retain legislative autonomy over foodstuffs regulation was legitimate, in principle, as many foodstuff-related issues were, and still remain, unregulated by EU law.[55] The hitherto 'vertical harmonisation' approach, as exemplified by Directive 74/329 which formed the backdrop to the *Muller* case, meant that EU legislation was slow to approve or prohibit individual additives. Member States should not be deprived of their ability to protect their citizens because of slow legislative progress within the EU. Whilst accepting this in principle, AG Slynn refuted Germany's *in terrorem* suggestion that it would create a Delaware effect on food safety, obliging all Member State to accept the weakest food safety standards. Instead, the Member States must adopt a more refined, concrete analysis of particular additives, rather than introduce an absolute a priori blanket prohibition.

Regarding the second factor, Germany did not argue that beers with additives were, *per se*, harmful to health. Instead, it argued that, as a matter of principle, the Member States have discretion to decide what additives may be used, in what foodstuffs, and in what quantities.[56] AG Slynn portrayed Germany's approach as being 'everything can be banned in beer until it is cleared and shown to be harmless both in itself and in relation to other substances ingested'.[57] With harmonisation proceeding at a snail's pace, given the unanimity requirement in Article 100 EC (now Article 115 TFEU),[58] this approach could have allowed Member States to obstruct the free movement of goods indefinitely.

---

[49] At p 1257 of the Opinion.

[50] At p 1253 of the Opinion. In Germany, beer was a 'staple food', accounting for an average of 26.7% of calorific intake of the male population.

[51] Case 247/84 *Motte* ECLI:EU:C:1985:492.

[52] Case 304/84 *Muller* ECLI:EU:C:1986:194.

[53] Council Directive 74/329/EEC of 18 June 1974 on the approximation of the laws of the Member States relating to emulsifiers, stabilizers, thickeners and gelling agents for use in foodstuffs [1974] OJ L189/1.

[54] AG Slynn referred to this as a 'serious risk' or 'real danger' to public health. In the Report for the Hearing, Judge Joliet asked about the 'objective necessity' of the measures (at p 1235).

[55] This remains true notwithstanding the entry into force, of Regulation (EC) No 178/2002 of the European Parliament and of the Council of 28 January 2002 laying down the general principles and requirements of food law, establishing the European Food Safety Authority and laying down procedures in matters of food safety [2002] OJ L31/1.

[56] At p 1253 of the Opinion.

[57] At p 1259 of the Opinion.

[58] Craig and de Búrca (n 8). Though what is now Art 114 TFEU entailing qualified majority voting was inserted into the EU Treaties at a later stage.

Germany's failure to discuss the health risks associated with particular additives led the Court to ask it to provide concrete evidence of the threat posed by the 27 additives authorised by other Member States for use in beer production. It transpired that the vast majority were permitted for use in German foodstuffs, other than beer. Despite highlighting the need for caution regarding the potential for harm when additives interact with alcohol, six of these additives were authorised for use in German wines, despite some regions consuming the equivalent amount of wine as beer.[59] The Commission accepted that legitimate arguments may exist to restrict one particular additive (glycyrrhizin), but these were based on scientific evidence, combined with the 'precautionary principle' margin of discretion which Member States enjoy in public health issues, and not a blanket ban such as that in German law. Neither the EU nor any international health organisations had identified credible health risks from beer additives,[60] and Germany had produced no credible evidence to establish an objective need for such restrictions. Conversely, additives were extensively used in non-German beers with no noticeable health problems, even in Member States with beer consumption rates similar to those in Germany.[61]

Germany's approach to additives was also inconsistent, rather than forming part of a coherent public health strategy. The restrictions did not apply to beers produced for export, or for consumption on the brewer's own premises. Additives could be used in almost all beverages other than beer. If additives posed genuine health risks, why would such exceptions exist? Germany allowed saccharine to be used in some beers, despite being considered unhealthy by other Member States. The Court noted that, contrary to the requirements established in *Muller*, Germany had no procedure for non-German traders to seek authorisation of particular additives. Germany's approach was, perhaps, not quite as blatant as the United Kingdom's when prohibiting the importation of turkeys before Christmas,[62] but it clearly aimed to protect Germany's domestic beer market. Unsurprisingly perhaps, as exported beer exceeded imports fourfold.[63] So, notwithstanding the merits of its philosophical viewpoint regarding Member States' autonomy over food regulation, the practical application of this philosophy to the facts left much to be desired. By way of analogy from criminal law, Germany eloquently extolled the *in abstracto* virtues of a self-defence principle, whilst trying to argue that they applied, *in concreto*, to an accused who took a baseball bat to the head of a sleeping victim. An unjustifiable concrete application of a justifiable philosophy.

Given the conclusion that Germany had failed to prove the need for its restrictions, it was inevitable that they would be found disproportionate, including in extreme situations involving people who consume 1,000+ litres of beer annually, or alcoholics with liver cirrhosis. AG Slynn's mischievous sense of humour was evident when he remarked that even such cases had more proportionate solutions, 'medical advice as to quantum and self-restraint to name only two'.[64] Germany's solution made as much sense as a drug dealer wishing to avoid his pure heroin being 'cut' with sugar, in case it harms diabetics. Alcoholism and related illnesses are extremely serious, but they cannot have been caused by non-German beers containing

[59] Report for the Hearing (n 28) p 1236.

[60] In para 44 of the Judgment the Court referred to the EU's Scientific Committee for Food, the Codex Alimentarius Committee of the Food and Agriculture Organization of the United Nations (FAO) and the World Health Organization (WHO).

[61] Beer consumption in Belgium, Denmark, and Ireland was almost 80% of that of Germany. See p 1257 of the Opinion.

[62] Case 40/82 *Commission v UK* ECLI:EU:C:1982:285.

[63] Report for the Hearing (n 28) p 1234.

[64] At p 1257 of the Opinion.

additives, given the existence of Germany's import restrictions. Hoisting Germany by its own petard, AG Slynn noted that, if Germany was correct in asserting that its consumers would avoid beers that contain additives, the consumption of foreign beers would remain insignificant and therefore unlikely to cause health risks. Whilst not articulating this *expressis verbis*, as happened in later cases,[65] his analysis indicates that *inappropriate* and *ineffective* national measures are, per se, disproportionate. Instead of adopting a 'finely tuned'[66] and nuanced analysis of individual additives, Germany's blanket prohibition was a sledgehammer used to crack the proverbial nut.

E. Effect on Future Case Law

Almost immediately after *Beer Purity*, a French brewer brought an action against Germany, seeking compensation for financial losses caused by Germany's unlawful restrictions. Together with persistent checks carried out by the German authorities at retailers' premises, these restrictions had led the sole German importer of the French brewer's beers to terminate a lucrative distribution contract. The brewer's claim failed before the lower courts, but the *Bundesgerichtshof* made a preliminary reference to the Court regarding EU law on state liability. This was conjoined with a case from an English court, forming part of the 'the well-known Factortame affair'.[67] The resulting *Brasserie du Pêcheur* judgment was the most significant development in state liability law since *Francovich*.[68] It clarified that Member States were liable for infringing a rule of law intended to confer rights on a claimant, if the breach was sufficiently serious, and directly caused the claimant's harm.[69] By this time, AG Slynn was Lord Slynn, and giving lead judgment in the House of Lords' case which applied the Court's ruling.

The Court contrasted Germany's 'manifest' infringement of EU law in preventing non-German beers being sold as 'bier',[70] with the 'less conclusive' situation of prohibiting additives. The latter was 'an excusable error', which did not give rise to state liability. However, the referring national court denied compensation for both breaches, arguing that no causal link existed between the breach and the French brewer's losses.[71] Nonetheless, the Beer Duty Act was eventually repealed, allowing non-German beers to be sold in Germany, provided that their ingredients were clearly marked.[72] Interestingly, the result of such repeal 'was *not* that production according to traditional German methods was no longer viable, but rather that such production would be – at long last – vulnerable to out-of-State competition'.[73] The fact that the Commission's challenge sought not to challenge the Reinheitsgebot's historical-cultural importance, but merely to uphold the internal market, was clear from the fact that the Reinheitsgebot, *per se*, was never challenged and, indeed, still remains in force. As AG Slynn

---

[65] See eg Case C-265/06 *Commission v Portugal* ECLI:EU:C:2008:210, para 44.

[66] P Craig and G de Búrca, *EU Law: Text, Cases and Materials*, 7th edn (Oxford, OUP, 2020) 761.

[67] Opinion of AG Tesauro in Joined Cases C-46/93 and C-48/93 *Brasserie du Pêcheur* ECLI:EU:C:1995:407, para 6.

[68] Joined Cases C-6/90 and C-9/90 *Francovich* ECLI:EU:C:1991:428.

[69] Para 51 of the *Brasserie du Pêcheur* Judgment.

[70] In para 59 of *Brasserie du Pêcheur* Judgment, the Court referred to *Cassis de Dijon*, and Case 193/80 *Commission v Italy* ECLI:EU:C:1981:298 as having made it clear that such restrictions were unlawful.

[71] See Barnard (n 47) 180–81; J Convery, 'State Liability in the UK after Brasserie Du Pêcheur' (1997) 34 *CMLRev* 603.

[72] See I Murray, 'German Beer Law Repealed' *The Times* (London, 2 June 1990) as referred to in Barnard (n 47) 180.

[73] S Weatherill, 'Pre-Emption, Harmonisation and the Distribution of Competence' in C Barnard and J Scott (eds), *The Law of the Single European Market: Unpacking the Premises* (Oxford, Hart Publishing, 2002) 41, 47.

noted, even in the sixteenth century, it was not intended as a public health measure but, rather, to preserve wheat so that it could be used to make bread.[74]

Beer Purity was an important contribution to the debate about the extent to which EU Member States may use public health justifications to regulate foodstuffs in areas that are not fully harmonised by EU law. Member States' concerns will be treated as legitimate if they are capable of being justified by scientific evidence demonstrating a genuine health risk or if there is a legitimate fear of such a health risk. If the concept of bad faith ran through EU law, as it does through the laws of its Member States,[75] it might be tempting to suggest say that only *mala fides* restrictions are prohibited, especially where the scientific evidence is debatable. *Beer Purity* sought to respect Member States' protective functions, whilst not allowing them to view the absence of harmonising legislation as an invitation to maintain legislation which aims to protect domestic products. The judgment came at a time when the EU was at a critical juncture. Achieving the single market required not only legislative reform, but also judicial support for the mutual recognition principle. If AG Slynn and the Court had accepted Germany's feeble justifications, the future of the internal market may well have been doomed.

The difficulty in achieving such balance was more apparent in later cases, when Member States' motivations seemed to be more *bona fides* than Germany's. Debates about food safety, and the number of related scientific studies, have proliferated. The diet industry has become more lucrative, more polarised and inundated with contradictory food safety studies. By way of example, whereas some studies consider dairy products necessary for healthy bones,[76] others suggest they are a leading cause of osteoporosis.[77] Studies commissioned by national food agencies lack credibility when their members have connections with food industries, or where such studies support measures that aim to protect domestic products. The Commission has even successfully challenged nutritional conclusions approved by the EU's own European Food Safety Authority (EFSA).[78]

Later cases have built on the foundations laid by *Sandoz* and *Beer Purity* by confirming that, where studies result in 'a high degree of scientific and practical uncertainty',[79] or where public health risks '... cannot be proved categorically, given the insufficiency, inconclusiveness or imprecision of the scientific results conducted', a Member State may apply the precautionary principle.[80] Such cases have clarified that, although the onus of justifying the necessity and proportionality of restrictive national laws originally lies with the Member State, the

---

[74] As noted by MacGregor, the Reinheitsgebot was 'an entirely political thing. It had nothing to do with consumer protection or stopping people from getting ill. It was simply to prevent them from brewing with wheat or rye because wheat and rye would be better used for bread. In other words, the Reinheitsgebot was originally connected to another abiding German memory – the fear of famine': MacGregor (n 3) 176.

[75] Of course, bad faith plays an important part in the EU law on trade marks. See N Dawson, 'Bad Faith in European Trade Mark Law' (2011) *Intellectual Property Quarterly* 3. More recently, the Commission accused the UK's of acting in bad faith in relation to the Northern Ireland Protocol forming part of the EU-UK Withdrawal Agreement (Agreement on the withdrawal of the United Kingdom of Great Britain and Northern Ireland from the European Union and the European Atomic Energy Community, [2020] OJ L 29/7). See J Bell, 'The Commission's argument for breach of good faith against the United Kingdom: an in-depth analysis from the standpoint of public international law', available at https://europeanlawblog.eu/2020/10/12/the-commissions-argument-for-breach-of-good-faith-against-the-united-kingdom-an-in-depth-analysis-from-the-standpoint-of-public-international-law/.

[76] R Kouvelioti et al, 'Effects of Dairy Consumption on Body Composition and Bone Properties in Youth: A Systematic Review' (2017) 1 *Current Developments in Nutrition* 1.

[77] RG Cumming and RJ Klineberg, 'Case-Control Study of Risk Factors for Hip Fractures in the Elderly' (1994) 139 *American Journal of Epidemiology* 493.

[78] See Case C-296/16 P *Dextro Energy* ECLI:EU:T:2016:150.

[79] Case C-192/01 *Commission v Denmark* ECLI:EU:C:2003:492, para 51.

[80] Case C-95/01 *Greenham and Abel* ECLI:EU:C:2004:71, para 48.

onus probandi reverts to the Commission if the Member State establishes a 'reasonably convincing case'.[81] They also continue the *Beer Purity* approach of referring to studies published by reputable international organisations.[82]

The foodstuff safety debate is destined to continue and evolve. In 2022, many would regard Germany's beer purity rules themselves as creating a health risk, especially to those with celiac disease or extreme gluten-intolerance. Maize and rice offer gluten-free, safe beer alternatives to the barley and wheat dictated by the Reinheitsgebot. As food-tech grows and innovates further, debates will flourish on laboratory-grown meats and fish, the use of DNA-infused micro-flora, insect-based meats,[83] and 3D-printed vegan 'steaks' being merely the tip of the iceberg (lettuce). Scientific literature will continue to produce contrary conclusions and provoke vociferous disagreements, both within and between Member States. New EU and national laws will be adopted and will, on occasions, inevitably lag behind technological developments or fail to anticipate future scientific creations which Member States fear may threaten human safety. In that sense, not much has changed from when the Reinheitsgebot was adopted, and when Mary Shelley wrote *Frankenstein*. None of this should be feared. It is an inevitable consequence of progression which will, in all likelihood, also lead to developments in EU jurisprudence. However, many of the core principles used to assess the legitimacy of national restrictions fears will remain the same as those discussed by AG Slynn in *Beer Purity*. Future food-tech and jurisprudential developments are as unforeseeable to us now as laboratory-grown meat would have been to Duke William IV in 1516. So, what else is there to do other than grab a beer, pick up a good book, and face the future with curiosity? It is a terrible shame that the Court will not have the assistance of an Advocate General from the United Kingdom as it faces those future challenges.

---

[81] P Oliver and M Martínez Navarro, 'Free Movement of Goods' in C Barnard and S Peers (eds), *European Union Law*, 3rd edn (Oxford, OUP, 2020) 365, 386.

[82] For a list see n 64. See also Case C-421/09 *Commission v France* ECLI:EU:C:2010:760. The Court also referred to Recommendation No R (95) 14 of the Committee of Ministers to the Member States of the Council of Europe.

[83] For a recent case discussing whether insects fall within the scope of Regulation 258/97 (Regulation 258/97 of the European Parliament and of the Council of 27 January 1997 concerning novel foods and novel food ingredients [1997] OJ L 43/1) see Case C-526/19 *Entoma* ECLI:EU:C:2020:769. In his Opinion in that case, AG Bobek expressed regret at feeling obliged to turn down an invitation concerning 'such culinary delights as those addressed by the present case' (Opinion of AG Bobek in Case C-526/19 *Entoma* ECLI:EU:C:2020:552, para 2).

Part IV

David Edward: Judge Acting as
Advocate General in the Court of
First Instance (1992)

23

Powers, Duties, and Responsibilities of the Commission When Dealing with Complaints about Infringements of EU Competition Law: Opinion of Judge Edward Acting as Advocate General in Automec *and* Asia Motor France

RICHARD WHISH

I. INTRODUCTION

ARTICLES 101 and 102 TFEU, formerly Articles 85 and 86 of the EEC Treaty, prohibit, respectively, agreements that have as their object or effect the prevention, restriction, or distortion of competition, and the abuse of a dominant position. The Commission was given wide-ranging powers to enforce Articles 101 and 102 by Regulation 17 of 1962,[1] including to impose significant penalties on recalcitrant undertakings and to issue directions as to their future behaviour. From the beginning, the Commission made frequent use of these powers, for example, condemning secret price-fixing and market-sharing cartels,[2] and applying Article 102 TFEU to exclusivity agreements, loyalty rebates, and predatory pricing practices when deployed by dominant firms.[3] The Commission was of the view that Article 101 TFEU could apply not only to horizontal agreements, that is to say to agreements between competitors, but also to vertical ones, for example, between a supplier and a distributor, and was upheld in the landmark judgment of the Court in *Consten and Grundig v Commission.*[4]

Article 101(2) TFEU provides that agreements that violate Article 101 TFEU 'shall be automatically void'. This clearly envisaged that the competition rules could have application in the 'private' sphere of litigation in addition to the powers of the Commission as a public authority to enforce the law: infringement of Article 101 TFEU could presumably be invoked as a defence in an action claiming breach of contract. In *BRT v SABAM*,[5] the Court held that

---

[1] EEC Council: Regulation No 17: First Regulation implementing Articles 85 and 86 of the Treaty [1962] OJ 13/204.

[2] See eg Case 48/69 *Imperial Chemical Industries* ECLI:EU:C:1972:70; Case 8/72 *Vereeniging van Cementhandelaren* ECLI:EU:C:1972:84.

[3] See eg Joined Cases 40–48, 50, 54–56, 111, 113 and 114–73 *Coöperatieve Vereniging 'Suiker Unie' UA* ECLI:EU:C:1975:174; Case 85/76 *Hoffmann-La Roche* ECLI:EU:C:1979:36; Case 62/86 *Akzo Chemie* ECLI:EU:C:1991:286.

[4] Joined Cases 56 and 58/64 *Consten and Grundig* ECLI:EU:C:1966:41.

[5] Case 127/73 *BRT* ECLI:EU:C:1974:25, para 16.

Articles 101 and 102 TFEU are directly applicable, and that they produce direct effects: they give rise to rights and obligations which national courts have a duty to safeguard and enforce. In due course (after the *Automec* and *Asia Motor France* litigation with which this chapter is concerned), the Court established in *Courage v Crehan*[6] that the victims of anti-competitive behaviour could bring an action for damages for loss caused by a contract, or by conduct liable to restrict or distort competition:

> the existence of such a right strengthens the working of the EU competition rules and discourages agreements or practices, which are frequently covert, which are liable to restrict or distort competition. From that point of view, actions for damages before the national courts can make a significant contribution to the maintenance of effective competition in the EU.[7]

The importance of the national courts in the enforcement of the competition rules led ultimately to the adoption of Directive 2014/14 on damages,[8] which required the Member States to amend their laws in such a way as to facilitate more effective private enforcement of the competition rules.

The fact that the competition rules can be enforced both by the Commission and national competition authorities, and by domestic courts as guardians of the rights derived from the direct effect of Articles 101 and 102 TFEU, provides an interesting factual matrix: specifically, what should a 'victim' of anti-competitive behaviour do? Should it complain to the Commission, in which case what rights does the complainant have in the event of inaction or a rejection of the complaint by the Commission? Or should the complainant raise any relevant competition law issues in domestic litigation, whether as a claimant or as a defendant? And what is the position where a complainant invokes competition law in private litigation while also complaining to the Commission? These were the issues that form the backdrop to the *Automec* and *Asia Motor France* cases.

II. BACKGROUND, CONTEXT, AND FACTS

The Court of First Instance, now the General Court, was created in September 1989.[9] Among its initial tasks was to hear appeals against decisions of the Commission in matters of competition law. Specifically, the General Court has unlimited jurisdiction in relation to penalties (Article 261 TFEU (formerly Article 172 of the EEC Treaty)); it hears actions for annulment of Commission 'acts' (Article 263 TFEU (formerly Article 173 EEC)); and it hears actions for failure to act (Article 265 TFEU (formerly Article 175 EEC)). Under the Rules of Procedure of the General Court (and the Court of First Instance before it), it is possible for the General Court to appoint one of its judges to act as an Advocate General (AG) in a particular case.[10] This may be done where it is considered that the legal difficulty or the factual complexity of the case so requires.[11] The decision to designate an AG is taken by the plenum of the General

---

[6] Case C-453/99 *Courage* ECLI:EU:C:2001:465.

[7] ibid, para 27.

[8] Directive 2014/14/EU of the European Parliament and of the Council on certain rules governing actions for damages under national law for infringements of the competition law provisions of the Member States and of the European Union, [2014] OJ L349/1.

[9] Council Decision 88/591/ECSC, EEC, Euratom of 24 October 1988 establishing a Court of First Instance of the European Communities [1988] OJ L319/1.

[10] Art 3(4)(3) of the Rules of Procedure of the General Court [2015] OJ L105/1.

[11] ibid, Art 30.

Court at the request of the Chamber hearing the case; and the President of the General Court selects the judge who is to act as AG.[12] This power has been used very rarely;[13] however Judge Edward was appointed to act as AG in two cases, *Automec v Commission* and *Asia Motor France v Commission*, in which he delivered a single Opinion.[14]

In *Automec*, Automec had been appointed as a distributor by BMW Italia in 1960 in the city and province of Treviso in Italy. In 1983, BMW Italia notified Automec that it would not be renewing its contract, which was due to expire on 31 December 1984. Automec brought an action in the District Court of Milan in which it unsuccessfully sought an order that BMW should continue the contractual relationship; Automec appealed to the Court of Appeal in Milan. Before the appeal was heard, Automec also made a complaint to the Commission, arguing that BMW Italia and its German parent BMW AG were infringing what is now Article 101 TFEU. Specifically it argued that the Commission had authorised BMW's selective distribution system, which was based on objective, qualitative criteria for the appointment of its distributors, and since Automec satisfied those criteria, the termination of Automec's distributorship was unlawful, and the Commission should order BMW to bring the infringement to an end and to resume the delivery of cars to Automec.

Protracted correspondence followed, culminating in a letter from the Member of the Commission responsible for competition of 28 February 1990, rejecting Automec's complaint. This was the 'act' that the General Court was asked to annul under what is now Article 263 TFEU. Two reasons were given by the Commission for the rejection of the complaint. First, even if it were to be the case that BMW had acted in breach of Article 101 TFEU, the Commission did not have an injunctive power under Regulation 17/62 to order BMW to deliver products to Automec. Secondly, the Italian courts were already seised with jurisdiction over the contractual relationship between BMW and Automec, and there was no reason why any competition law issues could not be considered in the context of that litigation. The Commission concluded by saying that it has a power of discretion when considering how to deal with complaints:

> This power allows it to apply different degrees of priority in dealing with the examination of alleged infringements brought to its notice. [Therefore] the Commission has come to the conclusion that there is no interest of the Community sufficient [to justify] going more deeply into the examination of the facts set forth in the present complaint.

Asia Motor France was an application for a declaration that the Commission had failed to act under what is now Article 265 TFEU. The applicants were engaged in importing, marketing, and distributing Japanese cars in France. These were cars that had already entered the EU and which the applicants usually sourced from Belgium and/or Luxembourg. Their complaint was that the French Government had entered into an agreement with a number of Japanese car manufacturers that led to quotas on the number of Japanese cars that would enter the French market. Specifically, this arrangement was made with Toyota, Nissan, Mazda, Honda, and Mitsubishi, whereas the applicants wished to sell cars produced by Suzuki, Daihatsu, Isuzu, and Subaru. They considered that Article 101 TFEU as well as Article 34 TFEU

---

[12] ibid, Art 31.

[13] It has only ever been used on four occasions: Case T-51/89 *Tetra Pak* ECLI:EU:T:1990:15, Opinion of Mr Kirschner, Judge in the Court of First Instance; Case T-120/89 *Stahlwerke Peine-Salzgitter* ECLI:EU:T:1991:6, Opinion of Judge Biancarelli of the Court of First Instance; Case T-1/89 *Rhône-Poulenc* ECLI:EU:T:1991:38, Opinion of Mr Vesterdorf acting as Advocate General; Case T-24/90 *Automec* and Case T-28/90 *Asia Motor France* ECLI:EU:T:1992:39, Opinion of Judge Edward acting as Advocate General.

[14] See R Greaves, 'Judge Edward Acting as Advocate General' in M Hoskins and W Robinson (eds), *A True European: Essays for Judge David Edward* (Oxford, Hart Publishing, 2003).

(formerly Article 30 EEC) on the free movement of goods were being infringed, and called on the Commission to act. Their first complaint was made in November 1985. There followed protracted correspondence with the Commission, culminating in a letter of 21 November 1989 in which the applicants again asked the Commission to act. *Asia Motor France* asserted that '[t]he Commission cannot continue to cover up the anticompetitive policy of a Member State within the meaning of Article [34 TFEU], effected by means of a cartel between undertakings contrary to the provisions of Article [101 TFEU], the consequence of which is to delay reparation of the loss suffered by the victim undertakings, which continues to get worse'.

Having received no reply to this letter the applicants brought an action for failure to act against the Commission on 20 March 1990 to the then Court of First Instance. They also asked for damages to be awarded against the Commission for the pecuniary loss that they had suffered.

III. THE OPINION OF JUDGE EDWARD ACTING AS ADVOCATE GENERAL

The *Automec* and *Asia Motor France* cases were not formally joined. However Judge Edward, appointed to act as AG in both of them, considered that the issues raised were sufficiently similar that they could be dealt with in a single Opinion. The cases had been heard in plenary session on successive days, and raised the same issue of principle: what was the nature and extent of the Commission's obligation to act on a complaint by someone under Article 3 of Regulation 17/62? Judge (AG) Edward set out the questions to be answered:

> Must the Commission investigate? If so, in what depth? Does it have a discretion not to proceed on the ground that it is not opportune to do so? Must it take a decision which the complainer can challenge before the Court under Article [263 TFEU]? Can the complainer use [Article 265 TFEU] to prod the Commission into action? Can the Commission justify inaction on the ground that relief is available in the national courts, that there is insufficient Community interest in pursuing the case, or that the Commission does not have the staff to deal with minor complaints?

The Opinion began by looking into the issues to be considered by reference to the Treaties, Regulation 17/62, comparable regulations, and the case-law of the Court. There had been a series of cases, *GEMA*,[15] *Metro 1*,[16] *Demo-Studio Schmidt*,[17] and *CICCE*,[18] in which aspects of the duties of the Commission in relation to complaints had been considered. The *Automec* litigation provided an opportunity to take a holistic view of the Commission's responsibilities. Presumably this is why the Chambers in *Automec* and *Asia Motor France* had asked for the appointment of an AG in the first place. Having reviewed the relevant legislation and case-law, Judge (AG) Edward then outlined the facts of each case, before considering the admissibility of the two appeals. In the case of *Asia Motor France*, he considered that there was no longer any purpose to the appeal, since the Commission had by then defined its position in relation to Asia Motor France's complaint. For Judge (AG) Edward, it had therefore not 'failed to act'; and therefore gave no opinion on the substance of this appeal. However, having decided that Automec's appeal was admissible, he proceeded to consider the substance of its application, which he proposed should be rejected for the reasons explained below.

[15] Case 125/78 *GEMA* ECLI:EU:C:1979:237.
[16] Case 26/76 *GEMA* ECLI:EU:C:1977:167.
[17] Case 210/81 *Demo-Studio Schmidt* ECLI:EU:C:1983:277.
[18] Case 298/83 *CICCE* ECLI:EU:C:1985:150.

As to the Treaty, Judge (AG) Edward noted that there was no specific provision requiring the Commission to act on individual complaints; however, the Commission did have a power under what is now Article 103 TFEU to adopt regulations and directives to give effect to the principles in Articles 101 and 102 TFEU, and Article 103(2)(a) TFEU (formerly Article 87 EEC), providing that such regulations should be designed to ensure compliance with the prohibitions that they contain. Article 105 TFEU (formerly Article 89 EEC) also refers to the Commission's duty to ensure compliance with Articles 101 and 102 TFEU, and that it should investigate suspected infringements and propose measures to bring them to an end. The Opinion then examined Regulation 17/62 as well as Regulation 1017/68,[19] which dealt with the application of Articles 101 and 102 TFEU to transport by rail, road and inland waterway, and Regulation 2423/88,[20] the anti-dumping regulation. Judge (AG) Edward noted that it could be deduced from these instruments that it was possible to make a distinction, in the event of a complaint that an undertaking had infringed the competition rules, between the existence of a *duty* to act on a complaint and a *discretion* as to whether to proceed with the matter to a final decision on substance.

Fast-forwarding to the outcome of *Automec*, as eventually decided by the then Court of First Instance, this is the critical issue of principle that the case established: that the Commission did have a 'duty of diligence' which required it to decide whether to reject a complaint or whether to proceed to a full investigation and to a final decision. However, it did not have a duty to make a decision on the substance of the case. The Commission's duty of diligence – its decision whether to investigate – was amenable to judicial review and must be exercised and reasoned properly. The Opinion noted that the case-law of the Court had already determined that 'the Commission must take complaints seriously: its discretion as to the action it will take in response to a complaint is not unfettered'. Furthermore, the Commission had conceded during the hearings in these two cases that a complainant was entitled to a decision capable of being challenged before the General Court: that is to say the decision whether to reject the complaint rather than a decision on its substance. What is now Article 265 TFEU was an important part of the reasoning in the Opinion, because it meant that the Commission could be 'prodded into activity': if it were to ignore a complaint or to reject it without defining its position it could be taken to the Court because of its failure to act.

The remainder of the Opinion of Judge (AG) Edward was concerned with the substance of Automec's application. The Commission's letter of 28 February 1990 rejecting Automec's complaint had given two reasons: first that it lacked the injunctive power to order BMW to resume delivery of cars to Automec, and secondly, that the Italian courts were seised of the dispute and the competition law issue could be dealt with in those proceedings. Before dealing with these specific points, Judge (AG) Edward addressed a general point that the Commission had made: that it lacked sufficient resources to follow up every complaint that it received. Having said that this could not, in itself, justify a refusal to consider how to proceed, he said that the scarcity of resources does justify defining priorities, since some cases may be more urgent than others. The Opinion then proceeded to address the two specific reasons given by the Commission for rejecting the complaint. In his Opinion, Judge (AG) Edward was dismissive of the first point: even if the Commission lacks the power to make a positive order to deliver

---

[19] Regulation (EEC) No 1017/68 of the Council of 19 July 1968 applying rules of competition to transport by rail, road and inland waterway [1968] OJ L175/1.

[20] Council Regulation (EEC) No 2423/88 of 11 July 1988 on protection against dumped or subsidized imports from countries not members of the European Economic Community [1988] OJ L209/1.

cars, it could adopt a decision that the BMW distribution system infringed Article 101 TFEU, and that the infringement must be terminated. In effect, this might have the same practical effect as a positive injunction.

As to the proceedings before the Italian courts, it would not be sufficient for the Commission simply to say that, because there is litigation in a national court, it declines to investigate a case. In Judge (AG) Edward's Opinion, the Commission must apply its mind properly to the question of whether adequate relief would be available to the complainant. Among the considerations would be whether a court competent and willing to assert jurisdiction is available; whether that court would be able to award interim measures pending the final outcome of the case; whether it would be able to obtain the necessary evidence, some of which might be in another jurisdiction; and whether any final judgment could be enforced. On the facts of the *Automec* case, Judge (AG) Edward was satisfied that the Commission had adequately addressed its mind to the availability of relief, and that therefore its decision not to proceed with the complaint was one that it was entitled to make.

IV. ANALYSIS

The application in the *Asia Motor France* case was dismissed. The Court agreed with Judge (AG) Edward that the Commission had defined its legal position, and therefore had not failed to act in the sense of Article 265 TFEU. The application in *Automec* was also dismissed, but the judgment shed important light on the role of the Commission under Regulation 17/62 when it was in receipt of a complaint.

A. The Commission's Powers under Article 3 of Regulation 17/62

The Commission had given, as one of its reasons for dismissing the complaint, that it lacked the power to make a positive order requiring BMW to supply Automec. Judge (AG) Edward had been unsympathetic to the Commission on this point, as an order to terminate any infringement of Article 101 TFEU might have the same effect as a positive injunction. The Court did not follow him here, deciding instead that the Commission had been correct. The Court's view was that freedom of contract is the general rule, and the Commission cannot be considered to have a power to order a party to enter into contractual relations.

The Court was of the view that there were other powers available to it to bring an infringement of Article 101 TFEU to an end. In so far as the Commission refused to act because it lacked the power to make a positive order, it had not committed an error of law. The judgment was perfunctory on this point, limited to three short paragraphs.[21] The Court said nothing about the power to make a positive order under Article 102 TFEU, because no complaint of infringement of that Article had been made. However, it had been established much earlier in *Commercial Solvents v Commission* in 1974 that a positive order can be made to bring an end to abusive behaviour such as a refusal to supply.[22]

---

[21] Case T-24/90 *Automec* ECLI:EU:C:1992:97, paras 51–53.
[22] Joined Cases 6/73 and 7/73 *Istituto Chemioterapico Italiano and Commercial Solvents* ECLI:EU:C:1974:18.

B. The Italian Litigation

The Court agreed with the Commission, and Judge (AG) Edward, that the Commission was entitled to reject Automec's complaint on the basis that the Italian courts were seised with jurisdiction and that the competition law issues could be dealt with in that litigation.[23] The Court noted that Articles 103 and 105 TFEU gave the Commission wide powers to enforce the competition rules, and that a supervisory role had been given to it in the field of competition law.[24]

However this did not mean that complainants have a right to a decision on whether there has been an infringement of the competition rules.[25] The Court noted that, as an authority with a public services task, the Commission was entitled to set priorities.[26] When it received a complaint, the Commission was obliged to examine the factual and legal particulars brought to its attention, and if it then decided to close the file, it had to give a statement of its reasons, and this was a decision which the Court could review. The Court said that the Commission had carried out a careful examination of the complaint and could not be accused of a lack of diligence.[27] It then specifically stated that the Commission was entitled to apply different degrees of priority in dealing with complaints submitted to it.[28]

The Court then considered whether, on the facts of *Automec*, the Commission had infringed EU law by rejecting the complaint. The Court stated that it was necessary to consider whether the Commission could refer to 'the Community interest' as a priority criterion (today we would say an 'EU interest').[29] It then stated, specifically, that the Commission, as an administrative authority, must act in the public interest in order to determine the degree of priority to be applied to the cases brought to its notice.[30] For the Court, it could not simply refer to the public interest in the abstract, but must set out the legal and factual considerations which led it to conclude that there was insufficient interest to justify an investigation of the case. As the Court put it:

> The Commission should in particular balance the significance of the alleged infringement as regards the functioning of the common market, the probability of establishing the existence of the infringement and the scope of the investigation required in order to fulfil, under the best possible conditions, its task of ensuring that Article[] [101 TFEU] and [102 TFEU] are complied with.[31]

The Court was satisfied that the Commission was entitled to take into account the fact that the Italian courts were considering the lawfulness of BMW Italia's behaviour. However it would not be sufficient for the Commission simply to refuse to investigate a case on the ground that a national court had jurisdiction, but on the facts of this case the Commission had not erred in law.[32]

---

[23] Case T-24/90 *Automec*, paras 71–98.
[24] ibid, paras 73–74.
[25] ibid, para 75.
[26] ibid, para 77.
[27] ibid, para 82.
[28] ibid, para 83.
[29] ibid, para 84.
[30] ibid, para 85.
[31] ibid, para 86.
[32] ibid, para 88.

C. The *Automec* Doctrine

The Court upheld the Commission's decision not to investigate the complaint because it agreed that the Commission could not make a positive order to supply Automec, and because the Commission had been correct to decide that the dispute could be adequately dealt with in the Italian courts. On the first point there was divergence between the position of Judge (AG) Edward and the Court's judgment; they were agreed on the second one.

However, the importance of the *Automec* judgment is what the Court said on prioritisation. As noted above, earlier cases had explored the duties of the Commission when in receipt of a complaint, but the *Automec* litigation entailed a holistic view of the position, and Judge (AG) Edward performed an important function in setting out the issues to be considered, beginning with an analysis of the provisions of the Treaties, and then examining a series of important considerations. It was not long before the competition law community started to refer to the '*Automec* doctrine', meaning that the Commission could reject a complaint where it was not a priority: a reasoned decision to this effect was required, and could be reviewed. However, the Commission could not be forced to investigate every case.

D. The Effect of the *Automec* Litigation

After *Automec*, it became possible for the Commission to systematise its approach to complaints. Today, various provisions in Regulation 1/2003,[33] the successor to Regulation 17/62, acknowledge that third parties with a sufficient interest have a right to participate in proceedings, although these rights are less than those of the undertakings accused of an infringement. Chapter IV of the Implementing Regulation, Regulation 773/2004,[34] also deals with the handling of complaints, and the Commission has published a Notice on the handling of complaints by the Commission under Articles [101 and 102 TFEU].[35] Part II of the Notice on Complaints discusses the complementary roles of public and private enforcement of the competition rules, pointing out the benefits for complainants, in some circumstances, of going to a court rather than a competition authority. For example, only a court can award damages or determine the effect on a contract of the voidness provided for by Article 101(2) TFEU.[36] It also explains the provisions on case allocation within the ECN, which should assist a complainant in deciding which public authority it would be sensible to approach if that is preferred to private litigation.[37] Part III of the Notice on Complaints explains, in detail, how the Commission goes about handling complaints, and specifies the information that must be supplied on Form C, the form that must be used when making a complaint.[38]

---

[33] Council Regulation (EC) No 1/2003 of 16 December 2002 on the implementation of the rules on competition laid down in Articles 81 and 82 of the Treaty [2003] L1/1.

[34] Commission Regulation (EC) No 773/2004 of 7 April 2004 relating to the conduct of proceedings by the Commission pursuant to Articles 81 and 82 of the EC Treaty [2004] OJ L123/18.

[35] Commission Notice on the handling of complaints by the Commission under Articles 81 and 82 of the EC Treaty [2004] OJ C101/65. See also European Commission, 'Manual of Procedures. Internal DG Competition working documents on procedures for the application' (2019) ch 21.

[36] Commission Notice, ibid, para 16.

[37] ibid, paras 19–25.

[38] ibid, paras 29–32.

The Notice discusses the well-established case law recognising the Commission's right to prioritise its enforcement efforts and to concentrate on cases that have an 'EU interest'.[39] As a result of *Automec*, it is well settled that complainants do not have a right to a final decision as to the existence or non-existence of an infringement of Articles 101 and/or 102 TFEU.[40] The final part of the Notice explains the Commission's procedure when dealing with complaints, including the procedural rights of complainants.[41] The judgments of the General Court in two third party appeals concerning De Beers' arrangements for the supply of diamonds provide a useful summary of the obligations owed by the Commission when deciding whether to reject a complaint.[42] Appeals against the rejection of complaints are not infrequent, but are usually unsuccessful, as the Commission is aware of its duty of diligence and the necessity to explain its motivation in accordance with the learning derived from *Automec*.[43]

The influence of *Automec* can also be detected in the Commission's Guidance on the Commission's Enforcement Priorities in applying Article [102 TFEU] to abusive exclusionary conduct by dominant undertakings of 2009.[44] The Commission was aware that there was widespread dissatisfaction with the law and practice of Article 102 TFEU. The Commission was not in a position to 'change' the law, which is contained in the jurisprudence of the Court. However, it was in a position to change its own practice, for example, as to the cases it chose to investigate. The result was that, instead of adopting 'Guidelines', which would have set out what the law says, it explained its 'Enforcement priorities', setting out the criteria that it would apply when deciding to investigate an alleged abuse of dominance. *Automec* can be seen to have prepared the way for this deft piece of work by the Commission.

The effect of *Automec* can also be seen in the UK, where the Competition and Markets Authority has adopted *Prioritisation Principles*,[45] in which it explains how it will make use of the resources at its disposal; its predecessor, the Office of Fair Trading, had first adopted this approach in 2008.[46] The *Automec* litigation provided an invaluable opportunity to define the responsibilities of the Commission in relation to competition complaints which the General Court seised, ably assisted by Judge Edward acting as AG. Its effects are clearly discernible today.

---

[39] ibid, paras 41–45.

[40] See also Case C-119/97 P *Ufex and Others* ECLI:EU:C:1999:116, para 87 and Case T-201/11 *Si.mobil* ECLI:EU:T:2014:1096, paras 79–108.

[41] Commission Notice (n 35), paras 53–81.

[42] Joined Cases T-104/07 and T-339/08 *BVGD* ECLI:EU:T:2013:366 and Joined Cases T-108/07 and T-354/08 *Spira* ECLI:EU:T:2013:367.

[43] Recent unsuccessful cases against the rejection of complaints include Case C-373/17 P *Agria Polska* ECLI:EU:C:2018:756; Case T-574/14 *EAEPC* ECLI:EU:T:2018:605; Case T-531/18 *LL-Carpenter* ECLI:EU:T:2020:91; and Case T-515/18 *Fakro* ECLI:EU:T:2020:620.

[44] Communication from the Commission – Guidance on the Commission's enforcement priorities in applying Article 82 of the EC Treaty to abusive exclusionary conduct by dominant undertakings [2009] OJ C45/7, para 5.

[45] Competition & Markets Authority, *Prioritisation principles for the CMA* (CMA16, 2014).

[46] Office of Fair Trading, *OFT Prioritisation Principles* (OFT 953, 2008).

Part V

Francis Jacobs: From European Communities to European Union (1988–2006)

24

The Rehabilitation of Trade Marks, the Demise of the Doctrine of Common Origin, and the Overruling of Prior Case Law: Opinion of Advocate General Jacobs in HAG II

DAVID T KEELING

I. INTRODUCTION

OVER THE LAST quarter of a century the Court has acquired a great deal of experience (and perhaps even expertise) in the field of trade mark law. The Court has delivered over 150 preliminary rulings interpreting the EU's trade mark legislation. It has also dealt with dozens of appeals against judgments of the General Court concerning decisions of the Boards of Appeal of the EU Intellectual Property Office (EUIPO). That workload has given the Court an opportunity to explore every aspect of the subject. The most arcane and intricate theories of trade mark law have been scrutinised by the great forensic minds of Europe's most senior judges. These men and women have had to familiarise themselves with the technical features of an IP registration system. In the course of those 25 years they have learnt one thing, if nothing else: trade mark law is not as simple and straightforward as it may appear to the uninitiated.

Before the 1990s, the Court had very little exposure to the legal aspects of trade mark protection. There was no trade mark directive for it to interpret. There was no Community trade mark and no Office in Alicante, with a strange name, churning out thousands of decisions appealable to the *juge communautaire*. From time to time, a trade mark would come to the Court's attention because it was exercised in a manner that allegedly collided with the principle of the free movement of goods, or with the competition rules of the EEC Treaty. As a result, the Court developed a slightly negative attitude towards trade marks; they were seen as troublesome things that threatened the integrity of the common market (because of their territoriality), or facilitated anti-competitive practices (because of their exclusivity).

II. BACKGROUND, CONTEXT, AND FACTS

The HAG story began in Bremen in the early years of the twentieth century when Ludwig Roselius set up a coffee-trading company called 'Kaffee-Handels-Aktien-Gesellschaft' or

'Kaffee HAG' for short.[1] For many decades, HAG was virtually the only brand of decaffeinated coffee on the market in Germany; it was a household name. HAG was registered as a trade mark in Germany and in many other countries. The registrations for Belgium and Luxembourg were transferred to a subsidiary of the Bremen company in 1935. After World War II, all the assets of that subsidiary, including the trade marks for Belgium and Luxembourg, were sequestrated as enemy property and sold to the highest bidder. The result was that, as from 1946, the Bremen company (HAG Bremen) retained the German trade mark, while in Belgium and Luxembourg the mark belonged to a different company (initially Van Oevelen, later Van Zuylen Frères).

In 1972, HAG Bremen started exporting HAG-branded coffee from Germany to Luxembourg. Van Zuylen Frères sued HAG Bremen for trade mark infringement in the Luxembourg Tribunal d'Arrondissement, which requested a preliminary ruling from the Court concerning the compatibility of the infringement suit with the competition rules of the EEC Treaty and with the rules on the free movement of goods. The Court, in what has come to be known as *HAG I*, gave the following ruling:

> To prohibit the marketing in one Member State of a product legally bearing a trade mark in another Member State for the sole reason that an identical trade mark, having the same origin, exists in the first State, is incompatible with the provisions for the free movement of goods within the Common Market.[2]

Superficially, that ruling gave victory to HAG Bremen; they could go on selling HAG coffee in Luxembourg. However, the ruling was drafted so widely that it seemed to entitle Van Zuylen Frères to sell their version of HAG coffee in Germany. HAG Bremen had gained access to the tiny Luxembourg market, but now risked losing their exclusivity in the much larger German market. It was, potentially, the most pyrrhic of victories.

A few years later, Van Zuylen Frères were taken over by Jacobs Suchard AG, a Swiss company that happened to be the market leader in coffee products (except for decaffeinated coffee) in Germany. The HAG trade mark registrations for Belgium and Luxembourg were transferred to SA CNL-Sucal NV, the wholly owned Belgian subsidiary of Jacobs Suchard. SA CNL-Sucal NV started to market HAG coffee in Germany, and was promptly sued for trade mark infringement by HAG Bremen. The litigation reached the German Supreme Court, which sought guidance from the Court, in a case that was to be known as *HAG II*.[3] Essentially, the German judges wanted to know whether HAG Bremen's infringement action was compatible with the free movement of goods.

III. THE OPINION OF AG JACOBS

AG Jacobs recognised from the outset that the Court was obliged to reconsider the so-called 'doctrine of common origin' laid down 15 years earlier in *HAG I*; the outcome of *HAG II* would depend on whether that doctrine was 'to be recognized as a legitimate child of Community law'.[4] He carried out an extensive review of the Court's case law, and discussed the nature and function of trade marks in a market economy. He analysed the reasoning of the judgment in *HAG I*, and criticised the Court's failure to justify the doctrine of common origin.

---

[1] I Berkemayer, *Die Entwicklung der Marke 'Kaffee HAG'* (Munich, GRIN Verlag, 2006) 4–6.
[2] Case 192/73 *Van Zuylen v Hag AG* ECLI:EU:C:1974:72 (*HAG I*).
[3] Case C-10/89 *CNL Sucal v HAG* ECLI:EU:C:1990:359 (*HAG II*).
[4] Opinion of AG Jacobs in Case C-10/89 *CNL Sucal v HAG* ECLI:EU:C:1990:112 (*HAG II*), para 13.

He concluded that the doctrine must be abandoned altogether, and advised the Court to recognise explicitly that *HAG I* had been wrongly decided; HAG Bremen should have the exclusive right to use the HAG trade mark in Germany, while CNL-Sucal should have a corresponding right in Belgium and Luxembourg.

The Court followed the AG's advice in its entirety. It accepted that the interpretation given in *HAG I* must be reconsidered, in the light of the subsequent case-law.[5] It recalled that in the intervening years it had held that the essential function of a trade mark was to enable consumers to distinguish products bearing the trade mark from products that had a different origin.[6] Trade marks enabled businesses to build up goodwill through the quality of their products and services. A trade mark could only fulfil that role if it offered a guarantee that all goods bearing it had been produced under the control of a single undertaking which was accountable for their quality.[7]

The Court concluded therefore that, where the mark originally had one proprietor and that single ownership was broken as a result of expropriation, each of the trade mark proprietors must be able to oppose the importation and marketing, in the Member State in which the trade mark belonged to it, of goods originating from the other proprietor, in so far as they were similar products bearing an identical mark or one which was liable to lead to confusion.[8]

IV. ANALYSIS

If the Opinion of AG Jacobs in *HAG II* had done nothing more significant than persuade the Court to abandon an irrational doctrine, and take the hitherto unprecedented step of reversing one of its earlier rulings, that alone would make it a milestone in the history of the Court's jurisprudence. However, a careful reading of the Opinion, some 30 years after it was delivered, suggests that the AG was attempting to achieve much more than that.

The Opinion was wide-ranging and did not confine itself to the specific problems that arise when ownership of a trade mark is fractured by an act of expropriation. The AG examined the relationship between intellectual property rights and the Treaty rules on the free movement of goods and competition in a market economy. He argued in favour of a holistic approach that took account of the nature and purpose of the different intellectual property rights. Above all, he sought to rehabilitate trade marks in the eyes of the Court. This involved undoing the negative image of trade marks that had been evident in *HAG I*, both in the judgment and in the Opinion of AG Mayras.

A. The Role of Trade Marks in a Market Economy

The disparaging attitude towards trade marks dated back to *Sirena v Eda*, where AG Dutheillet de Lamothe had stated:

> Both from the economic and from the human point of view the interests protected by patent legislation merit greater respect than those protected by trade marks.[9]

---

[5] Para 10 of the Judgment. R Joliet and DT Keeling, 'Trade Mark Law and the Free Movement of Goods: The Overruling of the Judgement in Hag I' (1991) 22 *International Review of Industrial Property and Copyright* 303.

[6] Para 16 of the Judgment.

[7] ibid, para 13.

[8] ibid, para 19.

[9] Opinion of AG Dutheillet de Lamothe in Case 40/70 *Sirena* ECLI:EU:C:1971:3, at p 87.

That case was about a trade mark for shaving cream which belonged to different entities in Germany and Italy, not as a result of an expropriation, but because the original proprietor had assigned one of the registrations to another undertaking in the 1930s. AG Dutheillet de Lamothe observed that society owed a much greater debt to the inventor of penicillin than to the creator of a trade mark for shaving cream. The Court adopted that negative view of trade marks, stating that the interests protected by patents 'are usually more important, and merit a higher degree of protection, than the interests protected by an ordinary trade-mark'.[10] That failure to understand the importance of trade marks in a market economy was still apparent three years later in *HAG I*, where the Court opined that an indication of the trade origin of goods might be 'useful', but that consumers could be given the necessary information by means that would not disrupt the free movement of goods.

In *HAG II*, AG Jacobs propounded a more positive view of trade marks. He stated:

> Like patents, trade marks find their justification in a harmonious dovetailing between public and private interests. Whereas patents reward the creativity of the inventor and thus stimulate scientific progress, trade marks reward the manufacturer who consistently produces high-quality goods and they thus stimulate economic progress. Without trade mark protection there would be little incentive for manufacturers to develop new products or to maintain the quality of existing ones.[11]

The Court endorsed this approach, stating:

> Trade mark rights are ... an essential element in the system of undistorted competition which the Treaty seeks to establish and maintain. Under such a system, an undertaking must be in a position to keep its customers by virtue of the quality of its products and services, something which is possible only if there are distinctive marks which enable customers to identify those products and services. For the trade mark to be able to fulfil this role, it must offer a guarantee that all goods bearing it have been produced under the control of a single undertaking which is accountable for their quality.[12]

In fact, the rehabilitation of trade marks, in the eyes of the Court, had started a mere three months after *HAG I*. The occasion for this was presented by *Centrafarm v Winthrop*, in which a trade mark owner attempted to rely on trade mark rights to block parallel imports into the Netherlands of products that it had marketed in the UK.[13] That was the first case in which the Court defined the *objet spécifique* of a trade mark, namely to protect the proprietor of the trade mark against competitors wishing to take advantage of the status and reputation of the trade mark by selling counterfeit products.[14] Two years later, in *Terrapin v Terranova*, the Court made its first reference to the 'essential function' of trade marks, namely 'to guarantee to consumers that the product has the same origin'.[15] The Court had finally discovered the origin function of trade marks – about 100 years after everybody else.

Terrapin v Terranova was a step forward inasmuch as the Court showed a basic understanding of trade marks, and refused to extend the *HAG I* 'free movement at all costs' philosophy to a situation in which the conflicting trade marks had been created independently. Regrettably though, the Court stubbornly insisted, in *Terrapin v Terranova*, that *HAG I* had been correctly decided. It even attempted to provide a rationale for the doctrine of common origin, stating

---

[10] Case 40/70 *Sirena* ECLI:EU:C:1971:18, para 7.

[11] Para 19.

[12] Para 13.

[13] Case 16/74 *de Peijper* ECLI:EU:C:1974:115.

[14] ibid, para 8.

[15] Case 119/75 *Terrapin* ECLI:EU:C:1976:94, para 6. The French version says *fonction essentielle*, which was incorrectly translated as 'basic function'.

that where the right relied on resulted from the subdivision, either by voluntary act or as a result of public constraint, of a trade-mark right which originally belonged to one and the same proprietor, the essential function of the trade mark to guarantee to consumers that products have the same origin was already undermined by the subdivision of the original right.

In *HAG II*, AG Jacobs described that as 'a valiant attempt to legitimize the doctrine of common origin', but pointed out that it was based on flawed logic. The essential function of a trade mark was to guarantee to consumers that products bearing it had the same origin. But the word 'origin' in this context referred, not to the historical origin of the trade mark, but to the commercial origin of the goods. He pithily observed:

> The consumer is not, I think, interested in the genealogy of trade marks; he is interested in knowing who made the goods that he purchases.[16]

The Court agreed. It recognised that the essential function of the trade mark would be jeopardised if its proprietor could not rely on it to oppose the importation from another Member State of similar goods bearing an identical or confusingly similar trade mark, because in such a situation consumers would no longer be able to identify for certain the origin of the marked goods and the proprietor of the trade mark could be held responsible for the poor quality of goods for which he was in no way accountable.[17] That analysis could not be altered by the fact that the marks in question originally belonged to the same proprietor, who was divested of one of them following expropriation prior to the establishment of the Community. From the date of expropriation and notwithstanding their common origin, each of the marks independently fulfilled its function, within its own territorial field of application, of guaranteeing that the marked products originated from one single source.[18]

HAG II was thus the case in which the Court finally showed a mature understanding of the role of trade marks in a market economy. The hesitations and prejudices of the past disappeared without trace. Trade marks were no longer viewed as second-class IP rights. They were now seen, not as a threat to the integrity of the common market, but as a vital element in the system of undistorted competition without which no market – common or otherwise – could function properly. *HAG II* came at just the right time. The Trade Mark Directive was being implemented, and a Community trade mark was about to become a reality.[19] The Court would soon see an avalanche of trade mark cases. Building on the insights acquired in *HAG II*, the Court was able to deepen its understanding of trade marks. In *HAG II*, the Court belatedly discovered the origin function of trade marks, as well as the quality-guarantee and goodwill functions. In its subsequent case law, it would have to grapple with further sophistications, such as the advertising and investment functions. *HAG II* was the beginning of a steep learning curve.

B. Trade Mark Conflicts in the Single Market

AG Jacobs rightly saw that *HAG II* raised issues going beyond the fate of a brand name whose unitary ownership was fractured by government decree. The *Terrapin v Terranova* case

---

[16] Para 24 of the Opinion.
[17] Para 16 of the Judgment.
[18] Paras 17–18 of the Judgment.
[19] First Council Directive 89/104/EEC of 21 December 1988 to approximate the laws of the Member States relating to trade marks [1989] OJ L40/1.

demonstrated that trade marks had huge potential to impede inter-state trade. It might not be a disaster if goods had to be rebranded before being exported, but it would be a major inconvenience – acceptable only where necessary to protect a trader's goodwill and save consumers from confusion about the origin of goods. Sections X to XII of the AG's Opinion examined the general problem of inter-state trade mark conflicts: that is to say, situations in which entirely separate undertakings in different Member States own identical trade marks registered in respect of identical goods, or trade marks that entail a likelihood of confusion on the part of the public due to the similarity/identity of the marks and the similarity/identity of the goods.

That part of the Opinion now reads a little dated. Some will say that it is largely of historical interest, in view of the developments that have taken place since (namely, the harmonisation of the national trade mark laws and the creation of the EU trade mark). That is true to some extent. The gradual replacement of national trade marks with EU trade marks means that more and more branded goods can be freely traded throughout the EU. Impediments to free movement caused by the territoriality of national trade marks will eventually become a thing of the past. Harmonisation means that the national courts are, at least in theory, all applying the same criteria when they try an infringement action. The fears of discrimination or asymmetrical trade barriers that caused AG Jacobs such concern seem not to have been realised.

That is not to say that everything is now fine and dandy as a result of harmonisation and the creation of the EU trade mark. In *HAG II*, the AG alluded to the distortions and barriers caused by an over-broad interpretation of the notion of confusingly similar trade marks. He cited a notorious judgment in which the German Federal Patent Court had held that LUCKY WHIP was likely to be confused with Schöller-Nucki, a decision that 'seems to postulate a body of consumers afflicted with an acute form of dyslexia'.[20] He suggested that an unduly broad interpretation of the likelihood of confusion might lead to unjustifiable barriers to trade between Member States but was optimistic that the Court would, 'by ensuring a uniform – and perhaps restrictive – interpretation of the concept of confusingly similar trade marks, be able to eliminate the abuses and discrepancies … alluded to …'.[21] Sadly, the EU Courts have not opted for a narrow view of the likelihood of confusion. Time and again, the General Court has given excessively broad protection to the earlier mark in opposition cases. It has repeatedly upheld oppositions where there was no real danger that reasonably attentive consumers would be confused. The Court has done nothing to correct this lamentable tendency. For a typical example we need only look at the case in which Yorma's AG, the owner of a chain of snack bars in Germany, attempted to protect its business name as an EU trade mark. To that end, it filed an application to register a figurative sign consisting of the word YORMA'S, in bright yellow letters inside a blue frame, together with three parallel blue lines and – in the background – a stylised letter 'y' in blue with a yellow frame. The application was opposed by a German supermarket owner on the basis of an earlier EU registration of the word mark NORMA. The OHIM Opposition Division sensibly decided that the marks were sufficiently different to preclude a likelihood of confusion. It rejected the opposition. That decision was annulled by the OHIM (now EUIPO) Board of Appeal, which produced a typically long, rambling decision full of the usual formalistic, pseudo-scientific gibberish about phonetic, visual and conceptual similarities, resulting in the conclusion that 'a likelihood of confusion cannot be excluded'.[22]

---

[20] Para 36 of the Opinion.
[21] Para 49 of the Opinion.
[22] R 1879/2007-1, 20 February 2009, para 53.

The Board of Appeal's decision was upheld by the General Court in a judgment full of the same formalistic reasoning.[23] A further appeal to the Court of Justice failed; the Court could see nothing wrong in that approach.[24] The fact that the two marks have co-existed in Germany for decades was considered irrelevant. The Board of Appeal stated that peaceful coexistence could not be taken into account in the absence of proof that the marks had been used alongside one another without any confusion arising. In fact, anyone who has set foot in Germany in the last 20 years will confirm that these two Bavarian companies and their respective trade marks have co-existed peacefully, with branches all over the country, and consumers do not walk into a YORMA'S snack bar thinking that it has anything to do with the NORMA supermarket two blocks away, where they did their shopping the day before. The proverbial 'moron in a hurry' would not confuse YORMA'S and NORMA.[25] No amount of trade mark pseudo-science will prove the contrary.

The fundamental problem in EU trade mark law is that oppositions are decided in a vacuum – in a hypothetical world divorced from reality and shorn of context. It is an artificial universe that bears little resemblance to the actual world in which real people walk into shops, or visit websites, and buy the stuff they need. It is a phony world into which common sense is not allowed to intrude and all awareness of life experience is discarded. That is a pity, because Wendell Holmes' aphorism ('The life of the law has not been logic: it has been experience') is as true in the trade mark field as in any other area of law. Legal formalism is a sterile doctrine at the best of times.[26] As a method of solving trade mark conflicts, it is catastrophically inappropriate.[27] Moreover, the brand of legal formalism practised by the General Court is especially grotesque. The judgments read as though they might have been produced by a machine, using a complex algorithm devised by a visitor from an exoplanet orbiting Alpha Centauri.

C. The Role of Precedent at the Court of Justice

It is often said that the Court is not bound by precedent under a formal doctrine of *stare decisis* similar to that of common-law jurisdictions.[28] The Court does, however, talk frequently of *jurisprudence constante*, and likes to give the impression that it strives to follow its own case law. To do otherwise would be to sacrifice two of its most cherished principles: legal certainty and equal treatment. But the Court does not handle case law in the same way as common law courts. The practice of the latter is to examine relevant precedents systematically, identifying contrasting strands in the case law, recognising conflicts, deciding which line to follow, seeking to build up a coherent body of law. The common-law courts will, if necessary, overrule a precedent if they consider it clearly wrong, though they prefer to avoid that extremity by recourse to artful devices such as 'distinguishing on the facts' or finding a narrow *ratio decidendi* in the inconvenient precedent, and discarding the rest as *obiter dicta*. The Court of Justice, by contrast, likes to pretend that there are no contradictions in its previous case law. It simply ignores any previous judgment that it chooses not to follow, in preference to expressly overruling it.

---

[23] Case T-213/09 *Yorma's* ECLI:EU:T:2011:37.

[24] Case C-191/11 P *Yorma's* ECLI:EU:C:2012:62.

[25] The 'moron in a hurry' test was first used by Foster J in *Morning Star v Express Newspapers* [1979] FSR 113.

[26] See DT Keeling, 'In Praise of Judicial Activism. But What Does it Mean? And Has the European Court of Justice Ever Practised It?' in *Scritti in onore di Giuseppe Federico Mancini*, vol II (Milan, Giuffrè Editore, 1998) 505, 507 ff.

[27] See R Morgan, 'Ensuring Greater Legal Certainty in OHIM Decision-taking by Abandoning Legal Formalism' (2012) 7 *Journal of Intellectual Property Law & Practice* 408.

[28] See chs 2 and 3.

HAG II is famed above all as the first case in which the Court expressly recognised that one of its earlier rulings was wrong. AG Jacobs strongly recommended that course of action, in particular on grounds of legal certainty. He thought that in an appropriate case the Court had an 'inescapable duty' to overrule an earlier decision and that the arguments for abandoning the doctrine of common origin were exceptionally strong.[29]

Anyone who thought that *HAG II* hailed the dawn of a new age in which the Court would ape the common law and develop a sophisticated doctrine of precedent, enabling it to confront its past mistakes honestly, has been disappointed. Explicit self-overruling has not become a regular practice at the Court; but it has happened occasionally. In the *Comitology* case, the Court held that the Parliament could not bring an action for annulment against the Council because the relevant provisions of the Treaties made no mention of the Parliament.[30] Less than two years later, in the *Chernobyl* case, the Court held that the absence in the Treaties of any provision allowing the Parliament to bring an action for annulment was a mere 'procedural gap', which could not prevail over the fundamental interest in the maintenance of the institutional balance laid down in the Treaties. The Parliament could therefore bring an action for annulment against an act of the Council or Commission in order to safeguard its prerogatives.[31]

In *Keck and Mithouard*, the Court decided that non-discriminatory national provisions restricting 'certain selling arrangements' should no longer be viewed as measures equivalent in effect to quantitative restrictions on trade between Member States. The Court recognised that this was 'contrary to what has previously been decided'; but it failed to specify which judgments were being overruled.[32] *Keck* was an example of how not to deal with precedent. Few of the judges had any understanding of the complex and contradictory case law that they had been producing throughout the 1980s.[33] Frustrated by their inability to deal satisfactorily with the 'Sunday Trading' cases (in spite of three attempts), they took a wrecking ball to their own case law without appearing to know what exactly they wanted to knock down. As AG Jacobs was to demonstrate a year later in *Leclerc-Siplec*, the distinction made in *Keck* between measures prohibiting the sale of certain goods and measures restricting the manner in which certain goods may be sold is as illogical as the doctrine of common origin.[34]

Perhaps the closest example of an explicit overruling since *HAG II* is the *Banco de Santander* judgment in which the Court held that a Spanish tax tribunal was not sufficiently independent to be a 'court or tribunal' empowered to request a preliminary ruling under Article 267 TFEU.[35] The Court recognised that in *Gabalfrisa* it had decided, 20 years earlier, that the same tribunal was sufficiently independent for that purpose.[36] As in *HAG II*, the case law had evolved in the time between the two judgments, so the overruling was not totally surprising.

More frequent than an explicit overruling is the practice of quietly forgetting a bad precedent. The infamous *Procter & Gamble v OHIM* ('BABY-DRY') judgment is a prime example.[37] That was the first OHIM case to work its way through to the Court. It was only the second

---

[29] Para 67 of the Opinion.

[30] Case C-302/87 *Parliament v Council* ECLI:EU:C:1988:461.

[31] Case C-70/88 *Parliament v Council* ECLI:EU:C:1991:373.

[32] Joined Cases C-267/91 and C-268/91 *Keck* ECLI:EU:C:1993:905, para 16.

[33] For a detailed review of the pre-*Keck* case law, see DT Keeling, 'The Free Movement of Goods in EEC Law; Basic Principles and Recent Developments in the Case Law of the Court of Justice of the European Communities' (1992) 26 *The International Lawyer* 467.

[34] Case C-412/93 *Leclerc-Siplec* ECLI:EU:C:1994:393, paras 38–40, see ch 35.

[35] Case C-274/14 *Banco de Santander SA* ECLI:EU:C:2020:17. See G Butler, 'Independence of Non-judicial Bodies and Orders for a Preliminary Reference to the Court of Justice' (2020) 45 *ELRev* 870.

[36] Joined Cases C-110/98 to C-147/98 *Gabalfrisa* ECLI:EU:C:2000:145.

[37] Case C-383/99 *Procter & Gamble* ECLI:EU:C:2001:461.

case in which the Court had occasion to deal with absolute grounds of refusal. A little caution was called for. Instead, just as in *HAG I*, the Court charged recklessly into an area of which it had neither knowledge nor experience, and made some disastrous mistakes. The then Court of First Instance (CFI) (now General Court) had agreed with the OHIM Board of Appeal that the word combination 'BABY-DRY' was not an inherently distinctive trade mark for nappies in the light of Article 7(1)(c) of the Community Trade Mark Regulation,[38] which prohibited the registration of marks consisting 'exclusively of signs or indications which may serve, in trade, to designate the kind, quality, … intended purpose … of the goods … or other characteristics of the goods'.[39]

Bearing in mind that one of the main functions of a nappy is to absorb urine and keep the baby dry, it is surely obvious that BABY-DRY falls squarely within the terms of Article 7(1)(c); it describes the intended purpose of the goods. Astonishingly, the Court thought otherwise. It held that BABY-DRY was a 'lexical invention' and a 'syntactically unusual juxtaposition' and that it was 'not a familiar expression in the English language, either for designating babies' nappies or for describing their essential characteristics'.[40] If that approach were correct, there would be no point in examining trade mark applications on absolute grounds at all; everyone might just as well be allowed to register everything they like, and then fight it out in the courts. The problem with that, of course, is that the freedom of honest traders to use plain words to describe their wares would be drastically curtailed. That is why Article 7(1)(c) of the Regulation exists.

Fortunately, the Court soon realised its mistake, but instead of expressly overruling *BABY-DRY*, it chose to ignore the judgment, and simply ceased to apply the *BABY-DRY* criteria in subsequent rulings. It stopped pretending that banal combinations of dictionary words are lexical inventions. It abandoned the idea that 'any perceptible difference' from the terms used in common parlance to designate the goods or their essential characteristics was sufficient to turn a word combination into a distinctive trade mark. The concept of the 'syntactically unusual juxtaposition' vanished from the Court's vocabulary. The rest of the world has also chosen to ignore *BABY-DRY* and its 'anything goes' approach.

In fact, the General Court has gone to the opposite extreme, refusing BigXtra (for travel services),[41] Clampflex (for medical clamps),[42] STEAM GLIDE (for irons),[43] and FOODLUBE (for chemicals used in industry).[44] All this suggests that an explicit overruling may not always be necessary; the Court can get rid of a bad precedent by ignoring it, and hoping that everyone else will do the same. However, in the interests of legal certainty, it would be better if the Court were to overrule explicitly a previous judgment that it no longer considers sound, instead of feigning amnesia. It would surely be better still if the Court, when faced with a novel issue in an area where it has little experience, thought deeply about the matter, did the necessary research, and got the law right in the first place.

---

[38] Council Regulation (EC) No 40/94 of 20 December 1993 on the Community trade mark (1994) OJ L11/1.
[39] Case T-163/98 Procter & Gamble ECLI:*EU*:*T*:1999:145.
[40] Paras 40–44 of the Judgment in Case C-383/99 *Procter & Gamble*.
[41] Case T-81/13 *FTI Touristik GmbH* ECLI:EU:T:2014:140.
[42] Case T-171/11 *Hans-Jürgen Hopf* ECLI:EU:T:2012:636.
[43] Case T-544/11 *Spectrum Brands* ECLI:EU:T:2013:20.
[44] Case T-200/08 *Interflon* ECLI:EU:T:2010:414.

25

'Civis Europeus Sum', Thirty Years On: Opinion of Advocate General Jacobs *in* Konstantinidis

DIMITRY KOCHENOV

I. INTRODUCTION

THE OVERWHELMING IMPACT of the UK Advocates General on the development of EU law notwithstanding, one erudite reference stands out as an unquestionable symbol of the British contribution to the shaping of EU law. Coined by AG Jacobs in the case of *Konstantinidis*,[1] it is one of the most quoted elements of any Opinion of an AG in the history of the Court – 'civis europeus sum' (I am a European citizen). Given how significant is the connection between the study of the classics and the British intellectual tradition, as amply illustrated subsequently by Eleanor Sharpston's brilliant Opinions, the phrase, as well as its actual and potential implications deserves a close scrutiny.

II. BACKGROUND, CONTEXT, AND FACTS

The case was referred to the Court under Article 177 EEC (now Article 267 TFEU) by a court in Tübingen (*Amtsgericht Tübingen*), Germany. The crux of the matter was a mistaken transliteration of a Greek name of the plaintiff in his wedding certificate issued in Germany. German law and German authorities thought that requiring a misspelling of a Greek name was fine. Germany at the time, was, for one view in the context of *Konstantinidis*, 'a country which has a reputation for being bureaucratically punctilious'.[2] However, the referring court wished to know if all of this was compatible with the principle of loyal cooperation,[3] the prohibition of discrimination on grounds of nationality,[4] free movement of workers and right of establishment.[5]

---

[1] Opinion of AG Jacobs in Case C-168/91 *Konstantinidis* ECLI:EU:C:1992:504.
[2] IS Forrester, 'Free Movement of Persons: The Right We Must Leave Behind?' (2018) 39 *European Competition Law Review* 379, 386.
[3] Art 5 EEC, now Art 4(3) TFEU.
[4] Art 7 EEC, now Art 18 TFEU.
[5] Arts 48 and 52 EEC, now Arts 45 and 49 TFEU.

The Opinion of AG Jacobs was hilarious in that it weaponized (then) limited EEC law and the brilliance of imagination, to defend fundamental rights (and common sense) against a smashingly thoughtless German legalistic assault on reason. It is a story of a good laugh meeting absurdly coherent Kafkaesque reality and winning by refusing to accept the claims of German law blindly, with no regard to their effects, resulting in setting German law aside. The good laugh (and EU law) is victorious, supplying a classical example of the humiliation of the Member State – Germany – as EU's key constitutional tactic, as Davies would put it.[6] A culture of authority is dismissed in the context of Socratic contestation,[7] fully rejecting the terms set by the Kafkaesque authority, which were by design oblivious of common sense. To many, *Konstantinidis* would be an illustration of what would actually be the core added value of EU law: questioning the key assumptions of national law from a perspective entirely external and necessarily sceptical of it.[8] The full context of the win-win quote of AG Jacobs was this:

> In the middle of the forum of Messana a Roman citizen, O judges, was beaten with rods; while in the meantime no groan was heard, no other expression was heard from that wretched man, amid all his pain, and between the sound of the blows, except these words, "Civis romanus sum (I am a citizen of Rome)." He fancied that by this one statement of his citizenship he could ward off all blows, and remove all torture from his person.[9]

To be absolutely clear: the quote is a hope being lost: 'civis romanus', although it sounds good, does not have mythical qualities and did not help. Let us go through the case's impact and place the idea of a supranational citizenship in action that the 'civis europeus sum' logic espoused in the context of European constitutionalism. This chapter revisits the hopes expressed 30 years ago from now, proceeding with little sections, each raising a slightly different point in connection to the hopes expressed by AG Jacobs.

The European Union, while heralding a break with at least some of the classical functions of citizenship, has indeed achieved a most radical break with the citizenship tradition. The question is, however, whether it is to the better or to the worse. This question remains open, as will be demonstrated. The hope vested in citizenship both by AG Jacobs and the poor Publius Gavius of Cicero's story is futile. EU citizenship – as a crucial element of EU constitutionalism – seemingly threatens too many basics, vital for the self-perpetuating of the constitutional order at the national level.[10] Once all the basics – 'the people', equality before the law, ability to regulate are denied by EU law with no regard to the national constitution, the question that arises is: 'In the name of what?'[11] By failing to give a convincing answer beyond an allusion to the supremacy of EU law the Union[12] – and the maxim of AG Jacobs – could not succeed.

---

[6] G Davies, 'Humiliation of the State as a Constitutional Tactic' in F Amtenbrink and PAJ van den Bergh (eds), *The Constitutional Integrity of the European Union* (The Hague, TMC Asser Press, 2010).

[7] M Cohen-Eliya and I Porat, 'Proportionality and the Culture of Justification' (2011) 59 *The American Journal of Comparative Law* 463.

[8] Davies (n 6).

[9] Marcus Tullius Cicero, *Against Verres* (CD Yonge, trans), Second pleading, book 5, para 62.

[10] See HU Jessurun d'Oliveira, 'Union Citizenship and beyond' in N Cambien et al (eds), *European Citizenship under Stress: Social Justice, Brexit, and Other Challenges* (Leiden, Brill-Nijhoff, 2020).

[11] D Kochenov, 'EU Law without the Rule of Law' (2015) 34 *YEL* 74; D Kochenov, 'The Oxymoron of "Market Citizenship" and the Future of the Union' in F Amtenbrink et al (eds), *The Internal Market and the Future of European Integration: Essays in Honour of Laurence W Gormley* (Cambridge, CUP, 2019).

[12] J Lindeboom, 'Why EU Law Claims Supremacy' (2018) 38 *OJLS* 328; AT Williams, 'Taking Values Seriously: Towards a Philosophy of EU Law' (2009) 29 *OJLS* 549.

III. THE OPINION OF AG JACOBS

AG Jacobs commenced by noting that the International Organization for Standardization (ISO) way of transliterating Greek names to the Roman alphabet would result in a written name that 'gives a highly misleading impression of their true pronunciation', and that 'some names will be distorted beyond recognition'.[13] For the applicant who was challenging the national authorities, the Opinion demonstrates extensive evidence of sympathy of the AG with the predicament in which Mr Konstantinidis found himself in.[14] As acknowledged by AG Jacobs, 'the inconvenience and unpleasantness thus inflicted on him are sufficient to entitle him to invoke the prohibitions laid down by the Treaty'.[15] Nic Shuibhne noted that AG Jacobs captured 'very well the idea that when movement occurs between Member States, this can involve movement between different systems or versions of rights'.[16]

For AG Jacobs, Mr Konstantinidis was clearly to suffer indirect discrimination[17] if his name was not registered properly. For him, fundamental rights for persons exercising free movement were to be embedded in their dealings with national authorities. As AG Jacobs put it, '[a] person's right to his name is fundamental in every sense of the word. After all, what are we without our name?'.[18] Then came the celebrated paragraph:

> In my opinion, a Community national who goes to another Member State as a worker or self-employed person under ... the Treaty is entitled not just to pursue his trade or profession and to enjoy the same living and working conditions as nationals of the host State; he is in addition entitled to assume that, wherever he goes to earn his living in the European Community, he will be treated in accordance with a common code of fundamental values, in particular those laid down in the European Convention on Human Rights. In other words, he is entitled to say 'civis europeus sum' and to invoke that status in order to oppose any violation of his fundamental rights.[19]

AG Jacobs therefore concluded, advising the Court, that

> Where a national of a Member State establishes himself, pursuant to Article 52 of the EEC Treaty, in another Member State which uses an alphabet different from the one used in his own State, Articles 7 and 52 of the Treaty [Articles 18 and 49 TFEU] are infringed by rules or practices of the host [s]tate which require his name to be entered in a register of civil status, against his wishes, in a transliteration which, as in circumstances such as those of the present case, seriously misrepresents the correct pronunciation of the name.[20]

Traces of the Opinion of AG Jacobs, it is argued,[21] can be seen in a book chapter that he had written, not long prior to its delivery.[22] Subsequently, the Court, rather simply and without

---

[13] Para 9.

[14] Interestingly, Mr. Konstantinidis was not represented by a lawyer and, at the hearing, pleaded by himself. This did not go unnoticed, as AG Jacobs remarked it was 'a rare opportunity to hear a litigant in person when he represented himself at the hearing. His essential argument, presented with a simple eloquence and brevity which many professional advocates would do well to emulate' (para 12 of the Opinion).

[15] Para 25.

[16] N Nic Shuibhne, 'Margins of Appreciation: National Values, Fundamental Rights and EC Free Movement Law' (2009) 34 *ELRev* 230, 245.

[17] In para 20 AG Jacobs called it 'covert discrimination'.

[18] Para 40.

[19] Para 46.

[20] Para 52.

[21] R Lawson, 'Case C-168/91, Christos Konstantinidis v. Stadt Altensteig-Standesamt, Judgment of 30 March 1993, [1993] 3 C.M.L.R. 401' (1994) 31 *CMLRev* 395, 405.

[22] See FG Jacobs, 'The Protection of Human Rights in the Member States of the European Community: The Impact of the Case Law of the Courts' in J O'Reilly (ed), *Human Rights and Constitutional Law: Essays in Honour of Brian Walsh* (Dublin, Round Hall, 1992).

deep reasoning, in essence followed the AG Jacobs, though on more narrow grounds, ruling that the national practice of registering names was incompatible with Article 52 EEC (now Article 49 TFEU) on establishment 'only in so far as their application causes a Greek national such a degree of inconvenience as in fact to interfere with his freedom to exercise the right of establishment enshrined in that article'.[23] This departure from a much broader approach suggested by the learned AG was one of the first steps towards the oxymoronic "market citizenship", which comes disassociated, per se, from even the most crucial rights, as such the right to a name.[24]

IV. ANALYSIS

A. *Civis … Sum*: An Opposition to Classical Constitutionalism?

Making a citizen is an ideology-inspired legal exercise, implying a choice among the available bodies, who could be useful or not for the achievement of the goals of the authority at any given time, whatever these are. Those bodies which are less useful are simply excluded and do not exist in the eyes of the law. Exclusions can run along any lines: geography of origin, race, religion, education, language, time; you name it, and a legal-historical example will be found. The citizenship's capacity to exclude is its core function, which means that, in the 'golden days' of citizenship – the mythical days of the concept's unquestioned authority – the exclusion at the level of the *legal status* could only rarely be questioned: equality is *among* citizens, remember? As a consequence, working with citizens, the authority enjoys an almost universal *carte blanche*: you create ethnic electorates,[25] you assign the status of those who are not white enough to your liking to the 'ancestral homelands',[26] you declare those you send away as ideologically,[27] or racially deficient – as non-citizens.[28] The long history of fragrant discriminations is rich and diverse. Under this paradigm, the core question before looking at rights, entitlements, duties and equality claims is *who* is a citizen in this society? Those who are not citizens are entitled to nothing, and this is legally and politically right, even if frequently also morally unjust. What AG Jacobs suggested cuts this logic short.

Indeed, if by its paramount nature, citizenship is the ultimate status of protection, the emanation of the love of the country by definition not extended to those without the status. It is in fact not what we see as the discrimination on the basis of nationality, but rather, the core normative ideal of citizenship allowing the bearers to bathe in the rays of their motherland's love, and look down at those who do not deserve this love by virtue of the place of birth, parentage, or both. This is outlawed in the European Union through the prohibition of discrimination on the basis of nationality.[29] *Civis europeus sum* is a cry in honour of the nationalist bonds lost. No, France does not love the Frenchmen more than Estonians. If it does,

---

[23] Case C-168/91 *Konstantinidis* ECLI:EU:C:1993:115, para 15 of the Judgment.

[24] Kochenov (n 11) 'The Oxymoron of Market Citizenship'.

[25] RC Visek, 'Creating Ethnic Electorate through Legal Restorationism: Citizenship Rights in Estonia' (1997) 38 *Harvard International Law Journal* 315.

[26] J Dugard, 'South Africa's Independent Homelands: An Exercise in Denationalization' (1980) 10 *Denver Journal of International Law & Policy* 11.

[27] L Chamberlain, *The Philosophy Steamer: Lenin and the Exile of the Intelligentsia* (London, Atlantic Books, 2006).

[28] K Rundle, 'The Impossibility of an Exterminatory Legality: Law and the Holocaust' (2009) 59 *The University of Toronto Law Journal* 65.

[29] Art 18 TFEU.

this could very well be a violation of EU law for the Commission to look into as a means of public enforcement, and bring to the Court to adjudicate.

The core issue of importance here is very basic and has to do with the traditional approaches to the core aspects of legitimacy in a political community: the justification of violence and of the obligation to submit to violence of the public authority as a necessary element of being 'free' going back to Jean Bodin[30] and rooted in the Christian soteriology of the day.[31] If only citizens and no one else are counted as the constituents of the group from which legitimacy emanates – call it *demos*, the nation, political community – then the picture of what the state and, necessarily, the law is about will be quite different, necessarily, compared with a situation when humans are counted, non-citizens included, like our EU-citizen Konstantinidis, a *civis europeus*. Indeed, why not put humans, persons, at the basis of *demos*, the nation, political community? While legal and social truths are bound to overlap for the law to be effective[32] – and knowing the bio-power of the contemporary state in shaping the life itself to the whims of fashion of the day[33] – making the citizens is still much easier and less problematic than acknowledging the humans. It was the second that EU law in the eyes of AG Jacobs clearly required Germany to do.

B. *Civis … Sum* as a Tool to Crack States Open?

One should not be too disappointed that the *'civis europeus sum'* logic did not actually work in the celebrated Opinion of AG Jacobs in *Konstantinidis*. Indeed, inspiration, the plight of Publius Gavius *'civis romanus sum'*, retold by Cicero in *In Verrem*, did not prevent torture and the cruci-fixion of that Roman citizen either. Indeed, as Beard rightly remarks pointing to the famous story, the most uses of *civis … sum*, predating AG Jacobs, are equally ironical. Beard wrote:

> when they chose to use this phrase, both Palmerton and Kennedy must have forgotten that its most famous ancient use was as the unsuccessful plea of an innocent victim under a sentence of death imposed by a rogue Roman governor.[34]

The same can be said about every textbook in EU law, while *civis … sum* in the EU is, of course, not at all out of context: appealing to it not infrequently has the same effect now as in the times when Gavius was ruthlessly beaten with rods: it would not help. Yet, the story of EU citizenship is infinitely more interesting when retold outside the context of troubling devia-tions from the norm when the law is not complied with and the expected outcomes are not reached. In fact, EU law as designed and as practiced, i.e., far from the realm of exceptions, plays the role which runs counter the normative foundations traditionally regarded as under-pinning the citizenship concept.

Such no doubt well-meaning[35] intrusion into the illusory, if not deceptive, as demonstrated above, garden of normative coherence is to the better, but also to the worse: besides opening

---

[30] JH Franklin, *Jean Bodin and the Sixteenth-Century Revolution in the Methodology of Law and History* (NY, Columbia University Press, 1963), discussed in detail in K Kim, *Aliens in Mediaeval Law* (Cambridge, CUP, 2000) 193.

[31] Kim, ibid.

[32] P Bourdieu, 'The Force of Law: Toward a Sociology of the Juridical Field' (1987) 38 *Hastings Law Journal* 805, 814.

[33] ML Flear, 'Developing Bio-Citizens through Migration for Healthcare Services' (2007) 14 *Maastricht Journal of European and Comparative Law* 239.

[34] M Bead, *SPQR: A History of Ancient Rome* (NY, Liveright, 2015) 254 (cross-reference omitted).

[35] On the positive potential, see eg FG Jacobs, 'Citizenship of the European Union – A Legal Analysis' (2007) 13 *ELJ* 591; F Wollenschläger, 'A New Fundamental Freedom beyond Market Integration' (2011) 17 *ELJ* 34.

up to Europeans new categories of rights outside the realm of their own states, just as the right not to have your name misspelled *sometimes*,[36] it has also questioned the essential elements of national citizenship, including the preferential relationship between the citizen and the state and, crucially, both aspects of Rogers Brubacker's now classical definition of citizenship. If citizenship is 'an instrument and an object of closure',[37] the EU deployed *civis europeus sum* logic of AG Jacobs to dismantle national citizenship as was known before Maastricht, by demanding inclusion of other EU citizens into the national community on the basis of the non-discrimination on the basis of nationality principle, thus 'abolishing'[38] the legal relevance of Member State nationalities in a huge array of crucial areas of human activity where EU law applies. The EU has also removed, to a great degree, the Member States' ability to regulate migration of EU citizens, with a very clear outcome for the relevance and function of the nationalities of the Member States to go beyond providing a bridge to the *ius tractum* status of EU citizenship.[39] As a consequence of non-discrimination on the basis of nationality, and rights distributed on the basis of non-discrimination of nationality and the possession of the formal status of EU citizenship, coupled with the evaporated ability not to allow EU citizens in, the standard normative correlation between national citizens and the societies in the Member States came under strong pressure. The ability of the French state to distribute the token of Frenchness, the French passport, in this context cannot possibly hide the fact that France does not control who is *de facto* French for pretty much all the purposes,[40] with the implications for the essence of the *demos* and the legitimation/justification of political power at both national and European level (especially given the exclusion of the European not-quite-foreigners from the national-level franchise). Ironically, this happens precisely at the time when the importance of *de facto* citizenship's recognition is growing exponentially, acquiring a radically new significance in the citizenship world as we have seen above.

This is not saying that deciding to crack states open in this way is a bad thing, but rather, it is that both aspects of the most accepted definition of citizenship in the literature today fail to find reflection in what the nationalities of the Member States have become after the advent of EU citizenship, which could probably provide one of the explanations for the gradual undermining of the latter, which we are facing coming both from the level of the national law, especially in the UK, and this is long before Brexit,[41] and also at the supranational level, where the Court seems to be minded to water down the core of the supranational legal status,[42] turning it, step-by-step, into a structural irrelevance in the context of the European law edifice.[43] In Nic Shuibhne's analysis[44] confined to the realm of EU law, such backlash was only to be expected, and is in fact nothing but a faithful adherence to the federalist principles.[45]

---

[36] Case C-391/09 *Runevič-Vardyn and Wardyn* ECLI:EU:C:2011:291. See A Łazowski et al, 'The Importance of Being Earnest: Spelling of Names, EU Citizenship and Fundamental Rights' (2015) 11 *Croatian Yearbook of European Law and Policy* 1.

[37] R Brubaker, *Citizenship and Nationhood in France and Germany* (Cambridge, MA, Harvard University Press, 1992) 34.

[38] G Davies, '"Any Place I Hang My Hat?" Or: Residence is the New Nationality' (2005) 11 *ELJ* 43.

[39] D Kochenov, '*Ius Tractum* of Many Faces: European Citizenship and the Difficult Relationship between Status and Rights' (2009) 15 *CJEL* 169.

[40] The exceptions include political rights at the national level and holding high offices.

[41] J Shaw et al, *Getting to Grips with EU Citizenship* (Edinburgh, University of Edinburgh, 2013).

[42] C O'Brien, '*Civis Capitalist Sum*: Class as the New Guiding Principle of EU Free Movement Rights' (2016) 53 *CMLRev* 937; E Spaventa, 'Earned Citizenship – Understanding Union Citizenship through Its Scope' in D Kochenov (ed), *EU Citizenship and Federalism: The Role of Rights* (Cambridge, CUP, 2017).

[43] D Kochenov, 'On Tiles and Pillars: EU Citizenship as a Federal Denominator' in Kochenov (n 42).

[44] N Nic Shuibhne, 'Recasting EU Citizenship as Federal Citizenship' in Kochenov (n 42).

[45] C Schönberger, 'European Citizenship as Federal Citizenship' (2007) 19 *European Review of Public Law* 63.

While inter-systemically this conclusion can be convincingly criticised, as Spaventa has shown,[46] it is beyond any doubt that the backlash can be explained in a sound way by looking at the overwhelming impact of EU law on what citizenship of the Member States is now about.

C. *Civis … Sum* as an Unjustifiable Take-over?

The main problem with citizenship in the EU at the moment, it seems, is not confined to pushing the Member States to rethink which communities of people they are in charge of. It goes even deeper, since the 'replacement' citizenship at the EU level – never mind the 'shall not replace'[47] language of the Treaty, which can only make legalistic, 'who issues the passport?' kind of sense, failing to capture the essence of the deeper on-going processes discussed in the preceding parts. While EU citizenship has the potential to 'take over', *de facto*, from the nationalities of the Member States, it seems to be based on entirely different principles, compared with any other citizenship in contemporary world. It is a citizenship conditioned on a market endorsement and the performance of objectively nonsense acts, like venturing out across the invisible inter-state borders within the Internal Market.[48]

Rather than a celebration of the abstract humanity of the bearer through the extension of rights based on a formal legal status aimed at ignoring the actual differences between the holders, EU citizenship, on the contrary, virtually never protects the weak and the needy based on their humanity and status,[49] but uniquely connects such protection with the perceived cross-border or economic aspects of the lives in question. In this sense, this is a 'citizenship of taking a bus',[50] which has legally dislodged in many respects ideologically sound national-level statuses, which are, precisely, *not* dependent on the performance of ideologised ethically and morally contingent acts. The supranational level citizenship undermining the national ones cannot, thus, withstand even the most basic criticism based on human dignity and human worth: these cannot depend on a used bus ticket – either you move in space or not is necessarily irrelevant from a moral or ethical perspective. Most reasonable suggestions voiced in the literature to disconnect the logics of citizenship and market-inspired movement in Europe by either making the latter irrelevant for the enjoyment of citizenship rights,[51] or, by giving the right *not* to move full recognition among the entitlements of EU citizenship deserving legal protection,[52] remained unanswered calls in a highly ideological context of European integration where the foundational ideal of the good, however ethically non-obvious, like the binding

---

[46] Spaventa (n 42).

[47] Art 20(1) TFEU makes the following clarification: 'Citizenship of the Union shall be additional to and not replace national citizenship'.

[48] Not all borders count, of course, as the Court explained: Case C-212/06 *Government of the French Community and Walloon Government v Flemish Government* ECLI:EU:C:2008:178. See also Opinion of AG Sharpston in Case C-212/06 *Government of the French Community and Walloon Government v Flemish Government* ECLI:EU:C:2007:398, especially paras 143–44. See P Van Elsuwege and S Adam, 'Situations purement internes, discriminations à rebours et collectivités autonomes après l'arrêt sur *l'Assurances soins flamande*' (2008) 44 *Cahiers droit européen* 655.

[49] C O'Brien, 'I Trade Therefore I Am: Legal Personhood in the European Union' (2013) 50 *CMLRev* 1643; P Caro de Sousa, 'Quest for the Holy Grail – Is a Unified Approach to the Market Freedoms and European Citizenship Justified?' (2014) 20 *ELJ* 499.

[50] Kochenov (n 43).

[51] E Sharpston, 'Citizenship and Fundamental Rights – Pandora's Box or a Natural Step Towards Maturity?' in P Cardonnel et al (eds), *Constitutionalising the EU Judicial System: Essays in Honour of Pernilla Lindh* (Oxford, Hart Publishing, 2012). See also S Iglesias Sánchez, 'Fundamental Rights and Citizenship of the Union at a Crossroads' (2014) 20 *ELJ* 464.

[52] S Iglesias Sánchez, 'A Citizenship Right to Stay?' in Kochenov (n 42).

requirement to move about, is predetermined and immune from contestation.[53] It is a citizenship without respect designed to bring down those whom the internal market does not need and thus perceives of as disposable and unworthy of protection, recognition and respect.[54] EU citizenship, in failing to endow with protections all those who possess the formal legal status and looking instead at the particular acts they engage in, emerges as the antithesis of what the notion of citizenship is usually about.[55] The worth of the legal truth of status assignment here frequently remains almost entirely inconsequential.

This being said, this is all about giving recognition to the person, of course, as opposed to the classical reality the departure from which was discussed in the preceding parts. The interesting thing with EU citizenship, however, is that the departure from the classical legalistic understanding of citizenship is actually used to the effect of *depriving* persons of rights under this pretext, rather than empowering them, which is the general constitutional trend outside the EU. Instead of using the logic the shift from the purely legal to social reality to extend additional protections to those whom the legalistic framework renders invisible, as the ECtHR, for instance,[56] EU citizenship deploys the same to the opposing end: to pre-empt the extension of rights. In this sense, EU citizenship is a negative departure from the abstract citizenship ideal, looking beyond the strictly legal truth of the supranational-level status only to undermine the latter's effects should the dogmatic ideal of a 'good market citizen',[57] which is by definition deprived of any moral or ethical *contenu* whatsoever not be satisfied.[58] This unexpected development demonstrates the attractiveness of the formal legalistic world of clearly formulated and meticulously enforced legal truths which citizenship has precisely been drifting away from over the last decennia, turning modern constitutionalism towards the person. How did the EU land with such an atypically modern and at the same time astonishingly denigrating citizenship on its hands, which is both in line with and, simultaneously, in contradiction with the global trends?

D. *Civis ... Sum* and the 'Market'

As the integration project matured, Europe's main strength became its chief weakness. Conceived as a market to serve the ideals grander than simple economic prosperity, thus intended to benefit each and every European through becoming part of our 'legal heritage', as the Court has amply noted in *Van Gend en Loos*,[59] EU law failed to move on with the

---

[53] G Davies, 'Social Legitimacy and Purposive Power: The End, the Means and the Consent of the People' in D Kochenov et al (eds), *Europe's Justice Deficit?* (Oxford, Hart Publishing, 2015); A Somek, 'Europe: Political, Not Cosmopolitan' (2014) 20 *ELJ* 142.

[54] O'Brien (n 49); O'Brien (n 42).

[55] D Kochenov, 'Neo-Mediaeval Permutations of Personhood in Europe' in L Azoulai et al (eds), *Constructing the Person in EU Law: Rights, Roles, Identities* (Oxford, Hart Publishing, 2016).

[56] The rise of Art 8 ECHR jurisprudence prohibiting, in numerous cases, deportations to the country of citizenship, has created something akin to a *de facto* nationality, altering the legal reality to a great degree. For one of the first notable examples, see the Concurring Opinion of Judge Martens in *Beldjoudi* (*Beldjoudi v France*, App No 12083/86, A/234-A (26 March 1992)); *Jeunesse v Netherlands*, App No 12738/10 (3 October 2014). This trend is deeply empowering at the individual level. *cf* S Adam and P Van Elsuwege, 'EU Citizenship and the European Federal Challenge through the Prism of Family Reunification' in Kochenov (n 42).

[57] For an overview of the relevant case-law of the CJEU, see L Azoulai, 'Transfiguring European Citizenship: From Member State Territory to Union Territory' in Kochenov (n 42).

[58] Caro de Sousa (n 49).

[59] Case 26/62 *Van Gend en Loos* ECLI:EU:C:1963:1. See also FG Jacobs (ed), *European Law and the Individual* (North Holland, 1976); O Due, 'The Law-Making of the European Court of Justice Considered in Particular from the Perspective of Individuals and Undertakings' (1994) 63 *Nordic Journal of International Law* 123.

times. Conceived once upon a time as a stepping stone to peace, and a bunch of other valuable ideals, now reflected in Article 2 TEU (but also colonialism[60] and building a unified nuclear force[61]) the Union gradually lowered its ambition: the means for greater progress, which was the market, fell on itself to take the chief place among the Union's ends.[62] This subtle taming of ambition, while sellable to an inattentive observer as a sign of respect vis-à-vis the Member States' sovereignty is in fact something else, it seems.

When the market is the means to achieve something greater, the limitations it imposes on the national authority are justifiable: as the official story goes, the Member States lost political and economic upper hand in the name of liberty – an insurance policy against totalitarian twists – and in the name of prosperity – a social Europe where tomorrow is better than today – which is to come through unity. Much has changed, however, since the first version of the story had been written. Prosperity is not on the horizon anymore, at least not for everyone,[63] liberty is none of the Union's business: the Union is not effective at all against Polish-Hungarian-style 'illiberal democracies' as is being discovered,[64] some commotion in high places notwithstanding.[65]

Instead of the optimism of a new beginning championed by the élites of the past, Union law is now a binding and directly effective tool to tame us, European citizens, in the name of a highly specific version of the market it cherishes. In the name of the internal coherence of the market we are shielded from human rights;[66] in the name of its smooth operation the market is 'apolitical.'[67] This is good for us, we are told, because the Treaties say so[68] and because politics, as much as the Treaties allow for it, is by definition the politics of means, not the politics of ends: the direction of European Unity is set in stone and not negotiable politically within the framework of the institutions the Treaties have created.

E. *Civis ... Sum* as a Utopia

Speaking of utopias, Sir Isaiah Berlin diagnosed that:

> in a society in which the same goals are universally accepted, problems can be only of means, all soluble by technological methods. That is a society in which the inner life of man, the moral and spiritual and aesthetic imagination, no longer speaks at all.[69]

Our supranational legal heritage lays claim to our imagination and fails, to which the rise of all kinds of extremist movements testifies. For the first time in its history the Union is routinely perceived as a potentially powerful agent of injustice not only by nationalists and outcast

---

[60] P Hansen and S Jonsson, *Eurafrica: The Untold History of European Integration and Colonialism* (London, Bloomsbury, 2015).

[61] G Mallard, *Fallout: Nuclear Diplomacy in an Age of Global Fracture* (Chicago, University of Chicago Press, 2014).

[62] G Peebles, '"A Very Eden of the Innate Rights of Man"? A Marxist Look at the European Union Treaties and Case Law' (1997) 22 *Law and Social Inquiry* 581.

[63] A J Menéndez, 'The Existential Crisis of the European Union' (2013) 14 *GLJ* 453.

[64] A von Bogdandy and M Ioannidis, 'Systemic Deficiency in the Rule of Law' (2014) 51 *CMLRev* 59.

[65] P Oliver and J Stefanelli, 'Strengthening the Rule of Law in the EU: The Council's Inaction' (2016) 54 *JCMS* 1075.

[66] *Opinion 2/13* ECLI:EU:C:2014:2454. See P Eeckhout, 'Opinion 2/13 on EU Accession to the ECHR and Judicial Dialogue – Autonomy or Autarky?' (2015) 38 *Fordham International Law Journal* 955. See also *Opinion 2/94* ECLI:EU:C:1996:140.

[67] MA Wilkinson, 'Politicising Europe's Justice Deficit: Some Preliminaries' in D Kochenov et al (eds), *Europe's Justice Deficit?* (Oxford, Hart Publishing, 2015) 111.

[68] For an analysis, see AT Williams, 'Taking Values Seriously: Towards a Philosophy of EU Law' (2009) 29 *OJLS* 549.

[69] I Berlin, *The Crooked Timber of Humanity* (NY, Alfred A Knopf, 1991) 15.

lunatics, but also by its own servants and facilitators, professors of law. Gráinne de Búrca is absolutely right pointing out that the EU can be perceived as 'patent injustice'.[70] Perceptions have changed, probably, because the market without a 'mantle of ideals' is not a pretty sight.[71]

The Union could try redeeming itself through making its law at least sensitive to human suffering: Sir Isaiah's 'first public obligation'. This can be done, at the very least, through allowing the *Van Gend en Loos* 'legal heritage' of the citizens to play a more significant role in the system than the market logic, which is absurd in the citizenship context as long as it shapes the formal status of citizenship which can be deactivated by the failure to engage with the market sufficiently, as explained above, forming the worst and the least humane blend of the legal truth and social reality paradigms of personhood in law. In a constitutional system – even where democracy as such is out of reach[72] – rights cannot be acquired by engaging in ethically and morally irrelevant acts, mothers are not punished when disability of their children prevents them from work;[73] and tax-breaks do not depend on the nationality of your former wife.[74]

The core problem with the EU today is precisely that the principle behind the application of the law directly penetrating countless lives is rather farcical and thus inexplicable at all from a rational humane perspective. Moreover, violence is done in the name of the perceived Member States' sensitivities, where in fact, this is the dull market-inspired sophistry that is at play: 'when he grows up, he might want to move across the non-existent border'.[75] Approached from this perspective the Union does not only have no democracy and no equality (the bus is sometimes late), but also no citizenship: the *Ruiz Zambrano* detour[76] was all too brief, and we seem to be back to square one, to Weiler's poignant criticism of the classical *status quo*: the Union 'precisamente omette di compiere la transizione concettuale da una libera circolazione basata sul mercato ad una libertà basata sulla cittadinanza.'[77] Now, 30 years on, the *civis ... sum* vision of AG Jacobs, regrettably, remains as utopian as it was at the moment of its original proclamation.

---

[70] G de Búrca, 'Conclusion' in D Kochenov et al (eds), *Europe's Justice Deficit?* (Oxford, Hart Publishing, 2015).

[71] JHH Weiler, 'Bread and Circus: The State of European Union' (1998) 4 *CJEL* 223, 231.

[72] But see, arguing the opposite, K Lenaerts and J A Gutiérrez-Fons, 'Epilogue on EU Citizenship: Hopes and Fears' in Kochenov (n 42).

[73] Case C-434/09 *McCarthy* ECLI:EU:C:2011:277; N Nic Shuibhne, '(Some of) The Kids Are All Right' (2012) 49 *CMLRev* 349.

[74] Case C-403/03 *Schempp* ECLI:EU:C:2005:446.

[75] Case C-148/02 *Garcia Avello* ECLI:EU:C:2003:539.

[76] Case C-34/09 *Ruiz Zambrano* ECLI:EU:C:2011:124. S Platon, 'Le champ d'application des droits du citoyen européen après les arrêts *Zambrano*, *McCarthy* et *Dereci*: de la boîte de Pandore au labyrinthe du Minotaure' (2012) 48 *Revue trimestrielle de droit européen* 23.

[77] JHH Weiler, 'Europa: "Nous coalisons des Etats noun n'unissons pas des hommes"' in M Cartabia and A Simoncini (eds), *La sostenibilità della democrazia nel XXI secolo* (Bologna, Il Mulino, 2009) 51, 82.

26

Don't Let Them Steal Our Music Away: Opinion of Advocate General Jacobs in the Legal Duet of Phil Collins and Cliff Richard

ADAM ŁAZOWSKI

I. INTRODUCTION

D ID copyright fall within the scope of founding EU Treaties? If so, could a domestic copyright law be discriminatory, and provide for a higher level of protection to a Member State's own nationals? Was Article 7(1) EEC (now Article 18(1) TFEU) directly effective, allowing the right holders to stop record labels from selling illegally released material? These, in a nutshell, were the main legal issues raised in two references for preliminary ruling submitted to the Court by the *Landgericht Munchen I* and *Bundesgerichtshof*. Due to their great similarity, the cases were joined for the proceedings at the Court, and thus – unintentionally and indirectly – created a legal duet of two famous artists at the time: Phil Collins and Cliff Richard.[1] Metaphorically, both sang from the same song book titled: 'Don't Let Them Steal Our Music Away'.[2] This, one should add, was a very successful collaboration, with far-reaching implications not only for the music stars involved and their record labels, but also for other performing artists affected by breaches of intellectual property rights.[3]

All of this happened at the Court in 1993. Since then, EU law – including intellectual property law – has evolved beyond recognition. Still, however, the Opinion of AG Jacobs and the judgment of the Court have aged well.[4] Put differently, in 2022 they remained a good law, especially as far as interpretation and direct effect of Article 18(1) TFEU was concerned.

---

[1] On 3 June 2002, Phil Collins and Sir Cliff Richard made a duet adequate to their professions by performing together at a concert in Buckingham Palace to celebrate the Golden Jubilee of HM Queen Elizabeth II. This time the singing was left to Sir Cliff Richard, while Phil Collins took the duties of a drummer, performing with almost all the artists listed on the bill for that special night (including the rock royalty, Queen). This was hardly surprising bearing in mind his prolific history of playing and singing with other musicians, which was duly reflected in a four-CD release aptly titled 'Phil Collins Plays Well with Others' (Atlantic/Rhino 2018). See P Collins, *Not Dead Yet. The Autobiography* (London, Penguin/Random House 2016) 348.

[2] This phrase, used also in the title of the present chapter, draws from Phil Collins and his song titled 'Don't Let Him Steal Your Heart Away' (P Collins, *Hello I Must Be Going*, 1984).

[3] This was not the first Sir Cliff Richard's case to have reached Court: see Case 341/87 *EMI v Patricia Im- und Export* ECLI:EU:C:1989:30.

[4] Joined Cases C-92/92 and C-326/92 *Collins v Imtrat and Patricia Im- und Export Verwaltungsgesellschaft Kraul v EMI* ECLI:EU:C:1993:847; Opinion of AG Jacobs in Joined Cases C-92/92 and C-326/92 *Collins v Imtrat and Patricia*

II. BACKGROUND, CONTEXT, AND FACTS

The Opinion of AG Jacobs was delivered on 30 June 1993, and the judgment of the Court on 20 October 1993. The timing mattered: this was an era of big transitions. Firstly, the Treaty on European Union was about to enter into force on 1 November 1993.[5] As is well-known, it was a watershed moment for European integration.[6] It was also the time when the EU citizenship, that is 'the fundamental status of nationals of the Member States',[7] was born. Furthermore, the European Community was busy implementing the White Paper of 1985.[8] This translated into plethora of new secondary legislation, aimed at turning what was originally the 'Common Market' into the 'Internal Market'.[9] The legislative bonanza extended to intellectual property, which was at the heart of the cases in question.[10] For Phil Collins and Cliff Richard, it was also a time of change. After the stratospheric successes their respective careers started to slow down, with record sales dwindling, and audiences turning their attention to other artists.[11] The globetrotting also became less frequent, even though the live performances have continued for years, with both artists filling in with faithful *afficionados* stadiums and arenas around the world.[12]

The two legal battles, which led to the references for preliminary ruling, started in German courts. Phil Collins submitted his claim against a local company, Imtrat, which – at the time – was notorious for releasing bootlegs: CDs which were not official recordings authorised by the artists themselves. On many occasions, poor quality live radio or TV broadcasts were used without consent of the performers, or any royalties filling their coffers.[13] This was the case

---

Im- und Export Verwaltungsgesellschaft Kraul v EMI ECLI:EU:C:1993:276. See L Flynn, 'Joined Cases C-92/92 and C-326/92, Collins v Imtrat Handelsgesellschaft mbH and Patricia Im- und Export Verwaltungsgesellschaft mbH and Leif Emanuel Kraul v EMI Electrola GmbH, Judgment of the Full Court of 20 October 1993' (1995) 32 *CMLRev* 997; LJ Smith, 'Rules of Reciprocity and Non-discrimination: National and International Copyright in a European Law Framework' (1994) 19 *ELRev* 405.

[5] Treaty on European Union [1992] OJ C191/1.

[6] For an appraisal see, inter alia, D O'Keeffe and PM Twomey (eds), *Legal Issues of the Maastricht Treaty* (Chichester, Chancery, 1994); M De Visser and A Pieter van der Mei (eds), *The Treaty on European Union 1993–2013: Reflections from Maastricht* (Cambridge, Intersentia, 2013); T Christiansen and S Duke (eds), *The Maastricht Treaty: Second Thoughts after 20 Years* (Abingdon, Routledge, 2013).

[7] Case C-184/99 *Grzelczyk* ECLI:EU:C:2001:458, para 31.

[8] Commission, 'Completing the Internal Market. White Paper from the Commission to the European Council', COM (1985) 310, p 37. See, also in relation to IP law, Commission, 'Green Paper on Copyright and the Challenge of Technology – Copyright Issues Requiring Immediate Action' COM (88) 172 final.

[9] It ought to be noted that the United Kingdom was a keen supporter and contributed to this project. See further A Łazowski, 'Goodbye but no good riddance: Internal Market with and without the United Kingdom' in A Łazowski and A Cygan (eds), *Research Handbook on Legal Aspects of Brexit* (Cheltenham, Edward Elgar, 2022).

[10] See J Pila and P Torremans, *European Intellectual Property Law*, 2nd edn (Oxford, OUP, 2019); C Seville, *EU Intellectual Property Law and Policy*, 2nd edn (Cheltenham, Edward Elgar, 2018).

[11] In case of Phil Collins, the peak came in 1980s when he led parallel lives of drummer/singer of the prog rock band Genesis, and – following the success of his first solo album 'Face Value' – of drummer/singer in his own right. One of the highlights was Live Aid in 1985, where – thanks to a combination of stamina and technology – Phil Collins performed at both Live Aid concerts. Following his stint at Wembley, he relocated – with a little help from supersonic Concorde – to Philadelphia to perform solo, and with Eric Clapton, and Led Zeppelin. For Sir Cliff Richard, the days of driving around Europe in London Routemaster were a remote past, however, in 1980s, his career was still in full swing. See, respectively, Collins (n 1); C Richard, *The Dreamer. An Autobiography* (London, Penguin, 2021).

[12] When the present chapter was finished, Phil Collins has completed mammoth 'Not Dead Yet' and 'Still Not Dead Yet' tours and again fronted Genesis during their sold out 'Last Domino?' tour.

[13] In order to appreciate the scale of the problem one needs to take a trip back into history of music business. Early 1990s were times of an industrial scale technological revolution. Introduction of CDs triggered a rapid demise of music cassettes and vinyl records. However, as hard as it is to believe for younger generations, YouTube channel or streaming services were, if at all, only in the minds of visionaries. Put differently, CDs were sold in huge numbers as the primary source of music entertainment. Bootlegs with live recordings flourished as most artists released primarily studio recorded material, with live recordings being rather sparce. Phil Collins, both as a solo artist and drummer/

here, and thus, Phil Collins applied for an interim injunction in the national court, requesting Imtrat to stop marketing a bootleg of concert recorded in the USA in 1983.[14]

The second case did not directly involve Sir Cliff Richard, but a label: EMI Electrola, which had exclusive rights to exploit some of his older recordings in Germany. It claimed that another local company released such a CD and this triggered the lawsuit. All appeared fine and straight forward, but alas, there was a fly in the ointment: Articles 96(1) and 125(1) of the then German Copyright Act.[15] A Rolls-Royce treatment was given to German artists who enjoyed full protection in respect of all performances, including recording of concerts which took place overseas. At the same time, non-German artists were only protected in relation to recordings made in Germany, with a higher level of protection available under international agreements. This, according to the referring courts, meant that neither of the plaintiffs could successfully file requests for injunctions, and let the court bailiffs seize the recordings.

III. THE OPINION OF AG JACOBS

The Opinion of AG Jacobs was divided into four main parts.[16] In the introductory section, the facts of both cases, as well as the German copyright law and its application to foreign artists were succinctly summarised. In a gentle nudge, hinting at lack of precision in the references, AG Jacobs noted that although the references *per se* dealt with copyright, the scope was wider and touched upon performers' rights too.[17] This set the stage for an in-depth analysis of the principle of non-discrimination on grounds of nationality.[18] With EU intellectual property law in its infancy, it all boiled down to the question whether the issue at hand fell within the scope of EEC Treaty allowing the plaintiffs to challenge the legality of the German rules due to their discriminatory character. With no specific prohibition of discrimination applicable to the area in question, the eyes of the referring courts, and consequentially, AG Jacobs, turned to Article 7(1) EEC containing a general prohibition of discrimination on grounds of nationality.

AG Jacobs rejected the argumentation submitted by both defendants, who claimed that neither of the cases fell within the scope of EEC Treaty, and thus, Article 7(1) EEC was not being applicable at all.[19] The role of international law, in particular the Rome Convention, was considered, but also dismissed by AG Jacobs.[20] Having concluded that matters of intellectual

---

singer with Genesis, was a good example in this respect. By 1993, he released 5 highly successful solo studio albums with only one live official recording (which was merely a compilation from several tours, not even a full concert). The situation was similar with Genesis. By 1993, it released 15 studio albums and only 4 live albums. Little wonder bootlegs were very popular. Over the years they have not disappeared, yet their share of the market has dwindled. Firstly, artists in many corners of the planet, kept on challenging breaches of IP rights by the bootleg labels. Secondly, several big acts saw releases of 'official bootlegs' as an opportunity, and financially viable proposition. The likes of Elton John, Genesis, Peter Gabriel or Mark Knopfler released via small labels, or their own websites, mixing desk quality recordings of all concerts with from several tours. And then came the YouTube channel. The rest is history.

[14] The title of the CD was 'Live and Alive', which – in hindsight – sits rather comically with the title of Phil Collins official autobiography and his final solo tours ('Not Dead Yet'). See Collins (n 1).

[15] Urheberrechtsgesetz vom 9. September 1965 (BGBl. I S. 1273).

[16] It should be noted that it was one of many opinions of AG Jacobs touching upon IP rights. See N Burrows and R Greaves, *The Advocates General and EC Law* (Oxford, OUP, 2007) 126–65; C Morcom, 'Intellectual Property' in P Moser and K Sawyer (eds), *Making Community Law: The Legacy of Advocate General Jacobs at the Court of Justice* (Cheltenham, Edward Elgar, 2008).

[17] Para 8.

[18] Paras 9–31.

[19] Paras 21–31.

[20] The Rome Convention for the Protection of Performers, Producers of Phonograms and Broadcasting Organisations, 496 UNTS 43. Paras 27–29 of the Opinion.

property did indeed fall under the remit of the EEC Treaty, AG Jacobs turned, albeit briefly, to direct effect of Article 7(1) EEC. A quick glance at existing jurisprudence of the Court led AG Jacobs to the inevitable conclusion that the provision in question was, indeed, capable of producing vertical and horizontal direct effect.[21] In a very subtle way, AG Jacobs acknowledged that in *Kenny* case, the Court referred to direct applicability instead of direct effect of Article 7(1) EEC.[22] In the final paragraph of the Opinion, AG Jacobs focused on the factual difference between the two cases, and its irrelevance for the conclusions. It was immaterial that Phil Collins was the plaintiff in the first case, while Cliff Richard was indirectly affected as the lawsuit was filed by the label to which the artist assigned his rights. The final conclusion reached by the AG Jacobs was unequivocal: Article 7(1) EEC Treaty precluded the German law as it stood at the time.

IV. ANALYSIS

The Opinion of AG Jacobs raised a number of fundamental issues, which merit closer analysis. Firstly, it extensively discussed the notorious question of what fell within the scope of EU Treaties, and what did not. Such competence battles are regularly fought and frequently reach the courtrooms at the Court on the Kirchberg plateau.[23] This time around, it was the question of copyright and performers rights. Secondly, the AG extensively discussed the role of the general prohibition of discrimination laid down in Article 7(1) EEC. Arguably, his conclusions were mindful of the forthcoming change at the time: the introduction of EU citizenship. Thirdly, the Opinion and the judgment had a considerable impact on performing artists. Here again, the 'transitional' character of both came to the surface as harmonisation of national IP laws by means of EU secondary legislation was gaining pace. The long-standing legacy of the cases was thus unequivocal confirmation of the constitutional position of Article 7(1) EEC and it its vertical and horizontal direct effect.

A. The Judgment

The Court followed AG Jacobs and reached conclusions along the same lines. It is interesting, though, to put the differences between the Opinion and the judgment under the microscope. Unlike AG Jacobs, the Court found it fitting to openly criticise the referring courts for the way they phrased the questions. It is a well-known rule that the Court has no jurisdiction to interpret national laws, or to rule on their compatibility with EU law.[24] National courts are requested to resort to creative ways of formulating questions with the view of keeping the Court within its jurisdiction under Article 267 TFEU.[25] This was not the case here. However, in

---

[21] Case 1/78 *Kenny* ECLI:EU:C:1978:140; Case 24/86 *Blaizot* ECLI:EU:C:1988:43; Case 309/85 *Barra* ECLI:EU:C:1988:42; Case C-357/89 *Raulin* ECLI:EU:C:1992:87; Case 13/76 *Donà* ECLI:EU:C:1976:115.

[22] Para 33.

[23] In the most recent jurisprudence this is particularly visible in the rule of law cases touching upon dismantling of independent judiciary in Poland. See, inter alia, Case C-619/18 *Commission v Poland* ECLI:EU:C:2019:531 para 52.

[24] See further M Broberg and N Fenger, *Broberg and Fenger on Preliminary References to the European Court of Justice*, 3rd edn (Oxford, OUP, 2021) 89–139.

[25] K Lenaerts et al, *EU Procedural Law* (Oxford, OUP, 2014) 216–41.

accordance with its well-established practice, the Court ruled that the references, despite their deficiencies, were admissible, but the questions had to be reformulated.[26]

Just like the AG Jacobs, the Court duly noted that the referring courts limited the references to copyright, while implicitly excluding the neighbouring rights. Following the plea submitted by the Commission, and allegedly in the spirit of cooperation with national courts, which is at the heart of Article 267 TFEU, the Court opted to skirt around the issue. On the one hand, the Court left it to the national courts to decide which rights were at stake. On the other hand, the answers covered both, the copyright and the neighbouring rights.[27] Not surprisingly, the Court dedicated a large part of its judgment to the question of discrimination. The analysis of the arguments submitted by Imtrat and Patricia was less extensive than in the Opinion, though, interestingly, the Court, unlike AG Jacobs, gave attention and rejected the plea claiming that the differentiation stemming from the German law was objectively justified.[28] Finally, in agreement the AG Jacobs, and following its previous case law, the Court ruled that Article 7(1) EEC was capable of producing direct effect. For unknown reason, and in typical fashion of its judgments on the provision in question, the Court avoided using the language of direct effect. The Court ruled instead:

> [...] the first paragraph of Article 7 of the Treaty should be interpreted as meaning that the principle of non-discrimination which it lays down may be directly relied upon before a national court [...].[29]

It is unclear whether this was just an example of sloppy drafting by the Court, or whether the lack of precision was purposeful. It is also interesting that the Court advised the referring courts that Article 7(1) EEC is a legal vehicle that may be employed by the parties filing requests to 'disapply the discriminatory provisions of national law'.[30] This, beyond doubt, was correct. However, for the sake of maintaining the principle of *effet utile*, it would be fitting to remind the German courts of their *Simmenthal* mandate,[31] and the inextricable link between the doctrines of primacy and direct effect.[32]

B. Non-discrimination and Scope of Application of the Founding Treaties

The two central issues for the cases at hand were the prohibition of discrimination on grounds of nationality laid down in Article 7(1) EEC, and the application of the then EEC law to the area of copyright and performers rights. Both were attended to in the Opinion of AG Jacobs and in the judgment of the Court. However, this was done in a different order and in a different fashion. In the Opinion, the centre of gravity was the prohibition of discrimination and its constitutional position in the EEC legal system. For the Court, the question of EEC competence was seemingly the priority.

---

[26] See para 16 of the Judgment. AG Jacobs also reformulated the questions without, however, criticising the referring courts. See paras 7-8 of the Opinion.

[27] Para 16.

[28] Para 29. The question whether any derogations from the general prohibition of discrimination returned in subsequent case law. See Opinion of AG Sharpston in Case C-73/08 *Bressol* ECLI:EU:C:2009:396 para 128.

[29] Para 35.

[30] Para 34.

[31] Case 106/77 *Simmenthal* ECLI:EU:C:1978:49. See W Phelan, *Great Judgments of the European Court of Justice: Rethinking the Landmark Decisions of the Foundational Period* (Cambridge, CUP, 2019) 171–84.

[32] In recent jurisprudence CJEU attended to these links in Case C-573/17 *Popławski* ECLI:EU:C:2019:530. See D Miąsik and M Szwarc, 'Primacy and Direct effect – Still Together: Poplawski II' (2021) 58 *CMLRev* 571.

AG Jacobs made a number of cardinal observations characterising the importance of Article 7(1) EEC. In his words:

> The prohibition of discrimination on grounds of nationality is the single most important principle of Community law. It is the leitmotiv of the EEC Treaty.[33]

This allowed AG Jacobs to link the importance of the principle in question with the economic objectives of what was then the EEC. He aptly noted that abolition of discrimination was the *conditio sine qua non* to achieve the high levels of integration envisaged by the drafters of the Treaty.[34] As already noted, AG Jacobs must have been clearly mindful of the inherent Copernican style revolution that would come with entry into force of TEU.[35]

At the same time with ratification troubles in Denmark, and trepidation with which the next step in the integration project was approached in the United Kingdom, AG Jacobs could not delve in his Opinion as what future would hold.[36] Interestingly, the famous 'civis europeus sum', originating in his earlier Opinion in case *Konstantinidis* was not repeated here.[37] Instead, the reference to symbolism of non-discrimination and the general status of nationals of Member States was more nuanced, yet more comprehensive:

> The prohibition of discrimination on grounds of nationality is also of great symbolic importance, inasmuch as it demonstrates that the Community is not just a commercial agreement between the governments of the Member States but it is a common enterprise on which all the citizens of Europe are able to participate as individuals.[38]

This took AG Jacobs to another important conclusion that such citizens of Europe 'must not simply be tolerated as aliens',[39] but must be entitled to all 'privileges and advantages enjoyed by the nationals of the host State'.[40] AG Jacobs ended this part of his Opinion with the following conclusion:

> No other aspect of Community law touches the individual more directly or does more to foster that sense of common identity and shared destiny without which the 'ever closer union among the peoples of Europe', proclaimed by the preamble to the Treaty, would be an empty slogan.[41]

Reading between the lines, this was an obvious allusion by AG Jacobs to what was lying ahead in terms of creation of the EU. Yet, even with the major hurdle in the ratification of TEU gone at the time when the Opinion was presented, AG Jacobs anchored his conclusions only in the rules applicable at the time.[42] Seemingly, two birds were killed with one stone, and the balance between the present and the future was found.

---

[33] Para 9.

[34] Para 10.

[35] The link between the EU citizenship and the prohibition of discrimination was established later, for instance, by AG Kokott. See Opinion of AG Kokott in Case C-164/07 *Wood* ECLI:EU:C:2008:135, para 32.

[36] Denmark held two referenda on ratification of the Treaty of Maastricht, only the second, which was held in 1993, gave a positive result. At the time of the Opinion, the ratification of the Treaty of Maastricht by the United Kingdom was still pending.

[37] Opinion of AG Jacobs in Case C-168/91 *Konstantinidis* ECLI:EU:C:1992:504, para 46. See ch 25.

[38] Para 11.

[39] ibid.

[40] ibid.

[41] ibid.

[42] The second referendum in Denmark on the Treaty of Maastricht was held on 18 May 1993, that is a few weeks before AG Jacobs presented the Opinion.

As to the next step, AG Jacobs turned to the relationship between Article 7(1) EEC and other provisions of the Treaty, which contained (and continue to contain) more specific prohibitions of discrimination. Without an in-depth analysis, he confirmed that Article 7 EEC was the gap filler. Put it more traditional fashion, it was *lex generalis*, while other provisions, for instance Article 39(2) EEC (now Article 45(2) TFEU), were *leges speciales*.[43]

The pertinent matter of the scope of the Treaty was attended in turn. At the meta level, the question was whether copyright and performers rights fell within the remit of Community law. With secondary legislation on the matters at hand only starting to emerge, these IP rights were protected under national law of the Member States, and international law binding upon them. This triggered a notorious question: if there was no harmonisation at the Community level, and the Member States benefited from the freedom to adopt national laws, could they resort to discriminatory legislation? According to Patricia, the defendant in the Sir Cliff Richard case, the Court should have answered this question in the positive. Neither AG Jacobs, nor the Court expressed a desire to entertain that claim.[44] The question had to be answered in the negative. The lack of EU legislation in a given field gave the EU Member States regulatory autonomy, which, however, could not be used in a discriminatory fashion.[45]

AG Jacobs gave a number of compelling reasons why the predicament in which Phil Collins, and the label to which Sir Cliff Richard assigned rights, found themselves in, fell within the scope of Article 7 EEC. First and foremost, intellectual property rights helped the right holders to benefit from the Common Market, in particular free movement of goods, right of establishment, and free movement of services.[46] Export of physical recordings, setting up of branches for their manufacturing or licensing of foreign companies for doing that, were aptly given as examples.[47] In the cases at hand, this was a matter of the exclusive right to authorise production of recordings, including live performances. As noted by AG Jacobs, this was not only a matter of economic importance. The moral rights of artists were also affected with recordings of poor technical quality or embodying performances which were not the artists' finest hour.[48] Interestingly, AG Jacobs also looked at the issue in question from the point of view of consumers. By purchasing CDs, many wrongly assumed that their musical treasures were produced with the consent of performers, thus the highest quality was guaranteed. Sadly, nothing could be further from the truth. Frequently bootlegs leave many very much disappointed, indeed. In this respect, a parallel with the economic significance of trademarks was drawn, and AG Jacobs referred to his own seminal opinion in *HAG II* case.[49] He also confirmed the well-established link between IP and EU competition law.[50]

---

[43] Paras 12–14.

[44] Para 23 of the Opinion; paras 18–19 of the Judgment.

[45] This is now a well-established principle of EU law. A very rich jurisprudence on, for instance, taxation of dividends is a living proof. In general terms, while direct taxation is a matter reserved for the EU Member States, they cannot use it in such a way as to introduce discriminatory tax rates (see, inter alia, Case C-292/04 *Meilicke* ECLI:EU:C:2007:132). See MJ Graetz and AC Warren Jr, 'Income Tax Discrimination and the Political and Economic Integration of Europe' (2006) 115 *Yale Law Journal* 1186.

[46] Para 15.

[47] Paras 17–18 of the Opinion; paras 23–24 of the Judgment.

[48] Para 19 of the Opinion; para 20 of the Judgment.

[49] Opinion of AG Jacobs in Case C-10/89 *HAG* ECLI:EU:C:1990:112. See ch 24.

[50] Para 25 of the Opinion in *Collins*.

C. Direct Effect of Article 18(1) TFEU

In hindsight, the judgment in question is referred to as the leading authority to confirm that Article 18(1) TFEU is capable of producing vertical and horizontal direct effect.[51] Interestingly enough, neither the Opinion of AG Jacobs, nor the judgment of the Court focused much on application of the key tenet of EU law to the provision in question.[52] Both, AG Jacobs and the Court dedicated only two paragraphs each to the matter.[53] It seems that the ability of Article 18(1) TFEU to produce vertical and horizontal effect was beyond any doubt. As already noted, the Court refrained from the language of direct effect, while AG Jacobs spelled it out rather clearly. It is interesting, though, that in the Opinion, the passages on the importance of Article 7(1) EEC and on its direct effect were not glued together. After all, without direct effect, the actual importance of the general prohibition of discrimination would have been rather modest.

D. Effect on Future Case Law

The Opinion of AG Jacobs and the judgment of the Court were period pieces. As already observed, Community law was in many respects at a turning point. A few days after the delivery of the judgment, the EU and its citizenship were created. The pertinent issues of IP law affected by the discussed cases became regulated in secondary legislation around the same time. The directive on renting and lending rights had already been adopted, however, the Member States still had time to turn it into national law.[54] In little over a week after the judgment was rendered, Directive 93/98 on term of protection was also approved.[55] As noted by Dworkin and Sterling, the judgment in question had repercussions for its implementation, and during its transposition period, also for national rules on the terms of protection and reciprocity which were now subject to directly effective prohibition of discrimination.[56] Still, however, the conclusions on the systemic position of Article 7(1) EEC and its direct effect continue to serve as points of reference for AGs,[57] and for the Court.[58]

---

[51] See D Martin, 'Article 18 TFEU' in M Kellerbauer et al (eds), *The EU Treaties and the Charter of Fundamental Rights: A Commentary* (Oxford, OUP, 2019) 413–23.

[52] See further on the doctrine of direct effect, inter alia, JM Prinssen and A Schrauwen (eds), *Direct Effect: Rethinking a Classic of EC Legal Doctrine* (Netherlands, Europa Law Publishing, 2002).

[53] Paras 32–33 of the Opinion; paras 34–35 of the Judgment.

[54] Council Directive 92/100/EEC of 19 November 1992 on rental right and lending right and on certain rights related to copyright in the field of intellectual property [1992] OJ L346/61.

[55] Council Directive 93/98/EEC of 29 October 1993 harmonizing the term of protection of copyright and certain related rights [1993] OJ L290/9.

[56] G Dworkin and JA Lawrence Sterling, 'Phil Collins and the Term Directive' (1994) 16 *European Intellectual Property Review* 187.

[57] See Opinion of AG La Pergola in Case C-435/95 *Forsberg* ECLI:EU:C:1996:212 paras 13–15; Opinion of AG La Pergola in Case C-323/95 *Hayes* ECLI:EU:C:1997:40, para 8; Opinion of AG Cosmas Case C-160/96 *Molenaar* ECLI:EU:C:1997:599, para 36; Opinion of AG Jacobs in Case C-274/96 *Bickel and Franz* ECLI:EU:C:1998:115 para 26; Opinion of AG Cosmas in Case C-309/96 *Annibaldi* ECLI:EU:C:1997:462, para 21; Opinion of AG Cosmas in Case C-412/97 *ED* ECLI:EU:C:1999:20 para 31; Opinion of AG Ruiz-Jarabo Colomer in Case C-360/00 *Hessen* ECLI:EU:C:2002:128 para 35; Opinion of AG Kokott in Case C-164/07 *Wood* ECLI:EU:C:2008:135 para 32.

[58] See Case C-435/95 *Forsberg* ECLI:EU:C:1996:357 para 14; Case C-323/95 *Hayes* ECLI:EU:C:1997:169 para 16; Case C-360/00 *Hessen* ECLI:EU:C:2002:346 para 31; Case C-28/04 *Tod's* ECLI:EU:C:2005:418 para 18; Case C-53/05 *Commission v Portugal* ECLI:EU:C:2006:448; Case C-427/06 *Bartsch* ECLI:EU:C:2008:517; Case C-581/18 *RB* ECLI:EU:C:2020:453 para 46.

A reminder is fitting that the provision in question is in nature lex specialis. Thus, as noted by AG Jacobs, 'one of the main functions of Article 7 [now Article 18 TFEU] is to close any gaps left by the more specific provisions of the Treaty'.[59] Its residual nature means that it is being employed as a last resort, which in turn means that litigants are more likely to invoke, for instance, what is now Article 34 TFEU in relation to free movement of goods, or today's Article 45(2) TFEU on free movement of workers. This, in turn, means that Article 18(1) TFEU is not as frequent a visitor in the Court as it is the case with other provisions prohibiting discrimination in more specific contexts. Yet, its constitutional value is unquestionable, it now has even a doppelganger in Article 21(2) of the Charter of Fundamental Rights.[60]

---

[59] Para 12 of the Opinion. This conclusion of AG Jacobs was later cited by AG Bobek. See Opinion of AG Bobek in Case C-581/18 *RB* ECLI:EU:C:2020:77, para 51.

[60] Charter of Fundamental Rights of the European Union [2016] OJ C202/391. See further C Kilpatrick and H Eklund, 'Article 21 – Non-Discrimination' in S Peers et al (eds), *The EU Charter of Fundamental Rights: A Commentary*, 2nd edn (CH Beck/Hart Publishing/Nomos, Munich/Oxford/Baden-Baden, 2021).

27

The Relationship between the Action for Annulment and Preliminary Reference Procedures: Opinion of Advocate General Jacobs in TWD

ANGELA WARD AND GRAHAM BUTLER

I. INTRODUCTION

THE complexity of the EU judicial architecture, and the consequences flowing from lacunae remaining therein, came into sharp view in *TWD v Bundesrepublik Deutschland*[1] (*TWD*, sometimes also known as the '*Deggendorf*' or '*TWD Deggendorf*' case). One procedure that was (and is) provided for in EU law is the right to petition the EU courts under the direct action procedures, such as that found in Article 173 EEC (now Article 263 TFEU) – an action for annulment. Another procedural way a case can arise at the EU courts was (and is) the possibility to plead before the judiciary in Member States – the national courts and tribunals – to activate the well-established mechanism of making a request for a preliminary ruling to the Court under Article 177 EEC (now Article 267 TFEU) and question the validity of the relevant EEC (now EU) measure.

Which route to be given priority, for cases to reach the docket of the EU courts,[2] was not addressed by the EU Treaties at the time of *TWD*, and nor has it ever been subsequently. As a result, there was an inevitability to the dispute which ultimately emerged in *TWD*, and which was subject to a classic judgment issued by the Court on 9 March 1994. The case concerned EU state aid law, in which a Commission Decision was addressed to the German Government declaring that state aid granted to a trader, and only that trader, was unlawful.[3] That trader, after having been notified of that Commission Decision by the competent German authorities, then challenged it before a national court in Germany, rather than at the Court through an action for annulment – a direct action – under Article 173 EEC (now Article 263 TFEU), or by seeking damages before the same court under Article 215 EEC (now Article 288 TFEU).

---

[1] Case C-188/92 *TWD* ECLI:EU:C:1994:90.

[2] At the time of *TWD*, the then Court of First Instance only had limited grounds to hear direct actions. Therefore, most direct actions under Article 173 EEC at the time were made to the Court, and not the Court of First Instance as it would today.

[3] Commission Decision 86/509/EEC of 21 May 1986 on aid granted by the Federal Republic of Germany and the Land of Bavaria to a producer of polyamide and polyester yarn situated in *Deggendorf* [1986] OJ L300/34.

The action for annulment procedure, not used in the case at hand, as a matter of primary law, sets down a two-month limit under which an action may be lodged.[4] For TWD, this time limit had expired, yet it still sought relief before the German courts. The EU Treaties were (and are) silent on whether this expiry, by definition, equally blocked any subsequent activation of the reference for preliminary ruling procedure under Article 177 EEC (now Article 267 TFEU).

Less inevitable than this conundrum, however, was the foresight with which this puzzle was addressed in the Opinion of Advocate General (AG) Jacobs[5] and its subsequent adoption by the Court. While the Opinion of AG Jacobs made no express reference to the right of access to a court as protected by Article 6(1) of the European Convention on Human Rights (ECHR), a provision which, by the time of the *TWD* judgment, was a source of general principles and fundamental rights protected by the EU legal order,[6] this imperative ran *sotto voce* beneath the Opinion of the AG, as did the established ECHR rule permitting justified limitations to it.[7]

In short, by advising the Court to rule that the mechanisms established under the reference for a preliminary ruling mechanism was blocked 'only in situations where *locus standi* under Article 173 [EEC (now Article 263 TFEU)] is clear beyond doubt',[8] AG Jacobs guaranteed, into the future, broad access to justice, all the while respecting Articles 173 and 177 EEC (now Articles 263 and 267 TFEU) as autonomous remedies, each of which were subject to their own conditions as to admissibility which were to be maintained and respected.[9] AG Jacobs noted in *TWD* that greater:

> damage to the coherence of the system of remedies would be done if an undertaking were allowed to challenge indirectly, under Article 177 [EEC (now Article 267 TFEU)], a decision against which the appropriate remedy is clearly a direct action under Article 173 [EEC (now Article 263 TFEU)].[10]

While this assertion continues to hold true, this chapter will examine whether the ruling in *TWD*, the essence of which AG Jacobs had proposed in his Opinion, is sufficient to guarantee legal certainty, and therefore, the necessary coherence in judicial remedies to guarantee right of access to a court, now guaranteed by Article 47 of the Charter of Fundamental Rights (CFR), first paragraph, in the complex rule making context of the modern EU. This is questionable, in particular, in the field of composite decision making involving both EU and Member State bodies (not to mention, also, the multi-body scenario that arises in rules into which multiple EU entities have had input). As forward looking as the Opinion of AG Jacobs and the judgment of the Court in *TWD* was, is it sufficient to guarantee rights of access to a court in the context of contemporary rule-making in the modern EU? Thus, consideration might be given, in the form of legislative intervention, or even amendment to the EU Treaties, to shore up a clearly articulated, and thus, accessible guarantee of a right of access to a court in the context of challenge to the legality of EU measures.[11]

---

[4] Article 173 EEC, third paragraph, now Article 263 TFEU, fifth paragraph.
[5] Opinion of AG Jacobs in Case C-188/92 *TWD* ECLI:EU:C:1993:358.
[6] See classically Case 222/84 *Johnston* ECLI:EU:C:1986:206.
[7] Para 18.
[8] Para 26.
[9] Para 13.
[10] Para 20.
[11] See eg the proposals made by S Alonso de Léon, *Composite Administrative Procedures in the European Union* (Madrid, Iustel Publicaciones, 2017) 357 ff. For a detailed analysis, with reference to further secondary sources, of the challenges arising with respect to the right to an effective remedy, as protected under Article 47 CFR, first paragraph, in the context of composite decision making, see the analyses by C Rauchegger and H Hofmann in S Peers, J Kenner, T Hervey, and A Ward (eds), *The EU Charter of Fundamental Rights: A Commentary*, 2nd edn (Oxford, Hart Publishing, 2021) at, respectively, paras 47.36–47.44 and 47.137–47.148.

II. BACKGROUND ISSUES

The first background issue which is essential to understanding the importance of *TWD* in the development of EU administrative law has already been alluded to; namely, the fact that the EEC Treaty was silent (as is the TFEU today) on the relationship between annulment (or nullity) proceedings (formerly Article 173 EEC, now Article 263 TFEU) to be brought directly before what is now known as the EU judicature, and references for a preliminary ruling (formerly Article 177 EEC, now Article 267 TFEU). Was recourse to one of these routes to be favoured over another, and if so, how, and why?

The second background issue concerned why a trader like TWD might have been reluctant to bring an action for annulment before the Court under Article 173 EEC (now Article 263 TFEU), within the two-month time limit set down in the third paragraph of that provision, and elect instead to seek to stop the German authorities from recovering from them the state aid at issue by petitioning the German courts, and seeking a reference for preliminary ruling under Article 177 EEC challenging the relevant Commission Decision, long after the expiry of the aforementioned two-month time limit for bringing proceedings?

Much has been written on the relative advantages and disadvantages of (direct) nullity review (through an action for annulment procedure) over (indirect) validity review (through the preliminary reference procedure).[12] For present purposes, it suffices to underscore that the requirement for establishing *locus standi* to bring nullity proceedings were interpreted, at the outset, by the EU judicature in a conservative manner. The pertinent text of Article 173 EEC through time (now Article 263 TFEU) has remained the same, save for an amendment introduced under the Treaty of Lisbon in 2009.[13] Article 263 TFEU reflects Article 173 EEC, in so far as it states that any 'natural or legal person may, under the conditions laid down in the first and second paragraphs, institute proceedings against an act addressed to that person or which is of direct and individual concern to them', and the interpretation of both 'individual' and 'direct' concern has barely altered since the early case law.[14]

With regard to the original Article 173 EEC, the Court issued its seminal ruling in *Plaumann* in 1963,[15] and has maintained its essence to date. For example, with regard to 'individual concern', the Court has reiterated as recently as 2021, that:

> it is apparent from the settled case-law of the Court that a natural or legal person can be individually concerned by a provision of general application only if that provision affects him or her by reasons of certain attributes which are peculiar to him or her or by reason of circumstances in which he or she is differentiated from all other persons, and by virtue of these factors distinguishes him or her individually just as in the case of a person to whom an act is addressed.[16]

---

[12] On the virtue of validity challenge brought under Article 267 TFEU see recently eg C-689/19 P *VodafoneZiggo Group* ECLI:EU:C:2021:142, paras 143–152. See also eg D Leczykiewicz, '"Effective Judicial Protection" of Human Rights After Lisbon: Should National Courts be Empowered to Review EU Secondary Law' (2010) 35 *ELRev* 326; S Peers and M Costa, 'Judicial Review of EU after the Treaty of Lisbon' (2012) 8 *EuConst* 82.

[13] Treaty of Lisbon amending the Treaty on European Union and the Treaty establishing the European Community, signed at Lisbon, 13 December 2007 [2007] OJ C306/1.

[14] For a recent exposition of the principles appertaining to direct concern see Opinion of AG Hogan in Case C-872/19 P *Venezuela v Council* ECLI:EU:C:2021:37.

[15] Case 25/62 *Plaumann* ECLI:EU:C:1963:17.

[16] Case C-297/20 *Sabo* ECLI:EU:C:2021:24, para 26, referring to Case 25/62 *Plaumann*; Case C-583/11 P *Inuit* ECLI:EU:C:2013:625, para 72. The case law was relaxed with respect to the loss of specific acquired rights C-309/89 *Codorníu* ECLI:EU:C:1994:197, referred to by the Court, recently, in, for example, Case C-297/20 *Sabo*, para 11. The Court has also held that 'where a decision 'affects a group of persons who were identified or identifiable when that measure was adopted by reason of criteria specific to the members of the group, those persons may be individually concerned by that measure inasmuch as they form part of a limited class of economic operators'. See Case C-362/06 P *Markku Sahlstedt* ECLI:EU:C:2009:243, para 30, referring to Case C-125/06 P *Infront WM AG* ECLI:EU:C:2008:159, para 71. Otherwise, the case law has remained, largely, static.

With respect to direct concern, the case law has remained similarly constant. The condition of 'direct concern' means that:

> the measure must, first, directly affect the legal situation of the individual and, second, leave no discretion to the addressees of that measure who are entrusted with the task of implementing it, such implementation being purely automatic and resulting from EU rules alone without the application of other intermediate rules.[17]

Both of these rules governed access to nullity proceedings under Article 173 EEC (now Article 263 TFEU) at the time of the litigation culminating in the ruling in *TWD*, and neither of them would have encouraged TWD to activate the direct route to the Court provided by the then Article 173 EEC (now Article 263 TFEU), within the two-month time limit provided by the third paragraph of that provision. Moreover, neither of them apply to validity proceedings brought before courts or tribunals in Member States.[18]

It is worth noting the high threshold for securing standing in nullity proceedings, which these two lines of case law embedded into the judicial architecture has, to date, not been attenuated by arguments appertaining to an applicant's right to effective judicial protection, by virtue of their right of access to a court or otherwise. Indeed, it is established in the case law that Article 47 CFR

> is not intended to change the system of judicial review laid down by the Treaties, and particularly the rules relating to the admissibility of direct actions brought before the Courts of the European Union, as is apparent also from the explanations relating to Article 47, which must, in accordance with the third subparagraph of Article 6(1) TEU and Article 52(7) of the Charter, be taken into consideration when interpreting the Charter.[19]

Even though it has been stated in the case law that the conditions of admissibility under the fourth paragraph of Article 263 TFEU 'must be interpreted in the light of the fundamental right to effective judicial protection, as enshrined in Article 47 [CFR]', the Court has underscored that 'such an interpretation cannot have the effect of setting aside those conditions, which are expressly laid down in the [TFEU]'.[20] According to the Court, the EU Treaties have established a complete system of legal remedies and procedures designed to ensure judicial review of the legality of EU acts.[21] Not even a claim that an act infringes fundamental rights is sufficient in itself for it to be established that an action brought by an individual is admissible,[22] and nor can concerns over access to justice in environmental matters modify the rules on admissibility for actions for annulment under the fourth paragraph of Article 263 TFEU.[23]

Finally, the only amendment to the text of the EU Treaties that relaxes the rules on *locus standi* for nullity proceedings has been interpreted by the Court in minimalist fashion.[24]

---

[17] Case C-352/19 P *Région de Bruxelles-Capitale* ECLI:EU:C:2020:978, para 30, referring to Case C-404/96 P *Glencore Grain* ECLI:EU:C:1998:196, para 41; Joined Cases C-663/17 P, C-665/17 P and C-669/17 P *ECB v Trasta Komercbanka* ECLI:EU:C:2019:923, para 103.

[18] In validity actions before courts and tribunals in Member States, procedural issues are governed by Member State law, subject to the principles of equivalence and effectiveness. See eg Case C-212/94 *FMC* ECLI:EU:C:1996:40. This includes *locus standi*, see eg Case C-510/13 *E.ON Földgáz Trade* ECLI:EU:C:2015:189.

[19] Case C-689/19 P *VodafoneZiggo Group*, para 136, referring to Case C-456/13P *T & L Sugars* ECLI:EU:C:2015:284, para 43, Case C-599/15 P *Romania v Commission* ECLI:EU:C:2017:801, para 68.

[20] Case C-461/18 P *Changmao Biochemical Engineering* ECLI:EU:C:2020:979, para 55.

[21] Case C-650/18 *Hungary v Parliament* ECLI:EU:C:2021:426, para 34 and the case law cited. The notion of 'complete system of legal remedies and procedures' originated in Case 294/83 *Les Verts* ECLI:EU:C:1986:166, para 23.

[22] Case C-297/20 *Sabo*, para 29 and the case law cited. See further Leczykiewicz (n 12).

[23] See eg Case C-352/19 P *Région de Bruxelles-Capitale*, para 26.

[24] See eg R Mastroianni, A Pezza, 'Striking the Right Balance: Limits on the Right to Bring an Action under Article 263(4) of the Treaty on the Functioning of the European Union' (2015) 30 *American University International*

The Treaty of Lisbon of 2009 added that any 'natural or legal person may, under the conditions laid down in the first and second paragraphs, institute proceedings ... against a regulatory act which is of direct concern to them and does not entail implementing measures'.[25] It suffices to say for present purposes that, had this amendment been in place at the time of the ruling in *TWD*, it would not have been relevant either to the Court's reasoning or the outcome of the case.

III. THE OPINION OF AG JACOBS

The Opinion of AG Jacobs commenced with the following:

> This case raises an important question of principle concerning the system of remedies established by the EEC Treaty: namely, whether a recipient of State aid which the Commission has declared unlawful may, when called upon by the national authorities to repay the aid in accordance with the Commission's decision, challenge the validity of that decision before the national courts and before the Court of Justice on a reference from the national court under Article 177 of the Treaty, even though it failed to challenge the Commission's decision in the Court of Justice directly under Article 173 of the Treaty.[26]

TWD was the recipient of state aid in the early 1980s. The Commission subsequently decided that, under Article 93(3) EEC (Article 108(3) TFEU), an unnamed 'producer of polyamide and polyester yarn situated in Deggendorf' had received aid that was incompatible with the internal market. TWD were made aware of the Commission Decision by the relevant German authorities, and the bases on which it might lodge an action for annulment against the Commission Decision under Article 173 EEC (now Article 263 TFEU). It did not do so, and nor did Germany, the recipient of the Commission Decision.

When Germany sought to recoup the aid that had been unlawfully provided to TWD, the latter applied to a German court seeking a judicial remedy against that national decision; a measure which was, in effect, following from the Commission Decision. In other words, the national decision and the Commission Decision were intertwined. The national court, the Higher Administrative Court for North Rhine-Westphalia (*Oberverwaltungsgericht für das Land Nordrhein-Westfalen*) referred two questions for preliminary ruling, the second concerning the substance of the case, with the first inquiring into its own authority to adjudicate on the dispute. That question was worded as follows:

> Is a national court bound by a decision of the EEC Commission adopted pursuant to Article 93(2) of the EEC Treaty when hearing an appeal regarding the implementation of that decision by the national authorities brought by the recipient of the aid and addressee of the implementation measures on the ground that the decision of the EEC Commission is unlawful in circumstances where the recipient of the aid did not institute proceedings under the second paragraph of Article 173 of the EEC Treaty, or did not do so in good time, even though it was informed of the Commission's decision in writing by the Member State?

Law Review 443; P-A Van Malleghem, N Baeten, 'Before the Law Stands & Gatekeeper-Or What is a 'Regulatory Act' in Article 263(4) TFEU? Inuit Tapiriit Kanatami' (2014) 51 *CMLRev* 1187.

[25] See eg Joined Cases C-622/16 P to C-624/16 P *Scuola Elementare Maria Montessori v Commission* ECLI:EU:C:2018:873. Among the numerous contributions on this topic see eg Van Mallegham, Baeten (n 24); DF Waelbroeck and T Bombois, 'Des requérants "privilégés et des autres ... À propos de l'arrêt Inuit et de l'exigence de protection juridictionnelle effective des particuliers en droit européen' [2014] *Cahiers de droit européen* 21.

[26] Para 1.

AG Jacobs observed that this problem was not resolved by pre-existing case law. On the one hand, *Universität Hamburg v Hauptzollamt Halburg-Kehrwieder*,[27] on which reliance has been placed by *TWD* and the French Government, differed from the proceedings in *TWD*, because the decision at issue in that case was addressed to all the Member States, and was of a general nature. But the decision at issue in the *TWD* case was addressed to a single Member State, and was concerned exclusively with aid granted to a single undertaking.[28] On the other hand, the judgment in *Commission v Belgium*, on which the Commission had relied to refute *TWD*'s interpretation of the remedies available to it, was viewed by AG Jacobs as having 'no direct bearing on the present case', because that ruling precluded validity challenge by a Member State with respect to a Commission Decision which had been addressed to it.[29]

For AG Jacobs, the basic principle had to be that Articles 173 and 177 (now Articles 263 and 267 TFEU) provided for autonomous remedies, each of which was subject to its own conditions of admissibility. If the addressee of an individual decision were allowed to challenge it in the national courts, the two month limitation period laid down in the third paragraph of Article 173 EEC (now Article 263 TFEU) would be deprived of any significance.[30] At the other extreme, an individual who was adversely affected by a general measure, but who might have difficulty in establishing direct and individual concern, as required by the second subparagraph of Article 173 EEC (now Article 263 TFEU), should not be prevented from challenging such a measure indirectly on the ground of failure to mount a direct challenge which might have been declared inadmissible.[31] This analysis was supported by the plea of illegality provided for in Article 184 EEC (now Article 277 TFEU), which the case law was already suggesting applied beyond EEC regulations, despite the wording of Article 184 EEC (now Article 277 TFEU), the plea being available with respect normative measures which natural or legal persons would not be able to attach under Article 173 EEC (now Article 263 TFEU).[32]

AG Jacobs concluded that the case was situated somewhere between these two extremes. The Commission Decision at issue was not addressed to TWD. At the same time; it was not a general measure, but was rather individual in nature. It was concerned solely with the aid granted by the German authorities to TWD in 1983 and 1984. Although not referred to in the Commission Decision, it was clearly identified in its terms. Thus, TWD was the only undertaking directly affected by the Commission's Decision, and not by virtue of its membership of a category of undertaking, so that,

> there cannot be any doubt that TWD would have been able to satisfy the requirements of direct and individual concern under the second paragraph of Article 173.[33]

AG Jacobs referred to *Philip Morris v Commission*,[34] and the Opinion of AG Darmon in *Deuful v Commission*,[35] in noting that the Court had expressly recognised that the recipient of

---

[27] Case 216/82 *Universität Hamburg* ECLI:EU:C:1983:248.

[28] Para 12.

[29] ibid.

[30] Para 13.

[31] Para 14.

[32] ibid. AG Jacobs referred, in this regard, to Case 216/82 *Universität Hamburg*; Case 92/78 *Simmenthal* ECLI:EU:C:1979:53, paras 39–40; Case 294/83 *Les Verts* ECLI:EU:C:1986:166.

[33] Para 15 of the Opinion.

[34] Case 730/79 *Philip Morris* ECLI:EU:C:1980:209, para 5.

[35] Opinion of AG Darmon in Case 310/85 *Deufil* ECLI:EU:C:1986:475, p 913.

aid is directly and individually concerned by a Commission Decision declaring the aid incompatible with the common market.[36] In consequence, for AG Jacobs:

> the present type of case should be treated as analogous to a case in which an individual measure is contested by the person to whom it is addressed, with the result that the failure to mount a direct challenge under Article 173 precludes an indirect challenge under Article 177.[37]

Thus, AG Jacobs stated that the two-month limitation period provided by the third paragraph of Article 173 EEC (now Article 263 TFEU) 'would be deprived of all sense and purpose if a person who undoubtedly has *locus standi* to challenge a decision under Article 173 could simply ignore the decision and contest its validity in subsequent proceedings brought to enforce the decision'.[38] For AG Jacobs, the purpose of this short limitation period was promoting legal certainty.[39] The principle that any measure, including normative ones, which produces binding legal effects, must be amenable to some form of challenge by persons who are adversely affected by it, did not justify derogating from the principle of legal certainty in favour of persons who 'undoubtedly had *locus standi* to contest an individual measure directly but omitted to do so'.[40]

Further, for AG Jacobs, there were no particular policy reasons militating in favour of permitting an undertaking in TWD's position to have a second opportunity to challenge a decision that it had failed to contest within the prescribed two month time limit. On the contrary, he stated that, 'the maximum *vigilantibus non dormientibus subveniunt jura* should be applied'.[41] There had been no denial of justice in the present case because TWD was informed of the Commission Decision by the German Government.[42] It was not necessary, therefore, to

> consider the difficult question whether the limitation period under Article 173 would have been set in motion by the publication of the decision in the Official Journal on 24 October 1986, even if TWD had not been expressly informed of it until a later date. What matters is that TWD had actual knowledge of the decision and failed to take the necessary steps to initiate the appropriate procedure for challenging it.[43]

The remainder of the Opinion of AG Jacobs was devoted to addressing the virtue of the Article 173 EEC (now Article 263 TFEU) procedure, as opposed to that established under Article 177 EEC (now Article 267 TFEU), for dealing with the circumstances of the case before him. He observed that an action for annulment under Article 173 EEC (now Article 263 TFEU) involved a full exchange of pleadings, as opposed to a single round of observations, as was the case under validity review as supplied under Article 177 EEC (now Article 267 TFEU), the latter procedure being essentially concerned with ruling on questions of law. Yet the validity on an individual decision, particularly concerning state aids, as was in issue in the *TWD* case, often depended on questions of fact, and sometimes complex issues entailing the assessment of economic data.[44] These considerations, along with 'the need to preserve the coherence of the system of remedies'[45] was strengthened by the creation of the Court of First Instance

---

[36] ibid, para 15.
[37] Para 16.
[38] Para 17.
[39] Para 18.
[40] ibid.
[41] Para 19.
[42] Para 24.
[43] ibid.
[44] Para 20.
[45] Para 22.

(now General Court), established for the specific purpose of reviewing individual decisions in proceedings initiated by natural and legal persons. Removal of proceedings from the competent court would result, if a decision which should in principle be reviewable in the Court of First Instance, could be challenged in the national court.[46]

AG Jacobs refuted arguments to the effect that the solution he was proposing would divest the national courts of their prerogative to refer questions to the Court under Article 177 EEC (now Article 267 TFEU). He took the view that such arguments disregarded the definitive character of an individual decision which had not been challenged under the appropriate procedure within the relevant time limit by any of the persons who had *locus standi* for such an action, and disregarded the fact that a direct action under Article 173 EEC was 'the proper remedy for contesting an individual decision that has no normative effects'.[47] At this juncture too, the theme of 'coherence' was evident. AG Jacobs concluded that it 'would be wrong to impair the coherence of the system of remedies for the sake of preserving the supposedly unfettered power of national courts to question the validity of any decision adopted by a Community institution'.[48]

Finally, AG Jacobs answered the objection to the effect that the '*TWD* rule', or the '*TWD* doctrine', as it became known, would oblige national courts to determine whether the person in question was directly and individually concerned by a decision before they will know whether they have jurisdiction to examine the decision's validity and refer the matter to the Court, thereby obliging the national court to resolve a complex preliminary issue.[49] There was no such difficulty in a case like the present one

> where TWD's *locus standi* under Article 173 cannot have been in any doubt. … it is only in situations where *locus standi* under Article 173 is clear beyond doubt that the availability of a direct action under that provision should preclude a natural or legal person from challenging indirectly a decision addressed to another person.[50]

There were certain decisions that could only be contested in a direct action under Article 173 EEC (now Article 263 TFEU),[51] and the approach advocated in the Opinion of AG Jacobs was 'further commended by the consideration that the rights of individuals should not be prejudiced as a result of uncertainty in the law'.[52]

IV. ANALYSIS

A. The Judgment

The Court ruled that if a Commission Decision can be challenged within the time limit imposed by Article 173 EEC (now Article 263 TFEU), then that time limit became definitive.[53]

---

[46] ibid, at para 23 the AG also referred to the, at the time, recent extension of the jurisdiction of the Court of First Instance, referring to Council Decision of 8 June 1993 amending Council Decision 88/591/ECSC, EEC, Euratom establishing a Court of First Instance of the European Communities (93/350/ECSC, EEC, Euratom) [1993] OJ L144/21.

[47] Para 25.

[48] ibid.

[49] Para 26.

[50] ibid.

[51] Para 25.

[52] Para 26.

[53] Para 13.

Echoing AG Jacobs, the Court held the case law to date had been guided by legal certainty.[54] However, whereas AG Jacobs said that challenging measures through the preliminary reference procedure, rather than a an action for annulment procedure, was not permissible when a party could use the direct action when '[a] producer was never in doubt' about the identity of a party that an EU legal act is targeted at,[55] or 'a person who undoubtedly has *locus standi*' to bring an action under Article 173 EEC (now Article 263 TFEU),[56] the Court, whilst agreeing in principle, opted for different language.

Instead, the Court stated it is not possible for parties

> who could have challenged that decision and who allowed the mandatory time-limit laid down in this regard by the third paragraph of Article 173 [EEC (now Article 267 TFEU)] to expire, to call in question the lawfulness of that decision before the national courts in an action brought against the measures taken by the national authorities for implementing that decision.[57]

Thereafter, the Court, again reasoning similarly to AG Jacobs, held that in the case at hand, the party, TWD, was 'fully aware'[58] of the Commission Decision, and that it was therefore possible for it to exercise rights available to it under Article 173 EEC (now Article 263 TFEU), yet did not do so. As per the Court, 'it is common ground that the applicant in the main proceedings was fully aware of the Commission's [D]ecision and of the fact that it could without any doubt have challenged it under Article 173 of the Treaty'.[59]

In essence, the Court, much like AG Jacobs, stood behind the legal certainty of the time limit established by Article 177 EEC (now Article 263 TFEU), and case-specific knowledge of the rights of the parties in such situations. The operative part of the Judgment stated that:

> The national court is bound by a Commission decision adopted under Article 93 (2) of the Treaty where, in view of the implementation of that decision by the national authorities, the recipient of the aid to which the implementation measures are addressed brings before it an action in which it pleads the unlawfulness of the Commission's decision and where that recipient of aid, although informed in writing by the Member State of the Commission's decision, did not bring an action against that decision under the second paragraph of Article 173 of the Treaty, or did not do so within the period prescribed.

B. Access to a Court in the EU Legal Order and a Question of Procedure

TWD was initially a state aid case, but in light of the finding that there was a bar to proceedings in a preliminary reference procedure if an action for annulment procedure was possible, the case lost its value as a state aid judgment. Instead, it has become a seminal doctrine of EU administrative law, and EU procedural law. Moreover, the case has come to be known as an essential part of the jurisprudence about access to a court of law, as a matter of EU law.

The right of access to a court is, perhaps, the most fundamental of all fundamental rights. For absent the backing of the rule of law, rights risk dilution to the status of aspiration, with those unpersuaded by the need for their observance left free to flout them with impunity.[60]

---

[54] Paras 16–17.
[55] Para 3.
[56] Para 17.
[57] Para 17.
[58] Para 24.
[59] ibid.
[60] As Lord Neuberger, the former President of the UK Supreme Court, aptly put it, 'Once you deprive people of the right to go to court to challenge the government, you are in a dictatorship'. See Opinion of AG Tanchev in

On numerous occasions, the Court has recognised the right of access to a court as a core component of the right to 'an effective remedy before a tribunal', as now protected by Article 47 CFR, first paragraph of the Charter of Fundamental Rights.[61] Yet, the question of such access was destined, at the outset, to be a more complex matter in the EU polity than it was in the Member States, largely due to certain enigmatically constructed elements of the judicial architecture of the EU, as drafted in the original treaties,[62] combined with the system of executive federalism equally established therein, in which Member States were primarily responsible for the implementation of EEC, then EC, then EU laws, with instances of centralised administration of EU rules remaining the exception.[63]

Whilst TWD were denied the right to challenge the validity of the pertinent EU legal act, the Opinion of AG Jacobs and the ruling of the Court crafted the *TWD* doctrine on ensuring that either direct (action for annulment procedure) or indirect (preliminary reference procedure) were available to parties that were affected by EU legal acts. Because of the specificity of the Commission Decision at issue, both were of the view that only one route was theoretically available. At the essence of the *TWD* case, therefore, was the right to judicial review, in some way or another; that is to say, parties have a right to a judicial remedy, but it is with every right for EU law to determine the modalities of procedure governing the possibility of such judicial review, and narrowing them to just one over another.

There is an additional element, however, along with the right of access to a court, which was equally prevalent in the Opinion of AG Jacobs. That was the need for legal certainty in the designation of judicial remedies. It has long since been established in the case law of the European Court of Human Rights (ECtHR), such as in its ruling in *de la Pradelle v France*,[64] that if a system of remedies is of 'such complexity' so as 'to create legal uncertainty' violation of Article 6(1) ECHR can result.[65] In short, applicants are 'entitled to expect a coherent system' of judicial review that achieves a fair balance between the authorities' interests and that of their own, resulting in 'a clear, practical and effective opportunity to challenge an administrative act'.[66] AG Hogan recently observed in *Bank Refah Kargaran* that such coherence is necessary and inherent in any system of effective judicial protection.[67]

Access to a court is not always a *de facto* given, even within the EU legal order. Outside the Court, EU institutions (and bodies, offices, and agencies) continue to try and deny individuals access to judicial remedies. A case in point here in that of *SatCen v KF*.[68] Here, the EU agency

---

Case C-824/18 *A.B.* ECLI:EU:C:2020:1053, para 1. See recently on 'the hurdle of justiciability' with respect to economic, social, and cultural rights, J Resnik, 'Courts and Economic, Social, and Cultural Rights' in KG Young (ed), *The Future of Economic and Social Rights* (Cambridge, CUP, 2019) 259.

[61] See classically Case 222/84 *Johnston* (n 6). See more recently, for example, *Opinion 1/17* ECLI:EU:C:2019:341, para 190; Case C-682/15 *Berlioz Investment Fund* ECLI:EU:C:2017:373; Case C-93/12 *ET Agrokonsulting-04* ECLI:EU:C:2013:432. For a detailed analysis of Article 47 CFR, including its role in protection rights of access to a court, see the chapter edited by A Ward in Peers, Hervey, Kenner, and Ward (n 11).

[62] See notably Articles 173, 177, and 215 EEC Treaty.

[63] M Eliantonio and N Vogiatzis, 'Judicial and Extra-Judicial Challenges in the EU-Multi- and Cross-Level Administrative Framework' (2021) 22 *GLJ* 315, 315, referring to R Schütze, 'From Rome to Lisbon: "Executive Federalism" in the (New) European Union' (2010) 47 *CMLRev* 1385.

[64] *De Geouffre de la Pradelle v France* App no 12964/87 (ECtHR, 16.12.1992).

[65] Para 33 of Judgment in *De Geouffre de la Pradelle*.

[66] ibid, para 34.

[67] Opinion of AG Hogan in Case C-134/19 P *Bank Refah Kargaran* ECLI:EU:C:2020:396, para 61, referring to the ruling of the Court in Case C-72/15 *Rosneft* ECLI:EU:C:2017:236, para 78. See G Butler and RA Wessel, 'Jurisdiction of the Court for Non-Contractual Liability and Actions for Damages Claims within the CFSP: *Bank Refah Kargaran*' in G Butler and RA Wessel (eds), *EU External Relations Law: The Cases in Context* (Oxford, Hart Publishing, 2022).

[68] Case C-14/19 P *SatCen v KF* ECLI:EU:C:2020:492, and previously Case T-286/15 *KF v SatCen* ECLI:EU:T:2018:718.

attempted to argue that the General Court had erred by accepting jurisdiction to review and annul a decision of an appeals board established by the Staff Regulations of the Agency. The Council intervened in support of the Agency, pleading inadmissibility. It was quite apparent that, other than going to the EU courts, the applicant had nowhere to turn to after the SatCen Appeal Board – an administrative review body – had decided the case before it. No national court could have jurisdiction over the EU Agency's appeal board, and thus, the General Court and Court ruled, in effect, that a judicial remedy had to be guaranteed, by insisting on the jurisdiction of the EU courts in such cases.[69]

In other cases, there can be difficulty in accessing the EU courts in other ways, such as where there is some level of discrepancy between contractual and non-contractual matters. For example, an action for annulment is a direct action mechanism in Article 263 TFEU concerning non-contractual matters. By contrast, there is the arbitration clause mechanism, another form of direct action in Article 272 TFEU concerning contractual matters. There are no provisions in the EU Treaties to delimit non-contractual matters from contractual matters, and the procedures that follow. This has given rise to difficulties about the appropriate basis upon which certain cases are to be litigated, such as *SC v Eulex Kosovo*,[70] but the issues go back further than that.[71] Such confusion continues, given there have been cases where applicants, as occured in *JF v EUCAP Somalia*,[72] have lodged a case on one basis, but offered an alternative legal basis if the former did not satisfy the General Court as regards its admissibility.

Moreover, what happens when the EU courts have only the ability to hear parts of a case, and national courts other parts of a case, owing to different clauses in different consecutive contractual arrangements? In *Jenkinson*, it was pleaded by several EU parties as respondents that part of the contractual arrangements between themselves and an individual would fall outside of the jurisdiction of the EU courts, and that national courts would instead have jurisdiction for part of the claims in issue.[73] In ensuring effective remedies at the EU courts, the Court was unwilling to entertain such a denial of protection for a person who was an employee of the Union; and ruled that the EU courts had jurisdiction to examine the entire period of time in which the applicant was employed on rolling contracts.

In *National Iranian Tanker Company v Council*,[74] the Court, although not seized of a problem with respect to right of access to a court, was asked to rule on the compatibility with Article 47 of the Charter, first paragraph, of a nullity remedy issued by the General Court, when the relevant EU institution had responded to the nullity declaration by re-taking a decision imposing restrictive measures against the Republic of Iran, thereby re-listing it as a person or entity whose assets had to be frozen. The Court held, *inter alia*, that

> [the] principle of effective judicial protection cannot prevent the Council from reinstating a person or entity on the lists of persons and entities whose assets are to be frozen on the basis of reasons other than those on which the initial listing was based, or for the same reason based on other evidence.

---

[69] See G Butler, 'Hidden Administrative Review in EU Law: The BoAs of EU Agencies in the Common Foreign and Security Policy' in M Chamon, A Volpato, and M Eliantonio (eds), *Boards of Appeal of EU Agencies: Towards Judicialization of Administrative Review?* (Oxford, OUP, 2022).

[70] See, in particular Opinion of AG Tanchev in Case C-730/18 P *SC v Eulex Kosovo* ECLI:EU:C:2020:176.

[71] For a fuller overview of the case law on this point see G Butler, 'The EU's Contractual Relations and the Arbitration Clause: Disputes at the Court of Justice of the European Union' (2021) 46 *ELRev* 345, 358–62.

[72] Case T-194/20 *JF v EUCAP Somalia*, ECLI:EU:T:2022:454.

[73] See Case C-43/17 P *Jenkinson* ECLI:EU:C:2018:531. See also Opinion of AG Szpunar in Case C-43/17 P *Jenkinson* ECLI:EU:C:2018:231.

[74] Case C-600/16 P *National Iranian Tanker Company* ECLI:EU:C:2018:966.

The purpose of that principle is to ensure that an act adversely affecting an entity may be challenged before the courts, and not to prevent the adoption of a new act adversely affecting that entity, based on different reasons or evidence.[75]

Alas, the complete system of legal remedies and procedures will continue to be an ongoing process of assessment and re-evaluation.

C. A 'Without Any Doubt' Test, and Complex Rule-making in the Modern EU

The terminology appearing in subsequent judgments of the Court reflecting on the *TWD* rule, or *TWD* doctrine, has not been entirely consistent over time. Sometimes, the Court is faithful to the text of its own case law by stating that 'it is only if it could be held that a legal person … is undoubtedly directly and individually concerned', that they will be entitled to institute validity review with respect to the same EU measure.[76] Whilst on occasion, however, it has ruled on whether the person concerned was 'indisputably' directly and individually concerned,[77] or whether or not a decision was 'unquestionably' of direct and individual concern to an applicant.[78]

However, whatever the terminology employed, the essence of the *TWD* rule has remained the same. The maximum *vigilantibus non dormientibus subveniunt jura* continues to prevail, so that those confronted with no apparent legal impediments to issuing nullity proceedings under Article 263 TFEU, fourth paragraph, will be stopped from pursuing their claim via the route of validity review under the preliminary reference procedure in Article 267 TFEU at a date subsequent to the two-month time limit still in place, but which now appears in Article 263 TFEU, fifth paragraph.

This interpretation of the term 'clear beyond doubt' is the fruit of academic analysis, rather than further elaboration in the case law of the Court. As pointed out, not long after the judgment in *TWD* was delivered, it was held that '[i]t is only really in the areas of anti-dumping, state aids and competition law that concrete principles have been established'.[79] It is perhaps fair to say that the same applies to date.[80] Aside from suggesting that it will be relevant whether an applicant seeking to rely on validity review is 'seeking to circumvent the definitive nature' of the decision it seeks to impugn,[81] it is difficult to discern any new principle elaborating upon the rule developed in *TWD*.

Moreover, it is important to underscore, as did AG Jacobs in his Opinion, that the facts of *TWD* made it an 'easy' case, in the sense that TWD was informed of a narrowly circumscribed Commission Decision of which it was the only trader affected. Yet lingering questions were evident about the precedential value of *TWD*. Did the *TWD* rule apply when two, three, or

---

[75] ibid, para 54. For a detailed analysis of the requirements in the context of the right to an effective remedy see Opinion of AG Tanchev in Case C-600/16 P *National Iranian Tanker Company* ECLI:EU:C:2018:227, paras 111–28.

[76] Case C-232/14 *Portmeirion Group* ECLI:EU:C:2016:180, para 24.

[77] Case C-550/09 *E and F* ECLI:EU:C:2010:382, para 50.

[78] Case C-414/18 *Iccrea Banca* ECLI:EU:C:2019:1036, para 65.

[79] M Hoskins, 'Case C-188/92, TWD Textilwerke Deggendorf GmbH v. Bundesrepublik Deutschland, Judgment of 9 March 1994, [1994] ECR I-833.' (1994) 31 *CMLRev* 1399, 1406. The distinctions in the field of dumping law can still, however, be fine. See Case C-143/14 *TMK Europe* ECLI:EU:C:2015:236, paras 22 ff. For a comprehensive analysis see Opinion of AG Pitruzzella in Case C-251/18 *Trace Sport* ECLI:EU:C:2019:295. The *TWD* rule continues to arise in disputes concerning state aid. See eg Case C-667/13 *Banco Privado Português* ECLI:EU:C:2015:151, para 29.

[80] See eg Case C-135/16 *Georgsmarienhütte* ECLI:EU:C:2018:582.

[81] Case C-667/13 *Banco Privado Português*, para 29.

more traders were affected by a Commission Decision addressed to a Member State? What was the position when a trader had not been informed of such a Commission Decision? Later, more difficult cases gave hints on how these questions would be answered.

Most importantly for the present chapter, the ruling in *TWD* was an example of 'simple' decision making, on which the only organ involved was the Commission, which issued a single definitive decision. How would the *TWD* rule apply in instances of complex decision making in which multiple EU bodies were involved, and/or Member State entities? The latter question was addressed by the Court in *Borelli v Commission* in 1992,[82] prior to *TWD*. This was a judgment that has remained pivotal in rulings concerning multi-body decision making in EU law.

In *Borelli*, the Italian authorities informed the Commission by letter of 19 January 1990 that the Regional Council of Liguria had issued an unfavourable opinion on 18 January 1990 (the 'national opinion') in respect of an application for aid from the European Agricultural Guidance and Guarantee Fund made by Borelli. By memorandum of 25 February 1992 ('the contested decision'), the Commission's Directorate-General (DG) for Agriculture informed Borelli that its project could not be admitted to the procedure for the grant of aid due to the unfavourable national opinion of Regional Council of Liguria. Because of this, the conditions laid in Article 13(3) of Regulation No 355/77[83] were not fulfilled. By order of 25 February 1992, the Court of First Instance (now the General Court) declared it did not have jurisdiction to hear the applicant in so far as it concerned the Regional Council of Liguria; a position that could not be altered by the fact that the national opinion formed part of a Community decision-making procedure, given that a national opinion was binding on the Community decision-taking authority and therefore determined the Community decision to be adopted. In other words, due to the binding nature of the national opinion, the CFI had no jurisdiction over the contested decision.

Any irregularity that might affect the national opinion could not affect the validity of the Commission Decision refusing aid. Thus, on the basis of the requirement of judicial control of any decision of a national authority, as established in *Johnston v RUC*,[84] and as reflected in Articles 6 and 13 ECHR,[85] it was for the national court, where appropriate, after obtaining a preliminary ruling from the Court, to rule on the lawfulness of the national opinion at issue on the same terms on which they review any definitive measure adopted by the same national authorities which are capable of adversely affecting third parties. That is so, even if the domestic procedure does not provide for it.[86] Since the opinion of the Regional Council of Liguria formed part of a procedure which led to the adoption of a Community decision, Italy was obliged to comply with the requirement of judicial control.[87] Or, as AG Darmon observed, the national opinion of the Regional Council of Liguria could not be construed as an intermediate measure against which redress is only available in an action brought against the final measure.[88]

---

[82] Case C-97/91 *Borelli* ECLI:EU:C:1992:491. See further eg F Brito Bastos, 'The Borelli Doctrine Revisited: Three Issues of Coherence in a Landmark Ruling for EU Administrative Justice' (2015) 8 *Review of European Administrative Law* 269; F Brito Bastos, 'Judicial review of composite administrative procedures in the Single Supervisory Mechanism: *Berlusconi*' (2019) 56 *CMLRev* 1355.

[83] Council Regulation (EEC) No 355/77 of 15 February 1977 on Common Measures to Improve the Conditions under Which Agricultural Products Are Processed and Marketed [1977] OJ L51/1.

[84] Case 222/84 *Johnston* (n 6).

[85] Para 14 of Judgment in *Borelli*.

[86] Para 13 of Judgment in *Borelli*.

[87] Para 15 of Judgment in *Borelli*.

[88] Opinion of AG Darmon in Case C-97/91 *Borelli* ECLI:EU:C:1992:254, para 32.

As was observed many years later by AG Campos Sánchez-Bordona in his Opinion in *Berlusconi and Fininvest*, the *Borelli* principle, combined with its mirror image ruling on EU competence, namely *Sweden v Commission*,[89] boiled down to the following:

> With regard to determining the applicable system of judicial review, both the *Borelli* case-law and the *Sweden* v *Commission* case-law address the specific distribution of competences between the national authorities and the EU institutions. Where the decision-making power lies with national authorities, the *Borelli* case-law applies; where it rests with the EU authority, the *Sweden* v *Commission* case-law applies.[90]

The tension, however, that this principle creates, in terms of legal certainty is starting to splinter through the case law of the Court, and is evidenced most notably in the rulings *Liivimaa Lihaveis MTÜ*,[91] and *Berlusconi and Fininvest*.[92]

In *Liivimaa Lihaveis MTÜ*, the Tartu Regional Court in Estonia posed the sensible question of whether it, or the General Court, should be hearing a challenge to refusal to award EU funding that was made by a joint Latvian/Estonian monitoring committee, a body that formed part of a complex and multi-stage decision-making process set up under EU legislation.[93] Moreover, the rules of the monitoring committee purported to preclude all judicial review of refusal of the EU aid in question, which was challenged by the applicants as being inconsistent with Article 47 of the Charter, first paragraph.

In *Liivimaa Lihaveis MTÜ*, the Court held, in reliance of the ruling in *Borelli*,[94] that a monitoring committee set as part of an operational programme to promote European territorial cooperation, is not an institution or a body, office or agency of the EU pursuant to the first paragraph of Article 263 TFEU,[95] so that the EU courts had no jurisdiction to rule on the lawfulness of a measure adopted by that monitoring committee.[96] However, the Court stated that given that adoption of a programme manual by the monitoring committee precluding judicial review implemented EU law within the meaning of Article 51(1) of the Charter,[97] the Court had jurisdiction, by way of reference for a preliminary ruling under Article 267 TFEU. This allowed it to rule that the parent Regulation establishing the procedure for the grant of aid in issue,[98] read in conjunction with Article 47 of the Charter, was to be interpreted as precluding a provision of a programme manual adopted by a monitoring committee in the context of an operational programme established by two Member States, and intended to promote European territorial cooperation, where that provision had not provided that a decision of that monitoring committee rejecting an application for aid could be subject to appeal before a court of a Member State.[99]

Thereafter, *Berlusconi and Fininvest*[100] hinged on whether a measure taken at Member State level was a preparatory act or a measure with legally binding effects. This is pivotal in

---

[89] Case C-64/05 P *Sweden v Commission* ECLI:EU:C:2007:802.

[90] Opinion of AG Campos Sánchez-Bordona in Case C-219/17 *Berlusconi* ECLI:EU:C:2018:502, para 103.

[91] Case C-562/12 *Liivimaa Lihaveis* ECLI:EU:C:2014:2229.

[92] Case C-219/17 *Berlusconi and Fininvest* ECLI:EU:C:2018:1023. See also Case C-414/18 *Iccrea Banca SpA Istituto Centrale del Credito Cooperativo*, paras 26–75.

[93] Namely Council Regulation (EC) No 1083/2006 of 11 July 2006 laying down general provisions on the European Regional Development Fund, the European Social Fund and the Cohesion Fund and repealing Regulation (EC) No 1260/1999 [2006] OJ L210/25.

[94] Case C-562/12 *Liivimaa Lihaveis MTÜ*.

[95] Para 47 of the Judgment in *Liivimaa Lihaveis MTÜ*.

[96] Para 48 of the Judgment in *Liivimaa Lihaveis MTÜ*.

[97] Para 65 of the Judgment in Case C-562/12 *Liivimaa Lihaveis MTÜ*.

[98] Council Regulation (EC) No 1083/2006 on the European Regional Development Fund, the European Social Fund and the Cohesion Fund and repealing Regulation OJ 2006 L 10, p 25.

[99] Paras 47 and 76 of the Judgment in *Liivimaa Lihaveis MTÜ*.

[100] Case C-219/17 *Berlusconi and Fininvest* ECLI:EU:C:2018:1023.

determining whether legal challenge should be instituted by way of nullity proceedings before the General Court, or by way of validity proceedings before a national court in a Member State, and reference to the Court under Article 267 TFEU. In the case, the European Central Bank (ECB) had found that the acquirers of the qualifying holding in an Italian bank did not meet a reputational requirement set by EU law, and that there were serious doubts as to the ability of the acquirers to ensure that that financial institution would be managed soundly and prudently in the future. The ECB consequently opposed the acquisition of the qualifying holding in issue.[101] The acquirers challenged the ECB's decision by bringing an action for annulment before the General Court.[102] Legal proceedings were also brought by the acquirers before the Italian courts, contesting, inter alia, a preparatory assessment of character made by the Bank of Italy, and which had formed part of the procedure leading to the aforementioned decision of the ECB.[103] Reliance was also placed on a prior ruling of the Italian courts that was alleged to be inconsistent with the ECB's decision on reputation.

The Court in *Berlusconi and Fininvest* recalled that Article 263 TFEU conferred exclusive jurisdiction upon the Court to review the legality of acts adopted by the EU institutions, one of which is the ECB. Thus, any involvement of the national authorities in the course of the procedure, leading to the adoption of such acts, cannot affect their classification as EU acts where the acts of the national authorities constitute a stage of a procedure in which an EU institution exercises, alone, the final decision-making power, without being bound by the preparatory acts or the proposals of the national authorities.[104] The Court therefore concluded that Article 263 TFEU was to be interpreted as precluding national courts from reviewing the legality of decisions to initiate procedures, preparatory acts, or non-binding proposals adopted by institutions such as the Bank of Italy, in procedures provided for in EU Regulations.[105] It was immaterial that a specific action for a declaration of invalidity on the ground of alleged disregard of the force of *res judicata* attaching to a national judicial decision had also been brought before a national court.[106]

Thus, central to this contemporary debate, long after the delivery of the Opinion of AG Jacobs and the judgment of the Court in *TWD* is, first, whether the entity issuing the measure challenged is an institution, body, office, or agency of the EU, within the meaning of the first sub-paragraph of Article 263 TFEU, and, secondly, whether an EU measure is intended to have binding legal effects, so that it has the status of a challengeable act; the latter being particularly important in complex administrative procedures involving a number of authorities.[107] However, as illustrated by *Borelli*, *Liivimaa Lihaveis MTÜ*, and *Berlusconi and Fininvest*, neither of these issues will always be easy to determine.

---

[101] Para 35 of the Judgment in *Berlusconi*.

[102] Case T-913/16 *Fininvest and Berlusconi v ECB* ECLI:EU:T:2022:279.

[103] Paras 36-37 of the Judgment in *Berlusconi*.

[104] Paras 42-43 of the Judgment in *Berlusconi*, referring to Case C-64/05 P *Sweden v Commission* ECLI:EU:C:2007:802, paras 93–94.

[105] Namely Articles 22 and 23 of Directive 2013/36/EU of the European Parliament and of the Council of 26 June 2013 on access to the activity of credit institutions and the prudential supervision of credit institutions and investment firms, amending Directive 2002/87/EC and repealing Directives 2006/48/EC and 2006/49/EC [2013] OJ L176/338; Articles 4(1)(c) and 15 of Council Regulation (EU) No 1024/2013 of 15 October 2013 conferring specific tasks on the European Central Bank concerning policies relating to the prudential supervision of credit institutions [2013] OJ L287/63; Articles 85 to 87 of Regulation (EU) No 468/2014 of the European Central Bank of 16 April 2014 establishing the framework for cooperation within the Single Supervisory Mechanism between the European Central Bank and national competent authorities and with national designated authorities (SSM Framework Regulation) [2014] OJ L141/1).

[106] Para 59 of the Judgment in *Berlusconi*.

[107] Joined Cases C-551/19 P and C-552/19 P *ABLV Bank AS* ECLI:EU:C:2021:369, para 66.

Such situations generate a multitude of questions concerning how to maintain the coherence and clarity of remedies, as required by Article 47 CFR, first paragraph.[108] Does the answer lie in developing special *ad hoc* rules on the allocation of jurisdiction as occurs under the statute of the ECB?[109] Could regulations setting up complex decision-making procedures stipulate the court that should be petitioned by way of nullity, or would this be inconsistent with the complete system of remedies set up in the EU Treaties? If the answer is treaty reform, what would such treaty reform look like? All the questions are ripe for further discussion and reflection, thanks, at least in part, to the foundational Opinion of AG Jacobs in *TWD*.

D. Effect on Future Case Law

TWD was, at a technical level, a case about state aid. But it was about much more. AG Jacobs recognised the importance of *TWD* beyond the case at hand. More fundamentally, it was about ensuring the *equity* of the system of remedies within the EU legal order.

Time limits are a strange thing in EU law. After all, they are generally applicable to EU legal acts that are not directed at specific individuals, and national courts remains empowered to refer questions on validity to the Court, and at any time, and indeed the latter can consider the issue of validity of any EU act, once seized, of its own motion. But if *TWD* had been decided differently, the preliminary reference procedure might have become an override to the time limit imposed under the direct action procedure under primary law, and in some circumstances to the point of rendering it null and void.

The immediate effect of *TWD*, after the judgment, was that, depending on the circumstances, an EU legal act could not be challenged by going to the national courts first. It was predicted that the scope of the principle established by *TWD* would 'remain narrow given the uncertainty in the case law concerning direct and individual concern'.[110] Elsewhere it was stated that the Court 'clearly had no wish to enlarge its discussion beyond the narrow points needed to reconcile its judgment with previous decisions'.[111]

Whilst the Court tried to limit the decision to 'factual and legal circumstances such as those of the main proceedings in this case',[112] it is apparent, however, that *TWD* has had a much broader impact. Indeed, the Opinion of AG Jacobs and the judgment of the Court established a much broader principle in EU procedural and administrative law. Recent jurisprudence demonstrates that the *TWD* doctrine is alive and well, and living in current case law.

---

[108] See above text fns 63–67.
[109] Opinion of AG Kokott in Joined Cases C-202/18 and C-238/18 *Rimšēvičs and ECB* ECLI:EU:C:2018:1030, para 36 ff.
[110] Hoskins (n 79) 1407.
[111] M Ross, 'Limits on Using Article 177 EC' (1994) 19 *ELRev* 640, 643.
[112] Para 25 of the Judgment.

28

Ulysses Unbound? Political Questions, Judicial Answers, and the Rule of Law in EU Foreign Policy: Opinion of Advocate General Jacobs in Commission v Greece (FYROM)

GEERT DE BAERE*

I. INTRODUCTION

T HE OPINION OF AG Jacobs discussed here examines the reliance by Greece on Articles 224 and 225 EC (now Articles 347 and 348 TFEU)[1] to justify various measures taken against the then Former Yugoslav Republic of Macedonia (FYROM) (since 2019, the Republic of North Macedonia).[2] While the provisions at issue are only rarely invoked, and are mentioned in only a handful of cases, their application can have a substantial impact on the functioning of the Union, in particular on the internal market and the common commercial policy (CCP). They also raise the fundamental issue of the scope of jurisdiction of the Court of Justice of the European Union to review the conditions for their application, and more generally, the possibility for courts, in particular international courts, to exercise judicial review over issues that are considered by at least some of the parties involved as essentially political.

---

* All opinions expressed herein are personal to the author.
[1] Article 347 TFEU provides an obligation for the Member States to consult each other with a view to taking together the steps needed to prevent the functioning of the internal market being affected by measures that a Member State may take in the event of serious internal disturbances affecting the maintenance of law and order, in the event of war, serious international tension constituting a threat of war, or in order to carry out obligations it has accepted for the purpose of maintaining peace and international security. Article 348 TFEU adds that if measures taken in the circumstances referred to in Article 347 TFEU have the effect of distorting the conditions of competition in the internal market, the Commission, together with the Member State concerned, is to examine how these measures can be adjusted to the rules laid down in the EU Treaties. However, by way of derogation from the infringement procedure laid down in Articles 258 and 259 TFEU, the Commission or any Member State can bring the matter directly before the Court if it considers that another Member State is making improper use of those powers, and the Court is to give its ruling in camera.
[2] Opinion of AG Jacobs in Case C-120/94 *Commission v Greece* ECLI:EU:C:1995:109 (*FYROM*).

II. BACKGROUND, CONTEXT, AND FACTS

While understanding the factual context of a case is invariably important, it is arguably particularly so in the present case, as a proper assessment of that context partly determines whether one agrees with the legal analysis put forward by AG Jacobs or not. More specifically, the present case cannot be understood without a basic grasp of the history of the break-up of what used to be Yugoslavia, and of the history of the Macedonian region ranging from what is currently northern Greece, into what is currently the Republic of North Macedonia.[3]

As the Opinion of AG Jacobs recalls, during the course of 1991, the Federal Socialist Republic of Yugoslavia began to break up into five parts. On 25 June 1991, Slovenia and Croatia declared independence. On 17 September 1991, the then former Yugoslav Republic of Macedonia did likewise. Greece complained of certain actions on the part of FYROM from the moment of its independence. It considered that FYROM had promoted the idea of a unified Macedonia, encompassing territories in Greece itself, including the city of Thessaloniki. In particular, Greece objected to FYROM's use of certain Macedonian symbols and of the name Macedonia, which Greece regarded as part of its own cultural patrimony. In August 1992, the parliament of FYROM adopted as the emblem on the national flag the Vergina sun, a 16-point motif that adorned the golden larnax containing the bones of Philip II of Macedon, found at the old Macedonian capital Αἰγαὶ (Aigai), now Vergina in Greek Macedonia. Greece regarded that symbol as quintessentially Greek, and in consequence, requested FYROM not to use it on its flag and repeated its requests that FYROM should renounce territorial claims against Greece and cease all hostile propaganda.

On 7 April 1993, the United Nations Security Council (UNSC) in Resolution 817 recommended to the General Assembly that FYROM should be admitted to the UN under the name of the Former Yugoslav Republic of Macedonia, pending settlement of the difference that had arisen regarding its denomination. On 16 February 1994, the Greek Government adopted measures prohibiting trade, in particular via the port of Thessaloniki, in products originating in, coming from, or destined for FYROM, and imports into Greece of products originating in or coming from that Republic, applying them to all goods except those vital for humanitarian purposes, such as food and pharmaceutical products, and closed its consulate in Skopje.[4]

The Greek Government subsequently informed the Council and other Member States of the measures taken, and explained the measures to the Commission, which had already expressed its serious doubts as to their compatibility with what was then Community law. The issue was discussed on 27 March 1994 at the informal Council meeting held at Ioannina, where the Greek Government maintained that no agreement was reached, and no decision taken. The Commission maintained, however, that the discussions showed that Greece had failed to establish that there existed a threat of war or a serious internal disturbance affecting the maintenance of law and order. On 22 April 1994, the Commission lodged the application that commenced the infringement proceedings discussed here, seeking a declaration from the Court, pursuant to the second paragraph of Article 225 EC, that Greece had made improper use of the powers provided for in Article 224 EC in order to justify the unilateral measures adopted on 16 February 1994, and that by so doing it had failed to fulfil its obligations under Article 113 EC and under various acts of secondary EU law.[5] The Commission also lodged,

---

[3] See also ICJ, *Application of the Interim Accord of 13 September 1995 (the former Yugoslav Republic of Macedonia v Greece)*, Judgment of 5 December 2011, ICJ Reports 2011, p 644, at pp 653–55, paras 15–22.

[4] Paras 2, 5, 13, 16–18 of the Opinion.

[5] Regulation (EEC) No 2603/69 of the Council of 20 December 1969 establishing common rules for exports [1969] OJ L324/25; Council Regulation (EEC) No 288/82 of 5 February 1982 on common rules for imports [1982] OJ L35/1;

on the same day, an application for an interim order to suspend the application of the Greek measures. The Court dismissed that application by order of 29 June 1994.[6]

III. THE OPINION OF AG JACOBS

At the outset, AG Jacobs announced that in order to determine whether the application should be granted, a number of issues must be examined. First, it was necessary to decide whether the action taken by Greece would, in the absence of the safeguard clause contained in current Article 224 EC, be contrary to EU law. Secondly, if so, it would be necessary to determine whether Greece could invoke Article 224 EC for the purpose of justifying its action on the ground that it was designed to counter serious internal disturbances affecting the maintenance of law and order or serious international tension constituting a threat of war. Thirdly, if so, it would be necessary to determine, in accordance with Article 225 EC, second paragraph, whether Greece had made improper use of the powers provided for under Article 224 EC.[7]

Regarding the first issue, AG Jacobs took the view that the embargo imposed by Greece on trade with FYROM was in principle incompatible with EU law, unless it could be regarded as falling within the scope of the safeguard clause contained in Article 224 EC. AG Jacobs stated that by conferring exclusive competence on the EU in the common commercial policy, the Member States had surrendered the power to adopt unilateral measures restricting trade with the outside world, except in certain circumstances defined by EU law. Greece had argued that the embargo on trade with FYROM fell outside the scope of Article 113 EC on the ground that it was not conceived as an instrument of commercial policy, but was designed to bring political pressure to bear on FYROM. However, according to AG Jacobs, the decisive element was not the purpose of the embargo, but its effects. For him, a measure that has the effect of directly preventing or restricting trade with a non-Member State came within the scope of Article 113 EC, regardless of its purpose.[8]

With respect to the second issue, AG Jacobs started by recalling the Court's holding at paragraph 27 of the judgment in *Johnston*,[9] that Article 224 EC concerned a wholly exceptional situation,[10] and adding that that provision, in fact, envisaged three exceptional situations in which a Member State may take measures that are capable of affecting the functioning of the Internal Market. The first two were both invoked by Greece.[11]

AG Jacobs then dismissed the analogy drawn by the Commission between Articles 36 and 224 EC, arguing that when the latter speaks of serious internal disturbances affecting the maintenance of law and order, it must be read as envisaging a breakdown of public order on a scale much vaster than the type of civil unrest that might justify recourse to Article 36 EC. What seems to be envisaged, according to AG Jacobs, would be a situation verging on a total collapse of internal security, for otherwise it would be difficult to justify recourse to a sweeping derogation which would be capable of authorising the suspension of all of the ordinary rules

---

Council Regulation (EC) No 3698/93 of 22 December 1993 concerning the arrangements applicable to the import into the Community of products originating in the Republics of Bosnia-Herzegovina, Croatia and Slovenia and the former Yugoslav Republic of Macedonia [1993] OJ L344/1; Council Regulation (EEC) No 2726/90 of 17 September 1990 on Community transit [1990] OJ L262/1.

[6] Case C-120/94 R *Commission v Greece* ECLI:EU:C:1994:275 (*FYROM*).

[7] Paras 29–32.

[8] Paras 40, 42.

[9] Case 222/84 *Johnston* ECLI:EU:C:1986:206.

[10] See Case C-273/97 *Sirdar* ECLI:EU:C:1999:523, para 19.

[11] Para 44 of the Opinion.

governing the internal market.[12] However, Greece's assertions were, according to the AG, not of such a nature as to establish that its authorities were actually faced with serious internal disturbances against which they would have been unable to take effective action without the adoption of economic sanctions against FYROM. Greece's claims regarding the organisation of massive demonstrations were vague and unsubstantiated. No details had been provided about specific disturbances of public order. AG Jacobs therefore concluded that Greece was not entitled to invoke that Article on such grounds.[13]

As the next step, AG Jacobs examined whether Greece was entitled to invoke Article 224 EC on the ground of war or serious international tension constituting a threat of war, acknowledging that that question was far more complex, and raised the fundamental issue of the scope of the Court's power to exercise judicial review in such situations. AG Jacobs emphasised that it was not for the Court to adjudicate on the substance of the dispute between Greece and FYROM, ie to determine who is entitled to the name Macedonia, the sun of Vergina and the heritage of Alexander the Great, whether FYROM was seeking to misappropriate a part of Greece's national identity, or whether FYROM had long-term designs on Greek territory or an immediate intention to go to war with Greece. Rather, what the Court had to decide was whether in the light of all the circumstances, including the geopolitical and historical background, Greece could have had some basis for considering, from its own subjective point of view, that the strained relations between itself and FYROM could degenerate into armed conflict.

AG Jacobs stressed that the question had to be judged from the point of view of Greece as a Member State, which was better placed than the EU institutions or the other Member States when it was a question of weighing up the dangers posed for it by the conduct of a third state.[14] The AG argued that it could not be said that Greece was acting wholly unreasonably by taking the view that the tension between itself and FYROM bore within it the threat of war. What mattered was not so much that Greece's fears might have been unfounded, but rather, that those fears appeared to be genuinely and firmly held by the Greek Government and by the bulk of the Greek people.[15] AG Jacobs concluded that, having regard to the extremely limited nature of the judicial review that could be carried out in this area, it would be wrong to rule that Greece could not invoke Article 224 EC on the ground that there was no serious international tension constituting a threat of war.[16]

As regards the third issue, AG Jacobs concluded that if a Member State considered, rightly or wrongly, that the attitude of a third state threatened its vital interests, its territorial integrity or its very existence, then it was for the Member State to determine how to respond to that perceived threat: for example, by diplomatic pressure, by the severing of sporting and cultural links, by economic sanctions, or even by military action. The sole limit placed on the autonomy of the Member States is that they may not make improper use of their powers, for example, if its real purpose in imposing an embargo on trade with a third state was not to prosecute any political dispute with the third state, but to protect its own economy or the interests of domestic traders. There was no suggestion that that is the purpose of the embargo imposed by Greece on trade with FYROM.[17]

---

[12] Paras 45–47.
[13] Paras 48–49.
[14] Para 54.
[15] Paras 56–58.
[16] Paras 59–60.
[17] Paras 65–67.

As to the Commission's argument that Greece was making improper use of its powers because the purpose of the embargo was not to repel a threat of war from FYROM, but simply to bring pressure to bear on FYROM in the political dispute between those states, the AG argued that that argument was misconceived; it sought to demonstrate, not that Greece was making improper use of its powers under current Article 224 EEC, but that Greece could not invoke that article at all because the requirement of serious international tension constituting a threat of war was not fulfilled. According to the AG, once it was accepted that that requirement was satisfied, it could not be argued that Greece was misusing its powers simply because it is attempting to bring pressure to bear on the third state with which it was in dispute. On the contrary, that was precisely the sort of purpose contemplated by current Article 224 EEC when it permits Member States to take measures which are capable of affecting the functioning of the internal market, in order to deal with serious international tension constituting a threat of war.[18]

IV. ANALYSIS

A. Articles 347 and 348 TFEU

As mentioned above, the two provisions of the EU Treaties are rarely invoked.[19] Article 347 TFEU forms part of a limited series of Articles in which the TFEU expressly provides for derogations applicable in situations that may affect law and order or public security,[20] and which deal with exceptional and clearly defined cases. In several instances the Court has held that although it is for the Member States to adopt appropriate measures to ensure law and order on their territory, and their internal and external security, it does not follow that such measures fall entirely outside the scope of EU law. Furthermore, it cannot be inferred from the explicit derogations provided for in the TFEU that the EU Treaties contain an inherent general exception excluding all measures taken for reasons of law and order or public security from the scope of EU law.[21]

According to the Court, the recognition of the existence of such an exception, regardless of the specific requirements laid down by the EU Treaties, might impair the binding nature of EU law and its uniform application.[22] In accordance with settled case law on such exceptions, Article 347 TFEU must be interpreted strictly. Furthermore, that Article cannot be read in such a way as to confer on Member States the power to depart from the provisions of EU law based on no more than reliance on the responsibilities incumbent upon Member States with regard to the maintenance of law and order and the safeguarding of internal security.[23]

Nevertheless, as the Court observed in the Order rejecting the interim measures requested by the Commission in the present case, the fact remains that Article 224 EC (now Article 347 TFEU) is a provision that permits a Member State in certain exceptional circumstances to

---

[18] Para 68.

[19] For an earlier survey see C Stefanou and H Xanthaki, 'Article 224 of the Treaty of Rome and the Repercussions of Case C-120/94' (1995) 1 *European Journal of Current Legal Issues* 1.

[20] The other provisions being Arts 36, 45, 52, 65, 72, and 346 TFEU. In general on Art 347 TFEU see M Trybus, *European Union Law and Defence Integration* (Oxford, Hart Publishing, 2005) 167–95.

[21] See eg Joined Cases C-715/17, C-718/17 and C-719/17 *Commission v Poland* ECLI:EU:C:2020:257 (*Temporary Relocation*), para 143 and the case law cited; Case C-808/18 *Commission v Hungary* ECLI:EU:C:2020:1029, para 214.

[22] ibid.

[23] Paras 144–45 of Judgment in Joined Cases C 715/17, C 718/17 and C 719/17 and para 215 of Judgment in Case C-808/18.

derogate even from fundamental EU rules. According to the Court, in order to ascertain whether the essential requirements for the application of that provision were met, and whether the Greek Government had made proper use of the powers referred to in that Article, it was necessary to consider complex legal questions, including the determination of the scope of the judicial review to be exercised in the context of the procedure laid down in Article 225(2) EC (now Article 348(2) TFEU).[24] In the present case, however, the Court had no further opportunity to delve into this matter. Following the withdrawal of the application by the European Commission, the case was removed from the register.[25]

B. The Scope of Judicial Review of the Conditions Posed by Article 347 TFEU

The possibility of judicial review of a Member State's reliance on Article 224 EC, and more generally of judicial review in EU external action, runs as a leitmotiv through the Opinion of AG Jacobs, who took the view that it could not be argued that the matter was non-justiciable.[26] It being plain from the terms of Article 225 EC that the Court has power to review the legality of action taken by a Member State under Article 224 EC, for AG Jacobs, that must logically include the power to review whether the conditions for invoking that Article are satisfied. The scope and intensity of that review are, however, severely limited on account of the nature of the issues raised. The AG highlighted in particular the paucity of judicially applicable criteria that would permit the Court, or any other court, to determine whether serious international tension exists and whether such tension constitutes a threat of war, and approvingly quoted Lord Wilberforce in *Buttes*:[27]

> [T]here are ... no judicial or manageable standards by which to judge these issues, or to adopt another phrase ... the court would be in judicial no-man's land.[28]

In turn, Lord Wilberforce had relied on the judgment of the US Fifth Circuit Court of Appeals in *Occidental of Umm al Qaywayn, Inc. v A Certain Cargo of Petroleum*,[29] which was based on what is known as the 'political question doctrine' in US constitutional law.[30] AG Jacobs also referred to the work of Franck on that doctrine,[31] as well as to case law of the German courts (not specifically identified), which was said to show substantial deference to the executive in matters of foreign policy for lack of judicial standards.[32] Furthermore, AG Jacobs recalled that the European Court of Human Rights (ECtHR) had likewise emphasised that issues of national security are primarily a matter for the appraisal of the authorities of the State concerned with respect to Article 15 of the European Convention on Human Rights (ECHR),

---

[24] Paras 68–69 of the Order.

[25] Case C-120/94 *Commission v Greece* ECLI:EU:C:1996:116 (*FYROM*), Order of the President of the Court of 19 March 1996.

[26] See also Opinion of AG La Pergola in Case C-273/97 *Sirdar* ECLI:EU:C:1999:523, paras 26–27.

[27] *Buttes Gas and Oil Co v Hammer* [1982] AC 888, 938.

[28] Para 50 of the Opinion.

[29] 577 F.2d 1196 (5th Cir. 1978), *cert. denied sub nom. Occidental of Umm Qaywayn, Inc. v Cities Serv. Oil Co*, 442 U.S. (1979).

[30] See L Collins, 'Foreign Relations and the Judiciary' (2002) 51 ICLQ 507. Collins suggests that all that *Buttes* decided is that where a case in a national court raises the issue of the territory of a foreign state, and the Foreign and Commonwealth Office refuses to certify what boundaries it recognises, then the issue is not justiciable.

[31] TM Franck, *Political Questions/Judicial Answers: Does the Rule of Law Apply to Foreign Affairs?* (Princeton, Princeton University Press, 1992).

[32] Para 51.

which allows Contracting Parties to take measures derogating from their obligations under the ECHR in time of war, or other public emergency threatening the life of the nation.[33]

AG Jacobs emphasised that it was not for the Court to decide on the substance of the dispute. Rather, it had to decide whether, taking into account all the relevant circumstances, including the geopolitical and historical context, Greece could have had a valid reason, *from its own subjective point of view*, to fear that the conflict with FYROM could degenerate into a full-blown war. This subjective point of view was taken to be all-important. Indeed, the Opinion points out, it was precisely the difference in subjective perceptions of certain circumstances that was decisive in the origin of armed conflicts. If such circumstances were exclusively interpreted from the vantage point of what objective external observers would consider a reasonable attitude, AG Jacobs remarked, wars would perhaps never occur.[34]

The Commission had argued that the embargo established by Greece would increase rather than decrease the tension, and would thus have detrimental consequences for the internal and external security of Greece. AG Jacobs remarked that such a line of argument was based on a political appreciation of an eminently political subject. It was simply not possible to apply any legal standards to determine what the wisest course of action for Greece under the circumstances would be.[35]

It was, according to the AG, not for the Court to criticise the appropriateness of the Member State's response, and to say that the chosen course of action was unlikely to achieve the desired aim or that the Member State would have a better prospect of successfully defending its interests by other means, as there are no judicial criteria by which such matters may be measured. It was difficult to identify a precise legal test for determining whether a trade embargo is a suitable means of pursuing a political dispute between a Member State and a third state. The decision to take such action was, in other words, essentially political. According to AG Jacobs, the sole limit placed on the autonomy of the Member States is that they may not make improper use of their powers.[36]

AG Jacobs no doubt rightly identified the assessment of whether the embargo would increase rather than decrease international tension as a clear example of a situation on which courts are not properly equipped to pass judgment. Indeed, it is probably fair to say that no institution is completely equipped to judge what the repercussions of such actions as taken by Greece would be on the international scene. However, the contrast with the stricter review applied by the AG as to the existence or otherwise of 'serious internal disturbances affecting the maintenance of law and order' was rather striking. On that issue, AG Jacobs concluded that Greece had not come anywhere near establishing the massive breakdown of public order needed to justify recourse to Article 224 EC on grounds of serious internal disturbances affecting the maintenance of law and order, and that Greece was hence not entitled to invoke that Article on such grounds.[37] The question may be asked why the subjective standpoint held to be of crucial importance for the assessment of international tension did not seem to matter all

---

[33] Para 55, referring to *Ireland v the United Kingdom* App no 5310/71 (ECtHR, 18 January 1978).

[34] Para 58.

[35] Paras 59 and 65. Compare Opinion of AG Kokott in C-420/07 *Apostolides v Orams* ECLI:EU:C:2008:749, paras 43–48. The issue there was whether the recognition of a judgment rendered by a court in the southern area of Cyprus but pertaining to real property in the northern area would imperil or help a final settlement of the 'Cyprus problem'. See further G De Baere, 'Case C-420/07, Meletis Apostolides v. David Charles Orams, Linda Elizabeth Orams, Judgment of the Grand Chamber of 28 April 2009, [2009] ECR I-3571' (2010) 47 *CMLRev* 1135.

[36] Paras 65–67.

[37] Paras 48–49.

that much with respect to internal disturbance.[38] An explanation may perhaps be found in the fact that, while Greece was not arguing that there *was* an armed conflict with FYROM (only that the actions of the latter made such a conflict likely), it was arguing that grave internal disturbances *did currently exist*. It seems logical that a claim that a certain situation existed can more readily be proved or disproved than the claim that a situation may occur in the future.

Nevertheless, it would clearly be saying too much to claim that no legal standards exist to assess the existence of a threat of force,[39] or, *a fortiori*, of the existence of an armed conflict.[40] Indeed, such a legal assessment is necessary to examine a potential breach of Article 2(4) of the UN Charter, which obliges UN states to refrain in their international relations from the *threat* or *use* of force against the territorial integrity or political independence of any state, or in any other manner inconsistent with the purposes of the United Nations, a prohibition recognised as a norm of customary international law, and even as a norm of *jus cogens*.[41]

C. EU External Action and Political Questions

Did AG Jacobs apply an EU law incarnation of the 'political question doctrine'?[42] That doctrine in US constitutional law affirms that some constitutional questions lie beyond judicial jurisdiction to resolve, and can in some instances be settled authoritatively by other branches of government,[43] most often the executive, as the original statement of the doctrine by Chief Justice Marshall of the Supreme Court of the United States (SCOTUS) in *Marbury v Madison* affirmed.[44] In essence, the political question doctrine marks some questions as ultra vires, or beyond the jurisdiction of courts to resolve. Nevertheless, even after denominating a question as political, courts typically retain a responsibility to check actions by other institutions that overreach the outer limits of those institutions' authority.[45]

Typologically, in the words of the useful summary by Justice William Brennan in *Baker v Carr*:

> It is apparent that several formulations which vary slightly according to the settings in which the questions arise may describe a political question, although each has one or more elements which identify it as essentially a function of the separation of powers. Prominent on the surface of any case held to involve a political question is found a textually demonstrable constitutional commitment of the issue to a coordinate political department; or a lack of judicially discoverable and manageable standards for resolving it; or the impossibility of deciding without an initial policy determination of a kind clearly for nonjudicial discretion; or the impossibility of a court's undertaking independent resolution without expressing lack of the respect due coordinate branches of government; or an unusual

---

[38] Similarly D Scannell, 'Legal Aspects of the European Union's European Security and Defence Policy' (PhD Dissertation, University of Cambridge, 2005) 236.

[39] See ICJ, *Legality of the Threat or Use of Nuclear Weapons (Advisory Opinion)* [1996] ICJ Rep 226, para 47; N Stürchler, *The Threat of Force in International Law* (Cambridge, CUP, 2007).

[40] See eg Case IT-94-1-AR72 *Prosecutor v Dusco Tadic a/k/a* 'Dule', Decision on the Defence Motion for Interlocutory Appeal on Jurisdiction, 105 ILR 453, para 70, in which the Appeals Chamber of the ICTY provided a definition of what amounted to an international armed conflict.

[41] ICJ, *Military and Paramilitary Activity in and against Nicaragua (Nicaragua v United States of America)* [1986] ICJ Rep 14, para 190. Further on the scope of Article 2(4) of the UN Charter see J Wouters, C Ryngaert, T Ruys and G De Baere, *International Law: A European Perspective* (Oxford, Hart Publishing, 2018) 604–07.

[42] Further on political questions in EU law, see K Lenaerts, *Le juge et la constitution aux États-unis d'Amérique et dans l'ordre juridique européen* (Brussels, Bruylant, 1988) 440–58.

[43] RH Fallon Jr , 'Political Questions and the Ultra Vires Conundrum' (2020) 87 *The University of Chicago Law Review* 1482.

[44] *Marbury v Madison* 5 US, 170.

[45] Fallon (n 43) 1485.

need for unquestioning adherence to a political decision already made; or the potentiality of embarrassment from multifarious pronouncements by various departments on one question.[46]

Justice Brennan also emphasised that while questions touching foreign relations frequently turn on standards that defy judicial application or involve the exercise of a discretion demonstrably committed to the executive or legislature, and that such questions uniquely demand single-voiced statement of the government's views, it was an error to suppose that every case or controversy that touches foreign relations lies beyond judicial cognisance.[47]

Nevertheless, foreign policy issues provide prime examples and a principal justification of the political question doctrine,[48] which in turn provides a technical legal basis for courts to refuse to consider the lawfulness of presidential action taken pursuant to either the wartime or foreign affairs powers.[49]

While the precise contours of the political question doctrine in US constitutional law are somewhat penumbral, there is not even an explicitly recognised political question doctrine in EU law, let alone a clearly circumscribed one. Nevertheless, a number of AGs have ventured to address and – to the extent possible – delineate, situations in which the jurisdiction of the Court would be excluded or severely limited. Whether such exercises, including the one discussed here, amount to the application of the EU equivalent of a political question doctrine, is a different matter.

Turning to the case discussed here, AG Jacobs referred to the paucity of judicially applicable criteria that would permit the Court to determine whether serious international tension exists, whether such tension constitutes a threat of war, and what the wisest course of action was for Greece under the circumstances. That could be an EU version of the 'lack of judicially discoverable and manageable standards' type of political question mentioned by Justice Brennan. Fallon has identified two elements to that type: first, a judicially manageable standard must give intelligible guidance and yield reasonably consistent, predictable outcomes when applied by different courts to different cases; and secondly, the term judicially manageable standards can refer either to the inputs (when an existing standard is applied to a constitutional controversy) or to the outputs (when a court successfully devises a new standard) of constitutional adjudication.[50] AG Jacobs appears essentially to have taken the view that neither were there existing standards to be applied nor was it possible to devise new standards to be applied in the instant case and in future cases. As mentioned above, one may question whether the legal standards were quite as undiscoverable and unmanageable for all the issues identified in the Opinion, in particular regarding the existence of a threat of war.

Nevertheless, if AG Jacobs applied an EU political question doctrine, it was arguably a '*lite*' version.[51] Indeed, while AG Jacobs emphasised that there are no legal standards to review the substance of Greece's action to avoid the threat of war, he seemed equally adamant that such legal standards did exist with regard to the possibility of internal disturbances and accordingly brushed aside Greece's claims. The same is no doubt true for independent measures that a Member State may be called upon to take in order to carry out obligations it has accepted for the purpose of maintaining peace and international security. Legal analysis is clearly required in determining Member States' obligations under international law, and there would seem to

[46] *Baker v Carr*, 369 US 186 (1962), para 50.

[47] ibid, para 44.

[48] L Henkin, *Foreign Affairs and the US Constitution*, 2nd edn (Oxford, OUP, 2002) 143.

[49] S Breyer, *The Court and the World: American Law and the New Global Realities* (New York, Vintage, 2016) 19.

[50] Fallon (n 43) 1500.

[51] G De Baere, 'European Integration and the Rule of Law in Foreign Policy' in J Dickson and P Eleftheriadis (eds), *Philosophical Foundations of European Union Law* (Oxford, OUP, 2012) 371.

be no reason why a court could not exercise judicial review in these circumstances, even if it would only be a marginal review.[52]

Two further examples illustrate that the Court and its AGs tread gingerly when venturing into political question territory. First, the Opinion of AG Darmon in *Maclaine Watson*,[53] a case concerning the responsibility of the then Community for its involvement in the International Tin Council, contained a fairly extensive exploration of the possibility for judicial review in external action, which included consideration of the political question doctrine (as well as of the act of state and act of the government doctrines). After careful and lengthy consideration of the Court's case law, and of the case law of the courts of the Member States, AG Darmon identified the extremely narrow confines of judicial control in the field of international relations as the thread running through the laws of the Member States.[54] AG Darmon concluded that the role of the courts is to ensure that the law is observed, and that there are certain acts that are based on assessments which positive law does not enable the court to review because it would be substituting its own decision for that of the institution whose conduct was in question. However, such refusal by or impossibility for the court to adjudicate ensued only from an examination of the substance of the claims put forward: 'it must, as it were, "look over the wall"'.[55]

Secondly, the Commission, the Council, and the UK had contended that the specific subject matter at issue in *Kadi I* did not lend itself to judicial review, claiming that the ECtHR took a similar position. The Commission specifically referred to the concept of 'political questions'. AG Poiares Maduro forcefully dismissed that claim:

> The implication that the present case concerns a 'political question', in respect of which even the most humble degree of judicial interference would be inappropriate, is, in my view, untenable. The claim that a measure is necessary for the maintenance of international peace and security cannot operate so as to silence the general principles of Community law and deprive individuals of their fundamental rights. This does not detract from the importance of the interest in maintaining international peace and security; it simply means that it remains the duty of the courts to assess the lawfulness of measures that may conflict with other interests that are equally of great importance and with the protection of which the courts are entrusted.[56]

He also approvingly quoted the dissenting opinion of SCOTUS Justice Murphy in *Korematsu*:

> Like other claims conflicting with the asserted constitutional rights of the individual, [that] claim must subject itself to the judicial process of having its reasonableness determined and its conflicts with other interests reconciled. What are the allowable limits of [discretion], and whether or not they have been overstepped in a particular case, are judicial questions.[57]

For their part, neither the Court of Justice nor the General Court has ever explicitly recognised a political question doctrine.

---

[52] P Eeckhout, *External Relations of the European Union: Legal and Constitutional Foundations*, 2nd edn (Oxford, OUP, 2011) 545.

[53] Opinion of AG Darmon in Case 241/87 *Maclaine Watson v Council and Commission* ECLI:EU:C:1989:229. Coincidentally, just like Case C-120/94 *Commission v Greece (FYROM)*, that case was likewise withdrawn before the Court proceeded to judgment.

[54] Paras 55–96 of the Opinion of AG Darmon.

[55] ibid, paras 99–100.

[56] Opinion of AG Poiares Maduro in Joined Cases C-402/05 P and C-415/05 P *Kadi* ECLI:EU:C:2008:11, para 34. See also Opinion of AG Sharpston in Case C-27/09 *France v People's Mojahedin Organization of Iran* ECLI:EU:C:2011:482, paras 253–55.

[57] *Korematsu v United States*, 323 US 214, 233–4 (1944). Note that Korematsu was finally explicitly overruled in *Trump v Hawaii*, 585 US (2018), Roberts CJ holding: 'The forcible relocation of U.S. citizens to concentration camps, solely and explicitly on the basis of race, is objectively unlawful and outside the scope of Presidential authority. [...] *Korematsu* was gravely wrong the day it was decided, has been overruled in the court of history, and – to be clear – "has no place in law under the Constitution."'

Furthermore, the need for the Court to expound a political question doctrine was arguably significantly diminished by the explicit exclusion of its jurisdiction in the area in which the need for such a doctrine would be most pressing. Pursuant to Article 24(1) TEU, second subparagraph, final sentence, and Article 275 TFEU, first paragraph, the Court does not, in principle, have jurisdiction with respect to the provisions relating to the Common Foreign and Security Policy (CFSP), or with respect to legal acts adopted on the basis of those provisions. However, the EU Treaties expressly lay down two exceptions to that principle. First, the Court has jurisdiction to monitor compliance with Article 40 TEU. Secondly, the Court has jurisdiction to review the legality of certain decisions referred to in Article 275 TFEU, second paragraph. That provision confers jurisdiction on the Court to give rulings on actions, brought subject to the conditions laid down in the of Article 263 TFEU, fourth paragraph, concerning the review of the legality of Council decisions, adopted on the basis of provisions relating to the CFSP, which provide for restrictive measures against natural or legal persons.[58]

In *Opinion 2/13*,[59] the Court explained that it had not yet had the opportunity to define the extent to which its jurisdiction is limited in CFSP matters as a result of those provisions, and that it was sufficient to declare that, as EU law stood at that point in time, certain acts adopted in the context of the CFSP fell outside the ambit of its judicial review, and that that situation was inherent to the way in which the Court's powers were structured by the EU Treaties.[60] Nevertheless, in subsequent case law, the Court has emphasised that Article 24(1) TEU, second subparagraph, final sentence and Article 275 TFEU, first paragraph, introduce a derogation from the jurisdiction of general scope that Article 19 TEU confers in order to ensure that in the interpretation and application of the EU Treaties the law is observed, and that, consequently, those provisions must be interpreted restrictively.[61]

The Court has notably held, first, in *Rosneft*, that the reference to the 'conditions laid down in the fourth paragraph of Article 263 [TFEU]' is to be understood as referring not to the type of procedure under which the Court may review the legality of certain decisions, but rather to the type of decisions whose legality may be reviewed by the Court, within any procedure that has as its aim such a review of legality.[62] Accordingly, since the same kind of decisions might be subject to a reference for a preliminary ruling on validity or an action for annulment and since these two procedures have as their aim a review of the legality of that decision, the Court concluded that it does have jurisdiction, under Article 267 TFEU, to give preliminary rulings on the validity of restrictive measures against natural or legal persons.[63] Secondly, the Court has clarified, as it did in *Bank Refah Kargaran*, that the principle of effective judicial protection of persons or entities subject to restrictive measures requires, in order for such protection to be complete, that the Court be able to rule on an action for damages brought by such persons or entities seeking damages for the harm caused by the restrictive measures taken in CFSP decisions, and that accordingly the GC and, on appeal, the Court of Justice, have jurisdiction to rule on an action for damages in so far as it seeks to obtain compensation for the harm allegedly caused by restrictive measures taken against natural or legal persons pursuant to CFSP decisions.[64]

---

[58] Case C-134/19 P *Bank Refah Kargaran* ECLI:EU:C:2020:793, paras 26–27.
[59] *Opinion 2/13* ECLI:EU:C:2014:2454.
[60] Paras 251–53 of the *Opinion 2/13*.
[61] Para 32 of the Judgment in Case C-134/19 P *Bank Refah Kargaran* and case law cited therein.
[62] Case C-72/15 *Rosneft* ECLI:EU:C:2017:236, para 70.
[63] Para 81 of the Judgment in Case C-72/15 *Rosneft*.
[64] Paras 43–44 of the Judgment in Case C-134/19 P *Bank Refah Kargaran*. See G Butler and RA Wessel, 'Jurisdiction of the Court for Non-Contractual Liability and Actions for Damages Claims within the CFSP: Bank Refah Kargaran' in G Butler and RA Wessel (eds), *EU External Relations Law: The Cases in Context* (Oxford, Hart Publishing, 2022) 991–1000.

On the one hand, this multistage rocket approach to an expansive interpretation of its jurisdiction in CFSP matters may help close the gap that, in the Court's own view,[65] still needs to be bridged before the EU can accede to the European Convention on Human Rights (ECHR). However, on the other hand, that expansive interpretation may, in turn, raise the issue of the need for a political question doctrine in EU law, given that cases in that area are arguably more likely to raise issues that could fall within the category of political questions.[66] That said, the need for that to happen should not be overstated. As AG Bobek argued in *SatCen*,[67] the Court's limited powers to review the lawfulness of certain CFSP acts:

> by no means implies that the EU judicature is capable of reviewing (or, for that matter, willing to review) choices of foreign policy or security that are eminently political. Regardless of whether Article 24(1) TEU and Article 275 TFEU codify a form of 'political question doctrine', the Court has shown that it is very mindful of the limits imposed on its constitutional role by the Treaties and, in particular, by the principle of the separation of powers.[68]

Of course, 'political' questions may also arise outside external action and outside the CFSP, yet the Court, having at its disposal an array of grounds of inadmissibility,[69] has until now not felt the need to expound an explicit political question doctrine.[70]

Instead, it has opted to modify the intensity of its review depending on the subject matter. For example, AG Jacobs gave a description of a marginal review with regard to whether the Court could get involved in assessing whether the export of certain dual-use goods could raise security concerns. Judicial review in such cases, AG Jacobs argued, 'is confined to ensuring that manifest errors of appraisal have not occurred and that national authorities have not abused the powers conferred …'.[71] Such an incremental and flexible approach based, in essence, on the presence or not of judicially cognisable criteria seems preferable to the drawing of bright lines[72] based on the determination that certain matters, in particular foreign policy, are simply too sensitive for judges to handle. As Franck put it:[73]

> What is the point of a carefully calibrated system of divided and limited power if those who exercise authority can secure an automatic exemption from its strictures merely by playing the foreign-affairs trump?'

D. Concluding Thoughts

While the difficulties in distinguishing what is 'legal' from what is 'political' are probably as old as the existence of judicial dispute settlement, they take a particular salience in

---

[65] Paras 254–57 of *Opinion 2/13*.

[66] See G Butler, *Constitutional Law of the EU's Common Foreign and Security Policy: Competence and Institutions in External Relations* (Oxford, Hart Publishing, 2019) 206–11; G Butler, 'In Search of the Political Question Doctrine in EU Law' (2018) 45 *Legal Issues of European Integration* 340, 352–53.

[67] Case C-14/19 P *SatCen v KF* ECLI:EU:C:2020:220, Opinion of AG Bobek.

[68] Para 78 of the Opinion of AG Bobek.

[69] See also J Odermatt, 'Patterns of avoidance: political questions before international courts' (2018) 14 *International Journal of Law in Context* 232–33.

[70] eg, regarding the 'EU-Turkey statement, 18 March 2016', see Case T-192/16 *NF* ECLI:EU:T:2017:128, paras 71–73. For criticism, see M Gatti, 'Attribution of Authorship of 'EU' Legal Acts: NF and Others v European Council' in Butler and Wessel (eds), *EU External Relations Law: The Cases in Context* (n 64) 861–70.

[71] Opinion of AG Jacobs in Case C-70/94 *Werner* ECLI:EU:C:1995:151, para 45.

[72] *cf* Breyer (n 49) 84.

[73] Franck (n 31) 5

international courts,[74] and regarding foreign policy more generally. As Sir Hersch Lauterpacht already observed in 1933:

> The consequences of the exclusion of 'political', i.e. important, issues from the domain of normal judicial settlement appear clearly from the consideration that, as a rule, every international dispute is of a political character, if by that is meant that it is of importance to the State in question.[...] Disputes between States, even if of a trifling origin, are important because the atmosphere of international relations, with the menacing shadow of force lurking behind a precarious recognition of the reign of law makes them so.[75]

However, at the same time, Lauterpacht observed, 'it is equally easy to show that all international disputes are, irrespective of their gravity, disputes of a legal character in the sense that, so long as the rule of law is recognized, they are capable of an answer by the application of legal rules'.[76]

International courts and tribunals, including the Court, adjudicate disputes not on the basis of political discretion, but on the basis of previously established rules, and thus contribute to a situation in which, contrary to what used to be the case in international relations, disputes are settled not through physical force and power contests but through a system of rules, thereby representing the normative ideal of the rule of law.[77]

In drawing a distinction between issues for which judicially discoverable criteria exist or do not exist, the Opinion of AG Jacobs in the case of *Commission v Greece (FYROM)* arguably reduced the scope of non-judicially cognisable issues in EU law to that specific type of political questions, irrespective of their politically sensitive nature.[78]

That appears by and large to accord with the position taken by the International Court of Justice (ICJ) when confronted with the argument that an issue brought before it is political rather than legal, holding, for example, that it 'has never shied away from a case brought before it merely because it had political implications',[79] and that it:

> considers that the fact that a legal question also has political aspects, 'as, in the nature of things, is the case with so many questions which arise in international life', does not suffice to deprive it of its character as a 'legal question' and to 'deprive the Court of a competence expressly conferred on it by its Statute ...'. Whatever its political aspects, the Court cannot refuse to admit the legal character of a question which invites it to discharge an essentially judicial task ....[80]

The ICJ had a chance to apply that case law in *FYROM v Greece*, in response to the argument by Greece that if the ICJ were to exercise its jurisdiction, it would interfere with the diplomatic process envisaged by the UN Security Council and this would be contrary to the ICJ's judicial function. The ICJ recalled that,

> as a judicial organ, the Court has to establish 'first, that the dispute before it is a legal dispute, in the sense of a dispute capable of being settled by the application of principles and rules of international

---

[74] Odermatt (n 69) 221–36.

[75] H Lauterpacht, *The Function of Law in the International Community*, 2011 edn (Oxford, OUP, 1933) 161.

[76] ibid, 165–66.

[77] G De Baere, A-L Chané and J Wouters, 'International Courts as Keepers of the Rule of Law: Achievements, Challenges, and Opportunities' (2016) 48 *New York University Journal of International Law & Politics* 754.

[78] On the distinction between 'political questions' and 'politically sensitive disputes', see Odermatt (n 69) 223.

[79] ICJ, *Case Concerning Military and Paramilitary Activities in and against Nicaragua (Nicaragua v United States of America)*, Jurisdiction and Admissibility, Judgment of 26 November 1984, 1984 ICJ Rep 293, para 96.

[80] ICJ, *Legal Consequences of the Construction of a Wall in the Occupied Palestinian Territory*, Advisory Opinion of 9 July 2004, 2004 ICJ Rep 136, para 41. In turn, that passage was quoted in the Opinion of AG Wathelet in Case C-104/16 P *Front Polisario* ECLI:EU:C:2016:677, para 142.

law, and secondly, that the Court has jurisdiction to deal with it, and that that jurisdiction is not fettered by any circumstance rendering the application inadmissible'.[81]

The ICJ determined that the question put before it, namely, whether Greece's conduct was a breach of Article 11, paragraph 1, of the Interim Accord signed by the Parties on 13 September 1995 and entered into force on 13 October 1995, was a legal question pertaining to the interpretation and implementation of a provision of that Accord, and that in accepting jurisdiction, the Court would be faithfully discharging its judicial function.[82]

Finally, a political question doctrine that would provide for all politically sensitive matters to be off limits for the judiciary and for all foreign policy issues to be politically sensitive would arguably be antithetical to the idea of European integration itself. Indeed, the development of the EU can be seen as an extraordinary attempt to bring foreign policy further within the realm of law, and thereby to constrain its possible destructive force. Having 'domesticated' the Member States' foreign policies with regard to each other, the EU is gradually bringing their foreign policies with regard to third countries within the constraining and enabling framework of EU law and hence under the rule of law at the EU level.[83] In limiting the scope of non-judicially cognisable issues in EU law to those for which no judicially discoverable criteria exist (and what belongs in that category is of course up for discussion), rather than encompassing all politically sensitive issues and ipso facto excluding all external issues from judicial review, the Opinion of AG Jacobs in *Commission v Greece (FYROM)* weds respect for the rule of law with respect for the separation of powers.

---

[81] ICJ, *Application of the Interim Accord of 13 September 1995 (the former Yugoslav Republic of Macedonia v Greece)*, Judgment of 5 December 2011, ICJ Rep 2011, p 644 at pp 663–64, paras 55–58.

[82] The ICJ concluded that it had jurisdiction, and that Greece had breached its obligations under the Interim Accord. Note that in his dissenting opinion, Judge ad hoc Roucounas referred to the Opinion of AG Jacobs discussed here, noting that it had found 'that the measures taken by Greece were legitimate and recommended that the Commission's request and application against Greece be dismissed': Diss Op Roucounas, para 5.

[83] De Baere (n 51) 356.

29

Effective Judicial Protection of EU Rights before National Courts: Opinion of Advocate General Jacobs in Van Schijndel

ANDREA BIONDI

I. INTRODUCTION

WALKING ALONG THE Grand Canal in Venice, three gentlemen were seen engulfed in deep conversation:[1] Simplicio defended Aristotelian and Ptolemaic cosmology as it provided certainty and stability; Salviati spoke for Copernicus and disparaged any other theory. Lastly, Sagredo listened attentively and committed to reason and truth only, attacking neither party. The Opinion of AG Jacobs in *Van Schijndel*[2] is the Sagredo in the debate on the relationship between the need to ensure a full and effective application of EU law, and the necessary reliance on national procedural machinery.

The Court, in its quest to provide equal remedies for equal rights, indeed had (and still continues to) rely upon national courts and tribunals as to provide specific judicial redresses for a breach of those rights. This meant, and still means, a process often slowed down by the mundane: time limits, appeals, paperwork, standing requirements, admissibility, detailed procedures often jealously guarded by centuries of traditions. In this context, it is easier for one to become embroiled in a dispute not dissimilar to that which troubled the Ptolemaics and Copernicans. The Opinion of AG Jacobs in *Van Schijndel* emphasised dialogue and finding a balanced solution. Mind you, balance is not synonymous with perfection. Rather, it is a continuous process of attempting to identify elements and patterns that may disrupt the equilibrium, and then devising ways in which to move back towards it.

II. BACKGROUND, CONTEXT, AND FACTS

The Opinion of AG Jacobs was delivered on 15 June 1995. Six months later, on 14 December 1995, the Court's judgment was handed down. At the time of this judgment, the Court was composed of 13 judges. Judge Rodriguez Iglesias was the President and Judge Mouthino Almedia

---

[1] Galile Galilei, *Dialogo sopra i due massimi sistemi del mondo* (1632).
[2] Opinion of AG Jacobs in Joined Cases C-430/93 and C-431/93 *Van Schijndel* ECLI:EU:C:1995:441.

the reporting judge (*juge rapporteur*) at hand. The case concerned whether the compulsory membership of a Dutch occupational scheme for physiotherapists could be considered to be preventing fair competition, and thus violating Articles 85, 86, and 90 EC (now Articles 101, 102 and 106 TFEU). Two physiotherapists wanted to join a different scheme provided by another operator. To achieve this, they asked for an exception to compulsory affiliation – which was denied. They challenged such decision, basing their claim on grounds related to the application of Dutch law. This action was dismissed twice, in the first instance, and then on appeal. Undeterred, they appealed to the Supreme Court of the Netherlands (*Hoge Raad*), this time relying on the application of EU competition law.

The case was, in short, an interesting contribution to the heated debate of the limits of competition law, the notion of economic activity, the duty of solidarity of the state, and so on. The intriguing point was, however, not of substance, but of procedure. Before the *Hoge Raad*, the claimants not only relied, for the first time, on EU law to defend their rights, but also contended that the Dutch courts should have considered of their own motion the question of the compatibility of the compulsory affiliation system with EU competition law. The *Hoge Raad* decided to refer a series of questions to the Court through the preliminary reference procedure, the most relevant here being:

(i)   whether the Supreme Court was obliged to apply the rules of European competition law *ex officio*,

(ii) on the role of a national court in applying EU law in the context of Dutch civil law procedure.

On this latter issue, the referring court observed that if it were obliged to apply *ex officio* EU competition rules, this would have meant for the court to:

> abandon the passive role which it should normally observe[,] in that it would have to (a) go outside the ambit of the legal dispute or/and (b) rely on facts and circumstances other than those which the party having an interest in the application of those provisions relies on in order to substantiate its claim.

Crucially, the application of EU law would have meant setting aside two rather basic principles of Dutch (or any) procedural system: that the perimeter of the claim has to be determined by the parties, and, hence, taking into account new grounds (and evidence) not previously raised on appeal, thus forcing the national court to go beyond its jurisdiction.

It is important to remember that similar issues were raised in another case pending at the time before the Court. In *Peterbroeck*,[3] the question was whether a national court must set aside a procedural rule preventing it from considering a point of EU law raised by one of the parties after the expiry date imposed by the relevant time limitations. AG Jacobs delivered his Opinion regarding that case on 4 May 1994, but the oral procedure was subsequently re-opened and the hearing was held jointly with that of *Van Schijndel*, followed by a second Opinion of AG Jacobs. This provided further evidence of the importance of the questions raised in those two cases as this was indeed a time of intense conversation between Simplicio and Salviati.[4]

---

[3] Opinion of AG Jacobs in Case C-312/93 *Peterbroeck* ECLI:EU:C:1994:184.

[4] See the *pro*, W van Gerven, 'Bridging the Gap between Community and National Law: Towards a Principle of Homogeneity in the Field of Legal Remedies' (1995) 32 *CMLRev* 679, and *contra*, J Coppell, 'Time's up for Emmott' (1996) 25 *Industrial Law Journal* 153.

III. THE OPINION OF AG JACOBS

As was customary, the Opinion of AG Jacobs was clear and straightforward, setting forth at the outset his conclusions: EU law does not require the national court to set aside its own procedural system, or to raise, *ex officio*, the EU legal element. Thus, there was no need to reply to the substantive question on competition law. His arguments were based on both an analysis of EU law, the case law of the Court – as to be expected – and on a rather detailed comparative law assessment of national procedural systems and their differences.

As regards the case law of the Court, AG Jacobs did not shy away from tackling its dichotomy: on the one hand, the Court has always acknowledged that enforcement of EU rights has to be reliant on national legal systems, and the rules of their procedural machinery. Such a national *procedural autonomy* test could be limited only in two respects: national procedural rules that do not have to render the exercise of EU rights impossible or excessively difficult (principle of effectiveness), and procedural rules used to enforce EU rights should not be less favourable than those used for similar claims under national law (principle of equivalence).[5] On the other hand, in several judgments such as *Simmenthal*[6] and *Factortame*,[7] the Court, to use the words of AG Jacobs, 'has given greater prominence to the need to ensure the effectiveness of Community law and proper judicial protection for individuals'.[8] For AG Jacobs, such a dichotomy was merely apparent. The principles of effectiveness and equivalence were also given a very prominent role, as they were defined as 'intended to establish a balance between the need to respect the procedural autonomy of the legal systems of the Member States and the need to ensure the effective protection of Community rights in the national courts'.[9] For him, *Simmenthal* and *Factortame* were not distinguished. They were simply examples where the Court had to intervene as the national law in question:

> would have deterred individuals from seeking enforcement of their rights under Community law; moreover, even where individuals were not deterred, Community law would have remained unapplied while the proceedings were pending.[10]

In the *Van Schijndel* case, according to AG Jacobs, none of these dangers materialised. The Dutch system worked properly, and offered all the possibilities for an EU claim to be heard, along with allowing the two litigants proper opportunities of doing so. Thus, for him on this point, there was no violation of EU law.

The second argument addresses the question of whether there was a duty placed on the national court to raise, *ex officio*, a point of EU law. First, according to AG Jacobs, ensuring the effective application of EU law did not mean that this principle was not subject to any limitation. In particular, he stated that:

> the interest in full application may need to be balanced against other considerations such as legal certainty, sound administration and the orderly and proper conduct of proceedings by the courts.[11]

As to decide how these two competing interests should be balanced, his Opinion relied on a comparative analysis of national procedural systems. Such analysis started with a traditional

---

[5] Case 33/76 *Rewe* ECLI:EU:C:1976:188. See ch 9.
[6] Case 106/77 *Simmenthal* ECLI:EU:C:1978:49.
[7] Case C-213/89 *Factortame* ECLI:EU:C:1990:257.
[8] Para 18 of the Opinion of AG Jacobs in *Van Schijndel*.
[9] ibid.
[10] ibid, para 19.
[11] Para 31.

view of the difference between continental civil law systems on the one hand, and the common law systems on the other. A civil law court would still rely on principles such as '*curia novit legem*' (the court knows the law), and that it must apply the appropriate legal rules to the facts as they are presented to the court by the parties ('*da mihi factum, dabo tibi jus*'); the common law system depended very much on the submissions advanced by the counsel for the parties, and its function was essentially to adjudicate on the exclusive basis of their submissions.

Then came the twist. For AG Jacobs, 'such contrasts between different categories of legal system often prove on closer examination to be exaggerated, and the present issue is no exception'.[12] Two lines to wipe away dusty and old-fashioned views (views that are still around) regarding the impossibility of comparing the civil and common law systems (another Ptolemaic and Copernican fight). Instead, the Opinion of AG Jacobs provided a more sophisticated and diverse account of how national systems really worked, and their common aspirations to provide an optimal and efficient composition of litigation. Because there was such a rich diversity, he stated that:

> to impose on all national courts a requirement to apply Community law of their own motion, although it might not be impossible to put into practice in any system, would cause a degree of disruption which might vary in different systems but would probably be significant in all of them.[13]

In short, it may be wiser to leave such matters to the expertise of national courts.

IV. ANALYSIS

A. The Judgment

The Court, in its judgment, substantially agreed with AG Jacobs, though using a slightly different approach.[14] It started with a rather empathic reaffirmation of the unique nature of EU law. In competition law rules were directly applicable within the national legal order, either when national law allowed it, or as part of the duty of loyal cooperation. Therefore, national courts were bound to raise, of their own motion, a point of EU law. That said, the Court fully embraced the 'balance approach' suggested by AG Jacobs.

In a now rather famous passage, the Court held that:

> whether a national procedural provision renders application of Community law impossible or excessively difficult must be analysed by reference to the role of that provision in the procedure, its progress and its special features, viewed as a whole, before the various national instances. In the light of that analysis the basic principles of the domestic judicial system, such as protection of the rights of the defence, the principle of legal certainty and the proper conduct of procedure, must, where appropriate, be taken into consideration.[15]

As regards the case at stake, the obligation to keep to the subject-matter of the dispute and to base the decision of the national court on the facts put before it was justified by the principle that, in a civil suit, it was for the parties to take the initiative. The Court essentially stated that a national court being able to act of its own motion was only appropriate in exceptional cases

---

[12] Para 34.
[13] Para 37.
[14] Joined Cases C-430/93 and C-431/93 *Van Schijndel* ECLI:EU:C:1995:441.
[15] Para 19 of the Judgment in *Van Schijndel*.

where the public interest required its intervention. The Court disposed the *Peterbroeck* case on the same day. Although the structure and rationale behind the Court's reasoning was essentially the same, the outcome was entirely different. Contrary to the Opinion of AG Jacobs, the Court found that a procedural rule barring appeal courts in national legal orders from the ability to raise their own motion points of EU law was preventing the full application of EU law, as it precluded parties obtaining adjudication over EU-derived rights.

B. A Question of Balance: National Procedural Law and EU Effectiveness

The Opinion of AG Jacobs on this matter has always been, in this author's view, the correct one. Even as a young academic, this author wrote an article[16] that had a *marked similarity* to the Opinion of AG Jacobs in *Van Schijndel*, albeit interspersed with ideas borrowed from another AG who this author very much admired: Walter van Gerven. Personal reminiscing and nostalgia aside, the balanced approach taken by AG Jacobs in *Van Schijndel* made good sense for several practical and principled reasons.

On the practical side, it prevented (and prevents) the Court from getting too entangled in the minutiae of national procedural law. In the cases where the Court did exactly that, it is doubtful that legal certainty is well served.[17] As put, '[t]he primacy of Community law does not require that they [national procedural rules] should be overridden in all circumstances so as to allow Community law to enter the arena at any stage in the proceedings',[18] forms the quotable passage from the Opinion of AG Jacobs in *Van Schijndel* which encapsulates a realistic idea of what the judicial process really entails. As AG Jacobs pointed out, any judicial resolution system, including the supranational one at the Court, would need to comply with certain rules as to guarantee an efficient composition of conflicting interests, access to justice, and the protection of the rights of the parties. At the same time, there needed to be measures to make sure that there was not a proliferation of unfounded suits or unending litigation. Thus, if it was true that any kind of remedy for a breach of right would have to go through a number of procedural hoops, why not go through the ones that already existed if they actually worked.

The 'balancing test' has also the advantage of being based on a presumption, and such a presumption can always be overturned, when necessary. The divergence in outcomes between *Van Schijndel* and *Peterbroeck* was exactly that: in the latter case, a 60-day limitation period was calculated after taking into account time spent before a tax authority, that was, of course, according to the Court case law, not a court or tribunal that could make a preliminary reference to the Court. When the case finally went before a court, the time had already elapsed, thus preventing the court from either raising an *ex officio* point of EU law, or make a preliminary reference to the Court. Thus, the time limit, although in theory necessary to provide legal certainty, would have made it impossible for the parties to rely on EU law.[19] If national law does not provide for either the right remedy to protect individual rights, or does not sufficiently guarantee the integrity of the EU legal order, the Court can escalate a response and sanction those inefficiencies.

---

[16] A Biondi, 'The European Court of Justice and certain national procedural limitations: not such a tough relationship' (1999) 36 *CMLRev* 1271.

[17] See Case C-208/90 *Emmott* ECLI:EU:C:1991:333 or Case C-326/96 *Levez* ECLI:EU:C:1998:577.

[18] Para 25 of the Opinion of AG Jacobs in *Van Schijndel*.

[19] As also discussed extra judicially by AG Jacobs himself. See F Jacobs, 'Enforcing Community rights and obligations in National Courts: striking the balance' in J Lonbay and A Biondi (eds), *Remedies for Breach of EC Law* (Chichester, Wiley, 1997).

The *Transportes Urbanos* judgment is a good example of this.[20] The Court was, in theory, asked to rule on whether certain complicated Spanish provisions, which required the exhaustion of remedies to bring a claim for damages against the state for a breach of EU law, did not respect the principle of equivalence, in so far as similar claims for damages against the state were based on national law infringements that were not subject to the same pre-condition. Despite speaking the language of equivalence, the Court eschewed any in-depth analysis of Spanish law. It simply found that the national law made it impossible to bring an action in damages for breaches of EU law before having exhausted the national remedies first, thus denying the full effective application of EU law and individual rights protection.[21]

C. Judicial Process and Ideologies

This chapter does not, however, try to argue that a judicial process is just a question of rules and hoops to jump through. Not only are substance and procedure often indistinguishable, but procedural systems are also heavily shaped by ideologies (not necessarily with negative connotations) as there is a close relationship between the generally prevailing ideology, and a state's law of procedure and evidence.[22] This is especially true in a supranational context such as the EU legal order. *Van Schijndel*, both judgment and Opinion, was indeed compliant with EU ideology in two respects: it left the effectiveness mantra intact, in addition to cleverly managing the expectations of national courts. As for this latter aspect, the emphasis was on the role of national courts as EU *juges du droit commun*, and on trusting them to maintain *judicial balancing*: the simultaneous consideration of both EU and national law. It was, to use an old expression, a 'Community method': a model essentially based on the coexistence of different regulatory levels.

Of course, such a method involved accepting, as AG Jacobs predicted, a certain degree of differentiation both in terms of application of EU law, and generally in taking into account different attitudes of national judges towards EU law. These attitudes should, however, not simply be measured in terms of their standing for or against EU ideology. Other important factors to take into account include issues such as workload, access to resources, chambers or monocratic decisions, seniority, and so on.[23] A lasting advantage of the balance test is the flexibility it offers, allowing the Court to be dynamic and open to the developments and transformations of national procedural systems. As predicted by AG Jacobs, terms such as 'continental', 'common law', 'adversarial', 'inquisitorial', 'private', and 'public' have become merely labels. Instead, the focus in most national procedural systems has shifted towards pragmatic solutions on how to facilitate optimal efficiency and the protection of rights in the organisation of the administration of justice.[24]

The Court itself has therefore gradually updated the list of 'good national procedural rules' that reflects the struggles and transformations of national procedural systems. Thus, elements that should be taken into account in evaluating the compliance of national procedural law with EU law now include the financial situation of the parties, rules to deal with the

---

[20] Case C-118/08 *Transportes Urbanos* ECLI:EU:C:2010:39.

[21] Case C-571/16 *Kantarev* ECLI:EU:C:2018:807.

[22] P Calamandrei, *"Procedure and Democracy* (New York, New York University Press, 1957).

[23] See the interesting data and observations in T Nowak and M Glavina, 'National courts as regulatory agencies and the application of EU law' (2021) 43 *Journal of European Integration* 739.

[24] See A Zuckerman, *Zuckerman on Civil Procedure* (London, Sweet & Maxwell, 2006) especially chs 2 and 3.

length of proceedings, the cost of litigation, or the potentially frivolous nature of the claim.[25] Whilst these elements can be relied upon to not necessitate the setting aside of the national rules in question, they contemporaneously form a de facto EU procedural code that applies across different jurisdictions, and against which national rules can be tested. In *Berliotz*,[26] for instance, the Court, in interpreting a directive on cooperation on fiscal matters,[27] held that a judge required to rule on the legality of a fine imposed at the end of a procedure of exchange of fiscal information between different national authorities was entitled to review preparatory acts, despite this being issued by a public authority of *another* Member State. This was in order to guarantee for the judge a full account of all possible evidence, and to conclude the process without any undue delay. Likewise in *DEB*, the restrictions imposed by German law on legal persons from applying for legal aid were assessed by the Court in terms of the evolution of legal aid in national systems, and the answer re-casted in the framework of the interpretation of the principle of effective judicial protection as enshrined in Article 47 of the EU Charter of Fundamental Rights.[28]

This leads to the second facet of *Van Schijndel*, which aligned ideologically with the EU. The balance test left the door open for the Court to intervene if it deemed necessary, but such intervention also renders visible the fundamental features of EU legal order. Let's take the *ex officio* question again. Although *not* raising a point of EU law, *ex officio*, is possible under the 'procedural autonomy' test,[29] the Court will impose such a duty if core EU provisions may be affected. Thus, the Court held that competition law or consumer protection are to be considered as rules of public policy, which national courts must examine, even *ex officio*.[30]

Likewise, this procedural supremacy[31] will always kick in if the institutional framework of the EU legal order is threatened. For instance, the Court is usually very respectful towards the principle of *res judicata* in reaffirming the importance of ensuring the finality of judgments as a tool to ensure the proper conduct of proceedings and legal certainty. It went as far as to hold that EU law does not require a national court to disapply domestic rules of procedure conferring finality on a decision, 'even if to do so would enable it to remedy an infringement of EU law by the decision at issue'.[32] However, the Court has shown no hesitation in setting aside a final judgment of a national court if this involved an *invasion* into an EU exclusive competence. For instance, in the *Lucchini* case,[33] an Italian civil court ordered the payment of a grant to the Lucchini company, despite the fact that the European Commission, in a decision that had not been appealed by the interested parties, considered such a grant as an unlawful state aid. In a subsequent action for recovery before the Italian administrative courts, the company opposed the finality of the judgment of the national court that ordered the payment as a bar to the recovery of the money. The Court, in a powerful yet concise judgment, held that

---

[25] Joined Cases C-317/08, C-318/08, C-319/08 and C-320/08 *Alassini* ECLI:EU:C:2010:146; Case C-260/11 *Edwards and Pallikaropoulos* ECLI:EU:C:2013:221.

[26] Case C-682/15 *Berlioz* ECLI:EU:C:2017:373.

[27] Council Directive 2011/16/EU of 15 February 2011 on administrative cooperation in the field of taxation and repealing Directive 77/799/EEC [2011] OJ L64/1.

[28] Case C-279/09 *DEB* ECLI:EU:C:2010:811.

[29] Case C-72/95 *Kraaijeveld* ECLI:EU:C:1996:404; Case C-564/15 *Farkas* ECLI:EU:C:2017:302 and also Opinion of AG Kokott in Case C-416/10 *Križan* ECLI:EU:C:2012:218, para 152.

[30] Case C-126/97 *Eco Swiss* ECLI:EU:C:1999:269; Case C-168/05 *Claro* ECLI:EU:C:2006:675; Case C-137/08 *VB Pénzügyi Lízing* ECLI:EU:C:2010:659.

[31] E Neframi, 'The Duty of Loyalty: Rethinking Its Scope Through Its Application In The Field of EU External Relations' (2010) 47 *CMLRev* 323, 330.

[32] Case C-2/06 *Kempter* ECLI:EU:C:2008:78.

[33] Case C-119/05 *Lucchini* ECLI:EU:C:2007:434. See also Case C-2/08 *Fallimento Olimpiclub* ECLI:EU:C:2009:506.

the principle of *res judicata* could not prevent the recovery of state aid which was granted in breach of EU law, and which had been found to be incompatible with the internal market, in a decision by the Commission that had become final.

In this context:

> a national court which is called upon, within the exercise of its jurisdiction, to apply provisions of Community law is under a duty to give full effect to those provisions, if necessary refusing of its own motion to apply any conflicting provision of national law.[34]

In areas such as state aid, which Member States have accepted as an institutionally exclusive competence conferred to the Commission along with a permanent limitation of their state powers, it is the duty of the national court to give *ex officio* precedence to EU law, and set aside any conflicting provisions.

D. Twenty-five Plus Years On

The *Van Schijndel* judgment has been cited 119 times by the Court and its AGs; a testament to the longevity of the approach taken. This 25-year plus longevity has, however, seen the constitutional landscape – in terms of the categories of EU rights to be guaranteed and of procedures available in areas such as consumer and environmental protection – change enormously. In particular, the binding effect of the Charter and the extended use by the Court of Article 47 of the Charter have provided a firm constitutional foundation for the right to an effective judicial remedy.

Quite rightly, an intense debate is ongoing over whether such a mutated landscape has led to the 'balanced approach' becoming rather outdated. Of course, Salviati was eventually proven right, and Sagredo was persuaded. Thus, certainly in many cases where a national procedural framework did not provide adequate forms of protection, the Court has not hesitated to wield Article 47 of the Charter to set aside those provisions.[35] Nevertheless, in a humble (and perhaps minority) view, the approach adopted by the Court can still be broadly assimilated to the one adopted in the context of *Van Schijndel*.

Today, the Court speaks of Article 47 of the Charter to be read in conjunction with Article 52 of the Charter as to ensure that such Charter rights 'may not affect genuine objectives of general interests'. This author would argue that these include respect for the essential (and EU approved) features of national procedural systems, such as the introduction of specific expedited procedures, or conditions on the right to be heard.[36]

A final, and perhaps more striking development, has been the combined use of Article 19 TEU in conjunction with Article 47 of the Charter. In a series of high-profile cases, the Court found that the judicial systems which do not comply with the requirements stemming from Article 19 TEU – in particular the independence of the members of judicial bodies – violate EU law.[37] The analysis of such case law goes beyond the scope of this chapter, but one cannot resist a final observation. Simplicio, Salviati, and Sagredo, despite their fierce divergences, all

---

[34] Para 61 of the Judgment in *Lucchini*.

[35] Case C-752/18 *Deutsche Umwelthilfe* ECLI:EU:C:2019:1114; Case C-556/17 *Torubarov* ECLI:EU:C:2019:626.

[36] Case C-418/11 *Texdata Software* ECLI:EU:C:2013:588.

[37] Case C-64/16 *Association of Portuguese Judges* ECLI:EU:C:2018:117; Case C-619/18 *Commission v Poland* ECLI:EU:C:2019:531; Case C-354/20 *Openbaar Ministerie* ECLI:EU:C:2020:1033.

agreed on the need to base their findings on the 'observation of nature and of the quest for scientific truth'. Likewise, *Van Schijndel* was predicated on a basic postulate: whatever the differences between national procedure systems are or their possible inefficiencies in term of effectiveness of EU rights' protections, independence of the judiciary and respect for the rule of law is (and always will be) non-negotiable, as is the basic assumption without which the system of cooperation between the Court and national courts cannot operate.

30

The Meeting of International Sanctions and European Human Rights: Opinion of Advocate General Jacobs in Bosphorus

PIET EECKHOUT

I. INTRODUCTION

THE Opinion of AG Jacobs in *Bosphorus* is one I had the enormous privilege to assist the AG with, as a *référendaire* in his Chambers.[1] This chapter therefore offers the opportunity to return to an Opinion I know well, including its gestation. Somewhat unavoidably, this means that the reader should not look for any trenchant criticism of the Opinion in the paragraphs that follow. Instead, what I want to do is to put the Opinion in context; to sketch the alternative approaches that were available; to discuss the main issues that were at stake; and to assess the effects of the Opinion on how EU law has evolved in the sensitive areas of foreign policy and restrictive measures (sanctions). I hope not to indulge in hagiography, but whether I do will be for the reader to decide.

II. BACKGROUND, CONTEXT, AND FACTS

Europe and the EU were ill-prepared for the conflict that engulfed Yugoslavia after the fall of the Iron Curtain. So was the international community. The UN Security Council (UNSC) attempted to ramp up the pressure on Serbia (hereafter the Federal Republic of Yugoslavia (Serbia and Montenegro)), regarded as a main culprit in the conflict. It imposed sanctions that were gradually tightened. The EU could not stand by, even if it failed to reach any real consensus on how to approach the break-up of Yugoslavia. At the time, UN sanctions were focused on severing trade and economic links. Those were blunt instruments, unavoidably affecting economic actors who played no part in the conflict. But trade is an exclusive EU competence, and EU trade regulations are an effective legal instrument, as they are directly applicable in all Member States, and need to be applied uniformly. The UN sanctions were

---

[1] Opinion of AG Jacobs in Case C-84/95 *Bosphorus* ECLI:EU:C:1996:179.

therefore implemented at EU level, essentially by way of carbon-copying the provisions of the relevant UN resolutions.[2]

At some point the UN ordered that all aircraft 'in which a majority or controlling interest is held by a person or undertaking in or operating from the Federal Republic of Yugoslavia (Serbia and Montenegro))' had to be impounded.[3] This affected Bosphorus Airways, a Turkish charter company which had leased two aircraft owned by Yugoslav Airlines (JAT). These were 'dry' leases, meaning that Bosphorus Airways had full day-to-day control over the aircraft. At some point, one of the aircraft was in Dublin for maintenance, and the Irish authorities decided to give effect to Resolution 820(1993), and indeed to the EU Regulation copying this provision into EU law.[4] They had sought the opinion of the UN Sanctions Committee, tasked with overseeing the Yugoslavia sanctions. That Committee considered that the aircraft needed to be impounded, and that was what the Irish authorities proceeded to do.

Bosphorus Airways challenged the Irish decision, implementing the Regulation in national court, and the High Court (Murphy J) found for the company on the basis that it was not controlled by JAT. The Minister appealed to the Supreme Court of Ireland, which referred the question of interpretation of the Regulation to the Court. Bosphorus Airways argued that the High Court interpretation was correct, and that a contrary interpretation would violate the principles of legal certainty and proportionality, and indeed its fundamental right to property.

III. THE OPINION OF AG JACOBS

AG Jacobs started his analysis by observing that the wording of the Regulation appeared to be clear, in the sense of extending to the aircraft in issue. JAT retained exclusive ownership, and the term 'interest' was a wide one, which encompassed all types of property interest. Other language versions referred to the notion of property. The preamble to the Regulation emphasised the need for a uniform application. The fact that JAT had no control over the aircraft appeared irrelevant, given the juxtaposition of 'a majority or controlling interest'. The question was therefore whether there were any compelling reasons to interpret the Regulation in a way which appeared to depart from its wording.[5]

First, AG Jacobs examined whether the UN Resolution that was at the basis of the Regulation could be such a reason. Textually, the two were identical. However, Murphy J had embraced a teleological interpretation, finding that it made no sense to extend the sanctions to an innocent party like Bosphorus Airways. He considered that the impounding of aircraft was targeted at avoiding that they be used to transport goods, circumventing the trade sanctions. But the AG did not find such a narrow construction of the Resolution compelling. It was not excluded that the UNSC intended to go further, depriving a Yugoslav undertaking even of the indirect benefit of the continued operation and maintenance of a means of transport. He also found it difficult to divine the precise purpose of the UNSC, 'an organ composed of many diverse States acting in highly charged political circumstances'.[6] AG Jacobs further

---

[2] For the contemporary analysis at the time, see PJ Kuijper, 'Trade Sanctions, Security and Human Rights and Commercial Policy' in M Maresceau (ed), *The European Community's Commercial Policy after 1992: The Legal Dimension* (Leiden, Martinus Nijhoff, 1993).

[3] UNSC Resolution 820(1993), para 24.

[4] Regulation (EEC) No 990/93 concerning trade between the European Economic Community and the Federal Republic of Yugoslavia (Serbia and Montenegro) [1993] OJ L102/14.

[5] Para 31.

[6] Para 40.

accepted the Commission's argument that the objective could be to impound means of transport at the earliest opportunity, so as to avoid that control was passed back to persons in the sanctioned Republic. He then looked at the language of the relevant Resolutions, and found that neither their aims nor text pointed in a different direction. He finally considered that due regard should be given to the concordant view of the UN Sanctions Committee, even if that Committee had no decision-making powers in this matter.[7]

Secondly, AG Jacobs examined whether the principles of legal certainty and proportionality were violated, and whether there was a breach of Bosphorus Airways' fundamental rights.[8] Legal certainty was not in issue, as the AG had established that the text of the Regulation was clear.[9] The proportionality and fundamental rights points could conveniently be taken together.

AG Jacobs started that analysis with a general description of how fundamental rights are protected in EU law – as guaranteed by the European Convention on Human Rights (ECHR) and as resulting from the constitutional traditions of the Member States. He then stated, firmly, that '[r]espect for fundamental rights is thus a condition of the lawfulness of Community acts',[10] with no qualifications whatsoever.

The AG then turned to the right to property as protected under the First Protocol to the ECHR. He analysed the relevant case law of the European Court of Human Rights (ECtHR), which showed that the kind of interest Bosphorus Airways had in the impounded aircraft was protected. States had a right to control the use of property in accordance with the general interest, but in doing so had to strike an appropriate and fair balance. After some further analysis of ECtHR's case law on the seizing and impounding of assets, the AG turned to the case law of the Court itself. Referring in particular to the Opinion of AG Capotorti and to the Court's judgment in *Hauer*,[11] AG Jacobs reiterated the proportionality analysis required in these types of cases: it was necessary to identify the aim pursued by the disputed regulation and to determine whether there was a reasonable relationship between the measures provided for and the aim pursued.

The AG then proceeded to apply those principles to the case at hand. Bosphorus Airways' interest in the aircraft was clearly protected by the right to property. The impounding was a severe restriction on the exercise by Bosphorus Airways of its property rights. On the other hand it was also clear that there was a particularly strong public interest in enforcing embargo measures decided by the UNSC. That did not mean that any type of interference with the right to property should be tolerated. The Court would have to intervene if the measure was wholly unreasonable. That was not the case, however, in light of the preceding analysis of the objectives pursued by the Resolution and the Regulation. AG Jacobs was also not convinced that the alleged drastic financial and commercial effects of the impounding could be given much weight. He questioned the reality of those effects, and in any event felt that the balance was right in light of the importance of the public interest involved. AG Jacobs concluded that there was no breach of the right to property and of the principle of proportionality.

---

[7] Para 46.
[8] Paras 48-69.
[9] Para 48.
[10] Para 53.
[11] Case 44/79 *Hauer* ECLI:EU:C:1979:290.

IV. ANALYSIS

A. Proportionality and Fundamental Rights

AG Jacobs was clearly of the view that *Bosphorus* was a hard case. He stated that the company's arguments on respect for proportionality and fundamental rights raised 'an important issue',[12] leading him to examine the question 'in some detail'.[13] For an AG rarely prone to hyperbole, that was a significant statement. The framing of the analysis is also notable, and should not be overlooked. AG Jacobs chose to treat the proportionality/fundamental rights question separately from the interpretative issue. He did not aim to colour the interpretation of the sanctions Regulation with concerns over Bosphorus Airways' right to property. He considered it more appropriate to interpret the Regulation on its own terms, and then to examine whether the interpretation withstood the test of respect for fundamental rights. That was a courageous and principled approach, because a conclusion that the Regulation did not withstand that test would have had to lead to a finding of invalidity. Such a finding (if also adopted by the Court) would have constituted significant judicial interference with a piece of general EU legislation in a highly charged and very sensitive political context.

It is further worth noting that the AG considered that respect for fundamental rights and for the principle of proportionality were interlinked. Any constitutional scholar will find this self-evident,[14] but as proportionality is also a self-standing principle of EU law, this correct framing is important. The case's balancing exercise, weighing up the sanctions' goals and the interference with Bosphorus Airways' interests in the impounded aircraft, cannot be dissociated from the right to property as a fundamental right.

Judicial texts are often important in what their authors do not voice and articulate, as opposed to what they do say. The Court's standard approach to reviewing the compliance of general legislation with the principle of proportionality is a limited one: it will only examine whether there is a *manifest* lack of proportionality.[15] This is not the place to examine whether that is the right approach. Clearly, AG Jacobs did not employ this test, and he was right not to do so in a hard fundamental-rights case. If legislation could only be struck down where the interference with fundamental rights is manifestly disproportionate, those rights would not be adequately protected.

However, it must also be recognised that AG Jacobs did not conduct an overly intrusive proportionality examination. He focused, first, on the question whether Bosphorus Airways' interest in the impounded aircraft was protected under the right to property, as articulated in ECHR and EU law. He examined that question with care, both as regards the types of interest involved and the acceptable reasons for interfering with those property interests.[16] He then turned to the public interest underpinning the sanctions, describing that as a particularly strong one:

> [i]ndeed, it is difficult to think of any stronger type of public interest than that of stopping a civil war as devastating as the one which engulfed the former Yugoslavia, and in particular Bosnia-Herzegovina.[17]

---

[12] Para 50.

[13] ibid.

[14] See eg A Barak, *Proportionality – Constitutional Rights and their Limitations* (Cambridge, CUP, 2012).

[15] See eg Case C-331/88 *Fedesa* ECLI:EU:C:1990:391, para 14; Case C-280/93 *Germany v Council* ECLI:EU:C:1994:367, para 90.

[16] Paras 55–63.

[17] Para 64.

Unavoidably, the sanctions imposed by the UNSC affected the property rights of innocent economic operators, and Bosphorus Airways was in no ways unique.[18] AG Jacobs then stated that this did not mean that any interference with property rights was acceptable. If it could be shown that the interference 'was wholly unreasonable in the light of the aims which the competent authorities sought to achieve, then it would be necessary for this Court to intervene'.[19] That was not the case here, in light of the reasons underpinning the extension of the sanctions to aircraft owned, but not controlled by a Yugoslav undertaking. Here, the AG referred back to his analysis of why the Regulation had to be interpreted in this wider sense.[20] He finally pointed out that the alleged 'drastic financial and commercial effects' on Bosphorus Airways could not be given the weight which the company suggested. Those financial consequences would vary from case to case, and it was not possible 'to set aside a general measure of this kind simply because of the financial consequences which it may have in a particular case'.[21] And even if it were relevant to take account of the losses incurred by Bosphorus Airways, the principle of proportionality would not be infringed 'in view of the importance of the public interest involved'.[22]

This is not a mechanical proportionality analysis, nor is it one that focuses on the standard components of the proportionality principle: adequacy, necessity, and strict proportionality. That is not a weakness of the Opinion. Both the adequacy and the necessity of these types of sanctions are difficult to assess. Do the sanctions assist in putting an end to a conflict such as the one in the former Yugoslavia? Are they necessary to that end, or could less restrictive measures be chosen? Those are hugely complex matters of judgement, and they are intensely political. Strict proportionality or balancing is even less conceivable. The public interest in stopping a civil war and the restrictions on an innocent company's right to property are incommensurable.[23] *Bosphorus* was clearly a case raising the issue whether EU law admits of something akin to the US political question doctrine.[24] Neither the AG nor the Court mentioned this concept, but the somewhat limited review which they exercised, and the focus on the importance of the public interest at stake, have overtones of such a doctrine.

Does this mean that AG Jacobs employed a weak, or even misconceived proportionality test? His claim that it would need to be shown that the interference with Bosphorus Airways' property rights was 'wholly unreasonable' may suggest this. Yet a more careful analysis of the Opinion shows that the AG took the fundamental rights at issue seriously. In one crucial respect, his Opinion offered more scrutiny than the Court's judgment. The Court confined itself to stating that what was at stake was:

> an objective of general interest so fundamental for the international community, which consists in putting an end to the state of war in the region and to the massive violations of human rights and humanitarian international law in the Republic of Bosnia-Herzegovina.[25]

---

[18] ibid.
[19] Para 65.
[20] ibid.
[21] Para 66.
[22] ibid.
[23] On incommensurability, see CR Sunstein, 'Incommensurability and Valuation in Law' (1993–94) 92 *Michigan Law Review* 779.
[24] See TM Franck, *Political Questions Judicial Answers: Does the Rule of Law Apply to Foreign Affairs?* (New Jersey, Princeton University Press, 1992).
[25] Case C-84/95 *Bosphorus* ECLI:EU:C:1996:312, para 26.

The AG, by contrast, was much more forensic in his analysis of the specific justifications for interpreting the Regulation as extending to a dry lease.[26] Whilst he recognised that the UNSC's reasons for such an extension could not be established, he also found that the impounding of leased aircraft was necessary because of their inherent mobility and the risk that, through an unexpected change of course, the aircraft could be returned to the Federal Republic of Yugoslavia (Serbia and Montenegro). Such a forensic analysis of the aim of specific sanctions was really indispensable in the face of an overriding public interest such as the one at stake in this case. Clearly, it is not for a court to decide whether or not sanctions are adequate or necessary to end a state of war. Nor is it possible to focus on the 'innocence' of those affected by the sanctions. But what a court can do is to scrutinise the scope of the overall sanctions and their specific components, and examine whether there is a reasonable justification for them.

B. The Status of the ECHR

The Opinion is also noteworthy for the emphasis it placed on the ECHR, next to the EU's own standards of fundamental rights protection. This calls for some 'law-in-context' analysis.[27] AG Jacobs has always been a jurist whose concepts of European law were as much inspired by the ECHR as they are by EU law. He worked at the ECtHR in Strasbourg in his younger days, and has always remained a strong advocate of the ECHR. The period over which he crafted the *Bosphorus* Opinion was a pivotal one in the development of the EU's approach to the protection of fundamental rights. Two years before, the Council had asked for an Opinion of the Court under what is now the Article 218(11) TFEU procedure, to inquire whether the EU could accede to the ECHR. The Court issued its negative Opinion just a month before the Opinion of AG Jacobs in *Bosphorus* was delivered.[28] It found that, in the then state of EU law, the EU lacked competence to accede to the ECHR. In those days, all the Advocates General (AGs) were 'heard' by the Court in proceedings for an Opinion. The practice was that they put their views in writing, but those writings were not public.[29] However, rumour has it that AG Jacobs advised the Court to rule that the EU did have competence to accede to the ECHR, and that such accession was compatible with the EU Treaties.

The Court's refusal to endorse accession to the ECHR in the mid-1990s did not kill the idea. The story is well-known. The ill-fated Constitution for Europe imposed an obligation on the EU to join,[30] and the Treaty of Lisbon copied the relevant provision, which is now situated in Article 6(2) TEU.[31] In the meantime, however, the EU had drafted its own Charter of Fundamental Rights, a development that might not have occurred had the Court accepted that ECHR accession was possible. Sadly, such accession continues to be a distant prospect because of the obstacles the Court put on the road in *Opinion 2/13*.[32]

---

[26] Paras 39–42.

[27] See W Twining, *Law in Context: Enlarging a Discipline* (Oxford, OUP, 1997).

[28] *Opinion 2/94* ECLI:EU:C:1996:140.

[29] In the past decade, this practice in the Opinion procedure has changed, and a single AG is assigned, who delivers an Opinion, like they would in normal cases. See eg ch 45.

[30] Treaty establishing a Constitution for Europe [2004] OJ C310/1, Article I-9(2).

[31] Treaty of Lisbon amending the Treaty on European Union and the Treaty establishing the European Community, signed at Lisbon, 13 December 2007 [2007] OJ C306/1.

[32] *Opinion 2/13* ECLI:EU:C:2014:2454. See P Eeckhout, 'Opinion 2/13 on EU Accession to the ECHR and Judicial Dialogue: Autonomy or Autarky?' (2015) 38 *Fordham International Law Journal* 955.

The ECHR analysis in the Opinion of AG Jacobs in *Bosphorus* cannot be dissociated from the broader debate about how best to protect fundamental rights in the EU. AG Jacobs was very clear about how he conceived of the role for the ECHR:

> for practical purposes the Convention can be regarded as part of Community law and can be invoked as such both in this Court and in national courts where Community law is in issue.[33]

His analysis of the right to property put the ECHR first, and he examined the relevant case law most carefully. He turned to relevant Court precedents as a matter of EU law in second order. The Court, by contrast, did not even mention the Convention.

The AG may have saved the Court the embarrassment of a genuine conflict with the ECtHR. The Bosphorus Airways case is of course best known for the judgment of the latter court, which followed the Court ruling.[34] In *Bosphorus v Ireland*, the ECtHR established that Ireland could rely on its obligations to respect EU law, provided that EU law guaranteed a level of protection of fundamental rights equivalent to that of the ECHR. The ECtHR found this to be the case, and stated that such equivalence created a presumption of compliance with the Convention – thus creating what has become known as the *Bosphorus* presumption. The presumption, however, is rebuttable, and in *Bosphorus v Ireland*, the ECtHR was satisfied that 'there was no dysfunction of the mechanisms of control of the observance of Convention rights'. It established this after having:

> had regard to the nature of the interference, to the general interest pursued by the impoundment and by the sanctions regime and to the ruling of the [Court] (*in the light of the opinion of the AG*).[35]

That is a remarkable statement, suggesting that the *Bosphorus* judgment was not, on its own, entirely persuasive, and needed the help of the AG's more careful and comprehensive scrutiny.

After having left the Court, AG Jacobs returned to the *Bosphorus* case and to the status of the ECHR in his Hamlyn Lectures.[36] He restated the idea that the ECHR, including the ECtHR case law, are fully part of EU law. He pointed out that, whereas the Court does not cite the case law of other courts, it makes few exceptions, such as the case law of the ECtHR. He discussed all this as evidence of a fundamental EU law openness towards other legal systems. It is clear, though, that not everyone will agree with this openness proposition. The more recent case law on the autonomy of EU law, particularly from the ECHR and from international investment arbitration, points in a different direction.[37] The Hamlyn Lectures are perhaps best read as making a normative as much as a descriptive claim. It can be argued that openness leads to a stronger and more effective rule of law, as elaborated below. The human-rights analysis in the Opinion of AG Jacobs in *Bosphorus* was definitely deeper and richer as a result of the inclusion of the ECHR provisions and the ECtHR case law.

C. The Role of the UN Security Council

The Yugoslavia sanctions emanated from the UNSC, and the relevant EU law instruments faithfully reflected the applicable UNSC Resolutions. AG Jacobs focused on those Resolutions,

---

[33] Para 53.
[34] *Bosphorus Hava Yolları Turizm ve Ticaret Anonim Şirketi v Ireland* [GC], no. 45036/98, ECHR 2005-VI.
[35] ibid, para 166, emphasis added.
[36] FG Jacobs, *The Sovereignty of Law* (Cambridge, CUP, 2007) 54–61.
[37] Opinion 2/13; Case C-284/16 *Achmea* ECLI:EU:C:2018:158; Case C-741/19 *Komstroy* ECLI:EU:C:2021:655.

and on the position taken by the UN's Sanctions Committee. He did not regard that position as in any way binding, but nevertheless looked at it as relevant context. He emphasised that, in the act of interpreting the relevant Regulation, one had to look at the objectives the UNSC sought to pursue – objectives which were difficult to establish in light of the inherently political nature of that UN institution. This led him to prefer a textual over a teleological interpretation.[38]

The Court was more perfunctory in its references to the relevant UNSC Resolution. It referred to it when considering 'context and aims' of the Regulation,[39] but ultimately limited the analysis to the mere wording of the relevant provision on impounding aircraft.[40] The focus was really on the interpretation of the Regulation in issue, and the Court also construed its own understanding of the overall objective of that EU foreign policy act: to put pressure on the Federal Republic of Yugoslavia (Serbia and Montenegro).

The Court would of course again be confronted with a UNSC sanctions resolution, implemented by the EU, in *Kadi*.[41] In the intervening period, UN sanctions had moved away from general sanctions targeted at states and regimes, to 'smart' sanctions focused on individuals and groups. In *Kadi*, the Court acted sharply, in light of the lack of due process in UN listing policies. Again, the Court did not formally review the UN Resolution, on the basis of a strict distinction between EU law and UN law. It construed its jurisdiction narrowly, as being confined to reviewing the lawfulness of the Regulation which copied the Resolution into EU law.[42] In substance, however, *Kadi* was indeed an act of judicial review of UN sanctions policies.

It is worth making some comments on these judicial review cases from the perspective of the plurality of the legal systems involved: UN law (embodying the policy decisions); EU law (implementing those decisions within the EU); Member States' domestic laws (applying EU law); and the ECHR (with which the sanctions need to comply). In this quadrangular relationship, EU law occupies a central position. UN law is not self-executing, even if it binds all states. EU Regulations, by contrast, have direct application and direct effect, and need to be applied uniformly. Member States need to respect and apply those Regulations, and the ECHR's function is one of further review. But the Regulation is the act with strongest legal authority. It is therefore not surprising that the Court plays such a significant role in the judicial review of international sanctions. Foreign and security policy may not be an area of strong and effective EU competence and activity, but that does not prevent EU law from stepping in.

D. Effect on Future Case Law

It is clear that *Bosphorus* has had significant effects on later case law. *Kadi* and *Bosphorus v Ireland* (of the ECtHR) were already touched upon above. The latter judgment was concerned with the equivalence between the ECHR and EU law systems of fundamental rights protection. That is a wider topic, beyond the scope of this chapter. But on *Kadi*, and judicial review of foreign policy sanctions, there is more to be said.

---

[38] Paras 40–47 of the Opinion. For criticism see I Canor, '"Can Two Walk Together, Except They Be Agreed?" The Relationship Between International Law and European Law: The Incorporation of United Nations Sanctions Against Yugoslavia Into European Community Law Through the Perspective of the European Court of Justice' (1998) 35 *CMLRev* 137. For a rebuttal of that criticism see P Koutrakos, *Trade, Foreign Policy and Defence in EU Constitutional Law: The Legal Regulation of Sanctions, Exports of Dual-use Goods and Armaments* (Oxford, Hart Publishing, 2001) 136.

[39] Para 13.

[40] Para 24.

[41] Joined Cases C-402/05 P and C-415/05 P *Kadi* ECLI:EU:C:2008:461.

[42] Para 288 of Judgment in *Kadi*.

Before exploring the effects of *Bosphorus*, it is perhaps worth sketching the counterfactual. AG Jacobs could have been less principled in his Opinion. He could have interpreted the Regulation in light of the right to property, and could even have found in favour of Bosphorus Airways (as did Murphy J in the High Court of Ireland). That would have meant, though, that no full judicial review would have been undertaken. The AG could also have operated the standard manifest-disproportionality test for review of general EU legislation. He could have preferred that test, in light of the UN origin of the sanctions and of the highly charged political context. The Court might have followed such an approach. Courts and judges are often receptive to 'political question' and 'act of state' doctrines. In such an outcome, *Bosphorus* would have been much more ambivalent about the very principle of full judicial review of foreign policy sanctions. Instead, the judgment, and particularly the Opinion, were clear about that principle.

A couple of years later, the Court was again faced with a sanctions review case. In *Racke*, and with AG Jacobs also involved, it was asked to review the EU's decision to suspend the Cooperation Agreement with Yugoslavia.[43] This was a further measure to put pressure on Serbia. The review was undertaken on the basis of customary international treaty law, more particularly the somewhat nebulous doctrine of *rebus sic stantibus*. Neither the AG nor the Court established a breach of that doctrine, and they did, in this instance, operate a limited type of review.[44] *Racke* is nonetheless a remarkable judgment, in which the Court showed a willingness to engage with an intensely political act of high foreign policy. It also showed the openness to international law, to which AG Jacobs referred in his Hamlyn Lectures.

But the real sequel came in *Kadi*. As is well known, Mr. Kadi has been listed by the UNSC shortly after 9/11, as a suspected supporter of Al Qaeda. No specific reasons had been given for his listing, and he had not been heard. The EU again implemented the relevant UN Resolution, and Mr Kadi challenged the EU Regulation in the EU courts. The Court of First Instance (now the General Court) found in favour of the EU institutions.[45] Mr Kadi appealed to the Court, and in that appeal relied heavily on the principle of full review as established in *Bosphorus*.

The Court was aided by another outstanding AG, Mr Poiares Maduro.[46] In his reasoning, *Bosphorus* was crucial for concluding that the UN origin of the Kadi sanctions did not preclude judicial review. He accepted the Commission's and the Council's argument 'that the judgment in *Bosphorus* is silent on the matter of the scope of the Court's jurisdiction, because, at any rate, the regulation did not infringe fundamental rights'.[47] However, he did not find that argument persuasive:

> I would suppose that, instead of deliberately leaving the matter undecided, the Court accepted as self-evident what the AG had felt useful to spell out, namely that 'respect for fundamental rights is ... a condition of the lawfulness of Community acts'.[48]

AG Poiares Maduro therefore took exactly the same approach as AG Jacobs. The Court followed suit. It stated that:

> the Community judicature must (...) ensure the review, *in principle the full review*, of the lawfulness of all Community acts in the light of the fundamental rights forming an integral part of the general

---

[43] Case C-162/96 *Racke* ECLI:EU:C:1998:293.
[44] Para 52 of the Judgment in *Racke*.
[45] Case T-315/01 *Kadi* ECLI:EU:T:2005:332.
[46] Opinion of AG Maduro in Joined Cases C-402/05 P and C-415/05 P *Kadi* ECLI:EU:C:2008:461.
[47] Para 27 of the Opinion of AG Maduro.
[48] ibid.

principles of Community law, including review of Community measures which, like the contested regulation, are designed to give effect to the resolutions adopted by the Security Council under Chapter VII of the Charter of the United Nations.[49]

Bosphorus has been cited in a string of further sanctions cases.[50] The principle of full review has been at work in many more cases. That does not mean that such review is straightforward.[51] The EU courts are struggling with issues such as access to secret evidence and the degree of discretion to be afforded to the EU's political institutions. There is definitely a willingness to accept that sanctions, and foreign policy decisions more generally, are complex terrain, and that the principle of full review needs to be adapted to that terrain.[52] The principle as such, however, continues to stand. This means two things: first, that the EU's Constitution does not stop at the water's edge:[53] a Turkish charter company and a Saudi Arabian business man are able to claim the protection of their fundamental rights in exactly the same way as an EU citizen. Secondly, the EU Constitution does not give way to high international politics, and to the institutions and actors (in the EU or elsewhere) involved in such politics. The path dependency of *Bosphorus* is a strong and intact EU rule of law.

---

[49] Para 326 of the Judgment in *Kadi*, emphasis added.

[50] See eg Case C-548/09 P *Bank Melli Iran* ECLI:EU:C:2011:735; Joined Cases C-539/10 P and C-550/10 P *Al-Aqsa* ECLI:EU:C:2012:711; Case C-72/15 *Rosneft* ECLI:EU:C:2017:236 and Case C-430/16 P *Bank Mellat* ECLI:EU:C:2018:668. See also A Ó Caoimh, 'Enforcement of International Sanctions within the EU Legal Order: Bosphorus' in G Butler and RA Wessel (eds), *EU External Relations Law: The Cases in Context* (Oxford, Hart Publishing, 2022).

[51] See eg C Eckes, 'EU Restrictive Measures Against Natural and Legal Persons: From Counterterrorist to Third Country Sanctions' (2014) 51 *CMLRev* 869.

[52] For a good example see the judgment in Joined Cases C-584/10 P, C-593/10 P and C-595/10 P *Kadi* ECLI:EU:C:2013:518.

[53] See P Eeckhout, *Does Europe's Constitution Stop at the Water's Edge? Law and Policy in the EU's External Relations* (Groningen, Europa Law Publishing, 2005).

31

The Game Over the Boards: Opinion of Advocate General Jacobs in Albany

CARL BAUDENBACHER

I. INTRODUCTION

IN ICE HOCKEY, playing the puck over the boards is a technique that requires considerable skill. You have to hit the playing device against the boards to trick the opponents, pick it up again when it bounces back further ahead and then pull on the goal.[1] That's what AG Jacobs achieved in *Albany* and related cases. He was not able to directly out-dribble his opponents in the European Commission and in certain EU Member States. But through a partner outside the EU, he still managed a great success.

In *Albany* and related cases, AG Jacobs addressed a fundamental problem of economic and social law that arises in all market-based systems: the question of the relationship between collective bargaining and competition law.[2] His sophisticated and nuanced considerations did not fall on fertile ground at the CJEU. AG Jacobs did, however, decisively influence the follow-up EFTA Court judgment on the same issue in the *LO* case.[3]

The decision of the EFTA Court in the *LO* case was in turn the basis for the judgment in the *Holship* case, a ruling in which the EFTA Court laid the groundwork for the termination of the Norwegian monopoly of organised dock workers in the loading and unloading of ships.[4] This ruling was implemented by the referring Supreme Court of Norway,[5] and in 2021 the European Court of Human Rights (ECtHR) found that no Convention provisions were violated in the process.[6] As similar monopolies exist in numerous EU Member States, it may be assumed that the EFTA Court's *Holship* verdict will also have an impact in this respect. This would mean that the Opinion of AG Jacobs would finally also have an impact in the EU, demonstrating that conclusions of Advocates General (AGs) may have a much more lasting effect on the development of European jurisprudence, beyond the EU, and beyond the cases in which courts of law have to adjudicate.

---

[1] Description available at www.hockeytutorial.com/ice-hockey-tips/pass-bank-boards-neutral-player-ice-hockey-offensive-play/.

[2] Opinion of AG Jacobs in Case C-67/96 *Albany*; Joined Cases C-115/97, C-116/97 and C-117/97 *Brentjens'*; Case C-219/97 *Drijvende Bokken* ECLI:EU:C:1999:28.

[3] Case E-8/00 *LO* [2002] EFTA Ct. Rep. 114.

[4] Case E-14/15 *Holship* [2016] EFTA Ct. Rep. 242.

[5] *LO v Norway* App no. 45487/17 (ECtHR, 10 June 2021).

[6] Supreme Court of Norway, Case HR-2016-2554-P *Holship*.

II. BACKGROUND, CONTEXT, AND FACTS

On 21 September 1999, the CJEU delivered its landmark judgment in *Albany* on the relation-ship between collective bargaining and competition law.[7] On the same day, two further rulings in *Brentjens' Handelsonderneming BV* and *Maatschappij Drijvende Bokken BV* were issued on the same subject.[8] These cases had all been referred by Dutch courts. At the centre was the question of whether sectoral pension systems based on collective bargaining were in violation of EU competition law.

The facts were mainly as follows: Under a Dutch law of 1949, company pension funds were established based on the principle of compulsory membership. The defendant compa-nies had found other pension solutions for their operations. Compulsory membership was then extended from what was originally a limited group of employees to all employees in the relevant sector of the economy. The exemption from compulsory membership demanded by the companies was rejected by the funds. For their part, the companies were unwilling to pay the contributions demanded. They claimed that EU competition law had been violated. Dutch courts referred a number of questions to the CJEU for a preliminary ruling.

In essence, the three cases were concerned, first, with whether social partners entering agreements on pensions in a particular sector of the economy, under which an occupational pension fund was set up for the entire sector, which all employees working in the sector in principle had to join, and which was granted the exclusive right to manage the pension monies accumulated in the sector, infringed what at the time was Article 85(1) EC (now Article 101(1) TFEU). Secondly, the national court wanted to know whether Article 86 EC (now Article 102 TFEU), in conjunction with Article 90 EC (now Article 106 TFEU), was to be interpreted as meaning that there was an infringement of those provisions when the state granted an exclusive right to an occupational pension fund that significantly restricted the freedom to agree on a pension scheme with a private insurer.

III. THE OPINION OF AG JACOBS

All these cases were assigned to AG Jacobs who wrote a single Opinion addressing them. Before going in *medias res*, the AG gave what he modestly called a 'comparative overview', in which he described the legal situation both on the books and in action (ie, including admin-istrative practice and case law of the courts) in Denmark, Finland, France, Germany, the UK, and – remarkably – the US. As far as the US Supreme Court was concerned, AG Jacobs also discussed dissents.[9] The results of the comparative analysis may be summarised as follows: in all the jurisdictions examined, as a general basic rule, collective bargaining was sheltered from competition law. However, the scope of the immunity, the legal mechanisms through which it was reached, and the extent of the immunity varied.

AG Jacobs then acknowledged that collective bargaining was, as a matter of principle, sheltered from the application of EU competition law. However, he argued for a limited antitrust immunity for collective agreements between management and labour.[10] In the

---

[7] Case C-67/96 *Albany* ECLI:EU:C:1999:430.
[8] Joined Cases C-115/97 to C-117/97 *Brentjens'* ECLI:EU:C:1999:434; Case C-219/97 *Drijvende Bokken* ECLI:EU:C:1999:437.
[9] Paras 80–112.
[10] Paras 183 and 186.

following, AG Jacobs proposed three conditions for ipso facto immunity: (1) there had to be a collective bargain between both sides of industry; (2) the agreement had to be concluded in good faith; and (3) the scope of the collective bargaining immunity had to be limited. A possible criterion could be that the agreement dealt with core subjects of collective bargaining such as wages and working conditions, and did not directly affect third parties such as clients, suppliers, competing employers, or consumers.[11] Accordingly, the conclusion of AG Jacobs was:

> that collective agreements between management and labour concluded in good faith on core subjects of collective bargaining such as wages and working conditions which do not directly affect third markets and third parties are not caught by Article 85(1) of the Treaty.[12]

AG Jacobs therefore made the primacy of collective bargaining subject to the proviso that the contractual regulations concerned the core area of the employment relationship, did not directly affect third parties, and were proportionate. Collective agreements on wages and working conditions were, in his view, excluded from the scope of Article 85 EEC, with contributions to supplementary old-age insurance being considered part of remuneration, and thus also excluded. AG Jacobs understood third parties to include, for example, customers, suppliers, competitors, and consumers. If third-party effects were to occur, the agreement would have to be examined in order to determine whether the interests it pursued were proportionate to the restrictions on competition. As far as the obligation to pay contributions to supplementary pension funds was concerned, the privilege ended, according to AG Jacobs, when contributions were to be made exclusively to a sectoral fund created for this purpose and the corresponding agreement was declared generally binding. This was because it directly interfered with relations with outsiders. Thus, this obligation was said not to fall under the core element of collective bargaining.

IV. THE COURT DOES NOT FOLLOW AG JACOBS

The CJEU dealt with the case in a composition of 11 judges which, at the time, was called the plenary session. The governments of Germany, France, and the Netherlands, as well as the European Commission submitted observations. The CJEU held that collective agreements concluded between employers' and employees' organisations inevitably involved certain restrictions on competition. However, the achievement of the social policy objectives sought by such agreements would be jeopardised if Article 85 EEC were applied. Contracts concluded within the framework of collective bargaining between the social partners with a view to achieving these objectives were therefore not covered by Article 85 EEC due to their nature and subject matter. With this, the CJEU followed the Commission's reasoning, rather than that of AG Jacobs. In contrast to the latter, the Court did not examine the limits of such immunity, nor did it adopt the 'good faith' requirement. The '*nemo propheta in patria*' concept, which is present in all four Gospels, applied to AG Jacobs.[13]

---

[11] Paras 190–93.

[12] Para 194.

[13] Compare HH Pope Benedict XVI, *Angelus* (8 July 2012) www.vatican.va/content/benedict-xvi/en/angelus/2012/documents/hf_ben-xvi_ang_20120708.html.

V. THE EFTA COURT'S *LO* CASE

A. Background, Context, and Facts

By a reference dated 27 September 2000, registered on 2 October 2000, the Labour Court of Norway submitted to the EFTA Court a request for advisory opinion in the *LO* case. The Norwegian Federation of Trade Unions (LO) and other unions instituted proceedings before the Labour Court of Norway against the Norwegian Association of Local and Regional Authorities (KS) and 11 of its member municipalities. The dispute concerned the interpretation and application of provisions of the Basic Collective Agreement for Municipalities.

At issue in the national proceedings was whether the defendant municipalities breached certain provisions of that collective agreement when they transferred their occupational pension insurance scheme from one supplier, KLP, a private mutual life insurance company, wholly owned by members of KS, to other insurance companies. The municipalities submitted that several provisions in the Basic Collective Agreement were void because they infringed Articles 53 and 54 of the Agreement on the European Economic Area (EEA),[14] which mirror Articles 101 and 102 TFEU. The contested provisions stated, in particular, that a plan to change the pension company should be discussed with union representatives; that before the decision-making body might begin to deal with a possible change of the pension company, relevant offers for a new occupational pension scheme should be put before those members of the pension committee who represented the parties to the collective agreement; that the occupational pension scheme had to be based on a financing system that was gender-neutral and did not have the effect of excluding older employees; that before the matter might be decided upon by the municipality there had to be approval from the Norwegian Public Service Pension Fund; and that the pension scheme had to be taken note of by the Norwegian Banking, Insurance and Securities Commission.

In its written submissions, the Norwegian Government, led by Jens Stoltenberg of the Labour Party, the future NATO Secretary General, urged the EFTA Court to stick to the line of argument followed by the CJEU in *Albany*. At the oral hearing, however, the Norwegian agent withdrew her government's written submissions, sided with the municipalities, and asked the EFTA Court to follow the Opinion of AG Jacobs in *Albany*. The Stoltenberg Government had shortly before been replaced by a new government, led by Kjell Magne Bondevik of the Christian Democratic Party. The new agent stated that according to the Norwegian authorities:

> the occupational pension market should be subject to free competition. Provisions regulating transfer of pension schemes from one company to another company are, in the opinion of the Norwegian Government, not covered by the exemption for social policy objectives.[15]

The Norwegian Government's *volte face* demonstrated the political explosiveness of the issue. The unions, for their part, pleaded unlimited immunity. This was in accordance with their belief that everything that concerns collective bargaining or industrial action was part of their core business. For them, it was also in line with the approach of the CJEU in *Albany*.

The EFTA Surveillance Authority (ESA) argued that the collective agreement could be applied to secure a monopoly, instead of opening up the area concerned for competition. For the ESA, to claim an upfront acceptance from the Banking Insurance Securities Commission for a new product could be contrary to EEA law. If the national court were to find that a refusal

---

[14] Agreement on the European Economic Area OJ 1994 L1/1.
[15] See C Baudenbacher, *Judicial Independence. Memoirs of a European Judge* (Cham, Springer, 2019) 215.

to transfer was based on the desire to protect KLP's dominant position, this would obviously be outside the scope of immunity. ESA was critical of the case law of the CJEU stating that the latter excluded the application of the cartel prohibition to collective agreements to a great extent, and thus made it easier to create monopolies in this field.

ESA finally argued that if a collective agreement was immune from Article 53 EEA, that exception did not extend to the prohibition of the abuse of dominance. Since KLP was a dominant undertaking, but not a party to the collective agreement, ESA recommended that the national court look into possible connections between KS and KLP and asked the EFTA Court to give guidance on this. It seemed possible that what was at issue was an example of exclusionary abuse. KS/KLP would enter into an agreement that purported to offer a freedom of choice, but in reality the agreement tied all the municipalities to KLP. Such a situation could also fall within the scope of Article 53 EEA. As regards the crucial question of which test was to be applied, ESA proposed a classical proportionality assessment: if the act in question went beyond what was necessary to attain the social policy objective and could not be justified otherwise, an abuse may well have occurred.[16]

The Commission was represented by the same pleader who had argued the *Albany* case before the CJEU. He did not share ESA's view, and instead defended the ruling in *Albany* and, as in the latter case, opted for a very limited test. He said at the hearing that the logic of *Albany* was:

> precisely to avoid in depth scrutiny under the competition rules of the outcome of the collective negotiations between the social partners.[17]

The Commission's man went on, stating that the CJEU in *Albany* had not followed the proposal of AG Jacobs to decompose the agreement into different constituent elements 'and then to look at the necessity and proportionality of these elements'.

Instead, for the Commission, the CJEU's approach was a very global and general one. It was astonishing. What the Commission was proposing was that the EFTA Court should not look into the clauses of the collective agreement themselves, nor look into whether these clauses went beyond a legitimate concept of social goals. At the hearing, this author, who was a sitting judge in the *LO* case, asked the Commission why the proportionality test was not agreeable. In reply, the representative of the Commission argued that instead of a full scrutiny it recommended:

> a marginal control of abuse. Pursuant to such marginal control of abuse, only specific provisions which are manifestly inappropriate or in relation to the social policy objectives pursued by the core of the agreement, or which are applied in a way which shows that they exclusively pursue other objectives, are excluded from immunity and fall within the scope of [the EU and EEA law cartel prohibition].[18]

Under this approach, there would only be a problem:

> when it turns out that a clause has no legitimate social purpose at all, has no other purposes than purposes which are not legitimate for social purposes. This is not the same as a proportionality test. Under a proportionality test, even if there is a legitimate social purpose, one would still look further and also look at other effects, other purposes or other effects, in particular the anti-competitive effect, and then one would have some weighing, some balance between the two.[19]

---

[16] ibid.
[17] ibid, p 216.
[18] Baudenbacher (n 15) 216.
[19] Baudenbacher (n 15) 216.

B. The EFTA Court's Judgment

In its ruling of 22 March 2002, the EFTA Court reproduced the central statement of the Opinion of AG Jacobs in *Albany*, almost verbatim, and cited the respective paragraph of his Opinion. It held that:

> legislatures and courts in most market economy oriented jurisdictions have drawn the conclusion that collective agreements between management and labour must to some extent be sheltered from the competition rules, without making that immunity unlimited (see the analysis in the Opinion of Advocate-General Jacobs in Case C-67/96 *Albany*, Joined Cases C-115/97 to C-117/97 *Brentjens'* and Case C-219/97 *Drijvende Bokken*, reported in [1999] ECR I-5751, at paragraph 109).[20]

AG Jacobs in his Opinion in *Albany* had stated:

> In all the systems examined collective agreements between management and labour are to some extent sheltered from the prohibition of anticompetitive cartels. However, that immunity is not unlimited.[21]

The EFTA Court also found that the good faith of the parties in concluding and implementing a collective agreement had to be taken into account.[22] AG Jacobs had pointed to this requirement in his Opinion in *Albany*.[23] Finally, the EFTA Court emphasised that the national court had to consider the aggregate effect of several elements of a collective agreement.[24] Even if individually they would not lead to any certain resolution of the status of the collective agreement in relation to the applicability of EEA competition law, their aggregate effect could bring the agreement within the scope of those rules. In other words, unlike the CJEU in *Albany*, the EFTA Court took a fact-based approach. A few years later, AG Miguel Poiares Maduro referred to *LO* in his Opinion in the *Viking Line* case, where he too argued in favour of a concept of limited antitrust immunity for collective agreements.[25]

The referring Norwegian Labour Court did not follow the EFTA Court's ruling, but in violation of its duty of loyalty, decided in favour of the unions. ESA, whose agent had, in a convincing line of argument, encouraged the EFTA Court to rule against the unions, remained inactive.

VI. THE EFTA COURT'S *HOLSHIP* CASE

A. Background, Context and Facts

The EFTA Court's *LO* ruling was, however, not in vain. On the one hand, it created the basis for a fruitful dialogue with AGs at the CJEU in the years to come.[26] AGs had from the outset

---

[20] Para 35 of the EFTA Court Judgment in *LO*.

[21] Para 109.

[22] Para 56 of the EFTA Court Judgment in *LO*.

[23] Para 192.

[24] Paras 57, 76–77, 79 of the EFTA Court Judgment in *LO* and answer No 4.

[25] Opinion of AG Maduro in Case C-438/05 *Viking* ECLI:EU:C:2007:292, fn 24.

[26] See C Baudenbacher, 'The EFTA Court's Relationship with the Advocates General of the European Court of Justice' in MT D'Alessio, V Kronenberger and V Placco (eds), *De Rome à Lisbonne: les juridictions de l'Union européenne à la croisée des chemins. Mélanges en l'honneur de Paolo Mengozzi* (Brussels, Bruylant, 2013); C Baudenbacher, 'The EFTA Court, the ECJ, and the Latter's Advocates General – a Tale of Judicial Dialogue' in A Arnull, P Eeckhout and T Tridimas (eds), *Continuity and Change in EU Law: Essays in Honour of Sir Francis Jacobs* (Oxford, OUP, 2008);

referenced EFTA Court rulings. It was in fact AG Jacobs who in 1996, two years after the establishment of the EFTA Court, in *De Agostini* opened this conversation.[27] On the other hand, the EFTA Court took into account Opinions of AGs. However, in the *LO* case, an Opinion of an AG was cited for the first time. Then CJEU President Vassilios Skouris has aptly written in his contribution to the *Festschrift* marking the EFTA Court's 20th anniversary that the *LO* judgment demonstrates the effective judicial dialogue between the two EEA courts. He noted that the EFTA Court referenced AG Jacobs' Opinion and thus followed an alternative authority to that of the CJEU.[28]

As indicated, the judgment in the *LO* case laid the foundation for the EFTA Court's later landmark ruling in the *Holship* case, in which this author acted as Reporting Judge and President.

The Norwegian Transport Workers' Union (NTF), a member of LO, and LO had concluded a collective framework agreement with the Confederation of Norwegian Enterprises (NHO) regarding a fixed pay scheme for dockworkers at 13 major ports in Norway, including the port of Drammen. The framework agreement included the right to permanent employment and better pay. Importantly, it also contained a clause obliging vessels of 50 deadweight tonnes and more sailing from a Norwegian port to a port in another state, and vice versa, to have any stevedoring, the loading and unloading work, performed by dockworkers. The framework agreement moreover established an administrative office for dock work at the port of Drammen (AO). This entity ran at cost, and its board of directors consisted of three representatives of port users and two representatives of dockworkers. All permanently employed dockworkers in the Drammen port were employed by AO.

Holship Norge AS (Holship), a wholly-owned Norwegian subsidiary of the global transport and shipping conglomerate Holship Holding A/S Denmark, was not a member of NHO and not a party to the framework agreement. Its workers in the Drammen port carried out stevedore operations. NTF asked Holship to accept the framework agreement, which would have meant priority engagement for AO's workers. After Holship failed to respond to these demands, NTF, by a letter of 11 June 2013, gave a notice of boycott. The purpose of the blockade was to secure a collective agreement containing the principle of priority of engagement in relation to Holship's unloading and loading activity. As regards the lawfulness of a blockade, NTF relied on the 1997 decision of the Supreme Court of Norway in the *Port of Sola* case – a matter essentially identical to the later *Holship* case.[29]

Holship lost on 19 March 2014 before Drammen City Court, and on 8 September 2014 before Borgarting Court of Appeal. The Supreme Court of Norway granted leave to appeal, and referred two sets of questions to the EFTA Court, one on the compatibility of the boycott with EEA competition rules, and the other one on its compatibility with the freedom of establishment.

J Kokott and D Dittert, 'European Courts in Dialogue' in EFTA Court (ed), *The EEA and the EFTA Court: Decentred Integration, Festschrift to mark the 20th anniversary of the EFTA Court* (Oxford, Hart Publishing, 2014); P Mengozzi, 'The Advocates General and the EFTA Court' in EFTA Court (ed), *The EEA and the EFTA Court: Decentred Integration* (Oxford, Hart Publishing, 2014).

[27] Joined Cases C-34/95, C-35/95 and C-36/95 *De Agostini* ECLI:EU:C:1996:333, paras 20, 21, 46, 63, 85, 88.

[28] The Role of the Court of Justice of the European Union in the Development of the EEA Single Market: Advancement through Collaboration between the EFTA Court and the ECJ, in EFTA Court (ed), *The EEA and the EFTA Court: Decentred Integration* (Oxford, Hart Publishing, 2014) 3, 12.

[29] Rt. 1997, 334; see para 14 of the judgment of Supreme Court of Norway in *Holship*.

B. The EFTA Court's Judgment

On 19 April 2016 the EFTA Court held in the *Holship Norge AS* case that the exemption of collective agreements from EEA competition rules did not cover a clause that obliged a port user to give priority to another company's workers over its own employees, or the use of a boycott in order to procure acceptance of the collective agreement containing said clause. The EFTA Court stated that a collective agreement falls outside the scope of EEA competition rules only if it was concluded following collective bargaining between employers and employees, and if it pursues the objective of improving work and employment conditions.

In the *Holship* case, the first requirement was fulfilled, but the second was not. The EFTA Court noted that the aggregate effect of two clauses of the framework agreement – the priority clause and the clause establishing the AO – was to guarantee AO's workers permanent employment and a certain wage. Their effect was, thus, to protect only a limited group of workers employed by AO to the detriment of Holship's workers, who were barred from performing similar work. Moreover, the boycott – while notified by the union – was to be attributed to AO, since it sought to compel Holship to observe the terms of the framework agreement. AO's system went beyond the improvement of conditions of work and employment.

For an entity such as AO to be regarded as an undertaking within the meaning of EEA competition law, it had to be engaged in an economic activity. The EFTA Court found the provision of stevedore services to constitute such an activity, since it consisted in offering a service on a market where AO, actually or potentially, competed with other providers. It was for the Supreme Court of Norway to assess whether this provision of stevedore services was attributable to AO. It was also for the Supreme Court of Norway to determine whether the conduct in question had an appreciable effect on trade between EEA Contracting Parties.[30]

As regards AO's possible dominant position, the Supreme Court of Norway had to determine whether the relevant geographic market was limited to the port of Drammen. Should it consider that AO held a dominant position on the relevant geographic market, it would need to determine whether that position covered a substantial part of the EEA territory. The EFTA Court noted that a single port may be regarded as a substantial part of the EEA territory. However, should the referring court find that the port of Drammen could not be regarded as a substantial part of the EEA, it would have to take into account identical or corresponding systems of the AO that might exist in other ports. As for the question of abuse, the EFTA Court directed the referring court to assess whether AO: (i) obliged customers to obtain all or most of their requirements for stevedore services from it, (ii) charged disproportionate prices, or (iii) refrained from using modern technology.

In relation to a possible infringement of the cartel prohibition laid down in Article 53 EEA, the EFTA Court held that the Supreme Court of Norway had to assess whether the 13 AOs were parties to an agreement or a concerted practice.

The EFTA Court relied on its *LO* precedent with regard to the following issues: that a collective agreement would only fall outside the scope of competition law if it has been concluded between employers and employees and pursues the objective of improving conditions of work and employment;[31] and that the first requirement was fulfilled in the present case, but that the second one was lacking so that it could not 'generally be exempted from the scope of the EEA

---

[30] The EEA Contracting Parties include the 27 EU Member States and the 3 EFTA-EEA states.
[31] Para 24 of the EFTA Court Judgment in *Holship*; reference to *LO*, paras 49 and 50.

competition rules'.[32] The EFTA Court underlined that the notion of 'conditions of work and employment' must be interpreted in a broad fashion. It held that:

> It relates to core elements of collective agreements, such as wages, working hours and other working conditions. Further elements may concern, *inter alia*, safety, the workplace environment, holidays, training and continuing education, and consultation and co-determination between workers and management.[33]

The EFTA Court added:

> In determining whether the second requirement is fulfilled, account must be taken of the form and content of the agreement and of its various provisions, and of the circumstances under which they were negotiated. The subsequent practice of the parties to the agreement may be of importance, as may be the effect, in practice, of its provisions. It is not sufficient that the broad objective of a collective agreement is recognised as seeking to improve conditions of work and employment, as individual provisions may be directed towards other purposes

> When examining the collective agreement's provisions, their aggregate effect must be considered. Even if individually the provisions would not lead to any certain resolution of the status of the collective agreement in relation to the applicability of Articles 53 and 54 EEA, their aggregate effect may bring the agreement within the scope of those Articles.[34]

These findings also reflected the spirit of the Opinion of AG Jacobs in *Albany*.

Interestingly in *Holship*, the Commission based its argumentation on the Opinion of AG Jacobs, and on the EFTA Court's *LO* ruling, and acknowledged that 'collective agreements between management and labour must not always be sheltered from the competition rules'. For the Commission, one criterion could be that the agreement deals with 'core subjects of collective bargaining such as wages and working conditions' and 'does not directly affect third parties or markets'.[35]

Upon a question from the bench, the Commission at the hearing put forward arguments on the basis of the ECtHR's 2006 judgment in *Sørensen and Rasmussen v Denmark*.[36] Here, the ECtHR held that a closed shop arrangement, whereby a specific employment was contingent on workers joining a union with which the employer had a special relationship, infringed Article 11 of the European Convention on Human Rights (ECHR). This provision guarantees, inter alia, the negative freedom of association. The EFTA Court affirmatively noted the Commission's argument.[37]

As regards the freedom of establishment, the EFTA Court found that the boycott constituted a restriction which might be justified either on the grounds laid down in Article 33 EEA[38] (public policy, public security or public health), or by overriding reasons of general interest, such as the protection of workers. These justifications had to be interpreted in light of fundamental rights. In the case at hand, a limited group of workers was protected to the detriment of other workers. There was nothing to indicate that the boycott aimed to improve the working

---

[32] Paras 43–52; reference to *LO*, paras 53, 51 and 57.

[33] Para 44 of the EFTA Court Judgment in *Holship*.

[34] Paras 45–46 of the EFTA Court Judgment in *Holship*.

[35] See points 12 and 13 of Observations to the EFTA Court submitted on behalf of the European Commission by L Malferrari and M Kellerbauer, www.kvale.no/wp-content/uploads/2019/03/08_european-commission_written-observations_original.pdf.

[36] *Sørensen & Rasmussen v Denmark* Apps no. 52562/99 and 52620/99 (ECtHR, 11 January 2006).

[37] 103 et seq and 123 of the EFTA Court Judgment in *Holship*.

[38] Article 33 EEA mirrors Article 52(1) TFEU.

conditions of Holship's employees. It was for the Supreme Court of Norway to determine, having regard to all the facts and circumstance before it and the guidance provided by the EFTA Court, whether the restrictive measure at issue could be justified.[39]

The EFTA Court also referred to the Opinion of AG Poiares Maduro in *Viking Line*,[40] and thus reiterated the importance it attached to the dialogue with the AGs of the CJEU.

C. The Supreme Court of Norway's Judgment

On 16 December 2016 the Supreme Court of Norway implemented the EFTA Court's ruling in a plenary decision with a 10 to 7 vote, finding the notified boycott unlawful. Justice Jens Edvin A Skoghøy, writing for the majority, underlined that the right to priority of engagement provided relatively indirect protection of employment conditions in that jobs were protected by effectively shielding AO from competition.[41] He added that, in his view, it was from:

> a human rights perspective [...] hard to argue that [the jobs generated within Holship] carry less weight than the jobs at the Administration Office.[42]

The Supreme Court's majority found that the boycott was unlawful because it violated the freedom of establishment. It therefore considered it unnecessary to extensively discuss the possible implications of EEA competition law. Nevertheless, the Supreme Court of Norway added that there were no sufficient grounds to depart from the conclusion reached by the EFTA Court in *Holship*.[43] Thereby, the Supreme Court made the EFTA Court's EEA competition law holdings an integral part of its judgment.

The outcome of the *Holship* case is particularly noteworthy since in its 1997 *Port of Sola* judgment, the Supreme Court of Norway had found that a boycott profited from the exemption of collective bargaining and industrial action from competition law.[44] The facts of the *Port of Sola* case were virtually identical to those in *Holship*. NTF had filed a lawsuit before Jæren District Court. On 4 February 1995 this Court found a notified blockade to be illegal because it aimed at forcing two free companies, Sola Havn AS and Stavanger Havnelager AS, to accede to a framework agreement for stevedore work. The single judge was the later Supreme Court Justice Magnus Matningsdal, who was part of the Supreme Court's majority in *Holship*.

By contrast, Gulating Court of Appeal ruled that the purpose of the boycott – to achieve a collective agreement – could not be considered unlawful even if the framework agreement would entail a certain monopolisation of stevedore work. Before the Supreme Court, the two companies invoked, inter alia, Articles 53 and 54 EEA prohibiting cartels and the abuse of dominance as a supporting argument for the boycott's alleged unlawful purpose. The NTF contended that the provisions of the EEA Agreement did not apply to pay and working conditions, and if they applied, they would not affect the preferential right of the unloading and loading office. It is notable that these pleadings were submitted long before the CJEU's judgment in *Albany*. The Supreme Court did not consider these arguments, but concluded that the balancing of interests could not lead to the announced boycott being qualified as unlawful.

---

[39] Paras 117 et seq and 123 et seq of the EFTA Court Judgment in *Holship*.
[40] ibid, paras 40, 73, 125.
[41] Para 103 of the Judgment of the Supreme Court of Norway in *Holship*.
[42] ibid, para 118.
[43] ibid.
[44] Supreme Court of Norway, *Port of Sola*.

VII. THE ECTHR'S *LO AND NTF* RULING

The Norwegian unions were not prepared to accept their defeat, but brought a case against Norway before the ECtHR claiming that their right to freedom of assembly and association in the meaning of Article 11 ECHR had been infringed. On 10 June 2021, the ECtHR found in the *LO and NTF* case that no human rights had been violated. At the core of the judgment were the considerations regarding the equivalence of fundamental rights protection in the EEA as compared to the EU. The relevant case law was laid down by the ECtHR in its 2005 *Bosphorus* judgment[45] and the recent *Konkurrenten.no* ruling.[46]

In *Bosphorus*, the Grand Chamber of the ECtHR held that if an organisation to which a Contracting State has transferred jurisdiction is found to protect fundamental rights in a manner which can be considered at least 'equivalent' to that of the ECHR, the presumption will be that that state has not departed from the ECHR's requirements when it merely implements legal obligations flowing from its membership in the organisation.[47] In *Konkurrenten.no*, the ECtHR's Second Section stated that the basis for the presumption established by *Bosphorus* was in principle lacking when it comes to the implementation of EEA law at domestic level within the framework of the EEA Agreement, due to the specificities of the governing treaties compared to those of the European Union.[48] Two features were highlighted. First, the Second Section noted that in contrast to EU law, direct effect and primacy were lacking within the framework of the EEA Agreement itself. Secondly, it opined that the EEA Agreement did not include the EU Charter of Fundamental Rights, or any reference to other legal instruments having the same effect, such as the ECHR.[49]

It is surprising that the ECtHR's Second Section did not take note of the EFTA Court's case law stating that the EEA Agreement provisions 'are to be interpreted in the light of fundamental rights',[50] in order to enhance coherence between EEA law and EU law. Moreover, the ECtHR seems to have overlooked that the principles of direct effect and supremacy were recognised in EU law by the CJEU by way of dynamic interpretation.[51] For its part, the EFTA Court has recognised EEA state liability in the same way.[52] State liability implies a certain degree of direct effect. On the question of the relevance of the EU Charter of Fundamental Rights in EEA law, the ECtHR's Second Section in *Konkurrenten.no* also failed to take into account the EFTA Court's *Deveci* ruling,[53] which was understood in academic literature to mean that the EFTA Court was evolving in that direction.[54]

---

[45] *Bosphorus v Ireland* App no 45036/98 (ECtHR, 30 June 2005).

[46] *Konkurrenten.no v Norway* App no 47341/15 (ECtHR, 5 November 2019).

[47] Paras 152 et seq and 155 et seq of ECtHR judgment in *Bosphorus*. Concerning potential EEA implications, see C Baudenbacher, 'Fundamental Rights in EEA Law or: How far from Bosphorus is the European Economic Area Agreement?' in S Breitenmoser, B Ehrenzeller and M Sassoli (eds), *Human Rights, Democracy and the Rule of Law: Liber Amicorum Luzius Wildhaber* (Baden-Baden, Nomos, 2007).

[48] Paras 155 et seq of ECtHR judgment in *Konkurrenten.no AS*.

[49] ibid, para 106.

[50] Case E-2/03 *Ásgeirsson* [2003] EFTA Ct. Rep. 185, para 23 and case law cited.

[51] Case 26/62 *Van Gend en Loos* ECLI:EU:C:1963:1; Case 6/64 *Costa v ENEL* ECLI:EU:C:1964:66.

[52] Case E-9/97 *Sveinbjörnsdóttir v Iceland* [1998] EFTA Ct. Rep. 95.

[53] Case E-10/14 *Deveci* [2014] EFTA Ct. Rep. 1364.

[54] See K Fløistad, *The EEA Agreement in a Revised EU Framework for Welfare Services* (New York, Springer, 2018) 21; H Haukeland Fredriksen, 'The EFTA Court' in R Howse, H Ruiz-Fabri, G Ulfstein, and MQ Zang (eds), *The Legitimacy of International Trade Courts and Tribunals* (Cambridge, CUP, 2018) 138, 165 et seq; R Spanó, 'The EFTA Court and Fundamental Rights' (2017) 13 *EuConst* 475, 480 et seq; E Pettinelli, 'The inter-courts interaction in Europe: the fruitful dialogue between the CJEU and the EFTA Court', http://tesi.luiss.it/25399/1/634312_PETTINELLI_ELEONORA.pdf; G Butler and M Meling, 'Horizontal Direct Effect of the Charter in EU Law: Ramifications for the European Economic Area' (2020) 3 *Nordic Journal of European Law* 1.

On the question of the equivalence of fundamental rights protection in the EEA, the Norwegian Government in *LO and NTF* before the ECtHR argued that while EU law and EEA law differ in certain respects, this may mean that EEA law, as such, could not benefit from the *Bosphorus* presumption of equivalent protection. The *LO and NTF* case concerned the application of the main part of the EEA Agreement. Its provisions corresponded to EU law, meaning the presumption should apply.

The ECtHR's Fifth Section held that, as clearly stated by the EFTA Court in its *Holship* decision, fundamental rights form part of the unwritten principles of EEA law. The Norwegian Government had provided several examples in this regard. The Fifth Section went on to note that this reflected the previous stance of EU law, where fundamental rights were also initially recognised as general principles of EU law through the CJEU. Thus, the absence of a codified fundamental rights charter in the EEA Agreement was irrelevant to deciding whether the *Bosphorus* case law applied to the implementation of the EEA Agreement or parts thereof.[55]

Perhaps most interesting are the remarks the ECtHR's Fifth Section made in passing regarding one of the two conditions for the application of the *Bosphorus* presumption – the existence of procedural mechanisms for ensuring the protection of substantive fundamental rights guarantees. It noted that there was an absence of direct effect and supremacy in EEA law, and that EFTA Court advisory opinions were legally non-binding. However, the ECtHR's Fifth Section left this issue to be reviewed in a future case concerning questions of procedural mechanisms under EEA law. Thus, for the purposes of the *Holship* case, it considered the *Bosphorus* presumption not to apply to EEA law.[56]

The Supreme Court of Norway's judgment had been somewhat mute on the issue of whether a 'closed shop' existed in the *Holship* case. The ECtHR therefore felt no need to examine whether a closed shop would be permissible. It limited its analysis to determining whether the restriction of the unions' rights as a result of the Supreme Court decision to declare the notified boycott unlawful was necessary for the purposes of Article 11 ECHR.

The ECtHR found that the Supreme Court of Norway had broadly assessed the conflicting fundamental right to collective action and the EEA law freedom of establishment. Its characterisation of the boycott as a means to compel acceptance of a right of priority engagement and with the desired effect to limit access of other operators to the market for loading and unloading services was central to its finding that a fair balance had been struck in the particular case. In addition, the fact that the announced boycott targeted a third party had also been considered. It then recalled that the ECHR Contracting States enjoy a wide margin of appreciation in this field, which would require strong reasons for the ECtHR to substitute its assessment for that of a national court.[57] As the ECtHR found no sufficiently strong reasons to do so, it concluded that no violation of Article 11 ECHR had occurred.

VIII. CONCLUSIONS

The series of rulings in the *Holship* matter has sealed the fate of the monopoly of organised dockworkers in the EFTA-EEA state of Norway. According to both the monopoly's opponents and defenders, the EFTA Court's *Holship* judgment was the decisive factor. Belgian lawyer and

---

[55] Para 107 of ECtHR judgment in *LO and NTF*.
[56] ibid, para 108.
[57] ibid, para 115.

professor Eric van Hooydonk, a renowned practitioner of port law – who wrote a comprehensive study of the international, EU and national policy and legal aspects of port labour in the EU for the European Commission[58] – characterised the ruling as 'crystal-clear' and remarked that it could impact EU ports.[59] *ANAVE*, the Spanish shipowners association, commented on 20 April 2016 that the EFTA Court's *Holship* ruling:

> considerably reinforces the effect of previous rulings by the EU Court of Justice and national courts of law, which declared that classic pooling systems in ports are contrary to the fundamental principles of the Treaty on the Functioning of the EU. To these rulings it adds the explicit confirmation that collective agreements for dockers' pools must be subject to competition rules; it impinges on the right to employment of workers who are not part of the pool and recognises the fundamental freedom of workers not to join a dockers' union.[60]

Even critics Hendy and Novitz described the EFTA Court's *Holship* judgment as 'one of the most significant cases in European labour law so far this century'.[61] The EFTA Court's ruling differs from judgments of the CJEU in that it is based both on competition law and the right to freedom of establishment, and that it also extensively discusses the implications of the negative freedom of coalition regulated in Article 11 ECHR. Moreover, the EFTA Court has in past cases chosen a different approach from EU courts as regards the application of competition law to collective bargaining matters.

The EFTA Court's *Holship* ruling is likely to have an impact on the situation in EU Member States where similar structures exist. The CJEU has so far mainly dealt with dockworkers' monopolies in Italy, Spain, and Belgium.[62] Its thrust is the same as that of the EFTA Court. But the approach in the various judgments is less broad. Labour unions have therefore been able to collude with certain politicians and bureaucrats with the result that liberalisation has only partially taken place. Whether the CJEU will one day also follow the EFTA Court's *LO* case law is an open question.

In ice hockey, playing the puck over the boards is a technique that only the greats can master. In the European judiciary, AG Jacobs was unquestionably one of the greats. The fact that with his *Albany* opinion he was supported by players who were not part of his team does not detract from his performance. In conclusion, it seems that Francis – via the EFTA Court – is becoming a prophet in *patria* after all. That his own state is no longer part of this '*patria*' is another matter.

---

[58] E Van Hooydonk, *Port Labour in the EU. Labour Market, Qualifications & Training. Health & Safety Vol 1-2* (Ghent, Portius 2013).

[59] E van Hooydonk, 'EFTA Court decision on Norway dockers could hit EU ports' Felixstowe Docker, www.felixstowedocker.com/2016/06/efta-court-decision-on-norway-dockers.html.

[60] Unofficial translation. In the original: '[...] refuerza considerablemente el efecto de los fallos anteriores del Tribunal de Justicia de la UE y los tribunales de justicia nacionales, que declararon que los sistemas clásicos de pool en los puertos son contrarios a los principios fundamentales del Tratado de funcionamiento de la UE. A estos fallos añade la confirmación explícita de que los convenios colectivos de los pools de estibadores deben estar sujetos a las normas de competencia; incide en el derecho al empleo de los trabajadores que no forman parte del pool y reconoce la libertad fundamental de los trabajadores a no afiliarse a un sindicato de estibadores' in 'El Tribunal de la EFTA condena a los pools de estibadores portuarios noruegos como contrarios a las normas sobre competencia, libre circulación y los derechos humanos' Asociación de Navieros Españoles, www.anave.es/ultimas-noticias/1307-el-tribunal-de-la-efta-condena-a-los-pools-de-estibadores-portuarios-noruegos-como-contrarios-a-las-normas-sobre-competencia-libre-circulacion-y-los-derechos-humanos#. See also 'Human Rights Court And Spanish High Court Deal New Blow To Dockworkers' Monopolies' (Port News, 11 June 2021, Online Daily Newspaper Hellenic Shipping News Worldwide) www.hellenicshippingnews.com/human-rights-court-and-spanish-high-court-deal-new-blow-to-dockworkers-monopolies/.

[61] J Hendy and T Novitz, 'The Holship Case' (2018) 47 *Industrial Law Journal* 315, 315.

[62] Case C-179/90 *Porto di Genova* ECLI:EU:C:1991:464; Case C-576/13 *Commission v Spain* ECLI:EU:C:2014:2430; Joined Cases C-407/19 and C-471/19 *Katoen Natie Bulk Terminals* ECLI:EU:C:2021:107.

32

The Virtue of Moderation: Opinions of Advocate General Jacobs in Oscar Bronner *and* PreussenElektra

LUCA RUBINI

I. INTRODUCTION

THIS CHAPTER BRINGS together two important Opinions delivered in two important cases. Both opinions 'made history' and are, still today, referred to as authoritative clarifications of the key principles of EU competition and internal market law. The Opinion delivered in *Oscar Bronner* was at the time highly anticipated and, since its delivery, it has been consistently regarded as the standard statement on the 'essential facility doctrine' in EU competition law, one of the most sensitive issues in any antitrust law system.[1] Quite similarly, the Opinion in *PreussenElektra*, delivered just a few years afterwards, had to deal with two other important questions, concerning the boundaries of the notion of state aid and the environmental justification in free movement.[2] By settling the two issues, it still stands as the watershed in the jurisprudence of the Court in the field.

Though they relate to distant areas – one antitrust, the other state aid/internal market – these two cases belong to that category of legal disputes where adjudicators have to respond to strong claims aimed at pushing the outer boundaries of the relevant disciplines, or to clarify previously inconsistent case law on defences, and, in the process, the fundamentals of the system are touched and re-defined. With a steady hand on the tiller, AG Jacobs rejected the expansionist claims of the parties, which would have significantly broadened the scope of antitrust and state aid law. By providing clear and reasoned guidance, he kept the ship stable and avoided navigating in unchartered waters. At the same time, his invitation to revisit the scope of the 'environmental justification' showed his promptness to steer the tiller gently and indicate a sensible and acceptable direction for the law, calling on the Court to clarify and consolidate it. The chapter will close by suggesting that these Opinions share one important feature, which is key to understanding the Opinions of AG Jacobs, which I call the virtue of moderation, the capacity to always keep the golden mean.

From the broader policy perspective, both cases are arguably defeats for the European Commission. Of different magnitude, but still defeats. *Oscar Bronner* (and probably more the

---

[1] Opinion of AG Jacobs in Case C-7/97 *Oscar Bronner* ECLI:EU:C:1998:265.
[2] Opinion of AG Jacobs in Case C-379/98 *PreussenElektra* ECLI:EU:C:2000:585.

Opinion of AG Jacobs than the judgment of the Court) is still to this day the most reasoned and authoritative warning against extending the reach of antitrust too much, and to carefully ensure that a duty to deal or an access to a facility is ordered only when strictly indispensable for the working of competition. Suffice to say, in this respect, that it was the Commission in its early 1990s practice to apply the 'essential facility doctrine'. What *Oscar Bronner* did was to impose clear discipline and limits. Arguably, the *PreussenElektra* case was a much bigger defeat because the clear expansionist strategy of the Commission in state aid control was strongly rejected.

II. OSCAR BRONNER

A. Background, Context, and Facts

More than any other case, *Oscar Bronner* goes to the very core of antitrust law, and to whether it can constitute the legal tool to intrude on fundamental tenets of public and private law. The issue was whether the dominant owner of a facility or infrastructure – the access to which is alleged to be necessary for competitors to carry out their activity – should give access to it. The 'essential facility' issue is nothing else than one, perhaps extreme, scenario of the more general question of whether antitrust law can impose a 'duty to deal or supply' on dominant undertakings. While the economic good or service to which access is claimed may differ – be it a raw material, proprietary information, intellectual property right or a physical or intangible infrastructure – the underlying economic and legal issues are the same.

Under which conditions does a refusal to deal with or to grant access to an 'essential' facility constitute an abuse of dominance? Since the beginning the jurisprudence had to deal with the dilemma a claim of access to someone's property or innovation brings with it: the interference with the right to property, freedom of contract, and the incentives to innovate. The first case where a duty to supply was imposed was *Commercial Solvents*.[3] Following AG Warner, the Court held that an undertaking with a dominant position with respect to the production of a raw material could not *cease supplying* an existing customer who manufactured a derivative product in a downstream market simply because it had decided to start manufacturing the derivative itself and wished to eliminate its former customer from the market. The Court underlined that the prohibition refers to those cases where the refusal would eliminate *all competition* in the downstream market.

To be sure, the judicial imposition of duties to deal or supply has been quite rare in the jurisprudence, reaching its climax in a trio of 'exceptional cases' (the Court itself dubbed them as such) which I analyse below.

The 'essential facility' doctrine is, by contrast, an 'import' of the Commission that has increasingly employed it in its decisions since the early 1990s.[4] I use the word 'import' because the 'essential facility' doctrine originated in US antitrust law where it has been applied to facilities as diverse as railroad bridges, telecommunication networks, or electricity networks.[5]

---

[3] Joined Cases 6/73 and 7/73 *Commercial Solvents* ECLI:EU:C:1974:18. It may be remembered that, at the time of this case, Francis Jacobs served as *référendaire* in the cabinet of AG Warner.

[4] The first two cases involved the port of Holyhead in Wales. See DG Goyder, *EC Competition Law* (Oxford, OUP, 1998) 347. For a very comprehensive and up-to-date list of cases see R Whish and D Bailey, *Competition Law*, 10th edn (Oxford, OUP, 2021) 739–41.

[5] H Hovenkamp, *Federal Antitrust Policy – The Law of Competition and Its Practice*, 4th edn (Saint Paul, West Academic, 2011) §7; Whish and Bailey, ibid.

Crucially, however, the doctrine had not received the endorsement of the US Supreme Court, being mostly a produce of lower courts.[6] Importantly, the doctrine itself has never been mentioned by the EU courts either.[7] Once again, we refer the reader to the analysis section.

The *Oscar Bronner* case came from a reference from the Higher Regional Court, Vienna, that asked the Court whether the refusal by a newspaper group holding a substantial share of the market in daily newspapers to allow the publisher of a competing newspaper access to its home-delivery network constituted an abuse of dominant position under what was then Article 86 EC (now Article 102 TFEU). The reference was soon perceived as a key case for the Court to clarify its position, especially after its delivery of judgment in *Magill* in which, because of 'expectational circumstances', it had imposed on a dominant undertaking the duty to share intellectual property to a competitor.[8]

B. The Opinion of AG Jacobs

After quickly disposing of the admissibility issue, and of the preliminary point of substance (the definition of the relevant market), AG Jacobs moved on to consider the questions of dominance and abuse together. In 18 paragraphs[9] he masterfully summarised the relevant case law and practice. He immediately noted that '[t]he Court has not as yet referred in its case-law to the essential facilities doctrine' but 'has ruled in a number of cases concerning refusals to supply goods or services'.[10] One by one, he eviscerated the principles outlined in *Commercial Solvents, United Brands*,[11] *Télémarketing*,[12] *GB-Inno-BM*,[13] *Volvo*[14] and *CICRA*,[15] to then reach the more recent and momentous Court's *Magill* decision,[16] and its consideration in the Court of First Instance's (now the General Court) *Tiérce Ladbroke* case.[17] Before quickly, but exhaustively, summarising the Commission's significant practice on refusal to supply,[18] AG Jacobs distilled the key legal principles arising from his case law review:

> It is clear from the above rulings that a dominant undertaking commits an abuse where, without justification, it cuts off supplies of goods or services to an existing customer or eliminates competition on a related market by tying separate goods and services. However, it also seems that an abuse may consist in mere refusal to license where that prevents a new product from coming on a neighbouring market in competition with the dominant undertaking's own product on that market.[19]

---

[6] As Justice Scalia underlined in the majority opinion in *Verizon Communications Inc v Law Offices of Curtis Trinko*, 540 US 398 (2004).

[7] This is certainly true for the Court of Justice of the European Union. One sporadic reference to the concept of 'essential facility' can be found in the decision of the Court of First Instance (now the General Court) in Joined Cases T-374/94, T-375/94, T-384/94 and T-388/94 *European Night Services* ECLI:EU:T:1998:198.

[8] See Goyder (n 4) 359. He refers to the anxiety caused in IP owners after *Magill* (see n 16 below). *Oscar Bronner* was the subsequent 'chapter' in the refusal to supply series.

[9] See paras 35–53 of the Opinion in *Oscar Bronner*.

[10] ibid, para 35.

[11] Case 27/76 *United Brands* ECLI:EU:C:1978:22.

[12] Case 311/84 *CBEM* ECLI:EU:C:1985:394.

[13] Case C-18/88 *RTT* ECLI: EU:C:1991:474.

[14] Case 238/87 *Volvo* ECLI: EU:C:1988:477.

[15] Case 53/87 *CICRA* ECLI:EU:C:1988:472.

[16] Joined Cases Case C-241/91 P and C-242/91 P *RTÉ and ITP* ECLI:EU:C:1995:98.

[17] Case T-504/93 *Ladbroke* ECLI:EU:T:1997:84.

[18] Para 19 of the Opinion in *Oscar Bronner*.

[19] ibid, para 43.

This analysis of the refusal to supply cases paved the way to the examination of the essential facility doctrine. After noting that 'commentators have seen the *Télémarketing* and especially the *Magill* rulings as an endorsement by the Court of the essential facility doctrine, increasingly employed by the Commission in its decisions',[20] AG Jacobs carried out a comparative overview of US law, '[s]ince that doctrine has its origins in US antitrust law',[21] and, crucially, of the Commission's practice. The latter's overview led him to conclude that 'the Commission considers that refusal of access to an essential facility to a competitor can of itself be an abuse even in the absence of other factors'[22] and that 'in the practice of the Commission in cases concerning refusal to supply the notion of essential facilities plays an important role'.[23] The very comprehensive and clear review was concluded by considering in the final paragraph the laws of the Member States which 'generally regard freedom of contract as an essential element of free trade', while, in some cases, 'explicitly provid[ing] that an unjustified refusal to enter a binding contract may constitute an abuse of dominant position'.[24] With more specific regard to the essential facility doctrine, AG Jacobs noted that in some Member States this access is granted by 'specific legislative provisions', while in other Member States the doctrine developed from 'more general principles'.[25]

After outlining the state of the art, AG Jacobs started his appraisal of the issues through findings which have become the standard definition of the doctrine in EU law. He noted that 'that question raises a general issue which can arise in a variety of different contexts'; this enabled him to make 'a number of general points'.[26] He first immediately noted how the 'right to choose one's trading partners and freely to dispose of one's property are generally recognised principles in the laws of the Member States, in some cases with constitutional status'.[27] This meant that '[i]ncursions on those rights require careful justification'.[28] The second caveat focused on the 'justification in terms of competition policy for interfering with a dominant undertaking's freedom to contract' which 'often requires a careful balancing of conflicting considerations'.[29] In this respect, the analysis should not be limited to increasing competition in the short term but most importantly to safeguarding the incentives to invest in the long term.[30] Thirdly, he warned that the 'primary purpose of Article [102 TFEU] is to prevent distortion of competition – and in particular to safeguard the interests of consumers – rather than to protect the position of particular competitors'.[31] After underlining the importance of the competition situation on the downstream market[32] (also through a reference to the Opinion of AG Warner in *Commercial Solvents*),[33] AG Jacobs carried on recognising that:

> refusal of access may in some cases entail elimination or substantial reduction of competition to the detriment of consumers in both the short and the long term. That will be so where access to a facility

[20] ibid, para 45.
[21] ibid, paras 45–47.
[22] ibid, para 50.
[23] ibid, para 52.
[24] ibid, para 53.
[25] ibid.
[26] Para 55 of the Opinion in *Oscar Bronner*.
[27] ibid, para 56.
[28] ibid.
[29] Para 57 of the Opinion in *Oscar Bronner*.
[30] ibid.
[31] Para 58 of the Opinion in *Oscar Bronner*.
[32] ibid.
[33] Opinion of AG Warner in Joined Cases 6/73 and 7/73 *Commercial Solvents* ECLI:EU:C:1974:5.

is a precondition for competition on a related market for goods or services for which there is a limited degree of interchangeability.[34]

He noted that in assessing the various, conflicting interests:

particular care is required where the goods or services or facilities to which access is demanded represent the fruit of substantial investment. That may be true in particular in relation to refusal to license intellectual property rights. Where such exclusive rights are granted for a limited period, that in itself involves a balancing of the interest in free competition with that of providing an incentive for research and development and for creativity.[35]

AG Jacobs then explained how the *Magill* ruling could be explained by the 'special circumstances of the case which swung the balance in favour of an obligation to licence'.[36] This led him to go deeper and analyse the relation between intellectual property rights and economic monopoly, notably:

While generally the exercise of intellectual property rights will restrict competition for a limited period only, a dominant undertaking's monopoly over a product, service or facility may in certain cases lead to permanent exclusion of competition on a related market. In such cases competition can be achieved only by requiring a dominant undertaking to supply the product or service or allow access to the facility. ...

It seems to me that intervention of that kind, whether understood as an application of the essential facilities doctrine or, more traditionally, as a response to a refusal to supply goods or services, can be justified in terms of competition policy only in cases in which the dominant undertaking has a genuine stranglehold on the related market. That might be the case for example where duplication of the facility is impossible or extremely difficult owing to physical, geographical or legal constraints or is highly undesirable for reasons of public policy. It is not sufficient that the undertaking's control over a facility should give it a competitive advantage.[37]

After these observations, and highlighting that the 'test' must be an 'objective one' ('in order for refusal to access to amount to an abuse, it must be extremely difficult not merely for the undertaking demanding access but for any other undertaking to compete'),[38] AG Jacobs duly concluded that it was clear that those conditions were not satisfied in the present case. Although probably 'uneconomic',[39] a duplication of the facility was not certainly impossible or extremely difficult. He concluded his reasoning with a gloss on the lack of desirability for 'Community and national authorities and Courts' to delve into the 'detailed regulation' of the market 'entailing the fixing of prices and conditions for supply in large sectors of the economy'.[40]

Since, in its decision of 26 November 1998, the Court essentially followed the Opinion of AG Jacobs, there is no need for a specific analysis.[41]

---

[34] Para 61 of the Opinion in *Oscar Bronner*.
[35] ibid, para 62.
[36] ibid, para 63.
[37] ibid, paras 64–65.
[38] ibid, para 66.
[39] ibid, para 68.
[40] ibid, para 69.
[41] Case C-7/97 *Oscar Bronner* ECLI:EU:C:1998:569. For a careful analysis of both Opinion and Court's judgment see G Monti, *EC Competition Law* (Cambridge, CUP, 2007) 224–26.

III. *PREUSSENELEKTRA*

A. Background, Context, and Facts

This case is one of the most important in state aid jurisprudence. The Court was called to clearly define the limits of the definition of state aid, by determining in particular whether to have state aid you need to have a transfer of 'state resources'. This has been an interpretative issue that has engaged the jurisprudence of the Court for many decades, especially from the 1970s onwards, and originates from the peculiar language of Article 107 TFEU which prohibits '… any aid granted by a Member State or through State resources in any form whatsoever …'. The expression 'by a Member State or through State resources' has been subject to debate and litigation in several cases before *PreussenElektra* with the Court fluctuating, in some cases not considering a use of public money an essential element of a state aid (*Commission v France*,[42] *Van der Kooy*,[43] *Greece v Commission*[44]), in other cases making it an essential requirement (*Van Tiggele*,[45] *Nord-deutsches Vieh- und Fleischkontor*,[46] *Sloman Neptun*,[47] *Kirsammer-Hack*,[48] *Viscido*,[49] *Ecotrade*,[50] *Piaggio*,[51] *Ladbroke*[52]).

As testament to the complexity of the question, it was not rare for the Court to disagree with its AGs (see eg AG VerLoren van Themaat in *Nord-deutsches Vieh- und Fleischkontor*, AG Mancini in *Commission v France*, and AG Darmon in *Sloman Netpun* and *Kirsammer-Hack*).

By settling a debate that lasted decades, the *PreussenElektra* case still stands as the watershed in the jurisprudence in the field. The case law has certainly developed since, but mostly attempting to clarifying the *dicta* of the Court, which found a powerful basis in the Opinion of AG Jacobs.

Interestingly, AG Jacobs already had to deal with the issue just a couple of years before the *PreussenElektra* case. In *Viscido*, he had observed:

> It might be asked why, given their potential effect on competition [Article 107(1) TFEU] does not cover all labour and other social measures which by virtue of being selective in their impact might distort competition and thereby have an equivalent effect to State aid. The answer is perhaps essentially a pragmatic one: to investigate all such regimes would entail an enquiry on the basis of the Treaty alone into the entire social and economic life of a Member State.[53]

The case was a preliminary reference from the Regional Court, Kiel. The German Court asked whether a law requiring regional electricity distributors to purchase at a fixed minimum price electricity produced from renewable energy sources in their area of supply amounted to state aid or, alternatively, constituted a measure equivalent to a quantitative restriction on imports. The German *Stromeinpeisungsgesetz* (*StrEG*), in its successive versions, has been one of the model and most successful price incentives (so called 'Feed-In Tariffs', 'FITs') to promote

---

[42] Case 290/83 *Commission v France* ECLI:EU:C:1985:37.
[43] Joined Cases 67/85, 68/85 and 70/85 *Van der Kooy* ECLI:EU:C:1988:38.
[44] Case 57/86 *Greece v Commission* ECLI:EU:C:1988:284.
[45] Case 82/77 *Van Tiggele* ECLI:EU:C:1978:10.
[46] Joined Cases 213/81, 214/81 and 215/81 *Norddeutsches Vieh- und Fleischkontor* ECLI:EU:C:1982:351.
[47] Joined Cases C-72/91 and C-73/91 *Sloman Neptun* ECLI:EU:C:1993:97.
[48] Case C-189/91 *Kirsammer-Hack* ECLI:EU:C:1993:907.
[49] Joined Cases C-52/97, C-53/97 and C-54/97 *Viscido* ECLI:EU:C:1998:209.
[50] Case C-200/97 *Ecotrade* ECLI:EU:C:1998:579.
[51] Case C-295/97 *Piaggio* ECLI:EU:C:1999:313.
[52] Case C-83/98P *France v Ladbroke Racing and Commission* ECLI:EU:C:2000:248.
[53] Opinion of AG Jacobs in Joined Cases C-52/97, C-53/97 and C-54/97 *Viscido* ECLI:EU:C:1998:78, para 16.

renewable energy generation. In questioning the legality of its core mechanism, the preliminary reference was thus very politically sensitive. Like in *Oscar Bronner*, the expectations for the Opinion and the judgment were very high. It is finally important to note that this was a very important case for the Commission that, through a broad interpretation of the concept of aid, wanted to have a major hold on the development of the green energy markets. To do so, not only did the Commission argue that the use of 'state resources' was not a necessary requirement but also, and alternatively, that the German incentive could amount to a 'measure equivalent to state aid' – a truly novel and innovative legal claim raised for the second (and, to the best of our knowledge, last) time in this case.

The case is also important because it provided the opportunity to clarify whether the 'environmental justification', initially developed under the *Cassis de Dijon* jurisprudence, could also apply to discriminatory measures. As noted in the Opinion of AG Jacobs, case law and literature had been showing openings in this respect. It was high time for a clearer statement of the law.

B. The Opinion of AG Jacobs

Setting aside various preliminary issues, AG Jacobs began his analysis on the issue of whether the German incentive scheme constituted state aid and immediately determined that 'only one element of the concept of State aid is disputed', that is the financing through state resources.[54] After conceding that the phrase 'granted by a Member State or through State resources' could be interpreted in two different ways, requiring (or not) a use of public money,[55] he highlighted that 'it is now well-established case-law that the second reading prevails and that only *advantages which are granted directly or indirectly through State resources* are to be regarded as State aid within the meaning of Article [107(1) TFEU]'.[56] What follows in the subsequent paragraphs[57] is then an exhaustive examination of the case law since the 1970s onwards, in the aforementioned cases.

After this review, AG Jacobs focused on whether the Court should reconsider its case law. Various arguments were being put forward in favour of an expansive interpretation. Both the language of Article 107(1) TFEU itself, by referring to aid granted 'in any form whatsoever', and the consideration of the importance of the goal that 'competition in the internal market is not distorted' would have supported a broad interpretation.[58] That argument was supported by the consideration that the 'distortion on competition might be greater when the cost of the measure is borne by competitors of the aided undertakings and not the general public', as was argued to happen in the case.[59] Finally, since 'all State revenue is ultimately provided by private individuals through taxes', requiring the financing through state resources would appear 'formalistic' and would have created opportunities for circumvention.[60]

Very interestingly, the Commission was strongly pushing for a reversal of the jurisprudence. After noting that, '[a]fter the completion of the internal market and with the beginning of monetary Union, selectively applied aid measures are the last remaining instrument which

---

[54] Para 112 of the Opinion in *PreussenElektra*.
[55] ibid, paras 114–16.
[56] ibid, para 117 (emphasis in the original).
[57] ibid, paras 118–33.
[58] ibid, paras 137–38.
[59] ibid, paras 139–42.
[60] ibid, paras 143–45.

the Member States can use to confer competitive advantages on their domestic undertakings', it noted that it was of 'paramount importance' to subject them to state aid control to guarantee the discipline and transparency.[61] Although 'accept[ing] that there is some force in the above arguments in favour of an extensive understanding of the concept of State aid', AG Jacobs remained of the opinion that 'financing through State resources is a necessary element of the concept of State aid and that the Court should adhere to its current case-law'.[62]

AG Jacobs' first argument was that the 'reading suggested by the Court in *Sloman Neptun*, *Kirsammer-Hack* and *Viscido* is more natural and raises fewer consequential problems'.[63] The first alternative ('aid granted by a Member State') would cover 'normal aid measures financed from public funds and granted directly by the State'. By contrast, the second alternative ('aid granted through State resources') would only cover 'the rarer and residual category of aid financed through State resources which is granted not directly by the State but by public or private bodies designated or established by the State'.[64] The alternative reading, whereby aid could be granted by the state without use of state resources, would lead to the incongruous situation where the authors of the Treaty [would have] put a residual category of cases (aid not financed through state resources) before the normal category of cases (aid financed through state resources). According to AG Jacobs, '[t]hat is neither the natural nor the usual way to proceed when drafting legislation'.[65] Finally, support would also be derived from the language of the heading of the Treaty section which refers to 'Aids granted by States' which should by definition cover both alternatives in Article 107(1) TFEU.

After these grounds based on semantics and drafting logic, AG Jacobs puts forward various arguments.[66] First, the extensive reading of Article 107(1) TFEU would 'run the risk of assuming what has to be proved, namely that the rules are intended to apply to all State measures'. It could equally be argued that Member States wanted to limit the scope of state aid control only to measures financed through public funds. Secondly, a systemic argument would favour the restrictive interpretation: if Article 107(1) TFEU covered also measures financed from private resources, one would expect that the private undertakings financing the aid had procedural rights and obligations under Article 108 TFEU, which was not the case. Thirdly, the restrictive interpretation would provide more legal certainty: the more extensive interpretation would oblige 'to decide in respect of all legislation regulating the relationship between enterprises whether it does confer selective advantages on certain undertakings within the meaning of Article 107(1) TFEU. Since such an assessment is a difficult exercise with an uncertain outcome, it seems preferable that legislation regulating the relationship between private actors is as a matter of principle excluded from the scope of the State aid rules'. Finally, AG Jacobs suggested that the risk of 'large scale support measures' financed through private resources should not have been exaggerated since the latter would have certainly resisted the introduction of such measures (as the case at issue, with legal proceedings launched before the German constitutional court, confirmed). In any event, other EU law provisions (such as Article 34 TFEU) could have applied.

After having advised not to depart from the current case law, AG Jacobs addressed various arguments put forward by the parties that would establish that, in the case at hand, there had

---

[61] ibid, para 146.
[62] ibid, para 150.
[63] ibid, paras 151–54.
[64] ibid.
[65] ibid.
[66] See paras 155–58 of the Opinion in *PreussenElektra*.

been a financing through state resources (through the potential loss in tax revenue, the conversion of private into public resources, the reduced earnings of publicly-owned undertakings) and rejected them all.[67]

AG Jacobs then addressed – and rejected – a very ambitious argument of the Commission pleading for the existence of a concept of a 'measure equivalent to aid'.[68] In other words, if the StrEG 1998 does not constitute state aid in the strict sense, because of the duty of cooperation of Article [4(3) TEU], it however 'constitutes a measure intended to circumvent the State aid rules' that could be pursue via Article 258 TFEU. Through this argument, the Commission wanted to introduce an anti-circumvention device that, when appropriate, the negotiators of the Treaty of Rome expressly introduced.[69]

Finally, after determining that the StrEG 1998 might well constitute a measure having an equivalent effect to a quantitative restriction under Article 34 TFEU,[70] AG Jacobs concentrated on another very important systemic legal issue, ie whether a discriminatory measure, such as the StrEG 1998, could be justified by the protection of environment reasons.[71] Two obstacles stood in the way. First, the possibility that EU legislation in the field pre-empted any action of the Member States. That, according to AG Jacobs, was not the case since 'specific Community measures on the promotion of electricity from renewable energy sources in the internal market are currently being discussed but have not yet been adopted'.[72]

The second obstacle depended on the fact that, while the protection of the environment was encompassed in the judicially-created *Cassis de Dijon* mandatory requirements, it was not listed in Article 36 TFEU which traditionally outlines the grounds for exception for discriminatory measures. Addressing an argument by the Commission, AG Jacobs analysed the *Commission v Belgium (Walloon Waste)* case,[73] criticised it, but found that it was showing 'something else, namely that it is desirable that even directly discriminatory measures can sometimes be justified on grounds of environmental protection'.[74] He then detected some 'indications that the Court is reconsidering its earlier case-law' (citing various cases and in particular *Dusseldorp*[75] and *Aher-Waggon*[76]) and also calls in the literature to overcome the distinction.[77] On this basis, and in view of the fundamental importance of the issue, he explicitly called on the Court to 'clarify its position in order to provide the necessary legal certainty' and offered two specific reasons for a 'more flexible approach': first, the Treaty of Amsterdam's introduction of the principle of integration of environmental protection requirements in all EU policies, and secondly the fact that 'national measures for the protection of the environment are inherently liable to differentiate on the basis of the nature and origin of the cause of harm, and are therefore liable to be found discriminatory'.[78]

The Court followed the Opinion on both counts, first, by confirming its prevailing case law that, in order to have a state aid, this has to be financed through state resources, secondly, by

---

[67] ibid, paras 160–79.

[68] ibid, paras 180–85.

[69] See, eg, Articles 28(1), 29, 30, 34, 35, 44.

[70] Ibid, paras 197–205.

[71] The defence on the basis of security of supply had been previously rejected because of the lack of proportionality (paras 207–210 of the Opinion in *PreussenElektra*).

[72] Para 219 of the Opinion in *PreussenElektra*.

[73] Case C-2/90 *Commission v Belgium* ECLI:EU:C:1992:310.

[74] Paras 222–26 of the Opinion in *PreussenElektra*.

[75] Case C-203/96 *Chemische Afvalstoffen Dusseldorp* ECLI:EU:C:1998:316.

[76] Case C-389/96 *Aher-Waggon* ECLI:EU:C:1998:357.

[77] Paras 227–28 of the Opinion in *PreussenElektra*.

[78] ibid, paras 230–33.

'clarifying' its case law.[79] In particular, the Court highlighted the connection between renewable energy incentives, such as the StrEG, and the protection of the environment.[80] It then noted that 'that policy is also designed to protect the health and life of humans, animals and plants'.[81] After referring to other principles (including the principle of integration), it concluded that 'in the current state of Community law concerning the electricity market, legislation such as the amended *Stromeinspeisungsgesetz* is not incompatible with Article [34 TFEU]'.[82]

IV. ANALYSIS

A. The Legacy of the Opinion in *Oscar Bronner*

As repeatedly noted, this Opinion has become (probably even more than the Court's decision) the official statement of the 'essential facility' doctrine in EU competition law. Throughout the Opinion, one can certainly feel a sense of scepticism towards a claim that would dramatically broaden the scope of competition law and, in doing so, significantly interfere with key legal and political principles (freedom of contract and right to property) and also manipulate the incentives to innovate and invest which are at the core of a functioning market. The importance of the Opinion is confirmed by how well received it has been in the literature. For example, Whish and Bailey introduce the lengthy and detailed analysis of refusals to supply with a quote and detailed analysis of the Opinion of AG Jacobs.[83] Jones and Sufrin note that *Bronner* was notable for the Opinion of AG Jacobs, urging the necessity of confining the essential facilities concept within strict limits.[84]

Even more significantly, the importance of the principles laid down by the Opinion, and, at its core, the requirement of 'indispensability', are confirmed by its relevance in the competition analysis of the digital economy. Essential facility claims that in the past focused on physical infrastructures are now directed towards digital platforms and data. AG Jacobs' caution, as expressed in his *Bronner* Opinion, is repeatedly referred to even in these new contexts.[85]

In setting forth, and developing, his standard of 'indispensability', AG Jacobs seems to have heavily drawn from the key conditions developed in the US (together with the 'indispensability', the fact that competitors are 'unable practically or reasonably to duplicate' the facility).[86] Across the Atlantic, we note a significant disdain for the doctrine, coming from the higher

---

[79] Case C-379/98 *PreussenElektra AG* ECLI:EU:C:2001:160.

[80] Paras 73–74 of the Judgment in *PreussenElektra*. The Court underlined that 'growth in that use is amongst the priority objectives which the Community and its Member States intend to pursue implementing' their UNFCCC commitments, the Kyoto Protocol and the European Parliament and Council Altener programme.

[81] Para 75 of the Judgment in *PreussenElektra*.

[82] ibid, para 81.

[83] Whish and Bailey (n 4) 732–33.

[84] A Jones and B Sufrin, *EU Competition Law: Text, Cases and Materials*, 5th edn (Oxford, OUP, 2014) 518.

[85] See eg the extensive analysis of the *Oscar Bronner* Opinion and Judgment in Case T-612/17 *Google LLC* ECLI:EU:T:2021:763, at paras 212–49. See also J Crémer, Y-A de Montjoye and H Schweitzer, *Competition Policy for the Digital Era – Final Report* (European Commission, Directorate General for Competition, Brussels, 2019) 99.

[86] Jacobs had the opportunity to further explain his viewpoint in the *Syfait* case, which concerned a refusal to supply to limit parallel trade in pharmaceuticals, where he further noted that 'any obligation to deal pursuant to Article 102 [TFEU] can be established only after a close scrutiny of the factual and economic context, and even then only within somewhat narrow limits'. See Opinion of AG Jacobs in Case C-53/03 *Syfait* ECLI:EU:C:2004:673, para 3.

levels. Hoverkamp, admittedly, the most authoritative textbook on US federal antitrust law, reads:

> The so-called 'essential facility' doctrine is one of the most troublesome, incoherent and unmanageable of bases for Sherman § 2 liability. The antitrust world would almost certainly be a better place if it were jettisoned, with a little fine tuning of the general doctrine of refusal to deal to fill any gaps.[87]

In the *Trinko* case, the US Supreme Court noted that the 'essential facilities' doctrine had been 'crafted by some lower courts.' Its laconic conclusion was:

> We have never recognized such a doctrine, and we find no need either to recognize it or to repudiate it here.[88]

Perhaps with a different language, the Opinion and judgment in *Bronner* share the same sentiments.

This is true if the standard statement of the law is contrasted with the 'exceptional cases' where the Court has imposed a duty to deal or supply. In the EU, that happened with the *Magill/IMS/Microsoft* trio (and it is interesting to note that the Court duly analysed the *Bronner* case, and painstakingly distinguished it, before reaching its conclusions). In the US, the 'ugly duckling' is represented by the *Aspen Skiing* decision[89] of the US Supreme Court which, according to it, is 'at or near the outer boundary of § 2 liability'.[90] We could safely say the same for *Magill/IMS/Microsoft*.[91]

One important point put forward in the Opinion of AG Jacobs was pragmatic and refers to the fact that the law, paraphrasing the expression of the dissenting opinion in the US *Leegin* case,[92] is an 'administrative system' which, beyond the validity of any point of principle, has to be managed. That is the deep meaning of his note about the lack of desirability for 'Community and national authorities and Courts' to delve into the 'detailed regulation' of the market 'entailing the fixing of prices and conditions for supply in large sectors of the economy'[93] which would inevitably derive if access to a facility were determined on the basis of an antitrust claim.

This leads to a more general comment. Like in trade, antitrust mostly deals with specific instances of distortions and does so *ex post*. It is reasonable to ask whether it is really suited to touch the very fundamental principles of a legal system. This should be left to the legislature or delegated independent authorities, defining the regulatory framework *ex ante*, and not to administrations or adjudicating bodies applying general principles in individual cases. A parallel with the *US Trinko* case is once again appropriate. One of the key arguments that led the US Supreme Court to reject the claim was that access was already granted and governed by

---

[87] Hoverkamp (n 5) 336.

[88] Para 6 of the Opinion delivered by Justice Antonin Scalia for the Court.

[89] *Aspen Skiing Co v Aspen Highlands Skiing Corp.*, 472 US 585 (1985).

[90] Para 5 the Opinion delivered by Justice Antonin Scalia for the Court in *Trinko*.

[91] For an interesting explanation of why the 'essential facility' doctrine has been so successful in EU Commission's practice, linked to the demonopolisation and liberalisation of various sectors of the economy, see Whish and Bailey (n 4) 742. For better understanding the methodology underlying the practice of the Commission see Communication from the Commission – Guidance on Article 102 Enforcement Priorities to Abusive Exclusionary Conduct of Dominant Undertakings [2009] OJ C45/7.

[92] *Leegin Creative Leather Products Inc v PSKS Inc*, 551 US 877 (2007), see Opinion of Justice Breyer.

[93] Para 69 of the Opinion.

sectoral regulation. In a passage, which was even quoted by AG Jacobs in his Opinion in *Syfait*, the US Supreme Court had said:

> Antitrust analysis must always be attuned to the particular structure and circumstances of the industry at issue. Part of that attention to economic context is an awareness of the significance of regulation.[94]

B. The Legacy of the Opinion in *PreussenElektra*

The main remark made with respect to *Bronner* could be made as regards *PreussenElektra*. In this case, AG Jacobs solved two issues in a way that, to this day, still constitutes the standard statement of the law in the two fields.

With respect to the financing through state resources, the Commission's practice and the jurisprudence have now focused on the different issue of when a certain practice involves a use of 'state resources' or, in another way, what makes certain resources 'public'. The statement that a measure needs to be necessarily financed through state resources has not been changed since the delivery of the Opinion of AG Jacobs in *PreussenElektra*. The case is regularly cited as the leading authority; as said, the true watershed in the jurisprudence. The need to have a use of public 'resources' has even been incorporated into the very recent EU-UK Trade and Cooperation Agreement (EU-UK TCA)[95] where the definition of subsidy, while largely following WTO jargon, does explicitly introduce that a subsidy 'means financial assistance which: (i) arises from the resources of the Parties …'.[96] This is a true innovation at the international level since WTO law does not require a 'cost to government'.[97]

This does not mean that no attempt to reconsider the case law has taken place. The most elaborate has probably been that of AG Maduro in his Opinion in *Enirisorse II* (which was, however, not followed by the Court).[98] Mostly with the benefit of hindsight (the actual application of the *PreussenElektra* test), many scholars, including this author, have criticised the *PreussenElektra* 'state resources' requirement (and, obviously, behind it, the Opinion of AG Jacobs).[99] But this criticism is partly unfair, precisely because it is based on *ex post* analysis. Neither the *PreussenElektra* Court nor certainly AG Jacobs can be held responsible for how the law has developed *afterwards*, through Byzantine and contradictory distinctions.[100]

Two powerful reasons supported the more conservative position of AG Jacobs. The strong perception that the requirement: (i) would have guaranteed legal certainty, and (ii) would have constituted the appropriate legal technique to distinguish between what should be subject to state aid control (hence, Commission's control) and what should have been left to Member

---

[94] Footnote 40 of the Opinion in *Syfait*.

[95] Trade and Cooperation Agreement between the European Union and the European Atomic Energy Community, of the one part, and the United Kingdom of Great Britain and Northern Ireland, of the other part [2021] OJ L149/10.

[96] Article 363 (1b) EU-UK TCA. See also Article 2.1(a) of the UK Subsidy Control Act 2022, which was awarded Royal Assent on 28 April 2022.

[97] It is also evidence that, despite language and political narratives, the EU-UK TCA does include a lot of EU law inspired regulation, subsidy disciplines being one notable example.

[98] Opinion of AG Maduro in Case C-237/04 *Enirisorse* ECLI:EU:C:2006:21.

[99] See eg A Biondi, 'State Aid is Falling Down, Falling Down: An Analysis of the Case Law on the Notion of Aid' (2013) 50 *CMLRev* 1719; T Jaeger, 'Goodbye Old Friend: Article 107's Double Control Criterion' (2012) 11 *European State Aid Law Quarterly* 533.

[100] See eg L Rubini, 'The Elusive Frontier: "Regulation" under EC State Aid Law' (2009) 8 *European State Aid Law Quarterly* 277. See also T Iliopoulos, 'Is *ENEA* The New *PreussenElektra*?' (2018) 17 *European State Aid Law Quarterly* 19.

States, and, if necessary, regulated under other EU provisions. They were – and still are – fundamental considerations shaping the law and policy of EU state aid. This strong precedent has not, however, stood the test of time with commentators mostly outlining the paradox of a requirement that was introduced to guarantee legal certainty and that has in fact contributed to some of the most confused case law of the Court (and we are still counting …).[101] Therefore, it is no surprise that many voices increasingly call for a reconsideration.[102]

The lack of application of EU state aid law was not the end of the story in *PreussenElektra* where the German purchase obligation was found to constitute a restriction on intra-EU trade and then eventually permitted in the name of the 'environmental justification'.

The Opinion of AG Jacobs is the path-opener in this respect too. As noted above, after a careful summary of the law, and in particular of the most recent openings that had shown the possibility of applying environmental protection as a justification even for distinctly applicable measures, he explicitly called on the Court to follow this path, through an evolutive interpretation of the law (justified by the changes that had occurred, and were occurring, more generally in EU law).[103] The *PreussenElektra* decision, which essentially followed the Opinion of AG Jacobs, is still the leading authority on the point,[104] the first case in a line of newer cases.[105]

Upon a closer look, however, it looks like the Court did not really do justice to Jacobs' call for clarification on the status of justifications to free movement restrictions. The only really significant *prescriptive* statement can be found in para 75 where, as noted, the Court finds:

> It should be noted that that policy is also designed to protect the health and life of humans, animals and plants.

This is the only passage which expressly refers to one of the grounds in Article 36 TFEU (the other *dicta* simply provide normative context by referring to the developments in EU and international law with respect to environmental protection, renewable energy, and climate change).

Although the Court reproduces one of the justifications of Article 36 TFEU, it is not clear what they make of it. Should this mean that the 1950s language 'health and life of humans, animals and plants' (directly originating from Article XX of the GATT 1947) should now also refer to the 'environment'? What does 'also' mean? And, drawing a parallel with the reasoned argumentation of AG Jacobs, what about the discussion and distinction between discriminatory and indistinctly applicable measures, and their justification? What about the proportionality of the national measure to achieve its goal? How has this been solved by the Court? What we know is that the German measures are justified for environmental reasons. The path and methodology that led the Court to the conclusion are still unknown.[106] Luckily, we still have a few directions to follow in AG Jacobs' Opinion.

What arises from the *PreussenElektra* case, in terms of the big picture, is that through a rejection of the state aid claim and the acceptance of the environmental defence, Member

---

[101] See eg Case T-251/11 *Austria v Commission* ECLI:EU:T:2014:1060; Case C-329/15 *ENEA* ECLI:EU:C:2017:671; Case C-405/16 *Germany v Commission* ECLI:EU:C:2019:268; Case C-434/19 *Poste Italiane* ECLI:EU:C:2021:162.

[102] See eg Biondi (n 99).

[103] See N Nic Shuibhne, 'Exceptions to the free movement rules' in C Barnard and S Peers (eds), *European Union Law*, 3rd edn (Oxford, OUP, 2020) 520.

[104] See eg P Craig and G de Búrca, *EU Law: Text, Cases, and Materials*, 7th edn (Oxford, OUP, 2020) 769.

[105] See eg Case C-142/05 *Mickelsson and Roos* ECLI:EU:C:2009:336.

[106] See L Rubini, 'Brevi note a margine del caso *PreussenElektra*, ovvero come 'prendere seriamente' le norme sugli aiuti di Stato e la tutela dell'ambiente nel diritto comunitario' [2001] *Diritto Comunitario e degli Scambi Internazionali* 473, 493–494.

States received a double-endorsement to their renewable energy policy, something which was probably very much needed at the time.[107]

C. Marking Boundaries in Competition and Internal Market Law

As has become evident by now, the two Opinions contributed to define, or re-define, the boundaries of EU antitrust law, EU state aid law and EU internal market law.

They did so in different ways. On the one hand, the 'outer' boundaries of EU competition law – be it antitrust or state aid – were significantly marked. Both AG Jacobs and the Court made it clear that, if there is anything like an 'essential facility doctrine' in EU law, it may be referred to only under very strict conditions, all summarised in the concept of objective 'indispensability'. Similarly, both AG Jacobs and the Court rejected the call to revisit the case law and broaden the definition of state aid (thus broadening the control of the Commission). From these perspectives, the two cases sounded like a definite 'no!' to the expansionist claims of the parties (including, especially for state aid, the Commission).

Quite different is the nature of the second issue in *PreussenElektra* which focused on the clarification of the availability of a defence. Here, once again, AG Jacobs and the Court concurred and pushed the boundaries of the law on the justifications to breaches of free movement of goods. Though the end result is the same, we have noted the (too) many ambiguities of the Court.

Trying to conceptualise, and loosely borrowing from Weatherill's *The Internal Market as a Legal Concept*,[108] one can identify three different scenarios. First, *Oscar Bronner* was really a 'switch' scenario: there is/there is not a breach of Article 102 TFEU, issue which is largely exhaustive: no other possible rules were at issue in the case (differently from the *Trinko* case). The limit drawn on EU antitrust law is therefore clear-cut. Secondly, *PreussenElektra*'s state aid part was more nuanced: a negative state aid decision would not have meant no liability; quite simply, other rules – notably internal market rules – would have been applicable, and that is exactly what happened in the case. In other words, *Oscar Bronner* and *PreussenElektra* responded differently to the question of definition/competence, the former by fully excluding the conduct from the reach of EU law, the latter by simply replacing the type of laws applicable. One limit was drawn narrowly, the other was possibly expanded. Thirdly, *PreussenElektra* (justification) is altogether another scenario. Using Weatherill's jargon, it is both about determining competence and also the appropriate interpretation of, and convergence between, similar rules.

D. The Virtue of Moderation

In his foreword to a collection in honour of AG Jacobs, Lord Bingham of Cornhill noted:

> ... the Advocate General has no licence to behave irresponsibly. He or she is bound to respect the existing case law of the Court and will be slow to suggest departures from existing authority or

---

[107] The hermeneutic irony is that this double-endorsement is reached by a broad interpretation of an exception, like Article 36 TFEU, and a narrow interpretation of a provision, like Article 107 TFEU, that is fundamental for EU competition policy. See Rubini, ibid, 495.

[108] S Weatherill, *The Internal Market as a Legal Concept* (Oxford, OUP, 2017) 49–93.

radical changes of direction. But the opportunity exists to nudge the Court towards new conclusions, to raise new ideas, to throw doubt on accepted orthodoxy, to bring a single judgment, coherent and informed, to bear on the complex and various problems which confront the Court.[109]

These words capture the essential characteristics of AG Jacobs as a jurist and member of the Court.

As anticipated in the introduction, there is a link between the, apparently different, cases of *Oscar Bronner* and *PreussenElektra* and, in particular, between the Opinions of AG Jacobs in those cases. We have called it the virtue of *moderation*, the capacity to always keep the 'golden mean'. Arguably, this is a useful key to understand more generally the several hundreds of Opinions of AG Jacobs and his inner legacy to EU law and policy.

The 'golden mean' or 'middle way' is a core concept in Western (but not only Western) philosophy. There have been famous restatements by the likes of Plato, Aristotle, and Saint Thomas Aquinas. Often phrased as 'nothing in excess', we believe that moderation is a crucial virtue for judicial activity – and AGs significantly contribute to the judicial activity of the Court, often providing the only – unrestrained, unconstrained – voice of reason.

In this context, moderation is not only about avoiding extreme solutions (whether too restrictive or too generous) but about understanding what to do in the precise case, in its precise circumstances, where the balance should be found and struck, in that particular moment in time and in the stage of evolution of EU law and policy and society. In a word, it is about *whether the boundaries of the law can be pushed or rather pulled*. The ability to distinguish these cases is moderation.

If AG Jacobs pulled the boundaries in *Bronner* and in the state aid part of *PreussenElektra*, it pushed them in the justification claim of the latter case. One can easily apply this heuristic to many other cases in this volume in fields as diverse as access to court, citizenship, fundamental rights.

This 'discretionary' exercise is made possible by the fact that the law, especially competition and internal market law, is ambiguous and is naturally open to different interpretations. But if interpretation is expected, over-reaching is not desirable.

Moderation also appears in more prosaic factors. The Opinion should strictly answer the questions asked and help in solving the case. It is not an academic piece. It is a fundamental document aiding the work of the Court. Verbosity should be avoided in favour of an efficient and clear style: to the point.[110] Words should be carefully chosen. So should the expression of legal concepts. One paragraph more than necessary is simply one too much. Moderation is a natural quality, not an art. AG Jacobs possessed it.

---

[109] A Arnull, P Eeckhout and T Tridimas, *Continuity and Change in EU Law: Essays in Honour of Sir Francis Jacobs* (Oxford, OUP, 2008).

[110] Speaking extra-judicially, Sir Francis Jacobs recalled to the present author how, when he was serving in AG Warner's cabinet, he very much admired the dry and confident style of AG Capotorti.

33

Protecting the Rights of Individuals: Opinion of Advocate General Jacobs in UPA

ANTHONY ARNULL

I. INTRODUCTION

Ｏ N 10 December 1952 in the Villa Vauban in Luxembourg, the seven members of the newly created Court of Justice of the European Coal and Steel Community were sworn in. The President of the Court, Massimo Pilotti, gave a speech in which he emphasised the importance of protecting the rights of litigants should the institutions of the Community exceed their powers. Some of the Court's early case law did indeed manifest a liberal approach to the admissibility of actions for annulment under Article 33 of the Treaty establishing the European Coal and Steel Community (ECSC). An example is *Assider*,[1] where the applicant challenged a number of decisions adopted by the High Authority on the basis that they were vitiated by misuse of powers and an infringement of the Treaty. The High Authority challenged the admissibility of the application on the basis that the applicant had failed to prove that a misuse of powers had been committed. The Court rejected the High Authority's argument. At the admissibility stage, it was enough for the applicant merely to allege that a misuse of powers had taken place. Proof was not necessary until the substance of the case was considered.

The climate changed following the entry into force of the EEC Treaty a number of years later. *Producteurs de Fruits*,[2] decided on 14 December 1962, was an action for the annulment under Article 173 EEC (now Article 263 TFEU) of a Council regulation on the establishment of a common organisation of the market in fruit and vegetables. It was dismissed as inadmissible on the basis that the regulation was not of individual concern to the applicants. AG Lagrange emphasised that there were 'important differences' between the EEC Treaty and the ECSC Treaty 'which have obviously been intended by the authors of the Treaty of Rome'.[3] The EEC

---

[1] Case 3/54 *Assider* ECLI:EU:C:1955:2.
[2] Joined Cases 16/62 and 17/62 *Producteurs de Fruits* ECLI:EU:C:1962:47.
[3] ibid, p 482.

Treaty was 'more strict than the ECSC Treaty with regard to the conditions which must be fulfilled before certain measures may be challenged'.[4] He reminded the Court that:

> these [legislative] texts have been arrived at only after considerable difficulty, and sometimes after a compromise reached in the Council, still wedded to the rule of unanimity ... we are presented here, by the authors of the Treaty, with a considered choice which it cannot be for the Court to correct.[5]

The Court accepted that the system established by the EEC Treaty laid down more restrictive conditions than did the ECSC Treaty for the admissibility of annulment actions brought by natural or legal persons. However, it did not consider it appropriate for the Court to pronounce on the merits of that system, which it said, 'appears clearly from the text under examination'.[6] The Court's restrictive approach was confirmed the following year in the famous 'clementines case', *Plaumann*.[7]

These cases established a pattern of reluctance on the part of the Court to entertain challenges to Community/Union acts by natural or legal persons. It reflected the Court's conviction that its task – perhaps even its principal task – was to help secure the achievement of the Community/Union's objectives. However, in a series of cases starting in the 1980s, the Court adopted some startling rulings on what is now Article 263 TFEU, which made it seem possible that a new dawn was breaking.

In *Les Verts*,[8] the Court held that 'an action for annulment may lie against measures adopted by the European Parliament intended to have legal effects vis-à-vis third parties'. That decision was reached notwithstanding the fact that at that time, the European Parliament was nowhere mentioned in the text of Article 263 TFEU as it then stood.[9] *Les Verts* was followed by the *Chernobyl* case,[10] where the European Parliament was accorded the right to bring annulment proceedings where the purpose was to protect its prerogatives. The decision in *Chernobyl* was all the more remarkable, in that the Court had only recently ruled in the *Comitology*[11] case that the Treaty did not permit it to recognise 'the capacity of the European Parliament to bring an action for annulment'.[12] In *Chernobyl*, the Court endorsed the conclusion it had reached in *Comitology*, but proceeded to create a new right of action to enable it to ensure that the prerogatives of the Parliament were respected.

Although these cases did not directly involve natural or legal persons, they created an atmosphere of possibility and promise around Article 263 TFEU. In *Extramet Industrie*[13] in 1991, the Court followed the advice of AG Jacobs, and accepted that a true regulation (ie, not merely a decision in the form of a regulation) could be challenged by private applicants who could show direct and individual concern. *Extramet* was followed by *Codorníu*,[14] where the Court found that an applicant was differentiated from all other traders and therefore

---

[4] ibid.
[5] ibid, pp 486–87.
[6] ibid, p 478.
[7] Case 25/62 *Plaumann* ECLI:EU:C:1963:17.
[8] Case 294/83 *Les Verts* ECLI:EU:C:1986:166.
[9] The Parliament became a privileged applicant following the entry into force of the Treaty of Nice on 1 February 2003.
[10] Case C-70/88 *Parliament v Council* ECLI:EU:C:1991:373.
[11] Case C-302/87 *Parliament v Council* ECLI:EU:C:1988:461.
[12] ibid, para 28.
[13] Case C-358/89 *Extramet Industrie* ECLI:EU:C:1992:257.
[14] Case C-309/89 *Codorníu* ECLI:EU:C:1994:197.

individually concerned because it was prevented by the contested regulation from continuing to use a long-held trade mark. One might therefore have been forgiven for thinking that the Court was progressively moving away from the restrictive approach exemplified in *Producteurs de Fruits* and *Plaumann*, in favour of a more liberal approach that offered non-privileged applicants greater access to justice.

However, a sign that the battle had yet to be won came in *Greenpeace*.[15] In that case, a coalition of individuals and associations concerned with the protection of the environment sought the annulment of a Commission decision granting Spain financial assistance for the construction of two electric power stations in the Canary Islands. The applicants specifically invited the Court of First Instance (CFI) (now, the General Court) to take a liberal approach on the question of admissibility, and to accept that standing could derive from a concern for the environment.

The CFI refused to accept that the standing of the applicants should be assessed on the basis of criteria, other than those laid down in the case law. It concluded that the individual applicants were affected by the contested measure in the same way as anyone living, working, or visiting the area concerned, and that they could not therefore be considered individually concerned. The same was true of the applicant associations, since they had been unable to establish any interest of their own distinct from that of their members, whose position was no different from that of the individual applicants.

On appeal to the Court, AG Cosmas maintained that, '[t]he significance and extent of mitigation by the Court, in *Extramet* and *Codorniu*, of the rigour of the case-law should not ... be overstated'.[16] He counselled against any modification of the existing case law which would permit environmental associations to be treated as a special case. The AG's advice, that the appeal should be dismissed, was followed by the Court, which declared that the approach taken by the CFI was 'consonant with the settled case-law of the Court'.[17]

II. BACKGROUND, CONTEXT, AND FACTS

This was the context in which *Unión de Pequeños Agricultores* (UPA) came before the Court. The facts were relatively straightforward. The applicant was seeking the annulment of an EU regulation withdrawing aid previously granted to producers of olive oil. It argued that, because the contested regulation did not call for any national measures of implementation, its validity could not be called into question in proceedings before a national court. Unless the applicant was granted standing to bring annulment proceedings in the Union Courts, it would be deprived of effective legal protection of its rights under Union law.

It was clear that the applicant was directly concerned by the contested regulation, so the case turned on the test for individual concern. Could an applicant be regarded as individually concerned on the ground that, in the absence of an alternative remedy before the national courts, it would otherwise be deprived of judicial protection? If not, could the applicant in this particular case be considered individually concerned? The case reached the Court by way of an appeal from the CFI, which had concluded that the applicant was not individually concerned: it was affected by the regulation in the same way as anyone else operating in the same market, then, or in the future.

---

[15] Case T-585/93 *Greenpeace* ECLI:EU:T:1995:147.
[16] Opinion of AG Cosmas in Case C-321/95 P *Greenpeace* ECLI:EU:C:1997:421, para 91.
[17] Case C-321/95 P *Greenpeace* ECLI:EU:C:1998:153, para 27.

III. THE OPINION OF AG JACOBS

AG Jacobs began his Opinion in *UPA* by pointing out that the Court had acknowledged that regulations might be challenged in proceedings instigated by individual applicants 'where they are of individual concern to the applicant, and that the test for establishing individual concern is in substance the same in the case of decisions and regulations'.[18] He noted, however, that the notion of individual concern had been interpreted strictly in the case law, and that applicants would be considered individually concerned by a measure only if it affected their legal position 'by reason of certain attributes peculiar to them, or by reason of a factual situation which differentiates them from all other persons and distinguishes them individually in the same way as the addressee'.[19]

This state of affairs had, AG Jacobs observed, 'been much criticised both by members of the Court of Justice in their individual capacities and by commentators', and was 'often regarded as creating a serious gap in the system of judicial remedies established by the EC Treaty'.[20] The present appeal, he said,

> which the Court has decided to hear in plenary session with a view to reconsidering its case-law on individual concern, raises an important question of principle: namely whether a natural or legal person ('individual') who is directly but not individually concerned by the provisions of a regulation within the meaning of the fourth paragraph of Article 230 EC as interpreted in the case-law should none the less be granted *locus standi* where that individual would otherwise be denied effective judicial protection owing to the difficulty of challenging the regulation indirectly through proceedings in national courts or whether *locus standi* under the fourth paragraph of Article 230 EC falls to be determined independently of the availability of such an indirect challenge ... I will argue that *locus standi* must indeed be determined independently and that moreover the only solution which provides adequate judicial protection is to change the case-law on individual concern.[21]

AG Jacobs sought to demonstrate that proceedings before national courts could not guarantee that individuals seeking to challenge the validity of Union measures were granted fully effective judicial protection.[22] He pointed out that the national courts could not declare measures of Union law invalid, but were limited to assessing whether the applicant's arguments raised 'sufficient doubts about the validity of the impugned measure to justify a request for a preliminary ruling from the Court of Justice'. It was therefore, he said, 'artificial to argue that the national courts are the correct forum for such cases'. While the national courts might fairly be described as 'the ordinary courts of [Union] law' in cases concerning the interpretation, application and enforcement of that law, that description was not appropriate for validity cases since the national courts did not have the power to decide the question at issue.

Moreover, the principle of effective judicial protection meant that applicants needed access to a court which could grant remedies capable of protecting them from the effects of unlawful measures. However, access to the Court through the preliminary reference procedure in Article 234 EC (now Article 267 TFEU) was not a remedy available as of right to individual applicants. National courts might decline to refer questions. Though courts of last instance were obliged to do so under the third paragraph of Article 234 EC, such courts might not

---

[18] Opinion of AG Jacobs in Case C-50/00 P *UPA* ECLI:EU:C:2002:197, para 2.
[19] ibid.
[20] ibid.
[21] ibid, para 3.
[22] ibid.

be asked to intervene until a considerable amount of time had elapsed. That might itself be incompatible with the principle of effective judicial protection and the need for legal certainty. Moreover, all national courts – even at the highest level – might decline to refer questions of validity to the Court in the mistaken belief that no such reference was necessary. Even where a reference was made, applicants might find that their claims were distorted by the way in which the questions were framed. The questions might, for example, limit the range of Union measures which an applicant had sought to challenge or the grounds of invalidity invoked.

In addition, it might prove difficult, even impossible, for individual applicants to challenge Union measures which did not require national implementation. This appeared to be the situation in the case of the regulation challenged by UPA. It could mean that there was no measure capable of forming the basis of an action before the national courts. As AG Jacobs pointed out:

> The fact that an individual affected by a Community measure might, in some instances, be able to bring the validity of a Community measure before the national courts by violating the rules laid down by the measures and rely on the invalidity of those rules as a defence in criminal or civil proceedings directed against him does not offer the individual an adequate means of judicial protection. Individuals clearly cannot be required to breach the law in order to gain access to justice.[23]

Finally, AG Jacobs demonstrated that proceedings before the national courts presented serious disadvantages for individual applicants compared to a direct action before the CFI. Proceedings in the national courts involving a preliminary reference would likely involve substantial extra delays and costs. The potential for delay made it likely that interim measures would be necessary. Although national courts were able to grant such measures, whether or not they did so was partly dependent on their discretion. In any event, AG Jacobs explained, 'interim measures awarded by a national court would be confined to the Member State in question, and applicants might therefore have to bring proceedings in more than one Member State. That would, given the possibility of conflicting decisions by courts in different Member States, prejudice the uniform application of Community law, and in extreme cases could totally subvert it'.[24]

In the AG's view, proceedings before the CFI under the action for annulment procedure were normally more appropriate for determining issues of validity than reference proceedings under the preliminary reference procedure. To his mind, the action for annulment procedure was more appropriate because the institution which adopted the contested measure was a party to the proceedings from beginning to end, and because a direct action involved a full exchange of pleadings, as opposed to a single round of observations followed by oral observations before the Court in reference cases. Moreover, '[t]he availability of interim relief under Articles 242 and 243 EC, effective in all Member States, was also a major advantage for individual applicants and for the uniformity of Community law'.[25]

Furthermore, the public was made aware of direct actions by means of a notice published in the Official Journal. This enabled third parties with a sufficient interest to intervene in the proceedings. By contrast, in preliminary reference proceedings, interested individuals were unable to submit observations unless they had intervened in the action before the national

---

[23] ibid, para 43.
[24] ibid, para 44.
[25] ibid, para 46.

court. That could be difficult, because individuals might not be aware of actions in the national courts at a sufficiently early stage to intervene.

In any event, the AG emphasised, it was 'manifestly desirable for reasons of legal certainty that challenges to the validity of Community acts be brought as soon as possible after their adoption'.[26] While direct actions had to be brought within the time-limit of two months laid down in the fifth paragraph of Article 230 EC, challenges to the validity of Community measures before the national courts were not subject to any time limit. He added that '[t]he strict criteria for standing for individual applicants under the existing case-law on Article 230 EC make it necessary for such applicants to bring issues of validity before the Court via Article 234 EC, and may thus have the effect of reducing legal certainty'.[27]

AG Jacobs concluded this part of his Opinion in the following terms:

> I consider, for all of those reasons, that the case-law on the locus standi of individual applicants as re-considered in the judgment in *Greenpeace* ... is incompatible with the principle of effective judicial protection. While review of Community measures through proceedings before national courts may be appropriate *where a case raises mixed issues of interpretation and validity* of Community law, proceedings before the Court of First Instance under the fourth paragraph of Article 230 EC are clearly more appropriate *where a case concerns exclusively the validity of a Community measure*. Since such cases will by definition raise questions of law, the possibility of an appeal on points of law provided by Article 225 EC would ensure that the Court of Justice could exercise effective ultimate control over the decisions adopted by the Court of First Instance (emphasis added).[28]

The AG therefore urged the Court to adopt a new, more liberal, test under which a person would be regarded as individually concerned by a Community/Union measure 'where, by reason of his particular circumstances, the measure has, or is liable to have, a substantial adverse effect on his interests'.[29] He saw 'no compelling reasons' to read into the notion of individual concern 'a requirement that an individual applicant seeking to challenge a general measure must be differentiated from all others affected by it in the same way as an addressee. On that reading, the greater the number of persons affected by a measure the less likely it is that judicial review under the fourth paragraph of Article 230 EC will be made available. The fact that a measure adversely affects a large number of individuals, causing wide-spread rather than limited harm, provides however to my mind a positive reason for accepting a direct challenge by one or more of those individuals'.[30]

Was the time ripe for an evolution in the interpretation of the concept of individual concern? This question was examined in detail by AG Jacobs.[31] He noted that the case law on standing had grown 'increasingly out of line with the administrative laws of the Member States'.[32] In French law, for example, 'practically any person adversely affected by a measure has standing to challenge it' while in English law 'the jurisdictional requirement of a "sufficient interest" for an applicant to apply for judicial review will rarely be an obstacle to access to the court'.[33] In other areas, 'the basic principles of judicial review' had been modelled on the laws of the Member States. When it came to standing, however, 'the position of the

---

[26] ibid, para 48.
[27] ibid.
[28] ibid, para 49.
[29] ibid, para 60.
[30] ibid, para 59.
[31] ibid, paras 82–99.
[32] ibid, para 85.
[33] ibid.

individual is far more restricted than in many, if not all, national legal systems'.[34] This, the AG said, was:

> a paradoxical situation, especially given the continuing concern about the lack of full democratic legitimacy of Community legislation, which exposes the Community to a risk of resistance by national courts which, it should not be forgotten, have repeatedly emphasised their resolve to ensure that developments in Community law do not undermine the judicial protection of individuals.[35]

The Court's stance was also hard to reconcile with 'the Court's evolving case law on the principle of effective protection of rights derived from Community law in national courts'.[36] While it was perhaps 'too harsh to speak of "double standards"', the arguments advanced by the Council and the Commission to justify the status quo seemed 'increasingly untenable in the light of the Court's case-law on the principle of effective judicial protection'.[37]

Before the Court gave judgment in *UPA*, the CFI had delivered another judgment of its own in *Jégo-Quéré*.[38] In that case, a fishing company sought the annulment of a regulation imposing minimum mesh sizes on certain fishing vessels in order to conserve fish stocks. Member States would be required to enforce the regulation, but it did not need to be transposed as such into national law. The CFI found that the applicant could not be regarded as individually concerned 'on the basis of the criteria hitherto established by [Union] case law'.[39] The applicant was affected by the contested provisions in the same way as any other economic operator, actually or potentially, in the same situation.

However, referring to Article 47 of the Charter of Fundamental Rights, the CFI proceeded to consider whether, 'where an individual applicant is contesting the lawfulness of provisions of general application directly affecting its legal situation, the inadmissibility of the action for annulment would deprive the applicant of the right to an effective remedy'.[40] The possibility that a reference for a preliminary ruling might be made by a national court was inadequate in a case such as this. Citing with approval the Opinion of Advocate General Jacobs in *UPA*, the CFI observed:

> The fact that an individual affected by a Community measure may be able to bring its validity before the national courts by violating the rules it lays down and then asserting their illegality in subsequent judicial proceedings brought against him does not constitute an adequate means of legal protection. Individuals cannot be required to breach the law in order to gain access to justice ....[41]

The 'inevitable conclusion' was that the other remedies, for which the Treaty provided, could 'no longer be regarded, in the light of Articles 6 and 13 ECHR and of Article 47 of the Charter of Fundamental Rights, as guaranteeing persons the right to an effective remedy enabling them to contest the legality of Community measures of general application which directly affect their legal situation'.[42] The CFI declared:

> ... in order to ensure effective judicial protection for individuals, a natural or legal person is to be regarded as individually concerned by a Community measure of general application that concerns

---

[34] ibid, para 86.
[35] ibid.
[36] ibid, para 97.
[37] ibid, para 98.
[38] Case T-177/01 *Jégo-Quéré* ECLI:EU:T:2002:112.
[39] ibid, para 38. See also Case C-565/19 P *Carvalho* ECLI:EU:C:2021:252.
[40] Case T-177/01 *Jégo-Quéré*, para 43.
[41] ibid, para 45.
[42] ibid, para 47.

him directly if the measure in question affects his legal position, in a manner which is both definite and immediate, by restricting his rights or by imposing obligations on him.[43]

The objection of inadmissibility raised by the Commission was therefore dismissed.

IV. ANALYSIS

A. The Judgment

The Court was not persuaded by the Opinion of AG Jacobs and gave judgment for the Council, reaffirming existing case law. Reform of the system currently in force, said the Court, would require an amendment to the Treaty. The Court acknowledged that individuals were 'entitled to effective judicial protection of the rights they derive from the Community legal order'.[44] However, it maintained that the Treaty provided various means of challenging the validity of Community/Union acts, devoting particular attention to the preliminary rulings procedure. The Court declared that it was the responsibility of the Member States 'to establish a system of legal remedies and procedures which ensure respect for the right to effective judicial protection'.[45] In particular, national courts were required:

> so far as possible, to interpret and apply national procedural rules governing the exercise of rights of action in a way that enables natural and legal persons to challenge before the courts the legality of any decision or other national measure relative to the application to them of a Community act of general application, by pleading the invalidity of such an act.[46]

The appeal was therefore dismissed. A surprising feature of the Court's judgment was the faith it placed in the Member States to 'establish a system of legal remedies and procedures which ensure respect for the right to effective judicial protection'. This would surely entail a level of supervision and enforcement which would not have been necessary had the Court followed the advice of AG Jacobs and relaxed the test for individual concern, a notion which, as he observed, 'is capable of carrying a number of different interpretations ...'.[47]

The Court later set aside the CFI's judgment in *Jégo-Quéré*.[48] In doing so, it emphasised that 'an action for annulment before the Community Courts should not on any view be available, even where it is apparent that the national procedural rules do not allow the individual to contest the validity of the Community measure unless he has first contravened it'.[49] This was a shocking statement that the Court would later repudiate.[50]

The Court ended its judgment in *UPA* with an olive branch, declaring:

> While it is, admittedly, possible to envisage a system of judicial review of the legality of Community measures of general application different from that established by the founding Treaty and never amended as to its principles, it is for the Member States, if necessary, in accordance with Article 48 EU, to reform the system currently in force.[51]

---

[43] ibid, para 51.
[44] Judgment in Case C-50/00 P *UPA*, para 39.
[45] ibid, para 41.
[46] ibid, para 42. Compare Case C-106/89 *Marleasing* ECLI:EU:C:1990:395.
[47] Para 75 of the Opinion. See also the judgment of the CFI in Case T-177/01 *Jégo-Quéré*, para 49.
[48] Case C-263/02 P *Jégo-Quéré* ECLI:EU:C:2004:210. See also, Case C-167/02P *Rothley* ECLI:EU:C:2004:193.
[49] Case C-263/02 P *Jégo-Quéré*, para 34.
[50] See Case C-432/05 *Unibet* ECLI:EU:C:2007:163, para 64.
[51] Case C-50/00 P *UPA*, para 45.

This pointed sentence was a reference to the Convention on the Future of Europe, which happened to be sitting when the *UPA* case was decided. When the Constitutional Treaty emerged, it contained a provision, Article III-365(4), which stated: 'Any natural or legal person may … institute proceedings against an act addressed to that person or which is of direct and individual concern to him or her, *and against a regulatory act which is of direct concern to him or her and does not entail implementing measures*' (emphasis added).[52] Curiously, the term regulatory act was not defined, but the *travaux préparatoires* suggested that it was intended to refer to any act other than a legislative act.

B. The Effect on Future Case Law

Although the Constitutional Treaty never entered into force, it influenced some of the provisions of the Treaty of Lisbon. Article 289(1) TFEU provides for an ordinary legislative procedure, which consists in 'the joint adoption by the European Parliament and the Council of a regulation, directive or decision on a proposal from the Commission'. The details of the procedure are set out in Article 294 TFEU. According to Article 289(2) TFEU, 'the adoption of a regulation, directive or decision by the European Parliament with the participation of the Council, or by the latter with the participation of the European Parliament, shall constitute a special legislative procedure'. Article 289(3) provides: 'Legal acts adopted by legislative procedure shall constitute legislative acts.'

There was still no definition of the term 'regulatory act'. However, an opportunity for the Union courts to address the matter arose in the *Inuit* case.[53] In that case, a number of private applicants asked the General Court to quash a regulation on trade in seal products. Having looked at the *travaux préparatoires* produced by the Convention on the Future of Europe, the General Court concluded that the term 'regulatory act' should be interpreted as covering 'all acts of general application apart from legislative acts'. As the contested regulation had been adopted under the ordinary legislative procedure, it constituted a legislative act, rather than a regulatory act. That conclusion was endorsed on appeal by both AG Kokott and the Court.

A remaining conundrum was the meaning of the phrase 'regulatory act which … does not entail implementing measures'. A leading case on that issue is *Telefónica*.[54] Referring specifically to the Opinion of AG Jacobs in *UPA*, AG Kokott reiterated that the introduction of the term 'implementing measures' in the Constitutional Treaty had been intended to apply only to litigants who would otherwise have to infringe the law in order to gain access to a court.[55] Where the contested act produced effects directly on the individual, there was no need for any implementing measures to be considered. That would be required only if the regulatory act itself produced definitive legal effects for the individual.

The Court observed:

> Where a regulatory act directly affects the legal situation of a natural or legal person without requiring implementing measures, that person could be denied effective judicial protection if he did not have a direct legal remedy before the European Union judicature for the purpose of challenging the

---

[52] Treaty establishing a Constitution for Europe [2004] OJ C310/1.
[53] Case T-18/10 *Inuit* ECLI:EU:T:2010:172.
[54] Case C-274/12 P *Telefónica* ECLI:EU:C:2013:852.
[55] See Opinion of AG Kokott in Case C-398/13 P *Inuit* ECLI:EU:C:2015:190, paras 39–40, and 44.

legality of the regulatory act. In the absence of implementing measures, natural or legal persons, although directly concerned by the act in question, would be able to obtain a judicial review of that act only after having infringed its provisions, by pleading that those provisions are unlawful in proceedings initiated against them before the national courts.[56]

The Court explained:

… where a regulatory act entails implementing measures, judicial review of compliance with the European Union legal order is ensured irrespective of whether those measures are adopted by the European Union or the Member States. Natural or legal persons who are unable, because of the conditions governing admissibility laid down in the fourth paragraph of Article 263 TFEU, to challenge a regulatory act of the European Union directly before the European Union judicature are protected against the application to them of such an act by the ability to challenge the implementing measures which the act entails.[57]

The glimpse of a better future revealed by the Opinion of AG Jacobs in *UPA* did not therefore materialise, at least not entirely. True, the intervention of the Convention on the Future of Europe was not helpful, but it was perhaps predictable in the circumstances that the Court would not wish to confront the issue of standing directly. Be that as it may, the introduction of a right under Article 263 TFEU, fourth paragraph, final limb, to challenge regulatory acts which are of direct concern to an applicant without entailing implementing measures is welcome, even if it has not so far been interpreted expansively by the Court.

---

[56] Case C-398/13 P *Inuit* ECLI:EU:C:2015:535, para 27.
[57] ibid, para 28.

34

Breaking New Ground on EU Fundamental Rights: Opinions of Advocate General Jacobs in Wachauf and Schmidberger

PETER OLIVER

I. *WACHAUF*: INTRODUCTION

O VER A PERIOD spanning some 20 years, milk – or rather, the EU's milk quota scheme designed to prevent over-production of the nutritious liquid – gave rise to a vast body of litigation before the Court. *Wachauf* was one of these cases. The applicant was a tenant farmer whose tenancy came to an end in 1985 because the lessor declined to extend it any further. Prior to the conclusion of the lease in 1959, the plot had not been used for dairy farming, and Mr Wachauf had built up dairy production at his own expense. In 1984, the Council had adopted complex legislation empowering Member States to grant compensation to producers who undertook to discontinue milk production definitively. Under the German implementing statute, tenant farmers who sought to benefit from this scheme were required to produce a written authorisation from their landlords. Unfortunately, the lessor declined to grant her consent when she realised that that would result in the farm losing its quota.

The two preliminary questions posed by the German court related to the arcane complexities of the EU's milk quota legislation. Since that legislation has long since ceased to have effect and to be of any legal interest, it is appropriate to concentrate instead on the crucial underlying question, namely: was such a national rule compatible with the general principles of EU law and with fundamental rights? This, it should be remembered, was well before the Charter of Fundamental Rights saw the light of day.

II. THE OPINION OF AG JACOBS

Generally speaking, the AG had no objection to a national requirement that the lessor consent to a tenant farmer's application for compensation for discontinuing dairy production definitively: it was right that the landlord should consent to the tenant's participation in the compensation scheme, since the consequence was the permanent loss of the quota to the holding.[1] However, to allow the landlord the unqualified power of veto might be inequitable in certain cases, as where the tenant had by his efforts attracted the quota to the holding in the first place.[2] In that event, the German measure would be unlawful for two separate reasons.

First, in the circumstances as mentioned above, it would run counter to what is now the second sub-paragraph of Article 40(2) TFEU, according to which common market organisations (CMOs) under the Common Agricultural Policy (CAP) may not discriminate between producers within the EU.[3] Secondly, as milk quotas are production licences and as such must be regarded as intangible assets, 'the permanent loss to the tenant of the use and value of the quota on expiry of the tenancy can be viewed [in certain circumstances] as a measure of expropriation'.[4] On this view, AG Jacobs stated that 'there may be cases where failure by a Member State to provide for compensation would amount to breach of the principle of respect for the right to property'.[5]

Then came the crucial innovative step in the AG's reasoning: he found that the Member States must respect the right to property when 'acting in pursuance of powers granted under Community law', since they must 'be subject to the same constraints ... as the Community legislator' in relation to fundamental rights.[6] To reach this conclusion, he relied on the ruling in *Klensch*, where the Court had held that, when implementing EU law, the Member States are bound by what is now the second sub-paragraph of Article 40(2) TFEU.[7] However, in the latter case, in keeping with its case law at the time,[8] the Court had regarded the prohibition of discrimination enshrined in that provision as nothing more than a general principle of EU law.[9] Finally, he stated that it was for the national court to determine in the case in point whether and to what extent account should be taken of the tenant's interest in the quota.[10]

III. THE JUDGMENT

The Court followed the same reasoning as AG Jacobs, except that it did not mention discrimination and did not directly address the question as to whether milk quotas were a form of property, while indirectly implying that they were. After summarising its case law on the right to property,[11] the Court stated:

> Community rules which, upon the expiry of the lease, had the effect of depriving the lessee, without compensation, of the fruits of his labour and of his investments in the tenanted holding would be incompatible with the requirements of the protection of fundamental rights in the Community legal order. Since those requirements are also binding on the Member States when they implement

---

[1] Opinion of AG Jacobs in Case 5/88 *Wachauf* ECLI:EU:C:1989:179, paras 21 and 23.
[2] ibid, para 22.
[3] ibid, para 23.
[4] ibid, para 24.
[5] ibid, para 27.
[6] ibid, para 22.
[7] Joined Cases 201/85 and 202/85 *Klensch* ECLI:EU:C:1986:439, para 10.
[8] T Tridimas, *The General Principles of EU Law*, 2nd edn (Oxford, OUP, 2006) 61–62.
[9] Joined Cases 201/85 and 202/85 *Klensch*, para 9. Of course, the principle of equality and non-discrimination has long since ripened into a fully-fledged fundamental right, which is now recognised in Articles 20 and 21 of the Charter of Fundamental Rights.
[10] ibid, para 30.
[11] Para 17–18 of the Judgment.

Community rules, the Member States must, as far as possible, apply those rules in accordance with those requirements.[12]

The message of this judgment was not lost on the referring court in Germany, which awarded compensation to Mr Wachauf.[13] This was significant in itself, given that at the time arguments based on the right to property were almost invariably rejected, especially in cases concerning the CAP.[14]

IV. ANALYSIS

By far the most important aspect of *Wachauf* is that in this case the AG and the Court first spelt out the principle that, when implementing EU law, the Member States are bound to respect the fundamental rights recognised by the EU. Some years after his departure from the Court, AG Jacobs wrote with habitual modesty that the *Wachauf* case was 'a step, perhaps small but certainly necessary' in the progression towards the establishment of a body of case law on fundamental rights protection.[15] That this step was necessary is beyond doubt, since otherwise the EU's fundamental rights would be easily circumvented. It is equally plain that this step was momentous, not merely because it establishes a major point of principle but also because of the very high proportion of legislative and regulatory acts adopted by the Member States which implement EU law.[16]

In any event, two years after *Wachauf*, the Court complemented that judgment with its ruling in *ERT*.[17] It was held there that the justification of restrictions on the provision of services under what is now Article 62 TEU must be determined 'in the light of the general principles of law and in particular of fundamental rights'.[18] Subsequently, the Court ruled to the same effect in *Vereinigte Familiapress* which concerned Article 36 TFEU;[19] and from then on (if not before) it was plain that the same applies to what are now Articles 45(3), 52 and 65 TFEU.

Writing in 2010 after leaving the Court, AG Jacobs criticised this case law on the grounds that in this context – in contrast to *Wachauf* – the issues raised by EU law and by human rights were separate and independent of one another.[20] Subsequently, Dougan also expressed concern that the Court might be overstretching the scope of EU law,[21] although in his view, the problem is rather due to the 'bloated interpretation' of the four fundamental freedoms in cases such as

---

[12] ibid, para 19.

[13] F Jacobs, '*Wachauf* and the Protection of Fundamental Rights in EC Law' in M Poiares Maduro and L Azoulai (eds), *The Past and Future of EU Law: The Classics of EU Law Revisited on the 50th Anniversary of the Rome Treaty* (Oxford, Hart Publishing, 2010) 133, 139.

[14] See eg Case 265/87 *Schräder* ECLI:EU:C:1989:303; Case C-177/90 *Kühn* ECLI:EU:C:1992:2; Case C-2/92 ECLI:EU:C:1994:116; Case C-280/93 *Germany v Council* ECLI:EU:C:1994:367); Joined Cases C-20/00 and C-64/00 *Booker Aquaculture and Hydro Seafood* ECLI:EU:C:2003:397, confirmed in Case C-56/13 *Érsekcsanádi Mezőgazdasági* ECLI:EU:C:2014:352.

[15] Jacobs (n 13) 139.

[16] V Trstenjak and E Beysen, 'The growing overlap of fundamental freedoms and fundamental rights in the case-law of the CJEU' (2013) 38 *ELRev* 296, 305.

[17] Case C-260/89 *ERT* ECLI:EU:C:1991:254.

[18] ibid, para 43.

[19] Case C-368/95 *Familiapress* ECLI:EU:C:1997:325, para 23.

[20] Jacobs (n 13) 137–38.

[21] M Dougan, 'Judicial Review of Member State Action under the General Principles and the Charter: Defining the "Scope of Union Law"' (2015) 52 *CMLRev* 1201, 1216.

Carpenter.[22] In any case, the Court has maintained the same trajectory in a long line of cases, including the well-known rulings in *Pfleger*[23] and *AGET Iraklis*.[24]

Article 51(1) of the Charter states that the provisions of that instrument 'are addressed … to the Member States only when they are implementing Union law'. Read literally, this language takes account of *Wachauf*, but not *ERT*: a national measure which imposes a restriction on one of the four fundamental freedoms, purportedly on the basis of one of the exceptions to those freedoms, cannot be said to implement EU law. Nevertheless, the official Explanations relating to the Charter[25] include *ERT* in the list of judgments implicitly enshrined in Article 51(1). These Explanations carry very considerable weight, since Articles 6(1) TEU and 52(7) of the Charter require the European and national courts to pay 'due regard' to them when interpreting the Charter. Indeed, Lenaerts has stated that the Court 'may not interpret the Charter in a way that conflicts with the Explanations'.[26] Accordingly, it is by no means surprising that in *Fransson* the Grand Chamber held that, pursuant to Article 51(1), the Charter applies whenever the Member States act within the 'scope' of EU law.[27] It reached this conclusion on the basis of the Court's earlier case law, including *ERT*, as well as the Explanations.

In recent years, the Court has continued to elaborate on the meaning of 'implementing Union law' in Article 51(1).[28] Indeed, in a very recent speech,[29] Lenaerts observed that, given the inherent complexity of the issue, several grey areas remain.[30] Needless to say, that by no means detracts from the force and clarity of *Wachauf*.

V. *SCHMIDBERGER*: INTRODUCTION

Every year, this author tells his students that everyone should be thankful to the Austrians for providing us with so many novel cases on free movement, partly because their Member State has imposed some unusual restrictions,[31] and partly because it has the Brenner pass.[32] *Schmidberger* – the first major case in which the Court had to grapple with a conflict between fundamental rights and the four fundamental freedoms – falls into the latter category. The plaintiff was a road haulage company engaged in transporting goods between Germany and Italy via the motorway through the Brenner pass, which was (and is) by far the most important route for road freight between those two Member States. The Austrian authorities had tacitly authorised an environmental demonstration, which resulted in that motorway

---

[22] Case C-60/00 *Carpenter* ECLI:EU:C:2002:434.

[23] Case C-390/12 *Pfleger* ECLI:EU:C:2014:281.

[24] Case C-201/15 *AGET Iraklis* ECLI:EU:C:2016:972. See P Oliver, *The Fundamental Rights of Companies: EU, US and International Law Compared* (Oxford, Hart Publishing, 2021) ch 4.

[25] Explanations relating to the Charter of Fundamental Rights [2007] OJ C303/17, 32.

[26] K Lenaerts, 'Exploring the Limits of the Charter of Fundamental Rights' (2012) 8 *EuConst* 375, 377.

[27] Case C-617/10 *Åkerberg Fransson* ECLI:EU:C:2013:105, paras 19–22.

[28] See eg Case C-258/14 *Florescu* ECLI:EU:C:2017:448; Joined Cases C-609/17 and C-610/17 *TSN* ECLI:EU:C:2019:981.

[29] K Lenaerts, 'La Charte dans l'ordre juridique de l'Union européenne' [2021] *Cahiers de droit européen* 29, 35.

[30] By way of illustration, he cites para 79 of the ruling in Case C-40/11 *Iida* ECLI:EU:C:2012:691. See also I Gambardella, 'L'application de la Charte des droits fondamentaux de l'Union européenne aux Etats members' [2021] *Cahiers de droit européen* 241.

[31] See eg Case C-368/95 *Familiapress*; Case C-169/07 *Hartlauer* ECLI:EU:C:2009:141; Case C-421/09 *Humanplasma* ECLI:EU:C:2010:760; Case C-382/08 *Neukirchinger* ECLI:EU:C:2011:27.

[32] See also Case C-320/03 *Commission v Austria* ECLI:EU:C:2005:684; Case C-28/09 *Commission v Austria* ECLI:EU:C:2011:854.

being closed for nearly 30 hours. Schmidberger claimed that this authorisation amounted to a breach of what are now Articles 34 and 35 TFEU concerning the free movement of goods, and consequently sought to recover damages.

VI. THE OPINION OF AG JACOBS

Three issues were raised by the reference for a preliminary ruling of the Austrian Court, namely:

(i) Did the tacit authorisation of the demonstration by the Austrian authorities amount to a measure of equivalent effect of imports and exports within the meaning of what are now Articles 34 and 35 TFEU?

(ii) If so, was the measure justified?

(iii) Could Schmidberger recover damages from the Austrian authorities for its loss of profit resulting from the closure of the motorway?

Since there was little doubt that the tacit authorisation was caught by Articles 34 and 35 TFEU,[33] the crucial issue was the second one. Austria maintained that the restriction was justified for the protection of the fundamental rights of freedom of expression and freedom of assembly, as recognised in its legal system. Stressing that this issue was quite different from that which had arisen in *ERT*, AG Jacobs accepted this contention on the basis that these fundamental rights were also recognised under the European Convention on Human Rights (ECHR) and in EU law.[34] He summarised this proposition as follows: 'where a Member State seeks to protect fundamental rights recognised in Community law the Member State necessarily pursues a legitimate objective'.[35]

However, AG Jacobs observed that it would be otherwise if (to take a purely hypothetical example) a Member State were to give constitutional protection to the right to be protected against competition, particularly from companies established abroad; such a right would be manifestly unacceptable in EU law.[36]

In addition, for AG Jacobs, the Court must have regard to the objective pursued by the Austrian authorities, and not to the aim of the demonstrators, which was 'of no significance when assessing the possible liability of the Member State'.[37] But at the same time, he also remarked that the demonstration was in no way motivated by protectionism, and that no violent acts or criminal offences were committed.[38]

As to proportionality, the AG observed that, 'as in the present case the restriction is primarily attributable to private individuals it is perhaps less justifiable to apply too strict a proportionality test'[39] and that Austria enjoyed 'a margin of discretion in determining

---

[33] Opinion of AG Jacobs in Case C-112/00 *Schmidberger* ECLI:EU:C:2002:437, paras 57–84. To be precise, following Case C-265/95 *Commission v France* ECLI:EU:C:1997:595 (*Spanish Strawberries*), AG Jacobs found that the measure was caught by Article 34 TFEU, read with what is now Article 4(3) TEU, rather than by Article 34 TFEU alone. However, this is of no significance in the present context.

[34] Paras 100–103 of his Opinion in *Schmidberger*.

[35] Para 102 of the Opinion of AG Jacobs in *Schmidberger*. In *Familiapress* (n 19), the Court had already held that the preservation of press diversity could justify restrictions on the free movement of goods on the basis that such diversity 'helps to safeguard freedom of expression' (para 18). However, this fell well short of the statement by AG Jacobs cited in the text accompanying the present footnote.

[36] Paras 97–98.

[37] Para 54.

[38] Paras 78–79. This stood in sharp contrast to the *Spanish Strawberries* case (n 33).

[39] Para 106.

when to take action and which measures are most appropriate to eliminate or limit that interference'.[40]

He then found that the authorisation of the demonstration was probably proportionate in view of the fact that it had lasted less than 30 hours.[41] No account should be taken, in his view, of the fact that the previous day, a Thursday, was a public holiday and that the two days following the demonstration were a Saturday and a Sunday, which meant that Schmidberger's vehicles were precluded from using the motorway for four days in total.[42] Accordingly, it was clearly arguable that the contested measure was justified.[43] Unsurprisingly, this finding led him to the conclusion as regards issue (iii) that the Austrian Court 'would be entitled to find' that the authorisation of the demonstration did not constitute a sufficiently serious breach of EU law such as to render them liable for damages.[44]

VII. THE JUDGMENT

In its judgment, the Court fully endorsed the approach taken by AG Jacobs. The Court also stressed that, 'unlike certain other fundamental rights enshrined in the ECHR such as the right to life and the prohibition of torture and inhumane or degrading treatment', the freedom of expression and freedom of assembly are not absolute, but are subject to various exceptions.[45] It added that 'the interests involved must be weighed [up] having regard to all the circumstances of the case in order to determine whether a fair balance was struck', and that the Member States enjoy a wide margin of discretion in this regard.[46] Although AG Jacobs did not employ precisely the same language, these statements are inherent in his approach.

Only in its conclusion did the Court differ from the AG, and then only slightly: it found that no breach of the provisions of the EU Treaties in issue had occurred, whereas he had proposed that this issue be left for the national court to determine.

VIII. ANALYSIS

How could it be seriously argued that the protection of legitimate fundamental rights should not justify restrictions on free movement? This all-important finding in the Opinion and the judgment seems unassailable.

A considerable amount of ink has been expended over the question whether the four fundamental freedoms, which are the basis of the internal market, are also to be regarded as fundamental rights.[47] The prevailing view is that these freedoms do not enjoy

---

[40] Para 106.

[41] Para 108.

[42] Para 108. Under Austrian law, lorries were prohibited from travelling on public holidays and at weekends.

[43] Para 112.

[44] Paras 113 ff.

[45] Para 80 of the Judgment.

[46] Paras 81–82 of the Judgment.

[47] See eg J Baquero Cruz, *Between Competition and Free Movement: The Economic Constitutional Law of the European Community* (Oxford, Hart Publishing, 2002) 81; A Biondi, 'Free Trade, a Mountain Road and the Right to Protest: European Economic Freedoms and Fundamental Individual Rights' [2004] *European Human Rights Law Review* 51, 53–54; U Everling 'Wirtschaftsfreiheit im europäischen Binnenmarkt – Anspruch und Realität' in J Schwarze (ed), *Wirtschaftsverfassungsrechtliche Garantien für Unternehmen im europäischen Binnenmarkt* (Baden-Baden, Nomos, 2001); P Oliver and W-H Roth, 'The Internal Market and the Four Freedoms' (2004) 41 *CMLRev* 407;

that status.[48] Moreover, one should bear in mind the assertion by AG Tesauro in *Hünermund* that Article 34 TFEU does not provide for a general right to trade[49] – a proposition which applies equally to the other fundamental freedoms, it is submitted.[50] Having said that, it is clearly otherwise where: (i) the free movement of natural persons is at stake, or (ii) a sale of goods or services involves the freedom of expression (eg books, or broadcasting);[51] but that was of no relevance in *Schmidberger*. On this view, free movement was of a lesser order in this case than fundamental rights.

In *Schmidberger*, a direct clash arose between the presumption in EU law that a restriction caught by Article 34 TFEU is not justified, and a similar presumption under Articles 10 and 11 of the ECHR and Articles 11 and 12 of the Charter that restrictions on the freedom of speech are not justified either.[52] As we have seen, both AG Jacobs and the Court deftly solved this conundrum by a relaxed application of the principle of proportionality. Undeniably, the outcome was satisfactory: the environmentalists were given adequate time to air their grievances and bring them to the notice of the authorities (their 30 hours on the motorway tarmac was the equivalent to the litigant's proverbial 'day in court'); and while this was of course unfortunate for road hauliers, the fact was that no major disruption occurred.

Accordingly, it is not surprising that this ruling has generally been well received. For instance, Bailleux hailed it as the first judgment in which the Court backed away somewhat from its traditional 'pro-economic' approach; and he also noted the Court's painstaking analysis of the facts.[53] Similarly, Weatherill commended the Court's 'sensitivity to the complexity of the calculations at stake in the interplay of economic integration with social and political freedoms'.[54] In the same vein, Biondi appeared to welcome the fact that the Court applied the proportionality test in a manner 'more accommodating to the Member States' than is usually the case.[55] By necessary implication, these comments apply equally to the Opinion of AG Jacobs, given that the judgment matched it so closely.

Turning to *Schmidberger*'s progeny, we cannot fail to mention *Viking*[56] and *Laval*,[57] given they are the most renowned – or rather, for the majority of scholars, the most notorious – examples. These judgments, in which the fundamental freedoms were held to prevail over basic social rights, cannot be discussed within the confines of this chapter. Suffice it to say that, while

---

M Poiares Maduro, *We the Court: The European Court of Justice and the European Economic Constitution* (Oxford, Hart Publishing, 1998) 166–68.

[48] Of the authors cited in footnote 47, only Everling took the opposite view. He regarded the four freedoms as part of the freedom of enterprise apart from the fact that they apply only to interstate transactions.

[49] Opinion of AG Tesauro in Case C-292/92 *Hünermund* ECLI:EU:C:1993:863, at p. I–6813; see also Opinion of AG Poiares Maduro in Joined Cases C-158/04 and C-159/04 *Alfa Vita Vassilopoulos* ECLI:EU:C:2006:212, paras 37 and 41.

[50] Admittedly, in Case C-228/98 *Dounias* ECLI:EU:C:2000:65, para 64, the Court referred to the free movement of goods as a 'fundamental right'; but we should not attach too much importance to an isolated statement such as this.

[51] Oliver and Roth (n 47) 408. As regards the free movement of workers, that is also Biondi's position (n 47) 54.

[52] While the Charter is mentioned in para 101 of the Opinion, no such mention is to be found in the judgment. Until Case C-540/03 *Parliament v Council* ECLI:EU:C:2006:429 (*Family reunification*), the Court was too coy to refer to the Charter, which only became binding when the Treaty of Lisbon came into force.

[53] A Bailleux, *Les interactions entre libre circulation et droits fondamentaux dans la jurisprudence communautaire* (Brussels, Bruylant, 2009) 285ff. However, he does describe the judgment as ambiguous in some respects. Similarly, see F Ronkes Agerbeek, 'Freedom of expression and free movement in the Brenner corridor: the *Schmidberger* case' (2004) 29 ELRev 255.

[54] S Weatherill, *The Internal Market as a Legal Concept* (Oxford, OUP, 2017) 138.

[55] Biondi (n 47) 59.

[56] Case C-438/05 *Viking* ECLI:EU:C:2007:772.

[57] Case C-341/05 *Laval* ECLI:EU:C:2007:809.

those rulings were undoubtedly controversial, we should spare a thought for the judges who found themselves in the invidious position of being required to determine an exceptionally thorny and essentially political issue which the old Member States had lacked the political courage to settle in the Act of Accession of 2003. While *Schmidberger* raised 'some fiendishly awkward questions of principle',[58] the task confronting the Court in *Viking* and *Laval* was of truly Herculean proportions. In these circumstances, it is hard to imagine how the Court could have found a genuinely satisfactory solution.[59]

Subsequently, AG Trstenjak sought to address the problem in *Commission v Germany (Old-age Pensions)*. In her view, there is no hierarchy between the fundamental freedoms and fundamental rights, since there is a 'broad convergence' between the two 'both in terms of structure and content'. Unsurprisingly, she added that the principle of proportionality enabled a fair balance to be struck, and 'the restriction on a fundamental right by a fundamental freedom [could never] go beyond what is appropriate, necessary and reasonable to realise the fundamental'.[60] In truth, this approach is very close to that adopted by AG Jacobs and the Court in *Schmidberger*.

In a separate development, the Court has delivered a very large number of judgments in which two fundamental rights have been pitted against one another,[61] especially since the Charter became a binding instrument pursuant to the Treaty of Lisbon. The Court's approach is encapsulated in *Sky Österreich*, where the Grand Chamber stated: 'the assessment of the possible disproportionate nature of a provision of European Union law must be carried out with a view to reconciling the requirements of the protection of those different rights and freedoms and a fair balance between them'.[62] One field in which this occurs particularly frequently is intellectual property law.[63]

The case law on balancing, whether between fundamental freedoms and fundamental rights or between conflicting fundamental rights, has attracted a considerable body of criticism for two reasons. First, several scholars claim that the Court gives priority to the four freedoms and other economic rights over social and labour rights.[64] With respect to numerous

---

[58] Weatherill (n 54) 137.

[59] In a similar vein, see eg Case C-346/06 *Rüffert* ECLI:EU:C:2008:189; Case C-201/15 *AGET Iraklis*. On the latter judgment, see P Oliver, 'How Social is the Social Market Economy Today?' in E Bribosia, N Joncheray, A Navasartian Havani and A Weyembergh (eds), *L'Europe au Kaléidoscope – Liber Amicorum Marianne Dony* (Brussels, Editions de l'Université de Bruxelles, 2019) 357, 362ff.

[60] Opinion of AG Trstenjak in Case C-271/08 *Commission v Germany* ECLI:EU:C:2010:183 (*Old-age Pensions*), paras 185ff. See also her Opinion in Case C-81/09 *Idryma Typou* ECLI:EU:C:2010:304, para 86.

[61] As the Court pointed out in para 80 of its judgment in *Schmidberger* (n 45), no balancing can take place where the fundamental right in issue is absolute or where the contested measure constitutes 'disproportionate and unacceptable interference' with that right such as to strike at the 'very substance' of that right. The latter rule is now enshrined in Article 52(1) of the Charter which speaks of the 'very essence' of the rights concerned; see Case C-362/14 *Schrems* ECLI:EU:C:2015:650.

[62] Case C-283/11 *Sky Österreich* ECLI:EU:C:2013:28, para 60.

[63] See eg Case C-275/06 *Promusicae* ECLI:EU:C:2008:54; Case C-70/10 *Scarlet Extended* ECLI:EU:C:2011:771; Case C-283/11 *Sky Österreich*; Case C-484/14 *Mc Fadden* ECLI:EU:C:2016:689. See S Garben, 'Fundamental rights in EU copyright harmonization: Balancing without a solid framework' (2020) 57 *CMLRev* 1909; J Griffiths, 'Constitutionalising or Harmonising? The Court of Justice, the Right to Property and European Copyright Law' (2013) 38 *ELRev* 65; T Mylly, 'The Constitutionalisation of the European Legal Order: Impact of Human Rights on Intellectual Property in the EU' in C Geiger (ed), *Research Handbook on Human Rights and Intellectual Property* (Cheltenham, Edward Elgar, 2015); P Oliver and C Stothers, 'Intellectual Property under the Charter: are the Court's Scales Properly Calibrated?' (2017) 54 *CMLRev* 517.

[64] See eg C Barnard, *The Substantive Law of the EU – the Four Freedoms*, 6th edn (Oxford, OUP, 2019) 449; F de Witte, 'The architecture of the EU' social market economy' in P Koutrakos and J Snell (eds), *Research Handbook on the Law of the EU's Internal Market* (Cheltenham, Edward Elgar, 2017) 117; S Giubboni, 'Freedom to Conduct a Business and EU Labour Law' (2018) 14 *EuConst* 172.

judgments (notably *Viking* and *Laval*), that is undeniably the case. To complete the picture, it should be noted that, in cases such as *Omega*,[65] non-economic fundamental rights have had the upper hand;[66] but that case had nothing to do with social rights. What is more, it is to be hoped that, when balancing two Charter rights against one another, the Court will adopt a genuinely neutral stance, now that it has finally held that at least one of the articles in Title IV of the Charter on social and labour rights is an enforceable right, and not a mere principle within the meaning of Article 52(5).[67]

Some authors also level this charge at the approach followed in *Schmidberger*, albeit without questioning the Court's conclusion on the facts.[68] In particular, while acknowledging that the Court now 'seems more genuinely committed to achieving a "fair balance"', Garben describes that ruling as 'rather unidirectional, tilting towards' giving preference to free movement.[69] She favours Schiek's 'bidirectional' approach under which equal weight is attached to the economic and the social or labour rights in any given case.[70]

To this author at least, Garben's criticism of *Schmidberger* appears somewhat harsh. Of course, having to treat the economic right to free movement as the prevailing right and the non-economic fundamental right as the exception is most unfortunate, a fact acknowledged by all the authors referred to here. However, by definition, the Court has to work within the framework set by the EU Treaties; to coin Reynolds' elegant phrase, the Court's approach in all these cases is 'inextricably linked to fundamentals of the Union's constitutional system'.[71] The reality is that in *Schmidberger*, by applying proportionality as flexibly as possible, AG Jacobs and the Court reached an entirely satisfactory solution. By this means, without referring to Schiek's bidirectional approach (which had presumably not yet been conceived), the Court in effect followed the same course of action.[72] Secondly, like the principle of proportionality of which it is a variant, balancing has one enormous quality: its flexibility, which enables its application to be tailored to the facts of each case. However, that is also its weakness; it is called legal uncertainty. Unsurprisingly, that is the other complaint raised by scholars.[73] With a view to overcoming this problem, Garben advocates a 'sensible hierarchical structure

---

[65] Case C-36/02 *Omega* ECLI:EU:C:2004:614.

[66] S de Vries, 'The Protection of Fundamental Rights within Europe's Internal Market after Lisbon – an Endeavour for more Harmony' in S de Vries, U Bernitz, and S Weatherill (eds), *The Protection of Fundamental Rights in the EU after Lisbon* (Oxford, Hart Publishing, 2013) 59, 93.

[67] Joined Cases C-569/16 and C-570/16 *Bauer* ECLI:EU:C:2018:871, which puts Article 31(2) of the Charter on the same footing as such economic Charter rights as the freedom to conduct a business and the right to property (Articles 16 and 17 respectively).

[68] C Brown, 'Case C-112/00, Eugen Schmidberger, Internationale Transporte und Planzüge v. Austria' (2003) 40 *CMLRev* 1499; Garben (n 63) 1910; and C Vial, 'Libre circulation des marchandises et protection des droits fondamentaux: à la recherche d'un équilibre' [2004] *Revue trimestrielle des droits de l'homme* 439.

[69] Garben (n 63) 1910.

[70] D Schiek, 'Towards more resilience for a social EU – the constitutionally conditioned Internal Market' (2017) 13 *EuConst* 611. More than 10 years earlier, Alemanno had proposed three alternative and more radical reforms in the case law to give greater weight to fundamental rights and in some cases to avoid such clashes between fundamental freedoms and fundamental rights. Two of these would have involved narrowing the scope of the concept of restrictions on free movement, while the third would have meant treating the 'mandatory requirements' differently from the express exceptions enshrined in Article 36 TFEU and its counterparts relating to the other freedoms. See A Alemanno, 'À la recherche d'un juste équilibre entre libertés fondamentales et droits fondamentaux dans le cadre du marché intérieur. Quelques réflexions à propos des arrêts « Schmidberger » et « Omega »' [2004] *Revue du droit de l'Union européenne* 709.

[71] S Reynolds, 'Explaining the Constitutional Drivers behind a Perceived Judicial Preference for Free Movement over Fundamental Rights' (2016) 53 *CMLRev* 643, 645.

[72] The same applies to AG Trstenjak's approach in Case 271/08 *Commission v Germany* (n 60).

[73] See eg Garben (n 63); Griffiths (n 63); Oliver and Stothers (n 63).

of EU law's plethora of constitutional values and norms'.[74] While this proposal may have much to commend it, it cannot be a panacea, since a given fundamental right will attract various degrees of protection depending on the circumstances.[75] For instance, freedom of speech covers a vast range of types of expression of which some (such as commercial expression) merit less protection than most speech, while others (such as racist or false and egregious political claims) deserve no protection whatsoever.

On any view, the cogent reasoning of judgments is indispensable if they are to be persuasive and ensure legal certainty.[76] Thus a high degree of consistency between judgments is required – and the Court must demonstrate that it is ensuring such consistency. The only effective way to achieve this is for the Court to compare the legal and factual issues of the case in hand with important precedents, and explain why it is following them or not, as the case may be. If this looks to many readers like a common lawyer's approach, it is none the worse for that! To be sure, balancing has its drawbacks,[77] but what alternative could there be?

In short, while these reproaches are undoubtedly warranted with respect to some cases, a comprehensive assault on the entire case law on balancing would be misplaced. In particular, *Schmidberger* stands out as a case in which, by giving the appropriate weight to the fundamental rights in issue, AG Jacobs and the Court reached a conclusion which cannot seriously be contested.

---

[74] Garben (n 63) 1928.

[75] As mentioned earlier in n 63, we are not concerned here with absolute fundamental rights.

[76] See T Kleinlein, 'Judicial Lawmaking by Judicial Restraint? The Potential of Balancing in International Economic Law' (2011) 12 *GLJ* 1141, 1167. Griffiths has written that 'the concept of "fair balance" is, without further elucidation, vacuous and unhelpful'. See Griffiths (n 63) 74.

[77] Garben (n 63) 1928.

35

Restrictions on Advertising and the Free Movement of Goods and Services: Opinions of Advocate General Jacobs in Leclerc-Siplec, De Agostini, and Gourmet

STEFAN ENCHELMAIER

I. INTRODUCTION

THE THREE OPINIONS discussed in this chapter address a question that arose from the *Keck* judgment of 1993.[1] AG Jacobs sought not only to clarify that judgment, but also explored whether and how the principles from *Keck* applied to restrictions on advertising. In the first two opinions, besides Articles 34 and 56 TFEU, the 'Television without Frontiers' Directive[2] also played a role (*Gourmet* concerned print media only.) Nevertheless, the focus in this chapter, in analysing the Opinions of AG Jacobs, will be on the articles in the EU Treaties.

II. BACKGROUND, CONTEXT, AND FACTS

In *Keck*, the Court had broken free from a development of the late 1980s in the case law on the free movement of goods. To put it briefly,[3] *Dassonville* had established that distinctly applicable measures (burdensome provisions that apply only to imported goods) require justification.[4] *Cassis de Dijon* extended this to indistinctly applicable measures (encompassing imports and domestic goods alike) that are in fact more difficult for imports to comply with.[5] This scheme

---

[1] Joined Cases C-267/91 and C-268/91 *Keck* ECLI:EU:C:1993:905.

[2] Council Directive 89/552/EEC of 3 October 1989 on the coordination of certain provisions laid down by law, regulation or administrative action in Member States concerning the pursuit of television broadcasting activities [1989] OJ L298/23.

[3] What follows above is more fully explained in S Enchelmaier, 'Free Movement of Goods: Evolution and Intelligent Design in the Foundations of the European Union' in P Craig and G de Búrca (eds), *The Evolution of EU Law*, 3rd edn (Oxford, OUP, 2021), 546.

[4] Case 8/74 *Dassonville* ECLI:EU:C:1974:82.

[5] Case 120/78 *Cassis de Dijon* ECLI:EU:C:1979:42.

left open how to deal with indistinctly applicable measures that also had the same factual repercussions on all goods. Such measures merely reduce the volume of goods sold overall, and not specifically in regard to imported goods. In a series of cases involving shop opening hours (the so-called 'Sunday trading' cases),[6] the Court had proceeded under the *Cassis de Dijon* doctrine. By the time *Keck* came along, the Court saw this development as erroneous.

In *Keck*, the Court revisited the question whether national provisions that merely reduce turnover across the board should be prohibited by Article 34 TFEU. Implicitly, it gave a negative answer, so that such provisions would no longer require justification. The Court's reasoning, however, threw up several new questions. In paragraphs 15 and 16 of the *Keck* judgment, respectively, it seemed to juxtapose 'requirements to be met by goods' with 'rules relating to certain selling arrangements'. The former called for a justification if obstacles specifically for imported goods arose as a 'consequence' of these requirements, even though the same rules applied to all goods. The latter did not require justification if they applied to all goods, and if they also affected all goods in the same way. This was followed by paragraph 17, explaining that rules of this kind were 'not by nature such as to prevent [goods] access to the market or to impede access any more than [they impeded] the access of domestic products'. The three cases at hand, *Leclerc-Siplec*, *de Agostini*, and *Gourmet* thus intersected with this matter, for which AG Jacobs provided his Opinions.

First, the preliminary reference in *Leclerc-Siplec* concerned the prohibition under French law of television advertisements by the (entire) distribution sector. This was meant to redirect advertisements that might have appeared on television towards the regional daily press instead. The Leclerc group of supermarkets sought to advertise its petrol prices on television, but the television companies approached refused to produce advertisements for broadcasting.

Secondly, other restrictions on television advertising gave rise to the preliminary reference in *de Agostini*. In this case, Swedish law prohibited television advertisements directed at children under the age of 12. Some of the television advertisements at the centre of the national litigation had been broadcast from other Member States. These adverts were, among others, for a children's magazine about dinosaurs, printed in Italy, and published in Sweden by de Agostini.

Thirdly, the preliminary reference in *Gourmet* arose from the near-complete prohibition on the advertising of alcoholic drinks in Sweden. This was part of a policy of moderating alcohol consumption in the interests of health and safety. Exceptions applied only to weak alcoholic drinks, mainly light beers, and it was permissible to praise any type of alcoholic drink in editorial pieces (so-called 'editorial publicity'). Such items appeared in, for instance, food magazines like *Gourmet*, published by the defendant, Gourmet International Products, in the national litigation. The restrictions did not apply to advertisements on the internet. The Swedish Consumer Ombudsman (*Konsumentombudsmannen*) had applied for an injunction against the distribution of an issue of *Gourmet* that contained advertisements for drinks with an alcohol content above the permissible threshold, namely, red wine and whiskey.

Another element of Sweden's policy *vis-à-vis* alcohol was (and is) the establishment of *Systembologet*, a state-owned company with the monopoly (except for light beers) of retail sales of alcoholic drinks for home consumption. *Systembolaget* ran (and runs) only a limited number of shops, with limited opening hours, strict enforcement of the statutory minimum

---

[6] Case 145/88 *Torfaen* ECLI:EU:C:1989:593; Case C-169/91 *B&Q* ECLI:EU:C:1992:519.

age for buying alcohol, and, finally, a restricted assortment of drinks, with only slow churn among products. Whoever wanted to try something not on offer in the shops, had to order it specifically through *Systembolaget*.[7]

III. THE OPINIONS OF AG JACOBS

The Opinions of AG Jacobs in *de Agostini*[8] and *Gourmet*[9] drew on his Opinion in *Leclerc-Siplec*,[10] and also on the judgment, in which the Court reached the same conclusions as AG Jacobs.[11] It is therefore apposite to deal with *Leclerc-Siplec* first, and in the greatest detail.

A. *Leclerc-Siplec*

AG Jacobs prefaced his legal assessment in *Leclerc-Siplec* with a reflection on 'the role of advertising'. This took, as its starting point, that, 'in a developed market economy based on free competition, the role of advertising is fundamental' and 'particularly important [...] in the launching of new products'.[12] This developed an idea from his Opinion in an earlier case, *HAG II*[13] – possibly his most influential opinion of all, because he convinced the Court to reverse its judgment in *HAG I*,[14] and inaugurated the modern jurisprudence on the exhaustion of trademarks following first marketing in the Internal Market. There, AG Jacobs had argued that, 'trade marks ... are, in the words of one author, "nothing more nor less than the fundament of most market-place competition".'[15] A trade mark is, so to say, an advertisement on the product itself.

This reflection from his earlier Opinion in *HAG II* led AG Jacobs in *Leclerc-Siplec* to conclude that, '[a] ban on advertising tends to crystallize existing patterns of consumption, to ossify markets and to preserve the *status quo*'.[16] The 'crystallisation' metaphor had its origins in the case law of the 1970s on internal taxation under what is now Article 110 TFEU (ex-Article 95 EC).[17] For AG Jacobs, this could be transferred to other handicaps that imported goods encountered while they were initially less well-known than their domestic counterparts,

---

[7] Separately, and beyond the scope of this case, the legality of *Systembologet* arise in, Case C-189/95 *Franzén* ECLI:EU:C:1997:504.

[8] Opinion of AG Jacobs in Joined Cases C-34/95, C-35/95 and C-36/95 *de Agostini* ECLI:EU:C:1996:333.

[9] Opinion of AG Jacobs in Case C-405/98 *Gourmet* ECLI:EU:C:2000:690.

[10] Opinion of AG Jacobs in Case C-412/93 *Leclerc-Siplec* ECLI:EU:C:1994:393.

[11] Case C-412/93 *Leclerc-Siplec* ECLI:EU:C:1995:26.

[12] Paras 19–20 of Opinion in *Leclerc-Siplec*.

[13] Opinion of AG Jacobs in Case C-10/89 *Hag* ECLI:EU:C:1990:112 (*HAG II*). See ch 24.

[14] Case 192/73 *Hag* ECLI:EU:C:1974:72 (*HAG I*).

[15] Para 17 of the Opinion in *Hag II*. AG Jacobs referred here to the textbook: WR Cornish, *Intellectual Property: Patents, Copyright, Trademarks and Allied Rights*, 2nd edn (London, Sweet & Maxwell, 1989) 393. The Court endorsed this view in para 13 of its Judgment by ruling that: 'Trade mark rights are [...] an essential element in the system of undistorted competition which the Treaty seeks to establish and maintain'. Most recently see also judgment of the General Court in Case T-663/19 *Hasbro v EUIPO* ECLI:EU:T:2021:211, para 49, with further references.

[16] Para 20, last sentence of Opinion in *Leclerc-Siplec*.

[17] Case 170/78 *Commission v UK* ECLI:EU:C:1980:53, para 14. The Court ruled that: '[...] the tax policy of a Member State must not [...] crystallize given consumer habits so as to consolidate an advantage acquired by national industries [...]'. See also Case C-230/89 *Commission v Greece* ECLI:EU:C:1991:156, para 9.

and which these other goods did not face (or not to the same extent). AG Jacobs therefore found it 'likely that the established brands will predominantly belong to domestic producers' so that, 'measures that prohibit or severely restrict advertising tend inevitably to protect domestic manufacturers and to disadvantage manufacturers located in other Member States'.[18]

Turning to Article 34 TFEU, AG Jacobs broached the concept of '(rules relating to certain) selling arrangements' from paragraph 16 of the *Keck* judgment, noting that:

> perhaps it is best understood as excluding from the scope of Article [34 TFEU] only measures of an entirely general character which do not preclude imports, which operate at the point of sale, and which have no effect on trade other than to reduce the overall quantity of goods sold and which in doing so affect imports and domestic products alike.[19]

Nevertheless, he emphasised that, '[f]or the reasons set out above, advertising restrictions may pose a particularly serious threat to the integration of markets'.[20] Applying the criteria from paragraph 16 of *Keck* – indistinct applicability and identical factual repercussions – AG Jacobs found that the French prohibition fell outside the scope of Article 34 TFEU.[21] All the same, he voiced two criticisms of the *Keck* judgment:

> 'First, it is inappropriate to make rigid distinctions between different categories of rules, and to apply different tests depending on the category to which particular rules belong ...'; '[s]econdly, ... [the *Keck* test] amounts to introducing, in relation to restrictions on selling arrangements, a test of discrimination. That test, however, seems inappropriate. ... If an obstacle to inter-State trade exists, it cannot cease to exist simply because an identical obstacle affects domestic trade.'[22]

In its stead, AG Jacobs suggested a *de minimis* threshold,[23] stating that '[f]rom the point of view of the Treaty's concern to establish a single market', it was immaterial whether a Member State similarly restricted the marketing of domestic goods. Equally irrelevant ought to be the local conditions which happened to prevail in each Member State. Rather, for him, 'the aim of access to the entire [Union] market' ought to guide the assessment. For AG Jacobs, a discrimination test was hence 'inconsistent as a matter of principle with the aims of the Treaty'.[24] On the contrary, all undertakings with lawful business in a Member State should have 'unfettered access to the whole of the Union market', unless there were a valid reason for denying them that access. In conclusion, once it was recognised that there was a need to limit the scope of Article 34 TFEU in order to prevent 'excessive interference in the regulatory powers of the Member States', a test based on the extent to which a measure hindered trade between Member States by restricting market access appeared the obvious solution.[25]

Concerning advertising bans, AG Jacobs argued, '[a] measure that constitutes such a significant barrier to the entry of goods from other Member States must surely be equivalent in effect to a quantitative restriction on trade between Member States'. Still, he stated that, 'even if the discrimination test formulated in *Keck* were applied, the same conclusion would be reached: an advertising ban, far from being neutral in its effects, tends to operate to the particular

---

[18] Para 21 of Opinion in *Leclerc-Siplec*.
[19] Para 34, last sub-para of Opinion in *Leclerc-Siplec*.
[20] ibid, para 37.
[21] ibid.
[22] Paras 38–39 of Opinion in *Leclerc-Siplec*.
[23] ibid, para 42.
[24] ibid, para 40.
[25] ibid, paras 41–42.

detriment of imported goods'.[26] In all, however, a ban on television advertising imposed on the entire distribution sector – all goods – fell outside the scope of Article 34 TFEU.[27]

B. *De Agostini*

Drawing on the judgment in *Leclerc-Siplec*, AG Jacobs submitted that '[a] measure prohibiting [televised] promotion in relation to a particular category of potential consumers, or a particular category of goods must on that basis be regarded as a selling arrangement, assuming that other forms of promotion are available and effective for the category concerned'.[28] This led him to apply the two *Keck* criteria of indistinct applicability and equal factual repercussions, and to refer to his Opinion in *Leclerc-Siplec*, to conclude that the effect of the prohibition of all television advertising directed at children might in fact be greater on products from other Member States.[29] Even under a discrimination test, the prohibition would 'almost certainly have a perceptible effect on imports'[30] – in light of the earlier opinion, this is presumably meant to say that imports suffer more from it than domestic products.

Under Article 56 TFEU's freedom to provide services, AG Jacobs suggested the prohibition was justified in the interest of the protection of children, as he had already found under Article 34 TFEU.[31] The freedom to provide services did not, however, enure to a broadcaster whose activities were in all aspects confined within a single Member State.[32]

C. *Gourmet*

Prompted by the Consumer Ombudsman's insistence that, by virtue of *Keck*, the advertising restrictions fell outside the scope of Article 34 TFEU, AG Jacobs summarised that pursuant to *Leclerc-Siplec*, advertising restrictions amounted to '(rules relating to) selling arrangements'. Nevertheless, the exception in *Keck* turned on equality in law and in fact.[33] While the prohibition of advertising directly to the public applied to all producers in equal measure, AG Jacobs found it inherent in such a prohibition that it would disproportionately affect imported products.

In the words of *Keck*, the prohibition would 'prevent their access to the market or [...] impede access [...] more than it impedes the access of domestic products'.[34] This was because a consumer accustomed to buying certain goods was unlikely to bother much to find out whether there might be any alternative goods to try. The foreseeable result was that the consumer would continue to purchase the same goods (and that these were in all likelihood domestic goods[35]). Echoing his Opinion in *Leclerc-Siplec*, AG Jacobs emphasised that the role of advertising was

---

[26] ibid, para 50.
[27] ibid, para 55.
[28] Para 97 of Opinion in *de Agostini*.
[29] ibid, paras 98–99.
[30] ibid, para 99 (after fn 60).
[31] ibid, paras 101–05, 110.
[32] ibid, paras 108–09.
[33] Paras 28–29 of Opinion in *Gourmet*.
[34] ibid, para 34.
[35] ibid, para 37.

primordial in launching a new product, or in penetrating a new market.[36] In light of the numerous exceptions, he found the prohibition disproportionate to its aim of reducing lawful alcohol consumption by adults.[37]

Regarding the freedom to provide services under Article 56 TFEU, the cross-frontier element was easily established since the products promoted in *Gourmet* came from other Member States, and the prohibition would also apply to providers of advertising from other Member States.[38] Some interveners contended that engagement of Article 56 TFEU required discrimination. AG Jacobs responded that according to the Court's jurisprudence, it was merely required that a restriction be liable to prohibit, impede or render less advantageous the activities of a provider of services established in another Member State where similar services were lawfully provided. According to *Alpine Investments*,[39] this applied to restrictions imposed by the Member State *from* which ('export' of services), as well as the one *to* which ('import'), the service was to be provided. What was more, according to the same judgment, the Member States did not benefit from an exception akin to that under *Keck*.[40]

IV. ANALYSIS

Throughout the three judgments, the Court came to the same conclusions as AG Jacobs, even though it did not always endorse his reasoning (below, Section IV.A), especially not the suggestion to introduce a *de minimis* threshold to the assessment under Article 34 TFEU (see Section IV.B). Likewise, one may wonder whether the concept of '(rules relating to certain) selling arrangements' is now sufficiently clear, or whether it is even useful at all (Section IV.C). In the background is the question of a common approach to all freedoms of the internal market, or at least to goods and services, as far as the presence of a restriction of the freedom is concerned (Section IV.D). Later, the Court would experiment with 'market access' to bring about such a unified approach (Section IV.E).

A. The Court's Judgments in *Leclerc-Siplec*, *De Agostini*, and *Gourmet*

The Court in *Leclerc-Siplec* held that,

> [the prohibition] concerns selling arrangements since it prohibits a particular form of promotion (televised advertising) of a particular method of marketing products (distribution). Furthermore, those provisions, which apply regardless of the type of product to all traders in the distribution sector, even if they are both producers and distributors, affect the marketing of products from other Member States and that of domestic products in the same manner.[41]

In *de Agostini*, the Court reiterated the first sentence quoted above. It warranted no discussion that the first criterion from paragraph 16 of *Keck*, indistinct applicability, was fulfilled. Regarding the second criterion, the Court found that it could not be excluded that an outright

---

[36] ibid, para 36.
[37] ibid, paras 43–63.
[38] ibid, paras 66–69.
[39] Case C-384/93 *Alpine Investments* ECLI:EU:C:1995:126.
[40] Paras 70–71 of Opinion in *Gourmet*.
[41] Paras 22–23 of Judgment in *Leclerc-Siplec*.

ban of a type of promotion for a product that was lawfully sold in that Member State might have a greater impact on products from other Member States. This was especially so because de Agostini had stated (and apparently convinced the Court) that television advertising was the only effective form of promotion, enabling it to penetrate the Swedish market. It had no other advertising methods for reaching children and their parents.[42]

The Court also said the prohibition also restricted the freedom to provide services. It limited the possibility for television channels established in other Member States to broadcast, for advertisers established in the receiving State, television advertising specifically directed at the public in that State.[43]

In *Gourmet*, taking its cue from paragraph 17 of *Keck*, the Court focused on the factual repercussions of the advertising prohibition for imports and domestic products, respectively. The Court found that,

> in the case of products like alcoholic beverages, the consumption of which is linked to traditional social practices and to local habits and customs, a prohibition of all advertising directed at consumers [...] is liable to impede access to the market by products from other Member States more than it impedes access by domestic products, with which consumers are instantly more familiar.[44]

Domestic producers were also more likely to have better access to the authors of 'editorial publicity', again placing their products at an advantage over imports.[45]

Likewise regarding the freedom to provide services, the Court stated that:

> A measure such as the prohibition on advertising [...], even if it is non-discriminatory, has a *particular effect on the cross-border supply of advertising space*, given the international nature of the advertising market in the category of products to which the prohibition relates, and thereby constitutes a restriction on the freedom to provide services within the meaning of Article [56 TFEU] (emphasis added).[46]

It had been established earlier that magazines published outside Sweden could be distributed in Sweden, even if they carried advertisements that would not have been allowed in Swedish magazines such as *Gourmet*.[47] The italicised passage above presumably means to say, therefore, that the Swedish provision put Swedish providers at a disadvantage on the advertising market outside of Sweden, compared to their competitors from other Member States. This is corroborated by the reference to *Alpine Investments*. That case dealt with the same paradigm of a Member State's 'making life harder' for its domestic industries in their efforts to find clients in other Member States, in competition with less-strictly regulated providers in other Member States.

B. A *De Minimis* Test for the Free Movement of Goods?

AG Jacobs went looking for an alternative test for the compatibility of national rules with Article 34 TFEU because he found a discrimination test 'inconsistent as a matter of principle' with the aims of the EU Treaties. It can only be remarked in passing that the second sentence

---

[42] Paras 39, 42–43 of Judgment in *de Agostini*.
[43] ibid, paras 50–51.
[44] Para 21 of Judgment in *Gourmet*.
[45] ibid, para 24.
[46] ibid, para 39, with reference to para 35 of Judgment in *Alpine Investments*.
[47] Para 24 of Opinion in *Gourmet*.

of Article 36 TFEU implies that Article 34 TFEU prohibits discrimination, if nothing else. On the grounds it lays down, Article 36 TFEU allows 'prohibitions or restrictions' that would otherwise be caught by Articles 34 and 35 TFEU, but makes a counter-exception for such national measures that constitute a means of 'arbitrary discrimination'. Such discrimination will, presumably, again (or still) be captured by the prohibition in Articles 34 and 35 TFEU. The same mechanism can be shown at work for all four freedoms, and for a number of related provisions.[48] It was therefore a bold proposition of AG Jacobs that a discrimination test should be 'inconsistent as a matter of principle' with the aims of the EU Treaties.

This does not mean, of course, that it can or ought not to be complemented by other tests. Whether *de minimis* should be that test, is yet another question. In the reasoning of AG Jacobs, it flowed from his postulate of 'unfettered access to the whole of the Union market'. The trouble is, however, that there is no 'Union market' in isolation. This is only the notional sum total of the individual Member States' markets, governed by national law (with some EU law on top). Article 26 TFEU envisages the continued existence of these markets when it demands that the 'internal frontiers' disappear, ie, those between the national markets. Article 26 TFEU therefore targets the various obstacles to free movement as proscribed in the four freedoms of the EU Treaties. Once the national markets are open *in law* (distance, and differences in consumer habits, cannot be decreed away) to all comers from anywhere else in the Member States, there is an internal market, but still made up of national markets.

If one wonders what amounts to a 'frontier', Article 36 TFEU provides a first answer: 'prohibitions and restrictions', especially discrimination, that is, unequal treatment in law or in fact without justification. There may be others, but AG Jacobs did not spell this out when he demanded 'unfettered' access. This only begs the question, what is a 'fetter'? AG Jacobs seemed to have in mind *any* restriction meaning, in the end, any and all national legislation. If according to this hypothesis, it cannot be EU law, only national law obstructs access to the purported 'Union market'.

What is more, by definition, the national law that was at issue was not discriminatory, neither in law nor in fact. It reduced the volume of sales evenly. In other words, the Advocate General's suggestion reintroduces the 'Sunday trading' conundrum that the Court had just overcome in *Keck*. AG Jacobs was well aware that his approach might lead to inacceptable 'interference in the regulatory powers of the Member States' ('exceed the scope' of Article 34 TFEU). That is why he wanted it to set in only above an as yet undefined threshold. Gormley's objection to this and similar suggestions is timeless:

> Several reasons militate against accepting a de minimis rule in the free movement of goods. Most practically, where should the line be drawn? A percentage of GDP; a percentage of the value of the market (and what would be the relevant market); the value of a daily penalty on the Commission's guideline scales for penalising Member States under Article [260 TFEU]; the value of a day's imports?[49]

C. The Elusive Concept of '(Rules Relating to Certain) Selling Arrangements'

Reflecting on the three Opinions of AG Jacobs, one is certainly left with the impression that, not least because paragraph 16 of *Keck* used the phrase '(rules relating to certain) selling

---

[48] See further Enchelmaier (n 3) 547–50.
[49] L Gormley, 'The Definition of Measures Having Equivalent Effect' in A Arnull, P Eeckhout, and T Tridimas (eds), *Continuity and Change in EU Law: Essays in Honour of Sir Francis Jacobs* (Oxford, OUP, 2009) 189, 202.

arrangements', they are of legal significance. One would expect a definition that helps the Court and the national courts gauge whether a given national provision counts as such a rule or not (whatever the import of 'certain'). Once this is done, the assessment of a case could move on to the remainder of the conditions stipulated in that passage of *Keck*, *viz* indistinct applicability and equal factual impact.

The closest AG Jacobs came to proposing a definition was in paragraph 34 of *Leclerc-Siplec*.[50] The passage, however, is only a precis of *Keck*. '[E]ntirely general character' seemed to be a reformulation of 'indistinctly applicable', the first of the conditions in *Keck*, paragraph 16. '[A]ffect imports and domestic products alike' was the second. '[D]o not preclude imports, [but merely] reduce the overall quantity of goods sold' echoed the Court's opening question from paragraph 13 of *Keck*, and was the outcome under the second condition. '[O]perate at the point of sale' was a factual characterisation of the prohibition of resale at a loss that was in issue in *Keck*. Whether this must always be so was not clear. At least, it did not easily fit advertising restrictions, which affect an earlier marketing stage.

AG Jacobs did not apply his formula, but merely asserted that advertising restrictions were 'particularly serious'. That, however, only ducked the question, and answered the next instead. Nevertheless, once the Court had (without a definition, either) held that advertising restrictions qualified, AG Jacobs in his subsequent Opinions did not revisit the question, but merely referred to the judgment. Next, in each of the Opinions, AG Jacobs applied the two aforementioned conditions, amounting in essence to a discrimination assessment.

The reason for the difficulties of a definition, but also its ultimate futility, appears on a closer reading of *Keck*. Paragraphs 15 and 16 ask, in substance, the same questions (indistinct applicability and uniform effects) in slightly varied wording. Only the answers are different. The rule in *Cassis de Dijon* applied to every liqueur equally (first question, positive answer), but not every producer found it equally easy to comply with it (second question, negative answer). In *Keck*, the prohibition of resale at a loss also encompassed all products (first question, positive answer), but no one in fact suffered more than anybody else (second question, positive answer). In *Dassonville*, the answer to the first question was negative: only imported products required a certificate of authenticity, and that without more triggered the need for a justification.

The initial categorisation of the rule as a 'product requirement' or a 'rule relating to certain selling arrangements' is immaterial for this. In fact, these labels are anticipated summaries of the result of the test that follow. The contrast in outcomes between *Leclerc-Siplec* on the one hand, and *de Agostini* and *Gourmet* (and, no less, *Cassis de Dijon*) on the other, shows that it is the two conditions that are decisive. For the same reason, the two criticisms[51] of AG Jacobs do not sink *Keck* altogether. There are no 'rigid distinctions between different categories of rules', with different tests attached to each. Moreover, the discrimination test was not 'introduced' in that judgment, let alone for 'rules relating to certain selling arrangements' only. The test was there even before *Dassonville*: it was laid down in the EU Treaties. It is conspicuous that in each of the three opinions, it yielded the same result as the assessment that included the prefatory categorisation.

Even though AG Jacobs did not sway the Court on this point, his Opinion had a lasting impact in the literature. This was especially true of his suggestion that rules of the *Cassis de Dijon*

---

[50] Para 34, last sub-para of Opinion in *Leclerc-Siplec*. For a discussion of other attempts at a definition, see Enchelmaier (n 3) 568–70.
[51] Paras 38, 39 of Opinion in *Leclerc-Siplec*.

type may be presumed to be in breach of Article 34 TFEU (unless justified),[52] while conversely, 'rules relating to certain selling arrangements' were not automatically caught.[53] Most commentators endorsed his criticisms, as well as the presumption mentioned, and even went so far as to stipulate a presumption against 'rules relating to certain selling arrangements' being caught by Article 34 TFEU.[54]

Nevertheless, doubts remain. Not only are the judgments in this area silent on any presumptions, *Gourmet* is, in substance, directly contrary. Their introduction would also fly in the face of the distribution of the burden of proof under Article 258 TFEU in particular: the Commission must not rely on any presumption that a Member State has failed in its obligations under EU law.[55] This is the procedural corollary to the substantive rule that, '[e]ven if a measure is not intended to regulate trade in goods between Member States, the determining factor is its effect, actual or potential, on intra-[Union] trade'.[56]

D. A Common Test for Restrictions of Free Movement?

The idea that there can be a test that applies to all freedoms, or at least to more than one, is known as the 'convergence' hypothesis. Most scholars remain to be convinced, and again it is AG Jacobs on whom they rely. Convergence is said to fall at the hurdle of the judgment in *Alpine Investments*. This comes from the Opinion in *Gourmet* where AG Jacobs had interpreted the *Alpine Investments* judgment to deny the Member States, under Article 56 TFEU, an escape of the sort that they enjoy according to *Keck*.

This starts from an interpretation of *Keck* whose difficulties have come to light above. Similar concerns arise with regard to judgment in *Alpine Investments*. The passage in the judgment that supposedly bars a transfer of the principles of *Keck* (whatever one understands these to be) is paragraph 36:

> Such a prohibition [of selling complex financial products in the course of unannounced telephone calls to consumers] is not analogous to the legislation concerning selling arrangements held in *Keck and Mithouard* to fall outside the scope of Article [34 TFEU] of the Treaty.

This tells a result. It does not say, 'goods and services follow different rules'. On the contrary, the question the Court here answers was familiar from *Keck*. From the context of *Alpine Investments*, it transpires that the reason why *Keck* did not apply was that the Dutch prohibition imposed an additional burden on those, such as Alpine Investments, who wanted to provide services across the border into another Member State. Alpine Investments had to overcome an obstacle its competitors were spared, namely, the prohibition on using its customary method of marketing over the telephone. Although the rule applied to all providers established and all services provided in the Netherlands, it affected those more gravely who sought business from an establishment in the Netherlands on more lightly regulated markets in other

---

[52] ibid, para 44.

[53] ibid, para 45.

[54] N Nic Shuibhne, *The Coherence of EU Free Movement Law* (Oxford, OUP, 2013) 215; C Barnard, *The Substantive Law of the EU*, 6th edn (Oxford, OUP, 2020) 130. According to Craig and de Búrca 'National rules concerning sales are not regarded *per se* as inhibiting market access'. Furthermore, 'the second choice is a test based on substantial hindrance to market access, subject to presumptions based on the type of case'. See P Craig and G de Búrca, *EU Law: Text, Cases, and Materials*, 7th edn (Oxford, OUP, 2020) 750, 755.

[55] Cases C-63/19 *Commission v Italy* ECLI:EU:C:2021:18, para 74; C-443/18 *Commission v Italy* ECLI:EU:C:2019:676, para 78; C-441/02 *Commission v Germany* ECLI:EU:C:2006:253, para 48.

[56] Case C-244/06 *Dynamic Medien* ECLI:EU:C:2008:85, para 27.

Member States (the 'export of services' paradigm). The second of the above conditions was not met, ie, equal factual repercussions for all. The situation was thus as in *Cassis de Dijon*, not as in *Keck*. *Alpine Investments* is, therefore, no obstacle to convergence.[57]

E. The Aftermath: The Emancipation of 'Market Access'

Keck was not the Court's last word on the assessment of cases under Article 34 TFEU. In *Commission v Italy ('Trailers')* of 2009, the Court seemed to promote 'market access' to the overarching test. This had already made an appearance in paragraph 17 of *Keck*, but was not explained further in that judgment, nor on the occasion when it was transferred to the other freedoms shortly afterwards.[58] At any rate, whatever it meant, it seemed subordinate to the discrimination test that kept on cropping up in the judgments as much as in Opinions of AG Jacobs.

Suffice it to say that 'market access' is just a different way of saying, 'free movement between Member States'. Article 26 TFEU shows that the law of free movement conceives of the Member States as legally constituted markets. To say that Member States must not restrict market access, therefore, begs the reply, 'granted – but what is it specifically that they must not do?'.[59] These developments took place after the retirement of AG Jacobs from the Court. Nevertheless, the questions that he discussed in his Opinions in *Leclerc-Siplec, de Agostini*, and *Gourmet* are still with us. Rarely have they been discussed in such depth, and with so much insight. Moreover, like every great teacher, AG Jacobs has enabled those who come after to disagree with him.

---

[57] Judgment in case *Alpine Investments* and convergence are more fully discussed in S Enchelmaier, 'The Development of the Free Movement Principles over Time' in S Garben and I Govaere (eds), *The Internal Market 2.0* (Oxford, Hart Publishing, 2020) 25, 51, 55–57.

[58] See eg in *Alpine Investments*, the Court ruled '… directly affects access to the market in services in the other Member States and is thus capable of hindering intra-Community trade in services' (para 38 of the Judgment).

[59] See Enchelmaier (n 3) 573–75.

36

Achtung Baby! Objectives of International Agreements Matter: Opinion of Advocate General Jacobs in Pokrzeptowicz-Meyer

I. INTRODUCTION

THE DISMANTLING OF communism in Central and Eastern Europe (CEE) marked the beginning of a new phase in modern history of the continent and the World. Many consider 1989 as an *annus mirabilis*,[1] when the transformation started and enabled gradual *rapprochement* between the states of the region and the then European Communities, now the European Union (EU). In the early 1990s, the face of Europe changed for good with a unified Germany, and with the radical development of market economies and reformed legal systems in the CEE states.[2] These unprecedented events did not go unnoticed by historians, politicians, and artists,[3] including the popular culture. In the case of the latter, it is worth noting that in the early 1990s, the Irish band U2 recorded the *Achtung Baby* album, identifying the transformation as one of their sources of inspiration.[4] While popular music can divide opinions,[5] there is one point that is worth exploring further before the analysis moves for good to the Opinion of AG Jacobs in *Pokrzeptowicz-Meyer*.[6]

---

[1] G Mak, *In Europe: Travels through the twentieth century* (New York, Vintage, 2008) 714.

[2] See T Garton Ash, *We The People: The Revolution of' 89 Witnessed in Warsaw, Budapest, Berlin & Prague* (London, Penguin, 1990); T Garton Ash, *History of the Present: Essays, Sketches and Despatches from Europe in the 1990s* (London, Penguin, 1999).

[3] One of the most symbolic performances to commemorate the historical events was a concert which took place on 25 December 1989 in Berlin. Combined orchestras of Symphonieorchester des Bayerischen Rundfunks, with musicians from Kirov Orchestra, St Petersburg, Orchestre de Paris, London Symphony Orchestra, and New York Philharmonic with soloists and Chor der Staatskapelle Dresden, conducted by Leonard Bernstein performed Ludwig van Beethoven's Symphony No 9. To mark the occasion the fourth movement 'Ode an die Freude' (Ode to Joy) became 'Ode an die Freiheit' (Ode to Freedom) and it was sung accordingly.

[4] J Rogers, 'New Year's Day – how U2's song was inspired by Lech Walesa and his wife' *Financial Times* (London, 26 December 2019) https://ig.ft.com/life-of-a-song/new-years-day.html; I Walker, 'U2 – Globalisation's poster boys' (*The New European*, London, 5 November 2020) www.theneweuropean.co.uk/brexit-news-globalisations-poster-boys-6148250/.

[5] PP, 'U2. Achtung Baby' (1992) *Stereo Review* 134.

[6] Opinion of AG Jacobs in Case C-162/00 *Pokrzeptowicz-Meyer* ECLI:EU:C:2001:474.

Context, aims, and interpretation matter. Just as it was with *Achtung Baby*, its message would not be clear without consideration of what led the artists to their choices of notes (or, as some would say, noises) and lyrics. U2 are known for their responsive take on human rights violations,[7] current developments,[8] and their reflections on Christianity.[9] However, a more careful analysis suggests that there are traces of Jewish thought in their work as well.[10] This is not surprising, bearing in mind the Judeo-Christian origins of Europe and its values.[11] This way the interpretation of their sounds yielded a richer, new dimension. 'One' is of the most prominent songs on the album, and it has generated a plethora of explanations of its meaning.[12] Using less obvious approaches, it can be said that in Hebrew 'one' is *echad* (אֶחָד) and it represents 'the fusion of diverse elements into a harmonious whole'.[13]

This is, symbolically, what the events of early 1990s have led to: unification of the West with the East, which culminated with the enlargements of 2004 and 2007 when Central and Eastern European states joined the EU. This historical context was taken on board by AG Jacobs. He approached *Pokrzeptowicz-Meyer* from a broader perspective, acknowledging the multifarious nature of the legal issues at hand. Above all, AG Jacobs carefully examined the impact that legal measures have on human beings, a theme which is very much present in many of his Opinions covering different areas of EU law, as demonstrated in other chapters of this book. Indeed, on a number of occasions, AG Jacobs presented his views on the importance of protection of rights of individuals.[14] In *Pokrzeptowicz-Meyer*, the leitmotif is clear: Achtung Baby, your rights matter, and 'regard must be paid to the spirit, the general scheme and the wording of the provision concerned'.[15]

II. BACKGROUND, CONTEXT, AND FACTS

The facts of the case were as follows. German Framework Law on Higher Education envisaged that fixed-term contracts of employment for certain members of staff at higher-education and research institutes were permitted. However, they had to be individually justified on objective grounds. At the same time, such grounds existed automatically in relation to foreign language teachers, who could be employed only for a maximum of five years. Not surprisingly, this solution led to litigation in German courts and – quite inevitably – a reference for preliminary ruling aiming at verification if it was compatible with Article 45(2) TFEU and the principle of non-discrimination laid down therein.

In *Spotti*, both AG Jacobs[16] and the Court[17] concluded that the German law in question amounted to indirect discrimination, especially bearing in mind that the majority of foreign

---

[7] A Greene, 'How Amnesty International Rocked the World: The Inside Story' (*The Rolling Stone*, London, 25 October 2013) www.rollingstone.com/music/music-news/how-amnesty-international-rocked-the-world-the-inside-story-61682/.

[8] L Filardo-Llamas, 'From Ireland to the States. The re-contextualisation of U2's "Sunday, Bloody Sunday" in different political contexts' (2019) 18(4) *Journal of Language and Politics* 509.

[9] See eg J Rothman, 'The Church of U2' (*The New Yorker*, New York, 16 September 2014) www.newyorker.com/culture/cultural-comment/church-u2.

[10] N Dinnen, 'You Don't See Me But You Will: Jewish Thought and U2' in S Calhoun (ed), *U2 and the Religious Impulse* (London, Bloomsbury, 2018) 152.

[11] N Davies, *Europe. A History* (Oxford, OUP, 1996).

[12] S Catanzarite, *U2's Achtung Baby* (London, Bloomsbury, 2007) 98.

[13] Tauber as quoted by Dinnen (n 10).

[14] See chs 25 and 26.

[15] Case 87/75 *Bresciani* ECLI:EU:C:1976:18, para 16.

[16] Opinion of AG Jacobs in Case C-272/92 *Spotti* ECLI:EU:C:1993:181.

[17] Case C-272/92 *Spotti* ECLI:EU:C:1993:848.

language teachers were not nationals of the host state (in this case Germany).[18] Bearing in mind that the plaintiff was Italian, the contested law fell foul of Article 45(2) TFEU. It was just a matter of time when citizens of third states would try their luck in contesting the regime laid down by the German law. This was done by Pokrzeptowicz-Meyer, a Polish national who lawfully resided in Germany.[19] In 1992 she found part-time employment as a Polish language assistant at the University of Bielefeld. Her contract stipulated that she was employed for a fixed term (8 October 1992–30 September 1996). The nature of her contract was influenced by her main duties of teaching the Polish language.[20]

In January 1996, as the date of expiration of her contract was approaching, Pokrzeptowicz-Meyer applied to the Labour Court in Bielefeld requesting that her contract would not be terminated at the end of its fixed term. The request was supported by the ruling in *Spotti*. Pokrzeptowicz-Meyer claimed that the prohibition of indirect discrimination the Court relied on should have been extended to nationals of third states, such as Poland. The Labour Court dismissed her claim; however, her appeal was allowed by the Higher Labour Court in Hamm.

The case eventually reached the Federal Labour Court, which submitted a reference for preliminary ruling as the interpretation of Community law was pivotal to the determination of the dispute. The Court requested guidance on the interpretation of Article 37(1) of the EC-Poland Europe Agreement and whether it precluded the application of the German law in question to Polish nationals.[21] It reads as follows:

> Subject to the conditions and modalities applicable in each Member State – the treatment accorded to workers of Polish nationality legally employed in the territory of a Member State shall be free from any discrimination based on nationality.

The German court also asked for a clarification if it was of relevance that the fixed-term employment contract was concluded before the entry into force of the Europe Agreement (EA), but came to an end at the time when the EA formed the main EU-Poland legal framework. The timing was important not only for Pokrzeptowicz-Meyer but, as explained further below, it was also of relevance for AG Jacobs and the Court. The big picture mattered.

The EA EC-Poland entered into force on 1 February 1994. A few months later on 5 April 1994, Poland applied for membership of the EU. The accession talks commenced in 1997, and were at advanced stages when the reference from the *Bundesarbeitsgericht* in *Pokrzeptowicz-Meyer* reached the Court. The Opinion of AG Jacobs in the case at hand was delivered on 20 September 2001, and the judgment of the Court was rendered on 29 January 2002.[22] At that point, *rapprochement* was entering the final stages with the conclusion of accession talks looming on the horizon. Thus, the interpretation of the EA was inextricably linked to the EU enlargement. With this in mind, it is fitting to have a brief recap as to what it entailed.

---

[18] See, in relation to a comparable Italian law, Case 33/88 *Coonan* ECLI:EU:C:1989:222.

[19] It is worth noting that the case at hand was not the only court adventure of Pokrzeptowicz-Mayer. In the years that followed she was embroiled in notorious litigation related to her personal life, which culminated with the European Arrest Warrant that was issued as she, allegedly, kidnapped her own child. See B T Wieliński, 'Najgłośniejszy przypadek polsko-niemieckiego sporu o dzieci' [The most famous case of the Polish-German dispute over children] (*Gazeta Wyborcza*, Warsaw, 7 December 2008).

[20] Para 14 of the Judgment.

[21] Europe Agreement establishing an association between the European Communities and their Member States, of the one part, and the Republic of Poland, of the other part [1993] OJ L 348/2 (hereinafter EA EC-Poland).

[22] At that point in time the Court had already delivered its judgment in Case C-63/99 *Gloszczuk* ECLI:EU:C:2001:488. It ruled that provisions of EA EC-Poland which meet the standard test could produce direct effect.

Enlargement has become a core element of the EU's development, and its impact is multidimensional.[23] The consecutive seven enlargements which took place in parallel to unprecedented deepening of integration within the EU significantly changed the European Communities and the EU. It also affected the way in which the Union's external borders are perceived, as noted by Zielonka, they are in constant flux that makes their perception softer.[24] New members change the internal dynamics of the EU, in that they bring their own interests influencing internal policies, as well as external relations with new neighbours as the borders of the EU move.[25]

It is notable that the legal bases of enlargement evolved from the focus on economic dimension of integration,[26] to a more holistic enlargement proviso, where the importance of values and solidarity is explicitly acknowledged. Article 49 TEU refers to 'conditions of eligibility', which were defined by the European Council in Copenhagen in 1993.[27] The fifth wave of enlargement, which materialised on 1 May 2004, marked the biggest of the EU expansions to date, when eight Central and Eastern European states, along with Malta and Cyprus, joined the ranks. Without a doubt, it tested the absorption capacity of the EU.[28] The membership of the new entrants in 2004 has been regarded as a vital contribution to a peaceful conclusion of the aforementioned East-West divide. It must be remembered that the accession process for this group of states had started in the late 1980s. It is also fitting to note that Europe Agreements,[29]

---

[23] On the impact of EU enlargements see A Dashwood, 'The Impact of Enlargement on the Union's Institutions' in C Hillion (ed), *EU Enlargement: A Legal Approach. Essays in European Law* (Oxford, Hart Publishing, 2004); M Cremona, *Enlargement: A Successful Instrument of EU Foreign Policy?* in P Matthews and P Nebbia (eds), *European Union Law for the Twenty-First Century* (Oxford, Hart Publishing, 2004); V Curzon Price, A Landau and RG Whitman, *The Enlargement of the European Union: Issues and Strategies* (Abingdon, Routledge, 1999); AF Tatham, *Enlargement of the European Union* (Alphen aan den Rijn, Kluwer Law International, 2009); A Ott and K Inglis (eds), *Handbook on European Enlargement* (The Hague, TMC Asser Press, 2002); C Preston, *Enlargement and Integration in the European Union* (Abingdon, Routledge, 1997); D Kochenov, *EU Enlargement and the Failure of Conditionality: Pre-accession Conditionality in the Fields of Democracy and the Rule of Law* (The Hague, Kluwer Law International, 2008).

[24] J Zielonka, *Europe as Empire* (Oxford, OUP, 2006) 143.

[25] M Comelli, E Greco and N Tocci, *From Boundary to Borderland: Transforming the Meaning of Borders in Europe Through the European Neighbourhood Policy* (Rome, Instituto Affari Internazionali, 2006).

[26] As per the now repealed Article 98 ECSC: 'Any European State may request to accede to the present Treaty. It shall address its request to the Council, which shall act by unanimous vote after having obtained the opinion of the High Authority; the Council shall also determine the terms of accession, likewise acting unanimously.'

[27] The political criteria are as follows: stable institutions guaranteeing democracy, compliance with the rule of law and human rights, respect for and protection of minorities. Economic criteria include a functioning market economy and the capacity to cope with competition and market forces in the EU. Capacity to take on the obligations of membership, including adherence to the objectives of political, economic and monetary union are also among the economic criteria. Adoption of the entire body of European legislation and its effective implementation through appropriate administrative and judicial structures is also required. See European Council, 'Conclusions of the Presidency', SN 180/1/93 REV 1. This general conclusion of the European Council paved the way for conditionality, which is now at the heart of the enlargement process. See E Gateva, *European Union Enlargement Conditionality* (London, Palgrave Macmillan, 2015).

[28] See A Łazowski, 'Treaty of Lisbon and EU's absorption capacity' (2011) 19 *Polish Quarterly of International Affairs* 56.

[29] Europe Agreement establishing an association between the European Communities and their Member States, of the one part, and the Republic of Hungary, of the other part [1993] OJ L347/2; Europe Agreement establishing an association between the European Communities and their Member States, of the one part, and the Czech Republic, of the other part [1994] OJ L360/2; Europe Agreement establishing an association between the European Communities and their Member States, of the one part, and the Slovak Republic, of the other part [1994] OJ L359/2; Europe Agreement establishing an association between the European Communities and their Member States, of the one part, and Romania, of the other part [1994] OJ L357/2; Europe Agreement establishing an association between the European Communities and their Member States, of the one part, and the Republic of Bulgaria, of the other part [1994] OJ L358/3; Europe Agreement establishing an association between the European Communities and their Member States, of the one part, and the Republic of Lithuania, of the other part [1998] OJ L51/3; Europe Agreement establishing an association between the European Communities and their Member States, of the one part, and

although not originally intended as enlargement tools, paved the way for the accession of the Central and Eastern European states to the EU.[30]

III. THE OPINION OF AG JACOBS

The Opinion of AG Jacobs focused on two main issues. First, AG Jacobs attended to the potential direct effect of Article 37(1) EA EC-Poland, enabling Pokrzeptowicz-Meyer to invoke it against her employer. Secondly, AG Jacobs assessed whether the contested German law was contrary to Article 37(1) EA EC-Poland, and amounted, similarly to *Spotti*, to prohibited indirect discrimination on grounds of nationality.

As far as the first issue is concerned, AG Jacobs firmly argued in favour of application of the doctrine of direct effect to the EA EC-Poland. Referring to the established case law on direct effect of international agreements,[31] AG Jacobs explored the wording of Article 37(1) EA EC-Poland, as well as the purpose and broader context of the Agreement itself. He noted that the Agreement created an association aimed at promotion of trade and political dialogue, leading to the facilitation of Poland's accession to the EU.[32] With this in mind, AG Jacobs argued that:

> the contention that Article 37(1) [of the EA EC-Poland] [was] incapable of having direct effect [was] also difficult to reconcile with the purpose and the context of the Agreement as a whole.[33]

AG Jacobs unequivocally demonstrated that the objectives of international agreements concluded by the EU with its neighbours matter, and determine their interpretation. This is particularly the case when one deals with an international agreement of a potential future Member State of the EU. However, in the case at hand, the devil was in the detail. As already mentioned, Article 37(1) EA EC-Poland prohibited discrimination 'subject to the conditions and modalities applicable in each Member State'. This, according to Land Nordrhein-Westfalen, precluded direct effect. While not dismissing this argument, AG Jacobs explained, step by step, why he could not agree with such interpretation, taking into account the wording of Article 37(2) EA EC-Poland, and the broader context of EA EC-Poland. This point was supported by the lack of a clause in the EA EC-Poland itself that would expressly deprive Article 37(1) of direct effect.[34]

Observations regarding direct effect of the provision opened the door to consideration of the principle of non-discrimination. This powerful pairing worked to the advantage of individuals, including Pokrzeptowicz-Meyer. AG Jacobs argued that provisions protecting against discrimination based on nationality played a vital role in agreements which did not aim at membership of third states in the EU. Therefore, it was even more significant to give effect

---

the Republic of Latvia, of the other part [1998] OJ L26/3; Europe Agreement establishing an association between the European Communities and their Member States, of the one part, and the Republic of Estonia, of the other part [1998] OJ L68/3; Europe Agreement establishing an association between the European Communities and their Member States, acting within the framework of the European Union, of the one part, and the Republic of Slovenia, of the other part [1999] OJ L51/3.

[30] K Inglis, 'The Europe Agreements Compared in the Light of Their Pre-Accession Reorientation' (2000) 37 *CMLRev* 1173.

[31] Case 12/86 *Demirel* ECLI:EU:C:1987:400, Case C-37/98 *Savas* ECLI:EU:C:2000:224.

[32] Para 40.

[33] Para 35.

[34] Para 36.

to such protection envisaged in international agreements paving the way to the EU.[35] The EA EC-Poland surely belonged to that category of agreements. Overall, the conclusions of AG Jacobs indicated that Article 37(1) EA EC-Poland produced direct effect, and as such the provision in question could be relied on in national courts of the Member States. Furthermore, it prohibited application of national [German] legislation stipulating those posts of foreign language assistants could be offered only on a fixed-term basis, while other teaching staff performing special duties could be offered such contracts only if individually justified by objective reasons. It amounted to indirect discrimination that could not be justified.[36]

Last but not least, AG Jacobs attended to the intertemporal matter raised by the referring court. A reminder is fitting that Mrs Pokrzeptowicz-Meyer had signed her fixed-term employment contract before the EA EC-Poland entered into force, but its termination was due when the EA EC-Poland was already in force. After a thorough analysis of existing case law on the application of new laws to future situations, AG Jacobs concluded that Article 37(1) EA EC-Poland was applicable to the case at hand.[37]

IV. ANALYSIS

At first sight, perhaps, the Opinion of AG Jacobs did not offer any new, ground-breaking, or daring views. However it was an important step forward, and of the highest quality. All these years later it serves as a reliable pillar supporting the application of the principle of direct effect to provisions of international agreements concluded by the EU with third states, and the protection against discrimination based on nationality laid down therein.

That said, the Opinion served as the beacon for navigation for the Court, which followed AG Jacobs in its judgment. The Opinion also emphasised that the objectives behind such international agreements matter and must be taken into account when it comes to their interpretation. Finally, the Opinion confirmed that regarding the prohibition of discrimination to work, a provision of EU law must produce direct effect. Without it, prohibition of discrimination may prove meaningless. From this perspective, both principles are interdependent to be able to serve an individual as one.

A. The Judgment

Pokrzeptowicz-Meyer falls into the category of cases where the Court generally agreed with its AG. While both were on the same page in principle, there are a few nuances that merit closer examination.

Just like AG Jacobs, the Court took as the point of departure the application of the doctrine of direct effect to Article 37(1) EA EC-Poland. Having recited the direct effect test,[38] the Court proceeded with its application to the provision in hand.[39] Following its AG, but without in-depth analysis of the matter at hand, the Court also dismissed the

---

[35] ibid.
[36] Para 52.
[37] Paras 54–67.
[38] Para 19.
[39] Paras 20–25.

argumentation pursued by the defending region of Germany that the caveat 'subject to the conditions and modalities applicable in each Member State' precluded direct effect. In the words of the Court:

> That proviso may not be interpreted in such a way as to allow the Member States to subject the principle of non-discrimination set forth in the first indent of Article 37(1) of the Europe Agreement to conditions or discretionary limitations. Such an interpretation would render that provision meaningless and deprive it of any practical effect.[40]

With this conclusion in place, the Court moved to the aims of the EA EC-Poland. It ruled:

> The purpose of the Europe Agreement, according to the 15th recital in its preamble and Article 1(2) thereof, is to establish an association designed to promote the expansion of trade and harmonious economic relations between the Parties, in order to foster dynamic economic development and prosperity in the Republic of Poland, with a view to facilitating its accession to the Community.[41]

While factually correct, the Court – unlike its AG – did not pay attention to detail. In the eyes of the European Community/the EU, the EA EC-Poland was not meant to serve as a vehicle for accession. The fifteenth recital in the Preamble was a one-sided declaration made by the Polish Government, and was not a bilateral commitment. Irrespective of that nuance, it is clear that the Court took the big picture into account when deciding whether Article 37(1) EA EC-Poland could produce direct effect. The Court's take on direct effect of provisions of international agreements confirmed a clear line of its jurisprudence recalling steppingstones such as *Głoszczuk* and *Sürül*.[42] It can be said that the Court eagerly confirmed the direct effect of Article 37(1) EA EC-Poland, and at the same time – just like AG Jacobs – dismissed the arguments of the defending region.

The first part of the judgment opened the door for consideration of substance of Article 37(1) and whether it precluded the German law at hand. It is interesting to note that in this respect, the judgment and the Opinion vary. For AG Jacobs, interpretation of Article 37(1) EA EC-Poland was of the essence. The Court focused more on exportability of *Spotti* and *Allué* to *Pokrzeptowicz-Meyer*. This aspect of the case was also in part of AG's assessment, however, it had slightly less prominence than in the judgment of the Court.[43]

On a matter of exportability of existing jurisprudence anchored in EU primary law, the main question was how to interpret provisions of EU international agreements with third states which are equally worded, or similar, to provisions of EU internal law. Arguably, the Court was mindful of the principle of *jurisprudence constante*, which it is governed by. Therefore, it started by restating the main parameters of the *Polydor* doctrine. It ruled:

> 32. According to settled case-law, a mere similarity in the wording of a provision of one of the Treaties establishing the Communities and of an international agreement between the Community and a non-member country is not sufficient to give to the wording of that agreement the same meaning as it has in the Treaties [...]

> 33. According to that case-law, the extension of the interpretation of a provision in the Treaty to a comparably, similarly or even identically worded provision of an agreement concluded by the Community with a non-member country depends on, *inter alia*, the aim pursued by each provision

---

[40] Para 24.
[41] Para 26.
[42] Case C-262/96 *Sürül* ECLI:EU:C:1999:228.
[43] Paras 49–52.

in its own particular context. A comparison between the objectives and context of the agreement and those of the Treaty is of considerable importance in that regard [...]

According to the *Polydor* doctrine, in its essence, provisions of international agreements which mirror the text of EU Treaties, do not warrant the same interpretation. In this case, however, the existing case law was exportable to Article 37(1) EA EC-Poland. The Court explained step-by-step why it was the case.[44] The Court noted that the main distinction between Article 37(1) EA EC-Poland and Article 45 TFEU was the general context. The latter provision laid down the principle of free movement of workers, while the former did not. Despite this distinction, the Court stressed that once workers of Polish nationality were lawfully employed within the territory of a Member State, Article 37(1) EA EC-Poland established their right to equal treatment similar to rights conferred by Article 45(2) TFEU. The Court then returned to the aims of the EA EC-Poland by pointing out that it sought to create appropriate framework for the progressive integration of Poland into the EU, and therefore permission of any form of direct or indirect discrimination affecting conditions of employment, would not sit comfortably with the objective of the EA.[45]

The Court used its findings in *Spotti* to confirm that the national [German] provisions placed the nationals of other states at a disadvantage, and as such constituted indirect discrimination, which was prohibited by Article 39(2) EC.[46] The Court pointed out that *Spotti* merely repeated the findings of *Allué*, in which the Court observed that the application of national provisions imposing a limit on the duration of the employment relationship between universities and foreign language assistants, if such limits were not applicable to contracts with other workers, were incompatible with Article 39(2) EC.[47] This is one of the most valuable parts of the judgment. Although Article 37(1) EA EC-Poland did not facilitate free movement of workers,[48] in the light of the views of AG Jacobs – as confirmed by the Court – the principle of non-discrimination not only applied to access *to* employment, but also to treatment *in* employment.

Thus, a clear message emerged: Polish nationals could not be offered worse terms and conditions of employment than EU citizens. The Court, just as AG Jacobs, noted that the specificity of the job of language assistants indicated that the majority of individuals employed in such capacity were nationals of states, and ruled to protect them against discrimination in the workplace by allowing the application of the interpretation of Article 39(2) EC *mutatis mutandis* to Article 37(1) EA EC-Poland.[49]

B. Direct Effect

Without a doubt, confirmation that EA EC-Poland could produce direct effect, and that it did so in relation to the prohibition of discrimination at the workplace, made *Pokrzeptowicz-Meyer* an important development, not only for the plaintiff, but also for other nationals of Central

---

[44] Paras 34–44.
[45] Para 42.
[46] Para 37.
[47] Para 36.
[48] Para 40.
[49] Para 44.

and Eastern European states with which the EU concluded Europe Agreements. As noted by AG Jacobs in his Opinion, all other EAs had provisions equally worded to Article 37(1) EA EC-Poland.[50] Seen through the prism of EU external relations, *Pokrzeptowicz-Meyer* was a pea in a pod and fitted perfectly into a well-established line of jurisprudence that many international agreements of the EU with neighbouring states, as well as legal acts adopted on their basis, can produce direct effect.[51]

The Opinion of AG Jacobs and the judgment of the Court in *Pokrzeptowicz-Meyer* reminded of the significance of the principle of direct effect. At that point in time, both confirmed the trend extensively supporting direct effect of provisions of international agreements. This progressing scope of application of the principle of direct effect clearly reflected the changing nature of EU law. Over the years, the system adapted to serve not only the internal organisation of the EU but, in equal terms, the developing forms of engagement with third states, where among them were the future Member States of the EU. As argued later in this chapter, the most recent developments, that see the persistent exclusion of direct effect of international agreements of the EU concluded with its neighbours, sit rather uncomfortably with this line of jurisprudence.

The approach to direct effect marked by *Pokrzeptowicz-Meyer* also confirmed the difference that the application of direct effect can make on lives of individuals. The Court eagerly continued with its empowerment of individuals, giving them this powerful tool to bring claims in national courts and tribunals. It appears that what was initiated by the seminal *Van Gend en Loos*[52] and *Costa v ENEL*[53] cases, has been – over time – meticulously developed by the Court to expand the catalogue of individuals eligible to seek justice using the sword of direct effect. With this in mind, *Pokrzeptowicz-Meyer* supports what is really at the core of the EU's existence – its legal system. It cannot be operational without measures supporting its effectiveness, and cases such as *Pokrzeptowicz-Meyer* in a direct manner secure that.

In constitutional terms, this course of interpretation provided by the Court falls rightfully within the foundations of the EU on the rule of law.[54] It is also a reminder that the rulings of the Court require cooperation and willingness of the national courts and tribunals of EU Member States to give effect to these developments. Once national courts and tribunals comply with their duties under EU law, only then can the rights of individuals be protected.

---

[50] Para 8, footnote 5 of the Opinion.

[51] See, inter alia, Joined Cases 21 to 24/72 *International Fruit* ECLI:EU:C:1972:115; Case 181/73 *Haegeman* ECLI:EU:C:1974:41; Case 104/81 *Kupferberg* ECLI:EU:C:1982:362; Case 192/89 *Sevince* ECLI:EU:C:1990:322. For an academic commentary see M Mendez, *The Legal Effects of EU Agreements: Maximalist Treaty Enforcement and Judicial Avoidance Techniques* (Oxford, OUP, 2013); N Zipperle, *EU International Agreements: An Analysis of Direct Effect and Judicial Review Pre-and Post-Lisbon* (Cham, Springer, 2017); J Klabbers, 'International Law in Community Law: The Law and Politics of Direct Effect' (2001) 21 *YEL* 263; F Martines, 'Direct Effect of International Agreements of the European Union' (2014) *EJIL* 129.

[52] Case 26/62 *Van Gend en Loos* ECLI:EU:C:1963:1. See further M Rasmussen, 'Law Meets History: Interpreting the Van Gend en Loos Judgment' in F Nicola and B Davis (eds), *EU Law Stories: Contextual and Critical Histories of European Jurisprudence* (Cambridge, CUP, 2017); W Phelan, *Great Judgments of the European Court of Justice: Rethinking the Landmark Decisions of the Foundational Period* (Cambridge, CUP, 2019) 31–57.

[53] Case 6/64 *Costa v ENEL* ECLI:EU:C:1964:66. See Phelan (n 52) 58–83.

[54] Opinion 1/91 of the Court of 14 December 1991. Opinion delivered pursuant to the second subparagraph of Article 228 (1) of the Treaty – Draft agreement between the Community, on the one hand, and the countries of the European Free Trade Association, on the other, relating to the creation of the European Economic Area ECLI:EU:C:1991:490, para 21.

C. Prohibition of Discrimination on Grounds of Nationality

Protection against discrimination constitutes one of the core elements of EU law. It falls within the general commitment to fundamental principles and values as guaranteed by the EU Treaties and interpreted by the Court. *Pokrzeptowicz-Meyer*, including the Opinion of AG Jacobs, provided another reminder of its key elements in pursuit of purposeful interpretation. Once again, the care for micro needs (as they may seem from the macro perspective) of individuals such as Mrs Pokrzeptowicz-Meyer was supported by the use of the broad interpretation of the principle in question. The examination of the aims and objectives of the EA EC-Poland enabled AG Jacobs, and in turn the Court, to confirm direct effect of Article 37(1) EA EC-Poland and protection against discrimination laid down therein. It was surely driven by the considerations falling under the umbrella of 'the spirit of the Treaties'.[55] This general commitment was also supported by the specific provisions of the Europe Agreement. As observed by AG Jacobs:

> The view that Article 37(1) is capable of directly governing the situation of individuals is, moreover, entirely consistent with the purpose and nature of the Agreement. As is apparent from the preamble and Article 1(2), that Agreement creates an association which, by providing a framework for political dialogue, aims to promote trade and harmonious economic relations between the parties as well as the prosperity of Poland in order to facilitate the accession of Poland to the European Union. It cannot be denied that that aim will be furthered if Polish migrant workers are afforded the possibility of relying directly on the equal treatment provisions laid down in the Agreement before the national courts in the Member States. Moreover, the Court of Justice has held that provisions laying down principles of equal treatment on grounds of nationality in agreements which, while establishing economic cooperation between the European Community and non-member countries, do not aim at the integration of those states into the Community, may have direct effect. The considerations which led the Court to take that view apply, perhaps even more strongly, in the context of agreements which aim to prepare States for membership of the Community.[56]

AG Jacobs relied heavily on the fact that the EA EC-Poland was reinvented into a vehicle for accession. Mindful of the big picture, he rightly noted that since international agreements which cannot lead to membership provide for directly effective prohibitions of discrimination, it would be rather illogical to rule otherwise in relation to Europe Agreements.[57] This plausible and rational take on direct effect is contemporarily being put to a test courtesy of practice of the European Commission and the Council of the EU. This is further explained in turn.

D. Effect on Future Case Law

Pokrzeptowicz-Meyer was, in a way, a period piece. This applies to both the Opinion of AG Jacobs and the judgment of the Court. As a consequence of accession to the EU

---

[55] Judgment in *Costa v ENEL*, p 593.

[56] Para 40.

[57] See FG Jacobs, 'Direct effect and interpretation of international agreements in the recent case law of the European Court of Justice' in A Dashwood and M Maresceau (eds), *Law and Practice of EU External Relations: Salient Features of a Changing Landscape* (Cambridge, CUP, 2008). By his successor, see E Sharpston, 'Different but (Almost) Equal – The Development of Free Movement Rights Under EU Association, Co-operation and Accession Agreements' in M Hoskins and W Robinson (eds), *A True European: Essays for Judge David Edward* (Oxford, Hart Publishing, 2003).

of 10 Central and Eastern European states, Europe Agreements of newly acceded states were terminated on 1 May 2004 and, in relation to Bulgaria and Romania, on 1 January 2007. This does not mean, however, that *Pokrzeptowicz-Meyer* did not influence future case law. Short term, it paved the way for the Opinion of AG Stix-Hackl[58] and the judgment of the Court in *Kolpak*.[59] The Court ruled that equally worded prohibition of discrimination laid down in Article 38(1) EA EC-Slovakia was also directly effective. In this particular case, unlike in *Pokrzeptowicz-Meyer*, it was a matter of horizontal direct effect. In a way then, *Kolpak* took the jurisprudence one step forward. However, it was the *Simutenkov*[60] case which demonstrated that the principles established by AG Jacobs and the Court in *Pokrzeptowicz-Meyer* survived the termination of Europe Agreements, and apply also to the Partnership and Cooperation Agreement (PCA) with Russia (and thus, at least potentially, to other agreements with third states).[61]

PCAs were concluded with several ex-Soviet Union countries for initial 10-year periods, and, unless replaced by new generation agreements, they have automatically renewed year by year. The PCAs were regarded to be entry-level agreements, and as such did not envisage membership in the EU. The term 'entry-level agreements' was introduced by Peers to describe PCAs as a way 'to assist with the integration of the ex-Soviet States into the world economy'.[62] Petrov added that '[they] do not envisage membership, but endorse the potential interest in developing further mutual cooperation between Parties'.[63] Their overall aim was to provide a basis for cooperation between parties. Their objectives included establishment of a framework for political dialogue; promotion of trade, investment, and economic relations; support for consolidation of democracy in transition to a market economy as well as completion of their transition into market economies; and enhancement of cultural, legislative economic, social, financial, civil, scientific and technological cooperation.

In *Simutenkov* the question emerged whether Article 23(1) of PCA EC-Russia could produce direct effect. It contained a prohibition of discrimination at the workplace drafted in such a way as to meet the requirements of the direct effect test. The Court ruled that indeed Mr Simutenkov could rely on the provision in question.[64] This was despite the fact that the PCA was not even an association agreement, however – in the words of the Court – it was 'designed to bring about the gradual integration between Russia and a wider area of cooperation in Europe'.[65] The Court explicitly relied on *Pokrzeptowicz-Meyer*, which proves the point made above that the latter judgment has had an impact going beyond the realm of Europe Agreements.[66]

Despite, or perhaps because of, well-settled case law on the direct effect of international agreements, later development demonstrates that the matter of direct effect of

---

[58] Opinion of AG Stix-Hackl in Case C-438/00 *Kolpak* ECLI:EU:C:2002:444.

[59] Case C-438/00 *Kolpak* ECLI:EU:C:2003:255.

[60] Case C-265/03 *Simutenkov* ECLI:EU:C:2005:213.

[61] Agreement on partnership and cooperation establishing a partnership between the European Communities and their Member States and the Russian Federation [1997] OJ L327/3.

[62] S Peers, 'From Cold War to lukewarm embrace: the European Union's agreements with the CIS' (1995) 44 *ICLQ* 845.

[63] R Petrov, 'Recent Developments in the Adaptation of Ukrainian Legislation to EU Law' (2003) 8 *EFARev* 127.

[64] Para 29.

[65] Para 35.

[66] See C Hillion, 'Case C-265/03, Igor Simutenkov v Ministerio de Educación y Cultura, Real Federación Española de Fùtbol, [2005] ECR I–2579' (2008) 45 *CMLRev* 815; A Łazowski, 'Direct Effect of the EU–Russia Partnership and Cooperation Agreement, Non-discrimination, and the Beautiful Game: Simutenkov' in G Butler and RA Wessel (eds), *EU External Relations Law: The Cases in Context* (Oxford, Hart Publishing, 2022).

international agreements is not settled for good. In its recent practice, the Commission and the Council have adopted a new paradigm by explicitly precluding direct effect of international agreements, either in decisions on their conclusion, or in the international agreements themselves.[67] While it could be justifiable in relation to agreements concluded with states which are geographically miles away from the EU, the application of this new paradigm to international agreements with its immediate neighbours goes against decades of the Court's jurisprudence. The consequences of such an approach are profound, as it puts nationals of some third states at a considerable disadvantage. For instance, the EU has – in the course of the past decade – upgraded its relations with Ukraine, Georgia, and Moldova. The aim was to replace respective PCAs[68] with much more robust Association Agreements (AAs).[69] Sadly, neither of the AAs is capable of being directly effective. Furthermore, in the EU-Georgia AA and the EU-Moldova AA, non-discrimination clauses are nowhere to be seen, even though the predecessor PCAs contained vaguely drafted (thus unlikely to produce direct effect) prohibitions of discrimination at the workplace. At the same time, the EU-Ukraine AA contains a non-discrimination clause, which at first sight looks clear, precise, and unconditional, thus meeting the direct effect test. Sadly, the general prohibition of direct effect, stemming from a Council Decision on the conclusion of the EU-Ukraine AA applies.[70] Even more surprising is the lack of a non-discrimination clause and general ban on direct effect laid down in Article 5(1) EU-UK TCA.[71]

All the above create a kaleidoscope effect. When it comes to the direct effect of neighbourhood agreements and prohibition of non-discrimination at the workplace of third country nationals, including many former EU citizens who hold a British passport, it is now a matter of playing with a toy consisting of a tube containing mirrors and pieces of coloured glass or paper, whose reflections produce changing patterns when the tube is rotated. Explained differently, the practice of EU decision-makers led to asymmetrical sets of rights which run against the well-established jurisprudence of the Court, where the Opinion of AG Jacobs in *Pokrzeptowicz-Meyer* and the subsequent judgment of the Court have a prominent place.

---

[67] A Semertzi, 'The preclusion of direct effect in the recently concluded EU free trade agreements' (2014) 51 *CMLRev* 1125; N Ghazaryan, 'Who Are the "Gatekeepers"?: In Continuation of the Debate on the Direct Applicability and the Direct Effect of EU International Agreements' (2018) 37 *YEL* 27.

[68] Partnership and Cooperation Agreement between the European Communities and their Member States, of the one part, and Ukraine, of the other part [1998] OJ L49/3; Partnership and Cooperation Agreement between the European Communities and their Member States, of the one part, and the Republic of Georgia, of the other part [1999] OJ L205/3; Partnership and Cooperation Agreement between the European Communities and their Member States, of the one part, and the Republic of Moldova, of the other part [1998] OJ L181/3.

[69] Association Agreement between the European Union and the European Atomic Energy Community and its Member States, of the one part, and Ukraine, of the other part [2014] OJ L161/3; Association Agreement between the European Union and the European Atomic Energy Community and their Member States, of the one part, and Georgia, of the other part [2014] OJ L261/4; Association Agreement between the European Union and the European Atomic Energy Community and their Member States, of the one part, and the Republic of Moldova, of the other part [2014] OJ L260/4.

[70] See Article 5 of Council Decision (EU) 2017/1247 of 11 July 2017 on the conclusion, on behalf of the European Union, of the Association Agreement between the European Union and the European Atomic Energy Community and their Member States, of the one part, and Ukraine, of the other part, with the exception of the provisions relating to the treatment of third-country nationals legally employed as workers in the territory of the other party [2017] OJ L181/1.

[71] Trade and Cooperation Agreement between the European Union and the European Atomic Energy Community, of the one part, and the United Kingdom of Great Britain and Northern Ireland, of the other part [2021] OJ L149/10. See further J Larik and RA Wessel, 'The EU-UK Trade and Cooperation Agreement: forging partnership or managing rivalry' in A Łazowski and A Cygan (eds), *Research Handbook on Legal Aspects of Brexit* (Cheltenham, Edward Elgar, 2022).

For the compatriots of AG Jacobs, who after Brexit decide to migrate to the EU, it sends a very clear signal: Achtung Baby, keep a watchful eye on what matters, your rights are not set in stone and may be easily taken away. It does leave one perplexed why citizens of a Member State would vote to deprive themselves of the protection from discrimination and the right to invoke relevant legal rules directly. A further warning comes for citizens of Central and Eastern European states. *Pokrzeptowicz-Meyer* was a taste of the levels of protection that soon became their everyday reality, which – in the light of recent events in Poland and Hungary – should not be taken for granted.

Part VI

Eleanor Sharpston: The Legal Order Pre-and Post-Lisbon (2006–2020)

37

When Security Trumped the Rule of Law: Opinion of Advocate General Sharpston in Heinrich

HELEN XANTHAKI AND ADAM ŁAZOWSKI

I. INTRODUCTION

O N 17 December 1903 a tiny and unconvincingly looking plane designed by the Wright brothers took off for its first, yet very short, flight in North Carolina.[1] Little did one know that this invention was a steppingstone for a Copernican style revolution of the ways we travel, ship cargo, or combat wars. Throughout the twentieth century air travel has gradually become a new normal. Without a doubt it was a catalyst for *travelitis furiosus*, a very contagious disease that many readers may be familiar with.[2] Its main symptom is an unstoppable urge to travel. Sadly, aircrafts have also served other, less peaceful, purposes. The events of 11 September 2001 have demonstrated repugnantly what happens when they fall into the wrong hands. Unfortunately, this was neither the first, nor the last time terrorists hijacked aircrafts to pursue their agenda.

Authorities around the globe for years now have worked on increasing the safety of air travel. Security checks at airports were introduced, including from the 1970s, x-ray screening of luggage. Following the events of 9/11 in New York and Washington, a new wave of measures followed. This included a series of EU regulations laying down the legal framework for the EU. However, in this justified pursuit of security the EU lawmakers opted, quite unjustifiably, to trump the rule of law. Put simply, they kept key parts of the legislation secret. In *Heinrich*, the Court was asked the fundamental question what was the status of such legislation. Not surprisingly, the case was assigned to the Grand Chamber of the Court. As it is traditionally the case when the Court sits in such composition, an Opinion of an Advocate General (AG) was required. AG Sharpston presented her Opinion on 10 April 2008,[3] and the judgment of the Court followed almost a year later, on 10 March 2009.[4]

---

[1] See, inter alia, RG Grant, *Flight: The Complete History of Aviation* (NY, Penguin Random House, 2017) 38–64.
[2] G Mikes, *How to be a Brit* (London, Penguin, 2015) 105.
[3] Opinion of AG Sharpston in Case C-345/06 *Heinrich* ECLI:EU:C:2008:212.
[4] Case C-345/06 *Heinrich* ECLI:EU:C:2009:140.

II. BACKGROUND, CONTEXT, AND FACTS

The facts of the case were quite straightforward, and easy to picture for those suffering from *travelitis furiosus*. On 25 September 2005, the plaintiff, Dr Gottfried Heinrich, was due to fly from Vienna Schwechat Airport. As part of the pre-flight routine his hand luggage was screened. At that stage, security personnel found tennis rackets in Heinrich's hand luggage and classified them as prohibited items. It is unclear what happened immediately afterwards. Whether a James Bond style chase took place, or Heinrich managed to leave the security point quietly and his disappearance was spotted with a bit of a delay, he somehow ended up boarding a plane with the tennis rackets still in his hand luggage. Eventually, the security staff forced him to disembark the plane. From the legal point of view, the situation was, at least prima facie, simple. Tennis rackets were listed in the legislation as dangerous items, therefore prohibited in hand luggage. A passenger refused to check-in the bag and, therefore, he was removed from the flight. The crux of the issue was, however, elsewhere. The list of prohibited items was neither available to Heinrich, nor to members of the public at large. It was included in the Annex to Commission Regulation 622/2003, which was not published in the Official Journal of the EU on the pretence of security.[5] In turn, Heinrich filed a case against Austria in a local court, which then submitted a request for a preliminary ruling. The Independent Administrative Chamber for the Land of Lower Austria wished to know if non-published legislation was covered by the notion 'documents' to which Regulation 1049/2001 on access to documents applied.[6] Furthermore, the referring court asked whether such legislation had binding force. Sadly, at this point, Dr Gottfried Heinrich turned into a part-time action hero. He did not submit written or oral pleadings at the Court.[7] This would have been tremendously helpful as it was unclear from the files of the case what kind of a claim he filed to the national court.

III. THE OPINION OF AG SHARPSTON

As a starting point, AG Sharpston provided a comprehensive overview of applicable rules.[8] It included not only the EU regulations at stake, but also the Treaty principles governing publication of EU legal acts, and the law drafting guidelines.[9] This led to the analysis of admissibility of the request for preliminary ruling. AG Sharpston did not proceed *ex officio*, but rather in reaction to submissions of several Member States, which argued that either the entire reference, or at least parts of it, should not be dealt with by the Court.[10] Application of the existing principles on admissibility[11] led AG Sharpston to the conclusion that the national court, despite some deficiencies in the reference, managed to prove that the questions bore the relation to the facts, and the answers were necessary to adjudicate in the domestic case. This conclusion

---

[5] Commission Regulation (EC) No 622/2003 of 4 April 2003 laying down measures for the implementation of the common basic standards on aviation security [2003] OJ L89/9.

[6] Regulation (EC) No 1049/2001 of the European Parliament and of the Council of 30 May 2001 regarding public access to European Parliament, Council and Commission documents [2001] OJ L145/43.

[7] Although, as noted by AG Sharpston, Dr Gottfried Heinrich was present at the hearing.

[8] Paras 2–28.

[9] European Parliament, Council, Commission, Interinstitutional agreement of 22 December 1998 on common guidelines for the quality of drafting of Community legislation [1999] OJ C73/1.

[10] For a summary see paras 36–38 of the Opinion and paras 25–29 of the Judgment.

[11] For an overview see M Broberg and N Fenger, *Broberg and Fenger on Preliminary References to the European Court of Justice*, 3rd edn (Oxford, OUP, 2021) 141–74.

paved the way for the assessment of the legal issues at stake. Bearing in mind the constitutional weight of the second question sent by the Austrian court, AG Sharpston opted to attend to it in the first place.

Not surprisingly Article 254(2) EC (now Article 297(2) TFEU), dealing with the publication regime for EU legal acts, was the point of departure. In its version applicable at the material time, it unequivocally provided that publication in the OJ of regulations adopted by the Commission was compulsory. Therefore, the crux of the issue was whether Regulation 622/2003 had been properly published in accordance with requirements laid down at the Treaty level. With annexes being integral parts of EU secondary legislation, the only conclusion that AG Sharpston could reach was that the failure to publish Regulation 622/2003 in full was in breach of Article 254(2) EC (now Article 297(2) TFEU).[12] According to AG Sharpston, the European Commission not only failed to provide adequate reasoning why the Annex was deemed unpublishable, but it also took a fundamentally absurd position. On the one hand, it relied on Article 8 of EP and Council Regulation 2320/2002 which required non-publication,[13] and, on the other hand, it published a press release with information about adopted measures.[14] Furthermore, the preamble to Commission Regulation 68/2004 (amending Regulation 622/2003) expressed the need to publish a harmonised list of prohibited items, while the annex remained secret. All of this, clearly, did not add up.[15]

Having concluded that Regulation 622/2003 had not been properly published, AG Sharpston turned to the resulting legal consequences. In this respect, she offered the Court a solution, supplemented by another, though less appealing options. As to the preferred outcome AG Sharpston argued:

> It seems to me that the irregularity that taints Regulation No 622/2003 (as amended) – persistent and deliberate disregard of the mandatory publication requirements in Article 254(2) EC in respect of the whole substance of the regulation – is one whose gravity is so obvious that it cannot be tolerated by the Community legal order. My preference is therefore to declare Regulation No 622/2003 (as amended) non-existent.[16]

This nuclear option was not only to the liking of the AG, but it had been also suggested by the Austrian court in its reference for preliminary ruling. However, bearing in mind how far reaching and consequential such a decision would be, AG Sharpston suggested that the Court could also consider invalidation of Regulation 622/2003.[17] She considered a breach of Article 254(2) EC to qualify as 'a violation of an essential procedural requirement, resulting, at the very least, in invalidity'.[18] Such invalidation would have immediate effect, with no temporal limitations to be introduced by the Court.[19]

AG Sharpston also anticipated a scenario whereby the Court would not follow her advice at all, and rule instead that Regulation 622/2003 was valid but unenforceable *vis-à-vis*

---

[12] Para 67 of the Opinion.

[13] Regulation (EC) No 2320/2002 of the European Parliament and of the Council of 16 December 2002 establishing common rules in the field of civil aviation security [2002] OJ L355/1.

[14] Commission, 'Air security: Commission draws up EU-wide list of prohibited articles on passenger aircraft' (16 January 2004) https://ec.europa.eu/commission/presscorner/detail/en/IP_04_59.

[15] Paras 65–66 of the Opinion. In para 112 AG Sharpston expressed, however, a bit of sympathy for the Commission's 'underlying predicament' and offered alternative, yet controversial solutions.

[16] Para 108.

[17] Paras 78–101.

[18] Para 91.

[19] Paras 92–101.

individuals. She put forward several arguments why the Court should resist the temptation to proceed in that direction. To begin with, the content of the Annex was not made available neither to the Austrian court, nor to the Court and its AG. She argued that it would be impossible for the Court to assess the exact scope of obligations imposed on individuals by the Annex.

The task at hand was not made easier by the fact that it was unclear from the reference on what legal basis the measures against Dr Gottfried Heinrich were taken. The fact there were no written or oral pleadings from the plaintiff did not assist either.[20] Thus, according to AG Sharpston, without having access to the Annex, the Court was not in a position to determine the exact nature of obligations stemming from Regulation 622/2003. She advised that the Court 'should restrict itself to holding in the abstract that the secret Annex cannot contain or be the source of *any* obligations for individuals'.[21] AG Sharpston also drew a line between the case at hand and an earlier judgment of the Court in *Skoma-Lux*.[22] The latter case also dealt with the status of non-published EU legal acts, however in a radically different factual context, making it not terribly relevant for *Heinrich*. In *Skoma-Lux*, there was a delay with publication of EU regulation in the language of a new Member State, which had just joined the EU.[23] Thus, the legal act itself was properly published in the Official Journal, however not in all official languages of the EU. The Court ruled that it was indeed unenforceable against individuals. By juxtaposing *Skoma-Lux* and *Heinrich*, one can easily spot the difference. In the former, the problem was caused by delays in translation, in the latter, the legal act at stake was intentionally kept secret.

Last but not least, AG Sharpston attended to the first question submitted by the referring court. She opined that such legal acts as Regulation 622/2003, which should be published in the Official Journal as per Article 254(2) EC, did not constitute documents that could be made accessible via Regulation 1049/2001 on access to documents. AG Sharpston argued that '[a]s a corollary, the Access to Documents Regulation cannot be used to restrict publication of a document falling within Article 254(1) or (2) EC'.[24] As aptly noted by Bobek:

> [...] there appears to be little point in requesting access via the Access to Documents Regulation for documents which should be publicly available in any case, due to their mandatory publication.[25]

This, however, was a rather secondary issue. The heart of the matter was, of course, the failure to publish the annex to Regulation 622/2003. As AG Sharpston concluded, it was done a fortiori and deliberately, and therefore it was 'unacceptable in the legal order of the European Union'.[26]

---

[20] As noted by AG Sharpston, three options were possible. The measures could have been taken on the basis of domestic law (Article 6 of Regulation 2320/2002 allowed the Member States to introduce stricter rules); or domestic powers derived potentially from the Annex, or directly on the basis of Regulation 622/2003. See para 73.

[21] Para 71.

[22] Case C-161/06 *Skoma-Lux* ECLI:EU:C:2007:773.

[23] See further, inter alia, M Bobek, 'The Binding Force of Babel: The Enforcement of EC Law Unpublished in the Languages of the New Member States' (2006–07) 9 *CYELS* 43; K Lasiński-Sulecki and W Morawski, 'Late publication of EC law in languages of new Member States and its effects: Obligations on individuals following the Court's judgment in Skoma–Lux' (2008) 45 *CMLRev* 705.

[24] Para 132.

[25] M Bobek, 'Case C-345/06. Gottfried Heinrich, Judgment of the Court of Justice (Grand Chamber) of 10 March 2019, not yet reported' (2009) 46 *CMLRev* 2077, 2081.

[26] Para 110.

IV. ANALYSIS

The Opinion of AG Sharpston made an impact even before the Court rendered its ruling. In anticipation of what was coming, the European Commission – after the delivery of the Opinion of AG Sharpston, but before the Court delivered its judgment – adopted Regulation 820/2008, which replaced Regulation 622/2003. The new legal act in its entirety was published in the Official Journal.[27] This included the annex with detailed requirements for security checks at airports. However, this is not where the importance of Opinion ends. *Au contraire*, it touched upon a number of fundamental legal issues, which merit further attention. Without a doubt, the respect for the rule of law, and all it entails, was the leitmotif throughout.

A. The Judgment

The judgment of the Court in *Heinrich* is a rather disappointing affair. It was shallow and underwhelming when juxtaposed with the rich and nuanced Opinion of AG Sharpston. In the operational part, the Court dedicated only 28 paragraphs to the matter at hand.[28] As argued by one of the present authors in an earlier publication, in cases where reasoning of the Grand Chamber of the Court is not terribly comprehensive, Opinions of Advocates General have the touch of substitution.[29] The Opinion of AG Sharpston in the case at hand belongs to this category. Furthermore, *Heinrich* was also one of those judgments where the Court decided not to follow its AG.

Not surprisingly, the starting point for the Court was the principle of legal certainty and the rules governing publication of EU secondary legislation. The Court, rightly, argued that '[i]ndividuals must be able to ascertain unequivocally what their rights and obligations are and take steps accordingly'.[30] Having confirmed that failure to publish the Annex to Regulation 622/2003 in the OJ, the Court turned to the consequences of non-publication. This is where the Court opted to go down the route AG Sharpston specifically advised it not to. The Court held that Regulation 622/2003 was valid, but not enforceable *vis-à-vis* individuals. Thus, despite the different factual contexts discussed earlier, the Grand Chamber followed its earlier ruling in *Skoma-Lux*.[31] The AG Sharpston's second best option of declaring the regulation in question invalid was dismissed.[32] Furthermore, it implicitly rejected the non-existent legal acts doctrine, which AG Sharpston recommended for application in *Heinrich*. If it could not be invoked in a case on a non-published regulation, then it is hard to imagine under what circumstances it would apply at all.[33]

One could argue that the Court opted for a less legally sound but – in abstract terms – a more pragmatic option. If it were not for adoption and publication of Regulation 820/2008,

---

[27] Commission Regulation (EC) No 820/2008 of 8 August 2008 laying down measures for the implementation of the common basic standards on aviation security [2008] OJ L221/8.

[28] Paras 41–69. The initial 15 paragraphs were dedicated to admissibility of the reference (see paras 25–40 of the Judgment).

[29] A Łazowski, 'Advocates General and Grand Chamber Cases: Assistance with the Touch of Substitution' (2011–12) 14 *CYELS* 635.

[30] Para 44.

[31] Para 43.

[32] Para 65.

[33] As noted by AG Sharpston in para 106 of the Opinion, the Court only on one occasion declared a legal act to be non-existent. See Joined Cases 1/57 and 14/57 *Société des usines à tubes de la Sarre* ECLI:EU:C:1957:13.

the Commission would have had to remedy the situation merely by publishing the Annex to Regulation 622/2003. To follow AG Sharpston's recommendation would have had far more reaching legal consequences as the Commission would have had to adopt the legislation again, and have it published in compliance with Article 254(2) EC. This, however, was a mute argument, as by the time of the Judgment, Regulation 820/2008 was published lock, stock, and barrel in the OJ. Thus reasons of pragmatism should have not stopped the Court from following AG Sharpston.

It should be added that the Court opted not to provide an answer to the first question submitted by the referring court. According to the Court, the answer to the second question made interpretation of Regulation 1049/2001 redundant.[34] While the practice of not answering all questions submitted by national courts is generally agreeable *modus operandi*, it is surprising in this instance. Written and oral pleadings submitted by several governments of the Member States demonstrated varied opinions on the role of access to documents legislation. This very fact persuaded AG Sharpston to delve into Regulation 1049/2001 in her Opinion.[35]

B. The European Union as a Polity Based on the Rule of Law: A Tale of Unknowns and Enforcement Asymmetry

Beginning with the big picture, there is no doubt that the EU is based on the rule of law. Respect for it lies at the core of the EU's polity, as clearly and expressly stated in Article 2 TEU.[36] This has been confirmed many a time by the Court in its jurisprudence.[37] However, when one takes a closer look, the picture becomes a bit blurry. First, the question is what exactly does the rule of law entail? Secondly, how do its principles apply to the EU itself and, above all, to its Member States? The EU model for the rule of law, when seen through the prism of enforcement *modi operandi*, gives a picture of considerable asymmetry, perhaps even bordering on different treatment of the EU and the Member States. While the parameters of this chapter do not permit for an in-depth exegesis of these issues, it is still rather fitting to make a number of general points before we return to Dr Gottfried Heinrich, his tennis rackets, the non-published Regulation, and the take on all of this by AG Sharpston and the Court.

A point of departure is a rather basic fact: EU law does not provide us with a definition of the rule of law.[38] This, in turn, triggers the following question which merits consideration:

---

[34] Para 70.

[35] Para 121.

[36] See, for instance, M Klamert and D Kochenov, 'Article 2' in M Kellerbauer, M Klamert and J Tomkin (eds), *The EU Treaties and the Charter of Fundamental Rights: A Commentary* (Oxford, OUP, 2019); W Schroeder, 'The Rule of Law As a Value in the Sense of Article 2 TEU: What Does It Mean and Imply?' in A von Bogdandy, P Bogdanowicz, I Canor, C Grabenwarter, M Taborowski and M Schmidt (eds), *Defending Checks and Balances in EU Member States: Taking Stock of Europe's Actions* (NY, Springer, 2021); L Pech, 'The Rule of Law' in P Craig and G de Búrca (eds), *The Evolution of EU Law*, 3rd edn (Oxford, OUP, 2021); W Schroeder (ed), *Strengthening the Rule of Law in Europe: From a Common Concept to Mechanisms of Implementation* (Oxford, Hart Publishing, 2016); C Closa and D Kochenov (eds), *Reinforcing Rule of Law Oversight in the European Union* (Cambridge, CUP, 2016).

[37] See Case 294/83 *Les Verts* ECLI:EU:C:1986:166. In the recent jurisprudence see Case C-64/16 *Association of Portuguese Judges* ECLI:EU:C:2018:117, para 30; Case C-216/18 *LM* ECLI:EU:C:2018:586, para 49. See further A von Bogdandy and LD Spieker, 'Protecting Fundamental Rights Beyond the Charter: Repositioning the Reverse Solange Doctrine in Light of the CJEU's Article 2 TEU Case-Law' in M Bobek and J Adams-Prassl (eds), *The EU Charter of Fundamental Rights in the Member States* (Oxford, Hart Publishing, 2020).

[38] In this respect, EU law is not unique by any stretch of imagination. Similar debates have been going on for years in the national legal contexts. See, for instance in relation to the UK, T Bingham, *The Rule of Law* (London, Penguin, 2010).

with the lack of an express definition of the rule of law in EU law, what exactly is it that the EU should be embracing and implementing? The issue, however, is not only what the rule of law entails but also to what extent the EU can intervene *qua* its legislation. As it is well known and documented in the literature, the EU operates under the principle of conferral. In a nutshell, it can only legislate, when permitted to do so.[39] The end result is not only the lack of definition of the rule of law, but also a system that is very patchy. Some matters, which are accepted to fall under the rule of law umbrella, are given general standing only in provisions of EU primary law, including the Charter of Fundamental Rights, and they are currently subject to deep, although incremental, exploration by the Court.[40] Furthermore, some rule of law matters have been given a proper framework in secondary legislation,[41] others not, either due to the lack of political will or the lack of legal basis in EU Treaties.[42]

As for the definition of the rule of law, an attempt was made by the Commission in its Communication of 2014 titled 'A new EU Framework to strengthen the Rule of Law'.[43] This has proven to be not an original concept, but rather an exercise in mimicking the Council of Europe's work, including the jurisprudence of the European Court of Human Rights (ECtHR). The Commission also built on six main principles already established in the jurisprudence of CJEU. The list of rule of law requirements includes legality,[44] legal certainty,[45] prohibition of arbitrariness of executive powers,[46] independent and effective judicial review, including respect for fundamental rights,[47] separation of powers,[48] and equality before the law.[49] Since the

---

[39] See T Tridimas, 'Competence after Lisbon. The elusive search for bright lines' in D Ashiagbor, N Countouris and I Lianos (eds), *The European Union after the Treaty of Lisbon* (Cambridge, CUP, 2012); P Craig, *The Lisbon Treaty: Law, Politics, and Treaty Reform* (Oxford, OUP, 2010) 155–92; M Claes and B de Witte, 'Competences: Codification and Contestation' in A Łazowski and S Blockmans (eds), *Research Handbook on EU Institutional Law* (Cheltenham, Edward Elgar, 2016).

[40] See, for instance, Case C-896/19 *Repubblika* ECLI:EU:C:2021:311.

[41] See the package of defence rights directives including Directive 2010/64/EU of the European Parliament and of the Council of 20 October 2010 on the right to interpretation and translation in criminal proceedings [2010] OJ L280/1; Directive 2012/13/EU of the European Parliament and of the Council of 22 May 2012 on the right to information in criminal proceedings [2012] OJ L 142/1; Directive 2013/48/EU of the European Parliament and of the Council of 22 October 2013 on the right of access to a lawyer in criminal proceedings and in European arrest warrant proceedings, and on the right to have a third party informed upon deprivation of liberty and to communicate with third persons and with consular authorities while deprived of liberty [2013] OJ L294/1; Directive (EU) 2016/343 of the European Parliament and of the Council of 9 March 2016 on the strengthening of certain aspects of the presumption of innocence and of the right to be present at the trial in criminal proceedings [2016] OJ L65/1.

[42] For instance, the EU has no competence to adopt binding legislation determining the basic parameters of independent judiciary. However, there is room for manoeuvre for the Court to do so in its jurisprudence based on Article 19 TEU and Article 47 of the Charter of Fundamental Rights. See Joined Cases C-585/18, C-624/18 and C-625/18 *A.K* ECLI:EU:C:2019:982; Case C-824/18 *A.B.* ECLI:EU:C:2021:153; Case C-619/98 *Commission v Poland* ECLI:EU:C:2019:531.

[43] Commission, 'A new EU Framework to strengthen the Rule of Law' COM (2014) 158 final, 1.

[44] Case C-496/99 P *Commission v CAS* ECLI:EU:C:2004:236, para 63.

[45] Joined Cases 212 to 217/80 *Vincenzo* ECLI:EU:C:1981:270, para 10.

[46] Joined Cases 46/87 and 227/88 *Hoechst* ECLI:EU:C:1989:337, para 19. See also see K Lenaerts, 'Upholding the Rule of Law within the EU' (Reconnect conference, Reconciling Europe with its Citizens through Democracy and Rule of Law, July 2019).

[47] Case C-583/11 P *Kanatami* ECLI:EU:C:2013:625, para 91; Case C-550/09 *Criminal proceedings against E and F* ECLI:EU:C:2010:382, para 44; Case C-50/00 P *Unión de Pequeños Agricultores* ECLI:EU:C:2002:462, paras 38–39; Case 26/62 *Van Gend en Loos* ECLI:EU:C:1963:1; Case 222/84 *Johnston* ECLI:EU:C:1986:206; Case 33/76 *Rewe-Zentralfinanz eG* ECLI:EU:C:1976:188, para 5; Case 45/76 *Comet* ECLI:EU:C:1976:191, para 16.

[48] Joined Cases C-174/98 P and C-189/98 P *Gerard van der Wal* ECLI:EU:C:2000:1, para 17. See also Case C-279/09 *DEB* ECLI:EU:C:2010:811, para 58.

[49] Case C-550/07 P *Akzo Nobel* ECLI:EU:C:2010:512, para 54; and Venice Commission, 'Report on the Rule of Law of 4 April 2011 Study No. 512/2009' (CDL-AD(20100)003rev), para 41.

Commission itself hinged the EU rule of law concept on the work of the Council of Europe, it is fitting to have a brief account of the Venice Commission's work on the matter in question. Its Report goes a bit further in exploring the content of the principle of the rule of law, as comprising accessibility of the law (that it be intelligible, clear, and predictable); questions of legal right should be normally decided by law and not discretion; equality before the law should be guaranteed; power must be exercised lawfully, fairly, and reasonably; human rights must be protected; means must be provided to resolve disputes without undue cost or delay; trials must be fair; and compliance with international and national obligations.[50]

As already alluded to, EU law, as interpreted and advanced by the Court, introduces the concept of the rule of law across the board.[51] The Court has long established the synergies between EU law and the Council of Europe in this field. Also, the Commission, in its 2014 Rule of Law Framework (borrowing from the Venice Commission's 2011 'Report on the Rule of Law'), declared the rule of law to be 'a fundamental and common European standard to guide and constrain the exercise of democratic powers'.[52] A conclusion to be drawn from this is that the rule of law standards are imposed on all actors – not only the Member States but also the EU as an organisation and its institutions. Sadly, the rule of law desiderata may not necessarily translate into the reality on the ground. As evidenced in course of the past decade, some teenage Member States have a loose relationship with the rule of law principles. Furthermore, the *Kadi* saga[53] or most recent *l'affaire* Sharpston[54] demonstrate that the European Union is not a saint either. *Heinrich*, which is at the heart of this chapter, was a good example, too.

This leads to the next point, that is the *modi operandi* available, should rule of law deficiencies occur. As already mentioned, this is precisely where asymmetry between the rules applicable to the Member States and to the EU, including its institutions, materialises. Both are presented in turn.

At the EU law level there are three main procedural vehicles that come into play in case of deficiencies of the application of the rule of law by the Member States, namely Article 7 TEU, the infringement procedures (Articles 258–260 TFEU), and the preliminary ruling procedure (Article 267 TFEU). Article 7 TEU introduces – respectively – a monitoring and an enforcement against Member States when their actions translate into a 'clear risk of a serious breach' or a 'serious and persistent breach' of the Union's founding values laid out in Article 2 TEU, inclusive – of course – of the rule of law. So, there is a political sanction in the case of risk, and a legal sanction in the case of an actual breach, albeit both are heavily drenched in big politics with key decisions belonging to the Council or the European Council. It is quite noteworthy that the initiators of the process can be one of the main EU institutions: the Commission, the European Parliament, and the Council. Sadly, Article 7 TEU – having been thus far invoked in two instances – has proven to be not fit for purpose.[55] The combination of politics with the unanimity requirement has properly de-activated the procedure in question. Not surprisingly, in relation to rule of law breaches allegedly attributable to authorities in Poland and

---

[50] ibid, para 37.

[51] Judgment in *Les Verts*, para 15.

[52] Judgment in *Les Verts*, para 16.

[53] For a comprehensive assessment see, inter alia, M Avbelj, F Fontanelli and G Martinico (eds), *Kadi on Trial: A Multifaceted Analysis of the Kadi Trial* (Abingdon, Routledge, 2014).

[54] See further D Kochenov and G Butler, 'Independence of the Court of Justice of the European Union: Unchecked Member States power after the Sharpston Affair' (2021) *ELJ* 262.

[55] See further D Kochenov, 'Article 7: A Commentary on a Much Talked-About 'Dead' Provision' in A von Bogdandy, P Bogdanowicz, I Canor, C Grabenwarter, M Taborowski and M Schmidt (eds), *Defending Checks and Balances in EU Member States: Taking Stock of Europe's Actions* (NY, Springer, 2021).

Hungary, the centre of gravity has moved in the last few years to Articles 258–60 TFEU. With several judgments in place the question remains how effective these tools can be. In the cases concerning Hungary and Poland, the judgments have not done the trick. Furthermore, so far, the Court has not been given an opportunity to use in rule of law cases its most powerful tool – financial penalties – which can be imposed under Article 260 TFEU. Finally, the national courts may submit requests for preliminary ruling touching upon the rule of law matters. In this respect, three main challenges may emerge, though. First, the litigation must first reach national courts where the doctrines of direct, indirect effect, and state liability are being invoked under the conditions laid down in case law of the Court.[56] Secondly, references may not deal solely with the rule of law matters, but they must be inextricably linked to matters covered by EU law.[57] Thirdly, with no financial penalties available to the Court, the Member States may be inclined to ignore the rulings coming from it.

As part of testing the water, there are a number of initiatives that have yet to bear fruit, such as the Rule of Law Framework, introduced by the Commission, or the new regime for requiring the respect for the rule of law as a criterion for the granting of EU funds.[58] Even if these instruments do bear fruit in the future, the same narrative is reflected in their conception, namely the rule of law is to be applied by Member States and monitored by EU institutions. This takes us to the next fundamental question: what about the EU, its institutions, and respect for the rule of law? What are the mechanisms available to the Member States or, for that matter, to individuals when the EU and its institutions do not respect the rule of law? They are – arguably – weaker and sparser, with only one common denominator: the preliminary ruling procedure, in particular references on validity of secondary legislation.[59] The others are bespoke for challenging the EU's actions, with the leading two including action for annulment (Article 263 TFEU) and action for damages (Article 340 TFEU). They are supplemented by a non-judicial remedy: complaints to the Ombudsman (Article 20(2) TFEU). But is this a complete system of remedies, as the Court tends to claim, that guarantees respect for the rule of law?[60]

To start with, the action for annulment is primarily available to the Member States and three key EU institutions, which – without the need to prove legal interest – may challenge any reviewable act. This may include a piece of EU secondary legislation adopted in breach of rule of law principles. The situation becomes much trickier when it comes to individuals. Unless a natural or legal person is the addressee of a legal act, the *locus standi* requirements – as interpreted by the Court – are an uphill struggle, frequently blocking access to justice.[61] Even if the action is admissible, its effect – at best – is annulment of an EU act, which is shy of any compensation for actual losses. While the action for damages is available, the amounts ordered by the Court are – sadly – symbolic. As *Gascogne* litigation proves, the Court may apply the right to effective remedy, so the right at the core of the rule of law,[62] to itself, yet

---

[56] See B de Witte, 'Direct Effect, Primacy and the Nature of the Legal Order' in Craig and de Búrca (n 36).

[57] For a rule of law reference that was not admissible see, inter alia, Joined Cases C-558/18 and C-563/18 *Miasto Łowicz* ECLI:EU:C:2020:234.

[58] Regulation (EU, Euratom) 2020/2092 of the European Parliament and of the Council of 16 December 2020 on a general regime of conditionality for the protection of the Union budget [2020] OJ L433I/1.

[59] See, for instance, Joined Cases C-293/12 and C-594/12 *Digital Rights* ECLI:EU:C:2014:238.

[60] See, for instance, Case C-583/11 P *Kanatami* ECLI:EU:C:2013:625, para 92.

[61] See P Craig and G de Búrca, *EU Law: Text, Cases, and Materials (UK Version)*, 7th edn (Oxford, OUP, 2020) 566–83. See ch 33.

[62] Case C-40/12 P *Gascogne* ECLI:EU:C:2013:768.

the damages for breach of Article 47 of the Charter may be symbolic.[63] Its soft approach to respect for rule of law in *Heinrich*, or the stance in the aforementioned *l'affair* Sharpston, also raise doubts. Arguably, it is time that the EU redresses this discriminatory procedural imbalance between the rule of law standards applicable to the Member States and to the EU, and its institutions. The EU should in all cases embrace the rule of law principle as a fundamental guiding light for its decision making and practices not only figuratively but also in action.

C. Security v Rule of Law: Uneasy Bedfellows?

The *tour d'horizon* presented in the previous section takes us back to Dr Gottfried Heinrich. Luck was on his side. The Austrian court decided to proceed with the reference for preliminary ruling and, potentially, the plaintiff was entitled to the remedy he sought.[64] It is highly debatable if he would have stood a chance of submitting a successful action for annulment or action in damages to the General Court. Thus, the preliminary ruling was the only option, though dependent on the will of the Austrian court.

As noted earlier, the meta question raised by *Heinrich* was how the prerequisites for a polity based on the rule of law, that is legal certainty, lack of arbitrariness, and accessibility could possibly be achieved when the regulators allowed themselves to refrain from publication of the legal act and, as in *Heinrich*, they did so intentionally and in flagrant breach of obligations laid down in Article 254(2) EC? It is impossible to perceive a concrete, full, and correct picture of the state of EU legislation, when some of it is not published.[65] In equal measure it is impossible to exclude arbitrariness (and possibly discrimination) when the applicable rules are not fully known to those to whom they apply, and indeed to those who are constitutionally tasked to monitor the accountability of the ones who exercise them. It is also impossible to conceive of accessibility of EU legislation when parts of it are not published. In view of this, how to establish respect for the rule of law when parts of EU legal acts remain secret?

Let us explore this further. The EU has served as a leader in the field of regulation. Better regulation requires an understanding of the use of legislation as the least desirable tool for the pursuit of regulatory aims. The EU is a traditional goal regulator, using its regulatory tools to set policy goals and to force Member States (in case of legislative acts, with their active participation in the decision-making process) to work with the EU institutions for the achievement of those regulatory goals. But what does regulation via legislation entail?

The EU legislates as a means of expressing to the addressees of the legal text what is the aim of the policy, what are the new obligations imposed by the legal text or what are the

---

[63] See Case T-577/14 *Gascogne* ECLI:EU:T:2017:1, quashed in the appeal in Joined Cases C-138/17 P and C-146/17 P *Gascogne* ECLI:EU:C:2018:1013.

[64] As already noted, it was unclear to AG Sharpston and to the Court what was the exact the nature of remedy the plaintiff asked for.

[65] In accordance with Article 297(2) TFEU:

'Regulations and directives which are addressed to all Member States, as well as decisions which do not specify to whom they are addressed, shall be published in the Official Journal of the European Union. They shall enter into force on the date specified in them or, in the absence thereof, on the twentieth day following that of their publication.

Other directives, and decisions which specify to whom they are addressed, shall be notified to those to whom they are addressed and shall take effect upon such notification.'

new rights to be enjoyed by means of the legal text. In other words, legislation is a means of communication with the addressees of legislation, a tool for instigating a change in behaviour that can bring about the desired regulatory results. So, if the goal of an EU directive is to ensure that EU citizens are not disadvantaged by a possible lack of understanding of the language of a Member State where they form part of a criminal process, then a directive communicates to its addressees that they now have the right to translation of all (or at least essential) documents in the language that they understand and speak, as well as interpretation of the oral part of proceedings.[66] This communication cannot take place where part of the legal act is secret. And so even partial secrecy of legal acts attacks their very role as regulatory tools. In that sense, it follows that secretive information cannot possibly be included in binding legal acts. It can be accommodated in non-binding communications, perhaps in internal documents, or in agreements. But not in binding legislation per se.

Thus, the alleged dilemma between security and the rule of law is rather false. The rule of law requires that all legislation is out in the open. It does so because it aims to promote accessibility, accountability, and legal certainty. It does so knowing that legislation is a channel of communication between regulator/legislator and the users/addressees of legislation, and in that sense there really is no space and scope for secrets. This explains why Article 297(2) TFEU and Regulation 1/58[67] require not only publication of various types of EU legal acts, but also provide that it has to be done in all official languages of the European Union. This takes place in a freely accessible OJ. The truth of the matter is that over the years, thanks to changes to Article 254(2) TFEU, but also to technical advances, EU law has become more available to members of the public than ever before. The unfortunate case of Commission Regulation 622/2003 was perhaps a blip, yet the Court failed to use this opportunity to follow AG Sharpston and take a firm and rule of law-based stance on the status of non-published legal acts. Instead, the Court offered a half-baked solution which did not reflect the importance of rule of law abuse that resulted from the decision to keep some parts of the directly applicable Regulation 622/2003 secret.

D. Long-term Implications

Heinrich has far reaching consequences for the future of the EU as an organisation, and as an ideal. By rejecting AG Sharpston's recommendations, the Court inadvertently placed sustainable integration in grave danger.[68] Legislation that is truly accessible (and this includes, but is not limited to, fully published legislation) can serve as the channel used by the EU to share its long-term regulatory vision, to explain the link between that vision and the legal acts, and to incite EU citizens to change their behaviour, and to comply with EU legislation. This inevitably enhances the implementation of EU law. But, much more importantly, it carries the capacity

---

[66] Directive 2010/64 on the right to translation and interpretation (n 41).

[67] Regulation of the EEC Council No 1 determining the languages to be used by the European Economic Community [1958] OJ 17/385; Regulation No 1 determining the languages to be used by the European Atomic Energy Community [1958] OJ 17/401.

[68] See K Nicolaïdis, 'EU 2.0? Towards Sustainable Integration" (*Open Democracy*, 12 July 2010) www. opendemocracy.net/en/can-europe-make-it/project-europe-2030-towards-sustainable-integration/; see also K Nicolaïdis, 'Sustainable Integration: Towards EU 2.0? – The JCMS Annual Review Lecture' (2010) 48 *Journal of Common Market Studies (Annual Review)* 21; K Nicolaïdis, 'Project Europe 2030: Reflection and Revival' (*Open Democracy*, 11 May 2010) www.opendemocracy.net/en/project-europe-2030-reflection-and-revival-part-one/.

to (re-)establish a direct relationship between EU citizens and the EU, and render them participants to EU legislation, and ultimately co-owners of the EU's long-term vision.[69]

The EU's measure of future success can only really be whether it survives the constant change of international and national environments within which it is placed, and whether it sustains its political, social, and economic following.[70] Conveying the regulatory rationale in EU legislative texts can render EU citizens participants (rather than suffering pawns) to the regulatory process. It can create collective ownership of the regulatory aims. If these aims continue to be acceptable and shared between the EU and its membership, they can enhance loyalty to the EU as an ideal and as a union.[71] And if the regulatory aims continue to be achieved, they can also enhance trust in the EU as an organisation capable of delivering the common aims to which EU citizens and EU Member States are now loyal.[72]

E. Conclusions

For a case that dealt, albeit partially, with the narrow point of non-publication due to security, *Heinrich* was a rather lost opportunity for the Court to contribute to the establishment of trust and loyalty to the organisation and, above all, it was a failure to take a firm stance on the respect for the rule of law. With the legislation published in its entirety after the Opinion of AG Sharpston but before the Court rendered the judgment, the CJEU would not lose much by declaring Commission Regulation 622/2003 non-existent. As argued earlier, the Court took a short cut and built its reasoning on *Skoma-Lux*, which was delivered against quite a different factual background.

At a time when authority is questioned worldwide, *Heinrich* could have served as a beacon of regulatory genius by placing EU citizens at the heart of regulatory and legislative initiatives. Alas, the decision of the Court was rather short sighted. One can debate whether it is the role of the Court to reaffirm the central role of the rule of law in the EU legal order. Indeed, there are strong arguments on both sides of the equation. But what cannot be questioned is the brilliant opportunity offered to the Court by AG Sharpston in *Heinrich*. Her Opinion was an invitation to move the cause of the rule of law further within the EU, its institutions, and to take a firm stance. One wonders whether it really is the British legal psyche that moves to push boundaries further. And who will take on that role now that the UK is, at least for now, no longer a Member State. In closing, one has to agree with Bobek (at the time of writing, a future AG), who argued that 'it might be, at the end of the day, an Advocate General who will in fact ensure that in the interpretation and application of the Treaty the law is observed'.[73]

---

[69] See J Black, 'Constructing and Contesting Legitimacy and Accountability in Polycentric Regulatory Regimes' (2008) 2 *Regulation & Governance* 137; see also K Murphy, TR Tyler and A Curtis, 'Nurturing regulatory compliance: Is procedural justice effective when people question the legitimacy of the law?' (2009) 3 *Regulation & Governance* 1.

[70] See Nicolaïdis (n 68).

[71] For an expert analysis on the link between trust, trustworthiness, and legislation (at RIA), see CM Radaelli and G Taffoni, 'The Trustworthiness Test for Regulatory Impact Assessment and Judicial Review' in M De Benedetto, N Lupo and N Rangone (eds), *The Crisis of Confidence in Legislation* (Oxford/Baden-Baden, Hart Publishing/Nomos, 2021).

[72] See YN Harari, *Sapiens: A Brief History of Humankind* (London, Harvill Secker, 2014).

[73] Bobek (n 25) 2094.

38

The Inconvenience of Names: Opinion of Advocate General Sharpston *in* Grunkin and Paul

I. INTRODUCTION

I T WOULD BE too predictable to begin this chapter on AG Sharpston's Opinion in *Grunkin and Paul* with the famous Shakespearean quote, 'What's in a name?',[1] though it is the obvious question to ask in such a context. Indeed, what is *in* the name in this case is pertinent – the referred question to the Court concerned whether a registered compound surname, made up of the child's maternal and paternal surnames, should be recognised uniformly across different EU Member States. This was despite the differing domestic naming conventions and the EU's principles of non-discrimination on nationality and equal treatment, protected by virtue of Union citizenship status.[2] Naming conventions fall under private international law, which AG Sharpston helpfully demystified as 'a branch of the domestic law of each legal system' and provides for a mechanism of determining 'what courts or other authorities should have jurisdiction, what substantive law should apply and what effects or recognition should be given to decisions taken'.[3] The Court has often had to grapple with questions of competence, and this is no exception in the context of rights under Union citizenship status.

The Opinion (and subsequent judgment) in *Grunkin and Paul* followed from only two earlier cases on names – *Konstantinidis* and *Garcia Avello*[4] – and became the third important decision in what is now a portfolio of cases on names and their recognition in light of EU citizenship rights. What is important in terms of the Opinion of AG Sharpston, however, is that whilst she pleaded for a more uniform approach to cases on names in anticipation of further similar questions arising before the Court, the Court nonetheless stuck to strictly deciding the case on its very specific facts in the Judgment. Therefore, as a whole, the judgment in *Grunkin and Paul* does contribute to the development of a judicial narrative in judgments on names. However, it was not before the Court delivered clarification on certain nuances in such

---

[1] W Shakespeare, *Romeo and Juliet* (London, Penguin, 2015).
[2] Treaty of Functioning of the European Union (TFEU) [2016] OJ C202/47, Articles 18 and 20 TFEU.
[3] Opinion of AG Sharpston in Case C-353/06 *Grunkin and Paul* ECLI:EU:C:2008:246, para 37.
[4] Case C-168/91 *Konstantinidis* ECLI:EU:C:1993:115; Case C-148/02 *Garcia Avello* ECLI:EU:C:2003:539. The Opinions in both cases were delivered by AG Jacobs. See ch 25.

questions, distinguishing the situation in particular from *Garcia Avello*. The lasting impression of AG Sharpston's Opinion in this area is of her mutual recognition approach to cases on names as a solution to the conflict of laws issue, which became more important in later cases.

II. BACKGROUND, CONTEXT, AND FACTS

The case concerned a child born in Denmark in 1998, Leonhard Matthias, to German parents, Stefan Grunkin and Dorothee Paul. Both parents had German nationality, as did the child. Leonhard Matthias lived most of his life in Denmark, initially with both parents, and then just with his mother, who remained in Denmark after the parents' separation. He regularly visited his father in Germany when the father moved. Leonhard Matthias, did not, however, have Danish citizenship, because of Denmark's *jus sanguinis* rather than *jus soli* rules on acquiring citizenship.[5]

Leonhard Matthias' surname was originally registered by the Danish authorities as Paul, with Grunkin as a middle name. After a few months this was changed in accordance with the Danish law to 'Grunkin-Paul'. In Denmark, jurisdiction over surnames is determined on the basis of the country of habitual residence (in this case, Denmark), rather than nationality of the individual concerned (German). For this reason, a compound surname with both maternal and paternal surnames was allowed, as per Danish law, for the German national.

However, the German authorities refused to register Leonhard Matthias' surname as Grunkin-Paul when the family sought to do so. The decision was based on the German law, dictating that surnames must be determined by the law of the country of the individual's nationality (in this case, Germany), and only exceptionally by another country if the parent (or other person conferring the name) holds that country's nationality. Neither parent had Danish nationality, so the German law applied. Furthermore, Germany did not allow for compound surnames like Grunkin-Paul, and required them to choose either Grunkin or Paul.

It is important to note that several years earlier, an Opinion had already been delivered by AG Jacobs involving the same family.[6] However, in case *Standesamt Stadt Niebüll*,[7] which was factually identical, the Court ruled that the reference for preliminary ruling did not meet the admissibility criteria. Accordingly the *Amtsgericht* had no jurisdiction to proceed with a reference under Article 267 TFEU when exercising administrative functions. The merits of recognising the surname Grunkin-Paul in Germany were not considered by the Court. However, AG Jacobs focused his Opinion on both the admissibility of the reference and the substance of the dispute.

Since the substantial questions on registration of names in *Standesamt Stadt Niebüll* and in *Grunkin and Paul* were the same, the Opinion of AG Jacobs in the former case was of particular interest. AG Sharpston referred to his Opinion in her own. Notably, having been the AG in the only other two cases on names, AG Jacobs maintained the position that whilst rules on surnames is an exclusive Member State competence, the exercise of this competence must be consistent with EU law.[8] He cited EU citizenship rights to non-discrimination and free

---

[5] *Jus sanguinis* determines nationality on the basis of one or both parent's own nationality, whilst *jus soli* bases nationality on the place of birth.

[6] Opinion of AG Jacobs in Case C-96/04 *Standesamt Stadt Niebüll* ECLI:EU:C:2005:419.

[7] Case C-96/04 *Standesamt Stadt Niebüll* ECLI:EU:C:2006:254.

[8] Opinion of AG Jacobs in Case C-168/91 *Konstantinidis* ECLI:EU:C:1992:504; Opinion of AG Jacobs in Case C-148/02 *Garcia Avello* ECLI:EU:C:2003:311.

movement as the principles underpinning this perspective, and that it would be 'totally incompatible' with the rights under this status not to maintain consistency between the surnames for Leonhard Matthias in Denmark and Germany.[9]

It was within this context that AG Sharpston then delivered her Opinion in case *Grunkin and Paul* just under three years later. The reference for preliminary ruling submitted to the Court in case *Grunkin and Paul* sought clarification on whether the principle of non-discrimination on the grounds of nationality (Article 12 EC, now Article 18 TFEU) as protected under EU citizenship (Article 18 EC, now under Article 20 TFEU) would render the German law on nationality and surnames in breach of EU law. If it was, it would allow Leonhard Matthias to have his surname registered as Grunkin-Paul in the Member State of his nationality consistent with what was already registered legally for almost a decade in Denmark.

III. THE OPINION OF AG SHARPSTON

The Opinion of AG Sharpston addressed the question referred to the Court above in three parts, with some extra embellishments as is the ways (and freedom) of AGs. First, she considered whether the question was within the scope of EU law; secondly, whether there was discrimination on the grounds of nationality, or an obstacle to free movement under EU citizenship; and thirdly, if there was discrimination or any obstacles to free movement, whether or not they were justified. It was a careful discussion of issues pertaining to principles related to the questions referred, as well as the subject matter of names and conflict of laws issues that are raised in this same context. The Judgment of the Court was structured in the same way, but it is notable that the reasoning provided by the Court was quite different from that of AG Sharpston.[10]

The judgment of the Court did not directly engage with all the points that AG Sharpston called for, such as offering a consistent approach to issues regarding conflict of laws on names. This was significant because the Court later revisited the same or similar issues raised in both *Garcia Avello* and *Grunkin and Paul* without necessarily having a consistent precedent in its approach to rely upon.[11] AG Sharpston opined that a legislative or conventional solution was preferable in the context of issues regarding registered names, but the Court did not clarify its position on this. By correctly predicting that these questions were likely to arise again in the future, there was greater depth in the discussion on the effect of this judgment and its Opinion on future case law on names below.

Overall, the Opinion of AG Sharpston focused on developing what can be conceived of as a mutual recognition approach to the recognition of names across Member States. She made a clear point to note the controversial boundaries that were potentially being pushed in terms of private international law matters (like names), which were complex, and advised not to intrude on these. Her way around this was to focus on precedent in case *Garcia Avello*, especially on the scope of the Treaty regarding these matters. She then went on to note that by expanding on the scope of the principle of mutual recognition to situations outside the Internal Market, the child's best interests in having a consistent surname across Member States could also be maintained, and would not cause undue inconvenience.

---

[9] Para 56 of the Opinion of AG Jacobs.
[10] Case C-353/06 *Grunkin and Paul* ECLI:EU:C:2008:559.
[11] See Case 208/09 *Sayn-Wittgenstein* ECLI:EU:C:2010:806; Case C-391/09 *Runević-Vardyn* ECLI:EU:C:2011:291; Case C-438/14 *Bogendorff von Wolffersdorff* ECLI:EU:C:2016:401.

The Court agreed with her analysis as to whether the question fell within the scope of the Treaty, which would only be logical given the previous Opinions of AG Jacobs and judgments on matters concerning names.[12] However, the judgment in *Grunkin and Paul* then diverged from AG Sharpston's discourse on questions of equal treatment in terms of the different rules chosen by the Member States when governing registration of names. Instead of adopting her mutual recognition approach, it determined the outcome entirely on the basis of free movement and obstacles to it under EU citizenship status.

IV. ANALYSIS

The Judgment of the Court did not place as much emphasis on the various questions of nationality law determining names that AG Sharpston considered important to avoid future situations of a similar nature. In particular, in lieu of the legislative or convention-based solution to recognition of names across Member States, as advocated by AG Sharpston,[13] the Court decided *Grunkin and Paul* on the quite specific fact-based scenario presented to it. AG Sharpston noted that it was not about adjudicating between two Member States' laws (like in *Garcia Avello* between the laws of Belgium and Spain). Instead, she argued that the Court should be concerned with considering the compatibility of German law on names with EU law.[14] Clearly, it was easier to satisfy the question of scope in this case, because of the cross-border element of the child moving between Denmark and Germany to see his parents.

This analysis considers the questions referred to in *Grunkin and Paul* in turn, first considering scope, then the two Articles in the Treaty most relevant to Union citizenship – Article 18 TFEU on non-discrimination on the grounds of nationality and Article 20 TFEU on rights to free movement and residence under Union citizenship status, respectively. The final section will conclude by considering the effect of this Opinion and judgment on future case law, which as alluded to above, is richer because of *Grunkin and Paul*.

A. Scope of the Treaty

The question of whether the reference fell within the scope of the Treaty was a simple and straightforward one. It was clearly indicative of the precedence also set by *Garcia Avello* as to competence over names under EU law, very much consistent with AG Sharpston's views that Leonhard Matthias' surname registration did fall squarely within the scope of EU law.[15] By recognising that names are an exclusive competence of Member States, the Court was able to respect the boundaries of private international law by requiring that national legal authorities respected EU law when exercising its exclusive competences, but not intruding in the substantive law concerning the competence itself.

---

[12] The exception is Case C-168/91 *Konstantinidis* (n 4) and its Opinion from AG Jacobs (n 8), where neither the Court nor the AG mentioned EU citizenship status, perhaps as they both preceded the Treaty of Maastricht coming into effect, where EU citizenship was first introduced.

[13] Para 45.

[14] Para 50.

[15] Para 55.

As already noted, AG Sharpston also cautioned against intrusion into private international law given that names are:

> clearly an area in which it behoves the Court to tread softly, and with care. But just because it must tread softly, that does not mean that it must fear to tread at all.[16]

This is certainly how the Court handled the question posed to it. AG Sharpston emphasised that there was no question of legality over dictating whether Germany should or should not allow compound names like Grunkin-Paul,[17] nor was it about the choice to use nationality or habitual residence to determine which jurisdiction applies for naming conventions. It was merely a question of compatibility of the German rules with EU law.

What was notable here was the factual situation of the child's parents being separated in different Member States. It meant that there was a clear cross-border element as Leonhard Matthias travelled between Denmark and Germany regularly. Criticism of the test applied by the Court of requiring a cross-border element before a situation falls within the scope of the Treaty aside,[18] it inherently made this case easier to justify coming under the scope of EU law. This was in stark contrast to *Garcia Avello*, where the Court spoke more of a potential obstacle to free movement between Member States. As noted earlier, there was no adjudication between which jurisdiction would apply as in *Garcia Avello* between the laws of Belgium or Spain. Therefore, the question of scope and jurisdiction was fairly straightforward in *Grunkin and Paul*, and the Opinion of AG Sharpston and judgment of the Court agreed it was within the scope of EU law.

B. Article 18 TFEU

In two short paragraphs, the Court plainly dismissed the idea that this had anything to do with non-discrimination on the grounds of nationality.[19] This was because other Germans determining their surnames on the basis of German law would be treated the same way. However, this fairly swift dismissal of issues of non-discrimination on nationality grounds belies the consideration of equal treatment more generally, which was made by AG Sharpston in her Opinion.

AG Sharpston considered an alternative scenario in which Denmark had *jus soli* rules for nationality, rather than *jus sanguinis*. In that case, Leonhard Matthias would be granted Danish nationality, as well as German, and there would be no question of conflict of laws. He would have had a valid surname under the Danish legal system, acceptable in Germany, by virtue of him holding Danish nationality. This alternative scenario thus raised the question of the equal treatment of Danish nationals in Germany, thus putting individuals who do not gain the nationality of their Member State of birth (as is the reality of the situation faced by Leonhard Matthias) at a disadvantage. AG Sharpston argued that this was why there would be an issue of equal treatment, and perhaps a breach of the principle.[20]

---

[16] Para 41.
[17] Para 48.
[18] AG Sharpston described the cross-border test as 'strange and illogical'. See Opinion of AG Sharpston in Case C-34/09 *Ruiz Zambrano* ECLI:EU:C:2011:560, para 86.
[19] Paras 24–25.
[20] M Lehmann, 'What's in a Name? Grunkin-Paul and Beyond' (2008) 10 *Yearbook of Private International Law* 135, 142.

Recognising a potential breach of equal treatment by the German authorities in their non-recognition of the Grunkin-Paul surname, AG Sharpston highlighted some precedence from other jurisdictions that may justify this. She cited Lithuanian naming conventions and the strong cultural values embedded in their policy which would not allow for the registration of a foreign name. She also focused on the European Court of Human Rights (ECtHR) juris-prudence which set a precedent for national linguistic rules that justified what may amount to discrimination on national language grounds.[21] None of this was addressed by the Court. Instead, it used free movement principles inherent in the Union citizenship case law to justify allowing the child to register his surname consistently in both his Member State of nationality, as well as his Member State of residence.[22]

C. Article 20 TFEU

Most of the Court's judgment was dedicated to elucidating the finer details of how the status of EU citizenship in this situation helped Leonhard Matthias in his parents' quest to have his compound surname recognised in Germany. In particular, as was commonplace for the Court in cases on EU citizenship during that decade, the focus was entirely on eliminating obstacles to free movement despite a quite clear link to the protection of fundamental rights, in this case, to the right to private and family life under Article 8 ECHR and later, Article 7 of the Charter of Fundamental Rights.[23] Reservations about this emphasis on free movement in lieu of fundamental rights aside, the Court heavily relied on the precedent set in case *Garcia Avello* as to what may amount to a 'serious inconvenience', administratively, on both a personal and professional level if surnames are not consistent in one legal system versus another.[24]

Agreeing with AG Sharpston that the case was not about the choice of domestic naming conventions being based either on habitual residence or nationality, the Court also agreed that there was a breach of EU law. It was as an obstacle to free movement, though, as opposed to equal treatment,[25] and thus required justification. The Court decided to focus on very specific observations raised by the German Government and intervening Member States, and meth-odologically dismissed each in turn.[26] Whilst this was painstakingly thorough, it did obscure the fact that AG Sharpston rightly called for a more unified approach, and it did not take away from the Court's contribution towards adding further clarification to what in later years becomes a more confusing situation.

The Court swiftly dealt with observations about the legitimacy and importance of using the 'connecting factor of nationality' to determine a surname.[27] In particular, it rejected the notion that this was to ensure continuity and stability – an easy dismissal given that there was no continuity if Leonhard Matthias was not able to bear the compound surname in both Denmark and Germany. It also dismissed the argument about ensuring siblings have the same

---

[21] Paras 84–85.

[22] Normally this would be considered his home State and host State respectively, but here does not reflect reality for Leonhard Matthias. As noted earlier, he has lived for most of his life – as a German national – almost exclusively in Denmark, a detail that has proven to be of importance later on.

[23] A Yong, *The Rise and Decline of Fundamental Rights in EU Citizenship* (Oxford, Hart Publishing, 2019) 71.

[24] Para 23 of the Judgment.

[25] Para 24 of the Judgment.

[26] Paras 30–38 of the Judgment.

[27] ibid, para 31.

name, for it was not relevant to the situation at hand, though this surely was a very possible future hypothetical the Court avoided getting into.

The heart of the analysis was in the specifics of German private international law on names, and the fact that the connecting factor of nationality for determination of surnames was 'not without exception'.[28] As the Court noted, had either of Leonhard Matthias' parents acquired Danish nationality, then the Grunkin-Paul surname would have been allowed.[29] AG Sharpston's similar point was made employing the well-known argument of a genuine link with the 'host' Member State (Denmark), to argue in favour of allowing Leonhard Matthias to register his surname consistently in his 'home' Member State (Germany).[30] Her considerations of the child's best interest, to allow him to register his surname uniformly across the EU, were entirely absent from the considerations in the Judgment itself, though perhaps implicit in the notion of it being a serious inconvenience to identity to have different surnames across Member States.

Finally, the Court found no public policy reason to disallow the surname Grunkin-Paul from being registered in Germany.[31] This was, perhaps, a very fleeting nod to the points raised by AG Sharpston on domestic naming conventions and linguistic culture before the ECtHR. The Court did not clearly accept an expanded scope of either Union citizenship rights nor fundamental rights protection so as to include mutual recognition of previously registered (and accepted) surnames, leaving the ground ripe for further case law on names. Only two years after the judgment in case *Grunkin and Paul*, AG Sharpston was asked again to deliver an opinion on names. This happened in *Sayn-Wittgenstein*, the next case in the saga.[32]

D. Effect on Future Case Law

Much of the commentary on *Grunkin and Paul*, before the next cases on names were decided,[33] focused on the question of how Member States should determine names – by habitual residence or by nationality.[34] As already noted, in her Opinion, AG Sharpston called for the extension of mutual recognition to situations concerning names to avoid any issues of conflict of laws,[35] which did not manifest in the judgment. However, what *Grunkin and Paul* did do was cement the fact that obstacles to free movement was the main way forward, according to the Court, when determining issues concerning names. Therefore, the three succeeding judgments are mostly on whether the relevant justifications to breaches of free movement were acceptable.

Sayn-Wittgenstein, which followed, concerned an adopted Austrian child in Germany inheriting a title of nobility in her surname, 'Fürstin von Sayn-Wittgenstein', from her adoptive German father. Such noble titles were banned in Austria and 15 years after the claimant had officially changed her name following her adoption, she was asked to correct it. AG Sharpston approached her analysis in this case slightly differently than *Grunkin and Paul*, perhaps as an acknowledgement to what the Court eventually decided in that Judgment itself.

---

[28] ibid, para 34.
[29] ibid, para 37.
[30] Para 87 of the Opinion.
[31] Para 38 of the Judgment.
[32] Opinion of AG Sharpston in Case 208/09 *Sayn-Wittgenstein* ECLI:EU:C:2010:608.
[33] Case 208/09 *Sayn-Wittgenstein*; Case C-391/09 *Runevič-Vardyn* ; Case C-438/14 *Bogendorff von Wolffersdorff*.
[34] Lehmann (n 20); C Honorati, 'Free Circulation of Names for EU Citizens?' (2009) 2 *Diritto dell'Unione Europea* 379.
[35] Honorati (n 34).

This time, AG Sharpston made more of the notion of a 'serious inconvenience' as an obstacle to free movement to the individual whose name would differ across Member States, if not recognised. A proportionality assessment was also suggested to determine whether it would be justified not to recognise their name consistently across Member States.[36] However, AG Sharpston stated that it may be disproportionate to require the claimant in question to change her name after 15 years, given how widely and how long she had used it. By contrast, the Court decided that whilst the Austrian rule was a breach of equal treatment, it could be justified on grounds of public policy.[37]

Subsequently, proportionality assessments and justifications became central to Court's judgments on names. The triptych of cases in the 2000s – *Garcia Avello*, *Grunkin and Paul*, and *Sayn-Wittgenstein* – effectively cemented the idea of serious inconveniences to free movement under Union citizenship as part of the adjudication around names before the Court.[38] Thereafter, in *Runevič-Vardyn and Wardyn*, this came to a head in light of the Lithuanian constitutional values in regard to names. It has been argued, however, that 'the usual distinction between strict and soft proportionality tests … [and] the seemingly random manner in which this distinction is being drawn is potentially problematic'.[39]

The problematic nature of this lack of consistency on the Court's part manifested in the latest case on names, *Bogendorff von Wolffersdorff*. Legal foundations were laid in the preceding case law for the Court to decide matters based on a serious inconvenience in terms of free movement under EU citizenship status. The reasoning used in the *Grunkin and Paul* case featured heavily, not only as to a serious inconvenience, but also when considering arguments concerning administrative convenience. It was not considered to be a sufficient reason to justify a breach of EU law under Article 20 TFEU to try to avoid creating an unduly long and unwieldy name. Whilst the Court was less partial as to the outcome in terms of whether or not recognising the six-part surname 'Graf von Wolffersdorff Freiherr von Bogendorff' for Peter Mark Emanuel and his daughter could be justified, it was clear this had to be subject to the relevant proportionality assessments.

An important feature of cases on names post-2010 is the fact that the Charter of Fundamental Rights became binding in 2009, that is, after the judgment in *Grunkin and Paul* had been handed down, but before *Sayn-Wittgenstein* was decided. The subsequent cases *Runevič-Vardyn* and *Bogendorff von Wolffersdorff* both refer to a person's identity as part of the right to private and family life under Article 7 of the Charter, and formed part of the proportionality assessments. Though free movement still reigns supreme as the main guiding principle under the status of EU citizenship, it is a noteworthy observation that fundamental rights are explicitly raised and highlighted.

Lastly, it is prudent to recall AG Sharpston's preference for a legislative or conventional approach to names in her Opinion in *Grunkin and Paul*. Her pleas for consistency have been lost to the Court's insistence on a 'stone-by-stone approach',[40] which may have provided some flexibility to the judges, but adds to the legal uncertainty in the area of names. As AG Sharpston

---

[36] Paras 62–68 of the Opinion.

[37] Para 94 of the Judgment.

[38] H van Eijken, 'Case C-391/09, *Malgožata Runevic-Vardyn and Lukasz Pawel Wardyn v. Vilniaus miesto savivaldybes administracija and Others*, Judgment of the Court (Second Chamber) of 12 May 2011' (2012) 49 *CMLRev* 809, 816.

[39] A Łazowski, E Dagilytė and P Stasinopoulos, 'The Importance of Being Earnest: Spelling of Names, EU Citizenship and Fundamental Rights' (2015) 11 *Croatian Yearbook of European Law & Policy* 1, 33.

[40] K Lenaerts, 'EU Citizenship and the European Court of Justice's 'Stone-by-Stone' Approach' (2015) 1 *International Comparative Jurisprudence* 1.

noted, names may be an area where the Court needs to tread carefully, not to mention that the Charter becoming binding raised the legal significance of national identity and cultural values as manifestations of fundamental rights. What this saga on names does show is how wide reaching the implications are in this area.[41] AG Sharpston's early contribution in her Opinion in *Grunkin and Paul* set an important and solid precedence, and her words have made a lasting impression.

---

[41] For example, recognition of names is compared with recognition of same-sex marriage across the Union, see M van den Brink, 'What's in a Name Case? Some Lessons for the Debate Over the Free Movement of Same-Sex Couples within the EU' (2016) 17 *GLJ* 421.

39

Legislation, Interpretation, and Equal Treatment: Opinion of Advocate General Sharpston in Sturgeon

PAUL CRAIG

I. INTRODUCTION

L EGAL DECISIONS CAN be of interest from a plethora of perspectives. This is exemplified by the subject matter of this chapter, which is the Opinion of AG Sharpston in the *Sturgeon* case,[1] and the ensuing decision of the Court.[2] The case raised issues at three different levels.

The initial issue raised by the litigation concerned the distinction between 'cancellation' and 'delay' for the purposes of claiming compensation in the context of air travel. This in turn raised questions as to whether the distinction between cancellation and delay in the enabling Regulation 261/2004 was sustainable in the light of the general principle of equality.[3] This then generated the third issue, which was how far the AG and the Court would go in interpreting the EU Regulation to be consistent with the general principle of equality, and hence preserve its validity. It is the conjunction of the second and third issues that made the case of more general interest within EU law.

II. BACKGROUND, CONTEXT, AND FACTS

The case arose out of Regulation 261/2004, which provided, inter alia, for a regime of compensation in the context of air travel. The immediate catalyst for the Regulation was the Montreal Convention to which the EU was a party.[4] The Regulation was enacted pursuant to

---

[1] Opinion of AG Sharpston in Joined Cases C-402/07 and C-432/07 *Sturgeon* ECLI:EU:C:2009:416.

[2] Joined Cases C-402/07 and C-432/07, *Sturgeon* ECLI:EU:C:2009:716.

[3] Regulation (EC) No 261/2004 of the European Parliament and of the Council of 11 February 2004 establishing common rules on compensation and assistance to passengers in the event of denied boarding and of cancellation or long delay of flights [2004] OJ L46/1.

[4] Convention for the Unification of Certain Rules for International Carriage by Air, Montreal, 28 May 1999, approved on behalf of the Community by Council Decision 2001/539/EC of 5 April 2001 on the conclusion by the European Community of the Convention for the Unification of Certain Rules for International Carriage by Air (the Montreal Convention) [2001] OJ L194/38.

Article 80(2) EC, which was concerned with air transport, and the Regulation was expressly predicated on the assumption that a high level of consumer protection should be afforded to passengers.[5]

However, the Regulation drew a sharp distinction between cases of 'cancellation' and 'delay': the former prima facie generated entitlement to compensation, while the latter did not. The airlines therefore had an incentive to categorise cases as involving delay, while passengers had the opposite incentive to regard them as entailing cancellation. The distinction between the two was rendered more difficult because, while the Regulation contained a definition of cancellation, there was no corresponding definition of delay.

The two cases arose out of instances where passengers on long-haul flights suffered considerable disruption to travel. The passengers alleged that this constituted cancellation, while the airlines predictably resisted this, and claimed that it was merely delay, which did not generate any right to compensation. The respective national courts framed a series of questions for the CJEU, which concerned the criteria that should be used to determine the divide between cancellation and delay, and whether a 'delay' could be treated as a 'cancellation' within the meaning of the Regulation after a certain amount of time had elapsed.

III. THE OPINION OF AG SHARPSTON

Legal reasoning is eternally fascinating for a concatenation of reasons. It was exemplified by the instant case, where the AG and the Court accorded differing weight to relevant lines of argument. The nub of the difference can be simply stated. The case raised two related, albeit distinct, issues.

The first concerned equality, more specifically whether the distinction between cancellation and delay in the Regulation was sustainable in the light of the general principle of equality. The second was whether the difficulty in this respect could be resolved through interpretation, or if this was not possible whether the relevant parts of the Regulation would have to be invalidated.

AG Sharpston was clear that there was a real problem with equal treatment in the provisions of the Regulation dealing with cancellation and delay. She was equally clear that it could not be resolved through creative interpretation. The Court agreed that there was an equality problem, but then, by way of contrast to AG Sharpston, it devoted the major part of its judgment to crafting an interpretive argument as to why the equality problem could be resolved, thereby obviating the need to invalidate the Regulation.

IV. ANALYSIS

A. AG Sharpston: The Equality Argument

Sturgeon was in many respects a classic equality case. The enabling Regulation drew a sharp distinction between cancellation, for which compensation was prima facie payable, and delay for which it was not. The problem was that the distinction lacked normative justification. The strengthening of consumer protection was, as stated in the then Article 3(1)(t) EC, an

---

[5] Para 1, Preamble of Regulation 261/2004.

objective that the Community was intended to pursue in accord with the then Article 2 EC. The dichotomy between cancellation and delay ran counter to this, in the sense that 'regardless of the seriousness of the inconvenience caused, the Regulation provides that the cancellation of a flight automatically triggers a right to compensation (under Article 7) while a delay never does'.[6] This was, as AG Sharpston stated, based on the assumption that a cancellation necessarily causes more inconvenience to passengers, and hence merits a stronger form of protection than a 'mere' delay, but 'it is wholly unclear to me why this should be so'.[7] She proffered the following telling example.

> Suppose passenger A and passenger B have both booked flights from Brussels to New York with different air carriers, both leaving at 08.30. When passenger A arrives at the airport, he is told that his flight has been cancelled. He is offered a place on another flight to New York departing one day later at 08.30. Passenger B is told upon arriving at the airport that his flight has been delayed. His flight finally takes off at the same moment as Passenger A's new flight, that is to say one day after the scheduled time of departure. Both passenger A and B arrive in New York at the same time. The two passengers are, in effect, in identical situations. Yet only passenger A is granted a right to automatic compensation under the Regulation.[8]

The distinction drawn between cancellation and delay in the Regulation was, therefore, at odds with its purpose, more especially because the Regulation could produce the perverse result that 'passengers who have suffered the greater inconvenience may be denied automatic compensation, while those who have suffered the lesser inconvenience may be granted it'.[9] This would be the case where, for example, the cancellation of a flight caused only minimal disruption, because the passenger was placed on alternative flight that left only one hour later, by way of contrast to a passenger who might be delayed for 12 hours.[10]

There was, moreover, no legitimate justification for the differential treatment. The Commission tried to defend the distinction on the ground that the airline was normally responsible for cancellation, but not always for delays. This did not, said AG Sharpston, withstand scrutiny. It amounted to saying that the airline operator was 'always responsible for cancellations (except when he is not); and that he is not always responsible for delays (except, presumably, when he is)',[11] which was a distinction without a difference. The AG then articulated a preferable touchstone:

> It seems to me that the underlying logic (again, against the background of enhanced consumer protection) must have been that, where the operator is not responsible for the inconvenience (whether caused by cancellation or long delay), he should not have to pay compensation; and that, conversely, where he is responsible, he should pay. Put another way, the criterion for compensation is not causation, but fault (broadly defined) on the part of the operator.[12]

This was not, however, the criterion on which the Regulation was based, since the distinction between cancellation and delay therein had nothing to do with the airline's responsibility or fault in the preceding sense. It was for this reason that the difference in treatment appeared to fall foul of the principle of equal treatment.[13]

---

[6] ibid, para 51.
[7] ibid, para 52.
[8] ibid, para 53.
[9] ibid, para 55.
[10] ibid, para 55.
[11] ibid, para 59.
[12] ibid, para 60.
[13] ibid, paras 61–62.

B. AG Sharpston: The Interpretive Argument

AG Sharpston then considered whether the equality problem could be resolved by creative interpretation. The focus of the inquiry was as to whether the Regulation could be interpreted in such a way that time was properly regarded as a factor in identifying cancellation. On this approach an inordinately long delay could become a de facto cancellation, thereby alleviating the equality problem adumbrated above. This view was supported by the claimants, and many Member States that took part in the preliminary reference proceeding and the Commission.[14]

The AG had no doubt that treating the passing of time as an important factor in identifying a cancellation would reinforce the Regulation's objective of increasing passenger protection. She, nonetheless, raised two difficulties with this approach. The first concerned the meaning of 'inordinate delay'. The second was whether it was permissible to interpret the Regulation in a way that classified inordinate delay as de facto cancellation.[15]

She was sceptical on the first issue, opining that it was impossible to 'identify, with any acceptable degree of precision, exactly what period of time must elapse before a delay become "inordinate"'.[16] The consequence was that it would then be for the 'national court, in each individual case, to evaluate the facts and reach a view – based on some mixture of national legal tradition, good sense and instinct rather than any precise Community legal norm – as to whether the delay in that instance had been 'inordinate' and should therefore be regarded as a de facto cancellation'.[17] The 'ensuing variability of results is likely to conflict with the principle of legal certainty'.[18]

AG Sharpston was equally sceptical on the second issue, concerning the legitimacy of this mode of interpretation. She acknowledged that if it were possible to identify a precise point in time at which delay became inordinate, or to construct a set of criteria that could serve as effective guidance to the national court, 'answering this question would involve choosing between a very teleological approach to consumer protection and the plain and literal wording of the Regulation'.[19]

However, she regarded the matter in starker terms and reasoned as follows. The legislator had the right to pick a figure as to the length of time that constituted inordinate delay, and defend it. It would be within the legislature's prerogative to make this choice. AG Sharpston felt, however, that the Court could not do so, because 'any figure one cared to pick would involve reading into the Regulation something it plainly does not contain and would be a judicial usurpation of the legislative prerogative'.[20] It would not, moreover, resolve the underlying equality issue. This was because it would still be the case that passengers of cancelled flights would continue to have an automatic right to compensation, 'while only passengers of inordinately delayed flights (however the Court chose to define that concept) would have such a right',[21] with the result that some passengers in objectively similar situations would still be treated differently. This led the AG to the following conclusion:

> It seems to me that, in seeking to avoid Scylla (obvious discrimination against passengers whose flights are inordinately delayed when compared to passengers who obtain automatic compensation

---

[14] ibid, paras 78–79.
[15] ibid, para 83.
[16] ibid, para 87.
[17] ibid, para 88.
[18] ibid, para 89.
[19] ibid, para 91.
[20] ibid, para 94.
[21] ibid, para 95.

for their cancelled flight), one is immediately swept into Charybdis (legal uncertainty). Moreover, the underlying difficulties that I have identified earlier in relation to the principle of equal treatment are unfortunately not solved by adopting a teleological approach towards 'inordinate delay'. They appear to me to be inherent in the structure of the Regulation as it presently stands.[22]

It was for this reason that AG Sharpston felt that the underlying problem with the Regulation could not be 'fixed' by interpretation, however constructive. This in turn informed the conclusion that the Court should reopen the oral procedure to see whether the Member States, Commission, Parliament, and Council could present arguments that might save those Articles of the Regulation that were predicated on the distinction between cancellation and delay from invalidation.

C. The Court: The Equality Argument

The Court's approach was somewhat different to that of AG Sharpston. It began by rejecting the argument that inordinate delay could constitute cancellation. It acknowledged that the Regulation did not define 'flight delay', but held that it could be discerned from the Regulation read as a whole. The concept could, however, be clarified in the light of the context in which it occurred. On this view, 'delay' related to a change in the scheduled departure time of a flight, assuming that other elements pertaining to the flight were unchanged. Cancellation, by way of contrast, meant the non-operation of a flight that was previously planned.

It followed, said the Court, that cancelled flights and delayed flights were two distinct categories, the corollary being that a flight which is delayed could not be classified as a 'cancelled flight' merely because the delay was lengthy.[23] It followed also that cancellation covered the situation in which the delayed flight for which the booking was made was 'rolled over' onto another flight, 'that is to say, where the planning for the original flight is abandoned and the passengers from that flight join passengers on a flight which was also planned – but independently of the flight for which the passengers so transferred had made their bookings'.[24]

The Court's reasoning heightened the contrast between delay and cancellation, and hence exacerbated the equality issue. Cancellation gave rise to compensation, delay did not. The argument that inordinate delay could be regarded as cancellation was designed to alleviate this tension, by providing an interpretive route for serious delay to be seen as cancellation, with the consequence that compensation would be available. AG Sharpston was sceptical about this argument for the reasons set out above. The Court unequivocally closed the door to the argument. It thereby highlighted the difference between delay and cancellation in terms of amenability to compensation.

This was accepted by the Court, in the sense that the remainder of its judgment was premised on the assumption that the differential treatment of delay and cancellation was problematic in terms of equality, and that certain provisions of the Regulation would be invalid as a consequence, unless they could be saved through interpretation. The Court then set to the task of constructing an interpretive argument that would obviate the need to invalidate the Regulation for infringement of the general principle of equality.

[22] ibid, para 96.
[23] Paras 33–34 of the Judgment.
[24] ibid, para 36.

D. The Court: The Interpretive Argument

The Court's reasoning in this respect warrants close attention, since it provided an object lesson as to how to deploy interpretive tools to 'cure' the inequality, and hence, avoid the need for invalidation. It may be helpful for explicatory purposes to disaggregate different stages in the Court's reasoning.

First, the Court, while acknowledging the Regulation's prima facie differential treatment of delay and compensation, stated that 'it is necessary, in interpreting a provision of Community law, to consider not only its wording, but also the context in which it occurs and the objectives pursued by the rules of which it is part'.[25] This included the reasons that led to the adoption of the Regulation.[26]

Secondly, the Court then forged an argument that the Regulation, notwithstanding appearances to the contrary, did contemplate compensation for delay. This argument was ingenious, and yet tenuous in equal measure. The Court reasoned as follows: the airline could be released from the obligation to pay compensation in the event of cancellation in the event of 'extraordinary circumstances'; however, Recital 15 in the preamble to the Regulation stated that that ground could also be relied on where an air traffic management decision in relation to a particular aircraft on a particular day gave rise to 'a long delay [or] an overnight delay'. It followed, stated the Court, that because the notion of long delay was mentioned in the context of extraordinary circumstances, 'it must be held that the legislature also linked that notion to the right to compensation'.[27]

Thirdly, the Court then reinforced this textual conclusion by reference to the general objectives served by Regulation 261/2004. It was, said the Court, readily apparent from Recitals 1 to 4 in the preamble, in particular from Recital 2, 'that the regulation seeks to ensure a high level of protection for air passengers regardless of whether they are denied boarding or whether their flight is cancelled or delayed, since they are all caused similar serious trouble and inconvenience connected with air transport'.[28] This was more particularly so since 'the provisions conferring rights on air passengers, including those conferring a right to compensation, must be interpreted broadly'.[29] It could not therefore 'automatically be presumed that passengers whose flights are delayed do not have a right to compensation and cannot, for the purposes of recognition of such a right, be treated as passengers whose flights are cancelled'.[30]

Fourthly, the Court then reinforced the preceding argument by recourse to general principles of interpretation. This meant that 'a Community act must be interpreted, as far as possible, in such a way as not to affect its validity', and that 'where a provision of Community law is open to several interpretations, preference must be given to that interpretation which ensures that the provision retains its effectiveness'.[31] All Community acts should be interpreted 'in accordance with primary law as a whole, including the principle of equal treatment, which requires that comparable situations must not be treated differently and that different situations must not be treated in the same way unless such treatment is objectively justified'.[32]

---

[25] ibid, para 41.
[26] ibid, para 42.
[27] ibid, paras 43, 62.
[28] ibid, para 44.
[29] ibid, para 45.
[30] ibid, para 46.
[31] ibid, para 47.
[32] ibid, para 48.

Fifthly, the Court then applied the preceding interpretive precepts to Regulation 261/2004. The Court accepted that passengers whose flight was cancelled and passengers whose flight was delayed could suffer similar damage. They were, therefore, to be regarded as in 'comparable situations for the purposes of the application of the right to compensation laid down in Article 7 of Regulation No 261/2004'.[33] This was more especially so given that delay could result in a similar, or greater, loss of time than cancellation, and thus if passengers whose flights were delayed did not acquire any right to compensation, they would be treated less favourably.[34] There was, moreover, 'no objective ground capable of justifying such a difference in treatment'.[35] The Court then drew out the consequences of this line of reasoning:

> Given that the damage sustained by air passengers in cases of cancellation or long delay is comparable, passengers whose flights are delayed and passengers whose flights are cancelled cannot be treated differently without the principle of equal treatment being infringed. That is a fortiori the case in view of the aim sought by Regulation No 261/2004, which is to increase protection for all air passengers.

> In those circumstances, the Court finds that passengers whose flights are delayed may rely on the right to compensation laid down in Article 7 of Regulation No 261/2004 where they suffer, on account of such flights, a loss of time equal to or in excess of three hours, that is to say when they reach their final destination three hours or more after the arrival time originally scheduled by the air carrier.[36]

Sixthly, the Court defended this conclusion against the argument that it was inconsistent with Article 6 of Regulation 261/2004, which provided for different forms of assistance under Articles 8 and 9 thereof for passengers whose flights were delayed. The Court's response echoes that used in other contexts. Regulation 261/2004 provided for 'various forms of intervention in order to redress, in a standardised and immediate manner, the different types of damage constituted by the inconvenience that delay in the carriage of passengers by air causes'.[37] Those measures were autonomous 'in the sense that they address different aims and seek to make up for various types of damage caused by such delay'.[38] The availability of other forms of redress for passengers who were delayed did not, therefore, undermine their right to compensation. The Court expressed its formal conclusion as follows:

> Articles 5, 6 and 7 of Regulation 261/2004 must be interpreted as meaning that passengers whose flights are delayed may be treated, for the purposes of the application of the right to compensation, as passengers whose flights are cancelled and they may thus rely on the right to compensation laid down in Article 7 of the regulation where they suffer, on account of a flight delay, a loss of time equal to or in excess of three hours, that is, where they reach their final destination three hours or more after the arrival time originally scheduled by the air carrier. Such a delay does not, however, entitle passengers to compensation if the air carrier can prove that the long delay was caused by extraordinary circumstances which could not have been avoided even if all reasonable measures had been taken, namely circumstances beyond the actual control of the air carrier.[39]

---

[33] ibid, para 54.
[34] ibid, para 58.
[35] ibid, para 59.
[36] ibid, paras 60–61.
[37] ibid, para 65.
[38] ibid, para 66.
[39] ibid, para 69.

E. Reflections: Text, Validity and Interpretation

The *Sturgeon* case does not have precedential value, such that it will be directly influential for later courts faced with analogous issues in other areas. It does, nonetheless, throw into sharp relief endemic issues concerning the relationship between text, validity, and interpretation. They arise in all legal systems, but have a special prominence in the EU. This follows from the very nature of general principles of law.

Their status in the hierarchy of norms means that they sit above legislative, delegated, and implementing acts. They can be used as tools of interpretation and of validity, as evidenced by *Sturgeon* itself, where it was accepted by all parties that the principles would result in the invalidation of provisions of the Regulation, if they could not be interpreted to be in conformity with them. The general principles of law can, in addition, be used as principles of interpretation in relation to the Treaty provisions, such that the Court will strive for an interpretation of the primary articles of the EU Treaties that are consistent with general principles of law.

It is not, however, merely the hierarchical status of such principles that serve to underline their importance. It is also their procedural and substantive reach. They include, but extend beyond, fundamental rights, and include many other precepts commonly found in systems of administrative law, such as proportionality and legitimate expectations.

The consequence of their hierarchical status and procedural/substantive reach means that they are a powerful tool, the disposition of which lies in the hands of the Court. This in turn has the consequence that certain options are literally taken off the legislative agenda, insofar as they are inconsistent with general principles of law. The only way in which such judicial decisions can be reversed is by amendment to the EU Treaties, which is for most practical purposes a non-starter.

It is axiomatic that the Court and the Advocates General (AGs) have inherent discretion as to how to deploy such principles, as forcefully exemplified by *Sturgeon* itself. There will, perforce, always be the possibility for differences of opinion as to how the Court applied such principles in a particular case, more especially the way in which it conceptualised what could be achieved through interpretation.

It was readily apparent that the AG was more cautious in this respect than the Court. This was manifest most notably in AG Sharpston's reticence as to what could legitimately be achieved by the judiciary, in the context of the discussion as to what would constitute inordinate delay.

The Court's approach, by way of contrast, was more interventionist, using that term to connote what could be achieved through interpretation, thereby obviating the need for invalidation. It is interesting to stand back from the Court's reasoning and reflect on the methodology therein.

It is clear that the Court felt the need to anchor its conclusions somewhere in the text of the Regulation. It considered that the starkly differential treatment of cancellation and delay insofar as compensation was concerned had to be 'dented' through a foothold found in the text itself. It was this impulse that drove the reasoning about Recital 15 of the Preamble adumbrated above, from which the Court concluded that the legislature did not intend compensation to be entirely foreclosed for cases of delay. Truth be told, it was pretty thin textual ground for this conclusion, given the dichotomy between cancellation and delay that runs through the entire Regulation. The Court's conclusions in this respect also sit uneasily with its reasoning earlier in the judgment, where it had emphasised the real divide between cancellation and delay when rebutting the argument that inordinate delay could constitute cancellation.

The interpretive reasoning in the remainder of the judgment was, however, more convincing. There is a strong presumption that legislation should be interpreted in accordance with general principles of law. There is an equally strong presumption that the particular wording of the Regulation should be interpreted to cohere with the objectives that informed the legislative initiative. The Court did, moreover, anchor its conclusions as to the effluxion of time whereby delay would count as cancellation for the purposes of compensation in the wording of the Regulation.

There will, as noted above, inevitably be differences of opinion as to whether the Court pushed too far in the name of interpretation. The choices in this respect are real. Invalidation places the matter back in the hands of the legislature. It would be for the Commission, Parliament, and Council to structure an amendment to the Regulation that removed the inequality between cancellation and delay. If it was unwilling to do so, then the relevant provisions concerning compensation for cancellation would have to be removed. However, this would then have created difficulties in terms of EU compliance with the underlying international obligations on which the Regulation was based, and it would have weakened the consumer protection that underpins this area of the law.

The interpretive route chosen by the Court forecloses this legislative inquiry. The Regulation now bears the meaning accorded to it by the Court. The EU legislature might try to amend the Regulation, but any such amendment would have to be consistent with the Court's reasoning in *Sturgeon* and with the general principles of law.[40]

---

[40] For a Commission proposal to amend Reg 261/2004, which would, inter alia, have incorporated the results of the *Sturgeon* case, see the Proposal for a Regulation of the European Parliament and of the Council amending Regulation (EC) No 261/2004 establishing common rules on compensation and assistance to passengers in the event of denied boarding and of cancellation or long delay of flights and Regulation (EC) No 2027/97 on air carrier liability in respect of the carriage of passengers and their baggage by air, COM(2013)0130 final.

40

'When Citizens Move, They Do So as Human Beings, Not as Robots': Opinion of Advocate General Sharpston in Ruiz Zambrano

NIAMH NIC SHUIBHNE

I. INTRODUCTION

AFTER A PARTICULARLY intensive day in the office (when it was possible to do such things prior to the COVID-19 pandemic), this author printed the Opinion of AG Sharpston in *Ruiz Zambrano* just before leaving Old College at the University of Edinburgh. Over two hours later, I was still sitting in my coat reading it. Arguably, it is one of the most significant Opinions ever delivered, not just in EU citizenship law, but in EU law more generally. Fulfilling the additional responsibility of paying tribute to the late AG Ruiz-Jarabo Colomer, to whom the case was originally assigned, but who sadly died while the case was in progress, AG Sharpston's text is a *tour de force* of analysis and insight, traversing the full span of EU free movement and citizenship law, and highlighting, in turn, the innate systemic connections between substantive EU law and the constitutional principles on which it stands. It did not go unnoticed that it was one of the most detailed Opinions delivered relative to the strikingly brief, cryptic judgment delivered by the Court.[1] Because AG Sharpston has done so herself when she speaks about *Ruiz Zambrano* at public events, the contribution of the *référendaires* should also be acknowledged.

The questions referred sat at the intersection of rights conferred by EU law on third country national family members of Union citizens, seen up to that point in free movement law only, and reserved national competence for immigration in situations outside of EU law. More specifically, the case highlighted the strain placed on the purely internal rule in free movement law by years of case law eroding what was needed to produce sufficient cross-border connections. In *Ruiz Zambrano*, AG Sharpston excavated the anomalies, contradictions, and legal fictions propagated as a result, asking, in essence: 'is the exercise of rights as a Union citizen dependent – like the exercise of the classic economic "freedoms" – on some trans-frontier free movement (however accidental, peripheral or remote) having taken place before the claim is advanced?'[2]

---

[1] N Nic Shuibhne, 'Seven Questions for Seven Paragraphs' (2011) 36 *ELRev* 161.
[2] Opinion of AG Sharpston in Case C-34/09 *Ruiz Zambrano* ECLI:EU:C:2010:560, para 3.

Above all, the case compelled the Court to consider what Union citizenship really means: is it 'merely the non-economic version of the same generic kind of free movement rights as have long existed for the economically active and for persons of independent means? Or does it mean something more radical: true citizenship, carrying with it a uniform set of rights and obligations, in a Union under the rule of law in which respect for fundamental rights must necessarily play an integral part?'[3] Building on *Rottmann*,[4] *Ruiz Zambrano* intensified a ground-breaking line of case law drawing profound (legal) implications from the deceptively simple statement in Article 20 TFEU that '[c]itizenship of the Union is hereby established'.

II. BACKGROUND, CONTEXT, AND FACTS

In *Saunders*, the Court held that '[t]he provisions of the Treaty on freedom of movement for workers cannot ... be applied to situations which are *wholly internal to a Member State, in other words*, where there is *no factor connecting them* to any of the situations envisaged by [Union] law' (emphasis added).[5] In *Uecker and Jacquet*, it confirmed that 'citizenship of the Union, established by Article [20 TFEU], *is not intended to extend the scope ratione materiae of the Treaty also to internal situations which have no link with [Union] law* ... Any discrimination which nationals of a Member State may suffer under the law of that State fall ... must therefore be dealt with within the framework of the internal legal system of that State' (emphasis added).[6] Reflecting these principles, Article 3(1) of Directive 2004/38/EC provides that the Directive applies 'to all Union citizens *who move to or reside in a Member State other than that of which they are a national*, and to their family members ... *who accompany or join them*' (emphasis added).[7]

Why, then, was a case involving the refusal of a residence permit in Belgium for the Colombian father of Belgian minor children, who had never moved anywhere within the Union, assigned to the Grand Chamber: to reverse the established approach to purely internal situations or to extinguish speculation that Union citizenship could justify a more radical approach once and for all?

Mr Ruiz Zambrano, his wife, and their eldest child, all Colombian nationals, arrived in Belgium in 1999. Applications for refugee status were refused in 2000, and they were ordered to leave Belgium, but with a *non-refoulement* clause that they should not be sent back to Colombia. In the years that followed, Mr Ruiz Zambrano and his wife remained in Belgium, and sought to regularise their situation. The couple had two more children, both of whom acquired Belgian nationality under the rules then applicable in Belgium. Mr Ruiz Zambrano was engaged in paid employment, providing sufficient resources to support his family, though without a work permit.

The proceedings concerned Mr Ruiz Zambrano's residence status in Belgium, and a refusal of unemployment benefits following the loss of his job. The questions referred to the Court asked whether 'the provisions of the TFEU on European Union citizenship are to be interpreted as meaning that they confer on a relative in the ascending line who is a third-country national,

---

[3] ibid.
[4] Case C-135/08 *Rottman* ECLI:EU:C:2010:104.
[5] Case 175/78 *Saunders* ECLI:EU:C:1979:88, para 11.
[6] Joined Cases C-64/96 and C-65/96 *Uecker and Jacquet* ECLI:EU:C:1997:285, para 23.
[7] Directive 2004/38/EC on the right of citizens of the Union and their family members to move and reside freely within the territory of the Member States [2004] OJ L158/77.

upon whom his minor children, who are European Union citizens, are dependent, a right of residence in the Member State *of which they are nationals and in which they reside*, and also exempt him from having to obtain a work permit in that Member State' (emphasis added).[8] All (eight) governments submitting observations, as well as the Commission, which argued that the family's circumstances did not constitute one of 'the situations envisaged by the freedoms of movement and residence guaranteed under European Union law' since the Union citizen children, from whom any rights under EU law for their third country national family members would have to be derived, 'reside in the Member State of which they are nationals and have never left the territory of that Member State'.[9]

III. THE OPINION OF AG SHARPSTON

AG Sharpston's expansive Opinion reached into the four corners of EU free movement law, interrogating both the logic and the viability of *Saunders* and *Uecker and Jacquet*, and connecting the analysis of economic free movement rights to the nature of Union citizenship and of the Union as a legal order producing that status.

Following reflections on admissibility (reverse discrimination was not permitted under Belgian law, and a ruling from the Court would therefore 'facilitate the referring court's task of comparing the position under EU law with the position under national law'[10]), AG Sharpston outlined three possible routes to determining the case, unfolding outwards in boldness: first, applying an already possible (though essentially fictional[11]) understanding of *potential* restrictions of free movement rights (paragraphs 75–122); secondly, engaging Union citizenship to resolve instances of reverse discrimination (paragraphs 123–150); and thirdly, reflecting on the implications of a polity rooted in respect for fundamental rights (paragraphs 151–177).

Points of detail in that analysis are returned to in Section IV, but two critical observations arguably frame the Opinion as a whole: first, that '[l]ottery rather than logic would seem to be governing the exercise of EU citizenship rights'; and secondly, that 'when citizens move, they do so as human beings, not as robots. They fall in love, marry and have families'.[12]

In the end, the Court opened a fourth dimension in its terse judgment, balanced precariously between meaningful Union citizenship and trampled Member State competence in internal situations. As will be seen below, however, the seeds of the Court's approach were evident in the Opinion of AG Sharpston all along.

IV. ANALYSIS

To the surprise of pretty much everyone, the Court articulated a new basis for derived residence rights in EU citizenship law by splitting the *Saunder* and *Uecker and Jacquet* reasoning

---

[8] Case C-34/09 *Ruiz Zambrano* ECLI:EU:C:2011:124, para 36.

[9] Para 37 of the Judgment.

[10] Para 43 of the Opinion.

[11] Para 77 of the Opinion: 'I do not think that exercise of the rights derived from citizenship of the Union is always inextricably and necessarily bound up with physical movement. There are also already citizenship cases in which the element of true movement is either barely discernible or frankly non-existent'; citing Case C-148/02 *Garcia Avello* ECLI:EU:C:2003:539; Case C-200/02 *Zhu and Chen* ECLI:EU:C:2004:639; and Case C-135/08 *Rottmann* ECLI:EU:C:2010:104 as examples.

[12] Paras 88 and 128 of the Opinion.

into two parts: in other words, situations that are purely internal to a single Member State do not necessarily have no (other) connection to EU law. First, the Court recalled that the status of Union citizen is conferred on Member State nationals – here, on Mr Ruiz Zambrano's younger children – by Article 20 TFEU and that Union citizenship is 'intended to be the fundamental status of nationals of the Member States'.[13] Secondly, 'Article 20 TFEU precludes national measures which have the effect of *depriving citizens of the Union of the genuine enjoyment of the substance of the rights* conferred by virtue of their status as citizens of the Union' (emphasis added).[14] Thirdly, '[a] refusal to grant a right of residence to a third-country national with *dependent* minor children in the Member State where those children are nationals and reside, and also a refusal to grant such a person a work permit, has such an effect',[15] as '[i]t must be assumed that such a refusal would lead to a situation where those children, citizens of the Union, *would have to leave the territory of the Union* in order to accompany their parents. Similarly, if a work permit were not granted to such a person, he would risk not having sufficient resources to provide for himself and his family, which would also result in the children, citizens of the Union, having to leave the territory of the Union. In those circumstances, those citizens of the Union *would, in fact, be unable to exercise the substance of the rights conferred on them* by virtue of their status as citizens of the Union' (emphasis added).[16]

But where did the Court's test *come from*, in legal terms? This question is examined in Section IV.A, finding the roots in the Opinion of AG Sharpston, before the discussion addresses her approach to movement as a legal fiction (Section IV.B) and to the significance of fundamental rights (Section IV.C); reflecting then on what her conclusions reveal about the nature of Union citizenship and the development of EU law (Section IV.D). The continuing influence of *Ruiz Zambrano* is then briefly considered in Section IV.E.

A. Origins of the 'Genuine Enjoyment of the Substance of the Rights' Test

Ruiz Zambrano was a game-changer on residence rights for third country national family members, but one legal step back to *Rottmann* is required better to understand the Court's thinking. As noted above, the Court invoked paragraph 42 of *Rottmann* to support the crucial finding in *Ruiz Zambrano* that 'Article 20 TFEU precludes national measures which have the effect of depriving citizens of the Union of the genuine enjoyment of the substance of the rights' conferred by Union citizenship.[17] In *Rottmann*, AG Poiares Maduro emphasised Mr Rottmann's *previous* exercise of free movement,[18] thereby engaging Article 21 TFEU, but the Court based its ruling on Article 20 TFEU, finding that 'the situation of a citizen of the Union who ... is faced with a decision withdrawing his naturalisation, adopted by the

---

[13] Paras 40–41 of the Judgment, citing, inter alia, Case C-184/99 *Grzelczyk* ECLI:EU:C:2001:458, para 31.

[14] Para 42 of the Judgment; citing, 'to that effect', Case C-135/08 *Rottmann*, para 42. This citation is returned to below.

[15] Para 43 of the Judgment.

[16] ibid, para 44. It was later confirmed that the fact that the third-country national parent was residing illegally in the home Member State is 'immaterial' for residence rights based on Article 20 TFEU; see Case C-82/16 *K.A.* ECLI:EU:C:2018:308, paras 78–81 and 89. In her Opinion for that case, AG Sharpston dismissed the idea of a 'general presumption of abuse when a family link arises at the point when a third-country national finds himself to be an irregular stayer' (Opinion of AG Sharpston in Case C-82/16 *K.A.* ECLI:EU:C:2017:821, para 65).

[17] Para 42 of the Judgment.

[18] Opinion of AG Poiares Maduro in Case C-135/08 *Rottmann* ECLI:EU:C:2009:588, paras 9–13.

authorities of one Member State, and placing him, after he has lost the nationality of another Member State that he originally possessed, in a position *capable of causing him to lose the status conferred by Article [20 TFEU] and the rights attaching thereto falls, by reason of its nature and its consequences, within the ambit of European Union law*' (emphasis added).[19]

The *Ruiz Zambrano* cross-reference to *Rottmann* was less instructive, at the time, than the Court might have assumed; but with the benefit of hindsight, the nature of Article 20 TFEU rights can be better appreciated: they manifest in exceptional circumstances, approaching a point of making it impossible to 'be' a Union citizen. Retaining Member State nationality – the precondition for Union citizenship and the context of the dispute in *Rottmann* – is an obvious exemplar of these criteria; but it was not clear which aspect or aspects of the situation in *Ruiz Zambrano* pushed that case across the same threshold.

Crucial further light can be found in the Opinion of AG Sharpston. Following her own reference to paragraph 42 of *Rottmann*, she continued:

> [The Ruiz Zambrano children] have not yet moved outside their own Member State. Nor, following his naturalisation, had Dr Rottmann. If the parents do not have a derivative right of residence and are required to leave Belgium, the children will, in all probability, have to leave with them. That would, in practical terms, place Diego and Jessica in a 'position capable of causing them to lose the status conferred [by their citizenship of the Union] and the rights attaching thereto'. It follows – as it did for Dr Rottmann – that the *children's situation* 'falls, by reason of its nature and its consequences, within the ambit of EU law (emphasis in the original).[20]

On this view, the practical impossibility of exercising Union citizenship rights – of genuinely enjoying the substance of those rights – could rationalise protection in Union law by analogy with losing the status of Union citizenship. Thus, while the Court did not choose one of the three *options* AG Sharpston had proposed, the option it adopted was grounded in her *reasoning*.

B. The Illusion of 'Movement'

For AG Sharpston, '[i]t is trite law that, in order to be able to claim classic economic rights associated with the four freedoms, some kind of movement between Member States is normally required'.[21] However, she emphasised the Court's willingness to accept disruption of the *potential* exercise of free movement as a sufficient trigger. Similarly, 'exercise of the rights derived from citizenship of the Union is [not] always inextricably and necessarily bound up with physical movement'.[22] She also noted 'the risk that "static" factors of production will be left in a worse position than their "mobile" counterparts, even though in all other respects their circumstances may be similar or identical. The outcome is reverse discrimination created by the interaction of EU law with national law – a discrimination that the Court has hitherto left each Member State to solve, notwithstanding that such a result is, *prima facie*, a breach of the principle of non-discrimination on the grounds of nationality'.[23] Reflecting that

---

[19] Case C-135/08 *Rottmann*, para 42.
[20] Paras 95–96 of the Opinion.
[21] ibid, para 69.
[22] ibid, para 77, discussing, inter alia, Case C-148/02 *Garcia Avello*.
[23] Para 133 of the Opinion.

understanding, 'the Member States that have submitted observations [and the Commission] argued, unanimously, that Mr Ruiz Zambrano's situation is one that is "purely internal" to Belgium and that EU law provisions, including those relating to citizenship of the Union, are therefore not triggered'.[24]

The next paragraph of the Opinion has just six words: 'I do not share their view'. AG Sharpston's perspective was already evident in *Government of the French Community and Walloon Government*:

> True, the Court has held that citizenship of the Union, as established by Article [20 TFEU], is not intended to extend the material scope of the Treaty to internal situations which have no link with [Union] law. However, that statement requires one to solve the logically prior question of which situations, internal or not, are deemed to have no link with [Union] law. The answer cannot be that all so-called 'internal situations' *are automatically deprived of any link to [Union] law* ... The question whether the situation is internal is therefore conceptually distinct from the question whether there is a link with [Union] law. Both questions must be answered in the light of the goals of the relevant Treaty provisions (emphasis added).[25]

In essence, Union citizenship 'challenge[s] the sustainability in its present form of the doctrine on purely internal situations'.[26] AG Sharpston progressed that analysis in *Ruiz Zambrano* – about as 'purely internal' as a case could get.

In her view, reverse discrimination should be addressed by Union law when three cumulative conditions are met: the situation of the static citizen should be comparable to citizens of other Member States protected by EU law in similar circumstances (family reunification providing a paradigmatic example); violation of a fundamental right protected under EU law should be present; and EU law – specifically Article 18 TFEU – should be triggered only as a subsidiary remedy when the violation could not be resolved by national law.[27]

The Court did not recalibrate its position on reverse discrimination in its judgment; but it did accept that purely internal situations could have links with EU law. Lenaerts and Gutiérrez-Fons thus suggested that *Ruiz Zambrano* 'served to emancipate EU citizenship from the constraints inherent in its free movement origins'.[28] However, the Court has since emphasised that residence rights conferred on the family members of Union citizens by Article 20 TFEU have 'an *intrinsic connection* with the freedom of movement of a Union citizen' (emphasis added).[29] Preserving a right to reside in the territory of the Union now, returned to below, facilitates freedom of movement in the future. It would seem, then, that the illusion of movement continues in some respects.

AG Sharpston also acknowledged a dimension of *Ruiz Zambrano* that the Court overlooked: that '[i]t is of course *theoretically possible* that another Member State might be prepared to take the family' (emphasis added).[30] The option (or obligation?) for a Union citizen to leave their home State and move to another State to generate residence rights for third

---

[24] ibid, para 91.

[25] Opinion of AG Sharpston in Case C-212/06 *Government of the French Community and Walloon Government* ECLI:EU:C:2007:398, paras 134–36.

[26] ibid, para 140.

[27] ibid, paras 144–48.

[28] K Lenaerts and JA Gutiérrez-Fons, 'Epilogue on EU Citizenship: Hopes and Fears' in D Kochenov (ed), *EU Citizenship and Federalism: The Role of Rights* (Cambridge, CUP, 2017) 751, 761.

[29] Case C-40/11 *Iida* ECLI:EU:C:2012:691, para 72.

[30] Footnote 76 of the Opinion.

country national family members featured more prominently in later case law.[31] However, the Court now engages more deeply with the *practical* and not just *theoretical* circumstances of affected Union citizens:[32] in other words, the option to move to another Member State 'cannot exist only in the abstract'.[33]

C. The Significance of Fundamental Rights

For AG Sharpston, protection of fundamental rights was the 'leitmotif' connecting the referring court's questions.[34] The systemic implications are returned to in Section IV.D below but, more concretely, she emphasised the significance of protecting fundamental rights in the context of exercising freedom of movement, especially in the Court's ruling in *Carpenter*,[35] and under Article 7 (respect for family life) and Article 24(2) (best interests of the child) of the Charter of Fundamental Rights (the Charter).

The judgment in *Ruiz Zambrano* was intensely recognized for its overreach into the sphere of national immigration competence,[36] leading initially to an impulse to contain its implications.[37] In that light, the Court held in *Dereci* that 'the mere fact that it might appear desirable to a national of a Member State, for economic reasons or in order to keep his family together in the territory of the Union, for the members of his family who do not have the nationality of a Member State to be able to reside with him in the territory of the Union, is not sufficient in itself to support the view that the Union citizen will be forced to leave Union territory if such a right is not granted'.[38]

Subsequently, in her joint Opinion for *O and B* and *S and G*, AG Sharpston remarked that 'the Court has yet to resolve whether one applies the same test in order to determine both whether EU law (and thus also the Charter) applies and whether a measure denying residence is contrary to Article 20 or 21 TFEU'.[39] She then continued:

> [A] provision such as Article 20 or 21 TFEU is not simply a basis for residence status separate from Article 7 of the Charter. Rather, *considerations regarding the exercise of the right to a family life permeate the substance of EU citizenship rights*. Citizenship rights under Article 20 or 21 TFEU must thus be interpreted in a way that ensures that their substantive content is 'Charter-compliant' ... Such an approach does not 'extend' the scope of EU law and thus violate the separation of competences between the Union and its constituent Member States. It merely respects the overarching principle that, in a Union founded on the rule of law, all the relevant law (including, naturally, relevant primary law in the shape of the Charter) is taken into account when interpreting a provision of that legal

---

[31] See especially, Case C-86/12 *Alokpa* ECLI:EU:C:2013:645, paras 32–35. That position was much criticised; see eg D Kochenov, 'EU Citizenship: From an Incipient Form to an Incipient Substance? The Discovery of the Treaty Text' (2012) 37 *ELRev* 369 at 393 ('[s]ince the Treaties do not connect the enjoyment of the substance of EU citizenship rights with movement or limit EU citizenship rights to the right not to leave the territory of the Union, the rights paradigm should not be artificially connected to movement .... It is quite sensible to expect that rights be sufficiently protected without taking a bus').

[32] See especially, Case C-133/15 *Chavez-Vilchez* ECLI:EU:C:2017:354, returned to below.

[33] Opinion of AG Wathelet in Case C-115/15 *NA* ECLI:EU:C:2016:259, para 114.

[34] Para 53 of the Opinion.

[35] Case C-60/00 *Carpenter* ECLI:EU:C:2002:434.

[36] Discussed in eg K Hailbronner and D Thym, 'Case C-34/09, Gerardo Ruiz Zambrano v. Office national de l'emploi (ONEm), Judgment of the Court of Justice (Grand Chamber) of 8 March 2011' (2011) 48 *CMLRev* 1253.

[37] For reflection of AG Sharpston post facto, see ch 52.

[38] Case C-256/11 *Dereci* ECLI:EU:C:2011:734, para 68.

[39] Opinion of AG Sharpston in Case C-456/12 *O* and Case C-457/12 *S* ECLI:EU:C:2013:837, para 58.

order. When viewed in that light, taking due account of the Charter is no more 'intrusive', or 'disrespectful of Member State competence', than interpreting free movement of goods correctly.[40]

In *Chavez-Vilchez*, the Court significantly advanced the role of the Charter in Article 20 TFEU cases compared to *Dereci*, absorbing the influence of AG Sharpston (and others[41]):

> [I]n order to assess the risk that a particular child, who is a Union citizen, might be compelled to leave the territory of the European Union and thereby be deprived of the genuine enjoyment of the substance of the rights conferred on him by Article 20 TFEU if the child's third-country national parent were to be refused a right of residence in the Member State concerned, it is important to determine ... which parent is the primary carer of the child and *whether there is in fact a relationship of dependency between the child and the third-country national parent. As part of that assessment, the competent authorities must take account of the right to respect for family life*, as stated in Article 7 of the Charter of Fundamental Rights of the European Union ... read in conjunction with the obligation to take into consideration the best interests of the child, recognised in Article 24(2) (emphasis added).[42]

A nuanced picture emerges above: the Charter is now a central part of an Article 20 TFEU assessment; but so too are conditions already evident (if implicitly at that point) in *Ruiz Zambrano*.

First, as AG Sharpston had observed, children 'cannot exercise their rights as Union citizens (specifically, their rights to move and to reside in any Member State) fully and effectively without the presence and support of their parents'.[43] The Court was less clear in its judgment, but it later confirmed that the relationship between the Union citizen and their third country national family member(s) must entail *dependency*.[44] Dependency is an expression of proportionality. It is not determined by whether a Union citizen lives with the person for whom a right to reside is sought or by a blood relationship,[45] though arrangements concerning the custody or primary care of minor children might be relevant.[46] Fundamentally, legal, financial or emotional dependency must be demonstrated, since that is what would lead, secondly, 'to the Union citizen being obliged, in fact, to leave not only the territory of the Member State of which he is a national but also that of the European Union as a whole'.[47]

In that light, 'an adult is, as a general rule, capable of living an independent existence apart from the members of his family' so that 'a relationship between two adult members of the same family as a relationship of dependency, capable of giving rise to a derived right of residence under Article 20 TFEU, is conceivable only in exceptional cases, where, having regard to all the relevant circumstances, there could be no form of separation of the individual concerned from the member of his family on whom he is dependent'.[48] Thus, while a theoretical prospect remains that dependency might be recognized in any relationship, *Ruiz Zambrano*

---

[40] ibid, paras 62–63.

[41] Expressly endorsing AG Sharpston's approach, see Opinion of AG Wathelet in Case C-115/15 *NA* ECLI:EU:C:2016:259, para 122. See also Opinion of AG Szpunar in Case C-165/14 *Rendón Marín* and Case C-304/14 *CS* ECLI:EU:C:2016:75, paras 119–22.

[42] *Chavez-Vilchez*, para 70.

[43] Para 96 of the Opinion; see similarly, para 102: 'Diego and Jessica cannot exercise such a right of residence without the support of their parents'.

[44] eg Joined Cases C-356/11 and C-357/11 *O. and S.* ECLI:EU:C:2012:776, para 50.

[45] ibid, paras 54–55.

[46] Case C-82/16 *KA*, para 71.

[47] Joined Cases C-356/11 and C-357/11, *O. and S.* ECLI:EU:C:2012:776, paras 54–56.

[48] Case C-82/16 *KA*, para 65.

has particular significance for protecting the rights of children.[49] What, though, does it mean to be *forced* to leave the territory of the Union?

D. Systemic Implications of Union Citizenship

Referencing the path-setting ideas of AG Jacobs,[50] AG Sharpston underlined in *Ruiz Zambrano* that 'by granting fundamental rights under EU law to its citizens, and stating that such rights are the very foundation of the Union [Article 2 TEU], the European Union committed itself to the principle that citizens exercising rights to freedom of movement will do so under the protection of those fundamental rights'.[51] She rejected 'the idea that one should simply follow, in respect of citizenship of the Union, the orthodox approach to free movement of goods and freedom of movement for employed and self-employed workers and capital' since '[c]itizens are not "resources" employed to produce goods and services, but individuals bound to a political community and protected by fundamental rights'.[52] In some respects, she then appeared to go further than the Court by calling for recognition of a 'free-standing right of residence' in EU law: a decoupling of the right to reside from the right to move.[53] But what emerges in the judgment and subsequent case law *does* come close to a 'free-standing right of residence' – just one framed as a right pertaining to the territory of the Union as a whole and not to a citizen's home State per se; as a 'right to stay'[54] within that wider territory.

In systemic terms, a 'right to stay' in the territory of the Union fosters an important, tangible connection between Member State nationals and something beyond the Member States. The threshold condition of being forced to leave the territory of the Union requires a decision of a public authority with implications for the residence status of a third country national family member on whom a Union citizen is dependent.[55] While *Ruiz Zambrano* addressed only the children's father, the approach to Article 20 TFEU developed more recently would assess separation from other family members in light of the child's best interests under Article 24(2) of the Charter.

It is arguable, though, that the dispute in *Ruiz Zambrano* was far more about the proportionality of a *national* decision affecting the right to family life of two of its own nationals than about Union citizenship. The case thus raised another important systemic question about balancing optimal protection of fundamental rights, on the one hand, and respect for conferral

---

[49] See further, H van Eijken and P Phoa, 'The Scope of Article 20 TFEU Clarified in *Chavez-Vilchez*: Are the Fundamental Rights of Minor Citizens Coming of Age?' (2018) 43 *ELRev* 949.

[50] Opinion of AG Jacobs in Case C-168/91 *Konstantinidis* ECLI:EU:C:1992:504, para 46: 'a [Union] national who goes to another Member State as a worker or self-employed person under ... the Treaty is entitled not just to pursue his trade or profession and to enjoy the same living and working conditions as nationals of the host State; he is in addition entitled to assume that, wherever he goes to earn his living in the European [Union], he will be treated in accordance with a common code of fundamental values, in particular those laid down in the European Convention on Human Rights. In other words, he is entitled to say "civis europeus sum" and to invoke that status in order to oppose any violation of his fundamental rights'. See ch 25.

[51] Para 129.

[52] ibid, paras 131 and 127.

[53] ibid, para 101. While AG Sharpston drew from Articles 20 and 21 TFEU, the Court has been careful to contain home State rights without movement (yet) to Article 20 TFEU.

[54] Case C-133/15 *Chavez-Vilchez*, para 42.

[55] A Union citizen can of course *choose* to leave the territory of the Union, but should not be forced to do so by a decision implementing national law, subject to the limits discussed further below. In other words, Union citizenship 'cannot amount to putting [Member State nationals] "under house arrest" in the territory of the European Union'. Opinion of AG Bot in Joined Cases C-356/11 and C-357/11 *O. and S.* ECLI:EU:C:2012:776, para 41.

of powers, on the other. AG Sharpston addressed both elements. She suggested, first, that 'in the long run, the clearest rule would be one that made the availability of EU fundamental rights protection dependent … on *the existence and scope of a material EU competence.* [P]rovided that the EU had competence (whether exclusive or shared) in a particular area of law, EU fundamental rights should protect the citizen of the EU *even if such competence has not yet been exercised*' (emphasis in the original).[56] However, secondly, she fully appreciated that introducing such an 'overtly federal element into the structure of the EU's legal and political system' would 'alter, in legal and political terms, the very nature of fundamental rights under EU law'.[57] In short, that would require Treaty change.

E. Effect on Future Case Law

It took some time for the *Ruiz Zambrano* case law to settle, and points of contraction and expansion have been identified above. The judgment exploded the potential of Union citizenship at one level, yet family residence rights in a Union citizen's home state are drawn from Article 20 TFEU only in exceptional circumstances: '[t]he mere possibility of losing the opportunity to quietly live with one's family does not trigger protection under EU law'.[58] It has also since been confirmed that the right to stay in the territory of the Union is not unlimited. The Court has applied free movement law by analogy for *Ruiz Zambrano* rights and ruled that 'Article 20 TFEU does not affect the possibility of Member States relying on an exception linked, in particular, to upholding the requirements of public policy and safeguarding public security'.[59]

Where the outer limits of *Ruiz Zambrano* rights might be fixed in other respects remains to be seen.[60] The question of entitlement to social assistance is likely to be referred to the Court in the future. Interestingly, the Court has suggested that it might ask more of a Union citizen's home state than it asks of host states,[61] noting its view that 'to refuse a third-country national who is a family member of a Union citizen a derived right of residence in the territory of the Member State of which that citizen is a national *on the sole ground* that the latter does not have sufficient resources, even though there is, between that citizen and that third-country national, a relationship of dependency … would constitute an impairment of the effective enjoyment of the essential rights deriving from the status of Union citizen' (emphasis added).[62] It is also likely that Article 20 TFEU will be drawn from to illuminate novel citizenship rights not yet activated,[63] though Brexit did not trigger Article 20 TFEU protection of *former* Union citizens, for example.

---

[56] ibid, para 163.

[57] ibid, paras 172–73.

[58] L Azoulai, 'Transfiguring European Citizenship: From Member State Territory to Union Territory' in D Kochenov (ed), *EU Citizenship and Federalism: The Role of Rights* (Cambridge, CUP, 2017) 178, 196.

[59] Case C-165/14 *Rendón Marín*, para 81.

[60] See also, D Sarmiento and E Sharpston, 'European Citizenship and its New Union: Time to Move On?' in Kochenov (n 58).

[61] eg Case C-333/13 *Dano* ECLI:EU:C:2014:2358.

[62] Case C-836/18 *Subdelegación del Gobierno en Ciudad Real* ECLI:EU:C:2020:119, para 48. Compare the focus on Mr Ruiz Zambrano's economic contributions in the Judgment (para 44), and in Opinion of AG Sharpston (para 120). Critiquing the narrow view taken by the UK Supreme Court in a pre-Brexit ruling, see C O'Brien, '*Acte Cryptique? Zambrano*, Welfare Rights, and Underclass Citizenship in the Tale of the Missing Preliminary Reference' (2019) 56 *CMLRev* 1697.

[63] See eg K Kalaitzaki, 'The Application of EU Fundamental Rights During the Financial Crisis: EU Citizenship to the Rescue? (2021) 27 *EPL* 331.

These choices, treading a delicate line between the reach of Union law and the preserve of national decision-making, were made possible by *Ruiz Zambrano*. Leaving the last word to AG Sharpston, '[t]he consequences of th[e] statement [in *Grzelczyk*] that Union citizenship "was destined to become the fundamental status of nationals of the Member States" are ... as important and far-reaching as those of earlier milestones in the Court's case-law. Indeed, I regard the Court's description of citizenship of the Union in *Grzelczyk* as being potentially of similar significance to its seminal statement *in Van Gend en Loos* that "the Community constitutes a new legal order of international law"'.[64] That is quite some legacy to live up to; and it was provoked in no small part by AG Sharpston herself.

---

[64] Para 68 of the Opinion; referring to Case 26/62 *Van Gend en Loos* ECLI:EU:C:1963:1.

41

Access to Administrative and Judicial Review in Public Interest Litigation: Opinion of Advocate General Sharpston in Slovak Bears

THEODORE KONSTADINIDES

I. INTRODUCTION

THE Aarhus Convention is a mixed agreement which was signed on 25 June 1998 by both the then European Community and the Member States and subsequently approved by Council Decision 2005/370/EC.[1] It was an important step in addressing the difficulties faced by individuals and non-governmental organisations when trying to protect the living environment. One of the key aims of the Aarhus Convention was to promote transparency in the way public authorities responded to a request for environmental information, including administrative measures, policies, and legislation, and make such information available to the public, subject to confidentiality and other restrictions (Article 4). Most importantly, for the purpose of this chapter, Article 9 of the Aarhus Convention provides the legal basis for public interest litigation in relation to access to justice in environmental disputes, and a right to judicial review at the national level where a request for environmental information has been ignored, refused, or there has been an inadequate response from national authorities.

Slovak Bears is a significant case for access to justice in environmental matters in relation to the effect of the Aarhus Convention at the national level, and the possibility for citizens to ensure the application of environmental law.[2] But beyond this, the case brought to the surface broader questions regarding whether individuals can rely directly on the rules of an international agreement in order to bring proceedings under EU law and challenge the decisions of national administrations in Member States. The case further revisited a much wider concern regarding the rules on the standing of individuals to challenge acts not addressed to them. Such rules have become the subject matter of a long saga ever since decisions such as *Plaumann*,[3] and *UPA*.[4] By contrast to these cases, however, which concerned challenging EU acts not addressed

---

[1] Council Decision 2005/370/EC on the conclusion, on behalf of the European Community, of the Convention on access to information, public participation in decision-making and access to justice in environmental matters [2005] OJ L124/1.

[2] Case C-240/09 *Lesoochranárske zoskupenie* ECLI:EU:C:2011:125.

[3] Case 25/62 *Plaumann* ECLI:EU:C:1963:17.

[4] Case C-50/00 P *UPA* ECLI:EU:C:2002:462. See ch 33.

to individuals, *Slovak Bears* was about a decision taken following administrative proceedings in a Member State which are liable to be in breach of international law. As will be discussed, the legacy of the case extends beyond environmental law and into constitutional law in relation to procedural autonomy, effective judicial protection and the right to an effective remedy. In this regard, the Opinion of the AG Sharpston was important as a reminder of the limits of EU competence and respect for national procedural autonomy, especially with regard to the freedom afforded to Member States to decide questions related to national conditions regulating access to justice and the granting of effective remedies to individuals whose interests have been adversely affected by administrative decisions.

II. BACKGROUND, CONTEXT, AND FACTS

The case was a preliminary reference to the Court made by the Supreme Court of Slovakia in a dispute concerning an environmental protection association (*Lesoochranárske zoskupenie VLK*, hereafter LZ) which sought recognition of its status as a 'party' to administrative proceedings brought under the Slovakian administrative procedure code by hunting associations requesting permission to derogate from the protective conditions accorded to the brown bear by the Habitats Directive.[5] The relevant district authority that allowed the hunting of the brown bear rejected LZ's request to participate in the proceedings despite the latter's claim that the proceedings directly affected its rights arising from the Aarhus Convention. The district authority replied that as a matter of national law LZ's status was rather that of an 'interested party', and as such, it could not directly challenge the legality of the administrative decision which granted the relevant derogations. It also argued that as an international agreement, the Aarhus Convention needed to be implemented in national law before it could take effect domestically. It added that Article 9 of the Convention did not provide a fundamental right which was directly effective to public authorities. LZ proceeded by challenging the district authority's decision unsuccessfully before the regional court in Bratislava, contending that the proceedings affected its rights as protected by Article 9(3) of the Aarhus Convention.

Following the adverse decision by the regional court, LZ appealed to the Supreme Court, which stayed the proceedings and sent a preliminary reference to the Court asking three questions concerning the interpretation of Article 9(3) of the Aarhus Convention. The first question was jurisdictional: is it for the Court or the national courts to determine whether Article 9(3) of the Aarhus Convention has direct effect? The Court was, in other words, asked to justify its jurisdiction in a national dispute concerning the enforcement of a provision of a mixed agreement. The second question was more substantive: Does Article 9(3) contain obligations that are sufficiently clear and precise to govern the legal position of individuals directly? This question concerned the self-executing character of a mixed agreement which relies on national legislation to implement the judicial review procedure under Article 9(3) of the Aarhus Convention. The third question was more procedural: does the wording 'an act of a public authority' under Article 9(3) include a decision taken by an administrative body for the purposes of the provision?

---

[5] Council Directive 92/43/EEC of 21 May 1992 on the conservation of natural habitats and of wild fauna and flora [1992] OJ L206/7, Article 12(1).

III. THE OPINION OF AG SHARPSTON

While the Aarhus Convention establishes that members of the public at large are entitled to access to administrative or judicial proceedings, a lot depends on the comprehensiveness of the transposition of Article 9(3) in the contracting state and the rigidity of the criteria that individuals and environmental protection associations need to meet as a matter of domestic law in order to bring a challenge in court against the acts of the national administration. The AG in the *Slovak Bears* case focused, in particular, on the extent to which the Aarhus Convention provides contracting parties with the necessary guidance as to what are the relevant criteria for environmental non-governmental organisations to access to administrative or judicial procedures.[6] The AG also shed some light on the issue regarding the appropriateness of the Court as a platform to decide whether national conditions regulating access to justice are compatible with the Aarhus Convention and EU law.

The AG opined that the neither the Court had jurisdiction to rule on Article 9(3) of the Aarhus Convention, nor did Article 9(3) produce direct effect. She argued that Article 9(3) does not produce obligations 'that are sufficiently clear and precise to govern the legal position of individuals directly, without further clarification or precision'.[7] Having said that, AG Sharpston stressed that LZ was correct in submitting that members of the public, by virtue of Article 9(3), are meant to be entitled to have access to administrative or judicial procedures. She underlined, however, that Article 9(3) entitles associations to have access to administrative or judicial procedures only once they meet the criteria laid down in national law. The Aarhus Convention does not give guidance as to what those criteria might or should be for the reason that the drafters intended this definition to be left to the contracting states. The AG appeared, therefore, cautious not to sideline the Member States' legislatures' ability to lay down the relevant criteria in their legislation and have them interpreted by their own courts. Intervention by the Court would in this context be equivalent to 'establishing an *actio popularis* by judicial fiat rather than legislative action'.[8]

The AG confirmed that mixed agreements, whose provisions fall within the scope of EU competence, have the same status as international agreements concluded solely by the EU. As to direct effect, she followed the lineage of Court's established case law and reaffirmed that what matters is that the provision under investigation (Article 9(3) of the Aarhus Convention in this case) falls within the broader scope of EU law – ie within an area that the EU has previously legislated. For AG Sharpston, once this connection has been established, then the Court has competence to evaluate the respective provision. In *Slovak Bears*, the only connecting tissue between Article 9(3) of the Aarhus Convention and EU law was the brown bear reference in the Habitats Directive under the list of protected species.[9] According to the AG, this reference in the Directive was of no direct relevance to the more specific exercise of determining whether Article 9(3) of the Aarhus Convention lies within a sphere falling within the scope of EU law, and whether it may as a result be given direct effect.

The above analysis led AG Sharpston to conclude that it is for the national court alone to determine whether Article 9(3) of the Aarhus Convention was directly effective within its own legal order under the current circumstances. This was insofar as the EU is party to an

---

[6] Opinion of AG Sharpston in Case C-240/09 *Lesoochranárske zoskupenie VLK* ECLI:EU:C:2010:436.
[7] Para 87 of the Opinion.
[8] ibid, para 89.
[9] Annex II of Directive 92/43/EEC.

international agreement, but has not legislated in order to incorporate the obligation under that agreement into EU law as far as the Member States' conduct is concerned. The AG also opined that the right of public access to judicial review should include the right to challenge a decision of an administrative body which is alleged to contravene provisions of a Member State's national law relating to environmental protection.

IV. ANALYSIS

The *Slovak Bears* judgment is most well-known for its contribution to public interest litigation and access to justice by citizens and environmental protection associations in relation to acts and omissions by public authorities.

It is worth noting that the Opinion of AG Sharpston was only partly followed by the Court, which held that while the dispute falls within the scope of EU law (contrary to the AG), Article 9(3) of the Aarhus Convention had no direct effect (in agreement with the AG). The Court took a broader approach compared to the AG's orthodox interpretation of the right to bring proceedings under EU law, having regard, in particular, to the provisions of Article 9(3) of the Aarhus Convention on direct effect. It stated that an issue which has not yet been subject to EU legislation may nonetheless fall within the scope of EU law, if it relates to a field covered in large measure by it. The Court therefore confirmed its jurisdiction to interpret Article 9(3) of the Aarhus Convention and, as it followed, to give a ruling on whether or not it has direct effect.[10]

Although at first glance it looked like the AG and the Court reached a similar conclusion (ie that Article 9(3) of the Aarhus Convention does not produce direct effect), the Court's assessment of the scope of EU law was much wider than the AG's assessment. The latter was mindful of the implications of the Court's decision to declare itself a gap-filler or 'referee' and enforce the obligations of a mixed agreement in the Member States in areas that have traditionally been off-limits for the Court. In the words of AG Sharpston:

> I do not think that the Court should ignore the absence of relevant Community legislation and allocate to itself the competence to rule on whether or not Article 9(3) has direct effect. If it does so, the Court will be stepping into the legislature's shoes. But the legislature has, thus far, intentionally chosen not to act.[11]

A. An *Actio Popularis* by Judicial Fiat

The big issue in *Slovak Bears* revolved around the following question touching upon the interaction between an international agreement and EU law: Is it a matter for the Court to attribute direct effect to a provision of a mixed agreement (such as the Aarhus Convention), and establish an *actio popularis* where the EU has not yet had the opportunity to adopt legislation that transposes the obligations of the Member States under this agreement into EU law?

By answering the question in the affirmative, the Court closed the second chapter of cases concerning the national implementation of Article 9 of the Aarhus Convention granting the right to access to justice for environmental protection associations in all circumstances, and

---

[10] Para 43 of the Judgment.
[11] Para 77 of the Opinion.

made a parallel between Article 9(2) which the EU legislature has implemented, and Article 9(3) which the EU legislature has not yet had the opportunity to implement.

Article 9 makes a distinction in paragraphs 2 and 3 between 'the public concerned', which covers only 'the public affected or likely to be affected by, or having an interest in, the environmental decision-making' (according to paragraph 2(5)) including non-governmental organisations and the public at large (in paragraph 3) which means everyone including both natural and legal persons. The first chapter of Article 9 litigation concerning paragraph 2 was written in the *Djurgården-Lilla Värtan* judgment, where the Court held that it has jurisdiction to adjudicate on the compatibility of national conditions regulating access to justice with the Aarhus Convention and EU law, insofar as they concerned the implementation of Article 9(2) of the Aarhus Convention.[12] This was the case in *Djurgården-Lilla Värtan*, although the Aarhus Convention and Directive 2003/35 on public participation which incorporates Article 9(2) of the Aarhus Convention into EU law provide that the right to access justice is only granted to NGOs 'meeting any requirements under national law'.[13]

The *Slovak Bears* judgment went a step further in the interpretation of Article 9(3) of the Aarhus Convention, which provided that members of the public shall have access to administrative or judicial procedures to challenge acts and omissions by private persons and public authorities which contravene provisions of national law relating to the environment. This provision had broad scope and granted rights to the members of 'the public', including associations, without further qualifications. It set the standard high in terms of the signatory states providing, according to the Aarhus Convention preamble, access to 'effective judicial mechanisms' so that 'legitimate interests are protected, and the law is enforced'. It is worth noting that such enforcement rights have been incorporated into EU law by Regulation 1367/2006, but only insofar as they concerned the obligations of EU Institutions. Conversely, there has been no EU legislation to date which binds Member States in relation to access to justice in environmental matters as prescribed by Article 9(3) of the Aarhus Convention.[14] Hence, the Opinion of AG Sharpston was correct to highlight that contracting states, in this regard, enjoy wide discretion about how to ensure procedures to challenge the relevant acts or omissions and grant effective remedies. As she stressed: 'in so far as Article 9(3) imposes obligations on a Member State, it is a matter of international law for the Member State to comply with those obligations'.[15]

No doubt, the outcome of the Court's judgment in *Slovak Bears* was an achievement for the standing of environmental protection associations to challenge national measures, which are in breach of international obligations that have become part of the EU *acquis* by approval. While, however, it enhanced the legal position of environmental protection associations at the EU level, the judgment did not leave a glimpse of hope in terms of revisiting the current position under Article 263 TFEU, fourth paragraph, insofar as the Court is also subject to the requirement under Article 9(3) of the Aarhus Convention (now part of EU law). One can therefore see common sense in the Opinion of the AG leaving matters, such as the possibility of action against public administrations, to the political institutions.

---

[12] Case C-263/08 *Djurgården-Lilla Värtans Miljöskyddsförening* ECLI:EU:C:2009:631.

[13] Directive 2003/35/EC providing for public participation in respect of the drawing up of certain plans and programmes relating to the environment and amending with regard to public participation and access to justice Council Directives 85/337/EEC and 96/61/EC [2003] OJ L156/17.

[14] See example of enforcement rights in Directive 2004/35/CE of the European Parliament and of the Council of 21 April 2004 on environmental liability with regard to the prevention and remedying of environmental damage [2004] OJ L143/56.

[15] Para 80 of the Opinion.

This was especially since it was highly unlikely that, for the sake of parity, the Court would be keen on revisiting the *Plaumann* doctrine, to grant direct access in actions for annulment to private applicants as a matter of its newly established Aarhus-proof interpretation. After *Slovak Bears*, it cannot be helped but be noticed that the locus standi conditions of individual applicants under EU law are somewhat different for those challenging the legality of acts of the EU institutions, as opposed to national administrative measures. This problem has been further exacerbated by recent litigation where the Court does not seem ready to adhere to the guidance it has given to national courts when it comes to challenges against EU secondary legislation by citizens or non-governmental bodies.[16]

B. Jurisdiction of the Court to Interpret the Provisions in Question

AG Sharpston refrained from construing national law in the light of EU law in this case. Had she accepted that the matter fell within the jurisdiction of the Court, she would have validated the claim that Article 9(3) had direct effect as a matter of EU law. The AG rightly stressed that the protection of the brown bear by the Habitats Directive fell within the scope of EU law. At the same time, however, she established that the rules concerning the right to access the national court in order to challenge the legality of the district authority's decision to grant a derogation on the hunting of the brown bear fell within the contours of national law. The AG's stance is clear and unequivocal in this regard: in the absence of EU legislation, the implementation of Article 9(3) of the Aarhus Convention was for the Member States to decide. Likewise, it was for the national courts to set the standards for access to justice at the domestic level in actions against public administrations.

By confirming that national courts were responsible for ensuring that international obligations are properly performed, the AG was mindful of the limits to the autonomy of the Member States in setting their own procedural rules for the enforcement of rights which citizens derive from international law. In this regard, AG Sharpston was correct in *Slovak Bears* to establish that the Court had no jurisdiction to intervene and rule on national legislation. She based her conclusion as regards the absence of a legal hook for the EU to intervene in this case by pointing to the silence of the case law of the Court with regard to the degree of exercise of EU power needed in order to firmly establish that the EU has legislated in a particular sphere as a prerequisite for establishing its jurisdiction to intervene.[17]

Despite the opposite conclusion reached by the Court, it is not difficult to see why the AG concluded that the existence of EU legislation on protected species was in no shape or form related to access to justice under the Aarhus Convention. As argued by Jans, in one of the many annotations of the case: 'The ECJ's mistake is that it looked at access to justice in environmental matters as being auxiliary to the substantive standards of the Habitats Directive. The Aarhus Convention shows that access to justice in environmental matters is not just supplementary, but rather has a value of its own.'[18] This was true, especially since the Habitats

---

[16] See Joined Cases C-401/12 P to C-403/12 P *Vereniging Milieudefensie and Stichting Stop Luchtverontreiniging Utrecht* ECLI:EU:C:2015:4. The Court held that the General Court erred in holding that Article 9(3) of the Aarhus Convention could be relied on in order to assess the legality of Article 10(1) of Regulation No 1367/2006.

[17] Case C-431/05 *Merck Genéricos* ECLI:EU:C:2007:496.

[18] JH Jans, 'Who is the Referee? Access to Justice in a Globalised Legal Order: A Case Analysis of ECJ Judgment C-240/09 Lesoochranárske Zoskupenie of 8 March 2011' (2011) 1 *Review of European Administrative Law* 85, 94.

Directive did not provide the legal framework for matters relating to access to justice. The Court should have therefore followed the Opinion of AG Sharpston in this regard, to allow breathing space to the national courts to determine whether Article 9(3) should be given direct effect as a matter of national law in an area where the national legislature has chosen to remain idle.

C. The Limits of Consistent Interpretation

The Opinion of the AG constituted a sobering reminder of the limits of the principle of consistent interpretation and sincere cooperation under Article 4(2) TEU and the responsibility under Article 19 TEU to ensure the full application of EU law in the Member States and judicial protection of the rights of individuals in the national courts. While the Court held, in chorus with the AG, that Article 9(3) of the Convention does not have direct effect, it nonetheless underlined the Member States' duty of consistent interpretation which provided a powerful alternative for ensuring the application of international law: '... [I]n so far as concerns a species protected by EU law, and in particular the Habitats Directive, it is for the national court, in order to ensure effective judicial protection in the fields covered by EU environmental law, to interpret its national law in a way which, to the fullest extent possible, is consistent with the objectives laid down in Article 9(3) of the Aarhus Convention'.[19] The Court, therefore ensured that the obligation under the Aarhus Convention was made effective in the national legal order, leading to a result which was similar to that of direct effect. Conversely, by opining that Article 9(3) was not part of EU law, the AG appeared to suggest that principle of subsidiarity would win over the duty of consistent interpretation in the case.

The contribution of the Court to the international rule of law was important in this case. At the same time, the Court's judgment was less concerned with the limits of consistent interpretation, especially with regard to the separation of powers which are also crucial for the adherence of the EU to the rule of law. To that extent, the Opinion of AG Sharpston in *Slovak Bears* stands as an important reminder of the jurisdictional boundaries of the EU. Perhaps the AG did not delve into a deductive discussion about consistent interpretation out of consideration of the fact that the result it can produce may often be not too different to that of direct effect. Judging from the outcome of the case, one can even argue that consistent interpretation and direct effect are 'barely distinguishable' in the Court's ruling.[20] By contrast in the Opinion of AG Sharpston, the principle of consistent interpretation fell short of providing a shortcut to guarantee the fulfilment of the Member States' international obligations under the Aarhus Convention.

D. Effect on Future Case Law

Despite the disagreement between the AG and the Court, the *Slovak Bears* case is a point of reference, especially as regards future disputes related to standing rules at national and European level. This is particularly important for the role of the Court in the enforcement of rights which citizens derive from international law, especially defending international values

---

[19] Para 50 of the Opinion.
[20] A Nollkaemper, *National Courts and the International Rule of Law* (Oxford, OUP, 2012) 141, 165.

such as the right to an effective legal remedy when the objectives of international law that have become part of the EU *acquis* by approval are in sync with EU fundamental values, such as effective judicial protection.

The above trend became obvious in the *Strážov Mountains* case, which was the second instalment of the *Slovak Bears* litigation.[21] The Court there, once again, brought together the Aarhus Convention and the Habitats Directive, and established that the right to participation and the manner in which it has been implemented fall under EU law. The novelty in *Strážov Mountains* was that such implementation subjects the national law in question to the scrutiny of the EU Charter of Fundamental Rights (CFR), especially Article 47 CFR, which is linked to the standard under Article 9 of the Aarhus Convention. As it has so far been argued, through this approach the Court has considerably minimised the margin of appreciation regarding standing that has traditionally been allowed to Member States. At the same time, the Court uses the full stealth of the Aarhus Convention in order to grant greater access to justice to environmental associations.[22]

Beyond establishing that the Court shall not interpret international law on which there are no EU measures in place, the Opinion of AG Sharpston in *Slovak Bears* was mindful of avoiding the formation of double standards for access to justice at the national and EU level, which undermines the idea of a complete system of remedies and procedures at the EU level.[23] It appears that the Aarhus Convention Compliance Committee (ACCC) is aware of this reality, and has found that the Court's case law on standing requirements under Article 263 TFEU, fourth paragraph, is in breach of Article 9(3) of the Aarhus Convention. In 2017, it criticised the EU in respect of the scope of reviewability of EU acts: 'in so far as Article 10(1) of Regulation No 1367/2006 limits the concept of "acts", as used in Article 9(3) of the Aarhus Convention, to "administrative act[s]" defined in Article 2(1)(g) of Regulation No 1367/2006 as "measure[s] of individual scope", it is not compatible with Article 9(3) of the Aarhus Convention'.[24] The *Slovak Bears* case has therefore generated a wind of change in the EU system of remedies, which has been propelled by none other than the Court's own jurisprudence on the protection of the environment against administrative inaction in the Member States. Standing for individuals and environmental protection associations is a work in progress, but a work where the EU needs to show good intentions with what it has been preaching.

---

[21] Case C-243/15 *Lesoochranárske zoskupenie VLK* ECLI:EU:C:2016:838.

[22] M van Wolferen, 'Comment on Case C-243/15 Lesoochranárske zoskupenie VLK v Obvodný úrad Trenčín' (2017) 14 *Journal For European Environmental & Planning Law* 136.

[23] This was elaborated by the Court in Case 294/83 *Les Verts* ECLI:EU:C:1986:166, para 23.

[24] Draft findings and recommendations of the compliance committee with regard to Communication ACC/C/2008/32 concerning compliance by the EU. Available at https://unece.org/fileadmin/DAM/env/pp/compliance/C2008-32/Findings/C32_EU_Findings_as_adopted_advance_unedited_version.pdf.

42

The Notion of 'Court or Tribunal of a Member State': Opinion of Advocate General Sharpston in Miles

TAMARA ĆAPETA

I. INTRODUCTION

MILES IS ONE of those cases in which the Court did not follow its AG. Does this mean that one of the two was 'wrong'? The present author would not claim so. As argued in this chapter, if the law is observed through the prism of legal realism, two different interpretations of the same legal rule in the same situation can be legally perfectly correct, even if only one will be applicable. Legal realism explains law as being indeterminate. The same legal text, depending on the interpreter, can therefore be given different meanings. The meaning of the law, thus, depends on the choice made by the interpreter. Within the limits allowed by the text,[1] none of the multiple possible choices is 'right' or 'wrong'.

Therefore, when the Court and its Advocate General diverge in their interpretation of the same legal rule in the same situation, this does not mean that the Court is 'right' and the AG is 'wrong', or vice versa. The observer might find one of the interpretations more to his or her liking, but this does not make the other interpretation legally incorrect. Of course, the Court's interpretations of EU law, coming from the highest authority in the EU legal order, will trump other equally possible interpretations, including those of its AGs. The Court's choices thus become the law to be applied to a case and constrain future interpretation of the same legal rule in novel situations.

Although there might be different interpretive choices, some may be better elaborated and justified than others, and could therefore be more persuasive. The Court's choice in *Miles* became binding interpretation due to the Court's authority,[2] but the Opinion of AG Sharpston would win the contest in persuasiveness.[3]

---

[1] If they see the law as indeterminate, legal realists do not claim that there are no constraints imposed on possible interpretations. Even critical legal studies (CLS) scholars admit the need for the interpreter to remain faithful to the body of law, including its text. See in that respect D Kennedy, *A Critique of Adjudication (fin de siècle)* (Cambridge, MA, Harvard University Press, 1997) 13. There are, therefore, certain interpretations that simply do not fit the text, or the clear purpose of the law.

[2] Case C-196/09 *Miles* ECLI:EU:C:2011:388.

[3] Opinion of AG Sharpston in Case C-196/09 *Miles* ECLI:EU:C:2010:777.

II. BACKGROUND, CONTEXT, AND FACTS

The case concerned the meaning of the expression 'court or tribunal of a Member State', as envisaged in Article 267 TFEU. More concretely, the question was whether this expression encompassed a body which possessed all the required qualities to be a 'court or tribunal', but was not a body established by a single Member State, but rather by all Member States acting together.

The body at issue was the Complaints Board established under the 1994 European Schools Convention.[4] The European Schools were (and are) educational institutions established with the purpose of providing multicultural and multilingual education to children of staff of EU institutions and other EU bodies. There are currently 13 such schools, situated in seven EU Member States.[5] Teachers are seconded to the European Schools by their respective Member States. Their salaries are set by staff regulations adopted by the Board of Governors of the European Schools. Under the staff regulation in force at the time of the facts in *Miles*,[6] the teachers' basic national remuneration was provided by their respective Member States and the difference between the national remuneration and the salary envisaged by the Staff Regulation (the so-called, European supplement[7]) was paid by the European School. If the teacher was from a Member State that did not have the euro as its currency, her/his national salary had to be converted into euro in order to calculate the amount of the European supplement. This was the situation of Mr Miles and other teachers seconded to the European Schools from the UK. For calculating the supplement, the exchange rates between the respective national currencies and the euro were set on 1 July each year. At the time when the facts of *Miles* occurred, no possibility of intermediate adjustments during the reference year was envisaged.[8]

Inconveniently for the UK teachers, in the period between July 2007 and July 2008, the pound sterling had depreciated approximately 7.4 per cent against the euro.[9] Mr Miles and several other UK teachers therefore lodged a request for the adjustment of their European supplements in order to cover for sterling's depreciation. The request was rejected by the Secretary General of the European Schools. The teachers consequently raised an appeal against the decision rejecting their request in front of the Complaints Board, which in turn, referred to the Court those questions of interpretation of EU law it deemed relevant for the resolution of the dispute. This reference resulted in the Court's decision to reject the Complaints Board's reference for not being issued by a 'court or tribunal of a Member State', contrary to the advice of AG Sharpston.

Before this chapter proceeds to the description and analysis of the differing positions of AG Sharpston and the Grand Chamber of the Court, a few additional explanations are in order. The Complaints Board was established by the 1994 European Schools Convention. This Convention, which entered into force only in 2002, was an international agreement to

---

[4] Convention defining the Statute of the European Schools [1994] OJ L212/3.

[5] Five Schools are in Belgium, (of which four in Brussels), three in Germany, two in Luxembourg, and one in Italy, the Netherlands and Spain respectively. All information on the European Schools as well as the founding legal documents can be found on the European Schools website.

[6] For the Staff Regulation in force at the time, see paras 19–26 of the Opinion. These rules were amended several times in the meantime. The current version of the staff rules for seconded staff, 'Regulations for members of the seconded staff of the European Schools' can be found on www.eursc.eu/BasicTexts/2011-04-D-14-en-15.pdf.

[7] Para 31 of the Opinion.

[8] Soon after, still during the adjudication of *Miles*, the rules were changed in order to allow for such intermediate adjustments. See para 34 of the Opinion.

[9] Para 32 of the Opinion.

which the EU was a party.[10] The 1994 Convention replaced earlier international treaties – the Statute of the European School signed at Luxembourg on 12 April 1957 and the Protocol of 13 April 1962 on the setting-up of European Schools with reference to the Statute of the European School signed in Luxembourg on 12 April 1957. These founding international agreements were concluded among Member States only, and the EU was not party to them. They were, there-fore, not part of EU law, which means that the Court lacked jurisdiction to interpret them under Article 267 TFEU. This was indeed the position of the Court expressed in its judgment in case *Hurd*.[11] However, as of 2002, when the 1994 Convention entered into force, the inter-national instrument founding the European Schools became part of EU law as the EU became a party. Therefore, as confirmed by the Court in *Oberto and O'Leary*,[12] the Court had gained the jurisdiction to interpret the basic act establishing the European Schools system.

III. THE OPINION OF AG SHARPSTON

The main issue in *Miles* was whether the Complaints Board could be qualified as a 'court or tribunal of a Member State' as understood under Article 267 TFEU. None of the participants in the proceedings before the Court disputed that the Complaints Board satisfied all the require-ment deemed necessary for being qualified as a 'court or tribunal' by the case law,[13] but rather, the case turned on whether it was 'of a Member State'. Both the AG in her Opinion[14] and the Court in its judgment[15] acknowledged this. The Complaints Board was established by law: the 1994 European Schools Convention which replaced the previous international agreements. It was established as a permanent body. It had compulsory, indeed even exclusive, jurisdiction in disputes such as the one in *Miles*.[16] Its decisions were binding.[17] It conducted procedures *inter partes* and applied the rules of law for deciding disputes, including, as confirmed by its case law, EU law. Finally, and crucially for a body to be qualified as a 'court', it was independent,[18] and acted as a third party in relation to the organs of the European Schools. The independ-ence of its members, elected from a list of persons compiled by the Court, was guaranteed by the provisions of the 1994 Convention,[19] and the Statute and the Rules of Procedure of the Complaints Board.[20] It was therefore not disputed that the Complaints Board was a 'court or tribunal', but only that it was a court or tribunal of 'a Member State'. The language used in Article 267 TFEU, referring to a single Member State, seemed to point to the conclusion that

---

[10] This was enabled by Council Decision 94/557/EC of 17 June 1994 authorizing the European Community and the European Atomic Energy Community to sign and conclude the Convention defining the Statute of the European Schools [1994] OJ L212/1.

[11] Case 44/84 *Hurd* ECLI:EU:C:1986:2, para 20.

[12] Joined Cases C-464/13 and C-465/13 *Oberto* ECLI:EU:C:2015:163, paras 29–31.

[13] Case C-54/96 *Dorsch Consult* ECLI:EU:C:1997:413, para 23; for recent confirmation see eg Case C-274/14 *Banco de Santander* ECLI:EU:C:2020:17, para 51.

[14] Paras 51–54 of the Opinion.

[15] Paras 37–38 of the Judgment.

[16] Article 27(2) of the 1994 European Schools Convention.

[17] ibid, Article 27(6).

[18] About the importance and the meaning of the requirement of independence, see Case C-896/19 *Repubblika* ECLI:EU:C:2021:311, paras 51–57 and the case law cited therein.

[19] Article 27(3) of the 1994 European Schools Convention.

[20] The Statute and the Rules of Procedure of the Complaints Bord are published at www.schola-europaea.eu/cree/textes.php.

the Complaints Board could not be qualified as a 'court or tribunal' for the purpose of initiating preliminary ruling proceedings. Such a textual argument was indeed put forward by the European Schools.[21]

AG Sharpston, however, considered that textual interpretation is not the only method for understanding the meaning of the law. More often than not, the Court has preferred the teleological method, which pays respect to the purpose of legal rules. To uphold the appropriateness of such interpretation in the case at hand, AG Sharpston quoted the *Broekmoelen* case,[22] explaining that already in this early case, the Court was willing to give a broad interpretation to the notion of 'court or tribunal' in order to ensure the proper functioning of EU law. Article 267 TFEU had the function of securing the uniformity of EU law in all its Member States. For AG Sharpston, this purpose had to be taken into consideration in interpreting the notions it used in its text.

AG Sharpston further noted that the circumstance that led the Court to acknowledge the status of court to the appeals committee established by the Royal Netherlands Society for the Promotion of Medicine, the body that referred the *Broekmoelen* case, was that there was no right of appeal against the decisions of that body. She observed that the analogy (another important tool in legal interpretation) with the position of the Complaints Board was obvious. There was no right of appeal against its decisions to any court in Member States either.[23] AG Sharpston thus convincingly established the preference for the purposive approach to interpret the notion of 'court or tribunal of a Member State', backing this up with the past practice of the Court itself.

The textual obstacle, the 'a' in the text of Article 267 TFEU, was already dismantled by the Court relying on purposive interpretation in *Christian Dior*.[24] In that case, the Court accepted that the Benelux Court, common to three Member States, was to be regarded as a 'court or tribunal of a Member State'.[25] AG Sharpston observed that in *Christian Dior*, the Court was guided by two reasons: first, the procedure in front of the Benelux Court, which had the task of ensuring uniformity of the rules common to the Benelux States, was only one step within proceedings before national courts; and, secondly, if the Benelux Court were entitled to refer to the Court, this would contribute to ensuring the uniform interpretation of EU law.[26] Whereas the first reason influenced the Court's decision in *Miles* (as will be demonstrated later), the second reason – the purpose of a preliminary ruling – was more important to AG Sharpston.

Making a parallel to *Christian Dior*, AG Sharpston concluded that the same purposive approach as applied in that case required that the Complaints Board also be qualified as a body which may refer under Article 267 TFEU. Whereas the Benelux Court was granted the right to refer, because the Court found 'no good reason why such a court, common to a number of Member States, should not be able to submit questions to this Court',[27] the Complaints Board, as a court common to all Member States, was 'the ultimate expression of that concept'.[28]

---

[21] Para 55 of the Opinion.

[22] Case 246/80 *Broekmeulen* ECLI:EU:C:1981:218.

[23] Paras 58–59 of the Opinion.

[24] Case C-337/95 *Dior* ECLI:EU:C:1997:517.

[25] The Court confirmed this position in subsequent cases in which it accepted references from the Benelux Court without questioning their admissibility. See eg Case C-265/00 *Campina Melkunie* ECLI:EU:C:2004:87.

[26] Para 60 of the Opinion.

[27] Para 21 of the Judgment in Case C-337/95 *Dior*.

[28] Para 65 of the Opinion.

Additionally, its judgments, in which it might need to apply EU law, were binding and enforceable in Member States. AG Sharpston therefore concluded that:

> [i]t would be paradoxical if, when applying EU law, the Complaints Board were unable to refer questions to the Court when the Member States are then obliged, through their national courts, to enforce its decisions.[29]

An additional argument was offered by AG Sharpston through an analogy between disputes about the meaning of the Convention that arise between its parties, and disputes about the meaning of the same provisions if they arise between the staff of the European Schools and its bodies. Under Article 26 of the 1994 Convention, the Court was given the exclusive jurisdiction to resolve disputes between the State parties to the Convention relating to its interpretation. AG Sharpston concluded that:

> [i]t would be anomalous if an equivalent question arising in a challenge brought by individuals against a decision taken by the Secretary-General could not also be referred by the Complaints Board to this Court for an authoritative ruling when it raises issues involving the interpretation of EU law.[30]

This argument was backed up by drawing a parallel with the complementarity between direct actions and preliminary references in the Treaty-based system of judicial protection.[31]

Finally, AG Sharpston added that depriving the Complaints Board of the possibility to refer would be contrary to the spirit of judicial cooperation, and could also be seen as depriving the applicant of his right to a judicial remedy.[32] One may disagree with these arguments, especially the latter, as individuals cannot themselves make preliminary references. On the other hand, the obligation of last-instance courts – and the Complaints Board would be such a court – does in practice result in individuals having a position similar to that of being granted this right. In any case, these were only additional arguments to strengthen the previously offered reasons based on the teleological approach to the interpretation of Article 267 TFEU in favour of acknowledging the possibility for the Complaints Board to refer.

After adducing a number of convincing arguments in favour of finding that the Complaints Board was allowed to refer, AG Sharpston continued her analysis by looking into the possible adverse consequences of such an interpretation. She contended that there was no reason to believe that admitting the status of 'court or tribunal' to the Complaints Board would significantly increase the workload of the Court, as there were not many comparable bodies.[33] In addition, she expressed her view that a possible increase in workload was, in any case, not a valid legal argument for a narrow interpretation of the term 'court or tribunal of a Member State'.[34] After stating all these arguments, AG Sharpston advised the Court to admit the reference and provide answers to the questions submitted by the Complaints Board.

The Court did not follow. In a short judgment, the Grand Chamber rejected the reference considering that the Complaints Board was not a court of 'a Member State', or common to the Member States acting together, but rather of the European Schools, 'an international organisation which, despite the functional links which it has with the Union, remains formally distinct

---

[29] ibid.
[30] Para 66.
[31] Paras 67–71.
[32] Paras 75–76.
[33] Paras 83–87 of the Opinion.
[34] Paras 81–82 of the Opinion.

from it and from those Member States'.[35] In line with its established method of reasoning, the Court did not engage with the arguments offered by AG Sharpston.[36]

IV. ANALYSIS

A. The Judgment

To return to the introductory statement, neither the solution suggested by AG Sharpston nor the one endorsed by the Court could, per se, be characterised as right or wrong. The text of Article 267 TFEU was open enough to allow for it to be decided that the Complaints Board is a body that may refer, or that it is not. What is striking in this case, however, is the obvious contrast between the well-elaborated proposal of the AG Sharpston, on the one hand, and the clear, but poorly reasoned, rejection of such a proposal by the Court, on the other.[37]

AG Sharpston clearly and openly opted to give preference to an interpretation that would best serve the purpose of a preliminary ruling procedure. She offered a number of arguments guided by such purposive logic, backed by case law. She then performed a sort of reality check, or cost-benefit analysis, by looking into possible adverse effects, which the proposed broad interpretation of the notion of 'court or tribunal of a Member State' could have on judicial practice. As she found none, she proposed to the Court the solution she considered to be both possible and most advantageous for the EU legal system. One need not agree with all her arguments, but the Opinion can still be described as coherent, well elaborated and logically structured. Legal commentators were indeed surprised that the Court did not follow, since they found AG Sharpston's Opinion convincing.[38]

The Court's reasons, on the other hand, were difficult to understand. As explained above, the main argument of the Court was that the Complaints Board was a body of the European Schools and not of the Member States. Although it is undisputable that the Complaints Board was a body of the European Schools, it was also a body common to the Member States. Similarly, the Benelux Court was at the same time a body of Benelux,[39] and a court common to the Member States. The Court has not explained in what way the European Schools system, as an international organisation distinct from the EU, was different from Benelux, which was (and continues to be) an international organisation distinct from the EU. And yet, the Benelux Court was considered to be a court common to several (but not all) Member States and able to refer, whereas the Complaints Board, even if common to *all* the Member States, was only considered to be a body of the European Schools.

---

[35] Para 42 of the Judgment. See also para 39 of the Judgment.

[36] For criticism, see T Ćapeta, 'The AG: Bringing Clarity to ECJ Decisions? A Case Study of Mangold and Kücükdeveci' (2011–12) 14 *CYELS* 563.

[37] This contrast can also be quantified. It took AG Sharpston 39 paragraphs to explain her position. There were just nine paragraphs in the relevant part of the judgment of the Court.

[38] 'Notion de juridiction', commentaire par S Denys, Europe n° 8, Août 2011, comm. 288, at 2; N Wahl and L Prete, 'The Gatekeepers of Article 267 TFEU: On Jurisdiction and Admissibility of References for Preliminary Rulings' (2018) *CMLRev* 511, at 529.

[39] The Benelux Court of Justice is, however, established by its own Treaty: le Traité du 31 mars 1965 relatif à l'institution et au statut d'une Cour de Justice Benelux, modified in 2012. The Treaty establishing the economic union of Benelux did not explicitly mention the Benelux Court as one of its organs until the reform of 2008: Traité portant révision du traité instituant l'Union économique Benelux. See M Belkahla, 'Benelux Court of Justice' www.mpi.lu/fileadmin/mpi/medien/research/MPEiPro/EiPro_Sample_Benelux_Court_of_Justice_2017-Feb.pdf.

The present author can agree that denying bodies of international organisations created by the Member States the status of 'court' capable of referring was one legally possible approach. If the European Schools were seen as a legal entity separate from the EU, it might not be important, from the point of view of the EU, how its law would be applied by such an entity. A parallel might be made with international agreements signed by the EU with a third state. It is for the third state to apply such an agreement, including the possible EU law concepts it contains, according to its own methods. Even if this may result in different interpretations in the third state and in the EU, it does not influence the effectiveness or uniformity of the EU legal order, which has to satisfy such requirements within the field of its application. However, even if it is possible to create a fiction of the European Schools as 'third states', the fact remains that the European Schools were created by an agreement concluded among the EU Member States, with no participating third states. The EU itself acceded to it in 1994, with effect as of 2002. Thus, the way that EU law would be construed for the purposes of applying the European Schools Convention would be applied in the same territory and by the same bodies which have the obligation to apply EU law according to EU law standards. The Court's aim of insisting that the Complaints Board was a body of the European Schools, and not of the Member States, was not clear if assessed in this context.

The Court offered one difference between the two judicial organs that it found to be of crucial importance. The decisions of the Benelux Court were, according to the Court, 'a step in the proceedings before the national courts leading to definitive interpretations of common Benelux legal rules',[40] whereas 'the Complaints Board does not have any such links with the judicial systems of the Member States'.[41] Indeed, such a difference between the two systems existed. The Benelux system envisaged that disputes were resolved by national courts, which are empowered to refer to the Benelux Court questions of interpretation of common Benelux law, similar to the way in which the preliminary ruling procedure functions under the EU Treaties. Interpretations provided by the Benelux Court were binding on the deciding national court. By contrast, national courts of the parties to the 1994 Convention did not have jurisdiction over disputes between teachers and the European Schools' bodies relating to the application of the Convention. The Complaints Board had exclusive jurisdiction. It thus replaced Member States' courts. However, its decisions were binding on national organs, including the national courts, and were enforceable in all Member States. The Court pointed to this difference as crucial, but did not explain why and how it decided the question on whether these bodies could refer under Article 267 TFEU. It is true that the AG said nothing about this difference, but one possible reason would be that she did not find it important, and did not therefore anticipate that the Court would base its decision on it.

As the Court did not explain, the reader of its judgment is left to wonder why it considered this difference so important. Arguably, if it had any influence on the decision, it should have been opposite to what the Court concluded. For the sake of the effectiveness and uniformity of EU law, it was more important to allow references from the Complaints Board than from the Benelux Court. In the Benelux system, the national court to which the case returns after an interpretation given by the Benelux Court will have the power, or indeed the obligation if its decision is not appealable, to refer the question of interpretation to the Court. This is so, even if this results in a finding that the Benelux Court's interpretation is contrary to EU law.

---

[40] Para 41 of the Judgment.
[41] ibid.

On the other hand, with no national courts involved, EU law may end up wrongly applied if the Complaints Board would not be allowed to refer.

This author is not saying that allowing references from the Benelux Court was not a good choice. On the contrary, it was. However, this was more important for the Benelux system itself, rather than for the system of EU law. In EU law, the mechanism for its uniform interpretation would exist, as explained, even if the Benelux Court could not refer. However, in denying it, such a possibility might have created a situation where the Benelux Court's interpretations, supposed to be authoritative and binding on national courts, could not be applied by the latter if they were found to be contrary to EU law. In the system of the European Schools Convention, such a safeguard for the effectiveness and uniformity of EU law was lacking, as national courts do not have jurisdiction over disputes which fall under the Complaints Board's competence. Thus, excluding the Complaints Board from the preliminary ruling mechanism would be more damaging for EU law than excluding the Benelux Court. However, this purposive way of thinking, which underlined the Opinion of AG Sharpston, was not present in the judgment. Given that the (meta) teleological interpretive method was not uncommon in the Court's reasoning, the lack of any explanation about why it was neglected in this case was surprising.

It is possible to speculate why the Court was so unwilling to disclose its reasons in *Miles*. It might be that the judges sitting in the Grand Chamber were not in agreement. The collegiate nature of decision-making in the Court results in judgments which contain only the reasoning which all judges can endorse. The Court never discloses which opposing arguments were offered during deliberation, nor does it justify the majority position in relation to minority arguments.[42] What, therefore, remained in the text of the judgment in *Miles* were a few de-contextualised reasons and an enigmatic message for the Member States, which, as will be presented under the next heading, has not yet been deciphered.

B. Implications for the Future: Judicial Protection in the European Schools System

Miles left many questions up in the air, which has had an influence on later developments. In the analysis that follows, the consequences of *Miles* for the system of the European Schools itself is discussed as a starting point. It will pave the way for assessment of how *Miles* relates to other developments in the case law, especially *Opinion 1/09*[43] and *Achmea*.[44]

As already mentioned, the judgment in *Miles* ended with a message addressed to the Member States as parties to the 1994 Convention. In one of the last paragraphs, the Court, citing its (unfortunate!) judgment in *UPA*,[45] rejecting the position that it can be blamed for a lack of uniformity of EU law, or a lack of effective judicial protection for teachers, stated:

> (…) it must be observed that while it is possible to envisage a development, along the lines described in the previous paragraph, of the system of judicial protection established by the European Schools' Convention, it is for the Member States to reform the system currently in force.[46]

---

[42] For criticism from this author of such an adjudication method, see T Ćapeta, 'EU Judiciary in Need of Reform?' in A Łazowski and S Blockmans (eds), *Research Handbook on EU Institutional Law* (Cheltenham, Edward Elgar, 2016) 263. See also N Bačić Selanec and T Ćapeta, 'The Rule of Law and Adjudication of the Court of Justice of the EU' in T Ćapeta, I Goldner Lang and T Perišin (eds), *The Changing European Union: A Critical View on the Role of Law and the Courts* (Oxford, Hart Publishing, 2022).

[43] *Opinion 1/09* ECLI:EU:C:2011:123.

[44] Case C-284/16 *Achmea* ECLI:EU:C:2018:158.

[45] Case C-50/00 P *UPA* ECLI:EU:C:2002:462.

[46] Para 45 of the Judgment.

In other words, presenting its choice of a narrow interpretation of Article 267 TFEU as the only possible reading of the EU Treaties, the Court refused to take any responsibility for the potentially wrong application of EU law to migrant UK teachers. If the present author's starting proposal is accepted: that AG Sharpston's interpretation was just as possible under the law as that opted for by the Court, then clearly it was the Court, by accepting the AG's interpretative choice, and not only the State parties to the 1994 Convention, that could have made the difference.

In *UPA*, the Court addressed a message to the Member States inviting them to change the text of the EU Treaties.[47] In *Miles*, the message was also sent to the Member States, but it invited them not to change the EU Treaties, but rather, to adjust the system of judicial protection in the European Schools so as to fulfil the requirements imposed by Article 267 TFEU. Unfortunately, however, the Court did not give any indication as to which changes would transform the Complaints Board into a 'court or tribunal of a Member State'. It resulted from the case that a body would be able to refer if it was a court common to the Member States. However, when a body can precisely be considered common to Member States was left open.

This, as well as other questions, thus remained unanswered. Should the European Schools system replicate the Benelux system, so as to bestow on the Complaints Board only interpretive jurisdiction, while making national courts competent to adjudicate disputes between staff and the European School bodies? Would other models also be acceptable? Do national courts always have to be involved, or can a court common to the Member States replace national courts, and under what conditions? Would an express provision enabling references to the Court of Justice help, or would it not make any difference?

The Board of Governors of the European Schools heard the Court's invitation for a revision of the system. On the initiative of the European Commission,[48] a working group was set up with a mandate to work on strengthening legal protection in the European Schools system.[49] However, possibly as a consequence of uncertainty as to what should be done after *Miles*, it seemed that the group concentrated on finding a solution for adding possibilities of appeal to decisions of the Complaints Board, rather than finding a way to allow for communication with the Court. So far, no change to the jurisdiction or organisation of the Complaints Board has been proposed.

C. Implications for the Future: Repercussions of the Subsequent Case Law on the Lawfulness of the Complaints Board

In her Opinion, AG Sharpston did not find that the bestowal on the Complaints Board of exclusive jurisdiction for a certain category of cases, divesting national courts of such jurisdiction, represented an obstacle for considering that body a 'court or tribunal' in the sense of Article 267 TFEU. The exclusion of national courts was not a problem, as she was of the view

---

[47] The provision at issue was Article 230 EC (now Article 263 TFEU), or more precisely the requirement that individuals show individual concern in order to be allowed direct access to the Court in order to ask for the annulment of an EU act. See ch 33.

[48] 'Reflection on the appeals system established by the Convention defining the Statute of the European Schools', Meeting of the Board of Governors of the European Schools on 16, 17 and 18 April 2013, Brussels, Ref: 2013-04-D-4-en-1.

[49] Report of the Secretary-General to the Board of Governors of the European Schools for the year 2013 (2014-01-D-23-en-2), presented to the Board of Governors of the European Schools at its meeting of 8, 9 and 10 April 2014, in Sofia, 16.

that the Complaints Board could and must refer if necessary. However, the circumstance that the Complaints Board replaced, instead of being built within the jurisdiction of the Member States' courts, seems to have motivated the Court's judgment in *Miles*. The result is that, today, national courts are divested of their jurisdiction over cases between teachers and the bodies of the European Schools, even when such cases involve issues of EU law,[50] while at the same time the only judicial body with jurisdiction over such cases is prevented from referring to the Court. Is such a situation possible under EU law? Or should the establishment by Member States of the Complaints Board, divesting their own courts of jurisdiction, be considered contrary to EU law? This question was not posed in *Miles*, but cannot be circumvented in light of the Court's decision in *Opinion 1/09* on the European Patent Court and its judgment in *Achmea*.

Opinion 1/09 of the Court preceded the judgment in *Miles* by a few months. Acting in its Full Court composition in *Opinion 1/09*, the Court considered that:

> the Member States cannot confer the jurisdiction to resolve (...) disputes on a court created by an international agreement which would deprive [national] courts of their task, as "ordinary" courts within the European Union legal order, to implement European Union law and, thereby, of the power provided for in Article 267 TFEU, or, as the case may be, the obligation, to refer questions for a preliminary ruling in the field concerned.[51]

This was one of the reasons why the Court considered that the proposal for the agreement creating a Unified Patent Litigation System was contrary to EU law. Only a few months later, the Grand Chamber in *Miles* did not even mention *Opinion 1/09*.

The prohibition to deprive national courts of jurisdiction in cases which may involve EU law also played an important part in the Court's reasoning in *Achmea*. The Court considered that an investment treaty concluded between two Member States and divesting national courts of jurisdiction over investment disputes by providing for the exclusive jurisdiction of an arbitral tribunal:

> call[s] into question not only the principle of mutual trust between the Member States but also the preservation of the particular nature of the law established by the Treaties, ensured by the preliminary ruling procedure provided for in Article 267 TFEU.[52] .

The Arbitral Tribunal envisaged by the Bilateral Investment Treaty (BIT) at issue was not considered a body capable of referring under Article 267 TFEU, just as the Complaints Board was denied such a possibility in *Miles*.

Applying the reasoning of *Opinion 1/09* and *Achmea* to the Complaints Board leads to the conclusion that the Member States acted contrary to EU law when they created this judicial body. Such a conclusion would not have been obtained had the Court followed the Opinion of AG Sharpston in *Miles*. If the Complaints Board can, and indeed must, refer under Article 267 TFEU, the particular nature of EU law ensured by the preliminary ruling procedure would be preserved. It remains surprising that, given *Opinion 1/09* was decided by the same judges a few months before, the Court decided as it did, or did not at least explain the consequences of its decision for the system established under the European Schools system.

---

[50] The Court confirmed this in Joined Cases C-464/13 and C-465/13 *Oberto and O'Leary*. AG Mengozzi, who was asked for an opinion in that case, suggested differently. He held that national courts cannot be deprived of jurisdiction over disputes between part-time teachers and the European Schools bodies as there is no guarantee that the Complaints Board will provide them with the protection they are entitled to under EU law. See Opinion of AG Mengozzi in Joined Cases C-464/13 and C-465/13 *Oberto* ECLI:EU:C:2014:2169, paras 64–65.

[51] Para 80 of the *Opinion 1/09*.

[52] Para 58 of the Judgment in *Achmea*.

D. The Influence of *Miles* on the Proposal for a Unified Patent Court

After the rejection of the Patent Court as proposed in the agreement under scrutiny in *Opinion 1/09*, the new agreement on a Unified Patent Court (UPC) was drafted.[53] Its features were influenced by *Opinion 1/09*, as well as by *Cristian Dior* and *Miles*.[54]

The lesson learned by the Member States from the Court's case law was that the new court had to be seen as a court common to the Member States, rather than as a court of an international organisation. In *Opinion 1/09*, the Court explained:

> (...) that the situation of the [Patent Court] envisaged by the draft agreement would differ from that of the Benelux Court of Justice (...). Since the Benelux Court is a court common to a number of Member States, situated, consequently, within the judicial system of the European Union, its decisions are subject to mechanisms capable of ensuring the full effectiveness of the rules of the European Union.[55]

How could a court established by an international agreement concluded among Member States be made a court common to Member States, if this court were to be given exclusive jurisdiction in certain types of disputes over patents, divesting Member States' courts of their jurisdiction over such cases? After *Miles*, this does not seem easy, or even possible.

The solution offered by the draft UPC Agreement was first to expressly state that the new court was a court common to Member States.[56] This would make it difficult for the Court to conclude differently. Secondly, the new UPC agreement also introduced the express obligation for the new court to respect the primacy of EU law,[57] and to engage in preliminary ruling proceedings.[58] Finally, in order to show a connection to the Member States' legal systems, the draft UPC agreement provided for a way in which Member States might become liable under EU law for damages caused by the decisions of the Court of Appeal of the UPC.[59] It also envisaged which state is to be prosecuted in infringement proceedings.[60] Thus, the missing feature of the Complaints Board, characterised in *Miles* as the lack of a link to Member States' judicial systems,[61] was established in relation to the UPC by establishing the possibility to sue Member States in the case of errors committed by the newly established judicial body. Whether this was indeed what the Court failed to find in *Miles* when looking for the link to Member States' judicial systems, is impossible to tell. *Opinion 1/09* can be read as upholding such a conclusion.[62] On the other hand, if the obligation to refer imposed on an international tribunal in which the EU and its Member States participate has to be coupled with the existence of Member States' liability in case of failure of such a body to refer to the Court, this may put the legality of judicial bodies created by several recent international agreements under question. This includes arbitral panels established under the EU-Ukraine Association Agreement,[63]

---

[53] Agreement on a Unified Patent Court (Proposed UPC Agreement) [2013] OJ C175/1.

[54] See eg a paper prepared by the Benelux countries 'Creating a Unified Patent Litigation System – Reflections on the Benelux Court of Justice', Council of the EU, 13984/11, Brussels, 9 September 2011.

[55] Para 82 of the *Opinion 1/09*.

[56] Article 1(2) of the Proposed UPC Agreement.

[57] ibid, Article 20.

[58] ibid, Article 21.

[59] ibid, Article 22.

[60] ibid, Article 23.

[61] Para 41 of the Judgment.

[62] Paras 86–88 of the *Opinion 1/09*.

[63] Association Agreement between the European Union and its Member States, of the one part, and Ukraine, of the other part, (2014) OJ L 161/3. Article 322(2) provides that the interpretation and application of provisions of the Agreement that relate to regulatory approximation cannot be decided by the Arbitration Panel but have to be referred by that body to the Court to give a ruling on the question.

the EU-Moldova Association Agreement,[64] and the EU-UK Withdrawal Agreement.[65] These agreements envisage the obligation of the established arbitral panels to refer to the Court on (certain) issues of EU law. Of course, the question that might arise in relation to these judicial bodies is not the same as the one relating to the Complaints Board, as first, they are not only the bodies of Member States, but bodies created between the EU, Member States and third states. Secondly, their obligation to refer to the Court is not imposed by Article 267 TFEU, but rather by the international agreement itself.

Member States and the Council believe that a system envisaged by the draft UPC agreement would satisfy the conditions imposed by the case law to consider an international court, in which only Member States participate, capable of engaging in the preliminary ruling mechanism. The new draft agreement has not yet been subject to scrutiny by the Court. The German Federal Constitutional Court decided not to refer in a case where the constitutionality of the proposed agreement was challenged under the German Constitution,[66] nor has a request so far been made for an Opinion on the new draft agreement under Article 218(11) TFEU.[67] Uncertainty created by the unclear judgment in *Miles* continues and complicates any move to establish international courts by Member States. One can wonder whether this issue could have been made much simpler had the Court accepted the Opinion of AG Sharpston in *Miles*.

---

[64] Association Agreement between the European Union and the European Atomic Energy Community and their Member States, of the one part, and the Republic of Moldova, of the other part, (2014) OJ L 260/4. Article 403(2) provides a similar obligation for the Arbitral Tribunal established by this Agreement to refer to the Court, as the one in the Agreement with Ukraine.

[65] Agreement on the withdrawal of the United Kingdom of Great Britain and Northern Ireland from the European Union and the European Atomic Energy Community, (2019) OJ C 384/1. Under Article 174 of the Withdrawal Agreement, the Arbitration Panel is obliged to refer to the Court questions of interpretation of a concept of Union law and questions of interpretation of a provision of Union law referred to in the Agreement if they arise in a dispute which the Arbitration Panel is invited to resolve.

[66] Bundesverfassungsgericht, Order of 23 June 2021, 2 BvR 2216/20, 2 BvR 2217/20.

[67] This, however, does not mean that the challenge will not arise. See A Plomer, 'The Unified Patent Court and the Transformation of the European Patent System' (2020) 51 *International Review of Intellectual Property and Competition Law* 791.

43

Mutual Recognition, Mutual Trust, and EU Criminal Law: Opinion of Advocate General Sharpston in Radu

I. INTRODUCTION

THE APPLICATION of the principle of mutual recognition in the field of criminal law has been the motor of European integration in criminal matters.[1] The principle has been attractive to those resisting further harmonisation or unification in European criminal law as mutual recognition was thought to enhance inter-state cooperation in criminal matters without Member States having to change their national laws to comply with EU harmonisation requirements.[2] Rather, a system has been created whereby the outcomes of national legal orders – in the form largely of judicial decisions – are required to be recognised and executed by the authorities in another Member State with automaticity and speed. Mutual recognition thus creates extraterritoriality in a transnational field,[3] and is based upon interaction between national authorities on the basis of a high level of presumed mutual trust.[4]

The adoption of this system as the central plank of European integration in criminal matters, involving the interaction between national legal orders where there is limited harmonisation and a limited EU level playing field in terms of procedural law, has raised a number of questions regarding the meaning, extent, and limits of mutual trust in the operation of mutual recognition. Would and could mutual trust lead to automaticity in mutual recognition, or should there be limits to recognition and trust on the basis of fundamental rights considerations? And if the latter is the case, what is the extent of the power of the executing authority to refuse recognition and execution, and what is the extent of scrutiny which should

---

[1] Of the now voluminous literature on mutual recognition, see the following monographs: C Janssens, *The Principle of Mutual Recognition in EU Law* (Oxford, OUP, 2013); E Xanthopoulou, *Fundamental Rights and Mutual Trust in the Area of Freedom, Security and Justice* (Oxford, Hart Publishing, 2020); A Willems, *The Principle of Mutual Trust in EU Criminal Law* (Oxford, Hart Publishing, 2021).

[2] V Mitsilegas, 'The Constitutional Implications of Mutual Recognition in Criminal Matters in the EU' (2006) 43 *CMLRev* 1277.

[3] K Nicolaidis and G Shaffer, 'Transnational Mutual Recognition Regimes: Governance without Global Government' (2005) 68 *Law and Contemporary Problems* 263.

[4] V Mitsilegas, 'The Limits of Mutual Trust in Europe's Area of Freedom, Security and Justice. From Automatic Inter-state Cooperation to the Slow Emergence of the Individual' (2012) 31 *YEL* 319.

take place in the interaction between national authorities? It is precisely these fundamental questions which AG Sharpston addressed head-on in her Opinion in *Radu*.[5]

II. BACKGROUND, CONTEXT, AND FACTS

The emblematic and most widely implemented instrument of mutual recognition in European criminal law has been the Framework Decision on the European Arrest Warrant (hereinafter FD EAW).[6] The EAW system has been designed in a way that the space for mutual accommodation or consideration of the interests and values of the Member State whose authorities are asked to execute a Warrant is extremely limited. This model has become increasingly challenging to uphold, in particular in cases where concerns on the protection of fundamental rights in the operation of the EAW system came into the fore. The design of this system envisaged an extremely limited role for fundamental rights considerations in the execution of the EAW. The basis of this model of mutual recognition is the presumption of a high level of mutual trust between national authorities, some would call this trust blind, premised upon the fact that all EU Member States, being signatories to the European Convention on Human Rights (ECHR) and subsequently bound by the Charter, in principle and save in exceptional circumstances, comply with fundamental rights.[7] This presumption of trust is reflected in the very limited, and mostly procedural, grounds for refusal to execute set out in the mutual recognition instruments, culminating into non-compliance with fundamental rights not being included as a ground to refuse to execute a EAW.[8]

From the outset, the Court has demonstrated strong support for this vision of mutual trust, stating the fundamental rights considerations are to be considered by the issuing authority.[9] This support has been maintained after the entry into force of the Treaty of Lisbon in 2009,[10] notwithstanding the constitutionalisation of EU criminal law and of the Charter this entailed,[11] and notwithstanding gradual judicial developments in fundamental rights scrutiny and the emergence of legal avenues to refuse to co-operate in the system of mutual recognition established by the Dublin system in EU asylum law.[12] In the field of asylum law, the Court held that a conclusive presumption of compliance with fundamental rights, could itself be regarded as undermining the safeguards which are intended to ensure compliance with fundamental rights by the European Union and its Member States,[13] and that such presumption is

---

[5] Opinion of AG Sharpston in Case C-396/11 *Radu* ECLI:EU:C:2012:648.

[6] Council Framework Decision of 13 June 2002 on the European Arrest Warrant and the surrender procedures between Member States [2002] OJ L190/1.

[7] Mitsilegas (n 2).

[8] The Framework Decision merely includes a general provision – Article 1(3) – according to which it will 'not have the effect of modifying the obligation to respect fundamental rights and fundamental legal principles as enshrined in Article 6 of the TEU' See also Preamble, recital 12. For further analysis see V Mitsilegas, 'Mutual Recognition, Mutual Trust and Fundamental Rights After Lisbon' in V Mitsilegas, M Bergström, and T Konstadinides (eds), *Research Handbook on EU Criminal Law* (Cheltenham, Edward Elgar, 2016).

[9] Case C-303/05 *Advocaten voor de Wereld* ECLI:EU:C:2007:261.

[10] Treaty of Lisbon amending the Treaty on European Union and the Treaty establishing the European Community, signed at Lisbon, 13 December 2007 [2007] OJ C306/1.

[11] V Mitsilegas, *EU Criminal Law After Lisbon. Rights, Trust and the Transformation of Justice in Europe* (Oxford, Hart Publishing, 2016) 124–52.

[12] Joined Cases C-411/10 and C-493/10 N.S. ECLI:EU:C:2011:865.

[13] ibid, para 100.

rebuttable,[14] leading to calls for the application of this approach to the field of mutual recognition in criminal matters.[15]

The question of the extent to which the executing authority can refuse to execute a EAW when there are concerns that execution and surrender will have adverse fundamental rights consequences arose in the case of *Radu*. The case involved prosecution warrants issued by German authorities, and addressed to their Romanian counterparts. Following challenges to the execution of these warrants in the issuing state, the Court of Appeal, Constanța, decided to stay the proceedings, and refer a number of questions to the Court for a preliminary ruling. These included in particular questions on the legal status and force of fundamental rights provisions of the ECHR and the Charter under EU primary law; whether the execution of a EAW entailing deprivation of liberty and forcible surrender without the consent of the requested person constituted interference with these rights; whether such interference satisfied the requirements of necessity in a democratic society and of proportionality in relation to the objective pursued; and, crucially, whether the executing authority could refuse to execute a EAW on the grounds of fundamental rights while being in compliance with EU law.

III. THE OPINION OF AG SHARPSTON

AG Sharpston started her Opinion with an important finding of admissibility.[16] She noted that the national court made it plain in its order for reference that it saw the answers to its questions as being essential to the resolution of the dispute before it, and that no fewer than seven governments, together with the Public Prosecutor and the Commission, have lodged observations before the Court.[17] This finding enabled the AG and Court to address directly the question on whether a judicial authority could refuse to execute a EAW. The AG then addressed, in detail, the fundamental rights questions at three levels: on the status of fundamental rights under EU law; on the place of fundamental rights in the system of mutual recognition in criminal matters; and on whether execution of a EAW could be refused on fundamental rights grounds.

The AG Sharpston held that rights under the EU's Charter form part of the primary law of the EU, and that ECHR rights constitute general principles of Union law.[18] She noted that while the obligations imposed on the Member States by the FD EAW related to matters that are essentially procedural, that did not mean that the legislature failed to take fundamental and human rights into account when enacting the FD.[19] The FD incorporated express references to fundamental rights in the Preamble and in Article 1(3),[20] and specific provisions on the rights of the requested persons,[21] while also intended to protect victims.[22] Moreover, the high level of mutual trust underpinning the operation of the FD *was predicated on* the observance by each of the Member States of the rights enshrined in the ECHR and the Charter, and of

---

[14] ibid, para 104.
[15] Mitsilegas (n 4).
[16] Paras 26–31.
[17] Para 30.
[18] Para 52.
[19] Para 36.
[20] Para 37.
[21] Para 39.
[22] Para 40.

the rights which form part of the constitutional traditions common to the Member States.[23] AG Sharpston thus elevated the protection of fundamental rights as an element underpinning the system of mutual recognition based on mutual trust, while, following the *N.S.* case, affirming that the presumption of Member States' compliance with fundamental rights was rebuttable.[24]

This approach to mutual recognition and mutual trust led to the acknowledgement by AG Sharpston that it was possible for an authority to refuse to execute a EAW on fundamental rights grounds. The AG did not confine herself into a narrow textual interpretation of the FD EAW, which as seen above, did not contain an express ground of refusal to execute on fundamental rights grounds. Such a narrow approach which would exclude human rights considerations altogether was not supported, in her view, by the wording of the FD, or by the case law.[25] AG Sharpston went on to essentially construct a ground for refusal to execute on fundamental rights grounds implicitly from Article 1(3) of the FD EAW, although this provision was specifically included in a part of the FD other than the specific provisions on grounds for refusal.[26] She also drew support from other Opinions of AGs on EAW cases,[27] notwithstanding the fact that the part of these Opinions had not been endorsed expressly by the Court itself, which insisted in favour of a law enforcement-heavy, blind trust approach on the EAW.

AG Sharpston held that it was clear that the judicial authorities of an executing Member State are bound to have regard to the fundamental rights set out in the Convention and the Charter when considering whether to execute a EAW,[28] and went on to assess when must executing authorities refuse to execute, and what factors they should take into account. The AG started by referring to the ruling of the Court in *N.S.*,[29] and the case-law of the European Court of Human Rights (ECtHR).[30] She went on to differentiate the fundamental rights test employed by executing authorities under EU law, from the test developed by the ECtHR, in particular as regards 'flagrant denial'.[31] AG Sharpston then proceeded to give concrete answers as to the criterion to be employed by the executing authority, that the deficiency or deficiencies in the trial process should be such as fundamentally to destroy its fairness,[32] and on the standard and burden of proof.[33] Importantly, the AG extended the fundamental rights ground to refuse to execute a EAW also if it is proved that there has been a breach of a fundamental procedural requirement as *to the issuing* of the Warrant.[34]

AG Sharpston also addressed, in detail, questions related, but also distinct, from the broader issue of fundamental rights grounds for refusal, namely questions related to the parameters of the principle of proportionality in the operation of the European Arrest

---

[23] Para 38.

[24] Para 41 of the Opinion. The AG acknowledged that the record of the Member States in complying with their human rights obligations is 'not pristine'.

[25] Para 69 of the Opinion.

[26] According to the AG Sharpston, Article 1(3) permeates the Framework Decision – it is implicit that fundamental rights may be taken into account in founding a decision not to execute a warrant (para 70 of the Opinion).

[27] In paras 71–72 of the Opinion AG Sharpston referred to Opinion of AG Cruz Villalón in Case C-306/09 I.B. ECLI:EU:C:2010:404.

[28] Para 73.

[29] Para 76.

[30] Paras 74–75.

[31] Paras 79–83.

[32] Para 83.

[33] Paras 84–89.

[34] Para 95.

Warrant. AG Sharpston addressed two different aspects of proportionality: proportionality in detention and proportionality in the issuing of warrants. In terms of proportionality of detention, the AG held that to avoid being arbitrary, such detention must be carried out in good faith; it must be closely connected to the ground of detention relied on by the executing judicial authority; the place and conditions of detention should be appropriate; and the length of the detention should not exceed that reasonably required for the purpose pursued (thus satisfying the proportionality test). For AG Sharpston, Article 6 of the Charter was to be construed in the same way as Article 5(1) ECHR in this context.[35] The AG also addressed proportionality concerns with regard to the decision to issue a EAW. These concerns were prominent at the time in Member States such as the UK, where executing authorities were of the view that EAWs were issued for offences which would be considered minor or not be prosecuted under the system of the executing Member State, yet which would fall within the broad scope of the FD EAW.[36] Elsewhere, calls for the introduction of a proportionality check in the operation of the EAW system have been put forward in order to ensure that pressure to the criminal justice systems of executing Member States and disproportionate results for the requested individuals are avoided.[37] This concern regarding the proportionality of issuing EAWs was also raised by AG Sharpston,[38] from the perspective of its compliance with Article 49 of the Charter. The AG stated eloquently, as an obiter, that:

> I would add one thing. At the hearing, counsel for Germany used the example of a stolen goose. If that Member State were asked to execute a European arrest warrant in respect of that crime where the sentence passed in the issuing Member State was one of six years, she thought that execution of the warrant would be refused. She considered that such a refusal would be justifiable on the basis of the doctrine of proportionality and referred the Court to Article 49(3) of the Charter, according to which 'the severity of penalties must not be disproportionate to the criminal offence'. This Court has yet to rule on the interpretation of that article. In the context of the Convention, the Court of Human Rights has held that while, in principle, matters of appropriate sentencing largely fall outside the scope of the Convention, a sentence which is 'grossly disproportionate' could amount to ill-treatment contrary to Article 3 but that it is only on 'rare and unique occasions' that the test will be met. It would be interesting to speculate as to the interpretation to be given to Article 49(3) of the Charter having regard to the interpretation given by the Court of Human Rights of the provisions of Article 3 of the Convention.[39]

IV. ANALYSIS

In her Opinion in *Radu*, AG Sharpston put forward a detailed and coherent approach on the place of fundamental rights within the system of mutual recognition in criminal matters, and addressed the question of whether mutual trust should be presumed head on. The Opinion was bold in departing from settled case law of the Court on mutual trust in EU criminal law at the time, most notably in stressing that mutual trust is rebuttable, and that fundamental rights should underpin the operation of the EAW, and that effective scrutiny of fundamental rights

---

[35] Para 62.

[36] For an overview of the debate, see T Ostropolski, 'The Principle of Proportionality under the European Arrest Warrant – with an Excursus on Poland' (2014) 5 *New Journal of European Criminal Law* 167.

[37] For a discussion, see Joint Committee on Human Rights, *The Human Rights Implications of UK Extradition Policy (fifteenth report)* (2010–12, HL 156, HC 767) 40–43; Sir Scott Baker, *A Review of the United Kingdom's Extradition Arrangements*, presented to the Home Secretary on 30 September 2011, paras 5.120–5.155.

[38] Para 60.

[39] Para 103.

does not undermine, but rather ensures the legitimacy and credibility of mutual recognition in criminal matters. The Opinion also brought clearly into the fore the ongoing debate on the meaning and parameters of proportionality in the operation of mutual recognition in criminal matters.

A. Judgment of the Court

In its ruling in *Radu*,[40] the Court did not follow the Opinion of AG Sharpston. The Court answered the question on whether mutual recognition could be refused on fundamental rights grounds in the negative.[41] It reaffirmed the adoption of a teleological interpretation, reiterating the purpose of establishing a simplified and more effective system of surrender based on mutual recognition.[42] Such system, for the Court, would contribute to the Union's objective of becoming an area of freedom, security and justice by basing itself on the high degree of confidence which should exist between the Member States.[43] In its judgment, the Court stated that a refusal to execute can only take place on the basis of the mandatory and optional grounds for refusal set out in the FD.[44] On the basis of this presumption of mutual trust, the Court found that the observance of Articles 47 and 48 of the Charter did not require that a judicial authority of a Member State should be able to refuse to execute a EAW issued for the purposes of conducting a criminal prosecution on the ground that the requested person was not heard by the issuing judicial authorities before that warrant was issued.[45]

Once again, the Court placed effectiveness considerations at the forefront of its reasoning. It pointed out that such an obligation would inevitably lead to the failure of the very system of surrender,[46] and added that in any event, the right to be heard would be observed in the executing Member State in such a way as not to compromise the effectiveness of the EAW system.[47] *Radu* thus followed the Court's earlier case law in two respects: it confirmed that it was satisfied with the provision of fundamental rights protection in one of the two Member States which take part in the cooperative mutual recognition system, in that the executing Member State which is under the duty to uphold the right to be heard; and it placed the protection of fundamental rights within a clear framework of effectiveness of the enforcement cooperation system which is established by the FD EAW. For the Court, too extensive a protection of fundamental rights (in both the issuing and the executing Member State) would undermine the effectiveness of law enforcement cooperation in this context.

B. Mutual Trust and Fundamental Rights

The reluctance of the Court to recognise the existence of fundamental rights grounds for refusal to execute a EAW came as a disappointment to many, with the ruling being deemed

---

[40] Case C-396/11 *Radu* ECLI:EU:C:2013:39.
[41] The CJEU did not engage with the question of proportionality in the issuing of EAW.
[42] Paras 33–34.
[43] Para 34.
[44] Para 36. The Court referred here to its earlier case law: Case C-388/08 PPU *Leymann and Pustovarov* ECLI:EU:C:2008:669, para 51; Case C-261/09 *Mantello* ECLI:EU:C:2010:683, para 37.
[45] Para 39.
[46] Para 40.
[47] Para 41.

as a missed opportunity to seriously engage with fundamental rights in the context of the operation of mutual recognition in criminal matters.[48] Things did not change in the immediate aftermath of *Radu*: on the contrary, the Court entrenched its position in favour of enforcement in mutual recognition based on uncritical mutual trust, linking the effectiveness of enforcement with the broader constitutional objectives of the primacy and autonomy of EU law.

In *Melloni*, the Court held that secondary EU law on criminal enforcement (the FD EAW) has primacy over national constitutional law granting rights to affected individuals.[49] Internal primacy considerations were coupled with the objective ensuring the autonomy of EU law externally vis-à-vis the legal order of the ECHR. In *Opinion 2/13*, rejecting the terms of accession of the EU to the ECHR, the Court questionably elevated the principle of mutual trust into a fundamental principle of EU law, and interpreted trust as the basis of its enforcement-focused reasoning in *Melloni*.[50] Member States were required to presume that fundamental rights have been observed by the other Member States, so that not only may they not demand a higher level of national protection of fundamental rights from another Member State than that provided by EU law, but, save in exceptional cases, they may not check whether that other Member State has actually, in a specific case, observed the fundamental rights guaranteed by the Union.[51]

The unwavering emphasis of the Court on a concept of uncritical, and for many, blind mutual trust in these cases caused a backlash in national courts, and in particular by the certain national courts, which responded by triggering a constitutional identity review on the operation of the EAW.[52] Such responses of national courts led the Court to reconsider its approach, and to accept for the first time, in the seminar ruling in *Aranyosi* and *Caldararu*, that the execution of a EAW can be suspended on fundamental rights grounds,[53] which was more in line with what AG Sharpston had originally proposed in *Radu*. This change of heart – reflected also in the statement of the President of the Court that the approach of the Court is not one of blind trust[54] – has led to the evolution, via extensive judicial dialogue, of meaningful and substantive criteria on assessing fundamental rights in the context of the execution of EAW requests, and setting the parameters of mutual trust in this process.[55] The Opinion of AG Sharpston in *Radu* remains significant in this context, as it constitutes the first detailed engagement in Luxembourg with the question of how should executing authorities assess the implications of the execution of a EAW for fundamental rights and what is required for the execution to be refused.

---

[48] R Raffaelli, 'C-394/11 – *Radu*' in V Mitsilegas, A Di Martino and L Mancano (eds), *The Court of Justice and European Criminal Law: Leading Cases in a Contextual Analysis* (Oxford, Hart Publishing, 2019).

[49] Case C-399/11 *Melloni* ECLI:EU:C:2013:107.

[50] *Opinion 2/13* ECLI:EU:C:2014:2454.

[51] *Opinion 2/13*, paras 191–192. For a critical view, see V Mitsilegas, 'The Symbiotic Relationship between Mutual Trust and Fundamental Rights in Europe's Area of Criminal Justice' (2015) 6 *New Journal of European Criminal Law* 460.

[52] For example, the German Federal Constitutional Court (*Bundesverfassungsgericht*) in Order of the Second Senate of 15 December 2015, 2 BvR 2735/14.

[53] Joined Cases C-404/15 and C-659/15 PPU *Aranyosi and Căldăraru* ECLI:EU:C:2016:198.

[54] K Lenaerts, 'La Vie Après L'Avis: Exploring the Principle of Mutual (Yet Not Blind) Trust' (2017) 54 *CMLRev* 806.

[55] See V Mitsilegas, 'Judicial Dialogue, Legal Pluralism and Mutual Trust in Europe's Area of Criminal Justice' 46 (2021) *ELRev* 579. On the challenges that national judges face in applying the Aryanosi test see: A Łazowski, 'The Sky Is Not the Limit: Mutual Trust and Mutual Recognition aprés Aranyosi and Căldăraru' (2018) 14 *Croatian Yearbook of European Law and Policy* 1.

C. Proportionality

A further issue which is relevant for setting the parameters of mutual trust is giving meaningful effect to the principle of proportionality in the operation of the EAW, and in particular at the issuing stage. The Opinion of AG Sharpston in *Radu* highlighted two important aspects of proportionality in this context, with the insights provided in the Opinion continuing to be relevant for addressing and interpreting proportionality today. The first aspect involves the emphasis on procedural aspects of proportionality in the issuing of a EAW – an issue which is inextricably linked with the protection of fundamental rights of the requested person and the acknowledgement that triggering the EAW mechanism will result in deprivation of liberty. The importance of ensuring effective scrutiny of proportionality in the issuing of the EAW has been reflected clearly in the case law of the Court on defining the concept of 'judicial authority' for the purposes of issuing a EAW as an autonomous concept of EU law: the Court has held that a key constituent element of this concept is the availability of an effective remedy against the decision to issue a EAW, including the proportionality of such decision.[56]

The second aspect of proportionality involves the question of issuing a EAW for minor offences. There has been recognition by EU institutions that proportionality must be taken into account in the operation of mutual recognition in criminal matters, but that this should occur at the stage of issuing a judicial decision. The requirement to introduce a proportionality check in the issuing Member State has also been introduced at EU level in the Directive on the European Investigation Order, which states that the issuing authority may only issue a European Investigation Order where the issuing of the latter is necessary and proportionate, and where the investigative measures indicated in the European Investigation Order could have been ordered under the same conditions in a similar domestic case.[57] Although such a clause is absent from the FD EAW, the Commission Guidance on how to issue and execute a EAW includes a proportionality check in the issuing Member State.[58]

The discussion on proportionality remains relevant in the relations between the EU and the UK after Brexit. Before Brexit, the UK had digressed from the Commission Guidance by amending domestic law (the Extradition Act 2003) to extend proportionality control to the executing Member State and treat non-compliance with proportionality as a ground of refusal to execute a Warrant.[59] This broader approach underpins the provisions on

---

[56] Joined Cases C-508/18 and C-82/19 PPU *OG and PI* ECLI:EU:C:2019:456. As the Court ruled in para 75 of this Judgment: 'the decision to issue such an arrest warrant and, inter alia, the proportionality of such a decision must be capable of being the subject, in the Member State, of court proceedings which meet in full the requirements inherent in effective judicial protection'.

[57] Directive 2014/41/EU of the European Parliament and of the Council of 3 April 2014 regarding the European Investigation Order in criminal matters [2014] OJ L130/1, Article 6(1).

[58] Commission Notice – Handbook on how to issue and execute a European arrest warrant [2017] OJ C335/1. In para 2.4 the Commission provided detailed guidance on factors to be taken into account by the issuing authority in this context including: '(a) the seriousness of the offence (for example, the harm or danger it has caused); (b) the likely penalty imposed if the person is found guilty of the alleged offence (for example, whether it would be a custodial sentence); (c) the likelihood of detention of the person in the issuing Member State after surrender; (d) the interests of the victims of the offence. Furthermore, issuing judicial authorities should consider whether other judicial cooperation measures could be used instead of issuing an EAW.'

[59] Section 157 of the Anti-Social Behaviour, Crime and Policing Act 2014 has amended s 21A of the Extradition Act 2003 to treat lack of proportionality as a ground for refusal (s 21A(1)(b)). See also the ruling of the Higher Regional Court of Stuttgart of 25 February 2010, reported by Vogel (J Vogel, 'Introduction to the Ruling of the Higher Regional Court of Stuttgart of 25 February 2010 – The Proportionality of a European Arrest Warrant' (2010) 1 *New Journal of European Criminal Law* 145). See also J Vogel and J Spencer, 'Proportionality and the European arrest warrant (Case Comment)' [2010] *Criminal Law Review* 474.

surrender in the EU-UK Trade and Cooperation Agreement (TCA).[60] Article 597 TCA provides:

> Cooperation through the arrest warrant shall be necessary and proportionate, taking into account the rights of the requested person and the interests of the victims, and having regard to the seriousness of the act, the likely penalty that would be imposed and the possibility of a State taking measures less coercive than the surrender of the requested person particularly with a view to avoiding unnecessarily long periods of pre-trial detention.

Mirroring domestic UK law, non-compliance with the proportionality principle may constitute a ground of refusal to recognise and execute an arrest warrant.[61] Thus, the EU has introduced a higher degree of scrutiny of proportionality in its external relations compared with the internal functioning of mutual recognition in criminal matters.

D. Impact of the Opinion

The Opinion of AG Sharpston in *Radu* was ahead of its time. AG Sharpston engaged in detail with the question of the parameters of mutual trust and provided concrete and detailed answers on how fundamental rights should be assessed by executing authorities. The Opinion was also insightful in terms of the different guises of the proportionality principle in the operation of the EAW system. it took some time for the Court to take fully into account the points raised in the Opinion of AG Sharpston, with the immediate reaction in *Radu* and the subsequent leading case of *Melloni* being to retrench in favour of a paradigm of blind trust. Yet in the face of sustained reactions in EU Member States, including by the judiciary, the Court has had to change its approach, and thus, be more in line with the approach to mutual trust that was offered by AG Sharpston in *Radu*. In the development of a more fundamental rights-friendly approach, and in the challenging task of defining the parameters of mutual trust on that basis, the Opinion of AG Sharpston in *Radu* remains influential and relevant in terms of the framing of the issues and the insights it provides.

---

[60] Trade and Cooperation Agreement between the European Union and the European Atomic Energy Community, of the one part, and the United Kingdom of Great Britain and Northern Ireland, of the other part [2021] OJ L149/10.

[61] Article 597(1) of the EU-UK TCA.

44

Discrimination on Grounds of Religion or Belief and Neutrality Requirements: Opinion of Advocate General Sharpston in Bougnaoui

RONAN McCREA

I. INTRODUCTION

THE QUESTION OF how best to regulate the role of religion in society in the context of increasing religious diversity has been one of the most controversial questions in European life in recent times. The choices made by states in this area have been challenged before the European Court of Human Rights (ECtHR) on several occasions, but until 2016, the Court of Justice of the European Union (the Court) had not had an opportunity to issue a major ruling in this area.[1] It is often said that you wait for ages for a bus, then two come along at once, and this was the experience of the Court in the area of religion. After waiting for decades to receive a major case, 2016 saw not one, but two landmark disputes come before the Court,[2] both in relation to the compatibility of rules that restricted the wearing of religious symbols by employees in the workplace, with the prohibition of discrimination on grounds of religion or belief contained in the framework directive on discrimination in employment.[3]

The question of religion's role in society is an emotive topic in its own right. In contemporary Europe, it is made all the more controversial so by the fact that this question has come to be mixed up with a host of other 'hot-button' issues such as migration, multiculturalism, national identity, feminism, and sexual orientation discrimination. States have taken very different approaches to these matters, often influenced by foundational constitutional principles ranging from recognition of state churches in a number of Member States, to strict separation of religion and state in others. Some states have followed an approach that facilitates individuals in expressing and adhering to the requirements of their religious identity

---

[1] See eg *Eweida and Others v United Kingdom* [2013] ECHR 37, and *Ebrahimian v France* [2015] 1041.
[2] Case C-157/15 *Achbita* ECLI:EU:C:2017:203 and Case C-188/15 *Bougnaoui* ECLI:EU:C:2017:204.
[3] Council Directive 2000/78/EC of 27 November 2000 establishing a general framework for equal treatment in employment and occupation [2000] OJ L303/16.

in a wide range of contexts. Others have taken the view that coexistence is best pursued by encouraging and sometimes enforcing reticence in relation to religious expression in certain shared contexts.

Therefore, in interpreting Directive 2000/78 in these cases, the Court was faced with the difficult task of interpreting legislation that applied in 28 Member States, all of which have their own particular approach to regulating the role of religion in society, approaches which are often linked to fundamental constitutional and political principles. Writing in 1994, Mancini and Keeling noted how the Court was changed by the arrival of the British and Irish members, who brought their common law traditions with them, and 'enriched the conceptual patrimony of the Court with rules and notions drawn from the common law, sometimes with surprisingly positive results'.[4]

As the presence of the word 'sometimes' indicates, blending legal traditions in a single institution can be a challenge. But it can also be an advantage. Humans have a tendency to regard what they are used to as acceptable and normal, and they can struggle to see how established ways of doing things are not inevitable nor necessarily fair. Viewed in this light, while the diversity of Member States arrangements in relation to religion made the Court's task of interpreting Directive 2000/78 difficult, the multinational nature of the Court also had the potential to be a major asset. Debate on this issue is all too often a dialogue of the deaf, in which people from different intellectual and constitutional traditions fail to realise that their way of looking at the issues is not the only one, and thereby talk past each other. An international court made up of lawyers from a range of legal and constitutional traditions could be particularly well-placed to come up with an approach that takes due account of the strengths and weaknesses of different approaches to religion, rather than being blinkered by their familiarity with particular national ways of doing things.

In debates around religion, two of the most prominent alternative ways of looking at the role of religion in society are represented by an approach predominant in France, which is based on the tradition of *laïcité*, which, despite the fact that this tradition focuses on the relationship between religion and the state, combines with the French republican ideas on citizenship to produce a broader suspicion of identitarian politics and of religious expression in non-state shared contexts, such as the workplace; and an Anglosphere approach which places greater emphasis on multiculturalism and facilitation of the expression of identity. Mutual incomprehension is a key feature of many of the disagreements between these two poles. For many Anglophone critics, the French approach is unduly restrictive, and insufficiently cognisant of the discriminatory impact of facially neutral rules against religious expression in certain contexts.[5] For many French critics, much Anglophone commentary is based on ignorance and mischaracterisation of French traditions of secularism and citizenship, as well as a regrettable tendency to apply an American (and sometimes, but less often, British) frame of reference to all situations.[6]

In these circumstances it was fortunate that, when faced with its first two major cases on religious expression at work, a francophone court such as the Court which is likely to be well-acquainted with French approaches, allocated one of the two cases (*Bougnaoui*) to an AG from the Anglophone world, AG Sharpston,[7] thus ensuring that the eventual decision would benefit

---

[4] GF Mancini and DT Keeling, 'Language, Culture and Politics in the Life of the European Court of Justice' (1995) 1 *CJEL* 397, 403.

[5] See JW Scott, *The Politics of the Veil* (Princeton, Princeton University Press, 2010).

[6] See B Haddad, 'France's War on Islamism Isn't Populism. It's Reality' (*Foreign Policy*, 3 November 2020). There are, of course, supporters and opponents of each approach in the US, the UK, and France.

[7] Opinion of AG Sharpston in Case C-188/15 *Bougnaoui* ECLI:EU:C:2016:553.

fully from common law and Anglosphere insights, and holding out the prospect that the Court may have been able to come up with a ruling that drew on the strengths of both approaches (the other case (*Achbita*) was allocated to AG Kokott, who is German).

II. BACKGROUND, CONTEXT, AND FACTS

Both cases related to the provisions of the framework directive on discrimination in employment – Directive 2000/78. The facts of the two cases were similar, but subtly different. In *Achbita*, the claimant, who worked as a receptionist at G4S, informed her employers in April 2006 that she intended to wear an Islamic headscarf at work, and was told that she could not do so because this violated G4S's unwritten rule requiring philosophical and religious neutrality in their employees' attire. In May 2006, G4S adopted a written rule banning visible signs of political, philosophical or religious belief a written rule, and in June 2006, Ms. Achbita was dismissed for her insistence on wearing the headscarf at work.[8]

In *Bougnaoui*, the claimant was informed by a representative of Micropole at an October 2007 student recruitment fair that wearing an Islamic headscarf may pose problems when she was in contact with customers. She began to work at Micropole in February 2008, initially wearing a bandana, and then a headscarf. In May 2009, a customer of Micropole's with whom Ms Bougnaoui had worked, informed her employers that Ms Bouganoui's wearing of the headscarf had upset some of their employees, and requested that there be 'no veil next time'. Ms Bougnaoui refused her employers request to confirm that she would agree not to wear the headscarf on future occasions, and was dismissed in June 2009.[9]

The Belgian and French Courts of Cassation both referred questions relating to the prohibition on discrimination in employment on grounds of religion or belief to the Court, which, given their importance, decided to attribute both cases to the Grand Chamber.

In *Achbita*, the Belgian court asked whether a ban on a female Muslim employee wearing the headscarf at work should be regarded as direct discrimination when the employer in question bans all employees from wearing any outward sign of political, philosophical or religious beliefs at work. This was important as under the Directive, a directly discriminatory rule can only be justified by a 'genuine and determining occupational requirement'.[10] Indirectly discriminatory rules, on the other hand, can be accepted if it is shown that they serve a legitimate aim, and are pursued by proportionate and necessary means.[11]

In *Bougnaoui*, the French court asked the Court whether the wish of a customer not to have services supplied by an employee in an Islamic headscarf could be seen as a genuine and determining occupational requirement under the Directive (seemingly, assuming that the restriction in question was directly discriminatory). Therefore, both claims focused on the issue of direct discrimination. However, in addition to ruling on the issue of direct discrimination, the Court decided to give significant guidance in relation to the question of justification of bans on religious symbols as indirectly discriminatory measures.

Given the similarity of the issues at stake, the Grand Chamber of the Court heard both cases jointly, and delivered its ruling in respect of each on the same day but, interestingly, the two Advocates General (AGs) came to sharply differing conclusions on key issues.

---

[8] Case C-157/15 *Achbita*, paras 10–21.
[9] Case C-188/15 *Bougnaoui*, paras 13–19.
[10] Article 4(1) of Directive 2000/78.
[11] Article 2(2)(b)(i) of Directive 2000/78.

III. THE OPINIONS OF AGS SHARPSTON AND KOKOTT

Both AGs were of the view that, where a ban on religious symbols at work is found to be indirectly discriminatory, a balancing exercise had to be carried out. However, they proposed giving contrasting indications to the national courts as to whether, on the facts, the actions of the employers ought to be found to have been proportionate. The AGs also disagreed as to whether such a ban could be found to constitute direct discrimination. Notably, the contrasting conclusions on both of these points were underpinned by very different characterisations of religion, a difference that reflects wider debates about the role of religion in contemporary Europe.

IV. ANALYSIS

A. Neutrality as an Occupational Requirement

As noted above, whether a ban on religious symbols at work amounts to direct or indirect discrimination is of considerable importance, as, under Directive 2000/78, if a measure is found to be directly discriminatory, it can only be justified if it represents a 'genuine and determining occupational requirement'. For AG Sharpston, the answer in this case was clear. She noted that the Court has held that the derogation from the prohibition on direct discrimination in respect of genuine and determining occupational requirements must be interpreted strictly and, according to the recital of the Directive should apply only 'in very limited circumstances'.[12] Thus, she argued, the derogation 'must be limited to matters which are absolutely necessary in order to undertake the professional activity in question'.[13] AG Sharpston therefore concluded that:

> There is nothing in the order for reference or elsewhere in the information made available to the Court to suggest that, because she wore the Islamic headscarf, she was in any way unable to perform her duties as a design engineer – indeed, the dismissal letter expressly refers to her professional competence. Whatever the precise terms of the prohibition applying to her, the requirement not to wear a headscarf when in contact with customers of her employer could not in my view be a 'genuine and determining occupational requirement.[14]

AG Kokott, found that in Ms Achbita's case, the refusal to allow her to wear her headscarf, belief amounted to indirect discrimination because:

> [T]he ban at issue applies to all visible religious symbols without distinction. There is therefore no discrimination *between religions*. In particular, all of the information available to the Court indicates that the measure in question is *not* one directed specifically against employees of Muslim faith, let alone specifically against *female* employees of that religion. After all, a company rule such as that operated by G4S could just as easily affect a male employee of Jewish faith who comes to work wearing a kippah, or a Sikh who wishes to perform his duties in a Dastar (turban), or male or female employees of a Christian faith who wish to wear a clearly visible crucifix or a T-shirt bearing the slogan 'Jesus is great' to work.[15]

---

[12] Para 95 of Opinion of AG Sharpston.
[13] ibid, para 96.
[14] ibid, para 102.
[15] Para 49 of Opinion of AG Kokott (italicisation in the original).

Contrary to AG Sharpston in *Bougnaoui*, AG Kokott in *Achbita* also concluded that, even if the ban were found to be directly discriminatory, it could be said to amount to a genuine and determining occupational requirement on the basis that a neutrality policy was in principle legitimate and because:

> an employer may require its workers to behave and dress in a particular way at work in other circumstances too, which may be part of a company policy which it has formulated. This is particularly true if the work of the employees concerned – like that of Ms Achbita here – brings them into regular face-to-face contact with customers.[16]

AG Kokott therefore concluded that:

> taking into account the employer's discretion in the pursuit of its business, by no means unreasonable for a receptionist such as Ms Achbita to have to carry out her work in compliance with a particular dress code – in this case, by refraining from wearing her Islamic headscarf. A ban such as that laid down by G4S may be regarded as a genuine and determining occupational requirement.[17]

B. Neutrality as a Proportionate Aim?

The disagreement of the AGs also extended to the question of justification of indirectly discriminatory measures. Under Directive 2000/78, indirect discrimination occurs where 'an apparently neutral provision, criterion or practice would put persons having a particular religion or belief (...) at a particular disadvantage compared with other persons'. However indirect discrimination will not be found to have occurred if 'that provision, criterion or practice is objectively justified by a legitimate aim and the means of achieving that aim are appropriate and necessary'.[18]

Both AGs recommended giving a clear steer to the respective national courts as to how it should exercise its power to apply the Court's ruling to the facts before each of them. AG Sharpston stated that:

> Whilst the question is ultimately one for the national court having the responsibility for reaching a final decision in the matter and while there may be other matters relevant to any discussion on proportionality of which this Court has not been informed, I consider it unlikely that an argument based on the proportionality of the prohibition imposed under Micropole's workplace regulations – whether the ban involved the wearing of religious signs or apparel generally or the Islamic headscarf alone – would succeed in the case in the main proceedings.[19]

In this regard, AG Sharpston distinguished between the headscarf and face veils, and between customer and non-customer facing roles, stating:

> Western society regards visual or eye contact as being of fundamental importance in any relationship involving face-to-face communication between representatives of a business and its customers. It follows in my view that a rule that imposed a prohibition on wearing religious apparel that covers the eyes and face entirely whilst performing a job that involved such contact with customers would be proportionate. The balancing of interests would favour the employer. Conversely, where the employee in question is asked to work in a role which involves no visual or eye contact with customers, for

---

[16] ibid, para 82.
[17] ibid, para 84.
[18] Articles 2.2(b) and 2.2.(b)(i) of Directive 2000/78.
[19] Para 132 of Opinion of AG Sharpston.

example in a call centre, the justification for the *same rule* would disappear. The balance will favour the employee. And where the employee seeks to wear only some form of headgear that leaves the face and eyes entirely clear, I can see no justification for prohibiting the wearing of that headgear.[20]

Having found that a ban on all religious symbols satisfied the much more demanding test of being a 'genuine and determining occupational requirement', it was not surprising that AG Kokott concluded that such a ban could satisfy the less demanding test set out for indirect discrimination. On her analysis, neutrality was a legitimate aim for businesses, other approaches (such as an option for a uniform with a hijab) would not achieve neutrality, the ban in question was capable of affecting both men and women and those of all ethnic backgrounds and required merely neutrality from employees, it did not involve an active obligation to espouse particular views or act in accordance with a particular doctrine.[21]

C. What is Religion?

The divergent approaches of the two AGs flowed from their differing characterisations of what religion is. Scholars of religion and law have noted that our concept of religion covers two rather different phenomena.[22] Religion can be seen as a set of beliefs that are chosen, can be changed, and which can be analogised to other kinds of philosophical or political beliefs. It can also be seen as a form of identity that is rarely changed or chosen (it is usually inherited from parents), and which overlaps with other identities such as racial, ethnic, and national identities. Which definition one adopts will largely determine one's conclusion as to whether restrictions on religious expression are legitimate. If one regards religion as a form of belief, then restricting an employee from wearing a headscarf or crucifix is no different from restricting an employee from wearing the badge of a political party while working. On the other hand, if you regard religion as a form of largely immutable identity, then a 'no religious symbols at work' rule appears little different from a rule excluding a particular racial group from a particular job.

For AG Sharpston:

> to someone who is an observant member of a faith, religious identity is an integral part of that person's very being. The requirements of one's faith – its discipline and the rules that it lays down for conducting one's life – are not elements that are to be applied when outside work (say, in the evenings and during weekends for those who are in an office job) but that can politely be discarded during working hours. Of course, depending on the particular rules of the religion in question and the particular individual's level of observance, this or that element may be non-compulsory for that individual and therefore negotiable. But it would be entirely wrong to suppose that, whereas one's sex and skin colour accompany one everywhere, somehow one's religion does not.[23]

AG Kokott, on the other hand, characterised religion as a matter of belief and ideology, thereby distinguishing it from other protected characteristics such as gender or race. She noted that the ban in question covered all religious and political signs and that:

> That requirement of neutrality affects a religious employee in exactly the same way that it affects a confirmed atheist who expresses his anti-religious stance in a clearly visible manner by the way he

[20] ibid, para 130.
[21] Paras 112–25 of Opinion of AG Kokott.
[22] See C Laborde, *Liberalism's Religion* (Cambridge, MA, Harvard University Press, 2017).
[23] Para 118 of Opinion of AG Sharpston.

dresses, or a politically active employee who professes his allegiance to his preferred political party or particular policies through the clothes that he wears (such as symbols, pins or slogans on his shirt, T-shirt or headwear).[24]

This allowed her to distinguish between:

immutable physical features or personal characteristics – such as gender, age or sexual orientation – rather than with modes of conduct based on a subjective decision or conviction, such as the wearing or not of a head covering at issue here.[25]

The Court therefore benefitted from two contrasting opinions, each flowing from a view of religion that makes sense in its own terms. However, the real trick for multi-national courts, whose members come from a variety of different legal traditions, is not just to be open to the different perspectives that those members bring, but to be able to synthesise a coherent and fair approach that takes on board the insights of those different perspectives. From this point of view, the two Opinions leave one with a sense of a missed opportunity. The main reason so many of the issues arising in the regulation of the role of religion in society are so tricky is that religion is both a set of beliefs, and a form of identity, and the form of treatment that is appropriate for a set of beliefs is often very different to the form of treatment appropriate for a form of identity.

AG Sharpston argued that religion is a form of immutable identity, and set out the conclusions that flow from that characterisation. AG Kokott characterised religion as a form of belief and ideology, and set out the conclusions that flow from that view. This leaves one with the impression of two intelligent people talking past each other. Because religion is *both* identity *and* belief, what was needed were criteria to work out when it is right to treat religion as belief, and when it is right to treat it as identity. Both approaches can be appropriate at times. In relation to laws criminalising apostasy, it is probably best to treat religion as a form of chosen belief. In relation to the right to receive goods and services, it is probably best to see it as a form of identity. In relation to the wearing of religious symbols at work, what was needed were reasons why, in this instance, religion ought to be treated as either opinion or identity (and reasons why the Directive should or should not be seen as requiring a uniform approach from member states in this area).

D. The Judgments

The Court issued its rulings in the two cases on the same day, and though not joined, it indicated that the two should be read together by engaging in a significant degree of cross-referencing between the two rulings. Citing the right to conduct a business covered by Article 16 of the Charter of Fundamental Rights (the Charter),[26] the Court found that, in principle, an employer's wish to project an image of neutrality 'must be considered legitimate' (...) 'notably' when the restriction on religious expression only applies to workers who are 'required to come into contact with [...] customers'.[27]

---

[24] Para 52 of Opinion of AG Kokott.
[25] ibid, para 45.
[26] Charter of Fundamental Rights of the European Union [2016] OJ C202/391.
[27] Case C-157/15 *Achbita*, para 38.

However, in order to be indirectly rather than directly discriminatory, a restriction on religious symbols or attire had to be part of a neutrality policy that 'is genuinely pursued in a consistent and systematic manner' that covered all symbols of religious, philosophical or political belief'.[28] As this approach sees restrictions on religious and political symbols as equivalent, it is much closer to AG Kokott's characterisation of religion than AG Sharpston's.

However, the Court also found that a policy that targeted the symbols of one particular faith (Ms. Bougnaoui had been told 'no veil next time'), would amount to direct discrimination that could only be justified if it was regarded as fulfilling a 'genuine and determining occupational requirement'. On this point, the Court preferred the approach AG Sharpston, finding that it was that only in very limited circumstances can characteristics related to religion constitute a genuine and determining occupational requirement. Compliance with a client request, such as that made in Ms Bougnaoui's case, did not meet the Directive's requirement that a discriminatory rule be justified 'by reason of the nature of the particular occupational activities concerned or of the context in which they are carried out'.[29]

In common with the AGs, the Court gave a strong steer to the national courts as to how they ought to apply the legal tests it had set out. Though emphasising that the application of the rulings was a matter for the national court, the ruling nevertheless stated explicitly that if a genuinely and systematically applied (and therefore indirectly discriminatory) prohibition on the wearing of symbols of religious or philosophical belief was applied only to workers with customer facing roles, then 'the prohibition must be considered strictly necessary for the purpose of achieving the aim pursued'. On the other hand, it was also clear that in the case of a directly discriminatory rule that targeted the symbols of one faith, then compliance with client desires could not be seen as the 'genuine and determining occupational requirement' required to justify such a directly discriminatory approach.[30]

Overall, the Court went further than AG Kokott had suggested in protecting religious expression at work, but not as far as AG Sharpston would have liked. The Court upheld the compatibility of rules prohibiting the wearing of religious symbols at work with the Directive, thus making room for an approach that sees reticence about religion in certain contexts as the best way of coexisting, while leaving states free to adopt other approaches if they choose to do so. But, by ruling that any restrictions must cover all religions and beliefs equally, the Court also took steps to ensure that such rules do not become a means to target adherents to minority or unpopular faiths.

E. Reaction and Effect on Future Case Law

The Court's two rulings have been criticised by a number of scholars who felt that the Court ought to have been less accommodating of attempts to restrict the wearing of religious symbols at work. Spaventa argued that the Court's analysis of the discriminatory nature of restrictions on religious symbols was 'rather superficial', and gave insufficient thought to the fact that protecting a principle of neutrality might have 'a more pronounced effect on people from a certain ethnic background or a certain gender'.[31] In a similar vein, Weiler criticised the

---

[28] ibid, para 40.

[29] Case C-188/15 *Bougnaoui*, paras 30–40.

[30] ibid, para 40.

[31] E Spaventa, 'What Is the Point of Minimum Harmonization: Some Reflections on the Achbita Case' (*EU Law Analysis*, 21 March 2017).

failure of the Court to engage in meaningful analysis of whether the goal of neutrality satisfied the third limb of the proportionality test, faulting the ruling for failing to 'explore and weigh the value of the company policy of neutrality as against at least the presumed liberty of *manifesting* one's religious beliefs if not *practising* them. And [...] in addition, if the company policy actually creates a discrimination among religions to further weigh whether the importance of the policy is such as to justify such discrimination'.[32]

AG Sharpston herself was critical of the Court's approach. For her, the ruling 'confused mandatory requirements of practising certain (non-Christian) religions with the optional choice of manifesting (or not manifesting) one's Christian belief in an overt way in the workplace'.[33] A similar point was also made by Weiler, who felt that the Court ought to have distinguished between expression of one's religion (as in the case of a Christian who wishes to express their faith by wearing a cross at work), and observing one's religion (as in the case a Muslim or Jew for whom wearing a headscarf or yarmulke is part of their faith).[34]

AG Sharpston also contrasted the approach in *Achbita* and *Bougnaoui* with the much more restrictive approach taken by the Court in cases such as *Egenberger* and *IR v JQ*,[35] in which it imposed a test of proportionality that was much more demanding in relation to rules on the part of employers that required employees either to be of a particular faith, or to live in accordance with the tenets of the ethos of the employer.[36]

Spaventa further worried that the invocation of the right to run a business in Article 16 of the Charter as a reason to permit employers to pursue a neutrality policy may limit the scope of Member States to pursue policies more protective of religious rights in the workplace.[37] This concern was also expressed in the aftermath of a subsequent Opinion on the question of religious symbols at work from AG Rantos.[38] Van den Brink notes how the Court's approach in *Achbita*, which sees neutrality as a goal that can be pursued partly to avoid offence to customers, influenced AG Rantos, and that small, discreet signs ought to be permitted, as they would not cause offence to customers, a view that for Van den Brink amounts to holding that 'it is not the perpetrator of discrimination who must change his intolerant attitudes, but rather the victim of discrimination who must change her religious practices'.[39] Similar criticisms were made by Sharpston when she took the unusual step of authoring a 'shadow opinion' on this case which she published online after AG Rantos had delivered his advice to the Court.[40]

There is something to some of these criticisms. The treatment of the right to be free of discrimination on grounds of religion, as equal in importance to the right to run a business, is somewhat troubling. On the other hand, much of the responsibility for this lies with those who insisted on including a very broad range of rights in the Charter. With such a range, the potential for them to come into conflict is high, with the result that, as in these cases, everything becomes a matter of balancing, and the narrower range of rights previously seen as fundamental, ironically, lose their fundamental status to some degree.

---

[32] JHH Weiler, 'Je Suis Achbita' (Editorial) (2017) 28 *EJIL* 989.

[33] E Sharpston, 'Religion in the Workplace: When is Enforcing a Religious Ethos Acceptable? and When is Neutrality Discrimination?' in K Lenaerts, J-C Bonichot, H Kanninen, C Naômé and P Pohjankoski (eds), *An Ever-Changing Union? Perspectives on the Future of EU Law in Honour of Allan Rosas* (Oxford, Hart Publishing, 2019) 248, 255.

[34] Weiler (n 32) 991.

[35] Case C-414/16 *Egenberger* ECLI:EU:C:2018:257; Case C-68/17 *IR* ECLI:EU:C:2018:696.

[36] Sharpston (n 33) 257–60.

[37] Spaventa (n 31).

[38] Opinion of AG Rantos in Joined Cases C-804/18 and C-341/19 *WABE* ECLI:EU:C:2021:144.

[39] M Van den Brink, 'Preserving Prejudice in the Name of Profit: AG Rantos' Opinion in IX v Wabe and MH Müller Handels GmbH' (*Verfassungsblog*, 1 March 2021).

[40] E Sharpston, 'Shadow Opinion of former Advocate-General Sharpston: Headscarves at Work (Cases C-804/18 and C-341/19)' (*EU Law Analysis*, 23 March 2021).

However, the Court is responsible for the emphasis it places on the question of customer preferences, something which raises more questions than it solves. For one thing, it fails to take account of the fact that employers' desire to restrict religious (or philosophical) expression at work may as often be motivated by a desire to avoid conflict or harassment between employees as to avoid difficulties with customers. In the well-known case of *Ladele* before the ECtHR, for example, the objection to accommodating the religious beliefs of a civil registrar who refused to register same-sex couples came from gay fellow employees, rather than any couple.[41]

Even focusing on customers alone, taking offence at a symbol of religious or other belief can be a matter of pure bigotry, but as religion and belief can encompass beliefs and opinions that a customer might legitimately find offensive, it is wrong to suggest, as Van den Brink does, that the Court's approach is equivalent to allowing businesses to pander to the prejudice of racist customers. It may often be the case that a customer's negative reaction to a religious symbol amounts to bigotry, but there may be circumstances when a belief is legitimately seen as offensive, and therefore negative reaction to that symbol would be understandable.

Indeed, despite her criticism of the Court's more permissive approach to restrictions on religious expression at work, the Opinion of AG Sharpston stated that customer preferences and upholding cultural norms could be relied on to prohibit the wearing of face-veils at work. If cultural norms can be relied on to prohibit the wearing of face-veils, why can a cultural norm that religious and political expression at work is to be avoided not be similarly enforced? There may be good reasons to distinguish between these situations, but the answers are not easy or obvious and the case for a multi-national Court making that determination is far from conclusive. That said, having invoked customer preferences, it was incumbent upon the Court to give guidance as to when it may or may not be legitimate to cater to customer preferences and its failure to do so in *Bougnaoui* and *Achbita* is regrettable. While the rulings in *Egenberger* and *IR v JQ* do indeed, as AG Sharpston noted, require much stronger justifications from employers for rules requiring employees to adhere to the employer's ethos, it is surely relevant that these cases related to attempts to regulate employee behaviour away from work, while *Achbita* and *Bougnaoui* related exclusively to conduct while on the job.

Weiler and Spaventa are correct that the Court could have provided more justification for its conclusion that the pursuit of a neutrality policy can satisfy the third limb of the proportionality test. On the other hand, this third limb is where judges engage in a form of merits review, by assessing whether the objective pursued by the restriction of the right justifies the restriction in question. This reluctance of the judges of the Court to definitively pronounce on whether a policy of neutrality can justify restrictions on religious expression at work is understandable. There are good reasons why the judges in such a court might be reluctant to pronounce on the merits of whether the goal of neutrality is sufficiently weighty to outweigh any indirect discrimination or restriction on religious liberty.

There is no consensus in Europe about what is the best way to manage the increase in religious diversity and the rising salience of religion as an issue in public life, and understandably so. Europe is living through the rapid rise of non-believers, the rapid decline of Christianity, and the rapid rise in the Muslim population, all at the same time. As these are all unprecedented developments, a store of precedents for how best to ensure coexistence in this situation does not exist. Different states have adopted different approaches. In the UK, the approach has been to permit religious expression in a wide range of contexts, whereas in France, the authorities have seen coexistence as best achieved by requiring a degree of reticence in relation to religious

---

[41] *Eweida and Others* (n 1). Ladele's case was one of the four cases decided together in the *Eweida* decision.

expression in non-private contexts. Each approach has its critics. Some in France see the French approach as illiberal and conducive to alienation of minorities, while some in Britain feel that cohesion and coexistence have not been well-served by the UK's more permissive approach. Other states, such as the Netherlands, have switched from one approach to another in recent decades.[42] In a situation of unprecedented change and shifting political approaches, it would be immodest for the judges of the Court to decide that they knew best what approach will work for a Union of 27 (then 28) different Member States, especially given that particular approaches to religion are woven deeply into the constitutional orders of many of those states.

That said, it is easy to see why treating the wearing of a religious symbol simply as an expression of a political belief is unsatisfactory from the perspective of the person who may have no expressive intent in wearing that symbol. On the other hand, it is not clear how a religion-specific right to wear symbols reasonably associated with certain beliefs can be reconciled with the consistent commitment to equality of religious and non-religious beliefs seen in the Article 9 jurisprudence of the ECtHR.[43]

The Opinions in these cases show the loss that will be incurred by the loss of the British voice in EU law. The voice of the Anglosphere will sound less loudly in the Court going forward (and the Irish approach to these issues, which is influenced both by the English-speaking world and the French republican tradition within Irish nationalism, may be less divergent from the francophone approach than the British approach).[44] AGs Sharpston and Kokott each gave an analysis that made perfect sense in its own terms, and each of which influenced the ruling of the Court in some aspects. Though the way in which the two Opinions talked past each other does give a sense of a missed opportunity, this talking past each other was also in some ways, helpful, as it underlined the degree to which debates in this area can all too easily fall into a dialogue of the deaf. Religion is both opinion and identity, and any durable solution will have to cope with the reality that these different elements of religion often pull the law in opposite directions. By provided eloquent reasons for prioritising each element, the two AGs have helped to ensure that whatever solution ultimately emerges will take some account of each.

Perhaps the most revealing feature of these cases is the fact that two distinguished AGs disagreed so sharply on the key issues. Ideally the Opinions would each have synthesised different national approaches and ways of looking at religion into a coherent EU approach. While neither Opinion managed to do that, the fact of their sharp disagreement itself gave useful advice to the Court, as it gave eloquent testimony to the lack of certainty in this area and the need for a pan-European court of law to tread carefully. That two experienced and longstanding members of the Court disagreed so profoundly shows perhaps that the Court was right to take the cautious approach of permitting different states to take different approaches in this developing area, though it ought perhaps to have been clearer about the fact that it was doing so. Given the increasing opportunistic use of secularist principles by those with exclusionary agendas to target religious minorities, the Court was also right not to be entirely permissive and to insist that any neutrality rules be applied in a way that does not target any individual faith. In an era of rapid change and uncertainty, that kind of gradualist, step by step approach to building a pan-European approach in this area is perhaps the most that can be expected.

---

[42] I Buruma, *Murder in Amsterdam: The Death of Theo Van Gogh and the Limits of Tolerance* (London, Penguin, 2006).

[43] *Eweida and Others* (n 1) and *Ebrahimian v France* (n 1).

[44] R McCrea, 'Rhetoric, Choices and the Constitution' in E Carolan (ed), *The Constitution of Ireland: Perspectives and Prospects* (Dublin, Bloomsbury Professional, 2013).

45

EU Competence to Conclude Trade Agreements: Opinion of Advocate General Sharpston in Opinion 2/15

PANOS KOUTRAKOS

I. INTRODUCTION

I T was the Court of Justice itself that laid the foundation for the law governing EU external relations in the early 1970s, in the seminal *ERTA* judgment.[1] The long and complex case law that has ensued notwithstanding,[2] significant questions about the Union's competence to conclude trade agreements have remained subject to legal controversy. These are about the scope of the EU's competence, the conditions under which this becomes exclusive, and the implications of the co-existence of the EU and the Member States on the international scene. Legal disputes about these issues keep arising despite the efforts of the drafters of the Treaty of Lisbon to codify and clarify the principles that govern the EU's external action. In fact, it is nothing short of staggering that the EU should have become an important international trade actor on the basis of internal rules and procedures, the precise scope and implications of which have been shrouded in ambiguity and clarified gradually following inter-institutional litigation and requests for an Opinion by the Court of Justice in accordance with Article 218(11) TFEU. It is in the light of this context that *Opinion 2/15* on the conclusion of the Free Trade Agreement between the European Union and Singapore (EUSFTA)[3] has shed light on a number of aspects of the EU's external competence, for which AG Sharpston offered her Opinion.

II. BACKGROUND, CONTEXT, AND FACTS

Negotiated for four and a half years, the EUSFTA (the Agreement) is a deep and comprehensive free trade agreement:[4] its content goes beyond the traditional tariff and non-tariff

---

[1] Case 22/70 *Commission v Council* ECLI:EU:C:1971:32 (*ERTA*).
[2] See further P Koutrakos, *EU International Relations Law*, 2nd edn (Oxford, Hart Publishing, 2015) chs 2–3.
[3] *Opinion 2/15* ECLI:EU:C:2017:376.
[4] Free trade Agreement between the European Union and the Republic of Singapore [2019] OJ L294/3.

barriers to trade in goods and services, and covers areas such as intellectual property rights, public procurement, competition, sustainable development and investment.[5]

The request for an Opinion under Article 218(11) TFEU was made by the Commission and was about the Union's competence to conclude the EUSFTA. In particular, the Court was asked to identify the provisions of the Agreement that fell within the Union's exclusive and shared competence, as well as those, if any, that fell within the exclusive competence of the Member States.

This request was made in a politically charged environment. Following the negotiation of the controversial and now doomed Transatlantic and Investment Partnership between the US and the EU (TTIP), the long and unpredictable process of the ratification of the Comprehensive Economic and Trade Agreement between the EU and Canada (CETA)[6] had raised the profile of trade agreements amongst the citizens of the Member States who became absorbed by an increasingly vociferous debate of a wide scope that included the impact of trade agreements on environmental and labour standards, and the regulatory autonomy of states. The latter controversy also highlighted the significance of domestic parliaments and their power to derail the ratification process and prevent the application of trade agreements negotiated by the EU.[7]

However, it was not only the political climate about trade agreements that made *Opinion 2/15* highly anticipated. The question that the Court was asked to address about the nature of the competence of the EU and the Member States was important for two main reasons. First, the Opinion was expected to shed light on the reforms that the Treaty of Lisbon introduced regarding external relations in general and, in particular, trade policy. Secondly, it would have implications for the form of trade agreements negotiated by the EU, given the emergence of domestic parliaments as powerful players in the process of the ratification of mixed agreements. In fact, so significant were these issues that it was the Full Court that rendered the Opinion, a composition that is rarely convened and only for the most important matters, while the governments of 25 Member States made submissions.

III. THE OPINION OF AG SHARPSTON

In the past, when the Court dealt with a request for an Opinion under Article 218(11) TFEU, the practice was that the AGs did not deliver a View or an Opinion. Instead, they were heard collectively, within the Court, with no published output. This changed in subsequent years following amendments to the Court's Rules of Procedure.[8]

The Opinion by AG Sharpston in *Opinion 2/15* is long, detailed, and of wide scope.[9] In fact, it reads as if it were set out to provide a systematic and comprehensive overall analysis of the legal issues raised by the EU competence to negotiate and conclude international agreements.

---

[5] For the policy shift towards such agreements, see BA Melo Araujo, *The EU Deep Trade Agenda: Law and Policy* (Oxford, OUP, 2016).

[6] Comprehensive Economic and Trade Agreement (CETA) between Canada, of the one part, and the European Union and its Member States, of the other part [2017] OJ L11/23.

[7] See G Van der Loo and RA Wessel, 'The non-ratification of mixed agreements: legal consequences and solutions' (2017) 54 *CMLRev* 735; R Quick and A Gerhäuser, 'The Ratification of CETA and other Trade Policy Challenges after Opinion 2/15' (2019) 22 *Zeitschrift für Europarechtliche Studien* 505.

[8] The first published 'View' of an AG was by AG Jääskinen, *Opinion 1/13* ECLI:EU:C:2014:2292.

[9] Opinion of AG Sharpston in Case 2/15 ECLI:EU:C:2016:992.

AG Sharpston made three main points. First, she argued that a significant part of the EUSFTA fell within the EU's exclusive competence. This was, on the one hand, as part of the Common Commercial Policy (CCP), such as trade in goods, trade and investment in renewable energy generation, trade in services and public procurement, foreign direct investment, the commercial aspects of intellectual property rights, competition, and trade and sustainable development in so far as its provisions relate primarily to commercial policy instruments. It was also, on the other hand, in the context of the conservation of marine biological resources as well as trade in rail and road transport services. Secondly, a considerable number of provisions fell within the EU shared competence: these would include trade in air, maritime and inland waterway transport services, indirect investment, public procurement provisions applicable or inherently linked to transport services, non-commercial aspects of intellectual property rights, labour and environmental standards. Thirdly, she also argued that Member States which had concluded bilateral investment agreements with Singapore retained exclusive competence to terminate them.

IV. ANALYSIS

While both AG Sharpston and the Court concluded that the EUSFTA did not fall within the EU's exclusive competence in its entirety, their approach differed considerably.

This author has analysed the Opinion of the Court elsewhere.[10] The following analysis of the Opinion of AG Sharpston will focus on three main issues where the Court departed from her Opinion. These are about the EU's exclusive competence to conclude the EUSFTA trade and investment provisions in the context of CCP, the EU's implied exclusive competence under Article 3(2) TFEU, and whether the Member States retained their power to terminate their bilateral investment agreements with Singapore.

In order to capture the difference of views between the Court and its AG, it is worth underlying at the outset the different vantage point from which they assessed the EUSFTA: the Court viewed the Agreement as, essentially, about trade,[11] whereas AG Sharpston stressed its multifarious objectives and pointed out that it was not 'homogeneous'.[12] These two positions, articulated early on in both documents, inform the different stance that the Court and AG Sharpston would take on the central issues that this chapter will explore.

A. Trade and Sustainable Development: A More Granular Analysis

The Court held that the trade and sustainable provisions laid down in Chapter 13 EUSFTA were about ensuring that trade between the two parties would be in compliance with the obligations that they had undertaken in relation to social protection of workers and environmental protection.[13] AG Sharpston had taken a more nuanced approach. While some provisions had

---

[10] P Koutrakos, 'The EU's Competence to Conclude Trade Agreements: The EU-Singapore Opinion' in F Amtenbrink, G Davies, D Kochenov and J Lindeboom (eds), *The Internal Market and the Future of European Integration: Essays in Honour of Laurence W. Gormley* (Cambridge, CUP, 2019) 651.

[11] The Court focuses on the establishment of a free trade area and the liberalisation and facilitation of trade and investment between the parties as the main subject-matter and objectives of the Agreement under Articles 1.1 and 1.2 (para 32).

[12] Paras 3 and 123 of the Opinion of AG Sharpston.

[13] ibid, para 152.

a direct and immediate link with trade regulation,[14] others were about setting standards '*in isolation* from their possible effects on trade'.[15]

These different conclusions may be explained on two grounds. The first is about legal reasoning. AG Sharpston carried out a granular analysis of Chapter 13 EUFSTA and engaged in a detailed interpretation of its specific provisions. The Court, instead, adopted a broader approach which appears somewhat untroubled by the need for detailed legal reasoning. For instance, the Court pointed out that a material breach of the sustainable development commitments could lead to a suspension of provisions about trade liberalisation. It made this point without referring to any specific EUSFTA provision,[16] and even though the dispute settlement procedure of the latter does not apply to Chapter 13.[17]

The second reason that may explain the different conclusion concerned context. The analysis in the Court's Opinion of the trade implications of the sustainable development provisions was preceded by an examination of the position of CCP within the broader set up of the EU's external action. Having referred to the common principles and objectives of the EU's external action set out in Article 21 TEU and their application to the CCP under Articles 21(3) TEU and 205 and 207(1) TFEU, the Court held that there is an 'obligation on the European Union to integrate those objectives and principles [set out in Article 21 TEU] into the conduct of its common commercial policy', of which 'the objective of sustainable development henceforth forms an integral part'.[18] This constitutional approach was significant: it gave specific meaning to the reorganisation of the primary rules on external action introduced at the Treaty of Lisbon by signalling that neither the provision of common principles and objectives in Article 21 TEU, nor the cross-references to them in other parts of primary law[19] would be merely rhetoric. Instead, they had specific legal implications which the Court itself was prepared to monitor.

On the other hand, whilst referring to Article 21 TEU, along with other primary law provisions about sustainable development in EU's policies, such as Article 3(5) TEU and Articles 9 and 11 TFEU, AG Sharpston argued that they 'cannot affect the scope of the common commercial policy' and that the compatibility of fundamental rights referred to in Article 13.3.3. EUSFTA with the EU's Charter is 'immaterial' as it 'cannot modify the scope of the European Union's competence'.[20]

The constitutional approach adopted by the Court may appear desirable in policy terms: it would make for a richer and more dynamic CCP which is therefore construed within the context of a multidimensional and evolving international economic policy that places increasing emphasis on sustainable development. It also appeared to strengthen the effect of sustainable development provisions in trade agreements. However, it highlights a degree of conceptual incoherence that emerged from the line of reasoning in the Opinion of the Court: as Cremona puts it, 'if the possibility of conditionality-based suspension is

---

[14] For instance Article 13.1.11 EUSFTA about trade and investment in environment-friendly goods and services.

[15] Para 491 of the Opinion of AG Sharpston (emphasis in the original).

[16] Para 161 of the Opinion of the Court, where reference is only made to Article 60(1) VCLT.

[17] Article 13.16(1) EUSFTA. For a criticism of this view, see G Marín Durán, 'Sustainable Development Chapters in EU Free Trade Agreements: Emerging Compliance Issues' (2020) 57 *CMLRev* 1031, 1046–48. She considers the proposition 'simply wrong' (at p 1046) and the Court's overall conclusion regarding sustainable development 'flawed' (at p 1048).

[18] Paras 143, 147 of the Opinion of the Court.

[19] Article 205 TFEU in relation to external action in general, and Article 207(1) TFEU in relation to CCP. See also Article 23(1) TEU in relation to CFSP.

[20] Para 496 of the Opinion of AG Sharpston.

taken seriously then the Court's contention that chapter 13 does not affect the scope of the obligations under the international agreements it refers to, and therefore does not impose new obligations on the parties, becomes harder to maintain'.[21]

There is also another implication from the difference of approach between the Court and its AG. The Opinion of the Court entailed considerable discretion in construing the EU's CCP: the price to pay for flexibility in defining the scope of a dynamic CCP is a degree of uncertainty as to the outer limits of the policy and greater reliance on the role of the Court. The latter approach, on the other hand, was more firmly embedded on the specific function of the provisions of the Agreement, and put greater pressure on treaty negotiators to be more explicit about the role of sustainable development.

B. Implied Exclusive Competence: A More Balanced Approach

In a similar vein to her approach to CCP, AG Sharpston's analysis of the Union's exclusive implied competence under Article 3(2) TFEU was granular, detailed, and rich in substantiating its conclusions. For instance, in dealing with EUSFTA provisions on maritime transport services, her Opinion engaged in a forensic examination of the relevant secondary EU measures,[22] and observed that, while there was a degree of overlap between their provisions and Chapter 8 EUFSTA, the area of liberalisation of maritime transport services was not already largely covered by common rules. Therefore, for her, the latter provisions did not fall within the EU's exclusive competence under the third limb of Article 3(2) TFEU.

The Court followed a different approach and reached the opposite conclusion. Its Opinion construed implied exclusivity in broad terms, and justified it on the basis of a line of reasoning that was characterised by analytical sparseness. For instance, in relation to commitments on transport services and public procurement on such services, it held that the Union's implied competence was exclusive because the Agreement established a set of rules which either differed from these set out in internal common rules,[23] or overlapped with them to a large extent.[24]

This approach is not novel: in earlier case law, the Court had already held that the provisions of an international agreement need not coincide fully with internal common rules in order to risk affecting the latter or altering their scope;[25] it had also held that a contradiction

---

[21] M Cremona, 'Shaping EU Trade Policy post-Lisbon: Opinion 2/15 of 16 May 2017' (2018) 14 *EuConst* 231, 245.

[22] Council Regulation 4055/86 applying the principle of freedom to provide services to maritime transport between Member States and between Member States and third countries [1986] OJ L378/1; Directive 2014/66/EU on the conditions of entry and residence of third-country nationals in the framework of an intra-corporate transfer [2014] OJ L157/1.

[23] This was the case in maritime transport and the impact of the Agreement on Council Regulation (EEC) 4055/86 applying the principle of freedom to provide services to maritime transport between Member States and between Member States and third countries [1986] OJ L378/1.

[24] This was the case in rail transport (covered by Directive 2012/34/EU establishing a single European railway area [2012] OJ L343/32); road transport (covered by Regulation (EC) 1071/2009 establishing common rules concerning the conditions to be complied with to pursue the occupation of road transport operator [2009] OJ L300/51; Regulation (EC) 1072/2009 on common rules for access to the international road haulage market [2009] OJ L300/72; Regulation (EC) 1073/2009 on common rules for access to the international market for coach and bus services [2009] OJ L300/88); and public procurement in transport services (covered by Directive 2014/24/EU on public procurement [2014] OJ L94/65. As for internal waterways transport, the commitments introduced by the Agreement were held to be of such narrow scope as to be irrelevant for the assessment of the overall competence of the Union in the area of transport.

[25] See *Opinion 1/03* ECLI:EU:C:2006:81, para 126; Case C-114/12 *Commission v Council* ECLI:EU:C:2014:2151, paras 69–70; *Opinion 1/13* ECLI:EU:C:2014:2303, paras 72–73; *Opinion 3/15* ECLI:EU:C:2016:657, paras 106–107.

between an international agreement and internal common rules is not necessary for exclusivity to be triggered, as long as the meaning, scope and effectiveness of the latter might be affected.[26]

What *Opinion 2/15* did, however, was to apply it with considerable force, a feature that is highlighted further by the analytical sparseness of the Court's line of reasoning. For instance, the references to the specific provisions of the Agreement and those of the internal secondary legislation were lacking in detail. This is noteworthy, given that, in *Opinion 1/03*, the Court had held that the assessment of the Union's implied external competence to conclude an agreement ought to rely upon a 'comprehensive and detailed analysis' of both its provisions and the internal common rules in the area.[27] Such analysis was not present in *Opinion 2/15*. While the Court took the Chapters of the Agreement with Singapore in turn, and examined them against EU secondary legislation, it did so in only broad terms. All in all, it becomes clear that the threshold to meet the *ERTA* test and its codification in Article 3(2) TFEU is by no means high, and neither is it subject to the detailed and extensive analysis of the kind we find in the Opinion of AG Sharpston.

C. The Power to Terminate Member States' Bilateral Investment Treaties: Acknowledging the Role of the Member States in International Treaty-making

Article 9(10) EUSFTA provided that, upon the entry into force of the Agreement, all bilateral investment treaties between Member States and Singapore would cease to have effect and would be replaced and superseded by EUSFTA.[28] In addressing the question whether that provision fell within the exclusive powers of the Member States, the Court and AG Sharpston reached different conclusions on the basis of fundamentally different approaches.

The latter focused on 'the fundamental rule of consent in international law-making',[29] and pointed out that the locus of the power to terminate an agreement concluded by a Member State with a third country remained with the Member State. In her view, this position was based on EU law, in particular the duty of sincere cooperation under Article 4(3) TEU, as well as Article 351 TFEU which applied specifically to treaties concluded by Member States prior to their accession to the EU. In her Opinion, she noted that, even in cases of incompatibility between such agreements and EU law, it is for the Member State in question to eliminate the incompatibility, even by terminating the agreements, 'irrespective of whether the European Union enjoys exclusive or shared competences over the area covered by those agreements'.[30]

However, what is striking about the Opinion of the AG is her emphasis on international law. She referred to Article 59 VCLT[31] and argues that there is 'no basis in international law

---

[26] Paras 143, 151–53 of Opinion 1/03; Paras 84–90 of *Opinion 1/13*; Case C-66/13 *Green Network* ECLI:EU:C:2014:2399, paras 48–49 and, even earlier, *Opinion 2/91* ECLI:EU:C:1993:106, paras 25–26; Case C-467/98 *Commission v Denmark* ECLI:EU:C:2002:625, para 82.

[27] Para 133 of *Opinion 1/03*.

[28] Such agreements had been concluded by Slovakia, Bulgaria, Slovenia, Latvia, Hungary, Czech Republic, Poland, Belgium-Luxembourg Economic Union, France, Germany, the Netherlands, as well as the UK.

[29] Para 396 of the Opinion of AG Sharpston.

[30] Para 387 of the Opinion of AG Sharpston.

[31] AG Sharpston to Article 59 VCLT dealing with the implied abrogation of a treaty between parties resulting from the conclusion by all of those parties of a later treaty and argues that it only applies if is accepted under international law that the EU has succeeded the individual Member states as regards their BITs referred to in Annex 9-D EUSFTA, a matter on which there is no practice that amounts to a rule of international law (paras 392–95 of the Opinion of AG Sharpston).

(as it currently stands) for concluding that the European Union may automatically succeed to an international agreement concluded by the Member States, to which it is not a party, and then terminate that agreement. Such a rule would constitute an exception to the fundamental rule of consent in international law-making' and 'would mean that, as a result of changes in EU law and (possibly) the European Union's exercise of its external competences, a Member State might cease to be a party to an international agreement, even though it was a State which had consented to be bound by that agreement and for which that agreement was in force'.[32]

This international law focus was entirely lacking in the Court's Opinion. Instead, the latter was confined to EU law in order to conclude that Article 9.10 EUSFTA (now Article 4.12 of the EU-Singapore Investment Protection Agreement) did not fall within the exclusive competence of the Member States. This was because the subject matter of that provision was about an area over which the EU was exclusively competent. As the Treaty of Lisbon conferred upon the EU such competence under Article 207 TFEU, from 1 December 2009, the EU had the power to insert a clause about the termination of bilateral agreements between Member States and a third country in an international agreement that it would conclude.

The Court justified this conclusion by reference to what is known as the doctrine of functional succession: it held that '[i]t has been undisputed ... that the European Union can succeed the Member states in their international commitments when the Member States have transferred to it, by one of its founding Treaties, their competences relating to those commitments and it exercises those competences'.[33] This conclusion was supported in the Opinion by reference to Joined Cases 21-24/72 *International Fruit* where the then European Economic Community (EEC) had been held to be bound by the General Agreement on Tariffs and Trade (GATT) 1947, given that all Member States had been bound by it, and that the latter had subsequently conferred on the EEC exclusive competence on trade.[34]

To argue that Member States should retain their right to terminate their investment treaties with Singapore even though all parties are in agreement that EUSFTA should replace those treaties may appear to have a whiff of formalism. However, the line of reasoning in the Court's *Opinion 2/15* raises a number of issues about the relationship between EU law and the power of Member States to terminate pre-existing agreements. First, it ignores the specific context within which the judgment in *International Fruit* was rendered, that is the binding effect of an agreement which all Member States had concluded and over which the nature of the EU's competence was not in dispute. In the case of EUSFTA, while the Court referred to succession by reference to foreign direct investment (which is covered by the EU's exclusive competence), it appeared to consider the distinction between exclusive and implied competence irrelevant in this context.[35]

Secondly, it does not consider the objective of functional succession in *International Fruit*, namely to ensure that the implementation of an agreement concluded by Member States would not be disrupted by the conferment of exclusive competence on the EU and that compliance with that agreement's obligations by the Member States would become fully a matter of EU law.

Thirdly, the Court's Opinion ignored the narrow construction of the doctrine of functional succession in its own case law.[36] Finally, the absence of an international law analysis

---

[32] Para 396 of the Opinion of AG Sharpston.

[33] Para 248 of the Opinion of the Court.

[34] Joined Cases 21-24/72 *International Fruit* ECLI:EU:C:1972:115, paras 10–18.

[35] Para 255 of the Opinion of the Court. See also Cremona (n 21) 253.

[36] See Case C-308/06 *Intertanko* ECLI:EU:C:2008:312, paras 47–52; Case C-301/08 *Bogiatzi* ECLI:EU:C:2009:649, paras 25–33; Case C-366/10 *Air Transport Association of America* ECLI:EU:C:2011:864; Case C-481/13 *Qurbani* ECLI:EU:C:2014:2101, para 24. For an analysis, see Koutrakos (n 2) 212–19.

notwithstanding, the Court's dismissal of the power of Member State to terminate their international agreements relies upon a somewhat one-dimensional reading of Article 351 TFEU. As the bilateral investment treaties (BITs) to which Article 9.10 EUSFTA (now Article 4.12 EU-Singapore Investment Protection Agreement) referred had been concluded with Singapore, and the latter had given its consent to their termination by concluding EUSFTA, the protection that Article 351 TFEU granted Member States was deemed unnecessary.[37] And yet, Article 351 TFEU has been interpreted consistently as requiring Member States to eliminate any incompatibilities between their agreements and EU law by taking all appropriate measures, including renegotiating with the other contracting parties.[38] The conceptual obscurity that characterises this part of the Court's Opinion disguised the specific context within which functional succession and Article 351 TFEU apply and ignored their underlying common function, which is how to ensure that the dynamic nature of the EU's external competence and the ensuing transfer of power from the Member States would not prevent the fulfilment of the international treaty obligations assumed by the latter.

The different conclusion reached by AG Sharpston and the Court on this matter did not have major practical implications in this specific context, given that they both agreed that not all EUSFTA provisions fell within the EU's exclusive competence. Their different approach, however, has implications for the role of the Member States as subjects of international law in the context of the EU's increasingly broad exclusive competence. The Opinion of the AG put emphasis on international law and acknowledged the continuing status of Member States, whereas the Court's Opinion relied on a bold reading of EU law in order to assert the Union's exclusive competence. The latter may end up depriving the Member States of their power to determine how to manage their international law obligations in a broader set of circumstances than those in *Opinion 2/15*. The former, on the other hand, was conceptually coherent in its interpretation of the relevant legal rules without dismissing practical arrangements that would facilitate EU action by enabling Member States to exercise their power to terminate their treaties by relying on the EU as the case may be.[39]

D. Effect on Future Case Law

Quite some time ago, this author pointed out the considerable complexity that underpins the exercise of the Union's competence to conclude international agreements and the choice of the appropriate legal basis, and called for greater clarity and pragmatism in the case law and institutional practice.[40] More recently, the request for *Opinion 2/15* was viewed as 'a unique yet challenging opportunity for the Court to refine its analytical standards and approaches with a view to generating legal certainty'.[41]

---

[37] Para 254 of the Opinion of the Court.
[38] See, for instance, Case C-62/98 *Commission v Portugal* ECLI:EU:C:2000:358, para 25; Case C-84/98 *Commission v Portugal* ECLI:EU:C:2000:359, para 35; Case C-249/06 *Commission v Sweden* ECLI:EU:C:2009:119, para 44. For an analysis of the relevant issues, see Koutrakos (n 36) 321–50.
[39] See Cremona (n 21) 254.
[40] P Koutrakos, 'Legal Basis and Delimitation of Competence in EU External Relations' in M Cremona and B De Witte (eds), *EU Foreign Relations Law: Constitutional Fundamentals* (Oxford, Hart Publishing, 2008) 171.
[41] D Kleimann, 'Reading Opinion 2/15: Standards of Analysis, the Court's Discretion, and the Legal View of the Advocate General', EUI Working Paper RWCAS 2017/23 at 35.

The Court's Opinion built on and developed the threads that had emerged in prior case law. The Opinion of AG Sharpston, and its contrast to the Court's subsequent stance, serves to highlight further the sharpness with which these threads are now apparent. In substantive terms, the strengthening of the Union's exclusive competence and its prevailing position in treaty-making appears inexorable. In terms of methodological approach, the centrality of contextual interpretation was further underlined by the distinctly constitutional approach that the Court has taken to the EU's principles and values as laid down in Article 21(3) TEU. As for judicial reasoning, the Court's *Opinion 2/15* has not rendered the quest for clarity any less relevant or urgent.

46

Horizontal Direct Effect of Directives Reconsidered: Opinion of Advocate General Sharpston in Farrell II

ELENI FRANTZIOU

I. INTRODUCTION

*U*bi jus, ibi remedium: where there is a right, there is a remedy.[1] This was, in summary, the driving principle in AG Sharpston's seminal Opinion in *Farrell II*,[2] which grappled with the vexed question of the horizontal direct effect of directives and, to be more precise, with the implications of its absence. The Opinion was largely followed by the Court, thus shedding much-needed light upon the question of which types of private actors can be considered 'public' for the purposes of the direct effect of EU law – a consideration which was crucial due to the *Marshall I* rule that directives lack horizontal direct effect, and can thus only be invoked in legal disputes with public actors.[3] Both the Opinion and the judgment confirmed that emanations of the state can be *functional*, rather than requiring state involvement or control.

This chapter approaches the Opinion of AG Sharpston and the judgment in *Farrell* as positive developments in the field of horizontal effect, both from the perspective of individuals seeking to draw a remedy for a violation of their rights, and as a matter of legal certainty and sound constitutional principle, more generally. Still, it will be argued that the Opinion of AG Sharpston went beyond the judgment in two important respects, which would have further improved the jurisprudence in this field. First, the AG was more eager than the Court to let go of the precise parameters of the *Foster* formula and its need for statutorily defined 'special powers' for a body to be considered an emanation of the state.[4] Secondly, in a noteworthy postscript at the end of her Opinion, she had anticipated and (in this author's view, correctly) criticised the Court's silence on the continuing problems posed by an obstinate reaffirmation of the non-horizontality of directives.

---

[1] Opinion of AG Sharpston in Case C-413/15 *Farrell* ECLI:EU:C:2017:492, para 32.
[2] The *Farrell (1)* case only concerned the interpretation of the Directive. See Case C-356/05 *Farrell* ECLI:EU:C:2007:229.
[3] Case 152/84 *Marshall* ECLI:EU:C:1986:84. See ch 20.
[4] Case C-188/89 *Foster* ECLI:EU:C:1990:313, para 20.

After laying down the factual and legal background of the case (Section II), this chapter analyses the main points of the Opinion of AG Sharpston in *Farrell II* (Section III). It then goes on to highlight the differences between the Opinion and the Court's judgment, as well as the constitutional and remedial implications of the case, both as the ruling now stands and in terms of the potential that the Opinion had engendered (Section IV).

II. BACKGROUND, CONTEXT, AND FACTS

In 1996, Ms Farrell was struck by bad luck, bad driving, and bad implementation of a Directive. As a passenger in a private vehicle, she suffered serious injuries in a car crash for which the driver of the vehicle, Mr Whitty, was responsible. As Mr Whitty was uninsured, Ms Farrell sought compensation for her injuries from the Motor Insurers' Bureau of Ireland (MIBI), which was the body to which Ireland had contracted out compulsory motor insurance. This seemingly simple claim led to a 20-year-long legal dispute about the nature and scope of Directive 90/232/EEC on insurance against civil liability in respect of the use of motor vehicles.[5]

In the first instance, the MIBI took the view that Ms Farrell was not entitled to compensation, as she had been seated in the back of a van, which was not fit for carrying passengers. In implementing the abovementioned Directive, Ireland had excluded liability for injuries sustained whilst travelling in parts of vehicles not intended to carry passengers. In *Farrell I*, therefore, the national court sought clarification on whether the Directive covered situations such as that of Ms Farrell. In that case, the Court found that Article 1 of the Directive did extend to her situation, so that the exclusion set out in Irish legislation amounted to an incorrect implementation of the Directive, and was thus a violation of EU law. This led to the deeper constitutional issue that became the subject of *Farrell II*.

Farrell II was about determining who was ultimately responsible for paying Ms Farrell's compensation under EU law: would it be the MIBI, under the direct effect principle, or the Irish Minister for the Environment, under the state liability principle? As is widely known, in paragraph 20 of its judgment in *Foster*, the Court had famously laid down its definition of emanations of the state, against whom direct effect was available despite their prima facie private law designation:

> a body, whatever its legal form, which has been made responsible, pursuant to a measure adopted by the State, for providing a public service under the control of the State and has for that purpose special powers beyond those which result from the normal rules applicable in relations between individuals is included in any event among the bodies against which the provisions of a directive capable of having direct effect may be relied upon.[6]

The MIBI and the Irish Minister for the Environment disagreed on the correct interpretation of the *Foster* test. The MIBI argued that, even though it had been given responsibility for overseeing insurance pay-outs, it was not caught by the *Foster* test, as it did not enjoy special powers beyond those applicable to ordinary disputes between individuals and was not directly controlled or financed by the state. In other words, the MIBI argued that it was a private entity

---

[5] Third Council Directive 90/232/EEC of 14 May 1990 on the approximation of the laws of the Member States relating to insurance against civil liability in respect of the use of motor vehicles [1990] OJ L129/33.

[6] Para 20 of the Judgment in *Foster*.

against which the provisions of a directive could not be directly invoked. By contrast, the Irish Minister for the Environment argued that the Court's test on emanations of the state in *Foster* comprised a body like the MIBI, simply because of the fact that the state had statutorily given it exclusive responsibility over motor insurance.

It is important to note that, by the time that the Opinion and judgment in *Farrell II* were decided in 2017, the parties had agreed an acceptable compensation amount with Ms Farrell, so that the substantive point about her access to a remedy had become moot. Despite this, the case retained its constitutional significance, as lack of clarity within the *Foster* test continued to elicit concerns over legal certainty and had stirred an important academic debate about whether state control was an essential or alternative criterion for a body to be designated as an emanation of the state.[7] Against this background, the Supreme Court of Ireland submitted three questions about the nature of the *Foster* test to the Court:

(1) Is the test in [*Foster*] as set out at paragraph 20 on the question of what is an emanation of a Member State to be read on the basis that the elements of the test are to be applied

  (a) conjunctively, or
  (b) disjunctively?

(2) To the extent that separate matters referred to in [*Foster*] may, alternatively, be considered to be factors which should properly be taken into account in reaching an overall assessment, is there a fundamental principle underlying the separate factors identified in that decision which a court should apply in reasoning an assessment as to whether a specified body is an emanation of the State?

(3) Is it sufficient that a broad measure of responsibility has been transferred to a body by a Member State for the ostensible purpose of meeting obligations under European law for that body to be an emanation of the Member State or is it necessary, in addition, that such a body additionally have (a) special powers or (b) operate under direct control or supervision of the Member State?

III. THE OPINION OF AG SHARPSTON

The Opinion of AG Sharpston in *Farrell II* was detailed and methodical. In response to the first of the national court's questions, she emphasised both the text of the *Foster* judgment and the broader background of the case.[8] In the context of the dispute between Ms Foster and British Gas, she argued, the Court did not need to proceed further than the authorities it mentioned in paragraph 19 of that judgment, such as *Becker* and *Fratelli Costanzo*,[9] as British Gas would have been covered by that case law anyway, due to the state-controlled character of the company at the time. Indeed, the Court chose in paragraph 20 of the judgment to use the words 'is included *in any event* among the bodies', which confirmed that it was not attempting to formulate a general test, but had specifically British Gas in mind, ie, a body which happened to display both responsibility for a public service and special powers uncharacteristic of the normal relations between individuals. However, AG Sharpston explained that, in a situation

---

[7] K Romanivna Bakhtina, '*Farrell II* and the Concept of an "Emanation of the State"' (2018) 18 *International and Comparative Law Review* 241, 245.

[8] Para 35 of the Opinion, citing para 18 of the Judgment in *Foster*.

[9] Case 8/81 *Becker* ECLI:EU:C:1982:7; Case C-221/88 *Busseni* ECLI:EU:C:1990:84; Case 103/88 *Costanzo* ECLI:EU:C:1989:256; cited in para 19 of Judgment in *Foster*.

that did not meet both of these criteria, paragraph 20 should be read in the light of paragraph 18 of the judgment, which was formulated disjunctively. She stated that:

> the Court has held in a series of cases that unconditional and sufficiently precise provisions of a directive could be relied on against organisations or bodies which were subject to the authority or control of the State *or* had special powers beyond those which result from the normal rules applicable to relations between individuals.

In light of this, the criteria should be seen as alternative, not as cumulative.[10]

AG Sharpston proceeded to offer extensive clarification to the national court in respect of its second question, regarding the underlying rationale and considerations that needed to be taken into account in assessing whether an actor amounted to an emanation of the state. After analysing the different types of bodies that have been considered emanations of the state after *Foster*, she concluded that the *Foster* criteria are '(i) whether the State has entrusted the body in question with the task of performing a public mission which the State itself might otherwise decide directly to perform; and (ii) whether the State has equipped that body with some form of additional powers to enable it to fulfil its mission effectively (this is merely a different way of saying, '"special powers beyond those that result from the normal rules applicable to relations between individuals")'.[11] The AG then proposed that the Court provide the following guidance to the national court:

(1)   The legal form of the body in question is irrelevant;

(2)   It is not necessary that the State should be in a position to exercise day-to-day control or direction of that body's operations;

(3)   If the State owns or controls the body in question, that body should be considered to be an emanation of the State, without it being necessary to consider whether other criteria are fulfilled;

(4)   Any municipal, regional or local authorities or equivalent body is automatically to be regarded as an emanation of the State;

(5)   The body in question need not be funded by the State;

(6)   If the State has both entrusted the body in question with the task of performing a public service which the State itself might otherwise need directly to perform; and has equipped that body with some form of additional powers to enable it to fulfil its mission effectively, the body in question is in any event to be regarded as an emanation of the State.[12]

In short, the AG's guidance rested upon the overarching fundamental principle that the state and its emanations must be prevented from benefitting from their own failure to comply with EU law.

In response to the third question, AG Sharpston felt that, 20 years after *Foster*, it was essential to ensure that the idea of 'special powers' acquired an autonomous, EU-wide meaning.[13] Having noted that EU case law after *Foster*, such as *Johnston* and *Portgás*, had associated special powers with the contracting out of state responsibility, but had not depended on that very terminology,[14] she suggested that EU law should recognise that emanations of the state do not necessarily require statutory 'special powers' (which are characteristic mainly of essential utilities). Rather, it is sufficient that such special powers be seen in the fact that the state has transferred 'a broad measure of responsibility to a body for the ostensible purpose of meeting

---

[10] Para 52 of the Opinion.

[11] ibid, para 119.

[12] ibid, para 120.

[13] ibid, para 135.

[14] ibid, para 137. See further Case 222/84 *Johnston* ECLI:EU:C:1986:206, para 56; Case C-425/12 *Portgás* ECLI:EU:C:2013:829, paras 30 and 31.

obligations under EU law'.[15] Despite assuming a broad construction of emanations of the state, though, AG Sharpston clarified that there were important limitations in that concept.[16] More specifically, acknowledging the need for legal certainty (not just for the claimant seeking to draw a remedy, but also for the body on which the obligation to observe a directive is thereby imposed), she noted that the body's 'public mission must be clearly defined as such by the relevant legislative or regulatory framework'.[17]

Last but not least, in a remarkable Postscript to her Opinion, AG Sharpston highlighted that her answers to the questions posed by the referring court were based on the assumption that the Court would not reopen the question of whether precise and unconditional provisions of directives ultimately should enjoy vertical as well as horizontal direct effect, thus truly resulting in a remedy against all actors after the time-limit for their implementation had expired. However, the AG (rightly, in this author's view) felt that it was ultimately this question that the Court should answer. As she put it:

> to the extent that the legal form of the defendant has been irrelevant – and that, since *Foster* itself – to the question whether that defendant is an emanation of the State, the Court has already accepted that a body governed by private law may be bound to give effect to directly effective rights contained in a directive at the suit of another private individual. In so doing, the Court has in reality itself already countenanced a limited form of horizontal direct effect.[18]

Lamenting the uncertainty and complexity that this situation had created, AG Sharpston thus joined 'earlier AGs in inviting the Court to revisit and review critically the justifications advanced in *Faccini Dori* for rejecting horizontal direct effect'.[19]

IV. ANALYSIS

The Court followed the crux of the Opinion of AG Sharpston. It found that the criteria in *Foster* are alternative, rather than cumulative, fully endorsing her reasoning on this point.[20] The Court also largely followed the AG's analysis – albeit in outline – regarding the main considerations that should be taken into account by national courts in assessing emanations of the state: the driving principle was that of preventing the state from benefitting from its own failure to observe EU law.[21] As the AG had predicted in her postscript, however, the Court was not prepared to reconsider the case law on the horizontal direct effect of directives, which it reaffirmed in its entirety.[22] Crucially, the Court was also not prepared to go as far as the AG in respect of the functional character of an emanation. In contrast with the response AG Sharpston had given to the third question, the Court found that it was essential that a body be given 'special powers' by statute in order to perform a task or service ceded to it by the state in the public interest.[23] Thus, even though the Court went on to define special powers broadly, eg, as including in that concept the MIBI's 'power to require all insurers to become members of

---

[15] Para 138 of the Opinion.
[16] ibid, paras 140–46.
[17] ibid, para 146.
[18] ibid, para 149.
[19] ibid, para 150. In this respect, AG Sharpston specifically endorsed the influential Opinion of AG Jacobs: Case C-316/93 *Vaneetveld* ECLI:EU:C:1994:32, paras 30–31.
[20] Paras 26–29 of the Judgment.
[21] ibid, para 32.
[22] ibid, para 31.
[23] ibid, paras 34–35.

it and to contribute funds for the performance of the task conferred on it by the Irish State',[24] the judgment still held on to the formal limitation of a statutory mandate. It thus came short of including other situations in which a public mission is being performed by an otherwise private body upon state instruction. Thus, while both the judgment and the Opinion offered a constitutionally and remedially sound compromise, the former arguably did not succeed in providing the level of coherence or certainty that the broader view, espoused by the AG, had entailed. Three more specific analytical points can be made in this respect, concerning the constitutional and remedial significance of *Farrell II*, as well as its fit in the overall framework of the direct horizontal effect of EU law. These are considered in turn, before briefly assessing the judgment's impact on future case law.

A. *Farrell II* as a Recognition of Private Expressions of Public Power

Farrell II amounts, in this author's view, to a constitutionally desirable clarification of *Foster*: it is a feature of the rule of law in any democratic society that infringements of the legal rights of private persons by public authorities are capable of effective redress. Of course, the conceptual viability of the distinction between the obligations of public and private actors is, in itself, a subject of intense debate, both in the EU and in other legal orders.[25] In outline, that basic distinction – marked in legal terms by the divide between public and private law – is theoretically justified by the fact that, because of its special powers as a policy-maker and law enforcer, the state owes its citizens duties both to observe the law and to apply it through fair and transparent procedures. These duties distinguish the state and its emanations from private actors who, albeit that they must comply with the law, are otherwise entitled to interact with others based on their rational self-interest.

Yet, in viewing public actors as duty-bearers and (all) private persons as right-holders, this paradigm is too reductionist as a descriptive account of the exercise of public power in modern states.[26] The extensive privatisation of essential services, in particular, renders it impossible to cabin off a 'pure' vision of the relations between individuals and the state as singular and distinct to those between – at least some – formally private entities.[27] In this sense, to extend duties akin to those of public actors to private parties that *function* as and in place of the state, as the Court did in *Foster* first, and unequivocally confirmed in *Farrell II*, is a pragmatic legal development that accommodates the need for state accountability in cases where the exercise of public tasks is simply not fulfilled by the state. By conceptualising the state functionally, rather than formalistically, *Farrell II* stands with an evolving theory of public law that pushes beyond traditional state boundaries.

But are 'special powers' always essential for finding oneself in the domain of public law, as opposed to the sphere of the 'normal rules applicable in relations between individuals', as the Court put it in *Foster*? From the perspective of constitutional coherence and future legal certainty, this author is of the view that AG Sharpston's response to that question (ie, that, as

---

[24] Para 40 of the Judgment.

[25] See further MA Wilkinson and MW Dowdle (eds), *Questioning the Foundations of Public Law* (Oxford, Hart Publishing, 2018); T Kahana and A Scolnicov (eds), *Boundaries of State, Boundaries of Rights* (Cambridge, CUP, 2016); G Teubner, *Constitutional Fragments: Societal Constitutionalism and Globalization* (Oxford, OUP, 2012).

[26] W Streeck, 'Citizens as Customers: Considerations on the New Politics of Consumption' (2012) 76 *New Left Rev* 27, 42ff.

[27] P Craig, 'Theory, "Pure Theory" and Values in Public Law' [2005] *Public Law* 440, 445–47.

long as state responsibility has been ceded, the granting of special powers is not essential) was preferable to the Court's approach (ie that special powers must be granted by statute). If, as both the Court and the AG reasoned, the driving consideration in cases concerning emana-tions of the state is to ensure Member State accountability in areas where an EU law obligation has been contracted out, then it appears to be problematic to insist – as the judgment did – upon 'special powers', rather than upon the performance of a public service, more broadly. In this sense, the Court's approach takes with one hand what it gives with the other, as it entails a continued questioning of the concept of 'special powers', rather than maintaining the same, functional reasoning that drove its approach towards the preceding questions.

B. The Remedial Significance of *Farrell II* for Claimants: Mitigating the Ineffectiveness of State Liability by Strengthening the Potential for Direct Effect

Beyond the questions of constitutional principle highlighted above, it is worth noting that the *Farrell II* case was especially desirable from a practical perspective within the specific context of EU law. It is impossible to assess the impact of *Farrell* by sectionally looking at the concept of direct effect, as that would forego its crucial remedial comparator: the fallback claim of state liability in damages, which would have been the only alternative available to the claimant if the MIBI had not been considered a public law entity. While, as noted earlier, Ms Farrell's luck improved as the dispute progressed, and she ultimately received compensa-tion by agreement between the parties, her situation could have been more complex if she had been forced to rely on state liability. Due to the strictness of the conditions of state liability, the latter can leave the individual without a sufficient remedy and, even, without a remedy at all in situations of non-quantifiable damage or where the link between the breach of EU law and the damage is unclear.[28] While it is likely that Ms Farrell's case could ulti-mately still be remedied through state liability in damages,[29] the difficulty of meeting the state liability conditions should not be overlooked, especially for claimants in factually more uncertain cases.

Indeed, as AG Jacobs previously noted in *Vaneetveld*, state liability in damages involves a procedurally complex process, which is simply not 'an adequate substitute for the direct enforcement of the directive'.[30] As he noted, in practice, state liability often requires 'the plain-tiff to bring two separate sets of legal proceedings, either simultaneously or successively, one against the private defendant and the other against the public authorities, which would hardly be compatible with the requirement of an effective remedy'.[31] State liability in damages is thus neither a fail-safe guarantee of state accountability, nor a clear enough prospect for an appli-cant in cases of non-pecuniary loss. The question of which actors form part of the state may thus be an important constitutional point for all legal orders, but it is essential to note that, in the specific context of the EU, it also has important practical implications for the availability and effectiveness of individual remedies.

---

[28] See eg Case C-176/12 *Association de médiation sociale* ECLI:EU:C:2014:2, para 50.
[29] Case C-122/17 *Smith* ECLI:EU:C:2018:631.
[30] Para 30 of Opinion in *Vaneetveld*.
[31] ibid.

Taking this point a step further, one could query whether the relationship between direct effect and state liability that the emanations of the state case law has sketched is constitutionally sound. Whereas a private actor upon whom an obligation has been imposed by EU law can normally reclaim the damage they have incurred as compensation from the state in cases where the damage they have sustained is attributable to the poor implementation of EU law in Member State legislation,[32] actors caught by the *Foster/Farrell II* test cannot do so. Later case law, such as *Smith*, demonstrates that this distinction can be largely artificial.

Smith concerned circumstances identical to *Farrell II*, but vis-à-vis an insurer that had not been given special powers by statute as the MIBI (yet practically fulfilled the same role). The Court held that the insurer, having in the meantime paid compensation, could recover that compensation from the state through the principle of state liability in damages. Thus, *Farrell II* made sense for those seeking a remedy for violations of a directive against entities with special powers, and it was clear in its attribution of responsibilities to those entities. However, at least in situations where – as was the case in *Farrell II* itself – it was the legislation that ultimately created the violation, and not its application by the relevant body, the concept of emanations of the state could be seen as contributing to two problems: first, it could leave the state *qua* legislator unaccountable for poor implementation of EU law, because it allows the emanation to be held responsible *in its place*. Secondly, it could result in significant remedial differences between factually similar claims, solely because of existence of 'special powers' (or lack thereof).

C. AG Sharpston's Postscript

It would, of course, be an oxymoron if an 'emanation of the state' were successful in a damages claim against the state in the same way as a private actor. The above analysis nevertheless highlights that coherence is lacking across the Court's horizontal effect jurisprudence, in that practically similar claims can still be treated very differently in EU law, due to the operation of the *Marshall I/Faccini Dori* rule. The more difficult and problematic aspects of *Farrell II*, therefore, arise from AG Sharpston's postscript, which put a further question mark over the continued salience of the non-horizontality of directives.

While *Farrell II* stands on its own terms as an endorsement of a functional definition of public power and, in its specific EU law context, struck the right balance between the remedial need for direct effect and the expectation of certainty and clarity by the parties, it still leaves much to be desired in respect of its fit within the broader jurisprudence on horizontal direct effect. Does *Farrell II* make sense as part of a principled – rather than casuistic – approach towards the obligations of private or regulatory entities more generally, based on a convincing overall understanding within EU constitutional law of the relations between individuals and the state, on the one hand, and of individuals *inter se*, on the other? Is it meaningful to continue to distinguish, eg, emanations of the state as defined in *Farrell II*, from bodies that fulfil a function of a public nature that was never under state control? Such issues, as AG Sharpston elegantly observed through her postscript, remain open for the Court to approach differently, and more holistically, in future case law on the horizontality principle itself.

---

[32] Case C-122/17 *Smith* ECLI:EU:C:2018:631; Opinion of AG Bot in Case C-122/17 ECLI:EU:C:2018:223. See further on this point Opinion of AG Bobek in Case C-193/17 *Cresco Investigation* ECLI:EU:C:2018:614, para 196.

D. Effect on Future Case Law

Despite its remarkable bearing on the judgment, the Opinion of AG Sharpston in *Farrell II* has not been extensively cited.[33] Nonetheless, the judgment itself has been mentioned in several Opinions and six judgments so far.[34] This line of case law has followed *Farrell II* regarding the concept of 'special powers',[35] by taking a reasonably broad approach towards what these powers might be (albeit still always requiring their existence). It is perhaps worth noting that, in *Balgarska Narodna Banka*, the Court referred to 'exorbitant powers', rather than 'special powers' in citing the *Farrell II* test,[36] but it is unclear for the time being whether this formulation should be read as a narrowing down of the 'special powers' requirement. Overall, then, *Farrell II* can be credited with improving the EU jurisprudence on horizontal direct effect in recent years. Its progeny has generally mitigated the effect of the non-horizontality of directives through the concept of emanations of the state, thus complementing other post-Lisbon case law that mitigates the effect of non-horizontality in specific fields (mainly the protection of human rights), as shown in cases such as *Egenberger*,[37] *Bauer*,[38] *IR*,[39] *Cresco*,[40] *Max-Planck*,[41] and *CCOO*.[42] The jury is still out on whether, even when combined, this case law succeeds in undoing the need for a broader revision of the *Marshall I/Faccini Dori* principle.

E. Author's Postscript

I am normally one for separating public from private. In a book such as this one, though, I hope that I will be forgiven for sharing a personal anecdote by way of a postscript of my own, after having spent a significant part of this chapter analysing AG Sharpston's far more remarkable one in *Farrell II*. I had the good luck of spending two weeks on 'detachment' to AG Sharpston's chambers during a longer 'stage' at Judge Schiemann's chambers more than 10 years ago. AG Sharpston's commitment to her work at the Court, as well as her innate and radiating kindness, have stayed with me throughout this time. In particular, I recall very vividly the warmth with which AG Sharpston looked after me when I was taken unexpectedly ill during a reception she was hosting. I was sorry to see that the sensitivity that characterised every aspect of AG Sharpston's presence at the Court could not be embedded in the treatment of her departure.

---

[33] See Opinion of AG Tanchev in Case C-414/16 *Egenberger* ECLI:EU:C:2017:851; Opinion of AG Sharpston in Case C-681/18 *JH* ECLI:EU:C:2020:300, Opinion of AG Wahl in Case C-706/17 *Achema* ECLI:EU:C:2019:38.

[34] Case C-688/15 *Anisimoviene* ECLI:EU:C:2018:209; Case C-17/17 *Hampshire* ECLI:EU:C:2018:674; Case C-122/17 *Smith* ECLI:EU:C:2018:631; Case C-168/18 *Pensions-Sicherungs-Verein* ECLI:EU:C:2019:1128; Case C-501/18 *Balgarska Narodna Banka* ECLI:EU:C:2021:249; and Case C-425/19 P *Commission v Italy* ECLI:EU:C:2021:154.

[35] NB: *Commission v Italy*, ibid, concerned a different issue, namely whether the *Farrell* test could be applied in assessing the existence of state aid (the Court found that it could not).

[36] Para 71 of the Judgment in *Balgarska Narodna Banka*.

[37] Case C-414/16 *Egenberger* ECLI:EU:C:2018:257.

[38] Joined Cases C-569/16 and C-570/16 *Bauer* ECLI:EU:C:2018:871.

[39] Case C-68/17 *IR* ECLI:EU:C:2018:696.

[40] Case C-193/17 *Cresco Investigation* ECLI:EU:C:2019:43.

[41] Case C-684/16 *Max-Planck* ECLI:EU:C:2018:874.

[42] Case C-55/18 *CCOO* ECLI:EU:C:2019:402.

47

The Rule of Law, Sincere Cooperation between Member States, and Solidarity: Opinion of Advocate General Sharpston in Temporary Relocation

MICHAEL-JAMES CLIFTON

I. INTRODUCTION

In her Opinion in *Temporary Relocation*,[1] AG Sharpston addressed the obligations borne by Member States in relocating some of the tremendous number of people seeking international protection within the European Union (EU) in 2015 as a result of the migration crisis resulting from, inter alia, the civil war in Syria. The relocation of these people by way of Decisions 2015/1523[2] and 2015/1601[3] (together 'the Relocation Decisions') was intended to alleviate the pressure on Italy and Greece, both of whose long coastlines were on the major routes of those making perilous voyages across the Mediterranean.

Temporary Relocation followed on from *Slovak Republic and Hungary v Council*, in which those two Member States had unsuccessfully challenged the validity of Decision 2015/1601.[4] In *Temporary Relocation*, AG Sharpston considered the obligations upon the Czech Republic, Hungary, and Poland to stand together in mutual support with other Member States in accordance with the Relocation Decisions in response to the sudden, tremendous influx of people seeking international protection, and the relationship between Articles 72 and 78 TFEU. AG Sharpston concluded that a Member State cannot disregard its EU law obligations based on its view of its national security or public order concerns. In the Opinion, which was delivered on a day that the UK had been due to withdraw from the EU, AG Sharpston was at pains to emphasise in her extraordinary and reflective concluding remarks, the necessity of the rule of law within the EU, the duty of sincere cooperation, and solidarity between Member States.

---

[1] Opinion of AG Sharpston in Case C-715/17 *Commission v Poland*, Case C-718/17 *Commission v Hungary*, and Case C-719/17 *Commission v Czech Republic* ECLI:EU:C:2019:917.

[2] Council Decision (EU) 2015/1523 of 14 September 2015 establishing provisional measures in the area of international protection for the benefit of Italy and of Greece [2015] OJ L239/146.

[3] Council Decision (EU) 2015/1601 of 22 September 2015 establishing provisional measures in the area of international protection for the benefit of Italy and Greece [2015] OJ L248/80.

[4] Joined Cases C-643/15 and C-647/15 *Slovakia and Hungary v Council* ECLI:EU:C:2017:631.

II. BACKGROUND, CONTEXT, AND FACTS

The background to *Temporary Relocation* is formed of many parts, some of which remain *loci* of tensions as to the nature of the EU and its future. These include the 'rule of law crisis' and the 'migrant crisis', each of which concerns a number of Member States, and, at one remove, the tensions pre- and post-Brexit. *Temporary Relocation* is a much more than a snapshot of those tensions. The Opinion sets out the obligations and responsibilities incumbent upon Member States in the immediate past: each must stand up, and stand together with, all other Member States. Although the full extent of these divisions exceeds the scope of this chapter, it is necessary to briefly sketch out these underlying geopolitical and societal tensions.

In 2015, the EU adopted emergency relocation measures in response to the extraordinary number of people seeking international protection in Europe, with 3,238 people recorded as perishing in the Mediterranean in 2015 alone.[5] As De Witte and Tsourdi put it, these measures 'highlighted the limitations inherent in the legal design and implementation modes of the EU asylum policy, and most notably a structural lack of solidarity'.[6] The application of the 'irregular crossing' criterion in the Dublin III Regulation led to the asylum systems of Greece and Italy being overwhelmed,[7] causing secondary migration movements towards northern Europe, which, in turn, prompted temporary border controls within the Schengen Area.[8] Emergency relocation measures were adopted and complemented by the 'hotspot' approach to migration management, which together sought to prevent the collapse of the EU's Common European Asylum System.[9]

On 20 July 2015, 27 Member States (excluding Hungary) and the EFTA States of Iceland, Liechtenstein, Norway, and Switzerland (described in this context as 'the Dublin States'), agreed to resettle 22,504 displaced persons who were in clear need of international protection.[10] The resettlement places were distributed between these States according to the commitments set out in the Resolution's Annex.[11] The Council subsequently adopted the two Relocation Decisions. Council Decision 2015/1523,[12] adopted by consensus, provided for a system

---

[5] Missing Migrants, *Tracking Deaths along Migration Routes*, available here: https://missingmigrants.iom.int/region/mediterranean.

[6] B De Witte and L Tsourdi, 'Confrontation on relocation – The Court of Justice endorses the emergency scheme for compulsory relocation of asylum seekers within the European Union: *Slovak Republic and Hungary v. Council*' (2018) 55 *CMLRev* 1457–94, at 1457.

[7] Article 13(1) of Regulation (EU) No 604/2013 of the European Parliament and of the Council of 26 June 2013 establishing the criteria and mechanisms for determining the Member State responsible for examining an application for international protection lodged in one of the Member States by a third-country national or a stateless person [2013] OJ L180/31.

[8] K Lenaerts, 'The Court of Justice of the European Union and the Refugee Crisis' in K Lenaerts, J-C Bonichot, H Kanninen, C Naômé and P Pohjankoski (eds), *An Ever-Changing Union? Perspectives on the Future of EU Law in Honour of Allan Rosas* (Oxford, Hart Publishing, 2019) 3.

[9] 'A "hotspot" is an area at the external border that is confronted with disproportionate migratory pressure'. See European Commission, 'Annex II to the Communication on managing the refugees crisis: Immediate operational, budgetary and legal measures under the European agenda on migration', COM (2015) 490 final, 2.

[10] Para 39 and footnote of the Opinion. See European Commission, 'Explanatory Memorandum to the Commission's proposal for a Council Decision amending Council Decision (EU) 2015/1601 of 22 September 2015 establishing provisional measures in the area of international protection for the benefit of Italy and Greece' COM (2016) 171 final, 2. The Dublin States participated with the EU Member States in the subsequent initiative.

[11] Council of the European Union, 'Conclusions of the Representatives of the Governments of the Member States meeting within the Council on resettling through multilateral and national schemes 20 000 persons in clear need of international protection' Council Document 11130/15.

[12] Footnote 31 of the Opinion. See Council of the European Union, 'Outcome of the Council Meeting' Council Document 11969/15.

of *voluntary* quotas in respect of 40,000 persons from Greece and Italy. It was followed by Council Decision (2015/1601), adopted only eight days later, which provided for the relocation of a further 120,000 applicants, primarily from Italy and Greece, using *mandatory* relocation quotas, with the possibility for Member States

> to meet their obligation by admitting to the territory Syrian nationals present in Turkey under national or multilateral legal admission schemes for persons in clear need of international protection.[13]

The mandatory relocation quotas were not uniformly supported within the Council, and the measure was adopted by qualified majority; the Czech Republic, Hungary, Romania, and Slovakia voted against, and Finland abstained. In accordance with Protocols Nos 21 and 22 of the Treaties, Denmark, Ireland, and the UK took no part in the adoption of the Relocation Decisions.[14] De Witte and Tsourdi observed that:

> [c]rossing this bridge [to create mandatory relocation quotas] led to a confrontation between, on the one side, the EU institutions and the majority of Member States [...] and, [...] a smaller number of Member States who refused to approve binding obligations in the name of their national autonomy. [...] The rift is political; at its heart lay contestations about the nature of the obligation to provide asylum (a common obligation at EU level or an obligation for each Member State individually?); about the limits of central EU action to enhance solidarity in the field of asylum; and about the use of 'people-sharing' as an appropriate tool for achieve a fair sharing of responsibilities between Member States.[15]

On 2 and 3 December 2015, respectively, the Slovak Republic and Hungary sought the annulment of Decision 2015/1601 in *Slovak Republic and Hungary v Council*. Poland intervened in their support; Belgium, France, Germany, Greece, Italy, Luxembourg, Sweden and the Commission intervened in support of the Council. On 15 and 16 June 2017, the Commission sent letters of formal notice to the Czech Republic, Hungary, and Poland concerning their inaction in implementing the Relocation Decisions. On 26 July, the Commission issued reasoned opinions to these Member States setting 23 August as the deadline for compliance.[16] On 6 September, the Grand Chamber of the Court of Justice dismissed the challenges in *Slovak Republic and Hungary v Council*. The same day, the Commission noted that the three countries had not complied with their obligations under the Relocation Decisions, and that they 'should start pledging and relocating immediately'.[17] On 17 September, Decision 2015/1523 expired pursuant to Article 13 thereof. Two days later, the Commission wrote to the Czech Republic, Hungary, and Poland, stating that the Court 'had recently confirmed the legality of the relocation measures', and invited those Member States 'to quickly initiate the steps needed to contribute to the relocation of the remaining eligible applicants in a timely manner'.[18] However, none of the three Member States replied to the Commission.[19] On 26 September, Decision 2015/1601 expired pursuant to Article 13 thereof.

On 21 December 2017, the Commission brought an infringement action in *Commission v Poland*, seeking a declaration that Poland had failed to comply with its obligations under Article 5(2), 5(4) to 5(11) of the Relocation Decisions to, inter alia, indicate regularly

[13] Article 4(3a) Decision 2015/1601.
[14] Footnote 32 of the Opinion.
[15] De Witte and Tsourdi (n 6) 1458.
[16] Para 82.
[17] Para 81.
[18] Para 83.
[19] Para 84.

the number of applicants who can be relocated to its territory.[20] The following day, the Commission brought infringement actions against Hungary[21] and the Czech Republic[22] for failure to comply with their respective obligations under Articles 5(2), and Articles 5(4) to 5(11) of Decision 2015/1601. On 31 October 2019, AG Sharpston issued her joint Opinion.

On 29 January 2020, the Conference of the Representatives of the Governments of the Member States adopted the Declaration on the consequences of the UK's withdrawal from the EU for the Advocates General of the Court. On 2 April 2020, the Third Chamber of the Court ruled, in the now joined cases, that the Member States had failed to fulfil their obligations.[23] On 2 September 2020, by decision of the representatives of the governments of the Member States appointing three Judges and an Advocate General to the Court of Justice, Mr Athanasios Rantos was appointed to the post of Advocate General at the Court of Justice from 7 September 2020. On 10 September 2020, AG Sharpston ceased to be a Member of the Court.

III. THE OPINION OF AG SHARPSTON

In her introduction, AG Sharpston concisely appraised the three applications observing that the defendant Member States:

> contest the admissibility of the applications. In the alternative, they argue that they may rely on Article 72 TFEU as justification for not applying those decisions (whose validity they do *not* now contest), since EU measures taken under Title V of Part Three of the TFEU (of which Article 78 TFEU, the basis of the Relocation Decisions, forms part) 'shall not affect the exercise of the responsibilities incumbent upon Member States with regard to the maintenance of law and order and the safeguarding of internal security'.[24]

AG Sharpston emphasised that the

> Relocation Decisions cannot be viewed in isolation. They were taken against the background of a (highly complex) set of obligations and consequent arrangements in international law and EU law, together with the Court's careful and detailed ruling in the judgment in *Slovak Republic and Hungary v Council*.[25]

Having set out the legal context concisely, but in depth,[26] AG Sharpston paid tribute to her 'esteemed and much regretted late colleague and friend' AG Bot,[27] referencing his 'careful and lengthy' Opinion in *Slovak Republic and Hungary v Council*.[28]

---

[20] Para 86.

[21] Para 87.

[22] Para 88.

[23] Joined Cases C-715/17, C-718/17 and C-719/17 *Commission v Poland, Hungary, and the Czech Republic* ECLI:EU:C:2020:257.

[24] Para 6, original emphasis.

[25] Para 8.

[26] The text of the various provisions accounts for 11 of the 34 pages of the Opinion.

[27] Para 66.

[28] Opinion of AG Bot in Joined Cases C-643/15 and C-647/15 *Slovakia v Council and Hungary v Council* ECLI:EU:C:2017:618.

A. Admissibility

AG Sharpston gave a preview to part of the procedural challenges, observing that the

> pre-litigation procedure in all three infringement proceedings began in the summer of 2017, that is, before the judgment in *Slovak Republic and Hungary v Council* was delivered. However … [a]t the time the written procedure before the Court began, the validity of [Decision 2015/1601] was therefore beyond dispute.[29]

This 'preview' enabled the matter before the Court to be recast succinctly as

> given that Decision 2015/1601 is valid and was therefore always binding on all the Member States to which it was addressed, are there legal arguments that the three defendant Member States can advance that absolve them of their obligations under the Relocation Decisions?[30]

The defendant Member States raised a battery of admissibility challenges, however AG Sharpston considered the cases admissible.[31] A couple of these admissibility points are considered below in order to illustrate the depth of the dispute: that there was a lack of purpose of these proceedings; a lack of legal interest in bringing the proceedings and a violation of the principle of sound administration of justice; and a breach of the principle of equal treatment.[32]

The defendant Member States contended that, because the Relocation Decisions had expired, they could no longer remedy their lack of compliance, and that consequently the actions were devoid of purpose.[33] Hungary contended that the case was '[i]mproper, [and] abusive' contrary to the principle of sound administration of justice, because it could only lead to a finding of principle without any actual legal effect. The Czech Republic argued that the proceedings were merely an 'academic discussion' of the question whether a Member State had previously breached EU law.[34] Additionally, the defendant Member States claimed that 'the Commission has not demonstrated sufficient legal interest in bringing these proceedings and that its action pursues a mere political goal, namely "stigmatising" the Member States that openly challenged the relocation mechanism',[35] and in so doing 'the Commission [had] disregarded the spirit of Article 258 TFEU'.[36]

AG Sharpston disagreed. Although the Relocation Decisions had expired, they were valid when the period laid down in the reasoned opinion expired. To paraphrase: Member States may not wait-out EU measures they dislike until their expiry. AG Sharpston stated that

> the Court has held that in the event of an infringement that took place in the past, it must examine 'whether the Commission still has a *sufficient* legal interest' in bringing proceedings.[37]

This was addressed as akin to a public interest test. With reference to the 1969 case of *Commission v France*,[38] and *Commission v Portugal*,[39] AG Sharpston agreed with the Commission that the

---

[29] Para 68.
[30] Para 69.
[31] Para 152.
[32] Para 91.
[33] Paras 93–94.
[34] Para 97.
[35] ibid.
[36] ibid.
[37] Para 104 (original emphasis).
[38] Case 26/69 *Commission v France* ECLI:EU:C:1970:67, para 10.
[39] Case C-34/11 *Commission v Portugal* ECLI:EU:C:2012:712, para 36.

cases raised important issues. However, AG Sharpston went substantially further, observing that:

> these proceedings raise legitimate and important questions about respect for the rule of law, the principle of solidarity, the common asylum policy and the role of the Commission as the guardian of the Treaties. Whether or not the infringement took place in the past, those questions retain all their relevance.[40]

Presciently – although arguably hypothetically as regards the 'sufficient interest test' that AG Sharpston observed, '[u]nfortunately, the future management of mass migration may well give rise to problems similar to those that led to the adoption of the Relocation Decisions'.[41]

Turning to the plea of a breach of the principle of equal treatment, Hungary and Poland asserted that by bringing infringement proceedings only against the three defendant Member States, although the vast majority of Member States did not fully comply with the obligations defined by the Relocation Decisions, the Commission had breached the principle of equal treatment laid down in Article 4(2) TEU and abused its discretion under Article 258 TFEU.[42] Despite rejecting that line of reasoning, and being in a position to end the analysis, AG Sharpston proposed the following test:

> can it reasonably be said that the three defendant Member States were in a situation *comparable* to that of the other Member States and that the Commission *manifestly* abused its margin of discretion, thus engaging in unjustified differential treatment at the expense of the three Member States in question?[43]

In her view,

> the three defendant Member States are in a situation that can be distinguished, by the gravity and persistence of their non-compliance, from the situation of the other Member States, which have at least pledged to relocate given numbers of applicants for international protection, even if (regrettably) those pledges have not in practice systematically materialised as effective relocations.[44]

This supplementary reasoning could perhaps have unfortunate consequences were it to promote mere lip service from Member States in order to avoid infringement proceedings. Indeed, Austria had made only one formal commitment to relocate involving '50 people from Italy, 15 of whom were actually relocated'.[45]

B. Substance

Based on the 'exhaustive analysis of Decision 2015/1601' in *Slovak Republic and Hungary v Council*, and noting that no challenge was brought within time against Decision 2015/1523, AG Sharpston emphasised that the 'Relocation Decisions are therefore to be considered as incontestably *intra vires* and valid. The three defendant Member States accept as much in the present proceedings'.[46]

---

[40] Para 105.
[41] ibid.
[42] Para 107.
[43] Para 115 (original emphasis).
[44] Para 118.
[45] Footnote 75 of the Opinion.
[46] Para 154.

The necessary substantive analysis was brief. Both Relocation Decisions were provisional measures adopted under Article 78(3) TFEU and, following *Slovak Republic and Hungary v Council*, must be classified as 'non-legislative acts'.[47] On the basis of Article 288 TFEU, the Relocation Decisions were binding in their entirety and 'clearly created legal obligations for the three defendant Member States'.[48] AG Sharpston considered that:

> Despite the (differing) latitude thus afforded to Member States in the two Relocation Decisions that I have identified, I have no hesitation in concluding that pledging to accept 100 applicants (Poland), 50 applicants (the Czech Republic) or indeed making no pledge at all (Hungary) cannot conceivably be regarded as complying with either the letter or the spirit of the obligations imposed by the Relocation Decisions.[49]

AG Sharpston considered that the Commission had made out its case, before turning to the defences raised.[50] The three Member States raised interrelated arguments. Poland contended that Article 72 TFEU is not a mere check on legality during the legislative process, but rather a conflict of laws rule which takes precedence over the Relocation Decisions and gives priority to Member State competence. Therefore, a Member State may rely on Article 72 TFEU to counter arguments about depriving the Relocation Decisions of *effet utile* or appeals to solidarity – there being no obligation to jeopardise internal security by showing solidarity with other Member States. Poland further contended that *Slovak Republic and Hungary v Council* did not (and could not) remove a Member State's inalienable right to rely on Article 72 TFEU, and was therefore not relevant to their defence.[51] Hungary's submissions were characterised as raising the following question:

> may a Member State rely on Article 72 TFEU to exclude or limit relocations under Decision 2015/1601 when they have reservations about the impact of such relocations on national security and public order within their territory?[52]

Meanwhile, the Czech Republic argued that:

> the relocation mechanism put in place by the Relocation Decisions is dysfunctional and that it has taken other, more effective, measures to help in the fight against the migration crisis.[53]

The Commission essentially relied on *Slovak Republic and Hungary v Council*, the need to give *effet utile* to the Relocation Decisions, and the principle of solidarity between Member States. It asserted that the Decisions contain adequate measures to enable the intended Member State of relocation to take the measures necessary to protect national security and public order within their territory as regards the individual applicant.[54] To that end, the Commission contended that Article 72 TFEU expresses a principle of law that must be taken into consideration whenever the EU legislature acts,[55] but that that provision is constrained in a similar manner to those limitations applicable to Articles 36, 45(3), and 52(1) TFEU.[56]

---

[47] Para 155, and Case Joined Cases C-643/15 and C-647/15 *Slovakia and Hungary v Council*, cited above, paras 66 and 70–74.
[48] Para 156.
[49] Para 168.
[50] Para 171.
[51] Para 172.
[52] Para 173.
[53] Para 174.
[54] Para 175.
[55] Para 186.
[56] Para 187.

AG Sharpston observed that Article 72 TFEU had been considered in *Adil*,[57] *A*,[58] and *Slovak Republic and Hungary v Council*, but that the latest judgment only 'foreshadowed' the arguments raised by the defendant Member States.[59] Therefore, AG Sharpston considered the concepts of public order, in *N*,[60] and security, in *Zh and O*,[61] and agreed with the Commission in general terms that the existing case law on the fundamental freedoms, in particular on the free movement of persons, provides a 'secure foundation' for approaching those concepts in the instant case.[62] She recalled that the explicit purpose of Article 78(3) TFEU is to enable the Council to adopt provisional measures to help a Member State that is 'confronted by an emergency situation characterised by a sudden inflow of nationals of third countries', and that it 'provides the necessary legal basis for appropriate measures to be taken that respect both Member States' international obligations under the Geneva Convention and all applicable fundamental principles of EU law' including the principles of solidarity and respect for the rule of law.[63]

An 'immediate answer,' to Poland and Hungary's submissions concerning Article 72 TFEU could be found in Article 5(4) and (7) of the Relocation Decisions. Read together, these paragraphs:

> *expressly recognised* that the Member State of relocation retained the right to refuse to relocate *a particular applicant* where (i) reasonable grounds existed for regarding that person as a danger to its national security or public order or (ii) serious reasons existed for thinking that that person could lawfully be excluded from the international protection sought.[64]

'On a restrictive view' this was sufficient to dispose of the defendant Member States' main line of defence.[65] However, AG Sharpston examined the matter more closely: 'can a Member State rely on Article 72 TFEU (read in conjunction, Hungary submits, with Article 4(2) TEU) in order simply to *disapply* a valid EU measure taken under Article 78(3) TFEU, with which it disagrees?'[66] Crucially, referring to the examples of the *Factortame* cases,[67] and the Member States' point to legislate in relation to direct taxation,[68] AG Sharpston was explicit that:

> Article 72 TFEU is therefore not [...] a *conflict of laws rule* that gives priority to Member State competence over measures enacted by the EU legislature or decision-maker; rather, it is a *rule of co-existence*. The competence to act in the specified area remains with the Member State [...] Nevertheless, the actions taken must respect the overarching principles that the Member State signed up to when it became a Member State and any relevant rules contained in the Treaties or in EU secondary legislation.[69]

---

[57] Case C-278/12 PPU *Adil* ECLI:EU:C:2012:508.
[58] Case C-9/16 *A* ECLI:EU:C:2017:483.
[59] Para 195.
[60] Case C-601/15 PPU *J. N.* ECLI:EU:C:2016:84, para 65.
[61] Case C-554/13 *Zh. and O.* ECLI:EU:C:2015:377, para 48.
[62] Para 199.
[63] Para 201.
[64] Para 204–05.
[65] Para 206.
[66] Para 208.
[67] Paras 214–17.
[68] Paras 218–19.
[69] Para 212 (original emphasis).

In this circumstance:

> EU secondary law within the asylum *acquis* provides an adequate legislative framework within which a Member State's legitimate concerns as to national security, public order and the protection of the community can be met *in relation to an individual applicant* for international protection. Against that background, I can find no scope for accommodating the argument that Article 72 TFEU gives Member States *carte blanche* to disapply a valid measure of EU secondary law with which they happen not to be in perfect agreement.[70]

In forthright terms, AG Sharpston stated 'EU law does not, however, permit a Member State peremptorily to disregard those obligations and, as it were, to put up a sign reading "*chasse gardée*" (roughly translatable as "private hunting – keep out")'.[71]

Short shrift was given to the arguments premised on a combined reading of Article 3(2) TEU and Article 72 TFEU entitling Member States to disapply the Relocation Decisions in order to ensure social and cultural cohesion, as well as to avoid potential ethnic and religious conflicts.[72] By analogy with *Commission v Luxembourg*,[73] a case concerning a nationality condition on civil-law notaries, AG Sharpston observed dryly, 'The Member States' legitimate interest in preserving social and cultural cohesion may be safeguarded effectively by other and less restrictive means than a unilateral and complete refusal to fulfil their obligations under EU law'.[74]

As regards the arguments that the Relocation Decisions allegedly created a 'dysfunctional system',[75] the consequence being that the defendant Member States were 'absolved'[76] from their legal obligations, AG Sharpston considered that the Court had given a complete answer to such an argument in *Slovak Republic and Hungary v Council*. The Court had held that:

> practical difficulties must 'be resolved in the spirit of cooperation and mutual trust between the authorities of the Member States that are beneficiaries of relocation and those of the Member States of relocation. That spirit [...] must prevail when the relocation procedure provided for in Article 5 of [Decision 2015/1601] is implemented'.[77]

The Relocation Decisions provided:

> an appropriate mechanism for addressing the complex issues and logistics of relocating very large numbers of applicants for international protection from the frontline Member States to other Member States. The decisions themselves cannot therefore sensibly be described as 'dysfunctional'. In what was clearly an emergency situation, it was the responsibility of *both* the frontline Member States *and* the potential Member States of relocation to make that mechanism work adequately, so that relocation could take place in sufficient numbers to relieve the intolerable pressure on the frontline Member States. That is what solidarity is about.[78]

Notably, 'for the sake of good order' AG Sharpston observed that:

> other Member States facing problems with their relocation obligations, such as Austria and Sweden, *applied for and obtained temporary suspensions of their obligations under those decisions,*

---

[70] Paras 220–21.
[71] Para 223.
[72] Paras 224–27.
[73] Case C-51/08 *Commission v Luxemburg* ECLI:EU:C:2011:336, para 124.
[74] Para 227.
[75] Paras 228–29.
[76] Para 230.
[77] Paras 233–34, and Joined Cases C-643/15 and C-647/15 *Slovakia and Hungary v Council*, para 309.
[78] Para 234.

as provided for by Article 4(5) and (6) thereof. If the three defendant Member States were really confronting significant difficulties, that – rather than deciding unilaterally not to comply with the Relocation Decisions was not necessary – was clearly the appropriate course of action to pursue in order to respect the principle of solidarity.[79]

C. Concluding Remarks

AG Sharpston issued her joint Opinion on 31 October 2019, at a time of great Brexit uncertainty. The heart of AG Sharpston's Opinion is to be found in her two-page long concluding remarks upon the critical nature of the rule of law,[80] the duty of sincere cooperation,[81] and solidarity[82] inserted as an obiter because 'these infringement proceedings raise fundamental questions about the parameters of the EU legal order and the duties incumbent upon Member States'.[83] It forms the quintessence of her views as to what is required '[i]f the European project is to prosper and go forward'.[84] At that tumultuous time, and with the consequences of Brexit yet to be resolved, including that of her own office, AG Sharpston's views are not so much charged as sharpened. These 'three important strands'[85] will be addressed in the following part.

IV. ANALYSIS AND REFLECTION

All aspects of the Opinion have been referred to by the Court and other AGs. The Court found in favour of the Commission, essentially agreeing with AG Sharpston's recommendations, and cited the Opinion in three paragraphs.[86] Specifically, the Court relied on AG Sharpston's extended admissibility analysis that:

> these three cases raise important questions of Union law, including whether and, if so, under what conditions a Member State may rely on Article 72 TFEU to disapply decisions adopted on the basis of Article 78(3) TFEU, the binding nature of which is not disputed, and which are aimed at relocating a significant number of applicants for international protection in accordance with the principle of solidarity and fair sharing of responsibility between Member States, which, in accordance with Article 80 TFEU, governs the Union's asylum policy ...[87]

Furthermore, the Court cited AG Sharpston's analysis of both Article 72 TFEU and her combined reading of Article 72 TFEU with Article 4(2) TEU. Referring to point 223 ('*chasse gardée*'), the Court stated:

> Thus, as the Advocate General also in essence observed in point 223 of her Opinion, [Article 5(4) and (7) of each of Decisions 2015/1523 and 2015/1601] precluded a Member State from peremptorily invoking Article 72 TFEU in that procedure for the sole purposes of general prevention and without establishing any direct relationship with a particular case, in order to justify suspending the

---

[79] Para 235.
[80] Paras 239–41.
[81] Paras 242–45.
[82] Paras 236–55.
[83] Para 238.
[84] Para 254.
[85] Para 238.
[86] Paras 70, 160, and 170 of the Judgment, referring to paras 105, 223, and 226–27 (respectively).
[87] Para 70 of the Judgment.

implementation of or even a ceasing to implement its obligations under Decision 2015/1523 and/or Decision 2015/1601.[88]

Finally, the Court found that:

> As the Advocate General also essentially observed, in points 226 and 227 of her Opinion, the arguments derived from a reading of Article 72 TFEU in conjunction with Article 4(2) TEU are not such as to call into question that finding. There is nothing to indicate that effectively safeguarding the essential State functions to which the latter provision refers, such as that of protecting national security, could not be carried out other than by disapplying Decisions 2015/1523 and 2015/1601.[89]

The Opinion of AG Sharpston in *Temporary Relocation* has been cited with approval by two other AGs since her departure from the Court. AG Pikamäe cited the entirety of AG Sharpston's analysis of Article 72 TFEU in his Opinion in *WM v Stadt Frankfurt am Main*,[90] noting that:

> The Advocate General rightly states that 'Article 72 TFEU most obviously serves to remind the EU legislature of the need to make appropriate provision, in any secondary legislation enacted under Title V, for Member States to be able to discharge those responsibilities' but that, when exercising those responsibilities in a particular area, the Member States must comply with the rules of EU law.[91]

AG Campos Sánchez-Bordona in *Germany v Poland, Commission*, a case concerning the existence of the principle of energy solidarity, cited part of the concluding remarks, observing: 'In her Opinion … Advocate General Sharpston stated that "solidarity is the lifeblood of the European project"'.[92]

A. Rule of Law

What makes *Temporary Relocation* stand apart and why, as Kirst contends, 'the opinion will likely find its way into the canon of significant AGs' opinions',[93] is the acuity of its concluding remarks. The term 'rule of law' is used differently across Europe. The scope of the rule of law in the common law tradition differs, for instance, from the German *Rechtsstaat*, the French *l'État de droit* and the Italian *Stato di diritto*. 'Although all adhere to the idea that the government's exercise of power should always be conditioned by law,[94] the precise convictions concerning the law vary.'[95] Sir Francis Jacobs wrote in his 2006 Hamlyn Lectures that:

> [t]he rule of law is today universally recognized as a fundamental value. But there is not universal agreement about what it means. Nor is there agreement about how it can be reconciled with other, competing values: notably, with the requirements of democratic government[96]

---

[88] Para 160.

[89] Para 170.

[90] Opinion of Advocate General AG Pikamäe in Case C-18/19 *WM* ECLI:EU:C:2020:130, fn 15.

[91] Case C-18/19 *WM* ECLI:EU:C:2020:511, para 70.

[92] Opinion of AG Campos Sánchez-Bordona in Case C-848/19P *Germany v Commission* ECLI:EU:C:2021:218, fn 53.

[93] N Kirst, 'The Three Villains and the Lifeblood of the European Union Project – Advocate General Sharpton's Opinion in C-715/17 (the asylum relocation mechanism)' (*EU Law Analysis*, 27 November 2019).

[94] G O'Donnell, 'The Quality of Democracy: Why the Rule of Law Matters' (2004) 15 *Journal of Democracy* 32, 33.

[95] H Addink, *Good Governance: Concept and Context* (Oxford, OUP, 2019) 75. Burgess contends that '[i]f "the Rule of Law" is invoked – in necessarily vague and undefined terms that cannot be verified – on both sides of an argument, any relative benefit that "the Rule of Law" brings is nullified; speaking of "the Rule of Law" is of little argumentative benefit'. He argues the term should be abandoned. P Burgess, 'Why we need to abandon "the Rule of Law"' (*IACL-IADC Blog*, 21 September 2021).

[96] F Jacobs, *The Sovereignty of Law: The European Way* (Cambridge, CUP, 2006) 7.

… It conveys the idea that the ultimate source of authority is no longer the sovereign in the shape of a monarch, or even in the shape of a Parliament; but rather certain values, or certain fundamental principles, which form an inherent part of a well-functioning legal system.[97]

In his seminal book, Lord Bingham defined the rule of law:

The core of the existing principle is, I suggest, that all persons and authorities within the state, whether public or private, should be bound by and entitled to the benefit of laws publicly made, taking effect (generally) in the future and publicly administered in the courts. This statement … is not comprehensive, and even the most ardent constitutionalist would not suggest that it could be universally applied without exception or qualification.[98]

AG Sharpston made similar points in *Temporary Relocation*, sketching out the rule of law's importance in three short paragraphs. AG Sharpston referred to the wording of the preamble of the TEU, observing that it 'stresses that the rule of law is a "universal value" that is part of "the cultural, religious and humanistic inheritance of Europe"',[99] given substantive effect by Article 2 TEU, and noting that the Court had first affirmed in *Les Verts*[100] the principle that the EEC (as it then was) 'is a Community based on the rule of law'.[101]

AG Sharpston referred to a couple of the rule of law's 'many important sub-components, such as respect for the proper balance of power between the different branches of government'.[102] She also referred to two contemporary national and European examples. First, reference was made to the UK Supreme Court's judgment in *R (Miller) v The Prime Minister* and *Cherry v Advocate General for Scotland*,[103] concerning the purported prorogation of Parliament, and secondly to *Commission v Poland (Independence of the Supreme Court)*[104] for the importance of 'ensuring the independence of the judiciary by protecting their tenure in office'.[105] Thus AG Sharpston contended, '[a]t a deeper level, respect for the rule of law implies compliance with one's legal obligations'.[106] Succinctly, AG Sharpston set out the insidious problems if a state or society departs from the rule of law:

Disregarding those obligations because, in a particular instance, they are unwelcome or unpopular is a dangerous first step towards the breakdown of the orderly and structured society governed by the rule of law which, as citizens, we enjoy both for its comfort and its safety. The bad example is particularly pernicious if it is set by a Member State.[107]

This ought ordinarily to be considered self-evident in case of a breakdown of the meta-principle of good governance,[108] however, what is most striking is that the point had to be made already in 2019.

---

[97] ibid, pp 61–62.
[98] T Bingham, *The Rule of Law* (London, Allen Lane, 2010) 8.
[99] Para 239, making a reference to the second and fourth recitals to the TEU.
[100] Case 294/83 *Les Verts* ECLI:EU:C:1986:166, para 23.
[101] Para 240.
[102] Para 241.
[103] [2019] UKSC 41.
[104] Case C-619/18 *Commission v Poland* ECLI:EU:C:2019:531.
[105] Para 241.
[106] ibid.
[107] ibid.
[108] Addink (n 95) 19.

B. Duty of Sincere Cooperation

The duty of sincere cooperation incumbent upon EU Member States pursuant to Article 4(3) TEU was addressed brusquely. AG Sharpston placed her own emphasis on the wording in *Achmea*[109] stating that:

> Member States are obliged, *by reason inter alia of the principle of sincere cooperation* set out in the first subparagraph of Article 4(3) TEU, to *ensure in their respective territories the application of and respect for EU law*, and to take for those purposes any appropriate measure, whether general or particular, to *ensure fulfilment of the obligations* arising out of the Treaties or *resulting from the acts of the institutions of the EU*.[110]

Furthermore, 'under the principle of sincere cooperation, each Member State is *entitled* to expect other Member States to comply with their obligations with due diligence'.[111]

C. Solidarity

The concerto closes with solidarity. AG Sharpston set out a brief history of the EU being imbued with the notion of solidarity beginning with the contention in the Schuman Declaration that 'Europe … will be built through concrete achievements which first create a de facto solidarity'.[112] Moving through the third recital to the Treaty establishing the European Coal and Steel Community[113] and Article 2 TEU, AG Sharpston turned to the Court's case law echoing 'that call to solidarity'.[114] The brief examination of the case law is personal and reflective. Referring to *Klöckner-Werke v Commission*,[115] AG Sharpston noted that 'paragraphs 18 to 20 also repay study';[116] touching on the principle of solidarity between producers of sugar in *Eridania zuccherifici nazionali and Others*[117] from 1986, AG Sharpston observed in a footnote that:

> [i]t has been my doubtful privilege since I joined the Court in 2006 to examine some aspects of those arrangements in a series of Opinions and the reader curious to discover more about the workings of the market in sugar is referred to those texts. See, for example, my Opinions in *Zuckerfabrik Jülich* (C-5/06 and C-23/06 to C-36/06, EU:C:1007:346), and in *Zuckerfabrik Jülich and Others* (C-113/10, C-147/10 and C-234/10, EU:C:2011:701).[118]

Paraphrasing the Court's findings in *Eridania zuccherifici nazionali and Others*, AG Sharpston considered that '[i]n so ruling, the Court made it clear that the principle of solidarity necessarily sometimes implies accepting burden-sharing'.[119] The examination concluded with the

---

[109] Case C-284/16 *Achmea* ECLI:EU:C:2018:158, para 34 and the case law cited.
[110] Para 243 (original emphasis).
[111] ibid, para 245 (original emphasis).
[112] Para 247.
[113] It read: 'recognising that Europe can be built only through practical achievements which will first of all create real solidarity, and through the establishment of common bases for economic development'.
[114] Para 249.
[115] Case 263/82 *Klöckner-Werke v Commission* ECLI:EU:C:1983:373, para 17.
[116] Footnote 148 of the Opinion.
[117] Case 250/84 *Eridania v Cassa Conguaglio Zucchero* ECLI:EU:C:1986:22.
[118] Footnote 49 of the Opinion.
[119] Para 251.

Court's use of EU citizenship in conjunction with solidarity in *Grzelczyk*,[120] and the requirements surrounding the need to show 'financial solidarity' for qualifying EU citizens from other Member States to obtain student loans in *Bidar*.[121]

Signing off, and perhaps presuming that she was signing out, AG Sharpston issued her *cri de coeur*:

> Solidarity is the lifeblood of the European project. Through their participation in that project and their citizenship of European Union, Member States and their nationals have obligations as well as benefits, duties as well as rights. Sharing in the European 'demos' is not a matter of looking through the Treaties and the secondary legislation to see what one can claim. It also requires one to shoulder collective responsibilities and (yes) burdens to further the common good.

> Respecting the 'rules of the club' and playing one's proper part in solidarity with fellow Europeans cannot be based on a penny-pinching cost-benefit analysis along the lines (familiar, alas, from Brexiteer rhetoric) of 'what precisely does the EU cost me per week and what exactly do I personally get out of it?' Such self-centredness is a betrayal of the founding fathers' vision for a peaceful and prosperous continent. It is the antithesis of being a loyal Member State and being worthy, as an individual, of shared European citizenship. If the European project is to prosper and go forward, we must all do better than that.

> Let me conclude by recalling an old story from the Jewish tradition that deserves wider circulation. A group of men are travelling together in a boat. Suddenly, one of them takes out an auger and starts to bore a hole in the hull beneath himself. His companions remonstrate with him. 'Why are you doing that?' they cry. 'What are you complaining about?' says he. 'Am I not drilling the hole under my own seat?' 'Yes,' they reply, 'but the water will come in and flood the boat for all of us.[122]

D. Beyond *Temporary Relocation*

In the two and a half years since the Opinion was rendered, so much and so little has changed. New conflicts, and new routes used by those seeking international protection have come into being, and new defensive measures have been conceived or imposed. Rule of law, sincere cooperation, solidarity – and indeed humanity or fellowship towards those in need – remain at issue today. However, compassion and generosity of heart has been shown to those seeking refuge from one invasion. In terms of legislation, reform of the Dublin III Regulation has stalled. 'The correct application of the Dublin III Regulation is neither always self-evident nor always easy to determine'.[123] The 2016 proposal for a Dublin IV regulation[124] expired on 23 April 2021, being replaced by a 'New Pact on Migration and Asylum' which was heavily criticised by Maiani.[125]

During the summer of 2021, the Greek Government sought to accelerate expulsions of migrants as it fears a new flow from Afghanistan following the US-led coalition's withdrawal

---

[120] Case C-184/99 *Grzelczyk* ECLI:EU:C:2001:458, paras 31–46, and especially para 44.

[121] Case C-209/03 *Bidar* ECLI:EU:C:2005:169. See, in particular, paras 56–63.

[122] Paras 253–255.

[123] E Sharpston, 'Shadow Opinion – Case C-194/19 *HA*, on appeal rights of asylum seekers in the Dublin system' (*EU Law Analysis*, 12 February 2021) para 91.

[124] Proposal for a Regulation of the European Parliament and of the Council establishing the criteria and mechanisms for determining the Member State responsible for examining an application for international protection lodged in one of the Member States by a third-country national or a stateless person (recast) COM (2016) 0270 final.

[125] Communication from the Commission to the European Parliament, the Council, the European Economic and Social Committee and the Committee of the Regions on a New Pact on Migration and Asylum COM (2020) 609 final. Bluntly characterised as 'ultra bureaucratic' by F Maiani, 'A "Fresh Start" or One More Clunker? Dublin and Solidarity in the New Pact' (*EU Immigration and Asylum Law and Policy*, 20 October 2020).

and disownment of the conflict, and the Taliban's return across the country in August 2021. The Greek Migration Minister pronounced 'Greece will not accept, as during the period 2015–19, to be the gateway to Europe for illegal immigration flows' with the Council of Europe observing that '[t]he draft law on deportations and returns raises serious concerns'.[126] Separately, 'forced migration' is coming from Belarus into Lithuania, Latvia, Estonia and Poland. On 23 August 2021, the Prime Ministers of those Member States declared that 'Using immigrants to destabilize neighbouring countries constitutes a clear breach of the international law and qualifies as a hybrid attack against the (sic) Latvia, Lithuania, Poland and thus against the entire European Union.'[127] On 2 September 2021, Poland declared a state of emergency in two regions bordering Belarus,[128] and intends to build a 'solid fence' along its border with Belarus.[129] On 8 September 2021, 31 NGOs wrote an open letter[130] to the European Parliament concerning the proposals to reform the EURODAC Regulation.[131] The NGOs contended that the proposed revised regulation following a 2018 political agreement between the Council and the European Parliament would lead EURODAC to becoming 'a powerful tool for the mass surveillance' of migrants enabling inter alia the fingerprinting and photographing of migrant children as young as six, compared with the current minimum age of 14.

Yet there are sparks of brightness. On 12 September 2021, Pope Francis visited Hungary, bound for Slovakia, and urged Hungary to 'extend its arms towards everyone'.[132] The following day, Olivér Várhelyi, European Commissioner for Neighbourhood and Enlargement, urged that the EU must learn from 2015 and 'needs to strengthen [its] work on migration, not only with Ankara, but also with the Western Balkans'.[133]

Russia's unprovoked large-scale invasion of Ukraine, which began on 24 February 2022,[134] has added another dimension. Member States and the EU have broadly shown tremendous compassion and support of all kinds to Ukraine and its people. On 4 March 2022, the Council, upon a Commission proposal, issued Council Implementing Decision (EU) 2022/382 establishing the existence of a mass influx of displaced persons from Ukraine within the meaning of Article 5 of Directive 2001/55/EC, and having the effect of introducing temporary protection.[135] On 8 April 2022, the President of the European Commission speaking in Kyiv, Ukraine declared that, 'Ukraine belongs in the European family' and asserted that '… we are with Ukrainians as they seek refuge within our borders. And I promise you

---

[126] 'Grèce: le Conseil de l'Europe s'inquiète d'une loi accélérant les expulsions de migrants' (*Le Figaro with AFP*, 3 September 2021).

[127] 'Statement of the Prime Ministers of Poland, Lithuania, Latvia and Estonia on the hybrid attack on our borders by Belarus' (23 August 2021).

[128] 'Poland declares state of emergency on Belarus border amid migrant surge' (*Reuters*, 2 September 2021).

[129] 'Poland to build Belarus border fence after migrant influx' (*BBC*, 23 August 2021).

[130] 'Fundamental rights concerns about the EURODAC reform' (*Amnesty*, 8 September 2021); J Rankin, 'EU seeking to turn migrant database into mass surveillance tool' (*The Guardian*, 8 September 2021).

[131] Regulation (EU) No 603/2013 of the European Parliament and of the Council of 26 June 2013 on the establishment of 'Eurodac' for the comparison of fingerprints for the effective application of Regulation 604/2013 and on requests for the comparison with Eurodac data by Member States' law enforcement authorities and Europol for law enforcement purposes, and amending Regulation (EU) No 1077/2011 establishing a European Agency for the operational management of large-scale IT systems in the area of freedom, security and justice [2013] OJ L180/1.

[132] T Kingston, 'Pope tells Viktor Orban to let migrants into Hungary' *The Times* (London, 13 September 2021); AP with Euronews, '"Open your arms to everyone", Pope tells Orban's Hungary' (*Euronews*, 12 September 2021).

[133] J Tamara, 'Várhelyi Olivér: „Tanulnunk kell a 2015-ös leckéből!"' [Olivér Várhelyi: "We have to learn from the 2015 lesson!"] (*Magyar Nemzet*, 13 September 2021).

[134] The war continues as of 16 May 2022.

[135] [2022] OJ L/71/1.

[President Zelenskyy of Ukraine]: We will take good care of them until it is safe to return home. Home to a free and prosperous Ukraine. We make sure, that they have access to housing, schools, medical care and work'.[136] As of 15 May 2022, the UNHCR calculated that 6.2 million people had fled Ukraine, with 3.4 million people arriving into Poland; 920,000 people into Romania; 605,000 people into Hungary; 422,000 people into Slovakia; and 463,000 people into Moldova, which like Ukraine and Georgia, also now seeks EU membership.[137]

Turning to the rule of law, there are many strains upon it both vertically and horizontally within the EU, and indeed elsewhere. Such problems are not limited to Hungary[138] and Poland,[139] but include the different perspectives on the role of the Court vis-à-vis national supreme courts,[140] and questionably, within the Court itself.[141]

E. Room for Hope, and Hard Work

In her State of the Union Address 2021, the President of the European Commission, declared that:

> [p]rotecting the rule of law is also hard work and a constant struggle for improvement ... there are worrying developments in certain Member States. Let me be clear: dialogue always comes first. But dialogue is not an end in itself, it should lead to results. This is why we take a dual approach of dialogue and decisive action. This is what we did last week.[142] And this is what we will continue to do.[143]

While it is unlikely that such actions will resolve the rule of law crisis, they are steps in the right direction.

Temporary Relocation is a landmark Opinion, as evidenced by its citations by the Court and AGs Pikamäe and Campos Sánchez-Bordona to-date. AG Sharpston's concluding remarks in *Temporary Relocation*, have been amplified in her 2021 Hamlyn Lectures,[144] and her 2021

---

[136] President von der Leyen, 'Statement by President von der Leyen with Ukrainian President Zelenskyy at the occasion of the President's visit to Kyiv' 8 April 2022.

[137] UNHCR Operational Data Portal – Ukraine Refugee Situation, accessed 16 May 2022. On 28 February 2022, President Zelenskyy signed an official request for Ukraine to join the EU Moldova and Georgia requested to accede to membership of the EU on 3 March 2022. All three countries currently have Deep and Comprehensive Free Trade Agreements and Association Agreements with the EU.

[138] European Commission, '2020 Rule of Law Report Country Chapter on the rule of law situation in Hungary' SWD (2020) 316 final.

[139] L Pech, P Wachowiec and D Mazur, 'Poland's Rule of Law Breakdown: A Five-Year Assessment of EU's (In)Action' (2021) 13 *Hague Journal on the Rule of Law* 1.

[140] eg BVerfG, Judgment of the Second Senate of 5 May 2020 – 2 BvR 859/15, and compare the judgment of 11 December 2018, *Weiss and others*, C-493/17 ECLI:EU:C:2018:1000; see also Court of Justice of the European Union PRESS RELEASE No 58/20, Press release following the judgment of the German Constitutional Court of 5 May 2020.

[141] Case C-684/20 P *Sharpston* ECLI:EU:C:2021:486, paras 40, 42, and 56; Case C-685/20 P *Sharpston* ECLI:EU:C:2021:485, paras 46–47, 49, and 61. For an analysis see D Kochenov and G Butler, 'Independence of the Court of Justice of the European Union: Unchecked Member States power after the Sharpston Affair' (2021) *ELJ* 262.

[142] Case C-121/21 R *Czech Republic v Poland* ECLI:EU:C:2021:420, Order of 20 September 2021 of the Vice-President, ordered Poland to pay a penalty payment of €500,000 per day, calculated from the date of notification of the order to Poland to the day when Poland complies with the Interim Measures.

[143] President von der Leyen, 'State of the Union Address 2021: Strengthening the Soul of Our Union' 15 September 2021.

[144] E Sharpston, *Taking Stock and Looking Forward*, The Hamlyn Lecture No. 3 (delivered on 23 November 2020, Honourable Society of Middle Temple).

Francqui Chair Lectures.[145] Once published, these Hamlyn Lectures may well be considered alongside Lord Bingham's great work on the *Rule of Law*, but provide a unique view into the construction of a Union under the rule of law.

Grimmel contends that:

> solidarity has to be thought of as the result of a process of constant conceptual application, ascertainment, adaption and refinement. Actions do not speak louder than words in this process, but they are absolutely necessary in order to develop a meaningful concept of solidarity.[146]

One imagines that the now former Advocate General would agree, but would consider that this does not go far enough: it is also essential for the rule of law, solidarity, and perhaps indeed for the 'conscience of mankind',[147] that Member States stand tall and stand together.

---

[145] E Sharpston, *Some reflections on the rule of law within the law of the EU: The rule of law and the refugee crisis, Francqui Chair 2021 Lecture No. 4* (delivered on 9 March 2021, Université Libre de Bruxelles).

[146] A Grimmel, 'Solidarity in the European Union: Fundamental Value or "Empty Signifier"' in A Grimmel and S My Giang (eds), *Solidarity in the European Union: A Fundamental Value in Crisis* (NY, Springer, 2017) 161, 174.

[147] Second recital to the Preamble of the Universal Declaration of Human Rights (adopted 10 December 1948) UNGA Res 217 A(III).

.

48

Homophobic Speech and its Prohibition under EU Anti-discrimination Law: Opinion of Advocate General Sharpston in NH

ALINA TRYFONIDOU

I. INTRODUCTION

IN the *NH* case,[1] the Court was faced, once more, with homophobic speech and its prohibition under EU anti-discrimination law. The first time that the Court had to consider this issue was in 2013, when it was asked to interpret Directive 2000/78,[2] in the *Asociaţia Accept* case,[3] which originated in Romania and which, also, involved homophobic remarks in the context of employment. As noted elsewhere,[4] although the ruling in *NH* was not particularly ground-breaking given that it mostly affirmed the principles established in *Asociaţia Accept*, it nonetheless offered useful clarifications regarding the reach of EU anti-discrimination law in situations involving homophobic speech where there is no identifiable victim. This chapter will present the facts of the case and the Court's ruling, with emphasis being placed on the Opinion of AG Sharpston.[5] It will also consider the implications of the ruling and the gaps in protection persisting even after its delivery.

II. BACKGROUND, CONTEXT, AND FACTS

When – what is today – the EU was established back in the 1950s in the form of three economically-orientated Communities, discrimination on the ground of sexual orientation was not prohibited by the Treaties. It was only in 1999, with the introduction of – what is now – Article 19 TFEU by the Treaty of Amsterdam, that the EU acquired competence to

---

[1] Case C-507/18 *NH* ECLI:EU:C:2020:289.

[2] Council Directive 2000/78/EC of 27 November 2000 establishing a general framework for equal treatment in employment and occupation [2000] OJ L303/16.

[3] Case C-81/12 *Asociaţia Accept* ECLI:EU:C:2013:275. For analysis see U Belavusau, 'A Penalty Card for Homophobia from EU Non-discrimination Law: Comment on *Asociaţia Accept*' (2015) 21 *CJEL* 353.

[4] A Tryfonidou, 'Case C-507/18 *NH v Associazione Avvocatura per i diritti LGBTI – Rete Lenford*: Homophobic speech and EU anti-discrimination law' (2020) 27 *MJECL* 513.

[5] Opinion of AG Sharpston in Case C-507/18 *NH* ECLI:EU:C:2019:922.

adopt legislation to prohibit discrimination on, inter alia, the ground of sexual orientation.[6] As a result of that, in 2000, the EU promulgated Directive 2000/78, which prohibits, among others, discrimination on the ground of sexual orientation in the context of employment and vocational training.[7] As explained by AG Sharpston in her Opinion in the *NH* case, Directive 2000/78 is a minimum harmonisation measure which, thus, allows Member States to introduce, or to maintain, more favourable provisions.[8] The AG also explained that the Directive offers protection at two different levels: the substantive level, by prohibiting direct and indirect discrimination on the ground of, inter alia, sexual orientation, and the level of enforcement, by providing a minimum standard for remedies that Member States must ensure are available in cases of discrimination.[9]

It was only in 2008 that the Court was given the opportunity, for the first time, to interpret the prohibition of discrimination on the ground of sexual orientation under Directive 2000/78.[10] And it was only five years later – in 2013 – that the Court provided an interpretation of the Directive in a case involving homophobic speech: *Asociaţia Accept*. In the latter case, the Court[11] held that homophobic statements in relation to the recruitment of gay footballers by a Romanian professional football club, which were made in an interview given to Romanian media by someone who presented himself – and was considered by public opinion – to play a leading role in that club, could amount to direct discrimination based on sexual orientation, contrary to Directive 2000/78.

Like in the *NH* case, which is under examination in this chapter, in *Asociaţia Accept*, the claim was not brought by a victim of the discrimination complained of but, rather, by an association (Asociaţia Accept) whose aim was to promote and protect LGBTI rights in Romania. Relying on the previous *Feryn* case,[12] which concerned the prohibition of racial discrimination laid down in Directive 2000/43,[13] the Court in *Asociaţia Accept* noted that in order for a finding of direct discrimination under Directive 2000/78 to be made, it was not necessary for there to be an identifiable complainant who claimed to be the victim of such discrimination.[14] The Court also held that Member States could give standing to associations with a legitimate interest in ensuring compliance with the Directive, when they did not act in the name of a specific complainant or in the absence of an identifiable victim.[15] Finally, the Court in *Asociaţia Accept* held that the fact that the employer associated with the person who made the statements might not have started any negotiations with a view to recruiting someone presented as being gay, did not preclude the possibility of establishing facts from which it might be inferred that that employer had been guilty of discrimination.[16]

---

[6] For analysis of the early steps taken by the EU to protect LGB rights see A Tryfonidou, 'Discrimination on the Grounds of Sexual Orientation and Gender Identity' in S Vogenauer and S Weatherill (eds), *General Principles of Law: European and Comparative Perspectives* (Oxford, Hart Publishing, 2017).

[7] For an analysis of the prohibition of discrimination on the ground of sexual orientation under the Directive see A Tryfonidou, 'The Impact of the Framework Equality Directive on the Protection of LGB Persons and Same-Sex Couples from Discrimination under EU Law' in U Belavusau and K Henrard (eds), *EU Anti-Discrimination Law Beyond Gender* (Oxford, Hart Publishing, 2018).

[8] Para 31 of the Opinion.

[9] ibid.

[10] Case C-267/06 *Maruko* ECLI:EU:C:2008:179.

[11] In *Asociaţia Accept*, the Court decided to proceed without an Opinion of an AG.

[12] Case C-54/07 *Feryn* ECLI:EU:C:2008:397.

[13] Directive 2000/43 implementing the principle of equal treatment between persons irrespective of racial or ethnic origin [2000] OJ L180/22.

[14] Para 36 of the Judgment in *Asociaţia Accept*.

[15] ibid, para 37.

[16] ibid, para 52.

Seven years had passed when the Court was confronted with similar issues in the *NH* case. This time, the reference was made by an Italian court. The reference arose from proceedings between NH – an Italian lawyer – and the Associazione Avvocatura per i diritti LGBTI – Rete Lenford ('the Associazione'), which is an Italian association of lawyers that defends the rights of LGBTI persons in court proceedings. At issue in these proceedings was the compatibility with Directive 2000/78 of the statements made by NH in a radio programme to the effect that he would not wish to recruit homosexual persons, nor to use the services of such persons, in his law firm. These statements, according to the Associazione, constituted conduct that was discriminatory on the ground of workers' sexual orientation, contrary to the Italian legislation (Legislative Decree No 216[17]) which implemented Directive 2000/78, and contrary to the Directive itself. As a result of this, the Associazione brought proceedings against NH before the District Court of Bergamo in Italy and the case ended up before the Italian Supreme Court of Cassation, which was the court that made the reference for a preliminary ruling to the Court.

The referring court expressed doubts as to whether the Associazione was a body which had a legitimate interest to bring proceedings *in the absence of an identifiable victim*. This was due to the fact that Article 9(2) of Directive 2000/78 grants standing only to bodies which bring an action either on behalf or in support of an identifiable complainant, as it provides that 'Member States shall ensure that associations, organisations or other legal entities which have, in accordance with the criteria laid down by their national law, a legitimate interest in ensuring that the provisions of this Directive are complied with, may engage, *either on behalf or in support of the complainant, with his or her approval*, in any judicial and/or administrative procedure provided for the enforcement of obligations under this Directive' (emphasis added).

The referring court also expressed doubts as to whether *in the absence of a current or planned recruitment procedure* NH's statements fell within the scope of Directive 2000/78 on the basis that they concerned 'employment' or whether they should be regarded as mere expressions of opinion unrelated to any recruitment procedure. The questions referred were, therefore: (1) whether Article 9 of Directive 2000/78 should be interpreted as meaning that an association composed of lawyers specialised in the judicial protection of LGBTI persons such as the Associazione automatically had standing to bring proceedings even in situations where there was no identifiable victim, and (2) whether a statement expressing a negative opinion with regard to gay persons, such as the one made by NH, fell within the material scope of Directive 2000/78, even if it did not relate to any current or planned recruitment procedure by the person who had made the statement.

III. THE OPINION OF AG SHARPSTON

AG Sharpston began her analysis by noting that the contested statement by NH amounted to direct discrimination on the ground of sexual orientation: 'It is evident that a homosexual person seeking employment in NH's law firm would be treated less favourably – that is, would not be hired – on the ground of his sexual orientation than another person in a comparable

---

[17] Decreto legislativo n. 216 – Attuazione della direttiva 2000/78 per la parità di trattamento in materia di occupazione e di condizioni di lavoro, GURI No 187, of 13 August 2003, p 4.

situation'.[18] Subsequently in the Opinion, the AG also held that none of the applicable derogations from the prohibition of direct discrimination provided by Directive 2000/78 were applicable on the facts of the case and, thus, if the contested statements were, indeed, found by the national court to fall within the scope of Directive 2000/78, they would amount to a breach of it.[19]

The first main issue that was examined by AG Sharpston was whether the facts of the case fell within the scope of Directive 2000/78, despite the fact that the referring court expressed doubts that there was a sufficient link between NH's statements and access to employment, as there was no current or planned recruitment procedure at the time that the statements were uttered. After considering the aims of the Directive and some of the Court's relevant case law (namely, *Feryn* and *Asociația Accept*) AG Sharpston formulated the following principles concerning the scope of 'access to employment' within the meaning of Article 3(1)(a) of Directive 2000/78: (i) that concept must be given an autonomous and uniform interpretation throughout the European Union; (ii) given the objective of Directive 2000/78 and the nature of the rights it seeks to safeguard, the scope of that concept cannot be defined restrictively; (iii) public declarations that persons belonging to a protected group will not be recruited are clearly likely to dissuade certain candidates from submitting their candidature and to hinder their access to the labour market; (iv) the specific method of recruitment is irrelevant (whether or not there has been a call for application, a selection procedure etc.); (v) provided that the person making the discriminatory statements regarding the selection criteria may reasonably be regarded as having an influence on the potential employer, it is irrelevant that that person is not legally capable of binding the actual employer in recruitment matters; (vi) the fact that the employer may not have started any negotiations with a view to recruiting a person presented as being a member of a protected group does not preclude the possibility of establishing discrimination; and (vii) a finding of discrimination is not dependent on identifying a complainant. Other relevant factors that may be considered are whether the actual employer clearly distanced itself from the statements and the perception of the protected groups concerned.[20]

The AG then noted that the above principles 'make it possible to derive a (non-exhaustive) list of criteria to establish when discriminatory statements present a sufficient link with access to employment to fall within the scope of Directive 2000/78'.[21] These criteria were: the status and capacity of the person making the statements,[22] the nature and content of the statements made,[23] the context in which the statements were made,[24] and the extent to which the nature, content and context of the statements made might discourage persons belonging to the protected group from applying for employment with that employer.[25] On that basis, AG Sharpston concluded that the contested statements were *capable* of falling within the scope of Directive 2000/78, but she left it to the referring court to make this decision on the facts of the case.

The next issue that the AG examined was whether NH's statements could be protected by the freedom of expression. AG Sharpston began by noting that 'by enacting Directive 2000/78 the EU legislature has expressed a clear choice. Statements that are discriminatory and that

---

[18] Para 33.
[19] ibid, paras 72–76.
[20] ibid, para 50.
[21] ibid, para 53.
[22] ibid, para 54.
[23] ibid, para 55.
[24] ibid, para 56.
[25] ibid, para 57.

fall within the scope of Directive 2000/78 may not be exonerated by invoking freedom of expression. Thus, an *employer* cannot declare that he would not hire LGBTI persons, or disabled persons, or Christians, or Muslims, or Jews, and then invoke freedom of expression as a defence. In making such a statement, he is not exercising his right to freedom of expression. He is enunciating a discriminatory recruitment policy'.[26] She then concluded that NH's statements could not be protected by freedom of expression, noting that the EU legislature's choice in limiting the freedom of expression through the prohibition laid down in Directive 2000/78 was a permissible choice, as it met the conditions laid down in Article 52(1) of the EU Charter of Fundamental Rights (the Charter) which permits limitations on the exercise of the rights and freedoms laid down in the Charter;[27] an interpretation which, according to the AG, was in line with the case law of the European Court of Human Rights (ECtHR).[28]

Finally, AG Sharpston considered the question whether a body such as the Associazione had standing to bring proceedings in a situation like the one at issue in the main proceedings. The AG began by recalling the Court's rulings in *Asociația Accept* and *Feryn* to the effect that a Member State was not precluded 'from laying down, in its national law, the right of associations with a legitimate interest in ensuring compliance with that directive to bring legal or administrative proceedings without acting in the name of a specific complainant or in the absence of an identifiable complainant'.[29] Thus, Article 8(1) of the Directive ('the non-regression clause')[30] read together with Article 9(2) of the same instrument allowed Member States to grant *additional* possibilities for legal enforcement.[31] The AG then moved on to clarify, however, that although in cases where there was no complainant or identifiable victim, the standing of associations to act was not governed by EU law (as it was up to the Member States to decide whether they would offer this additional possibility for legal enforcement), nonetheless, the substantive rights and obligations that they would be seeking to enforce *did* derive from Directive 2000/78.[32] For this reason, the principle of procedural autonomy together with its corollaries – the principles of equivalence and effectiveness – are triggered,[33] and, thus, although it is for national law to define the criteria that must be satisfied in order for an association to have a legitimate interest to bring actions to enforce the rights and obligations stemming from Directive 2000/78 in the absence of an identifiable victim, this must be done in a way which respects the principles of equivalence and effectiveness.[34]

IV. ANALYSIS

Delivering its judgment almost six months later, the Court was in agreement with AG Sharpston. It even followed the same structure, by considering, first, the second question referred (ie, whether the contested statements did, indeed, fall within the material scope of the Directive), and then proceeding to examine the first question (ie, the locus standi of the

---

[26] ibid, para 62.
[27] ibid, paras 64–69.
[28] ibid, para 70.
[29] ibid, para 83.
[30] Article 8(1) of Directive 2000/78 provides: 'Member States may introduce or maintain provisions which are more favourable to the protection of the principle of equal treatment than those laid down in this Directive'.
[31] Para 85 of the Opinion.
[32] ibid, para 90.
[33] ibid, para 92.
[34] ibid, para 104.

Associazione). Of course, in true fashion for Advocates General, the Opinion was much more detailed and analytical than the Court's judgment, but the conclusions of the two were, essentially, the same.

Hence, the Court held, first, that statements such as those made by NH could be covered by Article 3(1)(a) of Directive 2000/78 and could, thus, be considered to restrict access to employment even though no recruitment procedure had been opened, nor was planned, provided that the link between those statements and the conditions for access to employment or occupation within that undertaking was not hypothetical. Like AG Sharpston, the Court left it to the national court to determine whether the link was hypothetical on the facts of the case,[35] however, it also laid down a number of criteria – the same as those proposed by the AG – for determining whether the link was hypothetical.[36] The Court then also agreed with the AG as regards the fact that such an interpretation of the Directive did not violate the freedom of expression as, although there was an interference with the freedom of expression, the Court found that it was, nonetheless, justified.[37]

Finally, the Court examined the issue of the *locus standi* of the Associazione but its stance on this matter was expressed much more briefly – and cryptically – than were the views of AG Sharpston. The Court, in particular, concluded that Directive 2000/78 did not preclude national legislation under which an association such as the Associazione automatically had standing to bring legal proceedings for the enforcement of obligations under that Directive in the absence of an unidentifiable claimant.

A. Homophobic Speech and EU Anti-discrimination Law: Is the Court's Approach Satisfactory?

Asociaţia Accept and *NH* were, without a doubt, landmark cases where the Court's (and the AG's) approach showed a desire for achieving substantive – rather than formal – equality for LGB individuals in the context of employment, and which took into account the specific circumstances faced by LGB persons who often need to conceal their sexuality. This can be seen in two ways.

First, the rulings of the Court in these cases (and the Opinion of AG Sharpston in *NH*) ensured that even potential obstacles to access to the employment market which were liable to occur as a result of the employer's homophobia, which was demonstrated by oral statements made in public were prohibited, and this was so even in the absence of a formal recruitment policy which discriminated against LGB persons.[38] As explained elsewhere,[39] the reasoning of the Court in both cases – as was the Opinion of AG Sharpston in *NH* – demonstrated that the examination in a case involving homophobic speech should no longer be confined to a consideration of whether a specific person had been discriminated against in comparison with another person in similar circumstances at a particular instance. Rather, it should consider whether a certain practice or action of a person or body was such as to create a discriminatory climate against a segment of the population which shared a prohibited characteristic under Directive 2000/78, which resulted in a potential obstacle to access to the employment market.[40]

---

[35] Para 43 of the Judgment.
[36] ibid, paras 44–46.
[37] ibid, paras 47–55.
[38] Tryfonidou (n 7) 238.
[39] Tryfonidou (n 4) 518.
[40] Tryfonidou (n 7) 239.

Secondly, the Court's judgments in both cases and the Opinion of AG Sharpston in *NH* appeared to take into account the specific considerations that pertain to LGB individuals. By allowing actions to be brought by bodies such as Asociaţia Accept and the Associazione in the absence of an identifiable individual, it was ensured that homophobic statements could be condemned under the Directive without requiring LGB individuals who do not wish to 'come out' to do so by bringing an action claiming that they have been the victims of discrimination based on sexual orientation.[41] This is especially important for individuals who live in Member States where homophobia is still prevalent.

On the other hand, both the Court's and AG Sharpston's reading of the impact that the contested homophobic statements, in both cases, could have, was rather myopic. This is because, although the contested statements in both cases indicated that LGB persons would not be hired and, thus, at first glance they appeared to be discriminatory against LGB persons *with regard to access to employment*, nonetheless, such statements could clearly have a broader negative impact in the context of employment. In particular, if an existing employee becomes aware that their employer would not have hired them if he knew they are LGB, then they can probably expect that if their employer finds out about their sexuality, (s)he will discriminate against them with regard also to other issues such as pay and career progression or they may even lose their job – these matters are covered by 'employment and working conditions' which, also, fall within the material scope of Directive 2000/78 by virtue of Article 3(1)(c).

Although *NH* was, essentially, a confirmation of the Court's approach in *Asociaţia Accept*, it also went further, in that both the Court in its judgment and the Opinion of AG Sharpston took the opportunity – by laying down specific criteria for establishing a link between homophobic statements and access to employment – to sketch the outer limits of the material scope of Directive 2000/78 in situations involving homophobic speech made in public, at a time when there was no current or planned recruitment procedure by the said employer.

Such a clearer delimitation of the contours of the material scope of the Directive is particularly important in this context for ensuring that the Court is not castigated for over-expanding the scope of application of EU law, especially as here – as we shall see below – there was allegedly a clash with another fundamental right, namely, the freedom of expression. Nonetheless – as will be explained in the next part of this Section – the way that both the Court and the AG had navigated this conflict between the need to prohibit homophobic speech and the right to freedom of expression was one of the least satisfactory aspects of the *NH* case.

B. Homophobic Speech and Freedom of Expression

One of the issues that was not considered at all in *Asociaţia Accept*, but which was examined in both the Court's judgment and the Opinion of AG Sharpston in *NH* was the need to balance, on the one hand, the freedom of expression, which is protected by Article 11 of the Charter, with, on the other hand, the right to equality and to be free from discrimination on the ground of sexual orientation, which is, also, protected by Article 21 of the Charter as well as – in the context of employment – by Directive 2000/78.

As was noted above, both the Court and the AG found that reading the Directive as prohibiting homophobic statements in situations such as those in the main proceedings, constituted

---

[41] F Hamilton, '*NH v Lenford*: One further step in the continuing evolution of sexual orientation non-discrimination rights before the European Union' (2020) *GenIUS* 131.

a justified interference with the right to freedom of expression. And although the Court's approach to this issue has been characterised as 'lopsided',[42] favouring the protection of the right to non-discrimination over the freedom of expression, this view is not necessarily shared. On the contrary, in this author's view, it did not go far enough in the protection of the right to be free from discrimination based on sexual orientation. This is due to the fact that it appears to imply that the freedom to engage in homophobic speech needs to be protected as an aspect of the freedom of expression, which means that it can be deemed acceptable under certain circumstances. This approach appears to be in line with the approach of the ECtHR in *Vejdeland and others v Sweden*,[43] which was recently confirmed by the same Court in *Lilliendahl v Iceland*.[44]

Yet, in a democratic society, which is based on the protection of fundamental human rights and equality, there should be zero tolerance for homophobic (or any other type of hate) speech, and thus the right to freedom of expression should, simply, be read as not protecting homophobic speech *under any circumstances*.[45] As Judge Yudkivska, who was joined in her concurring opinion in the *Vejdeland* case at the ECtHR by Judge Villiger, has argued: 'cases like the present one should not be viewed merely as a balancing exercise between the applicants' freedom of speech and the targeted group's right to protect their reputation. Hate speech is destructive for democratic society as a whole, since "prejudicial messages will gain some credence, with the attendant result of discrimination, and perhaps even violence, against minority groups", and therefore it should not be protected'.[46]

The correct approach for the Court of Justice, as a matter of EU law, would have been to simply rule that homophobic speech is not protected under Article 11 of the Charter. This would mean that whenever the Court is confronted with homophobic speech, it will not need to engage in the balancing exercise between the right to freedom of expression and the right to be free from discrimination based on sexual orientation. In this way the Court would offer more protection from homophobic speech than the ECtHR, which is permitted under Article 52(3) of the Charter. The latter provision provides that in so far as the Charter contains rights which correspond to the rights guaranteed by the European Convention on Human Rights (ECHR), the meaning and scope of those rights shall be the same as those laid down by the ECHR, *without this, however, preventing Union law from providing more extensive protection*.

C. Homophobic Speech and EU Law: The Future

The above analysis leads to the conclusion that although the EU judiciary's approach to homophobic speech should be applauded as it shows a desire for achieving substantive equality for LGB individuals in the context of employment and for taking into account the specific circumstances faced by LGB persons who may wish to conceal their sexuality whether within or outside the employment context, nonetheless, it clearly leaves some gaps in protection.

---

[42] J Miller, 'In a Tight Spot, the Court of Justice Delivers a Lopsided judgment: NH v Associazione Avvocatura per I diritti LGBTI – Rete Lenford' (*EU Law Live*, 27 April 2020).

[43] ECtHR, *Vejdeland v Sweden*, Judgment of 9 February 2012, Application No. 1813/07.

[44] ECtHR, *Lilliendahl v Iceland*, Judgment of 12 May 2020, Application No. 29297/18.

[45] For a similar view see P Johnson, *Homosexuality and the European Court of Human Rights* (Abingdon, Routledge, 2014) 176–81.

[46] Para 9 of the Concurring Opinion of Judge Yudkivska in ECtHR, *Vejdeland v Sweden*.

In particular, the Court in both cases involving homophobic speech that reached it – *Asociaţia Accept* and *NH* – has taken a rather restrictive approach as to who can be affected by homophobic statements made in the context of employment. It is not only prospective employees who may decide not to apply for a position as a result of homophobic statements made by someone representing a business; it is, also, 'closeted' *current* employees who may realise that in case their sexuality is revealed to their employer they may lose their job or suffer other negative repercussions in their career. Accordingly, homophobic statements by an employer should not be taken to merely have an impact on *access* to employment but, also, on all aspects of employment, including working conditions: as a result of homophobic statements, an existing LGB employee may be faced with the dilemma of revealing his or her sexuality and suffering discrimination in relation to his or her working conditions or hiding his or her sexuality, with all the negative (psychological and other) repercussions that this may have.

Moreover, the EU judiciary should take a decisive step and rule that homophobic speech can under no circumstances be protected under the right to freedom of expression. The Commission has recently noted that sexual orientation is the most commonly reported ground of hate speech,[47] and in its first ever LGBTIQ Equality Strategy, which was published in November 2020, it announced a number of steps it will take which will aim to tackle homophobic speech. One of these steps will be to present 'an initiative to extend the list of "EU crimes" under Article 83(1) TFEU to cover hate crime and hate speech, including when targeted at LGBTIQ people'.[48] Accordingly, if homophobic speech will qualify as an EU crime, it will be incongruous to permit it in certain circumstances on the basis that it is necessary in order to protect the freedom of expression of its perpetrator.

---

[47] Commission, 'Countering illegal hate speech online: 5th evaluation of the Code of Conduct', 22 June 2020.

[48] Commission, 'Communication from the Commission to the European Parliament, the Council, the European Economic and Social Committee and the Committee of the Regions: Union of Equality: LGBTIQ Equality Strategy 2020–2025' COM (2020) 698 final, 14.

49

The Right to a Tribunal Established by Law: Opinion of Advocate General Sharpston in Simpson and HG

SÉBASTIEN PLATON

I. INTRODUCTION

IT was not very often that cases before the EU Civil Service Tribunal (hereinafter CST) led to rulings of the Court with constitutional relevance. As the CST ceased to exist on 1 September 2016, it will therefore not happen again, at least for the foreseeable future.[1] However, the cases of *Simpson* and *HG* are one of these rare instances. What started off as run-of-the-mill staff cases ended up with the Court adding a completely new branch to its growing case law on the protection of the rule of law.

The Opinion of AG Sharpston was instrumental in this respect.[2] AG Sharpston clearly exposed the constitutional issues of the cases. She proposed developing the right to a tribunal established by law, including the right to a regularly composed tribunal, as a standalone component of the right to a fair trial. She also insisted that a balance should be found between this right and the principle of legal certainty when determining the consequences arising from the irregular composition of a court. The Court followed the core, but not all of AG Sharpston's reasoning. It issued a ruling which, in all likelihood, is bound to have very far-reaching consequences, especially for national judicatures in the context of the rule of law backsliding that is currently unfolding in the European Union.

II. BACKGROUND, CONTEXT, AND FACTS

On 3 December 2013, a public call for applications was published in the Official Journal of the European Union (OJ), with a view to appointing two judges to the CST for a period of six years, commencing on 1 October 2014 and ending on 30 September 2020.[3] That call for

---

[1] On the rise and fall on the Civil Service Tribunal, see, G Butler, 'An Interim Post-Mortem: Specialised Courts in the EU Judicial Architecture after the Civil Service Tribunal' (2020) 17 *International Organizations Law Review* 586.

[2] Opinion of AG Sharpston in Cases C-542/18 RX-II and C-543/18 RX-II *Simpson* ECLI:EU:C:2019:977.

[3] Public call for applications for the appointment of judges to the European Civil Service Tribunal [2013] OJ C353/11.

applications was launched in view of the fact that, on 30 September 2014, the terms of office of two CST judges were due to come to an end. However, on 31 August 2015, the term of office of a third judge at the CST also ended. Given the imminent closure of the CST, the Council did not deem it appropriate to launch a new public call with a view to filling this post. Instead, in 2016, the Council adopted a decision appointing three judges to the CST on the basis of the 2013 call for applications, even though this call related only to two positions.[4]

FV, an unsuccessful applicant in a case before the CST,[5] brought an appeal before the General Court. She argued that the CST's judgment dismissing her claim had been delivered by a panel of judges which had been irregularly constituted. The General Court concluded that, 'having regard to the importance of compliance with the rules governing the appointment of a judge for the confidence of litigants and the public in the independence and impartiality of the courts, the judge at issue cannot be regarded as a lawful judge within the meaning of the first sentence of the second paragraph of Article 47 of the Charter [of Fundamental Rights of the Union]',[6] and set aside the CST's judgment.[7]

The Court of Justice did not review the General Court's judgment in *FV*.[8] Somewhat curiously, the then First Advocate General took the view that 'the judgment [in *FV*] does not (…) constitute a serious risk that the unity or consistency of EU Law may be affected', but nevertheless proposed that the Court should conduct a review.[9] Against that background, the Court decided that the formal conditions for review were not met.[10]

The cases in *Simpson* and *HG* were similar to *FV*, in that, in both cases, the applicants brought an appeal before the General Court against judgments of the CST, claiming that they had been judged by an irregularly composed panel, due to the same irregularity as in *FV*. The General Court thereupon set aside both CST decisions. Thereafter, on 20 August 2018, the First Advocate General recommended that the General Court judgments, on appeal in *Simpson* and *HG*, should be reviewed. The Reviewing Chamber of the Court held that there should be reviews of both those General Court judgments in order to determine whether they affected the unity or consistency of EU law.

III. THE OPINION OF AG SHARPSTON

From the outset, AG Sharpston was of the view that the appointment decision was irregular, since the call for applications concerned the replacement of two judges, yet the procedure led to the appointment of three judges. The main issue was, however, the consequences of this irregularity, and in particular, whether and to what extent a judgment of the CST should be set aside when issued by a panel which included irregularly appointed judges.

The cornerstone of the Opinion of AG Sharpston was the right to a tribunal established by law. This right is provided for in Article 47(2) of the Charter of Fundamental Rights (the Charter).[11] It not only means that there must be a legal basis for the existence of a

---

[4] Council Decision (EU, Euratom) 2016/454 of 22 March 2016 appointing three Judges to the European Union Civil Service Tribunal [2016] OJ L79/30.

[5] Case F-40/15 *FV* ECLI:EU:F:2016:137.

[6] Case T-639/16 P *FV* ECLI:EU:T:2018:22.

[7] Para 78 of Judgment in Case T-639/16P *FV*.

[8] Case C-141/18 RX *FV* ECLI:EU:C:2018:218.

[9] Para 4.

[10] Para 5.

[11] Charter of Fundamental Rights of the European Union [2016] OJ C202/391.

'tribunal', but also for the composition of the bench in each case, which includes the rules relating to the appointment of judges. Looking at the case law of the European Court of Human Rights (ECtHR) concerning Article 6(1) of the European Convention on Human Rights (ECHR) – which also contains the right to a tribunal established by law – she considered that the protection of this right corresponded to the growing importance of the separation of powers in the case law of the ECtHR. It was, in particular, necessary in her view to prevent the executive from exercising an unfettered discretion over the establishment of, or appointments to, a court or tribunal, in accordance with the principle of the rule of law, which is inherent in the entire ECHR.[12]

However, she considered that not every irregularity in a judicial appointment process is liable to affect that aspect of the right to a fair trial. Indeed, attention should also be paid, according to AG Sharpston, to the principle of legal certainty. The need for a balanced approach between the right to a tribunal established by law and the principle of legal certainty was supported by the case law of the ECtHR, which considers that only the most flagrant violations of domestic rules regarding the establishment of a court or tribunal can be regarded as violations of Article 6(1) ECHR. This view was also supported by a brief comparative law analysis, upon which AG Sharpston considered that several Member States had rules meant to mitigate the consequences of a violation of appointment rules on the principle of the authority of *res judicata*. She thus advocated for a balance between the right to a tribunal established by law, on one hand, and the principle of legal certainty, on the other hand. Only where the violation of appointment rules was sufficiently serious could the former outweigh the latter.[13]

Applying this reasoning to the cases at hand, AG Sharpston noted that the use of a call for applications for two positions to appoint three judges was the only irregularity vitiating the procedure. Furthermore, she considered that this irregularity was not to the detriment of 'the confidence that the judiciary in a democratic society must inspire in the public', since the executive did not, by way of the identified irregularity, exercise its power so as to undermine the entire appointment process.[14] Therefore, she considered that the General Court had erred in law by considering that any irregularity, regardless of its gravity, should automatically lead to the judgment being set aside.[15]

She also addressed the issue of the *ex officio* powers of an EU court to examine the lawfulness of judicial appointments. In this respect, the General Court had considered that the *Chronopost* precedent[16] was applicable.[17] In *Chronopost*, the Court had found that 'a ground of appeal alleging an irregularity in the composition of the Court of First Instance [...] must be regarded as involving a matter of public policy which must be raised by the Court of its own motion'.[18] However, AG Sharpston considered that *Chronopost* was only applicable when the alleged unlawfulness affects the independence or the impartiality of the court, which was not the case here.[19]

---

[12] Para 67.
[13] Para 88–111.
[14] Para 86.
[15] Para 142.
[16] Joined Cases C-341/06 P and C-342/06 P *Chronopost SA* ECLI:EU:C:2008:375.
[17] Case T-646/16 P *Simpson* ECLI:EU:T:2018:493 para 38 and 45; Case T-693/16 P *HG* ECLI:EU:T:2018:492 para 39.
[18] Para 48 of *Chronopost* (n 16).
[19] Para 126–36 of the Opinion.

IV. ANALYSIS

A. The Right to a Regularly Composed Tribunal as an Actionable Right under EU Law

The central question of the cases was whether an irregularity in the composition of the CST could justify that the General Court, as an appeal court, should set its judgments aside. Through the reasoning of AG Sharpston, followed by the Court in this respect, what could have been a procedural issue concerning purely EU courts was transformed into a constitutional issue, which is very likely to be applicable, to a large extent, to national courts and tribunals of Member States.

The cases acquired a constitutional status when AG Sharpston posited that it is through the lens of the Charter that they were to be resolved. This was, of course, where the major novelty of her Opinion lays. AG Sharpston considered that the right to a fair trial, as protected by Article 47 of the Charter, included the right to a tribunal established by law, which itself included the right to a regularly composed court or tribunal. Furthermore, this right, in certain circumstances, justified that a ruling be set aside if issued by (an) irregularly appointed judge(s).[20]

In doing so, AG Sharpston, just like the Court after her, followed the footsteps of the ECtHR in the case *Ástráðsson v Iceland*. In a judgment of the 12 March 2019,[21] the Second Section of the ECtHR found that the process by which a judge had been appointed to an Icelandic court amounted to a flagrant breach of the applicable rules at the material time. It was so because one of the judges had been appointed, even though his name was not on the list of selected candidates presented by the Evaluation Committee, in contradiction with Icelandic law. According to the ECtHR, this breach had been detrimental to the confidence that the judiciary in a democratic society must inspire to the public, and had contravened the very essence of the principle that a court or tribunal must be established by law.[22] On appeal of this judgment, but after the Court had issued its own ruling in the cases *Simpson* and *HG*, the Grand Chamber of the ECtHR in *Ástráðsson v Iceland* largely upheld, but also refined the position of the Second Section.[23]

In her Opinion in *Simpson* and *HG*, AG Sharpston heavily relied on the judgment of the Second Section – which was somewhat of a risk given that it was not definitive. On the basis, inter alia, of this precedent, and given the well-known relevance of the ECHR for the EU system of protection of fundamental rights, AG Sharpston, and the Court after her, took the view that a violation of appointment rules could also constitute a violation of Article 47 of the Charter.[24] This was obviously of major constitutional importance, not only at EU level, but also for the EU Member States. According to Article 51(1) of the Charter, the rights laid down therein apply not only to the European Union but also to Member States when they 'implement' EU Law. In *Åkerberg Fransson*,[25] the Court broadly interpreted this notion of implementation as including every situation that falls within the scope of application of EU law. Concerning Article 47 of the Charter, this meant that it would apply to all national judicial proceedings that concern rights granted by EU law.[26]

---

[20] Para 109 of the Opinion.

[21] *Guðmundur Andri Ástráðsson* CE:ECHR:2019:0312JUD002637418.

[22] Para 123 of the judgment.

[23] *Guðmundur Andri Ástráðsson* CE:ECHR:2020:1201JUD002637418.

[24] Para 62–87 of the Opinion.

[25] Case C-617/10 *Åkerberg Fransson* ECLI:EU:C:2013:105.

[26] See eg Case C-279/09 *DEB* ECLI:EU:C:2010:811.

Furthermore, in 2018, in its *Associação Sindical dos Juízes Portugueses* case,[27] the Court found that Article 19(1) TEU, second subparagraph ('Member States shall provide remedies sufficient to ensure effective legal protection in the fields covered by Union law') meant not only that Member States must provide judicial remedies for the protection of EU law, but also that those remedies must comply with the standards of good justice stemming from EU law, and in particular those set out in Article 47 of the Charter. This interpretation provided the Court with far-reaching jurisdiction to assess whether a measure adopted by a Member State was likely to affect the compliance with these standards of proceedings before national courts the jurisdiction of which is susceptible to include questions of EU law. Since the vast majority of national courts have jurisdiction, if only potentially, over questions relating to EU law, this meant that the Court enjoys a broad jurisdiction to review whether national measures concerning the domestic judicature comply with the standards set out in Article 47 of the Charter, via Article 19 TEU.

Thus far, this case law has mostly related to one specific aspect of the right to a fair trial, namely the right to an independent tribunal. In particular, to date,[28] the Court has issued two rulings in which it found that measures adopted by the Polish Government were jeopardising the independence of Polish courts and, thus, infringing Article 19 TEU.[29] It does not mean that the question of the appointment of judges has never been addressed by the Court. So far, however, the questions the Court had to deal with were whether appointment rules and procedures, taken in abstract, guarantee the independence and impartiality of judges.[30] The right to a tribunal established by law raises a connected but distinct question, which is whether *particular* national judges have been irregularly appointed and, if so, what consequences should arise from this. However, as the author of the present chapter and others have argued elsewhere,[31] there is no logical reason why Article 19 TEU would only 'contain' the right to an independent tribunal, and not the other standards protected under Article 47 of the Charter. This means that an irregular appointment of judges in a national court could constitute an infringement of Article 19 TEU.[32]

This conclusion is far from being of mere theoretical interest. As is now well known, a process dubbed 'rule of law backsliding'[33] is currently ongoing within certain EU Member States. Two of them, Hungary and Poland, are even currently subject to a procedure under Article 7 TEU in order to determine whether there is a clear risk of a serious breach of Union

---

[27] Case C-64/16 *Association of Portugueses Judges* ECLI:EU:C:2018:117.

[28] 24 June 2021 (time of writing).

[29] Case C-619/18 *Commission v Poland* ECLI:EU:C:2019:531; Case C-192/18 *Commission v Poland* ECLI:EU:C:2019:924.

[30] See, in particular, Case C-824/18 *A.B.* ECLI:EU:C:2021:153 and Case C-896/19 *Repubblika* ECLI:EU:C:2021:311.

[31] L Pech and S Platon, 'Judicial independence under threat: The Court of Justice to the rescue in the ASJP case' (2018) 55 *CMLRev* 1827, 1844–45; A Torres Pérez, 'From Portugal to Poland: The Court of Justice of the European Union as watchdog of judicial independence' (2020) 27 *MJECL* 105, 111. See also V Davio and C Rizcallah, 'L'article 19 du Traité sur l'Union européenne: sésame de l'Union de droit' (2020) 31 *Revue Trimestrielle des Droits de l'Homme* 156, 178–81.

[32] M Leloup, 'The appointment of judges and the right to a tribunal established by law: The ECJ tightens its grip on issues of domestic judicial organization: Review Simpson' (2020) 57 *CMLRev* 1139, 1155; K Bradley, 'Appointment and Dis-Appointment at the CJEU: Part I – The FV/Simpson Litigation' (2021) 20 *The Law & Practice of International Courts and Tribunals* 162; L Pech, 'Dealing with "fake judges" under EU Law: Poland as a Case Study in light of the Court of Justice's ruling of 26 March 2020 in Simpson and HG' (RECONNECT Working Paper No. 8 – May 2020); J Nowak, 'The staff case that you will never forget! The review judgment of the Court in Simpson and HG' (*EU Law Live*, 30 March 2020).

[33] L Pech and KL Scheppele, 'Illiberalism Within: Rule of Law Backsliding in the EU' (2017) 19 *CYELS* 3.

values, including the rule of law. In Poland, more particularly, one of the founding steps of the rule of law backsliding consisted in the governing party, called Law and Justice (PiS), taking control of the Polish Constitutional Tribunal via irregular appointments. In the case *Xero Flor*,[34] the ECtHR applied its *Ástráðsson* precedent, and found that the illegal appointment of three judges to that Tribunal had violated Article 6(1) ECHR. In a baffling move, the Polish Constitutional Tribunal later declared this ruling *'sententia non existens'* – which, as can be understood, is a sort of aggravated claim to ultra vires.[35] There is, however, a good chance that this situation also qualifies as a violation of Article 19 TEU.

B. The Connection between the Regularity of Judicial Appointment, the Right to an Independent and Impartial Tribunal and the Principle of Legal Certainty

One of the aspects on which the Opinion of AG Sharpston and the judgment differed significantly was the way three distinct principles were connected with one another: the principle of independence and impartiality of tribunals; the right to a tribunal established by law and the principle of legal certainty. This 'triangle' appeared, at times more or less clearly, in relation to two issues in both the Opinion and the judgment: the issue of whether an irregularity justifies setting aside a judgment and the issue of the power of the courts to raise *ex officio* the irregular composition of a tribunal.

On the first of these two issues, there is an important contrast between the Opinion of AG Sharpston's and the Court's ruling. Whereas the right to an independent and impartial tribunal had little bearing in AG Sharpston's reasoning, it was central in the reasoning of the Court. Conversely, whereas the principle of legal certainty is a key part in AG Sharpston's reasoning, it did not explicitly appear in the Court's reasoning – even though it could be argued that the Court applied it implicitly, and even more stringently than AG Sharpston.

When assessing whether an irregularity in the appointment of a judge can justify setting aside a judgment issued by an irregularly composed court, AG Sharpston considered that a balance must be struck between the right to a tribunal established by law, and legal certainty. This finding, in her view, was supported by the observation that, in several domestic legal systems, the possibly harsh consequences of an irregular appointment on the judgments issued by irregularly composed courts are often mitigated in the name of legal certainty. Thus, she proposed adapting the consequences of an irregularity depending on its gravity (para 109):

> Where there is a 'flagrant' breach of the right to a tribunal established by law that operates to the detriment of the confidence which justice in a democratic society should inspire in litigants, the judgments affected by that irregularity should evidently be set aside without more ado. Where, however, the irregularity in question is of a lesser nature and does not constitute such a breach, the principle of legal certainty does not allow those judgments to be set aside automatically. Rather, one should go on to examine the situation in greater detail, taking into account that important principle. In a particular case under scrutiny, it may be that that principle outweighs the right to a tribunal established by law. However, if it transpires that the substance of the right to a fair trial was adversely affected, it will become imperative to give that right precedence over the principle of legal certainty and set aside the judgment at issue.[36]

---

[34] *Xero Flor w Polsce sp. z o.o. v Poland*, CE:ECHR:2021:0507JUD000490718.

[35] R Lawson, '"Non-Existent": The Polish Constitutional Tribunal in a state of denial of the ECtHR Xero Flor judgment' (*Verfassungsblog*, 18 June 2021).

[36] Para 109 of the Opinion.

The Court's reasoning on the very same issue was significantly different. It seems that, for the Court, there can only be a breach of the right to a tribunal established by law in case of infringement of a fundamental appointment rule. More particularly, the Court considered that, for an irregularity to be serious enough to warrant setting aside a judgment, it must affect the appearance of independence and impartiality of the court or tribunal.[37] The Court did not seem to leave any room for balancing the breach of the appointment rules at issue with the principle of legal certainty, as proposed by AG Sharpston. Thus, the Court appeared even more protective of legal certainty than AG Sharpston, even though it did not explicitly mention it. As Pech notes, 'this approach may ... incentivise executive and other branches of the State to disregard non-fundamental rules for reasons of pure convenience',[38] something that the test put forward by AG Sharpston would have prevented.

This difference between AG Sharpston and the Court also appeared regarding the powers of the Court. One of the issues of the cases was whether the Court could, of its own motion, raise the issue of the irregular appointment of the court or tribunal that handed down the judgment under appeal. The question here was whether the *Chronopost* precedent[39] was applicable to this situation. AG Sharpston considered in her Opinion that the *Chronopost* case law was not applicable in the *Simpson and HG* cases. In support of this, she noted that, in *Chronopost*, the Court linked the regular composition of a court or tribunal with the independence and impartiality aspects of the right to a fair trial. She inferred from this that it only falls to a court or tribunal 'to verify that, taking account of the composition of that panel, on the one hand, and the particular characteristics of the case at issue, on the other, there can be no reasonable doubt as to the independence and impartiality of those called upon to give judgment in that case'. In other words, according to AG Sharpston, a court or tribunal can only raise, *ex officio*, the irregular composition of a court when this irregularity is likely to affect, even only in appearance, its independence or impartiality.

The Court did not endorse this distinction. In its ruling, and making explicit reference to the *Chronopost* ruling, the Court emphasised that 'the guarantees of access to an independent and impartial tribunal previously established by law, and in particular those which determine what constitutes a tribunal and how it is composed, represent the cornerstone of the right to a fair trial'.[40] This sentence was nearly the same as in *Chronopost*, except that, in *Chronopost*, the Court had not used the words 'previously established by law', thus insisting here that this was a separate, additional requirement. The Court then went on to infer from this finding that 'every court is obliged to check whether, as composed, it constitutes such a tribunal where a serious doubt arises on that point'. This obligation was significantly different from the one stated in *Chronopost*, in that there is no reference here to independence and impartiality. This clearly meant that the Court refused the proposal of its AG not to extend the *Chronopost* case to situations where an irregular appointment does not affect independence or impartiality.

In practice, however, the divergence was limited because, as seen, it is only when the irregularity was likely to affect the independence or impartiality of a court or tribunal that its judgments can be set aside. In other words, for the Court, even though *any* irregularity can be raised *ex officio*, only those irregularities that affect the independence or impartiality of the

---

[37] Para 75 of the Judgment.
[38] Pech (n 32) 13.
[39] *Chronopost* (n 16).
[40] Joined Cases C-542/18 RX-II and C-543/18 RX-II *Simpson* ECLI:EU:C:2020:232, para 57.

court that issued a judgment justify setting aside the judgment. This stands in contrast with the system suggested by AG Sharpston. If AG Sharpston had been followed, *only* irregularities affecting the independence or impartiality of a court could have been raised *ex officio*. However, *any* irregularity, even those which are not likely to affect the independence or impartiality of the court that has issued the judgment, could have potentially justified setting aside the judgment in question if, in the given case, the right to a tribunal established by law outweighed the principle of legal certainty.

This suggests a sort of paradox. Whereas AG Sharpston insists significantly on the principle of legal certainty in her Opinion, the solution she eventually suggested left the courts a substantial margin of appreciation when assessing whether an irregular appointment should lead to a judgment being set aside. Conversely, even though the Court puts the focus on Union values, including the rule of law, its solution seemed at the end more restrictive on the consequences that may arise from the irregular composition of a tribunal.

C. Effect on Future Case Law

It is too soon to fully assess the effect of AG Sharpston's opinion and the Court's ruling on posterior case law, but there is no doubt it will be significant. We can already observe that AG Tanchev heavily relied on the ruling of the Court in *Simpson and HG* in his Opinions in the pending[41] *W.Ż.*[42] and *Prokurator Generalny* cases.[43] Both cases are strongly connected with the ongoing rule of law backsliding in Poland. More precisely, these cases concern the irregular appointment of judges at the Disciplinary Chamber and at the Chamber of Extraordinary Control and Public Affairs of the Polish Supreme Court.

In both his Opinions, and more comprehensively in his opinion in *W.Ż.* to which he referred in his Opinion in *Prokurator Generalny*, AG Tanchev explicitly put the principles laid out by the Court in *Simpson and HG* at the centre of his reasoning. If followed by the Court, this would confirm the thesis developed above that the solution of the Court in *Simpson and HG* is applicable to national courts via Article 47 of the Charter and Article 19 TEU. AG Tanchev recalled that it will be for the referring court to assess, by reference to the judgment in *Simpson and HG*, whether the appointment of the judges of the Supreme Court at issue, namely A.S. and J.M., constitutes an irregularity which creates a real risk that other branches of the Member State, in particular the executive, could exercise undue discretion undermining the integrity of the outcome of the appointment process, and thus give rise to a reasonable doubt in the minds of individuals as to the independence and the impartiality of the judge concerned. However, AG Tanchev did not shy away from expressing his own findings in this respect.

In his Opinion in *W.Ż.*, he stated that:

> [T]he manifest and deliberate character of the violation of the order of the Supreme Administrative Court staying the execution of KRS Resolution No 331/2018, committed by such an important State authority as the President of the Republic, empowered to deliver the act of appointment to the post of judge of the Supreme Court, is indicative of a flagrant breach of the rules of national law governing the appointment procedure for judges.[44]

---

[41] At the time of writing (24 June 2021).
[42] Opinion of AG Tanchev in Case C-487/19 *W.Ż.* ECLI:EU:C:2021:289.
[43] Opinion of AG Tanchev in Case C-508/19 *Prokurator Generalny* ECLI:EU:C:2021:290.
[44] Para 87 of the Opinion in *W.Ż.*

He even went as far as saying that 'in relation to the criterion of gravity, to my mind, given the general context of the contentious judicial reforms in Poland, the gravity of the breaches in the present case is more serious than the irregularities at issue in *Ástráðsson v. Iceland*'.[45] Furthermore, in the next paragraph, he considered that 'the breaches committed in the present case in the course of the judicial appointment process and the risk of W.Ż. being without effective judicial protection constitute circumstances which justify the limitation of the binding character of the order of 8 March 2019, contrary to the principle of legal certainty'.

In the *Prokurator Generalny* case, AG Tanchev heavily referred to his 'parallel' Opinion in W.Ż. He considered at para 26 that 'it follows from the order for reference that there were numerous potentially flagrant breaches of the law applicable to judicial appointments in the appointment procedure in respect of J.M'.[46] It follows that:

[A] court, such as the court composed of J.M., does not meet the requirements to constitute such a tribunal established by law in a situation where the judge concerned was appointed to that position in flagrant breach of the laws of the Member State applicable to judicial appointments to the Supreme Court, which is a matter for the referring court to establish. The referring court must, in that respect, assess the manifest and deliberate character of that breach as well as the gravity of the breach and must take into account the fact that J.M. was appointed despite a prior appeal to the competent national court against the resolution of the KRS, which included a motion for the appointment of that person to the position of judge and which was still pending at the relevant time.[47]

Later in his Opinion, he added that:

[T]he national authorities may not take refuge behind arguments based on legal certainty and irremovability of judges. Those arguments are just a smokescreen and do not detract from the intention to disregard or breach the principles of the rule of law. It must be recalled that law does not arise from injustice (*ex iniuria ius non oritur*). If a person was appointed to such an important, institution in the legal system of a Member State as is the Supreme Court of that State in a procedure which violated the principle of effective judicial protection, then he or she cannot be protected by the principles of legal certainty and irremovability of judges.[48]

The wording used by AG Tanchev in both his Opinions is interesting. He assessed whether the alleged irregularity constitutes a 'flagrant breach' of national appointment rules, and weighted it against the principle of legal certainty. Yet, neither the notion of 'flagrant breach' nor the need for a balance with legal certainty appeared explicitly in the test designed by the Court in *Simpson and HG*. Both, however, are central to the test designed by AG Sharpston in her Opinion in these cases. Whatever the Court will decide on W.Ż. and *Prokurator Generalny*, this seems to suggest that AG Sharpston's rationale in her opinion in *Simpson and HG* has convinced other members of the Court, for the greater benefit of the rule of law.

---

[45] ibid, para 88.
[46] Para 26 of the Opinion in *Prokurator Generalny*.
[47] ibid, para 39.
[48] ibid, para 54.

Part VII

Afterwords

50

Reflections of an Advocate General: 1988–2006

FRANCIS G JACOBS

I. INTRODUCTION

THERE SEEMS LITTLE doubt that after the first enlargement of the Community in 1973, the development of European law by the Court was significantly influenced by the contribution of the AG and judge from the UK, by the contribution of counsel appearing before the Court, by the contribution of the UK in cases before the Court, and by the scholarship of authors from the new Member States (Denmark, Ireland, and the UK), to an extent which cannot of course be precisely quantified.

So far as the UK is concerned, my impression, initially as a *référendaire* to AG Warner (1973–74), later as counsel appearing before the Court, and subsequently as Advocate General (1988–2006), was that the quality of the proceedings before the Court benefited significantly from the contribution of the English Bar, and also the Irish Bar (there were very few cases from Scotland or Northern Ireland) from 1973 onwards. This might be regarded as contributing to the development of European law by the Court as a consequence of the UK's membership.

Often, counsel from the UK with their experience of oral advocacy were able to make what seemed useful contributions at the (relatively very short) hearings. The hearings became more interactive, and there was dialogue between Bench and Bar, a dialogue which was not usual, and was sometimes seen as improper since it contrasted greatly with practice in the national courts of some other Member States.[1]

It may be relevant to mention briefly, at the outset, my experience as counsel, before my appointment as AG. I had the good fortune to appear as counsel frequently before the Court, for (and against) the UK, and in many other cases.[2] From the outset, the UK itself

---

[1] That is not to accept that a full-scale hearing as featured in English courts should be adopted by the Court, if that would mean that the main arguments should be developed at the hearing rather than in writing beforehand. Often in important cases, to take just one point, many Member States will be represented, as well as the parties and the EU institutions; each Member State is, understandably, entitled to use its own language. Any new points which arose would have to be open to reply by all participants, with the consequent need for further rounds of reply. It may be thought that a reasonable compromise has evolved as the system now operates.

[2] Case 3/75 *Johnson & Firth Brown* ECLI:EU:C:1975:3; Case 104/75 *de Peijper* ECLI:EU:C:1976:67; Case 130/75 *Prais* ECLI:EU:C:1976:142; Case 103/77 *Royal Scholten-Honig* ECLI:EU:C:1978:186; Case 116/77 *Amylum* ECLI:EU:C:1979:273; Case 119/77 *Nippon Seiko* ECLI:EU:C:1979:93; Case 146/77 *British Beef* ECLI:EU:C:1978:127; Case 118/78 *Meijer* ECLI:EU:C:1979:97; Case 153/79 *Bowden* ECLI:EU:C:1981:184;

was an active participant in proceedings before the Court, the Member States having the right to take part in all cases. My impression is that throughout its membership, the UK's participation significantly assisted the Court. UK government lawyers, with their centre in the Treasury Solicitor's Department, were remarkably skilful in coordinating the UK government's interventions, especially on references from national courts – both UK courts, and courts elsewhere. All references from all national courts, on notification to the government from the Court, were scrutinised and passed to the relevant government departments. The Court's timetable was very tight, as there was a concern not to unduly delay the national court proceedings, which were suspended during the Court's proceedings. Written observations had to be submitted within the short period of two months from notification of the national court's reference. The Treasury Solicitor's lawyers often had to coordinate the positions of several government departments, with different priorities. Counsel were often consulted in this process, sometimes being required to moderate where there were different interests at stake, so as to aim for the most satisfactory solution.

The UK's own interests were in some cases defensive, to protect what were seen as UK interests: an example was the *Campus Oil* case, in which I pleaded before the Court, intervening in support of Ireland. My predecessor, Sir Gordon Slynn delivered his Opinion, as discussed in this book.[3] Another example was the arguably excessive UK contribution to the EU budget, where symbolic success was obtained in the Court,[4] and the main issue was ultimately resolved through a political settlement with the 'UK rebate'. In other cases, the UK was proactive in seeking the development of the Court's case law on the internal market, of which the UK was one of the architects, and was seen as a principal beneficiary.

II. THE ROLE OF THE ADVOCATE GENERAL AND THE QUESTION OF SEPARATE AND DISSENTING OPINIONS BY JUDGES

I start with some reflections on the role of the AG, as it might be seen from a UK perspective.

A. The Role of the Advocate General

The Opinion of the AG, as it has developed over the years, can be seen, in form if not in substance, as more like a judgment of an English or other common law court, than the

---

Case 154/79 *Biller* ECLI:EU:C:1981:185; Case 167/80 *Curtis* ECLI:EU:C:1981:131; Case 208/80 *Lord Bruce of Donington* ECLI:EU:C:1981:194; Case 84/81 *Staple Dairy Products* ECLI:EU:C:1982:187; Case 104/81 *Kupferberg* ECLI:EU:C:1982:362; Case 114/81 *Tunnel Refineries* ECLI:EU:C:1982:324; Case 230/81 *Luxembourg v Parliament* ECLI:EU:C:1983:32; Case 13/83 *Parliament v Council* ECLI:EU:C:1985:220; Case 72/83 *Campus Oil* ECLI:EU:C:1984:256; Case 120/83 *Raznoimport* ECLI:EU:C:1983:224; Case 44/84 *Hurd* ECLI:EU:C:1986:2; Case 174/84 *Bulk Oil* ECLI:EU:C:1986:60; Case 181/84 *Man* ECLI:EU:C:1985:359; Case 209/84 *Ministère public* ECLI:EU:C:1986:188; Case 222/84 *Johnston* ECLI:EU:C:1986:206; Case 84/85 *UK v Commission* ECLI:EU:C:1987:416; Case 93/85 *Commission v UK* ECLI:EU:C:1986:499; Case 150/85 *Drake* ECLI:EU:C:1986:257; Joined Cases 260/85 and 106/86 *TEC* ECLI:EU:C:1988:465; Joined Cases 273/85 and 107/86 *Silver Seiko* ECLI:EU:C:1988:466; Joined Cases 277/85 and 300/85 *Canon* ECLI:EU:C:1988:467; Case 297/85R *Towa Sandiken* ECLI:EU:C:1985:422; Case 301/85 *Sharp Corporation* ECLI:EU:C:1988:468; Case 384/85 *Clarke* ECLI:EU:C:1987:309; Case 23/86R *UK v Parliament* ECLI:EU:C:1986:125; Case 34/86 *Council v Parliament* ECLI:EU:C:1986:291; Case 141/86 *Imperial Tobacco* ECLI:EU:C:1988:12; Joined Cases 294/86 and 77/87 *Technointorg* ECLI:EU:C:1988:470. Note: this list of cases has been compiled by the editors.
[3] See ch 17.
[4] Case 23/86 R *UK v Parliament* ECLI:EU:C:1986:125.

judgment of the Court of Justice. The AG's Opinion generally sets out – and often rather fully – the facts, the issues, the main arguments, the relevant law, the analysis, and the conclusions, except that it ends with a *proposed* outcome. But it often does so more fully,[5] and occasionally more discursively, than the judgment of the Court. Sometimes it needs to consider different hypotheses and different ways of resolving the issues. The judgment of the Court, by contrast, once there is a decision on the outcome of the case, can often proceed more directly, and without distraction, to the goal.

The combination of Opinion of the AG and judgment of the Court can also be seen as having the advantage that the judgment in its form looks much like a judgment of some of the higher continental courts, while the Opinion often looks like a judgment of an English or other common law court, with the important exception that it does not decide the case.

But there are perhaps other advantages in this combination, or divisions of labour, between Opinions of the AGs and judgments of the Court. The fuller exposition and fuller reasoning in the AG's Opinions may compensate for a judgment which is understandably concise, and which is sometimes perhaps not fully coherent, given the need for a single judgment of the Court. A succinct judgment also has some obvious advantages. I suspect that all those familiar with the case law will, when reading a case, generally take the Opinion and the judgment into account together – and will do so even where the judgment does not follow the Opinion. It may be added, almost by way of a footnote, that AGs may also use footnotes, and sometimes do so to support their view with references to academic writings. That practice is not found in judgments of the Court.

B. Dissenting or Separate Opinions?

However, a view which has been widely held in the UK is that the Court should introduce dissenting or separate opinions in its judgments, an issue which is relevant to the relationship between the AG's Opinion and the judgment of the Court. At first sight, that might seem a useful innovation and might lead to clearer judgments, not concealing possible differences of view among the judges. It might also bring the Court closer to the common law model. I have not however found this idea convincing.[6]

First, as has been widely recognised, it would be difficult to introduce dissenting and separate opinions given the Treaty provision for a limited, renewable term of appointment of judges, currently a term of six years. In such a system, the renewal might become a political issue, which would be very damaging. Even if the present system were changed to introduce a longer, non-renewable term, it is doubtful whether the term would be longer than nine years (as was the term introduced in the European Court of Human Rights (ECtHR)). That would be undesirably short: continuity and institutional memory are of the greatest importance in the EU Court, especially given the increasing scope and increasing complexity of EU law. And it is unsatisfactory that, currently, the AGs from many Member States are appointed only for a single, non-renewable six-year term.

---

[5] Compare, just by way of illustration, my Opinion in Case C-168/91, *Konstantinidis*, to that of the judgment of the Court. See ch 25.

[6] For a similar viewpoint, see V Skouris, 'Judging at the Court of Justice of the European Union: Is There a Need for Dissenting Opinions?' in K Lenaerts, J-C Bonichot, H Kanninen, C Naômé and P Pohjankoski (eds), *An Ever-Changing Union?: Perspectives on the Future of EU Law in Honour of Allan Rosas* (Oxford, Hart Publishing, 2019).

Moreover, there are in any event strong intrinsic arguments against introducing dissenting and separate opinions, which are very much the exception in Europe. Even in the UK, there was, for many years, a requirement of a single opinion in the Judicial Committee of the Privy Council, and there is increasing use of a single judgment in the UK Supreme Court. Indeed recently, there has been a move towards a single judgment even in the US Supreme Court, which is notoriously divided ideologically. This exceptional character of dissenting or separate opinions of judges would reinforce the risk that judgments of the Court would carry less weight with national governments, and even with national courts. Judgments of the Court are still in need of unhesitating acceptance. There might even be an expectation that a decision with dissenting or separate opinions could be reversed in a future case.

A further point is that, if dissenting and separate opinions were introduced, individual judges on the Court would inevitably come to be identified with the views they had expressed there, and judges would be categorised accordingly; there could even develop, openly, separate factions within the Court. This would be undesirable in itself, and more seriously, it would probably also politicise the entire appointment process. Judges who had publicly taken a position might also find it difficult to change their position in future cases, whereas it is said that at present, dissenting judges can come round to the majority view in due course.[7]

Conversely, in the absence of dissenting or separate opinions, there may be a greater effort by the Court to achieve consensus.

The availability of dissent might, for the above reasons, encourage the adoption of more extreme positions. The existing requirement of a single judgment is more likely to lead to moderate positions being taken.[8] And perhaps there is a risk that, with dissenting or separate opinions, newly appointed judges would continue to think in terms of their national law, instead of contributing to a developing European approach, as is required by the need to adopt a single judgment.

In view of the above difficulties, an Opinion of the AG has distinct advantages: in some cases, it enables the development of fuller reasoning in the Opinion than is possible or appropriate in the judgment. The Opinion can also set out more fully the context in which the issues arise. In other cases, it may demonstrate that an alternative legitimate view is possible,[9] and it reduces the impression of EU law as a monolithic and impermeable structure. So in some cases, the Opinion of the AG could be seen as, de facto, a dissenting opinion. It also brings the EU system closer to those systems which do have dissenting and separate opinions. It represents an effective compromise between contrasting legal systems, both national and supranational.

The relationship between Opinion of the AG and judgment of the Court has various significant consequences. First, the Opinion is likely to be cited in future cases to illuminate, and occasionally perhaps to qualify, the effect of the judgment. Exceptionally, the Opinion may be cited to restrict the scope of the judgment, or even to seek a departure from it in a future case. It is also noteworthy that reviews of cases in EU law journals seem, quite often, to allot at least as much space to Opinions of the AGs as to judgments of the Court. No doubt this is due in part to the fuller reasoning of the Opinion.

---

[7] See eg the views of my colleague in ch 51.

[8] For this reason, it seems surprising that dissenting or separate opinions have been regarded as desirable by UK sources.

[9] On this, see ch 42.

It may also be significant in this context that in a high proportion of cases the judgment of the Court broadly follows, in substance, the Opinion of the AG. This should help to provide some measure of reassurance in demonstrating that different minds, working independently, have reached similar conclusions; but that also, of course, they can properly differ.

The Opinion of the AG can serve other valuable purposes, precisely when the judgment of the Court does not follow the Opinion: it could for example be relied on in future cases to argue for a qualified application, or even a reconsideration, of the law as laid down in the judgment. At the least, the Opinion of the AG demonstrates that EU law is not monolithic, even though there is no provision for separate and dissenting opinions by the judges. The 'separate Opinion' of the AG is particularly valuable if, as seems right, separate or dissenting opinions by the judges would not be appropriate for the Court. That question is of course of particular importance in any consideration of the role of the AG.

C. The EU and the Common Law: EU Law as a Case Law System?

How far can EU law be regarded as a case law system? How has that evolved following UK accession?

It would probably be generally agreed that the function of a court of law may go beyond seeking to find the solution to the case before it, and justifying that solution by appropriate reasons. A court's function may extend, especially in the highest courts, to placing a case in its context in the branch of the law concerned, and seeking to identify how to formulate the law in the way in which that branch of the law might best develop. That function may be particularly appropriate in the case of EU law, precisely because EU law is a system distinct from the systems of national law which national courts are generally applying, and in which the national courts have their particular expertise.

That function may also be particularly appropriate in the case of EU law in view of the special procedure of the reference for a preliminary ruling, under which the Court gives, not a decision on the case, but a general ruling on a question of law referred to it. That procedure, although it has some analogues in some of the Member States, is nevertheless wholly exceptional; but it is very understandable in the context of EU law: it requires the Court to give a ruling which is intended to govern not merely the instant case, but also any future case in which the same or a similar question of law arises before any court.[10]

That function is also particularly appropriate in the case of EU law because of the special situation of the Court. It is a single court for the whole of the EU; it is composed of lawyers from all the Member States; and it has the sole power to rule definitively on EU law. In addition, it is clearly of particular importance for the very functioning of the EU that EU law should be interpreted and applied uniformly in all Member States. For the above reasons, EU law may be regarded as having the foremost feature of a common law system, with a system of case law no less necessary – perhaps more necessary – than in national systems. But of course, other national systems, as well as the UK, may have areas in which case law predominates as a source of law.

Initially, and understandably, the Court was strongly influenced by the traditions of French law. There was therefore a reluctance to make explicit that case law was a source of law. On first reading the early case law in French (no English version was then available), it would be

---

[10] See eg my Opinion in Case C-188/92 *TWD*. See ch 27.

seen that the judgments did not explicitly cite previous judgments, but repeated propositions from them, in identical language, but without giving their source.

The Court subsequently went a little further, in that it was willing to cite previous cases by name, but it was reluctant ever to admit that it was departing from them. That led to some uncertainty; and it could have caused particular difficulties in *HAG II*,[11] as David Keeling has pointed out in this volume,[12] since *HAG I*[13] was by then generally recognised as mistaken. When in *HAG II*, the converse situation came to the Court, that mistake was widely recognised.[14]

I duly gave an Opinion stating that the decision in *HAG I* should not be followed in *HAG II*.[15] One difficulty was, however, that, as Keeling also points out, the Court, even when it departed from an earlier decision, was not inclined to state that the earlier decision was wrong. To make such a statement might be to accept explicitly that judicial decisions could 'make law', contrary to a basic conception which had had strong support in some Member States. However, if there were no indication that the previous decision had been overruled, the result might then be that where a similar situation arose again, there would be two conflicting past decisions from which the national courts were free to choose, and the very purpose of the preliminary ruling system would be defeated. The Court did in effect, if not explicitly, overrule *HAG I*.[16]

Overall, it seems that there has been a significant, and welcome, convergence in the Court between the common law and civil law traditions.

III. THE CONTRIBUTION OF UK AGS: GENERAL PRINCIPLES OF LAW, INCLUDING FUNDAMENTAL RIGHTS

As is well known, the 'general principles of law' can be invoked to interpret, to supplement, and even to invalidate, provisions of EU law. The Court has been able, by the use of general principles, not only to fill gaps in the law, but also to draw on the national law of the Member States, thereby seeking to ensure that EU law reflects fundamental European constitutional and legal values. General principles can perhaps be regarded as elements of a form of common law, both in the sense of shared values, and as an embodiment of a case law system.

The general principles of law have been a fruitful source for mutual influences, including notably: the common law's influence on EU law, and vice versa. Moreover the general principles of law can themselves be regarded as shared: they are a source of law in civilian systems, as well as in the common law, and in all systems they have evolved through case law of the national courts.

A. The Right to be Heard

A good illustration of a very early example of the consideration of the impact of UK law following the UK's accession to the Community is the Opinion of AG Warner in *Transocean*

---

[11] Case C-10/89 *HAG II* ECLI:EU:C:1990:359.

[12] See ch 24.

[13] Case 192/73 *HAG I* ECLI:EU:C:1974:72.

[14] Even by me. However, I should add that shortly after *HAG I*, and well before my time as an AG, I had written an academic article defending the Court's judgment in *HAG I*. See FG Jacobs, 'Industrial Property and the EEC Treaty: A Reply' (1975) 24 *ICLQ* 643.

[15] See Opinion of AG Jacobs in Case C-10/89 *HAG II* ECLI:EU:C:1990:112.

[16] The debate still continues on if, and how, the Court should overrule itself. See eg Opinion of AG Bobek in Case C-205/20 *Bezirkshauptmannschaft Hartberg-Fürstenfeld* ECLI:EU:C:2021:759.

Marine Paint Association, which was delivered in 1974.[17] The applicant complained that the Commission had imposed a condition when granting an exemption from the application of the competition rules, without giving the applicant the opportunity to comment on the matter.

The 'right to be heard' was regarded in English law as one of the principles of 'natural justice'. It was recognised also, if not always as broad in scope, in other national legal systems. The issue is addressed by AG Warner in characteristic style. Having accepted certain arguments advanced by the Commission, he continued:

> That, however, is, in my opinion, far from being the end of the question.

> There is a rule embedded in the law of some of our countries that an administrative authority, before wielding a statutory power to the detriment of a particular person, must in general hear what that person has to say about the matter, even if the statute does not expressly require it. 'Audi alteram partem' or, as it is sometimes expressed, 'audiatur et altera pars'. I say that the rule applies 'in general' because it is subject to exceptions, as are most legal principles.

> In the law of England the rule is centuries old, firmly established and of daily application. It is considered to be a 'rule of natural justice', a somewhat flamboyant and sometimes criticized phrase embodying a concept akin to what is, in French-speaking countries, more soberly and, I think, more accurately, referred to as *les principes généraux du droit*.[18]

Having started from 'the law of some of our countries', then from English law, AG Warner referred briefly to other national systems. He reached the conclusion that the applicant's right to be heard had not been respected, and that in consequence the relevant part of the Commission's decision had to be annulled. The Court took the same view. Similar issues arose subsequently in *Bearings I*.[19]

B. Legal Professional Privilege

A second potential example of 'general principles of law' which is of special interest is the principle of legal professional privilege. Again, it was a principle broadly recognised in English law, and it became especially important in the context of competition law, but it was recognised less widely in some other Member States.

The scope and applicability of the principle were considered in successive proceedings by AG Warner and again, unusually, in a further Opinion of an AG, by AG Slynn in *AM&S Europe*,[20] which makes the case of particular interest. However, as it has been analysed earlier in this book,[21] I need only refer to that discussion.

C. Proportionality

Notwithstanding the importance of fundamental rights, considered below, probably the most significant, the most pervasive and the most influential principle of EU law is the principle

---

[17] Opinion of AG Warner in Case 17/74 *Transocean Marine Paint Association* ECLI:EU:C:1974:91.
[18] Page 1088 of the Opinion.
[19] See ch 11.
[20] Opinion of AG Warner in Case 155/79 *AM&S* ECLI:EU:C:1981:9; Opinion of AG Slynn in Case 155/79 *AM&S* ECLI:EU:C:1982:17.
[21] See ch 14.

of proportionality, introduced partly under the influence of German law, as German courts would refer cases to the Court, and would question whether provisions of EU law might infringe that principle. The principle was subsequently spelt out in Article 5(4) TEU, second paragraph.[22]

The principle has also been making its way in English public law where proportionality is now seen by many as a more structured and more satisfactory guide to the validity of public measures than the traditional yardstick known as '*Wednesbury* unreasonableness'.[23]

D. Fundamental Rights

Fundamental rights have had a chequered career in EU law. The founding Treaties contained no provisions on fundamental rights, with certain provisions prohibiting specific forms of discrimination as a possible exception. Initially, the Court rejected challenges to Community measures on grounds of fundamental rights, possibly in the interest of preserving the primacy of Community law. But around 1970, shortly before UK accession, the Court changed its position, basing that change of position on the general principles of law. The Court held that 'respect for fundamental rights forms an integral part of the general principles of law protected by the Court of Justice'.[24]

Over the next 40 years, there was a gradually developing case law on fundamental rights. Both the Court and the ECtHR often followed, and remarkably, occasionally cited, each other's case law. However, the advent of the EU Charter of Fundamental Rights seemed to reduce references by the Court to the European Convention on Human Rights (ECHR) and to the ECtHR case law, even though the Charter expressly requires the provisions on the basic civil and political rights in the Charter to be interpreted in the same way as the corresponding provisions of the ECHR.[25]

The developing relations between the two courts were remarkably illustrated by the *Bosphorus* case.[26] Here the context was the seizure by the Irish authorities of an aircraft leased by the Turkish airline Bosphorus Airways from Yugoslav Airlines, pursuant to an EC Council Regulation giving effect to the United Nations sanctions regime against the Federal Republic of Yugoslavia (Serbia and Montenegro).[27] Bosphorus Airways considered that, as an innocent third party, it had been deprived of its property rights in breach of Article 1 of the First Protocol to the ECHR.

On a reference from the Supreme Court of Ireland, the Court held, broadly following my Opinion, as discussed by Piet Eeckhout,[28] and referring likewise to the ECHR, that the Council Regulation did not infringe the company's fundamental rights. When the company took its case to the ECtHR in Strasbourg, the ECtHR was able to take the view that the protection of fundamental rights in Community law was equivalent to that of the ECHR. Remarkably, the

---

[22] 'Under the principle of proportionality, the content and form of Union action shall not exceed what is necessary to achieve the objectives of the Treaties'.

[23] *Associated Provincial Picture Houses v Wednesbury Corporation* [1948] 1 KB 223.

[24] Case 11/70 *Internationale Handelsgesellschaft* ECLI:EU:C:1970:114, para 4.

[25] Charter of Fundamental Rights [2016] OJ C202/390, Article 52(3).

[26] Case C-84/95 *Bosphorus* ECLI:EU:C:1996:312.

[27] Regulation (EEC) No 990/93 concerning trade between the European Economic Community and the Federal Republic of Yugoslavia (Serbia and Montenegro) [1993] OJ L102/14.

[28] See my Opinion in Case C-84/95 *Bosphorus* ECLI:EU:C:1996:179, see ch 30.

ECtHR held that there would normally be no need for it to review measures taken in compliance with Community law: there was a presumption (but a rebuttable presumption) that action taken in compliance with Community law met the requirements of the Convention. This was the Bosphorus doctrine of Convention-compliance by the EU, which continues to this day. This judgment of the ECtHR, delivered on 30 June 2005, was to be the high point in the relations between the two courts.

E. Accession of the EU to the ECHR

From time to time, over a long period, the issue of possible EU accession to the ECHR surfaced and re-surfaced. I happened to come into it rather early, when the European Commission in 1979 made an unexpected proposal that the then European Community should accede to the ECHR. The House of Lords' very effective scrutiny committee, under the very able guidance of Sir Charles Sopwith, opened an examination of the proposal, and I was one of two advisers to the Committee. However, the issue may have seemed somewhat premature at that time, both because it was doubtful whether the Community had competence under the Treaties to accede to the ECHR, and because the Convention was open only to states. The proposal of the European Commission was not maintained.

Nevertheless, the idea continued to attract interest, and the issue came to the Court later, when I was AG. Some Member States (but not the UK) were, at that time, in favour of EU accession. Belgium, which held the presidency of the Union, referred to the Court the issue of the Community's competence under the Treaties to accede under the Opinion procedure, as set down in Article 228(6) EC (now Article 218(11) TFEU), and the case was lodged as *Opinion 2/94*.

At that time, the Court gave its opinion on such requests after *consulting* (or hearing) all the Advocates General,[29] but the procedure, at the time, did not require fully fledged opinions from AGs. The Opinion of the Court was negative:[30] the Community lacked the necessary competence to accede in the absence of amendment to the EC Treaty.

Subsequently the issue arose again in the context of the failed European Constitution and the subsequent Treaty of Lisbon, and the outcome was remarkable: the Treaty of Lisbon did not merely empower the EU to accede to the Convention, but imposed an obligation on the EU to do so;[31] and the Council of Europe (CoE), for its part, succeeded in obtaining an amendment to the Convention by all 47 states of the CoE, so as to enable the EU to accede to it. There followed detailed negotiations, in which both the ECtHR and the Court took an active part, and all significant outstanding issues seemed to be resolved in the agreement for accession of the EU to the ECHR.

However, when the Court was asked for an Opinion on that draft accession agreement, it stated several objections, some of which were considered by observers very difficult to resolve. That Opinion, *Opinion 2/13*,[32] has been much criticised. It is to be hoped that the matter can be satisfactorily resolved without further delay.

---

[29] At the time, there were nine AGs. My fellow colleagues were AGs Tesauro, Lenz, La Pergola, Cosmas, Léger, Elmer, Fennelly, and Ruiz-Jarabo Colomer. Much later, the Rules of Procedure of the Court were changed to allow a single AG to be heard, and thus, deliver a View/Opinion. This first occurred in View of AG Jääskinen in *Opinion 1/13* ECLI:EU:C:2014:2292.

[30] *Opinion 2/94* ECLI:EU:C:1996:140.

[31] Article 6(2) TEU.

[32] *Opinion 2/13* ECLI:EU:C:2014:2454.

F. Languages

An important change when Denmark, Ireland, and the UK joined the Community in 1973 was that English (and also Danish) became one of the official Community languages, and one of the languages used in cases before the Court. English is normally used in cases from Ireland, as well as from the UK.

In each case before the Court, one language is designated 'the language of the case', and is to be used by the parties and by the European institutions. The Member States have the right to use their own language. In references, the language of the case is the language of the national court making the reference. In direct actions, it is generally the language of the applicant, but in cases brought by the Commission against a Member State, it is the language of the Member State.

Before the first enlargement, the official languages were French, German, Italian, and Dutch. Currently there are more than 20 official languages. The successive enlargements have had the impact of reducing familiarity with French in the EU, and consolidating the role of English. A striking recent illustration of the growing significance of the English language in Europe is the announcement from Finland that Helsinki is to be considered as an English-speaking city.

At the Court, in 1973, when I was a *référendaire* for AG Warner, both the working language and the social language were French. The social language later changed to English, but the working language, in which the judges deliberate and the judgments are drafted, has remained French. That has relatively limited impact on AGs, and personally I have a strong affection for the French language; but it has considerable implications for judges and their *référendaires*, who are required to work in French, both in the preparation of draft judgments and in their deliberations together. The subject of the Court's working language has been addressed by my former colleague as UK judge on the Court, Sir Konrad Schiemann, in a publication written in French.[33]

IV. AFTERWORD

I see it as my great good fortune that I was able to play a part in what, on any view, was, and remains, a remarkable process of international cooperation. As I (and others) see it, the EU is very different from other forms of transnational organisation. As a broad generalisation, history suggests that states in the past were essentially concerned to damage other states, and indeed that this was one of their main objectives: either by waging war, if they considered themselves stronger, or by so-called 'diplomatic' means. Even in international organisations, which have developed greatly in recent years, major powers have sometimes frustrated their activities and taken advantage of their own political strength to harm other members.

The EU is different: experience has shown that the EU Member States benefit from each other's success. They avoid doing one another harm. They have conferred great financial advantages on less well-off Member States. They treat each other's nationals as genuine equals. Hostility between European nations, which many of us can vividly remember from the recent

---

[33] K Schiemann, 'La langue de travail de la Cour' in A Tizzano, A Rosas, R Silva de Lapuerta, K Lenaerts and J Kokott (eds), *La Cour de justice de l'Union européenne sous la présidence de Vassilios Skouris (2003–2015). Liber Amicorum Vassilios Skouris* (Brussels, Bruylant, 2015).

past, has largely been replaced by friendship. In the European institutions, there is a practice of avoiding measures which will harm a Member State. Indeed a very high proportion of measures are adopted without a vote being necessary; they are adopted by consensus.

A further and perhaps unique feature of the EU is that it is genuinely based on the rule of law. Its institutions and its Member States respect the decisions of the Court. While understandably not content with all its decisions, the Member States, in their capacity as authors of the Treaties, have regularly sought to amend the Treaties to strengthen the position of the Court: notably by extending its jurisdiction.

The Member States have also amended the Treaties to empower the Court to impose fines and periodic penalty payments on the Member States themselves where they fail to comply with judgments of the Court. This reform was under active consideration during my time as AG, and was supported by the UK. This too is a unique feature of the EU. It is a striking demonstration of concern for the rule of law.[34]

---

[34] Article 260 TFEU. See, for instance, Case C-278/01 *Commission v Spain* ECLI:EU:C:2003:635; Case C-304/02 *Commission v France* ECLI:EU:C:2005:444; C-568/07 *Commission v Greece* ECLI:EU:C:2009:342; Case C-496/09 *Commission v Italy* ECLI:EU:C:2011:740. Financial penalties may also be imposed as interim measures. See Case C-121/21 R *Czech Republic v Poland* ECLI:EU:C:2021:752.

51

Reflections of a Judge Acting as Advocate General in the Court of First Instance: 1990–1992

DAVID EDWARD

I. INTRODUCTION

I am very grateful to Richard Whish for setting out so clearly the essentials of these two cases – *Automec* and *Asia Motor France*.[1] I will begin by explaining the circumstances in which my single Opinion came to be written, leading into some thoughts about the difference between the roles of the judges and the AGs in the EU courts. I shall address the point identified by Whish on which the judgment of the Court of First Instance (CFI) may be thought to differ significantly from my Opinion, and finally add some additional reflections on the background to the two cases.

The circumstances in which my Opinion in *Automec* and *Asia Motor France* came to be written were unusual. The Opinion is dated 10 March 1992. That was the day I moved from the CFI to the Court of Justice (the Court). At 09:30, the First Chamber of the CFI, of which I was a member, delivered judgment in the last batch of the *Polyropylene* cases.[2] At 11:00, we delivered judgment in the *Italian Flat Glass* case, where I was Reporting Judge (*juge rapporteur*).[3] I delivered my Opinion in *Automec* and *Asia Motor France* that afternoon, and at 17:00, I was sworn in as a Judge of the Court.

Alongside my colleagues, I was one of the first members of the CFI upon its establishment in 1989.[4] Some two years later, just before Christmas 1991, I was nominated by the UK to succeed Sir Gordon Slynn at the Court. My appointment by the Member States was not made until 29 January 1992.[5] Consequently, all the cases in which I was involved in the CFI had to

---

[1] Opinion of Judge Edward acting as Advocate General in Case T-24/90 *Automec* and Case T-28/90 *Asia Motor France* ECLI:EU:T:1992:39. See ch 23.

[2] Cases T-9/89 *Hüls* ECLI:EU:T:1992:31; T-10/89 *Hoechst* ECLI:EU:T:1992:32; T-11/89 *Shell* ECLI:EU:T:1992:33; T-12/89 *Solvay* ECLI:EU:T:1992:34; T-13/89 *ICI* ECLI:EU:T:1992:35; T-14/89 *Montedipe* ECLI:EU:T:1992:36; and T-15/89 *Chemie* Linz ECLI:EU:T:1992:37.

[3] Joined Cases T-68/89, T-77/89 and T-78/89 *SIV* ECLI:EU:T:1992:38.

[4] My colleagues were José Luís da Cruz Vilaça, Donal Barrington, Antonio Saggio, Heinrich Kirschner, Christos Yeraris, Romain Schintgen, Cornelius Paulus Briët, Bo Vesterdorf, Rafael García-Valdecasas y Fernández, Jacques Biancarelli, and Koen Lenaerts.

[5] See Decision of the Representatives of the Governments of the Member States of the European Communities of 29 January 1992 appointing a Judge to the Court of Justice (92/74/EEC, Euratom, ECSC) [1992] OJ L30/22.

be completed and translated in the space of two months. The CFI had been set up to deal with 'actions requiring a close examination of complex facts'.[6] The *Polypropylene* and *Italian Flat Glass* cases certainly met that criterion, while *Automec* and *Asia Motor France* were not factually complex, but raised important legal issues.

Completion of the judgments in *Polypropylene* was thrown into disarray by the Second Chamber of the CFI's judgment on 27 February 1992 in the *PVC* cases, which had held that the Decision of the Commission was 'non-existent'.[7] This was immediately picked up by the parties in the *Polypropylene* cases, who applied for the procedure to be reopened, so that the Commission's Decision could be re-examined. By that time, judgment had been pronounced in all the preceding *Polypropylene* cases, and the judgments in this last batch had been agreed and were in the last stages of translation. We had therefore to reconvene, hear the AG (Judge Vesterdorf), decide how the application should be dealt with and approve three additional paragraphs refusing the application. Fortunately, the *juge rapporteur*, Judge Lenaerts, was a fast mover.

In these rather frantic weeks, I had to complete my draft judgment as *juge rapporteur* in *Italian Flat Glass*, and see it through deliberation and translation. So I did not have much time to write my Opinion in *Automec* and *Asia Motor France*. Fortunately, the logistical process of moving from one court to the other was in the capable hands of my *référendaire*, Elizabeth Willocks, and my secretary, Diane Ingram.[8] Our *stagiaire* at the time, Chris Thomas, had been working on *Automec* and *Asia Motor France*, and had compiled an exhaustive dossier of all the relevant texts and other materials, with helpful ideas as to how they might be handled. But it was for me to write the Opinion.

II. THE DIFFERENCE BETWEEN JUDGMENTS AND OPINIONS IN THE LUXEMBOURG COURTS

One of Dicey's lectures delivered at Harvard Law School in 1898 (later published as *Law and Opinion in England*)[9] was entitled – rather surprisingly – 'Judicial Legislation'. He began:

> As all lawyers are aware, a large part and, as many would add, the best part of the law of England is judge-made law .... Judicial legislation aims to a far greater extent than do enactments passed by Parliament, at the maintenance of the logic or the symmetry of the law.[10]

This contrasts with the approach of code-based systems, encapsulated, at its most brutal, in Article 5 of the French Civil Code (the *Code Napoléon*):

> It is forbidden for judges, in pronouncing on the cases submitted to them, to make rulings of general or regulatory application.[11]

---

[6] Council Decision 88/591/ECSC, EEC, Euratom of 24 October 1988 establishing a Court of First Instance of the European Communities [1988] OJ L319/1.

[7] Joined Cases T-79/89, T-84/89, T-85/89, T-86/89, T-89/89, T-91/89, T-92/89, T-94/89, T-96/89, T-98/89, T-102/89 and T-104/89 *BASF* ECLI:EU:T:1992:26.

[8] For an account of life at the Court, see D Hansen-Ingram 'Tales from the Tartan Chambers' in M Hoskins and W Robinson (eds), *A True European: Essays for Judge David Edward* (Oxford, Hart Publishing, 2004) 1.

[9] AV Dicey, *The Relation between Law and Opinion in England during the Nineteenth Century* (London, Macmillan, 1905), Lecture XI, 361 ff (in 2nd edn 1914).

[10] ibid, pp 361 and 364.

[11] 'Il est défendu aux juges de prononcer par voie de disposition générale et réglementaire sur les causes qui leur sont soumises'.

The latter approach to the business of judging is, to some extent, reflected in the practice of the EU courts, the essential task of the judges being seen as that of deciding the cases as pleaded. In direct actions, for example under Article 263 TFEU – unlike preliminary references under Article 267 TFEU – the normal practice is to organise the judgment according to the *conclusions* ('forms of order sought') and *moyens* ('pleas-in-law') advanced by the claimant/applicant. The English terminology disguises the underlying logic: the *moyens* are the route to the *conclusions* (*media concludendi*). The task of the judges is to determine whether the *moyens* have been established so that the *conclusions* have been made good, and not to proceed further to make a better case for the parties (*ne iudex ultra petita partium*).

It is true that the style of the judgments of the EU courts has changed considerably, with today's judgments being altogether different from those of the early years (arguably, for the better). Nevertheless, the writing style is designed to be dry and impersonal. As one of my colleagues in the CFI said when I presented my first draft judgment: 'This is a good opinion: now we must make it aseptic'.

The eventual judgment is the product of the process of deliberation, described to me by one of my then seniors as 'the heart of our activity'.[12] All Judges are sworn 'to preserve the secrecy of the deliberations of the Court'.[13] While some judgments are uncontentious, others may give rise to serious, sometimes heated, disagreements and, if necessary, a formal vote. In my time, the deliberations in very difficult cases stretched over many weeks with many fresh drafts, the aim being to achieve a legally coherent result (not, as is sometimes supposed, to achieve unanimity).[14] For me, presenting an argument to my colleagues could occasionally be as challenging as arguing a case before the House of Lords.[15] In the end, there could be so many changes in the draft that I was unable to remember how I had voted at the beginning.

A further constraint on the style of judgments at the EU courts is that they are drafted and agreed in a single language (normally French), and must then be translated into the other official languages. This leaves little scope for nuance, and sometimes leads to serious misunderstandings.[16]

Consequently, it is one of the penalties (and sometimes an advantage) of the life of judges at the EU courts that they cannot 'speak with their own voice' in the way that judges do in the common law system. Their influence can be traced in cases where they have been *rapporteur*[17] and they can, of course, express personal opinions in lectures, and in academic writings, as long as the secrecy of the deliberations is maintained.[18]

---

[12] Judge Grévisse (1981–82, 1988–94) said 'Le délibéré est le coeur de notre activité'. He was a fine gentleman, with none of the *hauteur* of the Enarch, but I did not know that he was a hero of the resistance until we learned that his funeral in 2002 began with full military honours at *Les Invalides*.

[13] Article 2 of the Statute of the Court of Justice of the European Union [2016] OJ C202/210.

[14] The judges' signatures at the end of the judgment signify only that the statutory quorum was present (see Article 17 of the Statute of the Court), not that all the judges agreed with the result.

[15] When I presented my first draft to the Court as a new member in 1992, Judge Joliet tore into it. The next day, he apologised, to which I replied 'Ce n'est rien. C'est la vie du barreau'. He replied, 'That's the difference between me and you. You are an advocate: I am a professor and a professor expects to be right'.

[16] See below for an example arising in this case. More serious examples are the English text of the judgment in Case 26/62 *Van Gend en Loos* ECLI:EU:C:1963:1, which loses the tautly drawn structure of the original French; and Joined Cases C-46/93 and C-48/93 *Brasserie du Pêcheur* ECLI:EU:C:1996:79, where crucial words appear as 'une violation suffisamment caractérisée' in French and the equivalent in some languages, by contrast with 'a sufficiently serious breach' in English and some others.

[17] A so-far-untilled field of enquiry for an aspiring academic, perhaps.

[18] See eg my contribution to a recent *Festschrift*. D Edward, 'What Was Keck Really About?' in F Amtenbrink, G Davies, D Kochenov, and J Lindeboom (eds), *The Internal Market and the Future of European Integration: Essays in Honour of Laurence W. Gormley* (Cambridge, CUP, 2018).

By contrast, the AGs speak with their own voice in their own language.[19] Their Opinions are the starting point of the judges' deliberations,[20] and will (ideally) show how the Court can, in Dicey's words, 'maintain the logic or the symmetry of the law'. A consequence is that, in the common law world at least:

> [T]he Opinion of the Advocate General, written by one individual in his/her mother tongue, is often seen as much more coherent, persuasive and logical exposition of reasoning than the judgment itself.[21]

My appointment by the President of the CFI to act as AG in *Automec* and *Asia Motor France* was an unusual opportunity to speak with my own voice in my mother tongue. I was the fourth and the last judge of the CFI (now General Court) to be given that opportunity.

III. ADVOCATES GENERAL IN THE COURT OF FIRST INSTANCE

When the CFI was set up in 1989, there were 12 Member States, with one judge being appointed from each. Our jurisdiction was limited to actions for annulment of Decisions of the Commission in competition cases, and to staff cases where the CFI played the role of employment appeal tribunal (a role that was transferred for a period to the EU Civil Service Tribunal).[22] Outstanding cases before the Court were transferred to the CFI, so we began with a ready-made caseload, with some of it several years behindhand.

The Court was organised into two Chambers (First and Second) for competition cases, and four for staff cases (Third, Fourth, Fifth, and Sixth). Initially, in some cases of general importance, the Court decided to sit in plenary formation. As there were 12 judges in all, and six in each of the larger Chambers, one had to be left out to maintain the principle that the Court is always composed of an uneven number of judges.

In four cases, the judge who was not sitting, was asked to act as AG: Judge Kirschner in *TetraPak*,[23] Judge Vesterdorf in the *Polypropylene* cases,[24] Judge Biancarelli in *Peine Salzgitter*,[25] and myself in *Automec* and *Asia Motor France*.[26] For an unexplained reason, we were styled differently in the reports of these cases.[27] The experiment has not been repeated ever since, and not even in the General Court, despite the increased number of judges. I do not know why.

---

[19] See ch 52 by AG Sharpston, who points out that whilst AGs can technically write in any language they wish, for the sake of expediency, they typically write in one of the Court's more mainstream languages, such as English or French. This practice began in my time at the Court when the mother tongue of some AGs was a minority language.

[20] 'Le commencement de notre délibéré', in Judge Grévisse's words.

[21] R Greaves, 'Judge Edward acting as Advocate General' in Hoskins and Robinson (n 8) 91.

[22] See G Butler, 'An Interim Post-Mortem: Specialised Courts in the EU Judicial Architecture after the Civil Service Tribunal' (2020) 17 *International Organizations Law Review* 586.

[23] Opinion of Mr Kirschner, Judge in the Court of First Instance in Case T-51/89 *Tetra Pak* ECLI:EU:T:1990:15.

[24] Opinion of Mr Vesterdorf acting as Advocate General in Case T-1/89 *Rhône-Poulenc* ECLI:EU:T:1991:38.

[25] Opinion of Judge Biancarelli of the Court of First Instance in Case T-120/89 *Stahlwerke Peine-Salzgitter* ECLI:EU:T:1991:6.

[26] Opinion of Judge Edward acting as Advocate General in Case T-24/90 *Automec* and Case T-28/90 *Asia Motor France* ECLI:EU:T:1992:39.

[27] See immediately preceding footnotes on the discrepancies.

IV. THE LEGAL BACKGROUND TO *AUTOMEC* AND *ASIA MOTOR FRANCE*

The EEC Treaty laid down in peremptory terms the role and obligations of the Commission:[28]

> In order to ensure the proper functioning and development of the Common Market, the Commission *shall*:
>
> — *ensure* that the provisions of this Treaty and the measures taken by the institutions pursuant thereto are applied; ...
> — *exercise the powers conferred on it* by the Council for the implementation of the rules laid down by the latter.[29]

Having set out the familiar competition rules in Articles 85 and 86 EEC (now Articles 101 and 102 TFEU),[30] the Treaty provided that:

> [T]he Commission *shall*, as soon as it takes up its duties, *ensure* the application of the principles laid down in Article 85 and 86. ...[31]

Regulation 17/62 implementing Articles 85 and 86 EEC (now Articles 101 and 102 TFEU) conferred on the Commission wide powers to enforce the Rules on Competition, referring to the Commission's '*duty* of ensuring that the provisions of the Treaty are applied'.[32]

For some years, the Commission actively encouraged complaints about anticompetitive practices falling within the scope of Articles 85 and 86 EEC (now Articles 101 and 102 TFEU). Indeed, there was a saying that the cost to the complainer was the price of a postage stamp. During the 1970s, the *Distillers* saga[33] and the *John Deere* saga[34] were instigated by a whisky bottler in Glasgow and a farmer in the Scottish Borders.

As late as 1989, a Commission publication addressed to Small and Medium Sized Enterprises claimed that:

> When a complaint is submitted by a party having a legitimate interest in the matter, the Commission will examine whether a violation of the competition rules is in fact taking place.[35]

In truth, the volume of work, and the failure of the Member States to fund sufficient staff, became such that the Directorate General for Competition (DGIV) in the Commission could no longer deal effectively with all the complaints that were made to it, let alone fulfil its other commitments in the field of competition, notably state aid. As a House of Lords Select Committee pointed out in 1985, DGIV had a staff of 140 lawyers and economists, respectively

---

[28] Articles 155–163 EEC, not replicated as such in the TEU or the TFEU.

[29] Article 155 EEC (emphasis added).

[30] Now Articles 101–109 TFEU.

[31] Article 89 EEC (emphasis added).

[32] EEC Council Regulation No 17, First Regulation implementing Articles 85 and 86 of the Treaty [1962] OJ 13/204, tenth recital.

[33] Commission Decision of 20 December 1977 (IV/28.282) upheld by the Court of Justice in Case 30/78 *Distillers* ECLI:EU:C:1980:186.

[34] Commission Decision of 17 February 1992 (IV/31.370 and 31.446) upheld by the CFI in Case T-35/92 *John Deere* ECLI:EU:T:1994:259, and on appeal by the Court in Case 7/95P *John Deere* ECLI:EU:C:1998:256.

[35] *EEC Competition Rules – Guide for Small and Medium Sized Enterprises*, November 1983, p 46, republished as *EEC Competition Policy in the Single Market*, March 1989, p 48.

one tenth and one half respectively of the number available to the federal anti-trust authorities of the United States and the German Cartel Office.[36]

A brief paragraph in the Commission's Report on Competition Policy published in 1988 set out its 'Criteria for selecting cases':

> In general where cases involve questions of broad political significance the Commission will afford them priority. For cases brought at the Commission's own initiative and for complaints, the seriousness of the alleged infraction will be considered. Additionally where complaints and notifications are involved the urgency of obtaining a quick decision requires to be taken into account. An example of this situation would be where national legal proceedings are pending ....[37]

As I observed in my Opinion in *Automec* and *Asia Motor France*,[38] these criteria were, to say the least, telegraphic, and they did not include any reference to the presence or absence of a 'Community interest' in prosecuting a case. It was therefore important to define more precisely the obligations of the Commission in dealing with competition complaints in such a way as to preserve the integrity of the Treaty texts, while recognising the practical reality of the Commission's position.

That is what I set out to do, as did the CFI with apparent success, and the '*Automec* doctrine' entered the language of EU competition law.

V. TWO POINTS ON THE COURT'S JUDGMENT

First, there is an apparent divergence between my Opinion and the CFI's Judgment. However, I think this reflects the difference between the function of the AG and that of the Court, which I discussed above. Secondly, there is an interesting problem of translation that may be obscured in the English translation of the Judgment.

In my Opinion, I had to consider the two reasons given by the Commission for rejecting Automec's complaint: first, the Commission's lack of power to issue a positive injunction requiring BMW to resume supplies to Automec, and secondly, the availability of relief in the Italian courts.[39]

On the first point, I stated:

> I do not find the argument based on the lack of a power of injunction convincing. In effect, the Commission says to Automec: 'You ask us to pronounce an order requiring BMW to resume supplies; we cannot pronounce such an order; therefore, we reject your complaint'. But the question for the Commission is not whether it has power to grant the order sought. The first question to be considered, as the Court said in *CICCE*, is whether the competition rules of the Treaty have been infringed. If, but only if, the Commission finds that the competition rules have been infringed, does any question arise as to the order to be pronounced. If the Commission, having established an infringement, cannot pronounce the order the complainer seeks, it can undoubtedly pronounce an order requiring the infringement to be brought to an end and impose fines and periodic penalty payments to enforce that order. Such an order may well have the same practical effect as a positive injunction.'[40]

---

[36] See the Report of the House of Lords Select Committee on the European Communities, *European Union*, 14th Report of Session 1984–85, para 51 at p xxi, and the evidence of Dr Ehlermann and Dr Glaesner at p 106, QQ.165-66.

[37] *Seventeenth Report on Competition Policy*, Office for Official Publications, Luxembourg, 1988, para 9, p 23.

[38] Para 104 of the Opinion.

[39] Para 106 ff of the Opinion.

[40] Para 107 of the Opinion.

I therefore took the view that the first reason for rejecting Automec's complaint was unsound, and that it was unnecessary to consider whether the Commission has power under Article 85 EEC (now Article 101 TFEU) to pronounce a positive injunction.

Whish says that the CFI did not follow me on this point,[41] and dealt with the issue in three perfunctory paragraphs, based on the principle of freedom of contract.[42] It is certainly true that that is what the Judgment appears to say in paragraphs 51–53. However, I think the apparent divergence is due to the way in which the Judgment is set out, although it is admittedly not entirely clear.

In paragraph 47, the CFI had said that it would deal first with Automec's contention that BMW Italia was obliged to take several specific steps to comply with Community law, notably to supply Automec with vehicles and spare parts and to appoint it as a distributor within its selective distribution system.[43] Paragraphs 51–53 of the Judgment, as I read them, address the limited point as to whether the Commission had power to order BMW to take those specific steps. In the immediately following paragraph (54), the Court went on to state:

> In particular, there cannot be held to be any justification for such a restriction on freedom of contract where several remedies exist for bringing an infringement to an end. This is true of infringements of Article 85(1) arising out of the application of a distribution system. Such infringements can also be eliminated by the abandonment or amendment of the distribution system. Consequently, the Commission undoubtedly has the power to find that an infringement exists and to order the parties concerned to bring it to an end, but it is not for the Commission to impose upon the parties its own choice from among all the various potential courses of action which are in conformity with the Treaty.

Whish considers that this approach was inconsistent with a judgment of the Court many years previously in *Commercial Solvents*, where a positive order was pronounced.[44] In that case, the Court held that:

> [Article 3 of Regulation 17] must be applied in relation to the infringement which has been established and may include an order to do certain acts or provide certain advantages which have been wrongfully withheld as well as prohibiting the continuation of certain acts, practices of situations which are contrary to the Treaty.[45]

In *Commercial Solvents*, which was a case under Article 86 EEC (now Article 102 TFEU), the Commission's order was that certain minimum quantities of raw material be supplied to make good the unlawful refusal of supply. There is, I think, a difference between an order requiring an undertaking that has been proved to hold a dominant position to make good an unlawful refusal to supply raw materials, and an order requiring a non-dominant undertaking to do what Automec wanted. (Automec did not invoke Article 86 EEC (now Article 102 TFEU), as it might possibly have done.)

Leaving aside that particular issue, it is worth drawing attention to a problem of translation in paragraph 76 of the CFI's judgment, which reads rather oddly in English:

> As the Commission is under no obligation to rule on the existence or otherwise of an infringement it cannot be compelled to carry out an investigation, because such investigation could have

---

[41] See ch 23.
[42] See s IV(A) of ch 23.
[43] See para 5 of the Judgment, last sentence.
[44] Joined Cases 6/73 and 7/73 *Commercial Solvents* ECLI:EU:C:1974:18.
[45] Para 17 of the Judgment in *Commercial Solvents*.

no purpose other than to seek evidence of the existence or otherwise of an infringement, which it is not required to establish. In that regard, it should be noted that, unlike the provision contained in the second sentence of Article 89(1) in relation to applications by Member States, Regulations Nos 17 and 99/63 do not expressly oblige the Commission to investigate complaints submitted to it.

The reasoning is not obvious and the reasoning in the next-but-one paragraph (78) to distinguish *Automec* from established case law of the Court, particularly *Demo-Studio Schmidt*,[46] may seem rather lame and unconvincing. However, the explanation lies, at least in part, in the words used in the original French text and the words of the English translation. The words used in the French text of the judgment corresponding to 'investigation' and 'investigate' are *mener une instruction* and *instruire*. The point being made is that the Commission cannot be compelled to proceed to the formal process of investigation provided for in Article 14 of Regulation 17, which is a necessary preliminary to a formal Decision. The obligations of the Commission are set out in paragraph 80 and following of the CFI Judgment.

VI. POSTSCRIPT

I have found it interesting when studying a procedural case to understand the underlying facts of the case and something of its historical context.[47] The procedural issues in *Automec* and *Asia Motor France* were incidental to two long-running disputes about the distribution of motor vehicles. *Automec* arose in the context of selective distribution agreements, *Asia Motor France* in the context of the French 'unofficial' quota on imports of Japanese cars.

A. *Automec*

The restriction of competition inherent in a selective distribution agreement is, in principle, contrary to Article 101(1) TFEU, unless the agreement is exempted, either individually or by category ('block exemption') under Article 101(3). As technology has advanced[48] and consumers have come to demand specialist service and maintenance and enforceable guarantees, the Commission has been favourable to selective agreements because the benefits to consumers outweigh the disbenefit of restricting competition. Apart from a series of general block exemption Regulations, a special Regulation (123/85) was enacted specific to the motor industry.[49] Inevitably, there were winners and losers, and Automec were one of the losers.

---

[46] Case 210/81 *Demo-Studio Schmidt* ECLI:EU:C:1983:277.

[47] AL Goodhart, 'Determining the *Ratio Decidendi of a Case*' (1930) 40 *Yale Law Journal* 161. This article sparked off a torrent of debate and philosophical argument about the way in which courts decide cases. See, for citation of some of the abundant literature, RG Scofield, 'Goodhart's Concession: Defending Ratio Decidendi from Logical Positivism and Legal Realism in the First Half of the Twentieth Century' (2005) 16 *King's Law Journal* 311.

[48] When I bought my first car in 1961, it could be repaired and serviced by the motor mechanic who had a small workshop in a nearby lane. It went to the dealer once a year for its check-up. Cars have developed to such an extent that electric cars have become 'computers on wheels', where the electronics are far more important than the mechanics and require the attention of specialists.

[49] Commission Regulation (EEC) No 123/85 of 12 December 1984 on the application of Article 85(3) of the Treaty to certain categories of motor vehicle distribution and servicing agreements [1985] OJ L15/16.

The effect of Regulation 123/85 was to grant exemption to agreements by which (in the words of the preamble[50]):

the supplying party entrusts to the reselling party the task of promoting the distribution and servicing of certain products of the motor vehicle industry in a defined area and by which the supplier undertakes to supply contract goods for resale only to the dealer, or only to a limited number of undertakings within the distribution network besides the dealer, within the contract territory.

The stated justification for the exemption was that:

Motor vehicle manufacturers cooperate with the selected dealers and repairers in order to provide specialized servicing for the product. On grounds of capacity and efficiency alone, such a form of cooperation cannot be extended to an unlimited number of dealers and repairers.[51]

One consequence of the exemption was to make it possible for a manufacturer like BMW to create a new distribution and repair network and, in so doing, to exclude established former dealers like Automec. Automec claimed to have been part of BMW's distribution system for 25 years and to have adapted its business to comply with the contractual requirements of BMW, including provision of an after sales service, a guarantee to the final purchaser, maintenance of a stock of cars and spare parts, and recruitment of suitably qualified staff, involving purchase of a large area of ground and construction of a new display and maintenance centre.[52]

Reliance on freedom of contract[53] was hardly a sufficient answer to Automec's complaint since, but for Regulation 123/85, BMW's exclusion of Automec and refusal to supply would have raised competition issues and might still have done so if Automec had approached its case differently.[54]

B. *Asia Motor France*

Our *Asia Motor France* case was only the second act in a long drama of litigation in which Asia Motor France, with others, tried to get the Commission to act against the 'unofficial' French quota on the import of Japanese vehicles.[55] The successive acts in the drama clarified some procedural points, without giving any satisfaction to the importers, and eventually reached a political solution with the Hague Declaration of 1991.[56]

---

[50] Para (1).

[51] Preamble, para (4).

[52] See paras 36 and 37 of my Opinion.

[53] See para 54 of the CFI judgment quoted above.

[54] For a contemporary explanation, for the benefit of American practitioners, of the mysteries of the EEC law of distribution agreements, see U Toepke, 'EEC Law of Competition: Distribution Agreements and Their Notification' (1985) 19 *The International Lawyer* 117.

[55] Case T-64/89 *Automec* ECLI:EU:T:1990:42; Case T-28/90 *Asia Motor France* ECLI:EU:1992:98; Case T-7/92 *Asia Motor France, Jean-Michel Cesbron* ECLI:EU:T:1993:52; Case T-387/94 *Asia Motor France* ECLI:EU:T:1996:120; Somaco's unsuccessful appeal in Case C-401/96P *Somaco* ECLI:EU:1998:208 (which Advocate General Tesauro optimistically described as 'the final round in a complex battle', see Opinion of AG Tesauro in Case C-401/96P *Somaco* ECLI:EU:C:1997:633, para 2); Case T-154/98 *Asia Motor France* ECLI:EU:T:2000:243 and the unsuccessful appeal Case C-1/01 P *Asia Motor France* ECLI:EU:C:2001:483.

[56] Joint Declaration on Relations between the European Community and its Member States and Japan, The Hague, 18 July 1991. For details of the history, see M Moguen-Toursel 'Defining a European vehicle' in HG Schroter (ed), *The European Enterprise: Historical Investigation into a Future Species* (NY, Springer, 2008) 67, 73.

There was undoubtedly a real (though perhaps exaggerated) concern in other Member States, as well as France, about the effect on domestic manufacturers of Japanese vehicle imports. This led to the imposition of national quotas. The French quota began 'unofficially' in 1978 and was announced publicly by President Giscard d'Estaing at the Paris Motor Show in 1980. It remained unofficial in the sense that it was handled in an opaque fashion by the Ministry of Industry in collaboration with the Ministry of Transport. Those responsible applied the quota, not only to direct imports from Japan, but also to imports from other Member States where they were already in free circulation. It was strongly felt in some quarters (inside the Commission too) that there was no conceivable legal reason why a Member State should be allowed to flout the fundamental principle of Community law against bans on parallel imports and, further, that the neutrality of the Commission as competition regulator was compromised by failure to act.

This raised a perennial problem about the position of the Commission as a political actor and, at the same time, the EU's competition regulator for the EU. The Commission is a political institution and must be aware of political realities and the practical consequences of any action it might take. On the other hand, public and business confidence in competition regulation requires that the regulator be, and be seen to be, politically neutral. The Member States, or some of them at any rate (the UK included), have established politically neutral competition regulators. For reasons best known to themselves, the Commission and the other EU institutions still refuse to bite the bullet.

I was aware of this problem as a former advocate with some experience in the field of competition. In my unusual capacity as AG, I felt it was important to ensure that that the Commission as regulator could not invoke vague concepts like 'political significance' or 'Community interest' as a fig leaf to conceal failure in analysis of the facts (as was later shown to have been the case in *CEAHR*)[57] or unwillingness to confront politically inconvenient facts.

The decisions in *Automec* and *Asia Motor France* may have offered little satisfaction to the litigants, but they did have the effect of imposing a legally enforceable discipline on the Commission as competition regulator.

---

[57] Case T-427/08 *CEAHR* ECLI:EU:T:2010:517.

52

'Can't Those European Judges Think for Themselves?' An Afterword on Why the Court (Still) Needs its Advocates General

ELEANOR SHARPSTON*

I. INTRODUCTION

I T is 2006, a few months after – to my astonishment and delight – I have been sworn in as an Advocate General (AG) to succeed Francis Jacobs. The scene is a university lecture hall somewhere in the UK. I am out 'on tour' ('en mission', to use the parlance of the Court), bringing the light of truth to the nations – or at least trying to help convey the message that the Court is modern, outgoing, and in touch with the citizen. I have done the main act and now it is question time. Always an awkward moment. Would some young student *please* pluck up the courage to ask me something? (Honestly: I do not bite, and I have *never* been known to eat a student alive, raw, and in public.) Ah, good, a hand goes up. I nod encouragingly. And then the question. 'Umm, I know it's not exactly what you were talking about ... but: why does the Court *need* Advocates General? Can't those European judges think for themselves?'

An unusual question, but a perfectly fair one.

In this afterword, I shall – as a renegade classicist – follow the lead given by Julius Caesar in *De Bello Gallico* ('Gallia est omnis divisa in partes tres' – 'All Gaul is divided into three parts')[1] and offer my commentary in three sections. I want first to look at some of the elements that (I hope) go into providing a plausible answer to the question put to me by that student

---

* I should like to thank two former members of 'team Sharpston' who responded valiantly to the familiar appeal, 'Could you possibly just have a quick look at this for me? It took me much longer to write than I had bargained for, so I am afraid that it's rather urgent (...)'. Appropriately, the two individuals in question represent, as it were, the early years and the final years of my time as an AG. Geert de Baere – now a distinguished judge at the General Court – spent three years with me as a *référendaire* from January 2007 to December 2009. Panagiota (Penny) Katsorchi joined the team as a *référendaire* in January 2017 and stuck with me to the bitter end: she is now (I am relieved to say) working as a *référendaire* with Judge Gervasoni at the General Court. I am extremely grateful to them both for their helpful critique of my draft. I am also grateful to my colleague and friend, Judge Ian Forrester (the former British judge at the General Court) for his characteristically pithy and accurate observations on an earlier draft.

[1] *De Bello Gallico*, 1.1.1. The statement may not have been entirely true at the time; but at least it has the merit of structural clarity and is blessedly easy to translate.

in 2006. Next, I shall highlight some aspects of actually doing the job of an AG, as it was done in 'team Sharpston' during my time at the Court. Finally, I shall ask some questions of my own (perhaps, typically awkward questions from an awkwardly independent AG) about the future of the AGs' role within the Court.

I emphasise that my remarks relate specifically to the court within the *institution* of the Court of Justice of the European Union in which I served – the Court of Justice ('the Court') – and *not* to the General Court. The work of the two jurisdictions is markedly different. The dossiers that the General Court handles are characterised by a very high level of technicality that is normally absent from the cases that come before the Court. Save exceptionally in its early years when judges acted as *ad hoc* AGs in select cases,[2] the General Court operates without AGs, and the full burden of shepherding a case through the system falls on the 'reporting judge' (*juge rapporteur*: 'JR') handling that case. That necessarily affects the role played by the JR in the General Court, which is therefore not identical to that of a JR in the Court.

II. SO – WHY BOTHER TO HAVE ADVOCATES GENERAL AT ALL?

There is of course a historical answer to this question. The legal systems of some of the original six Member States – notably, France – incorporated a role akin to that of the Advocate General in their structures.[3] When setting up a new legal system under the founding treaties, it was therefore natural enough to mimic a proven design. But to me, that is only the historical starting point.

If one looks at a system of national courts, the chances are that it will resemble a pyramid, with multiple first tier courts, then an appellate jurisdiction and, at the apex of the pyramid, the supreme court (or courts).[4] As a result, by the time that a case reaches the supreme court, several good judicial minds will have chewed it over. Whether the judges at last instance agree or disagree with their brethren below, much important judicial spadework has already been done. In contrast, of the three main categories of cases that the Court hears – direct actions, references for a preliminary ruling and appeals – in only the last-named category is there a detailed first-instance judgment (and Opinions for that category of case are correspondingly fewer in proportion). Having an Opinion is a neat way, using the same written and oral submissions, of having two 'goes' at a case within (essentially) the same time frame.

This does not – repeat and underline, *not* – mean that an Opinion of an Advocate General is the same as a judgment at first instance. Indeed, there is no better way of annoying an AG than to suggest that it is! The remark is usually made by a colleague from the common law

---

[2] See chs 23 and 51.

[3] N Burrows and R Greaves, *The Advocate General and EC Law* (Oxford, OUP, 2006) begin their work by excavating the historical origins of the role (pp 2–3). For a splendidly thoughtful review of their work, see G de Baere, *Aboli bibelot d'inanité sonore* (2006) 33 *ELRev* 927. See chs 1–2.

[4] There is no automatic reason why a given state should have only one supreme court – several EU Member States operate very satisfactorily with multiple supreme courts. Thus (for example) Belgium and France each have a *Cour constitutionnelle* (Constitutional Court), a *Cour de cassation* (Court of Cassation) and a *Conseil d'État* (Council of State). Germany – in addition to the venerated *Bundesverfassungsgericht* (the Constitutional Court) – has federal-level supreme courts for different branches of law: the *Bundesgerichtshof* (Federal Court of Justice – all matters of private law and criminal law), the *Bundesverwaltungsgericht* (Federal Administrative Court), the *Bundesarbeitsgericht* (Federal Labour Court), the *Bundessozialgericht* (Federal Social Court) and the *Bundesfinanzhof* (Federal Finance Court). This also applies to some Member States who joined later, such as Sweden, which has the *Högsta förvaltnings-domstolen* (Supreme Administrative Court) and the *Högsta domstolen* (Supreme Court).

tradition – perhaps an English 'silk' (QC). In *that* tradition, a good first instance judge does the best that he can, quickly, with the case before him. He then says, 'If I'm wrong and it matters, the boys and girls upstairs will put it right' and turns to the next case in his list. (Please note: I am *not* speaking here of what a JR working at first instance in the General Court does with the – sometimes enormous, and usually highly technical – cases that are in his or her docket.) To behave like an English first instance judge whilst serving as an AG at the Court would be a recipe for writing a relatively large number of bad Opinions.[5] If I may (rather) quote the wise advice given me, before I took up my post, by Judge David Edward (my mentor in EU law for longer than either of us probably cares to remember; and himself a former Judge both of the General Court and of the Court[6]): 'Your job as AG is to get in there and help the Court'.

Helping the Court has many facets. Drawing heavily on the talent and sheer hard work of your diligent *référendaires*, you comb the national file lodged with the Registry to try to decipher the more Delphic parts of the order for reference.[7] Then there is the painstaking research required to fill in the (sometimes striking) lacunae in the explanation of the current legal position proffered by the parties in their pleadings ('how *can* they have failed to mention three pertinent cases, one of them a Grand Chamber decision not three years old?'). You lay out clearly what you see as being the issues raised. That includes identifying what the Court does *not* have to decide in the instant case. You dissect certain superficially attractive, but specious, arguments. You endeavour to dispose of the various red herrings raised by the parties (or indeed by your dear judicial colleagues). Finally, you explain clearly and compellingly why you recommend that the Court should deal with the case in a particular way. I will unashamedly maintain that such an analysis, if properly done, adds real value: internally, for the Court in approaching the deliberation; and externally, for anyone who needs to understand the ensuing judgment and place it in context.

Another reason for having AGs is well documented in the literature.[8] In a collegiate court which does not cater for dissenting judgments, the 'public dialogue' between the Court and its AGs does provide some degree of openness, inasmuch as it enables one to see that there might have been different ways, of which the Court was aware, of approaching a particular problem. That said, the fact that the judgment does not *engage* with the Opinion of the AG – above all, does not condescend to explain to the reader why it is approaching matters differently – leaves both the outsider and the AG in question entirely in the dark as to what has really happened

---

[5] I once amused myself by estimating, for three cases in which I wrote Opinions, how long it would have taken me to write an English-style, common law first-instance judgment (based solely on the material submitted to the Court) in each of those cases. I assumed for the purposes of the exercise that – as for an Opinion – my *référendaire* and I would discuss the case, and then my *référendaire* would produce the first draft of the text which I would then revise. My estimates for that exercise (for *my* time) ranged from 25% to 35% of the time that in fact I spent working on the Opinions in each of those cases.

[6] Judge David Edward was the first judge nominated by the UK in 1989 to the newly created 'Court of First Instance of the European Communities', later re-christened the 'General Court of the European Union', before joining the Court as a judge, replacing Sir Gordon Slynn in 1992. See chs 5, 23, and 51.

[7] For the Court, the order for reference from a national court requesting a preliminary ruling arrives like a meteorite from a hitherto unknown controversy. Although the Court issues careful guidance on how such references should be presented (the 'Recommendations to national courts and tribunals in relation to the initiation of preliminary ruling proceedings', available in all the official languages on the Court's website: see https://eur-lex.europa.eu/legal-content/EN/TXT/PDF/?uri=OJ:JOC_2019_380_R_0001), the Court has no guarantee that the actual order for reference in a particular case will conform to those guidelines, or that the law, the pertinent facts and the issues requiring interpretation will be presented neatly and comprehensively to it.

[8] See chs 1 and 2.

and why.[9] This may be – indeed, this is – the sacred tradition of the institution; but that does not necessarily mean that it is a good tradition to preserve. As a working AG, I would have found it helpful to know *why* the Court had done something different (maybe I made an error in logic; maybe the judges placed a different emphasis on some aspect of the case; maybe they shied away from a solution that they regarded as too bold …?). Occasional snippets on the *'référendairenet'*[10] are an inadequate substitute for intelligent feedback.

A further – and in practical terms an important – reason for having AGs in a court with an ever-increasing workload that has become a little preoccupied by its statistics is that the AG conducts a detailed review, in parallel with the JR, of *every* case assigned to them, *even where* there is subsequently no Opinion. The AG is likewise involved, in *every* case that is assigned to them, in handling any procedural questions that arise during the period of gestation before the case-handling is determined by the Court's general meeting (the *'réunion générale'*: 'RG').[11] This is a time-consuming, although totally invisible, part of the AG's current work. I have always regarded it as a vital component of the job. Many cases go through the RG on 'list B' – which is to say that they go through on the nod, with the Court collectively blessing the case-handling recommendations made by the JR as discussed with/endorsed by the AG. As in *Animal Farm*,[12] all animals (for which, read judges) are equal, but some are more equal than others. Some JRs are reliably excellent and a pleasure to work with. Many others do a good workmanlike job. Yet others will occasionally produce a draft preliminary report (*'rapport préalable'*: 'RP') that needs a little friendly help before it accurately reflects the full extent and implications of the dossier before the Court. If the AG puts in the necessary diplomatic work to improve the RP before the case goes through the RG, he can then with a reasonably easy conscience leave it to the JR's colleagues in the chamber (the *formation de jugement*) to make sure that the case progresses smoothly to a sensible destination.

All cases, therefore, that are handled by the Court benefit from the contribution of the AG to whom that case is allocated, *not* just cases that end up with Opinions.

With the abolition (by the modifications introduced by the Treaty of Nice) of the previous rule that every case had an Opinion, deciding which cases should and should not get the 'extra' treatment of an Opinion has introduced an added level of complexity – and sometimes discord – into case handling. For a long time, there was a gentlemen's compromise (referred to as the *'règle* Cunha Rodriguez', in honour of its original proponent[13]) that if *either* the AG *or* the JR felt that a particular case merited an Opinion, the AG would write an Opinion. This courteous compromise has now been abandoned in the interests of 'efficiency'. Indeed, even if both JR and AG think that the case merits an Opinion, the RP recommending one may be met with the hackneyed phrase from a colleague anxious to cut corners and save time,

---

[9] My favourite example of this, amongst my own cases, would be *Ruiz Zambrano*. See ch 40. Rather to my surprise, the Court and I got to (vaguely) the same place; but I am no more able than any other commentator to explain how and why it got there.

[10] The corps of *référendaires* – past and present 'judicial assistants' working directly with individual Members of the Court (and the General Court) – has a strong sense of collegiality which, as a former *référendaire* myself, I proudly share. By 'référendairenet' is meant here both the constant informal exchange of useful information that takes place between *référendaires* and (nowadays) the private electronic network that links them and enables them to share news and other material.

[11] This is what lies behind the oft-repeated phrase in the official reports, 'l'avocat general entendu' ('having heard the advocate general'). The AG will have been asked formally to express his/her view on what should now be done, how some procedural difficulty should be resolved, what decision should now be taken. Having received this contribution from the AG, the Court then takes the actual decision.

[12] G Orwell, *Animal Farm* (London, Secker & Warburg, 1945). As the revolution progressed, pigs gradually became the 'more equal' species of animal.

[13] Judge Cunha Rodriguez served as a judge at the Court between 2000–2012. The biographies of former members of the Court are available on its website at https://curia.europa.eu/jcms/jcms/p1_217426/en/.

'*nous savons tous que les conclusions sont toujours utiles, mais est-ce qu'en l'espèce elles sont nécessaires?*' ('We all know that an Opinion is always useful; but is an Opinion necessary in this case?').

That will be the prelude to what is sometimes a slightly barbed fight, during which the AG will have to convince the sceptics within the RG that their contribution through an Opinion will shed additional light that is essential for the ensuing *délibéré*. Since the case is then perforce at an early stage, this sometimes requires the AG to go uncomfortably far in expanding upon their deep-seated gut feeling that the case really *does* need detailed and careful analysis by an AG before it falls into the rough and tumble of the *délibéré*. It is a fight that the AG does not always win. Although meeting the dear colleagues in the corridor looking haggard three months later and being told, 'We should have taken you up on your offer of an Opinion in that damn case!' generates a certain *Schadenfreude*, that is not a good substitute for appropriate case-handling. And whereas you can (in theory) see how much 'extra' time was added to the case after the hearing (or after the RG, if there was no hearing) by waiting for an Opinion from the AG,[14] no one has yet managed to quantify either how much time *en délibéré* is saved by having a good Opinion to use as the analytical starting point, or how much quality such an Opinion adds to the ensuing judgment.

Whether one is looking at the additional structural security afforded by having a system of 'double review' by two principal case-handlers (JR and AG), the quiet unpublicised contribution made to case-handling by the AG in cases that end up without an Opinion or the value-added that comes from a thoughtful Opinion in a difficult case, there are (still) I think good grounds for saying that AGs are *not* just there because 'European judges can't think for themselves' and that they continue to perform a useful function for the Court.[15]

III. INSIDE THE PRESSURE COOKER

When I joined the Court in 2006, I deliberately and gratefully took over all of Francis's team. With the team, I also adopted the basic *modus operandi* that Francis had developed and practised so successfully over the years. I had a profound sympathy for how Elisha must have felt as he watched Elijah being swept away to heaven in a chariot by the whirlwind and was left clutching the prophet's mantle.[16] So, to begin with, 'team Sharpston' was a close copy of 'team Jacobs'. We had only one quality for our output (the very best); only one approach (very careful and meticulous and comprehensive); only one type of quality control (a full and rigorous peer review of every draft Opinion by all the other *référendaires* and any *stagiaires* or visitors then working in chambers).

---

[14] Footnote for Court-watchers: the texts of Opinions are made available (in draft form) to the judges via the *site des présidents* at the point when the Opinion is sent across to be translated. If the draft text is in either English or French (as many are), the JR and their team are expected to start work on producing the draft reasoning of the judgment (the *projet de motifs*), using that draft text and that date (rather than the date on which the Opinion is actually delivered) as their base line. Applying the Court's formula for calculating translation time (the *délai de traduction standard*), a 45-page Opinion (in draft spacing: about 30 pages in final spacing) requires 20 working days of translation time, plus a week for final checking. So, in my example the date of delivery of the Opinion may well *overstate* the 'additional time' incurred by requesting an Opinion by nearly a month and a half.

[15] For the proposition that, on the contrary, the Court now no longer really needs Advocates General, see Burrows and Greaves (n 3) 297–99.

[16] See 2 Kings 2:9-13. In the months that followed my swearing in, I often (like Elisha) wished devoutly for a double portion of Francis's spirit, because taking over as the successor to such an outstanding AG was truly a daunting task. Indeed, Francis's apparent immortality as AG was exemplified when I was introduced in mid-2006 to a group of lawyers at an embassy reception in Luxembourg as 'the British AG at the Court'. Unanimously they responded, 'You can't be – that's Francis Jacobs'.

As time wore on and the pressure under which we were working crept relentlessly upwards, we discussed, agonised over, and gradually modified that *modus operandi* to the minimum extent necessary for our collective survival. Thus, we became stricter about not pursuing every hare running across our field of vision into its burrow: instead, we agreed that only hares deemed worthy for the pot were to be hunted. Only the very biggest and most difficult cases got a full team review by all the three other *référendaires*. Lesser cases got a one- or perhaps two-*référendaire* review. I made myself very unpopular with (successive) Presidents by defending our right *not* to issue an Opinion until we were satisfied with what we were saying in it; but we did also make – sometimes heroic – additional efforts within my chambers to cut back on length and respect the wretched *échéancier* (the Court's internal timetabling requirements).

Producing a decent Opinion involves a lot of very painstaking teamwork. As the duly appointed member, the AG is (naturally, we assume) knowledgeable, committed, hard-working. That said, it would be impossible for even a veritable phoenix of an AG to do their job without the unstinting support of their team. A single person has neither the sheer time required to burrow deeply enough into every single file, nor all the different talents that are needed to write consistently good, well-informed, and rigorous Opinions across all areas of EU law. This is the place to acknowledge the *immense* debt that I owe to former members of 'team Sharpston' of all vintages, from my first days back at the Court in 2006 (bright-eyed, bushy-tailed and eager: the new kid on the block) to the unbelievably stressful final year (and more), when we tried to carry on with 'business as usual' with the sword of Brexit hanging over our heads.

I am so proud of my team. They conducted reliable, detailed, quality research. They produced first drafts of everything from concise summaries of complicated case law to meticulously precise proposed answers to questions referred. They acted as sounding boards for ideas, pointing out gaps in my reasoning, commenting, critiquing. Occasionally, when my hot Irish temper threatened to get the better of my judgment in some internal tiff with someone-in-authority, they discreetly and gently reined me in and suggested a more diplomatic path forward. They undertook the tedious labour of checking everything, of giving each text its *toilettage*. They helped me revise the draft French translation (three pairs of eyes – assistant's, *référendaire*'s and my own – on every single text) to make sure that the *exact nuance* of what we wanted to say was conveyed across into the language in which the Court would be working. The tradition of the house is that the back-up team works unnamed, in the shadows. I should like nevertheless to pay tribute to their professionalism, idealism, and loyalty. It is a joy and a true privilege to have worked with them – and, alongside the unremitting effort, we also had a lot of fun together as a team.

I should also stress that an Opinion – or at least, a 'team Sharpston Opinion' – is a shared intellectual creation. The *référendaire* assigned that case is the initial draftsman and often remains the principal draftsman. In the nature of things, the *référendaire* spends longer than the AG crawling over every detail of the file, wondering how to deal with each facet of the problem and taking on board their colleagues' helpful critique of the intermediate draft. However much I also put into the case, the resulting text bears the *référendaire*'s stamp just as it does mine.[17]

---

[17] Thus, the Opinion in *Ruiz Zambrano* would have reached the same conclusion, but would have read differently, if I had written it with someone other than Daniel Sarmiento, a very bright Spanish constitutional lawyer who had studied in the US, whom I 'borrowed' from cabinet Ruiz Jarabo Colomer because *Ruiz Zambrano* was initially his case. My Opinions about refugees and the Dublin III Regulation owe a great deal to my wonderful, long-serving *chef de cabinet*, Doyin Lawunmi. The examples could be multiplied to encompass every single *référendaire* with whom I worked.

To be honest, I never thought of myself as 'the British AG'. Save for my passport, I am not perhaps very British; and I always saw myself as a European citizen who had the immense privilege of helping to shape the legal parameters of the European project. That said, it is true that I often found myself applying a very British pragmatism to draft texts. To my mind, the ultimate (acid) test was, 'Will this solution actually work when applied in a hurry on a Friday afternoon by a bored and not overly attentive clerk somewhere in a rather remote corner of the EU?' At the same time, the Opinion had to be intellectually rigorous. The reader had to see how what was being proposed fitted within the overall mosaic of EU law.

As a team, we cared deeply about writing Opinions that would assist the Court and those outside it. We had therefore to remain sensitive to the multi-lingual and multi-cultural aspect of what we were trying to do. Team Sharpston was never an all-British team. It drew heavily on the rich diversity of its membership (national, cultural, linguistic, professional) to try – precisely – to *avoid* expressing legal views that would only be comprehensible to those who shared this particular AG's common law background. It was a real delight to work with so many excellent younger colleagues from other legal traditions. I learnt so much from them. At the same time, I relied very heavily on the British component of the team for their sound common sense ('does this actually alter the price of fish?' became a sacred catchphrase within the team) and their linguistic rigour. Lord Denning has always been a hero of mine for the sheer, beautiful clarity of his writing. My team frequently teased me for my (repetitive) drafting recommendation, 'Why not shorten this? How about putting a full stop *here* and starting the new thought with a new sentence?'

I want to conclude this second section by stressing that in a collegiate court that operates by consensus, the qualities required of a good JR and those that make for a good AG are *not* necessarily the same. At the risk of slight over-simplification, it seems to me that a good JR at the Court[18] is essentially a good committee man, skilled at crafting consensus amongst a disparate group of colleagues in the Court's working language (French). He knows that the perfect is usually unattainable and that the almost-perfect may (still) be the enemy of the workmanlike 'good enough'. What matters is bolting together a text that can slip through the deliberation process smoothly and swiftly and then moving on to the next case. That is going to require compromise, adjustment, sometimes even deliberate concealment of inconsistencies.

In contrast, a good AG is an individualist with a strong individual vision of what the answer to the case should be (and why). He writes in his language of choice,[19] freed from the shackles of the Court's 'Vademecum' which lays down (in almost paralysing detail) precisely how draft judgments should be constructed. Ambiguity and fudge are – or should be – shameful words to hear applied to an Opinion.[20]

---

[18] Not every JR at my Court will recognise him- or herself in this description. Also, I do emphasise that, at the General Court, the (usually) higher degree of technicality and the greater sheer volume of the case files (partly due to the often elaborate and complex factual descriptions) gives the JR a greater degree of control in 'shepherding' the case through the judicial process.

[19] Out of kindness to the Court's hard-pressed translation services, the AGs on single six-year mandates from 'small- and medium-sized Member States' have charitably agreed *not* to exercise their right to write in their mother tongues, but instead write in a 'mainstream' language for which the Court already caters amply (usually, therefore, either French or English).

[20] Sir Gordon Slynn manifestly preferred the AG role to the JR role, although (wisely) he realised that to fulfil his ambition and enter the House of Lords after leaving the Court, he needed to be 'Judge' (a known quantity) rather than 'Advocate General' ('What's that?'). My first year with him as a *référendaire* was spent drafting Opinions, my second and third years preparing draft judgments. Working for Gordon as an AG was intensely exciting, like going hunting with a panther in the jungle (stay well behind the jaws, keep up, this is amazing fun). Working for Gordon as a JR was sometimes uncomfortably close to being shut up inside the over-small cage at the zoo in which a very frustrated – and consequently irritable – panther was pacing back and forth, lashing its tail.

Let me offer an illustration[21] of the difference between the resulting texts.

Luxembourg is a land of many castles, of which one of the best known (thanks to Victor Hugo) is Vianden Castle.[22] One of the largest fortified castles west of the Rhine, it was built between the eleventh to the fourteenth centuries on the foundations of a Roman castellum and a Carolingian refuge, fell into disrepair during the nineteenth century, and spent the first three-quarters of the twentieth century as an evocative ruin before being lovingly restored to its former glory by the Luxembourg State. Nowadays Vianden Castle is again a striking and distinctive shape, rearing over the picturesque little town at its feet.

A judgment of the Court that has been shepherded through the *délibéré* process by the JR looks like a model of Vianden Castle made out of Lego. If you know what Vianden Castle looks like, the model is – recognisably – a model of that particular castle. It is constructed out of standard plastic blocks that are then clipped together (sometimes a bit awkwardly) to create the necessary shapes. It is serviceable. It is also clunky and – to be honest – probably not a work of particular beauty. Along the way, the (necessary) fudges will have been concealed with greater or lesser skill.

In contrast, the AG is in the lucky position of a skilled photographer with first class digital equipment invited to present Vianden Castle to an expectant public. He determines precisely *what* he is going to present and precisely *how* he is going to present it. He is at total liberty to decide important factors like the time of day at which the photo is taken; how the photo is framed (cropped, wide-angle or somewhere in between); the aperture/focus/time exposure combination. The result is (or should be) a work of artistic creation, as close to perfection as the photographer can achieve – and it is a work for whose quality the photographer bears total responsibility. Just as there is total structural freedom, there is also no hiding place.

IV. THE FUTURE – ALL ABOUT RESOURCE MANAGEMENT?

I preface this final section with the usual caveat that I am not in possession of a crystal ball – either for the Court as an institution or for the role of AGs within it. There are, nevertheless, a few points that may bear to be made.

First, the Court has obviously changed since Jean-Pierre Warner joined it in 1973 as the first British AG upon UK accession to the (then) European Communities. It is two-tier (Court of Justice and General Court).[23] It has many more members (judges from 27 Member States, plus 11 Advocates General). Its jurisdiction extends over many more areas of law that was the

---

[21] I am of course not the first to attempt to explain by illustration. Thus, Judge David Edward once famously wrote that judgments of the Court sometimes bear a striking resemblance to camels – the proverbial horses designed by a committee (D Edward, 'How the Court of Justice works' (1995) 20 *ELRev* 539, 556–57); to which Anthony Arnull quipped in response that: 'If some of the Court's judgments are camels, Opinions are often jurisprudential racehorses, galloping directly to the finishing line decked out in vivid colours' (A Arnull, *The European Union and its Court of Justice*, 2nd edn (Oxford, OUP, 2006) 16.

[22] French: Château de Vianden; German: Burg Vianden; Luxembourgish: Buerg Veianen. Victor Hugo visited Vianden in 1862 and 1865 and spent a longer period there in 1871. He recorded its beauty and setting in prose, poetry, and sketches, including the series of poems *L'Année terrible*. A collection of his sketches and letters can be seen in the museum located in the house where he stayed, next to the bridge over the river Our. For a fuller description see https://castle-vianden.lu/gb/.

[23] At one stage, with the introduction by the Treaty of Nice of the possibility of specialist courts, the system looked to be headed towards being three-tier; and indeed the 'Civil Service Tribunal' did an excellent job and was much appreciated by its client base before it fell victim to the political manoeuvrings that saw its abolition in favour of doubling the number of judges in the General Court.

case in 1973 – including, importantly, areas of law that are *much* more sensitive politically (everything in the 'area of freedom, security and justice' (AFSJ), for a start) than was the case when it was 'merely' dealing with the bread-and-butter of the four freedoms and economic integration of a single market. It is dealing with a much (much) heavier case load.[24]

At the same time, what is to me remarkable – having seen the Court from the inside in 1982, from 1987 to 1990 and then from 2006 to 2020 – is how *little* the Court has changed. The Court's *basic thinking* about how to do its job has remained largely unaltered over that entire period. A kind of institutional sclerosis has set in. The Court has *not* (really) reviewed *all* aspects of its working methods. There are (still) some aspects of case handling that have become fossilised.

Let me give just one rather obvious example of Court practice that has remained unchanged, with a consequent real and significant cost to the Court in time and resources. In cases where there is an Opinion, the 'front part' of the Opinion and the 'front part' of the judgment present – essentially – the same material. Let's take the example of a reference for a preliminary ruling. After a short introduction, both the Opinion and the subsequent judgment will set out the relevant EU law and national law. Both will then narrate the facts, the procedural history, and the questions referred. Viewed objectively, this reduplication is unquestionably eccentric. Within the AG's chambers and the JR's chambers, much careful time and thought and skill goes into drafting these sections of respectively, the Opinion and the judgment. But in a court that is overburdened and that operates in 24 languages, with the concomitant translation requirements, it is bizarre that such an arrangement survives.

It would not be beyond the wit of man to devise a better system. The JR could write a shorter RP for the RG.[25] Once the RG had decided on the appropriate case-handling, in a case *with* an Opinion the AG would (as now) write the front end for his Opinion. The difference would be that the front end of the Opinion would then serve *both* for the Opinion *and* for the subsequent judgment.[26] The JR would *not* produce a separate text. (In a case with an Opinion, it would have to be that way round, for the simple and sufficient reason that the Opinion comes out first and is only intelligible if it has a front end setting out this material.[27]) The Court would then cross-refer to the front end of the Opinion in its judgment.[28] Conversely,

---

[24] In 2006, the year in which I joined the Court as an AG, 537 new cases were registered at the Court, 546 cases were completed and there were 731 cases pending (source: Annual Report 2006, Table 1, available at https://curia.europa. eu/jcms/upload/docs/application/pdf/2008-09/06_cour_stat_2008-09-29_13-30-8_188.pdf). In 2019, my last full year of service at the Court, 966 new cases were registered at the Court, 865 cases were completed and the 'stock' of pending cases stood at 1,102 (source: Annual Report 2019, Table 1, available at https://curia.europa.eu/jcms/upload/docs/ application/pdf/2020-05/qd-ap-20-001-en-n.pdf). The 2020 figures are – unsurprisingly – affected by the COVID-19 pandemic and therefore probably atypical. By way of comparison: in 1973, the first year of the UK's membership of the (then) European Communities, 192 new cases were brought and the Court delivered 80 judgments (source: Annual Report 1997, Table 16 ('General trend in the work of the Court up to 31 December 1997')), available at https://curia. europa.eu/jcms/upload/docs/application/pdf/2008-09/st97cr_2008-09-30_16-42-41_25.pdf.

[25] Currently, the RP is a heavy document, consisting of four sections: (i) a table showing case handling recommendations; (ii) the pre-draft of the front end of the judgment; (iii) a summary of the parties' arguments; and (iv) the JR's preliminary analysis. With a higher level of analysis and synthesis, it *would* often be possible to write a significantly shorter RP.

[26] For that reason, this would (probably) be done with collaborative input from the JR; but the AG would have the final word, because it would be the AG's text.

[27] If the Court wanted to have the 'front end' of the AG's draft Opinion available to it *in draft form* for use at a hearing, an appropriate timeframe could be agreed and a *provisional* translation into French prepared. The AG would (as now) fine-tune the draft text after the hearing and, when the draft opinion was sent over to translation, a track-change version of the (revised) front end would enable French translation to make the necessary adjustments.

[28] If the judges felt, as a result of the *délibéré*, that the Opinion had omitted some legal and/or factual element(s) on which they intended to rely later for their reasoning, they could cross-refer to the front end of the Opinion and then add, 'In the view of the Court, the following material is also pertinent' and set it out.

if in a particular case the Court decided to proceed to judgment without an Opinion, the JR would simply – as now – produce the front end of the judgment.[29]

To my knowledge, proposals to do (something like) this have never seriously been considered or properly discussed. If the Court wanted to make better/fuller use of its AGs, an obvious step would be to use the AG's text – the Opinion – in this way to lay the foundation for the subsequent judgment. The savings, in both drafting resources and translation resources, would be massive. Such a change would integrate the AG's work and the Court's subsequent work in a particular case; and the result would – I suspect – be clearer and more transparent for the reader. But the Court would have to be prepared to let go of its hallowed practices and *rely upon its AGs*.

Secondly, the Court does – ironically – now indeed rely upon its AGs to *write the legal reasoning* of orders based on Article 181 of the Rules of Procedure dismissing certain categories of appeal (notably, trademarks) as manifestly inadmissible and/or manifestly unfounded. This practice was introduced to free up judicial (judge) time to invest in deliberations in more difficult cases, and to improve the Court's performance statistics.[30] If you believe that AGs are there to advise and judges are there to write judicial decisions, the practice is questionable.[31]

I would compare and contrast this new practice for certain types of Article 181 order with what I believe to be an isolated instance where the Court in a *judgment* answering a request for a preliminary ruling comprehensively endorsed the Opinion presented by its AG, saying that 'For the reasons indicated in the Advocate-General's Opinion of [date], the reply to the question put by the national court must be that (...)'.[32] There, written observations had been lodged as usual (by the plaintiff in the national proceedings and by the European Commission) and the AG had delivered his Opinion in the normal way. There had then been a normal *délibéré* between the three members of the chamber, following which they accepted the draft *projet de motifs* presented by the JR (Judge David Edward). Clearly, therefore, a judicial deliberation and a judicial decision preceded the adoption of the judgment. It is perhaps noteworthy that the new model – if I may call it that – did not catch on with the Court as a whole: at all events, it did not become part of standard practice.

---

[29] As is currently the position with the draft RP shown to the AG for comments/acceptance before being submitted to the RG, the AG could make suggestions as to what should be included in the front end of a judgment-with-no-Opinion which the JR would be free to accept or disregard.

[30] Since the published statistics give the arithmetic average (mean) time for processing cases, if a trademark appeal can be turned round and thrown out very quickly (rather than languishing in the back of a judicial cupboard until someone has a quiet moment and digs it out), this has a favourable impact on the arithmetic mean. The Court's internal *échéancier* therefore has a very short deadline (15 days after the case goes through the RG) for the AG to write a mini-Opinion dismissing the appeal. On several occasions, I had to suspend work on a Grand Chamber Opinion to deal with such an order within the deadline. The AG's mini-Opinion is then quoted *in extenso* in the Court's order, with skeletal 'bookends' of judicial reasoning. Essentially, the shape of the order is, 'In this appeal ...', followed by the AG's contribution in quotations, followed by, 'For the reasons given by the AG, the Court dismisses the appeal'. For an example of such an order, see Case C-293/19 P *Et Djili Soy Dzhihangir Ibryam* ECLI:EU:C:2019:814, turned round in under 6 months.

[31] If the judges rubber-stamp the AG's reasoning *without* investing the necessary time themselves to read the file and arrive at a judicial conclusion, they are – arguably – shifting the judicial decision-making onto the AG. Conversely, if they *do* spend the necessary time themselves, the 'value-added' represented by having the AG's additional contribution is being squandered on (precisely) the category of cases that *least* need such value-added, because they are 'manifestly' inadmissible and/or unfounded. I note that if additional manpower is required to free the judges from the tedious and (by definition) not very innovative drafting work involved in such cases, Article 17 of the Court's Rules of Procedure contains a power to appoint 'Assistant Rapporteurs', to whom such work could be delegated under the supervision of the JR.

[32] Case C-59/92 *Hauptzollamt Hamburg-St. Annen* ECLI:EU:C:1993:167 (para 4 of the Judgment). See also Opinion of AG Darmon in Case C-59/92 *Hauptzollamt Hamburg-St. Annen* ECLI:EU:C:1993:128.

Thirdly, there is no point in having Opinions of Advocates General if these are reduced to a hasty attempt to pre-guess what the Court is going to do in its subsequent judgment. When I was working for him, Sir Gordon Slynn said crisply that 'an AG who is followed more than 7 or 8 times out of ten isn't doing his job – he's too close to the Court'. I firmly believe that he was right. For that reason, I have been very pleased, reading some of the draft contributions to this volume that discuss my Opinions as I prepared this afterword, to see commentators pick up occasions where the Court did not follow me, or followed me only partially, but where some of the ideas in those Opinions have had a life beyond the case in which they were expressed.[33]

I continue to believe – passionately – that the job of the AG is to have the courage to think round the immediate issues; and to be prepared where appropriate to put forward new, unorthodox, and possibly (yes) challenging solutions. After all – if the AG does not sometimes think outside the box, who else is going to do so? Almost certainly not a harassed JR who will have to rub along with his judge colleagues day in, day out, crafting consensual prose to get the next judgment written and dispatched to translation.

Fourthly, thinking requires time. Naturally it is necessary, within a court, to have targets for completing work. But the Court under successive presidents has become truly fixated by its statistics and tempted to apply double standards. If a case is causing trouble *en délibéré* (or that particular JR is over-burdened), it is an accepted part of life that a significant time may elapse between delivery of the Opinion and the ensuing judgment.[34] But if the AG is taking a bit longer than you would like to lay the golden egg that is the Opinion, that is unacceptable.[35]

If you want the AG to stand back, think seriously about the problem, and then recommend which of the possible solutions to adopt *and* explain convincingly why, you need to give them enough elbow room to do so. That is true in spades if – as you should – you want the Opinion to be the AG's own thoughtful recommendation rather than essentially that of the AG's *référendaire*. From what I have said earlier, I hope it is abundantly clear that I valued my *référendaires* (and the other efficient and helpful support staff within my team) extremely. But, at the end of the day, they were all there – paid for by the EU taxpayer – to put me in the best possible position to do *my* job as well and wholeheartedly as I possibly could. Sometimes, my team and I rewrote (and even re-rewrote) an Opinion before we got a text with which we were satisfied. If I, as its ultimate author, was not prepared to sign off on it, that Opinion was not (by definition) yet ready to leave the cabinet and take its chance in the unforgiving outside world. I think and believe that – where we did take additional time – that extra time was well invested.

In contrast, one of the most chilling snippets that reached me via the 'référendairenet' concerned an exchange between the JR's *référendaire* and the AG's *référendaire* involved in the work on a particular Grand Chamber case, after the Opinion in that case had been delivered.

---

[33] See chs 38, 42, and 43.

[34] The Court's case law does not lack examples, which the reader can deduce by comparing the various dates recorded in the preamble to the judgment. It would be unkind to single out particular illustrations for mention.

[35] Thus, the time taken to construct the Opinions in *Ruiz Zambrano* and in *Farrell II* made me deeply unpopular with, respectively, President Skouris and President Lenaerts. Both Opinions are discussed in detail in this volume. See chs 40 and 46. Should I have asked a nice *référendaire* to write something much more concise and superficial in each of those cases, given it a cursory read-through, and pushed it out over my signature within the *échéancier* deadline? In this respect, converting the deadlines in the *échéancier* into a three-track model (for 'straightforward', 'average' and 'complex' cases), where the target times for both the advocates general and the judges would vary realistically with the complexity of the case, would be a sensible step forward.

The JR's *référendaire* thanked his colleague politely for the Opinion; and then expressed surprise and disappointment that the AG had entirely failed to cover an important and difficult point that had emerged for the first time at the hearing and that was, the JR's *référendaire* foresaw, going to cause a lot of trouble and anxious discussion *en délibéré*. The AG's unfortunate *référendaire* wrung his hands. 'I know, I know', he said. 'I'm terribly sorry. *Of course* you needed us to cover that, properly and in detail, rather than pretend it had never been raised and just leave it out. I suggested to my AG that I should go away and research it all thoroughly and then do a first draft on that additional issue. But my AG told me we *had* to respect the '*échéancier*'; that there was no time for more research; and that I should just tweak a couple of sentences and get the pre-hearing draft of the Opinion over at once to translation'.

I do not enter here into the wider (and important, and difficult) question that, sooner or later, the Court is going to have to confront: how to make best use of its Advocates General? I confine myself to observing that the decision as to whether a given case needs an Opinion is taken at a *micro* level (case by case); and that there is *no mechanism* that links that individual decision, in any way, to the *macro* level. By '*macro* level', I mean the total number of Opinions that 11 Advocates General can reasonably be expected to write over the course of a year, taken in conjunction with the other (more invisible, but nevertheless valuable) work that they also do, such as the 'double review' of all cases to which I have already alluded. Of course, there is no such thing as a 'standard' Opinion (any more than there is a 'standard' judgment), and any mechanism would have to have built into it a degree of flexibility. But it is no good hoping that the solution lies merely in urging the Advocates Generals to greater efforts.[36]

Fifthly, whilst it is not perhaps possible to summon up wild enthusiasm for every single case in which one is asked to write an Opinion, *every such case* does have legal issues that are intellectually interesting and therefore intellectually satisfying to try to resolve. And sometimes, of course, you *will* feel real passion about a case. If so, in my book, you should not be afraid to express it. I remain proud of Opinions where that passion broke through the careful legal writing.[37] I am even prouder that members of team Sharpston of various vintages gave up their free time to help me research and write two 'shadow opinions' for Grand Chamber cases that were ours as a team, but that were mysteriously put on ice until after I had been ejected from the Court, and get them out into the public domain. They did so precisely because they were *not* mere electronic penpushers, but true professionals who cared about and took pride in what we created together.[38]

---

[36] I am again reminded of that loyal animal, Boxer the horse, in George Orwell's *Animal Farm* (after the show trial and execution of the four pigs following the destruction of the windmill): 'For some time no one spoke. Only Boxer remained on his feet. He fidgeted to and fro, swishing his long black tail against his sides and occasionally uttering a little whinny of surprise. Finally he said: 'I do not understand it. I would not have believed that such things could happen on our farm. *It must be due to some fault in ourselves. The solution, as I see it, is to work harder.* From now onwards I shall get up a full hour earlier in the mornings.' And he moved off at his lumbering trot and made for the quarry. Having got there, he collected two successive loads of stone and dragged them down to the windmill before retiring for the night' (Orwell (n 12) 59, emphasis added). Those who know the story will know the outcome. Boxer eventually collapsed from overwork and was shipped off to the knacker's, where he was slaughtered (Orwell (n 12) 77–81).

[37] For example, the three infringement proceedings involving the temporary mechanism for the relocation of applicants for international protection, Opinion of AG Sharpston in Case C-715/17 *Commission v Poland*, Case C-718/17 *Commission v Hungary* and Case C-719/17 *Commission v Czech Republic* ECLI:EU:C:2019:917 (*Temporary Relocation*). See my 'concluding remarks' at paras 238 et seq. See also ch 47.

[38] The 'shadow opinions' were written for Case C-194/19 *H.A.* (concerning a refugee's right of access to a court to challenge a transfer decision under the Dublin III Regulation) and for Case C-804/18 *Wabe* and Case C-341/19 *Müller Handels* (the two follow-up cases to Case C-157/15 *Achbita* and Case C-188/15 *Bougnaoui* about the dismissal of female Muslim employees for wearing the hijab). Both were kindly published by Professor Steve Peers on his blog.

V. CONCLUDING OBSERVATIONS

This afterword has been (as the reader will swiftly have realised) a swan song for my dream job. Being an AG at the Court is the best job on the planet for an EU lawyer. Despite the pressures and imperfections that I have highlighted just now, that remains emphatically the case. I was lucky enough to have that dream job, into which I could put my heart and my soul and all my energy, for 14 and a half years. Leaving the Court in 2021 at the end of my standard six-year mandate because of Brexit, rather than having the possibility of being renewed, was always going to be sad. The actual circumstances of my departure on 10 September 2020 were deeply painful; but this is not the place to enter into that saga.[39] Let me conclude instead with another image, another analogy, which encapsulates how I see the role that my three predecessors and I were privileged to play as 'the British AGs' during the years that the UK belonged to the 'European project', and which is explored in this book.

Imagine an army marching through unfamiliar terrain. Night is drawing on. They come to a place where there are three possible routes to take. Sensibly, the general orders the army to camp for the night. Then he asks his trusted colleague – a man of his own experience and seniority, who specialises in reconnaissance – to go forward and scout out the lie of the land. When the colleague returns, the general asks him for his opinion.

'Well', says the scout, 'the *left-hand path* is fine for the first 300m. Then it turns a sharp corner and goes straight into a bog. You'll never get any tracked vehicle through there – or get them out again once they've sunk in. Forget it. The *central path* starts off reasonably clear. However, after about 600m it passes into a narrow ravine which stretches onwards for at least a further 900m. There are cliff faces steep-to either side of the path and plenty of bushes too. I didn't *see* anything, but a couple of times I heard a little trickle of falling stones that shouldn't have been there. It's the perfect place for a very effective ambush. We might be ok, but person-ally I wouldn't risk taking the army through that way. That leaves the *right-hand path*. The first 500m are going to be tedious (the ground is a bit soft), but if we go steadily there shouldn't be a real problem. And after that the path widens out. It's good going, with no risk of ambush. My recommendation: *take the right-hand path*.'

Obviously, the scout is only giving his analysis and his opinion. The decision as to which way to march in the morning is up to the general. But a wise general will listen hard to what his scout is saying.

The links are, respectively, http://eulawanalysis.blogspot.com/2021/02/case-c19419-h.html (*H.A.*, 12 February 2021) and http://eulawanalysis.blogspot.com/2021/03/shadow-opinion-of-former-advocate.html (the two 'veils' cases, 23 March 2021).

[39] Anyone interested in reading my assessment of the *dénouement* of that story will find my statement dated 6 August 2021, commented on by Joshua Rozenberg QC under his 'A Lawyer Writes' rubric, via this link: https://rozenberg.substack.com/p/eu-court-undermines-its-independence (the link to my statement is embedded in his text). Once my website akulith.eu is up and running (probably, during the latter part of 2022), there will be a tab on that site with a bit more information: notably, the pleadings lodged on my behalf before the General Court and the Court by my wonderful *pro bono* team of lawyers, which explore the issues raised with rigour and precision. I hasten to add that there will also be a lot up there that is *not* about '*l'affaire Sharpston*' – and that (I hope) will be a lot more interesting!

Part VIII

EU Law without UK Advocates General

53

Neither Advocates, Nor Generals: The UK Advocates General and the Shaping of EU Law

GRAHAM BUTLER AND ADAM ŁAZOWSKI

I. INTRODUCTION

I N 1962, a special Common Market Law Advisory Committee was set up by the UK government. It mandated a group of distinguished members of the legal profession to attend to several pertinent questions as to the legal implications of UK's potential accession to the European Communities.[1] One of the dossiers put under scrutiny was future relations between the UK courts and the Court of Justice (the Court). What would the cooperation look like? Would the UK Courts and the Court speak – formatively and figuratively – the same language? The recommendation of the Committee was to do nothing, as 'any problems should be left to work themselves out in time'.[2] And they did, with no small input of UK courts, the Court, its UK judges, and its AGs.

To have the full picture merits not one, but a series of books, and such a comprehensive tale is for others to tell. The editors of this volume opted to focus on one aspect of this fascinating story. Together with the team of authors, they put under the scientific microscope the work of four consecutive UK AGs – AG Warner, AG Slynn, AG Jacobs, and AG Sharpston (as well as Judge Edward, who delivered a single opinion acting as an AG at the then Court of First Instance (now the General Court)). As argued in the title of the present book, they shaped EU law the British way, and – even despite the great misfortune of Brexit – they continue doing so. In this closing chapter of this book, the editors piece the narrative together, and bring it all home. They demonstrate how the UK AGs shaped EU law, and what was so British about it. Arguably, the UK AGs were British as far as their state of nomination was concerned, though above all, they were European through and through. At the same time, though, they came from a background of a Member State with different legal traditions. This influenced how they adapted to the idiosyncratic legal habitat at the Court on Kirchberg plateau in Luxembourg.

---

[1] See K Newman, CB, 'Legal problems of British accession' in G Wilkes (ed), *Britain's Failure to Enter the European Community 1961–63. The enlargement negotiations and crises in European, Atlantic and Commonwealth relations* (Abingdon, Routledge, 1997).

[2] ibid, p 127.

II. THE CONTRIBUTION OF UK AGS TO THE SHAPING OF EU LAW

'Shaping' is defined as giving shape to something and developing it further.[3] This is precisely what the UK AGs have been doing during their time at the Court and since – focusing on the present but also looking into the future. As this book has demonstrated, the UK AGs may now have left the bench in Luxembourg, but their contribution stands tall thanks to the legacy of Opinions delivered for the benefit of the Court, and invaluable fruits of other activities, including educational and academic endeavours.

First and foremost are the Opinions, which were the very essence of UK AGs' work at the Court. As highlighted already in the Introduction to this book, AG Warner, AG Slynn, AG Jacobs, and AG Sharpston delivered over 1,440 Opinions covering most, if not all areas of EU law. Many offered landmark and ground-breaking analyses and solutions which were followed by the Court, some leading to changes of EU secondary legislation. However, as in the case of AGs from other Member States, in many instances, the UK AGs were not followed. But a followed/not followed narrative is simplistic and misleading. As any EU lawyer knows, often it is close to impossible to determine whether the AGs and the judges were on the same page.

As Ćapeta, an AG herself, asked earlier in this volume,[4] does it mean that the AGs are wrong if the Court follows a different line of reasoning, or reaches a different conclusion than an AG? Arguably, to settle for a binary choice between 'yes' and 'no' may – for the convenience of ease and simplicity – be tempting, yet it would not be a prudent trajectory to embark on. There is much more nuance to the story of AGs, their Opinions, and judgments of the Court. Be it as it may, Opinions of the AGs, despite not being utilised by the Court in a given case, may nonetheless still have a long shelf life.

The decisions of the Court – in most cases – bring the matter at hand to a closure. *Au contraire*, however, for Opinions of the AGs, as they can have a life of their own, which frequently goes on after a case is closed. As noted by Dashwood, '[O]pinions of Advocates General stand as legal authorities in their own right'.[5] Judgments often serve as catalysts for debates, in which the Opinions of the AGs are essential ingredients. When not agreed with by the Court, AGs may be ahead of their time, offering solutions which are not always to the immediate liking of the judges of the day. But then, years later, they may return like a boomerang, be given justice, by their successors, and still influence the shaping of EU law.

UK AGs and their Opinions were no exception in this respect. This is demonstrated in several chapters of this book, where the authors made it clear that the capacity of Opinions of UK AGs to shape EU law was not only a short-term affair (when their Opinions were in one way or another adopted by the Court), but also a long-term phenomenon (where proposals of AGs were rejected in a given case, but then ideas laid down therein were picked up in subsequent cases). Therefore, Brexit or not, Opinions of UK AGs continue to radiate and to shape the future of EU law. They may inspire present and future judges and AGs and the Court. A recent Opinion of AG Emiliou in *CC v Pensionsversicherungsanstalt* is a good example to prove this point.[6] Needless to say, that Opinions of UK AGs have for years also inspired practising lawyers, and many members of the academic community. It is enough to mention the

---

[3] R Allen, *The Penguin Pocket English Dictionary* (London, Penguin Books, 2008) 470.

[4] See ch 42.

[5] A Dashwood, 'The Advocate General in the Court of Justice of the European Communities' (1982) 2 *Legal Studies* 202, 214.

[6] Opinion of AG Emiliou in Case C-576/20 *CC* ECLI:EU:C:2022:75. To support his point of view, AG Emiliou approvingly cited, in fns 38–39, the Opinion of AG Sharpston in Case C-465/14 *Wieland and Rothwangl*

Opinions of AG Jacobs in *UPA*,[7] and AG Sharpston in *Ruiz Zambrano*,[8] both of which kept the academic community in a state of frenzy for months on end. Many other Opinions of UK AGs have also done so and they are likely to continue for years to come.

Before select Opinions of UK AGs are put under the spotlight, it is worth looking at other ways in which UK AGs shaped EU law. To begin with, when AG Warner (and for that matter, the first UK judge at the Court, Alexander Mackenzie Stewart) joined the bench in January 1973, the Court was a well-established institution, heavily influenced by the legal cultures of the EEC founding states, France in particular. This was reflected in many aspects of the Court's work, including the style of Opinions of the AGs and judgments of the Court. According to Mancini and Keeling, 'throughout the 1950s and early 1960s the judgment of the European Court looked like a carbon copy of the judgments of the great French courts'.[9] The static nature of hearings was also one of such idiosyncrasies, which may have taken the new members of the Court, who came from the common law tradition, by surprise. This is when shaping of EU law, the British way, started in the early days of the UK's membership. As noted by several commentators, AG Warner and Judge Mackenzie Stewart brought more dynamism to the oral part of Court proceedings which initially had not been terribly friendly to direct interaction between bench and bar. A good example of the incoming change was the hearing in *Bouchereau*, when – according to Tobler – AG Warner 'entered into a regular "dialogue" with the representative of the UK'.[10] In his afterword to the present book, Jacobs added that UK counsel also played their part in giving life to courtrooms at the Court.[11] No surprise there, as lively exchanges are the cut and thrust of litigation in front of UK (or, for that matter, Irish courts), where *oral* advocacy skills, in addition to *written* advocacy skills, are an essential part of the game.

When the UK joined the European Communities, the Court had four AGs delivering Opinions. Thus, the style of Opinions was – in general terms – established. It is clear though that it has evolved since, and surely the UK AGs had a role to play in this regard. As Moser and Sawyer noted in 2008:

> It may well be that the more 'English' style of opinions is due in no small part to the contributions of Francis Jacobs and his two UK predecessors, Gordon Slynn and Jean-Pierre Warner.[12]

This apt conclusion applies, of course, also to AG Sharpston and her Opinions. And then there is the British sense of humour with its inextricably linked touch of lightness, which UK AGs brought to the Court, and which – as AG Szpunar once argued – non-British members of the public are not expected to understand.[13] The British sense of humour was visible not only

---

ECLI:EU:C:2016:77) and the Opinion of AG Jacobs in Case C-195/98 *Österreichischer Gewerkschaftsbund* ECLI:EU:C:2000:50). See, furthermore, the Opinion of AG Medina in Case C-344/20, *LF v SCRL* ECLI:EU:C:2022:328, referring the 'Shadow Opinion' of AG Sharpston in Joined Cases C-804/18 and C-341/19, *WABE*.

[7] Opinion of AG Jacobs in Case C-50/00 P *UPA* ECLI:EU:C:2002:197. See ch 33.

[8] Opinion of AG Sharpston in Case C-34/09 *Ruiz Zambrano* ECLI:EU:C:2010:560. See ch 40.

[9] GF Mancini and DT Keeling, 'Language, Culture and Politics in the Life of the European Court of Justice' (1995) 1 *CJEL* 397, 399.

[10] See ch 10.

[11] See ch 50.

[12] P Moser and K Sawyer, 'Introduction: Making Community Law: The legacy of Advocate General Jacobs at the European Court of Justice' in P Moser and K Sawyer (eds), *Making Community Law: The Legacy of Advocate General Jacobs at the European Court of Justice* (Cheltenham, Edward Elgar, 2008) 1, 6.

[13] Introductory speech at the University of Westminster, 16 February 2016, www.youtube.com/watch?v= nCZAHIJMDMk.

at hearings, as attested by Laurence Gormley earlier in this book,[14] but also in the Opinions themselves. For example, in *Kali*, the Opinion of AG Warner opened as follows:

> My Lords,
>
> When I first saw the names of these cases, I wondered how a Hindu goddess, even one with such a reputation for ag[g]ressiveness, could have come into conflict, not once but twice, with Community law. On opening the papers I discovered that she had not, Kali is also German for potash, and these cases are about fertilizers.[15]

The following passage from the Opinion of AG Jacobs in *Gourmet* may serve as another good example.[16] When considering whether the ban on the advertising of alcoholic goods in Sweden was justifiable under the free movement of goods, AG Jacobs argued:

> it seems to me highly unlikely that a reader – who has presumably made a conscious choice to read the magazine [addressed to alcohol merchants] unless it is common in dentists' waiting rooms – will be incited to drink alcohol to any greater extent as the result of the presence of commercial advertising material than he or she would otherwise have been after reading the editorial content.[17]

Readers will be excused for their loud 'hear hear' at this juncture. Such a tiny breath of fresh air is always very much welcome, especially when reading about tedious and technical nuances of EU law which are anything but easy to digest or exciting in nature.[18]

The UK AGs have also contributed to ongoing discussions on the functioning of the Court. For instance, AG Sharpston was involved internally at the Court in re-designing the appeal system, in the wake of the reform of the General Court and closure of the Civil Service Tribunal (CST) as the sole specialised court. AG Jacobs in his interventions played a role in advocating for a green light system in preliminary rulings, encouraging national courts to suggest answers to their queries in references to the Court.[19] Today, the Court very much welcomes suggestions from national courts on what they think is the proper interpretation of EU law.

The UK AGs have been also known for wearing the hats of educators. By the same token, they indirectly shaped EU law, its reception at the national level, and the way it is perceived by society at large. This was of particular importance in their own Member State, where Euroscepticism had been in abundance, and had even preceded accession to the European Communities. Such interventions were welcome as, in the words of Mummery:

> Good teachers dispel the ignorance and stupidity in which suspicion flourishes and they replace it with knowledge, understanding and wisdom.[20]

The UK AGs spent ample time popularising and explaining their own role at the Court,[21] as well as the function that the Court plays in the EU legal order.[22] Such educational activities

---

[14] See ch 21.

[15] Opinion of AG Warner in Joined Cases 19/4 and 20/74 *Kali* ECLI:EU:C:1975:37.

[16] Opinion of AG Jacobs in Case C-405/98 *Gourmet* ECLI:EU:C:2000:690.

[17] Para 59 of the Opinion.

[18] See further A Arnull, 'Postscript' in Moser and Sawyer (n 12) 228, 230–231.

[19] Moser and Sawyer (n 12) 14–15.

[20] J Mummery, 'Links with national courts' in Moser and Sawyer (n 12) 103.

[21] See, inter alia, FG Jacobs, 'Advocates General and Judges in the European Court of Justice: Some Personal Reflections', in D O'Keeffe and A Bavasso (eds), *Liber Amicorum in Honour of Lord Slynn of Hadley: Judicial Review in European Union Law* (The Hague, Kluwer Law International, 2000).

[22] See, inter alia, G Slynn, 'The Court of Justice of the European Communities' (1984) 33 *ICLQ* 409; G Slynn, 'What is a European Community Law Judge?' (1993) 52 *CLJ* 234; D Edward, 'How the Court of Justice works' (1995) 20 *ELRev* 539; E Sharpston and G De Baere, 'The Court of Justice as a Constitutional Adjudicator' in A Arnull, C Barnard, M Dougan, and E Spaventa (eds), *A Constitutional Order of States? Essays in EU Law in Honour of Alan Dashwood* (Oxford, Hart Publishing, 2011).

started rather early, almost immediately after the UK's accession to the then European Communities. A good example was a talk given by AG Warner, followed by a publication of a very informative and educational set of reflections on the role of AG at the Court.[23] In this respect, the Hamlyn Lectures – addressed to the wider public – delivered by AG Slynn, AG Jacobs, and AG Sharpston, were intellectual blockbusters.[24] The UK AGs also regularly engaged in debates focusing on the impact of EU law on the UK legal orders,[25] as well as broader discussions about the shape of EU law, both in terms of future reforms of the Court,[26] but also a wide spectrum of areas regulated by EU law.[27] Last but not least, as Fritz notes in her chapter in this book, AG Slynn and AG Sharpston heavily contributed, *qua* their support for British Law Centres, as well as the Central and Eastern European Moot Court Competition, to education of young lawyers to the East of the river Elba.[28]

III. THE JURY IS OUT: OPINIONS OF UK AGS

For reasons that deserve no further explanation, it would be impossible to analyse all the Opinions of the UK AGs in a single volume. Choices had to be made. As explained in the Introduction, the editors were governed by the words of the great Spanish writer Miguel de

---

[23] J-P Warner, 'Some Aspects of the European Court of Justice' (1976) 14 *Journal of the Society of Public Teachers of Law* 14.

[24] G Slynn, *Introducing a European Legal Order* (London, Stevens and Sons, 1992); FG Jacobs, *The Sovereignty of Law. The European Way* (Cambridge, CUP, 2007); E Sharpston, *The Great Experiment: Constructing a European Union under the Rule of Law from a Group of Diverse Sovereign States* forthcoming.

[25] See, inter alia, M Andenas and FG Jacobs (eds), *European Community Law in the English Courts* (Oxford, OUP, 1998); FG Jacobs, 'Influence of European Community Law on Public Law in the United Kingdom' (1999–2000) 2 *CYELS* 1.

[26] See, inter alia, C Barnard and E Sharpston, 'The Changing Face of Article 177 References' (1997) 34 *CMLRev* 1113; FG Jacobs, 'Recent and ongoing measures to improve the efficiency of the European Court of Justice' (2004) 29 *ELRev* 823; E Sharpston, 'The Changing Role of the Advocate General' in A Arnull, P Eeckhout, and T Tridimas (eds), *Continuity and Change in EU Law: Essays in Honour of Sir Francis Jacobs* (Oxford, OUP, 2008); D Edward, 'Reform of Article 234 Procedure: the Limits of the Possible' in in O'Keeffe and Bavasso (n 21); FG Jacobs, 'The Lisbon Treaty and the Court of Justice' in A Biondi, P Eeckhout, and S Ripley (eds), *EU Law After Lisbon* (Oxford, OUP, 2010); FG Jacobs, 'The Court of Justice in the twenty-first century. Challenges ahead for juridical system?' in A Rosas, E Levits, and Y Bot (eds), *The Court of Justice and the Construction of Europe* (The Hague, Asser Press/Springer, 2013).

[27] See, inter alia, E Sharpston, 'Milk Lakes, SLOMs, and Legitimate Expectations – a Paradigm in Judicial Review' in O'Keeffe and Bavasso (n 21); D Edward and J Bengoetxea, 'The Status and Rights of Sub-state Entities in the Constitutional Order of the European Union', in Arnull, Barnard, Dougan, and Spaventa (n 22); D Edward and N Nic Shuibhne, 'Continuity and Change in the Law Relating to Services' in Arnull, Eeckhout, and Tridimas (n 26); FG Jacobs, 'The Internal Legal Effects of the EU's International Agreements and the Protection of Individual Rights' in Arnull, Barnard, Dougan, and Spaventa (n 22); E Sharpston, 'Different but (Almost) Equal – The Development of Free Movement Rights Under EU Association, Co-operation and Accession Agreements' in M Hoskins and W Robinson (eds), *A True European: Essays for Judge David Edward* (Oxford, Hart Publishing, 2003); D Sarmiento and E Sharpston, 'European Citizenship and its New Union: Time to Move On?' in D Kochenov (ed), *EU Citizenship and Federalism: The Role of Rights* (Cambridge, CUP, 2017); E Sharpston, 'Religion in the Workplace: When is Enforcing of Religious Ethos Acceptable? and When is Neutrality Discrimination?' in K Lenaerts, J-C Bonichot, H Kanninen, C Naômé, and P Pohjankoski (eds), *An Ever-Changing Union? Perspectives on the Future of EU Law in Honour of Allan Rosas* (Oxford, Hart Publishing, 2019); E Sharpston, 'About that Sunday Trading Mess ...' in F Amtenbrink, G Davies, D Kochenov, and J Lindeboom (eds), *The Internal Market and the Future of European Integration: Essays in Honour of Laurence W. Gormley* (Cambridge, CUP, 2019); FG Jacobs, 'The Role of the EU Court and National Courts in Developing the EU's Internal Market: a Paradigm for Other Regional Organisations?' in Amtenbrink, Davies, Kochenov, and Lindeboom (ibid); D Edward, 'What Was *Keck* Really About?' in Amtenbrink, Davies, Kochenov, and Lindeboom (ibid).

[28] See ch 5.

Cervantes, who famously said that 'by a small sample we may judge of the whole piece'.[29] In these conclusions it is only apt, in a true European spirit, to marry this wise proposition with an idea which came from a quintessentially British figure – Sherlock Holmes. According to his Second Law of Life, 'it is a capital mistake to theorise before one has the data'.[30] In late 2020, when this book was conceptualised, all the data needed for assessment of Opinions of the UK AGs was in place, ready to be analysed and theorised. During 47 years of UK membership of the EEC/EC/EU, its AGs delivered hundreds of Opinions, leaving commentators with an abundance of evidence to choose from and to comment on. And then came Brexit.

The UK's withdrawal from the EU has been a watershed moment at many levels. A cut off point, save only by the terms of the EU-UK Withdrawal Agreement (EU-UK WA),[31] and the EU-UK Trade and Cooperation Agreement (EU-UK TCA).[32] It translated, among others, into termination of mandates of UK judges on 31 January 2020. This was followed by a legally questionable termination of mandate of AG Sharpston in September 2020.[33] Consequentially, and to much regret, it is unlikely any new contributions of UK AGs to the judicial discourse at the Court will be seen. This chapter of the UK's active involvement in the shaping of EU law is, if not definitely, then at least temporarily, closed.[34] Put differently, an important era came to an end. This is even though, as already argued, many Opinions of the UK AGs delivered between 1973–2020 are likely to radiate in the future.

This combination of prolific background material and, to use the words of Barnes,[35] the sense of an ending, made it fitting to pause and to indulge in legal peregrinations in time, all the way back to 1973. For aficionados, the contribution of the UK AGs to EU judicial and academic discourse has been unquestionable, and it is already sadly missed. However, it stands at risk of being overshadowed by the Brexit clout, bad blood, and partisanship that UK's withdrawal has brought. Therefore, in a way, the *raison d'être* behind this volume was to set the record straight.

As *cliché* as it may be, it is crucial to emphasise that AG Warner, AG Slynn, AG Jacobs, and AG Sharpston served in different eras. This, as alluded to previously, allowed AG Jacobs and AG Sharpston to soar at higher altitudes, giving them ample opportunities to explore and to shape many other areas of EU law that did not even exist when AG Slynn and AG Warner were members of the Court. Simply, the times and the surrounding circumstances were different. Their lengthier terms of office also contributed to this. Therefore, the records of four UK AGs should not be juxtaposed with one another, and their Opinions need to be analysed in the context of the era that they each belonged to. When AG Warner joined the bench, EEC law was in its early days. It was, in the words of Dashwood, 'the Court's "heroic age"'.[36] This was

---

[29] M de Cervantes, *D Quixote de la Mancha* (1605–1615), Part I, Book I, Ch. 4.

[30] H Rawson, *The Unwritten Laws of Life* (Carbolic Smoke Ball Co, 2008) 136.

[31] Agreement on the withdrawal of the United Kingdom of Great Britain and Northern Ireland from the European Union and the European Atomic Energy Community [2020] OJ L29/7.

[32] Trade and Cooperation Agreement between the European Union and the European Atomic Energy Community, of the one part, and the United Kingdom of Great Britain and Northern Ireland, of the other part [2021] OJ L149/10.

[33] See further D Kochenov and G Butler, 'Independence of the Court of Justice of the European Union: Unchecked Member States power after the Sharpston Affair' (2021) *ELJ* 262.

[34] Bearing in mind the contemporary shape of EU pre-accession policy it is highly unlikely that the UK would return to the European Union.

[35] J Barnes, *The Sense of an Ending* (London, Jonathan Cape, 2011).

[36] See ch 9.

an era of *Dassonville*,[37] *Cassis de Dijon*,[38] and *Simmenthal*,[39] amongst many other classics of the day.

However, despite all these great judgments, EEC law back then was really about the common market, its four freedoms, the customs union, and the beginnings of a common commercial policy. Consequentially, the Court's docket was filled with cases which, from today's perspective, look painfully technical, and perhaps slightly monotonous. Neither AG Warner, nor AG Slynn could have been given opportunities to venture into meanders of, to name a few, EU citizenship, EU environmental law, EU criminal law, or EU asylum legislation. But they had their share of foundational cases, for instance, on enforcement of the then EEC law in national courts.[40]

Furthermore, it needs to be remembered that during their respective tenures at the Court (and also AG Jacobs for a large part of his tenure), Opinions of AGs were required in *every* case. Consequentially, the record of AG Warner, AG Slynn, and – up to a point – of AG Jacobs covers not only ground-breaking cases, some of which were analysed earlier in this book, but also fairly pedestrian straightforward infractions,[41] or staff cases.[42] It proves, in hindsight, that the decision to allow the Court to engage AGs only in selected and important cases was fit for purpose.[43] Though, as noted by Sharpston, in her chapter, it is not without risks as expediency may trump the real need for an Opinion in a given case.[44]

During their tenures, AG Jacobs and AG Sharpston experienced, and contributed to, tectonic changes to European integration through law. When AG Jacobs joined the Court in 1988, the Communities were undergoing the first major treaty revision since their creation,[45] the White Paper on the Completion of the Internal Market was being implemented,[46] the talks between European Free Trade Association (EFTA) and the Communities on the creation

---

[37] Case 8/74 *Dassonville* ECLI:EU:C:1974:82.

[38] Case 120/78 *Cassis de Dijon* ECLI:EU:C:1979:42.

[39] Case 106/77 *Simmenthal* ECLI:EU:C:1978:49.

[40] Opinion of AG Slynn in Case 152/84 *Marshall* ECLI:EU:C:1985:345. See ch 20.

[41] See, inter alia, Opinion of AG Slynn in Case 280/83 *Commission v Italy* ECLI:EU:C:1984:279; Opinion of AG Warner in Case 163/78 *Commission v Italy* ECLI:EU:C:1979:27. In the latter case AG Warner reduced his Opinion to the following:

> 'In this case there is little that I can usefully say. The Italian Republic admits that it has failed to bring into force the national legislation necessary to comply with the Directive. It explains that the delay is due to internal difficulties, but recognizes that such difficulties cannot be invoked to justify a failure by a Member State to fulfil an obligation under the Treaty.

> In my opinion, in those circumstances, Your Lordships can but make the declaration sought by the Commission, and order the Italian Republic to pay the costs of the action.'

[42] See, inter alia, Opinion of AG Warner in Case 58/72 *Perinciolo* ECLI:EU:C:1973:43; Opinion of AG Warner in Joined Cases 112/73, 144/73 and 145/73 *Campogrande* ECLI:EU:C:1974:78, Opinion of AG Slynn in Case 47/87 *Lucas* ECLI:EU:C:1988:144; Opinion of AG Slynn in Case 12/84 *Kypreos* ECLI:EU:C:1985:76.

[43] The reform was brought by the Treaty of Nice (Treaty of Nice amending the Treaty on European Union, the Treaties establishing the European Communities and certain related acts, signed at Nice, 26 February 2001 [2001] C80/1). See further N Burrows and R Greaves, *The Advocate General and EC Law* (Oxford, OUP, 2007) 20–22.

[44] See ch 52.

[45] Single European Act [1987] OJ L169/1. See further, inter alia, D Swann (ed), *The Single European Market and Beyond. A Study of the Wider Implications of the Single European Act* (Abingdon, Routledge, 1992).

[46] European Commission, 'Completing the Internal Market; White Paper from the Commission to the European Council (Milan, 28-29 June 1985)' COM (85) 310 final. The White Paper was prepared by Lord Cockfield, a UK member of the European Commission. See further A Łazowski, 'Goodbye but no good riddance: Internal Market with and without the United Kingdom' in A Łazowski and A Cygan (eds), *Research Handbook on Legal Aspects of Brexit* (Cheltenham, Edward Elgar, 2022).

of a European Economic Area (EEA) were in full swing,[47] and the Iron Curtain was starting to crumble.[48] The Court had rejected the existence competence of the EU to accede to the European Convention on Human Rights (ECHR) in *Opinion 2/94*, whilst at the same time, the role of the ECHR in the case law of the Court continued to rise.[49]

In 2006, when AG Jacobs retired from the Court, things were very different. The European Union was in place, with new areas of EU law rapidly emerging, and waves of enlargements bringing the number of Member States to 25 and beyond. In legal terms, seismic changes also took place when AG Sharpston served at the Court. The entry into force of the Treaty of Lisbon[50] was a breakthrough: the EU's own Charter of Fundamental Rights became binding,[51] EU criminal law was given a chance to evolve like any other area of EU law, and the EU became more ambitious in terms of its common commercial policy. All these changes, quite inevitably, have led to a lot of litigation, both at the national level, and at the Court. As one would expect, they made the docket of AG Jacobs and AG Sharpston way more multifarious than it had been the case during the tenures of AG Warner and AG Slynn.[52] The selection of Opinions in this book mirrors this phenomenon rather well.

Admittedly, Opinions of the AGs may be analysed and assessed in lots of different ways. The ways in which the authors in this book have gone about their analysis proves this. In this respect though, of course, UK AGs and their Opinions are not completely different to Opinions of AGs coming from other Member States. As hinted at already, a common point of departure is whether AGs are followed or not by the Court in a case at hand. Such an approach is, however, when viewed alone, based on a nuance-shy assumption that such a binary choice exists. As noted earlier, frequently it does not. Put differently, while in some cases it is possible to conclude that, indeed, an AG is being followed,[53] in others it is not so easy to detect. Even when AGs are followed, questions emerge to what extent judges may be driven by the advice of their AG, or – perhaps – they are already on the same page. As it is well known, the secrecy of Courts *délibéré*, combined with the tradition of mere *en passant* references to Opinion of the AG in the case at hand, means that for outsiders, or even for AGs themselves (as they are not part of the deliberations) the truth is preciously kept away from the outside world. Still, however, in the case of several Opinions of the UK AGs analysed in this volume, it is possible to conclude that the AGs and judges shared the same approach to the matter at hand. The Opinions of AG Slynn in *Commission v Germany (Beer Purity)*[54] and in *Klopp*[55] may serve as good examples. The same goes, *exempli gratia*, for the Opinion of AG Jacobs in *Pokrzeptowicz-Meyer*.[56]

---

[47] See, inter alia, M Robinson and J Findlater (eds), *Creating a European Economic Space: Legal Aspects of EC-EFTA Relations* (Irish Centre for European Law, 1990).

[48] For a historical account see, inter alia, T Garton Ash, *We the People: The Revolution of '89 Witnessed in Warsaw, Budapest, Berlin and Prague* (London, Penguin, 1990).

[49] Opinion of AG Jacobs in Case C-84/95 *Bosphorus* ECLI:EU:C:1996:179. See ch 30.

[50] Treaty of Lisbon amending the Treaty on European Union and the Treaty establishing the European Community, signed at Lisbon, 13 December 2007, [2007] OJ C 306/1.

[51] Though fundamental rights were part of the Court's case law. See Opinion of AG Jacobs in Case 5/88 *Wachauf* ECLI:EU:C:1989:179; Opinion of AG Jacobs in Case C-112/00 *Schmidberger* ECLI:EU:C:2002:437. See ch 34.

[52] For example, it is hard to imagine the issue of last names coming before the Court in earlier times. See Opinion of AG Sharpston in Case C-353/06 *Grunkin and Paul* ECLI:EU:C:2008:246. See ch 38.

[53] For example, see Opinion of AG Sharpston in Case C-507/18 *NH* ECLI:EU:C:2019:922. See ch 48.

[54] Opinion of AG Slynn in Case 178/84 *Commission v Germany* ECLI:EU:C:1986:324 (*Beer Purity*). See ch 22.

[55] Opinion of AG Slynn in Case 107/83 *Klopp* ECLI:EU:C:1984:174. See ch 18.

[56] Opinion of AG Jacobs in Case C-162/00 *Pokrzeptowicz-Meyer* ECLI:EU:C:2001:474. See ch 36.

When judges concur with Opinions of AGs, for either of the two reasons mentioned above, this may have far reaching consequences not only for the cases at hand, but also for the future shape of EU law. For example, the Opinion of AG Warner in *Bearings I*[57] influenced the revision of the then EU Antidumping Regulation.[58] It led to enhancement of rights of undertakings in antidumping investigations. There is no doubt here that the common law principle of access to justice was the factor behind the thinking of AG Warner. It had already been evident in 1974 in his Opinion in *Transocean Marine Paint Association*.[59]

As much as it is considered a rarity, Opinions of the AGs may inspire the Court to depart openly from its *jurisprudence constante*. The Court is known for its attachment to this desideratum, making a 'reverse ferret' an unlikely scenario. Put differently, the Court is not exactly known for its willingness to overturn itself – explicitly or implicitly – though it will occasionally do so. One of the first, if not the first, to achieve such a milestone was AG Jacobs in *HAG II*.[60] The Court, encouraged by AG Jacobs, openly declared that the previous take on trademarks in *HAG I* had not been a sound judgment.[61] Admittedly, the Court does turn its back on some of its old case law, but rarely does so, and sometimes it takes the reasoning of an AG to detail why such a change in approach is needed.[62]

In many instances, the AGs and the Court reach the same destination but having travelled on different trajectories. This happened, for instance, in *Henn and Darby*, where AG Warner and the Court reached the same conclusions, however some of the accents were put in different places.[63] Similarly, in the words of Butler, 'by-and-large AG [Slynn] and Court were in agreement, though differing somewhat' in *Campus Oil*.[64] The Opinion of AG Jacobs in *Van Schijndel* is yet another example.[65] Furthermore, they might reach a similar conclusion, but use different language to explain their own. The Opinion of AG Jacobs in *TWD*,[66] and the judgment of the Court in that case illustrate this point quite vividly.

Naturally, the Court does not have to follow its AGs and thus, the judges are free to disagree with the Opinion offered. For instance, in *Miles*, the Court disagreed with AG Sharpston and ruled, contrary to her persuasive recommendation, that the reference for preliminary ruling submitted by the Complaints Board of the European Schools was not admissible.[67] The Opinion of AG Sharpston in *Radu* also belongs to the same category.[68] Whilst opting

---

[57] Opinion of AG Warner in Case 113/77, 118/77, 119/77, 120/77, 121/77 *Bearings I* ECLI:EU:C:1979:39. See ch 11.

[58] See Commission, 'Proposal for a Council Regulation (EEC) amending Regulation (EEC) No 459/68 on protection against dumping or the granting of bounties or subsidies by countries which are not members of the European Economic Community' COM (1979) 304 final; Council Regulation (EEC) No 1681/79 of 1 August 1979 amending Regulation (EEC) No 459/68 on protection against dumping or the granting of bounties or subsidies by countries which are not members of the European Economic Community [1979] OJ L 196/1.

[59] Opinion of AG Warner in Case 17/74 *Transocean Marine Paint Association* ECLI:EU:C:1974:91.

[60] Opinion of AG Jacobs in Case C-10/89 *HAG* ECLI:EU:C:1990:112 (*HAG II*). See ch 24.

[61] Case 192/73 *HAG* ECLI:EU:C:1974:72 (*HAG I*).

[62] See, for example, Opinion of AG Hogan in Case C-274/14 *Banco de Santander SA* ECLI:EU:C:2019:802, in which he argued that the Court should overturn its case law on admissibility of preliminary references from tribunals which are not independent. In doing so, he cited specifically a prior Opinion of one of his predecessors, Opinion of AG Saggio in Joined Cases C-110/98 to C-147/98 *Gabalfrisa* ECLI:EU:C:1999:489 (AG was not followed in this instance). In *Banco de Santander*, the Court agreed with AG Hogan, and *post facto*, AG Saggio, and overturned its *Gabalfrisa* judgment on admissibility of such requests.

[63] Opinion of AG Warner in Case 34/79 *Henn and Darby* ECLI:EU:C:1979:246. See ch 12.

[64] Opinion of AG Slynn in Case 73/82 *Campus Oil* ECLI:EU:C:1984:154. See ch 17.

[65] Opinion of AG Jacobs in Joined Cases C-430/93 and C-431/93 *Van Schijndel* ECLI:EU:C:1995:441. See ch 29.

[66] Opinion of AG Jacobs in Case C-188/92 *TWD* ECLI:EU:C:1993:358. See ch 27.

[67] Opinion of AG Sharpston in Case C-196/09 *Miles* ECLI:EU:C:2010:777. See ch 42.

[68] Opinion of AG Sharpston in Case C-396/11 *Radu* ECLI:EU:C:2012:648. See ch 43.

for a different course however, the Court never responds to *why* it has not opted for the same reasoning or approach.

It may well happen that the AGs are ahead of their time, which – as alluded to earlier in this chapter – may mean that Opinions, or some parts of the AGs reasoning – continue to shape EU law years later and are eventually picked up by the Court. As argued by Sarmiento in this volume, the Opinion of AG Slynn in *Foglia II* may serve as a very good example.[69] The Opinion of AG Slynn in *Cinéthèque* belongs to the same category.[70] The Opinions of AG Jacobs in *Leclerc-Siplec*, *De Agostini*, and *Gourmet* continue to resonate years later.[71] As shown by the Opinion of AG Warner in *Manghera*, it may well be *obiter dictum* that stands out in a longer-term perspective.[72] Alas, one of the most important and commented Opinions of AG Jacobs, which was in *UPA*, is still waiting for better days in terms of its adoption by the Court. Despite advances brought by the Treaty of Lisbon to relax the strict criteria for *locus standi* of individuals under Article 263 TFEU, the door to the Court remains merely ajar to natural and legal persons seeking judicial review of acts which are not addressed to them.[73]

In some cases, the AGs do not go as far as the Court eventually does. This may take place when both the AGs and the Court are asked to deal with an unexplored matter of EU law, neither properly regulated, nor touched upon before. Such novel matters may, indeed, lead to divergence of views. Several examples to evidence this phenomenon can be found in the wide suite of Opinions delivered by the UK AGs. For instance in *Rewe*, the Court went further than AG Warner and proclaimed the principles of equivalence and effectiveness that national provisions governing enforcement of law must comply with.[74] This was one of the first instances of the Court broaching the procedural autonomy of the Member States. In *AM&S*, both the AGs in the case, and the Court, were taking a leap into the unknown. The extent to which legal privilege was to apply to antitrust procedures was not regulated in EEC law, and at the same time, the standards applicable in the then nine Member States varied. Fate had it that two AGs were asked to deliver Opinions on the matter, given AG Slynn succeeded AG Warner. This was and continues to be a rarity.[75] Their paths crossed again, albeit in two separate, though inextricably linked *Foglia I* and *Foglia II* cases, where AG Warner and AG Slynn delivered rather contrasting Opinions.[76]

The other UK AGs also had their share of similar experiences in the Court, going further than they had concluded. For instance, in *Gascogne*, AG Sharpston argued that delays in the General Court may result in breach of the principle of effective legal protection guaranteed by the Charter of Fundamental Rights.[77] The Court went one step further. Not only did it agree with its AG, but it also applied the EU liability test laid down in *Bergaderm*,[78] with the view of concluding that the General Court was indeed in breach of the Charter, and thus

---

[69] Opinion of AG Slynn in Case 244/80 *Foglia II* ECLI:EU:C:1981:175. See ch 15.

[70] Opinion of AG Slynn Joined Cases 60 and 61/84 *Cinéthèque* ECLI:EU:C:1985:122. See ch 19.

[71] Opinions of AG Jacobs in Case C-412/93 *Leclerc-Siplec* ECLI:EU:C:1994:393; Joined Cases C-34/95, C-35/95 and C-36/95 *De Agostini*, ECLI:EU:C:1996:333; Case C-405/98 *Gourmet* ECLI:EU:C:2000:690. See ch 35.

[72] Opinion of AG Warner in Case 59/75 *Manghera* ECLI:EU:C:1976:1. See ch 8.

[73] See, inter alia, S Peers and M Costa, 'Judicial Review of EU acts After the Treaty of Lisbon' (2012) 8 *EuConst* 82. See ch 4.

[74] Opinion of AG Warner in Case 33/76 *Rewe* ECLI:EU:C:1976:167. See ch 9.

[75] Opinion of AG Warner in Case 155/79 *AM&S* ECLI:EU:C:1981:9; Opinion of AG Slynn in Case 155/79 *AM&S* ECLI:EU:C:1982:17. See ch 14.

[76] Opinion of AG Warner in Case 104/79 *Foglia I* ECLI:EU:C:1980:22; Opinion of AG Slynn in Case 244/80 *Foglia II*.

[77] Opinion of AG Sharpston in Case C-58/12 P *Gascogne* ECLI:EU:C:2013:360.

[78] Case C-352/98 *Bergaderm* ECLI:EU:C:2000:361.

the EU should be liable in damages in case the applicants submit their application under Article 340 TFEU to that end.[79] Similarly, the Court went further than AG Sharpston in *Opinion 2/15* on post-Lisbon scope of the common commercial policy, in particular in relation to the scope of the exclusive competence laid down in Article 207 TFEU.[80]

It may well be the other way around: the Court does not go as far as suggested by its AG. For instance, in *Heinrich*, the Court was asked to determine the status of unpublished EU secondary legislation. AG Sharpston, mindful of the importance of the rule of law for the EU, advised the judges to declare Regulation as non-existent.[81] This far-reaching proposition was not entertained by the Court, which ruled instead that unpublished legal acts were not enforceable vis-à-vis individuals. As argued by Xanthaki and Łazowski, it was an unfortunate turn of events, and ultimate failure of the Court to put a firm mark on respect for the rule of law. However, a few years later, the era of rule of law jurisprudence eventually reached the Court courtesy of several Member States which stepped on the path of constitutional vandalism. Questions also emerged about the lawful composition of the Court's sole specialised court – the CST.[82]

Sometimes, it impossible to tell whether an AG was followed or not. It happens in cases of poorly reasoned judgments when the only source of legal analysis is the Opinion of the AG in a given case. On such occasions, quite naturally, questions are raised as to where to draw the line between assistance, which is an AG's job, and substitution, which is not part of an AG's job description. As noted earlier, *Ruiz Zambrano* is the textbook example of such a case.

Another situation is when a case is withdrawn after the Opinion of the AG is delivered, but before the Court is given a chance to render a judgment. Such a scenario is not unheard of.[83] This happened, for instance, in *Commission v Greece (FYROM)* when following the Opinion of AG Jacobs, the case was withdrawn by the applicant.[84] Another scenario is when the Opinion of the AG presents on the substance of the case, which is subsequently declared inadmissible by the Court. A reminder is fitting that some AGs, even when cases are quite obviously inadmissible, do provide analysis of the substance. This, arguably, serves two purposes. First, in case the Court is willing to proceed with a case regardless of questionable admissibility, the judges have an Opinion to rely on. Secondly, even if the final decision on admissibility is negative, an Opinion may still have a role to play until the law is clarified at a later stage, for instance, by the Court in subsequent jurisprudence. This was the case with the Opinion of AG Jacobs in *Syfait*.[85] It proved to be of fundamental importance for interpretation of Article 102 TFEU, its application to pharmaceutical industry, and obstacles to parallel trade.[86]

Opinions of the AGs should be read and analysed in context. EU law, just like any other legal order, is in a state of constant flux. Thus, some Opinions in which AGs excel and take shaping of EU law to new levels turn out to be period pieces. They are no doubt important at

---

[79] Case C-58/12 P *Gascogne* ECLI:EU:C:2013:770.

[80] Opinion of AG Sharpston in *Opinion 2/15* ECLI:EU:C:2016:992. See ch 45.

[81] Opinion of AG Sharpston in Case C-345/06 *Heinrich* ECLI:EU:C:2008:212. See ch 37.

[82] Opinion of AG Sharpston in Cases C-542/18 RX-II and C-543/18 RX-II *Simpson* ECLI:EU:C:2019:977. See ch 49.

[83] Indeed, after AG Collins got to deliver his first Opinion as a member of Court in 2021, the case was withdrawn in 2022, before the Court had rendered its judgment. See Opinion of AG Collins in Case C-235/20 P *ViaSat* ECLI:EU:C:2021:941.

[84] Opinion of AG Jacobs in Case C 120/94 *Commission v Greece* ECLI:EU:C:1995:109 (*FYROM*). See ch 28.

[85] Opinion of AG Jacobs in Case C-53/03 *Syfait* ECLI:EU:C:2004:673.

[86] See R Whish, 'Competition Law' in Moser and Sawyer (n 12) 115, 120–22.

the time, but can be overshadowed later by developments in EU primary and secondary law, and in some cases, confined to history books in the end. The Opinion of AG Jacobs in *Collins* is very instructive in this respect.[87] It was of fundamental importance for Phil Collins, Cliff Richard, and many other artists as it allowed them to block distribution of illegally released bootlegs in Germany. This was back in the 1990s, which was before a flurry of EU secondary legislation providing for more comprehensive intellectual property rights were drafted. These days, indeed, musicians finding themselves in a comparable predicament to Phil Collins and Cliff Richard have EU secondary law to rely on. Despite this, the legacy of the Opinion of AG Jacobs in that case remains. It may be a period piece, but the direct effect of Article 18(1) TFEU, containing the general prohibition of discrimination on grounds of nationality, is standing strong.

Depending on circumstances, the Opinions of the AGs may remain important only for the case at hand, and be largely forgotten thereafter. The Opinion of AG Warner in *Ireland v Council* is a very good example in this respect.[88] Other Opinions of the AGs make a long-lasting impact and remain points of reference years, or even decades, later. This may be confined to the European Union and the Court. The Opinions of the AGs may also cross outside external borders of the EU, and be picked up in other jurisdictions. As Baudenbacher argued earlier in this volume, the Opinion of AG Jacobs in *Albany*,[89] while not followed by Court, decisively influenced the EFTA Court in *LO*.[90]

Opinions of the AGs are, of course, scrutinised by the academy. They are also on the radars of practitioners. Consequentially, the Opinions of AGs are praised and criticised in equal measure. While the Opinion of AG Sharpston in *Ruiz Zambrano* was acclaimed by many for its robustness and clarity of legal analysis,[91] the thinness of the Opinion of AG Warner in *Walrave and Koch* – contrasted with the importance of this case – was not terribly well received.[92] A similar fate was also shared regarding the Opinion of AG Warner in *Foglia I*,[93] which – as noted by Bradley – received a barrage of criticism.[94] As regards an Opinion that had both positives and negatives, the Opinion of AG Slynn in *Levin* is of particular note.[95] For the long-term implications of Opinions of the AGs, the Opinion of AG Slynn in *Marshall I* on the lack of horizontal direct effect of directives was not praised either.[96]

---

[87] Opinion of AG Jacobs in Joined Cases C-92/92 and C-326/92 *Collins* ECLI:EU:C:1993:276. See ch 26.

[88] Opinion of AG Warner in Case 151/73 *Ireland v Council* ECLI:EU:C:1974:14 (see ch 6). In that case, after the Court agreed on the same outcome as AG Warner – which saw a Regulation voided – AG Warner later remarked, 'I have it on the authority of the President of Ireland that the Court's health was drunk in the pubs of Dublin that night. I suspect he had in mind some near the Four Courts'. J-P Warner, 'The evolution of the work of the European Court of Justice' in Court of Justice of the European Communities (eds), *Judicial and Academic Conference 27-27 September 1976* (Luxembourg, 1976), p 7. The President of Ireland at the time, to whom AG Warner was referring to, was Cearbhall Ó Dálaigh, a judge at the Court from 1973–74, whom at that time, was a fellow member of the Court with AG Warner.

[89] Opinion of AG Jacobs Case C-67/96 *Albany*; Joined Cases C-115/97, C-116/97 and C-117/97; Case C-219/97 ECLI:EU:C:1999:28. See ch 31.

[90] Case E-8/00 *Norwegian Federation of Trade Unions and Others v Norwegian Association of Local and Regional Authorities and Others* [2002] EFTA Ct. Rep. 114.

[91] See ch 40.

[92] Opinion of AG Warner in Case 36/74 *Walrave* ECLI:EU:C:1974:111. See ch 7.

[93] Opinion of AG Warner in Case 104/79 *Foglia I* ECLI:EU:C:1980:22.

[94] See ch 13.

[95] Opinion of AG Slynn in Case 53/81 *Levin* ECLI:EU:C:1982:10. See ch 16.

[96] Opinion of AG Slynn in Case 152/84 *Marshall* ECLI:EU:C:1985:345. See ch 20. For a more open approach to horizontal effect, see Opinion of AG Sharpston in Case C-413/15 *Farrell* ECLI:EU:C:2017:492. See ch 46.

The long-term importance of the Opinions of the AG may lie not only in the substance of a given case and robustness of the legal analysis, but in a bold statement, or argument, made by an AG which becomes a beacon for navigation. For any EU law specialist, the nuances of national rules on spelling of names may not be something one rehearses on a daily basis. However, a simple mention of *Konstantinidis* immediately brings to one's mind the Opinion of AG Jacobs, and his famous 'Civis Europeus Sum' remark.[97] Equally poignant are the closing words in the Opinion of AG Sharpston in *Temporary Relocation*.[98] At the time of Brexit, and fully blown cases of constitutional vandalism in certain Member States, a reminder that solidarity is 'the lifeblood of the European project'[99] resonated with great power and, above all, it was very poignant. The beauty of the job of an AG is the unlimited freedom to speak openly, to use microscope and telescope in the same case, and to determine where the law should lead. This may happen in full knowledge, or an assumption, that the Court may not follow now but, perhaps, it may do so in the future when the winds are more permitting.

As this volume shows, it demonstrates how the advisory role of AGs has evolved over decades. As noted by Dashwood '[i]t was not his [AG Warner's] style to speculate as to how the law should develop in the future, but to help the Court find the right answer before it'.[100] His successors at the bench followed suit, but also adjusted to changing times and needs.[101] Several Opinions discussed in this book show how important AGs are when faced with novel questions raised by secondary legislation, especially when the latter suffers from constructive ambiguity, the price being paid for approval of a new legal act by the decision-making institutions. Here the role of the AGs is to advise, but also to warn. No other case proves it as well as *Sturgeon*.[102] AG Sharpston, and rightly so, felt compelled to draw the attention of the judges to poorly shaped Regulation 261/2004 on compensation for flight delays and cancellations.[103] Yet, despite the obvious flaws of the legislation, she issued a stark warning to the Court asking for prudence and reserve. After all, she argued, it is not the task of the Court to redraft the law adopted by EU institutions which are empowered to do so in EU Treaties. Alas, as it is well known, the Opinion of AG Sharpston did not trigger flashing red lights at the Court, which opted to proceed regardless, and quite predictably exposed itself to severe critique.[104]

Readers should not be under the impression that novel questions are a *spécialité de la maison* of legislation adopted by EU institutions at the time, which is not their finest hour. Even in the case of well-crafted EU regulations and directives, disputes arise as to the exact meaning of particular provisions, and the compatibility of national laws and practices with the EU standards. AGs are often called to assist, to take the bull by its horns. This, inevitably, may even lead to dialogue between several AGs acting in different cases pending in parallel. The Opinion of AG Sharpston in *Bougnaoui*[105] and the Opinion

---

[97] Opinion of AG Jacobs in Case C-168/91 *Konstantinidis* ECLI:EU:C:1992:504. See ch 25.

[98] Opinion of AG Sharpston in Case C-715/17 *Commission v Poland*, Case C-718/17 *Commission v Hungary*, and Case C-719/17 *Commission v Czech Republic* ECLI:EU:C:2019:917 (*Temporary Relocation*). See ch 47.

[99] Paras 253–255 of the Opinion.

[100] See ch 9.

[101] See eg Opinion of AG Jacobs in Case C-7/97 *Oscar Bronner* ECLI:EU:C:1998:265; Opinion of AG Jacobs in Case C-379/98 *PreussenElektra* ECLI:EU:C:2000:585. See ch 32.

[102] Opinion of AG Sharpston in Joined Cases C-402/07 and C-432/07 *Sturgeon* ECLI:EU:C:2009:416. See ch 39.

[103] Regulation (EC) No 261/2004 of the European Parliament and of the Council of 11 February 2004 establishing common rules on compensation and assistance to passengers in the event of denied boarding and of cancellation or long delay of flights, and repealing Regulation (EEC) No 295/91 [2004] OJ L 46/1.

[104] A similar warning was sent by AG Sharpston in para 77 of her Opinion in *Slovak Bears*. See ch 41.

[105] Opinion of AG Sharpston in Case C-188/15 *Bougnaoui* ECLI:EU:C:2016:553.

of AG Kokott in *Achbita*,[106] the so-called headscarf cases, are excellent examples in this respect.[107]

In the early days of 1973, when AG Warner joined the Court, European Court Reports, where judgments of the Court and Opinions of the AGs were published, were reduced to a single or a maximum of two modest volumes. At the time when AG Sharpston delivered her last Opinion, European Court Reports were a thing of the past, and no longer published. If their publication continued in the current era, they would have spanned dozens of volumes every year. These days, judgments of the General Court and the Court, and Opinions of the AGs, cover hundreds and thousands of pages. Consequentially, in all areas of EU law, one can easily detect lines of jurisprudence.

Despite the already mentioned desideratum of *jurisprudence constante*, the role of AGs is not to assure the judges that their interpretation of EU law is always correct. *Au contraire*, the task of AGs is also to ponder whether previous case law is in fact any good, or, to put it differently, to question a line of case law that is going in the wrong direction, or needs better steering towards a future course. They may do so even if it puts them on a collision course with other members of the Court. This is what characterised the contribution of UK AGs to the judicial discourse going on at the Court. As noted by Ritter, 'AG Jacobs distinguishe[d] himself by his habit of directly criticizing the Court's conscious policy choices'.[108] However, this was also the case with other UK AGs who challenged the Court when the shape of EU law and direction of travel was not, in their perspective, plausible. As AG Slynn told future AG Sharpston at the time when she was his *référendaire*, the role of the AG is not to anticipate what the Court will say. In his words 'an AG who is followed more than 7 or 8 times out of ten isn't doing his job – he's too close to the Court'.[109]

IV. BRITISH AND EUROPEAN: THE LEGACY OF UK ADVOCATES GENERAL

In the midst of Brexit turmoil, the then UK Prime Minister argued in her speech in Florence that: 'the United Kingdom has never totally felt at home being in the European Union'.[110] This is an obvious generalisation, which – perhaps – may be an accurate observation applicable to some circles, but not to others, and certainly not with regard to many lawyers. As this book demonstrates, all four UK AGs and Judge Edward (who acted as AG in the Court of First Instance, now the General Court)[111] found their new legal habitat most appealing. This started with AG Warner who joined the Court without any prior experience in a continental system. In the words of Brown, AG Warner 'was a common lawyer through and through'.[112] This view is also shared by Dashwood in the present volume.[113] Yet, it is clear that his mission was not to parachute common law concepts for the sake of doing it. He brought them forward when he believed that they were beneficiary to what was then EEC law.

---

[106] Opinion of AG Kokott in Case 157/15 *Achbita* ECLI:EU:C:2016:382.
[107] See ch 44.
[108] C Ritter, 'A New Look at the Role and Impact of Advocates-General – Collectively and Individually' (2006) 12 *CJEL* 751, 769–70.
[109] See ch 52.
[110] PM's Florence speech, 22 March 2017: a new era of cooperation and partnership between the UK and the EU.
[111] See chs 23 and 51.
[112] L Neville Brown, 'The Influence of the Conseil d'Etat on English Administrative Law and the European Court of Justice' in M Andenas and D Fairgrieve (eds), *Liber Amicorum in Honour of Lord Slynn of Hadley: Judicial Review in International Perspective, vol II* (The Hague, Kluwer Law International, 2000) 293, 298.
[113] See ch 9.

Commentators seem to be in unison that the changed nature of the oral part of the procedure and more lively hearings are a part of his legacy (and that of the first UK judge, Alexander Mackenzie Stuart).[114] As already mentioned, the Opinions of AG Warner in *Transocean Marine Paint Association* and in *Bearings I* demonstrate that the rights of individuals (in this case the right to be heard) were also close to his heart, and were where his contribution made the difference. His successor, AG Slynn, is also credited with advancing a more dynamic nature of hearings,[115] and bringing to the Court the principles of procedural fairness, known from common law.[116] Both AG Warner and AG Slynn found their way around in, at first sight, alien habitat. Their personal reflections show two common law lawyers coming to the Court with open minds, and eagerness to contribute to the European judicial discourse, but also to embrace its multinational character in which they were called to serve.[117] As aptly noted by Edward:

> the bringing together of lawyers from widely differing backgrounds is part of the richness of the Community system, and there is no country (including the most recent accessions) whose legal culture has not influenced the Court's jurisprudence).[118]

When AG Jacobs in 1988 and AG Sharpston in 2006 joined the Court, they were operating in more familiar territory. Both benefited from their earlier experience at the Court as *référendaires* of AG Warner and AG, later judge Slynn (respectively), not to mention that they regularly pleaded before the Court themselves thereafter. They too embraced their new legal habitat as AGs, which AG Sharpston hailed earlier in this book as a 'dream job'.[119]

This, obviously, takes us back to the title of this book: Shaping EU Law the British Way. In this context, the notion 'British' can be understood at least in two ways. *Sensu stricto*, it refers to the simple fact that AG Warner, AG Slynn, AG Jacobs, AG Sharpston, and Judge Edward were nominated for their posts by the UK. *Sensu largo*, it implies that there was something particularly idiosyncratic in the Opinions of the UK AGs that make them stand out. As this book demonstrates, their contribution was both British and European. It proves that contrary to the beliefs of some, being British does not exclude being European. *Au contraire*, as AG Sharpston argued in her chapter, save for her one of her passports, she did not see herself as a British AG, but a European one.[120]

The uniqueness of the contributions of UK AGs, alongside the contributions of – thus far – three Irish AGs,[121] has been the common law factor.[122] Many commentators have noted that, both procedurally and in substantive terms, the presence of a fundamentally different legal background of UK and Irish AGs and judges enriched the Court, and, more broadly, EU law.[123] It was not only the substance but also the style of their Opinions, but common law pragmatism and a sense of justice were, according to Terrett, visible in the Opinion of AG Slynn in *Commission v Germany (Beer Purity)*.[124] As Tridimas noted, the Opinion of AG Slynn in

---

[114] AG Warner himself was very open about it. See Warner (n 23) 28–29.

[115] See ch 18. See also Slynn (n 24) 155–56.

[116] J Guth, 'The EU legal order without the UK: a pity to lose the contribution?' in SL Greer and J Laible (eds), *The European Union after Brexit* (Manchester, Manchester University Press, 2020) 113, 122.

[117] See Warner (n 23); Slynn (n 24).

[118] D Edward, 'Reform of Article 234 Procedure: the Limits of the Possible' in O'Keeffe and Bavasso (n 21) 119, 132.

[119] See ch 52.

[120] ibid.

[121] AG Fennelly (1995–2000), AG Hogan (2018–21), and AG Collins (2021–present).

[122] That said, the common law aspects are just one of many ways of analysing the particular subject. See ch 2.

[123] See Preface and ch 3.

[124] See ch 22.

Klopp 'has all the hallmarks of an Opinion delivered by a common lawyer [...] [c]oncise but thorough, it is dispute-centred rather than principle setting'.[125] At the same time, the UK AGs were mindful of potential common law overload. For instance, Jacobs in his chapter in this book, argues that it would not be recommended to 'accept that a full-scale hearing as featured in English courts should be adopted by the Court'.[126] Such prudence was also exercised by AG Sharpston whose cabinet, as she herself noted:

> [...] was never an all-British team. It drew heavily on the rich diversity of its membership (national, cultural, linguistic, professional) to try – precisely – to *avoid* expressing legal views that would only be comprehensible to those who shared this AG's common law background.[127]

The Opinion of AG Sharpston in *Heinrich* is a stark example of how this worked in practice. Faced with a conundrum of status of non-published EU regulation, AG Sharpston based her recommendation to the Court on the German doctrine of non-existent legal acts, rather than UK rules on access to legal acts where a promulgation gazette does not exist.[128] Arguably, when it had merits, all UK AGs have successfully attempted to bring common law flavours to the mix, yet with prudence and caution, will full respect for the unique character of EU law. The Opinion of AG Warner in *AM&S*, and his peregrinations into legal standards on legal privilege in different legal systems of the Member States, including the UK, is a good example of this phenomenon.[129]

As Weatherill argued in his contribution in a Liber Amicorum for AG Jacobs, a successful AG needs to have five qualities: clarity of expression, clarity of vision, contextual richness, leadership, and capacity to inspire.[130] In his view, AG Jacobs passed this test with flying colours. The same test applies to all other UK AGs who served to the benefit of the Court. Many of their Opinions quite effortlessly meet these rather demanding benchmarks. This conclusion is not undermined, one should emphasise – by any stretch of imagination – by the fact that UK AGs also leave behind Opinions which were either not their best work, or where the pedestrian character of cases left no room for them to shine. This, inevitably, was a part of the game. The legacy of UK AGs also demonstrates their tireless ability to continue to contribute to the debate and broader engagement with EU law.

As editors, and on behalf of all the other contributing authors to this book, we thank them for their work, guidance, and inspiration.

---

[125] See ch 18.

[126] See ch 50.

[127] See ch 52.

[128] See further M Bobek, 'Case C-345/06. Gottfried Heinrich, Judgment of the Court of Justice (Grand Chamber) of 10 March 2019, not yet reported' (2009) 46 *CMLRev* 2077.

[129] See ch 14.

[130] S Weatherill, 'A consumer's appreciation of the contribution of Advocate General Francis Jacobs to the shaping of the EC's legal order' in Moser and Sawyer (n 12) 28, 30–31.

Index